Margaret Bartram

MALLETT'S INDEX OF ARTISTS

MALLETT'S INDEX OF ARTISTS

INTERNATIONAL – BIOGRAPHICAL

INCLUDING PAINTERS, SCULPTORS, ILLUSTRATORS, ENGRAVERS AND ETCHERS OF THE PAST AND THE PRESENT

By

DANIEL TROWBRIDGE MALLETT

NEW YORK
PETER SMITH
1948

Reprinted 1948 by
special arrangement with
R. R. BOWKER COMPANY

FOREWORD

This Index brings under one alphabet for the first time a biographical record of the leading artists of all countries, about 27,000 in all. It contains the basic data as to each artist and provides a key to the most authoritative sources of further information.

The Index is intended for use in libraries and museums and by students, art dealers and collectors and should supply first aid in the search for biographical material.

The list covers all the artists whose works are exhibited in leading galleries or inquired about by modern students, and, in checking the dates and biographical facts, the author has had the cooperation of museums, galleries and collectors. The catalogs of museums and of the latest gallery exhibits have been a valuable source for names and facts as have the extensive card indexes of the Metropolitan Museum of Art, the Frick Art Reference Library and the New York Public Library, which have been constantly consulted.

The Index gives the artist's full name, pseudonym, pre-marriage name in the case of women, nationality, place and year of birth and death, active years and place of residence.

By a system of key letters and numbers the reader is guided to more extended sources of biographical information. The key letters A to Y refer to material in standard reference books commonly found on the shelves of all libraries (see Sources of Biographical Information: I), and the key numbers 1 to 957 refer to individual volumes of biographical information, titles which have been selected for their usefulness from the extensive literature of art history (see Sources of Biographical Information: II).

Several thousand names are included in the Index which have never before been listed in any previous reference work on art and artists. The list of "Masters," for example, is the most complete in any reference book, about 160 names.

Especial effort has been made to make the lists of American artists complete and up-to-date.

A typical example of the form of entry is as follows:

AUDUBON, John James [Laforest]. (P-Birds)
Am. Les Cayes, Haiti 1785-1851 New York.
B-C-DAB-E-F-T-4-15-45-98-636.

Full name: Audubon, John James
[*Laforest*]*:* Signature used on early paintings
(P-Birds): Painter of birds
Nationality: American
Place and year of birth: Les Cayes, Haiti, 1785
Place and year of death: New York, 1851

General Reference Works (see Sources of Biographical Information I):

B: Bénézit, E., Dictionnaire critique et documentaire des peintres, etc., Paris, 1911-1923, 3 vols.
C: Champlin, J. D. jr., and Perkins, C. C., Cyclopedia of painters and paintings, New York, 1885-1887, 4 vols.
DAB: Dictionary of American biography, New York, 1928-1935, 16 vols. (work not yet completed)
E: Encyclopedia Britannica, 14th edition, London and New York, 1929, 24 vols.
F: Fielding, M., Dictionary of American painters, sculptors and engravers, Philadelphia, 1926
T: Thieme, U., and Becker F., Allgemeines Lexikon der bildenden Künstler von der Antike bis zur Gegenwart. Leipzig, 1907-1934, 28 vols.

Volumes of Biographical Data (see Sources of Biographical Information II; also Authors' Index to Sources of Biographical Information):

4: Tuckerman, H. T., Book of the Artists. New York, 1867
15: Clement, C. E., and Hutton, L., Artists of the nineteenth century. 3rd ed., Boston, 1885 and 1907, 2 vols.
45: Bolton, T., Early American portrait draughtsmen in crayons. New York, 1923
98: Herrick, F. H., Audubon, the naturalist. New York, 1917, 2 vols.
636: Audubon, J. J., Life of John James Audubon [Edited by Mrs. L. R. Audubon]. New York, 1869

The author owes a debt of gratitude to the many museums, libraries and galleries and to the large number of individuals who have so willingly assisted him in the preparation of this volume and have helped in making more complete the listings in the Index. To all of these he wishes to express his fullest appreciation and his sincere thanks.

The author would be glad to receive in care of his publishers, R. R. Bowker Company, 62 West 45th Street, New York, any corrections of data or suggestions of names to be added.

DANIEL TROWBRIDGE MALLETT

CONTENTS

ABBREVIATIONS

(For complete titles of reference works *see* Sources of Biographical Information: I)

A	American art annual	Gr.	Greek
ac.	active	Hs	History of sculpture (Chase & Post)
Am.	American	Hun.	Hungarian
Auc.	Auction	Ill	Illustrator
Aus.	Austrian	Ind.	Indianapolis
Aust.	Australian	Ir.	Irish
b.	born	It.	Italian
B	Bénézit Dictionnaire	J	Morrison's painters of old Japan
Balt.	Baltimore	Jap.	Japanese
Bav.	Bavarian	M	Mallett Library
Bd	Bryan's Dictionary	Med	Medallist
Belg.	Belgian	Mex.	Mexican
Biog.	Biography	Min	Miniaturist
Br.	British	Minn.	Minneapolis
C	Champlin & Perkins' Cyclopedia	Ms	Müller-Singer Lexikon
Can.	Canadian	Mu	Mural
Cari.	Caricaturist	Nor.	Norwegian
Cart.	Cartoonist	O.	Obituary
Cinn.	Cincinnati	P	Painter
Cs	Contemporary Am. sculpture	Per.	Persian
Czec.	Czecho-Slovakian	Phila.	Philadelphia
d.	died	Pol.	Polish
DAB	Dict. of Am. biography	Por.	Portuguese
Dan.	Danish	Prov.	Providence
DBA	Dictionnaire biographique des artists	Rus.	Russian
Dict.	Dictionary	S	Sculptor
DNB	Dict. of national biography	San Fran.	San Francisco
Dut.	Dutch	Scot.	Scottish
E	Encyclopedia Britannica	Sp.	Spanish
Eg	Engraver	Swe.	Swedish
Eng.	English	Swi.	Swiss
Et	Etcher	T	Thieme-Becker Lexikon
ex.	exhibition	Ta	Taft's History of Am. sculpture
F	Fielding's Dictionary	V	Vasari's Lives of eminent painters
Fa.	Frick Art Reference Library	W	Who's Who in America
Fin.	Finnish	WA	Who's Who in Art (London)
Flem.	Flemish	Wash.	Washington
Fr.	French	Wi	Witt Art Library
Ger.	German	Y	Year's Art (London)

SOURCES OF BIOGRAPHICAL INFORMATION: I

General reference works referred to in the Index by letters.

A American art annual. v. 1-31 (1898-1934). Washington, D. C.
Contains biographical data regarding living American artists, lists of associations, sales, obituary notices, etc. Reference is to vol. 30, [1933] unless another year is indicated. i.e. AXI refers to Amer. Art Annual Vol. XI.

AO The letter O indicates that the obituary section of the volumes should be consulted.

B Bénézit, E. Dictionnaire critique et documentaire des peintres, sculpteurs, dessinateurs & graveurs, de tous les temps et tous les pays. Paris, 1911-23. 3 vols.

Bd Bryan, M. Bryan's dictionary of painters and engravers. New ed., rev. and enl. under the supervision of G. C. Williamson. London; New York, 1903-05. 5 vols.

C Champlin, J. D., Jr., and Perkins, C. C. Cyclopedia of painters and paintings. New York, 1885-87. 4 vols.

Cs Contemporary American sculpture. [Exhibition of the National Sculpture Society. New York, 1929.]

DAB Dictionary of American biography. v. 1-15. New York, 1928-35. 15 vols. Work not yet completed.

DBA Dictionnaire biographique des artistes contemporains. 1910-1934. Paris, 1930-34. 3 vols.

DNB Dictionary of national biography [and supplements]. London and New York, 1885-1927. 70 vols.

E Encyclopædia Britannica. 14th edition. London and New York [1929]. 24 vols.

F Fielding, M. Dictionary of American painters, sculptors and engravers. Philadelphia [1926].

Fa Frick Art Reference Library, New York City.
An extensive and growing collection of photographs of painting and sculpture and a large library of art books, catalogues, museum bulletins, periodicals, etc. Its remarkable and valuable card index systems are of particular assistance as sources of information.

Hs Chase, G. H., and Post, C. R. History of sculpture. New York and London, 1925.

J Morrison, A. The painters of old Japan. New York [1911]. 2 vols.

M Mallett Library of Reproductions, Hackensack, N. J.
The author's file of biographical material about artists, not generally listed in other reference books.

Ms Müller, H. S., and Singer, H. W. Allgemeines Künstler-Lexikon. Frankfurt a. M., 1895-1922. 7 vols.

T Thieme, U., and Becker, F. Allgemeines Lexikon der bildenden Künstler von der Antike bis zur Gegenwart. Leipzig, 1907-1934. 28 vols.
Not yet completed.

Ta Taft, L. History of American sculpture. New York, 1st ed., 1924; new ed., 1930. 2 vols.

V Vasari, G. Lives of the most eminent painters, sculptors, and architects. London, 1912[-1915]. 10 vols.
Has appeared in many other editions.

W Who's who in America. v. 1-18, 1899/1900-1934/35. Chicago [1899-1934]. 18 vols.
Reference herein is to vol. 18, 1934/35, unless another year is noted, i.e. WXI refers to Who's Who in America Vol. XI.

Wa Who's who in art. London [1927-1934]. 3 vols.
Reference herein to third volume [1934] unless otherwise noted.

Wi Witt Art Library, London, England.
Founded by Sir Robert and Lady Witt, who started with three hundred photographs of paintings and by the year 1921 had a total number of 150,000 of photographs and prints. The collection has now expanded to more than 400,000 reproductions, illustrating the work of over 18,000 artists. This valuable collection, with accumulated data, is open to the public and is a remarkable source of information regarding artists and their work. It will eventually be installed in the Courtauld Institute, London.

Y The Year's Art. . . . A concise epitome . . . relating to . . . painting, sculpture, engraving and architecture. v. 1-55, 1880-1934. London, 1880[-1933]. 55 vols.

YO The letter O indicates an obituary notice in the volume for the year indicated.

For PERIODICAL references to artists consult The Art Index, New York, a cumulative author and subject index to periodicals and museum bulletins, both domestic and foreign.

SOURCES OF BIBLIOGRAPHICAL INFORMATION: II

Selected volumes of biographical and critical data referred to in the Index by numbers

1 Isham, S. History of American painting. New York, 1905; with supp. chapters, by R. Cortissoz. New York, 1927.

2 Dunlap, W. History of the rise and progress of the arts of design in the United States. New York, 1834. 2 vols.; new ed., by F. W. Bayley and C. E. Goodspeed. Boston, 1918. 3 vols.

3 French, H. W. Pioneers of art in America; art and artists in Connecticut. Boston, 1879.

4 Tuckerman, H. T. Book of the artists. New York, 1867.

5 McSpadden, J. W. Famous painters of America. New York, 1907.

6 Bolton, T. Early American portrait painters in miniature. New York, 1921.

7 Stauffer, D. M. American engravers upon copper and steel. New York, 1907. 2 vols.

8 Linton, W. J. History of wood-engraving in America. Boston, 1882.

9 Harper, J. H. House of Harper. New York, 1912.

10 Durtain, L. Frans Masereel. Paris, 1931.

11 Cummings, T. S. Historic annals of the National Academy of Design. Philadelphia, 1865.

12 Fielding, M. American engravers upon copper and steel. Philadelphia, 1917.

13 Flagg, J. B. Life and letters of Washington Allston. New York, 1892.

14 Burr, F. M. Life and works of Alexander Anderson. New York, 1893.

15 Clement, C. E., and Hutton, L. Artists of the nineteenth century. 3d ed. Boston, 1885. 2 vols.; also, Boston, 1907. 2 vols.

16 Hitchcock, J. R. W. Etching in America. New York, 1886.

17 Pennell, J. Pen drawing and pen draughtsmen. London and New York, 1889; New York, 1920.

18 Taft, L. Modern tendencies in sculpture. Chicago, 1921.

19 Caffin, C. H. American masters of sculpture. New York, 1903.

20 Maurice, A. B., and Cooper, F. T. History of the nineteenth century in caricature. New York, 1904.

21 Lafond, P. Degas. Paris, 1918-19. 2 vols.

22 Sheldon, G. W. American painters. New York, 1879.

23 Montgomery, W. American art and American art collections. Boston, 1889. 2 vols.

24 Bellows, E. S. George W. Bellows: his lithographs. New York, 1927.

25 Bayley, F. W. Little known early American portrait painters. 1915-1917[?]

26 Fairman, C. E. Art and artists of the capitol of the United States. Washington, D. C., 1927.

27 Rusk, F. H. George Caleb Bingham, the Missouri artist. Jefferson City, Mo., 1917.

28 Redgrave, S. Dictionary of artists of the English school. London, 1874.

29 Foster, J. J. Miniature painters, British and foreign. New York, 1903.

30 Wharton, A. H. Heirlooms in miniatures. Philadelphia, 1898.

31 Daingerfield, E. Ralph Albert Blakelock. New York, 1914.

32 Sherman, F. F. Landscape and figure painters of America. New York, 1917.

33 Blashfield, E. H. Mural painting in America. New York, 1913.

34 Hart, C. H. Browere's life masks of great Americans. New York, 1898.

35 Benjamin, S. G. W. Art in America. New York, 1880.

36 Radcliffe, A. G. Schools and masters of sculpture. New York, 1902.

37 Perkins, F. B. The picture and the men. New York, 1867.

38 Champney, B. Sixty years' memories of art and artists. Woburn, Mass., 1900.

39 Benjamin, S. G. W. Our American artists. Boston, 1886.

40 Baker, W. S. American engravers and their works. Philadelphia, 1875.

41 Roof, K. M. Life and art of William Merritt Chase. New York, 1917.

42 Cheney, E. D. Memoir of John Cheney. Boston [?], 1889.

43 Koehler, S. R. Catalogue of the engraved and lithographed work of John Cheney and Seth Wells Cheney. Boston, 1891.

44 Cahill, H. American folk art. [Museum of Modern Art, New York.] New York, 1932.

45 Bolton, T. Early American portrait draughtsmen in crayons. New York, 1923.

46 Michigan State Library. Biographical sketches of American artists. [Comp. by H. L. Earle.] 5th ed. Lansing, 1924.

47 Robinson, F. T. Living New England artists. Boston, 1888.

48 Knowlton, H. M. Art-life of William Morris Hunt. Boston, 1899.

49 Cole, T. The Course of empire, Voyage of life, and other pictures, with selections

from his letters and miscellaneous writings by L. L. Noble. New York, 1853.
50 Tuckerman, H. T. Artist-life; or, Sketches of American painters. New York, 1847.
51 Caffin, C. H. Story of American painting. New York, 1907.
52 Clark, W. J., Jr. Great American sculptures. Philadelphia, 1878.
53 Lester, C. E. Artists of America. New York, 1846.
54 Weaver, W. A. Lithographs of N. Currier and Currier & Ives; and supps. 1-2. New York, 1925-26. 3 vols.
55 Weitenkampf, F. American graphic art. New York, 1924.
56 Allen, C. D. American book-plates. New York, 1905.
57 Durand, J. Life and times of A. B. Durand. New York, 1894.
58 Jarves, J. J. The art-idea. New York, 1864.
59 Heermann, N. Frank Duveneck. Boston, 1918.
60 Bryant, L. M. What pictures to see in America. New York, 1915.
61 Sherman, F. F. American painters of yesterday and today. New York, 1919.
62 Fielding, M. Catalogue of the engraved work of David Edwin. Philadelphia, 1905.
63 Laver, J. History of British and American etching. London, 1929.
64 Bernard, J. Retrospections of America. New York, 1887.
65 Smith, A. R. H., and D. E. H. Charles Fraser. New York, 1924.
66 Wehle, H. B. American miniatures, 1720-1850; and a biographical dictionary of the artists, by T. Bolton. New York, 1927.
67 Price, S. W. Old masters of the Bluegrass. Louisville, Ky., 1902.
68 Millet, J. B. George Fuller, his life and works. Boston, 1886.
69 Van Rensselaer, Mrs. Schuyler. Six portraits. Boston, 1889.
70 Caffin, C. H. American masters of painting. New York, 1902.
71 Cortissoz, R. American artists. New York. 1923.
72 Colden, C. D. Life of Robert Fulton. New York, 1817.
73 Dickinson, H. W. Robert Fulton, engineer and artist. London, 1913.
74 Pennell, J. Modern illustration. London, 1895.
75 Gay, F. L. John Gay of Dedham, Mass., and his descendants. (New-England Historical and Genealogical Register. Boston, 1879. v. 33, p. 45-57.)
76 Wilson, C. C. John Gibson of Cambridge, Mass., 1900.
77 Adams, J. C. William Hamilton Gibson. New York, 1901.
78 Berenson, B. Italian pictures of the Renaissance. London, 1932.
79 Arkell, W. J. Old friends and some acquaintances. Los Angeles, 1927.
80 Stewart, F. H. History of the first United States mint. Philadelphia, 1924.
81 Simpson, H. Lives of eminent Philadelphians. Philadelphia, 1859.
82 Herbermann, C. G. Sulpicians in the United States. New York, 1916.
83 Scharf, J. T. History of Baltimore city and county. Philadelphia, 1881.
84 Scharf, J. T., and Westcott, T. History of Philadelphia. Philadelphia, 1884.
85 Mason, G. C. Life and works of Gilbert Stuart. New York, 1879.
86 Jarves, J. J. Art thoughts. New York, 1869.
87 Mitchell, W. D. American art in bronze and iron. v. 1, no. 1-7. New York, 1907-10. 7 nos.
88 Cossio, M. B. El Greco. Madrid, 1908.
89 National Academy of Design, New York. National Academy notes; ed. by C. M. Kurtz. no. 56-64. New York, 1881-89.
90 Andrews, H. F. The Hamlin family. Exira, Ia., 1902.
91 Neuhaus, E. Appreciation of art. New York, 1924.
92 Harrison, B. Landscape painting. New York, 1909.
93 Breckinridge, Mrs. I. D., and Desha, M. "The work shall praise the master"; a memorial to Joel T. Hart. Cincinnati, 1884.
94 Biographical encyclopædia of Kentucky. Cincinnati, 1878.
95 Ranck, G. W. History of Lexington, Kentucky. Cincinnati, 1872.
96 Gallatin, A. E. Whistler's pastels, and Other modern profiles. New York, 1912.
97 Prideaux, S. T. Aquatint engraving. London, 1909.
98 Herrick, F. H. Audubon the naturalist. New York, 1917. 2 vols.
99 Goodspeed, W. A. History of the Goodspeed family. Chicago, 1907.
100 Healy, G. P. A. Reminiscences of a portrait painter. Chicago, 1894.
101 Biographical sketches of the leading men of Chicago. Chicago, 1868.
102 Yarrow, W., and Bouche, L., eds. Robert Henri: his life and works. New York, 1921.
103 Henri, R. Robert Henri; comp. by N. Pousette-Dart. New York, 1923.
104 Hartmann, S. History of American art; rev. ed. Boston, 1932.
105 Neuhaus, E. History & ideals of American art. Stanford University, Cal., 1931.
106 Drepperd, C. W. Early American prints. New York, 1930.
107 Hill, J. H. John William Hill; an artist's memorial. New York, 1881.
108 Downes, W. H. Life and works of Winslow Homer. Boston, 1911.
109 Cox, K. Winslow Homer. New York, 1914.
110 Representative men and old families of Rhode Island. Chicago, 1908. 3 vols.
111 Hosmer, H. Letters and memories; ed. by C. Carr. New York, 1912.
112 American Art Association, New York. Illustrated catalogue of oil paintings by

the late Alfred Cornelius Howland; catalogued by C. De Kay. New York, 1910.
113 Hoxie, R. L. Vinnie Ream. Washington, D. C., 1908.
114 Hubbard, F. M. ("Kin"). Abe Martin's wisecracks; selected by E. V. Lucas. London, 1930.
115 Day, E. W. One thousand years of Hubbard history. New York, 1895.
116 Graves, A. The Royal Academy of Arts. London, 1906.
117 Orcutt, W. D. Good old Dorchester. Cambridge, Mass., 1893.
118 Stokes, I. N. P. Iconography of Manhattan Island. New York, 1915-28. 6 vols.
119 Bolton, E. S. American wax portraits. Boston, 1929.
120 Angell, H. C. Records of William M. Hunt. Boston, 1881.
121 Van Dyke, J. C. Text-book of the History of painting. New York, 1894.
122 Lübke, W. Outlines of the history of art; rev. by R. Sturgis. New York, 1904.
123 Salmon, A. Kisling. Paris, 1928.
124 The Huntington family in America. Hartford, Conn., 1915.
125 Ehrich Galleries, New York. One hundred early American paintings. [New York], 1918.
126 Inness, G., Jr. Life, art, and letters of George Inness; intro. by E. Daingerfield. New York, 1917.
127 Van Dyke, J. C. American painting and its tradition. New York, 1919.
128 Downes, W. H. Twelve great artists. Boston, 1900.
129 Inness, G. Fifty paintings; intro. by E. Daingerfield. New York, 1913.
130 Stevens, W. B. Halsey Cooley Ives. St. Louis, 1915.
131 Peters, H. T. Currier & Ives, print-makers to the American people. Garden City, N. Y., 1929-31. 2 vols.
132 Crouse, R. Mr. Currier and Mr. Ives. Garden City, N. Y., 1930.
133 Bland, J. C. Currier & Ives; a manual for collectors. Garden City, N. Y., 1931.
134 Grünewald, M. Der Maler des Eisenheimer Alters; mit einer einführung von W. Niemeyer. Berlin, 1921.
135 Beaux, C. Background with figures. Boston, 1930.
136 Morse, E. L. Samuel F. B. Morse, his letters and journals. Boston, 1914. 2 vols.
137 Commemorative biographical record of New Haven County, Connecticut. Chicago, 1902.
138 Bryant, L. M. American pictures and their painters. New York, 1917.
139 Brown, T. A. History of the American stage. New York, 1870.
140 Seilhamer, G. O. History of the American theatre. Philadelphia, 1888-91. 3 vols.
141 Wilson, Rev. R. Art and artists in provincial South Carolina. Charleston, S. C., 1899.
142 Richmond, L. Technique of the poster. London, 1933.
143 Cook, C. Art and artists of our time. New York, 1888. 3 vols.
144 Cline, I. M. Art and artists in New Orleans during the last century. New Orleans, La., 1922.
145 Koehler, S. R. Frederick Juengling. Roxbury, 1890.
146 Grolier Club, New York. Catalogue of an exhibition of early American engraving upon copper. New York, 1908.
147 New York Public Library. One hundred notable American engravers. New York, 1928.
148 Hay, E. P. B. William Keith as prophet painter. San Francisco, 1916.
149 Keppler, J. Selection of cartoons from Puck; [text] by H. C. Bunner. New York, 1893.
150 Kingsley, E. Catalogue of the works of Elbridge Kingsley; comp. for Mt. Holyoke College. [New York?] 1901.
151 Grolier Club, New York. Wood-engraving; three essays by A. V. S. Anthony, T. Cole, and E. Kingsley. New York, 1916.
152 Book of Minnesotans; ed. by A. N. Marquis. Chicago, 1907.
153 Smith, R. C. Gustav Kruell. Champlain, 1929.
154 Besnard, A. La Tour; la vie et l'œuvre de l'artiste. Paris, 1928.
155 Cortissoz, R. John La Farge; a memoir and a study. Boston, 1911.
156 Waern, C. John La Farge. London, 1896.
157 Wilson, E. Standard history of Pittsburgh, Pennsylvania. Chicago, 1898.
158 Prang, L., and Company. Collection of monuments and head stones designed by R. E. Launitz. Boston, 1866.
159 Rathbun, R. The National Gallery of Art. Washington, D. C., 1909.
160 Hart, C. H. Catalogue of the engraved portraits of Washington. New York, 1904.
161 Leslie, C. R. Autobiographical recollections. Boston, 1860.
162 Paine, A. B. Th. Nast, his period and his pictures. New York, 1904.
163 Youmans, W. J. Pioneers of science in America. New York, 1896.
164 Henderson, H. W. The art treasures of Washington. Boston, 1912.
165 Mott, F. L. History of American magazines. New York, 1930.
166 Fitch, C. E. Encyclopedia of biography of New York. v. 1-8. New York, 1916-25. 8 vols.
167 New York City Art Commission. Works of art belonging to the City of New York. New York, 1909.
168 Clark, E. M. Ohio art and artists. Richmond, Va., 1932.
169 Belknap, H. W. Artists and craftsmen of Essex County, Massachusetts. Salem, Mass., 1927.
170 Cousins, F., and Riley, P. M. The woodcarver of Salem, Samuel McIntire. Boston, 1916.
171 Piers, H. Robert Field. New York, 1927.

172 Mather, F. J., Jr. American spirit in art. New Haven, Conn., 1927.
173 Martin, E. G. Homer Martin; a reminiscence. New York, 1904.
174 Mather, F. J., Jr. Homer Martin, poet in landscape. New York, 1912.
175 Saint-Gaudens, A. Reminiscences; ed. by H. Saint-Gaudens. New York, 1913.
176 King, P. American mural painting. Boston, 1902.
177 Melchers, G. Gari Melchers, painter; foreword by H. Lewis-Hind. New York, 1928.
178 Brinton, C. Modern artists. New York, 1908.
179 Foster, J. J. Dictionary of painters of miniatures; ed. by E. M. Foster. London, 1926.
180 American Federation of Arts. Francis Davis Millet. Washington, D. C., 1912.
181 Burnet, M. Q. Art and artists of Indiana. New York, 1921.
182 Morgan, J. H. Early American painters. New York, 1921.
183 Cline, I. M. Contemporary art and artists in New Orleans. New Orleans, La., 1924.
184 Kelby, W. Notes on American artists. New York, 1922.
185 Woodberry, G. E. History of wood-engraving. New York, 1883.
186 Pennell, E. R., and J. Lithography and lithographers. New York, 1915.
187 Low, W. H. A painter's progress. New York, 1910.
188 Munn, C. A. Three types of Washington portraits. New York, 1908.
189 Johnston, E. B. Original portraits of Washington. Boston, 1882.
190 Cortissoz, R. Guy Pène du Bois. New York, 1931.
191 Cortissoz, R. Painter's craft. New York, 1930.
192 Cortissoz, R. Personalities in art. New York, 1925.
193 Shaw, C. B. American painters. Greensboro, N. C., 1927.
194 Fry, R. Cézanne. London, 1927.
195 Balch, E. S. Art in America before the Revolution. [Philadelphia?] 1908.
196 Sartain, J. Reminiscences of a very old man. New York, 1899.
197 Arnold, J. N. Art and artists in Rhode Island. Providence, R. I., 1905.
198 Book of American figure painters. Philadelphia, 1886.
199 Allen, E. B. Early American wall paintings. New Haven, Conn., 1926.
200 Hale, G. Fresco painting. New York, 1933.
201 Lucas, E. V. Edwin Austin Abbey. London, 1921.
202 Abdy, R. M. Old California; foreword by G. Piazzoni. San Francisco, 1924.
203 Fine Arts Federation of New York. Address of Mr. John G. Agar, and resolutions adopted at the testimonial to John W. Alexander. New York, 1916.
204 Sick, I. von. Nicholaes Berchem. Berlin, 1930.
205 Metropolitan Museum of Art, New York. Memorial exhibition of the work of George Bellows. New York, 1925.
206 Park, L. Joseph Blackburn, a colonial portrait painter. Worcester, Mass., 1923.
207 Young, J. W. Catalogue of the works of R. A. Blakelock, N.A., and his daughter Marian Blakelock [containing "Blakelock, his art and his family"]; foreword by Mrs. R. A. Blakelock, Chicago, 1916.
208 Segard, A. Un peintre des enfants et des mères: Mary Cassatt. Paris, 1913.
209 Metropolitan Museum of Art, New York. Paintings of Frederic E. Church. New York, 1900.
210 Amory, M. B. Domestic and artistic life of John Singleton Copley. Boston, 1882.
211 Bayley, F. W. Life and works of John Singleton Copley. Boston, 1915.
212 Perkins, A. T. Sketch of the life and a list of some of the works of John Singleton Copley. Boston, 1873.
213 Phillips Memorial Art Gallery, Washington, D. C. Arthur B. Davies; essays. Cambridge, Mass., 1924.
214 Cortissoz, R. Arthur B. Davies. New York, 1931.
215 Price, L. Immortal youth. [Memoir of Fred A. Demmler.] Boston, 1919.
216 Gallatin, A. E. Charles Demuth. New York, 1927.
217 Gibbes, R. W. Memoir of James De Veaux. Columbia, S. C., 1846.
218 Fuchs, E. With pencil, brush and chisel. New York, 1925.
219 Metropolitan Museum of Art, New York. A memorial catalogue of the paintings of S. R. Gifford, with a biographical and critical essay by J. F. Weir. New York, 1881.
220 Pousette-Dart, N. Childe Hassam; intro. by E. Haskell. New York, 1922.
221 Bigot, M. Life of George P. A. Healy. [Chicago, 1913?]
222 Wilson, M. Life of William Blake. New York, 1933.
223 Century Association, New York. Proceedings at a meeting held in memory of John F. Kennsett, December, 1872. New York, 1872.
224 Fitzgerald, D. Dodge Macknight. Brookline, Mass., 1916.
225 Carroll, D. H. Fifty-eight paintings by H. D. Martin. New York, 1913.
226 Sutro, T. Thirteen chapters of American history represented by the Edward Moran series of thirteen historical marine paintings. New York, 1905.
227 Munn, M. C., and Cabot, M. R. The art of George Frederick Munn. New York, 1916.
228 American Art Association, New York. Paintings and drawings by J. Francis Murphy. New York, 1926.
229 Pennsylvania Academy of the Fine Arts, Philadelphia. Catalogue of an exhibition

of portraits by John Neagle. Philadelphia, 1925.

230 Oertel, J. F. A vision realized; a life story, of Rev. J. A. Oertel. Milwaukee, Wis., 1917.

231 Pennsylvania Academy of the Fine Arts, Philadelphia. Catalogue of an exhibition of portraits by Charles Willson Peale and James Peale and Rembrandt Peale. Philadelphia, 1923.

232 Abbott, C. D. Howard Pyle, a chronicle. New York, 1925.

233 Cunningham, H. W. Christian Remick, an early Boston artist. Boston, 1924.

234 Morris, H. S. William T. Richards. Philadelphia, 1912.

235 Bartlett, T. H. Art life of William Rimmer. Boston, 1882.

236 Cortissoz, R. Augustus Saint-Gaudens. Boston, 1907.

237 Sherman, F. F. Albert Pinkham Ryder. New York, 1920.

238 Charteris, E. John Sargent. New York, 1927.

239 Sargent, J. S. Work of John S. Sargent, R.A.; intro. by J. B. Manson & Mrs. Meynell. London, 1927.

240 Metropolitan Museum of Art, New York. Memorial exhibition of the work of John Singer Sargent. New York, 1926.

241 Museum of Fine Arts, Boston. Catalogue of the memorial exhibition of the works of the late John Singer Sargent. Boston, 1925.

242 Downes, W. H. John S. Sargent, his life and work. Boston, 1925.

243 Pousette-Dart, N. John Singer Sargent; intro. by L. W. Zeigler. New York, 1924.

244 Wood, T. M. Sargent. New York, 1909.

245 Wildenstein, G. Lancret. Paris, 1924.

246 Sellstedt, L. G. From forecastle to academy. Buffalo, N. Y., 1904.

247 Simmons, E. From seven to seventy; memories of a painter and a Yankee. New York, 1922.

248 Gallatin, A. E. John Sloan. New York, 1925.

249 Fielding, M. Gilbert Stuart's portraits of George Washington. Philadelphia, 1923.

250 Park, L. Gilbert Stuart; an illustrated descriptive list of his works by L. Park; an account of his life by J. H. Morgan; and an appreciation by R. Cortissoz. New York, 1926.

251 Biddle, E., and Fielding, M. Life and works of Thomas Sully. Philadelphia, 1921.

252 Hart, C. H. Register of portraits painted by Thomas Sully. Philadelphia, 1909.

253 Pennsylvania Academy of the Fine Arts, Philadelphia. Catalogue of the memorial exhibition of portraits by Thomas Sully. Philadelphia, 1922.

254 Brawley, B. G. Negro in literature and art in the United States. New York, 1934.

255 Carnegie Institute: Fine Arts Department, Pittsburgh. Exhibition of paintings by Abbott H. Thayer. Pittsburgh, 1919.

256 Metropolitan Museum of Art, New York. Memorial exhibition of the work of Abbott Henderson Thayer. [Intro. by C. Cortissoz.] New York, 1922.

257 Pousette-Dart, N. Abbott H. Thayer. New York, 1923.

258 Art work of Louis C. Tiffany. Garden City, N. Y., 1914.

259 Trumbull, J. Autobiography. New York, 1841.

260 Morgan, J. H. Paintings by John Trumbull. New Haven, Conn., 1926.

261 Weir, J. F. John Trumbull, a brief sketch. New York, 1901.

262 Coffin, C. H. Art of Dwight W. Tryon. New York, 1909.

263 Vedder, E. Digressions of Vedder. Boston, 1910.

264 Phillips Memorial Art Gallery, Washington, D. C. Julian Alden Weir. New York, 1922.

265 Farington, J. The Farington diary; ed. by J. Grieg. London, 1922-28. 8 vols.

266 Galt, J. Life, studies, and works of Benjamin West. London, 1820.

267 Galt, J. The progress of genius; or, Authentic memoirs of the early life of Benjamin West. Boston, 1832.

268 Hart, C. H. Benjamin West's family. Philadelphia, 1908.

269 Jackson, H. E. Benjamin West, his life and work. Philadelphia, 1900.

270 Seitz, D. C. Writings by and about James Abbott McNeill Whistler. Edinburgh, 1910.

271 Bacher, O. H. With Whistler in Venice. New York, 1908.

272 Holme, G. British book illustration, yesterday and to-day; with commentary by M. G. Salaman. London, 1923.

273 Menpes, M. Whistler as I knew him. New York, 1904.

274 Pennell, E. R., and J. Life of James McNeill Whistler. Philadelphia, 1911.

275 Pousette-Dart, N. James McNeill Whistler; intro. by J. and E. R. Pennell. New York, 1924.

276 Sellstedt, L. G. Life and works of William John Wilgus. Buffalo, N. Y., 1912.

277 Devereux, H. K. "The Spirit of '76". Cleveland, 1926.

278 Hodges, W. R. Carl Wimar. Galveston, Tex., 1908.

279 British Museum. Catalogue of drawings by British artists and artists of foreign origin working in Great Britain. By L. Binyon. London, 1898-1907. 4 vols.

280 Clark, E. Alexander Wyant. New York, 1916.

281 Sievers, J. Pieter Aertsen. Leipzig, 1906.

282 Standing, P. C. Sir Lawrence Alma-Tadema. London, 1905.

283 Sparrow, W. S. Henry Alken; intro. by Sir T. Cook. New York, 1927.

284 Waldmann, E. Albrecht Altdorfer. London, 1923.

285 Douglas, L. Fra Angelico. London, 1900.

286 Hausenstein, W. Fra Angelico. München, 1923.

287 Hale, G. Fra Angelico. Boston, 1932.

288 Archipenko, A. Alexandre Archipenko, son oeuvre; intro. par H. Hildebrandt. Berlin, 1923.

289 Tuer, A. W. Bartolozzi and his works. London, 1882.

290 De Kay, C. Life and works of Antoine Louis Barye. New York, 1889.

291 Macfall, H. Aubrey Beardsley. New York, 1927.

292 Roberts, W. Sir William Beechey. London, 1907.

293 Eggers, G. W. George Bellows. New York, 1931.

294 Dobson, A. Thomas Bewick and his pupils. London, 1884.

295 Figgis, D. Paintings of William Blake. London, 1925.

296 De Selincourt, B. William Blake. London, 1909.

297 Gardner, C. William Blake, the man. London, 1919.

298 Werth, L. Bonnard. Paris, 1920.

299 Dubuisson, A. Richard Parkes Bonington. London, 1924.

300 Bode, W. von. Sandro Botticelli, by W. Bode. London, 1925.

301 Cartwright, J. Life and art of Sandro Botticelli. London, 1904.

302 Macfall, H. Boucher: the man, his times, his art, and his significance. London, 1908.

303 Julia, E. F. Antoine Bourdelle. Paris, 1930.

304 Sparrow, W. S. Frank Brangwyn and his work, by W. Shaw-Sparrow. London, 1910.

305 Furst, H. Decorative art of Frank Brangwyn. New York, 1924.

306 Vachon, M. Jules Bréton. Paris, 1919.

307 Jewell, E. A. Alexander Brook. New York, 1931.

308 Hueffer, F. M. Ford Madox Brown. London, 1896.

309 Bode, W. von. Adriaen Brouwer. Berlin, 1924.

310 Tolnai, K. Die Zeichnungen Pieter Bruegels. München, 1925.

311 Bell, M. Edward Burne-Jones. London, 1892.

312 Zahn, L. Die Handzeichnungen des Jacques Callot. München, 1923.

313 Hind, A. M. Etchings of D. Y. Cameron. London, 1924.

314 Zahn, L. Caravaggio. Berlin, 1928.

315 Fiocco, G. Carpaccio. Paris, 1931.

316 Watson, F. Mary Cassatt. New York, 1932.

317 Cellini, B. Memoirs; trans. by T. Roscoe. New York, 1845. 2 vols.

318 Meier-Graefe, J. Cézanne; trans. by J. Holroyd-Reece. London, 1927.

319 Chagall, M. Ma vie; trad. par B. Chagall. Paris, 1931.

320 Pascal, A., *pseudo.*, and Gaucheron, R. Documents sur la vie et l'œuvre de Chardin. Paris, 1931.

321 George, W. Chirico. Paris, 1928.

322 Nicholson, A. Cimabue. Princeton, N. J., 1932.

323 Dilke, E. F. (S.), Lady. Claude Lorraine, sa vie et ses œuvres, par Mme. M. Pattison. Paris, 1884.

324 Moreau-Nélaton, É. Les Clouet et leurs emules. Paris, 1924. 3 vols.

325 Henderson, M. S. Constable. London, 1905.

326 Lucas, E. V. John Constable. London, 1924.

327 Meier-Graefe, J. Corot. Berlin, 1930.

328 Faure, É. Corot. Paris, 1931.

329 Thomson, D. C. Corot. London, 1892.

330 Moore, T. S. Correggio. New York, 1906.

331 Cotman, J. S. Etchings of old English buildings. London, 1838. 2 vols.

332 Cranach, L. Die Gemälde von Lucas Cranach; hrsg. von. M. J. Friedländer und J. Rosenberg. Berlin, 1932.

333 Glaser, C. Lukas Cranach. Leipzig, 1921.

334 Crane, W. An artist's reminiscences. New York, 1907.

335 Baker, C. H. C. Crome. London, 1921.

336 Theobald, H. S. Crome's etchings. London, 1906.

337 Cohn, A. M. Bibliographical catalogue of the printed works illustrated by George Cruikshank. London, 1914.

338 Offner, R. Critical and historical corpus of Florentine painting. vol. 3, sec. 3. [Bernardo Daddi.] New York, 1930.

339 Delteil, L. Honoré Daumier. Paris, 1925-26. 11 vols. (His: Le peintre-graveur, t. 20-29.)

340 Klossowski, E. Honoré Daumier. München, 1908.

341 Holme, C. Daumier and Gavarni; notes by H. Frantz and O. Uzanne. London, 1904.

342 Meier-Graefe, J. Degas; trans. by J. Holroyd-Reece. London, 1923.

343 Escholier, R. Delacroix. Paris, 1926-29. 3 vols.

344 Piot, R. Les palettes de Delacroix. Paris, 1931.

345 Murrell, W. Charles Demuth. New York, 1931.

346 Williamson, G. C. John Downman, his life and works. London, 1907.

347 Balcarres, D. A. E., Lord. Donatello. London, 1903.

348 Schottmüller, F. Donatello. München, 1904.

349 Martin, W. Gérard Dou; trad. du hollandais, avec un avant-propos, par L. Dimier. Paris, 1911.

350 Duchamp-Villon, R. Raymond Duchamp-Villon. [Incl.: Notice biographique, par W. Pach.] Paris, 1924.

351 Friedländer, M. J. Albrecht Dürer. Berlin, 1919.

352 Moore, T. S. Albert Dürer. New York, 1905.

353 Goodrich, L. Thomas Eakins, his life and work. New York, 1933.

354 Powell, L. B. Jacob Epstein. London, 1932.

355 Foote, H. W. Robert Feke. Cambridge, Mass., 1930.
356 Ffoulkes, C. J., and Maiocchi, R. Vincenzo Foppa of Brescia. London, 1909.
357 Taylor, T. Birket Foster's pictures of English landscape, engraved by the Brothers Dalziel. London, 1881.
358 Cox, T. Jehan Foucquet. London, 1931.
359 Graber, H. Piero della Francesca. Basel, 1922.
360 Drinkwater, J., and Rutherston, A. Claud Lovat Fraser. New York, 1923.
361 Lanier, H. W. A. B. Frost, American sportsman artist. New York, 1933.
362 Armstrong, Sir W. Gainsborough, his place in English art. New York, 1906.
363 Mourey, G. Gainsborough. Paris, 1905.
364 Salaman, M. C. Graphic arts of Great Britain; ed. by C. Holme. London, 1917.
365 Becker, B. Paul Gauguin, the calm madman. New York, 1931.
366 George, W. Karl Geiser. Paris, 1932.
367 Leemann-Van Elck, P. Solomon Gessner. Zürich, 1930.
368 Tipping, H. A. Grinling Gibbons. London, 1914.
369 Gill, E. Engravings by Eric Gill. Bristol, 1929.
370 Conway, Sir M. Giorgione; a new study, by M. Conway. London, 1929.
371 Hermanin, F. Il mito di Giorgione. Spoleto, 1933.
372 Gielly, L. Giotto. Paris, 1931.
373 Hausenstein, W. Giotto. Berlin, 1923.
374 De Selincourt, B. Giotto. New York, 1905.
375 Sirén, O. Giotto and some of his followers. Cambridge, Mass., 1931.
376 Du Bois, G. P. William J. Glackens. New York, 1931.
377 Long, B. S. John Glover. London, 1924.
378 Goya y Lucientes, F. J. de. Goya. [Museo del Prado, Madrid.] v. 1. Madrid, 1928.
379 Rothenstein, W. Goya. New York, 1901.
380 Stokes, H. Francisco Goya; a study. New York, 1914.
381 Stokes, H. Benozzo Gozzoli. New York, 1904.
382 Calvert, A. F., and Hartley, C. G. El Greco; an account of his life and works. London, 1909.
383 Theotocopuli, D. (El Greco). Siete reproducciones en color; con una nota preliminar [von] A. L. Mayer; trad. de R. Gomez de Ortega. Leipzig, 1931.
384 Hagen, O. Matthias Grünewald. München, 1920.
385 Caw, J. L. Sir James Guthrie. London, 1932.
386 Grappe, G. Constantin Guys. London, 1908 [?]
387 Baudelaire, C. P. The Painter of Victorian life; a study of Constantin Guys; intro. and trans. of Baudelaire's Peintre de la vie moderne, by P. G. Konody; ed. by C. G. Holme. London, 1931.
388 Kuhn, A. Der Bildhauer Hermann Haller. Zürich, 1927.
389 Dülberg, F. Frans Hals; ein Leben und ein Werk. Berlin, 1930.
390 Hals. (Masters in art.) Boston, 1900.
391 Harding, C. Sketch of Chester Harding; ed. by M. E. White; new ed., by W. P. G. Harding. Boston, 1929. (Also earlier eds.)
392 Haydon, B. R. Autobiography and memoirs; comp. by A. P. D. Penrose. London, 1927; New York, 1929.
393 Thormaehlen, L. Erich Heckel. Berlin, 1931.
394 Graefe, F. Jan Sanders van Hemssen. Leipzig, 1909.
395 Read, H. A. Robert Henri. New York, 1931.
396 Gilbert, J. Memoir of J. F. Herring. London, 1848.
397 Loosli, C. A. Ferdinand Hodler. Paris, 1931.
398 Theile, A., ed. Bernhard Hoetger, von G. Biermann, K. Edschmid, M. Osborn, L. Roselius, A. Theile [und] L. Vauxcelles. Bremen, 1930.
399 Alexandre, A. Malvina Hoffman. Paris, 1930.
400 Dobson, A. William Hogarth. London, 1907.
401 Nichols, J. B. Anecdotes of William Hogarth. London, 1933.
402 Davies, G. S. Hans Holbein the younger. London, 1903.
403 Glaser, C. Hans Holbein der Ältere. Leipzig, 1908.
404 Douce, F. Holbein's Dance of death. London, 1858.
405 Homer, W. Winslow Homer; comp. by N. Pousette-Dart. New York, 1923.
406 Du Bois, G. P. Edward Hopper. London, 1931.
407 Hart, C. H., and Biddle, E. Memoirs of the life and works of Jean Antoine Houdon. Philadelphia, 1911.
408 Field, H. The races of mankind. Chicago, 1933.
409 Rowland, B., Jr. Jaume Huguet. Cambridge, Mass., 1932.
410 Williamson, G. C. Life and works of Ozias Humphry. New York, 1918.
411 Spinden, H. J. Fine art and the first Americans. New York, 1931.
412 Fröhlich-Bume, L. Ingres, his life & art; trans. by M. V. White. London, 1926.
413 Trumble, A. George Inness, N.A. New York, 1895.
414 Basily-Callimaki, Mme. de. J. B. Isabey; sa vie. Paris, 1909.
415 Marriott, C. Augustus John. London, 1917.
416 Dodgson, C. Catalogue of etchings by Augustus John. London, 1920.
417 Grohmann, W. Wassily Kandinsky. Leipzig, 1924.
418 Slusser, J. P. Bernard Karfoil. New York, 1931.
419 Kent, R. Rockwellkentiana. New York, 1933.
420 Grohmann, W. Paul Klee. Paris, 1929.
421 Hausenstein, W. Kairuan oder eine Ge-

schichte vom Maler Klee und von der Kunst dieses Zeitalters. München, 1921.
422 Klimt, G. 25 Handzeichnungen. Wien, 1919.
423 Kollwitz, K. Mappe. Hrsg. vom Kunstwart. München, 1924.
424 Justi, L. George Kolbe. Berlin, 1931.
425 Šafařík, E. Joannes Kuptezky. Prag, 1928.
426 Isay, R. Paul Landowski. Paris, 1932[?].
427 Ronot, H. La démence sénile de Maurice-Quentin de La Tour. Paris, 1932.
428 Leroy, A. A. Maurice-Quentin de La Tour. Paris, 1933.
429 Laurencin, M. Marie Laurencin; préf. par M. Jouhandeau. Paris, 1928.
430 Sparrow, W. S. John Lavery and his work, by W. Shaw-Sparrow; pref. by R. B. C. Graham. London, 1911.
431 Armstrong, Sir W. Lawrence. New York, 1913.
432 Du Bois, G. P. Ernest Lawson. New York, 1932.
433 Frith, W. P. John Leech, his life and work. London, 1891. 2 vols.
434 Waldmann, E. Wilhelm Leibl. Bielefeld, 1930.
435 Coleman, M. Amboise et Léonard de Vinci à Amboise; préf. de P. de Nolhac. Tours, 1932.
436 McCurdy, E. Mind of Leonardo da Vinci. New York, 1928.
437 Vinci, Leonardo da. Les manuscrits de Léonard de Vinci; préf. par C. Ravaisson-Mollien. Paris, 1881-91. 6 vols.
438 Müntz, E. Leonardo da Vinci. London, 1898.
439 Sirén, O. Leonardo da Vinci, the artist and the man. New Haven, 1916.
440 Mauclair, C., *pseud.* Henri Le Sidaner. Paris, 1928.
441 Lewis, M. Martin Lewis; intro. by M. C. Salaman. New York, 1931.
442 Schneider, H. Jan Lievens, sein Leben und seine Werke. Haarlem, 1932.
443 Russow, K. E. Bruno Liljefors. Stockholm, 1929.
444 Story, A. T. Life of John Linnell. London, 1892. 2 vols.
445 Meiss, M. Ugolino Lorenzetti. Chicago, 1931.
446 Beets, N. Lucas de Leyde. Bruxelles, 1913.
447 Cary, E. L. George Luks. New York, 1931.
448 Soupault, P. Jean Lurçat. Paris, 1929.
449 Maeterlinck, L. Le genre satirique dans la peinture flamande. 2e éd. Bruxelles, 1907.
450 Dussler, L. Benedetto da Majano. München, 1924.
451 Mander, K. van. Het leven der doorluchtige Nederlandsche en eenige Hoogdeuitsche schilders, voormaals beyeen-vergaderd en beschreeven door K. van Mander, door wylen J. de Jongh. Amsterdam, 1764.
452 Duret, T. Manet and the French impressionists; trans. by J. E. C. Flitch. Philadelphia, 1910.
453 Rey, R. Edward Manet. Paris, 1932.
454 Manning-Sanders, J. Drawings and paintings; pref. by R. H. Wilenski. New York, 1929.
455 Vitry, P. Paul Manship. Paris, 1927.
456 Mantegna, A. Andrea Mantegna, des meisters Gemälde und Kupperstiche in 200 Abbildungen, hrsg. von F. Knapp. Stuttgart, 1910.
457 Marc, F. Briefe, Aufzeichnungen und Aphorismen. Berlin, 1920.
458 Meier-Graefe, J. Hans von Marées, sein leben und sein werk. München, 1909-10. 3 vols.
459 Marin, J. Letters; intro. by H. J. Seligmann. New York, 1931.
460 Lindberg, H. To the problem of Masolino and Masaccio. Stockholm, 1931. 2 vols. [Swedish text.]
461 Barnes, A. C., and De Mazia, V. Art of Henri-Matisse. New York, 1933.
462 Thorpe, J. Phil May. London, 1932.
463 Buonarroti, M. A., the Elder. Rime di M. B. raccolte da Michelagnolo suo nipote. Firenze, 1623.
464 Holroyd, Sir C. Michael Angelo Buonarroti; with trans. of the life of the master by his scholar, A. Condivi, and three dialogues, by F. d'Ollanda. [2d ed.] London, 1911.
465 Knapp, F. Michelangelo. München, 1922.
466 Steinmann, E., and Wittkower, R. Michelangelo Bibliographie. Leipzig, 1927.
467 Millais, J. G. Life and letters of Sir John Everett Millais. New York, 1899.
468 Burroughs, A. Kenneth Hayes Miller. New York, 1931.
469 Waldmann, E. Edouard Manet. Berlin, 1923.
470 Verneuil, M. P. Carl Milles, sculpteur suédois. Paris, 1929.
471 Puyvelde, L. van. George Minne. Bruxelles, 1930.
472 McBey, J. Etchings and dry points; a catalogue by M. Hardie. London, 1925.
473 Barker, V. Henry Lee McFee. New York, 1931.
474 Marius, G. H. De hollandsche schilderkunst in de negentiende eeuw. 's-Gravenhage, 1920.
475 Voll, K. Work of Hans Memling. [By K. Voll.] New York, 1913.
476 Scalia, N. Antonello da Messino e la pittura in Sicilia. Milano, 1914.
477 Biermann, G. Paula Modersohn mit einem Beitrage "Erinnerungen an Paula Modersohn," von B. Hoetger. Berlin, 1927.
478 Pfannstiel, A. Modigliani; préf. de L. Latourrettes. Paris, 1929.
479 Saintenoy, P. Le statuaire Jan Mone. Bruxelles, 1931.
480 Marie, A. Henry Monnier. Paris, 1931.
481 Wildenstein, G. Un peintre de paysage au XVIIIe siècle. Paris, 1923.
482 Angoulvent, M. Berthe Morisot; préf. de R. Rey. Paris, 1933.
483 Dawe, G. Life of George Morland. London, 1904.
484 Gilbey, Sir W., and Cuming, E. D. George

Morland, his life and works. London, 1907.
485 Vallance, A. William Morris, his art, writings, and public life. New York, 1897.
486 Prime, S. I. Life of Samuel F. B. Morse. New York, 1901.
487 Trowbridge, J. Samuel Finley Breese Morse. Boston, 1901.
488 Calvert, A. F. Murillo. London, 1907.
489 Nolhac, P. de. J. M. Nattier. Paris, 1905.
490 Gwynn, S. Memorials of an eighteenth century painter. London, 1898.
491 Orozco, J. C. José Clemente Orozoco; intro by A. Reed. New York, 1932.
492 Konody, P. G., and Dark, S. Sir William Orpen, artist & man. London, 1932.
493 Schmidt, H. Jürgen Ovens. Kiel, 1920.
494 Hempel, E. Michael Pacher. Wien, 1931.
495 Stein, H. Augustin Pajou. Paris, 1912.
496 Palmer, A. H. Life and letters of Samuel Palmer. London, 1892.
497 Pascin, J. Pascin; préf. de P. Morand. Paris, 1931.
498 Biermann, G. Max Pechstein. Leipzig, 1919.
499 Whitmore, W. H. Notes concerning Peter Pelham. Cambridge, Mass., 1867.
500 Pennell, E. R. Life and letters of Joseph Pennell. Boston, 1929. 2 vols.
501 Bombe, W. Perugino. Stuttgart, 1914.
502 Canuti, F. Il Perugino. Siena, 1931.
503 Uhde, W. Picasso and the French tradition. Paris; New York, 1929.
504 Zervos, C. Picasso (1920-1926). Paris, 1932.
505 Miscattelli, P. La Libreria Piccolomini nel duomo di Siena. Siena, 1922; Engl. trans., by L. E. Hunter, Siena, 1926.
506 Hill, G. F. Pisanello. London, 1905.
507 Venturi, A. Giovanni Pisano, his life and work. New York, 1929.
508 Swarzenski, G. Nicolo Pisano. Frankfurt am Main, 1926.
509 Cruttwell, M. Antonio Pollaiuolo. London, 1907.
510 Pompon, F. François Pompon; notice de R. Brielle. Paris, 1930[?].
511 Clapp, F. M. Jacopo Carucci da Pontormo; forew. by F. J. Mather, Jr. New Haven, Conn., 1916.
512 Friedlaender, W. Nicolas Poussin. München, 1914.
513 Stuart, H. L. W. H. Powell's historical picture of the Mississippi by De Soto. New York, 1854.
514 Breuning, M. Maurice Prendergast. New York, 1931.
515 Roget, J. L. History of the "Old Water-Colour" Society. London, 1891. 2 vols.
516 Barnes, A. C., and Mazia, V. de. Art of Renoir. New York, 1935.
517 Brion, M. Pierre Puget. Paris, 1930.
518 Laran, J. Puvis de Chavannes; study by A. Michel; notes by J. Laran. London, 1912.
519 Raeburn, Sir H. Sir Henry Raeburn, his life and works; with a catalogue of his pictures by J. Greig. London, 1911.
520 Holmes, Sir C. J. Raphael and the modern use of the classical tradition, by Sir C. Holmes. London, 1933.
521 Oppé, A. P. Raphael. London, 1909.
522 Gronau, G., ed. Raffael; mit einer biographischen Einleitung von A. Rosenberg; hrsg. von G. Gronau. Stuttgart, 1909.
523 Müntz, E. Raphael, his life, works, and times. London, 1882.
524 Mellerio, A. Odilon Redon. Paris, 1913.
525 Brown, G. B. Rembrandt. New York, 1907.
526 Dülberg, F. Rembrandt Harmensz van Rijn und sein Werk. Berlin, 1931.
527 Hind, A. M. Catalogue of Rembrandt's etchings. [2d ed.] London, 1923. 2 vols.
528 Meldrum, D. S. Rembrandt's paintings. London, 1923.
529 Van Dyke, J. C. Rembrandt and his school. New York, 1923.
530 Rembrandt van Rijn. Rembrandt's paintings in America, by W. R. Valentiner. New York, 1931.
531 Meier-Graefe, J. Renoir. Leipzig, 1929.
532 Renoir, P. A. Renoir; préf. d'O. Mirbeau. Paris, 1913.
533 Roger-Marx, C. Renoir. Paris, 1933.
534 Vollard, A. Auguste Renoir. Paris, 1920; Eng. tr. by H. L. Van Doren and R. T. Weaver. New York [cop. 1925], 1934.
535 Andrews, W. L. Paul Revere and his engraving. New York, 1901.
536 Goss, E. H. Life of Colonel Paul Revere. Boston, 1891. 2 vols.
537 O'Brien, H. E. Paul Revere's own story. Boston, 1929.
538 Armstrong, Sir W. Sir Joshua Reynolds. New York, 1905.
539 Cotton, W. Sir Joshua Reynolds and his works. London, 1856.
540 Phillips, C. Sir Joshua Reynolds. New York, 1894.
541 Knapp, F. Tilman Riemenschneider. 2. Aufl. Paderborn, 1931.
542 Mayer, A. L. Jusepe de Ribera (Lo Spagnoletto). Leipzig, 1923.
543 Fourcaud, L. de. Théodule Ribot. Paris, 1885.
544 Ricketts, C. Charles Ricketts; intro. by T. S. Moore. London, 1933.
545 Rivera, D. Frescoes; pref. by E. Evans. New York, 1933.
546 Marquand, A. Luca della Robbia. Princeton, N. J., 1914
547 Cladel, J. Rodin, the man and his art; trans. by S. K. Star; intro. by J. Huneker.
548 Riotor, L. Rodin. Paris, 1927.
549 Nolhac, P. de. Hubert Robert. Paris, 1910.
550 Florentin, L. Théophile Robert. Neuchâtel, 1933.
551 Ward, T. H., and Roberts, W. Romney. New York, 1904. 2 vols.
552 Rousseau, H. J. Henri Rousseau; étude critique par A. Basler. Paris, 1929.
553 Gottschalk, H. Antonio Rossellino. Berlin, 1830.
554 Marillier, H. C. Dante Gabriel Rossetti; 2d ed., rev. New York, 1901.

555 Rothenstein, W. Portrait drawings of William Rothenstein, 1889-1925, an iconography by J. Rothenstein; pref. by M. Beerbohm. London, 1926; New York, 1927.
556 Oppé, A. P. Thomas Rowlandson. London, 1923.
557 Bertram, A. Life of Sir Peter-Paul Rubens. London, 1928; New York, 1929.
558 Fierens, P. Rubens. Paris, 1931.
559 Michel, É. Rubens, his life, his work, and his times. New York, 1899.
560 Rooses, M. L'oeuvre de P. P. Rubens. Anvers, 1886-92. 5 vols.
561 Sanisbury, W. N. Original unpublished papers illustrative of the life of Sir Peter Paul Rubens. London, 1859.
562 Rude, F. François Rude; notice de A. H. Martinie. Paris, 1930[?].
563 Rosenberg, J. Jacob van Ruisdael. Berlin, 1928.
564 Simon, K. E. Jacob van Ruisdael. Berlin, 1930.
565 Collingwood, W. G. Life and work of John Ruskin. Boston, 1893. 2 vols.
566 Wilenski, R. H. John Ruskin; an introduction. London, 1933.
567 Price, F. N. Ryder (1847-1917). New York, 1932.
568 Esdaile, Mrs. Arundell. The art of John Michael Rysbrack. London, 1932
569 Erasmus, K. Roelant Savery. Salle a. S., 1908.
570 Wellisz, L. Les amis romantiques; Ary Scheffer et ses amis polonais; précédé d'une étude de G. Sarrazin. Paris, 1933.
571 Goodrich, L. H. E. Schnakenberg. New York, 1931.
572 Schongauer, M. Descriptive catalogue of an exhibition of engravings; intro. by R. Ederheimer. New York, 1911.
573 Segantini, G. Giovanni Segantini. Milan, 1925.
574 Seurat, G. P. Georges Seurat. [Text in Fr.], by A. Lhote. Rome, 1922.
575 Maritain, J. Severini. Paris, 1930.
576 Cole, R. V. Art & life of Byam Shaw. Philadelphia, 1932.
577 Knox, K. M. The Sharples, their portraits of George Washington and his contemporaries. New Haven, Conn., 1930.
578 Armitage, H. Henrietta Shore; an article by E. Weston; appraised by R. Poland. New York, 1933.
579 Auroil, G. Steinlen. Paris, 1930.
580 Loos, V. Carl Skånberg; hans liv och verk. Norrköping, 1928.
581 Kurth, J. Sharaku. München, 1922.
582 Du Bois, G. P. John Sloan. New York, 1931.
583 Troescher, G. Claus Sluter. [1. Bd.] Freiburg im Breisgau, 1932.
584 Bosch, E. van den. Jakob Smits. Antwerp, 1930.
585 Mather, F. J., Jr. Eugene Speicher. New York, 1931.
586 Lecomte, G. Steinlen. Chats et autres bêtes. Paris, 1933.
587 Flint, R. Albert Sterner. New York, 1927.
588 James, H. William Wetmore Story. Boston, 1903.
589 Coxhead, A. C. Thomas Stothard. London, 1906.
590 Eisen, G. A. Portraits of Washington. New York, 1932. 3 vols.
591 Gilbey, Sir W. Life of George Stubbs. London, 1898.
592 Hellens, F. Gérard Terborch. Bruxelles, 1911.
593 Rosenberg, A. Thorwaldsen. Bielefeld, 1896.
594 Oppermann, T. Thorvaldsen. Kjøbenhavn, 1930.
595 Tiepolo, G. B. Drawings, by D. baron von Hadeln. Paris, 1928. 2 vols.
596 Sack, E. Giambattista und Domenico Tiepolo. Hamburg, 1910.
597 Bercken, E. von der, and Mayer, A. L. Jacopo Tintoretto. München, 1923. 2 vols.
598 Duret, T. Lautrec. Paris, 1920.
599 Wiles, B. H. Tribolo in his Michelangelesque vein. Chicago, 1932.
600 Levinger, M. Félix Trutat. Paris, 1932.
601 White, H. C. The life and art of Dwight William Tryon. Boston, 1930.
602 Watson, F. Allen Tucker. New York, 1932.
603 Babelon, J. Germain Pilon. Paris, 1927.
604 Turner, J. M. W. Autotype reproductions. The Liber Studiorum. Ed. by S. Brooke. London, 1882.
605 Tucker, A. John H. Twachtman. New York, 1931.
606 Utrillo, M. Maurice Utrillo; notice de F. Fels. Paris, 1930.
607 Tabarant, A. Utrillo. Paris, 1926.
608 Renders, É., and others. Hubert van Eyck, par É. Renders, avec la collaboration de J. de Smet et R. De Pauw. Bruges, Belg., 1933.
609 Weale, W. H. J. The Van Eycks and their art, by W. H. J. Weale, with the co-operation of M. W. Brockwell. London, 1912.
610 Schmarsow, A. Hubert und Jan van Eyck. Leipzig, 1924.
611 Weale, F. C Hubert & John van Eyck. London, 1903.
612 Meier-Graefe, J. Vincent Van Gogh; trans. by J. Holroyd-Reece. New York, 1933.
613 Coquiot, G. Vincent Van Gogh. Paris, 1923.
614 Spahn, A. Palma Vecchio. Leipzig, 1932.
615 Armstrong, Sir W. Art of Velasquez. London, 1896.
616 Stevenson, R. A. M. Velasquez. London, 1906.
617 Lucas, E. V. Vermeer of Delft; intro. by Sir C. J. Holmes. 2d ed. London, 1922.
618 Westphal, D. Bonifazio Veronese. München, 1931.
619 Fiocco, G. Paolo Veronese und Farinati. Wien, 1926.
620 [Wilder, E.] The unfinished monument by

Andrea del Verrocchio to the Cardinal Niccolo Forteguerri at Pistoia. [Florence, 1932.]
621 Cruttwell, M. Verrochio, London, 1904.
622 Nolhac, P. de. Madame Vigée-Le Brun. Paris, 1912.
623 Adams, A. John Quincy Adams Ward. New York, 1912.
624 Watteau, A. Handzeichnungen; notizen hrsg. von C. Gurlitt. Berlin, 1909.
625 Parker, K. T. The drawings of Antoine Watteau. London, 1931.
626 Carson, H. L. Life and works of Benjamin West. Philadelphia, 1922[?].
627 West, L. Catalogue of etchings of Levon West; comp. by O. M. Torrington; intro. by E. L. West, New York, 1930.
628 Lafond, P. Roger van der Weyden. Bruxelles, 1912.
629 Burroughs, A. Campin and van der Weyden again. (Metropolitan Museum studies. New York, 1933. v. 4, p. 131-150.)
630 Cary, E. L. Works of James McNeill Whistler. New York, 1907.
631 Simpson, A. L. Story of Sir David Wilkie. New York, 1879.
632 Ord, G. Sketch of the life of Alexander Wilson. Philadelphia, 1828.
633 Manners, Lady V., and Williamson, G. C. John Zoffany, R.A., his life and works. London, 1920.
634 Bénédite, L. Ignacio Zuloaga. Paris, 1912.
635 Kehrer, H. Francisco de Zurburán. München, 1918.
636 Audubon, J. J. Life of John James Audubon. [Ed. by Mrs. L. B. Audubon.] New York, 1869.
637 Brinton, S. Bartolozzi and his pupils in England. London, 1904.
638 Benton, T. The arts of life in America; a series of murals. [Whitney Museum of American Art.] New York, 1932.
639 Schevill, F. Karl Bitter. Chicago, 1917.
640 Brion, M. Botticelli. Mulhouse-Dornach; Paris, 1932.
641 Bourdery, L., and Lachenaud E. Léonard Limosin. Paris, 1897.
642 Léger, C. Antoine Bourdelle. Paris, 1930.
643 Turner, J. M. W. J. M. W. Turner; intro. by G. S. Sandilands. London, 1928.
644 Delacroix, E. Eugène Delacroix; Zeichnungen, Aquarelle und Pastelle. Text von C. Baudelaire und H. Graber. Basel, 1929.
645 Whitmore, W. H. Abel Bowen, engraver. Boston, 1884.
646 Bril, P. Studien zur Entwicklungsgeschichte der Landschaftsmalerei um 1600. (Von R. Baer.) München, 1930.
647 Delteil, L. Meryon. Paris, 1927; Eng. tr. by G. J. Renier. New York, 1928.
648 Bergmans, S. Catalogue critique des oeuvres de peintre Denis Calvert. Bruxelles, 1931.
649 Destrée, J. Le Maître dit de Flemallé. [Campin R.] Brussels, 1930.
650 Meyer, A. G. Canova. Leipzig, 1898.
651 Connor, R. D. W. Canova's statue of Washington. Raleigh, N. C., 1910.
652 Canova, A. Works; biographical memoir by Count Cicognara. London, 1876.
653 Holland, J. Memorials of Sir Francis Chantrey. London, 1851.
654 Claudel, P. Jean Charlot. 3. éd. Paris, 1933.
655 Courthion, P. Claude Gellée dit le Lorrain. Paris, 1932.
656 Bradley, J. W. Life and works of Giorgio Giulio Clovio. London, 1891.
657 Steinbart, K. Die Tafelgemälde des Jakob Cornelisz. Strassburg, 1922.
658 Bell, C. F. John Sell Cotman. London, 1926.
659 Aubert, L. F. Peintures de Charles Cottet; préf. de L. F. Aubert. Paris, 1928.
660 Keller-Dorian, G. Antoine Coysevox; catalogue raisonné de son œuvre; intro. par P. Vitry. Paris, 1920.
661 Zimmermann, H. Lukas Cranach, der Ältere. Halle a. Sa., 1929.
662 Friedländer, M. J. Die altniederländische Malerei. 9 Bd.: Joos van Cleve; Jan Provost; Joachim Patenier. Berlin, 1931.
663 Hardie, M., and Clayton, M. Thomas William Daniell. (Walker's Quarterly. London, 1932. no. 35/36, p. 1-106.)
664 Schubring, P. Work of Donatello. New York, 1913.
665 Pigler, A. Georg Raphael Donner. (Aus dem Ungarischen von J. Fleischer.) Wien, 1929.
666 Coad, O. S. William Dunlap. New York, 1917.
667 Delarue, H. Albert Durer. Geniève, 1921.
668 Ensor, J. James Ensor, von P. Colin. Berlin, 1931.
669 Poland, W. C. Robert Feke. Providence, R. I., 1907.
670 Quenzel, K. Der Maler Feuerbach. Leipzig, 1919.
671 Feuerbach, A. F. Feuerbach; beschreibender Katalog seiner sämtlichen Gemälde, von H. Uhde-Bernays. München, 1929.
672 Adams, A. Daniel Chester French. Boston, 1932.
673 Reigart, J. F. Life of Robert Fulton. Philadelphia, 1856.
674 Green, S. A. John Foster. Boston, 1909.
675 Vallon, F. Falconet. Paris, 1927.
676 Amiet, C. Cuno Amiet, par G. Charensol. Paris, 1932.
677 Plan, D. A. Constantin. Genève, 1930.
678 Leclerc, M. Une artiste angevine: Louise Desbordes-Jouas. Angers, 1927.
679 Mauclair, C., *pseud.* Marie Duhem, Rémy Duhem. Hommage. Paris, 1924[?].
680 Willoch, S. Maleren Thomas Fearnley. Oslo, 1932.
681 Giacometti, A. Augusto Giacometti, par G. Charensol. Paris, 1932.
682 Hubacher, H. Hermann Hubacher, par P. Fierens. Paris, 1932.
683 Scandinavian art; illustrated [by] C. Lauren, E. Hannover, J. Thiis; intro. by C. Brinton. New York, 1922.

684 Fischer, O. Karl Knappe. Augsburg, 1929.
685 Marque, A. Albert Marque; notice de G. Chérau. Paris, 1930[?].
686 Rivière, G. Cézanne, le peintre solitaire. Paris, 1933.
687 Fierens, P. Henry Parayre. Paris, 1927.
688 Brigham, C. S. John Rogers' Groups. Boston, 1934.
689 Milman, L. Sir Christopher Wren. New York, 1908.
690 Blacker, J. F. The ABC of Indian art. London, 1922.
691 Hartley, M. Adventures in the arts. New York, 1921.
692 Frobenius, L. Madsimu Dsangara. Südafrikanische Felsbilderchronik. Berlin, 1931-32. 2 vols.
693 Jackman, R. E. American arts. New York, 1928.
694 Narodny, I. American artists. New York, 1930.
695 Museum of Modern Art, New York. American painting & sculpture. [Includes "American art," by H. Cahill.] New York, 1932.
696 Museum of Modern Art, New York. American sources of modern art. New York, 1933.
697 Gallatin, A. E. American water-colourists. New York, 1922.
698 Baessler, A. Ancient Peruvian art; trans. by A. H. Keane. New York, 1902-03. 4 vols.
699 Cumberland, R. Anecdotes of eminent painters of Spain. London, 1782. 2 vols.
700 Bulliet, C. J. Apples & madonnas. New ed. New York, 1934.
701 La Follette, S. Art in America. New York, 1934.
702 Baker, C. H. C. Lely & the Stuart portrait painters. London, 1912.
703 Parkes, K. Art of carved sculpture. London, 1931. 2 vols.
704 Bulley, M. H. Art and counterfeit. London, 1925.
705 Maspero, G. Art in Egypt. New York, 1912.
706 Ross, Sir E. D. Art in Egypt through the ages. New York, 1931.
707 Grimsditch, H. B. William Hogarth. London, 1926.
708 Hourticq, L. Everyone's history of French art; trans. by M. Herbert. Paris, 1919.
709 Carls, C. D. Ernst Barlach. Berlin, 1931.
710 Horne, C. F. Great men and famous women. New York, 1894. 4 vols.
711 Armstrong, Sir W. Art in Great Britain and Ireland. New York, 1909.
712 Ridder, A. de, and Deonna, W. Art in Greece. New York, 1927.
713 Robinson, R. Thomas Bewick; his life and times. Newcastle, 1887.
714 Walters, H. B. Art of the Greeks. 3d ed. New York, 1934.
715 Mühlestein, H. Ferdinand Hodler. Weimar, 1914.
716 Ricci, C. Art in Northern Italy. New York, 1911.
717 Strong, E. Art in ancient Rome. New York, 1928. 2 vols.
718 Walters, H. B. Art of the Romans. New York, 1911.
719 Dieulafoy, M. Art in Spain and Portugal. New York, 1913.
720 Art studies, medieval, renaissance and modern. v. 1-8, no. 2. Princeton, N. J., 1923-31. 8 vols.
721 Gardner, H. Art through the ages. New York, 1926.
722 Blanc, C. Histoire des peintres de toutes les écoles. Paris, 1861-76. 14 vols.
723 McKay, W., and Roberts, W. John Hoppner, R. A. London, 1909; Supplement and index. London, 1914.
724 James, E. E. C. Bologna: its history, antiquities, and art. London, 1909.
725 Menpes, M. Gainsborough; text by J. Greig. London, 1909.
726 Holme, C. G. British marine painting; with articles by A. L. Baldry; ed. by G. Holme. London, 1919.
727 Baker, C. H. C. British painting; with a chapter on primitive painting by M. R. James. London, 1933.
728 Sparrow, W. S. Book of sporting painters. New York, 1931.
729 Mengin, U. Benozzo Gozzoli. Paris, 1909.
730 Robson, A. H. Canadian landscape painters. Toronto, 1932.
731 Bushell, S. W. Chinese art. London, 1906-07. 2 vols.
732 Giles, H. A. Chinese biographical dictionary. Fasc. 1-2. London, 1898.
733 Meyer, A. E. Chinese painting. [2d ed.] New York, 1923.
734 Waley, A. Introduction to the study of Chinese painting. London, 1923.
735 Siltzer, F. Story of British sporting prints. London, 1929.
736 Eddy, A. J. Cubists and post-impressionism. Rev. ed. Chicago, 1919.
737 Matějček, A., and Wirth, Z. Modern and contemporary Czech art. London, 1924.
738 Flint, W. R. W. Russell Flint; intro. by G. S. Sandilands. London, 1928.
739 Hourticq, L. Hollande. Paris, 1932.
740 Lees, F. The art of the great masters exemplified by drawings in the collection of Emile Wauters. Boston, 1913.
741 Stokes, M. Early Christian art in Ireland. London, 1887.
742 British Museum. Catalogue of early German and Flemish woodcuts. London, 1903-11. 2 vols.
743 Dalton, O. M. East Christian art. Oxford, 1925.
744 Worringer, W. Egyptian art; ed. by B. Rackham. London, 1928.
745 Grundy, C. R. English art in the XVIII century. London, 1928.
746 Gardner, S. English Gothic foliage sculpture. Cambridge, Eng., 1927.
747 Baker, C. H. C., and Constable, W. G. English painting in the sixteenth and seventeenth centuries. Firenze, 1930[?].
748 Mather, F. J., Jr. Estimates in art. New York, 1931.

749 Hamerton, P. G. Etching and etchers. Boston, 1902.
750 Royal Academy of Arts, London. Commemorative catalogue of an exhibition of Italian art held in the galleries of the Royal Academy, Burlington House, London, 1930. Edited by Lord Balniel and K. Clark in consultation with E. Madigliani. Oxford, 1931. 2 vols.
751 Hind, A. M. History of engraving and etching. London, 1929.
752 Bonington, R. P. Richard Parkes Bonington; intro. by G. S. Sandilands. London, 1929.
753 Mourey, G. French art in the XIX century. London, 1928.
754 Dilke, E. F. (S.)., Lady. French painters of the XVIIIth century. London, 1899.
755 Dimier, L. French painting of the sixteenth century. New York, 1904.
756 Macfall, H. The French pastellists of the eighteenth century. London, 1909.
757 Friends of American Art. Yearbook. No. 1-5. (1910/11-1914/15.) Chicago, 1911-15. 5 vols.
758 Wildenstein, G. Chardin: Biographie et catalogue critique. Paris, 1933.
759 Heidrich, E. Die altdeutsche Malerei. Jena, 1909.
760 Hoffman, W. J. Graphic art of the Eskimos. Washington, D. C., 1897.
761 Michel, É. Great masters of landscape painting. Philadelphia, 1910.
762 Abbot, E. R. Great painters. New York, 1927.
763 Fleury, J. Histoire de la caricature, par Champfleury. 3. éd. Paris, 1879.
764 Murrell, W. History of American graphic humor; forew. by C. Morley. New York, 1933-34. 2 vols.
765 Cundall, H. M. History of British water colour painting; forew. by Sir H. Hughes-Stanton. 2d ed., rev. London, 1929.
766 History of design in mural painting; intro. by N. H. J. Westlake. London, 1902-05. 2 vols.
767 Sirén, O. History of early Chinese painting. London, 1933.
768 Post, C. R. History of European and American sculpture. Cambridge, Mass., 1921.
769 Seidlitz, W. von. History of Japanese colour-prints. Philadelphia, 1910.
770 Mather, F. J., Jr. History of Italian painting. New York, 1923.
771 Crowe, J. A., and Cavalcaselle, G. B. History of painting in Italy; ed. by E. Hutton. New York, 1908-09. 3 vols.
772 Douglas, L. History of Siena. London, 1902.
773 Jackson, E. N. History of silhouettes. London, 1911.
774 Post, C. R. History of Spanish painting. Cambridge, Mass., 1930-34. 5 vols.
775 Justi, L. Von Corinth bis Klee. Berlin, 1931.
776 Sheldon, G. W. Hours with art and artists. New York, 1882.
777 Havell, E. B. Ideals of Indian art. London, 1920.
778 Spurrier, S. Illustration. London, 1933.
779 College Art Association: Research Institute. Index of twentieth century artists. (Oct., 1933-June, 1935.) New York, 1933-35.
780 Pope, A. U. Introduction to Persian art. New York, 1931.
781 Cortissoz, R. Art and common sense. New York, 1913.
782 Morelli, G. Italian painters. London, 1892-93. 2 vols.
783 Craven, T. Modern art. New York, 1934.
784 Venturi, L. Pitture italiane in America. Milano, 1931. 2 vols.
785 Lawrence, A. W. Later Greek sculpture. London, 1927.
786 Morgan, J. H., and Fielding, M. Life portraits of Washington. Philadelphia, 1931.
787 Cunningham, A. Lives of the most eminent British painters; rev. ed. [With life of A. Cunningham, by Mrs. C. Heaton] London, 1879-80. 3 vols.
788 Brown, F. P. London paintings. London, 1933.
789 Lethaby, W. R. Mediæval art. New York, 1904.
790 Craven, T. Men of art. New York, 1931; London, 1933.
791 Brenner, A. Idols behind altars. New York, 1929.
792 Furtwängler, A. Masterpieces of Greek sculpture; ed. by E. Sellers. London, 1895.
793 Masters of English landscape painting; ed. by C. Holme. London, 1903. (Studio, v. 29, special summer number.)
794 Joyce, T. A. Maya & Mexican art. London, 1927.
795 Boehn, M. von. Miniatures and silhouettes; trans. by E. K. Walker. London, 1928.
796 Aumonier, W. Modern architectural sculpture. New York, 1930.
797 Raynal, M. Modern French painters. New York, 1928.
798 Maryon, H. Modern sculpture. London, 1933.
799 Jackson, F. H. Mural painting. London, 1904.
800 Blochet, E. Musulman painting, XIIth-XVIIth century. London, 1929.
801 Singer, H. W. Stories of the German artists. London, 1911.
802 Cole, T. Old English masters. New York, 1902.
803 Reitlinger, H. S. Old master drawings. London, 1922.
804 Holmes, Sir C. J. Old masters and modern art, by Sir C. Holmes. New York, 1924.
805 Cole, T. Old Spanish masters; historical notes by C. H. Caffin. New York, 1907.
806 Orpen, Sir W. Outline of art. New York, 1923-24. 2 vols.
807 Pattison, J. W. Painters since Leonardo. Chicago, 1904.
808 Binyon, L., and others. Persian miniature painting, including a critical and descriptive catalogue of the miniatures exhibited at Burlington House, 1931; by L. Binyon, J. V. S. Wilkinson, and B. Gray. London, 1933.

809 Cheney, S. Primer of modern art. New York, 1924.
810 Carrington, F. Prints and their makers, by Fitz Roy Carrington. New York, 1912.
811 Rutter, F. Evolution in modern art. New York, 1926.
812 McKay, W. D. Scottish school of painting. New York, 1906.
813 Rindge, A. M. Sculpture. New York, 1929.
814 Marcel-Reymond, C. La sculpture italienne. Paris, 1927.
815 Parkes, K. Sculpture of to-day. London, 1921. 2 vols.
816 Davies, R. Six centuries of painting. New York, 1914.
817 Gardner, E. A. Six Greek sculptors. London, 1910.
818 Wedmore, F. Some of the moderns. London, 1909.
819 Metropolitan Museum of Art, New York. Catalogue of an exhibition of Spanish paintings. New York, 1928.
820 Bell, C. Landmarks in nineteenth-century painting. New York, 1927.
821 Adams, A. Spirit of American sculpture. New York, 1923.
822 Chandler, A. C. Story-lives of the master artists. New York, 1933.
823 Caffin, C. H. Story of Spanish painting. New York, 1910.
824 Roosval, J. Swedish art. Princeton, N. J., 1932.
825 Duveen, Sir J. Thirty years of British art; intro. by Sir M. Conway. New York, 1930.
826 Irwin, G. Trail-blazers of American art. New York, 1930.
827 Bell, C. Since Cézanne. New York, 1922.
828 Sparrow, W. S. Women painters of the world. New York, 1905.
829 Clement, C. E. Women in the fine arts. Boston, 1904.
830 Asplund, K. Anders Zorn; his life and work; ed. by G. Holme. London, 1921.
831 Bell, C. Account of French paintings. New York, 1932.
832 Harris, S. H. Art of H. Anglada-Camarasa. London, 1929.
833 Parker, L. Art and people. Toronto, 1934.
834 Block, M. Francois Boucher and the Beauvais tapestries. Boston, 1933.
835 Mumford, L. The Brown Decades. New York, 1931.
836 Hall, L. A. Catalogue of dramatic portraits. [Harvard University Library Theatre Collection.] Cambridge, Mass., 1930-34.
837 Manson, J. B. Life and work of Edgar Degas. London, 1927.
838 Sherman, F. F. Early American painting. New York, 1932.
839 Lee, C. Early American portrait painters. New Haven, Conn., 1929.
840 Sherman, F. F. Early American portraiture. New York, 1930.
841 Murray, M. A. Egyptian sculpture; pref. by E. A. Gardner. London, 1930.
842 Morse, H. K. Elizabethan pageantry. London, 1934.
843 Hoeber, A. Barbizon painters. New York, 1915.
844 Binyon, L. English water-colours. London, 1933.
845 Holme, C. G. Favourite British paintings; intro. by A. Bertram. London, 1934.
846 Wiles, B. H. Fountains of Florentine sculptors. Cambridge, Mass., 1934.
847 Wilenski, R. H. French painting. London, 1931.
848 McComb, A. Agnolo Bronzino. Cambridge, Mass., 1928.
849 Michel, A. Histoire de l'art. Paris, 1905-1929. 13 vols. in 17.
850 Cotterill, H. B. History of art. New York, 1922-23. 2 vols.
851 Kramrisch, S. Indian sculpture. Calcutta; London, 1933.
852 Kunstwissenschaftliche Forschungen. [Hrsg. von] O. Pächt. Bd. 1-2. (1931-33.) Berlin, 1931-33.
853 Bax, C. Leonardo da Vinci. London, 1932.
854 Lemoisne, P. A. Gavarni. Paris, 1924-28. 2 vols.
855 Wilenski, R. H. Meaning of modern sculpture. London, 1932.
856 Gerstenberg, K. Hans Multscher. Leipzig, 1928.
857 Lászaló de Lombos, P. A. Painting a portrait; recorded by A. L. Baldry. London, 1934.
858 Clarke, T. B. Portraits by American artists, exhibited at the Philadelphia Museum of Art. Philadelphia, 1928.
859 Fry, R. Giovanni Bellini, by R. E. Fry. London, 1899.
860 Bucklin, C. Nebraska art and artists. Lincoln, Neb., 1932.
861 Eglinton, G. Reaching for art. Boston, 1931.
862 Laurie, A. P. Brush work of Rembrandt and his school. Oxford, 1932.
863 Reynolds, Sir J. Letters; ed. by F. W. Hilles. Cambridge, Eng., 1930.
864 Underwood, E. G. Short history of English sculpture. London, 1933.
865 Underwood, E. G. Short history of French painting. London, 1931.
866 Papini, G. Ardengo Soffici. Milano, 1933.
867 Pach, W. Masters of modern art. New York, 1924.
868 Mann, H. Technique of portrait painting. London, 1933.
869 Davidson, M. Understanding modern art. New York, 1931.
870 Rothenstein, J. Nineteenth-century painting. London, 1932.
871 Marriott, C. Modern movements in painting. New York, 1920.
872 Montmorency, M. F. de. Short history of painting in England. London, 1933.
873 Westwood, H. R. Modern caricaturists. London, 1932.
874 Breuning, M. Exploring New York's art galleries. New York, 1928.
875 Faure, É. History of art; trans. by W. Pach. New York, 1921-30. 5 vols.

876 Furst, H. Art of still-life painting. New York, 1927.
877 Gardner, E. A. Art of Greece. London, 1925.
878 Gerwig, H. Fifty famous painters. New York, 1926.
879 Smith, S. C. K. Outline history of painting in Europe. Boston, 1928.
880 Slater, J. H. Engravings and their value. 6th ed. New York, 1929.
881 Aldin, C. C. W. Time I was dead. New York, 1934.
882 Bliss, D. P. History of wood-engraving. New York, 1928.
883 Capart, J. Egyptian art; tr. by W. R. Dawson. London, 1923.
884 Casson, S. Some modern sculptors. London, 1928.
885 Casson, S. XXth century sculptors. London, 1930.
886 Clayton, M. Print collector. New York, 1930.
887 Clutton-Brock, A. F. Introduction to French painting. London, 1932.
888 Cohn, W. Chinese art. New York, 1930.
889 Colnaghi, Sir D. E. Dictionary of Florentine painters; ed. by P. G. Konody and S. Brinton. London, 1928.
890 Fry, R. Flemish art. New York, 1927.
891 Grosse, E. Beginnings of art. New York, 1928.
892 Landgren, M. E. Towards romanticism. New York, 1934.
893 MacTavish, N. Fine arts in Canada. Toronto, 1925.
894 Munro, T. Great pictures of Europe. New York, 1930.
895 Newmarch, R. Russian arts. New York, 1916.
896 Poore, H. R. Modern art. New York, 1931.
897 Reinach, S. Apollo. New York, 1924.
898 Tonks, O. S. History of Italian painting. New York, 1927.
899 Short, E. H. The painter in history. London, 1929.
900 Neville, R. French prints of the 19th century. London, 1908.
901 Wilenski, R. H. Introduction to Dutch art. London, 1929.
902 Bode, W. von. Great masters of Dutch and Flemish painting; tr. by M. L. Clarke. New York, 1928.
903 Valentiner, W. R. The art of the Low Countries. New York, 1914.
904 Read, H. Art now. New York, 1934.
905 Edgell, G. H. History of Sienese painting. New York, 1932.
906 Price, F. N. Eric Hudson (1864-1932). New York, 1934.
907 Ticknor, C. May Alcott. Boston, 1934.
908 Rivera, D. Portrait of America; explanatory text by B. D. Wolfe. New York, 1934.
909 Fry, R. Reflections on British painting. London, 1934.
910 Smart, B. Technique of seascape painting; forew. by J. Olsson. New York, 1934.
911 Simonson, L. Theatre art. London, 1934.
912 Almanac [of] Russian artists in America. v. 1. [Eds.: N. Martinoff and M. A. Stern.] New York, 1932.
913 Muratoff, P. Fra Angelico; trans. by E. Law-Gisiko. London, 1930.
914 Anesaki, M. Art life, and nature in Japan. New York, 1933.
915 Preyer, D. C., and Adlow, D. Art of the Metropolitan Museum of New York. New ed. Boston, 1933.
916 Hay, G. Bellini. London, 1908.
917 Brooks, A. M. From Holbein to Whistler; notes by A. M. Brooks. New Haven, Conn., 1920.
918 Crastre, F. Rosa Bonheur. Paris, 1912; trans. by F. T. Cooper. New York, 1913.
919 Ferguson, J. C. Chinese painting. Chicago, 1927.
920 Ricci, C. Correggio. New York, 1930.
921 Hay, G. Carlo Dolci. London, 1908.
922 Johnson, C. English painting from the seventh century to the present day. London, 1932.
923 Carrington, F. Engravers and etchers. Chicago, 1917.
924 Hogarth, W. The works of William Hogarth; with an essay by C. Lamb. London, 1872. 2 vols.
925 Beaume, G. Fromentin; trans. by F. T. Cooper. New York, 1913.
926 Alexandre. A. Paul Gauguin. Paris, 1930.
927 Keim, A. Gérôme. Paris, 1911.
928 Greenaway, K Kate Greenaway pictures; with an appreciation by H. M. Cundall. New York, 1921.
929 Bode, W. von. Frans Hals. Hrsg. von W. von Bode; text von M. J. Binder. Berlin, 1914.
930 Moes, E. W. Frans Hals (trad. par J. de Bosschere). Bruxelles, 1909.
931 Morice, C. Paul Gauguin. Paris, 1919.
932 McSpadden, J. W. Famous sculptors of America. New York, 1924.
933 Coleridge, M. E. Holman Hunt. New York, 1908.
934 Waley, A. Index of Chinese artists represented . . . in the British Museum. London, 1922.
935 Rooses, M. Jacob Jordaens. New York, 1908.
936 Armitage, M. Rockwell Kent. New York, 1932.
937 Lehmbruck, W. Wilhelm Lehmbruck, von A. Hoff. Berlin, 1933.
938 Baldry, A. L. Leighton. New York, 1908.
939 Crastre, F. Bastien-Lepage. Paris, 1913; trans. by F. T. Cooper. New York, 1914.
940 Brown, F. P. London sculpture. London, 1934.
941 Valentiner, W. R. Nicolaes Maes. Stuttgart, 1924.
942 Barbusse, H. Meissonier. New York, 1912.
943 Cartwright, J. Jean François Millet. London, 1910.
944 Turner, P. M. Millet. London, 1934.
945 Hymans, H. Antonio Moro. Bruxelles, 1910.

946 Paris, W. F. Personalities in American art. New York, 1930.
947 Carstairs, C. Postscript to criticism. London, 1934.
948 Cecchi, E. Trecentisti senesi. Roma [1928]; also Fr. tr., Paris, 1928.
949 Poore, H. R. Thinking straight on modern art. New York, 1934.
950 Bensusan, S. L. Titian. London, 1909.
951 Turner, P. M. Van Dyck. London, 1934.
952 Staley, E. Watteau and his school. London, 1902.
953 Hare, W. L. Watts. New York, 1910 [?]
954 Benoit, F. Blake le visionnaire. Lille, 1906.
955 Calvert, A. F. Goya. London, 1908.
956 Mayer, A. L. Francisco de Goya; trans. by R. West. London, 1924.
957 Glassgold, C. A. Glenn O. Coleman. New York, 1933.

AUTHORS' INDEX TO SOURCES OF BIOGRAPHICAL INFORMATION

Numbers refer to volumes of biographical and critical data; letters to general reference works.

A

B

D

E

F

N

O

P

T

U

V

W

Y

Z

INDEX OF ARTISTS

(Painter unless stated otherwise in ( ) following name.)

AA, Dirk van der.
Dut. The Hague, 1731-1809. B-T.
AA, Hildebrand van der. (Eg.)
Dut. Leyden 1659/60-1722 Batavia, Java. B-T.
AACHEN, Johann von. *see* Achen, J.
AADNÄS, Peder Pedersen.
Nor. 1739-1792. B-T.
AAGAARD, Carl Frederic.
Dan. Odense 1833-1895 Copenhagen. B-C-T.
AALST, Willem van. *see* Aelst, W. van.
AARESTRUP, Marie Helene.
Nor. b. Flekkefjord 1829; ac. 1856 Paris. C.
AARON, [Mrs.] May Todd.
Am. b. La Celle, Ia.; ad. 1934 Pawhuska, Okla. A.
AARTSEN, Pieter. *see* Aertsz, P.
AARTZOON, Lambert Ryck. *see* Aerts, L. R.
ABACCO, Antonio dall'.
It. Verceilli 1495-1559. T-V.
ABAISE [or da Baisio], Tommasino (S).
It. d. 1423 Ferrara. B-T.
ABA-NOVÁK, Vilmos.
Hun. b. Hungary 1894; ex. 1934 London. M.
ABARCA, Maria de.
Sp. d. 1656 Madrid. B-T.
ABATE, Ciccio L'. *see* Solimena, F.
ABATE, Ercole dell'. *see* Abbate, E. dell'.
ABATE [or dell' Abbato], Niccolò dell.
It. Modena 1512-1570/1 Paris. B-C-E-T-V-722.
ABATI [or Abbati], Pietro Giovanni.
It. ac. 1700-1733. B-T.
ABBAL, André.
Fr. b. Montech 1876. DBA.
ABBASI, Riza.
Pers. ac. 17th century in Persia. M.
ABBATE [or Abate or Abati], Ercole dell'.
It. Modena 1563-1613. C.
ABBATE, Paolo Salvatore. (S)
Am. b. Italy 1884; ad. 1934 New York. A-Cs-F-Hs-W.
ABBATI, Giuseppe [di Vincenzo].
It. Naples 1836-1868 Florence. B-T.
ABBATI, Pietro Giovanni. *see* Abati, P. G.
ABBATO, Niccolò dell'. *see* Abate, N. dell'.
ABBATT, Agnes Dean.
Am. New York 1847-1917. A12-F-T.
ABBÉ, Salomon van. *see* Van Abbé, S.
ABBÉMA, Louise.
Fr. Estampes 1858-1927. B-DBA.
ABBEY, Edwin Austin.
Am-Br. Phila., Pa. 1852-1911. London. A09-B-C-DAB-DNB-E-F-T-5-15-46-71-201-272-748.
ABBEY, Iva L.
Am. b. Chester, Conn. 1882; ad. 1935 Wilkes-Barre, Pa. A20-F.
ABBEY, N.
Am. ex. 1935 New York. M.
ABBOT, Agnes Anne.
Am. b. Potsdam, Ger. 1897; ad. 1934 Brookline, Mass. A.
ABBOT, Katherine G.
Am. b. Zanesville, O., 1867. B.
ABBOT, Lilian Moore.
Am. b. Fairfax Co., Va.; ad. 1934 Wash., D. C. A.
ABBOTT, Anne Fuller.
Am. b. Brandon, Vt.; ad. 1934 Wash., D. C. A-F.
ABBOTT, Berenice.
Am. b. Springfield, O., 1898; ad. 1934 New York. M.
ABBOTT, Edith R.
Am. ad. 1934 New York. M.
ABBOTT, Elenore Plaisted. (Ill.)
Mrs. C. Yarnall Abbott.
Am. b. Lincoln, Me., 1875; ad. 1934 Moylan, Pa. A-F.
ABBOTT, Francis [Lemuel].
Eng. Leicestershire, Eng., 1760-1803 London. B-DNB-T.
ABBOTT, Francis R.
Am. b. Phila., Pa.; d. 1925 same. A20-B-F.
ABBOTT, Harold.
Aust. ad. 1935 Sydney, N. S. Wales. M.
ABBOTT, Samuel Nelson.
Am. b. 1874; ad. 1934 Stone Ridge, N. Y. M.
ABBOTT, Yarnall.
Am. b. Phila., Pa., 1870; ad. 1934 Same. A-F.
ABDO, Alexander.
Eng. b. Buckhurst Hill 1865; ad. 1934 Southall. Wa.
ABDULLAH ibn Al-Fadl. (Min).
Pers. ac. 1222 in Persia. M.
ABDY, [Mrs.] Rowena Meeks.
Am. b. Vienna, Aus. 1887; ad. 1934 San Fran., Calif. A-F-202.
ABEL, Louise. (S)
Am. b. Mt. Healthy, O., 1894; ex. 1934 Cincinnati, O. F.
ABEL, Myer.
Am. ad. 1935 Cuin, O. M.
ABEL DE PUJOL, Alexandre Denis.
Fr. Valenciennes, 1785-1861 Paris. C.
ABEL-TRUCHET, Louis.
Fr. Versailles, 1857-1918. B-DBA.
ABELE, Lanier Bradfield.
Am. ad. 1934 Atlanta, Ga. M.
ABELL, Margaret. (S)
Am. ad. 1934 New York. M.
ABERCROMBIE, Gertrude.
Am. ad. 1934 Chicago. M.
ABERLI, Jean [or Johann] Ludwig.
Swi. Winterthur, 1723-1786 Berne. B-T.
ABERNETHIE. (Eg.)
Am. ac. 1780-85 Charleston, S. C. B-F-T-2-7-147.
ABILDGAARD, Nikolaj Abraham.
Dan. Copenhagen 1743-1809. B-E-T.
ABLETT, Thomas Robert.
Eng. b. London; ad. 1929 Surrey, Eng. Wa.
ABLETT, William Albert.
Eng. b. Paris 1877. B-DBA.

ABRAHAMS, Dora.
Am. ex. 1935 New York. M.
ABRAHAMSEN, Christian.
Am. b. Bergen, Nor. 1887; ex. 1933 Chicago. F.
ABRAMOFSKY, Israel.
Am. b. Kiev, Rus. 1888; ad. 1934 Toledo, O. A.
ABRAMS, Eleanor.
Am. b. Karns City, Pa.; ad. 1935 Butler, Pa. F.
ABRAMS, Lucien.
Am. b. Lawrence, Kan.; ac. 1934 Lyme, Conn. A-B-F.
ABRAMS, Ruth.
Am. ex. 1935 New York. M.
ABRAMSON, Rosalind.
Am. b. Norfolk, Va. 1901. A20-F.
ABSOLON, John.
Eng. ac. Lambeth 1815-1895. B-T.
ABT, [or Apt] Ulrich. [The Elder]
Ger. ac. 1486-1532 Augsburg. T.
ACCARD, Eugène.
Fr. Bordeaux 1824-1888 Paris. B-T.
ACHEN, Johann [or Hans von].
Ger. Cologne 1552/62-1615 Prague, Czec. B-Bd-C-T.
ACHENBACH, Andréas.
Ger. Cassel 1815-1910 Düsseldorf. B-Bd-C-E-T.
ACHENBACH, Oswald.
Ger. Düsseldorf 1827-1905 Same. B-Bd-C-T.
ACHENER, Maurice Victor. (Et)
Fr. b. Mülhouse 1881. B-DBA-T.
ACHESON, [Mrs.] Alice Stanley.
Am. b. Charlevoix, Mich. 1895; ad. 1934 Wash., D. C. A.
ACHILLE-FOULD, [Mlle.] Georges.
Fr. b. Asnières 1865. B-T.
ACHMANN, Gustave.
Ger. ac. 1714. B-T.
ACHTSCELLINCK, Lucas.
Flem. Brussels 1626-1699 Same. B-T.
ACKE, Johan Axel Gustaf.
Swe. b. Stockholm 1859-1924 Vaxholm. B-M-T.
ACKEIN, Marcelle.
Fr. b. Algiers 1882; ex. 1930 London. DBA.
ACKER, Herbert van Blarcom.
Am. b. Pasadena, Calif. 1895; ad. 1934 San Marino, Calif. A.
ACKER, Rose M.
Am. ad. 1935 Rochester, N. Y. M.
ACKERMAN, [Mrs.] Carl.
Am. ad. 1934 New York. M.
ACKERMAN, Harry Gregory.
Am. ad. 1934 Marble Hill, N. Y. M.
ACKERMANN, Arthur Gerald.
Eng. b. Biddeford; ad. 1934 Same. B-T-Wa.
ACKERMANN, John J.
Am. ex. 1935 New York. M.
ACKERS, Charles. *see* Akers, C.
ACKERSON, Floyd Garrison.
Am. b. Portage, Mich. 1883; ad. 1934 Wilkensburg, Pa. A.
ACKLAND, Judith.
Eng. b. Biddeford; ex. 1934 London. Wa.
ACTON, John Adams. *see* Adams-Acton, J.
ADAM, Albrecht.
Ger. Nordling 1786-1862 Munich. B-Bd-C-T.
ADAM, Benno.
Ger. Munich 1812-1892 Kehlheim. Fa-M.
ADAM, David Livingston.
Am. Glasgow Scot. 1883-1924 Chicago. A021-F.
ADAM, Denovan.
Scot. d. 1896. M.
ADAM, Emile.
Ger. Munich 1843-1924. B-T.
ADAM, Frantz B.
Ger. Milan, It. 1815-1886 Munich. B-C-T.
ADAM, Jean Victor.
Fr. Paris 1801-1867 Viroflay. C.
ADAM, Joseph Donovan.
Scot. Glasgow 1842-1896 Same. B-T.
ADAM, Julius [The Elder].
Ger. Munich 1826-1874 Same. B-T.
ADAM, Julius [The Younger].
Ger. Munich 1852-1913. B-T.
ADAM, Lambert Sigisbert. (S)
Fr. Nancy 1700-1759 Paris. B-E-T.
ADAM, Patrick William.
Scot. Edinburgh 1854-1929. B-T.
ADAM, Stephen.
Scot. b. Glasgow; ac. 1892-1899. B-T.
ADAM, Wilbur G.
Am. b. Cincinnati, O. 1898; ad. 1934 Chicago. A.
ADAM, William.
Am. b. England 1846. A28-F.
ADAM-SALOMON, Anthony Samuel. (S)
Fr. 1818-1881 Paris. B-T.
ADAMS, Ansel.
Am. ad. 1935 San Fran., Calif. M.
ADAMS, Charles Laden.
Am. New York 1857-1914 Antwerp, Belg. A12-T.
ADAMS, Charles Partridge.
Am. b. Franklin, Mass. 1858; ad. 1934 Los Angeles, Calif. A-B-F-T.
ADAMS, Charles W.
Am. ex. 1934 New York. M.
ADAMS, Chauncey M.
Am. b. Unadillo Forks, N. Y. 1895; ad. 1934 Utica, N. Y. A.
ADAMS, Clifton E. (S)
Am. b. La Place, Ill. 1904; ad. 1934 Lohrville, Ia. M.
ADAMS, Douglas.
Eng. 1853-1920. B-T.
ADAMS, Edith Gordon.
Am. b. Shelbyville, Ind. 1870; ad. 1934 Same. A.
ADAMS, Frank. (Ill)
Eng. ex. 1935 London. M.
ADAMS, George Gammon. (S)
Eng. Staines 1821-1898 Chiswick. B-T.
ADAMS, Harry William.
Eng. b. Worcester 1868; ad. 1934 Same. Wa.
ADAMS, Herbert. (S)
Am. b. Concord, Vt. 1858; ad. 1934 New York. A-B-Cs-E-F-W.
ADAMS, Hervey.
Br. b. 1903; ex. 1934 London. M.
ADAMS, Jean Crawford.
Am. b. Chicago 1890; ad. 1934 Same. A.

ADAMS, John.
Am. ad. 1935 Cleveland, O. M.
ADAMS, John Clayton.
Eng. Guildford. 1840-1906. B-T.
ADAMS, John Ottis.
Am. Amity, Ind. 1851-1927 Indianapolis, Ind. A025-F-W14.
ADAMS, John Quincy.
Aus. Vienna 1874-1933. A030-B-T.
ADAMS, John Wolcott.
Am. Worcester, Mass. 1874-1925 New York. A022-B-F.
ADAMS, Joseph Alexander. (Eg)
Am. New Germantown, N. J. 1803-1880 Same. B-DAB-F-T-2-8-9-185.
ADAMS, Katherine Langhorne.
Mrs. Benjamin P. Adams.
Am. b. Plainfield, N. J.; ad. 1934 Palisades, N. Y. A-F.
ADAMS, Kenneth Miller.
Am. b. Topeka, Kan. 1897; ad. 1934 Taos, N. M. A.
ADAMS, Lawson.
Eng. ac. London 1834. B-T.
ADAMS, [Mrs.] Marjorie Nickles.
Am. b. Shippensburg, Pa. 1898; ad. 1934 Swarthmore, Pa. A.
ADAMS, Mary Crosjean. (Ill.)
Am. ad. 1934 Chicago. M.
ADAMS, Maurice Bingham. (S)
Eng. 1876-1933 London. B-T.
ADAMS, Nancy.
Am. ad. 1934 Cleveland, O. M.
ADAMS, Phillip.
Am. b. Honolulu, Hawaii 1881; ad. 1935 Wash., D. C. A20-F.
ADAMS, Sally.
Am. ex. 1933 New York. M.
ADAMS, Walter Burt.
Am. b. Kenosha, Wis. 1903; ad. 1934 Evanston, Ill. A.
ADAMS, Wayman.
Am. b. Muncie, Ind. 1883; ad. 1934 New York. A-F-W-46-181.
ADAMS, William Dacres.
Eng. ac. 1909-1927, London. B-T.
ADAMS, Willis Seaver.
Am. 1842-1921. M.
ADAMS, Winifred Brady.
Mrs. John Ottis Adams.
Am. b. Muncie, Ind. 1871; ad. 1934 Brookville, Ind. A-181.
ADAMS-ACTON, John. (S)
Eng. Acton Hill, 1830-1910 Isle of Arran. DNB.
ADAMSEN, Amandus Heinrich. (S)
Esthonian (Port Baltic). b. Hunkas 1855. B-T.
ADAMSON, Penryhn Stanley. *see* Stanlaws, Penryhn.
ADAMSON-ERIC, Karl Hugo.
Fr. b. Tartu, Esthonia 1902. DBA.
ADAN, Émile Louis.
Fr. b. Paris 1839. B-C-T.
ADDAMS, Clifford Isaac.
Am. b. Woodbury, N. Y. 1876; ad. 1934 New York. A-F.
ADDAMS, J. Howard.
Am. d. 1924. A022.
ADDISON, Julia de Wolf.
Mrs. D. D. Addison.
Am. b. Boston 1866; ad. 1934 Brookline, Mass. A.
ADELE, Lanier Bradfield.
Am. b. Atlanta, Ga.; ad. 1935 Same. M.
ADEMOLLO, Carlo.
It. Florence, 1825-1911. B-T.
ADERENTE, Vincent.
Am. b. Naples, It. 1880. A12.
ADIE, Edith Helena.
Eng. ac. 1892-1909 London. B-T.
ADLER, Émile.
Swi. b. Zurich; d. 1933. DBA.
ADLER, J. C.
Am. d. 1915 Charleston, W. Va. A013.
ADLER, Jules.
Fr. b. Luxeuil, 1865. B-DBA.
ADLER, Salomone.
It. ac. 1675-1691 Milan. B-T.
ADNEY, Edwin Tappan.
Am. b. Athens, O. 1868. B-F-T-W12.
ADOLPHE, Albert Jean.
Am. b. Phila., Pa. 1865; ad. 1934 Same. A-F-W.
ADOMEIT, George Gustav.
Am. b. Germany 1879; ad. 1934 Cleveland, O. A.
ADRIANCE, [Mrs.] Mary Horton.
Am. ad. 1934 New York. M.
ADRIANE, van Utrecht.
Flem. 1599-1652. Fa.
ADRION, Lucien.
Fr. b. Strassburg 1889. DBA.
ADSIT, Susan.
Am. ex. 1934 New York. M.
AEKEN, Hieronymus van. *see* Bosch, H.
AELST [or Aalst], Evert van.
Dut. Delft 1602-1658 Same. B-T.
AELST, Pieter Coecke [or Cock] van.
Flem. Aelst 1502-1550 Brussels. B-T.
AELST [or Aalst], Willem van.
Dut. Delft 1626-1683 Amsterdam. B-C-T.
AELZHEIMER, Adam. *see* Elsheimer, A.
AERTS [or Arts], Hendrik.
Dut. ac. 1553-1575. Fa.
AERTSZ [or Aartsen], Pieter [Lange Pier].
Dut. Amsterdam 1507/08-1573/5. B-C-E-281.
AERTZ [or Aartszen], Rijkert.
Dut. Wyck 1482-1577 Antwerp, Belg. B-Bd-T.
AETION [or Eetion].
Gr. ac. 350 B. C. E.
AGACHE, Alfred Pierre.
Fr. Lille 1843-1915 Cours-Cheverny. C-T.
AGAR, John Samuel.
Eng. ac. 1795-1835 London. B-T.
AGASIAS OF EPHESUS. (S)
Gr. ac. 100 B. C. Ephesus. B-E-Hs-T.
AGASSE, Jacques Laurent.
Swi. Geneva 1776-1849 London. B-DNB-T.
AGATE, Alfred T.
Am. Sparta, N. Y. 1812-1846 Wash., D. C. B-DAB-F-T-2-4-11.
AGATE, Frederick Styles.
Am. Sparta, N. Y. 1803-1844 Same. B-DAB-F-T-2-4-11.

AGATHARCHUS.
Gr. ac. 435 B. C. Athens. E.
AGATHON, [Mrs.] O. (Min.)
Am. ex. 1934 New York. M.
AGELADES [or Hagelaidas]. (S)
Gr. ac. 520-485 B. C. E-Hs-T.
AGELÜ. *see* Aguéli.
AGESANDROS. (S)
Gr. ac. 21-42 B. C. Rhodes. E-Hs.
AGGAS [or Angus], ROBERT. (Scene P.)
Br. d. 1679. DNB.
AGLIO, AUGUSTINE.
It. Cremona 1777-1857 England. DNB.
AGNOLO, BACCIO D' [Baglioni].
It. Florence 1462-1543 Same. T-V.
AGNOLO, DOMENICO DI DONNINO.
It. Florence 1466-1513 Same. T-V.
AGNOLO DEL MORO. *see* Angolo de Moro.
AGNOLO DI VENTURA. (S)
It. ac. 1325; d. 1350 Siena. B-E-Hs-T-V.
AGORACRITOS DE PAROS. (S)
Gr. ac. 488-432 B. C. Athens. B-E-Hs-T.
AGOSTINO DA LODI, GIOVANNI. *see* Boccaccino, B.
AGOSTINO DI BUSTI [or Bambaja]. (S)
It. Milan 1480-1548. Hs-T-V.
AGOSTINO DI DUCCIO [Antonio]. (S)
It. Florence 1418-1498 Same. B-Hs-T.
AGOSTINO DI GIOVANNI. (S)
It. Siena 1269-1348 Same. B-E-Hs-T-V.
AGRICOLA, CHRISTOPHER LUDWIG.
Ger. Ratisbonne 1667-1719 Same. B-E-T.
AGÜ, CORDELLE. *see* Previtali, Andrea.
AGUA, BERARDINO DEL.
It. ac. 1587. T.
AGUÉLI, IVAN GUSTAVE [assumed name of John Gustave Agelii].
Swe. 1869-1917. Fa.
AGUTTE, GEORGETTE [Marcel Sembat].
Fr. Paris 1867-1922 Chamonix. B-DBA.
AHL, HENRY HAMMOND.
Am. b. East Hartford, Conn. 1869; ad. 1934 Newburyport, Mass. A-F-W.
AHLBORN, LEA [née Lundren]. (S)
Swe. 1826-1897. B-T.
AHLEFELDT, [Countess] INGEGARD.
Swe. ex. 1934 London. M.
AHLQUIST, F. J.
Br. ac. 1932 London. M.
AHRENS, CARL.
Can. b. Winfield, Ont. 1867; ad. 1934 Galt, Ont. M-893.
AHRENS, ELLEN WETHERALD.
Am. b. Balt., Md. 1859; ad. 1934 Lansdowne, Pa. A-B-F-T-46.
AHRENS, HOWARD.
Am. ad. 1935 Hartford, Conn. M.
AID, GEORGE CHARLES.
Am. b. Quincy, Ill. 1872; ad. 1934 Tryon, N. C. A-F-46.
AIELLO, MARIO.
Am. ad. 1935 Coney Island, N. Y. M.
AIGUIER, LOUIS AUGUSTE LAURENT.
Fr. Toulon 1819-1865 Marseilles. B.
AIKEN, CHARLES AVERY.
Am. b. Georgia, Vt. 1872; ad. 1934 New York. A-F-W.
AIKEN, FRANK. (Min.)
Am. New York 1859-1933 Mamaroneck, N. Y. A030.
AIKMAN, GEORGE W.
Scot. Edinburgh 1830-1905 Same. B-E.
AIKMAN, WALTER MONTEITH. (Eg.)
Am. b. New York 1857; ad. 1934 Brooklyn, N. Y. A-F-W.
AIKMAN, WILLIAM.
Scot. Gairney 1682-1731. B-E.
AIMO, DOMENICO [Vecchio of Bologna].
It. ac. 1506-1537 Bologna. T-V.
AINMILLER, MAX EMANUEL.
Ger. Munich 1807-1870 Same. C.
AIRY, ANNA.
Eng. ac. 1907-1927 London. B.
AIRY, HUBERT.
Eng. ex. 1934 London. M.
AIRY, JACK.
Eng. ex. 1934 London. M.
AITKEN, PETER. (Eg)
Am. b. Dundas, Can. 1858. A12-B-F-T-W9.
AITKEN, ROBERT. (Eg)
Am. Scotland 1734-1802 Phila., Pa. B-DAB-F-T-7-12.
AITKEN, ROBERT INGERSOLL. (S)
Am. b. San Fran., Calif. 1878; ad. 1934 New York. A-B-Cs-F-Hs-T-W-46.
AITKEN, RUSSELL BARNETT. (S)
Am. ad. 1934 Cleveland, O. M.
AIVAZOFFSKI, IVAN CONSTANTNOVITSCH.
Rus. b. Tedosie 1817; d. 1900. B-T.
AIZELIN, EUGÈNE ANTOINE. (S)
Fr. Paris 1821-1902. B-T.
AKELEY, CARL ETHAN. (S)
Am. Clarendon, N. Y. 1864-1926 Kabale, Africa. A025-F.
AKEN, HIERONYMUS VAN. *see* Bos [Bosch] Jerome.
AKEN, JAN VAN.
Dut. 1614?-1661? B-T.
AKEN, JOHANN VON.
Ger. Cologne 1552-1615. M.
AKEN, JOSEF VAN.
Flem. Antwerp 1709-1749 London. B-T.
AKERS, BENJAMIN PAUL. (S)
Am. Westbrook, Me. 1825-1861 Phila., Pa. B-DAB-F-T-Ta-4.
AKERS, CHARLES. (S)
Am. Hollis, Me. 1835-1906 New York. A06-B-F-T-3-15-45.
AKIN, JAMES. (Cari)
Am. So. Car. 1773-1846 Phila., Pa. B-F-T-2-6-7-169.
AKIN, [Mrs.] JAMES. (Eg)
Am. ac. 1804 Newburyport, Mass. 7-147.
AKIN, LOUIS B.
Am. Portland, Ore. 1868-1913 Flagstaff, Ariz. A011-B-F.
AKKERINGA, EVERT.
Dut. ac. 1804 Holland. B-T.
AKKERINGA, JOHANN.
Dut. b. Banka, Formosa 1864; ac. 1910 Paris. B-T.
AKKERSDIJK, JACOB.
Dut. Rotterdam 1815-1862. B-T.
ALAJÁLOV, CONSTANTIN. (Ill.)
Am. b. Russia; ad. 1934 New York. 912.

ALART, Claeszson [called Aertgen van Leyden].
see Claessen [or Class], Alaert.
ALAUX, François.
Fr. b. Bordeaux 1878. DBA.
ALAUX, Guillaume.
Fr. Bordeaux; ac. 1883-1907. B-T.
ALAUX, Jean [The Roman].
Fr. Bordeaux; 1786-1864 Paris. B-T.
ALBA, Macrino. *see* D'Alba, Macrino.
ALBACH, George.
Am. ad. 1934 Buffalo, N. Y. M.
ALBANI [or Albane], Francesco.
It. Bologna 1578-1660 Same. B-C-E-T-722.
ALBANO, Salvatore Florenti. (S)
It. Oppido 1841-1893 Florence. B-T.
ALBEE, Grace Arnold. (Eg.)
Mrs. Percy F. Albee.
Am. ad. 1935 New York. A.
ALBEE, Percy F.
Am. b. Bridgeport, Conn. 1883; ad. 1934 New York. A-F.
ALBEREGNO [or Alberagno], Jacopo.
It. ac. Venice; d. 1397. B.
ALBERS [Prof.] Joseph. (Eg.)
Am. ex. 1935 Andover, Mass. M.
ALBERT, Drussilla. (S)
Am. ex. 1934 Seattle, Wash. M.
ALBERT, Ernest.
Am. b. Brooklyn, N. Y. 1857; ad. 1934 New Rochelle, N. Y. A-F-W.
ALBERT, E. Maxwell.
Am. b. Chicago 1890; ad. 1934 New Canaan, Conn. A.
ALBERT, Joseph.
Belg. ad. 1934 Brussels. M.
ALBERTI, Cherubino [Borgheggiano].
It. Borgo San Sepolero 1553-1615 Rome. B-T.
ALBERTI, Léon Battista. (S)
It. Florence 1404-1484. B-Hs-T-V.
ALBERTI, Michele.
It. b. 1527?; ac. 1550 Florence. T-V.
ALBERTINELLI, Biagio di Bindo [Mariotto].
It. Florence 1474-1515. B-Bd-C-E-T-V-722.
ALBERTO DI ARNOLDO. (S)
It. ac. 1350 in Florence. T.
ALBERTS, Jacob.
Ger. b. Westerhever 1860. B-T.
ALBERTS, John Bernhard.
Am. b. Louisville, Ky. 1886. A20-F.
ALBINI [or Albano], Francesco. *see* Albani, F.
ALBINSON, Dewey.
Am. b. Minn., Minn. 1898; ad. 1934 So. Minn. A.
ALBOY-REBONET. *see* Rebonet-Alboy.
ALBRECHT, Carl.
Ger. b. Hamburg 1862. B-T.
ALBRIGHT, Adam Emory.
Am. b. Monroe, Wis. 1862; ad. 1934 Warrenville, Ill. A-F-W.
ALBRIGHT, [Mrs.] Gertrude Partington.
Am. b. Heysham, Eng.; ad. 1934 San Fran., Calif. A-F.
ALBRIGHT, H. Oliver.
Am. b. Mannheim, Ger. 1876; ad. 1934 San Fran., Calif. A-F.
ALBRIGHT, Henry James.
Am. b. Albany, N. Y. 1887; ad. 1934 Glenmont, N. Y. A-F.
ALBRIGHT, Ivan Le Lorraine.
Am. b. Chicago 1897; ad. 1934 Warrensville, Ill. A-W.
ALBRIGHT, Lloyd Thron.
Am. b. Cleburne, Tex. 1897; ad. 1934 Dalhart, Tex. A.
ALBRIGHT, Malvin Marr. (S)
Am. b. Chicago 1897; ad. 1934 Warrensville, Ill. A-Cs-W.
ALBRIZIO, Conrad.
Am. ex. 1934 New York. M.
ALBRIZIO, Humbert. (S)
Am. ad. 1934 New York. M.
ALBRO, Maxine.
Mex. ex. 1932 New York. M.
ALCAMENES. *see Alkamenes.*
ALCATI, Andrea.
It. 1492-1550 Milan. T.
ALCHIMOWICZ, Kasimir.
Pol. Dziembrow 1840-1900. B.
ALCOTT, May.
Am. Concord, Mass. 1840-1879. C-F-15-907.
ALDEGREVER [or Aldegraf], Heinrich.
Ger. Paderborn 1502-1558 Soest, Westphalia. B-C-E-T-V-722.
ALDI, Pietro.
It. Manciano 1852-1888. B.
ALDIN, Cecil Charles Windsor.
Eng. Slough 1870-1935 Reading. B-M-Wa-881.
Obit. N. Y. papers, 1, 7, 1935.
ALDINI, Guiseppe.
It. ac. 1670 Bologna. B.
ALDRICH, Clarence N.
Am. b. Milford, Me. 1893; ad. 1934 Long Beach, Calif. A.
ALDRICH, George Ames.
Am. b. Worcester, Mass. 1872; ad. 1934 Chicago. A-F-W15.
ALDRICH, M. Azzi.
Am. ex. 1934 Cincinnati, O. M.
ALDRICH, Mary Austin.
Mrs. Malcolm Fraser.
Am. b. New York 1884; ad. 1934 Brookhaven, N. Y. A.
ALDRIDGE, Frederic James.
Eng. 1850-1933 London. B.
ALDRIDGE, John.
Br. ac. 1932. M.
ALEF, Torwald. (S)
Swe. ad. 1934 Stockholm. M.
ALEFOUNDER, John. (Min)
Br. 1730-1795 Calcutta, India. B-DNB.
ALEGRE, A. Villamor.
Am. b. Manila, P. I. 1909; ad. 1934 Chicago. M.
ALEMANNO, Pietro.
It. ac. 1471-1489. B-Bd-T.
ALENIS, Tomasco [Il Fadino].
It. ac. 1500-1515. V.
ALENZA Y NIETO, Leonardo.
Sp. Madrid 1807-1845 Same. T.
ALEOTTI, Antonio [or Argenta].
It. ac. 1498 Ferrara. T.
ALEXANDER, Anita Venier.
Am. b. Italy; ad. 1934 Chicago. M.
ALEXANDER, Arthur Hadden.
Am. b. Decatur, Ill. 1892; ad. 1934 Cleveland, O. A.

ALEXANDER, CLIFFORD GREAR.
Am. b. Springfield, Mass. 1870; ad. 1934 Brighton, Mass. A-F.
ALEXANDER, COSMO.
Scot. ac. 1763-1770 Edinburgh. B-T-2-182.
ALEXANDER, EDWIN G.
Scot. Edinburgh 1870-1926. B.
ALEXANDER, FRANCIS.
Am. Killington, Conn. 1800-1881 Florence, It. B-DAB-E-F-T-1-2-3-4-5-6-15.
ALEXANDER, FRANKLIN OSBORNE. (Cart)
Am. b. St. Louis, Mo. 1897; ad. 1934 Phila., Pa. M.
ALEXANDER, HENRY.
Am. San Fran., Calif. 1860-1895 New York. B-T.
ALEXANDER, JOHN WHITE.
Am. Allegheny, Pa. 1856-1915 New York. A012-B-DAB-E-F-T-1-5-46-127-203-757-844.
ALEXANDER, JULIA STANDISH. (S)
Am. b. Springfield, Mass.; ad. 1934 Mt. Vernon, N. Y. A.
ALEXANDER, MARIE DAY.
Mrs. Ernest R. Alexander.
Am. b. Greenfield, Mass. 1887; ad. 1934 Same. A.
ALEXANDER, MARY LOUISE. (S)
Am. ad. 1934 Cinn., O. A-F.
ALEXANDER, ROBERT L.
Scot. Kibwinning 1840-1923. B.
ALEXANDER, SARA DORA BLOCK.
Mrs. Max Alexander.
Am. b. Suwalki, Pol. 1888; ad. 1934 Mission Beach, Calif. A.
ALEXANDER, WILLIAM. (Eg.)
Eng. Maidstone 1767-1816. B-DNB.
ALEXANDER, WILLIAM HENRY SNOWDON. (Ill.)
Am. b. Haddonfield, N. J. 1883; ad. 1934 Same. A.
ALFANI, DOMENICO DI PARIDE [The Elder].
It. Perugia 1479/1480-1553 Same. B-C-E.
ALFANI, ORAZIO.
It. Perugia 1510-1583 Rome. B-T.
ALFANO, VINCENZO. (S)
Am. b. Naples, It. 1854; ac. 1915 New York. A12-B-T-Ta.
ALFARO Y GÁMEZ, JUAN DE.
Sp. Cordova 1640-1680 Madrid. B-T.
ALFRED, PAUL.
Can. b. Hanley, Eng.; ac. Ontario. 893.
ALFSEN, JOHN.
Can. ac. 1932. Fa.
ALGARDI, ALESSANDRO. (S)
It. Bologna 1602-1654 Rome. B-E-Hs-T.
ALGER, JOHN.
Am. b. Boston 1879; ad. 1933 New York. F.
ALIENSE, ANTONIO VASSILACCHI.
It. Milo 1556?-1629 Venice. C-722.
ALIGHIERI, DANTE.
It. ac. 14th century Naples. M.
ALIGHIERI, GIOVANNI. (Min)
It. ac. Padua 1543. B-T.
ALIGNY, CLAUDE-FÉLIX THÉODORE.
Fr. Chaumes 1798-1871 Lyons. B-T.
ALISON, DAVID.
Scot. b. Dysart 1882; ad. 1934 Edinburgh. B-Wa.
ALIX, JEANNE.
Fr. b. Paris 1884. DBA.
ALIX, PIERRE MICHEL. (Eg)
Fr. Honfleur 1762-1817 Paris. B-T.
ALIX, YVES.
Fr. b. Fontainebleau 1890; ad. 1934 Paris. DBA-797.
ALKAMENES. (S)
Gr. ac. 480-445 B. C. Athens. B-E-Hs-T.
ALKE, [Mrs.] ELIZABETH HEIL.
Am. ad. 1934 New Richmond, O. M.
ALKEN, HENRY. (Eg)
Eng. ac. 1816-1831. DNB.
ALKEN, HENRY GORDON. ["Ben Tally Ho"]
Eng. 1784-1850 London. B-283.
ALKEN, HENRY THOMAS.
Eng. 1800-1875. DNB.
ALKEN, SAMUEL.
Eng. 1750-1825 London. B-T.
ALLAIRE, LOUISE.
Am. ad. 1934 Brooklyn, N. Y. M.
ALLAIS, JEAN ALEXANDRE.
Fr. Paris 1792-1850 Same. B.
ALLAIS, LOUIS JEAN.
Fr. Paris 1762-1839 Same. B.
ALLAIS, PROSPER PAUL.
Fr. b. Paris 1827. B-T.
ALLAN, DAVID.
Scot. Alloa 1744-1796 Edinburgh. B-DNB-E-722.
ALLAN, ROBERT WEIR.
Scot. b. Glasgow 1852. B-T.
ALLAN, [Sir] WILLIAM.
Scot. Edinburgh 1782-1850 Same. B-C-DNB-E.
ALLARD-L'OLIVER, FERNAND.
Fr. b. Tournai, Belg. 1883. DBA.
ALLARDICE [or Allerdice], SAMUEL. (Eg)
Am. d. 1798. B-F-T-2-7-147.
ALLEAUME, LUDOVIC.
Fr. Angers 1859; ac. 1910. B-DBA.
ALLEGRAIN, ETIENNE.
Fr. Paris 1644-1736 Same. B-T.
ALLEGRAIN, GABRIEL CHRISTOPHE. (P, S)
Fr. Paris 1679-1748 Same. B-Hs-T.
ALLEGRI, ANTONIO. *see* Correggio.
ALLEN, ANNE HUNTINGTON.
Mrs. Thomas W. Allen.
Am. b. New York 1858; ad. 1935 Cinn., O. A20-F.
ALLEN, CHARLES CURTIS.
Am. b. Leominster, Mass. 1886; ad. 1934 Waban, Mass. A-F-W.
ALLEN, CHARLES JOHN. (S)
Eng. b. Greenford 1862; ad. 1934 Liverpool. B-T-Wa.
ALLEN, DAPHNE CONSTANCE.
Eng. b. 1899; ad. 1934 London. Wa.
ALLEN, FRANK LEONARD.
Am. b. Portland, Me. 1884; ad. 1934 Teaneck, N. J. A.
ALLEN, FREDERICK WARREN. (S)
Am. b. No. Attleboro, Mass. 1888; ad. 1934 Boston. A-F.
ALLEN, GEORGE. (Ill)
Eng. Newark 1832-1907 Orpington. DNB.
ALLEN, GREGORY SEYMOUR. (S)
Am. b. Orange, N. J. 1884; ad. 1934 Glendale, Calif. A-F.

ALLEN, Hazel Leigh. (S)
Am. b. Morrilton, Ark. 1892; ad. 1934 Milwaukee, Wis. A.
ALLEN, James. (Et)
Am. b. Louisiana, Mo. 1894; ad. 1934 Larchmont, N. Y. A.
ALLEN, James Baylis. (Eg)
Eng. Birmingham 1803-1876. Bd-DNB-T.
ALLEN, James C. (Eg)
Eng. b. London; d. 1831. DNB-T.
ALLEN, James Junius.
Am. b. Summit, N. J. 1898; ad. 1934 Same. A.
ALLEN, James Latimer.
Am. b. New York 1907; ad. 1934 Same. M.
ALLEN, Jane Mengel.
Am. b. Louisville, Ky. 1888; ad. 1934 Provincetown, Mass. A.
ALLEN, Joel Nott. (Eg)
Am. Farmington, Conn. 1755-1825. F-2-7.
ALLEN, John Donn [Jawne Allen].
Am. b. Norfolk, Va. 1893; ad. 1934 Wash., D. C. A.
ALLEN, John H.
Am. ad. 1934 Portland, Me. M.
ALLEN, Joseph William.
Eng. Lambeth. 1803-1852. DNB-T.
ALLEN, Louise. (S)
Mrs. A. H. Atkins.
Am. b. Lowell, Mass.; ad. 1934 Gloucester, Mass. A28-Cs-F.
ALLEN, Luther.
Am. Enfield, Conn. 1780-1821 Ithaca, N. Y. F-2-7.
ALLEN, Margaret Newton. (P, S)
Am. b. Lincoln, Mass. 1894; ad. 1934 Boston. A-Cs.
ALLEN, Marion Boyd.
Mrs. William A. Allen.
Am. b. Boston 1862; ad. 1934 Same. A-F-W.
ALLEN, Mary Cecil.
Am. ex. 1935 New York. M.
ALLEN, Mary Coleman.
Am. b. Troy, O. 1888; ad. 1934 Same. A.
ALLEN, [Mrs.] Mary Gertrude. (P, S)
Am. b. Mendota, Ill. 1869; ad. 1934 Lake Stevens, Wash. A.
ALLEN, Pearl Wright.
Mrs. J. G. Allen.
Am. b. Kossuth, Miss. 1880; ad. 1934 Muskogee, Okla. A.
ALLEN, Sarah Lockhart. (Min)
Am. Salem, Mass. 1793-1877 Same. F-2-45-169.
ALLEN, Thomas.
Am. St. Louis, Mo. 1849-1924 Worcester, Mass. A025-B-F-W13-47.
ALLEN, Thomas.
Eng. ac. 1767-1772. B-T.
ALLENBACH, Anna.
Am. ad. 1935 Kansas City, Mo. M.
ALLENDER, [Mrs.] Nina E.
Am. b. Auburn, Kan., ad. 1934 Wash., D. C. A.
ALLERS, Christian Wilhelm.
Ger. Hamburg 1857-1909/11? B-T.
ALLESIO, Gregory d'. (Cart)
Am. ad. 1934 Chicago. M.

ALLEY, James Pinckney. (Cart)
Am. Benton, Ark. 1885-1934 Memphis, Tenn. Obit. N. Y. papers. 4, 7, 1934. M-W.
ALLI, Aino Sofia.
Fin. b. Uleaborg 1879. DBA.
ALLINGHAM, [Mrs.] A.
Eng. ac. 1900. B.
ALLINGHAM, Charles.
Eng. ac. 1802-1812 London. B.
ALLINGHAM, [Mrs.] Helen.
Eng. Burton 1848-1926. B.
ALLINSON, Adrian. (P-S)
Eng. b. London 1890; ad. 1934 Same. Wa.
ALLIS, C. Harry.
Am. b. Dayton, O., ad. 1934 New York. A.
ALLIS, Genevieve.
Am. Derby, Conn. 1864-1914 Same. A011-B-T.
ALLISON, John William.
Eng. b. Bath; ad. 1934 Birmingham. B-T-Wa.
ALLISON, William Merle. (Ill)
Am. b. Kansas 1880; ad. 1934 New York. A.
ALLMOND, Katherine. *see* Hulbert, [Mrs.] Charles A.
ALLOM, Thomas. (Eg)
Eng. London 1804-1872 Barnes. B.
ALLONGÉ, Auguste.
Fr. Paris 1833-1898 Marlotte. B.
ALLORI, Angelo di Cosimo. *see* Bronzino, Il.
ALLORI, Cristofano.
It. Florence 1577-1621 Same. B-C-T-722.
ALLORI DEL BRONZINO, Alessandro.
It. Florence 1535-1607 Same. B-C-E-T-V-722.
ALLOU, Gilles. (S)
Fr. Paris 1670-1751 Same. B-T.
ALLOUARD, Émile Henri. (S)
Fr. Paris 1844-1929. B-DBA-T.
ALLSTON, Washington.
Am. Waccamaw, So. Car. 1779-1843 Cambridge, Mass. B-Bd-C-DAB-E-F-T-1-2-4-6-13-15-46-179-182-701-722.
ALLWARD, Walter S. (S)
Can. b. Canada 1876; ac. 1934 England. M.
ALLWORTHY, Joseph.
Am. b. Pittsburgh, Pa. 1897; ad. 1934 Chicago. A.
ALMA-TADEMA, [Lady] Laura Theresa.
Eng. London 1852-1909. B-Bd-C-DNB-T-282.
ALMA-TADEMA, Sir Lawrence.
Eng. Holland 1836-1912 Wiesbaden, Ger. B-Bd-C-DNB-E-T-282.
ALMANNO, Pietro. *see* Alemanno, P.
ALMELOVEEN, Jan van. (Eg)
Dut. Mijdrecht 1652-1700 Utrecht. B-T.
ALMOND, W. Douglas.
Eng. b. London 1866. B.
ALQUIST. *see* Schnars-Alquist.
ALSLOOT, Denis van.
Flem. Brussels 1570-1628. B-T.
ALST, Pieter Cock van. *see* Aelst, P. C. van.
ALSTON, Frederick Cornelius. (Ill)
Am. ad. 1934 St. Louis, Mo. A29.
ALT, Rudolf von.
Ger. Vienna, Aus. 1812-1905 Same. B-T.
ALTDORFER, Albrecht.
Ger. 1480?-1538 Ratisbonne. B-C-E-T-284-801.

ALTEN, Mathias Joseph.
Am. b. Gusenburg, Ger. 1871; ad. 1934 Grand Rapids, Mich. A-F-T-46.
ALTHEIM, Wilhelm.
Ger. b. Grand Gerau (Hesse) 1871. B-T.
ALTICHIERO [or Aldighiero] DA ZEVIO.
It. Zevio 1320-1385. B-T.
ALTISSIMO, Cristofano di Papi Dell'.
It. Florence 1550-1605. B-V.
ALTMANN, Aaron.
Am. b. San Fran., Calif. 1872; ad. 1934 Same. A.
ALTMANN, Alexandre.
Rus. b. Odessa; ac. 1930 Paris. B-DBA.
ALTMANN, Nathan.
Rus. ac. 19th-20th Cent., Russia. Fa.
ALUNNO, Niccolo.
It. Foligno 1430-1502. C-V-722.
ALVAREZ, Catalo Luis.
Sp. 1841-1901. Fa-M.
ALVAREZ, Don Manuel [El Griego]. (S)
Sp. Salamanque 1727-1797. B-E-T.
ALVAREZ, Mabel.
Am. b. Oahu, Hawaii; ad. 1934 Los Angeles, Calif. A.
ALVAREZ Y CUBERO, Don José. (S)
Sp. Priego 1768-1827 Madrid. B-E-T.
ALVARUS [or Alvario]. (Min)
Por. ac. 1527. B-T.
ALY, Gustave.
Fr. b. Arras; ac. 1930 Paris. B-DBA.
ALYWARD, William James *see* Aylward, W. J.
AMADEO, [or Amadei], Giovanni Antonio. (S)
It. Pavia 1447-1522. B-Hs-T-V.
AMALTEO, Pomponio.
It. Motta 1505-1584 San Vito. B-C-E-V.
AMAN-JEAN, Edmond François.
Fr. b. Chevry-Cossigny 1860. B.
AMANS, Jacques.
Am. b. 1801; d. 1888 Paris. B-F-T.
AMATEIS, Edmond Romulus. (S)
Am. b. Rome, It. 1897; ad. 1934 New York. A-Cs-F-W.
AMATEIS, Louis. (S)
Am. Turin, It. 1855-1913 Wash., D. C. A011-F-T-W6.
AMATO, Giovanni Antonio de [The Elder].
It. Naples 1475?-1555. B-T.
AMATRICE, Colo dall' [Nicoló di' Filotesio].
It. Amatrice 1480/90-1547 Ascoli. B.
AMBERG, August Wilhelm.
Ger. Berlin 1822-1899. B.
AMBERGER, Christoph.
Ger. Augsburg 1490/1500-1562/3 Same. B-T.
AMBERGER, Fritz Ludwig. (Ill)
Swi. b. Zurich 1899; ad. 1934 New York. M.
AMBERLING, Friedrich von.
Aus. Vienna 1803-1887 Same. C-T.
AMBROGIO DA MILANO. (S)
It. ac. 1472-1516/7 Venice. B-Hs-T.
AMBROGIO DE BALDESE.
It. Florence 1352-1429. B-T.
AMBROSE, C.
Eng. ac. 1824-1848 London. B-Fa
AMENDOLA, Giambattista. (S)
It. Salerno 1848-1887 Naples. T.
AMENDOLA, Robert Felix Phillip. (S)
Am. ad. 1934 Natick, Mass. M.
AMENKOFF, Georges.
Rus. b. Kamchatka 1890; ex. 1933 New York. M.
AMENT, Robert Selfe.
Am. b. Brooklyn, N. Y. 1879; ad. 1934 New York. A-F.
AMERIGHI [Merisi], Michel Angelo. *see* Caravaggio, M. A.
AMERO, Emilio.
Mex. ex. 1935 New York. M.
AMES, Arthur.
Am. ad. 1934 Santa Ana, Calif. M.
AMES, Edwin Isaac.
Am. b. Loda, Ill. 1862. B-T.
AMES, Ezra.
Am. Framingham, Mass. 1768-1836 Albany, N. Y. B-DAB-F-T-2-6-7.
AMES, Jessie T.
Am. ad. 1934 New York. M.
AMES, Joseph Alexander.
Am. Roxbury, Mass. 1816-1872 New York. B-C-DAB-F-T-4-15.
AMES, May.
Am. b. Cleveland, O.; ad. 1934 Same. A.
AMES, Sarah Fisher. (S)
Am. Lewes, Del. 1817-1901 Wash., D. C. F.
AMICK, Robert Wesley.
Am. Canon City, Colo. 1879; ad. 1934 Old Greenwich, Conn. A-F.
AMIENS SCHOOL.
Fr. ac. 16th century.
AMIET, Cuno [or Kuno].
Swi. b. Soleure 1868. B-676.
AMIGONI [or Amiconi], Jacopo.
It. Venice 1675-1752 Madrid, Sp. B.
AMMAN, Johann.
Ger. 1695-1751. B-T.
AMMAN, Jost [or Jobt].
Ger. Zurich, Swi. 1539-1591 Nüremberg. B-E.
AMMANNATI, Bartolomeo. (S)
It. Florence 1511-1592 Same. B-E-Hs-T-V.
AMOSSOFF, Sergius S.
Rus. 1837-1886 Moscow. B-T.
AMSCHEWITZ, John Henry.
Eng. b. Ramsgate 1882; ad. 1934 London. Wa.
AMSLER, Samuel.
Swi. Schinznach 1791-1849 Munich, Ger. B-E.
AMSTERDAM [or Oostzanen], Jacob Cornelisz van. *see* Cornelisz, Jacob van Amsterdam.
AMURY-DUVAL, Eugène Emmanuel.
Fr. d. 1885 Paris. C.
ANASTASI, Auguste Paul Charles.
Fr. Paris 1820-1889 Same. B.
ANCHINI, Pietro.
It. Florence 1610-1645. B-T.
ANDERLONI, Pietro. (Eg)
It. Brescia 1775-1849 Milan. B-T.
ANDERS, Ernst.
Ger. b. Magdeburg 1845. B-T.
ANDERSEN, Andreas Martin.
Am. Bergen, Nor. 1869-1903 Boston, Mass. A04-B.
ANDERSEN, Christian Schmidt.
Am. 1879-1931. W16.
ANDERSEN, Hendrick Christian. (S)
Am. b. Bergen, Nor. 1872. A20-B-F-T-W14.

ANDERSEN, Martinus.
Am. b. Peru, Ind. 1878; ad. 1934 New York. A-F-181.

ANDERSON, Abraham Archibald.
Am. b. New York 1847; ad. 1934 Same. A-B-C-F-T-W-15.

ANDERSON, Alexander. (Eg)
Am. [First Am. wood engraver] New York 1775-1870 Jersey City, N. J. Bd-DAB-F-T-2-6-7-8-14-15-45-185

ANDERSON, Alice Sloan.
Am. ex. 1935 New York. M.

ANDERSON, Carl Thomas.
Am. b. Madison, Wis. 1865; ex. 1933 New York A28-M.

ANDERSON, C. W. (Et)
Am. ad. 1935 New York. M.

ANDERSON, Dorothy Visju.
Am. b. Oslo, Nor.; ad. 1934 Hollywood, Calif. A.

ANDERSON, Ernfrid. (S)
Am. b. Sweden 1896; ad. 1935 Elmira, N. Y. A.

ANDERSON, Florence Ann Mewhinney.
Am. b. Terre Haute, Ind. 1874; ad. 1934 El Paso, Tex. A.

ANDERSON, Frank Hartley. (Eg)
Am. ad. 1935 Birmingham, Ala. M.

ANDERSON, Frederic A. (Ill)
Am. ad. 1934 Phila., Pa. A.

ANDERSON, G. Adolph.
Am. b. Rochester, Minn. 1897; ad. 1934 Mt. Tremper, N. Y. A-F.

ANDERSON, [Miss] Heath.
Am. b. San Fran., Calif. 1903; ad. 1934 Same. A.

ANDERSON, J. H.
Eng. ac. 1892 London. B.

ANDERSON, James Bell.
Scot. b. Edinburgh 1886; ad. 1934 Glasgow. Wa.

ANDERSON, Joel Randolph.
Am. b. So. Britain, Conn. 1905; ad. 1934 Waterbury, Conn. A.

ANDERSON, John. (Eg)
Eng. ac. 1799. DNB.

ANDERSON, Julia.
Mrs. C. D. Doerfler.
Am. b. Milwaukee, Wis. 1871; ad. 1934 Wauwatosa, Wis. A.

ANDERSON, Karl.
Am. b. Oxford, O. 1874; ad. 1934 Westport, Conn. A-F-T-W-46-757.

ANDERSON, Martha Fort.
Mrs. Frank Hartley Anderson.
Am. b. Macon, Ga. 1885; ad. 1934 Birmingham, Ala. A.

ANDERSON, Martin ["Cynicus"]. (Cari)
Scot. 1854-1932. Y01933

ANDERSON, Nils.
Swe. Ostergötland. 1817-1865 Vaxholm. B.

ANDERSON, Oscar.
Am. b. Gotland, Swe. 1873; ad. 1934 Gloucester, Mass. A.

ANDERSON, Percy E. (Ill)
Am. Chicago 1881-1934 Westport, Conn. M.

ANDERSON, Peter Bernard. (S)
Am. b. Sweden 1898; ad. 1934 St. Paul, Minn. A-F.

ANDERSON, Ronald.
Am. Lynn, Mass. 1886-1926 So. Norwalk, Conn. A024-F.

ANDERSON, Ruth A.
Mrs. Samuel Temple.
Am. b. Carlisle, Pa.; ad. 1934 Boston. A.

ANDERSON, [Mrs.] Sophie.
Mrs. Walter Anderson.
Eng. b. 1847; ac. 1894 London. B-T.

ANDERSON, Stanley. (Et)
Eng. b. Bristol 1884; ex. 1934 London. B-Wa.

ANDERSON, Victor Coleman.
Am. b. Peekskill, N. Y. 1882; ad. 1934 White Plains, N. Y. A.

ANDERSON, W. (Eg)
Am. ac. Cincinnati, O. 1855. F-7.

ANDERSON, William.
Scot. 1757-1837. DNB-T.

ANDERTON, Henry.
Eng. 1630-1665? DNB-T.

ANDO, Kaigetsudo.
Jap. J. Vol. 2 pages 29 and 38.

ANDRÉ, Albert.
Fr. b. Lyons 1869. B-DBA-T.

ANDRÉ, Alexis.
Fr. b. Paris; ac. 1904 Same. DBA.

ANDRÉ, Jean Paul de.
Fr. ac. 1662-86 Grenoble. B-T.

ANDRE, John. (Min)
Am. London, Eng. 1751-1780 Tappan, N. Y. T-6-45.

ANDRÉ, Master. *see* Master André.

ANDRÉ, Michel François.
Fr. Aix 1700-1778 Paris. B.

ANDREA D'AGNOLO. *see* Sarto, A. del.

ANDREA DA FARENZE. *see* Andrea di Giusto [Manzini].

ANDREA DA FIRENZE [Bonaiuto].
It. ac. 1350-1387 Florence. B-T.

ANDREA DA FIRENZE [Ciccione]. (S)
It. ac. 1388-1453. B-Hs-T.

ANDREA DEL CASTAGNO. *see* Castagno, A. del.

ANDREA DEL SARTO. *see* Sarto, A. del.

ANDREA DI BARTOLO.
It. ac. 1371-1428. Siena. B.

ANDREA DI GIUSTO [Manzini].
It. b. Florence; ac. 1424-1498. B-T.

ANDREA DI NICCOLÓ DI GIACOMO.
It. Siena 1440-1514. B-T.

ANDREA, Zorn. *see* Zorn, Andrea.

ANDREANI, Andrea.
It. Mantua. 1540/60-1623. B-E-T.

ANDREASEN-LINDBORG, [Mrs.] Ingeborg.
Am. b. Denmark 1876. A20-T.

ANDREASI, Ippolito.
It. Mantua 1548-1608 Same. B-T.

ANDREONI, Orazio. (S)
It. ac. 1884-1893. B-T.

ANDREOTTI, Frederigo.
It. Florence 1847-1883. B.

ANDREOTTI, Libéro.
It. Pescia 1875-1933 Paris. B-T.

ANDRÉU, Mariano.
Sp. b. Barcelona 1888; ad. 1934 Paris. DBA.

ANDREW, John. (Eg)
Am. Hull, Eng. 1815-1870 Boston. B-F-T.

ANDREW, Richard.
Am. b. Ireland 1867; ad. 1934 Gloucester, Mass. A.
ANDREWS, Ambrose. (Min)
Am. ac. 1829-1831 Troy, N. Y. F-6.
ANDREWS, Bernice. *see* Fernow.
ANDREWS, Eliphalet Fraser.
Am. Steubenville, O. 1835-1915 Wash., D. C. A012-B-F-T-W7-15.
ANDREWS, George Henry.
Eng. Lambeth, 1816-1898 Hammersmith. B.
ANDREWS, Helen Frances.
Am. b. Farmington, Conn. 1872; ad. 1934 Same. A-F.
ANDREWS, J. Winthrop.
Am. b. Newton, Mass. 1879; ad. 1934, Yonkers, N. Y. M.
ANDREWS, Joseph. (Eg)
Am. Hingham, Mass. 1806-1873 Boston. B-F-T-2-7-15-40.
ANDREWS, Marietta Minnegerode.
Mrs. Eliphalet Fraser Andrews.
Am. Richmond, Va. 1869-1931. A. A20-F-W16.
ANDREWS, Sybil. (Eg)
Eng. ad. 1934 London. Wa.
ANDRIESSEN, Anthonie.
Dut. Amsterdam 1746-1813. B-T.
ANDRIEU, Jean Bertrand. (S)
Fr. Bordeaux 1761-1822. B-E-T.
ANDRIEU, Jules.
Am. New Orleans, La. 1844-1923 Same. B-183.
ANDRIEU, Pierre.
Fr. Paris 1821-1892 Same. B-T.
ANDROSTHENES. (S)
Gr. ac. 4th century B.C. in Athens. B-E-T.
ANDROUSOW, Vadime. (S)
Rus. b. 1895. Fa.
ANDRUS, Vera.
Am. ex. 1934 New York. M.
ANELLI, Francesco.
Am. ac. 1841-1878. M.
ANESI, Paulo.
It. Rome 1700-1761. B.
ANGAROLA, Anthony.
Am. Chicago 1893-1929. A026-F.
ANGAS, George French.
Eng. Durham 1822-1886 London. DNB-T.
ANGEL, John. (S)
Br. ac. 1934 New York. M.
ANGEL, Rifka.
Am. b. Russia 1899; ad. 1934 Chicago. A.
ANGELA, Emilio. (S)
Am. b. Italy 1889; ad. 1934 New York. A-Cs-F.
ANGELI. *see also* Angolo.
ANGELI, Filippo di Liano de [Le Napolitan].
It. Rome 1600-1640 Same. B-T.
ANGELI, Giuseppe.
It. Venice 1709-1798. B-T.
ANGELI, Heinrich von.
Aus. Sopron, Oldenburg, 1840-1925. B.
ANGELI, Marguerite de. (Ill)
Mrs. John D. de Angeli.
Am. b. Lapeer, Mich. 1889; ad. 1934 Jenkintown, Pa. M.
ANGELICO, Fra [Giovanni da Fiesole].
It. Vecchio 1387-1455 Rome. B-Bd-C-E-T-V-285-286-287-806-913.
ANGELIS [or Angillis], Pieter.
Flem. Dunkirk 1685-1734 Rennes. B-DNB-T.
ANGELO. *see* Michelangelo.
ANGELO DI PIETRO D'ASSISI. (S)
It. ac. 1362. T.
ANGELO, Emidio. (Cart.)
Am. ad. 1935 Phila., Pa. M.
ANGELO, Valenti. (Ill)
Am. ad. 1934 Bronxville, N. Y. M.
ANGERS, David d'. *see* David d'Angers, P. J.
ANGILLIS, Pieter. *see* Angelis, P.
ANGIOLONI, Roger.
Am. ex. 1934 New York. M.
ANGLADA-CAMARASA, Hermengildo.
Sp. b. Barcelona 1873. B-832.
ANGMAN, Alfons Julius.
Am. b. Stockholm, Swe. 1883; ad. 1934 Oklahoma City, Okla. A.
ANGOLO, André da. *see* Sarto, A. del.
ANGOLO DEL MORO [or Agnolo Battista].
It. b. Verona; ac. 1512-1515. B-V.
ANGRAND, Charles.
Fr. Paris 1887-1926 Same. B.
ANGUIER, François. (S)
Fr. Eu. 1604-1669 Paris. B-E-Hs-T.
ANGUIER, Michel. (S)
Fr. Eu. 1612-1686 Paris. B-E-Hs-T.
ANGUISCINOLA, Anna Maria.
It. ac. 1598 Cremona. T-V.
ANGUISCINOLA, Europa.
It. ac. 1568 Cremona. T-V.
ANGUISCINOLA, Lucia.
It. ac. 1565 Cremona. T-V.
ANGUISCINOLA, Minerva.
It. Cremona 1527-1623 Palermo. T-V.
ANGUISCINOLA [or Anguisciola], Sophonisba.
It. Cremona 1530/5-1620/6 Genoa. B-C-E-T-V.
ANGUS, Margaret.
Eng. ex. 1935 London. M.
ANGUSSOLA. *see* Anguiscinola.
ANICHINI, Luigi [Francesco A.] (Med)
It. ac. 1550 Venice. E-V.
ANISFELD, Boris Israelevich. (P-S) D. 1973 - Cox
Am. b. Russia 1879; ad. 1934 Chicago. M.
ANKENEY, John Sites.
Am. b. Xenia, O. 1870; ad. 1934 Dallas, Tex. A-F-W.
ANKER, Albert.
Swi. Berne 1831-1910 Anet. B-T.
ANNA, Baldasarre d'.
It. Venice 1560?-1640? B-E.
ANNAN, Alice Hawthorne.
Am. b. New York; ad. 1934 Same. A.
ANNEN, Helen Wann.
Mrs. Peter J. Annen.
Am. b. Fairplay, Mo. 1901; ad. 1934 Madison, Wis. A.
ANNENKOFF, Georges.
Rus. b. Kamchatka 1890; ex. 1933 New York. M.
ANNESLEY, Mabel. (Eg)
Eng. ex. 1933 London. M.
ANNIS, W. T.
Eng. ac. 1798-1811 London. B-T.
ANNOT, Madame [Mrs. Rudolph Jacobi].
[Real name Annot Krigar-Menzel, Jacobi.]
Ger. b. Berlin; ad. 1935 New York. DBA-M.

ANOLFO DI CAMBIO. *see* Cambio, A. di.
ANQUETIN, JULES LOUIS.
Fr. b. Etrépagny 1861. B-DBA.
ANREP, BORIS. (Mosaic)
Eng. ex. 1930 London. 825
ANROOY, ANTON VAN.
Dut. b. Zatbommel 1870. B-T.
ANRUYEN, H.
Fr. ac. 1753. M.
ANSANO DI PIETRO. *see* Pietro Sano, di M.
ANSBACHER, JESSIE.
Am. b. Wilkesbarre, Pa.; ad. 1934 New York. A.
ANSDELL, RICHARD.
Eng. Liverpool 1815-1885 Farnborough. B-DNB-E.
ANSELIN, JEAN LOUIS.
Fr. Paris 1754-1823. B.
ANSELMI, MICHELANGELO.
It. Lucca 1491-1554 Parma. C-V.
ANSHUTZ, THOMAS POLLOCK.
Am. Newport, Ky. 1851-1912 Ft. Wash., Pa. A010-C-DAB-F-T-W7-46.
ANSIAUX, JEAN JOSEPH ELÉNORE ANTOINE.
Flem. Liège 1764-1840 Paris. C.
ANSIGLIONE, LEOPOLDO.
It. Piedmont 1832-1894 Rome. B-T.
ANSINGH, [Miss] LIZZI.
Dut. b. Utrecht; ad. 1934 Amsterdam. DBA.
ANSUINO DA FORLI.
It. ac. 1438-1448 Padua. B-T.
ANTAKOLSKY, MARK MATVEICH. (S)
Rus. Wilna 1843-1902 Hamburg, Ger. T.
ANTELAMI, BENEDETTO. (S)
It. [Byzantine] ac. 1177-1233. B-Hs.
ANTENOR.
Gr. ac. 510-480 B.C. Athens. B-E-Hs-T.
ANTHONISSEN, HENDRIK VAN.
Dut. Antwerp 1605/6-1654/60 Amsterdam. B.
ANTHONISZ [of Teunissen], CORNELIS.
Dut. 1499-1553 Amsterdam. B-T.
ANTHONY, ANDREW VARICK STOUT. (Eg)
Am. New York 1835-1906 West Newton, Mass. A06-B-DAB-F-T-8-15-151-185.
ANTHONY, ELIZABETH M.
Am. b. 1903; ad. 1935 Hackensack, N. J. M.
ANTHONY, GEORGE WILFRED [Gabriel Tinto].
Eng. Manchester 1810-1859. B.
ANTHONY, HENRY MARK.
Eng. Manchester 1817-1886 London. B.
ANTICO [Riccio]. *see* Briosco, Andrea.
ANTIGNA, JEAN PIERRE ALEXANDRE.
Fr. Orléans 1817-1878. B.
ANTIGONUS [or Antiqonos]. (S)
Gr. ac. 240 B.C. Athens. T.
ANTIOCHOS. (S)
Gr. ac. 1st century B.C. B-Hs.
ANTIPHILUS.
Gr. ac. 3rd century B.C. B-E.
ANTLERS, MAX H.
Am. b. Berlin, Ger. 1873; ad. 1915 New York. A12.
ANTOKOLSKI, MARKUS. (S)
Rus. Wilna 1843-1902 Hamburg, Ger. T.
ANTOLÍNEZ, JOSÉ [The Younger].
Sp. Séville 1639-1676 Madrid. B-T.
ANTOLÍNEZ Y SARABIA, [Francesco] CLAUDIO JOSÉ VINCENTE.
Sp. Séville 1644-1700 Madrid. B-T.
ANTOMMARCHI, C. FRANÇOIS. (S)
It. Corse 1780-1838. B-T.
ANTONELLO DA MESSINA.
It. Messina 1422/30-1479 Venice. B-Bd-E-T-V-476.
ANTONIAZZO, ROMANO. *see* Romano, A.
ANTONIO, ANTONELLO. *see* Antonello da Messina.
ANTONIO, FEDERIGHI. (S)
It. 1420?-1490. Hs-T.
ANTONIO, ROSSELLINO. *see* Rossellino.
ANTONIO, VENEZIANO.
[Antonio di Francesco da Venzia.]
It. ac. 1313-1387 Florence. T-V.
ANTONIO DA TRENTO [Fantuzzi]. (Eg)
It. Trente 1508-1550 Bologna. B-T.
ANTONIO DA VITERBO [Pastura].
It. ac. Rome 1460-1516. B-T-V.
ANTONOV.
Rus. ex. 1935 London. M.
ANTRAL, LOUIS ROBERT.
Fr. b. Marne 1895. DBA.
ANTROBUS, JOHN.
Am. d. 1907 Detroit, Mich. A06.
ANTROPOV, ALEXEY PETROVITCH.
Rus. 1716-1795. B.
ANTUM, AERT [or Aart] VAN.
Dut. ac. 1604-1640 Amsterdam. B.
ANTWERP MANNERISTS.
[Hugo and Willem van Antwerp.]
Flem. ac. about 1520. V.
AOYAMA, YOSHIO.
Jap. b. Tokio 1894. DBA.
APELLES [or Apelle].
Gr. ac. 4th century B.C. Colophon. B-E.
APOL, LOUIS [or Lodewyck Franciscus Hendrik].
Dut. ac. The Hague 1850. B-T.
APOLLODORUS.
Gr. b. Athens; ac. 408 B.C. B-E.
APOLLONIOUS [of Tralles]. (S)
Gr. ac. 2d century B.C. B-E-Hs-T.
APPEL, CHARLES P.
Am. b. Brooklyn, N. Y. 1857; ad. 1934 East Orange, N. J. A20-F.
APPEL, VIOLA.
Am. ad. 1934 East Orange, N. J. M.
APPERLEY, GEORGE OWEN WYNNE.
Eng. b. Ventnor 1884; ad. 1934 Tangier, Africa. Wa.
APPIAN, JACQUES BARTHELEMY [or Jules].
Fr. Lyons 1818-1898. B-T.
APPIAN, JEAN LOUIS.
Fr. Lyons 1862-1896 Same. B-T.
APPIANI, ANDREA [The Elder].
It. Milan 1754/6-1817. B-C-E-T.
APPIANI, ANDREA [The Younger].
It. b. Milan 1817-1865. B-T.
APPIANI [or Appiano], GIUSEPPE.
It. d. Mayence, Ger. 1786. B-T.
APPLEBEE, FRANK WOODBERRY.
Am. b. Boston 1902; ad. 1934 Auburn, Ala. A.
APPLEBY, ERNEST W.
Eng. ac. 1886-1907 London. B.
APPLEGATE, FRANK G. (S)
Am. Atlanta, Ill. 1882-1931. A028-W16.

APPLETON, A.
Eng. ac. 1929. Fa.
APPLETON, ELIZA BRIDGHAM. (S)
Mrs. Everard Appleton.
Am. b. 1882; ad. 1934 Providence, R. I. A.
APPLETON, THOMAS GOLD.
Am. Boston 1812-1884 Same. B-F-T-15.
APT, ULRICH [The Elder].
Ger. b. Augsburg; ac. 1486-1532. T.
APTHROP, LOUISE L.
Am. b. Orange, N. J. 1878; ad. 1934 Cambridge, Mass. A.
AQUILA, ANDREA DALL'. (S)
It. ac. 15th century in Florence. B-Hs.
ARAKI, KWAMPO.
Jap. ac. 1860 Japan. J, Vol. 2, page 88.
ARANDA, JOSÉ [or Luis] JIMENÈZ.
Sp. Séville 1837-1903. B.
ARAPOFF, ALEXIS.
Am. ad. 1934 Boston, Mass. M.
ARBIT-BLATES, NICOLAI.
Lithuanian. ex. 1934 New York. M.
ARBORELIUS, OLOF PER ULRICK.
Swe. Orsa 1842-1915. B.
ARCA, NICCOLÒ DELL'. *see* Bari, N. da.
ARCANGELO DI COLA DA CAMERINO. *see* Camerino, A. di C. da.
ARCHAMBAULT, ANNA MARGARETTA.
Am. b. Phila., Pa.; ad. 1934 Same. A-B-F-T-W.
ARCHDEACON, SPENCER. (Cart.)
Am. ad. 1932 Phila., Pa. M.
ARCHER, EDMUND MINOR.
Am. b. Richmond, Va. 1904; ad. 1934 New York. A.
ARCHER, JAMES.
Scot. Edinburgh 1823-1904. Shian. DNB.
ARCHER, JOHN WYKEHAM.
Eng. 1808-1864 London. DNB.
ARCHERMUS OF CHIOS. (S)
Gr. ac. 580 B.C. B-E-Hs-T.
ARCHIPENKO, ALEXANDER. (P-S)
Am. b. Kiev, Ukraine; ad. 1934 New York. A-Cs-Hs-288-700.
ARCIERI, CHARLES F.
Am. b. San Fran., Calif. 1885; ad. 1934 Grantwood, N. J. A.
ARCT, EUGENJUSZ.
Pol. ad. 1934 Warsaw. M.
ARDELL, JAMES MARC.
Ir. Dublin 1710-1765 London. B.
ARDISSON, GAITAN. (S)
Am. b. Italy; d. 1925 Milford, Conn. A023.
ARDIZZONE, EDWARD JEFFREY IRVING.
Eng. ex. 1934 London. Wa.
ARELLANO, JUAN DE.
Sp. Santorca 1614-1676 Madrid. B-C.
ARENTINO, LEONE [or Lioni]. *see* Leoni, L.
ARENTINO, NICCOLÒ LAMBERTI. *see* Lamberti, N.
ARENTSZ, ARENT [or Cabel].
Dut. Amsterdam 1586-1635 Same. B-722.
ARETINO, SPINELLO. *see* Spinello.
ARETUSI, CESARE.
It. d. 1612 Bologna. B-722.
AREZZO DA MARGARITONE. *see* Margaritone da Arezzo.
AREZZO, NICCOLÒ D'. *see* Niccolò d' Arezzo.
ARFE Y VILLAFANE, JUAN DE. (S)
Sp. 1535-1603 Madrid. Hs-T.
ARGENT, MICHEL D.
Flem. Liége 1751-1842 Lüttich. B.
ARGENTI, GIOSUE [or Josua]. (S)
It. b. Vigiu 1819. B-T.
ARGUNOFF, IVAN PETROWITSCH.
Rus. 1727-1797. B.
ARGUNOFF, NICKOLAI IWANOWITSCH.
Rus. 1771-1829. B.
ARIA, MICHELE D' [or Daria]. (S)
It. ac. 1466-1502. B.
ARISTIDES OF THEBES.
Gr. ac. 360-330 B.C. B-E.
ARISTODEMUS [or Aristodemos]. (S)
Gr. ac. 320 B.C. in Sicyon. B-T.
ARISTOKLES. (S)
Gr. ac. 520 B.C. B-Hs-T.
ARKESILAOS. (S)
Roman. ac. 1st century B.C. B-Hs.
ARKHIPOV, ABRAM EFIMOVEITCH.
Rus. b. Egorievsk Ryazan 1862; d. 1933. B-T.
ARKHIPOV, SERGEI N.
Rus. b. 1882; ac. 1935 Russia. M.
ARLAUD, JACQUES ANTOINE.
Swi. Geneva 1668-1743/6 Same. B.
ARLAUD, MARC LOUIS.
Swi. Orbe 1772-1845 Lausanne. B.
ARLENT-EDWARDS, SAMUEL. *see* Edwards, S. A.
ARMAND-DUMARESQ, EDOUARD.
Fr. Paris 1826-1895 Same. B.
ARMBUSTER, OTTO HERMAN. (Ill)
Am. Cincinnati, O. 1865-1908 New York. A07-B.
ARMENISE, RAFFAELLO.
It. b. Bari 1852. B.
ARMER, [Mrs.] LAURA ADAMS. (Ill)
Am. b. Sacramento, Calif. 1874; ad. 1934 Berkeley, Calif. M.
ARMER, RUTH.
Am. b. San Fran., Calif. 1896; ad. 1934 Same. A.
ARMER, SIDNEY. (Ill)
Am. b. San Fran., Calif. 1871; ad. 1934 Berkeley, Calif. M.
ARMFIELD, GEORGE SMITH.
Eng. ac. 1840-1880 London. B.
ARMFIELD, MAXWELL.
Am. b. Ringwood, Eng. 1862; ad. 1935 New York. A20-B-F-T-272.
ARMIN, EMIL. d 1971 Chi.
Am. b. Radantz, Rumania 1883; ad. 1934 Chicago. A.
ARMINGTON, CAROLINE HELENA. (Et)
Am. b. Brampton, Can. 1875; ad. 1934 Paris. A-B.
ARMINGTON, FRANK MILTON.
Am. b. Fordwich, Can. 1876; ad. 1934 Paris. A-B.
ARMITAGE, EDWARD.
Eng. London 1817-1896 Tunbridge Wells. B-Bd-DNB.
ARMITAGE, THOMAS LIDDELL.
Eng. ac. 1885-1891. B.
ARMOUR, GEORGE DENHOLM. (Ill)
Scot. b. 1864. B.
ARMS, JESSIE. *see* Botke, [Mrs.] J. A.
ARMS, JOHN TAYLOR. (Et)
Am. b. Wash., D. C. 1887; ex. 1934 New York. A28-F-W.

ARMSTEAD, Henry Hugh. (S)
Eng. Bloomsbury 1828-1905 London. B-DNB-E-Hs-T.
ARMSTRONG, Amos Lee.
Am. b. Many, La. 1899; ad. 1934 Monroe, La. A.
ARMSTRONG, Arthur.
Am. b. Lancaster Co., Pa. 1798-1851. F.
ARMSTRONG, David Maitland.
Am. Newburgh, N. Y. 1836-1918 New York. A015-B-DAB-F-T-W10-15.
ARMSTRONG, Elizabeth Adela. *see* Forbes, E. A.
ARMSTRONG, Estelle Manon.
Am. b. Lincoln, Ill. 1884; ad. 1934 Nutley, N. J. A.
ARMSTRONG, Francis Abel William Taylor.
Eng. Malmesbury 1849-1920. B.
ARMSTRONG, Helen Maitland.
Am. b. Florence, It. 1869; ad. 1934 New York. F-W.
ARMSTRONG, John. (Mu.)
Eng. ad. 1935 London. Wa.
ARMSTRONG, Samuel John.
Am. b. Denver, Colo. 1893; ad. 1934 Santa Barbara, Calif. A-F.
ARMSTRONG, Thomas.
Eng. Manchester 1832-1911 Abbots Langley. DNB.
ARMSTRONG, Voyle Neville.
Am. b. Dobbin, W. Va. 1891; ad. 1934 Wichita Falls, Tex. A-F-181.
ARMSTRONG, William G. (Eg)
Am. b. Montgomery Co., Pa. 1823-1890. F-T-6-7-40-45
ARMSTRONG, William T. L.
Am. Belfast, Ir. 1881-1934 Nutley, N. J. A-M.
Obit. N. Y. papers. 6, 24, 1934.
ARNETT, Eleanor. (S)
Am. ad. 1935 Phila., Pa. M.
ARNHEIM, Hans. (S)
Ger. b. Berlin 1881; ex. 1934 New York. B-T.
ARNO, Peter. (Cart.)
[Curtis Armoux Peters, Jr.]
Am. ad. 1934 New York. M.
ARNOLD, Aden F.
Am. b. Jefferson, Ia.; ad. 1934 Same. A.
ARNOLD, [Mrs.] Clara Maxfield.
Am. b. East Providence, R. I. 1879; ad. 1934 Same. A.
ARNOLD, Dorothy J.
Am. ad. 1934 Princeton, N. J. M.
ARNOLD, Frank McIntosh.
Am. 1867-1932 Orlando, Fla. A029.
ARNOLD, Friedrich.
Ger. Zenlenroda 1831-1862 Florence, It. B-T.
ARNOLD, Johann Friedrich.
Ger. 1780-1809 Berlin. B-T.
ARNOLD, John Knowlton.
Am. 1834-1909 Providence, R. I. A07-F.
ARNOLD, Joseph.
Swi. Tyrol 1788-1879 Innsbrück. B.
ARNOLD, Mary E.
Am. ad. 1934 Toledo, O. M.
ARNOLFO OF FLORENCE. *see* Cambio, A. di.
ARNOULT, Nicolas.
Fr. ac. 17th century in Paris. B-T.
ARNOUX, Charles Albert. (Cari.)
[Pseudonym Bertall.]
Fr. Paris 1820-1883 Same. B-T.
ARNOUX, Michel.
Fr. Paris 1833-1877. B.
ARNULPHY, Claude.
Fr. Aix 1697-1786. B-T.
ARONSON, Boris.
Am. ac. 1934 Jerusalem, Palestine. M-892.
AROSENIUS, Ivar Axel Henrik.
Swe. 1878-1909. DBA-T.
ARP, Hans.
Ger. b. 1888; ex. 1934 New York. M.
ARPA, José.
Am. b. Séville 1868; ad. 1934 San Antonio, Tex. A.
ARPINO, Il Cavaliere d . *see* Cesari, Giuseppe.
ARRUE, Ramiro.
Sp. b. Bilbao; ac. 1934 Paris. M.
ARTAN, Louis. [St. Martin.]
Dut. The Hague 1837-1890 Nieuport. B.
ARTAUD, William.
Eng. 1776-1822 London. B.
ARTER, J. Charles.
Am. d. 1923 Alliance, O. A021-B-F.
ARTHOIS [or Artois], Jacques van.
Flem. Brussels 1613-1684/6. B-C-T-722.
ARTHUR, Revington.
Am. b. Glenbrook, Conn.; ad. 1934 Same. A.
ARTHUR, Robert.
Am. Phila., Pa. 1850-1914 New York. A012-F.
ARTHURS, Stanley Massey.
Am. b. Kenton, Del. 1877; ad. 1934 Wilmington, Del. A-B-F-T-W.
ARTIGUE, Jack.
Fr. ac. 1907 in Paris. B.
ARTIS, William Ellisworth. (S)
Am. b. No. Car. 1914; ad. 1934 New York. M.
ARTLETT, Richard Austin.
Br. 1807-1873. DNB-T.
ARTS, Hendrick. *see* Aerts, H.
ARTVELT, Andries van. *see* Ertvelt [or Artvelt], A. van.
ARTZ [or Arts], David Adolf Constant.
Dut. The Hague 1837-1890. B-T.
ARTZYBASHEFF, Boris. (Ill)
Am. b. Russia; ad. 1934 New York. M.
ARWIN, Emil.
Am. ad. 1934 Chicago. M.
ARX, Heinrich von.
Swi. Berne 1802-1858 Same. T.
ASAH, Kiowa.
Am. Indian. ex. 1930 New York. 411.
ASAH, Spencer.
Am. Indian. ex. 1930 New York. 411.
ASAM, Egid Quiren. (S)
Ger. Tegernsee 1692-1750 Manheim. T.
ASCENZI [or Assenzi], Carlo.
It. ac. 18th century Rome. B.
ASCH, Pieter Janszoon.
Dut. Delft 1603-1678 Same. B.
ASHBROOK, Paul.
Am. b. New York 1867; ad. 1934 Cinn. O. A.
ASHBURTON, Mary.
Mrs. Mary A. P. Emmerich.
Am. b. Staten Island, N. Y.; ad. 1934 Wash., D. C. A.

ASHBY, Henry.
Eng. Wotton 1744-1818. T.
ASHE, Edmund M.
Am. ad. 1934 Pittsburgh, Pa. A.
ASHER, Louis.
Ger. Hamburg 1804-1878 Same. C.
ASHERMAN, Edward H.
Am. b. Milwaukee, Wis. 1878; ad. 1934 New York. A.
ASHFIELD, Edward.
Br. ac. 1680-1700. DNB.
ASHFORD, Frank Clifford.
Am. ac. 1910 Paris, Fr. B.
ASHFORD, William.
Eng. Birmingham 1746?-1824 Dublin, Ir. DNB-T.
ASHLEY, Clifford Warren.
Am. b. New Bedford, Mass. 1881; ad. 1934 Wilmington, Del. A-B-F.
ASHLEY, L. Seymour.
Am. d. 1912. A010.
ASHLEY, William John.
Am. England 1868-1921 Mt. Vernon, N. Y. F.
ASHMORE, Charles.
Eng. d. 1925 London. B-Fa.
ASHTON, Ethel.
Am. ad. 1934 Phila., Pa. M.
ASHTON, James.
Br. b. Isle of Man 1860. M.
ASHTON, Julian Rossi.
Eng. b. Surrey 1851. B.
ASHTON, [Mrs.] May Malone.
Am. ad. 1934 Wash., D. C. A.
ASHTON, ["Will."] John William.
Eng. b. York 1881; ad. 1935 Sydney, Aust. B-Wa.
ASKEVOLD, Anders Monsen.
Swe. Askevold 1834-1900 Düsseldorf, Ger. B-T.
ASKEW, Richard. (P-Ceramics)
Eng. d. 1798 Bilston. T.
ASNE. *see* Lasne.
ASPER, Hans. [The Elder].
Swi. Zurich 1499-1571 Same. B-C-E.
ASPERTINI, Amico. (S)
It. Bologna 1475-1552. B-C-V.
ASPERTINI, Guido.
It. ac. 1491 Bologna. B-T-722.
ASPETTI, Tiziano. (S)
It. Padua 1565-1607. B.
ASSARETO, Giovacchino.
It. Genoa 1600-1649. Fa.
ASSELIN, Paul Maurice.
Fr. b. Orléans; ad. 1934 Neuilly. B-DBA.
ASSELT, Jan van der.
Flem. ac. 1364/96 Ghent, Belg. B-T.
ASSELYN [or Asselin], Jan van.
Dut. Amsterdam 1610-1660 Same. B-C-E-722.
ASSEN, Jan van.
Dut. Amsterdam 1635-1695 Same. B.
ASSMUS, Robert.
Ger. b. Stuhm, Prussia 1837. B.
ASTI, Angelo.
It. Paris 1847-1903 Mantua. B.
ASTLEY, John.
Eng. Shropshire 1730?-1787 Cheshire. DNB-T.
ATAMIAN, Charles.
Armenian. ac. 1930 Paris. DBA.
ATCHISON, Joseph Anthony. (S)
Am. b. Wash., D. C. 1895; ad. 1934 Same. A.
ATHENIS [or Athenaios]. (S)
Gr. (Chios); ac. 540 B.C. B-E-Hs.
ATHENODORUS. (S)
Gr. ac. 80 B.C. Rhodes. B-Hs.
ATHERTON, Ezra. (Min)
Am. ac. 1830-1842 Boston. B-F-T-6.
ATHERTON, John. (Ill.)
Am. ex. 1935 New York. M.
ATHEY, Ruth. *see* Vivash.
ATKINS, Albert Henry. (S)
Am. b. Milwaukee, Wis.; ad. 1934 Boston. A-Cs-F-W.
ATKINS, Florence Elizabeth.
Am. b. Pleasant Hill, La.; ad. 1934 San Fran., Calif. A.
ATKINS, [Mrs.] Louise Allen. (S)
Am. b. Lowell, Mass.; ad. 1934 Boston. A-W.
ATKINS, Mildred.
Am. ex. 1935 New York. M.
ATKINS, Samuel.
Eng. ac. 1787-1808 London. DNB-T.
ATKINSON, John Augustus.
Eng. London 1775-1831/3. B-DNB.
ATKINSON, Thomas Lewis.
Eng. b. Salisbury 1817. B.
ATKINSON, William E.
Can. Toronto, Ont. 1862-1926. B.
ATTAVANTE [or Vante], Gabriello. (Min)
It. 1452-1517? Florence. T-V.
ATTIRET, Claude François. (S)
Fr. Dôle 1728-1804 Same. B-T.
ATTWELL, Mabel Lucie. (Ill.)
Eng. ad. 1934 London M.
ATWATER, Grace Elizabeth.
Am. d. 1909 New York. A08-B-T.
ATWATER, Jean Howe. *see* Morse, J. H.
ATWELL, Julia Hill.
Am. 1880-1930. A027.
ATWOOD, Clare.
Mrs. F. W. Fitts.
Am. b. Worcester, Mass. 1874. A28.
ATWOOD, Gladys.
Am. ad. 1934 New York. M.
ATWOOD, Helen G.
Mrs. Helen A. Douglas.
Am. b. New Haven, Conn. 1878; ad. 1934 Phila., Pa. A.
ATWOOD, Mary Hall. (Ill)
Am. ad. 1934 Los Angeles, Calif. A.
ATWOOD, Robert.
Am. ad. 1934 Orange, N. J. M.
AUBÉ, Jean Paul. (S)
Fr. Longwy 1837-1916 Capbreton. B-DBA-E-T-798.
AUBERJONOIS, René Victor.
Fr. b. Montagny 1872. B-DBA.
AUBERT, Jean Ernest.
Fr. Paris 1824-1906. B-C-T.
AUBERT, Jean Louis.
Fr. Paris 1824-1906. M.
AUBERT, Joseph.
Fr. Nantes 1840-1924 Neuilly. B-DBA-T.
AUBERT, Michel.
Fr. Paris 1700-1757 Same. B-T.

AUBERTIN, François.
Ger. Metz 1773-1821 Ghent, Belg. B-T.
AUBIN. *see* Saint-Aubin.
AUBLET, Albert.
Fr. b. Paris 1851. B-DBA.
AUBREY, Charles. (Eg)
Fr. ac. 1822-1852. B.
AUBREY, Etienne.
Fr. Versailles 1745-1781. B-C-T.
AUBREY, Peter.
Ger. Openheim 1596-1668 Strasburg. B.
AUBREY-LECOMTE, Hyacinthe Louis Victor Jean Baptiste.
Fr. Nice 1787-1858 Paris. B.
AUBRY, Emile.
Fr. b. Setif, Algeria 1880; ac. 1905 Paris. B-DBA.
AUBURTIN, Jean François.
Fr. b. Paris 1866. B-DBA.
AUCELLO, Salvatore.
Am. b. Sicily 1904; ad. 1935 Pleasantville, N. Y. M.
AUCHIAH.
Am. Indian; ex. 1931 New York. 411.
AUDEBERT, Giraud. (S)
Fr. ac. 1757 Toulon. B-T.
AUDENAERDE [or Auden-Aert], Robert van.
Flem. Ghent, Belg. 1663-1743 Same. B-T.
AUDENAERT, August.
Belg. ex. 1934 New York. M.
AUDINET, Phillip. (Eg)
Eng. London 1766-1837 Same. DNB-T.
AUDOUIN, Pierre.
Fr. Paris 1768-1822 Same. B.
AUDRAN, Benoît [The Elder].
Fr. Lyons 1661-1721. B-T.
AUDRAN, Benoît [The Younger].
Fr. Paris 1698-1772 Same. B-T.
AUDRAN, Charles.
Fr. Paris 1594-1674. B-T.
AUDRAN, Claude I.
Fr. Paris 1597-1675 Lyons. B-T.
AUDRAN, Claude II.
Fr. Lyons 1639-1684 Paris. B-T.
AUDRAN, Claude III.
Fr. Lyons 1685-1734 Paris. B-T.
AUDRAN, Gérard [or Girard].
Fr. Lyons 1640-1703 Paris. B-E-T.
AUDRAN, Germain.
Fr. Lyons 1631-1710 Same. B-T.
AUDRAN, Jean.
Fr. Lyons 1667-1756 Paris. B-E-T.
AUDUBON, John James [Laforest]. (P-Birds)
Am. Les Cayes, Haiti 1785-1851 New York. B-C-DAB-E-F-T-4-15-45-98-636.
AUDUBON, John Woodhouse.
Am. 1812-1862 New York. B-F.
AUDUBON, Victor Gifford.
Am. 1809-1860; ac. New York. B-F-T.
AUENAERD [or Auden-Aert], Robert van.
Flem. Ghent, Belg. 1663-1743 Same. B-T.
AUER, Lili. (S)
Ger. b. 1904; ex. 1934 Chicago. M.
AUER, Peter [of Ulm]. (S)
Ger. ac. 1508-1535. B-T.
AUERBACH-LEVY, William. (Et)
Am. b. Russia 1889; ad. 1934 New York. A-F.
AUGUR, Hezekiah. (S)
Am. New Haven, Conn. 1791-1858 Same. B-DAB-F-Ta-2-3-15.
AUGUSTE, Jules Robert. (P-S)
Fr. 1789?-1850. T.
AUGUSTIN, Jean Baptiste Jacques.
Fr. St. Die 1759-1832 Paris. B.
AULICZEK, Dominik. (S)
Ger. Bohemia 1734-1804 Ger. B-T.
AULT, George C.
Am. b. Cleveland, O. 1891; ad. 1934 New York. A.
AUMONIER, James.
Eng. Camberwell 1832-1911 London. B-DNB.
AUNSPAUGH, Vivian Louise.
Am. b. Bedford, Va.; ad. 1934 Dallas, Tex. A.
AURIFABER, Christian. (Eg)
Ger. ac. 1511/17 Wittenberg. T.
AUROUX, Nicholas.
Fr. b. Pont St. Esprit; d. 1689. B.
AUS, Carol.
Am. b. Norway 1868; ad. 1934 Chicago. A.
AUSTEN, Winifred Marie Louise. *see* Frick, [Mrs.] W. M. L.
AUSTIN, Arthur Everett, Jr.
Am. b. Brookline, Mass. 1900; ad. 1934 Hartford, Conn. A.
AUSTIN, Frederick George. (Et).
Eng. B. Leicester 1902; ad. Hammersmith. Wa.
AUSTIN, Louise M.
Am. b. Shell, Wyo. 1903; ad. 1934 Lincoln, Neb. A.
AUSTIN, Margaret Baer.
Am. b. Baltimore, Md. 1897; ad. 1934 Same. A.
AUSTIN, Paul W.
Am. ad. 1934 Toledo, O. M.
AUSTIN, Robert Sargent. (Et)
Eng. b. Leicester 1895; ad. 1934 London. Wa-830.
AUSTIN, Samuel.
Eng. Liverpool 1796-1834 London. B-DNB.
AUSTIN, Sarah. (Min)
Am. d. 1909 New York. A08.
AUSTRALIAN ARTISTS.
Consult Story of Australian Art, 2 vols. Sydney 1935.
AUSTREIK, [Dr.] W. M. (S)
Am. ad. 1934 New York. M.
AUSTRIAN, Ben.
Am. Reading, Pa. 1870-1921 Kempton, Pa. A019-F.
AUSTRIAN, Florence Hochschild.
Mrs. Charles Robert Austrian.
Am. b. Baltimore, Md. 1889; ad. 1934 Same. A.
AUSUBEL, Sheva.
Am. ad. 1934 New York. M.
AUTISSIER, Louis Marie. (Min)
Fr. Vannes 1772-1830 Brussels, Belg. B.
AUTREAU, Louis.
Fr. Paris 1692-1760 Same. B-T.
AUVRAY, Joseph Félix Henry.
Fr. Cambrai 1800-1833. B.
AUVREST, Pierre Laurent. (Eg)
Fr. b. Paris 1736. B.

AUZOU, Pauline [Desmarquets].
Fr. Paris 1775-1835 Same. B.
AVANT, Mayna.
Am. ad. 1934 Nashville, Tenn. M.
AVANZINO, Nucci.
It. Castillo 1551-1629 Rome. B-V.
AVANZO, Jacopo [da Bologna].
It. 1367-1404 Bologna. T.
AVANZO, Jacopo [da Padova].
It. ac. late 14th century in Padova. T.
AVED, Jacques André Joseph Camelot.
Fr. Douai 1702-1766 Paris. B.
AVELINE, Pierre [The Elder].
Fr. Paris 1654-1722. B-T.
AVELINE, Pierre [The Younger].
Fr. Paris 1679-1742. B-T.
AVELINE, Pierre Alexandre.
Fr. Paris 1702-1760 Same. B.
AVELLAR, Gioseffo de.
Por. ac. 1640 in Lisbon. M.
AVELOT, Henri Louis.
Fr. ac. 1906-1930. B-DBA.
AVENT, Mayna Treanor.
Mrs. Frank Avent.
Am. b. Nashville, Tenn.; ad. 1934 Same. A.
AVERCAMP, Hendrick van.
[Called the "Mute of Kampen"].
Dut. Amsterdam 1585-1663 Kampen. B-C-T.
AVERY, Frances.
Am. ad. 1935 New York. M.
AVERY, Harold. (Ill)
Am. East Elmhurst, N. Y. 1858-1927. A024.
AVERY, Hope.
Mrs. Nelson Mead.
Am. ad. 1934 New York. M.
AVERY, Kenneth Newell.
Am. b. Bay City, Mich. 1883; ad. 1934, Pasadena, Calif. A.
AVERY, Milton C.
Am. b. Altmar, N. Y. 1893; ad. 1934 New York. A.
AVERY, Samuel Putnam. (Eg)
Am. New York 1822-1905 Same. A05-B-T.
AVEY, Martha.
Am. b. Arcola, Ill.; ad. 1934 Oklahoma City, Okla. A.
AVIAT, Jules Charles.
Fr. b. Aubé 1844; ac. 1876-1910 Paris. B-DBA.
AVIGDOR, René.
Fr. b. Nice; ac. 1891-1930 Paris. B-DBA.
AVIGNON SCHOOL.
Fr. ac. 1400.
AVISON, George. (Ill)
Am. b. Norwalk, Conn. 1885; ad. 1934 Same. A.
AVONT, Peeter van.
Flem. 1600-1632. B-T.
AVRAM, Nathaniel. (S)
Am. Roumania 1884-1907 New York. A07.
AVRIL, Jean Jacques [The Elder].
Fr. Paris 1744-1831. B.
AVRIL, Jean Jacques [The Younger].
Fr. Paris 1771-1835 Same. B.
AVRIL, Paul Victor.
Fr. b. Alger 1843. B-DBA.
AWA, Tsireh.
Am. Indian. b. Pueblo, N. M.; ad. 1934 Santa Fe, N. M. M-411.
AXELSSON, Axel.
Swe. Stockholm 1854-1892 Lund. T.
AXILETTE, Alexis.
Fr. b. Durtal; d. 1931 Paris. DBA.
AYER, James C.
Am. b. Lowell, Mass. 1862; ad. 1934 Glen Cove, N. Y. A.
AYER, Margaret. (Ill)
Am. ad. 1934 New York. M.
AYERS, John. (Pen Work)
Eng. ac. 1680. M.
AYLWARD, Ida.
Mrs. William James Aylward.
Am. b. Fairport, N. Y.; ad. 1934 Port Washington, N. Y. A.
AYLWARD, William James. (Ill)
Am. b. Milwaukee, Wis. 1875; ad. 1934 Port Washington, N. Y. A-B-F-T.
AYRES, Martha Oathout. (S)
Am. b. Elkader, Ia. 1890; ad. 1934 Inglewood, Calif. A-W.
AYRTON, Annie.
Eng. b. London; ac. 1878-1890. B.
AYTON, Charles William. (S)
Am. b. St. Louis, Mo.; ac. 1915. A12-B.
AYUKAWA. (Et)
Jap. b. Tokyo 1880; ex. 1934 New York. M.
AZAMBRE, Étienne.
Fr. b. Paris; ac. 1883-1907. B-DBA.
AZZARETTI, Faust.
Am. ad. 1934 Brooklyn, N. Y. M.
AZZI, Gabriel.
Egyptian. b. Alexandria 1904; ad. 1934 Paris. M.
AZZI, Marius A. (S)
Am. b. New Jersey 1892. A20-Cs-F.

BAADE, Knud.
Nor. Stavenger 1808-1879 Munich. C.
BAAR, Stanfield Marion.
Am. b. New York 1895; ad. 1934 Westport, Conn. A.
BAARGELD.
Ger. d. 1927. M.
BABCOCK, Dean.
Am. b. Canton, Ill. 1888; ad. 1935 Denver, Colo. A28-F.
BABCOCK, Elizabeth Jones.
Mrs. J. W. Babcock.
Am. b. Keokuk, Ia. 1887; ad. 1934 New York. A-F.
BABCOCK, Ida Dobson.
Am. b. Darlington, Mo. 1870; ad. 1934 Redlands, Calif. A.
BABCOCK, [Mrs.] Perez R. *see* Barton, L. R.
BABCOCK, Richard. (Ill)
Am. b. Denmark, Ia. 1887. A20-F.
BABCOCK, Thomas.
Am. 1850-1899. A02.
BABCOCK, William P.
Am. Boston 1826-1899 France. B-F-T.
BABOCCIO [or Babosius] Antonio Piperno.
It. Naples 1351-1435. T.
BACA-FLOR, Cárlos.
Peruvian. b. 1869; ad. 1934 Paris. Fa-M.
BACARISAS, Gustavo.
Sp. ac. 1897-1905. B-T.
BACCANTE, Enzo.
ex. 1935 New York. M.

BACCHELLI, Mario.
It. ac. 1932 Rome. DBA.
BACCHIACA, Francesco Ubertini Verdi.
It. Florence 1494/5-1557 Same. B-C-T-V.
BACCI, Baccio Maria.
It. ad. 1934 Fiesole. M.
BACCICCIO, Gaulli. *see* Gaulli, G. B.
BACH, Alois.
Bav. Eshelkamm 1809-1893 Munich, Ger. C-T.
BACH, Florence Julia.
Am. b. Buffalo, N. Y. 1887; ad. 1934 Same. A-F.
BACH, Guido.
Ger. Annaberg 1828-1905 London. T.
BACH, Marcel.
Fr. b. Bordeaux 1879. B-DBA.
BACHARACH, Elsie.
Am. ex. 1935 New York. M.
BACHARACH, Herman J.
Am. b. Las Vegas, N. M. 1899. A28.
BACHE, Otto.
Dan. b. Roskilde 1839; ac. 1924. B-Fa.
BACHELIER, Jean Jacques.
Fr. Paris 1724-1806 Same. B-C-T-722.
BACHELIER, Nicolas. (S)
Fr. Toulouse 1485-1566/72. B-Hs-T.
BACHELIER, Sebastiano. (S)
It. ac. 17th Century. B.
BACHER, Otto Henry. (Et)
Am. Cleveland, O. 1856-1909 Bronxville, N. Y. A07-B-DAB-T-16-17-46.
BACHER, Rudolf.
Ger. b. Vienna, Aus. 1862. B-T.
BACHER, Will Low.
Am. b. Bronxville, N. Y.; ad. 1934 Rock Tavern, N. Y. A.
BACHMAN, Max. (S)
Am. d. 1921 New York. A018-Ta.
BACHMANN, Hans.
Swi. b. Winikon 1852; ac. 1874 Düsseldorf, Ger. B-T.
BACHOFEN, Max Albin.
Am. b. Neubrunen, Swi. 1903; ad. 1934 Castroville, Tex. A.
BACHRACH. *see* Bacharach.
BACICCIO. *see* Gaulli, G. B.
BACKER, Jacob Adriaensz.
Dut. Haerlingen 1608/9-1651 Amsterdam. B-T.
BACKHMYSEN, Ludolf [or Ludwick].
Dut. Embden 1631-1708 Amsterdam. B-C-E-T-722.
BACKHMYSEN, Ludolf [The Younger].
Dut. Amsterdam 1717-1782 Rotterdam. B-E-T-722.
BACKUS, Joseafa Crosby.
Am. b. Brooklyn, N. Y. 1875; ad. 1934 Dublin, N. H. A.
BACLER d'Albe, Louis Albert Guillian.
Fr. St. Pol. 1761/2-1824 Sèvres. C-T.
BACO, Jacomart. *see* Jacomart, J. B.
BACON, Beth Driggs.
Am. d. 1928 Indianapolis, Ind. A028.
BACON, Charles Roswell.
Am. New York 1868-1913 Same. A011-B.
BACON, Frederick. (Eg)
Eng. London 1803-1887 Calif. B-Bd-T.
BACON, George C.
Am. 1855-1883 Malden, Mass. B-T.
BACON, Henry.
Am. Haverhill, Mass. 1840-1924 Cairo, Egypt. A010-B-F-T-15.
BACON, Irving R.
Am. b. Fitchburg, Mass. 1875; ad. 1934 Detroit, Mich. A.
BACON, John [The Elder]. (S)
Eng. Southwark 1740-1799 London. B-DNB-E-Hs-T.
BACON, John [The Younger]. (S)
Eng. 1777-1859 London. B-DNB-Hs-T.
BACON, John Henry Frederick.
Eng. 1865-1914 London. B-Fa.
BACON, Julia.
Am. b. Boston; d. 1901. A04-B.
BACON, Kate L. *see* Bond, [Mrs.] K. B.
BACON, [Sir] Nathaniel.
Eng. 1585-1640. B-DNB.
BACON, Peggy.
Mrs. Alexander Brook.
Am. b. Ridgefield, Conn. 1895; ad. 1935 New York. A28-F.
BACON, Thomas. (S)
Eng. ac. 1795 London. DNB.
BACQUÉ, Daniel J. (S)
Fr. b. Isère 1874; ac. 1900 Paris. DBA-798.
BADALOCCHIO, Sisto [Rosa].
It. Parma 1581/5-1647 Ordogno. B-E-T.
BADALONI. *see* Stefano, P. di.
BADELEY, Henry John Fanshawe. (Eg)
Eng. b. Elswick 1874; ad. 1934 London. Wa.
BADEN-POWELL, Frank Smyth.
Eng. b. Oxford 1850. B.
BADGER, Joseph.
Am. Charleston, Mass. 1708-1765 Boston. DAB-F-2-182.
BADGER, Thomas.
Am. ac. 1836-1859. F-T.
BADIER, Florimond.
Fr. ac. 17th Century. T.
BADILE, Antonio IV.
It. Verona 1516-1560. B-T.
BADILE, Bartolomeo [The Elder].
It. ac. 1445-1451 in Verona B-T.
BADILE, Giovanni Antonio.
It. Verona 1516/17-1560. B.
BADITZ, Otto von.
Hun. 1849-1908 Budapest. B.
BADMIN, Stanley R.
Eng. b. London 1906; ad. 1934 Sydenham. Wa.
BADURA, Bernard.
Am. b. Milwaukee, Wis. 1896; ad. 1934 New Hope, Pa. A.
BAEHR, Francine.
Am. b. Chicago 1898; ad. 1934 New York. A.
BAEKELAND, Celine.
Am. b. Belgium; ad. 1934 Yonkers, N. Y. M.
BAELLIEUR [or Balju], Cornelis de [The Elder].
Flem. Antwerp, Belg. 1607-1671. B-T.
BAELLIEUR [or Balju], Cornelis de [The Younger].
Flem. Antwerp, Belg. 1642-1687. B-T.
BAEN, Jan [or Johannes] de.
Dut. Haarlem 1633-1702 The Hague. B-DNB-T.

BAER, George.
Am. b. Chicago 1895. DBA.
BAER, Herbert M.
Am. b. New York 1879. A20-F.
BAER, Howard. (Cart)
Am. ad. 1935 New York. M.
BAER, Kurt.
Am. b. Arbon, Swi. 1905; ad. 1934 Los Angeles, Calif. A.
BAER, Lillian. (S)
Am. b. New York 1887. A12-F.
BAER, Martin.
Am. b. Chicago 1894. DBA.
BAER, William Jacob.
Am. b. Cincinnati, O. 1860; ad. 1934 New York. A-B-E-F-T-W-46.
BAERER, Henry. (S)
Am. b. Kirchlin, Ger. 1837-1908 U. S. A08-B-F-Ta.
BAERMAN, Lucius E.
Am. b. Antwerp, N. Y. 1879. A12.
BAES, Émile.
Belg. b. Brussels 1879. B-DBA.
BAESEMANN, Margaret Maassen. *see* Maassen, M.
BAESTEN. *see* Myin.
BAGDATOPOULOS, William Spencer.
Am. b. Zante, Gr. 1888; ad. 1934 Santa Barbara, Calif. A.
BAGG, Henry Howard.
Am. 1852-1928 Lincoln, Neb. A025.
BAGG, Louise Eleanor.
Am. b. Springfield, Mass. A12.
BAGLIONI, Baccio. *see* Agnolo, B.
BAGLIONI, Cesare.
It. b. Cremona; d. 1790 Parma. B-T-722.
BAGNACAVALLO, Il, Bartolomeo [Ramenghi].
It. Bagnacavallo 1484-1542 Bologna. B-C-E-T-V-722.
BAHNC, Salcia.
Am. b. Dukla, Pol.; ad. 1934 France. A-700.
BAIL, Jean Antoine.
Fr. Chasseley 1830-1919. B-Fa.
BAIL, Joseph Claude.
Fr. Limonest 1862-1921 Paris. B-C-DBA.
BAILEY, Carden.
Am. ex. 1934 Houston, Tex. M.
BAILEY, Caroline Baskerville.
Am. b. Baltimore, Md. 1905; ad. 1934 Corbin, Ky. A.
BAILEY, Cora Louise.
Am. b. West Newton, Mass. 1870. A12.
BAILEY, Harry L.
Am. St. Louis, Mo. 1879-1934 Beverly Hills, Calif. A.
BAILEY, Henrietta Davidson.
Am. b. New Orleans, La.; ac. 1933. A28-183.
BAILEY, Henry Turner.
Am. b. No. Scituate, Mass. 1865; d. 1931. A20-B-F.
BAILEY, James Edward.
Am. b. Baltimore, Md. 1885. A28.
BAILEY, La Force.
Am. b. Joliet, Ill. 1893; ad. Urbana, Ill. A.
BAILEY, Vernon Howe. (Et)
Am. b. Camden, N. J. 1874; ad. 1935 New York. A28-B-F-T-W.
BAILEY, Walter Alexander.
Am. b. Wallula, Kan. 1894; ad. 1934 Kansas City, Mo. A.
BAILEY, Whitman. (Ill)
Am. b. Providence, R. I. 1883. B-T.
BAILLARGÉ, Jean François. (S)
Can. b. Quebec, Can. 1759; ac. 1780 Same. B.
BAILLIE, James S.
Am. ac. 1838-1855 New York. M.
BAILLIE, [Captain] William.
Ir. Killbride 1723-1810 London. B-DNB.
BAILLOT-JOURDAN, Cécile.
Fr. b. Troyes 1889. DBA.
BAILLOT-JOURDAN, Claire.
Fr. b. Paris 1910. DBA.
BAILLY, David.
Dut. Leyden 1584-1657 Same. B-T-722.
BAILLY [or Bailey], Edward Hodges. (S)
Eng. Bristol 1788-1867 Holloway. B-DNB-E-Hs-T.
BAILLY, Joseph Alexis. (S)
Am. Paris 1825-1883 Phila., Pa. B-DAB-F-T-Ta-15.
BAIN, Harriet F.
Am. b. Kenosha, Wis.; ad. 1934 Same. A.
BAIN, Lilian Pherne.
Am. b. Salem, Ore.; ad. 1934 Long Island City, N. Y. A.
BAINES, Thomas.
Eng. Kingslyn 1822-1875 Durban, Natal. DNB.
BAINS, Ethel Franklin Betts. (Ill)
Am. ad. 1934 Phila., Pa. A-F.
BAINSFATHER, Arthur L. (Ill)
Am. ad. 1934 So. Birmingham, Ala. A.
BAIRD, Eugene Quentin.
Am. b. Asia 1897; ad. 1934 East Orange, N. J. A.
BAIRD, Nathaniel Hughes John.
Scot. b. Yedholm 1865. B.
BAIRD, William Baptiste.
Am. b. Chicago 1847; ac. 1872-1899 Paris. B-T.
BAIRNSFATHER, Bruce. (Cari)
Scot. b. Murree, India 1887. M.
BAISCH, Hermann.
Ger. Dresden 1846-1894 Carlsruhe. B-T.
BAISDEN, Frank.
Am. b. Atlanta, Ga. 1904; ad. 1934 Chattanooga, Tenn. M.
BAISIO, Tommasino da. *see* Abaise, T.
BAIXERAS-VERDAGUER, Dionisio.
Sp. b. Barcelona 1862. B-T.
BAIZERMAN, Saul. (S)
Am. ex. 1934 New York. M.
BAKALOWICZ, Ladislaus.
Pol. Chzanow 1833-1904. T.
BAKALOWICZ, Stephan Wladisláwowitsch.
Pol. b. 1857. T.
BAKER, Adelaide Clarissa.
Am. b. Cleveland, O.; ad. 1934 Same. A.
BAKER, Anselm.
Eng. 1834-1885. DNB.
BAKER, Bryant [Percy]. (S)
Am. b. London 1881; ad. 1934 New York. A-F-Cs-W.

BAKER, CATHERINE ISABELLE.
Am. b. Columbus, O. 1905; ad. 1934 Same. A.

BAKER, CHARLES.
Am. 1844-1906 Lake George, N. Y. A06-B-F-T.

BAKER, CHELLIS.
Am. ad. 1934 New York. M.

BAKER, ELIZABETH GOWDY.
Am. Xenia, O. 1860-1927. A024-B-F-T-W14-46-829.

BAKER, ELLEN KENDALL.
Mrs. Harry Thompson.
Am. b. Fairfield, N. Y.; d. 1913 St. Giles, Eng. A011-B-F.

BAKER, FREDERIC VAN VLIET.
Am. b. New York 1876. A28-F.

BAKER, GEORGE AUGUSTUS, JR. (Min)
Am. New York 1821-1880 Darien, Conn. B-C-DNB-F-T-3-4-6-15-179.

BAKER, GEORGE HERBERT.
Am. b. Muncie, Ind. 1878; ad. 1934 Centerville, Ind. A-F-181.

BAKER, GEORGE O.
Am. b. Mexico, Mo. 1882; ad. 1935 Chicago, Ill. A20-F.

BAKER, GRACE M.
Am. Annawan, Ill. 1876; ad. 1934 Greeley, Colo. A.

BAKER, HELEN JOSEPHINE. (Min)
Am. b. Phila., Pa. 1869. A12.

BAKER, HELENA SEYMOUR.
Am. b. Laporte, Ind. 1900; ad. 1934 Same. A.

BAKER, HORACE. (Eg)
Am. No. Salem, N. Y. 1833-1918 Great Neck, N. Y. A015-B-F-T.

BAKER, JAMES H. (Eg)
Eng. b. Beaconsfield 1829. B-T.

BAKER, JEAN.
Am. b. Arcadia, Neb. 1903; ad. 1934 Hollywood, Calif. A.

BAKER, LAURA.
Mrs. A. T. Baker.
Am. ad. 1934 Princeton, N. J. M.

BAKER, M. LOUISE.
Eng. ac. 1934. M.

BAKER, MARIA MAY.
Am. b. Norfolk, Va. 1890; ad. 1934 Same. A-F.

BAKER, MARTHA SUSAN. (Min)
Am. Evansville, Ind. 1871-1911 Chicago. A010-B-F-T-46-181.

BAKER, MARY FRANCES.
Am. b. New Orleans, La. 1879; ad. 1934 Same. A.

BAKER, NATHAN. (S)
Am. ac. 1841 Cinn., O. M.

BAKER, ORA PHELPS.
Am. b. Stevens Point, Wis.; ad. 1934 Same. A.

BAKER, ROBERT P. (S)
Am. b. London, Eng. 1886. A28.

BAKER, SAMUEL BURTIS.
Am. b. Boston 1882; ad. 1934 Wash., D. C. A-B-F-W.

BAKER, SARAH M.
Am. b. Memphis, Tenn. 1899; ad. 1934 Balt., Md. A.

BAKER, VIOLET TWATCHMAN.
Am. ad. 1935 Greenwich, Conn. M.

BAKER, WILLIAM BLISS.
Am. New York 1859-1887. B-C-F-T.

BAKER, WILLIAM H.
Am. 1825-1875 Brooklyn, N. Y. B-C-F-T-144-183.

BAKEWELL, ROBERT.
Am. ac. New Haven, Conn. M.

BAKHUYSEN. *see* Backhmysen, L.

BAKHUYZEN, HENDRIK VAN DE SANDE.
Dut. The Hague 1795-1860. B-T.

BAKKER-KORFF, ALEXANDER HUGO.
Dut. The Hague 1824-1882 Leyden. B-T.

BAKOS, JOSEPH G.
Am. b. Buffalo, N. Y. 1891; ad. 1934 Same. A-F.

BAKST, LÉON [Rosenberg]. (Theatrical)
Rus. Leningrad 1866-1924 Paris. DBA-E-T.

BAKSTEEN, DIRK. (Et)
Belg. ac. 1921. M.

BALACA Y CANSECO, RICARDO.
Sp. Lisbon 1844-1880. T.

BALANO, PAULA HIMMELSBACH.
Mrs. Cosme Balano.
Am. b. Leipzig, Ger. 1878; ad. 1934 Phila., Pa. A-B-F-T.

BALBUENA, ROBERTO FERNÁNDEZ.
Sp. ad. 1934 Madrid. M.

BALCH, VISTUS. (Eg)
Am. Williamstown, Mass. 1799-1884 Johnstown, N. Y. B-F-T-2-7.

BALCOM, LOWELL LEROY.
Am. b. Kansas City, Mo.; ad. 1934 Norwalk, Conn. A-F.

BALDASSARE, ESTENSE [da Reggio]. *see* Estense, B.

BALDASSARE DA SIENA. *see* Peruzzi, B.

BALDAUGH, ANNI [or Amie].
Mrs. von Westrum.
Am. b. Holland 1886; ad. 1934 San Diego, Calif. A.

BALDESE, AMBROGIO DI. *see* Ambrogio di Baldese.

BALDINI, BACCIO BARTOLOMEO.
It. ac. 1460-1485 Florence. B-T.

BALDINUCCI, FILIPPO.
It. Florence 1624-1696. B-E-T.

BALDOVINETTI, ALESSO.
It. Florence 1425-1499. B-Bd-E-T-V-722.

BALDREY, HAYNSWORTH. (S)
Am. b. Cortland, N. Y. 1885; ad. 1934 Newton, N. J. A-Cs.

BALDREY, JOSHUA KIRBY. (Eg)
Br. 1754-1828. DNB.

BALDRIDGE, CYRUS LEROY. (Ill)
Am. b. Alton, N. Y. 1889; ad. 1934 New York. A28-F-W.

BALDRIGHI, GIUSEPPI.
It. Stradella 1723-1802. B-T.

BALDUCCIO, GIOVANNI DI. (S)
It. Pisa 1300-1347. B-Hs-T.

BALDUCCIO, MATTEO [di Giuliano di Lorenzo].
It. ac. 1490-1554. T.

BALDUNG, HANS. [Grien].
Ger. Weyersheim 1484-1545 Strassburg. B-C-E-T-801.

BALDWIN, ALBERTUS H. (Ill)
Am. b. Branford, Conn. 1865; ad. 1935 West Falls Church, Va. M.

BALDWIN, BURTON CLARKE. (Ill)
Am. b. Danville, Ill. 1891; ad. 1934 Chicago. A.
BALDWIN, CHARLES BOOTH.
Am. b. Derby, Conn.; ad. 1934 Same. A.
BALDWIN, CLIFFORD PARK.
Am. b. Cincinnati, O. 1889; ad. 1934 Montrose, Calif. A.
BALDWIN, [Mr. and Mrs.] R. ROBERTS. (Ill)
Am. ad. 1934 New York. M.
BALDWIN, THOMAS FREDERIC.
Am. b. Dublin, Ir. 1867; ad. 1935 Whitestone Landing, L. I., N. Y. M.
BALEN, HENDRIK VAN [The Elder].
Flem. Antwerp, Belg. 1575-1632 Same. B-C-T-722.
BALESTRA, ANTONIO.
It. Verona 1666-1740 Same. B-C-T-722.
BALESTRIERI, LIONELLO.
It. b. Siena 1874. B-T.
BALJU, CORNELIS DE. *see* Baellieur, C. de.
BALL, ALICE WORTHINGTON. (S)
Am. b. Boston; d. 1929. A026-B.
BALL, [Mrs.] CAROLINE PEDDLE. (S)
Am. b. Terre Haute, Ind. 1869; ad. 1934 Torrington, Conn. A-F-T-W15.
BALL, HUGH SWINTON.
Am. d. 1838. B-T.
BALL, L. CLARENCE.
Am. Mt. Vernon, O. 1858-1915 South Bend, Ind. A013-B-F-T-181.
BALL, ROBERT.
Am. b. Kansas City, Mo. 1890; ad. 1934 Provincetown, Mass. A.
BALL, RUTH NORTON. (S)
Am. b. Madison, Wis.; ad. 1934 San Diego, Calif. A-Cs-F.
BALL, SEYMOUR. (Ill)
Am. ad. 1934 New York. M.
BALL, STANLEY CRITTENDEN.
Am. b. Shelburne Falls, Mass. 1885; ad. 1934 New Haven, Conn. A.
BALL, THOMAS. (S)
Am. Charleston, Mass. 1819-1911 Montclair, N. J.
A010-B-DAB-E-F-Hs-T-Ta-W6-6-15-46.
Ball, THOMAS WATSON.
Am. New York 1863-1934 Old Lyme, Conn. A-B-F. Obit. N. Y. papers 1-25-1934.
BALL, WILFRID WILLIAMS.
Eng. London 1853-1917. B-Fa.
BALL-DEMONT, ADRIENNE ELODIE CLÉMENCE.
Fr. b. Montgeron 1886. DBA.
BALL-HUGHES, GEORGIANA.
Am. d. 1911 Dorcester, Mass. A010-B.
BALLA, GIACOMO.
It. b. Turin; ac. 1934 Rome DBA-T.
BALLANTINE, JAMES.
Eng. 1808-1877. DNB.
BALLANTYNE, KENNETH M.
Am b. New Zealand 1886; ad. 1934 Baldwins, N. Y. A.
BALLAVOINE, JULES FRÉDÉRIC.
Fr. b. Paris; ac. 1880-1900. B-T.
BALLERINI-BALL, N.
Am. b. Pittsfield, Mass. 1899; ad. 1934 Hartford, Conn. A.
BALLIN, FLORENCE. *see* Cramer, F. B.
BALLIN, HUGO. (Mural)
Am. b. New York 1879; ad. 1934 Santa Monica, Calif. A-B-F-T-W-46.
BALLINGER, HARRY RUSSELL. (Ill)
Am. b. Port Townsend, Wash. 1892; ad. 1934 New York. A-F.
BALLOU, BERTHA.
Am. b. Hornby, N. Y. 1891; ad. 1934 Spokane, Wash. A.
BALMER, CLINTON.
Am. ad. 1934 Long Island City, N. Y. M.
BALMER, GEORGE.
Eng. No. Shields 1806-1846 Ravensworth. DNB-T.
BALMER, PAUL FRIEDRICH WILHELM.
Ger. b. Basel, Swi. 1885. B-T.
BALUNIN, M.
Rus. b. 1875; ac. 1935 Russia. M.
BAMBAJA, AGOSTINO BUSTI. *see* Busti, A.
BAMBINO, VISPO. *see* Master of the Bambino Vispo.
BAMBOCCIO. *see* Laar.
BANASEWICZ, IGNATIUS.
Am. b. Leningrad, Rus. 1903; ad. 1934 Brooklyn, N. Y. A.
BANCEL, HENRY A.
Am. ad. 1934 New York. M.
BANCK [or Bank], JOHN VAN DER.
Eng. 1694-1739 London. B-DNB.
BANCK [or Banc], PIETER VAN DER. (Eg)
Eng. Paris 1649-1697 Bradford, Eng. DNB-T.
BANCO, NANNI D' ANTONIO DI. (S)
It. Florence 1373/83-1420/30. B-Hs-V.
BANCROFT, ALBERT.
Am. ex. 1935 Denver, Colo. M.
BANCROFT, HESTER. *see* Berry, H. B.
BANCROFT, MILTON HERBERT.
Am. b. Newton, Mass. 1867; ad. 1934 Sandy Spring, Md. A-B-F-W.
BANCROFT, RAYMOND.
Am. ad. 1934 Collingswood, N. J. M.
BANCROFT, THOMAS FORMAN.
Am. Troy, N. Y. 1864-1934 Collingswood, N. J. Obit. N. Y. papers 5-7-1934. M.
BANDEL, ERNEST VON.
Ger. Aüsbach 1800-1876. T.
BANDINELLI, BARTOLOMMEO [or Baccio]. (S)
It. Florence 1487/93-1559/60. B-E-Hs-T-V.
BANDINELLI, CLEMENTE.
It. b. Florence 1534; d. Rome. T-V.
BANDINI, GIOVANNI DI BENEDETTO [dell' Opera]. (S)
It. Florence 1540-1599. B-Hs-T-V.
BANDROLLEN. *see* Master of the Bandrollen.
BANEVER, GILBERT.
Am. b. New Haven, Conn. 1913; ad. 1934 Same. M.
BANFIELD [Mrs.], ELIZABETH S.
Am. ad. 1934 West Hartford, Conn. M.
BANGEMANN, OSKAR. (Eg)
Ger. b. 1882 in Germany. M.
BANKS, THOMAS. (S)
Eng. Lambeth 1735-1805 London. B-DNB-E-T.
BANKSON, GLEN PAYTON.
Am. b. Mt. Hope, Pa. 1890; ad. 1934 Spokane, Wash. A.
BANNERMAN, ALEXANDER.
Eng. Cambridge 1730-1780 London. DNB-T.

BANNERMAN, W. W. (Et)
Am. ac. 1829-1845. B-F-T-2-7.
BANNING, BEATRICE HARPER. (Et)
Mrs. Waldo Banning.
Am. b. Staten Island, N. Y. 1885; ad. 1934 Old Lyme, Conn. M.
BANNING, WILLIAM J.
Am. Lyme, Conn. 1810-1856. B-F-T.
BANNISTER, EDWARD M.
Am. Canada 1833-1901. A05-B-F-T-15.
BANNISTER, ELEANOR CUNNINGHAM.
Am. b. New York; ad. 1934 Brooklyn, N. Y. A-F.
BANNISTER, JAMES. (Eg)
Am. England 1821-1901 Brooklyn, N. Y. A04-F-T-7.
BANTZER, CARL LUDWIG NOAH.
Ger. B. Ziegenhain 1857. B-T.
BANVARD, JOHN.
Am. 1815-1891 Watertown, So. Dak. DAB-F-181.
BAPTIST, JOHN GASPARS.
Br. Antwerp, Belg. 1620-1691 London. DNB-T.
BAPTISTE. *see* Monnoyer.
BAR, BONAVENTURE DE.
Fr. Paris 1700-1729 Same. B-T.
BARABINO, NICCOLÒ.
It. Sampierdarena 1832-1891 Florence. B-T.
BARAGWANATH, [Mrs.] JOHN G. *see* McMein, N. M.
BARANCEANU, BELLE. (Mu)
Am. ad. 1934 San Diego, Calif. M.
BARATELLI, CHARLES. (S)
Am. b. Italy; d. 1925 Milford, Conn. A023.
BARATTA, PIETRO. (S)
It. ac. 1695 Venice. B-Hs.
BARAU, ÉMILE.
Fr. b. Reims 1851. B.
BARBA, JACOPO DELLA.
It. ac. 16th Century in Florence. T-V.
BARBARELLI, GIORGIO. *see* Giorgione.
BARBARI, JACOPO DE.
It. Venice 1440/50-1511/15. B-C-T.
BARBARINI, FRANZ.
Fr. Lorraine 1804-1873 Vienna, Aus. B-T.
BARBEDIENNE, BERNARD. (P-S)
Fr. b. Paris 1909; d. 1929 Gargan, Fr. DBA.
BARBEE, WILLIAM RANDOLPH. (S)
Am. b. Randolph, Va. 1868. B-F-T.
BARBER, CHARLES BURTON.
Eng. Yarmouth 1845-1894 London. B.
BARBER, CHARLES E. (Eg)
Am. London 1840-1917 Phila., Pa. A014-F-T-7.
BARBER, CHARLES VINCENT.
Eng. Birmingham 1783/4-1854 Liverpool. B-DNB.
BARBER, CHRISTOPHER. (Min)
Eng. Marylebone 1736-1810 London. DNB-T.
BARBER, DONN.
Am. d. 1925. M.
BARBER, JOHN.
Am. b. Galati, Fr. 1898; ex. 1935 New York. M.
BARBER, JOHN JAY.
Am. b. Sandusky, O. 1840; ac. 1871 Columbus, O. M.
BARBER, JOHN VINCENT.
Eng. b. Birmingham; d. 1830 Rome, It. DNB-T.
BARBER, JOHN WARNER. (Eg)
Am. E. Windsor, Conn. 1798-1885 New Haven, Conn. B-DAB-F-T-2-7-8.
BARBER, JOSEPH.
Eng. 1737-1811. DNB.
BARBER, WILLIAM. (Eg)
Am. London, Eng. 1807-1879 Phila., Pa. F-T-2-7.
BARBET, JEAN [de Lyon]. (S)
Fr. ac. 1475-1514 Lyons. B.
BARBIER, GEORGE. (Ill)
Fr. ac. 1934. DBA.
BARBIERE, DOMENICO DEL.
It. Florence 1506-1575 Same. T-V.
BARBIERI, GIOVANNI FRANCESCO. *see* Guercino ["Squint Eye"].
BARBIÈRRE-WALBONNE, JACQUES. (Min)
Fr. Nimes 1769-1860 Passy. B-F-T.
BARBIÈRS, PIETER.
Dut. Amsterdam 1717-1780 Same. B-T.
BARBUDO-SÁNCHEZ, SALVADOR.
Sp. b. Seville 1858. B-DBA-T.
BARCLAY, J. EDWARD.
Am. [No dates]. F-M.
BARCLAY, JOHN RANKINE. (Et)
Eng. b. Prescot 1876. Wa.
BARCLAY, McCLELLAND.
Am. b. St. Louis, Mo. 1891; ad. 1935 New York. A-F-W.
BARCLAY, WILLIAM. (Min)
Eng. Tottenham 1797-1859. DNB-T.
BARCLAY, WILLIAM.
Scot. ac. 1873-1917 Edinburgh. B.
BARCONS, ZULA ZULEMA.
Am. ad. 1934 New York. M.
BARCY, INEZ.
Fr. b. Rome; ac. 1930 Paris. DBA.
BARD, SARA FORESMAN.
Am. b. Slippery Rock, Pa.; ad. 1934 Ind., Ind. A.
BARDI, DONATO DI NICCOLÒ DI BETTO. *see* Donatello.
BARDI, GIOVANNI D' ANTONIO MINELLI DE. (S)
It. Padua 1460-1527. T.
BARDIN, MAURICE. (S)
Fr. b. 1890; ex. 1934 Chicago. M.
BARDWELL, THOMAS.
Eng. d. about 1780. DNB-T.
BARENGER, JAMES [The Younger].
Eng. London 1780-1831 Same. B-DNB.
BARENTSZ, DIRCK.
Dut. Amsterdam 1534-1592. T.
BARFORD, GEORGE. (Ill)
Am. ad. 1935 Milwaukee, Wis. M.
BARGUE, CHARLES.
Fr. b. Paris; d. 1883 Same. B-M.
BARHYDT, JEAN K.
Mrs. George Weed Barhydt.
Am. b. Brooklyn, N. Y.; ad. 1934 West Hartford, Conn. A.
BARI, NICCOLÒ DA. (S)
It. b. 1414; d. 1494. Hs-V.
BARILE, GIOVANNI DA FIRENZE.
It. ac. 1486 Florence. T-V.

BARILE, GIOVANNI DA SIENA.
It. ac. 1514-1530 Siena. T-V.
BARILE, XAVIER J.
Am. b. Italy 1891; ad. 1934 New York. A-F-W.
BARILLOT, LÉON.
Fr. Montigny 1844-1901 Paris. B-T.
BARISANUS DA TRANI. (S)
It. ac. 1180 Monreale. B-Hs-T.
BARJANSKY, CATHERINA. (S, Wax)
Pol. ex. 1931 New York. M.
BARKER, ALBERT WINSLOW. (Et)
Am. b. Chicago 1874; ad. 1935 Hingham, Mass. A28-M.
BARKER, BENJAMIN.
Eng. 1776-1838 Totness. DNB-T.
BARKER, GEORGE.
Am. b. Omaha, Neb. 1882; ad. 1934 Palisades, Calif. A.
BARKER, J. E.
Eng. ex. 1934 London. M.
BARKER, MARY CHAMBERLAIN. (Min)
Am. New York 1856-1914 Same. A011.
BARKER, OLIVE R.
Mrs. George Barker.
Am. b. Chicago 1885; ad. 1934 Palisades, Calif. A.
BARKER, ROBERT.
Scot. Kells 1739-1806 Lambeth. DNB-T.
BARKER [of Bath], THOMAS.
Eng. Portypool 1769-1847 Bath. B-DNB.
BARKER, WRIGHT.
Eng. b. Bradford; ac. 1893. B.
BARKSDALE, GEORGE EDWARD.
Am. b. Charlotte Co., Va. 1869; ad. Asheville, N. C. A.
BARLACCHI, TOMMASO.
It. ac. 16th century in Rome. T-V.
BARLACH, ERNST. (S)
Ger. b. Wedel 1870. B-E-T-709-798.
BARLOSIUS, GEORGE.
Ger. Magdeburg 1864-1908. B-T.
BARLOW, FRANCIS.
Eng. Lincolnshire 1626?-1702/4 London. B-E-T-Wi-803.
BARLOW, JOHN NOBLE.
Eng.-Am. Manchester 1861-1917 St. Ives. A014-B-F-T.
BARLOW, MYRON A.
Am. b. Ionia, Mich. 1873; ad. 1934 Detroit, Mich. A-B-F-46.
BARLOW, THOMAS OLDHAM.
Eng. Oldham 1824-1889 London. B-DNB-T.
BARNA [or Berna], DA SIENA.
It. [Lorenzetti]; ac. 1369-1380 Siena. B-T-V.
BARNABA DA MODENA.
It. b. Modena; ac. 1367-1383. B-Fa-T.
BARNARD, EDWARD HERBERT.
Am. Belmont, Mass. 1855-1909 Westerly, R. I. A07-B-F-T.
BARNARD, ELINOR M.
Mrs. Manuel Komroff.
Am. b. London 1872; ad. 1934 New York. A-F.
BARNARD, FREDERICK [Fred]. (Ill)
Eng. London 1846-1896 Wimbledon. B-DNB.
BARNARD, GEORGE GREY. (S)
Am. Bellefonte, Pa. 1863; ad. 1935 New York. A-B-E-F-Hs-T-W-46-701-783-813-884.
BARNARD, JOSEPHINE W.
Am. b. Buffalo, N. Y. 1869; ad. 1934 New York. A-F.
BARNARD, WILLIAM. (Eg)
Eng. London 1774-1849 Same. B-T.
BARNARDO DA FIRENZE. *see* Daddi, B.
BARNES, ERNEST HARRISON.
Am. b. Portland, N. Y. 1873; ad. 1934 Detroit, Mich. A-F.
BARNES, GERTRUDE JAMESON.
Mrs. Henry A. Barnes.
Am. b. Tyngsboro, Mass. 1865; ad. 1934 Minn., Minn. A-B-F.
BARNES, GUSTAVE A.
Eng. London 1878-1921 Adelaide, So. Aust. M.
BARNES, HIRAM PUTNAM. (Ill)
Am. b. Boston 1857; ad. 1935 Waltham, Mass. F-W8.
BARNES, MATTHEW.
Am. ex. 1934 San Fran., Calif. M.
BARNES, VIRGINIA WHITE.
Mrs. Robert H. Barnes.
Am. b. Livingston, Ala. 1895; ad. 1934 Eutaw, Okla. A.
BARNES, WILFRED M.
Can. b. Montreal; ad. 1935 Same. M.
BARNET, WILL. (Et.)
Am. ad. 1935 New York. M.
BARNETT, EUGENE A.
Am. b. Atlanta, Ga. 1894; ad. 1934 New York. A.
BARNETT, HERBERT PHILLIP.
Am. b. Providence, R. I. 1910; ad. 1934 Cambridge, Mass. A.
BARNETT, THOMAS P.
Am. St. Louis, Mo. 1870-1929. A026-B-F-W14.
BARNEY, [Mrs.] ALICE PIKE.
Am. Cincinnati, O. 1860-1931 Los Angeles, Calif. A028-B-F-W16.
BARNEY, ARTHUR L.
Am. ad. 1934 New York. M.
BARNEY, FRANK A.
Am. b. Union Springs, N. Y. 1862. A28-B-F.
BARNEY, [Mrs.] MAGINEL WRIGHT. (Ill)
Am. ad. 1934 New York. M.
BARNEY, MARIAN GREENE.
Mrs. W. Pope Barney.
Am. b. St. Paul, Minn.; ad. 1934 Moylan, Pa. A.
BARNHART, NANCY. (Ill)
Am. ad. 1934 New York. M.
BARNHORN, CLEMENT JOHN. (S)
Am. b. Cincinnati, O. 1857; d. 1935 Same. A-B-F-T-W.
BARNITZ, HENRY WILSON.
Am. b. Berwick, Pa. 1864. A12.
BARNITZ, MYRTLE TOWNSEND.
Am. b. Greensburg, Pa.; ad. 1934 Glen View, Ill. A.
BARNOIN, CAMILE.
Flem. ac. 1869-1879 Paris. B.
BARNOUW, NICOLAS.
Dut. Schiedam 1809-1873/4 Overschie. B.

BARNS, Cornelia.
Am. b. New York 1888; ad. 1934 Berkeley, Calif. A.
BARNSLEY, James Macdonald.
Can. Toronto, Ont. 1861-1929. B-893.
BARNUM, Emily Keene.
Am. b. New York 1874; ad. 1934 Lausanne, Swi. A-B-F-T.
BARNUM, Jay Hyde. (Ill)
Am. ad. 1934 Norwalk, Conn. A.
BARNUM, [Mrs.] Kay.
Am. ad. 1934 Norwalk, Conn. M.
BAROCCI, Ambrogio di Federico. (S)
It. ac. 15th Century Milan and Urbino. B-C.
BAROCCI [or Baroccio], Federico.
It. Urbino 1526/8-1612 Same. B-Bd-C-E-T-V-722.
BARON, A. (Min)
Fr. ac. 1800. Fa.
BARON, Bernard.
Eng. Paris 1696-1762/6 London. B-DNB.
BARON, Henri Charles Antoine.
Fr. Besançon 1816-1885 Geneva, Swi. B-T.
BARON, Théodore.
Belg. Brussels 1840-1899 St. Servan, Fr. C-T.
BARONE, Antonio.
Am. b. Sicily 1889; ad. 1935 New York. A20-B-F.
BARONINO, Bartolommeo.
It. ac. 1535-1554 Rome. T-V.
BARONZIO, Giovanni da Rimini. [School of the Marches]
It. ac. 1280; d. 1361. B-Fa.
BAROZZI, Jacopo [Vignuola]. *see* Barocci, Federico.
BARR, Joseph R.
Am. ad. 1934 Bronxville, N. Y. M.
BARR, Paul E.
Am. b. Goldsmith, Ind. 1892; ad. 1934 Tipton, Ind. A.
BARR, Robert Allan.
Can. b. London 1890; ad. 1934 Toronto, Ont. M.
BARR, William.
Am. Glasgow, Scot. 1867-1933 San Fran., Calif. A030-F.
BARRALETT, John James. (Eg)
Am. Ireland 1747-1815 Phila., Pa. B-Bd-F-T-2-6-7-184.
BARRATT, Reginald.
Eng. London 1861-1917. B.
BARRATT, Thomas E. (Min)
Am. ac. 1837-1854. F.
BARRAU, Laureano.
Sp. b. Caldatas 1864; ac. 1904 Madrid. B.
BARRAU, Théophile Eugène Victor. (S)
Fr. ac. 1900 Paris. B.
BARRAUD, Francis [or François].
Eng. London 1856-1924 Same. B.
BARRAUD, Henry.
Eng. 1811-1874 London. DNB-T.
BARRAUD, William.
Eng. 1810-1850. B-DNB-T.
BARRÉ, Jean Aguste. (S)
Fr. Paris 1811-1896. B-T.
BARRÉ, Jean Batiste. (S)
Fr. Nantes 1807-1877. B-T.
BARRÉ, Jean Jacques. (Med)
Fr. Paris 1793-1855. B-T.
BARREAUX, Adolphe.
Am. b. Orange, N. J. 1900; ad. 1934 New York. A.
BARRENSCHEEN, Herman.
Swi. b. Zurich 1909; ad. 1932 Munich, Ger. M.
BARRETT, Elizabeth Hunt.
Mrs. Edward N. Barrett.
Am. b. New York 1863. A12-F.
BARRETT [or Barret], George [The Elder].
Ir. Dublin 1728/32-1784 Paddington, Eng. B-DNB.
BARRETT [or Barret] George [The Younger].
Eng. London 1767-1842 Same. B-DNB.
BARRETT, Jerry.
Eng. 1814-1906 London. B.
BARRETT, Laura A.
Am. b. West New Brighton, N. Y.; d. 1928 New York. A025.
BARRETT, Lisabeth Stone. (Min)
Am. ad. 1934 Devon, Pa. M.
BARRETT, O. O'Connor. (S)
Eng. ex. 1934 London. M.
BARRETT, Robert P.
Am. ad. 1934 New York. M.
BARRETT, Thomas Weeks, Jr.
Am. b. Poughkeepsie, N. Y. 1902; ad. 1934 Same. A.
BARRETTO, Ann.
Am. ad. 1935 Goshen, N. Y. M.
BARRIAS, Félix Joseph.
Fr. Paris 1822-1907. B-C.
BARRIAS, Louis Ernest. (S)
Fr. Paris 1841-1905. B-Hs.
BARRIE, Erwin S.
Am. b. Canton, O. 1886; ad. 1934 New York. A-F.
BARRINGTON, Amy L.
Am. b. Jersey City, N. J.; ad. 1934 Worcester, Mass. A.
BARRON, Grace.
Am. ad. 1935 Buffalo, N. Y. M.
BARRON, Hugh.
Eng. London 1745-1791 Same. B-DNB
BARRON, William Augustus.
Eng. ac. 1764-1791 London. DNB-T.
BARROW, John Dobson.
Am. 1823-1907. F-M.
BARRY, Charles A.
Am. b. Boston 1830; ac. 1860. B-T-45.
BARRY, Edith Cleaves. (P, S)
Am. b. Boston; ad. 1934 Montclair, N. J. A.
BARRY, Eleanor E.
Am. ad. 1934 Melrose, Mass. M.
BARRY, Gerard.
Am. b. Ireland 1864; ac. 1926 New York. F.
BARRY, James.
Ir. Cork 1741-1806 London. B-C-DNB-E-T-722.
BARRY, John Joseph. (Et)
Am. b. Hamilton, Can. 1885. A28-F.
BARRY, Timothy.
Am. ac. 1845. M.
BARSE, George Randolph, Jr.
Am. b. Detroit, Mich. 1861; ad. 1934 Katonah, N. Y. A-B-F-T-W-46.
BARSKY, Syble. (S)
Am. ad. 1935 Pittsburgh, Pa. M.

BART-GERALD, ELIZABETH.
Am. b. Cleveland, O. 1907; ad. 1934 Toronto, Can. A.
BARTELS, HANS VON.
Ger. Hamburg 1856-1913 Munich. B-E.
BARTH, EUGENE FIELD.
Am. b. St. Louis, Mo. 1904; ad. 1934 Teaneck, N. J. A.
BARTH, FERDINAND.
Ger. Bavaria 1842-1892. B-C.
BARTH, PAUL BASILIUS.
Swi. b. Basel 1881. B.
BARTHE, RICHMOND. (S)
Am. b. Bay St. Louis, Miss. 1901; ad. 1934 New York. A.
BARTHÉLEMY [or Berthelemy] DE CLERC.
Fr. ac. 1447-1476 Anjou. M-T.
BARTHOLD, MANUEL.
Am. b. New York 1874. A12.
BARTHOLDI, FRÉDÉRIC AUGUSTE. (S)
Fr. Colmar 1834-1904 Paris. B-F-T.
BARTHOLDI, GIOVANNI DI. (S)
It. 1410-1491. M.
BARTHOLOMÉ, PAUL ALBERT. (P, S)
Fr. 1848-1928. B-C-DBA-Hs-T.
BARTHOLOMEUS DE BRYN. *see* Bruyn, B.
BARTHOLOMEW, DONALD C. (Cart)
Am. d. 1913 White Plains, N. Y. A011.
BARTHOLOMEW, EDWARD SHEFFIELD. (S)
Am. Colchester, Conn. 1822-1858 Naples, It. B-DAB-F-Hs-T-3-15.
BARTHOLOMEW, WILLIAM N. (Eg)
Am. 1856-1919 Brooklyn, N. Y. A016.
BARTL, JOHANN.
Aus. Tarvis 1765-1830. B-T.
BARTLE, GEORGE P.
Am. Wash., D. C. 1853-1918 Phalanx, N. J. A016-F-T.
BARTLE, SARAH NORWOOD. (Min)
Am. b. Wash., D. C.; ad. 1935 Same. A20-F.
BARTLETT, BENJAMIN PARRIS.
Am. ac. 1828. M.
BARTLETT, DANA.
Am. b. Ionia, Mich. 1878; ad. 1934 Los Angeles, Calif. A-F.
BARTLETT, EVELYN.
Am. ad. 1935 Beverly, Mass. M.
BARTLETT, FREDERIC CLAY.
Am. b. Chicago 1873; ad. 1935 Beverly, Mass. A-B-F-W.
BARTLETT, FREDERICK EUGENE.
Am. West Point, N. Y. 1852-1911 Highland Falls, N. Y. A010-B-T.
BARTLETT, GRACE LANDELL.
Am. b. Colorado Springs, Colo. 1907; ad. 1934 Same. A.
BARTLETT, JULIA MCMAHON.
Am. b. New York 1899; ad. 1934 Same. A.
BARTLETT, M. ELLSWORTH.
Am. b. Seymour, Ind. 1890. A12.
BARTLETT, MADELEINE ADELAIDE. (S)
Am. b. Woburn, Mass.; ad. 1934 Boston. A-B-Cs-F.
BARTLETT, PAUL.
Am. b. Taunton, Mass. 1881; ad. 1934 Ogunquit, Me. A.
BARTLETT, PAUL WAYLAND. (S)
Am. New Haven, Conn. 1865-1925 Paris. A023-B-DAB-E-F-Hs-T-Ta-18-19-46.
BARTLETT, TRUMAN HOWE. (S)
Am. Dorset, Vt. 1835-1923. B-F-T-3-15.
BARTLETT, WILLIAM HENRY. (Eg)
Eng. Kent 1809-1894 Marseilles, Fr. B-T.
BARTLETT, WILLIAM HENRY.
Eng. b. London 1858. B-T.
BARTLEY, HAZEL E.
Am. ad. 1934 Toledo, O. M.
BARTLOMIEJCZYK, EDMUND. (Eg)
Pol. 1885; ex. 1934 New York. M.
BARTOLI, J.
Am. ac. 1796 New York. B-T.
BARTOLINI, LORENZO. (S)
It. Vernio 1777-1850 Florence. B-E-Hs-T.
BARTOLO, ANDREA. *see* Andrea di Bartolo.
BARTOLO, DOMENICO DI. *see* Domenico di Bartolo.
BARTOLO, F.
It. ac. 1783-1796 London. B-T.
BARTOLO DI FREDI [Manfredi].
It. Siena 1330-1409/10 Same. B-C-T.
BARTOLO, MATTEO DI GIOVANNI. *see* Matteo di Giovanni.
BARTOLO DI TADDEO.
It. Siena 1363-1422. B-T-V.
BARTOLOMMEO, BOLGARINI [or Bolghini].
It. ac. 1347-1378 Siena. T-V.
BARTOLOMMEO, FRA.
It. Florence 1472-1517. T-V-722.
BARTOLOMMEO, JACOPO DI MARTINO.
It. ac. 1409. B.
BARTOLOMMEO, MASTER.
It. ac. 1236 Florence. T.
BARTOLOMMEO, RAMENGHI. *see* Bagnacavallo, Il, B.
BARTOLOMMEO, VENETO. *see* Veneto.
BARTOLOMMEO DI GIOVANNI. *see* Giovanni, B. di.
BARTOLOMMEO DI MANFREDI. *see* Bartolo di Fredi.
BARTOLOMMEO DI PAGHOLO, FRA [Baccio della Porta].
It. 1472/5-1517 Florence. B-Bd-C-E-T-722.
BARTOLOMMEO DI PAOLO.
It. ac. 1404 Venice. B-T.
BARTOLOZZI, FRANCESCO. (Eg)
Eng. Florence 1725/7-1815 Lisbon, Por. B-Bd-DNB-E-T-289-637-880.
BARTOLOZZI, GAETANO STEFANO. (Eg)
Eng. 1757-1821 Paris. Bd-DNB-T-637.
BARTON, CATHERINE GRAEFF.
Am. b. Englewood, N. J. 1904; ad. 1934 Same. A.
BARTON, DONALD BLAGGE.
Am. b. Fitchburg, Mass.; d. 1934 Same. A.
BARTON, LOREN ROBERTA.
Mrs. Perez R. Babcock.
Am. b. Oxford, Mass.; ad. 1934 Rome, It. A-F-W.
BARTON, MACENA.
Am. b. Union City, Mich. 1901; ad. 1934 Chicago. A.
BARTON, MARIE TAYLOR.
Am. ad. 1934 Nashville, Tenn. M.
BARTON, MINETTE.
Mrs. Charles H. Barton.
Am. b. Minn. Minn.; ad. 1934 Colorado Springs, Colo. A.

BARTON, Ralph. (Ill)
Am. Kansas City, Mo. 1891-1931.
A20-F-W16.
BARTOO, Catherine R.
Am. b. Williamsport, Pa.; ad. 1934 Binghampton, N. Y. A.
BARTSCH, Adam von. (Eg)
Aus. Vienna 1757-1821 Same. B-T.
BARTSCH, G. (Eg)
Am. ac. 1934. M.
BARWIG, Franz.
Aus. b. Schönau, 1868. T.
BARY, Hendrik.
Dut. b. Gouda 1640-1707? T.
BARYE, Antoine Louis. (S)
Fr. Paris 1796-1875 Same.
B-E-Hs-T-290-884.
BARZAGHI, Francesco. (S)
It. Milan 1839-1892. B-T.
BAS, Edward le.
Eng. ex. 1932 London. M.
BASAITI [or Baxaiti], Marco.
It. ac. 1470; d. 1521 Venice.
B-C-T-V-722.
BASAN, Pierre François. (Eg)
Fr. Paris 1723-1797. B-T.
BASÁWAN.
Pers. ac. end of 16th Century Persia. M.
BASCHET. Marcel André.
Fr. b. Gagny 1862. B-DBA.
BASHKIRTSEFF, Mario Konstantinowna.
Rus. 1860-1884 Paris. B.
BASING, Charles.
Am. Aust. 1865-1933 Morocco.
A030-F-W16.
BASIRE, James [The Elder]. (Eg)
Eng. London 1730-1802 Same. B-DNB.
BASIRE, James [The Younger]. (Eg)
Eng. London 1769-1822. DNB.
BASIRE, James [The Third]. (Eg)
Eng. London 1796-1869. DNB.
BASKERVILLE, Charles, Jr.
Am. b. Raleigh, N. C.; ad. 1934 New York.
A.
BASKETT, Charles Henry. (Et)
Eng. ac. 1893-1927 London. M.
BASKY, L. Marie.
Am. ad. 1934 New York. M.
BASSA, Ferrer.
Sp. 1290-1348. T.
BASSAN, Salomon.
It. 1696-1770. B-T.
BASSANO, Francesco da Ponte [The Elder].
It. Bassano 1470/75-1539/41 Same.
B-C-T-722.
BASSANO, Francesco da Ponte [The Younger].
It. Bassano 1549-1592 Venice. B-C-T-722.
BASSANO, Giacomo [Jacopo da Ponte].
It. Bassano 1510/15-1592 Same.
B-C-E-T-V-722.
BASSANO, Leandro da Ponte.
It. Bassano 1557-1622 Venice. B-C-T-722.
BASSEN, Bartholomeus van.
Dut. d. 1652 The Hague. C.
BASSET, Louis Charles.
Fr. b. Paris; ex. 1935 Same. DBA.
BASSETT, Carroll K. (S)
Am. ex. 1935 New York. M.
BASSETT, H. Ellsworth.
Am. b. Wash., D. C. 1875. A12-B.
BASSETT, Reveau.
Am. b. Dallas, Tex. 1897; ad. 1934 Same.
A.
BASSETTI, Marcantino.
It. Verona 1588-1630. T.
BASSFORD, Wallace.
Am. b. St. Louis, Mo. 1900; ad. 1934 Same.
A.
BASTERT, Nicolas.
Dut. b. Maarseven 1854. B.
BASTIAN, Dorcas Doolittle.
Am. b. Phila., Pa. 1901; ad. 1934 Same. A.
BASTIANINI, Giovanni. (S)
It. Camerata 1830-1868 Florence. B-T.
BASTIANNA, Lazaro [Scarpaccia]. *see* Sebastianni, L. B.
BASTIDA. *see* Sorolla.
BASTIEN-LEPAGE, Jules.
Fr. Damvillers 1848-1884 Paris.
B-Bd-C-E-T-939.
BATCHELDER, [Mrs.] Nathaniel Horton. *see* Longman, M. E. B.
BATE, Rutledge.
Am. b. Brooklyn, N. Y. 1891; ad. 1935 Same.
A.
BATEMAN, Charles. (S)
Am. b. Minn., Minn. 1890. A28-F.
BATEMAN, James. (Eg)
Eng. b. Kendal 1893; ad. 1934 London. Wa.
BATEMAN, John M. (S)
Am. b. Cedarville, N. J. 1877; ad. 1934 Haddonfield, N. J. A-B-F-W.
BATES, Bertha Corson Day.
Mrs. D. M. Bates.
Am. b. Phila., Pa. 1875; ad. 1934 Greenville, Del. A-B-F.
BATES, David.
Eng. b. Birmingham; ac. 1868-1910. M.
BATES, Dewey.
Am. Phila., Pa. 1851-1899 Rye, Eng.
B-C-F-T-15-181.
BATES, Earl Kenneth.
Am. b. Haverhill, Mass. 1895; ad. 1934 Mystic, Conn. A-F.
BATES, Gladys Bergh.
Am. b. London 1898; ad. 1934 Brooklyn, N. Y. A.
BATES, Gladys Edgerly. (S)
Am. b. Hopewell, N. J. 1896; ad. 1934 Mystic, Conn. A.
BATES, Henry. (S)
Eng. Stevenage 1850-1899 London.
B-DNB-E-Hs.
BATHURST, Clyde C. (S)
Am. b. Mt. Union, Pa. 1883; ad. 1934 Rockport, Mass. A-B-F.
BATHYCLES. (S)
Gr. (Ionian); ac. 550 B.C. E.
BATIST, Karel.
Dut. ac. 1659 Amsterdam. B.
BATONI, Pompeo Girolano.
It. Lucca 1702/8-1787 Rome.
B-Bd-C-E-T-722.
BATOWSKI-KACZOR, Stanislaus.
Pol. b. Lemberg 1866; ex. 1934 Chicago.
B-T.
BATTEM, Gérard [or Gerrit] van.
Dut. Rotterdam 1636-1684. B-T.

BATTEN, John Dickson. (Ill)
Eng. b. Plymouth 1871; d. 1932.
B-T-Wa-Y01933.
BATTHYÁNY, Gyula.
Hun. b. 1892; ex. 1934 London. M.
BATTILORE. *see* Bartolo di Fredi.
BATTISTA DA CITTÀ DI CASTELLO.
It. ac. 1530. T-V.
BATTISTA DA VICENZA.
It. ac. 1366-1408. T-V.
BATTISTA DI GIOENALE.
It. ac. 1432-1458 Rome. B-M.
BATTISTELLO, Il. *see* Caracciolo, G. B.
BATTISTINO. *see* Battista.
BATTONI, Pompeo Girolamo. *see* Batoni, P. G.
BAUCH, Solomon Stan.
Am. b. Podul-Illoiet, Roumania 1883; ad. 1934 New York. A.
BAUCHANT, André.
Fr. Châteaurenault 1873; ex. 1934 New York.
DBA-797.
BAUCK, Jeanna Maria Charlotte.
Swe. b. Stockholm, 1840. B-T.
BAUCK, John van der.
Dut. 1694-1739. M.
BAUCK, Peter van der. (Eg)
Eng. 1649-1697. DNB.
BAUD, Maurice.
Swi. Geneva 1866-1915. B-T.
BAUD, Max.
Lithuanian; ac. 1935 Paris. DBA.
BAUD-BOVY, Aguste.
Swi. Geneva 1848-1899 Davos. T.
BAUDE, Charles. (Eg)
Fr. b. Paris 1853. B-DBA.
BAUDE, François Charles.
Fr. b. Houplines 1880. B-DBA.
BAUDET, Étienne. (Eg)
Fr. Blois 1636/43-1711 Paris. B.
BAUDOUIN, Pierre Antoine.
Fr. Paris 1723-1769 Same. B-T-722-900.
BAUDRY, Paul Jacques Aimé.
Fr. La Roche 1828-1886 Paris. B-C-E-M-T.
BAUDUINS, Adrien François. *see* Boudewyns, A. F. [The Elder].
BAUER, Conrad.
[Swabian Monogrammist C. B.]
Ger. ac. 1530. M.
BAUER, Félix.
Fr. b. Lyons 1854. DBA.
BAUER [or Baur], Johann Wilhelm.
Ger. Strassburg 1600?-1640/2 Vienna, Aus.
B-T.
BAUER, Karl Conrad Friedrich.
Ger. b. Stuttgart 1868. B-T.
BAUER, Marius Alexander Jacques (Et)
Dut. The Hague 1864-1932.
B-T-Y01933-830.
BAUER, Sol A. (S)
Am. b. Cleveland, O. 1898; ad. 1934 Shaker Heights, O. A.
BAUER, Theodore. (S)
Am. ac. 1925 New York. F-Ta.
BAUER, William.
Am. b. St. Louis, Mo. 1888; ad. 1934 Same.
A-F.
BAUERFEIND, Gustave.
Aus. Sulz 1848-1904 Jerusalem, Palestine.
B-T.

BAUFFE, Victor.
Dut. ac. 19th Century Holland. B-T.
BAUGIN, Lubin.
Fr. Loiret 1610-1663 Paris. B-T.
BAUGNIET, Charles.
Belg. Brussels 1814-1886 Sèvres, Fr. B.
BAUM, Mark.
Am. b. Sanok, Pol. 1903; ad. 1934 New York.
A.
BAUM, Paul.
Ger. Meissen 1859-1932. B-T.
BAUM, Walter Emerson.
Am. b. Sellersville, Pa. 1884; ad. 1934 Same.
A-F.
BAUMANN, Gustave. (Eg)
Am. b. Ger. 1881; ad. 1934 Santa Fe, N. M.
A-F-W-181.
BAUMEISTER, Karl. (Eg)
Ger. b. Zwiefall 1840. B-T.
BAUMEISTER, Willi.
Ger. b. 1889. M.
BAUMER, Julius H.
Am. Muenster, Westphalia 1848-1917 Chicago.
A014-F.
BAUMER, Lewis.
Eng. b. London 1870; ad. 1934 Same. Wa.
BAUMGARTNER, Peter.
Ger. b. Munich 1834. B-T.
BAUMGARTNER, Warren. (Ill)
Am. ad. 1934 New York. M.
BAUMGRAS, Peter.
Am. Bavaria 1827-1904 U. S. A05-B-T.
BAUR, Albert.
Ger. Aix-la-Chapelle 1835-1906. B-T.
BAUS, Paul J. (S)
Am. ad. 1934 Indianapolis, Ind. M.
BAUS, Simon Paul.
Am. b. Indianapolis, Ind. 1882; ad. 1934 Same. A-F.
BAUSMAN, Marian D. *see* Walker, [Mrs.] Otis L.
BAUSS, Rudolph.
Ger. ex. 1935 New York. M.
BAWDEN, Edward. (Mu.)
Eng. b. Braintree 1903; ad. 1934 London.
Wa.
BAXAITI, Marco. *see* Basaiti, M.
BAXLEY, [Mrs.] Ellen Cooper.
Am. b. Lancaster, Pa. 1860; ad. 1934 Santa Barbara, Calif. A.
BAXTER, Bertha.
Am. b. Alexandria, Ind.; ad. 1934 New York.
A-F.
BAXTER, Charles.
Eng. London 1809-1879 Lewisham. DNB-T.
BAXTER, Elijah.
Am. b. Hyannis, Mass. 1849; ad. 1934 Newport, R. I. A-B-F-T-15.
BAXTER, George. (Eg)
Eng. Lewes 1804-1867 Sydenham. B-880.
BAXTER, Martha Wheeler. (S)
Am. b. Castleton, Vt. 1869; ad. 1934 Santa Barbara, Calif. A-B-F-T-W-46.
BAYARD, Clifford Adams.
Am. b. McKeesport, Pa. 1892; ad. 1934 Wilmington, Vt. A.
BAYARD, Émile Antoine.
Fr. 1837-1891 Cairo, Egypt. B.

BAYER, August von.
Ger. Rorschach 1803-1875 Carlsruhe. B-T.
BAYERLEIN, Fritz.
Ger. b. Bamberg 1872. B-T.
BAYES, Alfred Walter.
Eng. 1832-1909 London. B-M.
BAYES, Gilbert. (S)
Eng. b. London 1874. B-T.
BAYES, Jessie. (Min)
Eng. ac. 19th-20th Centuries in London. B.
BAYES, Walter John.
Eng. b. London 1869; ad. 1934 Same. Wa.
BAYLEY, Marguerite. (Eg)
Eng. ex. 1935 London. M.
BAYLINSON, A. S.
Am. b. Moscow, Rus. 1882; ad. 1934 New York. A-F-701.
BAYLISS, Lillian. (Min)
Am. b. Massillon, O. 1875. B.
BAYLISS, [Sir] Wyke.
Eng. Mandalay, India 1835-1906 London. B-DNB.
BAYLOR, Edna Ellis.
Mrs. Armistead K. Baylor.
Am. b. Hartford, Conn. 1882; ad. 1934 Ipswich, Mass. A.
BAYLOS, Zelma.
Am. b. Butka, Hun. 1867; ad. 1934 Lake Mahopac, N. Y. A-B-F-T.
BAYMAN, Leo. (S)
Am. ad. 1935 New York. A20-F.
BAYNES, James.
Eng. Lonsdale, Eng. 1766-1837. DNB-T.
BAYNES, Keith.
Eng. b. 1887; ad. 1935 London. Wa.
BAZ, Ben Hur. (Ill)
Mex. ac. 1934 New York. M.
BAZE, Willi. [Mrs. Lane.]
Am. b. Mason, Tex. 1896; ad. 1934 Oklahoma City, Okla. A.
BAZILLE, Frédéric.
Fr. Montpelier 1841-1870. B-T.
BAZIN, Nicholas. (Eg)
Fr. Troyes 1636-1710 Same. B-T.
BAZZANI, Guiseppe.
It. Reggio 1690/1710-1769 Mantua. B.
BAZZANI, Luigi.
It. b. Bologna 1836; ac. 1883 London. B.
BAZZANTI, Niccolò. (S)
It. ac. 1843 Florence. B-T.
BAZZI, Giovanni Antonio de. *see* Sodoma, Il.
BAZZOLI, Umberto.
It. ac. 19th Century Italy. B.
BEACH, Chester. (S)
Am. b. San Fran., Calif. 1881; ad. 1934 New York. A-B-Cs-F-W-46.
BEACH, Thomas.
Eng. Milton Abbas 1738-1806 Bath. B-DNB.
BEACHAM, Oliver Conley.
Am. b. Xenia, O. 1862; ad. 1934 Dayton, O. A.
BEAL, Gifford.
Am. b. New York 1879; ad. 1934 Same. A-B-F-T-W-757.
BEAL, Reynolds.
Am. b. New York 1867; ad. 1934 Rockport, Mass. A-B-F-T-W.
BEAL, William Goodrich. (Et)
Am. ac. 1887. B-T.
BEALE, Charles.
Eng. ac. 1689 London. DNB.
BEALE, Mary Cradock.
Mrs. Charles Beale.
Eng. Suffolk 1632-1697 London. B-DNB-702.
BEALL, Cecil Calvert. (Ill)
Am. b. Saratoga, Wyo.; ad. 1935 New York. M.
BEALS, Gertrude. *see* Bourne, G. B.
BEALS, Victor. (Ill)
Am. ad. 1934 Tuckahoe, N. Y. A29.
BEAMES, Stephen. (S)
Am. b. Multan, India 1896; ad. 1934 Evanston, Ill. A-Cs.
BEAN, Carolina Van Hook.
Mrs. Algernon H. Binyon.
Am. b. Wash., D. C.; ad. 1934 Same. A.
BEAN, Mary.
Mrs. Richard Rogers.
Am. b. Norristown, Pa. 1904; ad. 1934 Sumneytown, Pa. A.
BEARBLOCK [or Bereblock]. (Et)
Eng. ac. 1566. DNB.
BEARD, Adelia Belle. (Ill)
Am. b. Painesville, Ohio; d. 1920 Flushing, L. I., N. Y. A017-F.
BEARD, Alice.
Am. b. Cincinnati, O.; ad. 1934 New York. A.
BEARD, Beatrice.
Mrs. J. Allen Grover.
Am. ad. 1934 New York. M.
BEARD, Daniel Carter. ["Dan Beard"]. (Ill)
Am. b. Cincinnati, O. 1850; ad. 1934 Suffern, N. Y. A29-B-F-T-W.
BEARD, James Carter. (Ill)
Am. Cincinnati, O. 1837-1913 New Orleans, La. A011-B-DAB-T-W7.
BEARD, James Henry.
Am. Buffalo, N. Y. 1814-1893 Flushing, L. I., N. Y. B-C-DAB-F-T-4-15.
BEARD, Lina. (Ill)
Am. b. Cincinnati, O.; ac. 1933 Flushing, L. I., N. Y. A20 W.
BEARD, Mary Caroline. (Ill)
Am. Cincinnati, O. 1852-1933 Flushing, L. I., N. Y. A036.
BEARD, Thomas Francis [or Frank]. (Ill)
Am. Cincinnati, O. 1842-1905 Chicago. A05-B-DAB-F-T-W3-20.
BEARD, William Holbrook.
Am. Painesville, O. 1824-1900 New York. A02-B-Bd-C-DAB-E-F-T-4-15-22-39.
BEARDSLEY, Aubrey Vincent. (Et)
Eng. Brighton 1872-1898 Menton, Fr. B-DNB-E-291.
BEARDSLEY, Rudolph.
Am. b. 1875; d. 1921 New York. A018.
BEATO, Angelico. *see* Angelico, Fra.
BEATRICIO, Niccolò [Beautrizet].
It. ac. 1540-1565 Rome. T-V.
BEATTIE, Robert.
Eng. Preston 1810-1874 Same. M.
BEATTIE-BROWN, William.
Scot. Haddington 1831-1909 Edinburgh. DNB.

BEATTY, HETTY. (S)
Am. ad. 1934 Gloucester, Mass. M.
BEATTY, JOHN WESLEY.
Am. Pittsburgh, Pa. 1851-1924 Clifton Springs, N. Y. A021-B-F-T-46.
BEATTY, JOHN WILLIAM.
Can. b. Toronto 1869; ac. 1933 Same. M.
BEATTY, W. GEDNEY.
Am. ad. 1935 New York. M.
BEAUBRUM [or Bobrun], CHARLES.
Fr. Amboise 1604-1692 Paris. B-T-722.
BEAUCHAMP, JOHN W.
Am. ex. 1935 Phila., Pa. M.
BEAUCLERK, [Lady] DIANA. (Ill)
Eng. 1734-1808. B-DNB.
BEAUDIN, ANDRÉ.
Fr. b. Mannecy 1895; ex. 1934 London. DBA-797.
BEAUDUIN [or Beaudouin], JEAN.
Fr. Verniers 1851-1916 Paris. B-DBA.
BEAUFRÈE, ADOLPHE MARIA TIMOTHÉE. (Et)
Fr. b. Quimperlé 1876. B-DBA.
BEAUGRANT, GUYOT DE. (S)
Sp. d. 1551 Bilbao. Hs-T.
BEAULEY, WILLIAM JEAN.
Am. b. Joliet, Ill. 1874; ad. 1934 New York. A-F.
BEAUME, JOSEPH.
Fr. Marseilles 1796/8-1885 Paris. B.
BEAUME, SERGE. (Ill)
Fr. ac. 1933 Paris. DBA.
BEAUMONT. *see also* De Beaumont.
BEAUMONT, [Sir] ALBAINS.
Br. b. Piedmont, It.; d. 1810? DNB.
BEAUMONT, ARTHUR.
Am. b. Bradford 1879; ad. 1934 Stapleton, S. I., N. Y. A-F.
BEAUMONT, ARTHUR EDWAINE.
Am. b. Norwich, Eng.; ad. 1934 Los Angeles, Calif. A.
BEAUMONT, ERNEST.
Am. Huddersfield, Eng. 1871-1933 New York. A030.
BEAUMONT, FREDERICK SAMUEL.
Eng. b. Lockwood 1861; ex. 1934 London. Wa.
BEAUMONT, [Sir] GEORGE HOWLAND.
Eng. Dunnow 1753-1827 Cole. DNB-T-722.
BEAUMONT, [Mrs.] HENRIETTA E.
Am. b. York, Eng.; ad. 1934 Stapleton, S. I., N. Y. A.
BEAUMONT, HUGUES DE.
Fr. b. Chouzzy 1874. B-DBA.
BEAUMONT, LEONARD. (Eg)
Eng. ex. 1934 Brooklyn, N. Y. Wa.
BEAUMONT, LILIAN ADELE.
Am. b. Jamaica Plains, Mass. 1880; d. 1922. A020-F.
BEAUNEVEU, ANDRÉ. (S)
Fr. ac. 1360-1403 Bourges. B-Hs-T.
BEAUQUESNE, WILFRED CONSTANT.
Fr. Rennes 1847-1913 Montegeron. B-DBA.
BEAUREGARD, DONALD.
Am. b. 1884; d. 1915 Fillmore, Utah. A012.
BEAUVAIS, NICOLAS DAUPHIN DE. (Eg)
Fr. Paris 1687-1753 Same. B-T.
BEAUVARLET, JACQUES FIRMIN. (Eg)
Fr. Abbeville 1731-1797 Same. B-T.
BEAUX, CECILIA.
Am. b. Phila., Pa. 1863; ad. 1934 New York. A-B-E-F-T-W-1-828.
BEAVIS, RICHARD.
Eng. Exmouth 1824-1896 London. B-Fa.
BÉCAT, PAUL ÉMILE.
Fr. b. Paris 1885. DBA.
BECCAFUMI, DOMENICO DI PACE.
It. Siena 1486-1551 Same. B-Bd-C-E-T-V-722.
BECCI, LUIGI. *see* Bechi. *see also* Bezzi.
BECERI, DOMENICO [Benci].
It. ac. 1565 Florence. T-V.
BECERRA, GASPAR [or Jaspar]. (S)
Sp. Baeza 1520-1570 Madrid. B-E-Hs-T-722.
BECHER, ARTHUR E.
Am. b. Freiburg, Ger. 1877; ad. 1934 Ardsley, N. Y. A.
BECHI [or Becci], LUIGI.
It. b. Florence 1830. B.
BECK, CAROL H.
Am. Phila., Pa. 1859-1908 Same. A07-B-F-T.
BECK [or Beek], DAVID.
Dut. Delft 1621-1656 The Hague. B-DNB-E.
BECK, DUNBAR DYSON.
Am. b. Delware, O. 1902; ad. 1934 New York. A.
BECK, J. AUGUSTUS.
Am. ac. 19th Cent. F-Fa.
BECK, LEONHARD HANS.
Ger. Augsburg 1480-1542 Same. B-T.
BECK, MINNA MCLEOD.
Am. b. Atlanta, Ga. 1878; ad. 1934 Montevallo, Ala. A-F.
BECK, RAPHAEL.
Am. ad. 1935 Buffalo, N. Y. A12-F.
BECK, WALTER.
Am. b. Dayton, O. 1864; ad. 1934 Millbrook, N. Y. A-B-F-T-W.
BECKER, CARL LUDWIG FRIEDRICH.
Ger. Berlin 1820-1900 Same. B-Bd-C-T.
BECKER, EULABEE DIX.
Am. b. Greenfield, O.; ad. 1935 New York. M.
BECKER, FREDERICK.
Am. b. Vermilion, S. D. 1888; ad. 1934 Oklahoma City, Okla. A-F.
BECKER, GEORGES.
Fr. b. Paris 1845. C.
BECKER, JOSEPH. (Ill)
Am. Pottsville, Pa. 1841-1910 Brooklyn, N. Y. A08.
BECKER, [Mainz], JOSEPH FERDINAND.
Ger. Gonsenheim 1846-1877 Munich. B-T.
BECKER, MAURICE. (Cart)
Am. b. Rus. 1889; ad. Tioga, Pa. A.
BECKER, PAULA MODERSOHN.
Ger. 1876-1907. T.
BECKERATH, MORITZ VON.
Ger. Crefeld 1838-1896 Munich. T.
BECKERATH, WILLY VON. (Et)
Ger. b. Crefeld 1868. T.
BECKETT, ISAAC. (Eg)
Eng. Kent 1653-1719 London. B-DNB-T.
BECKHOFF, HARRY. (Ill)
Am. ad. 1934 New York. M.
BECKINGTON, ALICE. (Min)
Am. b. St. Charles, Mo. 1868; ad. 1934 New York. A-F-T-W-46.

BECKMAN, CONRAD.
Ger. Hanover 1846-1902 Munich. B-T.
BECKMANN, [Prof.] MAX.
Ger. b. Leipzig 1884; ad. 1934 Berlin. B-T.
BECKWITH, ARTHUR.
Am. London 1860-1930 U. S. A027-F.
BECKWITH, JAMES CARROLL.
Am. Hannibal, Mo. 1852-1917 New York. A015-B-C-DAB-E-F-T-W9-15.
BECQUER, JOAQUIN D.
Sp. Sèville 1805-1841. T.
BECQUER, JUSTIN. (S)
Fr. Besançon 1829-1907 Paris. B-E-T.
BEDFORD, FRANCIS DONKIN. (Ill)
Eng. b. London 1864; ex. 1934 Same. Wa.
BEDFORD, HENRY EDWARD.
Am. Brooklyn, N. Y. 1861-1932. A029-B.
BEDINI, POLICARPO.
It. Piove di Sacco 1818-1883. B-T.
BEDORE, SIDNEY NELSON. (S)
Am. b. Stephenson, Mich. 1883; ad. 1934 Green Bay, Mich. A-F.
BEEBE, [Miss] DEE.
Am. b. New Orleans, La.; ad. 1934 Brooklyn, N. Y. A-F.
BEECHEY, GEORGE DUNCAN.
Eng. b. 1798; d. 1852 Lucknow, India. DNB-T.
BEECHEY, HENRY WILLIAM.
Eng. d. 1870 New Zealand. DNB.
BEECHEY, [Sir] WILLIAM.
Eng. Buford 1753-1839 London. B-Bd-DNB-E-T-292-722.
BEEK, [Mrs.] ALICE D. ENGLEY.
Am. b. Prov., R. I. 1876; ad. 1934 Tacoma, Wash. A-F-W.
BEEK, BERNARDUS ANTOINE VAN.
Dut. b. Amsterdam 1875. B-T.
BEEKEN, WILLIAM S.
Am. ad. 1934 New York. M.
BEEKMAN, HENRY RUTGERS.
Am. b. New York 1880; ad. 1934 Same. A-F.
BEELDEMAKER, JOHANNES.
Dut. The Hague 1630/6-1710 Same. B-T.
BEEM, PAUL E.
Am. b. Ind., Ind. 1908; ad. 1934 Same. A.
BEER, FREDERICK. (S)
Aus. b. 1846. T.
BEERBOHM, MARVIN.
Am. ad. 1935 Detroit, Mich. M.
BEERBOHM, MAX. (Cart)
Eng. b. London 1872. E-272-825.
BEERS, JAN VAN.
Belg. b. Lierre 1852. B-T.
BEERSTRATEN, JAN ABRAMHAMSZ.
Dut. 1622-1666 Amsterdam. B-C-T.
BEERSTRATEN, JOHANNES.
Dut. ac. 1658-1668 Amsterdam. B-T.
BEESON, BETTY ZIMMERMAN.
Am. b. Atlanta, Ga. 1897; ad. 1934 Chicago. A.
BEEST, ALBERT VON.
Am. Rotterdam, Holland 1820-1860 New York. B-C-F.
BEETON, ALAN.
Eng. b. London 1880; ad 1934 Checkendon. Wa.
BEGA, ABRAHAM CORNELISZ. *see* Begeyn, A. C.
BEGA, CORNELIS PIETERSY.
Dut. Haarlem 1620-1644. B-C-T-722.
BEGARELLI, ANTONIO. (S)
It. Modena 1479-1565. B-Hs-T-V.
BEGAS, KARL JOSEPH. [The Younger].
Ger. Hainsburg 1794-1854 Berlin. B-C-E-T-722.
BEGAS, REINHOLD. (S)
Ger. Berlin 1831-1911 Same. B-E-Hs-T.
BEGEYN, [or Bega], ABRAHAM CORNELISZ.
Dut. Leyden 1637/8-1697/8 Berlin. B-C-T.
BEGGS, THOMAS MONTAGUE.
Am. b. Brooklyn, N. Y. 1899; ad. 1934 Claremont, Calif. A.
BEHAM, [or Baehm], BARTHEL. (Eg)
Ger. Nüremberg 1502-1540 Italy. B-C-T.
BEHAM [or Böhm], HANS SEBALD. (Eg)
Ger. Nüremberg 1500-1550 Frankfort. B-C-T-V.
BEHME, GUSTAVUS A.
Ger. b. Nordhausen, Prussia; d. 1895 Munich. M.
BEHN, FRITZ. (S)
Ger. b. Grabow 1878; ad. 1935 Munich. B-T.
BEHNCKE, NILE JURGEN.
Am. b. Oshkosh, Wis. 1894; ad. 1934 Same. A.
BEHNES [or Burlowe], HENRY. (S)
Ir. Dublin 1796-1837 Rome. DNB-T.
BEHNES, WILLIAM. (S)
Eng. London 1790-1864 Middlesex. B-DNB.
BEHRENDSEN, AUGUST.
Swi. d. 1886 Meran, Tyrol. C.
BEHZAD. (Min) ["Marvel of the Age"]
Per. ac. 1478-1500 in Persia. M.
BEIKWA, YAMAOKA.
Jap. ac. 1900. J, Vol. 2, page 89.
BEILBY, RALPH. (Eg)
Eng. Newcastle 1744-1817. DNB-T.
BÉJOT, EUGÈNE. (Et)
Fr. Paris 1867-1931. B-DBA.
BEKE, JOOST VAN DER.
see Cleves, J. van [The Elder].
BELANGER [or Bellangé], LOUIS.
Fr. Paris 1736-1816 Stockholm. B.
BELAY, PIERRE DE.
Fr. b. Quimper 1890. Fa.
BELCHER, GEORGE FREDERICK ARTHUR.
Eng. b. 1875; ad. 1934 London. Wa.
BELCHER, HILDA.
Am. b. Pittsford, Vt. 1881; ad. 1934 New York. A-F-W-46.
BELCHER, MARTHA WOOD.
Am. b. Eng. 1884; ad. 1935 New York. A20-F.
BELDY, [Mrs.] Mabel Maugham.
Eng. ex. 1933 London. M.
BELIN DE FONTENAY, JEAN BAPTISTE.
see Blain de Fontenay, J. B.
BELINE, GEORGE.
Am. b. Minsk, Rus. 1887; ad. 1934 New York. A.
BELL, ANDREW. (Eg)
Br. 1726-1809. DNB.
BELL, BLANCHE BROWNE.
Am. b. Helena, Tex. 1881; ad. 1934 San Antonio, Tex. A.

BELL, Carl. (S)
Am. b. Ger. 1858-1927 Chicago. A024.
BELL, Caroline M.
Am. ad. 1934 Mattituck, L. I., N. Y. M.
BELL, Clara Louise. (Min)
Am. b. Newton Falls, O. 1886; ad. 1934 New York. A-F.
BELL, Corydon.
Am. b. Tiffin, O. 1894; ad. 1934 Cleveland, O. M.
BELL, E. Hamilton.
Am. ac. 1890-1920. M.
BELL, Edith Marion.
Am. b. Cushing, Ia.; ad. 1934 Iowa City, Ia. A.
BELL, Edward. (Eg)
Eng. ac. 1794-1847. B-T.
BELL, Edward August.
Am. New York 1862; ad. 1934 Peconic, L. I., N. Y. A-B-F-T-W.
BELL, Enid. (S)
Mrs. Missak Palanchian.
Eng. b. London 1904; ad. 1935 Newark, N. J. M.
BELL, George.
Aust. ac. 1933. M.
BELL, Helen K.
Am. Franklin, Pa. 1902; ad. 1934 Same. A.
BELL, John. (S)
Eng. Norfolk 1811-1895. DNB-T.
BELL, [Lady] Maria.
Eng. d. 1825 London. DNB-T.
BELL, Robert Anning.
Eng. Soho 1863-1933 London.
B-Wa-272-Obit. Art News 12-30-1933.
BELL, Robert Charles. (Eg)
Scot. Edinburgh 1806-1872. DNB-T.
BELL, Sidney.
Am. ac. 1931. Fa.
BELL, [Mrs.] Vanessa.
Eng. b. London 1879; ex. 1934 Same. Wa-825.
BELL, Wenonah.
Am. b. Trenton, N. J.; ad. 1934 Greenville, Ga. A.
BELL, William.
Eng. Newcastle 1740-1804? DNB-T.
BELL-SMITH, Frederick M.
Can. London, Eng. 1846-1923 Toronto, Ont. Y01924-893.
BELL-SMITH, John.
Can. London, Eng. 1810-1883 Toronto, Ont. M.
BELLA, Francesco della. (S)
It. d. 1612 Florence, It. B-T.
BELLA, Stefano della. (Et)
It. Florence 1610-1664 Same. B-T.
BELLANGÉ, Jacques.
Fr. ac. 1602-1617 Nancy. B.
BELLANGÉ, Joseph Louis Hippolyte.
Fr. Paris 1800-1866 Same. B-T.
BELLANGER. *see* Bellangé.
BELLANO [or Vellano], Bartholommeo. (S)
It. 1434-1496 Padua. B-Hs-T.
BELLE. *see also* De Belle.
BELLE, Alexis Simon. (S)
Fr. Paris 1674-1734 Same. B-T.
BELLE, André.
Fr. b. Paris; ac. 1930 Same. B-DBA.
BELLE, Charles Ernest de.
see De Belle, C. E.
BELLECOUR, Berne. See Berne-Bellecour.
BELLEGAMBE, Jean.
Flem. Douai 1470/80-1535. B-V.
BELLENGER, Clement Edouard.
Am. Paris 1851-1898 U. S. A01-B-T.
BELLENGER, Georges. (Eg)
Fr. Rouen 1847-1915. B-T.
BELLEROCHE, Albert Gustave de.
Eng. b. Swansea; ad. 1935 Sussex. B-DBA-Wa.
BELLERS, William.
Eng. ac. 1761-1774 London. DNB-T.
BELLET, André.
Fr. ac. Genoble 1646. B.
BELLET, Anna.
Fr. b. Guipry; ac. 1931 Paris. DBA.
BELLET DU POISAT, Jean Pierre Joseph Alfred.
Fr. Bourgoin 1823-1883 Paris. B-T.
BELLEUSE, Carrier. *see* Carrier-Belleuse.
BELLEW, Frank Henry Temple. (Cari)
Am. Hindustan 1828-1888 New York. DAB-F.
BELLEW, Frank P. W. ["Chip"]. (Cari)
Am. 1862-1894. DAB.
BELLI, Valerio [Vicentino].
It. Venice 1468-1546. T-V.
BELLIN, Samuel. (Eg)
Eng. London 1799-1893 Same. B-DNB.
BELLING, Rudolph.
Ger. b. 1886; ad. 1934 New York. M-798.
BELLINI, Gentile.
It. Venice 1426/30-1507 Same.
B-Bd-C-E-T-V-722-916.
BELLINI, Giovanni.
It. Venice 1428/30-1516 Same.
B-Bd-C-E-T-V-722-859-916.
BELLINI, Jacopo.
It. Venice 1400?-1470/1 Same.
B-C-E-T-V-916.
BELLINIANO [Bellini], Vittore.
It. Venice 1450-1529 Same. B-T-V.
BELLIS, Daisy Maud.
Am. b. Waltham, Mass.; ad. 1934 Same. A.
BELLIS, Herbert.
Belg. Brussels 1831-1902 Paris. T.
BELLO, [or Belli], Marco.
It. 1477-1576. B-T-V.
BELLO, Raffaello.
It. ac. 1530 Florence. T-V.
BELLOC, Jean Hilaire.
Fr. Nantes 1786-1866 Paris. B-T.
BELLONI, Giorgio.
It. b. Codogno 1861; ad. 1934 Milan. B.
BELLOTTO, Bernardo. *see* Canaletto, B.
BELLOWS, Albert Fitch.
Am. Milford, Mass. 1829-1883 New York.
C-DAB-E-F-T-3-4-15-22-23.
BELLOWS, George Wesley.
Am. Columbus, O. 1882-1925 New York.
A022-B-DAB-E-F-W13-1-24-39-46-71-105-138-172-191-205-293-700-701-721-779.
BELLUCI, Antonio.
It. Trévise 1654-1726 Same. B-C-T.
BELLUCI, Giovanni Battista.
It. San Marino 1506-1554. T-V.
BELLUCI, Marzocchi de. *see* Marzocchi de B.

BELLVER Y RAMÓN, Ricardo. (S)
Sp. b. Madrid 1845. Hs-T.
BELLY, Léon Adolphe Auguste.
Fr. St. Omer 1827-1877 Paris. B-T.
BELMONDO, Paul. (S)
Fr. b. Algiers; ac. 1934 Paris. DBA.
BELMONT, Ira Jean.
Am. b. Kaunas, Lithuania, 1885; ad. 1934 New York. A.
BELOT, Gabriel.
Fr. b. Paris 1882. DBA.
BELSKIE, Abram.
Am. ad. 1935 Closter, N. J. M.
BELTRAFFIO [or Boltraffio], Giovanni Antonio.
It. Milan 1467-1516 Same. B-T-V-722.
BELTRAM-MASSES, Federico.
Sp. b. Barcelona 1885. DBA.
BELTRAND, Jacques.
Fr. b. Paris 1874. B-DBA-T.
BEMAN, Jean. *see* Cook-Smith, J. B.
BEMBO [or Bembi], Bonifazio.
It. ac. 1475 Cremona. T-V.
BEMBO, Giovanni Francesco [Vetraio].
It. ac. 1514-1524 Cremona. B-V.
BEMENT, Alon.
Am. b. Ashfield, Mass. 1876; ad. 1934 New York. A28-B-F-W.
BEMUS, [Mrs.] Mary B.
Am. b. Leicester, N. Y. 1849. A12-F.
BENADE, James A.
Am. Bethlehem, Pa. 1823-1853 Reading, Pa. M.
BENAGLIO, Francesco.
It. ac. 1432-1487 Verona. B.
BENARD [or Besnard], Jean Baptiste.
Fr. ac. Paris 1751; d. 1789 Same. B.
BENAZECH, Charles.
Eng. London 1767?-1794 Same. B-DNB-T.
BENAZECH, Peter Paul. (Eg)
Eng. 1730-1783 London. B-DNB-T.
BENAZECH [or Benezech], René.
Fr. ac. 1930 Paris. M.
BENBRIDGE, Henry.
Am. Phila., Pa. 1744-1812 Norfolk, Va. DAB-F-T-2-4-6-179-182.
BENCZUR, Gyula Julius de.
Hun. Nyiregyhaza 1844-1920. B-C-T.
BENDA, Wladyslaw Theodore. (Masks)
Am. b. Poznan, Pol. 1873; ad. 1934 New York. A28-E-F-W.
BENDEMANN, Edouard Jules Frédéric.
Ger. Berlin 1811-1889 Düsseldorf. B-C-T.
BENDEMANN, Rudolph Christian Eugène.
Ger. Dresden 1851-1884 Pegli, It. B-T.
BENEDETTO DA MIANO [Leonardo]. (S)
It. 1442-1497. B-T.
BENEDETTO OF PARMA. *see* Antelami.
BENEDETTO DA ROVEZZANO. (S)
It. Pistoia 1474-1552 Vallomtresa. B-T.
BENEDICT, Augusta Burke.
Mrs. Stewart Benedict.
Am. b. New York 1897; ad. 1934 Cleveland, O. A.
BENEDICT, Frank M.
Am. 1840-1930. M.
BENEDICTER, Alois Josef.
Ger. b. 1843. T.
BENEDITO-VIVES, Manuel.
Sp. b. Vives; ac. Madrid 1929; d. Valencia. DBA.
BENEDUCE, Antimo.
Am. b. Naples, It. 1900; ad. 1934 Cleveland, O. A-F.
BENEKER, Gerritt Albertus.
Am. Grand Rapids, Mich. 1882-1934 Truro, Mass.
A-B-F-W-Obit. N. Y. papers 10-23-1934.
BÉNET, Eugène Paul. (S)
Fr. b. Dieppe 1863; ac. 1884-1905 Paris. B-DBA-798.
BENETT, Newton.
Eng. London 1854-1922 Dorchester. B.
BENETTINI, Pietro. *see* Cortuna, P. da.
BÉNÉZIT, Emanuel Charles Louis.
Fr. b. Paris 1887. B-DBA.
BENGO, John. (Eg)
Scot. ac. 1796-1830 Edinburgh. B.
BENGTSSON, Sven.
Swe. b. Lund 1843; ac. 1920. T.
BENING, Alexander. (Min)
Flem. ac. 1469-1519. B-T.
BENING [or Beninc], Simon. (Min)
Flem. Ghent, Belg. 1483/4-1561 Bruges, Belg. T-V
BENITO, Éduardo G.
Fr. ex. 1935 New York. M.
BENJAMIN, Gershon.
Am. ex. 1935 New York. M.
BENJAMIN, [Mrs.] Lucile Joullin.
Am. Geneseo, Ill. 1876-1924 San Fran., Calif. A021.
BENJAMIN, Nora.
Am. ex. 1935 New York. M.
BENJAMIN, Paul.
Am. ex. 1935 New York. M.
BENJAMIN, Samuel Greene Wheeler.
Am. Argos, Gr. 1837-1914 Burlington, Vt. A011-B-C-DAB-F-T-W8-15.
BENJAMIN-CONSTANT, Jean Joseph.
Fr. Paris 1845-1902 Same. B-Bd-C-T.
BENJONI, Giovanni Maria. (S)
It. 1809-1873 Rome. B-T.
BENLLIURE Y GIL, José.
Sp. b. Valencia 1855/8. B-E-T.
BENN, Ben.
Am. Rus. 1884; ad. 1934 New York. A-F.
BENNECKE, D.
Am. ac. 1853 New York. M.
BENNER, Emanuel [or Jean].
Fr. Mulhouse 1836-1909 Paris. B-C-T.
BENNER, Emanuel Michel Many.
Fr. b. Capri, It. 1873. B-DBA.
BENNERS, Ethel Ellis de Turck.
Mrs. Alfred Eugène Benners, Jr.
Am. ad. 1934 Phila., Pa. A.
BENNETT, Charles Henry. (Eg)
Eng. 1829-1867. DNB.
BENNETT, Emma Dunbar. (S)
Mrs. Harrison Bennett.
Am. b. New Bedford, Mass.; ad. 1934 Paris. A.
BENNETT, [Mrs.] Emma-Sutton Carter.
Am. b. 1902; ad. 1934 St. Louis, Mo. A.
BENNETT, Francis I.
Am. b. Phila., Pa. 1876; ad. 1934 Nutley, N. J. A.

BENNETT, Frank Moss.
Eng. b. Liverpool; ac. 1930. DBA.
BENNETT, Franklin.
Am. b. Greenport, N. Y. 1908; ad. 1934 New York. A.
BENNETT, Gertrude.
Am. b. Monterey, Calif. 1894; ad. 1934 Pleasanton, Calif. M.
BENNETT, Rainey.
Am. b. 1907; ex. 1934 Chicago. M.
BENNETT, Reginald Osborn.
Am. b. Devils Lake, N. D.; ad. 1934, Detroit, Mich. A.
BENNETT, Ruth M. (Carver)
Am. ad. 1934 Hollywood, Calif. A.
BENNETT, William James. (Eg)
Am. London 1787-1844 New York. B-F-T-2-7.
BENNEY, Ernest Alfred Sallis.
Eng. b. Bradford 1894; ad. 1929 Cheltenham. Wa1929.
BENOIS, Alexander Nikolaivitch.
Rus. b. Leningrad 1870; ac. 1911. B.
BENOIS, [Mrs.] Nadia.
Rus. ad. 1934 London. M.
BENOIST, Antoine. (Eg)
Eng. Soissons, Fr. 1721-1770 London. DNB-T.
BENOIST, Marie Guilhelmine.
Fr. Paris 1768-1826 Same. B-T.
BÉNOUVILLE, François Léon.
Fr. Paris 1821-1859 Same. B-T-722.
BÉNOUVILLE, Jean Achille.
Fr. Paris 1815-1891 Same. B-T.
BENOZZO, Gozzoli. *see* Gozzoli, B. di L.
BENSA [or Benja] Ernesto.
It. ac. 1897 in Florence. B.
BENSELL, George Frederick.
Am. Phila., Pa. 1837-1879. B-F-T-45.
BENSHERTEN, Clara D. van.
Am. ad. 1934 New York. M.
BEN-SHMUEL, Ahron. (S)
Am. ex. 1934 New York. M.
BENSING, Frank C. (Ill)
Am. ad. 1934 New York. A29
BENSINGER, Anne Mosejiere.
Am. b. Topeka, Kan. 1906; ad. 1934 Los Angeles, Calif. A.
BENSON, [or Bentsoen], Ambrosius.
[Master of the Deipara Virgo of Antwerp.]
Flem. 1495/1500-1550 Bruges. B-Fa.
BENSON, Eda Spoth.
Am. b. Brooklyn, N. Y. 1898; ad. 1934 Danbury, Conn. A.
BENSON, Eugene.
Am. Hyde Park, N. Y. 1839-1908 Venice, It. B-C-DAB-F-T-1-3-4-15.
BENSON, Frank Weston.
Am. b. Salem, Mass. 1862; ad. 1934 Same. A-B-E-F-T-W-1-46-757-830.
BENSON, John P.
Am. b. Salem, Mass. 1865; ad. 1934 Kittery, Me. A.
BENSON, John William.
Am. b. Brooklyn, N. Y.; ad. 1934 Same. A.
BENSON, Leslie L.
Am. ad. 1934 Norwalk, Conn. M.
BENSON, Stuart. (S)
Am. b. Detroit, Mich.; ad. 1934 Clos du Père, Fr. M.
BENSON, Tressa Emerson.
Am. b. Bucksport, Me.; 1896; ad. 1934 Chicago. A.
BENT, Johannes van der. (P, S)
Dut. Amsterdam 1650-1690 Same. B-T.
BENTHAM, George. (Ill)
Am. Ir. 1850-1914 Fordham, N. Y. A011.
BENTLEY, Charles.
Eng. 1806-1854 London. DNB-T.
BENTLEY, John Woodstock.
Am. b. Paterson, N. J. 1880; ad. 1934 Monroe, N. Y. A-F.
BENTLEY, Joseph Clayton.
Eng. Bradford 1809-1851 Sydenham. B-DNB-T.
BENTLEY, Joseph Herbert.
Eng. b. Lincoln 1866; ad. 1934 Sheffield. Wa.
BENTLEY, Richard.
Eng. d. 1782. T.
BENTON, Dwight.
Am. b. New York 1834. B-T.
BENTON, Harry Stacey.
Am. b. Saratoga Springs, N. Y. 1877; ad. 1934 Norwalk, Conn. A-B-F.
BENTON, Thomas Hunt. (Mu)
Am. b. Neosho, Mo. 1889; ad. 1934 New York. A-F-6-38-701-779-783.
BENTUM, Christian Philipp.
Aus. d. 1750 Silesie. B-T.
BENTZ, John.
Am. b. Columbus, O.; ac. 1934 Leonia, N. J. A.
BENVENUTI, Augusto (S)
It. Venice 1839-1899 Same. B-T.
BENVENUTI, Giovanni Baptista [Ortolano].
It. Ferrara 1460/90-1525/9 Same. B-T.
BENVENUTO DI GIOVANNI [Guasta].
It. Siena 1436-1518. B-T.
BENVENUTO DI GIROLAMO.
see Girolamo di Benvenuto del Gusta.
BENVENUTO DA SIENA.
see Benvenuto di Giovanni.
BENVENUTO TISI [or Tisio].
see Garofolo, Il, B. da T.
BENWELL, John Hodges.
Eng. Blenheim 1764-1785 London. B-DNB.
BENWELL, Mary. [Mrs. Code.]
Eng. ac. 1761-1800 London. DNB-T.
BENZ, Séverin.
Swi. St. Gall 1834-1898 Munich, Ger. B-T.
BENZIGER, August.
Am. b. Swi. 1867; ad. 1934 Same. A12-B-T-W.
BENZONI, Giovanni Maria. (S)
It. Songavazzo 1809-1873 Rome. B-T.
BÉRAIN, Claude.
Fr. ac. 1726. T.
BÉRAIN, Jean [The Younger].
Fr. Paris 1678-1726 Same. B-T.
BÉRANGER, Gabriel.
Br. b. Rotterdam; d. 1817 Ireland. DNB.
BÉRANGER, Jean Baptiste Antoine Émile.
Fr. Sèvres 1814-1882. B-T.

BÉRARD, Christian.
Fr. ex. 1934 Paris. M.
BÉRAUD, Jean.
Fr. Leningrad, Rus. 1849-1910 Paris. B-DBA.
BERCHEM [or Berghem], Claes Pieteray Nicolaes.
Dut. Haarlem 1620-1683 Amsterdam. B-Bd-C-E-T-204-722.
BERCHER, Henri Edouard.
Fr. b. Vevey 1877. DBA.
BERCHÈRE, Narcisse.
Fr. Estampes 1819-1891 Asnièrs. B-T.
BERCHET, Peter.
Br. France 1657/9-1720 England. DNB-T.
BERCKHEYDE, Gerrit Andriaensz.
Dut. Haarlem 1638-1698 Same. B-T-722-803.
BERCKHEYDE, Job. Andriaensz.
Dut. Haarlem 1630-1693 Same. B-C-T.
BERCKMANS, [Mrs.] Elizabeth.
Am. Plainfield, N. J. 1842-1915 Brooklyn, N. Y. A012.
BERDANIER, Paul Frederick. (Et)
Am. b. Frackville, Pa. 1879; ad. 1934 Jackson Heights, N. Y. A-W.
BEREND, Charlotte.
Ger. b. Berlin 1886; ad. 1935 Same. M.
BERENGER, Émile.
Fr. 1814-1883. M.
BERESFORD, Frank Ernest. (Mu)
Eng. b. Derby 1881; ad. 1934 London. Wa.
BERG, Claus. (S)
Swe. ac. 1520 Lübeck, Ger. T-824.
BERG, George Lewis.
Am. b. McGregor, Ia. 1870; ad. So. Norwalk, Conn. A-F.
BERG, Hans Johan Fredrik.
Nor. Näsne 1813-1874. T.
BERG, Jacobus Evaudus Josephus van den.
Dut. Rotterdam 1802-1861 The Hague. B-T.
BERGAMASCO, Il. *see* Castello, G. B.
BERGAMASCO, Guglielmo.
It. ac. 1515-1550 Venice. T-V.
BERGCRANTZ, Lloyd.
Am. ad. 1934 Toledo, O. M.
BERGE, Augustus Charles de la.
Fr. Paris 1807-1842 Same. B-T-722.
BERGE, Edward. (S)
Am. Baltimore, Md. 1876-1924 Same. A021-B-F.
BERGE, Olaf A.
Am. b. St. Paul, Minn. 1898; ad. 1934 Same. A.
BERGE, Pieter van den.
Dut. ac. 1689-1737 Amsterdam. B-T.
BERGE, Stephens.
Am. ex. 1934 Baltimore, Md. M.
BERGEN, Claus von.
Ger. ac. 1909 Munich. B-T.
BERGEN [or Berghan], Dirck Theodore van.
Dut. Haarlem 1645-1689/90. B-T-722.
BERGEN, George.
Eng. ex. 1930 London. M.
BERGEN, Karl von.
Ger. Hamburg 1794-1835. B-T.
BERGER, Daniel R. (Eg)
Am. Berlin, Ger. 1744-1824 U. S. B-M.
BERGER, Frank W. (S)
Am. d. 1916 Minn., Minn. A013.
BERGER, Jacques.
Fr. b. Lyons 1834; ac. 1902 Paris. DBA-T.
BERGER, William Merritt. (Ill)
Am. b. Union Springs, N. Y.; ad. 1934 New York. A.
BERGH, Richard Swén.
Swe. Stockholm 1858-1919. B-C-DBA-T.
BERGHE, Fritz van den.
Flem. b. Ghent, Belg. 797.
BERGHEM, Claes Pietersy Nicolaes.
see Berchem, C. P. N.
BERGLER, Ettore de Maria.
see Maria Bergler, E. de.
BERGMAN, Karola.
Am. b. Prague, Czec. 1902; ad. 1934 New York. A.
BERGMANN, Frank W.
Am. ex. 1933 San Fran., Calif. M.
BERGMANN, Julius Hugo.
Ger. b. Nördhausen 1861. B-T.
BERGSTRÖM, Alfred Maurits.
Swe. b. Stockholm 1869. B-DBA.
BERGSTRÖM, Elizabeth T. B.
Am. b. Stockholm; ad. 1934 Chicago. A.
BERGSTRÖM, Sigge. (Eg)
Swe. b. Finshyttau 1880. T.
BERHOEVEN-BALL, Adrien Joseph.
Belg. b. Antwerp 1824; ac. 1856-1873. M.
BERHOLZ, E.
Rus. 1860-1909. M.
BERJOLE, Pierre.
Fr. b. Saumur; ac. 1929 Paris. DBA.
BERJON, Antoine.
Fr. Lyons 1754-1843 Same. B.
BERKAM, Otto.
Am. 1832-1906 Passaic, N. J. A06-F.
BERKMAN, Aaron.
Am. ex. 1935 New York. M.
BERLANDINA, Jane.
Fr. ex. 1935 New York. M.
BERLIN, Andreas.
Ger. ac. 1867 Berlin. B-T.
BERLIN, Harry.
Am. b. New York 1886. A12-B.
BERLINGHIERI, Berlinghiero.
It. b. Milan; ac. 1228 Lucca. B-T.
BERLINGHIERI, Bonaventura.
It. ac. 1228-1244 Lucca. B-T.
BERMAN, Eugène.
Rus. b. Leningrad 1899; ad. 1934 Paris. M.
BERMAN, Harry G.
Am. Phila., Pa. 1900-1932. A029-F.
BERMAN, Léonide.
Rus. b. Leningrad 1896. M.
BERMAN, Sam. (Cart.)
Am. ad. 1934 New York. M.
BERMAN, Sarah.
Am. b. Rus. 1895; ad. 1934 New York. A.
BERMAN, Saul.
Am. b. Rus. 1899; ad. 1934 New York. A.
BERMEJO, Bartolemé. *see* Vermejo, B.
BERNA da Siena. *see* Barna da S.
BERNAERTS, Nicasius.
Flem. Antwerp, Belg. 1620-1678 Paris. B-722.
BERNARD, Émile.
Fr. b. Lille 1868. B-DBA.

BERNARD, Jean.
Dut. Amsterdam 1765-1833. B-T.
BERNARD, Jean Joseph.
Fr. 1740-1809. T.
BERNARD, Joseph Antoine. (S)
Fr. Vienna, Aus. 1866-1931 Paris. B-DBA-798.
BERNARDEAU, Henri Marie Georges.
Fr. b. Orléans 1867. DBA.
BERNARDI, Giovanni Battista. (S)
It. ac. 1700 Venice. B.
BERNARDI, Giovanni da Castel.
It. 1496-1553 Faenza. T-V.
BERNARDINO, di Betto. *see* Pinturicchio.
BERNARDINO di Mariotto [della Stagno].
It. Pérouse 1478-1566. B.
BERARDINO Perugino. *see* Perugino.
BERNATZ, Max.
Ger. b. Aitrang 1862. B-T.
BERNAZZANO, Cesare.
It. ac. 1536 Milan. T-V.
BERNE-BELLECOUR, Étienne Prosper.
Fr. Boulogne-sur-Mer 1838-1910 Paris. B-T.
BERNE-BELLECOUR, Jean Jacques.
Fr. b. St. Germain-en-Laye 1874. B-DBA.
BERNEKER, Louis Frederick.
Am. b. Clinton, Mo. 1876; ad. 1934 New York. A-F-W.
BERNEKER, Maud Fox.
Mrs. Louis F. Berneker.
Am. b. Memphis, Tenn. 1882; ad. 1934 New York. A.
BERNEZ, Theresa. (Et)
Am. ad. 1934 Baltimore, Md. A29.
BERNHARD, Bernardus.
Ger. ac. 1476 Augsburg. B-T.
BERNINGHAUS, J. Charles.
Am. b. St. Louis, Mo. 1905; ad. 1934 Taos, N. M. A.
BERNINGHAUS, Oscar Edward.
Am. b. St. Louis, Mo. 1874; ad. 1934 Taos, N. M. A.
BERNINI, Giovanni Lorenzo. (S)
It. Naples 1598-1680 Rome. B-E-Hs-T.
BERNOUARD, Suzanne.
Fr. ac. 1930 Paris. DBA.
BERNSTEIN, Edna L.
Am. ad. 1935 New York. M.
BERNSTEIN, Elizabeth.
Mrs. Milton L. Bernstein.
Am. ad. 1934 New York. M.
BERNSTEIN, Meyer. (Et)
Am. ad. 1934 New York. M.
BERNSTEIN, Norma Jeanne.
Am. ad. 1934 New York. M.
BERNSTEIN, Saul.
Am. b. Poswol, Rus. 1872-1905 Baltimore, Md. A06-B.
BERNSTEIN, Theresa F.
Am. b. Phila., Pa.; ad. 1934 New York. A-F.
BERNSTEIN, Walter.
Ger. b. 1901; ad. 1935 Berlin. M.
BERNSTROM, Victor. (Eg)
Am. Sweden 1845-1907 Nyack, N. Y. A06-B-F-T.
BERNWARD [Bishop of Hildesheim]. (S)
Ger. 930-1022. Hs-T.
BERNÝ, Pierre Jean Paul. (Pen Work)
Fr. Chartres 1722-1779 Strasburg. T.
BÉROUD, Louis.
Fr. b. Lyons 1852; ad. 1908 Paris. B-DBA-T.
BERRÉ, Jean Baptiste.
Flem. Antwerp, Belg. 1777-1838 Paris. B-T.
BERRESFORD, Virginia.
Am. ex. 1934 New York. M.
BERRETTINI, Pietro da Cortona.
It. Cortona 1596-1669 Rome. B-C-T-722.
BERRIE, John Archibald Alexander.
Eng. b. Fallowfield 1887. Wa.
BERRONE, Giovanni. (S)
It. ex. 1932 Venice. M.
BERRONE, John. (S)
Br. b. Buenos Aires, Argentine 1893; ac. 1929 Rome. Wa.
BERRUER, Pierre François.
Fr. Paris 1733-1797. B-T.
BERRUGUETE Y GONZALES, Alonzo. (S)
Sp. Paredes 1480-1561 Alcalá. C-Hs-722.
BERRUGUETE, Pedro.
Sp. b. Paredes de Nava; d. 1503. B-T.
BERRY, Corinna de.
Mrs. Antonio Salemme.
Am. b. Nice, Fr. 1908; ad. 1934 New York. M.
BERRY, Erick. (Ill)
Mrs. Allena C. Best.
Am. ad. 1934 New York. A20.
BERRY, Hester Bancroft. (S)
Mrs. Romeyn Berry.
Am. b. Ithaca, N. Y. 1889; ad. 1934 Same. Cs-F.
BERRY, K. W. (Ill)
Am. ad. 1934 Newton Upper Falls, Mass. M.
BERRY, Patrick Vincent.
Am. Troy, N. Y. 1843-1913 New York. A011-B.
BERRYMAN, Clifford Kennedy. (Cart)
Am. b. Versailles, Ky.; ac. 1933 Wash., D. C. A28-F-W.
BERRYMAN, James T. (Cart)
Am. ad. 1934 Wash., D. C. M.
BERSANI, Stefano.
It. Melegnano 1872-1910. B-T.
BERSUGLIA, Giovanni Domenico.
It. ac. 1545-1573 Carrara. T-V.
BERTA, Edourdo [or Edoarta].
Swi. b. Guibiasco 1867. B.
BERTALL [or Berthall]. *see* Arnoux, C. A.
BERTALON, Albert.
Hun. b. Iaszberény 1899. DBA.
BERTANI, Giovanni Battista.
It. Mantua 1516-1596. T-V.
BERTHELON, Eugène.
Fr. b. Paris 1829; ac. 1864-1910. B-C.
BERTHELOT [or Bertolet], Guillaume. (S)
Fr. Paris 1576-1648. B-Hs.
BERTHELSEN, Johann.
Am. b. Copenhagen, Den. 1883; ad. 1934 New York. A-F.
BERTHOLD VON NÖRDLINGER.
Ger. ac. 1420-1430. M.
BERTHOLET. *see* Master Flemale.
BERTICHEN, P. G.
Dut. b. 1796; ac. 1814-1852 Amsterdam. B.

BERTIER, FRANCISQUE ÉDOUARD.
Fr. b. Paris 1847; ac. 1875 in Geneva, Swi. B.
BERTIERI, PILADE.
It. b. Turin 1874. B.
BERTIN, ÉMILE.
Fr. b. Suresnes 1878. DBA.
BERTIN, JEAN VICTOR.
Fr. Paris 1775-1842. B-T.
BERTOLDO DI GIOVANNI. (S)
It. 1410-1491 Caiano. B-Hs-T-V.
BERTOLT, CUSTOS. (Min)
Aus. ac. 11th century in Salzburg. T.
BERTON, ARMAND.
Fr. Paris 1854-1927 Same. B-DBA-T.
BERTON, PAUL ÉMILE.
Fr. d. Chartrettes 1909; ac. 1874 Paris. T.
BERTONNIER, PIERRE FRANÇOIS. (Eg)
Fr. b. Paris 1791; ac. 1819-1847. B.
BERTRAM, ABEL.
Fr. b. St. Omer 1871. B-DBA.
BERTRAM OF MINDEN. *see* Master Bertram.
BERTRAND, [James] JEAN BAPTISTE.
Fr. Lyons 1823-1887 Orsay. B-C-T.
BERTUCCI, GIOVANNI BATTISTA. [The Elder].
It. ac. 1475-1516 Faenza. B-T.
BERTUCCI, GIOVANNI BATTISTA.
[The Younger.]
It. Faenza 1540-1614 Same. B-T.
BERUETE Y MORET, AURELIANO DE.
Sp. Madrid 1845-1912. B.
BERUGUETTE, PEDRO.
Sp. ac. 16th century. M.
BERVIC, CARLES CLÉMENT. (Eg)
Fr. Paris 1756-1822. B-T.
BERWICK, C. M.
Eng. ac. 1926. M.
BERZEVIZY, JULIUS.
Am. b. Homona, Hun. 1875; ad. 1934 Buffalo, N. Y. A.
BESCHEY, BALTASAR.
Flem. Antwerp, Belg. 1708-1776 Same. B-C-T.
BESCHEY, JACOB ANDRIES.
Flem. Antwerp, Belg. 1710-1786 Same. B.
BESNARD, [Paul] ALBERT.
Fr. Paris 1849-1934 Same.
B-DBA-E-T-Obit. N. Y. papers 12-5-1934.
BESSE, RAYMOND.
Fr. b. Niort 1871. DBA.
BESSELL, EVELYNE BYERS.
Am. b. Houston, Tex. 1900. M.
BESSIRE, DALE PHILIP.
Am. b. Columbus, O.; ad. 1934 Nashville, Ind. A.
BEST, EDWARD S. (Eg)
Am. London 1826-1865 Phila., Pa. B-F-T-7-40.
BEST, HARRY CASSIE.
Am. b. Peterboro, Can. 1863; ac. Calif. A.
BEST, WILLARD SEWELL.
Am. b. Albany, Mo. 1872; ad. 1915 Chicago. A12.
BESTLAND, CHARLES.
Eng. ac. 1783-1836 London. B.
BETHAM, MARY MATILDA. (Min)
Eng. London 1776-1852. DNB-T.
BETHEA, F. ELIZABETH.
Am. b. Birmingham, Ala. 1902; ad. 1934 Ruston, Ala. A.
BETTANIER, ALBERT.
Fr. b. Metz; ac. 1881-1891. B.
BETTELHEIM, JOLAN GROSS.
Am. ad. 1935 Cleveland, O. M.
BETTES, JOHN. (Min)
Eng. ac. 1530-1580 London. DNB-T.
BETTI, BIAGIO [Carigliano].
It. Milan 1545-1615 Rome. B-T-V.
BETTINARDI, JOHN.
Am. b. Venice, It. 1885; ad. 1934 Hasbruck Heights, N. J. M.
BETTINGER, HOYLAND B.
Am. b. Lima, N. Y. 1890; ad. 1934 Waltham, Mass. A.
BETTO, BERNARDINO DE. *see* Pinturiccho.
BETTS, ANNA WHELAN.
Am. b. Phila., Pa.; ad. 1934 New Hope, Pa. A-F-W9.
BETTS, E. C. (Mural)
Am. Hillside, Mich. 1856-1917 Denver, Colo. A014-F.
BETTS, EDITH F. (Ill)
Am. ad. 1934 Wilmington, Del. M.
BETTS, EDWIN DANIEL, JR.
Am. b. St. Louis, Mo. 1879; ad. 1915 Chicago. A12-B.
BETTS, EDWIN DANIEL, SR.
Am. 1847-1915 Chicago. A012-F.
BETTS, GRACE MAY.
Am. b. New York 1885; ad. 1915 Chicago. A12-B.
BETTS, HAROLD HARINGTON.
Am. New York 1881; ad. 1915 Chicago. A12-F.
BETTS, LOUIS.
Am. b. Little Rock, Ark. 1873; ad. 1934 New York. A-B-F-W-46-757.
BETZLMANN, [Mrs.] FERDINAND.
see Reisner, I. V.
BEUCKELAER [or Bueckelaer], JOACHIM.
Flem. Antwerp, Belg. 1530/5-1575/8. B.
BEURDELEY, JACQUES. (Et)
Fr. b. Paris 1874; ex. 1934 Minn., Minn. B-DBA-880.
BEVAN, ROBERT POLHILL.
Eng. Hove, Sussex 1865-1925 London. T-825.
BEVERIDGE, KUEHUE. (S)
Am. b. Springfield, Ill. 1877. B-F-T-W12
BEVERLEY, WILLIAM ROXBY.
Eng. Richmond 1824-1889 Hampstead. B-E.
BEVIN, ALICE CONKLIN.
Mrs. George J. Leevitz.
Am. b. East Hampton, Conn.; ad. 1934 Same. A.
BEW, [Mrs.] MATTIE CLOVER. *see* Clover-Bew, (Mrs.) M. M.
BEWICK, JOHN. (Eg)
Eng. Cherryburn 1760-1795. DNB-T.
BEWICK, ROBERT ELLIOT. (Eg)
Eng. 1788-1849. DNB-T.
BEWICK, THOMAS. (Eg)
Eng. Newcastle 1753-1828 Gateshead. B-Bd-DNB-E-T-294-713.

BEWLEY, MURRAY PERCIVAL.
Am. b. Fort Worth, Tex. 1884; ad. 1934 New York. A-B-F-W.
BEYER, GEORGE ALBERT.
Am. b. Minn., Minn. 1900; ad. 1934 Same. A.
BEYEREN, ABRAHAM HENDRICKSZ VAN.
Dut. The Hague 1620/1-1690 Overschie. B.
BEYLE, PIERRE MARIE.
Fr. Lyons 1838-1902. B.
BEYNON, JOHN.
Can. b. Minnedosa, Man.; ac. 1933 Toronto. 893.
BEYSCHLAG, ROBERT.
Ger. Nördlingen 1838-1903 Munich. B.
BEZARD, JEAN LOUIS.
Fr. b. Toulouse 1799; ac. 1829-1861. B.
BEZZI. *see also* Bechi.
BEZZI, BARTHOLOMEO.
It. b. Trente 1851. B-M.
BEZZUOLI, GIUSEPPE.
It. Florence 1784-1855. B-T.
BHIWANDIWALA, ERACH A.
["Orpen of India."]
Br. ac. 1934 in India and China. M.
BHORA.
Per. ac. late 16th century Persia. M.
BIAFORA, ENEA G. (S)
Am. b. Calabria, It. 1892; ad. 1934 New York. A-Cs-F.
BIAGIO, BERNARDINO DI. *see* Pinturicchio.
BIAGIO, VINCENZIO DI. *see* Catena, V. di B.
BIALA.
Rus. b. Biala, Rus.-Pol. 1903; ad. 1935 Toulon, Fr. M.
BIANCHI, BALDASSARE.
It. Bologna 1614-1678 Modena. B-T.
BIANCHI, FRANCESCO. (S)
It. ac. 17th century in Italy. Bd-M.
BIANCHI [or Bianco], GIOVANNI PAOLO.
It. ac. 1621-1646 in Milan. B.
BIANCHI, GIUSEPPE. (Eg)
It. ac. 1829-1845 in Rome. B-T.
BIANCHI, MOSÈ DI GIOSUÈ.
It. Monza 1845-1904. B-T.
BIANCHINI, CHARLES.
Fr. Lyons 1860-1905 Paris. T.
BIANCO, PAMELA.
Eng. b. England 1906; ad. 1935 N. Y. Fa-M.
BIBBY, H.
Br. ac. 19th century. Fa.
BIBERMAN, EDWARD.
Am. b. Phila., Pa. 1904; ad. 1934 New York. A.
BIBIENA, FERDINANDO GALLE. [The Younger]
It. Bologna 1657-1743 Same. B-722.
BIBIENA, FRANCESCO GALLI.
It. Bologna 1659-1739 Same. B-T-722.
BICCHI, SILVIO.
It. b. Leghorn 1874-. B-M.
BICCI DI LORENZO, SR.
It. Florence 1350-1427. B-V.
BICCI DI LORENZO, JR.
It. Florence 1373-1450. B-T-V.
BICCI DI NÉRI.
It. Florence 1419-1491 Same. B-T-V.
BICENKO, ANDRÉ.
Rus. b. Koursk 1886. DBA.
BICHITR. (Min)
Per. ac. 1650 in Persia. M.
BICKFORD, NELSON H. (S)
Am. ac. 1915-1926 Paris. A12-F.
BICKHAM, GEORGES [The Elder]. (Eg)
Eng. London 1684-1769 Richmond. B-DNB.
BICKHAM, GEORGES [The Younger]. (Eg)
Eng. d. 1758. DNB-T.
BICKNELL, ALBION HARRIS.
Am. Turner, Me. 1837-1915 Malden, Mass. A012-F.
BICKNELL, EVELYN M.
Am. ad. 1934 New York. M.
BICKNELL, FRANK ALFRED.
Am. b. Augusta, Me. 1866; ad. 1934 Old Lyme, Conn. A-B-F-W.
BICKNELL, WILLIAM HARRY WARREN. (Et)
Am. b. Boston 1860; ad. 1934 Winchester, Mass. A28-B-F-W.
BIDA, F. ALEXANDRE.
Fr. Toulouse 1813-1895 Bühl, Ger. B.
BIDAULD, JEAN JOSEPH XAVIER.
Fr. Carpentras 1743-1813 Lyons. B-T.
BIDDLE, GEORGE.
Am. Phila., Pa. 1885; ad. 1934 Croton, N. Y. A-F-W-779.
BIDDLE, LAURENCE.
Eng. b. Sussex 1888; ad. 1934 London. Wa.
BIDDLE, R. S.
Am. ac. 1830 Phila., Pa. M.
BIDEAULT, LOUIS.
Fr. b. Lyons; d. 1928. DBA.
BIDUINUS, DA PISA. (S)
It. ac. 12th century Pisa. B-Hs-T-V.
BIDWELL, ALICE L.
Mrs. Charles W. Bidwell.
Am. ad. 1934 Chicago. M.
BIEL, JOSEPH.
Am. b. France; ex. 1934 New York. M.
BIENNAIS, MARTIN GUILLAUME. (Metal-Ware)
Fr. ac. 1800-1832 Paris. T.
BIENNOURRY, VICTOR FRANÇOIS ELOI.
Fr. Bar-sur-Aube 1823-1893 Paris. B.
BIERHALS, OTTO.
Am. ad. 1935 Tenafly, N. J. M.
BIERMANN [or Birman], GOTTLIEB PETER.
Ger. Dez 1758-1844. T.
BIERSTADT, ALBERT.
Am. Germany 1830-1902 New York. A04-B-Bd-C-DNB-E-F-T-1-4-26-46.
BIESEL, CHARLES.
Am. b. New York 1865; ad. 1934 Chicago. A-F.
BIESEL, FRED.
Am. b. Phila., Pa.; ad. 1934 Chicago. A.
BIESHOECKE, J. VAN. (S)
Belg. ac. Ghent, Belg. 798.
BIESTER, ANTHONY.
Am. Cleves, Ger. 1837-1917 Madisonville, O. A014-B-F-T.
BIETRY, PAUL.
Fr. b. Verrières; ac. 1927 Paris. DBA.
BIFFIN [or Beffin], SARAH. (Min)
Eng. Bridgewater 1784-1850 Liverpool. DNB-T.
BIGARI, VITTORIO MARIA.
It. Bologna 1692-1776. B-T.

BIGELOW, Charles C.
Am. b. Buffalo, N. Y. 1891; ad. 1934 Same. A.
BIGELOW, Constance.
Am. ex. 1935 New York. M.
BIGELOW, Daniel Folger.
Am. Peru, Ind. 1823-1910 Chicago. A08-B-F-T-181.
BIGELOW, Olive.
Mrs. Herbert C. Pell.
Am. ad. 1934 Newport, R. I. M.
BIGG, William Redmore.
Eng. 1755-1828 London. B-DNB-T.
BIGGS, Esther.
Am. ad. 1934 Toledo, O. M.
BIGGS, Walter. (Ill)
Am. b. Elliston, Va. 1886; ad. 1934 New York. A-F.
BIGIO, Francia. *see* Franciabigio, M.
BIGIO, Nanni di Baccio.
see Nanni di Baccio, B.
BIGONET, Charles. (S)
Fr. b. Paris; d. 1931. DBA.
BIGORDI, Domenico. *see* Ghirlandajo, D. B.
BIGOT, Raymond. (Carver)
Fr. b. Orbec (Calvados) 1872. DBA.
BIHARI, Sandor Alexander.
Hun. Réybanya 1856-1906 Budapest. B.
BIHZAD. *see* Behzad.
BIJUR, Nathan I.
Am. ad. 1935 New York. M.
BILBAO Y MARTINEZ, Gonzalo de.
Sp. b. 1860. Fa.
BILCOQ, Marie Maro Antoine.
Fr. Paris 1755-1838 Same. B-T.
BÎLEK, Františěk. (S)
Pol. b. 1872. T-798.
BILINSKA, Anna.
Pol. Ukraine 1857/8-1893 Warsaw. T.
BILL, Carroll.
Am. b. Phila., Pa. 1877; ad. 1934 Boston. A-F.
BILL, Sally Cross.
Mrs. Carroll Bill.
Am. b. Lawrence, Mass.; ad. 1934 Boston. A.
BILLE, Edmond.
Swi. b. Valangin 1878. B-DBA.
BILLET, Pierre Celestin.
Fr. Cantin 1837-1922 Same. B-C-DBA.
BILLETE, Aimé Émile Raymond.
Fr. b. Paris 1875. DBA.
BILLINGS, A. W. K., Jr.
Am. ad. 1934 Boston. M.
BILLINGS, Edwin T.
Am. 1824-1893. F.
BILLINGS, Hammatt.
Am. Milton, Mass. 1818-1874 Boston. B-T-15.
BILLINGS, Henry.
Am. b. New York 1901; ad. 1934 Woodstock, N. Y. A.
BILLINGS, Mary Hathaway.
Am. b. Brooklyn, N. Y.; ad. 1934 Same. A-B-F.
BILLINGTON, Jules.
Am. ex. 1934 New York. M.
BILLMYER, Charlotte Post. (Ill)
Mrs. James Irwin Billmyer.
Am. b. Brooklyn, N. Y. 1901; ad. 1934 New York. A.
BILLMYER, James Irwin. (Ill)
Am. b. Union Bridge, Md. 1897; ad. 1934 New York. A.
BILLOTTI, René.
Fr. Tarbes 1846-1915. B-DBA.
BILLOTTI, Salvatore F. (S)
Am. b. Cosenja 1879; ad. 1934 New York. A-Cs-F.
BINCK [or Bink], Jacob. (Eg)
Ger. Cologne 1500-1568/70. B-T.
BINDER, Carl F.
Am. b. Ger. 1887; ad. 1934 Cleveland Heights, O. A.
BINDER, Jacob.
Am. b. Kreslavke, Rus.; ad. 1934 Boston. A.
BINDER, Josef.
Aus. Vienna 1805-1863. B.
BINDERS, Josef. (Posters)
Aus. b. 1902; ad. 1934 Vienna. M.
BINET, Adolphe Gustave.
Fr. La Rivière 1854-1897. B.
BINET, Victor Jean Baptiste Barthélemy.
Fr. Rouen 1849-1924 St. Aubin. B-DBA.
BINFORD, Julian.
Am. ad. 1935 Atlanta, Ga. M.
BINGHAM, George Caleb.
Am. Virginia 1811-1879 Kansas City, Mo. DAB-F-4-27W.
BINGHAM, Lavina.
[Countess of Spencer]
Eng. ac. 1787; d. 1831 London. Fa.
BINK, Jacob. *see* Binck, J.
BINKS, R. Ward. (Et)
Eng. ex. 1934 New York. M.
BINNS, Charles F. (Stoneware)
Am. b. 1857; d. 1934. M.
BINTLIFF, [Mrs.] Martha Bradshaw.
Am. b. Superior, Wis. 1869; ad. 1934 La Jolla, Calif. A.
BINYON, [Mrs.] Algernon H. *see* Bean, C. van H.
BINYON, Edward.
Br. 1830?-1876 Capri, It. B-DNB-T.
BION, Cyril.
Br. ex. 1935 London. M.
BIONDI, Ernesto. (S)
It. b. Morolo 1855. B.
BIONDO, Giovanni. *see* Giovanni del B.
BIORN, Emil.
Am. b. Christiania, Nor. 1864; ac. 1915 Chicago. A12-B.
BIORSHI, Charles. (S)
Am. ac. 1934 St. Paul, Minn. M.
BIOT, Gustave. (Eg)
Belg. Brussels 1833-1905 Antwerp. B.
BIRCH, Charles Bell. (S)
Eng. London 1832-1893. B-E-Hs.
BIRCH, Geraldine. (Et)
Mrs. G. R. Duncan.
Am. b. Eng. 1883; ad. 1934 Pasadena, Calif. A29.
BIRCH, Reginald Bathurst. (Ill)
["Little Lord Fauntleroy"]
Am. b. London 1856; ad. 1934 New York. A20-B-F-W16.

BIRCH, Samuel J. Lamorna.
Eng. b. Egremont 1869. Wa.
BIRCH, Thomas.
Am. London 1779-1851 Phila., Pa.
B-C-DAB-F-T-2-4-6-7-15.
BIRCH, William Russell.
Am. Warwick, Eng. 1755-1834 Phila., Pa.
B-DAB-DNB-F-T-2-6-7-28-29-30-40-45.
BIRD, Edward.
Eng. Wolverhampton 1772-1819 Bristol.
B-DNB-T.
BIRD, Francis. (S)
Eng. London 1667-1731. DNB-Hs-T.
BIRD, [Mrs.] Mary Holden.
Scot. ad. 1934 Morar. Wa.
BIRDSALL, Amos, Jr.
Am. b. Waretown, N. J. 1865; ad. 1934 Melrose Park, Pa. A.
BIRGE, Mary Thompson.
Mrs. Edward Birge.
Am. b. 1872 New York; ad. Bloomington, Ind.
A12-F.
BIRKBECK, Geoffrey.
Eng. b. Norwich 1875; ex. 1934 London.
Wa.
BIRKENBERGER, William.
Am. ex. 1935 New Haven, Conn. M.
BIRKLE, Albert.
Ger. ex. 1930 Berlin. M.
BIRLEY, Oswald.
Aust. b. Auckland, N. Z. 1880. B-Fa.
BIRNBAUM. (Eg)
Ger. ac. 1531 in Nüremburg. B-T.
BIRNBAUM, A.
Am. ad. 1934 New York. M.
BIRNEY, William Verplanck.
Am. Cinn., O. 1858-1909. B-T.
BIRREN, Joseph P.
Am. Chicago 1865-1933 Milwaukee, Wis.
A030-B-F-W17.
BISBING, Henry Singlewood.
Am. Phila., Pa. 1849-1933 Ledyard, Conn.
A030-B-F-T.
BISCAINO, Bartolomeo.
It. ac. 1632-1657 Genoa. T.
BISCHOFF, Franz A.
Am. Austria 1864-1929 Calif. A026.
BISCHOFF, Henry.
Fr. b. Lausanne; ac. 1930 Paris. DBA.
BISCHOFF, Ilse Marthe. (Ill)
Am. ad. 1934 New York. A29.
BISCHOFF, Théophile.
Fr. b. Lausanne 1847. B-T.
BISEO, Cesare.
It. Rome 1843/4-1909 Same. B.
BISET, Karel Emanuel.
Flem. Mechlin 1633-1680 Breda, Belg. C.
BISHOP, Emily Clayton. (S)
Am. d. 1912 Smithburg, Md. A06.
BISHOP, [Mrs.] Flora Melissa.
Am. b. Minn., Minn.; ad. 1934 Seattle, Wash.
A.
BISHOP, Harold S.
Am. b. 1884; ad. 1934 Rochester, N. Y. A.
BISHOP, Harry [or Henry].
Eng. ad. 1934 London. B-Wa.
√ BISHOP, Isabel.
Am. b. Cinn., O. 1902; ad. 1934 New York.
A.
BISHOP, John.
Eng. Liverpool 1810-1858 Birmingham. M.
BISHOP, [Mrs.] Morris. *see* Kingsbury, A. M.
BISHOP, Richard Evett. (Et)
Am. b. 1877; ad. 1934 Phila., Pa. F-M.
BISHOP, William Follen.
Eng. b. Liverpool 1856; ad. 1934 St. Helier.
Wa.
BISHOP, William James.
Eng. Manchester 1805-1888. M.
BISI, Fra Bonaventura.
[Il Padre Pettorini]
It. Bologna, 1612-1659 Modena. B-T.
BISI, Luigi.
It. Milan 1814-1886 Same. B-C.
BISMARCK, Jack Reppert von.
see Reppert-Bismarck, Jack von.
BISPHAM, Henry Collins.
Am. Phila., Pa. 1841-1882 Rome, It.
B-F-T-4-15.
BISSCHOP, Christoffel.
Dut. Leewarden 1828-1904 The Hague.
B-T-474.
BISSCHOP, Cornelis.
Dut. Dordrecht 1630-1674. B-T.
BISSCHOP, Jan de [Episcopius].
Dut. The Hague 1628-1686 Same. B-T.
BISSCHOP, Richard.
Dut. b. Leewarden 1849. T-474.
BISSELL, Edgar Julian.
Am. b. Aurora, Ill. 1856-. A20-B-F.
BISSELL, George Edwin. (S)
Am. New Preston, Conn. 1839-1920 Mt. Vernon, N. Y.
A016-B-DNB-E-F-T-Ta-W11.
BISSEN, Herman Wilhelm. (S)
Dan. Slesvig 1798-1868 Copenhagen.
B-Hs-T.
BISSET, James.
Eng. 1760-1832 Leamington. B-DNB.
BISSIÈRE, Roger.
Fr. b. Sittereal 1888; ex. 1934 London.
DBA.
BISSILL, George William.
Eng. b. Fairford 1896; ex. 1933 London.
Wa.
BISSOLO [or Bissuolo], Francesco Pietro.
It. Trévise 1492-1554. B-C-T.
BISSON, Edourd.
Fr. b. Paris 1856. B-DBA.
BISSTRAN, Emil James.
Am. b. Hun. 1895; ad. 1934 Taos, N. M.
A-F.
BISSUOLO, Francesco, Pietro.
see Bissolo, F. P.
BISTOLFI, Leandro. (S)
It. b. Trieste 1859. B-Hs-T-798.
BITKENBERGER, William.
Am. ad. 1935 Waterbury, Conn. M.
BITTER, Karl Theodore Francis. (S)
Am. Vienna, Aus. 1867-1915 New York.
A012-B-DAB-E-F-Hs-T-Ta-18-46-639
BITTINGER, Charles.
Am. b. Wash., D. C. 1879; ad. 1934 Same.
A-B-F-W.
BIVA, Henri.
Fr. b. Paris; d. 1929 Same. B-DBA.

BIXBEE, William Johnson.
Am. Manchester, N. H. 1850-1921 Lynn, Mass. A018-B-F-T.
BIZEMONT-PRUNELÉ, André Gaspard Parfait. (Eg)
Fr. Tignoville 1752-1837 Orléans. B.
BIZETTE-LINDET, André. (S)
Fr. ad. 1935 Paris. DBA.
BJORCK, Gustaf Oskar.
Swi. b. Stockholm 1860. B.
BJORKMAN, Olaf. (S)
Am. b. Sweden 1886; ad. 1934 New York. W.
BJURMAN, Andrew. (S)
Am. b. Sweden 1876; ad. 1934 Alhambra, Calif. A-Cs-F.
BLAAS, Eugène Ritter von.
Aus. b. Albano, It. 1843. B-T.
BLAAS, Giulio da.
It. Venice 1888-1934 New York. DBA-M-Obit. N. Y. papers 5-15-34.
BLAAS, Karl von.
Aus. Nauders 1815-1894 Vienna. B-T.
BLACK, Eleanor Simms.
Mrs. Robert M. Black.
Am. b. Wash., D. C.; ad. 1934 Pittsburgh, Pa. A.
BLACK, John Lorin.
Am. b. 1895. M.
BLACK, [Mrs.] Kate Eleanor.
Am. London, Eng. 1855-1924 U. S. A022-F.
BLACK, Mary C. W.
Mrs. Clarence A. Black.
Am. b. Poughkeepsie, N. Y.; ad. 1934 Monterey, Calif. A.
BLACK, Miriam H. (Min)
Am. ad. 1934 East Cleveland, O. M.
BLACK, Norman I. (Ill)
Am. b. Chelsea, Mass. 1883; ad. 1934 Casco Bay, Me. A-F.
BLACK, [Mrs.] Norman I.
Am. b. Prov., R. I. 1884; ad. 1934 Casco Bay, Me. A-F.
BLACK, Olive Parker.
Am. b. Cambridge, Mass. 1868; ad. 1934 New York. A.
BLACK, Richard B.
Am. Greenfield, Ind. 1888-1915 Same. A012-181.
BLACKBURN, Joseph [or Jonathan].
Am. England 1700?-1763 Boston, Mass. C-DAB-E-F-T-1-2-3-182-206.
BLACKBURN, Morris Atkinson.
Am. b. Phila., Pa. 1902; ad. 1934 Oakmont, Pa. A.
BLACKLOCK, William James.
Br. 1816-1858 Brampton. B-DNB.
BLACKMAN, Carrie Horton.
Mrs. George Blackman.
Am. b. Cinn., O.; ad. 1934 Carmel, Calif. A.
BLACKMAN, Walter.
Am. New York 1847-1928. A026-B-F-15.
BLACKMORE, Arthur Edward.
Am. Bristol, Eng. 1854-1921 U. S. A019-B-F.
BLACKMORE, Thomas. (Eg)
Eng. 1740?-1780? London. B-DNB-T.
BLACKSHEAR, Annie Laura Eve.
Am. b. Augusta, Ga., 1875; ad. 1934 Athens, Ga. A-F.
BLACKSHEAR, Kathleen.
Am. b. Navasota, Tex. 1897; ad. 1934 Chicago. A.
BLACKSTONE, Harriet.
Am. b. New Hartford, N. Y.; ad. 1934 New York. A-B-F.
BLADA, V. *see* Volck, A. J.
BLADEN, Alfred.
Eng. ad. 1934 Derby. Wa.
BLAI, Boris. (S)
Am. b. Rowno, Rus. 1893; ad. 1934 Phila., Pa. A.
BLAIN, [or Belin] DE FONTENAY, Jean Baptiste.
Fr. b. Caen 1653; d. 1715 Paris. B-T.
BLAINVILLE, Henri Marie Ducrotay de.
Fr. 1777-1850. M.
BLAIR, Elizabeth.
Am. ex. 1933 New York. M.
BLAIR, Lee Everett.
Am. b. Los Angeles, Calif. 1911; ad. 1934 Glendale, Calif. A.
BLAIRSY, Leo. (S)
Fr. ac. 19-20th centuries France. M.
BLAISDELL, Elinore ["Blaisie"].
Mrs. Melrich V. Rosenberg.
Am. ad. 1934 New York. M.
BLAKE, Benjamin.
Eng. d. 1830. B-T.
BLAKE, Charles B.
Am. ad. 1934 New York. M.
BLAKE, Donald. (Ill)
Am. b. Tampa, Fla. 1899; ad. 1934 Same. A-F.
BLAKE, James Edward.
Am. Peru, Ind. 1864-1912 Cinn., O. A010.
BLAKE, James Henry.
Am. b. Boston 1845. A28-B-F-T.
BLAKE, William. (P-Poet)
Eng. London 1757-1827 Same. B-Bd-C-DNB-E-T-222-272-295-296-297-364-790-844-880-909-922-954.
BLAKELOCK, Ralph Albert.
Am. New York 1847-1919 Adirondacks, N. Y. A016-B-C-DAB-E-F-T-31-32-46-71-207.
BLAKELY, Dudley Moore.
Am. b. Harriman, Tenn. 1902; ad. 1934 New York. A.
BLAKEMAN, Thomas Greenleaf. (Et)
Am. ad. 1934 Provincetown, Mass. A.
BLAKESLEE, Walter.
Am. d. 1902 New Haven, Conn. A04.
BLAKEY, Nicholas. (Eg)
Ir. ac. 1752-1758. DNB-T.
BLAMPIELD, Clifford George.
Eng. b. Jersey 1875. M.
BLAMPIELD, Edmund. (Et)
Eng. b. 1886; ad. 1935 London. M-830.
BLANC, Charles.
Fr. b. Limoges 1896. DBA.
BLANCH, Arnold.
Am. b. 1896; ad. 1934 New York. A.
BLANCHE, Lucile.
Am. b. Hawley, Minn. 1895; ad. 1934 Woodstock, N. Y. A.

BLANCHARD, AUGUSTE JEAN BAPTISTE MARIE. (Eg)
Fr. Paris 1792-1849 Same. B-T.
BLANCHARD, GABRIEL LOUIS.
Fr. Paris 1630-1704 Same. B-T.
BLANCHARD, JACQUES.
Fr. Paris 1600-1638 Same. B-C-T-722.
BLANCHARD, MARIA.
Fr. b. Spain; ac. Paris. 797.
BLANCHARD, MAURICE FÉLICIEN JULES PAUL.
Fr. b. Paris 1903. DBA.
BLANCHARD, THOMAS MARIE AUGUSTE. (Eg)
Fr. Paris 1819-1898 Same. B-T.
BLANCHARD, WASHINGTON. (Min.)
Am. ac. 1831/49 Boston. F-2-6.
BLANCHE, JACQUES ÉMILE.
Fr. b. Paris 1861; ad. 1934 Same. B-DBA-E-M.
BLANCHET, THOMAS.
Fr. Paris 1614-1689 Lyons. B-T-722.
BLANCHETIERRE, HENRI ÉMILE.
Fr. Paris 1881-1933. DBA.
BLAND, E. BEATRICE.
Eng. ad. 1934 London. Wa.
BLANEY, DWIGHT.
Am. b. Brookline, Mass. 1865; ad. 1934 Boston. A-B-F-W.
BLANEY, HENRY ROBERTSON.
Am. b. Dedham, Mass. 1885. B-T.
BLANKE, MARIE ELSA.
Am. b. Chicago; ad. 1934 Same. A-F.
BLARENBERGHE, HENRI DÉSIRÉ VAN.
Fr. Lille 1734-1812 Paris. B-T.
BLARENBERGHE, HENRI JOSEPH VAN.
Fr. Lille 1741-1826 Same. B-T.
BLARENBERGHE, LOUIS NICOLAS VAN.
Fr. Lille 1716/19-1794 Fontainebleau. B-T.
BLÄSER, GUSTAF. (S)
Ger. Düsseldorf 1813-1874 Cannstadt. B-Hs-T.
BLASHFIELD, EDWIN HOWLAND. (Mu.)
Am. b. New York 1848; ad. 1934 Same. A-B-C-E-F-T-W-1-15-33-46.
BLASINGAME, [Mrs.] MARGUERITE LOUIS.
Am. b. Honolulu, Hawaii 1906; ad. 1934 Same. M.
BLASINGHAM, KATHERINE GROH.
Mrs. H. E. Blasingham.
Am. b. Logansport, Ind. 1893; ad. 1934 Canton, O. A.
BLAU, DANIEL. (Et.)
Am. ac. 1934 Dayton, O. A29.
BLAU-LANG, TINA.
Ger. Vienna, Aus. 1845/7-1916 Munich. B-T.
BLAUVELT, CHARLES F.
Am. New York 1824-1900 Greenwich, Conn. A2-B-C-F-T-4-15.
BLAY Y FABREGA, MIGUEL. (S)
Sp. b. Olot 1866. Hs-T.
BLAYN, FERNAND.
Fr. ac. 1878-1892 Paris. C-T.
BLAZEK, ANTON.
Am. b. Vienna, Aus. 1902; ad. 1935 Los Angeles, Calif. M.
BLAZEY, LAWRENCE E.
Am. b. Cleveland, O. 1902; ad. 1934 Same. A.
BLAZICEK, OLDRICH.
Czec. b. 1890; ad. 1935 Prague, Czec. M.
BLAZY, STERLING.
Am. b. Cleveland, O. 1904; ad. 1934 New York. A.
BLAZYS, ALEXANDER. (S)
Am. b. Lithuania 1894; ad. 1934 Cleveland, O. A.
BLECHER, KARL EDUARD FERDINAND.
Ger. Kottbus 1798-1840. B-T.
BLEIL, CHARLES GEORGE. (Et.)
Am. b. San Fran., Calif. 1893; ad. 1934 Same. A29-F.
BLEKER [or Bleyker], GERRIT CLAESZ.
Dut. b. Haarlem; ac. 1625-1664. B-T.
BLENNER, CARL JOHN.
Am. b. Richmond, Va. 1864; ad. 1934 New York. A-B-F-T-W.
BLERY, EUGÈNE STANISLAS ALEXANDER. (Eg.)
Fr. b. Fontainebleau 1805. B-T.
BLES, DAVID JOSEPH.
Dut. The Hague 1821-1899 Same. B-T-474.
BLES, HENRI MET DE [Civetta].
Flem. Dinant 1480-1550. B-C-T-722.
BLEUMMER, OSCAR.
Am. ex. 1934 New York. M.
BLIND, RUDOLPH.
Eng. 1846-1889. B.
BLINKS, THOMAS.
Eng. 1860-1912 London. B.
BLISS, ALMA HIRSIG. (Min.)
Am. b. Berne, Swi.; ad. 1934 New York. A.
BLISS, DOUGLAS PERCY. (Eg.)
Eng. b. India 1900; ex. 1933 London. Wa.
BLOCH, ALBERT.
Am. b. St. Louis, Mo. 1882; ad. 1934 Lawrence, Mass. A-F-W.
BLOCH, ARMAND LUCIEN. (S)
Fr. b. Montbéliard [Doubs] 1866; d. 1932 Paris. B-DBA-T.
BLOCH, CARL HEINRICH.
Dan. Copenhagen 1834-1890. T.
BLOCH, JULIUS THIENGEN.
Am. b. Kehl, Baden, Ger. 1888; ad. 1934 Phila., Pa. A-F.
BLOCHE, ROGER. (S)
Fr. b. Paris 1865. DBA-E.
BLOCHERER, KARL.
Ger. ex. 1930 Munich. M.
BLOCK, ADOLPH. (S)
Am. b. New York 1906; ad. 1934 Same. A-Cs.
BLOCK [or Blok], BENJAMIN VON.
Ger. Lübeck 1631-1690 Ratisbonne. T.
BLOCK, EUGENIUS FRANS DE.
Flem. Grammont 1812-1893 Antwerp, Belg. B-T.
BLOCK, HENRY.
Am. b. Lithuania 1875; ad. 1934 New York. A.
BLOCK, LUCIENNE. (Mu)
Am. ad. 1935 New York. M.
BLODGETT, GEORGE W. (S)
Am. ad. 1934 Santa Fe, N. M. M.
BLODGETT, WALTON.
Am. b. Cleveland, O. 1908; ad. 1934 Stamford, Conn. A.

BLOEMAERT, Abraham.
Dut. Gorcum 1564-1651 Herenthals. B-Bd-C-E-T-722.
BLOEMAERT, Cornelis II. (Eg)
Dut. Utrecht 1603?-1680/4 Rome, It. B-T.
BLOEMAERT, Frédéric. (Eg)
Dut. Utrecht 1610-1669. B-T.
BLOEMAERT, Hendrik I.
Dut. Utrecht 1601-1672 Same. B-T.
BLOEMEN, Jan Frans van [Orizonte].
Flem. Antwerp, Belg. 1662-1740 Rome, It. B-E-722.
BLOEMEN, Peeter van [Standard].
Flem. Antwerp, Belg. 1657-1720 Same. B-C-T.
BLOM, Jan.
Dut. Amsterdam 1622-1689? B-T.
BLOMMERS, Bernardus Johannes [or Berend].
Dut. The Hague 1845-1914. B-T-474.
BLOMSTROM, Anna.
Am. ex. 1934 New York. M.
BLONDEEL, Lancelot. (S)
Flem. Bruges, Belg. 1495/6-1581. B-C-Hs-V-722.
BLONDEL, Jacob. D.
Am. New York 1817-1877. B-F-T.
BLONHEIM, Adolphe W. (Et)
Am. b. Balt., Md. 1888; ad. 1934 New Hope, Pa. A-F.
BLOODGOOD, Morris Seymour.
Am. Cinn., O. 1845-1920 New York. A017-B.
BLOODGOOD, Robert Fanshawe.
Am. New York 1848-1930. A027-B-T.
BLOOM, Hyman.
Am. b. 1913; ad. 1934 Boston. M.
BLOOMER, Hiram Reynolds.
Am. b. New York 1845; ex. 1877 Paris. B-C-F-T-15.
BLOOT, Pieter de.
Dut. 1601/2-1658 Rotterdam. B-T.
BLOOTELING [or Blotoeling], Abraham.
Dut. Amsterdam 1640-1690. B-T.
BLOS, Carl.
Ger. b. Manheim 1860. B-T.
BLOSER, Florence Parker.
Am. b. Los Angeles, Calif. 1889; ad. 1934 Same. A.
BLOSSOM, Earl. (Et)
Am. ac. 1934 New York. M.
BLOT, Maurice. (Eg)
Fr. Paris 1753-1818 Same. B-T.
BLOW, Thomas Richeson. (Et)
Am. ad. 1934 St. Louis, Mo. A.
BLOWER, David Harrison.
Am. b. Fontanet, Ind. 1901; ad. 1934 Detroit, Mich. A.
BLUCK, J. (Eg)
Eng. ac. 1791-1819 London. B-T.
BLUE EAGLE.
Indian [Am.]; ex. 1934 New York. 411.
BLUEMNER, Oscar Florianus.
Am. b. Ger. 1867; ad. 1934 So. Braintree, Mass. A.
BLUM, Alexander A.
Am. b. Hungary 1888; ad. 1934 New York. A-F.
BLUM, Edith C.
Am. ad. 1934 New York. M.
BLUM, Jerome S.
Am. b. Chicago 1884; ex. 1934 New York. M.
BLUM, John J.
Am. ad. 1934 Toledo, O. M.
BLUM, Maurice.
Fr. b. Lyons 1832; ac. 1850-1875 Paris. B.
BLUM, Robert Frederick.
Am. Cinn., O. 1857-1903 New York. A04-B-C-DAB-E-F-T-1-17-46-192.
BLUMBERG, Feiga.
Am. b. Lithuania 1894; ad. 1934 New York. M.
BLUME, [Mrs.] Melita.
Am. b. Ger.; ad. 1934 Brookhaven, N. Y. A-F.
BLUME, Peter.
Am. b. Rus. 1906; ad. 1934 New York. A.
BLUMENSCHEIN, Ernest Leonard.
Am. b. Pittsburgh, Pa. 1874; ad. 1934 Taos, N. M. A-B-F-T-W-46.
BLUMENSCHEIN, Mary Shepard Green. (P, S)
Mrs. E. L. Blumenschein.
Am. b. New York; ad. 1934 Taos, N. M. A-B-F-W-46.
BLUMENTHAL, Moses Lawrence. (Ill)
Am. b. Wilmington, N. C. 1879; ad. 1934 Elkins Park, Pa. A-F.
BLUMERT, Johanne Marie.
Am. b. Fresno, Calif. 1901; ad. 1934 Oakland, Calif. A.
BLUNDELL, Alfred Richard. (Et)
Eng. b. Edmunds 1883; ac. 1929 Suffolk. Wa-825.
BLUNDSTONE, Ferdinand Victor. (S)
Eng. b. Swi. 1882; ad. 1934 London. Wa-798.
BLY, Morton H.
Am. ac. 1900. Fa.
BLYTH [or Blythe], A.
Am. d. 1850 New York. Fa.
BLYTH, Benjamin. (Et)
Am. Salem, Mass. 1740-1781. F-T-2-7-45.
BLYTHE, David G.
Am. East Liverpool, O. 1815-1865. M.
BOADEN, John.
Eng. ac. 1812/39 London. B-DNB-T.
BOADLE, William Barnes.
Ir. Dublin 1840-1916 Birkenhead, Eng. B.
BOARD, Ernest. (Mu)
Eng. Worchester 1877-1934 Albury. B-T-Wa.
BOARDMAN, Frank Crawford. (S)
Am. b. Hartford, Conn.; ac. 20th Century. M.
BOARDMAN, Rosina Cox. (Min.)
Am. b. New York; ad. 1934 Huntington, L. I., N. Y. A-F.
BOAS, [Mrs.] Simone Brangier. (S)
Am. b. France 1895; ad. 1934 Balt., Md. M.
BOATRIGHT, Elizabeth Kiefer. (Et)
Am. ad. 1934 Austin, Tex. M.
BOBBS, Ruth Pratt.
Am. b. Ind., Ind. 1884; ad. 1934 Same. A-F.
BOBERG, Anna.
Mrs. Ferdinand Boberg.
Swe. b. 1864; ex. 1912 New York. Fa-M.
BOBRITSKY [Bobri], Vladimir.
Am. b. Rus. 1898; ad. 1934 New York. 912.
BOCCACINO, Boccaccio. [The Elder.]
It. Ferrara 1467-1524/5 Cremona. B-T-V.

BOCCACINO, Camillo.
It. Cremona 1501-1546. T-V.
BOCCALINO, Giovanni [Ribaldi].
It. ac. 1494 in Cremona. T-V.
BOCCARDI, Giovanni di Giuliano. (Min.)
It. Florence 1460-1529 Same. T-V.
BOCCATI [or Boccato], Giovanni.
It. Camerino 1420-1480. B-V.
BOCCHI, Amedeo.
It. b. 1883. M.
BOCCIONI, Umberto. (S)
It. 1882-1916. Hs-798.
BOCHOLT, Frans van. *see* Master, F. V. B.
BOCK, Charles Peter.
Am. b. Germany 1872; ad. 1935 Manvel, Tex. A12-B-F.
BOCK, Hans [The Elder].
Swi. Alsace, Fr. 1550-1624 Basle. B-T.
BOCK, Hans [The Younger].
Swi. Basle 1573/5-1626 Same. B-T.
BOCK, Richard W. (S)
Am. b. Germany 1865; ad. 1934 River Forest, Ill. A-Cs-F-Ta-W.
BOCK, Théophile Émile Achille de.
Dut. The Hague 1851-1904 Haarlem. B-Bd-C-T-474.
BOCK, Vera. (Ill.)
Am. ad. 1934 New York. M.
BOCKHORST, Gerard van. *see* Bronckhorst, G. van.
BÖCKLIN, Arnold.
Ger.-Swi. Basel, Swi. 1827-1901 Fiesole, It. B-Bd-C-E-T.
BODDINGTON, Henry John Williams.
Eng. 1811-1865 Bornes. B-DNB-T.
BODEBENDER, Laura.
Am. b. New Orleans, La. 1900; ad. 1934 Same. A.
BODELL, Mark Robinson.
Am. b. Lafayette, Ind. 1891; ad. 1934 Glen Ellyn, Ill. A.
BODENMÜLLER, Alfons.
Ger. Munich 1847-1886 Same. B-C-T.
BODINE, Helen.
Am. b. Phila., Pa.; ac. 1905-1915 Same. A12-B.
BODINIER, Guillaume.
Fr. Angers 1795-1872 Same. B-T.
BODLEY, Josselin Réginald Courtenay.
Eng. b. Veaux, Fr. 1893; ad. 1934 London. DBA.
BODMER, Karl.
Swi. Riesbach 1809-1893 Barbizon, Fr. [Came to U. S. 1832]. B-T.
BOEBINGER, Charles William.
Am. b. Cincinnati, O. 1876. A28-F.
BOECKL, Herbert.
Aus. ac. 1934. M.
BOECKLIN. *see* Böcklin.
BOECKMAN, Carl L.
Am. b. Nor.; ad. 1934 So. Minn., Minn. A.
BOEHLE, Fritz Friedrich.
Ger. Emmendingen 1873-1916. B-T.
BOEHM, Hans Sebald. *see* Beham, H. S.
BOEHM, Henry Richard.
Am. Illinois 1870-1914 Briarcliff, N. Y. A011.
BOEHM, [Sir] Joseph Edgar. (S)
Eng. Vienna, Aus. 1834-1890 London. B-DNB-E-Hs-T.
BOEHME, Hazel Fetterley.
Am. b. Minn., Minn. 1900; ad. 1934 Los Angeles, Calif. A.
BOEHME, Karl Theodor.
Ger. b. Hamburg 1866. B-T.
BOEHMER, Fritz.
Am. ad. 1934 Toledo, O. M.
BOEHMER, Margaret Huntington.
Am. ad. 1934 Syracuse, N. Y. M.
BOEL [or Bol], Pieter.
Flem. Antwerp 1622/25-1674/80 Amsterdam. B-722.
BOEL, Quirin [or Coryn].
Flem. Antwerp 1620-1688 Brussels. T.
BOENISCH, Gustav Adolf.
Ger. Soppau 1802-1887 Breslau. C-T.
BOERICKE, Johanna Magdalene.
Am. b. Phila., Pa. 1868; ad. 1934 Same. A.
BOESCHENSTEIN, Hugo.
Ger. ac. 1934 in Germany. M.
BOETHUS OF CHALCEDON. (S)
Gr. (Hellenistic); ac. 2nd century B. C. E-Hs.
BOETTICHER, [Major] Otto.
Am. ac. 1862. M.
BOETTÓ, Giovenal.
It. ac. 1642-1682 Turin. B.
BOEYERMANS, Théodore.
Flem. Antwerp 1620-1677/8 Same. C-722.
BOGACZYK, Wincenty. (S)
Pol. ac. Warsaw. 798.
BOGAERTS, C. (Eg)
Dut. ac. 18th century Amsterdam. B-T.
BOGAIEWSKY, Constantin.
Rus. ad. 1934 Moscow; ex. 1934 Pittsburgh, Pa. M.
BOGAILEI, Kleofas.
Fr. ex. 1935 Paris. M.
BOGARDUS, James. (Eg)
Am. Catskill, N. Y. 1800-1875 New York. F-2-6-7.
BOGARDUS, [Mrs.] William. (Min)
Am. 1804-1878. F-6.
BOGARDUS, William. (Min)
Am. ac. 1843. F.
BOGDANI [or Bogdone], Jakob [or James].
Hun. Hungary 1660-1724 London. B.
BOGDANOFF-BJELSKI, Nikolai Petrovitsch.
Rus. b. Gouvern, Smolensk 1868; ex. 1935 New York. B-T.
BOGDANOVE, Abraham Jacobi.
Am. b. Minsk, Rus. 1887; ad. 1934 New York. A-F.
BOGER, Fred.
Am. b. Balt., Md. 1857; ad. 1934 Detroit, Mich. A-F.
BOGERT, George Hirst.
Am. New York 1864; ad. 1934 Lyme, Conn. A-B-F-T-W14-46.
BOGGS, Frank Meyers.
Am. Springfield, O. 1855-1926 France. A023-B-C-F-T.
BOGLE, James.
Am. So. Car. 1817-1878 Brooklyn, N. Y. B-C-F-T-15.

BOGOLYUBOFF, Alexei Petrovitsch.
Rus. Pomeranje 1824-1896 Paris. B-T.
BOGUET, Nicolas Didier.
Fr. Chantilly 1755-1839 Rome. B-T.
BOHLAND, Gustav. (S)
Am. b. Austria 1897; ad. 1934 New York. A-Cs.
BOHLEMAN, Herman T.
Am. b. Portland, Ore. 1872; ad. 1934 Same. A.
BOHLMAN, Edgar Lemoine.
Am. b. Oregon 1902; ad. 1934 Fez, Morocco. A.
BOHM, C. Curry.
Am. b. Nashville, Tenn. 1894; ad. 1934 Chicago. A.
BOHM, Max.
Am. Cleveland, O. 1868-1923 Provincetown, Mass. A020-B-DAB-F-T.
BOHNENBERGER, Theodor.
Ger. b. Munich 1868. B-T.
BOHNERT, Herbert.
Am. b. Cleveland, O. 1890; ad. 1934 Greenwich, Conn. A.
BOHRDT [or Boys], Hans.
Ger. b. Berlin 1857. B-T.
BOHROD, Aaron.
Am. b. Chicago 1907; ad. 1934 Same. A.
BOICHOT, Jean Guillaume. (S)
Fr. Chalon 1735-1814 Paris. B-T.
BOILEAU, Phillip.
Am. Quebec, Can. 1864-1917 New York. A014-B-F.
BOILLY, Alphonse. (Eg)
Fr. Paris 1801-1867. B-T.
BOILLY, Julien [or Jules] Léopold.
Fr. Paris 1796-1874. B-T.
BOILLY, Louis Léopold.
Fr. La Basée 1761-1845 Paris. B-C-T-722.
BOILVIN, Émile.
Fr. Metz 1845-1899. B-T.
BOILY, Charles Ange. (Eg)
Fr. Paris 1735/9-1813 Lyons. B-T.
BOIS. *see* Du Bois.
BOISSIEU, Jean Jacques de.
Fr. Lyons 1736-1810 Same. B-T-880.
BOIT, Charles. (Enamel)
Swe. Stockholm 1663?-1727 Paris. B-T.
BOIT, Edward Darley.
Am. Boston 1840-1915 Rome, It. A013-B-C-F-15.
BOITARD, Louis Pierre. (Eg)
Fr. b. France; d. 1770 England. B-DNB.
BOIZOT, Louis Simon. (S)
Fr. Paris 1743-1809 Same. B-T.
BOKELMANN, Christian Ludwig.
Ger. St. Jürgen 1844-1894 Berlin. B-C-T.
BÔKHTÏSO. (Illuminator)
Syrian Monk. Martyred 1241 Zerne, Syria. M.
BOL. *see also* Boel.
BOL [or Boel], Cornelis.
Flem. b. Antwerp, Belg. 1576/80; ac. 1614. B-T.
BOL, Cornelis IV.
Dut. Holland 1589-1666 London. B-T.
BOL, Ferdinand.
Dut. Dordrecht 1616-1680 Amsterdam. B-Bd-C-T-722.
BOL, Hans.
Dut. Mechlin 1534-1593 Amsterdam. B-C-T-V.
BOLANDER, Karl S.
Am. b. Marion, O. 1893. A28-F.
BOLDEN, Joseph E. (Et)
Am. ad. 1935 Phila., Pa. M.
BOLDINI, Jean Giovanni.
It. Ferrara 1844/5-1931 Paris. B-DBA-T.
BOLDRINI, Niccolò. (Eg)
It. b. Vicenzo; ac. 1492-1498. B-T.
BOLESLAW-JAN, Czedekowski.
Pol. b. 1885. M.
BOLLES, Francisca. (Ill.)
Am. ad. 1934 New York. M.
BOLLES, [Mrs.] Ida Randall.
Am. ad. 1934 Laguna Beach, Calif. A.
BOLLING, Leslie Garland. (S)
Am. b. Dendron, Va. 1898; ad. 1934 Richmond, Va. A.
BOLLINGER, Friedrich Wilhelm. (Eg)
Ger. Berlin 1777-1825. B-T.
BOLMAR, Carl Pierce.
Am. b. 1874; ad. 1934 Topeka, Kan. A.
BOLMER, M. De Forest.
Am. Yonkers, N. Y. 1854-1910. A09-B-F.
BOLOGNA, Andrea da.
It. ac. 14th century in Italy. B-T.
BOLOGNA, Giovanni da. (P-S)
It. Douai 1524-1608 Florence. B-E-Hs-T-V.
BOLOGNA, Niccolò di Giacomo da.
It. ac. 1374-1400 Rome. B.
BOLOGNA, Simone da [Crocefissi].
It. ac. 1370 in Italy. M.
BOLOGNESE, Il. *see* Grimaldi.
BOLOGNINI, Bartolommeo. *see* Bartolommeo, B.
BOLOGNINI, Giovanni Battista.
It. Bologna 1611-1688 Same. B-T.
BOLSWERT, Schelte Adams.
Dut. Bolswert 1586-1659. B.
BOLTON, Hale William.
Am. Honey Grove, Tex. 1885-1920 Dallas, Tex. A017.
BOLTON, Theodore. (Et)
Am. b. Columbia, S. C. 1889; ad. 1934 New York. W.
BOLTON, William Jay.
Am. Bath, Eng. 1816-1884 U. S. M.
BOLTON-JONES. *see* Jones, H. Bolton.
BOLTRAFFIO. *see* Beltraffio.
BOLTZ, H. Emerson.
Am. ad. 1934 No. Baltimore, O. M.
BOMBOIS, Camille.
Fr. b. Laumes 1883. DBA-797.
BOMMER, Marie A.
Am. b. Brooklyn, N. Y. 1905; ad. 1934 Babylon, L. I., N. Y. A.
BOMPARD, Maurice.
Fr. b. Rodez 1857; ac. 1929 Paris. B-C-DBA.
BOMPIANI, Roberto.
It. Rome 1821-1908 Same. B-T.
BONACOLSI, Pier Jacopo Ilario (L'Antico). (S)
It. 1450-1528 Mantua. M.
BONAGUIDO, Pacino di.
It. ac. 1310. Fa.

BONAMICI, Louis.
Fr. ac. 1930 in Paris. DBA.
BONANNUS OF PISA. (S)
It. ac. 12th century in Pisa. Hs.
BONASCIA [or Bonasci], Bartolommeo.
It. Modena 1450-1527. B-M.
BONASONE, Giulio di Antonio.
It. Bologna 1498-1580. B-V.
BONAVENTURA, Segna di. *see* Segna di B.
BONAWIT, G. Owen.
Am. ad. 1934 New York. M.
BONAWITZ, George.
Am. ad. 1934 New York. M.
BOND, John Daniel.
Eng. 1725-1803 Birmingham. B-DNB.
BOND, Kate Lee Bacon.
Am. b. Topeka, Kan., 1890; ad. 1934 Winnetka, Ill. A.
BOND, William Joseph.
Eng. Liverpool 1833-1926. B.
BONDOL [or Bandol], Jean de.
[Called "Maitre aux Bouquetaux"].
Fr. ac. 1368-1381 Bruges, Belg. T.
BONDONE, Giotto de. *see* Giotto di B.
BONE, Freda. (Eg)
Eng. ex. 1933 London. M.
BONE, Henry [The Elder].
Eng. Truro 1755-1834 London. B-DNB-E-T.
BONE, Henry Pierce [The Younger].
Eng. London 1779-1855. B-DNB.
BONE, Herbert Alfred.
Eng. 1853-1931. Fa.
BONE, Muirhead. (Et)
Scot. b. Glasgow 1876. B-T-818-825.
BONE, Robert Trewick.
Eng. London 1790-1840. B-DNB.
BONFIELD, George R.
Am. Portsmouth, Eng. 1802-1898 Phila., Pa. F.
BONFIGLI [or Buonfiglio], Benedetto.
It. Perouse 1420-1496. B-E-T.
BONFILS, Gaston.
Fr. ac. 1878-1897 in Paris. B.
BONFILS, Robert.
Fr. b. Paris 1886. DBA.
BONHAM, Horace.
Am. West Manchester, Pa. 1835-1892. F.
BONHEUR, Auguste François.
Fr. Bordeaux 1824-1884 Bellevue. B-T.
BONHEUR, Isadore Jules. (S)
Fr. Bordeaux 1827-1901. B-T.
BONHEUR, Juliette [Mme. Peyrol].
Fr. Paris 1830-1891 Same. B-T.
BONHEUR, Marie Rosa [or Rosalie]. (P-S)
Fr. Bordeaux 1822-1899 Thomery. B-Bd-C-E-T-918.
BONHEUR, Raymond B.
Fr. ac. in Paris 1831; d. 1849 Same. B-T.
BONI, Michele Giovanni. *see* Giambono.
BONIFAZIO, Veneziono. *see* Veneziono, B.
BONIFAZIO, Veronesè. *see* Veronesè, B.
BONINGER, Robert.
Ger. b. 1869. T.
BONINGTON, Richard Parkes.
Eng. Arnold 1801-1828 London. B-Bd-C-DNB-T-299-722-752-844-870-909.
BONINI, Giralamo [Anconitano].
It. ac. 1660-1680 Ancona. B-T.
BONIROTE, Pierre.
Fr. Lyons 1811-1891 Orléans. B-T.
BONNANO. (S)
It. ac. 1180 in Pisa. M.
BONNAR, William.
Scot. Edinburgh 1800-1853. DNB-T.
BONNARD, Pierre.
Fr. b. Fontenay 1867. B-DBA-298-827.
BONNAT, Léon Joseph Florentin.
Fr. Bayonne 1833/4-1922 Paris. B-Bd-C-E-T.
BONNER, Emma Alice Henriette.
Belg. b. Brussels 1857. B-T.
BONNER, Mary.
Am. b. Bastrop, La. 1885; d. 1935 San Antonio, Tex. A-Obit. N. Y. papers 6-28-1935.
BONNER, Thomas.
Eng. b. Gloucestershire; d. 1812 London. T.
BONNESEN, Carl Johan. (S)
Dan. b. Alborg 1868. T-798.
BONNET, Leon.
Am. b. Phila., Pa. 1868; ad. 1934 Bonita, Calif. A.
BONNET, Louis Marin. (Eg)
Fr. Paris 1743-1793. B-T.
BONNET, Rudolf.
Dut. ac. 1934 The Hague. M.
BONO, Bartolommeo. *see* Buon, B.
BONO DA FERRARA.
It. ac. 1450/61 Verona. B-T.
BONOME, Santiago P. (S)
Sp. ac. in Madrid. 798.
BONOMI, Joseph [The Younger]. (S)
Eng. Rome 1796-1878 London. DNB.
BONONI, Bartolommeo da Pavia.
It. d. 1514 Paris. B-T.
BONSALL, Elizabeth Fearne.
Am. b. Phila., Pa. 1861; ad. 1934 Same. A-B-F-T.
BONSALL, Mary Waterman.
Am. b. Fernwood, Pa.; ad. 1934 Phila., Pa. A-B-F-T.
BONSIB, Louis W.
Am. b. Vincennes, Ind. 1892; ad. 1934 Ft. Wayne, Ind. A.
BONSIGNORI, Fra Cherubino. (S)
It. b. 1479. B-V.
BONSIGNORI, Francesco.
It. Verona 1455-1519 Caldero. B-Bd-T-V.
BONTA, Elizabeth Brainard.
Am. b. Syracuse, N. Y.; ad. 1934 Brooklyn, N. Y. A.
BONTE, George Willard. (Ill.)
Am. b. Cinn., O. 1873; ad. 1934 New York. W.
BONTEMPS, Pierre. (S)
Fr. ac. 1552. B-Hs-T.
BONUSAMICUS da Pisa. (S)
It. ac. 12th century in Pisa. Hs.
BONVICINO, Alessandro. *see* Moretto da Brescia.
BONVIN, François.
Fr. Paris 1817-1887 St. Germain. B-DBA.
BONZI [or Bonsi], Pietro Paolo [Gobbo].
It. b. Cartone ac. 1623-1644. B.
BOOG, Carle Michel.
Am. b. Switzerland 1877; ad. 1934 Brooklyn, N. Y. A.
BOOMERS, Bernardus Johannes. *see* Blommers, B. J.
BOON [or Boone], Daniel.
Flem. Antwerp, Belg. 1630/1-1700 London. B.

BOONE, Peggy.
Am. ad. 1934 Wilton, Conn. M.

BOONEN, Arnold van.
Dut. Dordrecht 1669-1729 Amsterdam. B-C-T.

BOORAEM, [Mrs.] Laura Fulton.
Am. b. St. Paul, Minn. 1890; ad. 1934 Minn., Minn. M.

BOORSMA, Jay.
Am. b. Grand Rapids, Mich. 1893; ad. 1934 Detroit, Mich. M.

BOOTH, Cameron.
Am. b. Erie, Pa. 1892; ad. 1934 Minn., Minn. A-F.

BOOTH, Eunice Ellenetta.
Am. b. Goshen, N. H.; ad. 1934 Stockton, Calif. A.

BOOTH, Franklin. (Ill.)
Am. b. Indiana 1874; ad. 1934 New York. A-W.

BOOTH, Hanson.
Am. b. Noblesville, Ind. 1885; ad. 1934 Woodstock, N. Y. A28-F.

BOOTH, James Scripps.
Am. Detroit, Mich. 1888; ad. 1934 Same. A-F.

BOOTH, [Mrs.] Nina Mason.
Am. b. Gilbert Mills, N. Y. 1884; ad. 1934 Batavia, N. Y. A.

BOOTH, T. D. (Eg)
Am. ac. 1830-1857 New York. F-7-40.

BOOTT, Elizabeth.
Am. b. Cambridge, Mass. 1846; ac. 1886. B-C-F-15.

BOQUILLON. (S)
Fr. av. 1934 in Paris. M.

BORCH. *see* Terborch.

BORCHARDT, Félix.
Ger. b. Berlin 1857. B.

BORCHARDT, Norman. (Ill.)
Am. ad. 1934 New York. M.

BORCHT, Pieter van der [The Elder].
Flem. 1540/5-1608 Antwerp, Belg. B-T.

BORCKMANN, August.
Ger. Berlin 1827-1890. T.

BORDE, André.
Fr. b. Avignon 1480. T.

BORDES, Ernest.
Fr. Pau 1852-1914 Same. B-DBA.

BORDONE, Benedetto. (Min.)
It. ac. 1480-1539 Venice. T-V.

BORDONE [or Bordon], Paris Paschalinus.
It. Trévise 1500-1570/1 Venice. B-Bd-C-E-T-V-722.

BOREIN, Edward. (Et)
Am. b. San Leandro, Calif. 1872; ad. 1934 Santa Barb., Calif. A.

BOREL, André Marie Paul.
Fr. b. Lyons 1828; ac. 1850-1908. B-T.

BORÈS, Francisco.
Sp. b. Madrid 1898; ad. 1934 Paris. M.

BORG, Carl Oscar.
Am. b. Sweden 1879; ad. 1934 Hollywood, Calif. A-DBA-F-W.

BORGEAUD, Marius.
Fr. Lausanne 1861-1924. B-DBA.

BORGHUM, John Gutzon [de la Mothe]. (S)
Am. b. Idaho 1867; ad. 1934 Stamford, Conn. A-B-E-F-Hs-T-W-46-932.

BORGHUM, Solon Hannibal. (S)
Am. Ogden, Utah 1868-1922 Stamford, Conn. A019-B-DAB-F-Hs-T-Ta-19-46-798.

BORGMANN, Paul.
Ger. b. Berlin 1851. T.

BORGOGNONE, Ambrogio Stefani da Fossano.
It. Fossano 1455-1535 Milan. B-Bd-C-E-T.

BORGOGNONE, Guillaume Courtois.
see Courtois [or Cortese] Jacques.

BORGONA, Juán de.
Sp. b. 1495; d. 1533 Toledo, Sp. T.

BORGORD, Martin. (P, S)
Am. Gausdal, Nor. 1869-1935 Riverside, Calif. A-F-M-Obit. N. Y. papers 3-6-1935.

BORIE, Adolphe.
Am. b. Phila., Pa. 1877-1934 Same. A-B-F-M-Obit. N. Y. papers 5-16-1934.

BORKMAN, Gustaf. (Eg)
Am. Sweden 1842-1921 Brooklyn, N. Y. A018-F.

BORN, Ernest Alexander.
Am. b. San Fran., Calif. 1898; ad. 1934 New York. A.

BORNEMANN, Heinrich.
Ger. Hamburg 1450?-1499? T.

BORON, Vivian Browne.
Am. b. Harbor Beach, Mich. 1902; ad. 1934 Detroit, Mich. A.

BORONDA, Beonne. (S)
Am. b. Monterey, Calif. 1911; ad. 1934 New York. A.

BORONDA, Lester D.
Am. b. Reno, Nev. 1866; ad. 1934 New York. A-F.

BOROUGH-JOHNSON, Ernest.
Br. b. Shifnal 1867; ac. 1930 Bayswater. Wa.

BOROVIKOWSKY, Vladimir Lukitch.
Rus. Mirgorod 1757-1825 Leningrad. B-T.

BOROWSKI, Waclaw.
Pol. b. 1885; ad. 1934 Warsaw; ex. 1934 Pittsburgh, Pa. M.

BORRAS, Fray Nicolas.
Sp. Cocentayna 1530-1610 Gandia. C.

BORRÁS Y MOMPÓ, Vicente.
Sp. b. Olleria 1837; ac. 1873 Madrid. B-T.

BORRASSÁ, Luis.
Sp. ac. Barcelona; d. 1434 Mallorca. T.

BORREMANS [or Borman], Jan. (S)
[Family of Carvers ac. 15-16 Cent.]
Flem. ac. 1479-1522 Brussels, Belg. B-Hs-T.

BORRO, Giovanni Battista.
It. ac. 1550 Florence. T-V.

BORSSON [or Borssum], Anthonie van.
Dut. Rotterdam 1629/30-1677 Amsterdam. B-T.

BORST, George H. (S)
Am. b. Phila., Pa. 1889; ad. 1934 Same. A-Cs.

BORTHWICK, Alfred E.
Scot. ac. 1895 in Edinburgh. M.

BORZO, Karel.
Am. b. Hertogenbosch, Holland 1888; ad. 1934 Seattle, Wash. A.

BOS. *see* Bosch.

BOSBOOM, Johannes.
Dut. The Hague 1817-1891 Same. B-T-474.

BOSCH [or Bos], Balthazer van den [The Elder].
Flem. ac. 1551-1555 Antwerp. B-T.

BOSCH [or Bos], BALTHAZAR VAN DEN [The Younger].
Flem. Antwerp 1675/81-1715 Same. B-T.
BOSCH [or Bos], CORNELIS [or Sylvius].
Dut. 1506/10-1564. B-T.
BOSCH, ERNEST.
Ger. b. Krefeld 1834; ac. 1869 Düsseldorf. B-T.
BOSCH [or Bos], HIERONYMUS [Van Aeken].
Flem. Bois-le-Duc 1460/2-1516/8 Same. B-Bd-C-E-T-V.
BOSCHER, JEAN EDOUARD FERDINAND.
Fr. b. Paris 1888. DBA.
BOSCO, JEROME.
see Bosch [or Bos] Hieronymus.
BOSCOLI, GIOVANNI DI TOMMASO.
It. 1524-1589 Parma. T-V.
BOSCOLI, MASO DEL BOSCO.
It. Fiesole 1503-1574 Florence. T-V.
BOSE, NORMA.
Am. ad. 1935 Wash., D. C. M.
BOSER, FRIEDRICH KARL ADOLPH.
Ger. Düsseldorf 1809-1881 Halbau. B-T.
BOSIO, FRANÇOIS JOSEPH. (S)
Fr. Monaco 1768-1845 Paris. B-Hs-T.
BOSLEY, FREDERICK ANDREW.
Am. b. Lebanon, N. H.; ad. 1934 Concord, Mass. A-F-W.
BOSLEY, SYLVIA. (S)
Eng. ex. 1935 London. M.
BOSS, EDOURD.
Swi. b. Berne 1873. B.
BOSS, HOMER.
Am. b. Blanford, Mass. 1882; ad. 1934 Santa Cruz, N. M. A-F.
BOSSCHAERT, THOMAS. *see* Willebort, T.
BOSSCHE, BALTHASAR VAN DEN.
Flem. Antwerp 1681-1715 Same. C.
BOSSCHÈRE, JEAN DE. (Ill)
Fr. ac. 1934 Paris. M.
BOSSE, ABRAHAM.
Fr. Tours 1602-1676 Paris. B-T-880.
BOSSHARD, RODOLPHE THÉOPHILE.
Fr. b. Morges 1889. DBA-797.
BOSSHARDT, KASPAR.
Ger. Zurich, Swi. 1823-1887 Munich. C-T.
BOSSI, FAMILY. (S)
It. ac. 17th-18th cenutries in Italy. T.
BOSSI, FRANÇOIS JOSEPH. *see* Bosio, F. J.
BOSSI, GIUSEPPE.
It. Milan 1777-1815 Same. B-E-T.
BOSSUET, FRANÇOIS ANTOINE.
Belg. Ypres 1800-1889 Brussels. B-T.
BOSTELMANN, ELSE. (Ill)
Am. ad. 1934 New York. M.
BOSTICK, ALMA.
Am. b. Monroe, La. 1891; ad. 1934 Wash., D. C. A.
BOSTON, FREDERICK JAMES.
Am. Bridgeport, Conn. 1855-1932. A029-B-F.
BOSTON, JOSEPH H.
Am. b. Bridgeport, Conn.; ad 1934 New York. A-B-F-W.
BOSTWORTH, WINIFRED.
Am. b. Elgin, Iil. 1885. A20-F.
BOSWELL, HELEN.
Am. b. Chicago 1906; ad. 1935 New York. M.
BOSWELL, NORMAN GOULD.
Am. b. Halifax, N. S. 1882; ad. 1934 San Jose, Calif. A.
BOTH, ANDRIES DIRKSZ.
Dut. Utrecht 1608/12-1644/50 Venice, It. B-C-T-722.
BOTH, ARMAND. (Ill)
Am. Portland, Me. 1881-1922 New York. A019-F.
BOTH, JAN DIRKSZ.
Dut. Utrecht 1610/18-1652 Same. B-C-T-722.
BOTH, WILLIAM C. (Ill)
Am. b. Chicago 1880; ad. 1934 Same. A.
BOTHWELL, DORR.
Am. ad. 1934 Los Angeles, Calif. M.
BOTKE, CORNELIUS. (Et)
Am. b. Holland 1887; ad. 1934 Santa Paula, Calif. A-F.
BOTKE, [Mrs.] JESSE ARMS.
Am. b. Chicago 1883; ad. 1934 Santa Paula, Calif. A-B-F-T.
BOTKIN, HENRY ALBERT.
Am. b. Boston 1896; ad. 1934 New York. A.
BOTT, EARLE WAYNE.
Am. b. Ind., Ind. 1894; ad. 1934 Same. A.
BOTTIAN, ALFRED A. (S)
Fr. b. Valenciennes 1889. DBA.
BOTTICELLI, SANDRO [Alessandro di Mariano del Filipepi].
It. Florence 1444/7-1510 Same. B-Bd-C-E-T-V-191-300-301-640-722-748.
BOTTICINI, FRANCESCO.
It. Florence 1446-1497/8 Same. T.
BOTTICINI, RAFFAELLO.
It. Florence 1477-1520? B-T.
BOTTIGHEIMER, ERNA.
Am. ad. 1935 Cinn., O. M.
BOTTINELLI, ANTONIO. (S)
It. b. Viggiu 1827; d. Rome. B-T.
BOTTINI, GEORGE ALFRED.
Fr. Paris 1874-1906/7. B-DBA.
BOTTO, OTTO.
Am. ex. 1935 New York. M.
BOTTON, JEAN. *see* Jean de B.
BOTTUME, GEORGE F.
Am. Baltic, Conn. 1828-1846 Norwich, Conn. F.
BOUCART, GASTON HIPPOLYTE AMBROSE.
Fr. b. Angoulême 1878. B-DBA.
BOUCHARD, HENRI LOUIS. (S)
Fr. b. Dijon 1875. DBA-Hs.
BOUCHARD, PAUL LOUIS.
Fr. b. Paris; ac. 1900-1908. B-DBA.
BOUCHARDON, EDMÉ. (S)
Fr. Chaumont 1698-1762 Paris. B-E-Hs-T.
BOUCHARDY, ÉTIENNE.
Fr. Paris 1797-1849 Same. B-T.
BOUCHÉ, GEORGES PIERRE HIPPOLYTE.
Fr. b. Lyons 1874. B-DBA.
BOUCHÉ, LOUIS.
Am. b. New York 1896; ad. 1934 Same. A.
BOUCHÉ, LOUIS ALEXANDRE.
Fr. Luzancy 1838-1911. B-T.
BOUCHER, ANDRÉ. (S)
Fr. Nogent 1850-1934 Aix. B-DBA-T-Obit. Art News, 10-6-1934.

BOUCHER, François.
Fr. Paris 1703-1770 Same. B-Bd-C-E-T-302-722-756-834.
BOUCHER, Graziella V.
Am. b. Detroit, Mich. 1906; ad. 1934 Portland, Ore. A.
BOUCHER, Jean Marie. (S)
Fr. b. Cesson 1870. B-DBA.
BOUCHER-DESNOYERS, Auguste Gaspard Louis.
Fr. Paris 1779-1857 Same. B-T.
BOUCHET, Auguste.
Fr. b. Bordeaux 1876. DBA-T.
BOUCHET, Louis André Gabriel.
Fr. Paris 1759-1842. B-T.
BOUCHOR, Joseph Félix.
Fr. b. Paris 1853. B-DBA.
BOUCHOT, François.
Fr. Paris 1800-1842 Same. T-722.
BOUCK [or Boucle] van.
Flem. d. 1673 Paris. B-T-722.
BOUCQUET, Victor.
Flem. Furnes 1619-1677. T.
BOUDA, Cyril. (Eg)
Czec. ad. 1934 Prague-Dejvice. M.
BOUDEWYNS, Adriaen Frans [The Elder].
Belg. 1644-1711. T-722.
BOUDIN, Eugène Louis.
Fr. Honfleur 1824-1898 Deauville. B-DBA-E-T.
BOUDRY, Alois.
Belg. b. Antwerp 1851; ac. 1910 Brussels. B-T.
BOUE, Adolphe.
Am. d. 1934 Phila., Pa. M-Obit. N. Y. papers, 10-13-1934.
BOUGH, Samuel.
Scot. Carlisle 1822-1879 Edinburgh. B-DNB-T.
BOUGHTON, George Henry.
Br.-Am. Norwich, Eng. 1833-1905 London. A05-B-C-DNB-E-F-T-1-4-15.
BOUGUEREAU, Elizabeth Jane Gardner.
Mrs. William Adolphe Bouguereau.
Am. Exeter, N. H. 1851-1922 St. Cloud, Fr. A019-B-C-F-T-46.
BOUGUEREAU, William Adolphe.
Fr. La Rochelle 1825-1905 Same. B-Bd-C-DBA-E-T.
BOUILLARD, Jacques.
Fr. Versailles 1774-1806 Paris. B-T.
BOUILLON, Henry Théophile.
Fr. St. Front 1864-1933. B-DBA-T.
BOULANGER, Clément.
Fr. Paris 1805-1842 Magnésie. B-E-T.
BOULANGER, Gustave Clarence Rodolphe.
Fr. Paris 1824-1888 Same. B-C-E-T.
BOULANGER, Jean.
Fr. Troyes 1606-1660 Paris. B-E-T.
BOULANGER, Louis.
Fr. Verccil 1806/7-1867 Dijon. B-E-T.
BOULARD, Auguste [The Elder].
Fr. Paris 1827-1897. B-T.
BOULARD, Auguste [The Younger].
Fr. b. Paris 1852. B-T.
BOULARD, Émile Alexandre.
Fr. b. Paris; ac. 1889 Same. DBA.
BOULET, Cyprien Eugène. *see* Cyprien-Boulet.
BOULLAIRE, Jacques.
Fr. b. 1893 Paris. DBA.
BOULLANGER, Jean. *see* Boulanger, J.
BOULLOGNE, Louis de [The Elder].
Fr. Paris 1609-1674 Same. B-C-E-T-722.
BOULLOGNE, Louis de [The Younger].
Fr. Paris 1654-1733 Same. B-C-T.
BOULLOGNE, Valentin de. *see* Valentin, Jean de B.
BOULLONGE, Jean de. *see* Valentin, Jean de B.
BOULLONGUE, Bon.
Fr. Paris 1649-1717 Same. C-722.
BOULT, F. C.
Br. 1819-1887. M.
BOULTON, Frederick William.
Am. b. Mishawaka, Ind. 1904; ad. 1934 Chicago. A.
BOULTON, Joseph Lorkowski. (P-S)
Am. b. Fort Worth, Tex. 1896; ad. 1934 Ridgefield, Conn. A-F.
BOULY, Louis Alexis Achille. (S)
Fr. b. Paris 1805; ac. 1825-1840 Same. B.
BOUNDEY, Burton Shepard.
Am. b. Oconomowoc, Wis. 1879; ad. 1934 Monterey, Calif. A.
BOUNEAU, Émile.
Fr. b. Avignon 1902; ac. 1934 Paris. DBA.
BOUNETHEAU, Henry Brintnell. (Min)
Am. Charleston, S. C. 1797-1877 Same. DAB-F-6.
BOUNIEU, Michel Honoré.
Fr. Marseilles 1740-1814 Paris. B-T.
BOUPALOS. *see* Bupalus.
BOUQUET, Michel.
Fr. Lorient 1807-1890. B-T.
BOURASSA, Napoleon.
Can. 1827-1916 Canada. M.
BOURCARD, Emmanuel André. (S)
Fr. b. Guebviller; ac. 1930 Paris. DBA.
BOURDELLE, Émile Antoine. (S)
Fr. Montauban 1861-1929 Vesinet. B-DBA-Hs-T-303-642-798-884.
BOURDICHON, Jean [or Jehan].
Fr. Tours 1457-1521 Same. B-T.
BOURDON, Sébastien.
Fr. Montpelier 1616-1671 Paris. B-C-T-722.
BOURET, Germaine [or Marcel].
Fr. ad. 1929 Paris. DBA.
BOURET, Pierre. (S)
Fr. b. Paris; ac. 1930 Same. DBA.
BOURGEOIS, Léon Pierre Urbain.
Fr. b. Nevers; ac. 1877-1884. C.
BOURGEOIS, [Sir] Peter Francis.
Eng. London 1756-1811. B-DNB-722.
BOURGUIGNON, Guillaume Courtois.
see Courtois, G.
BOURGUIGNON, Hubert François.
see Gravelot, H. F.
BOURGUIGNON, Jacques Courtois.
see Courtois, J.
BOURGUIGNON, Perrier François.
see Perrier, F.
BOURILLON-TOURNAY, Jeanne.
Fr. Paris 1867-1932. DBA.
BOURNE, Evelin Bodfish.
Am. ad. 1934 Boston. M.

BOURNE, GERTRUDE BEALS.
Mrs. Frank A. Bourne.
Am. b. Boston; ad. 1934 Same. A.
BOUROGH-JOHNSON, ERNEST.
Eng. ad. 1934 London. M.
BOURSSE, [or Boutze] ESAIAS.
Dut. Amsterdam 1630/1-1672/3. B-E-T.
BOUSSINGAULT, JEAN LOUIS.
Fr. b. Paris 1883. DBA.
BOUT, PIETER.
Flem. Brussels 1658-1719 Same. B-T.
BOUTELLE, DEWITT CLINTON.
Am. Troy, N. Y. 1817-1884 Bethlehem, Pa. F-T-15.
BOUTET, HENRI. (Eg)
Fr. St. Hermine 1851-1919. B-DBA.
BOUTET DE MONVEL, BERNARD.
Fr. b. Paris 1884; ad. 1934 Same; ex. 1934 Pittsburgh, Pa. B-DBA.
BOUTET, DE MONVEL, LOUIS MAURICE.
Fr. Orléans 1851-1913 Paris. B-DBA-128.
BOUTIBONNE, CHARLES EDOUARD.
Hun. Pest 1816-1897 Wilderswil. B.
BOUTIGNY, PAUL ÉMILE.
Fr. Paris 1854-1929 Same. B-DBA.
BOUTS, ALBERT [or Aelbrecht].
[Master of the Assumption].
Dut. 1455/60-1549. B-T.
BOUTS, DIRK [or Dierick de Louvain].
Dut. Haarlem 1410/20-1475 Louvain, Belg. B-Bd-T-722.
BOUTWOOD, CHARLES EDWARD.
Am. b. Eng. ad. 1934 Chicago, Ill. A.
BOUVÉ, [Mrs.] ROSAMOND SMITH.
Am. ad. 1934 New York. A.
BOUVIER, ARTHUR.
Belg. b. Brussels 1837. B-T.
BOUWERT. *see* Dagman-Bouwert, Pascal.
BOUZONNET, STELLA ANTOINE.
Fr. Lyons 1637-1682 Paris. B-T.
BOUZONNET, STELLA CLAUDINE.
Fr. Lyons 1636-1697 Paris. B-T.
BOUZONNET, STELLA FRANÇOISE.
Fr. Lyons 1638-1691/2 Paris. B-T.
BOVI [or Bova] MARINO. (Eg)
Eng. b. Naples, It. 1758; ac. 1805 London. B-M-T.
BOWATER, EARL.
Am. ad. 1934 Redwood City, Calif. M.
BOWCHER, FRANK. (S)
Eng. ac. 1899-1926 London. B-Y1929.
BOWDEN, BEULAH.
Am. ad. 1934 Mars Hill, N. C. M.
BOWDISH, EDWARD ROMAINE.
Am. b. Richfield Springs, N. Y. 1856; ad. 1934 Skaneateles, N. Y. A.
BOWDISH, NELSON S.
Am. b. New Lisbon, N. Y. 1831; d. 1916 Skaneateles, N. Y. A013.
BOWDITCH, MARY O. (S)
Am. ad. 1934 Boston. A20-F.
BOWDOIN, HARRIETTE.
Am. b. Mass.; ad. 1934 New York. A-F.
BOWEN, ABEL. (Eg)
Am. b. Greenbush, N. Y. 1790-1850 Boston. DAB-F-T-2-7-8-12-645.
BOWEN, BENJAMIN JAMES.
Am. Boston 1859-1930. A027-B-F-46.
BOWEN, JAMES.
Eng. d. 1774 Shropshire, Eng. DNB.
BOWEN, JOHN.
Eng. Shropshire 1756-1832 Same. DNB.
BOWER, ALEXANDER.
Am. b. New York 1875; ad. 1934 Portland, Me. A-B-T.
BOWER, JOHN. (Eg)
Am. ac. 1815. T-2-7.
BOWER [or Bowers], GEORGE. (Eg)
Eng. d. 1690. DNB.
BOWER, [Mrs.] LUCY SCOTT.
Am. Rochester, Ia. 1867-1934 Paris.
A-W-Obit. N. Y. papers 11-15-1934.
BOWER, MAURICE L. (Ill.)
Am. ad. 1934 Phila., Pa. A.
BOWER, PHILLIP FREDERICK. (Mu)
Am. b. Astoria, Ore. 1895-1935 Malaga, Sp.
A-M-Obit. Art Digest, 3-15-1935.
BOWERS, EDWARD.
Am. ac. 1854-1858. F-45.
BOWES, JULIAN. (S)
Am. b. New York 1893; ad. 1934 Saybrook, Conn. A-F.
BOWLER, HAROLD THOMAS.
Am. b. Syracuse, N. Y. 1903; ad. 1934 New York. M.
BOWLER, HENRY ALEXANDER.
Eng. Kensington 1824-1903 Same. DNB.
BOWLER, THOMAS WILLIAM.
Eng. d. 1869. B-DNB.
BOWLES, THOMAS. (Eg)
Eng. b. London 1712; ac. 1753. T.
BOWLES-CARINGTON. (Eg)
Eng. ac. 1777 London. B.
BOWMAN, CHARLOT. (Ill.)
Am. ad. 1934 Rochester, N. Y. M.
BOWMAN, DOREEN.
Am. ad. 1934 Boston, Mass. M.
BOWMAN, FRANCES T.
Am. ad. 1934 Evanston, Ill. M.
BOWNESS, WILLIAM.
Eng. Kendal 1809-1867 London. B-DNB-T.
BOWYER, ROBERT.
Br. 1758-1834 Surrey. B-DNB-T.
BOXALL, SIR WILLIAM.
Eng. b. Oxford 1800-1879 London. B-DNB-T.
BOYCE, RICHARD AUDLEY.
Am. b. Brooklyn, N. Y. 1902; ad. 1934 Ridgewood, N. J. A.
BOYD, BYRON BENNETT.
Am. b. Wichita, Kan. 1887; ad. 1934 Des Moines, Ia. A.
BOYD, CLARENCE.
Am. Ironton, O. 1855-1883 Louisville, Ky. M.
BOYD, CLARE SHENAHAN.
Mrs. Fiske Boyd.
Am. ad. 1934 Summit, N. J. M.
BOYD, FISKE. (Et)
Am. b. Phila., Pa. 1895; ad. 1935 New York. A.
BOYD, FRANK. (Ill.)
Am. ad. 1934 Yonkers, N. Y. M.
BOYD, MARY.
Am. ad. Toledo, O. M.
BOYD, PENLEIGH.
Aust. d. 1924 Adelaide, So. Aust. M.

BOYD, Phoebe Amelia.
Am. b. Phila., Pa. 1875; ad. 1934 Germantown, Pa. A.
BOYD, Rutherford. (Ill.)
Am. ad. 1934 Leonia, N. J. A.
BOYD, William.
Am. b. Glasgow, Scot. 1882; ad. 1934 Pittsburgh, Pa. A.
BOYDELL, John. (Eg)
Eng. b. Dorington 1719-1804. B-T.
BOYDELL, Josiah.
Eng. Stanton 1752-1817 Hatford. B-DNB.
BOYDEN, Dwight Frederick.
Am. Boston 1860-1933 Balt., Md. A030-B-F-T-Obit. Art Digest, 6-1-1933.
BOYER, Émile.
Fr. b. Paris 1877. DBA-797.
BOYER, Ida F.
Am. d. 1915 New York. A013.
BOYER, Ralph L. (Et)
Am. b. Camden, N. J. 1879; ad. 1934 Westport, Conn. A.
BOYLE, Charles Washington.
Am. New Orleans, La. 1861-1925 Same. A023-F.
BOYLE, Ferdinand Thomas Lee.
Am. Ringwood, Eng. 1820-1906 Brooklyn, N. Y. A06-C-F-T.
BOYLE, John J. (S)
Am. New York 1851-1917 Same. A014-B-DAB-E-F-Hs-T-Ta-19-46.
BOYLE, John Joseph. (S)
Am. Pittsburgh, Pa. 1874-1911 Ocean View, N. J. A09-B-T.
BOYLE, Sarah Yocum McFadden. (Min.)
Am. b. Germantown, Pa.; ad. 1934 West Phila., Pa. A.
BOYNE, John.
Br. 1750-1810. B-DNB.
BOYNTON, George Rufus.
Am. b. Pleasant Grove, Wis. 1866; ad. 1934 New York. A-F.
BOYNTON, Ray. (Mu.)
Am. b. Whitten, Ia.; ad. 1934 San Fran., Calif. A.
BOYS, Thomas Shotter.
Eng. b. 1803-1874 London. B-DNB.
BOYVIN, René. [Renato.]
Fr. Angers 1525-1598 Rome, It. T.
BOZA, Daniel.
Am. ad. 1935 Cleveland, O. M.
BOZE, Joseph. (Min.)
Fr. Martigues 1744-1826 Paris. B-T-756.
BOZNANSKA, [Mme.] Hélène Olga.
Pol. b. Krakow 1865. B-DBA.
BOZZA, Bartolommeo.
It. 1532-1594. T-V.
BOZZACCO [or Brazzacco]. *see* Ponchino.
BRABANT der Perle.
see Master of the Pearl.
BRABAZON, Hercules Brabazon.
Eng. Paris 1821-1906 Oaklands, Eng. B-DNB-T.
BRABO, Albert.
Fr. b. Alais [Gard.] ex. 1935 New York. DBA-M.
BRACCI, Pietro. (S)
It. 1700-1733. Hs-T.
BRACCINI. *see* Tribolo.
BRACHERT, Hermann. (S)
Ger. b. 1890. Fa.
BRACHETTI, P.
Ger. ex. 1930 Munich. M.
BRACHT, Félix Prosper Eugène.
Swi. Morges 1842-1921. B-T.
BRACKEN, Clio Hinton Huneker. (S)
Mrs. William Barrie Bracken.
Am. Rhinebeck, N. Y. 1870-1925 New York. A022-B-F-T-Ta.
BRACKEN, Julia M. *see* Wendt, [Mrs.] William.
BRACKETT, Edward Augustus. (S)
Am. Vassalboro, Me. 1818-1908. B-DAB-F-Hs-T-Ta-4-15.
BRACKETT, Francis W.
Am. ad. 1934 Bellmore, L. I., N. Y. M.
BRACKETT, Walter M.
Am. Unity, Me. 1823-1919 Boston. A016-C-F-T-4-15.
BRACKMAN, Robert.
Am. b. Odessa, Rus. 1896; ad. 1934 New York. A-F.
BRACOUY, Leopold. (S)
Am. b. Rome, It.; ac. 1926 U. S. B-F.
BRACQUE. *see* Braque.
BRACQUEMOND, Félix Henri. (Et)
Fr. Paris 1833-1917 Paris. B-E-T-880.
BRACQUEMOND, Pierre.
Fr. b. Paris 1870. B-DBA.
BRADBURY, Arthur Royce.
Eng. ad. 1934 Bournemouth. Wa.
BRADBURY, Charles Earl.
Am. b. North Bay, N. Y. 1888; ad. 1934 Champaign, Ill. A-F.
BRADBURY, Leone C.
Am. b. 1907 Denver, Colo.; ac. 1934 Same. M.
BRADDOCK, Effie Francis. (S)
Am. b. Phila., Pa. 1866; ad. 1934 Warren, Pa. A.
BRADDON, Charles Edwin.
Am. b. Cleveland, O. 1906; ad. 1934 Same. A.
BRADFORD, Francis Scott.
Am. b. Appleton, Wis. 1898; ad. 1934 New York. A.
BRADFORD, Myrtle Taylor.
Am. ad. 1934 Miami, Fla. M.
BRADFORD, William.
Am. Fairhaven, Mass. 1823-1892 New York. B-C-DAB-E-F-T-1-4-15.
BRADISH, Alvah.
Am. Sherburne, N. Y. 1806-1901 Detroit, Mich. A04-F-2.
BRADLEY, Anne Cary.
Am. b. Fryeburg, Me. 1884; ad. 1934 Same. A.
BRADLEY, Basil.
Eng. London 1842-1904. B-T.
BRADLEY, Carolyn Gertrude.
Am. b. Richmond, Ind.; ad. 1934 Same. A.
BRADLEY, Susan H.
Mrs. Leverett Bradley.
Am. Boston 1851-1929. A026-B-F.
BRADLEY, William.
Eng. Manchester 1801-1857 Same. B-DNB-T.
BRADLEY, ["Will"] William H. (Ill.)
Am. b. Boston 1868; ad. 1934 Short Hills, N. J. A-B-F-W.

BRADSHAW, Alexander Christine.
Am. b. Nova Scotia; ad. 1934 Fresno, Calif. A.
BRADSHAW, George A. (Et)
Am. b. Trenton, N. J.; ad. 1934 Same. A28-F.
BRADSTREET, Edward D.
Am. Meriden, Conn. 1878-1921 Same. A018-F.
BRADWAY, Florence Dell.
Am. b. Phila., Pa. 1898; ad. 1934 Same. A.
BRADY, William J.
Am. ad. 1935 New York. M.
BRAECKE, Pierre. (S)
Belg. b. Nieuport, Belg. 1859. Hs-T-798.
BRAEDAEL, Jan Frans Van.
see Bredael, J. F. van.
BRAEKELEER, Adrien Ferdinand de.
Belg. Antwerp 1848-1904. B-T.
BRAEKELEER, Ferdinand de [The Elder].
Flem. Antwerp 1792-1883. B-C-T.
BRAEKELEER, ~~Henri~~ Jean Augustin de.
Flem. Antwerp 1830-1888. B-E-T.
BRAGADIN, Donato di Giovanni.
see Donato, Veneziano.
BRAHDY, Dorothy Kohnstamm.
Am. ad. 1934 New York. M.
BRAILES, William de. (Illuminator)
Eng. ac. 1220-1240. M.
BRAILOWSKY, Leonid.
Rus. ac. 20th century. M.
BRAILOWSKY, Rimma.
Rus. ac. 1927. M.
BRAINARD, [Mrs.] Elizabeth Holmes.
Am. b. Middleboro, Mass.; d. 1905 Boston. A05-F.
BRAITH, Anton.
Ger. Biebrich 1836-1905 Munich. B-T.
BRAKENBURG, Richard [or Renier].
Dut. Haarlem 1650-1702/3 Same. B-T-722.
BRALEY, Margaret Temple. (Ill.)
Am. ad. 1934 New York. M.
BRALEY, Norman R. (Ill.)
Am. ad. 1934 New York. M.
BRAMANTE, Donato da Urbino.
It. ac. 1492 in Urbino. T.
BRAMANTI, Bruno. (Eg)
It. b. Florence 1896; ad. 1935 Same. M.
BRAMANTINO, Bartolommeo Suardi.
see Suardi, B.
BRAMBILLA, Francesco.
It. ac. 1571-1599 in Milan. T-V.
BRAMER, Léonard.
Dut. Delft 1595/6-1674 Same. B-C-T-722.
BRAMLEY, Frank.
Eng. Boston, Eng. 1857-1915 Grasmere. B-DBA-T.
BRAMMER, L. G. (Et.)
Eng. ad. 1934 London. M.
BRAMTOT, Alfred Henri.
Fr. Paris 1852-1894 Garennes. B-T.
BRANCACCIO, Giovanni.
It. b. Pozzuoli 1903; ac. 1932 Naples. M.
BRANCHARD, Emile Pierre.
Am. b. New York 1881; ad. 1934 Same. A-F.
BRANCUSI, Constantin. (S)
Rumanian. b. 1876; ex. 1933 New York. B-DBA-Hs-798.
BRAND. *see also* Brandt.
BRAND, Christian Hülfgott.
Aus. Frankfort, Ger. 1695-1756 Vienna, Aus. B-T.
BRAND, Friedrich Auguste.
Aus. Vienna 1755-1806. B-T.
BRAND, Johann Christian.
Aus. Vienna 1723-1795 Same. B-T.
BRANDARD, Robert.
Eng. Birmingham 1805-1862. B-DNB-T.
BRANDEGER, Robert Bolling.
Am. Berlin, Conn. 1848-1922 Farrington, Conn. A025-F-T-3.
BRANDENBURG, Martin.
Pol. b. 1870; ac. 1934 in Berlin, Ger. B-T.
BRANDI, Giacinto.
It. Poli 1623-1691 Rome. B-T.
BRANDNER, Karl C.
Am. b. Berwyn, Ill. 1898; ad. 1934 Same. A.
BRANDOIN, Michel Vincent [L'Anglais].
Fr. Vevey 1733-1807. B-M.
BRANDRIFF, George Kennedy.
Am. b. Millville, N. J. 1890; ad. 1934 Beverly Hills, Calif. A.
BRANDT, Carl Ludwig.
Am. Holstein, Ger. 1831-1905 Savannah. Ga. A05-F-T-15.
BRANDT [or Brand], Heinrich Carl.
Aus. Vienna, Aus. 1724-1787 Munich, Ger. B.
BRANDT, Henry.
Am. b. Germany 1862; ad. 1934 Chicago. A.
BRANDT, Josef von.
Pol. Szczebreszyn 1841-1914. B-C-T.
BRANDT, Rexford.
Am. ad. 1934 Berkeley, Calif. M.
BRANGWYN, Frank. (Et.-S)
Eng. b. Bruges, Belg. 1867; ad. 1935 Ditchling, Sussex. B-DBA-E-T-Wa-304-305-825-830-871.
BRANN, Esther. (Ill.)
Am. ac. 1933. M.
BRANNAN, Sophie Marsten.
Am. b. Mountain View, Calif.; ad. 1934 New York. A-F.
BRANNAN, William Penn.
Am. d. 1866 Cincinnati, O. F.
BRANNIGAN, Gladys.
Mrs. Robert Brannigan.
Am. b. Hingham, Mass. 1882; ad. 1934 New York. A-F.
BRANSGROVE, Stephen Alfred.
Am. b. Hobart, Tasmania 1900; ad. 1934 Sydney, N. S. W., Aust. A.
BRANSOM, Paul. (Ill.)
Am. b. Wash., D. C. 1885; ad. 1934 Green Lake, N. Y. A-F.
BRANSON, Edith.
Am. ad. 1935 New York. M.
BRANSON, Isabel Parke.
Am. b. Coatsville, Pa. 1886; ad. 1915 Same. A12.
BRANSON, Lloyd.
Am. 1861-1925 Knoxville, Tenn. A023-F.
BRANSTON, Allen Robert. (Eg)
Eng. Lynn 1778-1827 London. B-DNB.
BRANT, Sebastian. [Cari.]
Ger. ac. in 1507 Strasburg. M.
BRANTLY, Benjamin D.
Am. b. Little Rock, Ark.; ad. 1934 Same. A.

BRANTONNE, René Louis.
Fr. ac. 1930 in Paris. DBA.
BRANWHITE, Charles.
Eng. Bristol 1817-1880. B-DNB-T.
BRANWHITE, Charles Brooke.
Eng. Bristol 1851-1929 Same. B.
BRANWHITE, Nathan Cooper.
Eng. Suffolk 1775-1857 Bristol. B-DNB.
BRAQUAVAL, Louis.
Fr. Lille 1853?-1919. B.
BRAQUE, Georges.
Fr. b. Argenteuil 1882. B-DBA-797-867.
BRASCASSAT, Jacques Raymond.
Fr. Bordeaux 1804-1867 Paris. B-E-T.
BRASHER, Rex.
Am. ad. 1934 Kent, Conn. M.
BRASS, Italico [or Italo].
It. b. Corizia 1870. B-DBA.
BRASZ, Arnold Franz.
Am. b. Wisconsin 1888. A20-F.
BRAUGHT, Ross Eugène.
Am. b. Carlisle, Pa. 1898; ad. 1934 Woodstock, N. Y. A-F.
BRAUN, Esther. (Ill.)
Mrs. Richard Schorr.
Am. b. New York; ad. 1934 Same. M.
BRAUN, Katalin.
Am. ad. 1934 Jackson Heights, N. Y. M.
BRAUN, Maurice.
Am. b. Hungary 1877; ad. 1934 Point Loma, Calif. A-F-W.
BRAUNER, Olaf Martinius.
Am. b. Christiania, Nor. 1869; ad. 1934 Ithaca, N. Y. A-B-F-W.
BRAUNFEL, Charles.
Am. ex. 1935 New York. M.
BRAUWER, Adriaen. *see* Brouwer, A.
BRAXTON, William Ernest.
Am. b. Wash., D. C. 1878; ad. 1934 Brooklyn, N. Y. A-F.
BRAY, Dirk de.
Dut. ac. Amsterdam 1664. B-T.
BRAY, Jan de.
Dut. Haarlem 1627-1697 Same. B-T.
BRAY, Salomon de.
Dut. Haarlem 1597-1664 Amsterdam. B-T.
BRAYER, Yves.
Fr. b. Versailles 1907; ex. 1935 Paris. DBA.
BRAYMER, L. E. (Ill.)
Am. b. Chicago 1901; ad. 1934 Phila., Pa. A.
BRAZINGTON, William Cary.
Am. Westfield, Ind. 1865-1914 Ind., Ind. A011.
BRCIN, John David. (S)
Am. b. Serbia 1899; ad. 1934 Chicago. A-Cs-F-W.
BRÉA [or Bré] de.
Fr. ac. 1780 in Paris. B-T.
BRÉA, Lodovico [or Louis].
It. 1443-1520. B-T.
BREAKSPEARE, William A.
Eng. b. Birmingham 1856. B.
BREANSKI, Alfred de.
Eng. ac. 1869-1893 Greenwich, Eng. B.
BRÉARD, Henri Georges.
Fr. b. Paris 1873. DBA.
BRECHER, Samuel.
Am. b. Austria 1897; ad. 1934 New York. A.
BRÉCHERET, Victor. (S)
Brazilian. b. San Paulo; ac. 1932 Paris. DBA.
BRECK, George William. (Mu.)
Am. Wash., D. C. 1863-1920 Flushing, L. I., N. Y. A017-B-DAB-F-T-W11-33.
BRECK, John L.
Am. d. 1899 Boston, Mass. A01.
BRECK, Robert Evans.
Am. b. White Plains, N. Y. 1907; ad. 1934 Boston. A.
BRECKELENKAM, Quiryn.
see Brekelenkam, Q.
BRECKENRIDGE, Hugh Henry.
Am. b. Leesburg, Va. 1870; ad. 1934 Fort Wash., Pa. A-B-F-T-W-46.
BREDA, Carl Fredrik von.
Swe. Stockholm 1759-1818. B-T.
BREDAEL [or Breda], Jan Frans van.
Flem. Antwerp 1683-1750 Same. C-E-722.
BREDEMEIER, Carl.
Am. b. Chicago 1892; ad. 1934 Buffalo, N. Y. A.
BREDIN, Christine. (S)
Am. ad. 1934 Phila., Pa. A.
BREDIN, R. Sloan.
Am. Butler, Pa. 1881-1933 New Hope, Pa. A030-B-F-W.
BREDT, Ferdinand Max.
Ger. b. Leipzig 1860. B-T.
BRÉE, Joseph von.
Dut. ac. 1675. B-T.
BRÉE, Mattheus Ignatius van.
Flem. Antwerp, Belg. 1773-1839. B-C-T.
BRÉE, Phillip Jacob van.
Flem. Antwerp, Belg. 1786-1871. B-T.
BREEN, Katherine.
Am. ex. 1934 New York. M.
BREENBERGH, Bartholomeus.
Dut. Deventer 1599/1600-1655/9 Amsterdam. B-C-T-722-880.
BREGNO, Lorenzo di Roberto [or Alberto]. (S)
It. d. 1523 Venice. B-T.
BREGY, Edith Maurice.
Am. b. Phila., Pa.; ad. 1934 Same. A.
BRÉHAN, Marquise de.
Fr. ac. 1786-1789 Wash., D. C. 786.
BREHM, Adam. (S)
Am. b. Ger. 1901; ad. 1934 Kansas City, Mo. A.
BREHM, George. (Ill.)
Am. b. Anderson, Ind. 1878; ad. 1934 New Rochelle, N. Y. A.
BREIDVIK, Mons. (Et.)
Am. ad. 1934 New York. A29.
BREIDWISER, Theodor.
Aus. b. Vienna 1847. B-T.
BREISACH, Paul.
Am. b. Waterville, O. 1906; ad. 1934 Maumee, O. M.
BREITBACH, Carl.
Ger. Berlin 1833-1904 Cassel. T.
BREITMAYER, M. V. (Et.)
Am. b. Mich. 1889; ad. 1934 Jackson, Mich. A-F.
BREITNER, Georg Hendrik.
Dut. Rotterdam 1857-1923 Amsterdam. B-E-T.

BREKELENKAM, Quieringh Gerrttsz van.
Dut. Zwammerdam 1620?-1668 Leyden. B-C-T-722.
BRÉLÉVÉNEZ, Eglise de.
Fr. ex. 1934 London. M.
BRELING, Heinrich.
Ger. b. Burgdorf 1849. B-T.
BREMEN, Meyer von. *see* Meyer, Johann George.
BREMER, Anne M.
Am. b. San Fran., Calif.; d. 1923 Same. A025-F.
BREMER, Hester. (S)
Am. b. Germany 1887; ad. 1935 Dayton, O. A20-Cs.
BREMOND, Marie Jeanne.
Fr. b. Paris; d. 1926. DBA.
BRENAN.
Ir. ac. 1756 Dublin. DNB.
BRENDEL, Albert Heinrich.
Ger. Berlin 1827-1895 Weimar. B-T.
BRENEISER, Stanley Grotevent.
Am. b. Reading, Pa. 1890; ad. 1934 Santa Maria, Calif. A.
BRENNAN, Alfred Laurens. (Ill.)
Am. Louisville, Ky. 1853-1921 Brooklyn, N. Y. A018-DAB-F-T-W4-17.
BRENNER, Carl Christ. (Et.)
Am. Bavaria 1838-1888 Louisville, Ky. T.
BRENNER, Carlos.
Am. b. Louisville, Ky.; d. 1924 Chicago. M.
BRENNER, Victor David. (Med.-S)
Am. Rus. 1871-1924 New York. A025-DAB-F-T-Ta.
BRENNERMAN, George W.
Am. New York 1856-1906 Same. A06-F.
BRENSON, Theodore.
Br. ac. 1928. M.
BRESCIA. *see* Giovanne Antonio da.
see Moretto da Brescia.
BRESCIANNO DA SIENA.
It. ac. 1520. T-V.
BRESDIN, Rodolphe. (Et.)
[Called "Chien Caillou".]
Fr. Ingrande 1825-1885. B-T.
BRESLAU, Leo.
Am. b. Brooklyn, N. Y. 1909; ad. 1934 Same. A.
BRESLAU, Marie Louise Catherine.
Ger. Munich 1856-1927. B-T.
BRESSLERN-ROTH, [Mrs.] Norbertine.
Aus. b. Graz 1891; ad. 1934 Same. Wa.
BRET, Paul Marie Léonce.
Fr. b. Draguignan 1902. DBA.
BRETEGNIER, Georges.
Fr. Héricourt 1863-1892. B.
BRETLAND, Thomas W.
Eng. Nottingham 1802-1874 Same. B.
BRÉTON-DEMONT. *see* Demont-Bréton.
BRÉTON, Émile Adelard.
Fr. Courrières 1831-1902. B-C-T.
BRÉTON, Jules Adolphe Aimé Louis.
Fr. Courrières 1827-1906 Paris. B-Bd-C-DBA-E-T-306.
BRETT, Dorothy Engeme.
Am. b. London; ad. 1934 Taos, N. M. A.
BRETT, Harold M. (Ill.)
Am. b. Middleboro, Mass. 1880; ad. 1935 Boston. A.
BRETT, John.
Eng. Bletchingley 1831-1902 Putney. B-Bd-DNB-T.
BRETT, Rosa.
Eng. ac. 1867-1881 London. B-T.
BREU, Jörg [The Elder].
Ger. 1480-1537 Augsburg. B-C-T.
BREU, Jörg [The Younger].
Ger. 1510-1547 Augsburg. B-C-T.
BREUER, Henry Joseph.
Am. b. Phila., Pa. 1860. F-46.
BREUGHEL. *see* Bruegel.
BREUIL. *see* Dubreuil.
BREUL, Harold Guenther. (Ill.)
Am. b. 1889; ad. 1935 Prov., R. I. A28-F.
BREUL, Hugo.
Am. b. Saalfield, Ger. 1854-1915 Prov., R. I. A08-B-T.
BRÉVANNES, Maurice.
Am. ex. 1932 New York. M.
BREVOORT, James Renwick.
Am. Yonkers, N. Y. 1832-1918 Same. A016-B-C-DAB-F-T-W9-4-15-184.
BREWER, Adrian Louis.
Am. b. St. Paul, Minn. 1891; ad. 1934 Little Rock, Ark. A.
BREWER, Alice Ham. (Min.)
Mrs. F. Layton Brewer.
Am. b. Chicago 1872; ad. 1934 Montclair, N. J. A.
BREWER, [Mrs.] Harriet E.
Am. ad. 1934 Norwich, Conn. A.
BREWER, Nicholas Richard.
Am. b. Minn. 1857; ad. 1934 St. Paul, Minn. A-F-W.
BREWSTER, Anna Richards.
Mrs. William T. Brewster.
Am. Germantown, Pa. 1870; ad. 1934 Scarsdale, N. Y. A-F.
BREWSTER, Earl H.
Am. b. Chagrin Falls, O. 1879; ad. 1915 Paris. A12.
BREWSTER, George Thomas. (S)
Am. b. Kingston, Mass. 1862; ad. 1934 Cos Cob, Conn. A-B-F-T-Ta-W.
BREWTNALL, Edward Frederick.
Eng. London 1846-1902 Bedford Park. DNB.
BREYDEL, Karel [Cavalier].
Flem. Antwerp 1678-1733 Same. B-T-722.
BREYFOGLE, John Winstanley.
Am. b. Louisville, Ky. 1874; ad. 1915 New York. A12-B.
BRIANCHON, Maurice.
Fr. b. Fresnay 1899; ad. 1934 Paris. DBA.
BRICARD, François Xavier.
Fr. ac. 1904-1927 in Paris. B-DBA.
BRICHER, Alfred Thompson.
Am. Portsmouth, N. H. 1837-1908 New Dorp, N. Y. A07-C-F-T-15-169.
BRICKDALE. *see* Fortescue-Brickdale.
BRIDAHAM, Lester.
Am. ex. 1932 New York. M.
BRIDELL, Frederick Lee.
Eng. Southampton 1831-1863. B-DNB.

BRIDGEMAN, FREDERICK ARTHUR.
Am. Tuskegee, Ala. 1847-1927 France.
A025-B-C-DAB-E-F-T-W14-1-15-22-46.
BRIDGEMAN, GEORGE B.
Am. b. Bing, Can. 1864; ad. 1934 Pelham, N. Y. A.
BRIDGES, CHARLES.
Am. b. Eng. d. Virginia; ac. 1730-1750.
F-T-2-182.
BRIDGES, FIDELIA.
Am. Salem, Mass. 1834-1924 New Canaan, Conn. A021-B-C-F-T-15-46-169.
BRIDPORT, HUGH.
Am. London 1794-1832 Phila., Pa.
F-T-2-6-7-179.
BRIEM, GOTTLOB. (Et.)
Am. b. Stuttgart, Ger.; ad. 1935 New York.
M.
BRIEN, G. L. (Et.)
Am. ex. 1933 New York. M.
BRIERLY, [Sir] OSWALD WALTERS.
Eng. Chester 1817-1894 London. B-DNB-E-T.
BRIET, ARTHUR H. C.
Dut. b. Java 1867. B.
BRIFFANET. [Cari.]
Fr. ac. 1844 Paris. M.
BRIGDEN, FREDERICK H.
Can. b. London, Eng.; ad. 1935 Toronto. M.
BRIGGS, BERTA.
Mrs. William Harlowe Briggs.
Am. b. St. Paul, Minn. 1884; ad. 1934 New York. A.
BRIGGS, CLARE A. (Cart.)
Am. 1875-1930. A027.
BRIGGS, GERTRUDE RUSSELL.
Am. b. Lexington, Mass. 1899; ad. 1934 New York. A.
BRIGGS, HENRY PERRONET.
Eng. Walworth 1791/3-1844 London.
B-Bd-T-722.
BRIGGS, IRLAM.
Eng. ad. 1935 London. M.
BRIGGS, WARREN C.
Am. Brooklyn, N. Y. 1867-1903 New York.
A025.
BRIGHAM, W. COLE.
Am. b. Balt., Md. 1870; ad. 1934 Shelter Is., N. Y. A.
BRIGHT, HENRY.
Eng. Saxmundham 1814-1873 Ipswich.
B-DNB-T.
BRIGHT, JOHN IRWIN.
Am. b. Phila., Pa. 1869; ad. 1915 Same. A12.
BRIGHTWELL, CECILIA LUCY. (Et.)
Eng. 1811-1875 Norwich, Eng. DNB-T.
BRIGHTWELL, L. R. (Et.)
Am. ex. 1934 New York. M.
BRIGSTOCKE, THOMAS.
Eng. London 1809-1881 B-DNB-T.
BRILL, GEORGE REITER.
Am. Allegheny, Pa. 1867-1918 Florida.
A025-T.
BRILL [or Bril] MATTHAUS [The Younger].
Flem. Antwerp 1550-1583/4 Rome. B-C-T.
BRILL, PAUL [or Paulo].
Flem. Antwerp 1554/6-1626 Rome.
B-C-E-T-646-722.
BRILLOUIN, LOUIS GEORGES.
Fr. St. Jean d'Angély 1817-1893 Melle. B-T.

BRINDESI, OLYMPIO. (S)
Am. b. Abruzzi, It. 1897; ad. 1934 New York. A-Cs-F.
BRINGHURST, ROBERT PORTER. (S)
Am. Jerseyville, Ill. 1855-1925 Univ. City, Mo. A022-F-T-Ta.
BRINI [or Brina], FRANCESCO.
It. ac. 1570 in Florence. T-V.
BRINKERHOFF, ROBERT MOORE. (Ill.)
Am. b. Toledo, O. 1879. A28-F.
BRINLEY, DANIEL PUTNAM. (Mu.)
Am. b. Newport, R. I. 1879; ad. 1934 New York. A-B-F.
BRINSON, J. PAUL.
Eng. d. 1927. Obit. Wa. 1929.
BRINTON, CAROLINE PEART.
Mrs. Christian Brinton.
Am. ac. 1926 West Chester, Pa. A12-F-178.
BRION, GUSTAVE.
Fr. Rothau 1824-1877 Paris. B-C-T.
BRIOSCHI, CARLO.
It. Milan 1826-1895 Vienna, Aus. T.
BRIOSCO, ANDREA [or Il Riccio]. (S)
It. Padua 1470-1532. E-Hs-T.
BRISAC, EDITH MAE.
Am. ad. 1934 New York. M.
BRISCOE, ARTHUR JOHN TREVOR. (Et)
Eng. b. Birkenhead 1873; ex. 1935 New York. Wa-830.
BRISCOE, FRANKLIN D.
Am. Balt., Md. 1844-1903 Phila., Pa. A04.
BRISÉ [or Brize], CORNELIS.
Dut. Haarlem 1622-1670 Amsterdam. B-T.
BRISGAND, GUSTAVE.
Fr. ac. 1930. B-DBA.
BRISLEY, ETHEL C.
Eng. ad. 1934 London. Wa.
BRISLEY, JOYCE LANKESTER. (Ill.)
Eng. ad. 1934 London. Wa.
BRISLEY, NINA KENNARD. (Ill.)
Eng. ad. 1934 Richmond. Wa.
BRISPOT, HENRI.
Fr. b. Beauvais 1846. B-DBA.
BRISSAUD, PIERRE. (Ill.)
Fr. b. Paris 1885; ac. 1935 Same. B-DBA.
BRISSOT DE WARVILLE, FÉLIX SATURNIN.
Fr. Véron 1818-1892. B-T.
BRISTOL, JOHN BUNYAN.
Am. Hillsdale, N. Y. 1826-1909 New York.
A07-B-C-DAB-F-T-1-3-4-15.
BRISTOL, RENÉ. (S)
Fr. Thiviers 1888-1934. DBA.
BRISTOW, EDMUND.
Eng. Windsor 1787-1876 Eton. B-DNB-T.
BRISTOWE, [Mrs.] SYDNEY.
Br. ex. 1934 in London. M.
BRITON-RIVIERE. *see* Riviere, Briton.
BRITT, RALPH M.
Am. b. Winchester, Ind. 1895; ad. 1934 Atlanta, Ga. A.
BRITTAN, CHARLES EDWARD.
Eng. b. Plymouth; ad. 1934 Lewdown.
B-Wa.
BRITTON, EDGAR.
Am. b. 1901; ad. 1934 Chicago. M.
BRITTON, HARRY.
Can. b. Cambridge, Eng. 1878; ad. 1934 Parrsboro, N. S. M.

BRITTON, JAMES.
Am. b. Hartford, Conn. 1878; ad. 1934 New York. A20-F-M.
BRIZE, CORNELIS. *see* Brise, C.
BRIZZI, FRANCESCO [Briccio Nosadella].
It. Bologna 1574-1623/5 Same. B-T.
BROAD, HARRY ANDREW.
Am. b. Chicago 1910; ad. 1934 Same. A.
BROADHEAD, W. SMITHSON. (Ill.)
Am. ad. 1934 New York. M.
BROCAS, MAURICE.
Belg. b. 1892 in Belgium; ad. 1935 Brussels. M.
BROCK, CHARLES EDMUND.
Eng. b. Holloway 1870. Wa.
BROCK, EDMOND.
Eng. ex. 1934 in London. Wa.
BROCK, EMMA L. (Ill.)
Am. b. Fort Shaw, Mont.; ad. 1934 St. Paul, Minn. A.
BROCK, [Sir] THOMAS. (S)
Eng. Worcester 1847-1922 London. B-E-Hs-Y01923.
BROCKBANK, ALBERT ERNEST.
Eng. ac. 1886-1927 London. B.
BROCKEDON, WILLIAM.
Eng. Devon 1787-1854 London. B-DNB-T.
BROCKHURST, GERALD LESLIE. (Et.)
Eng. b. 1890; ad. 1934 London. Wa-825-830.
BROCKMAN, ANN.
Mrs. William McNulty.
Am. b. Alameda, Calif. 1899; ad. 1934 New York. A.
BROCKMAN [or Brokman], HENRI JACOB.
Dan. Copenhagen 1868-1933. DBA-T.
BROCKY, CHARLES.
Hun. Hungary 1807/8-1855 London. B-DNB.
BROD, FRITZI.
Am. ad. 1935 Chicago, Ill. M.
BRODEUR, PAUL A. (S)
Am. b. Webster, Mass. 1894; ad. 1935 Wellesley Hills, Mass. M.
BRODHEAD, GEORGE HAMILTON.
Am. b. Boston; ad. 1934 Rochester, N. Y. A.
BRODIE, ALEXANDER. (S)
Scot. 1830-1867 Edinburgh. B-DNB.
BRODIE, WILLIAM. (S)
Scot. 1815-1881 Edinburgh. B-DNB.
BRODOSKI, ANTON.
Pol. Warsaw 1784-1832 Same. B.
BRODOSKI, HORACE.
Am. b. Melbourne, Aust. 1855; ad. 1935 New York. A20-F.
BRODOSKI, ISAAC.
Rus. ad. 1934 Leningrad. M.
BROECK, ELIAS VAN DEN.
Dut. Amsterdam 1650-1708 Same. B-T.
BROEDEL, MAX. (Ill.)
Am. b. Leipzig, Ger. 1870; ad. 1935 Balt., Md. A28-F.
BROEDERLAM, MELCHIOR.
Fr. b. Ypres, Belg.; ac. 1381-1409. B-T.
BROEMEL, CARL WILLIAM.
Am. b. Cleveland, O. 1891; ad. 1934 Same. A.
BROEUCQ, JACQUES DU. *see* Dubroeucq.
BROKAW, IRVING.
Am. b. New York 1871; ad. 1934 Same. A.
BROMBERGER, DORA.
Ger. ad. 1934 Bremen, Ger. M.
BROMLEY, JOHN MALLORD.
Eng. ac. 1880-1903 London. T.
BROMLEY, VALENTINE WALTER.
Eng. 1848-1877 Harpenden. B-DNB.
BROMLEY, WILLIAM. (Eg.)
Br. 1769-1842 Isle of Wight. B-DNB.
BROMPTON, RICHARD.
Br. 1734-1782 Leningrad, Rus. B-DNB.
BRONCKHORST, GERARD VAN.
Dut. Utrecht 1637-1673 Same. B-C-T.
BRONCKHORST, JAN GERRITS VAN.
Dut. Utrecht 1603-1661/78 Amsterdam. B-C-T-722.
BRONZINO, IL. [Angolo di Cosimo di Mariano].
It. Monticelli 1502/3-1572 Florence. B-Bd-C-E-T-V-722-848.
BROOK, ALEXANDER.
Am. b. Brooklyn, N. Y. 1898; ad. 1935 New York. A-F-307-700-779.
BROOK, [Mrs.] ALEXANDER. *see* Bacon, Peggy.
BROOKE, HENRY.
Ir. Dublin 1738-1806 Same. B-DNB.
BROOKE, RICHARD NORRIS.
Am. Warenton, Va. 1847-1920 Same. A-17-F-T.
BROOKE, WILLIAM HENRY.
Eng. 1772-1860 London. B-DNB.
BROOKER, BERTRAM.
Can. ad. 1935 Toronto, Ont. M.
BROOKING, CHARLES.
Eng. 1723-1759 London. B-DNB-T.
BROOKS, ADELE RICHARDS.
Am. b. Buffalo, N. Y. 1873; ad. 1934 St. Louis, Mo. A.
BROOKS, ALDEN FINNEY.
Am. b. West Williamsfield, O. 1840; ad. 1933 Chicago. A-F.
BROOKS, ARTHUR D.
Am. b. Cleveland, O. 1877; ad. 1934 Same. A.
BROOKS, BERNICE ANN.
Am. ex. 1934 N. Y. M.
BROOKS, CAROLINE SHAWK. (S)
Am. b. Cinn., O. 1840; ac. 1880. F.
BROOKS, CORA SMALLEY.
Am. d. 1930. A027.
BROOKS, ERICA MAY. (P-S)
Am. b. London, Eng. 1894; ad. 1934 New York. A.
BROOKS, HENRY HOWARD.
Am. b. Bedford, Mass. 1898; ad. 1934 Concord, Mass. A.
BROOKS, ISABEL.
Am. b. Balt., Md.; ad. 1934 Same. A.
BROOKS, MARJORIE.
Eng. b. Hornsley 1904; ad. 1934 Same. Wa.
BROOKS, MARY MASON.
Am. Salem, Mass. 1860-1915 Jamestown, N. Y. A013.
BROOKS, MATILDA.
Am. England 1837-1913 New York. A011.
BROOKS, MILDRED BRYANT. (Et.)
Am. ad. 1935 So. Pasadena, Calif. M.
BROOKS, RICHARD EDWIN. (S)
Am. Braintree, Mass. 1865-1918 Wash., D.C. A16-B-DAB-F-T-Ta.
BROOKS, ROMAINE. (Et)
Am. ad. 1935 New York. M.
BROOKS, THOMAS.
Eng. Hull 1818-1891. B-T.

BROOME, Isaac. (S)
Am. Canada 1835-1922 U. S. F-T.
BROSAMER, Hans. (Eg.)
Ger. Fulda 1480/1500-1554 Erfurt. B-T.
BROUET, Auguste. (Et.)
Fr. b. Paris 1872; ex. 1934 New York. DBA.
BROUGH, Robert.
Scot. Invergordon 1872-1905 London. B-DNB-E.
BROUGH, Walter W.
Am. b. Phila., Pa. 1890; ad. 1934 Cleveland, O. A.
BROUGIER, Rudolphe W.
Am. b. Swi.; d. 1926 Santa Barbara, Calif. A23.
BROUILLET, Pierre Aristide André.
Fr. Charroux 1857-1914. B-DBA-T.
BROUN, Heywood Campbell. (Writer-P)
Am. b. Brooklyn, N. Y. 1888; ad. 1935 New York. W.
BROUWER [or Brauwer], Adriaen.
Flem. Oudenarde 1605/8-1638/40 Antwerp. B-Bd-C-E-T-309-722-902.
BROWERE, Abertis.
Am. Tarrytown, N. Y. 1814-1887 Catskill, N. Y. F.
BROWERE, John Henri Isaac. (S)
Am. New York 1792-1834 Same. DAB-F-T-Ta-34.
BROWN. *see also* Browne.
BROWN, Abigail Keyes.
Am. b. Rockford, Ill. 1891; ad. Same. A.
BROWN, Agnes.
Am. b. Newburyport, Mass.; ac. 1926. B-F-T-W8-15.
BROWN, Alexander Kellock.
Scot. Edinburgh 1849-1922 Lamlash. B-T.
BROWN, Alice Van Vechten.
Am. b. Hanover, N. H. 1862; ad. 1934 Wellesley, Mass. A.
BROWN, Arnesby.
Eng. b. Nottingham 1866; ad. 1934 Haddiscoe. B-T-825.
BROWN, Arthur William. (Ill.)
Am. b. Hamilton, Can. 1881; ad. 1934 New York. A28-B-F-W.
BROWN, Benjamin Chambers.
Am. b. Marion, Ark. 1865; ad. 1934 Pasadena, Calif. A-F-W.
BROWN, Bolton Coit. (Et.)
Am. b. Dresden, N. Y. 1865; ad. 1934 New York. A-B-F-T-W.
BROWN, Caroleen Ackerman.
Mrs. Egbert Guernsey Brown.
Am. b. New York; ad. 1934 Brooklyn, N. Y. A.
BROWN, Charles V.
Am. b. Phila., Pa. 1848; ac. 1926. B-F-T.
BROWN, Charlotte Harding. (Ill.)
Mrs. James A. Brown.
Am. b. Newark, N. J. 1873; ad. 1934 Smithtown, N. Y. A-B-F-W.
BROWN, David.
Eng. ex. 1772-1797 in London. B-DNB.
BROWN, Dorothy Hunter.
Am. ad. 1934 Prov., R. I. A.
BROWN, ["Ted"] Edward Scott. (Cart.)
Am. b. Stillwater, Minn.; ad. 1934 Norwalk, Conn. W.
BROWN, Elmore. (Ill.)
Am. ad. 1934 New York. M.
BROWN, Ford Madox.
Eng. Calais, Fr. 1821-1893 London. B-Bd-DNB-E-T-1-308-922.
BROWN, Francis Clark.
Am. ad. 1934 Richmond, Ind. M.
BROWN, Francis F.
Am. b. Glassboro, N. J. 1891; ad. 1934 Muncie, Ind. A.
BROWN, Frank A.
Am. b. Beverly, Mass.; ad. 1934 New York. A.
BROWN, Frederick.
Eng. b. Chelmsford 1851; ad. 1934 Richmond. B-T-Wa.
BROWN, George Bacon.
Am. Ogdensburg, N. Y. 1893-1923 Mankato, Minn. A020.
BROWN, George Loring.
Am. Boston 1814-1889 Malden, Mass. B-C-F-T-4-6-7-15-39-40.
BROWN, Glenn Madison. (Ill.)
Am. Hartford, Conn. 1876-1932. A-B-F.
BROWN, Grace Evelyn.
Am. b. Beverly, Mass. 1873; ad. 1934 Newton, Mass. A-F.
BROWN, Harold Haven.
Am. Malden, Mass. 1869-1932. A029-B-F-W17-181.
BROWN, H. Harris.
Eng. b. 1864; ad. 1934 Chelsea. M.
BROWN, Harrison B.
Am. Portland, Me. 1831-1915 London. A012-F.
BROWN, Harrison Paul.
Am. b. Waterloo, Ind. 1889; ad. 1934 Mt. Clemens, Mich. A.
BROWN, Helen Paxton.
Eng. ac. 1883-1887 in London. B.
BROWN, Henry Kirke. (S)
Am. Leyden, Mass. 1814-1886 Newburgh, N. Y. DAB-E-F-Hs-T-Ta-4-15-19-26-35-36-182-701.
BROWN, Horace.
Am. b. Rockford, Ill. 1876; ad. 1934 Springfield, Vt. A.
BROWN, Howard V. (Ill.)
Am. b. Lexington, Ky.; ad. 1934 New York. A.
BROWN, Howell Chambus. (Et.)
Am. b. Little Rock, Ark. 1880. A28-F.
BROWN, Irene.
Am. b. Hastings, Mich. 1881. A12-F.
BROWN, [Mrs.] James A. *see* Brown, C. H.
BROWN, James Francis.
Am. b. Niagara Falls, N. Y.; ad. 1934 New York. A-B.
BROWN, John.
Scot. Edinburgh 1752-1787 Leith. T.
BROWN, John. (Heraldic P.)
Eng. ac. 1502-1532 in London. B-DNB-T.
BROWN, John Appleton.
Am. Newburyport, Mass. 1844-1902 New York. A04-DAB-F-T-W1-1-15-47-169.
BROWN, John Crawford.
Br. 1805-1867. Fa.
BROWN, John George.
Am. Durham, Eng. 1831-1913 New York. A011-DAB-E-F-T-1-4-15-22-46-182.

BROWN, JOHN HENRY. (Min.)
Am. Lancaster, Pa. 1818-1891. F-6-15-179.
BROWN, JOHN LEWIS.
Fr. Bordeaux 1829-1890 Paris. B-T.
BROWN, JOSEPH RANDOLPH.
Am. b. Port Huron, Mich. 1861; ad. 1934 Sharon, Mass. A.
BROWN, LUCILLE ROSEMARY.
Am. b. Hollywood, Calif. 1905; ad. 1934 Venice, Calif. A.
BROWN, LYDIA M.
Am. b. Waterman, N. Y.; ad. 1934 Atlanta, Ga. A.
BROWN, MATHER.
Am. Boston 1761-1831 London, Eng. B-Bd-DAB-F-T-2-6-182-184.
BROWN, M. E. D. (Eg.)
Am. ac. 19th century Phila., Pa. T.
BROWN, OLIVER MADOX.
Eng. London 1855-1874. B-DNB.
BROWN, OZNI C.
Am. ad. 1934 New Canaan, Conn. M.
BROWN, PAUL. (Ill.)
Am. b. Mapleton, Minn. 1893; ad. 1934 Garden City, L. I., N. Y.
BROWN, [Miss] PLUMA.
Am. ad. 1934 New York. M.
BROWN, RAY. (Ill.)
Am. b. Groton, Conn. 1865. B.
BROWN, ROBERT.
Eng. d. 1753 in London. B-DNB-T.
BROWN, ROY HENRY.
Am. b. Decatur, Ill. 1879; ad. 1934 New York. A-F-W.
BROWN, SONIA F. (S)
Mrs. Gordon Brown.
Am. b. Moscow, Rus. 1890; ad. 1934 New York. A.
BROWN, THOMAS AUSTEN.
Am. Edinburgh, Scot. 1859-1924 San Antonio, Tex. A14-B.
BROWN, THOMAS E.
Am. b. Wilmington, N. C. 1881; ad. 1934 Wash., D. C. A.
BROWN, WALTER FRANCIS.
Am. Prov., R. I. 1853-1929. A027-B.
BROWN, WILLIAM ALDEN.
Am. b. Prov., R. I. 1877; ad. 1934 Same. A.
BROWN, WILLIAM G.
Am. ac. 1844 in Virginia. Fa.
BROWN, WILLIAM MASON.
Am. Troy, N. Y. 1830-1895 Brooklyn, N. Y. A01-F.
BROWNE, ALEXANDER. (Min.)
Eng. ac. 1660-1667 London. DNB-T.
BROWNE, BELMORE.
Am. b. Tomkinsville, L. I., N. Y. 1880; ad. 1934 Banff, Alberta, Can. A-F-W.
BROWNE, BYRON.
Am. ac. 1934 New York. M.
BROWNE, CHARLES FRANCIS.
Am. Natick, Mass. 1859-1920 Waltham, Mass. A017-B-F-T.
BROWNE, GEORGE ELMER.
Am. b. Gloucester, Mass. 1871; ad. 1934 New York. A-B-F-T-W-46.
BROWNE, HABLOT KNIGHT. ["Phiz".] (Cari)
Eng. Lambeth 1815-1882 Brighton. B-DNB-E.
BROWNE, HAROLD PUTNAM.
Am. Danvers, Mass. 1894-1931. A028-F.
BROWNE, HENRIETTÉ SOPHIE.
Mrs. Jules de Saux.
Fr. Paris 1829-1901. B-T.
BROWNE, ISAAC. (S)
Am. 1836-1922 Trenton, N. J. A-19.
BROWNE, J. ARCHIBALD.
Can. b. Liverpool, Eng. 1862; ad. 1935 Lancaster, Ont., Can. M.
BROWNE, JOHN. (Eg.)
Eng. Essex 1741-1801 Walworth. DNB-T.
BROWNE, MARGARET FITZHUGH.
Am. b. Boston 1884; ad. 1934 Boston. A-F.
BROWNE, MATILDA.
Mrs. Frederick Van Wyck.
Am. b. Newark, N. J. 1869; ad. 1934 New York. A-B-F-T.
BROWNE, SYD.
Am. ad. 1934 New York. M.
BROWNE, THOMAS [or Tom]. (Ill.)
Eng. Nottingham 1870-1910 London. B-DNB.
BROWNELL, CHARLES DE WOLF.
Am. b. Prov., R. I., 1822; ac. 1854-1865. B-F-3-15.
BROWNELL, FRANKLIN.
Can. b. New Bedford, Mass. 1857; ac. 1916 Canada. B.
BROWNELL, MATILDA AUCHINLOSS.
Am. b. New York; ad. 1934 Same. A.
BROWNING, AMY KATHERINE.
Mrs. A. K. Dugdale.
Eng. ad. 1934 Suffolk. Wa.
BROWNING, AMZIE DEE.
Am. b. Kent, Wash. 1892; ad. 1934 Tacoma, Wash. A.
BROWNING, G. WESLEY.
Am. b. Salt Lake City, Utah 1868; ad. 1934 Same. A.
BROWNING, ROBERT BARRETT.
Eng. 1848-1912 London. B.
BROWNLEE, ALEXANDER.
Am. d. 1905 Cleveland, O. A6.
BROWNSCOMBE, JENNIE AUGUSTA.
Am. b. Honesdale, Pa. 1850; ad. 1934 New York. A-B-F-T-W-15.
BROXTON, MARGARET KALB. (S)
Am. b. Shrewsbury, Eng. 1909; ad. 1934 Clarendon, Va. A.
BROZIK, JAROSLAV. (Et.)
Am. ad. 1934 Flint, Mich. A.
BROZIK, WENZEL VON [Vacslaw].
Czec. Pilsen 1851-1901 Paris. B-T.
BRUAUDET, LAZARE.
Fr. Paris 1755-1804 Same. T-722.
BRUBAKER, JOHN O. (Ill.)
Am. b. Dixon, Ill. 1875; ad. 1934 Greenport, N. Y. A.
BRUCE, BLANCHE CANFIELD.
Am. b. Wells, Minn. 1880; ad. 1934 Terre Haute, Ind. A.
BRUCE, EDWARD.
Am. b. Dover Plains, N. Y. 1879; ad. 1934 New York. A-F-105-779.
BRUCE, JOSEPH A.
Am. England 1838-1908 Brooklyn, N. Y. A07-B.
BRUCE, WILLIAM BLAIR.
Can. Hamilton, Ont. 1857/9-1906. B.
BRUCE-JOY, ALBERT. *see* Joy, A. B.

BRUCKE-LAJOS, Ludwig.
Hun. Poza 1846-1910. B-T.
BRUCKMAN, W. L.
Dut. b. The Hague 1866; ad. 1934 London. B.
BRUCKNER, C. W.
Am. ac. 1865 in New York. F.
BRUCKNER, Gustav. (Glass-P.)
Am. ex. 1934 New York. M.
BRUEGEL, Abraham [Ryngraaf].
Flem. Belg. 1631-1690 Naples, It. B-T.
BRUEGEL, Ambrosius.
Flem. Antwerp 1617-1675. B-T.
BRUEGEL, Jan [The Elder; called "Velvet"].
Flem. Brussels 1568-1625 Antwerp. B-Bd-C-T-310-722.
BRUEGEL, Jan [The Younger].
Flem. Antwerp 1601-1678. B-Bd-C-T-310-722.
BRUEGEL, Pieter [The Elder].
Flem. Breda 1525-1569 Brussels. B-Bd-C-E-T-V-310-449-722.
BRUEGEL, Pieter [or "Hell"] [The Younger].
Flem. Brussels 1564-1638 Antwerp. B-Bd-C-T-310-722.
BRUEHL, Anton.
Am. ad. 1935 New York. M.
BRUEN, Elizabeth Dorsey.
Am. b. Savannah, Ga. 1908; ad. 1934 Same. A.
BRUESTLE, Bertram G.
Am. b. New York 1902; ad. 1934 Frederick, Md. A.
BRUESTLE, George Matthew.
Am. b. New York 1872; ad. 1934 Same. A-B-F-W.
BRUGES [or Bondol] Jean. (Min)
Flem. ac. 1368/81. B-T.
BRUGES, Master. *see* Master of the Legend of St. Ursula.
BRUGGE, F. van. *see* Master F. V. B.
BRUGGE, Roget van. *see* Weyden, R. van der.
BRÜGGEMANN, Hans. (S)
Ger. Silesia 1480-1540 Same. B-Hs-T.
BRUGGEN, Jan [or Gaspar] van der.
Flem. b. Brussels 1649-1714. B-T.
BRUGGER, Dorothy.
Am. ad. 1934 St. George, S. I., N. Y. M.
BRUGNOLI, Bernardino.
It. ac. 1541-1582 in Verona. T-V.
BRULOTS, Germain.
Fr. Hamburg, Ger. 1902-1932 Marseilles. DBA.
BRULOV, Karl Pavlovitch.
Rus. b. Leningrad 1799; d. 1853 Rome, It. B.
BRUMBACK, [Mrs.] Louise Upton.
Am. Rochester, N. Y. 1872-1929. A026-F.
BRUMIDI, Constantino.
Am. Rome, It. 1805-1880 Wash., D. C. DAB-F-T-26.
BRUMIDI, Lawrence.
Am. 1862-1920 Wash., D. C. A017.
BRUN, Le Charles. *see* Lebrun, C.
BRUN, Le Vigee. *see* Vigee, Lebrun.
BRUNDAGE, William Tyson.
Am. New York 1849-1923. A020-F.
BRUNDRIT, Reginald Grange.
Eng. b. Liverpool 1883; ad. 1934 Skipton, Yorks, Eng. Wa.
BRUNELLESCHI, Filippo. (S)
It. Florence 1377-1446. B-Hs-T-V.
BRUNELLESCHI, Umberto.
It. b. Florence; ac. 1907-1930. B-DBA-T.
BRUNET, Adele Laure.
Am. b. Austin, Tex. 1879; ad. 1934 Dallas, Tex. A.
BRUNET, Jean Jacques Baptiste.
Fr. b. Poitiers 1854; ac. 1930 Paris. DBA-T.
BRUNET, Lorenzo. (Et.)
Sp. ac. 1932. M.
BRUNET-DESBAINES, Louis Alfred.
Fr. b. Havre 1845. B-DBA-T.
BRUNHOFF, Jean de. (Ill.)
Fr. ad. 1934 Paris. M.
BRUNIN, Léon de Meutter.
Belg. b. Antwerp 1861. B-T.
BRUNK, Ann.
Am. ad. 1935 Des Moines, Ia. M.
BRUNNER, Arnold W.
Am. New York 1857-1925. M.
BRUNNER, Bruce Christian.
Am. b. New York 1898; ad. 1934 Flushing, L. I., N. Y. A.
BRUNNER, Ferdinand.
Ger. b. 1870; ad. 1909 Berlin. B-T.
BRUNNER, Karl.
Swi. Berne 1796-1867 Same. B.
BRUNNER, Rudolph.
Am. 1860-1931 New York. A028.
BRUNTON, [Mrs.] Winifred Mabel.
Eng. b. London 1880; ad. 1934 Cairo, Egypt. Wa.
BRUNTON-ANGLESS, [Mrs.] Violet.
Eng. b. Brighouse 1878; ad. 1934 London. Wa.
BRUSASORCI, Domenico Ricci [The Elder].
It. Verona 1494-1567 Same. B-T-722.
BRUSASORCI, Felice Ricci [The Younger].
It. Verona 1540/2-1605 Same. B-T.
BRUSH, George de Forest.
Am. b. Shelbyville, Tenn. 1855; ad. 1934 New York. A-B-C-F-T-W-7-46-71.
BRUSH, Gerome. (P-S)
Am. b. New York; ad. 1934 Dublin, N. H. M.
BRUSSEL, Hermanus van.
Dut. Haarlem 1763-1815 Utrecht. B-T.
BRUYCKER, François Antoine de.
Belg. Ghent 1816-1882. B-T.
BRUYCKER, Jules de. (Et.)
Belg. b. Ghent 1870; ad. 1935 Same. B-T.
BRUYER, Georges Léon.
Fr. b. Paris 1883. DBA.
BRUYN, Bartholomaeus [The Elder].
Ger. Cologne 1493-1553/6. B-T-897.
BRUYN, Bartolomeus [The Younger].
Ger. Cologne 1530-1610. B-T-897.
BRUYN, Theodore de.
Flem. Antwerp 1726-1804 London. B-DNB-T-897.
BRY, Adolf.
Ger. Danzig 1612-1680. M.
BRY, Edith. [Mrs. Benjamin.]
Am. ad. 1935 New York. M.
BRY, Johann Theodor de.
Ger. 1561-1623 Frankfort. T.
BRY, Theodorus [Dirk] de. (Eg.)
Ger. Liége, Belg. 1528-1598 Frankfort. E.

BRYAGIN, A. I.
Rus. ac. 1931. Fa.
BRYAN, William Edward.
Am. b. Iredell, Tex. 1876. M.
BRYANT, [Mrs.] Annie [Nanna] B. Mattheus. (S)
Am. 1871-1933 Waltham, Mass. A030-F.
BRYANT, Charles David Jones.
Aust. b. N.S.W. 1883; ad. 1934 Sydney, N.S.W. Wa.
BRYANT, Everett Lloyd.
Am. b. Galion, O. 1864; ad. 1934 Los Angeles, Calif. A-B-F-T.
BRYANT, Henry.
Am. Hartford, Conn. 1812-1881. B-F-T-3-15.
BRYANT, Henry G.
Am. ad. 1934 New York. M.
BRYANT, [Mrs.] Maude Drew.
Am. b. Wilmington, Del. 1880; ad. 1934 Hendricks, Pa. A.
BRYANT, Wallace.
Am. b. Boston; ad. 1935 Wash., D. C. A12-F.
BRYAXIS. (S)
Gr. ac. 350-312 B.C. in Athens. E-Hs.
BRYDEN, Olivia Mary.
Eng. ad. 1935 Hampstead. Wa.
BRYMNER, William.
Can. Greenock, Scot. 1855-1925 Canada. B-Y01926.
BRYNE, Anne Frances.
Eng. 1775-1837 London. B-DNB.
BRYNE, Letitia. (Eg.)
Eng. 1779-1849 London. B-DNB.
BRYNE, William. (Eg.)
Eng. London 1743-1805 Same. B-DNB.
BRYON, Robert. (Chalks)
Eng. b. Wembley 1905; ad. 1935 Savernake, Marlbough, Eng. M.
BRYSON, Hope Mercereau.
Am. b. St. Louis, Mo. 1887; ad. 1934 San Diego, Calif. A.
BRYSON, James Rose.
Am. ac. 1933 in Chicago. M.
BRYSON, Marion.
Am. ad. 1934 Cleveland, O. M.
BRYSON, Robert Alexander.
Am. b. Marshallton, Del. 1906; ad. 1934 Wilmington, Del. M.
BRYSON, Robert M.
Eng. ac. 1863-1876 in London. B.
BRZESKA. *see* Gaudier-Brzeska.
BUBERL, Caspar. (S)
Am. Bohemia 1834-1899 New York. A1-F.
BUCCI, Anselmo.
It. b. Fossombrone 1887; ad. 1934 Milan. B-DBA.
BUCHANAN, Ella. (S)
Am. b. Preston, Can.; ad. 1934 Los Angeles, Calif. A.
BUCHANAN, Laura.
Ad. 1934 Dallas, Tex. M.
BUCHBINDER, Simon.
Pol. Radzyn 1853-1900 Kracow. T.
BUCHELE, William.
Am. ad. 1934 Toledo, O. M.
BUCHHOLZ, Emmaline.
Am. ad. 1935 Sarasota, Fla. M.
BUCHHOLZ, Fred.
Am. b. Springfield, Mass. 1901; ad. 1935 New York. M.
BUCHNER, Johann Georg.
Ger. Nüremburg 1815-1857 Stuttgart. B-T.
BUCHSBAUM, Elizabeth Mable.
Am. b. Philippine Islands 1909; ad. 1934 Gary, Ind. A.
BUCHTERKIRCH, Armin.
Am. b. Corning, N. Y. 1859; ad. 1915 Rochester, N. Y. A12-B.
BUCK, Adam. (Min.)
Ir. Cork 1759-1853 London. B-M-T.
BUCK, Carl.
Am. ex. 1935 New York. M.
BUCK, Claude.
Am. b. New York 1890; ad. 1934 Chicago. A.
BUCK, Lawrence.
Am. 1865-1929. A026.
BUCK, Roger. (Eg.)
Am. ad. 1934 New York. M.
BUCK, Samuel. (Eg.)
Eng. 1696-1779. B-DNB-T.
BUCK, Walter. (Eg.)
Am. ex. 1934 New York. M.
BUCK, William H.
Am. Norway 1840-1888 New Orleans, La. F-144-183.
BUCKLER, John.
Eng. Calbourne 1770-1851 London. B-DNB-T.
BUCKLER, John Chesrel.
Eng. 1793-1894. B-T.
BUCKLEY, Jeanette.
Am. ac. 1900 in Chicago. B.
BUCKLEY, John Michael.
Am. b. Boston 1891; ad. 1934 Rockfort, Me. A.
BUCKLIN, Bradley A.
Am. Little Falls, N. Y. 1824-1915 Troy, N. Y. A012.
BUCKLIN, William Savery.
Am. Phalanx, N. J. 1851-1928 Same. A025-B-F.
BUCKNER, Richard.
Eng. ac. 1840-1879 in London. B-T.
BUCKSHORN, Joseph.
Dut. ac. 1670 in London. DNB.
BUDAGOSSKY.
Rus. ex. 1935 London. M.
BUDD, Charles Jay.
Am. So. Shadock, N. Y. 1859-1926 New York. A13-B-F-W14.
BUDD, George.
Eng. ac. 1756 in London. B-DNB.
BUDD, Herbert Ashwin.
Eng. b. Ford Green 1881; ad. 1934 London. Wa.
BUDELL, Ada.
Am. b. Westfield, N. J. 1873; ad. 1934 Same. A-F.
BUDELL, Hortense. (S)
Am. b. Lyons, Fr.; ad. 1934 Westfield, N. J. A-F.
BUDWORTH, William Sylvester.
Am. b. Brooklyn, N. Y. 1861; ad. 1934 Mt. Vernon, N. Y. A-B-F-T.
BUECKELAER, Joachim. *see* Beuckelaer, J.
BUEHLER, Lytton Briggs.
Am. b. Gettysburg, Pa. 1888; ad. 1935 Provincetown, Mass. A12-F.

BUEHR, KARL ALBERT.
Am. b. Ger. 1866; ad. 1934 Chicago. A-B-F-W.
BUEHR, MARY G. HESS. (Min.)
Mrs. Karl Albert Buehr.
Am. b. Chicago; ad. 1934 Same. A.
BUELL, ABEL. (Ag.)
Am. Killingsworth, Conn. 1742-1825 New Haven, Conn. F-2-7.
BUELL, ALICE STANDISH. (Et)
Am. b. Oak Park, Ill.; ex. 1935 New York. M.
BUELL, HORACE HENRY.
Am. d. 1919 New York. A17.
BUENA, VILLEGES.
Sp. ac. 19th century in Spain. M.
BUERGEL [or Bürgel] HUGO.
Ger. Landshut 1853-1903 Munich. T.
BUFANO, BENIAMINO. (S)
Am. ex. 1935 San Fran., Calif. M.
BUFF, CONRAD.
Am. b. Swi. 1886; ad. 1934 Los Angeles, Calif. A.
BUFFALMACCO, BUONAMICO.
It. Florence 1262-1340. T-V.
BUFFINGTON, ELIZA.
Am. b. Springfield, Mass. 1883; ad. 1934 Madison, N. J. A.
BUFFORD, J. H. (Eg.)
Am. ac. 1850-1871. F.
BUFFUM, KATHERINE G. (Et.)
Am. Prov., R. I. 1884-1922 Phila., Pa. A019-F.
BUGATTI, REMBRANDT. (S)
It. b. 1883. B.
BUGBIRD, MARY BAYNE.
Am. ad. 1934 Madison, N. J. M.
BUGIARDINI, GIULIANO [or Giulio].
It. Florence 1475-1554 Same. B-C-T-V-722.
BUGLINO, JOSEPH. (S)
Am. b. Palermo, It. 1878; ad. 1934 New York. A.
BUGLIONI, BENEDETTO.
It. Florence 1461-1521. T.
BUGLIONI, SANTI. (S)
It. 1494-1576 Florence. T.
BUHLER, AUGUSTUS.
Am. d. 1920 Gloucester, Mass. A017.
BUHLER, ZUBER. *see* Zuber-Buhler.
BUHOLZ, FRANCES.
Am. ex. 1934 Minn., Minn. M.
BUHOT, FÉLIX HILAIRE. (Et.)
Fr. Valogones 1847-1898 Paris. B-T-880.
BUISSERET, LOUIS.
Belg. ad. 1934 Brussels; ex. 1934 Pittsburgh, Pa. M.
BUK, ULRICH.
Am. b. 1889; ad. 1935 New York. M.
BUKOVAC, BLAISE.
It. b. Ragusa, 1884. B.
BULAND, JEAN EUGÈNE.
Fr. Paris 1852-1926 Same. B-DBA.
BULCOCK, PERCY.
Eng. Norton 1877-1914 Liverpool. M.
BULL, CHARLES LIVINGSTON.
Am. 1874-1932. A28-B-F-W17.
BULL, JOHAN. (Ill.)
Am. b. Oslo, Nor. 1893; ad. 1934 New York. M.
BULLARD, [Mrs.] MARION R.
Am. b. Middletown, N. Y.; ad. 1934 Woodstock, N. Y. A.
BULLEID, GEORGE LAWRENCE.
Eng. 1858-1934 Bath, Eng. T-Wa.
BULLER, AUDREY.
Am. ad. 1934 New York. M.
BUMSTEAD, ETHEL QUINCY.
Am. b. London 1873; ad. 1915 Cambridge, Mass. A12-F.
BUNAND-SEVASTOS, FANNY.
Am. b. France 1905; ad. 1934 Wash., D. C. A.
BUNBURY, HENRY WILLIAM. (Cari.)
Eng. Suffolk 1750-1811 Keswick. B-DNB-E-T.
BUNCE, JOHN OSCAR. (S)
Am. b. New York 1867; ad. 1934 Ridgewood, N. J. W.
BUNCE, LOUIS DEMOTT.
Am. ad. 1934 Portland, Ore. M.
BUNCE, WILLIAM GEDNEY.
Am. Hartford, Conn. 1840-1916 Same. A014-B-C-DAB-F-T-3-15-71.
BUNCHO, TANI.
Jap. ac. 1804. J., Vol. 2, page 51.
BUNDASZ, RUDOLF.
Am. ex. 1933 Cleveland, O. M.
BUNDEL, WILLEM VAN DEN.
Dut. 1575-1653 Delft. B-T.
BUNDY, EDGAR.
Eng. Brighton 1862-1922. B.
BUNDY, JOHN ELWOOD.
Am. No. Car. 1853-1933 Cinn., O. A030-B-F-W16.
BUNEL, JACOB.
Fr. Mai 1558-1614 Paris. T-722.
BUNGER, FRANCES.
Am. b. New York 1911; ad. 1934 Mt. Vernon, N. Y. A.
BUNKER, DENNIS MILLER.
Am. New York 1861-1890 Boston. F-T.
BUNKER, PHOEBE A.
Am. b. Brooklyn, N. Y. 1863; ad. 1915 Merrick, L. I., N. Y. A12-B.
BUNKYO, NORMURA.
Jap. d. 1910. J., Vol. 2, page 105.
BUNNER, ANDREW FISHER.
Am. New York 1841-1897. B-T.
BUNNER, RUDOLPH F.
Am. ad. New York. A28-B-F.
BUNNEY, JOHN WHARLTON.
Eng. England 1828-1882 Venice, It. B.
BUNNY, RUPERT CHARLES WOLSTON.
Aust. b. Victoria 1864; ad. 1934 Same. B.
BUNRIN, SHIOGAWA.
Jap. d. 1877. J., Vol. 2, page 105.
BUNYEI, YAMAMOTO.
Jap. ex. 1930 Tokyo. M.
BUON, [or Buono], BARTOLOMMEO. (S)
It. Venice 1410-1464/70. B-Hs-T.
BUON [or Buono], GIOVANNI. (S)
It. ac. 1281 in Venice. B-Hs.
BUONACCORSI, PERINO [or Piero] DEL VAGA. (P-S)
It. Florence 1500-1547 Rome. B-C-E-Hs-T-V-722.
BUONACCORSO, NICCOLÒ DI.
It. Siena 1348?-1388 Same. T.
BUONARROTI. *see* Michelangelo.

BUONAVENTURA. *see* Segna di B.
BUONCONSIGLIO, GIOVANNI [Marescalco].
It. ac. 1495/7-1535/7 Venice. B-T-V.
BUONGIORNO, DONATUS. (Mu.)
Am. b. Solofra, It. 1865. A20-B-F.
BUONI [or Buono] SILVESTRO DE.
It. Naples 1420-1480. B-T.
BUONINSEGNA, DUCCIO DI.
It. Siena 1260?-1339? B-T-V.
BUONTALENTI, BERNARDO TIMANTE.
It. Florence 1536-1608. B-T-V.
BUPALUS [Son of Archermus]. (S)
Gr. ac. 540 B.C. at Chios. E-Hs.
BURBANK, ELBRIDGE AYER.
Am. b. Harvard, Ill. 1858; ad. 1934 Muskogee, Okla. A20-B-F-T-W.
BURBANK, WILLIAM EDWIN.
Am. Boston, Mass. 1866-1922. A020-B-F.
BURCH, EDWARD.
Eng. London 1730-1814. DNB-T.
BURCH, HENDRIK VAN DER.
Dut. ac. 1650-1660 Delft. T.
BURCHARD, ALFRED WILLIAM.
Am. b. Falls City, Neb. 1901; ad. 1934 Same. A.
BURCHELL, NATHANIEL J.
Am. New York 1866-1934 New Rochelle, N. Y. M-Obit. N. Y. papers 7-11-1934.
BURCHFIELD, CHARLES E.
Am. b. Ashtabula Harbor, O.; ad. 1934 Gardenville, N. Y. A-F-779.
BURCK, JACOB.
Am. ex. 1934 Woodstock, N. Y. M.
BURCKEL, HEINRICH.
Ger. 1802-1869. T.
BURCKMAIR. *see* Burgkmair.
BURCKMANN, J.
Bav. 1761; ac. 1806 Amsterdam. T.
BURD, CLARA MILLER.
Am. b. New York; ad. 1934 Same. A.
BURDETTE, HATTIE E.
Am. ad. 1934 Wash., D. C. A-B.
BURDICK, HORACE ROBBINS.
Am. b. East Killingly, Conn. 1844; ad. 1934 Malden, Mass. A-B-F-15.
BUREAU, LÉON. (S)
Fr. b. Limoges 1866. T.
BURFORD, ROBERT.
Eng. 1791-1861 London. B-DNB.
BURFORD, THOMAS. (Eg.)
Eng. ac. 1740-1765 in London. B-DNB.
BURGDORFER, RENÉ H.
Am. b. Paris 1908; ad. 1934 Kansas City, Mo. A.
BURGDORFF, FERDINAND.
Am. b. Cleveland, O. 1881; ad. 1934 Pebble Beach, Calif. A-F.
BURGER, ANTON.
Ger. Frankfort 1824-1905 Cronberg. B-T.
BURGER, FRANCES.
Am. b. New York 1911; ad. 1934 Mt. Vernon, N. Y. A.
BURGER, JOHANNES. (Eg.)
Swi. ac. 1859 in Munich, Ger. B-T.
BURGERS, HENRICUS JACOBUS.
Dut. Arnheim 1834-1899 Paris. B-C-T.
BURGES [or Bondol], JEAN DE. (Min.)
Flem. ac. 1368/81. B-T.
BURGESS, ALICE LINGLOW.
Mrs. Wilson Harley Warner.
Am. b. St. Louis 1880; ad. 1934 New Haven, Conn. A.
BURGESS, GELETT. (Ill.)
Am. b. Boston 1866; ad. 1934 New York. A.
BURGESS, HENRIETTA.
Am. b. Auburn, Calif. 1899; ad. 1934 Seattle, Wash. A.
BURGESS, IDA JOSEPHINE.
Am. b. Chicago; ad. 1934 Woodstock, N. Y. A-F-T-W.
BURGESS, JOHN BAGNOLD.
Eng. Chelsea 1829-1897 London. B-C-DNB-T.
BURGESS, JOHN CART.
Eng. 1798-1863 Leamington. B-DNB.
BURGESS, RUTH PAYNE.
Mrs. John W. Burgess.
Am. b. Montpelier, Vt.; d. 1934 New York. A-B-F-M-W-Obit. Art News, 3-17-1934.
BURGESS, THOMAS.
Eng. ex. 1766-1786 London. B-DNB.
BURGESS, THOMAS.
Eng. 1784?-1807 London. B-DNB.
BURGESS, WILLIAM.
Eng. 1749?-1812 London. B-DNB.
BURGESS, WILLIAM. (Eg.)
Eng. 1755-1813 Fleet. B-DNB.
BURGESS, WILLIAM OAKLEY. (Eg.)
Eng. d. 1844 England. B-DNB.
BURGH, HENDRIK VAN DER.
Dut. The Hague 1769-1858 Same. B-T.
BURGHERS [or Burgers], MICHIEL. (Eg.)
Dut. Amsterdam 1653?-1727 Oxford, Eng. B-DNB.
BURGIS, WILLIAM. (Eg.)
Am. b. London; ac. 1718-1731 New York. DAB-F-T-2-7.
BURGKMAIR, HANS [The Elder].
Ger. Augsburg 1473-1531 Same. B-Bd-C-E-T-722-801.
BURGKMAIR, HANS [The Younger].
Ger. Augsburg 1500?-1559. C-T-801.
BURGKMAIR, THOMAN.
Ger. ac. 1460-1480 Augsburg. C.
BURGOS, JUAN DE. *see* Juan de B.
BURI, MAX ALFRED.
Swi. Berhoud 1868-1925 Interlaken. B-DBA-T.
BURKE, MARJORIE.
Am. ad. 1934 Louisville, Ky. M.
BURKE, MAY CORNELIA.
Am. b. Brooklyn, N. Y. 1903; ad. 1934 New York. A.
BURKE, ROBERT E.
Am. b. Winsted, Conn. 1884; ad. 1934 Nashville, Ind. A.
BURKE, RUTH.
Am. b. Canada; ad. 1934 New York. M.
BURKE, THOMAS. (Eg.)
Ir. Dublin 1749-1815 London. B-DNB-T.
BÜRKEL, HEINRICH.
Ger. Pirmasens 1802-1869. B-T.
BURKHARD, HENRI.
Am. b. New York 1892; ad. 1934 Leonia, N. J. A.
BURKHARD, VERONA LORRAINE.
Am. ex. 1934 in Cinn., O. M.

BURLEIGH, Averil M.
Eng. ex. 1934 in London. M.

BURLEIGH, Sidney Richmond.
Am. Little Compton, R. I. 1853-1931. A028-B-F-W16.

BURLEIGH-BRUHL, Louis.
Eng. b. Bagdad, Turkey; ad. 1934 London. Wa.

BURLIN, [Mrs.] Natalie Curtis.
Am. d. 1921 in Paris. A18.

BURLIN, Paul.
Am. New York 1886; ad. 1934 Paris. A-DBA-F-W.

BURLING, Gilbert.
Am. 1843-1895. B-F-T-15.

BURLINGAME, Charles Albert.
Am. Bridgeport, Conn. 1860-1930. A28-B-F.

BURLINGAME, G.
Am. ex. 1935 New York. M.

BURLINGAME, Sheila. (S)
Am. b. Kansas 1894; ad. 1934 Clayton, Mo. A.

BURLIUK, David.
Am. b. Rus. 1882; ad. 1934 New York. A.

BURMAN, Thomas. (S)
Br. d. 1674. DNB-T.

BURN, Rodney Joseph.
Eng. b. Palmer's Green 1899; ad. 1935 London. Wa.

BURNAND, Eugène Charles Louis.
Swi. London 1850-1921 Paris. B-C-DBA-T.

BURNARD, Nevill Northey. (S)
Eng. 1818-1878 London. B-DNB.

BURNE, Harry. (Ill.)
Am. ad. 1934 New York. M.

BURNE-JONES, [Sir] Edward Coley.
Eng. Birmingham 1833-1898 London. B-Bd-C-DNB-E-T-311.

BURNE-JONES, [Sir] Philip.
Eng. ac. 1886 in London. B-T.

BURNET, James M.
Eng. 1788-1816 London. B-DNB-722.

BURNET, John.
Scot. Edinburgh 1784-1868 London. B-DNB-722.

BURNEY, Edward Francis.
Eng. Worcester 1760-1848 London. B-T.

BURNHAM, Anita Willets.
Mrs. Alfred Newton Burnham.
Am. b. Brooklyn, N. Y. 1880; ad. 1934 Winnetka, Ill. A-B.

BURNHAM, Roger Noble. (S)
Am. b. Boston 1876; ad. 1934 Los Angeles, Calif. A-Cs-F-W.

BURNIER, Richard.
Dut. The Hague 1826-1884 Düsseldorf, Ger. B-T.

BURNITZ, Karl Peter.
Ger. Frankfort 1824-1886 Same. B-C-T.

BURNS, Jean Douglas.
Br. b. Cumbernauld 1903; ad. 1934 Same. Wa-Y1928.

BURNS, Maurice King.
Am. ad. 1934 New York. M.

BURNS, Michael J. (Ill.)
Am. ac. 1898 in Boston, Mass. B-T.

BURNS, Robert.
Scot. b. Edinburgh 1869; ad. 1934 Same. Wa.

BURNSIDE, Cameron.
Am. b. London 1887; ad. 1934 Paris. A-DBA-F-W.

BURNSIDE, [Mrs.] Lucile Hitt.
Am. d. 1921 Wash., D. C. A24.

BURPEE, William Partridge.
Am. b. Rockland, Me. 1846; ad. 1934 East Orange, N. J. A-B-F-T-W.

BURR, Alexander Holenlohe.
Scot. Edinburgh 1835-1899. B-T.

BURR, Frances.
Mrs. Frances Burr Ely.
Am. b. Boston 1890; ad. 1934 New York. A.

BURR, George Brainerd.
Am. b. Middletown, Conn.; ad. 1934 Old Lyme, Conn. A.

BURR, George Elbert. (Et.)
Am. b. Cleveland, O.; ad. 1934 Phoenix, Ariz. A-F-W.

BURR, Harold Saxton.
Am. b. Lowell, Mass. 1889; ad. 1934 New Haven, Conn. A.

BURR, John.
Scot. Edinburgh 1831-1892 London. B-T.

BURRAGE, Mildred Giddings.
Am. b. Portland, Me. 1890; ex. 1934 New York. A28.

BURRIDGE, Frederick Vango. (Et.)
Eng. ad. 1934 London. M.

BURROUGHS, Bryson.
Am. Hyde Park, Mass. 1869-1934 New York. A-B-F-T-W-1-Obit. N. Y. papers, 11-7-1934.

BURROUGHS, Dorothy.
Eng. ex. 1935 London. M.

BURROUGHS, Edith Woodman. (S)
Mrs. Bryson Burroughs.
Am. Riverdale, N. Y. 1871-1916 Flushing, L. I., N. Y. A13-B-F-46-701.

BURROUGHS, Edward R.
Am. ad. 1935 Dayton, O. M.

BURROWS, H. L.
Am. ad. 1935 New York. M.

BURT, Albin R.
Br. d. 1842. DNB.

BURT, Charles. (Eg.)
Am. Edinburgh, Scot. 1822-1892 Brooklyn, N. Y. F-T-7-40.

BURT, Charles Thomas.
Eng. Birmingham 1823-1902. B-T.

BURT, John.
Am. d. 1745 in Boston, Mass. T.

BURT, Louis.
Am. b. New York 1900; ad. 1934 Bronx, N. Y. A.

BURT, Mary Theodora.
Am. b. Phila., Pa.; ad. 1934 Same. A.

BURTON, Arthur Gibbs.
Am. ex. 1934 Manchester, Vt. M.

BURTON, [Sir] Frederick William.
Ir. Limerick 1816-1900 Kensington, Eng. B-DNB-E-T.

BURTON, Harriet B. (S)
Mrs. Crawford Burton.
Am. b. Cinn., O. 1893; ad. 1934 New York. A.

BURTON, [Mrs.] MARJORIE DE KRAFT.
Am. b. Germantown, Pa. 1886; ad. 1934 Winchester, Mass. A.
BURTON, SAMUEL CHATWOOD.
Am. b. Manchester, Eng. 1881; ad. 1934 Minn., Minn. A.
BURTON, WILLIAM SHAKESPEARE.
Eng. London 1825-1916 Same. B-Y01917.
BURY, ADRIAN.
Eng. b. 1895; ac. 1933 London. M.
BURY, GAYNER ELIZABETH.
Eng. b. London 1890; ad. 1934 Same. Wa.
BUSBEE, JACQUES.
Am. b. Raleigh, N. C. 1870; ad. 1934 Steeds, N. C. W.
BUSBY, JANET.
Am. ad. 1934 Chicago. M.
BUSCH, CLARENCE FRANCIS.
Am. b. Phila., Pa. 1887; ad. 1934 Babylon, N. Y. A.
BUSCH, PAUL.
Am. ex. 1935 New York. M.
BUSCH, WILHELM.
Ger. Hanover 1832-1908 Mechtshausen. B-E-T-880.
BUSENBENZ-SCOVILLE, VIRGINIA.
Am. b. Chicago 1896; ad. 1934 Salisbury, Conn. A.
BUSH, CHARLES GREEN. (Cari.)
Am. Boston 1842-1909 Camden, So. Car. A07-B-2.
BUSH, DACRE.
Am. ad. 1934 Boston, Mass. M.
BUSH, ELLA SHEPARD.
Am. b. Galesburg, Ill.; ad. 1934 Sierra Madre, Calif. A-B.
BUSH, [Mrs.] IRVING T.
Am. ex. 1934 New York. M.
BUSH, JOSEPH H.
Am. Frankfort, Ky. 1794-1865. F.
BUSH, MARGARET S.
Am. ad. 1934 Boston, Mass. M.
BUSH, NORTON.
Am. b. Rochester, N. Y. 1834; ac. 1878 San Fran., Calif. B-C-F-T-15.
BUSH, REGINALD E. J.
Eng. b. 1869; ad. 1934 Bristol. M.
BUSH-BROWN, HENRY KIRKE. (S)
Am. Ogdensburg, N. Y. 1857-1935 Wash., D. C.
A-B-Cs-F-T-W-Obit. N. Y. papers, 3-2-1935.
BUSH-BROWN, MARGARET LESLEY.
Mrs. Henry Kirke Bush-Brown.
Am. b. Phila., Pa. 1857; ad. 1934 Wash., D. C. A-B-F-T.
BUSH-BROWN, MARJORIE. *see* Conant, Marjorie.
BUSHBY, ASA.
Am. 1834-1896. Fa.
BUSHNELL, JOHN. (S)
Eng. 1640?-1701 London. DNB.
BUSI, GIOVANNI DE'. *see* Cariani, G. de' B.
BÜSINCK, LUDWIG [or Louis].
Ger. b. Allemagne 1590; ac. 1643. B-T.
BUSON, YOSA.
Jap. 1716-1783. J., Vol. 2, page 76.
BUSS, ROBERT WILLIAM.
Eng. London 1804-1875 Same. B-DNB-T.
BUSSCHE, JOSEPH EMANUEL VAN DER.
Belg. Antwerp 1837-1908 Brussels. B-T.
BUSSON, CHARLES.
Fr. Montiore 1822-1908 Paris. B-C-DBA-T.
BUSSON, GEORGE LOUIS CHARLES.
Fr. Paris 1859-1933 Versailles. B-DBA-T.
BUSSY, ALBERT SIMON.
Fr. b. Dóle 1869. B-DBA.
BUSTELLI, FRANCESCO ANTONIO. (S)
Swi. b. near Locarno; ac. 1754. M.
BUSTI, AGOSTINO. *see* Agostino di B.
BUTADES, [Called Dibutades]. (S)
Gr. Sicyon; ac. 600 B.C. B-E.
BUTCHER, ENID. (Et.)
Eng. ac. 1930. M.
BUTENSKY, JULES LÉON. (S)
Am. b. Russia 1871; ad. 1935 Ramah, Romona, N. Y. A20-F.
BUTERA, JOSEPH.
Am. ex. 1935 Boston. M.
BUTIN, ULYSSE LOUIS AUGUSTE. (Et.)
Fr. St. Quentin 1838-1883 Paris. C.
BUTINONE, BERNARDINO [Jacopi].
It. Treviglio 1435/6-1507/8. T.
BUTLER, ANDREW R.
Am. b. Yonkers, N. Y. 1896; ad. 1934 New York. A.
BUTLER, CHARLOTTE W.
Am. b. Boston 1872; ad. 1934 Same. M.
BUTLER, EDWARD BURGESS.
Am. Lewiston, Me. 1853-1928. A24-F.
BUTLER, [Lady] ELIZABETH SOUTHERDEN THOMPSON.
Eng. Lausanne, Swi. 1851-1933 Ireland. B-C.
BUTLER, GEORGE BERNARD.
Am. New York 1838-1907 Croton Falls, N. Y. A07-B-F-T-15.
BUTLER, GEORGE EDMUND.
Eng. b. Southampton 1872; ad. 1934 Richmond. Wa.
BUTLER, HOWARD RUSSELL.
Am. New York 1856-1934 Princeton, N. J. A-B-F-T-W.
BUTLER [or Büttler], JOSEPH NIKLAUS.
Swi. Küssnach 1822-1885 Düsseldorf, Ger. B-T.
BUTLER, LEONARD C.
Am. ad. 1935 Buffalo, N. Y. M.
BUTLER, MARGARET. (S)
Aust. b. Hellington, N. Z. 1890. DBA.
BUTLER, MARY.
Am. b. Phila., Pa.; ad. 1934 Same. A-F-W.
BUTNER, ["Kitty"] KATHRYN ELIZABETH.
Am. b. Phila., Pa. 1914; ad. 1935 Atlanta, Ga. M.
BUTTAR, EDWARD JAMES.
Eng. b. London 1873; ad. 1934 Cricklade. Wa-Y1929.
BUTTERFIELD, FRANCIS.
Eng. b. Bradford, Eng.; ex. 1934 London. M.
BUTTERI, GIOVAN MARIA.
It. 1540-1606. T-V.
BUTTERSACK, BERNHARD.
Ger. Württemberg 1850-1899. B-T.
BUTTERWORTH, JAMES E.
Am. b. Isle of Wight 1817; ac. 1850 New York. T.
BUTTERWORTH, THOMAS.
Eng. ac. 1813-1827 in London. B-T.

BUTTINONE, Bernardino Jacobi. (Min.)
It. Treviglio 1436-1507 Milan. B-T.
BÜTTNER, G. H.
Ger. ac. 1883-1891 in Munich. B-T.
BUTTON, Albert Prentice.
Am. b. Lowell, Mass. 1872. A28-B.
BUTTON, Joseph P.
Am. Germantown, Pa. 1864-1931 Phila., Pa. A028.
BUTTRE, John Chester. (Eg.)
Am. Auburn, N. Y. 1821-1893 Ridgewood, N. J. F-T.
BUTTS, John.
Ir. b. Cork; d. 1764 Dublin. B-DNB-T.
BUVELOT, Abraham Louis.
Swi.-Aust. Swi. 1814-1888 Melbourne, Aust. T.
BUXTON, Robert Hugh.
Eng. b. Harrow; ad. 1934 London. Wa.
BUXTON, William Graham.
Eng. ac. 1855-1892 in London. B.
BUYCK, Edward P.
Belg. b. Bruges 1888. M.
BUYER, Bernice E.
Am. b. Cleveland, O. 1903; ad. 1934 Dayton, O. M.
BUYLE, Robert.
Belg. b. Flanders 1895. DBA.
BUYS, Cornelis I.
Dut. ac. 1516-1524. B-T.
BUYS, Cornelis, II.
Dut. ac. 1524-1546 Alkmaar. B-T.
BUYS, Cornelis, III.
Dut. Amsterdam 1745-1826. B-T.
BUYS, Jacobobus.
Dut. Amsterdam 1724-1801. B-T.
BUYTEWECH, Willem [The Elder].
Dut. Rotterdam 1585/90-1630. B-T.
BUYTEWECH, Willem [The Younger].
Dut. Rotterdam 1625/6-1670. B-T.
BYARD, Dorothy Randolph.
Am. b. Germantown, Pa.; ad. 1934 Norwalk, Conn. A.
BYE, Arthur Edwin.
Am. b. Phila., Pa. 1885; ad. 1934 Holicong, Pa. A.
BYE, Marcus de.
Dut. The Hague 1639-1688. T.
BYER, Alexander.
Am. ex. 1935 New York. M.
BYER, Nicholas.
Eng. b. Norway; d. 1681 Richmond, Eng. B-DNB.
BYER, Samuel.
Am. b. Warsaw, Pol. 1885; ad. 1934 Chicago. A.
BYERS, Maryhelen.
Am. b. Seattle, Wash. 1902; ad. 1934 Same. A.
BYERS, Ruth Felt.
Am. b. Council Bluffs, Ia.; ad. 1934 Same. A.
BYFIELD, John. (Eg.)
Eng. ac. 1830/5 London. B-DNB-T.
BYLERT, Jan van.
Dut. Utrecht 1603-1671 Same. B-T.
BYLINA, Michal. (Eg.)
Pol. b. 1904; ac. 1934 Warsaw. M.
BYNG [or Bing], Edward and Robert [Brothers].
Eng. ac. 1723-1781 in England. T.
BYRAM, Ralph Shaw.
Am. b. Germantown, Pa. 1881; ad. 1934 Same. A-B.
BYRNE, Ellen Albert.
Am. b. Fort Moultrie, S. C.; ad. 1934 Wash., D. C. A.
BYRON-BROWNE, George.
Am. b. Yonkers, N. Y. 1908; ad. 1934 New York. A.
BYRUM, Ruthven Holmes.
Am. b. Grand Junction, Mich. 1896; ad. 1934 Anderson, Ind. A.
BYSS [or Biss], Johann Rudolf.
Swi. Soleure 1660-1738 Würzburg. B-T
BYSTROM, Johan Niklas. (S)
Swe. Philipstad 1783-1838 Rome, It. B-E-T.
BYWATERS, Jerry.
Am. b. Paris, Tex. 1906; ad. 1934 Dallas, Tex. A.
BYZANTIOS. (S)
Swe. ac. 1120-1165. 824.

CABANE, Edourd.
Fr. b. Paris 1857. B-DBA.
CABANEL, Alexandre.
Fr. Montpelier 1823-1889 Paris. B-Bd-C-E-T.
CABANISS, Lila Marguerte.
Am. b. Savannah, Ga.; ad. 1934 Same. A.
CABANISS, Mary Hope.
Am. b. Savannah, Ga.; ad. 1934 Same. A.
CABAT, Louis.
Fr. b. Paris 1812-1893 Same. B-T.
CABEL, A. *see* Arentsz, Arent.
CABIANCA, Francesco. (S)
It. 1665-1737. Fa.
CABIANCA, Vincenzo.
It. b. Verona 1827; d. Rome 1902. B-T.
CABOT, Amy.
Am. ad. 1934 Boston, Mass. M.
CABOT, W. Channing.
Am. 1868-1932 New Haven, Conn. A029.
CABRERA, Miguel.
Mex. Oaxaca 1695-1768 Same. M.
CACHOUD, François Charles.
Fr. b. Chambéry 1866. B-DBA-T.
CADDICK, Richard.
Eng. Liverpool 1750-1823. B.
CADDICK, William.
Eng. Liverpool 1719-1794. B-T.
CADDY, Alice. (Ill)
Mrs. Ben Lucien Burman.
Am. ad. 1935 Hollywood, Calif. M.
CADEL, Eugène.
Fr. b. Paris; ac. 1899-1929 Same. B-DBA.
CADEL, G. M. (Eg.)
Am. b. Italy; ad. 1934 Chicago. M.
CADELL [or Catell], Arnaldo [or Arnolfo]. (S)
Sp. ac. 12-13 centuries in Spain. Fa.
CADELL, Francis Campbell Bolleau.
Scot. b. Edinburgh 1883; ad. 1934 Same. Wa.
CADENA, Luis.
So. Amer. Quito, Equador 1830-1899 Same. M.

CADENASSO, Giuseppe.
Am. Genoa, It. 1858-1918 San Fran., Calif. A15.

CADENHEAD, James.
Scot. Aberdeen 1858-1927. Wa01929.

CADES, Giuseppe.
It. Rome 1750-1799 Same. B-T.

CADMUS, Egbert.
Am. b. Bloomfield, N. J. 1868; ad. 1934 Hadlyme, Conn. A.

CADMUS, Paul.
Am. b. 1905; ad. 1934 New York. A29-M.

CADORIN, Ettore. (S)
Am. b. Venice, It. 1876; ad. 1934 Santa Barbara, Calif. A-B-Cs-F-T-W.

CADORIN, Guido.
It. b. 1892. M.

CADWALADER-GUILD, Emma Marie. (S)
Am. b. Zanesville, O. 1843. T.

CADY, Henry.
Am. b. Warren, Pa. 1849; ad. 1934 Same. A.

CADY, Walter Harrison. (Ill.)
Am. b. Gardner, Mass. 1877; ad. 1934 Brooklyn, N. Y. A-F-T-W.

CADZOW, James.
Scot. b. Carluke 1881; ad. 1934 Dundee. Wa.

CAESAR, [Mrs.] Doris Porter. (S)
Am. ad. 1934 New York. M.

CAFFERTY, James H.
Am. Albany, N. Y. 1819-1869 New York. B-F-T-15.

CAFFI, Cavaliere Ippolito.
It. Bellune 1809-1866. B-T.

CAFFIÉRI, Hector.
Eng. b. Cheltenham 1847; d. 1932. B-Y01933.

CAFFIÉRI, Jean Jacques. (S)
Fr. Paris 1725-1792 Same. B-Hs-T.

CAGGIANO, Joseph A.
Am. ad. 1927 New York. M.

CAGLE, Charles.
Am. b. Beersheba Springs, Tenn. 1907; ad. 1934 Nashville, Tenn. A.

CAGLIARI, Carlo [or Carletto].
It. Venice 1570-1596. C-T.

CAGLIARI FAMILY.
It. ac. 16-17th centuries in Italy. T.

CAGLIARI, Gabriele.
It. Venice 1568-1631. C-T.

CAGNACCI [or Caulassi], Guido.
It. Rimini 1601-1681 Vienna, Aus. B-C-T-722.

CAHILL, Arthur.
Am. b. San Fran., Calif.; ad. 1934 Pasadena, Calif. M-722.

CAHILL, Katherine Kavannaugh.
Am. b. Four Oaks, Ky.; ad. 1934 Los Angeles, Calif. A.

CAHILL, Paul T.
Am. ad. 1934 Toledo, O. M.

CAHILL, William Vincent.
Am. b. Syracuse, N. Y.; d. 1924 Chicago. A21-B-F.

CAILLE, Léon.
Fr. Merville 1836-1907. B-T.

CAILLEBOTTE, Gustave.
Fr. 1848-1894 Paris. B-T.

CAIN, Auguste. (S)
Fr. Paris 1822-1894 Same. B-Hs-T.

CAIN, Charles William. (Et.)
Eng. b. Surrey 1893; ad. 1934 Beckenham. Wa.

CAIN, Georges Jules Auguste.
Fr. Paris 1856-1919 Same. B-DBA-T.

CAIN, Joseph ["Jo"].
Am. b. New Orleans, La. 1904; ad. 1934 New York. A.

CAINELLI, Carlo. (Et.)
It. Riverto 1896-1925 Florence. M.

CALABRESE, Il, Cavaliere [Mattia Preti].
It. Taverna 1613-1699 Malta. B-Bd-C-T-722.

CALAME, Alexander.
Swi. Vevey 1810-1864 Menton, Fr. B-C-T-722.

CALAMIS. *see* Kalamis.

CALANDRA, David. (S)
It. b. Turin 1856. T-798.

CALAPAI, Letterio.
Am. b. Roxbury, Mass. 1902; ad. 1934 New York. A.

CALBET, Antoine.
Fr. b. Engayrac 1860. B-DBA.

CALCAGNI, Tiberio. (S)
It. Florence 1532-1565 Rome. B-Hs-T.

CALCAR [or Kalcker], Johan Stephan van.
Dut. Calcar 1499-1546/50 Naples, It. B-E-T-V-722.

CALDARA, Polidoro. *see* Caravaggio, P. C.

CALDECOTT, Randolph. (Ill.)
Eng. Chester 1846-1886 St. Augustine, Fla. B-DNB-E-T.

CALDENBACH. *see* Kaldenbach.

CALDER, Alexander. (S)
Am. Phila., Pa. 1898; ad. 1934 Roxbury, Conn. M.

CALDER, Alexander Milne. (S)
Am. Scot. 1846-1923 Phila., Pa. A20-B-F-T-Ta.

CALDER, Alexander Stirling. (S)
Am. b. Phila., Pa. 1870; ad. 1934 New York. A-B-Cs-F-T-W-46-779.

CALDER, Josephine Ormond.
Mrs. John R. Calder.
Am. ad. 1934 Toledo, O. M.

CALDERON, Ludmilla.
Am. ex. 1935 West New York, N. J. M.

CALDERON, Phillip Hermogenes.
Eng. Poitiers, Fr. 1833-1898 London. B-Bd-C-T.

CALDWELL [or Cadwall], James. (Eg.)
Eng. London 1739-1789 Same. B-DNB-T.

CALDWELL, Edmund.
Eng. ac. 1880 in London; d. 1930. Y01931.

CALDWELL, William H. (Et.)
Am. Rochester, N. Y. 1837-1899. A1.

CALET. *see* Callet.

CALIARI, Benedetto.
It. Verona 1538?-1598. B-T-722.

CALIARI, Carlo [or Carletto].
It. Verona 1510-1596 Zani. B-T.

CALIARI, Gabriele. (S)
It. Verona 1568-1631. B-T-722.

CALIARI, Paolo. *see* Véronèse, Paolo.

CALIFANO, Michael.
Am. b. Italy; ad. 1935 New York. M.

CALIGA, Isaac Henry.
Am. b. Auburn, Ind. 1857; ad. 1934 Provincetown, Mass. A-B-F-T-47-181.
CALIGIANI, Alberto.
It. ad. 1934 Fiesole; ex. 1934 Pittsburgh, Pa. M.
CALLAHAN, Kenneth L.
Am. b. Boston 1907; ad. 1934 Seattle, Wash. A.
CALLAIS, Horace de.
Fr. ac. 1880. M.
CALLCOTT, [Sir] Augustus Wall.
Eng. London 1779-1844 Same. B-C-DNB-E-T.
CALLCOTT, Frank.
Am. b. San Marco, Tex. 1891; ad. 1934 New York. M.
CALLENDER, Benjamin. (Eg.)
Am. Boston 1773-1856 Northfield, Mass. F-T-7.
CALLENDER, F. Arthur.
Am. b. Boston, Mass.; ac. 1909-1923. A12-B.
CALLENDER, Joseph. (Eg.)
Am. Boston, Mass. 1751-1821 Same. F-T.
CALLET, Antoine François.
Fr. Paris 1741-1823 Same. B-T.
CALLIMACHUS. (S)
Gr. ac. 5th century B.C. in Athens. E.
CALLOT, Henri Eugène.
Fr. b. La Rochelle 1875. B-DBA.
CALLOT, Jacques. (Eg.)
Fr. Nancy 1592-1635 Same. B-E-T-312-722.
CALLOW, John.
Eng. 1822-1878 Lewisham. B-DNB.
CALLOW, William.
Eng. Greenwich 1812-1908 London. B-DNB-T.
CALMA, Monico C.
Am. b. Anda, P. I. 1907; ad. 1934 Chester Springs, Pa. A.
CALMAN, Edward.
Am. ad. 1934 New York. M.
CALOSCI [Prof.], Arturo.
It. ad. 1935 Florence. B-T.
CALRAET, Abraham. *see* Kalraet, A.
CALS, Adolphe Félix.
Fr. Paris 1810-1880 Honfleur. B-T.
CALVAERT, Denys [Dionisio Fiamingo].
Flem. Antwerp, Belg. 1540-1619 Bologna, It. B-E-T-648-722.
CALVERLEY, Charles. (S)
Am. Albany, N. Y. 1833-1914 Essex Fells, N. J. AXI-DAB-F-T-Ta-15.
CALVERT, Charles.
Eng. Glossop Hall 1785-1852 Bowness. B-E.
CALVERT, Edward.
Eng. Devonshire 1799-1883 Hackney. B-DNB-E-T.
CALVERT, Raisley. (S)
Br. d. 1794. DNB.
CALVI di Bergolo, Grogorio.
It. b. Turin 1904. DBA.
CALVIN, Katherine.
Am. ad. 1934 Akron, O. M.
CALVIN, Mildred Bell.
Am. b. New York 1908; ad. 1934 Fairfield, Conn. M.
CALYO, Niccolino Vicomte.
Am. Naples, It. 1799-1884 New York. F-6.
CAMAINO, Tino da Siena. (S)
It. 1315-1337 Naples. B-Hs.
CAMALDOLESE, Don Silvestro. (Illuminator)
It. b. 1350 in Florence. M.
CAMARASA, Hermengildo Anglade y.
Sp. ac. 1930. M.
CAMARENA, Jorge Gonzalez.
Mex. b. 1908. M.
CAMAX-ZOEGGER, Marie Anne.
Fr. Paris; ac. 1930 Same. DBA.
CAMBIASO, Luca [or Luchetto].
It. Moneglia 1527-1585 Madrid, Sp. B-C-E-T-722.
CAMBIO, Arnolfo di. (S)
It. 1260-1302 Florence. B-Hs.
CAMBON, Charles Antoine.
Fr. Paris 1802-1875 Same. B-T.
CAMBON, Henri Joseph Armand.
Fr. Montauban 1819-1885. B-T.
CAMDEN, Harry Poole. (S)
Am. b. Parkersburg, W. Va. 1900; ad. 1934 Ithaca, N. Y. A-Cs.
CAMERINO, Arcangelo di Cola da.
It. ac. 1416-1430 in Florence. M.
CAMERMIO, Boccato de. *see* Boccatis.
CAMERON, Charles Scott. (Eg.)
Scot. ac. 1767-1772 in London. B-T.
CAMERON, [Sir] David Young. (Et.)
Scot. b. Glasgow 1865; ad. 1934 Kippen. B-T-313-825-880.
CAMERON, Edgar Spier. (Mu.)
Am. b. Ottawa, Ill. 1862; ad. 1934 Chicago. A-B-F-T-W.
CAMERON, Elizabeth Wallace.
Am. b. Woodland, Pa.; ad. 1934 Pittsburgh, Pa. A.
CAMERON, Hugh.
Scot. Edinburgh 1835-1918. B-T.
CAMERON, John.
Am. ac. 1876 New York. M.
CAMERON, Katherine. *see* Kay, Katherine.
CAMERON, Marie Gelon.
Mrs. Edgar Spicer Cameron.
Am. b. Paris, Fr.; ad. 1934 Chicago, Ill. A.
CAMERON, Mary.
Mrs. Alexis Miller.
Scot. b. Edinburgh; ac. 1900-1921. B-T-Y01922.
CAMERON, William Ross. (Et.)
Am. ad. 1934 Alameda, Calif. A.
CAMERON-MENK, Hazel.
Mrs. Oswen W. Menk.
Am. b. St. Paul, Minn. 1888; ad. 1934 Clarendon, Va. A.
CAMFFERMAN, Margaret Gove.
Am. b. Rochester, Minn.; ad. 1934 Langley, Wash. A.
CAMFFERMAN, Peter Marienus.
Am. b. The Hague, Holland 1890; ad. 1934 Langley, Wash. A.
CAMILLIANI Family [Gucci].
It. ac. 16th century in Florence. T.
CAMM, Robert.
Aust. b. England 1847; d. 1933 Adelaide, So. Aust. M.
CAMMARATA, Peter.
Am. ad. 1935 Union City, N. J. M.

CAMMILLIERI, NICOLAS.
It. ac. 18th century. M.
CAMOIN, CHARLES.
Fr. b. Marseilles 1879; ex. 1934 London. B-DBA-M.
CAMP, CAMILLE J. B. VAN.
Flem. Brussels 1834-1891. B-T.
CAMP, JEAN DE.
Belg. ac. 1517 Brussels. M.
CAMP, JOSEPH DE. *see* De Camp, J.
CAMPAGNA, GIROLAMO. (S)
It. Verona 1549/50-1626 Same. B-Hs-T.
CAMPAGNA, PEDRO. *see* Kempener, P.
CAMPAGNOLA, DOMENICO. (Eg.)
It. Padua 1482/4-1562/4. B-T-V-722.
CAMPAGNOLA, GUILIO. (Eg.)
It. 1482-1564. B-T-V-722.
CAMPANA, PEDRO DE. *see* Kempener, P.
CAMPBELL, ALEXANDER.
Am. ac. 1775. M-786.
CAMPBELL, ALICE.
Am. ad. 1934 Toledo, O. M.
CAMPBELL, ANNE BANNARD. (Min.)
Am. Virginia 1879-1927 New York. A24.
CAMPBELL, [Sir] ARCHIBALD.
Eng. 1739-1791 London. B-T.
CAMPBELL, BLENDON REED.
Am. b. St. Louis, Mo. 1872; ad. 1934 New York. A-B-F-T.
CAMPBELL, C. ISABEL.
Am. b. Brooklyn, N. Y.; ad. 1934 Phila., Pa. A.
CAMPBELL, CHARLES M.
Am. b. Dayton, O. 1905; ad. 1934 Cleveland, O. A.
CAMPBELL, CORA A.
Am. b. Phila., Pa.; ad. 1934 Same. A.
CAMPBELL, EDMUND SIMMS. (Cart.)
Am. b. Freehold, N. J.; ad. 1934 Charlottesville, Va. A.
CAMPBELL, EDWARD MORTON.
Am. Hannibal, Mo. 1858-1911. B.
CAMPBELL, FLOY.
Am. b. Kansas City, Mo. 1875; ad. 1934 Same. A.
CAMPBELL, GEORGINE.
Am. New Orleans, La. 1861-1931. M.
CAMPBELL, HARRIET DUNN.
Mrs. W. D. Campbell.
Am. b. Columbus, O.; ad. 1934 Same. A.
CAMPBELL, [Mrs.] HELENA EASTMAN OGDEN.
Am. b. Eastman, Ga. 1879; ad. 1934 New York. A-B-F.
CAMPBELL, INA CONNER.
Am. ad. 1934 Pittsburgh, Pa. M.
CAMPBELL, ISABELLA FROWE.
Am. b. Rockford, Ill. 1874; ad. 1934 Hollywood, Calif. A.
CAMPBELL, JAMES.
Eng. Liverpool 1828-1903 London. B-T.
CAMPBELL, JOHN HENRY.
Ir. Dublin 1757-1829. B-T.
CAMPBELL, MAUD HOSKINSON.
Am. b. Erie, Pa. 1865. B.
CAMPBELL, ORLAND.
Am. b. Chicago 1890; ad. 1934 New York. A.
CAMPBELL, ORSON D.
Am. Fillmore, Utah 1876-1933 Provo, Utah. M.
CAMPBELL, SARA WENDELL. (Ill.)
Am. ad. 1934 New York. A.
CAMPBELL, THOMAS. (S)
Scot. Edinburgh 1790-1858 London. B-DNB-Hs-T.
CAMPBELL, T. E.
Am. ad. 1934 Suffern, N. Y. M.
CAMPBELL, V. FLOYD. (Et.)
Am. b. Port Austin, Mich.; d. 1906 Morton, Pa. A6.
CAMPBELL-GRAY, IAN.
Scot. ex. 1934 New York. M.
CAMPDEN, HARRY P. (S)
Am. b. 1900; ad. 1934 Ithaca, N. Y. M.
CAMPELLO, ANTONIO EMMANUEL.
Por. ac. 1540 in Portugal. B.
CAMPEN [or Kampen], JACOB VAN.
Dut. Haarlem 1590-1657/8 Randenbroek. B-T.
CAMPENDONK, HEINRICH.
Ger. b. 1889; ad. 1934 Düsseldorf. M.
CAMPHAUSEN, WILHELM.
Ger. Düsseldorf 1818-1885 Same. B-C-E-T.
CAMPHUYSEN, GOVAERT DIRCKSZ.
Dut. Gorkum 1623/4-1672 Amsterdam. B-C-T.
CAMPHUYSEN, JOACHIM GOVERTSZ.
Dut. Gorkum 1601/2-1659 Amsterdam. B-C-T.
CAMPHUYSEN, RAPHAEL DIRKSZ.
Dut. Gorkum 1598-1657 Amsterdam. B-C-T-903.
CAMPI, CAVALIERE ANTONIO. (S)
It. Cremona 1536-1591. B-C-T.
CAMPI, BERNARDINO.
It. Cremona 1522-1590/5 Reggio. B-E-T.
CAMPI, GÌULIO.
It. Cremona 1500-1572. B-E-T.
CAMPIDOZLIO, MICHAEL ANGELO. *see* Pace, M. A.
CAMPIGLI, MASSIMO [or Maximo].
It. b. Florence 1895; ad. 1935 Paris. M.
CAMPIGLIA, GIOVANNI DOMENICO.
It. Lucca 1692-1762/8. B-T.
CAMPIN, ROBERT.
[Master of Flémalla].
Flem. 1375-1444. B-T-629-649.
CAMPION, GEORGE BRYANT.
Br. England 1796-1870 Munich, Ger. B-DNB-T.
CAMPIONE [or Campo], GIOVANNI FILIPPO DEL.
Flem. ac. 1600-1638. T.
CAMPIONE [or Campo], GIOVANNI DI UGO DA. (S)
It. ac. 1348 in Bergamo. B-Hs-T.
CAMPO. *see* Campione.
CAMPOTOSTO, HENRY.
Belg. b. Brussels; ac. London 1870; d. 1910. B-T.
CAMPS. *see also* De Camps.
CAMPS, LEONARDO.
Sp. b. Malaga; ac. 1864 Barcelona. B-T.
CAMUCCINI, VINCENZO.
It. Rome 1771/3-1844 Same. B-E-T.
CANACHIUS OF SICYON. (S)
Gr. ac. 516 B.C. in Sicyon. B-E-Hs.
CANADÉ, VINCENT.
Am. b. Italy 1879; ad. 1934 New York. A-F.

CANADIAN ARTISTS. *see* books 730-893.
also consult Year Book of the Arts in Canada.
CANADIAN INDIAN SCULPTURE.
Totem Poles. 1850-1865. M.
CANAL, GILBERT VON.
Bavarian. b. Laibach 1849. B-T.
CANALE. *see* Canaletto.
CANALETTO [or Canale], ANTONIO.
It. Venice 1697-1768 Same. B-Bd-E-T-722.
CANALETTO [or Canale], BERNARDO BELLOTTO.
It. Venice 1720/4-1780 Warsaw, Pol. B-Bd-C-T.
CANALS Y LAMBI, RICARDO.
Sp. b. Barcelona 1876. B-T.
CANDEE, GEORGE EDWARD.
Am. b. New Haven, Conn. 1838. F-3.
CANDELL, VICTOR G. (Ill.)
Am. ad. 1934 New York. M.
CANDIDO [or Candid], PIETRO. (S)
Belg. Bruges 1548-1586 Munich, Ger. B-C-Hs-T.
CANDLIN, [Mrs.] ABBIE.
Am. b. Farmington, Wis. 1885; ad. 1934 Long Island City, N. Y. A.
CANE, ALICE NORCROSS.
Am. b. Louisville, Ky.; ad. 1934 Same. A.
CANE, ELSIE M.
Am. b. Brooklyn, N. Y. 1890; ad. 1934 Same. A.
CANEDO, ALEJANDRO DE.
Mex. ex. 1935 New York. M.
CANEVARI, GIOVANNI BATTISTA.
It. Genoa 1789-1876 Rome. T.
CANFIELD, BIRTLEY KING. (S)
Am. Ravenna, O. 1866-1912 Same. A10-B.
CANFIELD, [Mrs.] FLAVIA.
Am. 1844-1930. A027
CANGIASO, LUCA. *see* Cambiaso, Luca.
CANINI, GIOVANNI ANGELO.
It. Rome 1617-1666 Paris. B-E-T.
CANLASSI. *see* Cagnacci.
CANNING-FREEMAN, E.
Eng. ex. 1934 Lewes, Sussex. M.
CANNON, FLORENCE V.
Am. b. Camden, N. J.; ad. 1934 Same. A.
CANNON, HUGH. (S)
Am. b. Ireland; ac. 1926 Phila., Pa. F-Ta.
CANNON, [Mrs.] JENNIE VENNERSTROM.
Am. b. Albert Lea, Minn. 1869; ad. 1934 Berkeley, Calif. A.
CANO, ALONSO. (P-S)
Sp. Granada 1601-1667 Same. B-C-E-Hs-T-722-823.
CANO, JOACHÍN JOSÈ.
Sp. b. Sèville 1784. B-T.
CANO, DE LA PEÑA, EDUARDO.
Sp. Madrid 1823-1897. B-T.
CANON, HANS VAN STRASCHIRIPKA.
Aus. Vienna 1829-1885 Same. B-C-T.
CANONICA, PIETRO. (S)
It. b. Turin 1869/72. B-T.
CANOT, PIERRE CHARLES. (Eg.)
Fr. France 1710-1777 Kent, Eng. B-DNB.
CANOVA, ANTONIO. (S)
It. Possagna 1757-1822 Venice. B-E-Hs-T-651-652-660-849.
CANTALAMESSA-PAPOTTI, NICOLA. (S)
It. Ascoli 1833-1910 Rome. T.
CANTARINI, SIMON DE PESARO. [Il Pesarese].
It. Oropezza 1612-1648 Verona. B-E-T-722.
CANTER, ALBERT M.
Am. b. Norma, N. J. 1892; ad. 1934 New York. A.
CANTINE, "Jo."
Mrs. J. A. Cantine.
Am. ad. 1934 Woodstock, N. Y. M.
CANTRALL, HARRIET M.
Am. b. Springfield, Ill.; ad. 1934 Same. A.
CANTWELL, JAMES.
Am. Syracuse, N. Y. 1856-1926 Same. A025.
CANZIANI, ESTELLA L. M.
Eng. b. London 1887; ad. 1934 Same. Wa.
CAPARN [Miss] RHYS. (S)
Am. ex. 1935 New York. M.
CAPECCHI, JOSEPH. (S)
Am. b. Florence, It. 1889. Cs.
CAPEL, WILLEM ADRIAENSZ.
Dut. ac. 1639 in Utrecht. T.
CAPGRAS, GEORGES.
Fr. b. Joinville-le-Pont 1866. B-DBA.
CAPILELLI, BERNARDINO.
It. Siena 1589-1639. B-Bd-T.
CAPITANI, LORENZO.
It. b. Tuscany; ex. 1935 New York. M.
CAPOLINO, GERTRUDE ROWAN.
Am. b. Phila., Pa. 1899; ad. 1934 Same. A.
CAPOLINO, JOHN JOSEPH.
Am. b. Phila., Pa. 1896; ad. 1934 Same. A.
CAPON, GEORGES ÉMILE.
Fr. b. 1890; ex. 1933 Chicago, Ill. DBA-M.
CAPON, WILLIAM.
Eng. Norwich 1757-1827 Westminster. B-DNB.
CAPONE, GAETANO.
Am. Maiori, It. 1864-1920 New York. A017-B-T.
CAPORALI, BARTOLOMMEO.
It. ac. 1442-1509? in Perugia. T.
CAPPELLE, JAN VAN DE.
Dut. Amsterdam 1624/5-1679 Same. C-T.
CAPPIELLO, LEONETTO.
It. b. Leghorn 1875. B-DBA-T.
CAPPONI. *see* Raffaellino del Garbo.
CAPPS, CHARLES M. (Eg)
Am. ad. 1935 Wichita, Kan. M.
CAPRILE, VINCENZO.
It. b. Naples 1856. B-T.
CAPROTTI, GUIDO.
It. b. Milan; ac. 1929. DBA.
CAPUCCINO, IL. *see* Strozzi, Bernardo.
CAPUTO, ULISSE.
It. b. Salerno 1872. B-DBA.
CAQUET, JEAN GABRIEL.
Fr. Paris 1749-1802 Same. B-T.
CARABAIN, JACQUES FRANÇOIS.
Dut. b. Amsterdam 1834; ac. 1883 Brussels. B-C-T.
CARABELLI, JOSEPH. (S)
Am. Italy 1850-1911 Cleveland, O. A9.
CARACCI. *see* Carracci.
CARACCIOLO, GIOVANNI BATTISTA.
It. Naples 1570-1637 Same. B-T.
CARADOSSI, VITTORIO. (S)
It. ac. 1910 in Florence. T.
CARADOSSO. [Foppa Ambrogio]. (S)
It. Milan 1445?-1527. Hs-T-V.

CARAGLIO, Giovanni Jacopo.
It. 1500-1565 Verona. T-V.
CARAN D'ACHE, Emmanuel Poiré.
Rus. Moscow 1858-1909. B-E-T.
CARAVAGE. *see* Caravaggio.
CARAVAGGIO, Michel Angelo Merisi.
It. Caravaggio 1560/5-1609 Ponto. B-Bd-C-E-T-314-722.
CARAVAGGIO, Polidoro Caldara da.
It. Caravaggio 1490/1500-1543 Messina. B-Bd-C-E-T-V-722.
CARBEE, Scott Clifton.
Am. b. East Concord, Vt. 1860; ad. 1934 Boston. A-B-W.
CARBONATI, Antonio. (Et.)
It. b. Mantua 1893; ad. 1934 Rome. DBA-M.
CARBONELL Y SELVA, Don Miguel.
Sp. 1855-1896 Barcelona. C-T.
CARBONERO, José Moreno.
Sp. b. Malaga 1860. B-T.
CARD, Judson.
Am. d. 1933 New York. A030.
CARDELL, [Mrs.] Frank Hale.
Am. d. 1905 Boston, Mass. A06.
CARDELLA, Liberato.
It. ac. 1800-1850. M.
CARDELLO, Tomasco.
It. ac. 1468 in Romagna. Fa.
CARDI, Lodovico.
It. Cigoli 1559-1613 Rome. B-E-T.
CARDISCO, Marco [Calavrese].
It. 1486-1542 Naples. T-V.
CARDON, Anthony [or Antoine]. (Eg.)
Eng. Brussels, Belg. 1772-1813 London. B-DNB-T.
CARDON, Phillip. (Eg.)
Eng. d. 1817? in London. DNB-T.
CARDOSO. *see* Souza-Cardoso.
CARDUCCI, [or Carducho], Bartolomé.
Sp. Florence, It. 1560-1608/10 Madrid. B-C-E-T-722.
CARDUCCI [or Carducho], Vincenzo.
Sp. Florence, It. 1578-1638 Madrid. B-C-T-722.
CAREL, Dorothy A.
Am. ex. 1934 Cincinnati, O. M.
CARENA, Felice.
It. b. 1880; ad. 1934 Florence, It. M.
CARENO [or Carreno] DE MIRANDA, Juan.
Sp. Ociedo 1614-1685 Madrid. B.
CARÊSME, [or Carême], Philippe.
Fr. Paris 1734-1796 Same. B-T.
CAREVALE, Fra [Bartolommeo].
see Corradini, B.
CAREW, [Mrs.] Berta. (Min.)
Mrs. Frank Carew.
Am. b. Springfield, Mass. 1878; ad. 1934 Los Angeles, Calif. A.
CAREW, John Edward. (S)
Ir. Ireland 1785?-1868 London. B-DNB.
CAREW, Thomas A. (S)
Am. ac. in Boston 17th century. M.
CAREY, Constance Beddoe.
Mrs. H. K. Carey.
Am. b. Birmingham, Eng.; ad. 1934 Phila., Pa. A.
CAREY, Rosalie McGill.
Am. b. Baltimore, Md. 1898; ad. 1934 Riderwood, Md. A.
CARGILL, Jessie Taylor. (Cart.)
Am. b. Viola, Ark. 1885; ad. 1934 Cleveland, O. W.
CARI, G. de. (Ill.)
Fr. ac. 1820 in Paris. B-T.
CARIANI, Giovanni de Busi.
It. Fuipiano 1485/90-1547/8 Venice. B-T.
CARIANI, Varaldo J.
Am. b. Renazzo, It. 1897; ad. 1934 Springfield, Mass. A.
CARIATA, Giovanni. (S)
Am. Rome 1865-1917 New York. F.
CARINGS, Alexander. *see* Keerincx, A.
CARL, Katherine Augusta.
Am. b. New Orleans, La.; ad. 1934 New York. A-B-F-T-W11.
CARLAND, Dorothea Chandler.
Am. ad. 1934 Toledo, O. M.
CARLANDI, Onorato.
It. b. 1848. Fa.
CARLÈGLE, Émile Charles.
Fr. b. Aigle 1877. DBA.
CARLES, Arthur B. Jr.
Am. b. 1882; ad. 1934 Phila., Pa. A-F.
CARLETON, Anne.
Am. ad. 1934 Lynn, Mass. M.
CARLETON, Clifford. (Ill.)
Am. b. Brooklyn, N. Y. 1867; ad. 1934 New York. A-F-T-W13.
CARLETON, William T.
Am. d. 1890. M.
CARLEVARIS, Luca [Zenobio].
It. Udine 1665-1731 Venice. B-T.
CARLI, Auguste.
Fr. Marseilles 1868-1930. DBA.
CARLIER, Camille Marie Louise.
Fr. b. Villemomble; ac. 1904-1930. B-DBA.
CARLILE [or Carlisle] Anne. (Min.)
Br. ac. 1658-1680. DNB-T.
CARLIN, John.
Am. Phila., Pa. 1813-1891 New York. B-F-T-2-6.
CARLINE, Sydney William.
Br. 1888-1929. Wa1929-Y01929.
CARLINI, Agostino. (P-S)
It. b. Genoa; ac. 1760-1790 London. DNB.
CARLINO, Charles I.
Am. b. New York 1902; ad. 1934 Same. A.
CARLISLE. *see also* Carlile.
CARLISLE, George James Howard. [9th Earl].
Eng. 1843-1911 London. B-T.
CARLISLE, Mary Helen.
Am. b. South Africa; d. 1925 New York. A22-B.
CARLO [or Carletto].
(Son of Paul Véronèse).
It. 1572-1596. 722.
CARLONI, Giambattista.
It. Genoa 1594?-1680 Same. C.
CARLOS [King of Portugal].
[Ferdinand Louis Marie François].
Por. Lisbon 1863-1908 Same. B-T.
CARLSE, James. (Eg.)
Eng. Shoreditch 1798-1855. B-DNB.
CARLSEN, Dines.
Am. b. New York 1901; ad. 1935 Falls Village, Conn. A-F-W.

CARLSEN, EMIL.
Am. Denmark 1853-1932 New York.
A28-B-F-T-W16-46.
CARLSEN, FLORA BELLE.
Mrs. Harald Carlsen.
Am. b. Cleveland, O. 1878; ad. 1934 New York. A.
CARLSON, CHARLES JOSEPH.
Am. b. Eskilstuna, Swe. 1866; ad. 1934 Brooklyn, N. Y. A.
CARLSON, EDWARD W.
Am. b. Chicago 1883; ad. 1934 Same. A.
CARLSON, HARRY.
Am. b. Brooklyn, N. Y. 1895; ad. 1934 Same. A.
CARLSON, JOHN FABIAN.
Am. b. Sweden 1875; ad. 1934 Woodstock, N. Y. A-F-W-46.
CARLSUND, OTTO G.
Swe. b. Leningrad, Rus.; ad. 1929 Paris. DBA.
CARLU, NATACHA.
Fr. ac. 1930 Paris. Fa.
CARLYLE, FLORENCE.
Can. Galt, Can. 1864-1923. B-M.
CARMAN, ALBERT.
Am. ex. 1935 New York. M.
CARMAN, EVA L. (Min.)
Am. ad. 1934 New York. A.
CARMEN, ALBERT.
Am. ad. 1934 Jamaica, L. I., N. Y. M.
CARMER, DOROTHY ROSS.
Am. b. Somerville, N. J. 1883; ad. 1915 Elizabeth, N. J. A12.
CARMICHAEL, FRANKLIN.
Can. b. Orillia, Ont.; ad. 1935 Lansing, Ont. M.
CARMICHAEL, HERBERT.
Eng. b. Newcastle 1856; ad. 1935 London. M.
CARMICHAEL, JAMES WILSON.
Eng. Newcastle 1800-1868 Scarborough. B-E-T.
CARMICHAEL, [Miss] WARREE.
Am. b. Elba, Ala. 1910; ad. 1934 Montgomery, Ala. A.
CARMIENCKE, JOHN HERMANN.
Am. Hanover, Ger. 1810-1867 Brooklyn, N. Y. B-F-T.
CARMONA, MANUEL SALVADOR. (Eg.)
Sp. Madrid 1730-1807 Same. B-T.
CARMONTELLE, LOUIS CARROGIS DE.
Fr. Paris 1717-1806 Same. B-T.
CARNE, MICHELE FELICE [Abbé d'Carnel].
Fr. ac. 1879-1893 in Paris. B.
CARNEVALE, CARMEN RICHARD.
Am. ad. 1934 Pittsburgh, Pa. A.
CARNEVALE, FRA. *see* Corradini, Bartholommeo.
CARNEY, BETTY.
Am. ex. 1934 Minn., Minn. M.
CARNOVALE, DOMENICO.
It. b. Modena; ac. 1564. B-T.
CARO-DELVAILLE, HENRY.
Fr. Bayonne 1876-1928. B-DBA-T.
CAROLSFELD [or Karolsfeld]. *see* Schnorr von K.
CAROLUS-DURAN, CHARLES ÉMILE AUGUSTE.
Fr. Lille 1838-1917 Paris. B-C-DBA-E-T.
CARON, PAUL.
Can. ad. 1935 Montreal, Can. M.
CARONI, EMMANUEL. (S)
It. b. Rancate 1826; ac. 1867 Paris. B-T.
CAROSELLI, ANGELO.
It. Rome 1585-1652 Same. T.
CAROTO, GIOVANNI FRANCESCO.
It. Venice 1478/82-1555. B-T-V.
CAROZZI, GIUSEPPE.
It. b. 1864. M.
CARPACCIO, VITTORIO [or Vittore] SCARPAZA.
It. Venice 1450/5-1522/6.
B-Bd-C-E-T-V-315-722.
CARPEAUX, JEAN [or Jules] BAPTISTE. (P-S)
Fr. Valenciennes 1827-1875 Courbevoie.
B-E-Hs-T-191.
CARPENDER, ALICE PREBLE TUCKER DE HAAS.
Am. b. Boston; d. 1920 New York. A018.
CARPENTER, [Miss] A. M.
Am. b. 1887; ad. 1934 Abilene, Tex. A.
CARPENTER, BERNARD V.
Am. b. Foxboro, Mass.; ad. 1934 Buffalo, N. Y. A.
CARPENTER, DUDLEY SALTONSTALL.
Am. b. Nashville, Tenn. 1880; ad. 1935 La Jolla, Calif. B-F-T.
CARPENTER, ELLEN M.
Am. b. Killingly, Conn. 1831. B-F-T-15.
CARPENTER, FLETCHER H.
Am. b. Providence, R. I. 1879; ad. 1934 Rochester, N. Y. A.
CARPENTER, FRANCIS BICKNELL.
Am. Homer, N. Y. 1830-1900 New York.
A1-B-C-DAB-F-T-W1-4-15-37-46.
CARPENTER, FREDERICK GREENE.
Am. b. Nashville, Tenn. 1882; ad. 1934 Webster Groves, Mo. A-B-F-W.
CARPENTER, GEORGE MULFORD.
Am. b. Brooklyn, N. Y. 1875. B-T.
CARPENTER, MARGARET SARAH [née Geddes].
Mrs. William G. Carpenter.
Eng. Salisbury 1793-1872 London. B-DNB-T.
CARPENTER, MILDRED BAILEY.
Mrs. Frederick Greene Carpenter.
Am. b. St. Louis, Mo. 1894; ad. 1934 Webster Groves, Mo. A.
CARPENTIER, ADRIEN.
Swi.-Eng. b. Swi.; ac. 1760-1768 London. DNB.
CARPENTIER, EVARISTE.
Belg. b. 1845; ac. in Antwerp. B-T.
CARPI, ANTONIO MARIA DA.
It. ac. 1495 Venice. B-T.
CARPI, GIROLAMO DA.
It. Ferrara 1501-1556/69 Baruffalda.
B-E-T-V.
CARPI, UGO DA.
It. 1450-1525 Rome. B-E-T-V.
CARPIONE, GIULIO [The Elder].
It. Venice 1611-1674 Verona. B-T.
CARR, ALICE ROBERTSON. (S)
Am. b. Roanoke, Va.; ad. 1934 New York. A20-F-M.
CARR, DAVID.
Eng. b. London 1847; ac. 1890 Same. B-C-T.
CARR, GENE. (Cart)
Am. b. New York 1881. A20-F-W16.
CARR, JOHNSON.
Eng. England 1743/4-1765. B-DNB.

CARR, Lyell.
Am. Chicago 1857-1912 New York. A010-B-T.
CARR, Michael Carmichael.
Am. 1881-1929. A026.
CARRÀ, Carlo D.
It. b. 1881; ad. 1934 Milan. DBA.
CARRACCI, Agostino.
It. Bologna 1557-1602 Parma. B-Bd-C-E-T-722.
CARRACCI, Annibale.
It. Bologna 1560-1609 Rome. B-Bd-C-E-T-722.
CARRACCI, Antonio Marziale.
[Son of Agostino Carracci.]
It. Venice 1583-1618 Rome. B-T.
CARRACCI, Franceschino.
It. Bologna 1559-1622 Rome. B-T.
CARRACCI, Lodovico [or Ludovico].
It. Bologna 1555-1619 Same. B-Bd-C-E-T-722.
CARRAND, Louis Hilaire.
Fr. Lyons 1821-1899 Same. B-T.
CARRARI, Baldassare. [Il. Vecchio]
It. ac. 1354 Forli. B-T.
CARRÉ, Ben.
Am. b. Paris 1883; ad. 1934 Hollywood, Calif. M.
CARRÉ [or Carrée], Michel.
Dut. The Hague 1657-1727/47 Alkmaar. B-T.
CARREÑO DE MIRANDA, Juan.
Sp. Avila 1614-1685. B-C-T-722-823.
CARRERA, Augustin.
Sp. b. Madrid 1878; ac. in Paris. B-DBA.
CARRERE, John M.
Am. Rio de Janeiro, Brazil 1858-1911 New York. M.
CARRICK [or Craig], Edward A. (Eg.)
Eng. b. London 1904; ad. 1934 Same. Wa.
CARRICK, Thomas Heathfield. (Min.)
Eng. Carlisle 1802-1875 London. B-DNB.
CARRICK, Valery. (Ill.)
Rus. b. Russia; ac. 1934 Norway. M.
CARRIER, Aguste Joseph.
Fr. Paris 1800-1875 Same. B-T.
CARRIER-BELLEUSE, Albert Ernest. (S)
Fr. Anizy 1824-1887 Sèvres. B-T.
CARRIER-BELLEUSE, Louis Robert.
Fr. Paris 1848-1913 Same. B-DBA-T.
CARRIER-BELLEUSE, Pierre.
Fr. Paris 1851-1933 Same. B-DBA-T.
CARRIER-BELLEUSE, Victor Armand François. (S)
Fr. 1824-1887. B.
CARRIERA, Rosalba.
It. Venice 1675-1757 Same. B-Bd-C-T-722-756.
CARRIERÈ, Eugène.
Fr. Gournay 1849-1906 Paris. B-DBA-T-748.
CARRIERÈ, Jean René. (S)
Fr. ac. 1930 Paris. DBA-T.
CARRIÈS, Jean Joseph Marie. (S)
[Outstanding genius in pottery designing.]
Fr. Lyons 1855-1894. B-T.
CARRIGAN, William L.
Am. b. San Fran., Calif. 1868; ad. 1934 Falls Village, Conn. A.
CARRISS, Henry T.
Am. Phila., Pa. 1850-1903 Same. A04.
CARROLL, Harriet I.
Am. b. Erie, Pa. 1872; ad. 1934 Same. A.
CARROLL, John.
Am. b. Wichita, Kan. 1892; ad. 1934 Woodstock, N. Y. A.
CARROLL, Léon.
Am. ad. 1934 Darien, Conn. M.
CARROLL, Robert Joseph.
Am. b. Syracuse, N. Y. 1904; ad. 1934 Same. A.
CARROLL, [Mrs.] Ruth.
Am. b. Lancaster, Pa. 1899; ad. 1934 New York. M.
CARROTHERS, Grace Neville.
Am. b. Abbington, Neb. 1882; ad. 1934 Tulsa, Okla. A.
CARRUCCI, Jacopo [Il. Pontormo].
It. Pontormo 1493/4-1557/8 Florence. B-C-E-T-V-511-722.
CARRY, Marion Katherine.
Am. b. Newport, R. I. 1905; ad. 1934 Same. A.
CARSE, Alexander. [Old Carse].
Scot. ac. 1812-1820 Edinburgh. B-DNB-T.
CARSON, Frank. [E. Francis].
Am. b. Waltham, Mass. 1881; ad. 1934 Boston. A.
CARSPEKEN, George Lewis.
Am. Pittsburgh, Pa. 1884-1905 Burlington, Ia. A05-B.
CARSTAIRS, James Stewart.
Am. 1892-1932 New York. Y01933.
CARSTENS, Armus Jacob.
Dan. St. Jurgensby 1754-1798 Rome, It. B-C-E-T-722.
CARSTENS, Julius Victor.
Ger. d. 1849 Nusse, Aus. B-T.
CARTE, Anto [or Antoine].
Belg. b. Mons 1886; ad. 1934 Brussels. B.
CARTELLIER, Pierre. (S)
Fr. Paris 1757-1831/3 Same. B-Hs-T.
CARTER, Betty Miller.
Am. b. New York; ad. 1934 Same. A.
CARTER, Charles Milton.
Am. b. No. Brookfield, Mass. 1853. A20-B-T.
CARTER, Clarence Holbrook.
Am. b. Portsmouth, O. 1904; ad. 1934 Cleveland, O. A.
CARTER, Dennis Malone.
Am. Ireland 1827-1881 New York. B-F-T-15.
CARTER, Dudley C. (S)
Am. b. New Westminster, B. C., Can. 1892; ad. 1934 Everett, Wash. A.
CARTER, Ellen. [née Vavasour]. (Ill.)
Eng. 1762-1815 Lincoln. DNB.
CARTER, Fernando A.
Am. Boston 1855-1931 Syracuse, N. Y. A028.
CARTER, Gordon Knowles.
Am. b. St. Louis, Mo. 1902; ad. 1934 Webster Groves, Mo. A.
CARTER, Helene. (Ill.)
Am. ad. 1934 New York. M.
CARTER, Henry ["Frank Leslie"]. *see* Leslie, F.
CARTER, Hugh.
Eng. Birmingham 1837-1903 London. B-DNB-T.

CARTER, John.
Ir. Ireland 1748-1817 London. B-T.
CARTER, Mary Mein. (Min.)
Mrs. James Newman Carter.
Am. b. Phila., Pa. 1864; ad. 1934 Same. A.
CARTER, Norman.
Aust. ac. 1933 in Australia. M.
CARTER, Pruett A. (Ill.)
Am. b. 1891; ad. 1934 Los Angeles, Calif. A.
CARTER, Robert. (Cart.)
Am. 1873-1918 Phila., Pa. A015.
CARTER, Samuel John.
Eng. Norfolk 1835-1892. B-T.
CARTER, Thomas. (S)
Eng. d. 1795 Knightsbridge. B-DNB.
CARTIER, Victor Émile.
Fr. Versailles 1811-1866 Paris. B-T.
CARTOTTO, Ercole.
Am. b. Piedmonte, It. 1889; ad. 1934 New York. A-F-W.
CARTWRIGHT, [Mrs.] Isabel Branson.
Am. b. Coatesville, Pa. 1885; ad. 1934 Phila., Pa. A-F.
CARTWRIGHT, John.
Eng. ex. 1763-1808 London. B-DNB.
CARTWRIGHT, Joseph.
Eng. 1789?-1829. B-DNB-T.
CARTWRIGHT, Leo.
Am. ad. 1935 Boston, Mass. M.
CARVALHO, Gaspar.
Por. d. 1596 in Portugal. T.
CARVER, Robert.
Br. b. Ireland; d. 1791 London. B-DNB.
CARWITHAM, J. (Eg.)
Eng. ac. 1723-1741. B-Bd.
CARY, Francis Stephen.
Eng. 1808-1860 London. B-DNB-T.
CASADO DEL ALISAL, Don José.
Sp. Valencia 1832-1886 Madrid. C.
CASALI, Andrea [Cavaliere].
It. Italy 1720?-1783? London. B-DNB.
CASANOVA Y ESTORACH, Antonio.
Sp. Tortosa 1847-1896 Madrid. B-C-T.
CASANOVA, Francesco Giuseppe.
It. London 1727-1802/5 Vienna, Aus. B-C-DNB-T-722.
CASANOVA, Giovanni Battista.
It. Venice 1722/30-1795. B-T.
CASARIN, Alexander. (S)
Am. b. Mexico; d. 1907 New York. A06-F.
CASAS, Ramón.
Sp. Spain 1867-1932 Paris. B-DBA.
CASCIERI, Angelo. (S)
Am. ad. 1933 New York. M.
CASE, Richard.
Am. ad. 1934 Brooklyn, N. Y. M.
CASELLAS, Fernando Miranda. (S)
Am. Valencia, Sp. 1842-1925 New York. A22-F.
CASELLI, Christoforo [Temperilli].
It. Parma 1455?-1521. B-T.
CASENTINO. *see* Jacopo del C.
CASER, Ettore.
Am. b. Venice, It. 1880; ad. 1934 New York. A-F.
CASEY, Edward F.
Am. ad. 1934 Brooklyn, N. Y. M.
CASH, Harold Cheney. (S)
Am. b. Chattanooga, Tenn. 1895; ad. 1934 Paris, Fr. A-Cs-DBA.
CASH, William Edmund Jr. ["Bill Cash"].
Am. ad. 1934 Phila., Pa. A.
CASILEAR, John William.
Am. New York 1811-1893 Saratoga, N. Y. C-DAB-F-T-4-7-15.
CASOLANI, Alessandro di Agostino [Torre].
It. Siena 1552-1606. B-T.
CASORATI, Felice.
It. b. 1886; ad. 1934 Turin. M.
CASPAR-FILSER, Maria.
Ger. b. 1878; ad. 1934 Munich. M.
CASS, Caroline Pickands. (S)
Am. b. Euclid, O. 1902; ad. 1934 Same. A.
CASS, George N.
Am. d. 1882 Boston, Mass. F-T-15.
CASSADY, Edithe Jane.
Am. b. Chicago 1906; ad. 1934 Same. A.
CASSAGNE, Armand Théophile.
Fr. Landin 1823-1907. B-T.
CASSANA, Niccolò. [Nicoletto].
It. Venice 1659-1713/4 London. B-E-T.
CASSATT, Mary.
Am. Allegheny City, Pa. 1855-1926 Paris, Fr. A23-B-DAB-E-F-T-W14-1-15-46-71-138,208-316-700-701-779-828-880.
CASSE, Roger.
Fr. b. Paris 1880. DBA.
CASSEL, John Harmon. (Cart.)
Am. b. Neb. City, Neb. 1873; ad. 1934 New York. A28-F-W.
CASSIDY, Ira D. Gerald.
Am. Cinn., O. 1879-1934 Santa Fé, N. M. A-F-M-W-Obit. N. Y. papers, 2-13-1934.
CASSIE, James.
Scot. 1819-1879 Edinburgh. B-DNB.
CASSIERS, Hendrik. [Henri].
Belg. b. Antwerp 1858. B-DBA.
CASSIGNOLA, Giacomo da. (S)
It. ac. 1561 in Lombard. T-V.
CASSIGNOLA, Giovanni Battista da. (S)
It. ac. 1579 in Rome. T-V.
CASSON, Alfred Joseph.
Can. b. Toronto; ad. 1935 Same. M.
CASTAGNO, Andrea del.
It. Castagno 1390-1457 Florence. B-Bd-E-T-V-722.
CASTAIGNE, André.
Fr. ac. 1889-1930 Paris. B-DBA.
CASTAN, Edmond [Pierre Jean]. (Eg.)
Fr. b. Toulouse 1817; ac. 1882 Paris. B-T.
CASTAN, Gustave Eugène.
Swi. Geneva 1823-1892. B-T.
CASTANO, Giovanni.
Am. b. Italy 1896; ad. 1934 Cinn., O. A.
CASTEDO, Julian.
Sp. ad. 1934 Madrid. M.
CASTEELS, Peter Francicus.
Flem. ac. 1690-1698 in Antwerp. B-T.
CASTEELS, Pierre.
Flem. Antwerp 1684-1749 Eng. B-DNB.
CASTELFRANCO. *see* Giorgione, C.
see Ponchino, G. B.
CASTELL, Johann Anton.
Ger. b. Dresden 1810; [No death date]. B-T.
CASTELLAN, Antoine Laurent.
Fr. Montpelier 1772-1838 Paris. B-T.

CASTELLANI, Charles Jules
Fr. Brussels, Belg. 1838-1913 Bois-le-Roi, Fr. B-DBA-T.
CASTELLO, Augustin del.
Sp. Sèville 1564-1626 Cordova. B-T-722.
CASTELLO [or Castelli], Bernardo.
It. Genoa 1557-1629 Same. B-C-E-T-722.
CASTELLO, Eugène.
Am. Phila., Pa. 1851-1926 Same. A23-B-T-W14.
CASTELLO, Giovanni Battista [Bergamasco].
It. Gandino 1509-1569 Madrid, Sp. B-C-E-T.
CASTELLO, Valerio.
It. Genoa 1625-1659 Same. B-E-T.
CASTELLON, Frederic.
Am. ex. 1934 New York. M.
CASTELUCHO, Claudio.
Sp. Barcelona 1870-1927. B-DBA.
CASTERTON, [Mrs.] Eda Nemoede. (Min)
Am. b. Brillion, Wis. 1877; ad. 1934 Chicago. A-F.
CASTIGLIONE, Giovanni Benedetto. [Il. Grechetto].
It. Genoa 1616-1670 Paris. B-C-E-T-722.
CASTIGLIONE, Giuseppe.
[Chinese name: Lang Shih-ning.]
It. Milan, It. 1698-1768 Peking, China. T-919.
CASTILEDEN, George Frederick.
Am. b. Canterbury, Kent, Eng. 1861; ad. 1934 New Orleans, La. A.
CASTILLO, Antonio del.
Sp. 1603-1667. 722.
CASTILLO, Augustin del.
Sp. Sèville 1567-1626 Cordova. B-T-722.
CASTILLO, Juan del.
Sp. Sèville 1584-1640 Cadiz. B-T-722.
CASTREA, Edouard.
Swi. Genoa 1838-1902 Same. B-C-T.
CASTRO, Fabián de. [Gitano].
Sp. ac. 1926. Fa.
CASTRO, Juan Sanchez. *see* Sanchez de Castro.
CASTRO, Paul de.
It. b. Leghorn 1882; ex. 1930 London. DBA.
CASWELL, Edward C.
Am. b. New York 1879; ad. 1935 Same. A28-M.
CATALDI AMIETO [or Amleto]. (S)
It. Naples 1886-1930 Rome. DBA-T.
CATENA, Vincenzo di Biagio.
It. Treviso 1470-1531 Venice. C-722.
CATERINO, [Moranzone] Andrea. (S)
It. ac. 15th century in Venice. T.
CATERINO, Veneziano II.
It. ac. 1455 Venice. T.
CATHELL, Edna S.
Mrs. J. E. Cathell.
Am. b. Richmond, Ind. 1876; ad. 1934 Same. A.
CATLIN, George.
Am. Penn. 1796-1872 Jersey City, N. J. B-Bd-C-DAB-F-2-4-6-15-144-183.
CATS, Jacob.
Dut. Altona 1741-1799 Amsterdam. B-T.
CATTANEO, Danese [da Carrara]. (S)
It. Colonnata 1509-1573 Padua. Hs-V.
CATTERMOLE, George.
Eng. Norfolk 1800-1868 London. B-DNB-E-T.
CATTERMOLE, Lance.
Eng. ad. 1935 London. M.
CATTON, Charles [The Elder].
Eng. Norwich 1728-1798 London. B-DNB.
CATTON, Charles [The Younger].
Eng. London 1756-1818 U. S. B-DNB.
CAUCANNIER, Jean Denis Antoine.
Fr. b. Paris; ac. 1885-1905. B-T.
CAULDWELL, Leslie Giffen.
Am. b. New York 1861; ad. 1934 Paris. A-B-F-T-W7.
CAULITZ, Peter.
Ger. Berlin 1650-1719 Same. C.
CAVACOS, Emmanuel A. (S)
Am. b. Kythera, Gr. 1885; ad. 1934 Paris. A-Cs-F.
CAVAILLÈS, Jean.
Fr. b. Carmaux; ex. 1935 Paris. DBA.
CAVALIERE, Giovanni di Stefano. *see* Lanfranco, G.
CAVALIERE, R. J. (Ill)
Am. ad. 1934 New York. M.
CAVALLI, François Antoine.
It. b. Maggiore 1835?; d. Paris. B-T.
CAVALLINI, Pietro.
It. 1250-1330 Rome. B-E-T-V.
CAVALLITO, Albino. (S)
Am. b. Cocconato, It. 1905; ad. 1934 Woodbridge, N. J. A.
CAVALLON, G.
Am. ex. 1935 New York. M.
CAVALLUCCI, Antonio.
It. Sermoneta 1752-1795 Rome. B-T.
CAVAZZA, Giovanni Batista.
It. b. Bologna 1620. B-T.
CAVAZZOLA, Paolo [Il. Moranda].
It. Verona 1486-1522 Same. B-T-V.
CAVÉ. *see* also La Cavé.
CAVÉ, Jules Cyrille.
Fr. b. Paris 1859. B-C-DBA.
CAVE, Peter le.
Fr.-Eng. ac. 1769-1810 London. T.
CAVEDONE, Jacopo [or Giacomo].
It. Modena 1577-1660 Bologna. B-C-E-T-722.
CAWEIN, Fred W.
Am. d. Louisville, Ky. 1912. A10.
CAXES [or Caxesi or Caxete], Eugenio.
Sp. Madrid 1577-1642 Same. B-T.
CAXES [or Caxesi or Caxete], Patrico.
Sp. ac. 1567-1612 in Arezzo. B-T.
CAYLUS, Anne Claude Philippe. (Eg)
Fr. Paris 1692-1765 Same. B-T.
CAYRON, Jules.
Fr. b. Paris 1868. B-DBA.
CAZENAVE, J. François. (Eg)
Fr. b. Paris 1770. B-T.
CAZES, Pierre Jacques.
Fr. Paris 1676-1754 Same. B-C-E-T-722.
CAZIN, Jean Charles.
Fr. Samer 1841-1901 Lavan Dou. B-DBA-E-T.
CECCARELLI, Ezio. (S)
It. b. Montecatini 1865. T.
CECCARELLI, Naddo [or Nardo].
It. ac. 1347 in Siena. M.
CECCHI, Francesco Antonio.
It. Florence 1784-1812. B.
CECELIN, Frank. (Ill)
Am. ad. 1934 New York. M.

CECERE, Ada Rosario.
Mrs. Gaetano Cecere.
Am. b. New York; ad. 1934 Same. A.
CECERE, Gaetano. (S)
Am. b. New York 1894; ad. 1934 Same. A-Cs-F.
CECIL, Thomas. (Eg)
Eng. ac. 1627-1635 London. B-DNB.
CECIONI, Adriano. (S)
It. ac. 19th century in Italy. M.
CEDASPE, Pablo de. *see* Cespedes.
CEDERQUIST, Arthur E.
Am. b. Titusville, Pa. 1884; ad. 1934 Same. A.
CEDERSTROM, Gustaf Olaf.
Swi. b. Stockholm 1845. B-T.
CEDERSTROM, Thur Nikolaus von.
Swi. b. 1843. M.
CEIKE, Alfred.
Am. ex. 1934 New York. M.
CELESTI, Andrea.
It. Venice 1637-1700/6 Same. B-Bd.
CELESTINI, Celestino. (Et)
It. b. 1882. M.
CELLINI, Benvenuto. (S)
It. Florence 1500-1571 Same. B-Hs-T-V-317.
CENNINI [di Cinni], Bernardo [di Bartolomeo].
It. b. 1415; ac. 1483. T.
CEPHISODOTUS [Father and Son]. (S)
Gr. ac. 400-370 B. C. E.
CERACCHI [or Cerracchi], Giuseppie. (S)
It. Rome 1740/51-1801/2 Paris. B-Hs-T-2-184-786.
CERACCHINI, Gisberto.
It. ex. 1935 Rome. M.
CERAMANO, Charles Ferdinand.
Flem. Thielt 1828-1909. B-T.
CEREZO, Mateo [The Younger].
Sp. Burgos 1635-1685 Madrid. B-C-T-722.
CÉRIA, Edmond.
Fr. b. Evian 1884; ad. 1935 Paris. DBA.
CERISIER, Simonne Maris.
Fr. b. Anceenis 1903. DBA.
CERMAK, Jaroslav.
Aus. Prague, Czec. 1831-1878 Paris. B-T.
CERRACCHIO, Enrico Filiberto. (S)
Am. b. Italy 1880. F-W16.
CERRINI [or Cerini] Giovanni Domenico.
It. Perugia 1609-1681 Rome. T.
CERUTTI-SIMMONS, Teresa. (Et)
Am. ad. 1934 Roxbury, Conn. A.
CESARE DA SESTO. *see* Sesto, C. da.
CESARI, Giuseppe [Cavaliere d'Arpino].
It. Rome 1560/8-1640 Same. B-C-E-T-722.
CESATI, Alessandro. (Med)
It. ac. 1538-1564 in Milan. T-V.
CESI, Bartolommeo.
It. Bologna 1556/7-1629 Same. B-T-722.
CESPEDÈS, Pablo de [or Cedaspe].
Sp. Cordova 1538-1608 Same. B-C-E-T-722.
CEULEN, van. *see* Janssens, van C.
CEUNIS, Gérard.
It. ad. 1934 Hitchin, Eng. M.
CÉZANNE, Paul.
Fr. Aix 1839-1906 Same. B-DBA-T-192-194-318-686-700-790-811-827-847.
CHABANIAN, Arsène.
Turkish. b. Erzersum, Turkey; ac. 1896-1910. B-T.
CHABAS, Maurice.
Fr. b. Nantes; ac. 1904-1930. B-DBA.
CHABAS, Paul Émile Joseph.
Fr. b. Nantes 1869. B-DBA-T.
CHABAUD, Auguste Elisée.
Fr. b. Nîmes 1882; ex. 1930 Paris. DBA.
CHACE, Dorethea.
Am. b. Buffalo, N. Y. 1894; ad. 1934 New York. A.
CHADEAYNE, Robert O.
Am. b. Cornwall, N. Y. 1897; ad. 1934 Columbus, O. A.
CHADWICK, Arch. D.
Am. b. Ovid, N. Y. 1871; ad. 1934 Ithaca, N. Y. A.
CHADWICK, Charles Wesley. (Eg.)
Am. b. Red Hook, N. Y. 1861; ad. 1934 New York. A12-F-T-W.
CHADWICK, William.
Am. ac. 1934 Old Lyme, Conn. A18-F.
CHAFFEE, Olive.
Am. b. Paducah, Ky.; ad. 1934 St. Louis, Mo. A.
CHAFFEE, Oliver Newberry.
Am. b. Detroit, Mich. 1881; ad. 1934 Provincetown, Mass. F-M.
CHAFFETZ, Asa. (Et.)
Am. Auction sale New York 1934. M.
CHAGALL, Marc.
Rus. b. Vitebsk. DBA-319-700-797.
CHAHINE, Edgar.
Fr. b. Constantinople, Turkey 1874; ex. 1934 New York. B-DBA-T.
CHAIGNEAU, Jean Ferdinand.
Fr. Bordeaux 1830-1906. B-DBA-T.
CHAIX, Auguste.
Fr. 1861-1922 Bearlieu-sur-Mer. DBA.
CHALE, Ellen Wheeler.
Am. b. Faribault, Minn.; ad. 1915 Paris. A12.
CHALETTE, Jean.
Fr. Troyes 1581-1643/5 Toulouse. B-T.
CHALFANT, Jefferson Davis.
Am. Penn. 1856-1931 Wilmington, Del. A028.
CHALFIN, Paul. (Mu.)
Am. b. New York 1874; ad. 1934 Greenwich, Conn. A.
CHALLENER, Frederick Sproston.
Can. b. Whetstone, Eng. 1869; ad. 1935 Toronto, Ont. B.
CHALMERS, [Sir] George.
Scot. b. Edinburgh; d. 1791 Same. B-DNB.
CHALMERS, George Paul.
Scot. Montrose 1833/6-1878 Edinburgh. B-DNB-E-T.
CHALMERS, Helen Augusta.
Mrs. Stephen Chalmers.
Am. b. New York 1880; ad. 1934 Laguna Beach, Calif. A.
CHALMERS, W. A.
Eng. ac. 1790-1798 London. B-DNB.
CHALON, Alfred Edward.
Swi. Geneva 1780-1860 London. B-DNB-T-722.
CHALON, Henry Bernard.
Dut. Holland 1770-1849 London. B-T.

CHALON, JOHN JAMES.
Eng. Geneva, Swi. 1778-1854 London. B-T-722.
CHALON, LOUIS.
Fr. b. Paris 1866. B-T.
CHALONS, LOUIS.
Dut. Amsterdam 1687-1741 Same. B-T.
CHAM. *see* Noé Amédée Charles Henri.
CHAMBELLAN, RENÉ PAUL. (S)
Am. ad. 1934 New York. A.
CHAMBERLAIN, ARTHUR B.
Am. b. Kitchner, Can. 1860; ad. 1934 Rochester, N. Y. A-F.
CHAMBERLAIN, EMILY HALL. (Et.)
Am. b. Shelby, O.; d. 1916 New York. A013.
CHAMBERLAIN, JACK B. (Et.)
Am. 1881-1907 Lakewood, N. J. A06.
CHAMBERLAIN, K. (Ill.)
Am. ad. 1934 New York. M.
CHAMBERLAIN, NORMAN STILES.
Am. b. Grand Rapids, Mich. 1887; ad. 1934 Los Angeles, Calif. A.
CHAMBERLAIN, SAMUEL V. (Et.)
Am. b. Cresco, Ia. 1895; ad. 1934 Senlis [Oise], Fr. A28-M.
CHAMBERLAIN, WILLIAM.
Eng. ex. 1760-1787 London; d. 1817 Hull. B-DNB.
CHAMBERLIN, FRANK TOLLES. (S)
Am. b. San Fran., Calif. 1873; ad. 1934 Pasadena, Calif. A-B-Cs-F-W.
CHAMBERLIN, MASON.
Eng. ex. 1760-1787 London. B-DNB-T.
CHAMBERS, C. BOSSERON.
Am. b. St. Louis, Mo. 1883; ad. 1934 New York. A-F.
CHAMBERS, CHARLES EDWARD. (Ill.)
Am. b. Ottumwa, Ia. 1883; ad. 1934 New York. A-W.
CHAMBERS, GEORGE.
Eng. Whitby 1803-1840 London. B-DNB-E-T.
CHAMBERS, HALLIE WORTHINGTON.
Mrs. Kirby L. Chambers.
Am. b. Louisville, Ky. 1881; ad. 1934 Same. A.
CHAMBERS, J. K.
Am. b. Ireland; d. 1916 Boston, Mass. A013.
CHAMBERS, ROBERT WILLIAM. (Ill.)
Am. b. Brooklyn, N. Y. 1865; ad. 1934 New York. A-W.
CHAMPAIGNE [or Champagne], JEAN BAPTISTE DE.
Fr. Brussels, Belg. 1631-1681 Paris. B-Bd-C-T.
CHAMPAIGNE [or Champagne], PHILIPPE DE.
Flem. Brussels 1602-1674 Paris. B-Bd-C-E-T-722.
CHAMPCOMMUNAL, JOSEPH. (Eg.)
Fr. ac. 1906 in Paris. B.
CHAMPLAIN, DUANE. (S)
Am. b. Black Mountain, N. C. 1889; ad. 1934 New York. A-Cs-F.
CHAMPLIN, ADA BELLE.
Am. b. St. Louis, Mo.; ad. 1934 Pasadena, Calif. A.
CHAMPNEY, BENJAMIN.
Am. New Ipswich, N. H. 1817-1907 Woburn, Mass. A07-B-DAB-F-T-38.
CHAMPNEY, JAMES WELLS.
Am. Boston 1843-1903 New York. A04-B-C-DAB-F-T-15-39-46.
CHAMPOLLION, EUGÈNE ANDRÉ. (Et.)
Fr. Embrun 1848-1901 Lettret. T.
CHANDLER. *see also* Chanler.
CHANDLER, [Miss] CLYDE GILTNER. (S)
Am. b. Evansville, Ind.; ad. 1915 Chicago. A12-B.
CHANDLER, DIGBY W.
Am. 1856-1928. A026.
CHANDLER, GEORGE WALTER. (Et.)
Am. b. Milwaukee, Wis.; ac. 1926. A20-F-46.
CHANDLER, HELEN CLARK.
Am. b. Wellington, Kan. 1881; ad. 1924 Los Angeles, Calif. A.
CHANDLER, J. W.
Scot. 1769-1805 Edinburgh. B-DNB-T.
CHANDLER, WINTHROP.
Am. Woodstock, Conn. 1747-1790 Thompson, Conn. M-2.
CHANG CHU'AN-SHAN.
Chinese. Ching Period. M.
CHANG HSUAN.
Chinese. T'ang Dynasty. (618-906 A.D.) T.
CHANG SÊNG-YU [or Chōsōyu].
Chinese. ac. 502-550 A.D. T.
CHANG TA CHIEN.
Chinese. ad. 1935 Shanghai, China. M.
CHANIN, A. L.
Am. ex. 1934 Phila., Pa. M.
CHANLER, ROBERT WINTHROP.
Am. New York 1872-1930. A027-46.
CHANTREY, [Sir] FRANCIS LEGATT. (S)
Eng. Norton 1782-1841 Sheffield. E-Hs-653.
CHANTRON, ALEXANDRE JAQUES.
Fr. Nantes 1842-1918. B-DBA-T.
CHANTRON, ANTOINE.
Fr. Avignon 1771-1842 Same. B-T.
CHAO CH'ANG.
Chinese. Sung Period. [960-1260.] E.
CHAO MÊNG-CHIEN
Chinese. Sung Dynasty. 13th Cent. T.
CHAO MÊNG-FU.
Chinese. 1254-1322. E.
CHAO TA-NIEN.
Chinese. Sung Period. [960-1260.] E.
CHAPEL, GUY M.
Am. b. Detroit 1871; ad. 1934 Chicago. A.
CHAPERON, EUGÈNE.
Fr. b. Paris 1857. B-DBA-T.
CHAPIN, CHARLES.
Am. ad. 1934 Leonia, N. J. M.
CHAPIN, FRANCIS.
Am. b. Bristolville, O. 1899; ad. 1934 Chicago. A-DBA.
CHAPIN, JAMES ORMSBEE.
Am. b. West Orange, N. J. 1887; ad. 1934 New York. A-F-700.
CHAPIN, JOHN R.
Am. b. Providence, R. I. 1823; ac. 1908 Buffalo, N. Y. B-T.
CHAPIN, JOSEPH HAWLEY.
Am. b. Hartford, Conn. 1869; ad. 1934 New York. A.

CHAPIN, Lucy Grosvenor.
Am. b. Syracuse, N. Y. 1873; ad. 1934 Same. A.
CHAPIN, William. (Eg.)
Am. Phila., Pa. 1802-1888 Same. F-T-7.
CHAPLAIN, Jules Clément. (S)
Fr. b. Mortagne 1839; ac. 1900 in Paris. B-Hs.
CHAPLIN, Charles Joshua.
Fr. Andely 1825-1891 Paris. B-C-T.
CHAPLIN, Christine.
Mrs. C. C. Brush.
Am. b. Bangor, Me. 1842. B-T-15.
CHAPLIN, Elizabeth.
Fr. b. Fontainebleau; ad. 1934 Paris. DBA.
CHAPMAN, Carleton Theodore.
Am. New London, O. 1860-1925 New York. A22-B-F-T-W13.
CHAPMAN, Charles Shepard.
Am. b. Morristown, N. J. 1879; ad. 1934 Leonia, N. J. A-B-F-W.
CHAPMAN, Conrad Wise.
Am. Rome, It. 1842-1913 U. S. F.
CHAPMAN, Cyrus Durand.
Am. Irvington, N. J. 1856-1918 Same. A014.
CHAPMAN, Esther I. E. McCord.
Am. b. Neb.; ad. 1934 Wash., D. C. A.
CHAPMAN, Frederick. (Ill.)
Am. ad. 1934 Mahwah, N. J. M.
CHAPMAN, John Gadsby. (Et.)
Am. Alexandria, Va. 1808-1889 Brooklyn, N. Y. B-C-DAB-F-T-2-4-7-15-26-40-46.
CHAPMAN, Kenneth Milton.
Am. b. Ligonier, Ind. 1875; ad. 1934 Santa Fé, N. M. A24-F-W.
CHAPMAN, Minerva Josephine.
Am. b. Altmar, N. Y. 1858; ad. 1934 Palo Alto, Calif. A-B.
CHAPMAN, Walter H.
Am. ad. 1934 Toledo, O. M.
CHAPNEY, J. Wells.
Am. Boston 1843-1903 New York. A4.
CHAPPEL, Alonzo.
Fr. or Am. b. 1820; d. 1885. M-Wi.
CHAPPELL, Warren. (Ill.)
Am. ad. 1934 New York. M.
CHAPU, Henri Michel Antoine. (S)
Fr. Mée 1833-1891. B-Hs-T.
CHAPUY, Jean Baptiste.
Fr. Paris 1760-1802 Same. B-T.
CHARD, Walter Goodman. (S)
Am. b. Buffalo, N. Y. 1880. A20-F.
CHARDERON, Francine [Mlle.]
Fr. b. Lyons; ac. 1885-1902 Paris. B-T.
CHARDIGNY, Barthelémy François. (S)
Fr. Rouen 1757-1813 Paris. B-T.
CHARDIGNY, Pierre Joseph. (S)
Fr. Aix 1794-1866 Paris. B-T.
CHARDIN, Gabriel Gervais.
Fr. Paris 1814-1907. B-T.
CHARDIN, Jean Baptiste Simeon.
Fr. Paris 1699-1779 Same. B-Bd-C-E-T-191-320-700-722-756-758-847.
CHAREAU, François.
Fr. 1680-1729. M.
CHARENTON. *see* Charonton.
CHARES. (S)
Gr. ac. 300 B.C. Rhodes. E.
CHARLEMAGNE, Paul.
Fr. b. Paris 1892; ad. 1934 Same. DBA.
CHARLES, James.
Eng. Warrington 1851-1906 London. B-DNB-T.
CHARLES, Samuel ["Sam"].
Am. b. Agawan, Mass. 1887; ad. 1934 Wellesley, Mass. A.
CHARLES, William. (Cari.)
Am. Scotland 1776-1820 Phila., Pa. DAB-F-T-2-7.
CHARLET, Albert.
Fr. b. Xermanénil; ac. 1929 Paris. DBA.
CHARLET, Franz.
Belg. Brussels 1862-1928. B-DBA-T.
CHARLET, Nicolas Toussaint.
Fr. Paris 1792-1845 Same. B-C-E-T-722.
CHARLIER, Guillaume. (S)
Belg. b. Brussels 1854. Hs-T.
CHARLIER, Jacques.
Fr. 1720-1779 Paris. B-T.
CHARLOT, Jean.
Mex. b. Paris 1898; ad. 1934 Mexico. A-654-791.
CHARLOT, Louis.
Fr. b. Cussy-en-Morwan 1878. B-DBA.
CHARLTON, Edward William.
Eng. b. 1859; ad. 1934 Lymington. Wa.
CHARLTON, George.
Eng. b. London 1899; ad. 1934 Same. Wa.
CHARLTON, John.
Eng. Bamborough 1849-1917. B-T.
CHARMAN, Jessie Harris.
Am. ad. 1934 Syracuse, N. Y. M.
CHARMAN, Montague.
Am. b. London 1894; ad. 1934 Syracuse, N. Y. A.
CHARMY, Émilie.
Fr. b. 1880; ac. 1929 in Paris. B-DBA.
CHARNAY, Armond.
Fr. Charlieu 1844-1916. B-DBA-T.
CHARONTON [or Charton], Eguerrand.
Fr. Lyons 1410?-1461. B-Wi.
CHARPENTIER, Félix Maurice. (S)
Fr. Bolléne 1858-1925. B-DBA.
CHARPIN, Albert.
Fr. Grasse 1842-1924. B-DBA-T.
CHARRETIE, Anna Maria [née Kenwell]. (Min.)
Eng. 1819-1875 Kensington. B-DNB.
CHARRETON, Victor Léon Jean Pierre.
Fr. b. Bourgoin 1864. B-DBA.
CHARRIER, Pierre Edouard. (S)
Fr. b. Niort 1820; ac. 1880 Paris. T.
CHART, Daphne.
Eng. ex. 1934 London. M.
CHARTIER, Henri Georges Jacques.
Fr. Château Chinon 1859-1924 Paris. B-DBA-T.
CHARTRAN, Théobald.
Fr. Besançon 1849-1907. B-T.
CHARTRES, Edmund.
Fr. b. Val St. Pierre; ac. 1800 in Paris. B-T.
CHASE, Adelaide Cole.
Mrs. William Chester Chase.
Am. b. Boston 1868; ad. 1934 Same. A-B-F-T-W-829.
CHASE, Carl C.
Am. ex. 1935 New York. M.

CHASE, Clarence Melville.
Am. b. Auburn, Me. 1871; ad. 1934 Boston. A.

CHASE, Edward L.
Am. ad. 1933 New York. M.

CHASE, Ellen Wheeler.
Am. b. Faribault, Minn.; ad. 1934 New York. A.

CHASE, Elsie Rowland.
Mrs. Frederick S. Chase.
Am. b. Saratoga Springs, N. Y. 1863; ad. 1934 Waterbury, Conn. A.

CHASE, Frank Swift.
Am. b. St. Louis, Mo. 1886; ad. 1934 Woodstock, N. Y. A.

CHASE, Harry.
Am. Woodstock, Vt. 1853-1889 Suwanee, Tenn. B-C-F-T-15.

CHASE, Jesse Kalmbach.
Mrs. Wilfrid E. Chase.
Am. b. Bailey's Harbor, Wis. 1879; ad. 1934 Madison, Wis. A.

CHASE, John.
Eng. London 1810-1879 Same. B-DNB.

CHASE, Joseph Cummings.
Am. b. Kent Hill, Me. 1878; ad. 1934 New York. A-F-W.

CHASE, Marian Emma.
Eng. London 1844-1905 Same. DNB-T.

CHASE, Marion Monks.
Am. b. Boston; ad. 1934 Wellesley Hills, Mass. F-M.

CHASE, Sidney Marsh.
Am. b. Haverhill, Mass. 1877; ad. 1934 Same. A-F.

CHASE, [Mrs.] Susan Brown.
Mrs. V. O. Chase.
Am. b. St. Louis, Mo.; ad. 1934 Wash., D. C. A-F.

CHASE, William Merritt.
Am. Franklin, Ind. 1849-1916 New York. A014-B-C-DAB-E-F-T-5-15-39-41-46-127-181-701-748.

CHASLES, Albert.
Fr. b. Nogent; d. 1928. DBA.

CHASSAING, Edourd. (S)
Am. ad. 1935 Chicago. M.

CHASSAING, Olga. (S)
Am. b. 1897; ex. 1934 Chicago. M.

CHASSELAT, Charles Abraham. (Eg.)
Fr. Paris 1782-1843 Same. B-T.

CHASSÉRIAU, Théodore.
Fr. Panama 1819-1856 Paris. B-E-T-722.

CHASTEL, Daniel.
Fr. Montbéliard, France 1596-1679 Geneva, Swi. B.

CHASTILLON. *see* Châtillon.

CHATELAIN, Alfred Joseph.
Swi. b. Berne 1867. T.

CHATELAINE, John Baptist Claude.
Fr. Paris 1710-1771. B-DNB-T.

CHATFIELD, Edward.
Eng. 1802-1839. B-DNB-T.

CHÂTILLON [or Chastillon], Louis de.
Fr. Champagne 1639?-1688/1734. B-T.

CHÂTILLON, Zoé Laure de. [Delaune]
Fr. Chambray 1826-1908. B-T.

CHATOV, Roman. (Mu)
Am. b. Russia 1900; ad. 1934 New York. 912.

CHATTERTON, Clarence K.
Am. b. Newburgh, N. Y. 1880; ad. 1934 Poughkeepsie, N. Y. A.

CHATTIN, Lou-Ellen.
Am. b. Temple, Tex. 1891; ad. 1934 St. Petersburg, Fla. A.

CHAUDET, Antoine Denis. (S)
Fr. Paris 1763-1810 Same. B-Hs-T.

CHAUVEAU, François.
Fr. Paris 1613-1676 Same. B-T.

CHAUVEL, Théophile Narcisse.
Fr. Paris 1831-1910 Same. B-T.

CHAUVET, Jules Adolphe.
Fr. b. Péronne 1828; ac. 1896 Paris. B-T.

CHAVANNE, Pierre Salomon. *see* Domenchim de C.

CHAVANNES. *see* Puvis de C.

CHAVES. *see* Echave, Balthasar.

CHAVET, Victor Joseph.
Fr. Pourcieux 1822-1906. B-T.

CHAVICOKIOLI, William. (S)
Am. b. Venice, It. 1909; ad. 1934 New York. A.

CHAVIGNAUD, Georges.
Can. b. Britanny, Fr.; ad. 1934 Toronto. 893.

CHECA Y SANZ, Ulfiano.
Sp. Madrid 1860-1916 Paris. T.

CHEDANNE, Georges Paul.
Fr. b. Maromme 1861. DBA.

CHEERE, [Sir] Henry. (S)
Eng. 1703-1781 London. B-DNB-T.

CHEESEBOROUGH, Mary Hugger. (Min.)
Am. d. 1902 Saratoga, N. Y. A04.

CHEESEMAN, Thomas. (Eg.)
Eng. 1760-1820 London. B-DNB.

CHEFFETZ, Asa. (Eg.)
Am. ad. 1934 Springfield, Mass. A.

CHELMINSKI, Jan van.
Pol. Warsaw 1851-1925. B-T.

CHELMONSKI, Joseph [or Josef].
Pol. Betchki 1849-1914 Kirklowska. B-DBA.

C'HEN YUNG [or Jung].
Chinese. ac. 12th century. E-T.

CHÉNARD-HUCHÉ, Georges.
Fr. b. Nantes 1864. B-DBA.

CHENAVARD, Paul Marc Joseph.
Fr. Lyons 1807-1895 Paris. B-T.

CHENEY, John. (Eg.)
Am. So. Manchester, Conn. 1801-1885 Same. DAB-F-T-2-7-40-42-43.

CHENEY, Leo.
Eng. 1866-1928. Y01929.

CHENEY, Philip.
Am. b. Brookline, Mass. 1897; ad. 1934 New York. M.

CHENEY, Russell.
Am. b. So. Manchester, Conn. 1881; ad. 1934 Same. A-F-W.

CHENEY, Seth Wells. (Eg.)
Am. So. Manchester, Conn. 1810-1856 Same. DAB-T-2-3-4-7-15-42-43-45.

CHENEY, Warren. (S)
Am. b. Paris 1907; ad. 1934 Berkeley, Calif. A.

CH'ÊNG SSU-HSIAO.
Chinese. ac. Sung Dynasty 13-14th cent. T.
CHÉRET, JULES. (Posters)
Fr. Paris 1836-1932 Nice.
B-DBA-T-Y01933.
CHÉRON, ELIZABETH SOPHIE [née Le Hay].
Fr. Paris 1648-1711 Same. B-T.
CHÉRON, LOUIS. (Eg.)
Fr. Paris 1655-1715 London. B-DNB.
CHERRY, [Mrs.] EMMA RICHARDSON.
Am. b. Aurora, Ill. 1859; ad. 1934 Houston, Tex. A-F-T.
CHERRY, [Mrs.] KATHRYN E.
Am. Quincy, Ill. 1871-1931 St. Louis, Mo.
A028-W16.
CHERUBINI, ANDRÉ.
It. b. Rome; ac. 1883. T.
CHERUY, RÉNE [Mme.].
Am. ad. 1934 Windsor, Conn. M.
CHERVIN, LOUIS.
Fr. b. Paris; ad. 1934 Same. DBA.
CHÉRY, PHILIPPE.
Fr. Paris 1759-1858 Same. B-T.
CHESHAM, FRANCIS. (Eg.)
Br. 1749-1806 London. B-DNB.
CHESKIN, LOUIS.
Am. b. Russia 1907; ad. 1934 Chicago. A.
CHESNEY, LETITIA.
Am. b. Louisville, Ky. 1875; ad. 1934 Winslow, Wash. A.
CHESNEY, MARY.
Am. b. Louisville, Ky. 1872; ad. 1934 Winslow, Wash. A.
CHESNUT, [Mrs.] BILLIE.
Am. ad. 1934 New York. M.
CHESSE, RALPH.
Am. b. New Orleans, La. 1900; ad. San Fran., Calif. A.
CHESTON, CHARLES SUDNEY.
Eng. b. 1882; ex. 1933 London. Wa.
CHEVALIER, ÉTIENNE.
Fr. b. Paris; d. 1763. B-T.
CHEVALIER, NICOLAS.
Rus. Leningrad 1828-1902 London. B-T.
CHEVILLIARD, VINCENT JEAN BAPTISTE.
Fr. Italy 1841-1904 Paris. T.
CHIALIVA, LUIGI.
Swi. Caslano 1842-1914. B-T.
CHIAO PING-CHENG.
Chinese. ac. 1696. E.
CHICHARRO Y AGÜERA, EDUARDO.
Sp. b. Madrid 1873. B.
CHI-CHÊN.
Chinese. [Northern] Sung Dynasty (960-1127). M.
CHICHESTER, CECIL.
Am. b. New York 1891; ad. 1934 Woodstock, N. Y. A.
CHICKERING, CHARLES R. (Ill.)
Am. ad. 1934 New York. M.
CH'IEN LUNG. (P-S)
Chinese, 1736-1795. [Auc. sale, New York, 1934]. M.
CH'IËN SHUN-CHÜ.
Chinese. ac. 1235-1260. T.
CHIERICI, ALFONSO.
It. 1816-1873 Reggio. T.
CHIERICI, GAÉTANO.
It. b. Reggio 1838-1877. B-T.
CHIFFLART, FRANÇOIS NICOLAS. (Et)
Fr. St. Omer 1825-1901 Paris. B-T.
CHIKUDEN, TAKANORI [Tanomura].
Jap. 1777-1835 Osaka. T.
CHILD, CHARLES JESSE.
Am. b. Montclair, N. J. 1902; ad. 1934 Lumberville, Pa. M.
CHILD, EDWIN BURRAGE.
Am. b. Gouverneur, N. Y. 1868; ad. 1934 Dorset, Vt. A-F-T-W.
CHILDE, ELIAS.
Eng. ac. 1798-1848 London. B-DNB.
CHILDE [or Child], JAMES WARREN. (Min.)
Eng. 1780-1862 London. B-DNB.
CHILDREY, MERRIE PENDER.
Am. b. Richmond, Va. 1908; ad. 1934 Wash., D. C. A.
CHILDS, BENJAMIN F. (Eg.)
Am. Cambridgeport, Mass. 1814-1863. F-T.
CHILDS, CEPHAS GIOVANNI. (Eg.)
Am. Penn. 1793-1871 Phila., Pa.
F-T-2-7-40.
CHILDS, JOSEPH. (Ill.)
Am. d. 1909 Westport, Conn. A07.
CHILDS, LILLIAN E.
Am. b. Illinois; ad. 1934 New York. A.
CHILLMAN, JAMES, Jr.
Am. b. Phila., Pa. 1891; ad. 1934 Houston, Tex. A.
CHILTON, WILLIAM BRENT.
Am. b. Wash., D. C. 1856; ad. 1934 Same.
A.
CHIMENTI, JACOPO DA EMPOLI.
It. Florence 1554-1640. B-T.
CHINARD, JOSEPH [Pierre]. (S)
Fr. Lyons 1756-1813 Same. B-Hs-T.
CHIN CH'U-SHIK.
Chinese. ac. Sung Dynasty [960-1127]. M.
CHINESE ARTISTS. *see* Books No. 731-732-733-734-767-888-919-934.
CHINTEREUIL, ANTOINE.
Fr. Pont-de-Vaux 1814-1873 Septeuil. T.
CHIODAROLO, GIOVANNI MARIA.
It. Bologna 1500-1565? B-T-722.
CHIRICO, GIORGIO DE.
Gr.-It. b. Volo, Gr. 1888; ad. 1934 Paris.
DBA-321-797.
CHISHOLM, ALEXANDER.
Scot. Elgin 1792/3-1847 Rothesay.
B-DNB-T.
CHITTENDEN, ALICE BROWN.
Am. b. Brockport, N. Y. 1860; ad. 1934 San Fran., Calif. A.
CHLEBOWSKI, PORAJ STANISLAUS.
Pol. 1835-1884 Posen. T.
CHMIELEWSKI, JAN M. (Et.)
Am. ad. 1934 Phila., Pa. A.
CHOATE, FLORENCE. (Ill.)
Am. ad. 1934 New York. M.
CHOATE, NATHANIEL. (S)
Am. b. Southboro, Mass. 1899; ad. 1935 New York. Cs-M.
CHOCARNE-MOREAU, PAUL.
Fr. b. Dijon 1855. B-DBA-T.
CHO DENSU.
Jap. d. 1431. J., Vol. 1, page 55.

CHODOWIECKI, Daniel Nicolaus.
Ger. Danzig 1726-1801 Berlin.
B-C-E-T-722-801-803-880.
CHOFFARD, Pierre Philippe. (Eg.)
Fr. Paris 1730-1809. B-T-880.
CHOGA, Takuma [Kose Tamenobu].
Jap. J., Vol. 1, page 66.
CHÓKI, Yeishosai [Shiko].
Jap. J., Vol. 2, page 59-T.
CHOKUAN, Soga [Mokusuké].
Jap. d. about 1614 in Sakia.
J., Vol. 1, page 98.
CHÓSHUN, Mikagawa.
Jap. J., Vol. 2, pages 20 and 47-T.
CHOU CH'EN [or Shên].
Chinese. Ming Dynasty [1368-1644]. E.
CHOU CHIH-MIEN.
Chinese. ac. 16th century E.
CHOU FANG.
Chinese. ac. 8th century. E.
CHOU WÉN-CHÜ.
Chinese. ac. 900-960. E.
CHOUBINE, Theodor Ivanvitch. (S)
Rus. 1740-1805. B.
CHOUDHURY, S. (Mu.)
Br. b. India; ad. 1934 London. M.
CHOUINARD, Nelbert Murphy.
Am. b. Montevideo, Minn. 1879; ad. 1934 Los Angeles, Calif. A-W.
CHOULTSE, Iwan F.
Rus. b. Leningrad 1877; ex. 1932 New York. M.
CHÓUN, Yamazaki. (S)
Jap. ex. 1935 Tokyo. M.
CHOWNE, Gerard.
Br. 1875-1917. T.
CHRÉTIEN, Eugène Edmund Ernest. (S)
Fr. b. Elbeuf; ac. 1874-1930 in Paris.
B-DBA-T.
CHRISTENSEN, Ingelborg.
Am. b. Chicago; ad. 1934 Same. A.
CHRISTIAN, Barbara.
Eng. ex. 1934 London. M.
CHRISTIAN, Max. (S)
Aus. b. Vienna 1864. T.
CHRISTIE, Alexander.
Scot. Edinburgh 1807-1860 Same. B-DNB-T.
CHRISTIE, James Elder.
Scot. Fifeshire 1847-1914. T.
CHRISTMAS, E. W.
Eng. ac. 1915 in London. M.
CHRISTMAS, Gerard [or Gerrett]. (Carver)
Eng. ac. 1614-1634 in London. DNB-T.
CHRISTOPHORUS. *see* Master C.
CHRISTOPHSEN, Pieter. *see* Cristus, Petrus.
CHRISTUS, Petrus. *see* Cristus, P.
CHRISTY, Earl. (Ill.)
Am. b. Phila., Pa. 1883; ad. 1934 New York. W.
CHRISTY, Howard Chandler.
Am. b. Morgan Co., Ohio 1873; ad. 1935 New York. A-B-F-T-W-46.
CHROSTOWSKI-OSTOJA, Stanislaw. (Eg.)
Pol. ac. 1930. M.
CHURAZZI, Jonderia. (S). It. M.
CHURBUCK, Leander M.
Am. b. Wareham, Mass. 1861; ad. 1934 Brockton, Mass. A-B-F.
CHURCH, Angelica Schuyler. (S)
Am. b. Scarborough, N. Y. 1878; ad. 1934 Ossining, N. Y. A-F.
CHURCH, Charles F.
Am. ad. 1934 Chicago. A.
CHURCH, Frederic Edwin.
Am. b. Brooklyn, N. Y. 1876; ad. 1934 New York. A.
CHURCH, Frederick Edwin.
Am. Hartford, Conn. 1826-1900 New York.
A1-B-Bd-C-DAB-E-F-T-1-3-4-15-45-46-71-209-701.
CHURCH, Frederick Stuart.
Am. Grand Rapids, Mich., 1842-1924 New York. A21-B-C-DAB-T-WX1-15-46.
CHURCHILL, Alfred Vance.
Am. b. Oberlin, O. 1864; ad. 1934 Northampton, Mass. A-B-W.
CHURCHILL, William W.
Am. Boston, Mass. 1858-1926 Wash., D. C. A025-B-F.
CHURCHMAN, Ella Mendenhall.
Am. b. Brooklyn, N. Y.; ad. 1934 Brielle, N. J. A.
CHU TA.
Chinese. ac. 17th century. E.
CIAMPAGLIA, Carlo.
Am. b. Italy 1891; ad. 1934 New York. A-F.
CIANFARANI, Aristide Berto.
Am. b. Agnone, It. 1895; ad. 1934 Providence, R. I. A.
CIANI, Vittorio A. (S)
Am. Florence, It. 1858-1908 Perth Amboy, N. J. B-F-Ta.
CIARDA, Emma.
It. Venice 1879-1933. B-T.
CIARDI, Beppe [Giuseppe].
It. Venice 1875-1932. T.
CIARDI, Guglielmo.
It. Treviso 1843-1917 Venice. B-C-T.
CIAVARRA, Pietro. (S)
Am. b. Phila., Pa. 1891; ad. 1934 Same. A-F.
CIBBER [or Cibert], Caius [or Kai] Gabriel. (S)
Dan. Hensborg 1630-1700 London. B-E.
CICCIO, Abate. *see* Solimena, F.
CICCIO, Il. *see* Francanzano, F.
CICCIONE, Andrea. *see* Andrea da Firenze.
CICÉRI, Bernardino.
It. Pavia 1650-1718. B-T.
CICÉRI, Eugène.
Fr. Paris 1813-1890 Marlotte. B-T.
CICHONOVICH, Nikolai.
Rus. ad. 1935 Detroit, Mich. M.
CICOGNA, Maestro.
It. ac. 1300-1332 Verona. T.
CICOGNARA [or Cicognari], Antonio.
It. ac. 1480-1500 in Cremona. B-T.
CIESLEWSKI, Tadensz, Jr. (Eg.)
Pol. b. Warsaw 1895. T.
CIGNANI, Carlo.
It. Bologna 1628-1719 Forli. B-C-E-T-722.
CIGOLI [or Civoli], Lodovico Cardi da. *see* Cardi, L.
CIKOVSKY, Niccolai.
Am. b. Pinsk, Pol. 1894; ad. 1934 New York. A.

CIMA DA CONEGLIANO, GIOVANNI BATTISTA.
It. Friuli 1459-1517/18 Conegliano.
B-Bd-C-T-722.
CIMABUE [or Gualtier], GIOVANNI [or Cenni di Pepo].
[Considered the oldest painter on canvas.]
It. Florence 1240-1301/2.
B-Bd-C-E-T-V-322.
CIMAROLI, GIOVANNI BATTISTA.
It. b. Salo Brescia; d. after 1753 in Venice.
T.
CIMINO, HARRY D. (Eg.)
Am. b. Marion, Ind. 1898; ad. 1934 Falls Village, Conn. M.
CIMIOTTI, GUSTAVE.
Am. b. New York 1875; ad. 1934 Same.
A-B-F-W.
CIMMUTO, ARMANDO DEL. (Et.)
Am. ad. 1934 Aspinwall, Pa. M.
CIMON OF CLEONAE.
Gr. (Early Vase Painter.) E.
CINISELLI, GIOVANNI. (S)
It. Milan 1832-1883 Rome. B-T.
CIONE, ANDREA DI BERNARDO DI. *see* Orcagna, A.
CIONE, JACOPO DI.
It. 1308-1394. M.
CIPOLLA, FABIUS [or Fabio].
It. b. 1854; ac. 1902 Rome. B-T.
CIPOLLINI, BENEDICT R. (S)
Am. b. Carrara, It. 1889; ad. 1934 Somerville, Mass. A.
CIPPER, GIACOMO FRANCESCO [Tedesco].
It. ac. 1710-1736. T.
CIPRIANI, GIOVANNI BATTISTA. (Eg.)
It. Florence 1727-1785 London.
B-Bd-DNB-E-T.
CIRINO, ANTONIO.
Am. b. Italy 1889; ad. 1934 Providence, R. I.
A.
CISARI, GIULIO. (Et.)
It. ac. 1934 in Milan. M.
CISERI, ANTONIO.
It. Ascona 1821-1891 Florence. B-T.
CITRON, MINNA.
Am. b. Newark, N. J. 1896; ad. 1934 New York. A.
CITTADINI, TITO.
Sp. ex. 1933 Pittsburgh, Pa. M.
CIVERCHIO, VINCENZO [Il. Fanone].
It. Crema 1468/70-1544 Milan. B-Bd-E-T.
CIVETTA. *see* Bles, Henri Met de.
CIVILETTI, BENOÎT. (S)
It. b. Palermo 1846. B-T.
CIVITALI, MATTEO DI GIOVANNI. (S)
It. Lucca 1435/6-1501. B-Hs-T.
CLADEL, MARIUS. (S)
Fr. b. Sèvres 1883. DBA.
CLADIUS, WILHELM LUDWIG HEINRICH.
Ger. b. Altona 1854. T.
CLAESZ [or Claessens], PIETER II.
Flem. d. 1623 Bruges. B-T.
CLAESSEUS. *see* Utrecht, Jacob van.
CLAESZ, ALLAERT [or Wyert]. (Eg.)
Dut. 1498-1564 Amsterdam. B-T.
CLAESZ [or Claessens], PIETER III.
Dut. Haarlem 1600-1661 Same. B-T.
CLAGHORN, JOSEPH C. (Et.)
Am. ad. 1934 Cabin John, Md. A.

CLAGUE, RICHARD.
Am. La. 1816-1878 New Orleans, La.
F-144-183.
CLAIRIN, GEORGE JULES VICTOR.
Fr. Paris 1843-1919. B-C-DBA-T.
CLANCY, JOE. W.
Am. ad. 1935 Birmingham, Ala. M.
CLANEY, HOWARD.
Am. ad. 1933 New York. M.
CLAPP, MARCIA. (S)
Am. b. Hartsville, Ind. 1907; ad. 1934 New York. A.
CLAPP, WILLIAM HENRY.
Am. b. Montreal, Can.; ad. 1934 Oakland, Calif. A-F.
CLARA, JOSÉ [or Júan]. (S)
Sp. b. Olot 1878. DBA-Hs.
CLARE, JOSEPH.
Am. d. 1917 Central Islip, L. I., N. Y. A14.
CLARENBACH, MAXIMILIEN.
Ger. b. Neuss 1880. B-T.
CLARIN, PIERRE EUGÈNE.
Fr. b. 1897. M.
CLARK. *see also* Clarke.
CLARK, ADELE.
Am. ad. 1934 Richmond, Va. A-F.
CLARK, ALLAN. (S)
Am. b. Missoula, Mont. 1898; ad. 1934 Santa Fé, N. M. A-Cs-F.
CLARK, ALSON SKINNER.
Am. b. Chicago 1876; ad. 1934 Pasadena, Calif. A-B-F-T-W.
CLARK, ALVAN. (Min.)
Am. Ashfield, Mass. 1804-1887 Cambridge, Mass. F-2-4-6-169.
CLARK, BENTON. (Ill.)
Am. b. Coshocton, O. 1895; ad. 1934 New York. M.
CLARK, ELIOT CANDEE.
Am. b. New York 1883; ad. 1935 Charlottesville, Va. A-F-W.
CLARK, ELSIE SOUTHWICK.
Mrs. C. Waterbury Clark.
Am. ex. 1934 New York. M.
CLARK, [Mrs.] EMELIA M. GOLDWORTHY.
Am. b. Platteville, Wis. 1869; ad. 1934 Los Angeles, Calif. A.
CLARK, FLETCHER. (S)
Am. b. Kansas; ex. 1935 New York. M.
CLARK, FREEMAN.
Am. b. Holly Springs, Miss.; ad. 1934 Same.
A-F.
CLARK, HARRIETTE A. (Min.)
Am. b. Depere, Wis. 1876; ad. 1935 New York. A12-F.
CLARK, HERBERT WILLIS, JR. (S)
Am. 1877-1920. M.
CLARK, ISAAC C.
Am. ad. 1935 Haddam, Conn. M.
CLARK, JAMES.
Eng. b. Hartlepool 1858; ex. 1934 London.
B-Wa.
CLARK, JAMES LIPPITT. (S)
Am. b. Prov., R. I. 1883; ad. 1934 New York.
A-F.
CLARK, JOHN A.
Am. ad. 1934 New York. M.
CLARK, JOHN HEAVISIDE ["Waterloo"].
Scot. 1771/2-1863 Edinburgh. B-T.

CLARK, Joseph.
Eng. Dorchester 1834-1919. T.
CLARK, Matt. (Ill.)
Am. b. Coshocton, O. 1903; ad. 1934 New York. M.
CLARK, Roland. (Et.)
Am. ad. 1935 New York. M.
CLARK, Rose.
Am. ad. 1933 Buffalo, N. Y. B-M.
CLARK, Roy C.
Am. b. Sheffield, Mass. 1889; ad. 1934 Takoma Park, Md. A-F.
CLARK, Sally. (S)
Mrs. James Lippitt Clark.
Am. ad. 1934 New York. M.
CLARK, Sarah L.
Am. b. Phila., Pa. 1869; ad. 1934 Same. A.
CLARK, Thomas.
Scot. Whiteside 1820-1876 Dundarach. DNB-T.
CLARK, Virginia Keep.
Mrs. Marshall Clark.
Am. New Orleans, La. 1878; ad. 1934 New York. A-F.
CLARK, Walter.
Am. Brooklyn, N. Y. 1848-1917 Bronxville, N. Y. 1917. A014-B-F-T.
CLARK, Walter Appleton.
Am. Worcester, Mass. 1876-1906 New York. A06-B-F-T-46.
CLARK, Walter Leighton.
Am. Phila., Pa. 1859; ad. 1934 New York. A.
CLARKE, Dora. (S)
Eng. ad. 1934 London. Wa.
CLARKE, Frederick Benjamin. (S)
Am. b. Mystic, Conn.; ad. 1934 New York. A.
CLARKE, George. (S)
Eng. 1796-1842 Birmingham. B-DNB.
CLARKE, Gladys Dunham.
Am. Southington, Conn. 1899; ad. 1934 Weston, Conn. A.
CLARKE, Harriet Ludlow.
Eng. ac. 1837-1866 London. DNB-T.
CLARKE, Harry.
Eng. 1891-1931. Y01932.
CLARKE, John Lee, Jr.
Am. b. Albuquerque, N. M. 1907; ad. 1934 Springfield, Mass. M.
CLARKE, John Louis. (S)
Am. ex. 1934 New York. F-M.
CLARKE, René. (Ill.)
Am. ad. 1931 New York. M.
CLARKE, Theophilus.
Eng. 1776-1832 London. B-DNB.
CLARKE, Thomas. (Eg.)
Am. b. Ireland; ac. 1797 in Phila., Pa. DNB-F-T-2-7-147.
CLARKE, Thomas Shields. (P-S)
Am. Pittsburgh, Pa. 1860-1920 New York. A017-B-DAB-E-F-Hs-T-Ta-WX1-46.
CLARKE, William.
Am. ex. 1935 San Fran., Calif. M.
CLARKSON, Nathaniel.
Eng. Islington 1724-1795. B-DNB-T.
CLARKSON, Ralph Elmer.
Am. Amesbury, Mass. 1861; ad. 1934 Chicago. A-B-F-T-W-757.

CLARY, Jean Eugène.
Fr. Paris 1856-1929 Same. B-DBA.
CLASGENS, Fréderic. (S)
Am. b. Richmond, Ohio; ad. 1933 Paris. DBA.
CLATER, Thomas.
Eng. 1789-1867 London. B-DNB-T.
CLAUDE, Louis Michel. *see* Clodion.
CLAUDE, Maxime Jean.
Fr. Paris 1823/4-1904 Same. B-DBA.
CLAUDE OF LORRAINE [Gellée].
Fr. Charmes 1600-1682 Rome, It. B-Bd-C-E-T-323-655-722-748-870-917.
CLAUDEL, Camille. (S)
Fr. ac. 1888-1930 in Paris. B-DBA.
CLAUS, Émile.
Belg. Flanders 1849-1924 Astène. DBA-E.
CLAUS, William A. J.
Am. b. Maintz, Ger. 1862. A28-F.
CLAUSEN, [Sir] George.
Eng. b. London 1852; ex. 1934 Same. B-DNB-E-T-Wa-825.
CLAUSER [or Klauser], Jacob.
Swi. Zurich 1520/30-1578 Mülhausen. T.
CLAUSSELL, Joaquim.
Mex. ad. 1934 Mexico City, Mex. M.
CLAXTON, Virgie.
Am. b. Gatesville, Tex. 1883; ad. 1934 Houston, Tex. A.
CLAY, Alfred Borron.
Eng. Preston 1831-1868 Liverpool. B-DNB-T.
CLAY, Edward Williams. (Cart.)
Am. Phila., Pa. 1799-1857 New York. DAB-F-T-2-7-764.
CLAY, [Mrs.] Howard.
Br. ad. 1934 Halifax, N. S. M.
CLAY, [Mrs.] Mary F. R.
Am. b. Phila., Pa.; ad. 1934 Bar Harbor, Me. A-B.
CLAY, William.
Am. d. New York 1911. A010.
CLAYPOOLE, James.
Am. Phila., Pa. 1720-1795 Jamaica, West Indies. F-2-179-182
CLAYS, Paul Jean.
Belg. Bruges 1819-1900 Brussels. B-E-T.
CLAYTON, Alexander Benjamin.
Am. b. Chevy Chase, Md. 1906; ad. 1934 Same. A.
CLAYTON, Frances. (Ill.)
Am. ac. 1932. M.
CLAYTON, John.
Eng. 1728-1800 Enfield. B-DNB.
CLEAR, Charles Val.
Am. b. Albion, Ind.; ad. 1934 Wash., D. C. A.
CLEAVER, Alice.
Am. Racine, Wis. 1878; ad. 1934 Falls City, Neb. A.
CLEAVES, Muriel Mattocks.
Mrs. H. H. Cleaves.
Am. b. Hastings, Neb.; ad. 1934 Prince Bay, S. I., N. Y. A.
CLEEF, Joos. *see* Cleves, J.
CLELAND, Thomas Maitland.
Am. b. New York 1880; ad. 1934 Danbury, Conn. A-F.
CLEMENS, Wilhelm.
Ger. Munich 1847; ac. 1902 in Berlin. B-T.

CLÉMENT, ACHILLE.
Fr. b. Marseilles; ac. 1862. B-T.
CLEMENT, EDWARD HENRY.
Am. b. Chelsea, Mass. 1843; ad. 1915 Boston [deceased]. A12-B-F.
CLÉMENT, FÉLIX AUGUSTE.
Fr. Donzère 1826-1888 Alger. B-T.
CLÉMENT, JOSEPH MAXIME. (Ill.)
Fr. b. Chasseneuil; ac. 1934 Paris. DBA.
CLÉMENT, THÉRÈSE.
Fr. b. Paris 1889; ac. 1934 Same. DBA.
CLEMÉNTE, DON SALVADOR.
Sp. ac. 1883 in Cadiz. C.
CLEMÉNTI, PROSPERO. (S)
It. d. 1584. Hs.
CLEMENTS, GABRIELLE DE VEAUX.
Am. b. Phila., Pa. 1858; ad. 1934 Gloucester, Mass. A-B-F-T.
CLEMENTS, GEORGE H.
Am. b. La.; ad. 1934 New York. A-F.
CLEMENTS, GRACE.
Am. b. Oakland, Calif. 1905; ad. 1934 Los Angeles, Calif. A.
CLEMENTS, ROSALIE THOMSON.
Am. b. Wash., D. C. 1878; ad. 1934 Wiccopee, N. Y. A.
CLEMENTZ, HERMANN.
Ger. b. Berlin 1852. B-T.
CLEMINSON, ROBERT.
Br. ac. 1865-1868 in London. B.
CLENNELL, LUKE. (Eg.)
Eng. Ulgham 1781-1840 Newcastle. B-DNB-T.
CLEOMENES OF ATHENS. (S)
Gr. ac. 150 B.C. in Athens. Hs.
CLEPHANE, LEWIS PAINTER.
Am. b. Wash., D. C. 1869; ad. 1934 Same. A-F-184.
CLERC. *see* Le Clerc.
CLERC, BARTHÉLEMY DE. *see* Barthélemy de C.
CLERE, HAZEL. (S)
Am. ad. 1934 New York. M.
CLERE, VERE. (S)
Am. ad. 1934 New York. M.
CLERISSEAU, CHARLES [or Jacques] LOUIS.
Fr. Paris 1722-1820 Auteuil. B-T.
CLERMONT, GALLERANDE ADHEMAR DE.
Fr. d. 1895 France. M.
CLÉSINGER, JEAN BAPTISTE AUGUSTE. (S)
Fr. Besançon 1814-1883. B-T.
CLEVELY, JOHN. [The Elder.]
Eng. London 1747-1792 Same. B-DNB.
CLEVELY, ROBERT.
Eng. London 1747-1809 Douvres, Fr. B-DNB-T.
CLEVENGER, SHOBAL VAIL. (S)
Am. Middleton, Ohio 1812-1843 at sea. DAB-F-Hs-T-Ta-4.
CLÈVES [or Cleef], JOOS VAN DER BELE [The Elder].
[Called Master of the Death of the Virgin.]
Flem. Clèves 1485?-1540/1 Antwerp. B-T-662-722.
CLÈVES [or Cleef], JOOS VAN [The Younger].
Flem. Antwerp 1516?-1556? B-T-662-722.
CLÈVES [or Cleef], MARTIN VAN [The Elder].
[Master of the Ape.]
Flem. Antwerp 1527-1581 Same. B-C-T.
CLEYN [or Clein or Kleine], FRANZ.
Eng. Rostock 1582-1658 London. B-T.
CLIFFORD, EDWARD.
Eng. Bristol 1844-1907. B-T.
CLIFFORD, JOHN H. (Et)
Am. ad. 1935 New Bedford, Mass. T.
CLIFTON, ADELE ROLLINS.
Mrs. Henry Clifton.
Am. b. Brooklyn, N. Y. 1875; ad. 1934 Phila., Pa. A.
CLIME, WINFIELD SCOTT.
Am. b. Phila., Pa. 1881; ad. 1934 Old Lyme, Conn. A-F.
CLINEDINST, BENJAMIN WEST.
Am. Woodstock, Va. 1859-1931 Pawling, N. Y. A028-B-F-T-W16.
CLINKER, LEROY C. (Ill.)
Am. ad. 1934 New York. M.
CLINT, ALFRED. (Cart.)
Eng. London 1807-1883. DNB-T-Y01884.
CLINT, GEORGE.
Eng. London 1770-1854. B-DNB-T.
CLINT, SCIPIO. (Med.)
Eng. 1805-1839 London. DNB-T.
CLISBEE, GEORGE ["Kliz"]. (Ill.)
Am. ad. 1935 Westport, Conn. M.
CLIVETTE, MERTON.
Am. Wisconsin 1848-1931 New York. A028-M.
CLODION, LOUIS [Claude Michel]. (S)
Fr. Nancy 1738-1814 Paris. B-E-Hs-T.
CLOGSTON, EVELYN BELLE.
Am. Pomona, Calif. 1906; ad. 1934 Portland, Ore. A.
CLONNEY, JAMES GOODWYN.
Am. Liverpool, Eng. 1812-1867 Binghampton, N. Y. F-T-2-6.
CLOS, ANTOINE JEAN DU. *see* Duclos, A. J.
CLOSE, MARY LEWIS.
Am. b. Brooklyn, N. Y. 1886; ad. 1915 Same. A12.
CLOSS, GUSTAV PAUL.
Ger. Stuttgart 1840-1870. B-T.
CLOSSON, WILLIAM BAXTER PALMER. (Eg.)
Am. Thetford, Vt. 1848-1926 Hartford, Conn. A23-DAB-F-T-W14-8-46-47.
CLOSTERMAN, JOHANN BAPTIST.
Ger. Osnabrück 1660-1711 London. T.
CLOSTERMAN, JOHN.
Ger. Osnabrück 1656-1713 London. B-DNB-T-702.
CLOTZ [or Clots], Valentine [or Valentyn].
Dut. Maestricht 1669-1743. B-T-Wi.
CLOUET [or Cloet], FRANÇOIS [or Janet or Jehannet].
Fr. Tours 1505/10-1572 Paris. B-Bd-C-E-T-324-722-847.
CLOUET [or Cloet], JEAN [or Jehannet].
Flem. Brussels 1486-1546 Paris. B-C-E-T-324-722.
CLOUET DE NAVARRE [Brother François Clouet].
Fr. ac. 1529. B-T.
CLOUGH, GEORGE L.
Am. Auburn, N. Y. 1824-1901 Same. A04-T.

CLOUGH, Jane B.
Am. b. Chicago 1881; ad. 1934 Kansas City, Mo. A.
CLOUGH, Stanley Thomas.
Am. b. Cleveland, O. 1905; ad. 1934 Same. A.
CLOUZOT, [Mlle] Marianne.
Fr. ex. 1935 Paris. M.
CLOVER, Lewis P.
Am. New York 1819-1896. F-T-7.
CLOVER, Philip.
Am. 1842-1905 Columbus, O. A05-F-T.
CLOVER-BEW, [Mrs.] Mattie May. (S)
Am. b. Ind., Ind. 1865; ad. 1934 San Fran., Calif. A.
CLOVIO [or Macedo], Giorgio Giulio.
It. 1498-1578 Rome, It. B-E-T-V-656.
CLOWES, Butler. (Eg.)
Eng. ac. 1768-1782 in London. B-DNB-T.
CLUBB, John Scott. (Cart.)
Am. Hall, N. Y. 1875-1934 Rochester, N. Y. M-Obit. N. Y. papers, 1-29-1934.
CLUSMANN, William.
Am. North Laport, Ind. 1859-1927 Chicago. A024-B-F.
CLUTE, Beulah Mitchell.
Mrs. Walter Marshall Clute.
Am. b. Rushville, Ill. 1873; ad. 1934 Berkeley, Calif. A-F.
CLUTE, Carrie Elizabeth.
Am. b. Schenectady, N. Y. 1890; ad. 1934 New York. A.
CLUTE, Walter Marshall.
Am. Schenectady, N. Y. 1870-1915 No. Cucanonga, Calif. A012-B-F.
CLUTERBUCK, Julia. (Et.)
Eng. d. 1932. Y01933.
CLUVER, Bernt.
Am. b. Norway; ex. 1934 New York. M.
CLUZEAU, Pierre Antoine Marie.
Fr. b. St. Mandé 1884. DBA.
CLYMER, Edwin Swift.
Am. b. Cincinnati, O. 1871; ad. 1934 Gloucester, Mass. A-B-T.
CLYMER, James Floyd.
Am. b. Perkasie, Pa. 1893; ad. 1934 Provincetown, Mass. A-F.
CLYMER, John.
Can. ex. 1934 Toronto, Ont. M.
COADE, Eleanor. (S)
Eng. ac. 1773-1791 London. B-T.
COADY, Robert J.
Am. New York 1881-1921 Brooklyn, N. Y. A18.
COALE, Donald Vincent.
Am. b. Baltimore, Md. 1906; ad. 1934 Same. A.
COALE, Griffith Bailey.
Am. b. Baltimore, Md. 1890; ad. 1934 New York. A-F.
COAN, Frances C. Challenor. (Ill.)
Am. b. East Orange, N. J.; ad. 1934 Nyack, N. Y. A.
COAN, Helen E.
Am. ad. 1934 Los Angeles, Calif. A.
COAST, Oscar Regan.
Am. Salem, O. 1851-1931 Santa Barbara, Calif. A028-F.
COATE, Harry W.
Am. b. Ogden, O.; ad. 1915 New York. A12-B.
COATES, George James.
Aust. b. Melbourne; ad. 1934 Chelsea, Eng. B-T-Wa.
COATS, Randolph L.
Am. b. Richmond, Ind. 1891; ad. 1934 Ind., Ind. A.
COBB, Bert.
Am. ad. 1935 Harmon, N. Y. M.
COBB, Cyrus. (P-S)
Am. Malden, Mass. 1834-1903 Allston, Mass. A04-B-F-T-15.
COBB, Darius. (P-S)
Am. Malden, Mass. 1834-1919 Newton Falls, Mass. A016-B-F-T-Y01920-15.
COBB, H. I.
Am. ex. 1934 New York. M.
COBB, [Mrs.] Katherine M.
Am. b. Syracuse, N. Y. 1873; ad. 1934 Same. A.
COBB, Nathaniel.
Am. Danville, Vt. 1869-1932 Rome, It. *see* Art Digest 5-1-1935.
COBBETT, Edward John.
Eng. London 1815-1899 Same. B-T.
COBHAM, [Mrs.] Ethel R. (Ill.)
Am. ad. 1934 Fieldston, N. Y. M.
COBURN, Frederick Simpson.
Can. b. Montreal 1871; ad. 1935 Same. M.
COBURN, Frederick William. (Ill.)
Am. b. Nashua, N. H. 1870; ad. 1934 Lowell, Mass. A.
COCCETTI, Napoléon.
It. b. Florence 1850. B-T.
COCHEREAU, Léon Matthieu.
Fr. Montigny 1793-1817. T.
COCHET, Robert Eugène Joseph. (S)
Fr. b. Paris 1903. DBA.
COCHIN, Charles Nicolas [The Elder]. (Eg.)
Fr. Paris 1688-1754 Same. B-T.
COCHIN, Charles Nicolas [The Younger].
Fr. Paris 1715-1790 Same. B-T.
COCHRAN, Allen Dean.
Am. b. Cincinnati, O. 1888; ad. 1934 Woodstock, N. Y. A-F.
COCHRAN, William.
Scot. 1738-1785 Glasgow. B-DNB-T.
COCHRANE, Constance.
Am. b. Pensacola, Fla.; ad. 1934 Upper Darby, Pa. A.
COCHRANE, Josephine G.
Am. b. Phila., Pa.; ad. 1934 Wash., D. C. A28.
COCK, César de.
Flem. Ghent 1820-1904. B-T.
COCK, Hieronymus Wellens.
Flem. 1510-1570. B-E-T-V.
COCK, Jan de.
Flem. ac. 1506/27 in Antwerp. T.
COCK, Jan Claudius. (S)
Flem. Antwerp 1668/70-1736 Same. T.
COCK, Philbert.
Flem. b. 1879. Fa.
COCK VAN AELST, Pieter. *see* Aelst, P. C. van.
COCK, Xavier de.
Flem. Ghent 1818-1896 Deurle. B-T.

COCKBURN, James Pattison.
Eng. 1778-1847 Woolwich. B-T.
COCKCROFT, Edythe Varian.
Mrs. Charles L. Wayland.
Am. b. Brooklyn, N. Y. 1881; ad. 1934 Ramapo, N. Y. A12-F-M.
COCKER, Edward. [Pen Work.]
Eng. 1631-1675 London. DNB-T.
COCKERELL, Samuel Pepys. (S)
Eng. b. London 1844. T-798.
COCKRELL, Dura Brokaw.
Mrs. E. R. Cockrell.
Am. b. Liscomb, Ia. 1877; ad. 1934 Fulton, Mo. A.
COCKSON [or Coxon], Thomas. (Eg.)
Eng. ac. 1591-1636. B-T.
COCTEAU, Jean. (Ill.)
Fr. ad. 1934 Paris. DBA.
COCX. *see* Coques, Gonzalez.
CODDE [or Kodde], Pieter Jacobsz.
Dut. Amsterdam 1599-1678. B-C-T.
CODEZO, Thomas.
Am. b. Havana, Cuba; ac. 1869 U. S. B-F-T-15.
CODRINGTON, Isabel.
Eng. b. Devon; ad. 1934 Woldingham. DBA-Wa.
COE, Charles Martin.
Am. b. Massillon, O. 1902; ad. 1934 Cleveland Heights, O. A.
COE, Ethel Louise.
Am. b. Chicago; ad. 1934 Evanston, Ill. A-B-F-46.
COE, Richard B.
Am. ad. 1935 Birmingham, Ala. M.
COE, Theodore D.
Am. b. Suffern, N. Y. 1866; ad. 1934 Tampa, Fla. A.
COEBERGHEN, [or Koebergen] Wenceslas.
Flem. 1557/61-1634 Brussels. B-T-722.
COECKE VAN AELST, Pieter. *see* Aelst, P. C. van.
COELLO, Alónzo Sánchez.
Sp. Valencia 1515-1590 Madrid. B-E-T-722.
COELLO, Claudio.
Sp. Madrid 1630/5-1693 Same. B-C-T-722.
COEN, Robert.
Am. ad. 1934 Toledo, O. M.
COENE [or Cona or Cone], Jacques.
Fr. b. Paris 1398. [No death date.] T.
COENE, Jean Henri de.
Flem. Nederbrakel 1798-1866 Brussels. B-T.
COES, Kent Day.
Am. ad. 1934 Upper Montclair, N. J. M.
COESSIN DE LA FOSSE, Charles Alexander.
Fr. b. Lisieux 1829; ac. 1902 in Paris. C-T.
COETZER, W. H.
Br. b. Cape Colony, So. Africa 1900. M.
COFFEE, Thomas. (S)
Eng. ac. Charleston, S. C. 1850. F-M.
COFFEE, William J. [or W. T.]. (S)
Eng. ac. 1801-1816 in London. B-T.
COFFERMANS. *see* Koffermans.
COFFEY, Neva.
Am. ad. 1935 New York. M.
COFFIN, George Albert.
Am. 1856-1922 New York. A020-F.
COFFIN, Isabel C.
Am. b. Portland, Me.; d. 1912 Summit, N. J. A010.
COFFIN, J. Edward. (Cart.)
Am. Minn., Minn. 1860-1905 Manchester, N. H. A05.
COFFIN, Sarah Taber.
Mrs. William H. Coffin.
Am. Vassalboro, Me. 1844-1928. A26-B.
COFFIN, William Anderson.
Am. Allegheny, Pa. 1855-1925 New York. A22-B-C-DAB-F-T-W13.
COFFIN, William Haskell.
Am. ad. 1934 New York. A28-B-F-M.
COFFMAN, Charles W.
Am. ad. 1935 Waynesboro, Pa. M.
COGDELL, John Stevens. (P-S)
Am. Charleston, S. C. 1778-1847 Same. DAB-F-T-2.
COGELS, Joseph [Mabilde].
Flem. Brussels 1786-1831. C.
COGGLESHALL, John I.
Am. Fall River, Mass. 1856-1927 Lowell, Mass. A025.
COGNIET, Léon.
Fr. Paris 1794-1880 Same. B-T.
COGSWELL, William.
Am. Fabius, N. Y. 1819-1903 Pasadena, Calif. A06-F.
COHAN, Max Bernd.
Am. ex. 1935 New Orleans, La. M.
COHEN, Harry.
Am. 1824-1906 Amityville, L. I., N. Y. A18.
COHEN, Hy.
Am. b. London 1901; ad. 1934 New York. A.
COHEN, Isaac M.
Eng. b. Ballarat; ad. 1934 London. Wa.
COHEN, Isabel M.
Am. b. Charleston, S. C. 1867; ad. 1934 Same. A-F.
COHEN, Katherine M. (S)
Am. Phila., Pa. 1859-1914 Same. A012-F-T-Ta.
COHEN, Lewis.
Am. London 1857-1915 New York. A012-B-F-T.
COHEN, Nessa. (S)
Am. b. New York 1885; ad. 1934 Newark, N. J. A-F.
COHILL, Charles.
Am. ac. 1838 in Phila., Pa. [No death date.] F.
COHN, Ala. (S)
Aust. ac. 1933. M.
COHN, Max Arthur.
Am. ex. 1935 New York. M.
COIA. (Cari)
It. (Glasweigian); ac. 1933 London. M.
COIGNARD, Louis.
Fr. Mayenne 1810/2-1883 Paris. B-T.
COIGNET, Jules Louis Philippe.
Fr. Paris 1798-1860 Same. B-T.
COINER, Charles T. (Ill)
[Designed the Blue Eagle of the N.R.A.]
Am. b. Santa Barbara, Calif. 1898; ad. 1935 Mechanicsville, Pa. M.
COIT, Caroline.
Am. b. Cleveland, O.; d. 1934. M.

COL, David.
Belg. Antwerp 1822-1900 Antwerp. B-T.
COLA. *see* Camerino da.
COLA DI PETRUCCIOLO [da Orvieto].
It. ac. 1372-1408 in Italy. T.
COLAHAN, Colin.
Aust. b. Melbourne 1897. Y1922.
COLANTONIO, Niccolò Antonio [del Fiore].
It. ac. 1420-1460 in Naples. Fa.
COLBRON, Paul T.
Am. ad. 1934 New Canaan, Conn. M.
COLBURN, Eleanor.
Am. b. Dayton, O.; ad. 1934 Laguna Beach, Calif. A.
COLBURN, Eleanor Ruth.
Mrs. Joseph Elliott Colburn.
Am. Dayton, O. 1866-1929. A25-F.
COLBURN, Joseph Elliott.
Am. Massena, N. Y. 1853-1927. A026.
COLBY, George W.
Am. ex. 1934 New York. M.
COLBY, Homer Wayland. (Ill)
Am. b. No. Berwick, Me. 1874; ad. 1934 Arlington, Mass. A28.
COLBY, James M.
Am. Arlington, Mass. 1841-1909 Waltham, Mass. A8.
COLBY, Josephine Wood.
Mrs. Franklin G. Colby.
Am. New York 1864-1930 Andover, N. J. A28-F.
COLDSTREAM, William.
Eng. ad. 1934 London. M.
COLE, Adelaide.
Am. ac. 1888. M.
COLE, Alphaeus Philemon.
Am. b. Jersey City, N. J. 1876; ad. 1934 New York. A-F-T-W.
COLE, Annie Elizabeth.
Mrs. Myron Asa Cole.
Am. Prov., R. I. 1880-1932 Washington, D. C. A030.
COLE, Charles Octavius.
Am. b. Newburyport, Mass. 1814; ac. 1835 New Orleans, La. F-169.
COLE, Ernest A. (Et)
Eng. ac. 19th century. Wi.
COLE, Ethel Kathleen.
Eng. b. Beccles 1892; ad. 1934 London. Wa.
COLE, George.
Eng. Portsmouth 1808/10-1883 London. B-C-DNB-T.
COLE, George Vicat.
Eng. Portsmouth 1833-1893 London. B-C-DNB-T.
COLE, John Vicat.
Eng. b. London 1903; ad. 1934 Sussex. Wa.
COLE, Joseph Foxcroft.
Am. Jay, Me. 1837-1892 Winchester, Mass. B-DAB-F-T-4-15-47-48.
COLE, Joseph Greenleaf.
Am. Newburyport 1803-1858 Boston, Mass. F-2-169.
COLE, Margaret Ward. (S)
Mrs. Alphaeus Philemon Cole.
Am. b. Haslington, Eng.; ad. 1934 New York. A.
COLE, Reginal Vicat.
Eng. b. London 1870; ac. 1930. T.
COLE, Tennyson Philip.
Eng. ac. 1878-1889 in London. B-T.
COLE, Thomas.
Am. Bolton-le-Moors, Eng. 1801-1848 Catskill, N. Y. B-Bd-C-DAB-E-F-T-2-3-4-15-45-46-49-50.
COLE, Thomas Casilear.
Am. b. Stattsburg, N. Y. 1888; ad. 1934 New York. A-F.
COLE, Timothy. (Eg)
[Son of Thomas Cole 1801-1848.]
Am. London 1852-1931 Poughkeepsie, N. Y. A028-E-F-T-W16-1-8-151-185.
COLE, Virginia Thurman.
Am. b. Columbus, O.; ad. 1934 Same. A.
COLEMAN. *see also* Colman.
COLEMAN, Blanche E.
Am. ad. 1934 Boston, Mass. M.
COLEMAN, Charles Caryl.
Am. Buffalo, N. Y. 1840-1928 Capri, It. A026-B-C-DAB-F-T-W6-1-4-15-21.
COLEMAN, Enrico [Henry].
It. Rome 1846-1911. B-T.
COLEMAN, Glenn O.
Am. Springfield, O. 1887-1932 Long Beach, Calif.
A029-F-M-Y01933-Obit. N. Y. papers 5-9-1932.
COLEMAN, Herbert.
Am. Goshen, N. Y. 1833-1925 New York. A23.
COLEMAN, Mary Dartes.
Am. b. Ft. Worth, Tex.; ad. 1934 Los Angeles, Calif. M.
COLEMAN, Ralph Pallen. (Ill)
Am. b. Phila., Pa. 1892; ad. 1934 Same. A-F.
COLEMAN, William Stephen. (Ill)
Eng. Horsham 1829-1904 St. John's Woods. DNB-T.
COLERIDGE, Gilbert. (S)
Eng. b. London 1859; ad. 1934 Surrey. Wa.
COLES, Ann Cadwallader.
Am. b. Columbia, S. C. 1882; ad. 1934 New York. A.
COLES, Mary Drake.
Am. ex. 1935 New York. M.
COLETTI, Joseph Arthur. (S)
Am. b. Italy 1898; ad. 1934 Boston. A-Cs.
COLGATE, Edith Frances.
Mrs. Charles Baker Salsbury.
Am. ad. 1934 New York. M.
COLIBERT, Nicolas. (Eg.)
Fr. Paris 1750-1806 London. B-T.
COLIN. *see also* Collin.
COLIN, Alexandre. (S)
Flem. Mechlin, Belg. 1526-1612 Innsbruck, Aus. E-Hs.
COLIN, Alexandre Maria.
Fr. Paris 1798-1873/5 Same. B-T.
COLIN, Gustave Henri.
Fr. Arras 1828-1911. B-T.
COLIN, Paul.
Fr. Nimes 1838-1916 Paris. DBA.
COLIN, Paul Émile.
Fr. b. Lunéville 1877. DBA-T.
COLIN, Paul Hubert. (S)
Fr. b. Paris 1801; ac. 1840 Same. [No death date.] B-T.

COLL, Joseph Clement. (Et.)
Am. Phila., Pa. 1881-1921 Same. A018-B-C-F-T.
COLL, Madeleine Jeanne. *see* Lemaire, M. J.
COLLAERT, Adriaen. (Eg)
Flem. 1560-1618 Antwerp. B-T.
COLLAERT, Jan [or Hans Baptist]. (Eg)
Flem. 1540-1628. B-E-T.
COLLANTES, Francisco.
Sp. Madrid 1599-1656. B-C-T-722.
COLLART, Marie.
Belg. b. Brussels 1842. B-T.
COLLE RAFFAELLO DAL [Borgo].
It. Foligna 1490-1540 Rome. B-T-V.
COLLES, Gertrude.
Am. b. Morristown, N. J. 1869; ad. 1934 Same. A.
COLLET, Charles. (S)
Fr. b. Esternay; ac. 1889 Paris. B.
COLLET, John.
Eng. London 1725?-1780. B-DNB-T.
COLLETTE, Maurice.
Am. ad. 1934 New York. M.
COLLIER, Charles Myles.
Am. Hampton, Va. 1836-1908 Gloucester, Mass. A07-F.
COLLIER, Estelle Elizabeth.
Mrs. H. H. Collier.
Am. b. Chicago, 1881; ad. 1934 So. Tacoma, Wash. A.
COLLIER, Franklin Perry. (Cart)
Am. Beverly, Mass, 1881-1934 Brookline, Mass. M.
COLLIER, John.
Eng. London 1850-1934 Same. B-T-Wa-Obit. N. Y. papers, 4-12-1934.
COLLIER, John ["Tim Bobbin"]. (Cart)
Br. Warrington 1708-1786. B-DNB-T.
COLLIER, Nate. (Ill)
Am. b. Orangeville, Ill. 1883; ad. 1934 Leonia, N. J. A.
COLLIER, Thomas ["Tom"].
Eng. Glossop 1840-1892 London. B-T.
COLLIN, Dominique. (Eg)
Fr. Mirecourt 1725-1781 Nancy. B-T.
COLLIN, Louis Joseph Raphael.
Fr. Paris 1850-1916. B-T.
COLLIN DE VERMONT, Hyacinthe.
Fr. Versailles 1693-1761 Paris. B-T.
COLLINGS, Albert H.
Eng. b. London; ex. 1934 Same. Wa.
COLLINGS, Charles John.
Can. b. Devonshire, Eng. 1848-1931 Can. M-Obit. Art Digest, 9-1-1934.
COLLINGS, Samuel. (Cart.)
Eng. ex. 1780-1789 in London. B-DNB.
COLLINGWOOD, William.
Eng. Greenwich 1819-1903 Bristol. B-T.
COLLINS, Alfred Quinton.
Am. Portland, Me. 1855-1903 Cambridge, Mass. A04-F-T.
COLLINS, Archibald.
Eng. Worcester 1853-1922 Adelaide, So. Aust. T.
COLLINS, Benjamin Franklin.
Am. b. Phila., Pa. 1895. A28.
COLLINS, Charles Allston.
Eng. London 1828-1873. B-Bd-DNB-T.
COLLINS, Edward Quinton.
Am. Boston 1862-1913 Cambridge, Mass. A9.
COLLINS, John.
Eng. 1725?-1758/9 London. B-DNB-T.
COLLINS, John. (Eg.)
Eng. ac. 1670-1682 London. B-T.
COLLINS, John Walter.
Am. b. Naperville, Ill. 1897; ad. 1934 New York. A.
COLLINS, Julia Alice.
Am. b. Savannah, Ga.; ad. 1934 Same. A.
COLLINS, Mary Susan.
Am. b. Bay City, Mich. 1880; ad. 1934 East Cleveland, O. A.
COLLINS, Richard. (Min.)
Eng. Gosport 1755-1831 London. B-DNB-T.
COLLINS, Samuel. (Min.)
Eng. ac. 1750-1780 in Bristol. B-DNB.
COLLINS, Walter.
Am. Dayton, O. 1870-1933 Tampa, Fla. A030.
COLLINS, William.
Eng. London 1788-1847 Same. B-Bd-C-DNB-E-T-722.
COLLINS, William Wiehe.
Eng. b. Kensington 1862; ad. 1934 Holford. Wa.
COLLINSON, James.
Eng. 1825?-1881 London. B-DNB-T.
COLLVER, Ethel Blanchard.
Mrs. L. L. W. Collver.
Am. b. Boston; ad. 1934 Greenwich, Conn. A.
COLMAN. *see also* Coleman.
COLMAN, George Sumner.
Am. b. Elgin, Ill. 1881; ad. 1934 Balboa Beach, Calif. A.
COLMAN, R. Clarkson.
Am. b. Elgin, Ill. 1884; ad. 1934 La Jolla, Calif. A.
COLMAN, Samuel.
Am. Portland, Me. 1832-1920 New York. A017-B-C-DAB-E-F-T-WX1-4-15-22-39.
COLNOT, Arnout J. G.
Dut. ad. 1935 Amsterdam; ex. 1934 Pittsburgh, Pa. M.
COLOMBE [or Colomb], Michel. (S)
Fr. Nantes 1430-1512. B-Hs-T.
COLONIA, Adam de.
Dut. Rotterdam 1634-1685 London. B-DNB.
COLONIA, Adam Louisz de.
Flem. Antwerp 1574-1651 Rotterdam. B.
COLONNA, Michele Angelo. (Mu.)
It. 1600-1686/7 Bologna. B-T-722.
COLOQUHOUN, Archibald.
Ex. 1934 in London. M.
COLOTES. *see* Kolotes.
COLT, Arthur N.
Am. ad. 1934 Madison, Wis. M.
COLT, John [The Younger]. (S)
Eng. ac. 1618 in England. DNB-M.
COLT, Martha Cox.
Mrs. Guy Colt.
Am. b. Harrisburg, Pa.; ad. 1934 Same. A.
COLT, Maximilian. (S)
Eng. b. Arras, Fr.; ac. 1595-1618 in England. DNB-M.
COLT, Morgan.
Am. Summit, N. J. 1876-1926. A23.

COLTMAN, Ora.
Am. b. Shelly, O. 1858; ad. 1934 Cleveland, O. A.
COLTON, Gordon.
Am. b. Brooklyn, N. Y. 1877; ad. 1934 Same. A.
COLTON, Mary Russell Ferrell.
Mrs. Harold S. Colton.
Am. b. Louisville, Ky. 1889; ad. 1934 Flagstaff, Ariz. A.
COLTON, William Robert. (S)
Eng. b. Paris 1867; ac. 1910 London. B-DBA-E-T.
COLWELL, Elizabeth. (Et.)
Am. b. Mich. 1881; ad. 1934 Chicago. A.
COLYER, Vincent.
Am. Bloomingdale, N. Y. 1825-1888 Conn. C-F-T-3-15-45.
COLYNS DE NOLE, Jacob [or Jacques]. (S)
Flem. ac. 1520-1601 at Cambrai, Belg. Hs-T.
COLYNS DE NOLE, Robert.
Flem. Antwerp 1570-1635/6 Same. B-T.
COMACINI, Il. (S)
It. ac. 1321 in Italy. M.
COMAN, Charlotte Buell.
Am. Waterville, N. Y. 1833-1924 Yonkers, N. Y. A22-C-DAB-F-T-W13-15-46.
COMANTONIO, Alcamedos Gio. (S)
Am. ad. 1935 Jersey City, N. J. M.
COMBS, Frances Hungerford.
Am. ad. 1934 Wash., D .C. A.
COMERE, Léon François.
Fr. Trelou 1850-1916 Paris. B-C-DBA-T.
COMERFORD, John. (Min.)
Ir. Dublin 1762?-1832? DNB.
COMÉS, Marcella Rodange.
Am. b. Pittsburgh, Pa. 1905; ad. 1934 Same. A.
COMFORT, Charles Fraser.
Can. b. Edinburgh, Scot.; ad. 1935 Toronto, Can. M.
COMINS, [Mrs.] Alice R.
Am. ad. 1934 Carmel, Calif. M.
COMINS, Eben Farrington.
Am. b. Boston 1875; ad. 1934 Wash., D. C. A-F.
COMO, Guido da Pisa. (S)
It. Lombard; ac. 1250 in Italy. Hs.
COMPERA, Alexander.
Am. So. Bend, Ind. 1856-1906 Calif. A06-T.
COMPRIS, Maurice.
Am. b. Holland 1885; ad. 1934 Rockport, Mass. A.
COMPTON, Caroline R.
Ad. 1935 Vicksburg, Miss. M.
COMPTON, Edward Harrison.
Eng. b. Bavaria 1881; ad. 1934 Same. T-Wa.
COMSTOCK, Anna Botsford. (Eg.)
Mrs. John H. Comstock.
Am. Otto, N. Y. 1854-1930. A12-T-W15.
COMSTOCK, Enos Benjamin.
Am. b. Milwaukee, Wis. 1879; ad. 1934 Leonia, N. J. A-F.
COMSTOCK, Frances Bassett.
Am. b. Elyria, O. 1881. A28-F.
COMSTOCK, H. B. (Silhouette)
Am. ad. 1934 New York. M.
COMTE, Pierre Charles.
Fr. Lyons 1823-1895 Paris. B-T.
COMTE-CALIX, François Claudius.
Fr. Lyons 1813-1880 Chazay. C.
CONACHER, J.
Am. ad. 1935 Rowayton, Conn. M.
CONANT, Alban Jasper.
Am. Chelsea, Vt. 1821-1915 New York. A012-DAB-F-W8.
CONANT, Lucy A.
Am. ad. 1930 Phila., Pa. M.
CONANT, Lucy Scarborough.
Am. Brooklyn, N. Y. 1867-1921 Boston. A018.
CONANT, Marjorie.
Mrs. Harold Bush-Brown.
Am. b. Boston 1885; ad. 1934 Atlanta, Ga. A-F.
CONARD, Grace Dodge.
Am. b. Dixon, Ill. 1885; ad. 1934 River Forest, Ill. A.
CONARROE, George W.
Am. 1803-1882. F.
CONCA, Sebastiano.
It. Gaeta 1676/80-1764 Naples. B-Bd-C-E-T.
CONDÉ, John [or Jean]. (Eg.)
Eng. b. France; ac. 1785-1800 London. B-DNB-T-880.
CONDER, Charles.
Eng. London 1868-1909 Same. B-DNB-B-T.
CONDIT, [Mrs.] Charles L.
Am. b. Perrysburg, O. 1863; ad. 1934 Austin, Tex. A.
CONDON, Catherine E.
Am. ad. 1934 Syracuse, N. Y. M.
CONDY [or Cundy], Nicholas Matthew.
Eng. Plymouth 1799-1857 Same. B-DNB.
CONE, Joseph. (Eg.)
Am. ac. 1814-1830. F-T-2-7-40.
CONE, Marvin D.
Am. b. Cedar Rapids, Ia. 1891; ad. 1934 Same. A.
CONEGLIANO, Cima. *see* Cima da C.
CONEGLIANO, Giovanni Battista da. *see* Cima da C. G. B.
CONELY, William B.
Am. 1830-1911. M.
CONEY, John. (Eg.)
Eng. London 1786-1833. B-T.
CONGDON, Adairene Vose.
Mrs. Thomas R. Congdon.
Am. b. New York; ac. 1926. A12-F-T.
CONGDON, Allen.
Am. ad. 1935 Nantucket, Mass. M.
CONGDON, Thomas Raphael.
Am. Addison, N. Y. 1862-1917 Boston. A015-F-T.
CONGNET, Gillis [Vlek].
Flem. Antwerp, Belg. 1535-1599 Hamburg, Ger. C.
CONINCK. *see also* Koninck.
CONINCK, David de.
Flem. Antwerp, Belg. 1636-1687 Rome, It. C.
CONINCK, Pierre Louis Joseph de.
Fr. Meteren 1828-1910 Same. B-T.
CONINXLOO, Cornélis van.
Flem. ac. 1526/58 in Brussels. B-T.
CONINXLOO, Gilles I. van.
Flem. Antwerp, Belg. 1544-1607 Amsterdam, Holland. B-T.

CONIXLOO, Jan II. van.
Flem. Brussels, Belg. 1489?-1552 Antwerp, Belg. B-T.

CONKEY, Samuel. (P-S)
Am. New York 1830-1904 Brooklyn, N. Y. A5-T.

CONKLING, David Paul Burleigh. (P-S)
Am. New York 1871-1926 Same. A23-F.

CONKLING, Mable. (P-S)
Mrs. Paul B. Conkling.
Am. b. Boothbay, Me. 1871; ad. 1934 New York. A-Cs-F.

CONLEY, Sarah Ward.
Am. b. Nashville, Tenn. 1861; ad. 1934 Same. A.

CONLEY, William J.
Am. d. 1909 New York. A07.

CONLON, George. (S)
Am. b. Maryland; ac. 1926. A12-F.

CONNARD, Philip.
Eng. b. Southport 1875; ad. 1934 Richmond. T-Wa-825.

CONNAWAY, Jay H.
Am. b. Liberty, Ind. 1893; ad. 1934 New York. A.

CONNELL, Edwin D.
Am. b. New York 1859; ad. 1934 Clamert, Fr. A-F-T.

CONNELY, Pierce Francis. (S)
Am. b. La. 1841; ac. 1900 Florence, It. DAB-F-T-Ta-15.

CONNER, Albert Clinton.
Am. Indiana 1848-1929 Calif. A026.

CONNER, John Ramsey.
Am. b. Radnor, Pa.; ad. 1934 Bryn Athyn, Pa. A.

CONNER, Paul.
Am. b. Richmond, Ind. 1881; ad. 1934 Long Beach, Calif. A.

CONNICK, Charles J. (Glass-P)
Am. ad. 1934 Boston, Mass. M.

CONNOR, Charles.
Am. Richmond, Ind. 1857-1905 Same. A05-T.

CONNOR, Jerome Stanley. (S)
Am. b. Ireland 1876; ad. 1935 Wash., D. C. A20-F-T.

CONNY, John. (Eg.)
Am. Boston 1655-1722 Same. F-T-2-7.

CONOR, William.
Ir. b. Belfast; ad. 1934 Same. Wa-Y1928.

CONOVER, Alida. (Ill.)
Am. ex. 1935 New York. M.

CONOVER, Garrett V.
Am. ad. 1934 Riveredge, N. J. M.

CONRAD [or Conradus], Abraham. (Eg.)
Flem. Amsterdam, Holland 1612/3-1661 Same. B-T.

CONRAD VON CREUZNACH. *see* Faber, Conrad.

CONRAD-KICKERT.
Dut.-Fr. ad. 1934 Paris; ex. 1934 Pittsburgh, Pa. DBA-M.

CONRADS, Carl H. (S)
Am. b. Germany 1839. [No death date.] F-Ta.

CONROW, Wilford Seymour.
Am. b. So. Orange, N. J. 1880; ad. 1934 New York. A-F.

CONSANI, Vincenzo. (S)
It. Lucca 1818-1887 Florence. T.

CONSTABLE, John.
Eng. Suffolk 1776-1837 London. B-Bd-C-DNB-E-T-325-326-722-790-820-870-909-922.

CONSTANT, Benjamin. *see* Benjamin-C.

CONSTANT, George Z.
Am. b. Aijun, Greece 1892; ad. 1934 New York. A.

CONSTANT, Smith. *see* Smith-C.

CONSTANTINESCO, Marc. (S)
Fr. b. Charlottenburg 1900. DBA.

CONSTANTINI, Abraham.
It. Genoa 1785-1855 Same. B-T-677.

CONSTANZI, Placide.
It. 1688-1759. B.

CONSUELO-FOULD.
Fr. Cologne, Ger. 1862-1927 Paris. DBA.

CONTALI, A. (S)
It. ac. 19th century in Italy. M.

CONTARINI, Giovanni.
It. Venice 1549-1605 Same. C.

CONTEL, Jean Charles [Leconte].
Fr. Glos-Montfort 1895-1928. DBA.

CONTENT, Daniel ["Dan"]. (Ill.)
Am. ad. 1934 New York. M.

CONTI, Bernardino dei.
It. Pavia 1450-1525. B-T.

CONTI, Gino Emilio.
Am. b. Lucca, It. 1900; ad. 1934 Prov., R. I. A.

CONTI, Primo.
It. b. 1900; ad. 1934 Viarezzio. M.

CONTI, Tito.
It. b. Florence 1842. B-C-T.

CONTUCCI, Andrea. *see* Sansovino.

CONVERS, Louis J. (S)
Fr. Paris 1860-1915. B-DBA-T.

CONWAY, John Severinus. (S)
Am. Dayton, O. 1852-1925 Tenafly, N. J. A23-F-T-Ta.

CONWAY, William John. (S)
Am. b. St. Paul, Minn. 1872; ad. 1934 Same. A-F.

COOGHEN, Leendert van der.
Dut. Haarlem 1610-1681. T-803.

COOK. *see also* Cooke.

COOK, Clarence.
Am. Dorchester, Mass. 1828-1900 Fishkill, N. Y. A1.

COOK, Frances Kerr. (Ill.)
Mrs. David C. Cook, Jr.
Am. b. West Union, Ia.; ad. 1934 Elgin, Ill. A.

COOK, George E.
Am. d. 1930 Southern Pines, N. C. A027.

COOK, Hazelle Grace.
Am. b. Minn., Minn. 1899; ad. 1934 Milwaukee, Wis. A.

COOK, Howard Norton. (Et.)
Am. b. Springfield, Mass. 1901; ad. 1935 Same. A28-M.

COOK, Isabel Vernon.
Mrs. Jerome Cook.
Am. b. Brooklyn, N. Y.; ad. 1934 New York. A.

COOK, John A.
Am. b. Gloucester, Mass. 1870; ad. 1934 Same. A-F.

COOK, John William. (Eg.)
Eng. b. London; ac. 1820-1850 Same. B-T.
COOK, Lauren W. (Ill.)
Am. ad. 1934 New York. M.
COOK, Mary Elizabeth. (S)
Am. b. Chillicothe, O. 1881; ad. 1934 Columbus, O. A-Cs-F.
COOK, Nelson.
Am. ac. 1844. F-M.
COOK, Paul Rodda.
Am. b. Salina, Kan. 1897; ad. 1934 San Antonio, Tex. A.
COOK, Richard.
Eng. London 1784-1857 Same. B-DNB.
COOK, Robert.
Br. d. 1593? B-DNB-T.
COOK, Samuel.
Eng. 1806-1859 Plymouth. B-DNB.
COOK, Thomas. (Eg.)
Eng. 1744?-1818 London. B-DNB.
COOK, Walter.
Am. New York 1846-1916. M.
COOK, William Edwards.
Am. b. Independence, Ia. 1881; ad. 1915 Same. A12-T.
COOK-SMITH, Jean Beman. (S)
Am. b. New York 1865; ad. 1934 San Diego, Calif. A-F.
COOKE. *see also* Cook.
COOKE, Charles H.
Am. b. Toledo, O. 1859; ad. 1934 Chicago. A.
COOKE, Dorothea.
Am. b. Hollywood, Calif. 1908; ad. 1934 Same. A.
COOKE, Edward William.
Eng. London 1811-1880 Tunbridge Wells. B-DNB-T.
COOKE, George. (Eg.)
Eng. London 1781-1834 Barnes. B-DNB-T.
COOKE, Henry.
Eng. 1642-1700. B-T.
COOKE, Isaac.
Eng. Warrington 1846-1922 Wallasey. B-T.
COOKE, Jessie Day.
Am. b. Atchison, Kan. 1872; ad. 1934 Chicago. A.
COOKE, Regina Tatum.
Am. b. Corsicana, Tex. 1902; ad. 1934 Denver, Colo. A.
COOKE, William Bernard. (Eg.)
Eng. 1778-1855. B-DNB.
COOKE, William John. (Eg.)
Ir. Dublin 1797-1865 Darmstadt, Ger. B-DNB.
COOKMAN, Charles Edwin.
Am. Columbus, O. 1856-1915. A012-F.
COOL, Jan Daemen.
Dut. Rotterdam 1589-1660 Amsterdam. B-T.
COOLIDGE, Bertha. (Min.)
Am. b. Lynn, Mass. 1880; ad. 1934 New York. A-F.
COOLIDGE, Georgette E.
Mrs. Walter B. Coolidge.
Am. Brooklyn, N. Y. 1850-1929. A026.
COOLIDGE, John.
Am. b. Penn. 1882; ad. 1934 Los Angeles. A-F-W15.
COOLIDGE, John Templeman, Jr.
Am. b. Boston 1888; ad. 1934 Readville, Mass. A.
COOLIDGE, Mary Rosamond.
Am. b. Watertown, Mass. 1884; ad. 1934 Same. A28.
COOMANS, Pierre Olivier Joseph.
Belg. Brussels 1816-1889 Bologna, It. B-T.
COOMBS, Delbert Dana.
Am. b. Lisbon Falls, Me. 1850; ad. 1915 Auburn, Me. A12.
COON, Howard A.
Am. ad. 1934 Ballardvale, Mass. M.
COONSMAN, Nancy. *see* Hahn, N. C.
COOPER, Abraham.
Eng. London 1787-1868 Greenwich, Eng. B-C-DNB-E-T.
COOPER, Alexander. (Min.)
Eng. London 1605?-1660 Stockholm, Swi. DNB-E.
COOPER, Alexander Davis.
Eng. 1837-1888 London. E-T.
COOPER, Alfred Egerton.
Eng. b. Tettenhall 1883; ex. 1934 London. Wa.
COOPER, Alfred Heaton.
Eng. 1864-1929 London. T-Y01930.
COOPER, Alice. (S)
Am. b. Denver, Colo.; ac. 1926. F.
COOPER, Colin Campbell.
Am. b. Phila., Pa. 1856; ad. 1934 Santa Barbara, Calif. A-F-T-W.
COOPER, Emma Lampert.
Mrs. Colin Campbell Cooper.
Am. b. Nunda, N. Y.; d. 1920 Pittsfield, Mass. A017-F-T-46-829.
COOPER, Florence A.
Am. ad. 1934 Toledo, O. M.
COOPER, Ford H.
Am. ad. 1935 New Britain, Conn. M.
COOPER, Frederic G. (Cart.)
Am. b. McMinnville, Ore. 1883; ad. 1934 New York. W.
COOPER, George Victor.
Am. Hanover, N. J. 1810-1878 New York. Fa.
COOPER, Henry.
Am. b. Russia 1905; ad. 1934 Phila., Pa. A.
COOPER, James Davis. (Eg.)
Eng. Lambeth 1823-1904 London. DNB-T.
COOPER, Jane Farrow.
Mrs. John Cooper.
Am. b. Laurens, S. C. 1861; ad. 1934 Atlanta, Ga. A.
COOPER, John. (Eg.)
Eng. b. London 1894; ex. 1932 Same. B-T.
COOPER, Margaret Miller.
Mrs. Elisha H. Cooper.
Am. b. Terryville, Conn. 1874; ad. 1934 New Britain, Conn. A-F.
COOPER, Mario. (Ill.)
Am. ad. 1934 Bayside, L. I., N. Y. M.
COOPER, Marjorie E. (Mu.)
Am. ad. 1934 Great Falls, Mont. M.
COOPER, Peregeine F.
Am. ac. 1840-1890. F-6-15.
COOPER, Richard [The Elder]. (Eg.)
Eng. Yorkshire 1705-1764 Edinburgh, Scot. B-DNB-T.

COOPER, Richard [The Younger].
Scot. Edinburgh 1740?-1810/4 London. B-DNB-T.
COOPER, Robert. (Eg.)
Eng. ac. 1795-1836 in London. B-DNB-T.
COOPER, Samuel. (Min.)
Eng. London 1609-1672 Same. B-DNB-E-T.
COOPER, Thomas Sidney.
Eng. Canterbury 1803-1902 Same. B-Bd-C-DNB-E-T.
COOPER, William.
Am. ad. 1934 Memphis, Tenn. M.
COOPER, William Heaton.
Eng. b. Coniston 1903; ad. 1934 Sussex. Wa.
COOPER, William Henry.
Eng. b. Romsey 1858; ad. 1934 Sanhurst. Wa.
COOPER, Winifred.
Eng. ac. 1919 in England. Y1924.
COOPSE [or Coops], Pieter.
Dut. ac. 1668-1677 in Amsterdam. B-T.
COOSEMANS, Joseph Théodore.
Belg. Brussels 1828-1904 Same. C-T.
COOTES, F. Graham.
Am. b. Staunton, Va. 1879; ad. 1934 New York. A.
COOVER, Nell B.
Am. b. Wooster, O.; ad. 1934 Laguna Beach, Calif. A.
COPE, [Sir] Arthur Stockdale.
Eng. ac. 1875-1912 London. B-T.
COPE, Charles West.
Eng. Leeds 1811-1890 Bournemouth. B-DNB-T.
COPE, Margaretta P. (Min.)
Am. ad. 1934 Phila., Pa. M.
COPELAND, Alfred Bryant.
Am. b. Boston, Mass.; d. 1909 Same. A07-F-T-15.
COPELAND, Charles G.
Am. b. Thomaston, Me. 1858; ad. 1934 Newton Center, Mass. A-F-T-W.
COPELAND, Eleanor Rogers.
Mrs. Joseph Frank Copeland.
Am. b. London 1875; ad. 1934 Drexel Hill, Pa. A.
COPELAND, Joseph Frank.
Am. b. St. Louis, Mo. 1872; ad. 1934 Drexel Hill, Pa. A-F-T.
COPELAND, M. Baynon.
Am. b. El Paso, Tex.; ad. 1935 Paris. A12-F.
COPLEY, [Mrs.] John. *see* Gabain, Ethel.
COPLEY, John Singleton [The Elder].
Am.-Eng. Boston, Mass. 1737-1815 London. B-Bd-C-DAB-DNB-E-F-T-1-2-4-5-6-7-45-46-51-138-179-182-184-210-211-212-701
COPONIUS. (S)
Roman. ac. 80 B.C. in Rome. T.
COPPEDGE, [Mrs.] Fern.
Am. b. Decatur, Ill. 1888; ad. 1934 Phila., Pa. A-F-W.
COPPERMAN, Mildred Turner.
Am. b. New York 1906; ad. 1934 Gloucester, Mass. A.
COPPINI, Eliseo.
Am. ac. 1915. M.
COPPINI, Pompeo. (S)
Am. b. Moglia, It. 1870; ad. 1934 New York. A-Cs-F-T-W.
COPPOLI, Carlo.
It. Florence 1850-1933 Same. T.

COQUES [or Cocx], Gonzalèz.
Flem. Antwerp 1614-1684. B-C-E-T-722.
COQUIN [or Cossin], Louis.
Fr. Troyes 1627-1686 Paris. T.
CORABOEUF, Jean Alexander.
Fr. b. Pouillé; ac. 1896-1930 Paris. B-DBA.
CORAM, Thomas. (Eg.)
Am. Bristol, Eng. 1756-1810/2 U. S. F-2-4-7-182.
CORBAUX, Marie Françoise Cathern Doetter.
[Called Fanny Corbaux].
Eng. 1812-1883 Brighton. B-DNB.
CORBET, Matthew Ridley.
Eng. So. Willingham 1850-1902 London. B-DNB-T.
CORBETT, Edward J.
Eng. b. London 1815; ac. 1849 Paris. [No death date.] B-T.
CORBETT, Gail Sherman. (S)
Mrs. Harry Wiley Corbett.
Am. b. Syracuse, N. Y.; ad. 1934 New York. A-Cs-F-W.
CORBINO, Jon. (S)
Am. b. Italy 1905; ad. 1934 New York. M.
CORBOULD, Edward Henry.
Eng. London 1815-1905 Same. B-DNB.
CORBOULD, Henry. (Ill.)
Eng. London 1787-1844 Same. B-DNB.
CORBOULD, Richard.
Eng. London 1757-1831 Highgate. B-DNB-T.
CORCK, Albert H.
Am. ad. 1934 Brooklyn, N. Y. M.
CORCOS, Vittorio Matteo.
It. b. Leghorn 1859. B-T.
CORDAZZO. *see* Vivani.
CORDELLIAGHI, Andrea. *see* Previtali, A.
CORDEN, William [The Elder]. (Min.)
Eng. Ashbourne 1797-1867 Nottingham. DNB-T.
CORDEN, William [The Younger].
Eng. d. 1900. T.
CORDERO, Joséf.
Sp. Maria 1717-1797 Sèville. T.
CORDIER, Marie Louise.
Fr. Paris 1853-1927 Same. DBA.
CÒRDOBA, Pedro de.
Sp. ac. 1475 in Còrdova. T-774.
CORDONNIER, Alphonse Amédée. (S)
Fr. b. Madeleine 1848. B-DBA-T-798.
CÒRDOVA, Pablo de. *see* Cespedes.
CORELLI, Augusto.
It. Rome 1853-1910 Turin. B-C-T.
CORENZIO [or Corentio], Belisario [or Baldassare].
It. Greece 1558/60-1640/3 Naples. B-E-T.
CORINI, Margit de.
Am. b. 1902; ad. 1935 New York. M.
CORINTH, Joseph Lovis [or Louis].
Ger. Königsberg 1858-1925 Holland. B-E-T-775.
CORIOLANO, Bartolommeo. (Eg.)
It. Bologna 1599-1676 Same. B-T.
CORLEY, Viola.
Am. ad. 1935 Del Rio, Tex. M.
CORMON, Fernand Anne Piestre.
Fr. Paris 1845-1924 Same. B-C-DNB-E-T.

CORNE, Michele Felice.
Am. Italy 1752-1832 Newport, R. I. F-2-6-169.
CORNEAU, Eugène.
Fr. b. Vouzeron 1894. DBA.
CORNEILLE DE LYON, Claude.
Fr. The Hague, Holland 1500/5-1574/7. B-T.
CORNEILLE, Jean Baptiste [The Younger].
Fr. Paris 1649-1695 Same. B-T.
CORNEILLE, Michel [The Elder].
Fr. Orléans 1601/3-1664 Paris. B-C-T.
CORNEILLE, Michel. (Gobelins)
Fr. Paris 1642-1708 Same. B-T.
CORNELIS [or Cornelys], Albert.
Flem. ac. 1500-1532 in Bruges. B-T.
CORNELIS, Barent.
Dut. Amsterdam 1610-1661. T.
CORNELIS, van de Capelle. *see* Corneille de Lyon.
CORNELIS VAN CEULEN. *see* Ceulen, van.
CORNELIS VAN HAARLEM.
Dut. Haarlem 1562-1638 Same. B-C-T-722.
CORNELISZ, Jacob van Amsterdam.
[Called also Jacob van Oostsanen].
Dut. Oostsanen 1460/70-1533 Amsterdam. B-T-657.
CORNELISZ, Lucas de Kok.
Dut. Leyden 1493/5-1552 London. B-DNB-T.
CORNELIUS, Peter [Joseph] von.
Ger. Düsseldorf 1783-1867 Berlin. B-C-E-T-722.
CORNER, John. (Eg.)
Eng. ac. 1788-1825 in London. B-DNB-T.
CORNER, Thomas Cromwell.
Am. b. Baltimore, Md. 1865; ad. 1934 Same. A-F-T-W.
CORNETT, Robert Frank.
Am. b. Lafayette, La. 1867; ad. 1934 Woodridge, D. C. A.
CORNISH, John. (Eg)
Eng. ac. 1751-1825 in Oxford. [No death date.] Bd-T.
CORNOYER, Paul.
Am. St. Louis, Mo. 1864-1923 E. Gloucester, Mass. A020-DAB-F-T.
CORNWELL, Dean. (Ill.)
Am. Louisville, Ky. 1892; ad. 1934 New York. A-F-W.
CORNWELL, Martha Jackson. (P-S)
Am. b. West Chester, Pa. 1869; ad. 1934 Same. A-F.
CORNWELL, William Caryl.
Am. Lyons, N. Y. 1851-1932 New York. A029-F.
COROËNNE, Henri.
Fr. b. Valenciennes 1822; ac. 1883. [No death date.] B-T.
COROMALDI, Umberto.
It. b. Rome 1870. B-T.
COROT, Jean Baptiste Camille.
Fr. Paris 1796-1875 Ville d'Avray. B-Bd-C-E-T-327-328-329-820-843-847.
CORRADINI, Antonio. (S)
It. d. 1752. Hs-T.
CORRADINI, Bartolommeo [or Fra. Carnevale].
It. ac. in Urbino; d. 1478. B-T.
CORRADINI, Mara.
It. b. Naples 1910. DBA.
CORRADO, Giaquinto.
It. Molfetta 1693/9-1765 Naples. B-T.
CORREGGIO.
[Real name Antonio Allegri.]
It. Correggio 1494-1534 Same. B-Bd-C-E-T-V-330-722-920.
CORRENS, Erich.
Ger. Cologne 1822-1877 Munich. B-T.
CORRODI, Arnold.
It. Rome 1844/6-1874 Berlin, Ger. B-T.
CORRODI, Hermann David Salomon.
It. Rome 1844-1905 Same. B-T.
CORSON, Alice Vincent.
Am. b. Phila., Pa.; d. Paris, Fr. A012.
CORSON, Charles Schell.
Am. ac. in Phila., Pa.; d. 1921. A12.
CORSON, Emmasita Register.
Mrs. Walter Corson.
Am. b. Milford, Del. 1880; ad. 1915 Solesbury, Pa. A12.
CORSON, Katherine Langdon.
Mrs. Walter H. Corson.
Am. b. Eng.; ac. 1895-1925 Penn. A20-F.
CORT, [or Kort], Cornelis. (Eg)
Dut. Hoorn 1533/6-1578 Rome, It. B-E-T.
CORT, Hendrik Frans de.
Flem. Antwerp 1742-1810 London. B-DNB-T.
CORTAZZO, Oreste.
It. b. Rome 1836; ac. 1883 Paris. [No death date.] C-T.
CORTE, Júan de la.
Sp. Madrid 1597-1660 Same. B-T.
CORTESE. *see* Courtois.
CORTIGLIA, Niccolò.
Am. New York 1893; ad. 1934 Wilkes-Barre, Pa. A.
CORTONA, Pietro da. *see* Berrettini, P. da C.
CORTONA, Urbana da. (S)
It. d. 1504 Siena. M-T.
CORTOT, Jean Pierre. (S)
Fr. Paris 1787-1843. B-T.
CORVUS [or Korvus], Johannes [Jan Rave].
Flem. Bruges 1480/90-1554 London. B-DNB-T.
CORWAINE, Aaron H.
Am. Kentucky 1802-1830 Phila., Pa. F-2.
CORWIN, Charles Abel.
Am. b. Newburg, N. Y. 1857; ad. 1934 Chicago. A-F-T.
CORY, Kate T.
Am. b. Illinois; ad. 1934 Prescott, Ariz. A.
COSGROVE, Earle M.
Am. d. 1915 Los Angeles, Calif. A013.
COSIMINI, Roland Francis.
Am. b. Paris 1898; ad. 1934 Winthrop Highlands, Mass. A.
COSIMO, Andrea di. *see* Feltrini, A. di G.
COSIMO DI MARIANO, Angelo.
see Bronzino.
COSIMO, Piero di. *see* Piero di C.
COSMATI [or Cosma], Giovanni. (S)
It. ac. 1290-1304 in Italy. B-Hs-T.
COSSA, Francesco del.
It. Ferrara 1435-1480. B-Bd-T.
COSSARD, Adolphe.
Fr. ad. 1935 Paris. M.

COSSIERS [or Cotsiers or Causiers], JAN.
Flem. Antwerp 1600-1671 Same. C-722.
COSSIO DEL PORMAR, FELIPE.
Peruvian. b. Pinra 1889. DBA.
COSSON, J. L. MARCEL.
Fr. b. Bordeaux; ad. 1935 Paris; ex. 1934 Pittsburgh, Pa. DBA.
COSTA. *see also* Da Costa.
COSTA, ACHILLOPULO.
Gr. b. 1910 Paris; ex. 1934 Oxford, Eng. DBA.
COSTA, GIOVANNI.
It. Leghorn 1827-1903. B-Bd-E-T.
COSTA, HECTOR. (S)
Am. b. Caltanessetta, It.; ad. 1934 New York. A.
COSTA, LORENZO [The Elder].
It. Ferrara 1460-1535 Mantua. B-Bd-C-E-T-V-722.
COSTA, LORENZO [The Younger].
It. Mantua 1537-1583 Same. B-T.
COSTA, PILIDES.
Am. ad. 1935 Phila., Pa. M.
COSTAGNI, FILIPPO.
Am. Rome, It. 1839-1904 Maryland. A05-F-T.
COSTANTINI, VIRGILIO.
It. b. Cefalu 1882. DBA.
COSTELLO, LOUISA STUART. (Min)
Br. 1799-1870 Bologne, Fr. DNB-T.
COSTELLO, VAL.
Am. b. Marion, Kan.; ad. 1934 Los Angeles, Calif. A.
COSTIGAN, JOHN EDWARD.
Am. b. Prov., R. I. 1888; ad. 1934 Orangeburg, N. Y. A-F-W.
COSWAY, MARIA LOUISA CATHERINE CECILIA. [née Hadfield; Mrs. Richard Cosway.]
Eng. Florence, It. 1759-1838 Lodi. B-DNB.
COSWAY, RICHARD.
Eng. Tiverton 1740-1821 London. B-C-DNB-E-T-722.
COT, PIERRE AUGUSTE.
Fr. Bédarieux 1837-1883 Paris. B-Bd-C-T.
COTE, A. SUZOR. *see* Suzor-Cote.
COTER, COLIJN DE [or Colin].
Flem. Tournay, Fr. 1467?-1506/9 Brussels, Belg. B-T.
COTES, FRANCIS.
Eng. London 1726-1770 Same. B-DNB-T.
COTES, SAMUEL. (Min)
Eng. 1734-1818 Chelsea. B-DNB.
COTHARIN, KATE LEAH.
Am. b. Detroit, Mich. 1866; ad. 1934 Boston. A.
COTHER, DOROTHY MCVEY.
Am. b. Tenn.; ad. 1934 Brooklyn, N. Y. A.
COTIGNOLA, BERNARDINO DA. *see* Zaganelli, B.
COTIGNOLA, FRANCESCO DA ZAGANELLI. *see* Zaganelli, F. da C.
COTIGNOLA, GIACOMA. *see* Cassignola, G.
COTIGNOLA, GIOVANNI BATTISTA. *see* Cassignola, G. B.
COTIGNOLA, GIROLAMO DA MARCHESI. *see* Marchesi da C.
COTMAN, FREDERICK GEORGE.
Eng. Ipswich 1850-1920. B-T.
COTMAN, JOHN SELL.
Eng. Norwich 1782-1842 London. B-Bd-DNB-E-T-331-658-793-844-922.
COTMAN, JOSEPH JOHN.
Eng. 1814-1878 Norwich, Eng. B-DNB-T.
COTMAN, MILES EDMUND.
Eng. 1810-1858 London. B-DNB-T.
COTSWORTH, STAATS. (Ill)
Am. b. Oak Park, Ill. 1908; ad. 1934 Florence, It. A.
COTTER, EDWARD.
Am. b. Salem, Mass.; d. Ishpeming, Mich. 1917. A015.
COTTET, CHARLES.
Fr. Puy 1863-1925 Paris. B-DBA-E-T-659.
COTTET, RÉNE. (Eg)
Fr. b. Paris; ad. 1935 Same. DBA.
COTTIGNOLA. *see* Cotignola.
COTTON, JOHN WESLEY.
Can. Toronto 1868-1932 Same. A029-F.
COTTON, LILLIAN (Impey).
Am. b. Boston 1892; ad. 1934 Paris, Fr. A.
COTTON, MARIETTA.
Mrs. Leslie Cotton.
Am. b. New York; ac. 1889-1911 in London. T.
COTTON, WILLIAM H.
Am. b. Newport, R. I. 1880; ad. 1934 New York. A-F-W.
COUARD, ALEXANDER P.
Am. b. New York 1891; ad. 1934 Norwalk, Conn. F.
COUBINE, OTHON.
Czec. b. Moravia 1883. DBA-797.
COUDER, GUSTAVE ÉMILE.
Fr. b. Paris; d. 1903 Same. B-T.
COUDER, JEAN ALEXANDRE RÉMY.
Fr. Paris 1808-1879 Same. B-T.
COUDER, LOUIS CHARLES AUGUSTE.
Fr. Paris 1790-1873. B-T.
COUDERT, AMALIA KÜSSNER. (Min)
Mrs. Charles Duport Coudert.
Am. Terre Haute, Ind. 1876-1933. F-T-W8-46-181-Obit. Art Digest, 7-1-1933.
COUGHLIN, MILDRED MARION. (Et)
Am. b. Penn. 1895; ad. 1934 Roslyn Estates, L. I., N. Y. A.
COULAUD, MARTIN.
Fr. b. Cournon; d. 1906 Paris. B-T.
COULTANS, HARRY K. (Cart)
Am. 1863-1923 Phila., Pa. A020.
COULTER, [Mrs.] MARY J.
Am. b. Newport, Ky.; ad. 1934 Santa Barbara, Calif. A.
COUNTEE, SAMUEL ALBERT.
Am. b. Texas 1909; ad. 1935 Boston, Mass. M.
COUPER, [Mrs.] B. KING.
Am. b. Augusta, Ga. 1867; ad. 1934 Montreat, N. C. A-F.
COUPER, RICHARD HAMILTON.
Am. Norfolk, Va. 1886-1918 New York. A015.
COUPER, WILLIAM. (S)
Am. b. Norfolk, Va. 1853; ad. 1934 Montclair, N. J. A-F-Hs-T-WX1-46.
COURANT, MAURICE FRANÇOIS AUGUSTE.
Fr. Havre 1847-1925 Paris. B-DBA-T.

COURBET, GUSTAVE.
Fr. Ormans 1819-1877 Vevey, Swi. B-Bd-C-E-T-192-870.
COURCHÉ, FÉLIX.
Fr. b. Paris 1863. DBA.
COURT, JEHAN [Vigier].
Fr. b. Limoges; ac. 1572-1583. B-T.
COURT, JOSEPH DÉSIRÉ.
Fr. Rouen 1797-1865 Same. B-T.
COURT, SUZANNE DE.
Fr. ac. late 16th century in Limoges. B-T.
COURTAT, LOUIS.
Fr. ac. 1873-1885 in Paris. C.
COURTEN, ANGELO DE.
It. b. Bologna 1848. B-T.
COURTENAY, ZOFJA BAUDOUIN [Mlle].
Pol. ac. 1934 in Poland. M.
COURTENS, FRANZ.
Belg. b. Termonde 1854. B-DBA-T.
COURTEYS, JEAN [or Jehan]. (Enamel)
Fr. b. Limoges 1520; d. 1586. B-T.
COURTEYS [or Corteys], PIERRE. (Enamel)
Fr. b. Limoges 1520; d. 1591. B-T.
COURTNEY, CLARENCE. (S)
Am. ex. 1935 Pittsburgh, Pa. M.
COURTOIS, GUILLAUME.
Fr. St. Hippolyte 1628-1675 Rome. B-E-T.
COURTOIS, GUSTAVE CLAUDE ÉTIENNE.
Fr. b. Pusey 1852. B-DBA-T.
COURTOIS, JACQUES [Giacomo Bourguignon].
Fr. St. Hippolyte 1621-1676 Rome, It. B-C-E-T-722.
COUSE, EANGER IRVING.
Am. b. Saginaw, Mich. 1866; ad. 1934 Taos, N. M. A-F-T-W-46.
COUSE, WILLIAM P.
Am. ad. 1934 Asbury Park, N. J. M.
COUSEN, JOSEPH. (Eg.)
Eng. Bradford 1804-1880 London. B-DNB.
COUSIN, JEAN. (S)
Fr. Soucy 1500/1-1589/90 Paris. B-C-E-T-722.
COUSINS, CLARA LEA.
Mrs. William Douglass Cousins.
Am. b. Va. 1894; ad. 1934 Danville, Va. A.
COUSINS, HENRY. (Eg.)
Eng. d. 1864 Dorking, Eng. B-T.
COUSINS, SAMUEL. (Eg.)
Eng. Exeter 1801-1887 London. B-DNB-E-T-880.
COUSTOU, GUILLAUME, I. (S)
Fr. Lyons 1677-1746 Paris. B-E-Hs-T.
COUSTOU, GUILLAUME, II. (S)
Fr. Paris 1716-1777 Same. B-T.
COUSTOU, NICHOLAS. (S)
Fr. Lyons 1658-1733 Paris. B-E-Hs-T.
COUTAN, JULES FÉLIX. (S)
Fr. Paris 1876-1925 Same. DBA-798.
COUTTS, GORDON.
Am. b. Scotland 1880; ad. 1934 Palm Springs, Calif. B-F.
COUTTS-MICHIE, JAMES. *see* Michie, J. C.
COUTURE, THOMAS.
Fr. Senlis 1815-1879 Villiers-le-Bel. B-C-E-T.
COUTURIER, EDOUARD.
Fr. 1871-1903. T.
COUTURIER, HENRI.
Am. ac. 1660-1684. Fa-M.
COUTURIER, LÉON [Antoine Lucien].
Fr. b. Mâcon 1842; ac. 1864 Lyons. B-T.
COUTURIER, PHILIBERT LÉON.
Fr. Chalon 1823-1901 St. Quentin. B-T.
COVARRUBIAS, MIGUEL. (Ill.)
Mex. b. 1902; ex. 1935 New York. M.
COVENTRY, ROBERT MCGOWN.
Scot. Glasgow 1855-1914. T.
COVEY, ARTHUR SINCLAIR.
Am. b. Bloomington, Ill. 1877; ad. 1934 Torrington, Conn. A-F-W.
COVEY, LOIS LENSKI.
Am. b. Ohio 1893; ad. 1934 Torrington, Conn. W.
COVEY, MOLLY SALE.
Mrs. Arthur S. Covey.
Am. b. Dunedin, N. Z. 1880; ad. 1915 Englewood, N. J. A12.
COVIN, MO.
Am. ad. 1935 Brookline, Mass. M.
COVINGTON, WICKLIFFE COOPER.
Mrs. R. W. Covington.
Am. b. Ky. 1867; ad. 1934 Bowling Green, Ky. A.
COWAN, ELSIE.
Am. b. 1913; ex. 1934 Orlando, Fla. M.
COWAN, SARAH EAKIN. (Min.)
Am. ad. 1935 New York. A-F.
COWELL, JOSEPH GOSS.
Am. b. Peoria, Ill. 1886; ad. 1934 Boston. A-F.
COWEN, WILLIAM.
Eng. Rotherham 1787-1860/1 London. B-DNB-T.
COWLES, CLEMENT.
Eng. ad. 1934 London. M.
COWLES, EDITH V.
Am. b. Farmington, Conn. 1874. A-F.
COWLES, GENEVIEVE ALMEDA. (Mu.)
Am. b. Farmington, Conn. 1871. A-F-T-W-46.
COWLES, HAROLD H.
Eng. ex. 1934 London. M.
COWLES, MAUD ALICE. (Mu.)
Am. Farmington, Conn. 1871-1905. A04-B-T-46.
COWLES, MILDRED LANCASTER.
Am. Farmington, Conn. 1876-1929 Paris. A026.
COWLES, RUSSELL.
Am. b. Algona, Ill. 1887; ad. 1934 New York. A-F.
COWPER, DOUGLAS.
Eng. Gibraltar 1817-1839 Guernsey, Eng. B-DNB.
COWPER, FRANK CADOGAN.
Eng. b. Northamptonshire 1877; ad. 1934 Guernsey, Eng. T-Wa.
COX, ABBIE ROSE.
Am. ad. 1934 Port Arthur, Tex. M.
COX, ALBERT SCOTT.
Am. b. Randolph, Me. 1863. F-T-W9.
COX, ALLYN. (Mu.)
Am. b. New York 1896; ad. 1934 Same. A.
COX, CHARLES BRITTON. (S)
Am. d. 1905. Ta.
COX, CHARLES HUDSON.
Am. Liverpool, Eng. 1829-1901 Waco, Tex. A04-T.

COX, DAVID [The Elder].
Eng. Birmingham 1783-1859 Same. B-DNB-E-T-793.
COX, DAVID [The Younger].
Eng. Dulwich 1808/9-1885 London. B-DNB-T.
COX, DORIS E.
Am. b. Oshkosh, Wis. 1904; ad. 1934 Wauwatosa, Wis. A.
COX, E. ALBERT.
Eng. b. London 1876; ad. 1934 Halloway. Wa.
COX, GARSTIN.
Eng. b. Cambourne 1892. Wa1929.
COX, HELEN MORTON.
Am. b. New Orleans, La. 1869; ad. 1915 New York. A12.
COX, JACOB.
Am. Phila., Pa. 1810-1892 Ind., Ind. M-181.
COX, JAMES.
Am. England 1751-1834 Phila., Pa. F-T-2.
COX, JOHN.
Am. ex. 1934 in Paris. M.
COX, KENYON. (Mu.)
Am. Warren, O. 1856-1919 New York. A016-C-DAB-E-F-T-1-46-51-71-748.
COX, LOUISE [Howland King].
Mrs. Kenyon Cox.
Am. San Fran., Calif. 1865; ad. 1934 Honolulu, Hawaii. A-F-T-W-46-829.
COX, LYDA MORGAN.
Am. b. Depere, Wis. 1881; ad. 1934 Seattle, Wash. A.
COX, PALMER. (Cart.)
Am. Granby, Can. 1840-1924 Same. A21-DAB-F-W13.
COX, WALTER B. (Mu.)
Am. b. Miss. 1872; ad. 1915 New York. A12.
COX, WALTER I.
Am. England 1866-1930 Alexandria, Va. A027.
COX, WARREN EARLE.
Am. b. Oak Park, Ill. 1895; ad. 1934 New York. A.
COX-McCORMACK, [Mrs.] NANCY. (S)
Am. b. Nashville, Tenn. 1885; ad. 1934 New York. A-Cs-F-W.
COXE, MARY BOWMAN.
Am. d. 1921 Providence, R. I. A18.
COXE, REGINALD CLEVELAND.
Am. b. Baltimore, Md. 1855; ac. 1926 Seattle, Wash. A20-F-T.
COXIE [or Coxcien], MICHIEL FIAMINGO.
Flem. Mechlin 1499-1592 Same. B-C-E-T-722.
COXIE [or Coxcyen], RAPHAËL VAN.
Flem. Mechlin 1540-1616 Ghent. B-T.
COXON, RAYMOND JAMES.
Eng. b. Hanley; ad. 1934 Hammersmith. Wa.
COY, ANNA.
Am. b. Rockford, Ill.; ad. 1934 Same. A.
COY, C. LYNN. (S)
Am. b. Chicago 1889; ad. 1934 Brookfield, Ill. A.
COY, GUY.
Am. ad. 1935 New York. M.
COYLE, DEAN G. (Ill.)
Am. ad. 1934 Cleveland, O. M.
COYLE, JAMES.
Am. England 1798-1828 New York. F-T.
COYNE, ELIZABETH K.
Am. b. Phila., Pa.; ad. 1934 Same. A.
COYNE, JOAN JOSEPH.
Am. b. Chicago 1895-1930 Phila., Pa. A028.
COYNE, WILLIAM VALENTINE. (Ill.)
Am. ad. 1934 New York. A.
COYPEL, ANTOINE.
Fr. Paris 1661-1722 Same. B-C-E-T-722.
COYPEL, CHARLES ANTOINE.
Fr. Paris 1694-1752 Same. B-C-T-722.
COYPEL, NÖEL [The Elder].
Fr. Paris 1628-1707 Same. B-C-E-T-722.
COYPEL, NÖEL NICOLAS.
Fr. Paris 1690/2-1734 Same. B-C-E-T-722.
COYSEVOX, ANTOINE. (S)
Fr. Lyons 1640-1720 Paris. B-E-Hs-T-660.
COZE, PAUL. (Ill.)
Syrian. b. Beirut; ex. 1934 New York. DBA.
COZENS, ALEXANDER.
Eng. Russia 1700-1786 London. B-DNB-T.
COZENS, JOHN ROBERT.
Eng. London 1752-1799 B-DNB-T-844.
COZZA, FRANCESCO.
It. Calabre 1605-1682 Rome. B-T.
COZZARELLI, GIACOMO DI BARTOLOMEO. (S)
It. 1453-1515. Hs-T.
COZZARELLI, GUIDOCCIO [di Giovanni].
It. 1450-1516 Siena. B-T.
COZZENS, EVANGELINE C.
Am. ad. 1934 New York. M.
COZZENS, FREDERICK SCHILLER.
Am. 1856-1928 Livingston, N. Y. A025.
COZZOLINO, SALVATORE.
It. b. Naples; ac. 1883 in Milan. B-T.
CRABEELS, FLORENT.
Belg. Anversen 1835-1896. B-T.
CRADOCK, MARMADUKE ["Luke"].
Eng. Somerton 1660?-1716 London. B-DNB.
CRAESBECKE, JOOST VAN.
Flem. Neerlinter 1606-1661? Brussels. C-722.
CRAEYER [or Krayer], GASPARD DE.
Flem. Antwerp 1582-1669 Ghent. B-C-E-T-722.
CRAFT, PERCY ROBERT.
Eng. London 1856-1934 Same. T-Wa-Obit. N. Y. papers, 11-29-1934.
CRAIG, ANNA BELLE.
Am. Pittsburgh, Pa. 1878; ad. 1934 Same. A.
CRAIG, CHARLES.
Am. b. Ohio 1846. A20-F-T-W13-46.
CRAIG, COLIN S.
Am. b. 1872; d. 1914 New York. A012.
CRAIG, EDWARD GORDON. (Eg.)
Eng. b. England 1872; ad. 1934 London. Wa.
CRAIG, EMMETT JUNIUS. (S)
Am. b. DeWitt, Mo. 1878; ad. 1934 Kansas City, Mo. A.
CRAIG, FRANK.
Eng. Abbey 1874-1918. T.

CRAIG, J. HUMBERT.
Irish. ad. 1934 Donegal; ex. 1935 London. Wa.
CRAIG, ROBERT C.
Am. ad. 1934 Ind., Ind. M.
CRAIG, THOMAS.
Am. b. Upland, Calif. 1908; ad. 1934 Los Angeles, Calif. M.
CRAIG, THOMAS BIGELOW.
Am. Phila., Pa. 1849-1924 Woodland, N. Y. A21-F-T-W13.
CRAIG, WILLIAM.
Am. Dublin, Ir. 1829-1875 Lake George, N. Y. F-T-15.
CRAIG, WILLIAM MARSHALL.
Eng. b. Manchester; ex. 1788-1828 London. B-DNB-T.
CRAIGHILL, ELEANOR RUTHERFORD.
Am. b. Ft. Totten, N. Y. 1896; ad. 1934 Williamsburg, Va. A.
CRAM, ALLEN GILBERT.
Am. b. Wash., D. C. 1886; ad. 1934 Santa Barbara, Calif. A-F.
CRAM, LEIGHTON R.
Am. ad. 1934 Boston, Mass. M.
CRAMER, ALFONS VON.
Ger. Smyrna 1834-1884 Italy. C-T.
CRAMER, FLORENCE BALLIN.
Mrs. Konrad Cramer.
Am. b. Brooklyn, N. Y.; ad. 1934 Woodstock, N. Y. A.
CRAMER, KONRAD.
Am. ad. 1934 Woodstock, N. Y. A-F.
CRAMER, PETER.
Dan. Copenhagen 1726-1782. B-T.
CRAMPTON, ROLLIN MCNEIL.
Am. b. New Haven, Conn. 1886; ad. 1934 Same. A.
CRANACH, LUCAS MULLER [The Elder].
[Real Name Lucas Sunder.]
Ger. (Saxon) Kronach, Bav. 1472-1553 Weimar. B-Bd-C-E-T-332-333-661-722-801.
CRANACH, LUCAS [The Younger].
Ger. Wittenberg 1515-1586 Same. B-Bd-C-E-T-772-801.
CRANCH, CAROLINE A.
Am. ac. 1926 in Cambridge, Mass. F-T.
CRANCH, CHRISTOPHER PEARCE.
Am. Alexandria, Va. 1813-1892 Cambridge, Mass. C-F-T-4-15.
CRANCH, JOHN.
Am. Wash., D. C. 1807-1891 Urbana, O. F-T-2-15-45.
CRANCH, JOHN.
Eng. Devon 1751-1821 London. B-DNB.
CRANDELL, BRADSHAW. (Ill.)
Am. ad. 1934 New York. M.
CRANE, ALAN. (Ill.)
Am. ad. 1934 Brooklyn, N. Y. M.
CRANE, ALBERT.
Am. ex. 1933 Paris. M.
CRANE, ANN.
Mrs. Bruce Crane.
Am. b. New York; ad. 1934 Bronxville, N. Y. A-F.
CRANE, BRUCE [Robert].
Am. b. New York 1857; ad. 1934 Bronxville, N. Y. A-B-C-F-T-W-46.
CRANE, FRANK. (Et.)
Am. Rahway, N. J. 1857-1917 New York. A015.
CRANE, FREDERICK.
Am. Bloomfield, N. J. 1847-1915 Jamaica, L. I., N. Y. A012-F-T.
CRANE, MARIA LOUISA.
Mrs. Robert Treat.
Am. ad. 1934 New York. M.
CRANE, THOMAS. (Min.)
Eng. Chester 1808/9-1859 London. B-DNB.
CRANE, WALTER T.
Eng. Liverpool 1845-1915 Horsham. B-C-DNB-E-T-334.
CRANE, WILBUR.
Am. New York 1875-1934 New Rochelle, N. Y. A-M-Obit. N. Y. papers, 12-23-1934.
CRANKE, JAMES.
Eng. 1746?-1826 London. B-DNB.
CRANMER, FRANCES. *see* Greenman, Cranmer.
CRANOR, HELEN.
Am. ex. 1934 New York. M.
CRASKE, LEONARD. (S)
Am. b. London 1882; ac. 1926 U. S. A20-Cs-F.
CRATZ, BENJAMIN A.
Am. b. Shanesville, O. 1886; ad. 1934 Toledo, O. A.
CRAUCK [or Crauk], GUSTAVE ADOLPHE DÉSIRÉ. (S)
Fr. Valenciennes 1827-1905 Same. B-E-T.
CRAVATH, RUTH. (S)
Am. b. Chicago 1902; ad. 1934 San Fran., Calif. A.
CRAVEN, HAWES. [Scene-P].
Eng. 1837-1910 London. DNB-T.
CRAVEN, LAURA.
Am. b. Phila., Pa. 1874; ad. 1915 Same. A12.
CRAWFORD, ARTHUR ROSS.
Am. b. Marilla, Mich. 1885; ad. 1934 Niles, Ill. A.
CRAWFORD, BRENETTA HERMANN.
Mrs. Earl Stetson Crawford.
Am. b. Toledo, O. 1875; ad. 1934 Menton, Fr. A.
CRAWFORD, EARL STETSON.
Am. b. Phila., Pa. 1877; ad. 1934 Menton, Fr. A-F-W16.
CRAWFORD, EDMUND THORNTON.
Scot. Cowden 1806-1855 Lasswade. B-DNB-T.
CRAWFORD, ESTHER MABEL.
Am. Atlanta, Ga. 1872; ad. 1934 Los Angeles, Calif. A-F.
CRAWFORD, LESLEY.
Am. ex. 1935 New York. M.
CRAWFORD, RALLSTON.
Am. ad. 1935 New York. M.
CRAWFORD, THOMAS G. (S)
Am. New York 1813-1857 London. DAB-E-F-Hs-T-Ta-4-15-26-52-53.
CRAWFORD, WILL. (Ill.)
Am. ad. 1934 Scotch Plains, N. J. M.
CRAWFORD, WILLIAM. [Crayon-P]
Scot. Ayr 1825-1869 Edinburgh. B-DNB-T

CRAWHILL, JOSEPH.
Scot. Newcastle-on-Tyne, Eng. 1860-1913. B-T-825.
CRAWLEY, IDA JOLLY.
Am. b. Pond Creek, Tenn. 1867; ad. 1934 Asheville, N. C. A.
CRAYER, GASPARD DE. *see* Craeyer, G.
CREAL, JAMES PIRTLE, JR.
Am. b. Franklin, Ky. 1903; ad. 1934 Denver, Colo. A.
CREDI, LORENZO DI [Barducci]. (P-S)
It. Florence 1456/9-1537 Same. B-Bd-C-E-T-V-722.
CREEFT, JOSÉ DE.
Sp. b. Guadalajara 1884; ad. 1934 Paris. DBA-M.
CREEKMORE, RAYMOND. (Et.)
Am. b. Portsmouth, Va. 1905; ad. 1935 Balt., Md. M.
CREGAN, MARTIN.
Ir. Dublin 1788-1870. B-T.
CREIFELDS, RICHARD.
Am. b. New York 1853; ad. 1934 Same. A-F.
CREIGHTON, BESSY.
Am. ad. 1934 Swampscott, Mass. A.
CREMONA, TRANQUILLO.
It. b. Pavia 1837; d. 1878. T.
CREMONINI, GIOVANNI BATTISTA. *see* Zamboni, G. B.
CRENIER, CAMILLE HENRI. (S)
Am. b. Paris 1873; ad. 1934 Mamaroneck, N. Y. A-B-F-T-W.
CRESILES OF CYDON. (S)
Gr. ac. 450 B.C. E-Hs.
CRESPI, DANIELE.
It. Busto 1590-1630 Milan. B-C-E-T.
CRESPI, GIOVANNI BATTISTA [Il. Cerano].
It. Cerano 1557-1633 Milan. B-C-E-T.
CRESPI, PACHITA.
Am. ad. 1934 New York. M.
CRESPI, [Lo Spagnuolo], GIUSEPPE MARIA.
It. Bologna 1665-1747 Same. B-C-E-T.
CRESPO, JORGE JUÁN.
Mex. ex. 1935 New York. M.
CRESSON, MARGARET FRENCH. (S)
Am. b. Concord, Mass. 1889; ad. 1934 Glendale, Mass. A-Cs-F-W.
CRESSWELL, WILLIAM N.
Can. England 1822-1888 Canada. M.
CRESWICK, THOMAS.
Eng. Sheffield 1811-1869 London. B-Bd-DNB-E-T.
CRETIUS, KONSTANTIN FRANZ.
Ger. Brieg 1814-1901 Berlin. B-T.
CREUSS, MARIE.
Am. ac. 1934 Berkeley, Calif. M.
CREW, MAYO.
Am. b. Memphis, Tenn. 1903; ad. 1934 Schenectady, N. Y. A.
CREW [or Crewe], RANDOLF.
Eng. England 1631-1657 Paris. DNB.
CRIMI, ALFREDO DIGIORGIO.
Am. b. Messina, It. 1900; ad. 1934 Bronx, N. Y. A.
CRISLER, RICHARD MANNING.
Am. b. Dallas, Tex. 1908; ad. 1934 Chicago. A.
CRISP, ARTHUR. (Mu.)
Am. b. Hamilton, Can. 1881; ad. 1934 New York. A-F-W.
CRISP, FRANCIS.
Am. b. London 1901; ad. 1934 New York. A.
CRISSAY, MARGUERITE.
Fr. b. Mirecourt; ac. 1934 Paris. DBA.
CRISTALL, JOSHUA.
Eng. Camborne 1767-1847 London. B-DNB-T.
CRISTUS, PETRUS [or Pieter Christophsen].
Flem. Baerle 1400?-1472/3 Bruges. 722-870.
CRITCHER, CATHERINE CARTER.
Am. b. Virginia; ad. 1934 Wash., D. C. A-F-T-W.
CRITE, ALLAN ROHAN.
Am. ad. 1935 Boston, Mass. M.
CRITIUS OF ATHENS. (S)
Gr. ac. 485-478 B.C. E-Hs.
CRITTENDEN, [Mrs.] C. D.
Am. ad. 1934 Flushing, L. I., N. Y. M.
CRITTENDEN, [Mrs.] WALTER H.
Am. d. 1919 Brooklyn, N. Y. A16.
CRITZ. *see* De Critz.
CRIVELLI, CARLO [Chevalier].
It. Venice 1430/5-1493/5. B-Bd-C-E-T-78-722.
CRIVELLI, VITTORIO.
It. b. Venice; ac. 1480-1501. B-Bd-T-78.
CROCE. *see* Santa Croce.
CROCHEPIERRE, ANDRÉ ANTOINE.
Fr. b. Villeneuve-sur-Lot 1860. B-DBA-T.
CROCKER, MARIAN E.
Am. b. Boston; ad. 1934 Brookline, Mass. A.
CROCKER, MARTHA E.
Am. b. So. Yarmouth, Mass. 1883; ad. 1934 Paris. A.
CROCKER, WILLIAM H.
Am. New York 1856-1928 Clermont, Fla. A026.
CROCKET, HENRY EDGAR.
Eng. b. England 1870; ac. 1913 in London. T.
CRODEL, PAUL EDUARD VON.
Ger. b. Kottbus 1862. T.
CROFTS, ERNEST.
Eng. Leeds 1847-1911 London. B-C-T.
CROISY, ARISTIDE-ONÉSIME. (S)
Fr. Fagnon 1840-1889 Paris. B-T.
CROKER [or Crocker], JOHN [or Johann]. (Med.)
Br. Dresden, Ger. 1670-1741 England. DNB.
CROKER, MARIANNE.
Br. d. 1854. DNB.
CROLA [or Croll], GEORGE HEINRICH.
Ger. Dresden 1804-1879 Ilsenburg. B-T.
CROLA [or Croll], HUGO.
Ger. b. Ilsenberg 1841. B-T.
CROLARD, FRANÇOIS. (S)
Sp. ex. 1934 New York. M.
CROLL. *see also* Crola.
CROLL, CARL ROBERT.
Ger. Dresden 1800-1865. T.
CROLL, FRANCIS. (Eg.)
Scot. Edinburgh 1827-1854. B-DNB-T.

CROMARTY, Margaret A.
Am. b. Can. 1873; ad. 1934 Pensacola, Fla. A.
CROMBIE, Benjamin William.
Scot. Edinburgh 1803-1847. T.
CROME, John ["Old Crome"].
Eng. Norwich 1768-1821 Same. B-DNB-E-T-335-336-722-845-909-922.
CROME, John Bernay.
[Son of John Crome.]
Eng. Norwich 1793/4-1842 Yarmouth. B-DNB-T.
CROMEK, Robert Hartley. (Eg.)
Eng. Hull 1770-1812 London. B-DNB.
CROMMIE, Michael James.
Am. b. New York 1889; ad. 1934 Same. A.
CROMPTON, James Shaw.
Eng. Liverpool 1853-1916 London. T.
CROMWELL, Joane.
Am. b. Lewistown, Ill.; ad. 1934 Hollywood, Calif. A.
CRON, [Mrs.] Nina Nash. (Min.)
Am. b. Spokane, Wash. 1883; ad. 1934 Honolulu, Hawaii. A.
CRONACA, Il. [Simone del Pollaiuolo.]
It. Florence 1457-1508 Same. T-V.
CRONE, Robert.
Ir. b. Dublin; ex. 1768-1779 London. B-DNB.
CRONIN, David C.
Am. ac. 1891. M.
CRONK, Marian Truby.
Am. b. Kansas 1906; ad. 1934 Denver, Colo. A.
CRONYN, Randolph E.
Am. b. New York 1901; ad. 1934 Same. A.
CROOHE, [Mrs.] Lydia R.
Am. ad. 1935 New York. M.
CROOK, Alfred T.
Am. ac. 1869; d. Albany, N. Y. M.
CROOK, Thomas Mewburn. (S)
Eng. b. 1869 Bolton; ex. 1934 London. Wa-798.
CROOKS, Forrest C. (Ill.)
Am. ad. 1934 New York. M.
CROOKS, Mildred.
Am. ad. 1934 Paris, Fr. M.
CROOS [or Croost], Anthony Jansz van der.
Dut. 1606/8-1662/3 The Hague. B-T.
CROPSEY, Jaspar Francis.
Am. Rossville, N. Y. 1823-1900 Hastings on Hudson, N. Y. A1-B-C-DAB-E-F-T-1-4-15.
CROSBY, Caresse. (S)
Am. b. New York 1892; ad. 1928 Paris. DBA.
CROSBY, Frederick Gordon. (Ill.)
Eng. b. Sunderland 1885; ex. 1934 London. Wa.
CROSBY, Gertrude Volz. *see* Volz, G.
CROSBY, Katherine Van Rensellaer. (S)
Am. b. Colorado Springs, Colo. 1897. A20-Cs-F.
CROSBY, Percy Leo. (Cart.)
Am. b. Brooklyn, N. Y. 1891; ad. 1934 McLean, Va. A28-W.
CROSBY, Raymond Moreau. (Ill.)
Am. b. Grand Rapids, Mich. 1877. A28-F-T-W14.
CROSMAN. *see also* Crossman.
CROSMAN, Rose. (Et.)
Am. ad. 1934 Chicago, Ill. A.
CROSS. *see also* Crosse.
CROSS, Amy.
Am. b. Milwaukee, Wis. 1856; ad. 1934 New York. A.
CROSS, Anson Kent.
Am. b. Lawrence, Mass. 1862; ad. 1934 Boothbay Harbor, Me. A-F-T-W.
CROSS, Henri Edmond.
Fr. Douai 1856-1910 St. Clair. B-DBA-T.
CROSS, Henry H.
Am. Tioga Co., N. Y. 1837-1918 Chicago. A015.
CROSS, Herbert Richard.
Am. b. Prov., R. I. 1877; ad. 1934 New York. A.
CROSS, John.
Eng. Tiverton 1819-1861 London. B-DNB.
CROSS, Louise. (S)
Am. b. Rochester, Minn. 1896; ad. 1934 New York. A.
CROSS, Marian Leigh. (S)
Am. b. Minn., Minn. 1900; ad. 1934 Brookline, Mass. A.
CROSS [or Cruz], Michael.
Br. ac. 1630-1660 Madrid, Sp. B-Bd-DNB-T.
CROSS, Sally. *see* Bill, Sally Cross.
CROSS, Thomas. (Eg.)
Eng. ac. 1632-1682 London. B-DNB-T.
CROSSE, Lawrence. (Min.)
Br. 1650?-1724. DNB-T.
CROSSE, Richard. (Min.)
Eng. Devon 1742/5-1810 Knowle. B-DNB.
CROSSMAN. *see also* Crosman.
CROSSMAN, Abner.
Am. Vermont 1847-1932 Chicago, Ill. A030.
CROSSMAN, John H. (Ill.)
Am. ad. 1934 Boston, Mass. M.
CROSSMAN, William Henry.
Am. b. New York 1896; ad. 1934 Same. A.
CROTTI, Jean.
Fr. b. Bulle 1878. DBA.
CROW, Louise.
Am. ad. 1934 Seattle, Wash. M.
CROW, [Mrs.] Phil M.
Am. ad. 1934 Lima, O. M.
CROWE, Eyre.
Eng. Chelsea 1824-1910 London. B-C-T.
CROWELL, Reid Kendrick.
Am. b. Alta, Ia. 1911; ad. 1934 Dallas, Tex. A.
CROWINSHIELD, Frederic.
Am. Boston 1845-1918 Stockbridge, Mass. A015-C-DAB-F-T-15-46.
CROWLEY, Nicholas Joseph.
Ir. Dublin 1818-1857 London. B-DNB-T.
CROWTHER, Robert W. (Ill.)
Am. b. Phila., Pa. 1902; ad. 1934 Same. M.
CRUGER, William F. (Ill.)
Am. ad. 1934 New York. M.
CRUIKSHANK, George. (Cari.)
Eng. London 1792-1878 Same. B-DNB-E-T-20-272-337.
CRUIKSHANK, Isaac. (Cari.)
Scot. Edinburgh 1756?-1811 London. B-DNB.

CRUIKSHANK, Robert Isaac. (Cari.)
Eng. London 1789-1856. B-DNB-T.
CRUIKSHANK, William.
Can. b. Scotland 1844/8-1922 Canada. M.
CRUMB, Charles P. (S)
Am. b. Bloomfield, Mo. 1874; ad. 1934 Beechwood, Pa. A-F.
CRUMMER, Mary Worthington.
Am. b. Baltimore, Md.; ad. 1934 Same. A-F.
CRUMP, Leslie.
Am. b. Saugerties, N. Y. 1894; ad. 1934 Cranford, N. J. A.
CRUMPACKER, Grace Dauchy.
Mrs. S. J. Crumpacker.
Am. b. Troy, N. Y. 1881; ad. 1934 So. Bend, Ind. A.
CRUNELLE, Leonard. (S)
Am. b. Lens, Pa. 1872; ad. 1934 Chicago, Ill. A-F-T-Ta-W-46.
CRUZ. *see* Pantoja de la Cruz.
CRUZ, Martín, Miguel de la. (S)
Sp. Modern. 798.
CRUZ, Miguel de la. *see* Cross, Michael.
CRUZ Y RIOS, Luis de la.
Sp. Canaries 1815-1850 Malaga. B-T.
CRUZADO, Alonso.
Sp. d. 1791 Madrid. T.
CRUZADO, Joaquin Manuel Fernandez.
Sp. 1781-1856. M.
CSÁNKY, Dénes.
Hun. b. 1885 Hungary. M.
CSÓKA, István [or Stephen].
Hun. b. 1865; ad. 1935 Brooklyn, N. Y. M.
CSOSZ, John.
Am. b. Hungary 1897; ad. 1934 Cleveland, O. A.
CUBLEY, William Harold.
Eng. Heanor 1816-1896 Wales. B.
CUCCHI, Giovanni Antonio.
It. b. Campiglia Cervo 1674; ac. in Milan. T.
CUCUEL, Edward.
Am. b. San Fran., Calif. 1879; ad. 1934 New York. A-F-T.
CUEVAS, Pedro de las.
Sp. Madrid 1568-1635 Same. B-T.
CUIFFAGNI, Bernardo. (S)
It. 1385-1456. Hs.
CUIT [or Cuitt], George [The Elder].
Eng. Moulton 1743-1818 Richmond. B-DNB.
CUIT [or Cuitt], George [The Younger].
Eng. Richmond 1779-1854 Masham. B-DNB.
CULBERTSON, Josephine M.
Am. b. Shanghai, China 1852; ad. 1934 Carmel, Calif. A.
CULBERTSON, Linn.
Am. b. Princeton, Ia. 1890; ad. 1934 Des Moines, Ia. A.
CULBERTSON, Queenie.
Am. b. San Angelo, Tex.; ad. 1934 Cinn., O. A.
CULIN, Alice Mumford.
Mrs. Stewart Culin.
Am. b. Phila., Pa. 1875; ad. 1934 Coconut Grove, Fla. A28-F-W.
CULLEN, Maurice Galbraith.
Can. St. John's N. F. 1866-1934 Quebec, Can. B-M-Obit. N. Y. papers, 3-29-1934.
CULMBACH. *see* Kulmbach.
CULMER, Henry L.
Am. England 1854-1914 Salt Lake City, Utah. A011-T.
CULVERHOUSE, Johann Mongels.
Dut. ac. 1859-1891 in Rotterdam. B-T.
CUMING, Beatrice Lavis.
Am. b. Brooklyn, N. Y. 1903; ad. 1934 Same. A.
CUMMING, Charles Atherton.
Am. b. Illinois 1858; d. 1932. A28-F-W16.
CUMMING, William.
Ir. Dublin 1769-1852. B-DNB-T.
CUMMINGS, E. E.
Am. ex. 1935 New York. M.
CUMMINGS, Melvin Earle. (S)
Am. b. Salt Lake City, Utah 1876; ad. 1934 San Fran., Calif. Cs-F-T-W.
CUMMINGS, Thomas Seir.
Am. Bath, Eng. 1804-1894 Hackensack, N. J. C-DAB-F-T-1-2-3-4-15-45.
CUMMINS, Jane Catherine.
Can. Ontario 1842-1893. 893.
CUNDALL, Charles Ernest.
Eng. b. Stretford 1890; ad. 1934 Chelsea. Wa-825.
CUNDY, James. (S)
Br. 1792-1826. DNB-T.
CUNEO, Cyrus Cincinatto.
Am. San Fran., Calif. 1878-1916 London. A013-T.
CUNEO, Rinaldo.
Am. b. San Fran., Calif. 1877; ad. 1935 Same. A-F.
CUNGI, Giovanni Battista.
It. ac. 1538-1542 Sansepolcio. T-V.
CUNGI, Leonardo.
It. b. Sansepolcio; d. 1569 Rome. T-V.
CUNGI, Lodovico.
It. ac. 16th century in Sansepolcio. T-V.
CUNINGHAM [or Calze], Edmund Francis.
Scot. Kelso 1742?-1795 London. B-DNB.
CUNLIFFE, D.
Eng. ac. 1826 London. T.
CUNNING, John.
Am. b. Albany, N. Y. 1889; ad. 1934 Brooklyn, N. Y. A.
CUNNINGHAM, Ben.
Am. b. Colo. 1904; ad. 1934 San Fran., Calif. M.
CUNNINGHAM, Charles C.
Am. b. 1841; d. 1918 Brooklyn, N. Y. A016.
CUNNINGHAM, Cornelia.
Am. b. Savannah, Ga. 1903; ad. 1934 Atlanta, Ga. A.
CUNNINGHAM, Fern F.
Am. ad. 1935 Defiance, O. M.
CUNNINGHAM, John Wilton.
Am. b. St. Louis, Mo.; d. 1903 San Antonio, Tex. A04-B-T.
CUNNINGHAM, Mildred Cotman.
Mrs. O. D. Cunningham.
Am. b. St. Paul, Minn. 1898; ad. 1934 Rockford, Ill. A.
CUNY, Henry Pierre.
Fr. b. Concarneau 1880. DBA.
CUPRIEN, Frank W.
Am. b. Brooklyn, N. Y. 1871; ad. 1934 Laguna Beach, Calif. A-F.

CURE, CORNELIUS. (S)
Dut.-Eng.; ac. 1606/7. T.
CURE, WILLIAM. (S)
Dut.-Eng.; d. 1632. DNB-T.
CURLEY, VIRGINIA LEE.
Am. ad. 1934 Montclair, N. J. M.
CURNOCK, JAMES.
Eng. Bristol 1812-1869. B-T.
CURNOCK, JAMES JACKSON.
Eng. Bristol 1839-1891 London. T.
CURRAN, CHARLES COURTNEY.
Am. b. Hartford, Ky. 1861; ad. 1934 New York. A-F-T-W-46.
CURRAN, JANE.
Am. ad. 1934 Toledo, O. M.
CURRIER, ALGER V.
Am. 1862-1911. M.
CURRIER, CYRUS BATES.
Am. b. Marietta, O. 1868; ad. 1934 Los Angeles, Calif. A.
CURRIER, EDWARD WILSON.
Am. Marietta, O. 1857-1918 San Fran., Calif. A016.
CURRIER, J. FRANK.
Am. Boston 1843-1909 Same. A07-B-F-T.
CURRIER, NATHANIEL [of Currier & Ives]. (Eg)
Am. Roxbury, Mass. 1813-1888 New York. DAB-F-54-131-132-133.
CURRIER, RICHARD.
Am. ad. 1934 New York. M.
CURRIER, WALTER BARRON.
Am. b. Springfield, Mass. 1879; d. 1934 Santa Monica, Calif. A.
CURRY, JOHN STEWART.
Am. b. Dunavant, Kan. 1897; ad. 1934 Westport, Conn. A.
CURRY, ROBERT F.
Am. b. Boston 1872. T.
CURSITER, STANLEY.
Scot. b. Kirwall, Orkney Islands 1887; ad. 1934 Porto Bello, Midlothian. M.
CURTI, GIROLAMO [Dentone].
It. Bologna 1570/7-1631 Same. B-T-722.
CURTIS, CALVIN.
Am. b. Bridgeport, Conn. 1822; ac. 1886. [No death date.] C-F-T-3-15.
CURTIS, CONSTANCE.
Am. b. Wash., D. C.; ad. 1934 New York. A-F-T-W.
CURTIS, ELIZABETH.
Am. b. New York 1873; ad. 1934 Same. A-F.
CURTIS, GEORGE WASHINGTON.
Am. b. 1869; d. 1927 Southampton, N. Y. A24.
CURTIS, IDA MAYNARD.
Am. b. Lewisburg, Pa.; ad. 1934 Carmel, Calif. A.
CURTIS, JOHN. (Eg.)
Eng. ac. 1908 London. B-T.
CURTIS, JOHN I.
Eng. ac. 1790/9 London. B-T.
CURTIS, JOHN II. (Eg.)
Eng. Norwich 1791-1862 London. B-DNB-T.
CURTIS, LELAND.
Am. b. Denver 1897; ad. 1934 Los Angeles, Calif. A.
CURTIS, NATHANIEL CORTLANDT.
Am. b. Smithville, N. Y. 1881; ad. 1934 New Orleans, La. A.
CURTIS, [Mrs.] NORA. (Ill)
Eng. ex. 1934 London. M.
CURTIS, RALPH WORMSLEY.
Br. 1854-1922. B-T.
CURTIS, SARAH. *see* Hoadly, Sarah.
CURTIS, WILLIAM FULLER.
Am. b. Staten Island, N. Y. 1873; ad. 1934 Ashfield, Mass. A-F-T-W.
CURTIUS, JOHN CHRISTOPHER. (S-Wax)
Swi. b. Berne; d. 1794 in Paris. T-M.
CURZON, PAUL ALFRED DE.
Fr. Poitiers 1820-1895 Paris. T.
CUSHING, HOWARD GARDINER.
Am. Boston, Mass. 1869-1915 New York. A013-F-T-46.
CUSHING, LILY.
Mrs. William T. Emmet.
Am. ex. 1933 New York. M.
CUSHING, ROBERT. (S)
Am. 1841-1896. M.
CUSHMAN, ALICE.
Am. b. Phila., Pa. 1854; ad. 1934 Same. A.
CUSHMAN, CORDELIA H. (S)
Mrs. Paul Cushman.
Am. ad. 1934 New York. M.
CUSHMAN, GEORGE HEWITT. (Eg.)
Am. Windham, Conn. 1814-1876 Jersey City, N. J. F-T-3-6-7.
CUSHMAN, HENRY. (S)
Am. b. London 1859; ad. 1934 Los Angeles, Calif. A.
CUSTER, BERNARDINE.
Am. b. Bloomington, Ill.; ad. 1934 New York. M.
CUSTER, EDWARD L.
Am. Basle, Swi. 1837-1881 Boston, Mass. M.
CUSTIS, ELEANOR PARKE.
Am. b. Wash., D. C. 1897; ad. 1934 Same. A-F.
CUSUMANO, STEFANO.
Am. ex. 1935 New York. M.
CUTHBERT, VIRGINIA I.
Am. b. West Newton, Pa. 1908; ad. 1934 Pittsburgh, Pa. A.
CUTLER, CARL GORDON.
Am. b. Newtonville, Mass. 1873; ad. 1934 Same. A-F.
CUTLER, JERVIS. (Eg.)
Am. Martha's Vineyard, Mass. 1768-1846 Evansville, Ind. F.
CUTLER, MERRITT. (Ill.)
Am. ad. 1934 New York. M.
CUTTS, GERTRUDE SPURR.
Can. b. Scarborough, Eng.; ad. 1935 Port Perry, Can. M.
CUTTS, WILLIAM M.
Can. b. Allahabad, India; ad. 1935 Port Perry, Can. M.
CUVILLON, LOUIS ROBERT DE.
Fr. b. Paris 1848. B-T.
CUYLENBORCH [or Kuylenburg], ABRAHAM VAN.
Dut. ac. 1639-1664 in Utrecht. C.
CUYP, AELBERT [or Albert].
Dut. Dordrecht 1620-1691 Same. B-Bd-C-E-T-722.

CUYP, Benjamin Gerritsz.
Dut. Dordrecht 1612-1652 Same. B-T.
CUYP, Jacob Gerritsz.
Dut. Dordrecht 1594-1651/2 Same. B-C-T.
CYBIS, Boleslaw.
Pol. b. 1899; ad. 1935 Warsaw; ex. 1934 Pittsburgh, Pa. M.
CYPRIEN-BOULET, Eugène.
Fr. b. Toulouse; ad. 1934 Paris. DBA.
CZACHORSKI, Wladislaw von.
Pol. Lüblin 1850-1911 Munich, Ger. B-T.
CZAJKOWSKI, Joséf von.
Pol. b. Warsaw 1872. T.
CZAJKOWSKI, Stanislaw.
Pol. b. Warsaw 1878. T.
CZECHO-SLOVAKIAN Artists. *see* book 736.
CZEDEKOWSKI, Boleslaw Jan.
Pol. b. Woynilow 1885; ex. 1930 London. DBA.
CZENCZ, Janos.
Hun. b. 1885; ad. 1934 Budapest. M.
CZERMAK [or Cremak], Jaroslav.
Czec. Prague 1831-1878 Paris. B-C-T.
CZÓK, István. *see* Csóka.
DA ALBA, Macrino. *see* Macrino d'Alba.
DABO, Leon.
Am. b. Detroit, Mich. 1868; ad. 1934 New York. A-F-T-W-46.
DABO, Theodore Scott.
Am. b. New Orleans, La. 1877. F-46.
DABOS, Laurent.
Fr. Toulouse 1761-1835 Paris. T-T.
DABOUR, John.
Am. b. Smyrna, Turkey; d. 1905 New York. A05-C-F-T-15.
DA COSTA. *see also* Costa.
DA COSTA, John.
Eng. Teignmouth 1867-1931.
Wa1929-Obit. N. Y. papers, 5-28-1931.
DADD, Frank.
Eng. London 1851-1929. Y01930.
DADD, Richard.
Eng. Chatham 1817/9-1887. B-T.
DADDI, Bernardo [da Firenze].
It. Florence 1280?-1330/50. B-Bd-T-338-784.
DADDI [or Dado], Bernardo.
It. 1512-1570 Rome. B-T.
DADE, Ernest.
Eng. b. Kensington 1868; ad. 1934 St. John's Wood. B-Wa.
DADIE-ROBERG, Dagman. (S)
Swe. b. Stockholm 1897. DBA.
DADLEZ, Pawel.
Pol. ad. 1934 Cracow. M.
DAEGE, Eduard.
Ger. Berlin 1805-1883 Same. C.
DAEL, Jan Frans van.
Flem. Antwerp 1764-1840 Paris. B-C-T.
DAELEN, Edourd.
Ger. ac. 1876 in Dresden and Berlin. B-T.
DAFFINGER, Moritz Michael.
Aus. Vienna 1790-1849 Same. B-T.
DAGGETT, Alfred. (Eg)
Am. New Haven, Conn. 1799-1872 Same. F-T-7.
DAGGETT, Grace D. (Min)
Am. ad. 1934 New Haven, Conn. M.
DAGGETT, Maud. (S)
Am. b. Kansas City, Mo. 1883; ad. 1934 Pasadena, Calif. A-Cs-F.
DAGGY, Augustus Smith.
Am. ad. 1934 Norwalk, Conn. M.
DAGGY, Richard Smith.
Am. b. Chatham, N. J. 1892; ad. 1934 Norwalk, Conn. A.
DAGLEY, Richard.
Eng. 1765-1841 London. DNB-T.
DAGLISH, Eric Fitch. (Eg)
Eng. b. London 1894; ad. 1934 Same. Wa.
DAGNAC-RIVIÈRE, Charles Henri Gaston.
Fr. b. Paris 1864. B-DBA.
DAGNAN-BOUVERET, Pascal Adolphe Jean.
Fr. Paris 1852-1929 Quincey. B-DBA-T.
D'AGOSTINO, Vincent.
Am. b. Chicago 1896; ad. 1934 Same. A.
DAGUERRE, Louis Jacques Mandé.
[Inventor of the Daguerreotype Process.]
Fr. Carneilles 1787-1851 Marne. B-E-T.
DAHL, Hans.
Nor. Hardanger 1849-1910. B-E.
DAHL, Johan Christian Claussön.
Nor. Bergen 1788-1857 Dresden, Ger. B-E-T.
DAHL, Michael [The Elder].
Swe. Stockholm 1656-1743 London. B-DNB-E-T-702.
DAHL, Niels Carl Michaelis Flindt.
Dan. Faxborg 1812-1865 Copenhagen. B-T.
DAHLER, Warren.
Am. b. Helena, Mont. 1887; ad. 1934 New York. A.
DAHLGREEN, Charles W.
Am. b. Chicago 1864; ad. 1934 Oak Park, Ill. A-F-W.
DAHLING, Heinrich Anton.
Ger. Hanover 1773-1850 Potsdam. C.
DAHLSKOG, Ewald.
Swe. b. 1894; ex. 1929 Paris. DBA.
DAI LIBRI, Girolamo. *see* Libri, G. dai.
DAILEY, [Dr.] Wilbur Manton.
Am. b. Athens, N. Y. 1868; ad. 1934 New York. M.
DAINGERFIELD, Elliott.
Am. Harpers Ferry, Va. 1859-1932 New York. A029-B-E-F-T-W17-46.
DAINGERFIELD, Marjorie.
Am. ad. 1935 New York. M.
DAINTREY, Adrian Maurice.
Eng. b. London 1902; ac. 1932 New York. Wa.
DAINTY, John. (Eg)
Am. ac. 1840 in Phila., Pa. F-T-7-147.
DALBY, David [of York].
Eng. b. York 1790. M.
DALE [or Dalem] Cornelis van.
Dut. ac. 1545-1573/6. B-T.
DALE, [Mrs.] Gertrude.
Eng. 1851-1927. Y01928.
DALE, Maude.
[Mrs. Chester Dale.]
Am. ad. 1934 New York. M.
DALEM [or Dalen or Dale], Hans van.
Flem. ac. 1632-1649 in Antwerp. B-T.
DALEN, Cornelis van [The Elder].
Dut. Amsterdam 1602?-1665. B-T.

DALEN, CORNELIS VAN [The Younger].
Dut. Amsterdam 1638-1664?. B-T.
DALENS, DIRCK [or Dirk] I.
Dut. Dordrecht 1600-1676 Zierikzée. B-T.
DALENS, DIRCK [or Dirk] II.
Dut. Amsterdam 1658/9-1688. B-T.
DALENS, DIRK [or Dirk] III.
Dut. Amsterdam 1688-1753. B-T.
D'ALESSIO, GREGORY. (Cari)
Am. ad. 1935 New York. M.
DALGAS, CARLO EDURDO.
Dan. Naples, It. 1820/1-1851 Möllhorst, Den. B-T.
DALI, SALVADOR.
Sp. b. Figueras 1904; ex. 1934 New York. M-904.
DALLAM, ELIZABETH FORBES.
Am. b. Phila., Pa. 1875; ad. 1934 Same. A.
DALLAS, ELMSLIE WILLIAM.
Eng. London 1809-1879 Edinburgh, Scot. DNB-T.
DALLAS, JACOB A.
Am. Phila., Pa. 1825-1857. T.
DALLETT, LIZA. (S)
Am. ex. 1933 Paris. M.
DALLIN, CYRUS EDWIN. (P-S)
Am. b. Springville, Utah 1861; ad. 1934 Arlington Heights, Mass. A-B-Cs-E-F-Hs-T-W-46-798.
DALLMAN, JOSEPH.
Swi. Bellach 1828-1888 Montreux. B-T.
DALLMAN, OTTO.
Am. ex. 1934 Minn., Minn. M.
DALMATA, GIOVANNI [G. di Trau]. (S)
It. 1440-1509. T.
DALMAU, LUIS.
Sp. ac. 1428-1460. T.
DALOU, AIMÉ JULES. (S)
Fr. Paris 1838-1902 Same. B-E-Hs-T.
DALRYMPLE, AMY FLORENCE.
Am. b. Boston, Mass.; ad. 1934 Same. A.
DALRYMPLE, FREDERIC.
Am. ex. 1934 Chicago, Ill. M.
DALRYMPLE, LOUIS. (Cart.)
Am. Cambridge, Ill. 1865-1905 Amityville, L. I., N. Y. A06.
DALRYMPLE, LUCILLE STEVENSON.
Am. b. Sandusky, O. 1882; ad. 1934 Chicago. A.
DALSTROM, GUSTAF OSCAR.
Am. b. Gothland, Swe. 1893; ad. 1934 Chicago. A.
DALTON, PETER C. (S)
Am. b. Buffalo, N. Y. 1894; ad. 1935 New York. A.
DALTON, RICHARD. (Eg)
Eng. 1715?-1791 London. DNB-T.
DALY, DAVID RAYMOND.
Am. b. New York; ad. 1934 Same. A.
DALY, MATT. A.
Am. b. Cinn., O. 1860; ad. 1934 Same. A.
DALZIEL, EDWARD. (Eg)
Eng. Wooler 1817-1905 Hampstead. DNB-357.
DALZIEL, GEORGE. (Eg)
Eng. Wooler 1817-1905 Hampstead. DNB-357.
DALZIEL, THOMAS BOLTO GILCHRIST. (Ill)
Eng. Wooler 1823-1906 Kent. DNB-357.
DAMER, ANNA SEYMOUR. (S)
Br. 1749-1828. DNB.
DA MESSINA. *see* Antonello da M.
DAMIANAKES, CLEON.
Am. b. Berkeley, Calif.; ad. 1934 Oakland, Calif. A.
D'AMICO, VICTOR E. (Eg)
Am. ad. 1934 New York. A.
DA MILANO. *see* Solario, Andrea.
DAMMANN, HANS. (S)
Ger. b. Proskau 1867. T.
DAMMANN, PAUL MARCEL. (Med)
Fr. b. Montgeron 1885. DBA.
DAMON, LOUISE WHEELWRIGHT.
Am. b. Boston, Mass. 1889; ad. 1934 Prov., R. I. A.
DAMOPHON OF MESSENE. (S)
Gr. ac. 300 B.C. B-E-Hs.
DAMOYE, PIERRE EMANUEL.
Fr. Paris 1847-1916 Same. B-DBA-T.
DAMPT, JEAN AUGUSTE. (S)
Fr. b. Venarcy 1854; ac. 1919 Paris. DBA-T-798.
DAMSCHRODER, J. J. M.
Ger. ac. 1850-1909. B-T.
DANA, CHARLES EDMUND.
Am. Wilkesbarre, Pa. 1843-1924 Salt Lake City, Utah. A011-F.
DANA, WILLIAM PARSONS WINCHESTER.
Am. Boston, Mass. 1833-1927 London. A024-B-C-F-T-W14-4-15.
DANAHER, MAY.
Am. b. La Grange, Tenn.; d. 1931 Little Rock, Ark. A028.
DANBY, FRANK [or Francis].
Ir. Wexford 1793-1861 Geneva, Swi. B-DNB-E-T-722.
DANBY, THOMAS.
Eng. Bristol 1817-1886 London. B-C-DNB-T.
DANCE, ELIZABETH JENNINGS.
Am. b. Richmond, Va. 1901; ad. 1934 Same. A.
DANCE, [Sir] NATHANIEL [Holland].
Eng. London 1734-1811 Winchester. B-T.
DANCKERTS, HENRY [or Johan].
Dut. The Hague 1630?-1680? Amsterdam. DNB-T.
DANDINI, CÉSARE.
It. Florence 1595-1658. B-T.
DANDINI, PIETRE.
It. Florence 1646/7-1712. B-Bd-T.
DANDO, [Mrs.] SUSIE MAY.
Am. b. Odell, Ill. 1873; ad. 1934 Venice, Calif. A.
DANDRIDGE, BARTHOLOMEW.
Eng. ac. 1711-1750/1. B-DNB-T.
DANFORTH, MOSELEY ISAAC. (Eg)
Am. Hartford, Conn. 1800-1862 New York. DAB-F-T-2-3-7-15-40.
DANFRIE, PHILLIPE [The Elder].
Fr. 1531/5-1606 Paris. T.
D'ANGELO, BATTISTA. *see* Moro, G.
DANHAUSER, JOSEF.
Aus. Vienna 1805-1845 Same. C.
DANIEL, CLARK.
Am. ex. 1933 Paris. M.
DANIEL, LEWIS C. (Ill)
Am. b. New York 1901; ad. 1934 Same. A.
DANIELE DA VOLTERRA. *see* Volterra, D. da.

DANIELE DI LEONARDO [Orvieto].
It. ac. 1389-1441. T.
DANIELL, SAMUEL.
Br. England 1775-1811 Ceylon, India. DNB-T.
DANIELL, THOMAS.
Eng. Kingston, West Indies 1749-1840 London. B-DNB-E-T-663.
DANIELL, WILLIAM [The Elder].
Eng. 1769-1837 London. B-DNB-T-663.
DANIELL, WILLIAM SWIFT.
Am. b. San Fran., Calif. 1865; ad. 1934 Laguna Beach, Calif. A.
DANIELS, ELMER HARLAND.
Am. b. Owosso, Mich. 1905; ad. 1934 Westfield, N. J. A.
DANIELS, HARRY.
Am. ad. 1934 New York. M.
DANIELS, JOHN KARL. (S)
Am. b. Norway 1875; ad. 1934 Minn., Minn. A-W.
DANIELS, WILLIAM.
Eng. Liverpool 1813-1880 Same. B-T.
DANIELSON, ELIN KLEOPATRA.
Finnish. b. Norrmark 1861. T.
DANKMEYER [or Dankmeijer], CHARLES BERNARDUS.
Dut. b. Amsterdam 1861. B-T.
DANLOUX, HENRI PIERRE.
Fr. Paris 1753-1809 Same. B-C-T-722.
DANNAT, WILLIAM TURNER.
Am. Hempstead, N. Y. 1853-1929 Paris. A026-B-C-E-F-T-W14-1-15-46.
DANNECKER, JOHANN HEINRICH VON. (S)
Ger. Waldenbuch 1758-1841 Stuttgart. B-E-Hs-T.
DANNER, SARA KOLB.
Mrs. W. M. Danner.
Am. b. New York; ad. 1934 Santa Barbara, Calif. A.
DANSAERT, LÉON MARIE CONSTANT.
Belg. b. Brussels 1830. [No death date.] B-T.
DANTAN, ANTOINE LAURENT. (S)
Fr. St. Cloud 1798-1878 Paris. B-Hs-T.
DANTHON, GUSTAVE.
Fr. b. Nevers 1859. DBA.
DA PARMA, MICHELE. *see* Parmigianino, M.
DA PANICALE. *see* Masolino.
DAPOIGNY, ALBERT LOUIS.
Fr. b. Montesson 1885. DBA.
DA PONTE, FRANCESCO. *see* Bassano, F.
DARAGNÈS, JEAN GABRIEL.
Fr. b. Guéthary 1886; ex. 1935 Paris. DBA.
DARBEFEUILLE, PAUL. (S)
Fr. Toulouse 1852/5-1933. B-DBA.
DARBY, ELIZABETH.
Am. d. 1906 Brielle, N. J. A06.
DARBY, HENRY F.
Am. ac. 1853-1859 New York. F.
DARCIS, JEAN LOUIS. (Eg)
Fr. d. Paris 1801. B-T.
DARDÉ, PAUL. (S)
Fr. b. Olmet 1888. DBA.
DARDEL, NILS VON.
Swe. b. 1888; ex. 1929 Paris. DBA.
DARET, JACQUES [or James].
Flem. Tournay, Fr. 1404-1468. B-T.
DARET [de Cazeneuve], PIERRE. (Eg)
Fr. Paris 1604-1678 Dax. B-T.
DARGAUD, PAUL JOSEPH VICTOR.
Fr. Paris 1873-1921. B-T.
DARGELAS, ANDRÉ HENRI.
Fr. Bordeaux 1828-1906. B-T.
D'ARGENTA, MICHELE. *see* Argent, Michel d'.
DARIO DI GIOVANNI.
It. Pordone 1420-1498. T-V.
DARLEY, FELIX OCTAVIUS CARR. (Et)
Am. Phila., Pa. 1822-1888 Claymont, Del. B-C-DAB-T-4-7-15-40-45-55-880.
DARLEY, JAN COOPER [née Sully]. *see* Sully, J. C.
DARLEY, JOHN CLARENDON.
Am. ac. 1830-1840 in Phila., Pa. F.
DARLING, JAY NORWOOD ["J. N. Ding"]. (Cart)
Am. b. Norwood, Mich. 1876; ad. 1934 Des Moines, Ia. W.
DARLING, WILDER M.
Am. Sandusky, O. 1856-1933 Toledo, O. A030-B-T.
DARNAULT, FLORENCE MALCOLM. (S)
Am. b. New York 1905; ad. 1934 Same. M.
DARNAUT, HUGO.
Aus. b. Dessau 1850. B-T.
DAROUX, LEONORA.
Am. b. Sacramento, Calif. 1886; ad. 1934 Same. A.
D'ARPINO. *see* Cesari Giuseppe.
DARRAH, [Mrs.] S. T.
Am. b. Phila., Pa.; d. 1881 Boston. F-T-15.
DARRELL, [Mrs.] Edward. *see* Snyder, M. E.
DARROW, WILLIAM, JR. (Ill)
Am. ad. 1934 New York. M.
DART, HESTER WILSON.
Am. b. Pekin, Ill.; d. 1913 Ossining, N. Y. A0X1.
D'ARTHOIS. *see* Arthois.
DÁS, BISHAN and MANOHAR.
Persian ancient artists. M.
DASBURG, ANDREW MICHAEL.
Am. b. Paris 1887; ad. 1934 Santa Fé, N. M. A-F.
D'ASCENZO, MYRTLE GOODWIN.
Mrs. Nicola D'Ascenzo.
Am. b. No. Tunbridge, Vt. 1864; ad. 1934 Germantown, Pa. A.
D'ASCENZO, NICOLA.
Am. b. It. 1871; ad. 1934 Germantown, Pa. A-W.
DASHORST, MOOR. *see* Moro, [Sir] Antonio.
D'ASSISE, ANDREA DI LUIGI. *see* Ingegno, A. di L.
DASSONEVILLE [or Dassonville], JACQUES.
Fr. St. Ouen 1619-1653. B-T.
DASTUGNE, MAXIME.
Fr. ac. 1876-1908 in Paris. B-DBA.
DASWANTH.
Per. ac. 1542-1605 in Persia. T.
DATZ, A. MARK.
Rus. b. Chrenovna 1896; ad. 1935 New York. M.
DAUBER, [or Daucher] ADOLF. (S)
Ger. 1460/5-1523/4 Augsburg. T.
DAUBIGNY, CHARLES FRANÇOIS.
Fr. Paris 1817-1878 Same. B-Bd-C-E-T-128-843-880.

DAUBIGNY, Edmonde François.
Fr. Paris 1789-1843 Same. B-T.
DAUBIGNY, Karl [or Charles] Pierre.
Fr. Paris 1846-1886 Same. B-C-T.
DAUBIGNY, Pierre. (Min)
Fr. Paris 1793-1858 Same. T.
DAUCHEZ, André.
Fr. b. Paris 1870. B-DBA-T.
DAUER, Johannes.
Swi. ac. 1526. B-T.
DAUGHERTY, James Henry. (Ill)
Am. b. No. Car. 1886; ad. 1934 Westport, Conn. A20-F-W.
DAUGHERTY, Nancy Lauriene.
Am. b. Kittanning, Pa. 1890; ad. 1934 Same. A.
DAUHER, Adolf. (S)
Ger. 1460/5-1523/4 Ulm. Hs-T.
DAUHER, Hans Adolf. (S)
Ger. 1485-1538 Ulm. Hs-T.
D'AULAIRE, Edgar Parin. (Ill)
Am. ad. 1934 New York. M.
DAULAT.
Persian ancient artist. M.
DAULLÉ, Jean. (Eg)
Fr. Abbeville 1707-1763 Paris. B-T.
DAUMAS, Louis Joseph. (S)
Fr. Toulon 1801-1887 Paris. B-T.
DAUMIER, Honoré. (P-S)
Fr. Marseilles 1808-1879 Valmondois. B-E-T-192-339-340-341-790-820-847-870-880.
DAUPHIN, Eugène Baptiste Émile.
Fr. b. Toulon 1857. B-T.
DAUZATS, Adrien.
Fr. Bordeaux 1804-1868 Paris. B-T.
DA VENEZIA. *see* Veneto, B.
DAVENPORT, Carson Sutherlin.
Am. b. Danville, Va. 1908; ad. 1934 Same. A.
DAVENPORT, Edith Fairfax.
Am. b. Kansas City, Mo.; ad. 1934 New York. A-F-183.
DAVENPORT, Ethel.
Mrs. Don Abbott Davenport.
Am. b. Phila., Pa.; ad. 1934 New Hope, Pa. M.
DAVENPORT, Henry.
Am. b. Boston, Mass. 1882; ad. 1934 Paris. A.
DAVENPORT, Homer Calvin. (Cari)
Am. Silverton, Ore. 1867-1912 New York. A010.
DAVENPORT, Jane. (S)
Mrs. Reginald G. Harris.
Am. b. Cambridge, Mass. 1897; ad. 1934 Cold Spring Harbor, L. I., N. Y. A-Cs.
DAVENPORT, Samuel. (Eg.)
Eng. Bedford 1783-1867. DNB-T.
DAVERDOING, Charles Aimé Joseph.
Fr. Arras 1813-1895 Paris. B-T.
DAVESNE [or Davenne], P. (Eg.)
Fr. ac. 1764-1796 Paris. B-T.
DAVEY, Randall.
Am. b. East Orange, N. J. 1887; ad. 1934 Santa Fé, N. M. A-F-W.
DAVEY, Robert.
Eng. Cullompton 1735-1793 London. DNB-T.
DAVID D'ANGERS, Pierre Jean. (S)
Fr. Angers 1788-1856 Paris. B-E-Hs-T.
DAVID, Charles.
Fr. Cadenet 1797-1869 Avignon. T.
DAVID, Fernand. (S)
Fr. Paris 1872-1926. T.
DAVID, Geraerd [Gheeraert Davit].
Flem. Oudewater, Holland 1450/60-1523 Bruges. B-Bd-C-E-T.
DAVID, Giacomo [or Lodovico].
It. Lugano 1648-1728/30. B-T.
DAVID, Gustave.
Fr. Paris 1824-1891. B.
DAVID, Hermine.
Fr. b. Paris 1886. DBA.
DAVID, Jacques Louis. (P-S)
[Founder of the Modern French School of Painting.]
Fr. Paris 1748-1825 Brussels, Belg. B-Bd-C-E-T-191-192-722-820-847-849-867.
DAVIDS, Dorothy.
Am. ex. 1935 Pittsburgh, Pa. M.
DAVIDS, Renée. (Et.)
Fr. b. Paris 1877; ac. 1933 Same. DBA-T.
DAVIDSON, Allan Douglas.
Eng. 1874-1932. T-Y01933.
DAVIDSON, Bessie.
Aust. b. So. Aust. 1879. M.
DAVIDSON, Charles Grant.
Eng. London 1824-1902 Falmouth. B-DNB-T.
DAVIDSON, Clara D. [Mrs. Simpson].
Am. b. St. Louis, Mo. 1874; ad. 1934 Norwalk, Conn. A.
DAVIDSON, Daniel Pender.
Scot. Camelon 1885-1933. Wa1929.
DAVIDSON, George.
Am. b. Butka, Rus. 1889; ad. 1934 New York. A.
DAVIDSON, Harry. (Eg)
Am. Phila., Pa. 1858-1924 New York. A21-B-F-T.
DAVIDSON, Jo. (S)
Am. b. New York 1883; ad. 1934 Same. A-Cs-F-W-46-813.
DAVIDSON, McNeill.
Am. ad. 1934 Houston, Tex. M.
DAVIDSON, Ola McNeill.
Am. b. Brazoria, Tex.; ad 1934 Houston, Tex. A.
DAVIDSON, Oscar L.
Am. Fithian, Ill. 1875-1922 Ind., Ind. A019.
DAVIDSON, Robert. (S)
Am. b. Ind., Ind. 1904; ad. 1934 Same. A-Cs.
DAVIDSON [Mrs.], W. F.
Am. ad. 1934 Greenwich, Conn. M.
DAVIES, Arthur Bowen.
Am. Utica, N. Y. 1862-1928 Florence, It. A026-B-DAB-E-F-T-W13-1-46-71-191-213-214-701-748-757.
DAVIES, Charles William. (Eg)
Am. b. Whitesboro, N. Y. 1854. F-T-7.
DAVIES, David.
Am. b. 1876; d. 1921 Chicago, Ill. A18.
DAVIES, Edward.
Eng. London 1843-1912. B-T.
DAVIES, George O. (Ill)
Am. ad. 1933 New York. M.
DAVIESS, Maria Thompson.
Am. Harrodsburg, Ky. 1872-1924 New York. DAB-W13.
DA VINCI. *see* Leonardo da Vinci.

DAVIS, Alexander Jackson.
Am. New York 1803-1892. T.
DAVIS, Alice.
Am. b. Iowa City, Ia. 1905; ad. 1934 Same. A.
DAVIS [Mrs.], Cecil Clarke.
Am. b. Chicago 1877; ad. 1934 Marion, Mass. A-W-1.
DAVIS, Charles Harold.
Am. Amesbury, Mass. 1856-1933 Mystic, Conn. A030-B-E-F-T-W-1-46-Obit. Art Digest, 9-1-1933.
DAVIS, Charles Henry.
Am. Cambridge, Mass. 1845-1921. A12-B-F.
DAVIS, Charles Percy.
Am. b. Iowa City, Ia.; ac. 1931. A28.
DAVIS, [Mrs.] Cornelia Cassady.
Am. Cleveland, O. 1870-1920 Cinn., O. A018-F.
DAVIS, E. L.
Am. ex. 1934 Woodstock, N. Y. M.
DAVIS, Earl R.
Am. b. 1886; ad. 1934 Prov., R. I. A.
DAVIS, Edward.
Eng. Worcester 1833-1867 Rome, It. DNB-T.
DAVIS, Emma Earlenbaugh.
Mrs. William John Davis.
Am. b. Altoona, Pa. 1891; ad. 1934 Bala-Cynwyd, Pa. A.
DAVIS, Floyd. (Ill)
Am. ad. 1934 New York. M.
DAVIS, Fred W.
Eng. ac. 1890-1906 Birmingham. B-T.
DAVIS, Gladys Rockmore.
Am. ad. 1935 New York. M.
DAVIS, Helen Cruikshank. (Min)
Mrs. William B. Davis.
Am. b. Elizabeth, N. J.; ad. 1934 Houston, Tex. A.
DAVIS, Helen S. (S)
Am. b. Phila., Pa.; ad. 1934 New York. A.
DAVIS, Henry William Banks.
Eng. Finchley 1833-1914 Glaslyn. B-C-E-T.
DAVIS, Hubert.
Am. ad. 1935 New York. M.
DAVIS, James Edward.
Am. ex. 1935 New York. M.
DAVIS, Jesse.
Am. b. Texas 1887; ad. 1934 Dallas, Tex. A.
DAVIS, John Parker. (Eg)
Am. Meredith Bridge, N. H. 1832-1910 Elmhurst, L. I., N. Y. A08-F-T-8-185.
DAVIS [or Davies], John Scarlett.
Eng. Hereford 1804-1845/6. B-DNB-T.
DAVIS, John Steeple.
Am. Parkridge, Eng. 1844-1917 Brooklyn, N. Y. A015-T.
DAVIS, Leonard M.
Am. b. Winchendon, Mass. 1864; ad. 1934 Los Angeles, Calif. A-F.
DAVIS, Lew.
Am. ad. 1934 Plainfield, N. J. M.
DAVIS, Lucien.
Eng. b. Liverpool 1860. B-T-Wa.
DAVIS, Natalie Harlan. (Ill)
Am. b. Phila., Pa. 1898; ad. 1934 Same. A.
DAVIS, [Mrs.] Pinder.
Eng. ex. 1932 London. M.
DAVIS, Richard Barrett.
Eng. Walford 1782-1854. B-DNB-T.
DAVIS, Ronald Fremont. (Et)
Am. Worcester, Mass. 1887-1919 Mt. Vernon, N. Y. A016.
DAVIS, Stark.
Am. b. Boston, Mass. 1885; ad. 1934 Chicago. A.
DAVIS, Stuart.
Am. b. Phila., Pa. 1894; ad. 1934 New York. A-F.
DAVIS, Val [or Valentine].
Eng. b. Liverpool 1854; ac. 1916 London. B-T.
DAVIS, Warren. (Et)
Am. ad. 1934 New York. M.
DAVIS, Warren B.
Am. New York 1865-1928 Brooklyn, N. Y. A025-F.
DAVIS, Wayne Lambert. (Et)
Am. b. Oak Park, Ill. 1904; ad. 1934 Pelham, N. Y. M.
DAVIS, Will.
Am. b. Boston, Mass. 1879; ad. 1934 Same. A.
DAVIS, William.
Ir. Dublin 1812-1873 London. B-Bd-DNB-T.
DAVIS, William Arthur. (S)
Eng. ac. 1895 London. T.
DAVIS, William Steeple. (Et)
Am. b. Orient, N. Y. 1884; ad. 1934 Same. A-F.
DAVIS, Willis E.
Am. ac. 1900 San Fran., Calif.; d. 1910 at sea. A08.
DAVISON, Lucien Adelbert.
Am. b. Clay, N. Y. 1872; ad. 1934 Brooklyn, N. Y. A.
DAVISSON, Homer Gordon.
Am. b. Blountsville, Ind. 1866; ad. 1934 Fort Wayne, Ind. A.
DAVISSON, Oscar. (S)
Am. ex. 1932 New York. M.
DAVOL, Edith.
Am. ad. 1934 Fishkill, N. Y. M.
DAVOL, Joseph Benjamin.
Am. Chicago 1864-1923 Ogunquit, Me. A020-F.
DAVOL, Ralph. (Ill)
Am. b. Taunton, Mass. 1874; ad. 1934 Same. W.
DAWANT, Albert Alphonse Pierre.
Fr. Paris 1852-1923 Same. B-DBA-T.
DAWE, George. (Eg)
Eng. London 1781-1829 Same. B-DNB-T-722.
DAWE, Henry Edward. (Eg)
Eng. London 1790-1848 Windsor. B-DNB-T.
DAWE, Philip. (Eg)
Eng. London 1750-1785. DNB-T.
DAWES, Dexter B.
Am. b. Englewood, N. J. 1872; ad. 1934 Same. A.
DAWES, Edwin M.
Am. b. Boone, Ia. 1872; ad. 1934 Fallon, Nev. A-F.
DAWES, Pansy.
Am. b. Clay Center, Kan. 1885; ad. 1934 Colorado Springs, Col. A.

DAWKINS, HENRY. (Eg)
Am. ac. 1753-1776 in New York. DAB-F-T-2-7-56-184.
DAWLEY, HERBERT M. (S)
Am. b. Chillicothe, O. 1880; ad. 1934 Chatham, N. J. A.
DAWSON, ARTHUR.
Am. Crewe, Eng. 1859-1922 Richmond, Va. A019-F-T.
DAWSON, GEORGE WALTER.
Am. b. Andover, Mass. 1870; ad. 1934 W. Phila., Pa. A-F-T-W.
DAWSON, HENRY [or William].
Eng. Hull 1811-1878 Cheswick. B-Bd-DNB-T.
DAWSON, JOHN WILFRED.
Am. b. Chicago 1885; ad. 1934 Wickford, R. I. A.
DAWSON, MONTAGUE J.
Eng. b. at sea; ac. 1934. Wa.
DAWSON, NELSON.
Eng. ad. 1934 London. B-T-Wa.
DAWSON, WILLIAM. *see* Dawson, Henry.
DAWSON-WATSON, DAWSON.
Am. b. London 1864; ac. 1934 San Antonio, Tex. A-F-T-W.
DAY, ALEXANDRE. (Min)
Eng. 1773-1841 Chelsea. B-Bd-DNB.
DAY, BENJAMIN.
Am. New York 1838-1916 Summit, N. J. A13.
DAY, CLARENCE. (Author-Ill)
Am. b. New York 1874; ad. 1935 Same. M.
DAY, FORSHAW.
Can. England 1827-1903 Canada. M.
DAY, FRANCIS.
Am. b. LeRoy, N. Y. 1863; ad. 1934 Lanesboro, Mass. A-F-T-W.
DAY, FRANK MILES.
Am. Covington, Ky. 1848-1918. M.
DAY, HORACE TALMAGE.
Am. b. Amoy, China 1909; ad. 1934 Staten Island, N. Y. A.
DAY, KATHARINE SEYMOUR.
Am. b. Hartford, Conn.; ad. 1915 New York. A12.
DAY, MABEL K.
Am. b. Yarmouth, Nova Scotia 1884; ad. 1934 Schenectady, N. Y. A.
DAY, MARTHA B. WILLSON. (Min)
Am. ad. 1934 Prov., R. I. M.
DAY, RICHARD.
Am. b. Canada; ad. 1934 Hollywood, Calif. M.
DAYES, EDWARD.
Eng. 1763-1804 London. B-DNB-T.
DAYTON, F. E. (Ill)
Am. b. Hartford, Conn.; ad. 1934 New York. A.
DAZZI, ROMANO.
It. b. 1904 Italy. T.
DE. *see also* last names.
DEACON, JAMES. (Min)
Eng. 1728-1750 London. DNB-T.
DEAKIN, EDWIN.
Am. b. Sheffield, Eng. 1840; ac. 1925 Calif. F-46.
DEAN, ABNER. (Cart)
Am. ad. 1934 Chicago, Ill. M.
DEAN, ARTHUR.
Am. b. New York 1910; ad. 1934 Same. M.
DEAN, EDWARD CLARENCE.
Am. b. Wash., D. C. 1879; ad. 1934 Greenwich, Conn. M.
DEAN, ELIZABETH M.
Mrs. Samuel R. Dean.
Am. b. Cambridge, Mass.; ad. 1915 Roxbury, Mass. A12.
DEAN, EVA.
Am. b. Storm Lake, Ia.; ad. 1934 Los Angeles, Calif. A.
DEAN, GLADYS JESSIE. *see* Haesler, G. J.
DEAN, [Mrs.] GRACE RHOADES. (Et)
Am. ad. 1934 Toledo, O. A.
DEAN, HELGA HAUGAN.
Am. b. Milwaukee, Wis.; ad. 1934 Chicago. A.
DEAN, HUGH PRIMROSE.
[Called the "Claude of Ireland".]
Ir. ac. 1765-1784. B-T.
DEAN, JAMES ERNEST. (Et)
Am. East Smithfield, Pa. 1871-1933 Toledo, O. A030-F.
DEAN, T. A. (Eg)
Eng. ac. 1818-1840 in London. B-T.
DEAN, WALTER LOFTHOUSE.
Am. Lowell, Mass. 1854-1912 Gloucester, Mass. A010-T.
DEANE, CHARLES.
Eng. ac. 1815-1855. M.
DEANE, JOHN.
Eng. Liverpool 1759-1798 Rome, It. B-DNB-T.
DEANE, LILLIAN REUBENA. (Min)
Am. b. Chicago 1881; ad. 1934 Los Angeles, Calif. A.
DE ANGELI, MARGUERITE. (Ill)
Am. ad. 1934 Jenkintown, Pa. M.
DEARBORN, NATHANIEL. (Eg)
Am. Boston 1786-1852 So. Reading, Mass.
DEARE, JOSEPH. (S)
Eng. Liverpool 1804-1835 Same. DNB-T.
DEARMAN, JOHN.
Eng. b. London 1857; d. Guildford. B-T.
DEARTH, HENRY GOLDEN.
Am. Bristol, R. I. 1864-1918 New York. A015-B-DAB-F-T-W9-46.
DEAS, CHARLES.
Am. Phila., Pa. 1818-1867. B-F-T-4-15.
DE BAAN. *see* Baen.
DEBACQ, CHARLES ALEXANDRE.
Fr. Paris 1804-1853 Same. B-T.
DEBAINS, THÉRÈSE.
Fr. ex. 1934 in Paris. DBA.
DEBAR. *see* Bar, Bonaventure de.
DEBAT-PONSAN, EDOURD BENARD.
Fr. Toulouse 1847-1913 Paris. B-DBA-T.
DEBAY, AUGUSTE HYACINTHE. (S)
Fr. Nantes 1804-1865 Paris. B-T.
DEBAY, JEAN BAPTISTE JOSEPH. (S)
Fr. Mechlin, Belg. 1779-1863 Paris. B-T.
DE BEAUMONT, CHARLES EDOURD.
Fr. b. Lannion 1821; d. 1888. M.
DE BEAUMONT, W.
Eng. ac. 1832-1854. M.
DE BECK, WILLIAM. (Cart)
Am. b. Chicago 1890; ad. 1934 New York. W.
DE BELLE, CHARLES ERNEST.
Can. b. Budapest, Hun.; ad. 1934 Montreal, Can. M.

DEBEREINER, George.
Am. b. Arzberg, Ger. 1860; ad. 1934 Cinn., O. A.
DE BERNARDI, Domenico.
It. ad. 1934 Besozzo (Varese). M.
DE BEUL, Franz.
Belg. ac. 19th Cent. in Belgium. M.
DE BOCK. *see* Bock.
DEBONNET, Maurice G.
Am. b. Paris 1872; ad. 1934 Bayside, L. I., N. Y. A.
DE BRA, Mabel Mason.
Am. b. Milledgeville, O. 1899; ad. 1934 Columbus, O. A.
DEBRET, François. [S-Architect]
Fr. Paris 1777-1850 St. Cloud. T.
DEBRET, Jean Baptiste.
Fr. Paris 1768-1848. T.
DEBRIE, Dirk [or Théodore]. (Eg)
Dut. Liège, Belg. 1528-1598. DNB.
DE BRUYCKER. *see* Bruycker.
DE BRUYN, Théodore. *see* Bruyn, T. de.
DEBUCOURT, Louis Philibert. (Eg)
Fr. Paris 1755-1832 Belleville. B-T.
DECAISNÉ, Henri.
Flem. Brussels 1799-1852 Paris. C-T.
DE CAMP, Joseph Rodefer.
Am. Cinn., O. 1858-1923 Florida. A020-DAB-E-F-T-46.
DE CAMPS, Alexandre Gabriel.
Fr. Paris 1803-1860 Fontainebleau. B-Bd-C-E-T-722.
DECANIS, Théophile Henry.
Fr. Marseilles 1848-1917. B-T.
DECARIS, Albert. (Ill)
Fr. ad. 1934 Paris. M.
DECARIS, Johann Wilhelm.
Fr. 1747-1830. T.
de CELLE, Edmond Carl.
Am. b. New York 1889; ad. 1934 Mobile, Ala. A.
DECHAUME, Cecile Geoffrey.
Fr. ad. 1934 Paris. M.
DECHAUME, Charles Geoffrey.
Fr. ad. 1934 Paris. M.
DE CHELMINSKI, Jan V.
Am. b. Warsaw, Pol.; d. 1925 New York. A22.
DECHENAUD, Louis Adolphe.
Fr. St. Ambreuil 1868-1926 Paris. B-DBA-T.
DECHKOVITCH, Branko. (S)
Jugo-Slav. ad. 1919 Paris. M.
DECIO [or Desio] Family.
It. ac. 15-16th centuries in Milan. T.
DECISY, Eugène.
Fr. b. Metz 1866. B-DBA.
DECKER [or Dekker], Cornelis Gerritsz.
Dut. 1600?-1678 Haarlem. C-722.
DECKER [Mrs.] E. Bennett. (Min.)
Am. b. Wash., D. C. 1869; ad. 1934 Same. A.
DECKER, Joseph.
Am. Württemberg, Ger. 1853-1924 Brooklyn, N. Y. A21.
DECKER, Robert M.
Am. b. Troy, N. Y. 1847. T.
DE COCK. *see* Cock.
DECOMBES, Émilie Elizabeth.
Am. b. Paris; d. 1905 Boston, Mass. M.
DECOMPS, S. (S)
Am. ac. 1887. M.
DE CORDOBA, Mathilda J.
Am. b. New York; d. 1912 Same. A010-F.
de CORINI, Margit [or Margaret].
Am. b. Hungary 1902; ad. 1934 New York. A.
DE CORT, Henry Francis [or Hendrik Frans]. *see* Cort, H. F.
de COSSY, Ed. (Ill.)
Am. ad. 1934 New York. A.
DE CRAEYER [or Crayer], Gaspard [or Jasper]. *see* Craeyer, G.
DE CRANO, Fèlix.
Am. b. France; d. 1908 Wallingford, Pa. A07.
DE CRITZ, Emanuel.
Eng. 1605-1665 London. B-DNB-T.
DE CRITZ, John [The Elder].
Flem. Antwerp 1555-1641 London. B-DNB-T.
DE CRITZ, John [The Younger].
Eng. 1600-1644 London. B-DNB-T.
DE CUVILLON, Louis Robert. *see* Cuvillon, L. R.
DEDAESTS.
Belg. ac. 1850. *see* N. Y. Pub. Lib.
DEDINA, Jean.
Fr. b. Strals 1870. B-DBA.
DEDINA, Venceslas.
Czec. b. Prague 1872. DBA.
DEDREUX, Alfred.
Fr. Paris 1810-1860 Same. B-T-722.
DEELEN. *see* Delen.
DEERSON, Arthur.
Am. ad. 1934 New Canaan, Conn. M.
D'ÉSPAGNET, Georges.
Fr. b. 1870. M.
DEFAUX, Alexandre.
Fr. Bercy 1826-1900. B-T.
DEFENDENTE, Ferrari. *see* Ferrari, D.
DE FEO, Charles. (Ill.)
Am. ad. 1934 New York. M.
DE FILIPPIS, August.
Am. ad. 1934 Jersey City, N. J. M.
DE FIORI, Ernesto. (S)
Ger. b. 1884. M.
DE FOE, Charles.
Am. b. Wilmington, Del.; ad. 1935 New York. M.
DEFONTE, Edmond.
Fr. b. Paris 1862. B-DBA.
DE FOREST, [Mrs.] Cornelius W. *see* Morrow, Julie.
DE FOREST, Grace Banker.
Am. b. 1897; ad. 1934 Grosse Point, Mich. A.
de FOREST, Harriet Stanton.
Am. b. Milburn, N. J. 1909; ad. 1934 Greenwich, Conn. A.
DE FOREST, Julie Morrow. *see* Morrow, Julie.
DE FOREST, Lockwood.
Am. New York 1850-1932 Santa Barbara, Calif. A029-F-W.
DE FRANCA, Manuel Joachim.
Am. b. Oporto, Port.; d. 1865 St. Louis, Mo. F.
DEFRANCE. *see* France, Léonard de.

DE FRANCISCI, ANTHONY. (S)
Am. b. Italy 1887; ad. 1934 New York. A-Cs-F.
DEFREGGER, FRANZ VON.
Ger. (Bav.) Dolsach, Tyrol 1835-1921 Munich. B-C-T.
DEGAS, EDGAR HILAIRE GERMAIN. (P-S)
Fr. Paris 1834-1917 Same. B-E-T-21-192-342-837-847-849-947.
DE GAVERE, COR.
Am. b. Batavia, Java 1877; ad. 1934 Santa Cruz, Calif. A.
DEGENER, FAUSTINA MUNROE. (P-S)
Am. ad. 1934 Charlotte, N. C. M.
DEGEORGE, CHARLES JEAN MARIE. (S)
Fr. Lyons 1837-1889 Paris. B.
DEGEORGE, CHRISTOPHE THOMAS.
Fr. Blanzat 1786-1854 Clermon. B-T.
DEGER, ERNEST.
Ger. Bockenem 1809-1855 Düsseldorf. B-T.
DE GLEHN, WILFRED GABRIEL.
Eng. b. London 1870; ex. 1934 Same. Wa.
DEGLER, HANS. (Wood-S)
Bav. ac. 1590-1637 Munich. Hs-T.
DEGRAIN, ANTONIO MUNOZ.
Sp. ac. 19th Cent. in Spain. B.
DE GRAVE, JOSUA. *see* Grave, J.
DE GROOT, ADRIAAN MARTIN.
Am. b. Holland 1870; ad. 1935 New York. A20-F.
DEGROUX, CHARLES. *see* Groux, C.
DE HAAS. *see also* Haas.
DE HAAS, ALICE PREBLE TUCKER.
Mrs. M. F. H. de Haas.
Am. b. Boston, Mass.; ad. 1915 New York. A12.
DE HAAS, JOHANNES HUBERTUS LEONARDUS.
Belg. Kedel 1832-1908 Brussels. B-T.
DE HAAS, MAURITZ FREDERICK HENDRIK.
Am. Rotterdam, Holland 1832-1895 New York. B-C-E-F-T-4-15.
DE HAAS, WILLIAM FREDERICK.
Am. Rotterdam, Holland 1830-1880 Fayal, Azores. C-T-15.
DE HAVEN, FRANKLIN.
Am. Bluffton, Ind. 1856-1934 New York. A-F-M-W-46-181-Obit. N. Y. papers, 1-11-1934.
DE HELLEBRANTH, BERTHA.
Am. b. Budapest, Hun.; ad. 1934 Ventnor, N. J. A.
DE HELLEBRANTH, ELENA.
Am. b. Budapest, Hun.; ad. 1934 Ventnor, N. J. A.
DE HEUSCH. *see* Heusch, Willem de.
DEHN, ADOLF ARTHUR. (Et.)
Am. b. Waterville, Minn. 1895; ad. 1934 New York. A28.
DEHNER, WALT.
Am. b. Buffalo, N. Y. 1898; ad. 1934 Whitehouse, O. A.
DEHODENCQ, EDMÉ ALEXIS ALFRED.
Fr. Paris 1822-1882. B-T.
DE HOOG. *see* Hoog.
DEIGENESCH, HERMAN F.
Am. Phila., Pa. 1858-1921. A018-F.
DEIKE, CLARA L.
Am. b. Detroit, Mich. 1881; ad. 1934 Cleveland, O. A-F.
DEIKER, CARL FREDRICH.
Ger. Wetzlar 1836-1892 Düsseldorf. B-T.
DEINEKA [or Deyneka], ALEXANDRE.
Rus. b. Kursk 1899; ad. 1935 Moscow. M.
DEINES, E. HUBERT. (Eg)
Am. ad. 1935 Kansas City, Mo. M.
DE IVANOWSKY, SIGISMUND.
Am. b. Poland 1874; ad. 1934 Westfield, N. J. A.
DE JONG, BETTY.
Am. Paris 1886-1917 San Fran., Calif. A015.
DE KEYSER. *see* Keyser.
DEKHTEREV.
Rus. ad. 1935 Moscow. M.
DEKKER. *see* Decker.
DE KONNICK. *see* Koninck.
DE KOSENKO, STEPHAN. (S)
Am. b. Rus. 1865; ad. 1934 New York. A.
DE KRUIF, HENRI GILBERT.
Am. b. Grand Rapids, Mich. 1882; ad. 1934 Los Angeles, Calif. A.
DEL. *see also* last names.
DELABORDE, HENRI.
Fr. Rennes 1811-1899 Paris. B-T.
DELACROIX, FERDINAND VICTOR EUGÈNE.
Fr. Charenton 1798-1863 Paris. B-Bd-C-E-T-343-344-644-790-820-849-870.
DE LA CRUZ, PANTOJA. *see* Pantoja.
DELAGARDETTE, PIERRE CLAUDE. (Eg.)
Fr. Paris 1743/5-1782 Same. T.
DE LA HARPE, JOSEPH.
Am. Swi. 1850-1901 Brooklyn, N. Y. A4.
DELAHAYE, CLAUDE JACQUES ROBERT.
Fr. b. Paris; d. 1928. DBA.
DELAHAYE, ERNEST JEAN.
Fr. b. Paris 1855. B-T.
DE LA HYRE. *see* La Hire.
DE LAITRE, ELEANOR.
Am. ex. 1934 New York. M.
DELAMAIN, PAUL.
Fr. Paris 1821-1882 Ormans. B-T.
DE LA MARRE. *see* La Mare-Richart, Fl.
DE LA MOREUX, DWIGHT. (S)
Am. b. 1841; d. 1917 Chicago, Ill. A15.
DE LA MOTTE, WILLIAM ALFRED.
Eng. 1775-1863 Oxford. B-DNB-T.
DELANCE, PAUL LOUIS.
Fr. Paris 1848-1924. B-DNB-T.
DE LANCY, DARRAGH. (S)
Am. b. East Orange, N. J. 1870; ad. 1934 Waterbury, Conn. W.
DE LAND, CLYDE OSMER.
Am. b. Union City, Pa. 1872; ad. 1934 Phila., Pa. A-F-W.
DELANE, SOLOMON.
Scot. Edinburgh 1727-1784? London. DNB-T.
DELANO, ANNITA.
Am. b. Hueneme, Calif. 1894; ad. 1934 Los Angeles, Calif. A.
DELANO, GERARD C. (Ill.)
Am. ad. 1934 New York. M.
DELANOY, ABRAHAM [The Younger].
Am. New York 1740?-1786 Same. F-T-1-182-184.
DELANOY, HIPPOLYTE PIERRE.
Scot. Glasgow 1849-1899. B-T.
DELAPLANCHE, EUGÈNE. (S)
Fr. Belleville 1836-1891 Paris. B-E-T.

DELARAM, Francis. (Eg.)
Eng. 1590-1627 London. DNB-T.
DELAROCHE, Hippolyte Paul.
Fr. Paris 1797-1856 Same. B-Bd-C-E-T-722.
DELARUE. *see* La Rue.
DE LÁSZLÓ, Philipp A. *see* László, P.
DE LA TOUR. *see* La Tour.
DELATRE, Auguste. (Eg.)
Fr. Paris 1822-1907. B-T.
DELATRE, Eugène. (Eg.)
Fr. b. Paris 1864. B-DBA-T.
DELATRE [or Delattre], Jean Marie. (Eg.)
Fr. Abbeville 1745-1840 Fulham, Eng. DNB-T.
DELAUNAY, Jules Élie.
Fr. Nantes 1828-1891 Paris. B-C-DBA-E-T.
DELAUNAY, Nicolas. *see* Launay, N. de.
DELAUNAY, Robert. (Eg.)
Fr. Paris 1749-1814 Same. B-T.
DELAUNAY, Robert.
Fr. b. Paris 1882. DBA-797.
DELAUNE, Étienne.
Fr. Paris 1818/9-1883 Same. T.
DELAUNE, Zoé Laure. *see* Chatillon, Z. L.
DELAUNEY, Robert. (S)
Fr. ac. 14th Cent. in France. M.
DELAVANTE, S. (Ill)
Am. ad. 1935 New York. M.
DELAVILLE, Emily.
Am. ex. 1935 New York. M.
DELAW, Georges. (Ill.)
Fr. ac. 1930 in Paris. DBA.
DELBOS, G. Edmond.
Am. b. London 1879; ad. 1934 Grosse Point, Mich. A.
DELBOS, Julius M.
Am. b. London 1879; ad. 1934 New York. A.
DELBRIDGE, Thomas James.
Am. b. Atlanta, Ga. 1894; ad. 1934 New York. A.
DELCOUR, Jean. (S)
Flem. Hamoir 1627-1707 Liége. B-Hs-T.
DE LEEUW, Cateau.
Am. b. Hamilton, O. 1903; ad. 1934 Plainfield, N. J. A.
DELEGATOR, Maurice.
Rus. b. Novograd-Volynsk 1902; ad. 1934 New York. M.
DELEGUE, James. (Eg.)
Eng. ac. 1777 in England. M.
DELEN, Dirk van.
Dut. Heusden 1605-1671 Arnemuyden. B-T.
de LESLIE, Alexander Paulovitch.
Am. b. Moscow, Russ.; ad. 1934 Springfield Gardens, L. I., N. Y. A.
DELESSARD, Auguste Joseph.
Fr. Paris 1827-1890? B-T.
DELÉTANG, Robert Adrien.
Fr. b. Preuilly 1874. B-DBA.
DELEVANTE, S. (Ill.)
Am. ad. 1934 New York. M.
DELFF, Jacob Willemsz [The Elder].
Dut. Gouda 1550-1601 Delft. B-T.
DELFF, Jacob Willemsz [The Younger].
Dut. Delft 1619-1661 Same. B-T.
DELFF, Willem Jacobz.
Dut. Delft 1580-1638 Same. B-T.
DELFOS, Abraham.
Dut. Leyde 1729/31-1820 Same. B-T.
DELFOSSE, Georges.
Can. ad. 1935 Montreal, Can. M-893.
DELFT, van. *see* Vermeer.
DELGADE, L. F.
Am. ex. 1934 New York. M.
DELIN, Johannes Josephus Nicolaus.
Flem. Antwerp 1774/6-1811 Paris. B-T.
DELLA BELLA, Stefano. (Eg.)
It. Florence 1610-1664. E.
DELLA COLLE, Raffaellino.
It. Colle 1490-1540? E-V.
DELLA QUERCIA, Jacopo. *see* Quercia.
DELLA ROBBIA. *see* Robbia.
DELLENBAUGH, Frederick Samuel.
Am. b. McConnelsville, O. 1853; ad. 1934 Cragsmoor, N. Y. F-W.
DELLO, Antonio.
It. b. Florence 1603. [No death date.] M.
DELLO DI NICCOLÒ DELLI. [or Nicolás Florentino].
It. Florence 1404?-1466/77. M.
DEL MAR, Frances.
Am. b. Wash., D. C.; ad. 1934 New York. A-DBA.
DELMONT, Deodat [van der Mont].
Flem. St. Troud 1581/2-1644 Antwerp. B-T.
DEL MUE, Maurice August.
Am. b. Paris 1878; ad. 1934 Forest Knolls, Calif. A-F.
DEL NERO, Angelo. (S)
It. b. 1860 in Italy. M.
DELOBBE, François Alfred.
Fr. b. Paris 1835. B-C-T.
DE LONGPRÉ, Paul.
Am. Lyons, Fr. 1855-1911 Los Angeles, Calif. A09.
DELORME, Anthonie. *see* Lorme, Anton de.
DELORT, Charles Edouard [or Edmond].
Fr. Nimes 1841-1895 St. Eugène. B-T.
DE LOUTHERBOURG, Philip James.
Eng. Strassburg 1740-1812 London. E.
DÉLOYE, Gustave Jean Baptiste.
Fr. Sedan 1838-1899. B-T.
DELPÉRÉ, Émile.
Belg. Huy 1850-1896 Esneux. T.
DEL POLLAJUOLO, Antonio. *see* Pollajuolo, A.
DELPY, Hippolyte Camille.
Fr. Joigny 1842-1910. B-T.
DEL RIO, Cueva. (Mu.)
Mex. ac. 1934 Wash., D. C. M.
DELTOMBE, Paul.
Fr. b. Catillon 1878; d. 1916. B-DBA.
DE LUCE, Olive Susanna.
Am. b. Oswego, N. Y. 1894; ad. 1934 Maryville, Mo. A.
DE LUCE, Percival.
Am. New York 1847-1914 Same. A011-F.
DELUG, Alois.
Aus. b. Bozen 1859; ac. 1913. B-T.
DE LUNA, Francis P. (S)
Am. b. New York 1891; ad. 1934 Same. A-Cs.
DELVAILLE, Henry Caro. *see* Caro-Delvaille, H.

DELVAUX, Laurent. (S)
Flem. Ghent 1696-1778 Nivelles. DNB-T.
DEL VEROCCHINO, Andrea. *see* Verocchino, A.
DELYEN [or Deslyens], Jacques François.
Fr. Ghent, Belg. 1684-1761 Paris. B-T.
DEMACHY, Pierre Antoine.
Fr. Paris 1723-1807 London. B-T.
DE MAINE, Harry.
Am. b. Liverpool, Eng. 1880; ad. 1934 Brooklyn, N. Y. A.
DE MAIO, Salvatore.
It. ac. 1934 in Rome. M.
DE MANCE, Henri.
Am. b. Hamburg, Ger. 1871; ad. 1934 New York. A.
DEMANCHE, Blanche Marguerite.
Fr. b. Douai 1868. DBA.
DE MAR, John L. (Cart.)
Am. Phila., Pa. 1865-1926 Penfield, Pa. A23.
DE MARE, Georges.
Am. b. Lucca, It. 1863-1907 Kansas City, Mo. A06.
DEMAREST, Eda Lord. (S)
Mrs. Benjamin G. Demarest.
Am. ad. 1934 New York. M.
DEMARIA, Pierre Jean.
Fr. b. Paris 1896. DBA.
DE MARIS, Walter.
Am. b. Cedarville, N. J. 1877; ad. 1934 New Rochelle, N. Y. A.
DEMARNE [or Demarnette], Jean Louis.
Fr. Brussels, Belg. 1744-1829 Paris. B-T-722.
DEMARTEAU, Gilles Antoine [The Elder]. (Eg.)
Flem. Liége 1722/9-1776 Paris. B-T.
DEMARTEAU, Gilles Antoine [The Younger].
Flem. Liége 1750/6-1802/6 Paris. B-T.
DE MARTINI, Joseph.
Am. ex. 1935 New York. M.
DE MATTEIS, Paolo.
It. Cilento 1662-1728 Naples. M.
DEMETRIUS II.
Gr. ac. 4th Cent. B.C. E-T.
de MILHAU, Zella. *see* Milhau, Z.
DEMING, Adelaide.
Am. b. Litchfield, Conn. 1864; ad. 1934 Same. A-F-T.
DEMING, Edwin Willard. (P-S)
Am. b. Ashland, O. 1860; ad. 1934 New York. A-F-T-W-46.
DEMMLER, Fred A.
Am. Allegheny, Pa. 1888-1918 France. A016-215.
DE MOLL, Mary Hitchner.
Mrs. Carl De Moll.
Am. b. Clayton, N. J. 1884; ad. 1934 Swarthmore, Pa. A.
DEMONT, Adrien Louis.
Fr. Douai 1851-1928 Wissant. B-DBA-T.
DEMONT, Ball. *see* Ball-Demont.
DEMONT-BRÉTON, Virginie [Elodie].
Mrs. Adrien Louis Demont.
Fr. b. Courrières 1859. DBA-T.
DE MORGAN, Evelyn.
Mrs. William De Morgan.
Eng. 1850-1919 London. T.
DE MORGAN, William Frend.
Eng. London 1839-1917 Same. DNB.
DEMUTH, Charles.
Am. b. Lancaster, Pa. 1883; ad. 1934 Same. A-F-216-345-701.
DENBY, Edwin H.
Am. ad. 1934 New York. M.
DENBY, William.
Eng. Great Bookham 1819-1875 London. B.
DENEIKA, Alexander.
Rus. ad. 1935 Moscow, Rus. M.
DE NESTI, Adolfo. (S)
Am. b. Florence, It. 1870; ad. 1915 Phila., Pa. A12.
DE NEUVILLE. *see* Neuville.
DENGHAUSEN, Franz H. (S)
Am. b. Boston, Mass. 1911; ad. 1934 Same. A.
DENGLER, Francis [or Franz] Xavier. (S)
Am. Cincinnati, O. 1853-1879 Covington, Ky. F-T-Ta-15.
DENIERE, Jacques.
Fr. b. Paris; ac. 1930 Same. DBA.
DENIS, Maurice.
Fr. b. Granville 1870; ad. 1934 St. Germain-en-Laye. B-DBA-E-T.
DENIS-VALVERANE, Louis.
Swi. b. Manosque 1870. DBA.
DENISON, George H.
Am. ad. 1934 Pittsfield, Mass. M.
DENISON, Harold Thomas. (Et.)
Am. b. 1887; ad. 1934 Boston Corners, N. Y. A.
DENMAN, Herbert.
Am. Brooklyn, N. Y. 1855-1903 Calif. A05-B-F-T.
DENNER, Balthasar.
Ger. Hamburg 1685-1749 Rostock. B-T-722.
DENNER, Walt.
Am. ex. 1934 New York. M.
DENNEULIN, Jules.
Fr. Lille 1835-1904 Same. B-T.
DENNIS, Charles Warren.
Am. b. New Bedford, Mass. 1898; ad. 1934 Needham, Mass. A.
DENNIS, James Morgan. (Et.)
Am. b. Boston, Mass. 1891; ac. 1934. A28.
DENNISON, Dorothy.
Am. ad. 1935 Youngstown, O. M.
DENNISON, Lucy.
Am. b. Youngstown, O. 1902; ad. 1934 Same. A.
DENOTER, Pierre François.
Belg. Walheim 1778-1842 Ghent. B-T. A.
DENSLOW, Dorothea Henrietta. (S)
Am. b. New York 1900; ad. 1934 Brooklyn. A.
DENT, Lucian Minor.
Am. ad. 1934 Memphis, Tenn. M.
DENTE, Girolamo. *see* Tiziano, G.
DENTE, Marco [Ravenna].
It. b. Ravenna; d. 1527 Rome. T-V.
DENTONE. *see* Curti.
DENYS, Frans.
Flem. Antwerp 1610-1657. B-T-722.
DEODATUS [or Adeodatus]. Son of Cosmas II.
It. ac. 1294-1317 in Rome. T.
D'OGGINO. *see* Oggino, Marco d'.

DE PARIS, JEAN. *see* Perreal, Jehan.
DEPAULIS, ALEXIS JOSEPH. (Med.)
Fr. Paris 1790/2-1867 Same. B.
DE PAUW, VICTOR.
Am. ex. 1935 New York. M.
DE PEYSTER, GERARD BEEKMAN.
Am. ac. 1800 in U. S. F-2.
D'ÉPINAY. *see* Épinay.
DE POLGARY, GEZA.
Am. Hungary 1862-1919 Atlantic City, N. J. A016.
DE PRATERE, EDMUND J.
Belg. Courtrai 1826-1888. M.
DEQUEVAUVILLER, FRANÇOIS.
Fr. Abbeville 1745-1807 Paris. T.
DERAIN, ANDRÉ.
Fr. b. Chartres 1880; ad. 1934 Paris. DBA-E-797-827-847.
DERBY, ALFRED THOMAS.
Eng. London 1821-1873 Hammersmith. B-DNB-T.
DERBY, WILLIAM.
Eng. Birmingham 1786-1847 London. DNB-T.
DE REYN, JAN.
Flem. Dunkirk, Belg. 1610-1678 Same. M.
DERGANS, LOUIS S.
Am. Austria 1890-1930 Wash., D. C. A027.
DER GOES. *see* Goes, van der.
DE RIBCOWSKY, DEY.
Am. b. Bulgaria 1880; ad. 1934 New York. A.
D'ERLANGER, BARON RUDOLPHE.
Eng. b. 1872; d. 1932 London. Wa-Y01933.
DE ROCCO, JOVAN.
Am. ad. 1934 New York. M.
DERONICO, OTTO HIERL.
Ger. b. 1859. M.
DE ROSE, ANTHONY LEWIS.
Am. New York 1803-1836 Same. F.
DERRICK, THOMAS. (Cari.)
Eng. b. Bristol; ad. 1934 London. Wa-873.
DERRICK, WILLIAM ROWELL.
Am. b. San Fran., Calif.; ad. 1934 New York. A-F-T.
DERSO, ALOIS. (Cari.)
Hun. b. Baja, Hun. 1888. 873.
DERUJINSKY, GLEB W. (S)
Am. b. Smolensk, Rus. 1888; ad. 1934 Bronxville, N. Y. A-Cs-F.
DE RYCK, WILLIAM.
Flem. Antwerp 1635-1697. DNB.
DE SAISETT, ERNEST PIERRE.
Am. b. San Jose, Calif.; d. 1899 Same. A2.
DE SAULLES, GEORGE WILLIAM. (Med.)
Eng. Birmingham 1862-1903 Chiswick. DNB.
DE SAUX, JULES. *see* Browne, Henrietta.
DESBOEUFS, ANTOINE. (S)
Fr. Paris 1793-1862 Passy. B-Hs.
DESBOIS, JULES. (S)
Fr. b. Parsay 1851. B-DBA.
DESBORDES-JONAS, LOUISE ANGEVINE.
Fr. Angers 1848-1926 Paris. B-678.
DESBOUTIN, MARCELLIN GILBERT.
Fr. Cévilly 1823-1902 Nice. B-T.
DESBROSSES, JEAN ALFRED.
Fr. Paris 1835-1906 Same. B-T.
DESCAMPS, JEAN BAPTISTE [The Elder].
Fr. Dunkerque 1706-1791 Rouen. B-T.
DESCATOIRE, ALEXANDRE. (S)
Fr. b. Douai 1874. B-DBA.
DESCH, FRANK H.
Am. Phila., Pa. 1873-1934. A-F.
DESCHAMPS, LOUIS HENRI.
Fr. Montélimar 1846-1902. B-T.
DES CLAYES, ALICE.
Can. b. Aberdeen, Scot.; ac. 1935 Montreal, Can. M.
DES CLAYES, BERTHE.
Can. b. Aberdeen, Scot.; ac. 1935 Montreal, Can. 893.
DES CLAYES, GERTRUDE.
Can. b. Aberdeen, Scot.; ac. 1935 Montreal, Can. DBA.
DESCOMBES, ÉMILIE E.
Am. b. Paris, Fr.; d. 1906 Boston, Mass. A06.
DESCOURS [or Descourt], MICHEL HUBERT.
Fr. Bernay 1707-1775 Same. B-T.
DESCOURS, MICHEL PIERRE HUBERT.
Fr. Paris 1741-1814 Bernay. B-T.
DESCOURTIS, CHARLES MELCHIOR. (Eg.)
Fr. Paris 1753-1820/6 Same. B-T.
DESFONTAINES, CHARLES.
Fr. ac. 1884 in Paris. B-T.
DESFONTAINES, HENRI.
Fr. ac. 1904 in Paris. B-T.
DESFRICHES, AIGNAN THOMAS.
Fr. Orléans 1715-1800 Same. B-T.
DESGOFFE, ALEXANDRE.
Fr. Paris 1805-1882 Same. B-T.
DESGOFFE, BLAISE ALEXANDRE.
Fr. Paris 1830-1901 Same. B-T.
DES GRANGES, DAVID. (Min.)
Br. ac. 1625-1675. DNB.
DESHAYES, CHARLES FÉLIX EDOUARD.
Fr. b. Toulon 1831; ac. 1864 Paris. B.
DESHAYES, FRÉDÉRIC LÉON.
Fr. b. Paris 1883. DBA.
DESHAYES DE COLLEVILLE, JEAN BAPTISTE HENRI. [Called "Le Romain".]
Fr. Rouen 1729-1765/6. B-C-T-722.
DESIDERIO DA SETTIGANO. (S)
It. Settigano 1428-1464. B-E-Hs-T-V.
DÉSIRÉ [or Déziré], HENRI.
Fr. b. Libourne 1878; ad. 1934 Paris. B-DBA.
DÉSIRÉ-LUCAS, LOUIS. *see* Lucas, L. D.
DESJOBERT, LOUIS REMY EUGÈNE.
Fr. Châteauroux 1817-1863 Paris. B-T.
DESMARQUETS, PAULINE. *see* Auzou, P. D.
DE SMET, GUSTAVE.
Belg. ac. 1910 in Brussels. B.
DESMOND, CRESWELL HARTLEY.
Eng. b. Streatham 1877; ad. 1934 Paris. Wa.
DESNOYERS, A. G. L. *see* Bouche-Desnoyers.
DE SOTO, MINNIE B. HALL.
Mrs. Emilio Dominguez De Soto.
Am. b. Denver, Colo. 1864; ad. 1934 Same. A.
D'ESPAGNET. *see* Espagnet.
DESPIAU, CHARLES. (S)
Fr. b. Mont-de-Marsan 1875. B-DBA-884.
DESPORTES, ALEXANDRE FRANÇOISE.
Fr. Champagne 1661-1743 Paris. B-C-T-722.

DESPREZ, Louis. (S)
Fr. Paris 1799-1870/2. B-T.
DESPREZ, Louis Jean.
Fr. Lyons 1740/3-1804 Stockholm, Swe. B-T.
DESPUJOLS, Jean.
Fr. b. Salles 1886. DBA.
DESRAIS, Claude Louis.
Fr. Paris 1746-1816 Same. B-T.
DESSAIN, Émile François.
Fr. Valenciennes 1808-1882. Same. B.
DESSAR, Louis Paul.
Am. b. Ind., Ind. 1867; ad. 1934 Lyme, Conn. A-B-F-T-W-46.
DESSIN-FOURDANCHON. (S). Fr. B.
DESVALLIERS, Gaston [or Georges] Oliver.
Fr. b. Paris 1861. B-DBA-T.
DESVARREUX-LARPENTEUR, James.
Am. b. Balt., Md. 1847; ad. 1934 Paris. A-F-T.
DETAILLE, Jean Baptiste Édouard.
Fr. Paris 1848-1912 Same. B-C-DBA-T.
DETHLOFF, Peter Hans.
Am. b. Barnsdorf, Ger. 1869; ad. 1934 Los Angeles, Calif. A.
DETHOMAS, Maxime. (Ill.)
Fr. b. Garches; ad. 1934 Same. DBA.
DE THOREN. *see* Thoren, von.
DE THULSTRUP, Thure. *see* Thulstrup, T.
DETMOLD, Charles Maurice.
Eng. Putney 1883-1908 Hampstead. DNB.
DETROY. *see* Troy, de.
DETTHOW, Erik.
Swe. b. 1893; ad. 1935 Stockholm. DBA.
DETTI, Césare Auguste.
It. Spolèto 1847-1914 Paris. B-DBA-T.
DETTMANN, Ludwig Julius Christian.
Ger. b. Adelbye 1865. B-T.
DETURCK, Julien Jules Alphonse. (Eg.)
Fr. b. Bailleul 1862. B-DBA.
DETWILLER, Frederick Knecht.
Am. b. Easton, Pa. 1882; ad. 1934 New York. A-F-W.
DEULLY, Eugène Auguste François.
Fr. b. Lille 1860. B-DBA-T.
DEUTSCH, Boris.
Am. b. Russia 1895; ad. 1934 Los Angeles, Calif. A.
DEUTSCH, Ernest. (Et.)
Aus. b. Vienna 1883. T.
DEUTSCH, Hans Rudolf von.
Ger. Erlach 1525-1572. T.
DEUTSCH, Ludwig.
Aus. b. Vienna 1855. B-DBA-T.
DEUTSCH, Nicolas Manuel I.
Swi. Berne 1484-1530 Same. B-T.
DEUTSCH, Nicolas Manuel II.
Swi. Berne 1528-1588 Same. B-T.
DEVAL, Pierre Jean Charles.
Fr. b. Lyons 1897. DBA.
DEVAMBEZ, André Victor Édouard.
Fr. b. Paris 1867. B-DBA-T.
DÉVÉ, Eugène.
Fr. Rouen 1826-1887. B-T.
DE VEAUX, James.
Am. b. Charleston, S. C. 1812. F-2-217.
DEVÉDEUX, Louis.
Fr. Clermont-Ferrand 1820-1875 Passy. B-T.
DEVERELL, Walter Howell.
Eng. 1828-1854 London. B-Bd-T
DEVÉRIA, Achille Jacques Jean Marie.
Fr. Paris 1805-1857 Same. B-T
DEVÉRIA, Eugène François Marie Joseph.
Fr. Paris 1805-1865 Pau. B-C-T
DEVILLE, Joseph Henri.
Swi. Geneva 1803-1857 Same. B-T
DEVILLY, Théodore Louis.
Fr. Metz 1818-1886 Nancy. C-T
DE VINCI. *see* Leonardo da Vinci.
DEVINE, Bernard.
Am. b. Portland, Me. 1884; ad. 1915 Paris. A12-F.
DE VINEY, Jess E.
Am. ad. 1934 Toledo, O. M.
DEVIS, Anthony Thomas.
Eng. Albury 1729-1817. B-T.
DEVIS, Arthur William.
Eng. London 1763-1822. B-DNB-T.
DEVLAN, Daniel.
Am. New Jersey 1835-1870 Reading, Pa. M.
DE VOLL, Frederick Usher.
Am. b. Prov., R. I. 1873; ad. 1934 Same. A-F-T-W.
DEVOSGE, François.
Fr. Gray, Fr. 1732-1811. B-T.
DE WENTWORTH, Cecile. *see* Wentworth, C.
DEWEY, Charles Melville.
Am. b. Lowville, N. Y. 1849; ad. 1934 New York. A-B-C-F-T-W-46.
DEWEY, Julia Henshaw.
Mrs. Charles Melville Dewey.
Am. b. Batavia, N. Y.; d. 1928 New York. A026.
DEWHURST, Wynford.
Eng. b. Manchester 1864; ac. London. B-T.
DE WILDE, Samuel.
Eng. 1748-1832 London. B-DNB.
DEWING, Francis. (Eg.)
Am. b. London; ac. 1716-1745 Same. DAB-F-T-2-7-147.
DEWING, Maria Richards Oakey.
Mrs. Thomas Wilmer Dewing.
Am. New York 1857-1927 Same. A025-C-DAB-F-T-W14-46.
DEWING, Thomas Wilmer.
Am. b. Boston 1851; ad. 1934 New York. A-B-C-E-F-T-W-1-15-46-51-71-104-191-757.
DE WINT, Peter.
Eng. Stone 1784-1849 London. B-C-DNB-E-793-844.
DE WITT, Jerome Pennington.
Am. b. Newark, N. J. 1895; ad. 1935 New York. A.
DE WITTE, Emanuel and Jacob. *see* Witte, E. and J.
DE WOLF, Wallace L.
Am. Chicago, Ill. 1854-1930. A028-F.
DEXTER, Henry. (S)
Am. Nelson, N. Y. 1806-1876 Cambridge, Mass. DAB-F-Hs-T-Ta-4-15.
DEXTER, Walter.
Aust. b. Wellingboro 1876; ad. 1934 Norfolk. B-T-Wa
DEXTER, Wilson C. (Et.)
Am. b. 1881; d. 1921 New York. A018.

DEYGAS, Régis Jean Benjamin.
Fr. b. Lyons 1876. DBA.
DEYNEKA, Alexander.
Rus. ac. 1929 in Russia. M.
DE YONGH, John.
Am. d. 1916 New Rochelle, N. Y. A014.
DE YOUNG, Harry Anthony.
Am. b. Chicago 1893; ad. 1934 San Antonio, Tex. A-F.
DEYROLLE, Théophile Louis.
Fr. ac. 1876-1900 in Paris. B-T.
DEYRUP, Dorothy.
Am. ex. 1934 New York. M.
DE ZAYAS, George. (Ill.)
Am. b. Mexico City, Mex. 1895; ad. 1934 New York. A.
DEZIN, Fred.
Ger. ac. 1888 in Munich. M.
DÉZIRÉ, Henri. *see* Désiré, H.
D'HONECORTER. *see* Honecorter, Melchior d'.
D'HUE, Lambertus.
Dut. 1623-1681. M.
DHURMER. *see* Levy-Dhurmer.
DIAMANT, David S.
Am. Germany 1849-1912 New York. A010.
DIAMANTE, Fra.
It. Prato 1430-1498? Spoleto. B-E-T-V.
DIAMANTOPOULO, [Miss]. (Enamel)
Gr. ex. 1935 Athens, Gr. M.
DIAMONDSTEIN, David.
Am. b. Kurenitz, Rus. 1883; ad. 1934 New York. A.
DIANA, Benedetto.
It. Venice 1460-1525 Same. T-V.
DIAS [or Diaz] Gasper.
Por. d. 1571 in Lisbon. B-T.
DIAZ, Daniel Vazquez. *see* Vazquez Diaz, D.
DIAZ DE OVIEDO, Pedro.
Sp. ac. 1490 Oviedo. T-774.
DIAZ DE LA PENA, Narcisse Virgile.
Fr. Bordeaux 1807/9-1876 Mentone. B-Bd-C-E-T-843.
DIAZ Morante, Pedro. (Pen Work)
Sp. ac. 1616-1631 Madrid. T.
DIBBLEE, Anita L.
Am. ad. 1934 Bolinas, Calif. M.
DIBDEN, Thomas Colman.
Eng. 1810-1893 London. B-T.
di BONA, Anthony. (S)
Am. b. Quincy, Mass. 1896; ad. 1935 Trudeau, N. Y. A.
DIBUTADES DE SICYON. *see* Butades.
DICE, David A.
Am. 1856-1911 York, Pa. A08.
DICK, [Mrs.] Fairman R. [Gladys Roosevelt.]
Am. New York 1889-1926 Same. A024.
DICK, James T.
Am. New York 1834-1868 Brooklyn. T-7.
DICK, William Reid. (S)
Scot. b. Glasgow 1879. Wa-798.
DICKERSON, William.
Am. ad. 1934 Wichita, Kan. M.
DICKEY, Robert L. (Ill)
Am. ad. 1934 New York. M.
DICKINSON, Anson.
Am. Milton, Conn. 1779-1847 Same. DAB-F-2-3-6-184.
DICKINSON, Daisy.
Am. b. Bellingham, Wash. 1903; ad. 1934 Los Angeles, Calif. A.
DICKINSON, Daniel.
Am. Litchfield, Conn. 1795-1840? Same. F-2-3-6.
DICKINSON, Edwin W.
Am. b. Seneca Falls, N. Y. 1891; ad. 1934 Provincetown, Mass. A.
DICKINSON, Lowes Cato.
Eng. Kilburn 1819-1908 London. B-DNB-T.
DICKINSON, Preston.
Am. New York 1891-1930 Spain. A028-F.
DICKINSON, Ross.
Am. b. Santa Ana, Calif. 1903; ad. 1934 Los Angeles, Calif. A.
DICKINSON, Sidney Edward.
Am. b. Wallingford, Conn. 1890; ad. 1934 New York. A-F-W.
DICKINSON, William. (Eg.)
Eng. London 1746-1823 Paris. B-DNB-T.
DICKMAN, Charles John.
Am. b. Demmin, Ger. 1863; ad. 1934 San Fran., Calif. A.
DICKSEE, [Sir] Francis [or Frank], Bernard.
Eng. London 1853-1928. B-C-Wa01929-Y01929.
DICKSEE, Herbert Thomas.
Eng. b. London 1862; ad. 1934 Hampstead. Wa.
DICKSEE, Margaret Isabel.
Eng. 1859-1903. M.
DICKSEE, Thomas Francis.
Eng. London 1819-1895 Same. B-T.
DICKSON, Helen.
Am. ad. 1935 Boston, Mass. M.
DIDAY, François.
Swi. Geneva 1802-1877 Same. B-T.
DIDDEL, Norma Louise.
Am. b. Denver, Colo. 1901; ad. 1934 Same. A.
DIDIER, Adrien. (Eg.)
Fr. Gigors 1838-1924 Paris. B-DBA-T.
DIDIER, Jules.
Fr. Paris 1831-1892. B-T.
DIDIER-POUGET, William.
Fr. b. Toulouse 1864. B-DBA-T.
DIDO Master. (S)
It. ac. 1445 in Florence. V.
DIEDERICH, Wilhelm Hunt. (S)
Am. b. Hungary 1884; ad. 1934 New York. A-Cs.
DIEFENBACH, Anton Heinrich.
Ger. Wiesbaden 1831-1914. T-T.
DIEGHEM, A. van.
Dut. ac. 1864-1909 in London. B.
DIEGO, Julio de.
Am. b. 1900 Spain; ex. 1934 Chicago. M.
DIEGO DE TIEDRA. (S)
Sp. ac. 1525 in Salamanca. T.
DIELITZ, Konrad.
Ger. b. Berlin 1845. B-T.
DIELMAN, Ernest Benham. (S)
Am. b. New York 1893. A20-Cs-F.
DIELMAN, Frederick.
Am. b. Hanover, Ger. 1847; d. 1935 Ridgefield, Conn. Obit. N. Y. papers 8-16-1935. A-C-E-F-T-W-15-46.
DIEM, Peter.
Ger. b. 1890 in Germany. M.

DIEMAN, Clare Sorensen. (S)
Am. b. Ind., Ind.; ad. 1934 Houston, Tex. A.
DIEMER, Michael Zeno.
Ger. b. Munich 1867. B-T.
DIEPENBECK, Abraham van.
Flem. Boris-le-Duc 1596/9-1675 Antwerp. B-C-E-T-722.
DIEPRAAM, Abraham [or Arent].
Dut. Rotterdam 1622?-1670 Same. B-T.
DIERCKX, Pierre Jacques.
Belg. b. Antwerp 1855; ac. 1895 Paris. T.
DIES, Christoph Albert.
Aus. Hanover, Ger. 1755-1822 Vienna. B-E-T.
DIEST, Adriaen van.
Dut. The Hague 1655/6-1704 London. B-E-T.
DIEST, Johan van.
Dut. ac. 1750 in London. B-T.
DIEST, Willem van.
Dut. The Hague 1610; ac. 1650 London. DNB-T.
DIETERICH, Waldemar Franklin.
Am. b. Balt., Md. 1876; ad. 1934 Same. A-F.
DIETERLE, Marie [von Marcke].
Fr. b. Sèvres 1860. B-DBA-T.
DIETRICH, Adolf.
Swi. b. 1877. M.
DIETRICH, Carl J.
Am. b. Coburg, Ger. 1865-1914 Hartford, Conn. A012.
DIETRICH [or Dietricy], Christian Wilhelm Ernest.
Ger. Weimar 1712-1774 Dresden. B-C-E-T-722.
DIETRICH, George Adams.
Am. b. Indiana 1905; ad. 1934 Milwaukee, Wis. A.
DIETSCH, Clarence Percival. (S)
Am. b. New York 1881; ad. 1934 Saybrook, Conn. A-Cs-F-W.
DIETTERLEIN, Wendel.
Ger. Strasburg 1550-1599 Same. C.
DIETZ, Elmar Georg. (S)
Ger. b. Bamberg 1902; ad. 1935 Munich. M.
DIETZ, Feodor.
Ger. Baden 1813-1870 Gray, Fr. C.
DIETZI, Hans.
Swi. b. Berne 1864. B.
DIEZ, Julius.
Ger. b. Nürnberg 1870; ac. 1935 Munich. T.
DIEZ, Wilhelm von.
Ger. Bayreuth 1839-1907. B-T.
DIGGS, Arthur.
Am. b. Columbia, Mo. 1888; ad. 1934 Chicago. A.
DIGHTON, Denis.
Eng. London 1792-1827 Brittany. B-DNB-T.
DIGHTON, Robert. (Cari.)
Eng. 1752?-1814 London. B-DNB.
DIGHTON, William Edward.
Eng. 1822-1853 Hampstead. B.
DiGIOIA, Frank.
Am. b. Italy; ex. 1935 New York. M.
DIGNAN, Mary E.
Can. ex. 1935 New York. M.
DIGNIMONT, André.
Fr. b. Paris 1891. DBA.
DIKE, Philip Latimer.
Am. b. Redlands, Calif. 1906; ad. 1934 Los Angeles, Calif. A.
DIKE, Victoria.
Am. ad. 1934 New York. M.
DILL, Ludwig.
Ger. b. Baden 1848; ac. 1883 Munich. B-C-T.
DILL, Otto.
Ger. b. 1884 in Germany. M.
DILLAWAY, Theodore M.
Am. b. Somerville, Mass. 1874; ad. 1934 Phila., Pa. A.
DILLAYE, Blanche.
Am. b. Syracuse, N. Y.; d. 1931 Phila., Pa. A028-F-T-W-46.
DILLENS, Adolf Alexander.
Belg. Ghent 1821-1877 Brussels. B-T.
DILLENS, Julien. (S)
Belg. Antwerp 1849-1904 Brussels. B-E-T.
DILLER, Burgoyne.
Am. b. New York 1906; ad. 1935 Same. M.
DILLON, Corinne Boyd. (Ill.)
Am. ad. 1934 New York. M.
DILLON, Frank.
Eng. London 1823-1909 Kensington. B-DNB-T.
DILLON, Frank H.
Am. b. Evanston, Ill. 1886; ad. 1934 Chicago. A.
DILLON, Henri Patrice.
Fr. San Fran., Calif. 1851-1909 Paris. B.
DIMOCK, Edith.
Mrs. William J. Glackens.
Am. b. Hartford, Conn. 1876; ad. 1934 New York. M.
DIMOND, Jane. (P-S)
Am. ad. 1934 New York. M.
D'IMPERIO, Dominic. (S)
Am. b. Italy 1888; ad. 1934 Phila., Pa. A.
DINCKEL, George.
Am. ad. 1934 Toledo, O. M.
DINET, Alphonse Étienne.
Fr. b. Paris 1861. B-T.
DIOG [or Diogg], Félix Maria.
Swi. Urseren 1762/4-1834 Rappersvil. B-T.
DIONISO [or Dionysius]. (S)
Gr. ac. middle 5th Cent. B.C. B-T.
DIONYSIUS, Dooley.
Am. b. St. Louis, Mo. 1907; ad. 1934 Los Angeles, Calif. A.
DIPOENUS. (S)
Gr. ac. 580 B.C. in Crete. E-T.
DIRK, Nathaniel.
Am. b. Brooklyn, N. Y. 1895; ad. 1934 New York. A.
DISERTORI, Benvenuto. (Et.)
It. b. Italy 1896; ex. 1934 Chicago, Ill.; ad. 1935 Milan, It. M.
DISMUKES, Adolyn Gale.
Mrs. George E. Dismukes.
Am. b. Memphis, Tenn.; ad. 1934 Biloxi, Miss. A.
DISMUKES, Mary Ethel.
Am. b. Pulaski, Tenn.; ad. 1934 Biloxi, Miss. A.

DISNEY, Walt. (Cari.)
[Creator of "Micky-Mouse" pictures.]
Am. b. Chicago 1900; ad. 1934 Hollywood, Calif. W.

DITE, Emanuel.
Ger. b. 1862. T.

DIVINO, El. *see* Morales, Luis de.

DIX, Charles Temple.
Am. Albany, N. Y. 1838-1873 Rome, It. C-F-T-4-15.

DIX, Eulabee. (Min.)
Am. b. Greenfield, Ill. 1879; ad. 1934 New York. A-F-46.

DIX, [Miss] J. Alex.
Scot. ex. 1926 Edinburgh. M.

DIX, John A. (Et.)
Am. ex. 1934 New York. M.

DIX, Otto.
Ger. b. Géra 1891. DBA-700.

DIXEY, John. (S)
Am. b. Ireland; ac. 1789-1820 U. S. DNB-F-Hs-T-Ta-2.

DIXON, Alfred.
Eng. London 1842-1919. B-T.

DIXON, Charles.
Eng. Goring 1872-1934 Chichester. M-Wa-Obit. N. Y. papers, 9-13-1934.

DIXON, Francis Stillwell.
Am. b. New York 1879; ad. 1934 Same. A-F.

DIXON, John. (Eg.)
Ir. Dublin 1720-1780 London. B-DNB-T.

DIXON, John. (Min.)
Eng. d. 1715 in Bungay. B-DNB-T.

DIXON, Mabel Eastman.
Am. b. Auburn, Ia.; ad. 1934 Des Moines, Ia. A.

DIXON, Maynard.
Am. b. Fresno, Calif. 1875; ad. 1934 San Fran., Calif. A-F-W-46.

DIXON, Nathaniel.
Eng. [No dates known.] Bd.

DIZIANI, Gasparo.
It. Belluno 1689-1767 Venice. B-T.

DMOCHOWSKI. *see* Saunders, Henry D.

DOANE, Lucy. (Ill.)
Am. ad. 1934 Newton Upper Falls, Mass. M.

DOANE, Pelagie. (Ill.)
Am. b. Palmyra, N. J. 1906; ad. 1934 New York. M.

DOBBIN, John.
Eng. ac. 1842-1884 in London. B-T.

DOBIAS, Frank. (Ill.)
Am. ad. 1934 Larchmont, N. Y. M.

DOBKIN, Alexander.
Am. ex. 1935 New York. M.

DOBLER, Maud A.
Mrs. George Dobler.
Am. b. Rockford, Ill. 1885; ad. 1934 Same. A.

DOBOS, Andrew.
Am. b. Galicia, Pol. 1897; ad. 1934 Oak Park, Ill. A.

DOBOUJINSKY, M.
Rus. ex. 1935 London. M.

DOBSON, Arthur. (S)
Eng. ac. 1933 London. M.

DOBSON, Frank. (S)
Eng. b. London 1887; ad. 1934 Same. E-Wa-825-864.

DOBSON, Henry John.
Scot. Edinburgh 1858-1928. Wa01929.

DOBSON, Margaret A.
Am. b. Balt., Md. 1888; ad. 1934 Los Angeles, Calif. A.

DOBSON, [Sir] William.
Eng. Holborn 1610-1646 London. B-Bd-DNB-E-T-702.

DOBSON, William Charles Thomas.
Eng. Hamburg, Ger. 1817-1898 Ventnor, Eng. B-C-DNB-T.

DOCHARTY, James.
Scot. Bonhill 1829-1878 Glasgow. B-DNB-T.

DOD, Samuel Bayard. (Et.)
Am. Princeton, N. J. 1847-1907 So. Orange, N. J. A06.

DODD, Daniel.
Eng. ac. 1760-1790 in London. B-DNB-T.

DODD, Francis.
Scot. b. Holyhead 1874. B-Wa.

DODD, Jessie Hart.
Am. Cinn., O. 1863-1911 Same. A012.

DODD, Lamar.
Am. ad. 1935 Birmingham, Ala. M.

DODD, Mark Dixon.
Am. b. St. Louis, Mo. 1888; ad. 1934 St. Petersburg, Fla. A-F.

DODD, Robert.
Eng. 1748-1816 London. B-DNB-T.

DODD, Samuel. (Eg.)
Am. b. Bloomfield, N. J. 1797; d. 1862. F.

DODD, William Lamar.
Am. b. Fairburn, Ga. 1909; ad. 1934 La Grange, Ga. A.

DODDS, Peggy.
Mrs. Henry A. Williams.
Am. ad. 1934 Paterson, N. J. M.

DODGE, Chester L.
Am. b. Salem, Mass. 1880; ad. 1934 Prov., R. I. A.

DODGE, Francis F.
Mrs. A. C. Dodge.
Am. b. Lansing, Mich. 1878; ad. 1934 Chicago. A.

DODGE, John Wood.
Am. New York 1807-1893. F-T-2.

DODGE, Ozias. (Et.)
Am. Morrisville, Vt. 1868-1925 Norwich, Conn. A022-B-F.

DODGE, William de Leftwich. (Mu.)
Am. Liberty, Va. 1867-1935 New York. A-B-F-T-W-46-Obit. N. Y. papers, 3-26-1935.

DODGSON, George Haydock.
Eng. Liverpool 1811-1880 London. B-DNB-T.

DODSON, Nellie Plitt.
Am. b. Pilot Mountain, N. C. 1906; ad. 1934 Winston-Salem, N. C. A.

DODSON, Richard W. (Eg.)
Am. Cambridge, Md. 1812-1867 Cape May, N. J. F-T-2-7-40.

DODSON, Sarah Paxton Ball.
Am. Phila., Pa. 1847-1906 Brighton, Eng. A06-F-T-46.

DODS-WITHERS, [Mrs.] Isobelle Ann.
Scot. b. Congalton 1876; ad. 1934 London. B-Wa.

DOERR, JAMES EDWARD.
Am. b. Portsmouth, O. 1909; ad. 1934 Same. A.
DOES, ANTHONY [or Arnold] VAN DER.
Flem. Antwerp 1609-1680. B-T.
DOES, JACOB VAN DER [The Elder].
Dut. Amsterdam 1623-1673 Sloten. B-C-T-722.
DOES, SIMON VAN DER.
Dut. Amsterdam 1653/4-1718 Antwerp, Belg. B-C-T-722.
DOESBURGH, THÉODOR VAN.
Dut. b. Utrecht; d. 1931. DBA.
DOESBURGH, THOMAS.
Dut. b. 1692; d. 1714. T.
DOGGETT, ALLEN B.
Am. b. Groveland, Mass.; d. 1926 Brooklyn, N. Y. A023.
DOGGETT, RUTH.
Eng. ex. 1934 in London. M.
DOHANOS, STEVAN.
Am. b. Lorain, O. 1907; ad. 1935 Cleveland, O. M.
DOHN, ROBERT.
Am. ad. 1934 Toledo, O. M.
DOI, ISAMI. (Eg)
Am. b. Honolulu 1903; ad. 1934 New York. M.
DOIDALSOS. (S)
Gr. (Bithynian); ac. middle 3rd Cent. B.C. T.
DOLAN, ELIZABETH HONOR. (Mu)
Am. b. Fort Dodge, Ia. 1887; ad. 1934 Lincoln, Neb. A.
DOLCI, AGNESE. [Son of Carlo Dolci.]
It. d. 1689 in Italy. B-T.
DOLCI [or Dolce], CARLO [or Carlino].
It. Florence 1616-1686 Same. B-Bd-C-E-T-722-921.
DOLE, [Mrs.] MARGARET FERNALD.
Am. b. Melrose, Mass. 1896; ad. 1934 New York. A.
DOLECHECK, CHRISTINE A.
Am. b. Dubuque, Ia. 1894; ad. 1934 Ellsworth, Kan. A.
DOLINSKY, NATHAN.
Am. b. Russia 1889; ad. 1934 New York. A.
DOLL, FRANZ.
Ger. b. 1899; ad. 1935 Munich. M.
DOLLE, WILLIAM. (Eg)
Eng. ac. 1670-1680 London. B-DNB-T.
DOLLMAN, JOHN CHARLES.
Eng. Brighton 1851-1934 London. B-T-Wa-Obit. N. Y. Papers, 12-12-1934.
DOLPH, JOHN HENRY.
Am. Fort Ann, N. Y. 1835-1903 New York. A04-B-F-T-4-15-46.
DOMBROSKI, ANTOINE SAMUEL.
Pol. Tourovice 1774-1838 Warsaw. B.
DOMENCHIN DE CHAVANNE, PIERRE SALOMON.
Fr. Paris 1672/3-1744 Same. B-T.
DOMENICHINO [or Domenico], ZAMPIERI.
It. Bologna 1581-1641 Naples. B-Bd-C-E-T-722.
DOMENICO DI BARTOLO [Ghezzi].
It. Asciano 1400-1444/6 Siena. T-V.
DOMENICO DI MICHELINO.
[Real name: Domenico di Francesco.]
It. Toscano 1417-1491 Florence. B-T-V.
DOMENICO DI PIETRE. *see* Pietro di D.
DOMENICO VENEZIANO. *see* Veneziano, D. B.
DOMENJOZ, RAOUL.
Fr. b. Lausanne 1896; ex. 1930 Paris. DBA.
DOMERGUE, JEAN GABRIEL.
Fr. b. Bordeaux 1889; ad. 1934 Paris. B-DBA.
DOMINGO Y FALLOLA, ROBERTO.
Sp. b. Paris 1883. T.
DOMINGO Y MARQUÉS, FRANCISCO.
Sp. b. Valencia 1842-1920 Madrid. B-T-15.
DOMINGO Y MUNOZ, JOSÉ.
Sp. b. 1843 in Spain. M.
DOMINICK, GEORGE F., JR.
Am. ex. 1934 Greenwich, Conn. M.
DOMSCHEIT, FRANZ.
Ger. b. Cropiens 1880; ex. 1930 Berlin. T.
DOMVILLE, PAUL.
Am. b. Hamilton, Can. 1893; ad. 1934 Woodstock, N. Y. A.
DONAHEY, JAMES HARRISON. (Ill)
Am. b. Westchester, O. 1875; ad. 1934 Aurora, O. A28-F-W.
DONAHEY, WILLIAM. (Ill)
Am. b. Westchester, O. 1883; ad. 1934 Chicago. F-W.
DONAHUE, WILLIAM HOWARD.
Am. b. New York 1881; ad. 1934 Same. A.
DONALD, JOHN MILNE.
Scot. Nairn 1819-1866. B-T.
DONALDSON, ELISE.
Am. ad. 1934 Chicago, Ill. M.
DONATELLO, [Donato di Niccolò di Bardi]. (S)
It. Florence 1386-1466 Same. B-E-Hs-T-V-347-348-664-855.
DONATO, GIUSEPPE. (S)
Am. b. Calabria, It. 1881; ad. 1934 Phila., Pa. A-F-W.
DONATO DI MARTINI.
It. ac. 1464-1471 in Rome. T.
DONATO, VENEZIANO [Bragadin].
It. ac. 1438-1473 in Italy. T-V.
DONAUDI, MARIO.
Am. ad. 1934 West New York, N. J. M.
DONAUER [or Donnauer], JOHANNES.
Ger. b. 1521?; d. 1596 in Germany. T.
DONCKER [or Doncher], HERMAN MIJNERTS.
Dut. 1610-1656 Haarlem. B-T.
DONCRE, GUILLAUME DOMMIQUE JACQUES.
Fr. Zegers 1743-1820 Arras. B-T.
DONDO, MATHURIN M.
Am. b. 1884; ad. 1934 Berkeley, Calif. A.
DONDUCCI, GIOVANNI ADRÉA [Mastelletta].
It. Bologna 1575-1655 Same. B-T.
DONELSON, EARL TOMLINSON.
Am. b. Scranton, Pa. 1908; ad. 1934 Trenton, N. J. A.
DONELSON, MARY HOOPER. (S)
Am. ad. 1935 Hermitage, Tenn. M.
DONGEN, CORNELIS T. M. VAN.
Fr. ad. 1934 St. Cloud. M.
DONGEN, KEES VAN.
Dut. b. Delfslaven 1877. DBA-T-797.
DONGHI, ANTONIO.
It. b. 1897; ad. 1934 Rome. M.
DONIPHAN, DORSEY.
Am. b. Washington, D. C. 1897; ad. 934 Same. A.

DONLEVY, Alice Heighes.
Am. Manchester, Eng. 1846-1929 France. A026.
DONLY, Eva Brook.
Am. b. Simcoe, Can. 1867; ad. 1934 Same. A.
DONNE, Walter.
Eng. b. Surrey 1867; ac. 1905 London. B-T.
DONNELLY, Thomas J.
Am. b. Washington, D. C. 1893; ad. 1934 Valhalla, N. Y. A.
DONNER, Geog Raphaël. (S)
Aus. Essling 1692-1741 Vienna. B-Hs-T-665.
DONNER von RICHER, Otto. (P-S)
Ger. Frankfort 1828-1911 Same. B-C-T.
DONNINO, Agnolo di Domenico.
It. Florence 1466-1513. T.
DONO, Paolo. *see* Uccello, P.
DONOGHUE, John. (S)
Am. Chicago 1853-1903 New Haven, Conn. DAB-F-T-Ta-46.
DONOHO, Gaines Ruger. (P-S)
Am. Churchill, Miss. 1857-1916 New York. A013-B-F-T-46.
DONOHUE, Harry E. (S)
Am. ad. 1935 New York. M.
DONOVAN, Ellen.
Am. b. Phila., Pa. 1903; ad. 1934 Same. A.
DONTAS [of Sparta]. (S)
Gr. (Doric); ac. 500-465 B.C. B-Hs.
DOO, George Thomas. (Eg)
Eng. Christ Church 1800-1886 Sutton. B-T-880.
DOOLEY, [Mrs.] Eliza B. K.
Am. ad. 1934 San Juan, Porto Rico. M.
DOOLITTLE, Amos. (Eg)
Am. Cheshire, Conn. 1754-1832 New Haven, Conn. DAB-F-T-2-7-40-147.
DOOLITTLE, Edwin Stafford.
Am. Albany, N. Y. 1843-1879. F-T-15.
DOOLITTLE, Harold L. (Et)
Am. b. Pasadena, Calif. 1883; ad. 1934 Same. A28-F.
DOONER, Émilie Zeckner.
Mrs. Richard T. Dooner.
Am. b. Phila., Pa. 1877; ad. 1934 Merion, Pa. A.
DOONER, Richard T.
Am. b. Phila., Pa. 1878; ad. 1934 Merion, Pa. A.
DOORNHEIN, Jeannettie.
Am. b. Holland, Mich. 1906; ad. 1934 Chicago. M.
DOOYEWAARD, Jacob.
Dut. b. Holland 1876; ad. 1934 New York. B-M.
DÖRBECK, Franz Burkhard. (Cari)
Ger. ac. 1830 in Germany. [No death date.] M.
DORÉ, Gustave [Louis Cristophe Paul]. (P-S)
Fr. Strassburg 1832-1883 Paris. B-Bd-C-E-T-710.
DOREY, Elsie.
Am. ex. 1935 New York. M.
DORGAN, Thomas Aloysius ["Tad"]. (Cart)
Am. San Fran., Calif. 1877-1929 Great Neck, N. Y. A026-DAB.
DORIGNAC, Georges.
Fr. Bordeaux 1879-1925 Paris. DBA.
DORIGNY, Louis.
Fr. Paris 1654-1742 Verona, It. B-T.
DORIGNY, Michel.
Fr. St. Quentin 1617-1685 Paris. B-T.
DORIGNY, [Sir] Nicolas.
Eng. Paris 1658-1746 Same. B-DNB-T.
DÖRING, Willi.
Ger. ac. 1877-1889 in Carlsruhe. B-T.
DORN, Carl Heinrich. (S)
Ger. b. Berlin 1831; ac. 1897. T.
DORN, Joseph.
Ger. Sambach 1759-1841 Bamberg. B-T.
DORN, Leo F. (Eg)
Am. b. Louisville, Ky. 1879; ad. 1934 Rowayton, Conn. M.
DORNBUSH, Adrian J.
Am. ad. 1934 Des Moines, Ia. M.
DORNER, Johann Jacob [The Elder].
Ger. Ehrenbreitstein 1741-1813 Munich. B-T.
DORNER, Johann Jacob [The Younger].
Ger. Munich 1775-1852 Same. B-T.
DORPH, Anton Laurids Johanne.
Dan. Horsens 1831-1914. B-T.
DORSEY, Conte. *see* Orsay.
DORSEY, John Syng. (Et)
Am. Phila., Pa. 1783-1818 Same. F-2-7.
DORSEY, Stanton Lindsey.
Am. b. Frankfort, Ky. 1890; ad. 1934 Washington, D. C. A.
DOSKOW, Israel.
Am. b. Rus. 1881; ad. 1934 New York. A.
DOSSENA, Alceo. (S)
It. ac. 1880 in Italy. M.
DOSSI, Battista.
It. ac. 1548 in Italy. T-V.
DOSSI, Dosso.
[Giovanni di Nicolò de Lutero.]
It. Ferrara 1479-1542 Same. B-Bd-C-T-V.
DÖTEBER, Christian Julius. (S)
Swe. b. Leipzig, Ger.; ac. 1600 Stockholm. 824.
DOU [or Dow], Gérard [or Gerrit].
Dut. Leyden 1613-1675 Same. B-Bd-C-E-T-349-722.
DOUANIER. *see* Le Douanier.
DOUARD, Cécile.
Belg. b. Rouen, Fr. 1866. DBA-T.
DOUBA, Joseph.
Ger. ac. 1883-1889 in Prague and Munich. B-T.
DOUBLEMARD, Amédée Donatien. (S)
Fr. Beaurain 1826-1900 Paris. B.
DOUBTING, James.
Eng. Bristol 1841-1904. T.
DOUCET, Henri Lucien.
Fr. Paris 1856-1895. B-T.
DOUD, Isabel Cohen.
Mrs. G. C. Doud.
Am. ad. 1934 New York. M.
DOUDYNS [or Doedyns], Willem.
Dut. The Hague 1630-1697 Same. B-T.
DOUGHERTY, [Mrs.] Bertha H. (Et)
Am. ad. 1935 Glen Ridge, N. J. M.
DOUGHERTY, Louis R. (S)
Am. b. Phila., Pa. 1874. A20-F-T.

DOUGHERTY, PARKE CUSTIS.
Am. b. Phila., Pa. 1867. A20-F-T.
DOUGHERTY, PAUL.
Am. b. Brooklyn, N. Y. 1877; ad. 1934 Carmel, Calif. A-E-F-T-W-1-46.
DOUGHTY, JAMES.
Am. ac. 1829. [No death date.] M.
DOUGHTY, THOMAS.
Am. Phila., Pa. 1793-1856 New York. B-Bd-C-DAB-F-T-2-4-15.
DOUGHTY, WILLIAM.
Eng. b. York; d. 1782 Lisbon, Sp. B-DNB-T.
DOUGLAS, AARON. (Ill.)
Am. b. Topeka, Kan. 1898; ad. 1934 New York. M.
DOUGLAS, ARCHIBALD RAMSAY. (Min.)
Br. 1807-1886. DNB.
DOUGLAS, CHESTER.
Am. b. Lynn, Mass. 1902; ad. 1934 Same. A.
DOUGLAS, EDWARD BRUCE. (S)
Am. b. Minn., Minn.; ac. 1929. Cs.
DOUGLAS, [Sir] EDWIN. (Eg.)
Scot. Edinburgh 1848-1914. T-15.
DOUGLAS, HALDANE.
Am. b. Pittsburgh, Pa. 1893; ad. 1934 Hermosa Beach, Calif. A.
DOUGLAS, HARRY. (Mu.)
Am. ad. 1934 Los Angeles, Calif. A.
DOUGLAS, LUCILLE SINCLAIR.
Am. b. Tuskegee, Ala.; ad. 1934 New York. A.
DOUGLAS, WALTER.
Am. b. Cinn., O. 1868; ad. 1934 Morristown, N. J. A.
DOUGLAS, WILLIAM. (Min.)
Br. 1780-1832. DNB-T.
DOUGLAS, [Sir] WILLIAM FETTES.
Scot. Edinburgh 1822-1891. B-Bd-DNB-T.
DOUILLARD, ALEXIS MARIE LOUISE.
Fr. Nantes 1835-1905. B-T.
DOUROUZE, DANIEL URBAIN.
Fr. Grenoble 1874-1923 Paris. DBA.
DOUTHAT, MILTON.
Am. b. Kansas City, Mo. 1905; ad. 1934 Chicago. A.
DOUVEN, FRANS BARTHOLOMEUS.
Ger. Düsseldorf 1688-1726. B-T.
DOUVEN, JAN FRANS VAN.
Dut. Roermonde 1656-1727 Düsseldorf, Ger. B-C-T.
DOUW. *see also* Dou.
DOUW [or Dou or Dow], SIMON JOHANNES VAN.
Flem. Antwerp 1630-1677. B-T.
DOUWERMANN, HEINRICH. (S)
Ger. ac. 1510-1544 in Calcar. Hs-T.
DOUX, MARY F.
Am. ad. 1934 Brooklyn, N. Y. M.
DOVE, ARTHUR G.
Am. b. Canandaigua, N. Y. 1880; ad. 1934 Geneva, N. Y. A-F.
DOVE, WILLIAM C.
Am. ex. 1935 New York. M.
DOW, ARTHUR WESLEY. (Et.)
Am. Ipswich, Mass. 1857-1922 New York. A020-F-T.
DOW, GÉRARD. *see* Dou, G.
DOW, LELIA A.
Am. Cooksville, Wis. 1864-1930 Madison, Wis. A027.
DOWD, JAMES H. (Et.)
Eng. ac. 1927 in London. Wa1929.
DOWIATT, DOROTHY.
Am. b. Pittsburgh, Pa.; ad. 1934 Whittier, Calif. A.
DOWLING, COLISTA.
Am. b. Kansas City, Mo.; ad. 1934 Portland, Ore. A.
DOWLING, ROBERT.
Eng. 1827-1886 London. T.
DOWNES, BERNARD.
Br. ac. 1761-1775 London. B-T.
DOWNES, JOHN IRELAND HOWE.
Am. Derby, Conn. 1861-1933 New Haven, Conn. A030.
DOWNEY, ALFRED J. (Eg.)
Eng. ac. 20th Cent. M.
DOWNIE, JANET.
Am. b. Detroit, Mich. 1854; ad. 1934 Austin, Tex. M.
DOWNMAN, JOHN.
Eng. Devonshire 1750-1824 Wrexham. B-DNB-E-T-346.
DOWS [Stephen], OLIN.
Am. b. Irvington, N. Y. 1904; ad. 1934 Rhinebeck, N. Y. A.
DOYEN, GABRIEL FRANÇOIS.
Fr. Paris 1726-1806. B-C-E-T-722.
DOYEN, GUSTAVE.
Fr. b. Festieux 1837; ac. 1893 Paris. B-T.
DOYLE, ALEXANDER. (S)
Am. Steubenville, O. 1857-1922. A020-DAB-F-T-Ta-26.
DOYLE, HENRY EDWARD.
Eng. London 1827-1892 Same. B-T.
DOYLE, JAMES WILLIAM EDMUND.
Eng. 1822-1892 London. T.
DOYLE, JOHN. (Cari.)
Ir. Dublin 1797-1868 London. B-DNB-T.
DOYLE, RICHARD. (Cari.)
Eng. London 1824-1883 Same. B-DNB-E-T.
DOYLE, WILLIAM M. S.
Am. Boston, Mass. 1769-1828 Same. F-2-6-45.
DOZE, JEAN MARIE MELCHIOR.
Fr. b. Uzès 1827; ac. 1879 Paris. B-T.
DRABINOWICZ, STANLEY.
Am. b. Milwaukee, Wis. 1915; ad. 1935 Same. M.
DRABKIN, STELLA.
Am. ad. 1934 Phila., Pa. M.
DRADY, JOHN G. (S)
Am. 1833-1904 New York. A05-F-T.
DRAHONET, DUBOIS. *see* Dubois-D.
DRAKE, ALEXANDER WILSON. (Eg.)
Am. Westfield, N. J. 1843-1916 New York. A013.
DRAKE, BERTRAM DELANEY.
Am. 1880-1930 Garrison, N. Y. A027.
DRAKE, FRANK CORNELIUS. (Ill.)
Am. Palmyra, N. Y. 1868-1922. A020.
DRAKE, FRIEDRICH JOHANN HEINRICH.
Ger. Pyrmont 1805-1882 Berlin. B-Hs-T.
DRAKE, JOHN POAD.
Eng. Devonshire 1794-1883 Cornwall. DNB-T.

DRAKE, NATHAN.
Eng. York 1750-1783 London. B-T.
DRAKE, WILLIAM HENRY.
Am. New York 1856-1926 Los Angeles, Calif. A023-F-T.
DRAPENTIER, JAN [or Johannes]. (Eg.)
Eng. b. Dordrecht, Holland; ac. 1674-1713 London. B-Bd-E-T.
DRAPER, HERBERT JAMES.
Eng. London 1864-1920 Same. B-T.
DRAPER, WILLIAM FRANKLIN.
Am. ad. 1934 New York. M.
DRAYTON, GRACE GEBBIE. (Ill.)
Am. b. Phila., Pa. 1877; ad. 1934 New York. A-F-T-W.
DRAYTON, JOHN. (Eg.)
Am. ac. 1820 Phila., Pa. F-T-2-7-147.
DREIER, DOROTHEA A.
Am. b. New York 1870-1923 Saranac, N. Y. A020.
DREIER, KATHERINE SOPHIE.
Am. b. Brooklyn, N. Y. 1877; ad. 1934 West Redding, Conn. A-F-M.
DREIFOOS, BYRON GOLDING.
Am. b. Phila., Pa. 1890; ad. 1934 Newark, N. J. A.
DRENNAN, VINCENT JOSEPH.
Am. b. New York 1902; ad. 1934 Same. A.
DRESSER, [Mrs.] AILEEN KING.
Am. ad. 1935 New York. M.
DRESSLER, ADOLF.
Ger. Breslau 1833-1881 Same. B-T.
DRESSLER, CONRAD. (S)
Eng. b. London 1856. B-T.
DRESSLER, EDWARD JAMES.
Am. Centerville, Mich. 1859-1907 Chicago. M.
DREUX, ALFRED DE. *see* Dedreux, Alfred.
DREVET, PIERRE. (Eg.)
Fr. Loire 1663/4-1738 Paris. B-T.
DREVET, PIERRE IMBERT. (Eg.)
Fr. Paris 1697-1739 Same. B-Bd-T.
DREW, CLEMENT.
Am. 1807-1889 Boston, Mass. M.
DREW, JOHN. (Ill.)
Am. ad. 1934 New York. M.
DREW, LEWIS.
Am. 1885-1915 Saranac, N. Y. A012.
DREWES, WERNER. (Et.)
Am. b. Canig, Ger. 1899; ad. 1934 New York. A.
DREXEL, CHRISTOF.
Ger. b. 1886. M.
DREYER, GEORG LÉONHARD. (Ill.)
Swe. Harburg, Ger. 1793-1879 Stockholm. B-T.
DREYFOUS, FLORENCE.
Am. b. New York; ad. 1934 Same. A.
DREYFUSS, ALBERT.
Am. b. New York 1880. A.
DRIELST, EGBERT VAN.
Dut. Groningue 1746-1818. B-T.
DRIGGS, ELSIE.
Am. b. Hartford, Conn.; ad. 1934 New Rochelle, N. Y. A.
DRINKWATER, GEORGE CARR.
Eng. b. Oxford 1880; ad. 1934 London. Wa.
DRIVIER, LÉON ERNEST. (S)
Fr. b. Grenoble 1878. B-DBA.
DROELLING. *see* Drölling.
DROESHOUT, JOHN [or Johannes]. (Eg)
Eng. 1596-1652 London. DNB-T.
DROESHOUT, MARTIN [The Younger]. (Eg)
Eng. b. London; ac. 1620-1651. DNB-T.
DRÖLLING, MARTIN [The Elder].
Fr. Colmar, Ger. 1752-1817 Paris. B-C-T-722.
DRÖLLING, MICHEL MARTIN [The Younger].
Fr. Paris 1786-1851 Same. B-T-722.
DROOGSLOOT, JOOST CORNELISZ [The Elder].
Dut. Utrecht 1586-1666. B-T.
DROOGSLOOT, CORNELISZ [The Younger].
Dut. Utrecht 1630-1673? B-T.
DROST, CORNELIS [or Geraert] VAN.
Dut. b. Leyden; d. 1678 Amsterdam. B-T.
DROST, JACOB VAN.
Dut. Amsterdam 1638-1694. B-T.
DROUAIS, FRANÇOIS HUBERT.
Fr. Paris 1727-1775 Same. B-Bd-C-T-722-756.
DROUAIS, HUBERT.
Fr. La Rocque 1699-1767 Paris. B-T.
DROUAIS, JEAN GERMAIN.
Fr. Paris 1763-1788 Rome, It. B-C-E-T-722-756.
DROUART, MAURICE RAPHAËL.
Fr. b. Choisy-le-Roi 1884. DBA.
DROUET, BESSIE CLARK.
Mrs. Henry Drouet.
Am. b. Portsmouth, N. H. 1879; ad. 1934 New York. A.
DROUIN, JEAN PIERRE.
Fr. Besançon 1782-1861. T.
DROWN, W. STAPLES.
Am. b. Dorchester, Mass.; d. 1915 Prov., R. I. A012.
DROZ, JEAN PIERRE. (Med)
Sw. Switzerland 1746-1823 Paris. T.
DROZ, JULES ANTOINE. (S)
Fr. Paris 1804-1872 Same. B-T.
DRU, HILAIRE. *see* Le Dru, H.
DRUGGER, [Mrs.] MARIE R. (S)
Am. d. 1922 St. Louis, Mo. A019.
DRUMMOND, JAMES.
Scot. Edinburgh 1816-1877. B-T.
DRUMMOND, KATHERINE RUSSELL.
Br. b. Ceylon, India; ad. 1934 London. Wa.
DRUMMOND, SAMUEL.
Eng. London 1765-1844 Same. B-DNB-T.
DRURY, ALFRED. (S)
Eng. b. London 1859. B-Hs-T.
DRURY, HERBERT R.
Am. b. Cleveland, O. 1873; ad. 1934 Willoughby, O. A.
DRURY, HOPE CURTIS.
Mrs. William H. Drury.
Am. b. Pawtucket, R. I. 1889; ad. 1934 Newport, R. I. A.
DRURY, PAUL DALOU. (Et)
Eng. b. St. John's Woods, 1903; ex. 1934 London Wa.
DRURY, WILLIAM H.
Am. b. Fitchburg, Mass. 1888; ad. 1934 Newport, R. I. A-F.
DRYDEN, HELEN. (Ill)
Am. b. Balt., Md. 1887; ad. 1934 New York. A.
DRYER, DELLA.
Am. ad. 1935 Birmingham, Ala. M.

DRYER, JORGEN C.
Nor. b. Tromsol 1877. M.
DRYSDALE, ALEXANDER JOHN.
Am. b. Marietta, Ga. 1870; ad. 1934 New Orleans, La. A-F.
DUBBELS, HENDRIK JACOBSZ.
Dut. Amsterdam 1620/1676 Same. B-C-T-722.
DUBE, LOUIS THÉODORE.
Fr. b. Quebec, Can. 1861. DBA.
DUBE, [Mrs.] MATTIE.
Am. b. Florence, Ala. 1861. A12-B-T.
DUBOIS, AMBROISE.
Fr. Antwerp, Belg. 1543-1614 Fontainebleau. B-T-722.
DUBOIS, CHARLES EDOUARD.
Am. Hoboken, N. J. 1847-1885 France. C-F-T-15
DU BOIS, EDWARD.
Flem. Antwerp 1619-1699? London. B-DNB-T.
DUBOIS, ERNEST. (S)
Fr. b. Dieppe 1863; ac. 1911 Paris. DBA-798.
DUBOIS, EUGÈNE. (S)
Fr. Paris 1825-1893. B-T.
DUBOIS, FRANÇOIS.
Fr. Paris 1790-1868/71. B-T.
DUBOIS, GUILLIAM [or Willem].
Dut. Amsterdam 1622-1680 Same. T.
DU BOIS, GUY PÈNE.
Am. b. Brooklyn 1884; ad. 1934 New York. A-F-1-190-701.
DUBOIS, HIPPOLYTE HENRI PIERRE.
Fr. Rezé 1837-1890. B-T.
DU BOIS, PATTERSON.
Am. Phila., Pa. 1847-1917 Same. A015.
DUBOIS, PAUL. (S)
Fr. Nogent 1829-1905 Paris. B-E-Hs-T.
DUBOIS, PAUL ÉLIE.
Fr. b. Paris 1886. DBA.
DU BOIS, SIMON.
Flem. Antwerp 1632-1708 England. B-DNB-T.
DU BOIS, YVONNE PENE.
Am. ex. 1935 New York. M.
DUBOIS-DRAHONET, ALEXANDRE JEAN.
Fr. Paris 1791-1834 Versailles. T.
DUBORDIEU, PIETER.
Dut. Touraine 1609/10-1678 Amsterdam. B-T.
DU BOSC, CLAUDE. (Eg.)
Eng. France 1682-1745? England. DNB-T.
DUBOUCHET, HENRI JOSEPH.
Fr. Caluire 1833-1909. B-T.
DUBOURG, LODEWYK FABRICUS.
Dut. Amsterdam 1693-1775. B-T.
DUBOURG, M. (Eg)
Eng. ac. 1786-1838 in London. T.
DUBOURG, MAURICE. (Tapestry)
Fr. ac. 1584-1636 in Paris. T.
DUBOURJAL, SAVINIEN EDMÉ.
Fr. Paris 1795-1853 Same. B-F-T-6-45.
DU BRAU, GERTRUD MARGARETE.
Am. b. Ger. 1889; ad. 1934 Cumberland, Md. A.
DUBRAY, VITAL GABRIEL. (S)
Fr. Paris 1813-1892. B-T.
DUBREUIL [or Breuil], TOUSSAINT.
Fr. Paris 1561-1602 Same. B-T-722.
DUBROEUCQ, JACQUES. (S)
Flem. Mons 1500/10-1584 Rome, It. T.
DUBUCAND, ALFRED. (S)
Fr. b. Paris 1828; ex. 1890 Same. T.
DUBUFE, CLAUDE MARIE.
Fr. Paris 1790-1864 St. Cloud. B-T.
DUBUFE, ÉDOUARD MARIE GUILLAUME.
Fr. Paris 1853-1909 Buenos Aires, Arg. B-T.
DUBUFE, LOUIS ÉDOUARD.
Fr. Paris 1819/20-1883 Versailles. B-C-T.
DUBUISSON, ALEXANDRE.
Fr. Lyons 1805-1875 Versailles. B-T.
DUBUQUE, EDWARD WILLIAM.
Am. b. Moosup, Conn. 1900; ad. 1934 Prov., R. I. A.
DUBUS, HENRY BARTHELÉMY.
Fr. b. Évreux 1851. DBA.
DUBUT, FRIEDRICH WILHELM. (S)
Ger. Berlin 1711-1779 Danzig. T.
DUCASSE, MABEL LISLE.
Mrs. C. J. Ducasse.
Am. b. Colo. 1895; ad. 1934 East Prov., R. I. A.
DUCCIO, AGOSTINO DE. (S).
It. Siena 1418-1498. Hs.
DUCCIO DI BUONINSEGNA.
It. Siena 1255-1319. B-Bd-T-V-905.
DUCHAMP, SUZANNE CROTTI.
Fr. b. Rouen 1898; ad. 1934 Neuilly. DBA-M.
DUCHAMP-VILLON, MARCEL.
Fr. b. France 1887; ex. 1933 Chicago. M.
DUCHAMP-VILLON, RAYMOND. (S)
Fr. Damville 1876-1918. DBA-T-350.
DUCHÂTEL [or du Châtel], ÉDOUARD.
Fr. ac. 1889-1893 in Paris. B.
DUCHÂTEL [or du Châtel], FRANÇOIS.
Flem. Brussels 1616/25-1679/94. B-C-T-722.
DUCHÉ, THOMAS SPENCE.
Am. Phila., Pa. 1763-1790 England. F.
DUCIS, LOUIS.
Fr. Paris 1773-1847. B-T.
DUCK [or Duyck], JACOB A.
Dut. Utrecht 1600-1660 The Hague. B-T.
DUCLAUX, JEAN ANTOINE.
Fr. Lyons 1783-1868 Same. B-T.
DUCLOS, ANTOINE JEAN. (Eg)
Fr. Paris 1742-1795. B-T.
DUCORNET, LOUIS JOSEPH CÉSAR.
Fr. Lille 1806-1856 Paris. B-T.
DUCQ [or Duck], JAN [or Jean].
Dut. The Hague 1629/30-1676. B-T-722.
DUCREUX, JOSEPH.
Fr. Nancy 1737-1802 Paris. B-C-T-722.
DUDENSING, BIBI.
Am. b. San Fran., Calif. 1901; ad. 1934 New York. A.
DUDENSING, RICHARD. (Et)
Am. b. Ger. d. 1899 New York. F-T-7.
DUDLEY, CAROL R.
Am. ad. 1934 New York. M.
DUDLEY, DOROTHY.
Am. b. Somerville, Mass. 1892; ad. 1934 New York. A.

DUDLEY, Frank Virgil.
Am. b. Delavan, Wis. 1868; ad. 1934 Chicago. A-F-W.
DUDLEY, Howard. (Eg)
Eng. London 1820-1864. DNB-T.
DUDLEY, Katharine.
Am. b. 1884. A14.
DUDLEY, Thomas. (Eg)
Br. 1634-1680. B-DNB-T.
DUER, Henrietta A.
Am. b. Balt., Md. ad. 1934 Same. A.
DUEZ, Ernest Ange.
Fr. Paris 1843-1896 St. Germain. B-C-T.
DUFAU, Clémentine Hélène.
Fr. b. Quinsac 1879. B-DBA.
DUFAUX, Frédéric. (S)
Swi. Geneva 1830-1871 Same. B-T.
DUFEU, Jacques Édouard.
Fr. 1840-1900 Paris. B-T.
DUFF, John Robert Keitley.
Eng. b. London 1862; ex. 1934 Same. B-Wa.
DUFFAUD, Jean Baptiste.
Fr. Marseilles 1853-1927 Paris. B-DBA.
DUFFIELD, William.
Eng. Bath 1816-1863 London. B-DNB-T.
DUFFY, Edmund. (Cart)
Am. b. Jersey City, N. J. ad. 1934 Balt., Md. W.
DUFFY, Patrick Vincent.
Ir. Dublin 1836-1909 Same. DNB-T.
DUFFY, Richard H. (S)
Am. b. New York 1881; ad. 1915 New York. A12-F.
DUFLOS, Claude.
Fr. Paris 1662/5-1727 Same. B-T.
DUFNER, Edward.
Am. b. Buffalo, N. Y. 1872; ad. 1934 New York. A-B-DBA-F-T-W-46.
DUFOUR, Camille Émile.
Fr. b. Paris 1841. B-DBA-T.
DUFOUR, Jean Jules.
Fr. b. Toulouse 1889. DBA.
DUFRÉNOY, Georges Léon.
Fr. b. Thais 1871. B-DBA.
DUFRESNE, Charles Georges.
Fr. b. Millemont 1876; ad. 1934 Paris. B-DBA-797.
DUFRESNE, Maurice Charles.
[Supposed to be Charles Georges Dufresne].
DUFRESNOY. *see also* Fresnoy.
DUFRESNOY, Charles Alphonse.
Fr. Paris 1611-1668. B-T-722.
DUFY, Jean.
Fr. b. Havre 1888. DBA.
DUFY, Raoul.
Fr. b. Havre 1880; ex. 1934 New York. DBA-797.
DUGDALE, [Mrs.] Amy Katherine.
see Browning, A. K.
DUGDALE, Thomas Cantrell.
Eng. b. Blackburn 1880; ex. 1934 London. Wa.
DUGGAN, Peter Paul.
Am. Ireland 1810?-1861 Paris. B-Bd-F-T-4-15-45.
DUGHET [or Poussin], Gaspard.
It. Rome 1613/5-1675 Same. B-Bd-C-T-512-722.
DUGMORE, [Major] A. Radclyffe.
Am. ex. 1914 New York. M.
DUGOURC [or du Gour], Jean Démosthène.
Fr. Versailles 1749-1825 Paris. B-T.
DU GUERNIER, Louis. *see* Guernier, L.
DUHEM, Maris Genenève.
Fr. b. Guimps; ac. 1900 in Paris. B-T-679.
DUJARDIN, Karel. *see* Jardin, K.
DULAC, Charles Maris.
Fr. Paris 1865-1898. T.
DULAC, Edmund. (Ill)
Fr.-Eng. b. Toulouse, Fr. 1862; ac. 1934 London. B-Wa.
DULAC, [Jean] Guillaume. (Ill)
Fr. ex. 1929 in Paris. DBA.
DULCETUS. (S)
Sp. ac. 1251 in Spain. M.
DULL, Christian Lawton.
Am. b. Phila., Pa. 1902; ad. 1934 Same. A.
DULL, John J.
Am. b. Phila., Pa. 1862; ad. 1934 Same. A-F-T.
DULUARD, Hippolyte François Léon.
Fr. b. Paris; ac. 1910-1924 Same. B-DBA.
DU MARBORÉ, Pitsch Émile Jean.
Fr. b. Paris 1896. DBA.
DUMARESQ, Charles Édouard Armand.
see Armand-Dumaresq.
DUMAS, Michel Realier.
Fr. Lyons 1812-1885 Same. B-T.
DU MAURIER. *see* Maurier.
DUMLER, Martin George.
Am. b. Cinn., O. 1868; ad. 1934 Same. A.
DUMMER, H. Boylston.
Am. b. Rowley, Mass. 1878; ad. 1934 Rockport, Mass. A.
DUMMER, Jeremiah.
Am. Newbury, Mass. 1645-1718 Boston. DAB-F-T.
DU MOND, Frank Vincent.
Am. b. Rochester, N. Y. 1865; ad. 1934 Lyme, Conn. A-F-W.
DU MOND, Frederic Melville.
Am. New York 1867-1927 Monrovia, Calif. A024-B.
DU MOND, Helen Savier. (Min)
Mrs. Frank Vincent Du Mond.
Am. b. Portland, Ore. 1872; ad. 1934 Lyme, Conn. A.
DUMONS [or Dumont], Jean Joseph.
Fr. Tulle 1687-1779 Paris. B-E-T.
DUMONSTIER, Cosme.
Fr. ac. 1581 in Rouen. B-T-722.
DUMONSTIER, Daniel.
Fr. Paris 1574-1646 Same. B-T.
DUMONSTIER, Geoffroy.
Fr. ac. 1537/40 in Fontainebleau. B-T-722.
DUMONSTIER, Pierre II.
Fr. Paris 1565-1656 Same. B-T.
DUMONT, Augustin Alexander. (S)
Fr. Paris 1801-1884 B-E-Hs-T.
DUMONT, Edmé. (S)
Fr. Paris 1720-1775 Same. B-E-T.
DUMONT, François. (S)
Fr. Paris 1688-1726. B-E-T.
DUMONT, François. (Min)
Fr. Lunéville 1751-1831 Paris. B-E-T.
DUMONT, Jacques [le Romain].
Fr. Paris 1701-1781 Same. B-E-T.

DUMONT, Jacques Edmé. (S)
Fr. Paris 1761-1844 Same. B-E-T.
DUMONT, Pierre Jean.
Fr. b. Paris; ac. 1931. DBA.
DUN, John. (Min)
Scot. b. Edinburgh; ac. 1872-1907 London. B-T.
DUNAND [or Dunant], Jean François.
Fr. ac. 1806-1827 in Paris. B-T.
DUNBAR, Anna Glenny. (S)
Mrs. Davis T. Dunbar.
Am. b. 1888; ex. 1931 Buffalo, N. Y. M.
DUNBAR, F. A. T. (S)
Am. ac. 1877. M.
DUNBAR, Harold C.
Am. b. Brockton, Mass. 1882; ad. 1934 Chatham, Mass. A-F-T.
DUNBAR, Ulric Stonewall Jackson. (S)
Am. London, Can. 1862-1927 Wash., D.C. A025-F-T-W14.
DUNBIER, Augustus William.
Am. b. Osceola, Neb. 1888; ad. 1934 Omaha, Neb. A.
DUNCAN, Ann.
Scot. b. Glasgow; ex. 1932 in London. M.
DUNCAN, Charles Stafford.
Am. b. Hutchinson, Kan. 1892; ad. 1934 San Fran., Calif. A.
DUNCAN, Edward.
Eng. London 1804-1882 Same. B-Bd-DNB-T.
DUNCAN, Frederick Alexander.
Am. b. Texarkana, Ark. 1881; ad. 1934 New York. A.
DUNCAN, Gregor. (Ill)
Am. ad. 1934 New York. M.
DUNCAN, [Dr.] J. D. Campbell.
Br. ad. 1934 Rotorua, N. Z., Aust. M.
DUNCAN, Jean.
Am. b. St. Paul, Minn. 1900; ad. 1934 Same. A.
DUNCAN, John.
Scot. Edinburgh 1803-1882. B.
DUNCAN, John.
Scot. b. Dundee 1866; ad. 1934 Paul, Eng. Wa.
DUNCAN, Mary.
Eng. b. Bromley, Kent.; ad. 1935 Paul, near Penzance, Eng. Wa.
DUNCAN, Perry M. (Ill)
Am. ad. 1934 New York. M.
DUNCAN, Thomas.
Scot. Kinclaven 1807-1845 Edinburgh. B-DNB-E-T-722.
DUNCAN, Walter Jack.
[Official Artist Am. Forces in Fr. 1918].
Am. b. Ind., Ind. 1881; ad. 1934 New York. F-W.
DUNCANSON, Robert S.
Am. Cinn., O. 1821-1871. M.
DUNCOMBE, Susanna [née Highmore].
British. 1725-1812 London. DAB-T.
DUNIKOWSKI, Ksawery. [Carver]
Pol. b. Cracow 1876. T.
DUNKARTON, Robert. (Eg)
Eng. London 1744-1811. B-DNB-T.
DUNKEL, Eugène.
Rus.-Am. b. Samarkand 1890; came to U. S. 1922; ad. 1935 New York. DBA-M.
DUNKELBERGER, Ralph D.
Am. b. Reading, Pa. 1894; ad. 1934 Same. A.
DUNKER, Balthasar Anton. (Eg)
Swi. Saal, Ger. 1746-1807 Berne, Swi. B-T.
DUNLAP, Adele Helena.
Am. b. Los Angeles, Calif.; ad. 1934 Same. A-F.
DUNLAP, Edward.
Am. ex. 1934 Chicago, Ill. M.
DUNLAP, Mary Stewart.
Am. b. Ohio; ad. 1935 Pasadena, Calif. F-46.
DUNLAP, William. (P-Author)
Am. Perth Amboy, N. J. 1766-1839 New York. B-Bd-F-T-1-2-3-4-6-7-45-182-666-786.
DUNLAP, Zoe Fleming. (Min)
Am. b. Cinn., O.; d. 1927 Same. A024.
DUNLOP, R. O.
Ir. b. Dublin 1894; ex. 1934 London. Wa.
DUNN, Alan Cantwell. (Ill)
Am. ad. 1934 New York. A.
DUNN, Charles A. R.
Am. b. Wash., D. C. 1895; ad. 1934 Same. A.
DUNN, [Mrs.] Delphine.
Am. b. Rushville, Ind.; ad. 1934 Cambridge, Mass. A.
DUNN, Emelene Abbey.
Am. Rochester, N. Y. 1859-1929. A026.
DUNN, Harvey Hopkins. (Ill)
Am. b. Phila., Pa. 1879; ad. 1934 Same. A.
DUNN, Harvey T.
Am. b. Manchester, S. D. 1884; ad. 1934 Tenafly, N. J. A.
DUNN, [Mrs.] Louise M.
Am. b. East Liverpool, O. 1875; ad. 1934 Cleveland, O. A.
DUNNELL, John Henry.
Am. 1813-1904 New York. A05.
DUNNING, Robert S.
Am. Brunswick, Me. 1829-1905 Westport, Mass. A05.
DU NOUY. *see* Nouy.
DUNOYER DE SEGONZAG, André. *see* Segowzac, A. D.
DUNSMORE, John Ward.
Am. b. Cinn., O. 1856; ad. 1934 New York. A-B-F-T-W.
DUNSTALL, John. (Eg)
Eng. ac. 1644-1675 London. DNB-T.
DUNTHORNE, John [The Elder].
Eng. London 1770-1844. DNB-T.
DUNTHORNE, John [The Younger].
Eng. London 1798-1832. DNB-T.
DUNTHORNE, John [The Third].
Eng. ex. 1783-1792 in London. DNB-T.
DUNTLEY, Wilbur L.
Am. ac. 1890-1920. [No death date.] M.
DUNTON, William Herbert.
Am. b. Augusta, Me. 1878; ad. 1934 Taos, N. M. A-F-W.
DÜNWEGE, Victor [The Elder].
see Master of Coppenberg.
DUPAIN, Edmund Louis.
Fr. b. Bordeaux 1847. DBA.
DUPAS, Jean Théodore.
Fr. b. Bordeaux 1882. B-DBA-T.
DUPATZ, Louis Maris Charles Henri Mercier. (P-S)
Fr. Bordeaux 1771-1825 Paris. B-T.
DUPEE, Jeannie.
Am. ad. 1934 Boston. M.

DUPÉRAC, ÉTIENNE.
Fr. Bordeaux 1525-1601/4 Paris. B-Bd-T.
DUPHINEY, WILFRED ISRAEL.
Am. b. Central Falls, R. I. 1884; ad. 1934 Prov., R. I. A.
DUPLAIX, GEORGES. (Ill)
Fr. b. Nevers 1898; ad. 1935 New York. M.
DUPLESSIS, HENRY.
Fr. b. 1886; ac. 1932 London. T.
DUPLESSIS, JOSEPH SILFRÈDE.
Fr. Carpentras 1725-1802 Versailles. B-T.
DUPLESSIS-BERTAUX, JEAN.
Fr. Paris 1747/9-1813/9. B-T.
DUPON, JOSUÉ. (S)
Belg. b. Antwerp 1864. B-T.
DUPONT, GAINSBOROUGH.
[Nephew of Thomas Gainsborough].
Eng. 1754-1797 London. B-DNB-T.
DUPONT, HENRIQUEL. *see* Henriquel-D.
DUPONT, P.
Dut. Amsterdam 1870-1911 The Hague. B-T.
DUPONT, VICTOR FRANÇOIS EUGÈNE.
Fr. b. Bologne-sur-Mer 1875. DBA.
DUPRAY, HENRY LOUIS.
Fr. b. Sedan 1841. B-T.
DUPRÉ, AMALIA. (S)
It. Florence 1845-1928. T.
DUPRÉ, E.
Fr. ac. 1850. M.
DUPRÉ, GIOVANNI. (S)
It. Siena 1817-1882. Hs-T.
DUPRÉ, JULES.
Fr. Nantes 1811-1889 Paris. B-Bd-C-E-T.
DUPRÉ, JULIEN.
Fr. Paris 1851-1910 Same. B-Bd-C-T.
DUPRÉ, LÉON VICTOR.
[Brother of Jules Dupré].
Fr. Limoges 1816-1879 Paris. B-C-T.
DUPRESSOIR, JOSEPH FRANÇOIS.
Fr. Paris 1800-1859 Same. C.
DUPUY, ELLA M.
Am. ad. 1934 New York. M.
DUPUY, PAUL MICHEL.
Fr. b. Pau 1869; ex. 1934 Paris. B-DBA-T.
DUQUE, FRANCIS.
Am. Columbia, So. Am. 1832-1915 New York. A012-F.
DUQUESNOY, FRANÇOIS [Fiammingo]. (S)
Flem. Brussels 1594-1644 Leghorn, It. B-Hs-T.
DURAMEAU, LOUIS JEAN JACQUES.
Fr. Paris 1733-1796 Versailles. B-T.
DURAN [or Durand], CAROLUS.
see Carolus-Duran, C. E. A.
DURAND, AMÉDÉE. (S)
Fr. b. 1789; d. 1873 Paris. M.
DURAND, ASHER BROWN.
Am. Jefferson Village, N. J. 1796-1886 So. Orange, N. J. B-C-DAB-E-F-T-1-2-4-6-7-15-22-40-45-57-58-880.
DURAND, BENNETT.
Am. b. Wash., D. C. 1906; ad. 1934 Same. A.
DURAND, CYRUS. (Eg)
Am. Jefferson Village, N. J. 1787-1868 Irvington, N. J. F-T-2-7-57.
DURANGEL, LÉOPOLD VICTOR.
Fr. Marseilles 1828-1898 Paris. C-T.
DURANT, JOHN WALDO.
Am. West Indies 1774-1832 Phila., Pa. F-2.
DURDEN, JAMES.
Eng. b. Manchester 1878; ad. 1934 London. DBA-Wa.
DURENNES, EUGÈNE ANTOINE.
Fr. b. Paris 1860. DBA.
DÜRER, ALBRECHT.
Ger. Nüremberg 1471-1528 Same. B-Bd-C-E-T-V-191-192-351-352-667-710-722-801-880-904-917-923.
DURET, FRANCISQUE JOSEPH.
Fr. Paris 1804-1865 Same. B-Hs-T.
DURHAM, JOSEPH.
Eng. London 1814-1877 Same. B-DNB-Hs.
DURIG, ERNEST. (S)
Am. ac. 1934 in Wash., D. C. M.
DURKEE, HELEN WINSLOW. (Min)
Mrs. C. J. Mileham.
Am. b. New York; ac. 1934 Same. A.
DURKIN, JOHN. (Ill)
Am. 1868-1903 New York. A04.
DURNO, JAMES.
Eng. London 1745-1795 Rome, It. DNB-T.
DURRIE, GEORGE HARVEY.
Am. New Haven, Conn. 1820-1863 Same. F-3.
DURST, ALAN LYDIATE.
Eng. b. Alverstoke 1883; ad. 1934 London. Wa.
DURSTAN, ARTHUR.
Am. ad. 1934 Los Angeles, Calif. M.
DURY, ANTOINE [or Tony].
Fr. Lyons 1819-1878. B-T.
DURY, GEORGE.
Am. Ger. 1817-1894 Nashville, Tenn. F.
DUSART [or Du Sart], CORNELIS.
Dut. Haarlem 1660-1704 Same. B-C-T-722.
DUSART, FRANS [Wallon]. (S)
Dut. b. Holland; d. 1661 London. B-T.
DU SEIGNEUR, JEAN BERNARD. (S)
Fr. Paris 1808-1866. B-Hs-T.
DU SIMITIÈRE, PIERRE EUGÈNE.
Am. Geneva, Swi. 1736-1784 Phila., Pa. DAB-F-2-6-45-182-184-786.
DUSTIN, SILAS S.
Am. b. Richfield, O.; ad. 1934 Los Angeles, Calif. A.
DUTERTRE, ANDRÉ.
Fr. 1753-1842 Paris. B-T.
DUTILLEUX, HENRI JOSEPH CONSTANT.
Fr. Douai 1807-1865 Paris. B-T.
DUTTON, HAROLD JOHN.
Eng. b. Birmingham; ad. 1934 Notts. Wa.
DUVAL, CAROLINE.
Fr. ac. 1844-1848 in Paris. B-T.
DUVAL, CHARLES ALLEN.
Ir. Ireland 1808-1872 Cheshire, Eng. DNB-T.
DUVAL, CONSTANT LÉON.
Fr. b. Champlay 1877. B-DBA.
DUVAL, PHILIPPE.
Eng. b. France; ac. 1670-1709 London. B-DNB-T.
DUVAL, ROBERT [or Nicolas].
Dut. The Hague 1644/9-1732 England. B-DNB-T.
DUVAL-GOZLAN, LÉON. *see* Gozlan, L. D.

DUVALL, Fanny Eliza.
Am. b. Port Bryan, N. Y. 1861; ad. 1934 Los Angeles, Calif. A.
DUVEEN, Rhoda.
Am. ad. 1934 New York. M.
DUVENECK, Frank. (P-S)
Am. Covington, Ky. 1848-1919 Cinn., O. A016-B-C-DAB-E-T-Ta-1-15-46-59-60-71-701.
DUVENT, Charles Jules Walère.
Fr. b. Langres 1867. B-DBA-T.
DUVERGER, Théophile Emmanuel.
Fr. Bordeaux 1821-1901? B-T.
DUVET, [or Drout], Jean. (Eg) [Master of the Unicorn].
Fr. b. Langres 1481/5-1561. B-T.
DUVIVIER, Aimée.
Fr. ac. 1786-1824 in Paris. B-T.
DUWETT. *see* Wet.
DUXA, Karl.
Aus. b. Vienna 1871. B-T.
DUYCKINCK, Evert, 1st.
Am. 1621-1702 New York. F.
DUYCKINCK, Evert, 3rd.
Am. 1677-1727 New York. F-182-184.
DUYCKINCK, Gerardus.
Am. 1695-1742 New York. F.
DUYCKINCK, Gerret.
Am. 1660-1710? New York. F.
DUYNEN [or Duyn], Isaac van.
Dut. ac. 1630-1677/81 The Hague. B-T.
DUYSTER, Willem Cornelisz.
Dut. Amsterdam 1599?-1635 Same. B-T.
DVORAK [or Dworak], Franz.
Aus. b. Prelouc 1862. B-T.
DWIGGINS, William Addison. (Ill)
Am. b. Martinsville, O. 1880; ad. 1934 Boston. W.
DWIGHT, Julia S.
Am. b. Hadley, Mass. 1870; ad. 1915 Boston. A12-F.
DWIGHT, Mable. (Et)
Am. b. Cinn., O. 1876; ad. 1934 New York. A29-F.
DWYER, Adelaide.
Am. b. Wash., D. C.; ad. 1934 Same. A.
DWYER, James.
Am. ad. 1934 Dayton, Ohio. M.
DYCE, William.
Scot. Aberdeen 1806-1864 London. B-DNB-E-T-812.
DYCK, Anthony van. *see* Van Dyck, A.
DYCKMANS, Joseph Laurens.
Flem. Lierre 1811-1888 Antwerp. B-T.
DYCZKOWSKI, Eugène M.
Am. ad. 1934 Buffalo, N. Y. M.
DYE, Clarkson.
Am. b. San Fran., Calif. 1869. F.
DYE, [Mrs.] Olive Bagg.
Am. b. Lincoln, Neb. 1889; ad. 1934 Same. A.
DYER, Briggs (Et)
Am. b. Atlanta, Ga. 1911; ad. 1934 Chicago. A.
DYER, Charles Gifford.
Am. Chicago 1851-1912 Bavaria. A010-C-F-T-15.
DYER, Harry W.
Am. b. Portland, Me. 1871. A28.
DYER, Hezekiah Anthony.
Am. b. Prov., R. I. 1872; ad. 1934 Same. A-F-T-W.
DYER, Leonard.
Am. ex. 1935 New York. M.
DYER, Lowell.
Am. b. Brooklyn, N. Y. 1856; ad. 1915 St. Ives, Cornwall, Eng. A12.
DYER, Nancy A.
Am. b. Prov., R. I. 1903; ad. 1934 Same. A.
DYK [or Dyck], Philip van.
Dut. Amsterdam 1680-1753 The Hague. B-T.
DYKAAR, Moses Wainer. (S)
Am. Vilna, Rus. 1884-1933 New York. A030.
DYKE, Myrtle Parke.
Am. ad. 1934 Fort Smith, Ark. M.
DYONNET, Edmund.
Can. b. France 1875; ad. 1935 Montreal, Can. M.
DYSON, William H. ["Will"]. (Cart)
Aust. b. Ballarat 1883; ad. 1934 London. 873.
DYSSELHOFF, Gerrit William.
Dut. 1866-1925. T.
EAGAN, Joseph B. (Ill)
Am. ad. 1934 Cleveland, O. M.
EAGEL. (S)
Fr. ac. 1930 Paris. M.
EAGLES, John.
Br. 1783-1855. DNB.
EAKINS, Thomas W.
Am. Phila., Pa. 1844-1916 Same. A013-B-C-DAB-E-F-1-15-35-46-51-71-104-172-353-701-748-762-779.
EARHART, John Franklin.
Am. b. Ohio 1853; ad. 1934 Cinn., O. A-F.
EARL [or Earle], Maude.
Eng. ac. 1884-1934. F-M.
EARLE, Cornelia.
Am. b. Huntsville, Ala. 1863; ad. 1934 Columbia, S. C. A.
EARLE, Elinor.
Am. b. Phila., Pa.; ad. 1934 Same. A.
EARLE, James.
Am. Leicester, Mass. 1761-1796/8 Charleston, So. Car. B-F-T-2-6.
EARLE, Lawrence Carmichael.
Am. New York 1845-1891 Grand Rapids, Mich. A018-B-F-T.
EARLE, Olive.
Am. b. London, Eng. 1888; ad. 1934 New York. A.
EARLE, Paul Barnard.
Can. b. Montreal, Can.; ad. 1935 Same. M.
EARLE [or Earl], Ralph.
Am. Shrewsbury, Mass. 1751-1801 Bolton, Conn. B-Bd-DAB-E-F-T-1-2-3-4-6-144-182-701.
EARLE [or Earl], Ralph Eleaser Whitesides.
Am. b. England; d. 1837 New Orleans, La. F-2-6-144.
EARLE, Winthrop. (S)
Am. Yonkers, N. Y. 1870-1912 New York. A04.
EARLEY, James Farrington. (S)
Am. b. Birmingham, Eng. 1856; ad. 1915 Wash., D. C. [deceased]. A12.
EARLEY, James W. (Ill)
Am. ad. 1935 New York. M.

EARLOM, Richard. (Eg)
Eng. London 1743-1822 Same. B-DNB-E-T-917.
EAST, [Sir] Alfred.
Eng. Kettering 1849-1913 London. B-E-T.
EAST, Pattie Richardson.
Am. b. Okla. 1894; ad. 1934 Ft. Worth, Tex. A.
EASTLAKE, Charles Herbert.
Eng. ad. 1933 Croyden, Eng. Wa.
EASTLAKE, [Sir] Charles Lock.
Eng. Plymouth 1793-1865 Pisa, It. B-Bd-C-DNB-E-T.
EASTLAKE, [Mrs.] Mary Alexandra.
Can. b. Can.; ad. 1933 Croyden, Eng. Wa.
EASTLAKE, Mary Bell.
Can. b. Douglas, Can.; ad. 1935 Montreal. M-893.
EASTMAN, Ruth.
Am. ac. 1931. A28.
EASTMAN, [Col.] Seth.
Am. Brunswick, Me. 1808-1875. F.
EASTMAN, William Joseph.
Am. b. Cleveland, O. 1888; ad. 1934 Same. A-F.
EASTON, Linwood.
Am. ad. 1935 Portland, Me. M.
EASTWOOD, E. H.
Am. b. American Fork, Utah 1876; ad. 1934 Provo, Utah. M.
EASTWOOD, Raymond James.
Am. b. Bridgeport, Conn. 1898; ad. 1934 Lawrence, Kan. A.
EATON, Charles Frederick.
Am. b. Prov., R. I. 1842. [Deceased.] F-W14.
EATON, Charles Harry.
Am. Akron, O. 1850-1901 Leonia, N. J. A04-B-F-T-6.
EATON, Charles Warren.
Am. b. Albany, N. Y. 1857; ad. 1934 Bloomfield, N. J. A-B-F-T-W.
EATON, Dorothy.
Am. b. E. Orange, N. J. 1893; ad. 1934 New York. A.
EATON, Hugh McDougal.
Am. Brooklyn, N. Y. 1865-1924 Same. A021-B-F-T.
EATON, Joseph Oriel.
Am. Newark, O. 1829-1875 Yonkers, N. Y. B-Bd-C-DAB-F-T-15-181.
EATON, Louise Herreshoff.
Am. b. Prov., R. I.; ad. 1934 Same. A.
EATON, Malcolm. (Ill.)
Am. ad. 1934 New York. M.
EATON, Margaret Fernie.
Mrs. Hugh M. Eaton.
Am. b. Leamington, Eng. 1871; ad. 1934 Brooklyn, N. Y. A-B-F-T.
EATON, William Sylvester.
Am. b. Waltham, Mass. 1861; ad. 1934 Sag Harbor, N. Y. A.
EATON, Wyatt.
Can.-Am. Canada 1849-1896 Newport, R. I. B-C-DAB-E-F-T-15-22-46-61.
EBEL, Fritz Carl Werner.
Ger. Lauterbach 1835-1895 Düsseldorf. B-T.
EBERBACH, Alice Kinsey.
Mrs. Nelson F. Eberbach.
Am. b. Phila., Pa.; ad. 1934 Same. A.
EBERHARD, Konrad. (S)
Ger. Hindelang 1768-1859 Munich. B-Hs-T.
EBERHARD, Robert George. (S)
Am. b. Geneva, Swi. 1884; ad. 1934 New York. A-B-Cs-F.
EBERL, Christoph Ulrich.
Ger. 1566-1635. T.
EBERL, François Zdenck.
Czec. b. Prague 1888. DBA.
EBERLE, Abastenia St. Leger. (S)
Am. b. Webster City, Ia. 1878; ad. 1934 New York. A-B-Cs-F-W-46.
EBERLE, Adam.
Ger. Aix-la-Chapelle 1804-1832 Rome, It. C-T.
EBERLE, Adolf.
Bav. Munich, Ger. 1843-1914. B-T.
EBERLEIN, Gustav [Heinrich]. (S)
Ger. b. 1847; ac. 1893 in Berlin. T.
EBERSOLE, Mabel Ellen.
Am. b. Keokuk, Ia. 1885; ad. 1934 Same. A.
EBERT, Anton.
Bohemian. 1835-1896. B-T.
EBERT, Charles H.
Am. b. Milwaukee, Wis. 1873; ad. 1935 Old Lyme, Conn. A.
EBERT, Karl.
Ger. Stuttgart 1821-1885 Munich. C-T.
EBERT, Mary Roberts.
Mrs. Charles H. Ebert.
Am. b. Titusville, Pa. 1873; ad. 1935 Old Lyme, Conn. A.
EBY, Kerr. (Et.)
Am. b. Tokio, Jap. 1889; ex. 1934 New York. A28.
ECCLESINE, Joseph A.
Am. ad. 1934 Bronx, N. Y. M.
ECHAGUE, Antonio Ortiz.
Sp. ex. 1930 Pittsburgh, Pa. M.
ECHAVE [or Chaves], Balthasar.
Sp. b. Zumaya; ac. 1630. T.
ECHERT, Florence.
Am. b. Cinn., O.; ad. 1934 St. Augustine, Fla. A.
ECHTLER, Adolf.
Ger. Danzig 1843-1914. B-T.
ECKENBRECHER, Karl Paul Thémistocles von.
Ger. b. Athens, Gr. 1842. B-T.
ECKERSBERG, Christoffer Wilhelm.
Dan. Blaaskrog 1783-1853. B-E-T.
ECKERT, Katherine.
Mrs. Augustus Henry Fox.
Am. b. Cleveland, O. 1899; ad. 1934 Schenectady, N. Y. M.
ECKFORD, Jessijo.
Am. b. Dallas, Tex. 1895; ad. 1934 Same. A-F.
ECKHARDT, Hieronymus.
Dan. ac. 1552-1572 Freiburg. T.
ECKSTEIN, John. (P-S)
Am. Germany 1750-1817/22 Phila., Pa. B-Bd-DAB-F-T-2-7.
ED, Carl Frank Ludwig. (Cart.)
Am. b. Moline, Ill. 1890; ad. 1934 Evanston, Ill. W.
EDDIS, Eden Upton.
Eng. London 1812-1901 Shalford. B-DNB.
EDDY, Augustus.
Am. U. S. 1851-1921 Paris, Fr. A018.

EDDY, Henry B. (Ill.)
Am. b. New York 1872; d. 1935. A.
EDDY, Henry Stephens.
Am. b. Rahway, N. J. 1878; ad. 1934 Westfield, N. J. A-F-W.
EDDY, Isaac. (Eg.)
Am. Weathersfield, Vt. 1777-1847. F-2-7.
EDDY, James. (Eg.)
Am. b. 1806; ac. 1827-1881 Prov., R. I. F-T-2-7.
EDDY, Sarah James. (S)
Am. b. Boston, Mass. 1851. Cs-F.
EDELBAUM, Sam.
Am. ad. 1934 New York. M.
EDELFELT, Albert Gustaf Aristide.
Fin. Helsingfors 1854-1905. B-T.
EDELMANN, Charles Auguste.
Fr. b. Soult-sous-Forêts 1879. DBA.
EDELNICK [or Edelink], Gérard.
Flem. Antwerp 1640/4-1707 Paris. B-Bd-E-T-880.
EDEMA, Gérard.
Eng. Friesland, Holland 1652-1700? Eng. DNB.
EDERHEIMER, Richard.
Am. ad. 1934 New York. M.
EDGERLY, Beatrice. [Mrs. MacPherson.]
Am. ad. 1934 Trenton, N. J. M.
EDGERLY, Mira. *see* Korzybska.
EDHOLM, Charlton Lawrence.
Am. b. Omaha, Neb. 1879; ad. 1934 Dobbs Ferry, N. Y. A.
EDIE, Stuart Carson.
Am. b. Wichita Falls, Tex. 1908; ad. 1934 New York. A.
EDMISTON, Alice R.
Am. b. Monroe, Wis.; ad. 1934 Lincoln, Neb. A.
EDMOND, Elizabeth. (S)
Am. Portland, Me. 1887-1918 Pasadena, Calif. A016.
EDMONDS, Esther Topp.
Am. b. New York 1888; ex. 1933 Pittsburgh, Pa. F-M.
EDMONDS, Francis William. *see* Edmunds, F. W.
EDMONDSON, William John.
Am. b. Norwalk, O. 1868; ad. 1934 Cleveland, O. A-B-F.
EDMONSTONE, Robert.
Scot. Kelso 1794-1834 Same. B-DNB-T.
EDMUNDS, [or Edmonds], Francis William.
Am. Hudson, N. Y. 1806-1863 Bronxville, N. Y. B-Bd-C-DAB-F-T-4-15.
EDMUNDS, Hepburn. *see* Hepburn-Edmunds.
EDMUNDS, Paul.
Eng. b. Stroud 1873; ad. 1934 Brighton. Wa.
EDRIDGE, Henry. (Et.)
Eng. Paddington 1769-1831 London. B-DNB-T.
EDROP, Arthur Norman ["Topping"]. (Ill)
Am. b. Birmingham, Eng. 1884; ad. 1934 St. David's, Pa. A.
EDSON, A. Allan.
Can. Stanbridge, Que. 1846-1888. B-T.
EDSTROM, David. (S)
Am. b. Hvetlanda, Swe. 1873; ad. 1934 Los Angeles, Calif. A-F-T-W.
EDWARDS, Edward. (Et.)
Eng. London 1738-1806. B-DNB-T.
EDWARDS, Edward B.
Am. b. Columbia, Pa. 1873; ad. 1934 New York. A-F-W.
EDWARDS, Edwin. (Et.)
Eng. Frawlington 1823-1879 London. B-DNB-T.
EDWARDS, Emily.
Am. b. San Antonio, Tex.; ad. 1935 Same. M.
EDWARDS, George Wharton.
Am. b. Fair Haven, Conn. 1859; ad. 1934 Greenwich, Conn. A-B-F-T-W.
EDWARDS, Harry C.
Am. Phila., Pa. 1868-1922 Brooklyn, N. Y. A020-F.
EDWARDS, Joseph Lee.
Am. b. Culbert, Ga.; ad. 1934 Atlanta, Ga. A.
EDWARDS, Kate Flournoy.
Am. b. Marshallville, Ga. 1877; ad. 1934 Atlanta, Ga. A-F-W.
EDWARDS, Lionel Dalhousie Robertson.
Eng. b. Clifton 1877; ad. 1934 Salisbury. Wa.
EDWARDS, Mary Ellen.
Eng. b. Kingston 1839. [No death date.] T.
EDWARDS, Mary Stella.
Eng. ex. 1934 in London. M.
EDWARDS, Robert.
Am. b. Buffalo, N. Y. 1879; ad. 1934 New York. A.
EDWARDS, Samuel Arlent. (Eg.)
Am. b. Somersetshire, Eng. 1862; ad. 1935 Bruges, Belg. A20-B-F-T-7-880.
EDWARDS, Sydenham Teak. (Et.)
Eng. Usk 1768-1819 Chelsea. B-DNB-T.
EDWARDS, William Camden. (Eg.)
Br. Monmouthshire 1777-1855 Bungay. DNB-T.
EDWARDSON, Lawrence Christie.
Am. b. Waltham, Mass. 1904; ad. 1934 New Britain, Conn. A.
EDWIN, David. (Eg.)
Am. Bath, Eng. 1776-1841 Phila., Pa. B-Bd-DAB-F-T-2-7-40-62.
EDY-LEGRAND. *see* Legrand.
EDZARD, Dietz.
Ger. b. Bremen 1893; ad. 1934 Paris. DBA.
EECKHOUT [or Heckout], Gerbrandt van den.
Dut. Amsterdam 1621-1674 Same. B-Bd-C-E-T-722.
EEKMAN, Nicolas.
Dut. b. 1889 in Holland; ad. 1935 Paris. M.
EGAN, Beatrice. *see* Humphreys, B. J.
EGAN, Eloise.
Am. ad. 1935 New York. M.
EGAN, James. (Eg.)
Ir. Ireland 1799-1842 London. B-DNB-T.
EGAN, Joseph Byron.
Am. b. Cleveland, O. 1906; ad. 1934 Same. M.
EGAS, Camilo. (Mu.)
Ecuadorian b. Quito, Eq. 1897; ad. 1934 New York. M.
EGBERT, Henry. (Ill.)
Am. 1826-1900 Brooklyn, N. Y. A01.
EGELI, Bjorn P.
Am. b. Oslo, Nor. 1900; ad. 1934 Wash., D. C. A.

EGELMANN [or Engelmann], CARL FRIEDRICH. (Eg.)
Am. 1782-1860. F-2-7-147.
EGG, AUGUSTUS LÉOPOLD.
Eng. London 1816-1863 Algiers. B-Bd-DNB-E-T-722.
EGGEMEYER, MAUDE KAUFMAN.
Am. b. New Castle, Ind. 1877; ad. 1934 Richmond, Ind. A.
EGGENSCHUYLER, URS. (S)
Swi. b. Subingen 1849. B-T.
EGGENSCHUYLER, URS PANKRAZ. (S)
Swi. 1756-1821 Soleure. B-T.
EGGER-LIENZ, ALBIN.
Swi. Striebach 1868-1926. B-T.
EGGERS, BARTHOLOMEUS. (S)
Dut. d. 1692 in Amsterdam. B-T.
EGGERS, GEORGE WILLIAM.
Am. b. Dunkirk, N. Y. 1883. A28.
EGGERS, JOHANN CARL.
Ger. Neu-Strelitz 1787-1863 Same. B-T.
EGGERT, SIGMUND.
Bav. b. Munich, Ger.; ac. 1880-1886. B-T.
EGGLESTON, ALLEGRA.
Am. 1859-1933 Glens Falls, N. Y. M-Obit. N. Y. papers, 12-13-1933.
EGGLESTON, BENJAMIN.
Am. b. Belvidere, Mass. 1867; ad. 1934 Brooklyn, N. Y. A-B-F-T.
EGGLESTON, EDWARD M. (Ill.)
Am. b. Ashtabula, O. 1887; ad. 1934 New York. A.
EGINTON, FRANCIS. (Eg.)
Eng. Birmingham 1775-1823 Newport. DNB-T.
EGINTON, FRANCIS. (Glass-P)
Eng. 1737-1805 Birmingham. DNB-T.
EGINTON [or Egginton], WYCLIFFE.
Eng. b. Birmingham 1875; ad. 1934 So. Devon. Wa.
EGLEY, WILLIAM MAW. (Min.)
Eng. Doncaster 1798-1870 London. B-DNB-T.
EGMONT, JUSTUS [or Verus] VAN.
Flem. Leyden 1601-1674 Antwerp. B-Bd-C-T.
EGYPTIAN ARTISTS. *see* books 705-706-744-841-883.
EHLERS, KARL.
Ger. b. Altona 1854. T.
EHMSEN, HEINRICH.
Ger. ac. 1930 in Berlin. M.
EHNINGER, JOHN WHETTON.
Am. New York 1827-1889 Saratoga Springs, N. Y. B-DAB-F-T-4-15.
EHRENBERG, FREDERICK.
Am. b. Germany; d. 1910 New York. A08.
EHRICH, WILLIAM. (S)
Am. b. Koenigsberg, Ger. 1897; ad. 1934 Buffalo, N. Y. A.
EHRLICH, GEORG. (S)
Aus. b. 1897; ac. 1934. M.
EHRMAN, HYMAN M. (S)
Am. b. Russia 1884; ad. 1934 Portland, Ore. A.
EHRMANN, FRANÇOIS ÉMILE.
Fr. Strassbourg 1833-1910. B-T.
EICHBAUM, GEORGE CALDER.
Am. Bowling Green, Ky. 1837-1919 St. Louis, Mo. A016.
EICHBERG. *see* Kayser-Eichberg.
EICHELBERGER, ROBERT A. (Et)
Am. d. 1890 New York. M.
EICHENBAUM, [Miss] AUDREY. (S)
Am. ad. 1935 Chicago, Ill. M.
EICHENS [or Eithens], PHILIPP HERMANN.
Ger. Berlin 1812-1877. B-T.
EICHHOLTZ, JACOB.
Am. Lancaster, Pa. 1776-1842 Phila., Pa. DAB-F-2-6.
EICHSTEDT, RUDOLPH.
Ger. Berlin 1857-1926. B-T.
EIKYU, MATSUOKA.
Jap. b. Satsuma 1881; ad. 1934 Tokyo. M.
EILERS, EMMA.
Am. b. New York; ad. 1934 Brooklyn, N. Y. A-F.
EILSHEMIUS, LOUIS MICHEL.
Am. b. Arlington, N. J. 1864; ad. 1934 New York. A.
EISEN, CHARLES DOMINQUE JOSEPH.
Fr. Valenciennes 1720-1778 Brussels, Belg. B-T.
EISEN, FRANÇOIS.
Flem. Brussels 1695-1778 Same. B-T.
EISENBACH, DOROTHY L.
Am. b. Lafayette, Ind.; ad. 1934 Ind., Ind. A.
EISENBERG, LUCY.
Am. ex. 1934 New York. M.
EISENDIECK, SUZANNE.
Pol. b. Dantzig, Ger. 1908; ex. 1934 London. M.
EISENLOHR, EDWARD G.
Am. b. Cinn., O. 1872; ad. 1934 Dallas, Tex. A.
EISENSCHUTZ, WILLY.
Ger. ex. 1934 New York. M.
EISER, RAYMOND H.
Am. ad. 1934 Toledo, O. M.
EISNER, DOROTHY.
Am. b. New York 1906; ad. 1934 Same. M.
EITHENS. *see* Eichens.
EITNER, WILHELM HEINRICH ERNEST.
Ger. b. Hamburg 1867. B-T.
EKEGARTH, HANS.
Swe. b. Christianstad 1891. DBA.
EKENAES, JAHN.
Nor. b. Christiana 1847. B-T.
EKMAN, NICOLAS.
Belg. b. Brussels 1889. DBA.
EKSERZIAN, CARNIG.
Am. Constantinople, Turkey 1855-1931 U. S. M-Obit. Art Digest, 9-1-1931.
EKWALL, KNUT.
Swe. Säby, Sweden 1843-1912. B-T.
ELAND, JOHN SHENTON.
Am. England 1872-1933 New York. A030.
ELAUS. *see* Elouis.
ELBO, JOSÉ.
Sp. Ubeda 1804-1844 Madrid. T.
ELDER, ARTHUR JOHN.
Am. b. London, Eng. 1874; ad. 1934 Westport, Conn. A.
ELDER, INEZ STAUB.
Am. b. Kossuth, O. 1894; ad. 1934 Dallas, Tex. A.

ELDER, John A.
Am. Fredericksburg, Va. 1833-1895 Same. F.
ELDER, William. (Eg.)
Eng. ac. 1680-1700 in London. B-DNB-T.
ELDERSHAW, John R.
Aust. b. Sydney, N. S. W. 1896; ad. 1934 Richmond, Tasmania. Wa.
ELDH, Carl Johan. (S)
Swe. b. Film 1873; ex. 1929 Paris. DBA-T.
ELDRIDGE, Marion.
Am. ad. 1934 New York. M.
ELDRIDGE, Stuart.
Am. ad. 1935 New York. M.
ELGOOD, George Samuel.
Eng. b. Leicester 1851; ad. 1934 Same. B-T-Wa.
EL GRECO. *see* Greco.
ELIAS [or Eliasz], Nicolas. *see* Pickenoy, N. E.
ELIASOPH, Paula.
Am. b. New York 1895; ad. 1934 Same. A.
ELISCU, Frank. (S)
Am. b. New York 1912; ad. 1934 Same. A.
ELIZABETH, Princess of England. [Landgräfin of Hesse-Homburg].
Eng. Windsor 1770-1840 Frankfort, Ger. B-Bd-DNB-T.
ELKINS, Henry Arthur.
Am. Vermont 1847-1884 Georgetown, Colo. F.
ÉLLE, Louis Ferdinand [The Elder].
Fr. Paris 1612-1689 Same. B-T.
ÉLLE, Louis Ferdinand [The Younger].
Fr. Paris 1648-1717 Rennes. B-T.
ELLENRIEDER, Anna Marie.
Ger. Constance 1791-1863 Same. C-T.
ELLERHAUSEN, Florence Cooney.
Am. b. Canada 1888; ad. 1934 New York A-W.
ELLERHAUSEN, Ulric Henry. (S)
Am. b. Germany 1879; ad. 1934 New York. A-Cs-F-W.
ELLERSTON, Homer E.
Am. b. River Falls, Wis. 1892; ad. 1934 Tryon, N. C. A.
ELLERY, Richard Vanderford.
Am. b. Salem, Mass. 1909; ad. 1934 Danvers, Mass. A.
ELLFELDT, Walter Charles. (S)
Am. b. Kansas City, Mo. 1909; ad. 1934 Same. A.
ELLICOTT, Henry Jackson. (S)
Am. Ellicott, Md. 1848-1901 Wash., D. C. A04-B-F-T.
ELLIGER, Ottmar [The Elder].
Ger. Gothenburg 1633-1679 Berlin. B-C-T.
ELLIGER, Ottmar [The Younger].
Ger. Hamburg 1666-1732. B-C-T.
ELLIOTT, Charles Loring.
Am. Scipio, N. Y. 1812-1868 Albany, N. Y. B-Bd-C-DAB-F-T-1-3-4-6-15-46-51.
ELLIOTT, Elizabeth Shippen Green. (Ill.) Mrs. Huger Elliott. A-B-F-T-W-46.
Am. b. Phila., Pa.; ad. 1934 New York.
ELLIOTT, Hannah. (Min.)
Am. b. Atlanta, Ga. 1876; ad. 1934 Birmingham, Ala. A.
ELLIOTT, John.
Am. England 1858-1925 Charleston, S. C. A022-DAB-F-T-W13-46.
ELLIOTT, Ruth Cass.
Am. b. Los Angeles, Calif. 1891; ad. 1934 Brentwood Heights, Calif. A.
ELLIS, Charles. (Actor-P)
Am. ex. 1935 New York. M.
ELLIS, Clyde Garfield.
Am. b. Humboldt, Kan. 1879; ad. 1934 Los Angeles, Calif. A.
ELLIS, Edwin.
Eng. Nottingham 1841-1895. B-T.
ELLIS, Fremont F.
Am. b. Virginia City, Mont. 1897; ad. 1934 Santa Fé, N. M. A.
ELLIS, Harriet.
Am. b. Springfield, Mass. 1886; ad. 1934 Same. A.
ELLIS, Harvey.
Am. Rochester, N. Y. 1852-1904 Syracuse, N. Y. A05-B-T.
ELLIS, Joseph Bailey. (S)
Am. b. No. Scituate, Mass. 1890; ad. 1934 Pittsburgh, Pa. A.
ELLIS, Salathiel.
Am. ac. 1845/60 in New York. F-T-6.
ELLIS, William. (Eg.)
Eng. London 1747-1810. B-DNB-T.
ELLSWORTH, James Sanford.
Am. Windsor, Conn. 1802-1873 Pittsburgh, Pa. F-6.
ELLSWORTH, Wilson H.
Am. b. Glens Falls, N. Y. 1908; ad. 1934 New York. M.
ELLYS [or Ellis], John.
Eng. London 1700/1-1757. DNB-T.
ELMER, Stephen.
Eng. d. 1796 Farnham, Eng. DNB-T.
ELMER, William.
Ir. ex. 1783-1799 London. B-DNB-T.
ELMORE, Alfred.
Ir. Cork 1815-1881 London. B-C-DNB-T.
ELMORE, [Mrs.] Elizabeth Tinker.
Am. Clinton, Wis. 1874-1933. A030-F.
ELMQUIST, Hugo. (S)
Swe. b. Carlshaum; ac. 1895. B.
ELOUIS, Jean Pierre Henri.
Fr. Caen 1755-1843 Same. B-F-T-6.
ELSHEIMER, Adam.
Ger. Frankfort 1574/8-1620 Rome, It. B-C-T-722-801.
ELSHIN, Jacob. [Alexandrovitch].
Am. b. Leningrad, Rus. 1891; ad. 1934 Seattle, Wash. A.
ELSHOECHT, Jean Jacques Marie Carl Vital. (S)
Fr. Dunkirk 1797-1856 Paris. B-T.
ELSLEY, Arthur John.
Eng. b. London 1861. B-T.
ELST, van. *see* Verelst.
ELSTRACKE, Renold [Renier]. (Eg.)
Eng. ac. 1571-1625 in London. B-DNB-T.
ELWELL, D. Jerome.
Am. Gloucester, Mass. 1857-1912 Naples, It. A010-B-T.
ELWELL, Francis [or Frank] Edwin. (S)
Am. Concord, Mass. 1858-1922 Darien, Conn. A019-B-F-Hs-T-Ta-W10-19-46.

ELWELL, Frederick William.
Eng. b. 1870; ex. 1933 London. Wa.
ELWELL, John H.
Am. b. Marblehead, Mass. 1878. A28-F.
ELWES, Simon.
Eng. b. Rugby 1902; ad. 1934 London. Wa.
ELY, [Mrs.] Caro Weir.
Am. ad. 1935 Old Lyme, Conn. M.
ELY, [Mrs.] Dorothy Winship.
Am. ad. 1935 Old Lyme, Conn. M.
ELY, [Mrs.] Fanny G.
Am. b. New York 1877; ad. 1934 Same. A.
ELY, Francis C.
Am. ad. 1934 Avalon, N. J. M.
EMANUEL, Frank Lewis.
Eng. b. Bayswater 1865; ad. 1934 London. T-Wa.
EMANUELE, Romano. *see* Romano.
EMEREÈ, Berla Iyone.
Am. b. Wichita, Kan. 1899; ad. 1934 El Paso, Tex. A.
EMERSON, Arthur Webster.
Am. b. Honolulu, Hawaii 1885; ad. 1934 Same. A-F.
EMERSON, Charles Chase.
Am. d. 1922 Boston, Mass. A020-F.
EMERSON, Edith.
Am. b. Oxford, O.; ad. 1934 Phila., Pa. A.
EMERSON, Louise Harrington.
see Ronnebeck, L. H. E.
EMERSON, Sybil.
Am. b. Worcester, Mass.; ad. 1934 New York. M.
EMERSON, Sylvia Hathaway Watson.
Am. b. 1834. [No death date.] M.
EMERSON, W. C.
Am. ad. 1934 New Canaan, Conn. A.
EMERY, Irene. (S)
Am. b. Grand Rapids, Mich. 1900; ad. 1934 Same. A.
EMES, John. (Eg.)
Eng. ex. 1785-1805 in London. B-DNB-T.
EMMES, Thomas. (Eg.)
Am. ac. 1701 in Boston, Mass. F-T-2-7-147.
EMMET, Edith Leslie.
Am. ad. 1934 New York. A22-F.
EMMET, Ellen G. *see* Rand, E. G. E.
EMMET, Lydia Field.
Am. b. New Rochelle, N. Y. 1866; ad. 1934 New York. A-B-F-T-W-1-46-829.
EMMET, Rosina. *see* Sherwood, R. E.
EMMET, [Mrs.] William T. *see* Cushing, Lily.
EMMONS, [Mrs.] Chansonetta Stanley. (Min.)
Am. b. Kingfield, Me. 1858; ad. 1934 Newton, Mass. A.
EMMONS, Dorothy Stanley.
Am. b. Roxbury, Mass. 1891; ad. 1934 Newton, Mass. A.
EMORY, Hopper. (Ill.)
Am. b. Balt., Md. 1881; ad. 1934 Same. A.
EMPOLI, Jacopo Chimenti da.
It. Empoli 1554-1640 Florence. C-T-722.
EMPTAGE, Arthur.
Am. ex. 1934 New York. M.
EMRICH, Harvey.
Am. b. Ind., Ind. 1884; ad. 1934 Woodstock, N. Y. A.
EMSLIE, Alfred Edward.
Eng. b. London 1848; ac. 1929. B-DBA-T.
EMSLIE, John Philipps.
Eng. 1839-1885 London. B-T.
EMSLIE, Rosalie.
Eng. b. Hampstead 1891; ad. 1934 London. DBA-T-Wa.
ENCKE, Fedor.
Ger. b. Berlin 1851. B-T.
ENDE, Edgar.
Ger. ad. 1935 Munich; ex. 1934 Pittsburgh, Pa. M.
ENDE, Hans [or Am].
Ger. Trèves 1864-1918. B-T.
ENDE, Johann Heinrich.
Saxon. Pirma 1645-1695 Leipzig. T.
ENDER, Édouard.
Aus. Rome 1822-1883 London. B-T.
ENDOENUS [or Endoios]. (S)
Gr. ac. 516 B.C. in Athens, Gr. B-E.
ENGALIÈRE, Marius.
Fr. Marseilles 1824-1857 Paris. B.
ENGEL, Harry.
Am. b. Roumania 1901; ad. 1934 Bloomington, Ind. A.
ENGEL, Richard Drum.
Am. b. Wash., D. C. 1889; ad. 1934 Same. A.
ENGEL-GARRY, José.
Fr. b. Joinville-le-Pont 1873. DBA.
ENGELBACH, [Mrs.] Florence.
Eng. ex. 1934 in London. M.
ENGELBRECHTSZ [or Engelbertsz], Cornelis.
Dut. Leyden 1468?-1533 Same. B-C-T.
ENGELHARD, Elizabeth. (Et.)
Am. ac. 20th Cent. M.
ENGELHARDT, George B.
Ger. Mulhouse 1823-1883. B-T.
ENGELMANN, Gottfried. (Eg.)
Ger. Mulhouse 1788-1839 Paris. B-T.
ENGERTH, Éduard von Ritter.
Ger. Silesia 1818-1897 Vienna, Aus. C-T.
ENGL, Hugo.
Bav. ac. 1877 in Munich, Ger. B-T.
ENGLE, Harry Léon.
Am. b. Richmond, Ind. 1870; ad. 1934 Chicago. A-F-181.
ENGLEHARD, Anton Friedrich.
Ger. Murten 1821-1870 Same. B-T.
ENGLEHEART, Francis. (Eg.)
Eng. London 1775-1849. B-DNB.
ENGLEHEART, George. (Min.)
Eng. Kew 1752-1829 Blackheath. B-Bd-DNB-E-T.
ENGLEHEART, John Cox Dillman. (Min.)
Eng. 1783-1862 Tunbridge Wells. B-DNB.
ENGLEHEART, Thomas. (S)
Eng. 1745-1786 London. B-DNB.
ENGLEHEART, Timothy Stansfield. (Eg)
Eng. London 1803-1879 Same. B-DNB.
ENGLER, Arthur. (Eg)
Am. b. Jersey City, N. J. 1885. A20-F.
ENGLISH, Frank F.
Am. b. Louisville, Ky. 1854. A12-F.
ENGLISH, Harold.
Am. b. Omaha, Neb. 1890; ad. 1934 Paris. A.
ENGLISH, Henriette.
Am. b. Colfax, Wash. 1905; ad. 1934 Seattle, Wash. M.

ENGLISH, JOSIAS. (Et)
Eng. 1630-1718 Mortlake. B-DNB-T.
ENGLISH, MABLE BACON PLIMPTON.
Mrs. J. L. English.
Am. b. Hartford, Conn. 1861; ad. 1934 Same. A.
ENGSTRÖM, ALBERT LURENTIUS JOHANNES.
Swe. b. Lönneberga 1869. T.
ENGSTRÖM, LEANDER.
Swe. b. 1886; d. 1927. DBA.
ENHUBER, KARL VON.
Ger. Hof 1811-1867 Munich. B-C-T.
ENJOLRAS, DELPHIN.
Fr. b. Coucourou 1865. B-DBA.
ENNEKING, JOHN JOSEPH.
Am. Minster, O. 1841-1916 Boston, Mass. A014-B-C-DAB-E-F-T-W7-15-39-46-47.
ENNEKING, JOSEPH ELIOT.
Am. b. Hyde Park, Mass.; ad. 1934 Boston. A.
ENNIS, GEORGE PEARSE.
Am. b. St. Louis, Mo. 1884; ad. 1934 New York. A-F-W.
ENNIS, GLADYS ATWOOD.
Am. b. Natick, Mass.; ad. 1934 New York. A.
ENRICHUS DI PISTOJA. (S)
It. ac. 12th Cent. in Italy. Hs.
ENRICO DI TEDICE.
It. ac. 13th Cent. in Italy. T.
ENRIGHT, WALTER JOSEPH. (Cart.)
Am. b. Chicago 1879; ad. 1934 New York. A-W.
ENSER, JOHN F.
Am. b. Ennis, Tex. 1898; ad. 1934 Lexington, Mass. A.
ENSOM, WILLIAM. (Eg.)
Eng. 1796-1832 Wandsworth. B-DNB-T.
ENSOR, JAMES.
Belg. b. Ostend 1860. B-DBA-T-668.
ENTERS, ANGNA.
Am. ex. 1934 New York. M.
ENTLER, KATHERINE E.
Am. ad. 1935 Hagerstown, Md. M.
ENTRAYGUES, CHARLES BERTRAND D'.
Fr. b. Brives; ac. 1876-1904 in Paris. B-DBA-T.
ENTZING-MILLER, JOHANN MICHAEL. (Eg.)
Am. Germany 1804-1855 New York. F-T-7.
EPAGATUS. (S)
Gr. ac. 6th Cent. B.C. B-Hs-T.
EPINAY, MARIE DE. (S)
Fr. b. Rome, It.; ad. 1934 Paris. B-DBA-T.
EPINAY, PROSPER D'. (S)
Fr. 1836-1914. B-T.
EPP, RUDOLPH.
Ger. Eberbach, Baden 1834-1910 Munich. B-T.
EPPENSTEINER, JOHN JOSEPH.
Am. b. St. Louis, Mo. 1893; ad. 1934 Same. A.
EPPINK, NORMAN ROLAND. (Mu.)
Am. Cleveland, O. 1906; ad. 1934 Same. A.
EPPS, LAURA THERESA. *see* Alma-Tadema, L. T.
EPSTEIN, JACOB. (S)
Am. b. New York 1880; ad. 1935 London. Cs-E-Hs-T-W-354-701-783-798-813-825-855-884.
EPSTEIN, JEHUDO.
Pol. b. Poland 1870. T.

ERASMUS, DESIDERIUS.
Dut. Rotterdam 1467-1536 Basel, Swi. B-T.
ERBAUGH, [Mrs.] HUGH R.
Am. ad. 1935 Flint, Mich. M.
ERBAUGH, RALPH WALDO.
Am. b. Peru, Ind. 1885; ad. 1934 Flint, Mich. A.
ERBIT, JULES.
Am. ad. 1935 New York. M.
ERCEVILLE, WENCESLAS D.
Pol. b. 1888; ad. 1934 Paris. DBA.
ERCOLE DI GIULIO, CESARE GRANDI *see* Grandi, G.
ERDMANN, OTTO.
Ger. Leipzig 1834-1905. B-C-T.
ERDMANN, RICHARD F.
Am. b. Chillicothe, O. 1894; ad. 1934 Same. A.
ERESCH, JOSIE. (Ill.)
Am. ed. 1934 Beloit, Kan. A.
ERICHSEN, VIRGILIUS.
Dan. Copenhagen 1722-1782 Same. T.
ERICSON, DAVID.
Am. b. Motala, Swe. 1873; ad. 1934 Paris. A-B-DBA-F-T.
ERICSON, MAURITZ A. (S)
Am. 1836-1912 Pelham, N. Y. A0x.
ERIKSEN, JOHN M.
Am. Sweden 1844-1918 U. S. A016.
ERIKSON, CARL OLAF.
Am. ad. 1935 Chicago, Ill. F.
ERIKSON, OSCAR B.
Am. ad. 1934 Milwaukee, Wis. M.
ERIKSSON, CHRISTIAN. (S)
Swe. b. Areckna 1858. B-DBA-T.
ERISTOFF-KASAK, PRINCESS MARIA.
Rus. b. Leningrad; d. 1934. B.
ERLANGER, RODOLPHE.
Fr. b. Bologne 1872. DBA.
ERLER, FRITZ.
Ger. b. Frankenstein 1868. B-T.
ERNST, MAX.
Ger. b. Brühl 1891; ex. 1934 San Fran., Calif. DBA-M.
ERNST, RODOLPHE.
Aus. b. Vienna 1854. B-T.
ERRARD [or Hérard], GÉRARD LÉONARD. (S)
Fr. Liége 1630-1675. B-T.
ERSKINE, HAROLD PERRY. (S)
Am. b. Racine, Wis. 1879; ad. 1934 New York. A.
ERTÉ [Conte Romain de Tirtoff]. (Cari)
Fr. b. Russia; ad. 1934 Bologne-sur-Seine, Fr. M.
ERTVELT [or Artvelt], AANDRIES VAN.
Flem. Antwerp 1590-1652. B-T.
ERTZ, EDWARD FREDERICK.
Am. b. Canfield, Ill. 1862; ad. 1934 Sussex, Eng. A-B-F-T-W.
ES [or Essen], JACOB FOPSEN VAN.
Flem. 1596-1666 Antwerp. B-C-T-722.
ESCALANTE, JUÁN ANTONIO [de Frias].
Sp. Cordova 1630-1670 Madrid. B-C-T.
ESCALANTE, JUÁN DE SÈVILLE ROMERO Y.
Sp. 1627-1695. 722.
ESCALLIER, ELÉONORE.
Fr. b. Poligny; ac. 1857-1888 Paris. B-T.
ESCHBACH, PAUL ANDRÉ JEAN.
Fr. b. Paris 1881. B-DBA-T.

ESCHENBACH, PAUL.
Am. b. New York 1867; ad. 1915 Cinn., O. A12-B.
ESCHER, MAURITS CORNELIS. (Et.)
Dut. b. 1898; ad. 1934 Rome, It. M.
ESCHERICH, [Mrs.] ELSA F.
Am. b. Davenport, Ia. 1888; ad. 1934 Pasadena, Calif. A.
ESCHWEGE, F. A. ELMER [or Eilmar] VON.
Ger. b. Brunswick 1856. B-T.
ESCOSURA, IGNACIO LÉON Y.
Sp. Oviedo 1840-1901 Toledo. B-C-T.
ESHERICK, WHARTON.
Am. b. Phila., Pa. 1887; ad. 1934 Paoli, Pa. A.
ESKIMO ARTISTS. *see* book 760.
ESKRICH [or Cruche], VASE PIERRE.
Fr. Paris 1530-1590. B-T.
ESKRIDGE, ROBERT LEE.
Am. b. Philipsburg, Pa. 1891; ex. 1935 New York. A-M.
ESLEY, JOAN. (Ill.)
Am. ad. 1934 Walworth, N. Y. M.
ESNER, ARTHUR.
Am. ad. 1934 Boston, Mass. M.
ÉSPAGNAT. *see also* D'Éspagnat.
ÉSPAGNAT, GEORGES D'.
Fr. b. Melun 1870. B-DBA-T.
ESPAGNOLET. *see* Ribera.
ESPALARGUES, PERE [or Pedro].
Sp. (Catalan); ac. 1490 in Spain. M.
ESPALTER Y RULL, JOAQUIN.
Sp. Sitges 1809-1880 Madrid. T.
ESPINOSA, JACINTO JERÓNIMO DE.
Sp. Valencia 1600-1680 Same. C-T.
ESQUIVEL, ANTONIO MARÍA.
Sp. Sèville 1806-1857 Madrid. T.
ESSEN, HANS VAN.
Dut. ac. 1589-1636 Antwerp, Belg. T.
ESSEN, JACOB FOPSEN VAN. *see* Es, J. F.
ESSEN, JOHANNES CORNELIS JAN VAN.
Dut. b. Amsterdam 1854. B-T.
ESSER, MAX. (S)
Ger. b. Barth 1885; ac. 1915 Berlin. T.
ESSEX, ALFRED.
Br. ac. 1837. [No death date.] DNB-T.
ESSEX, WILLIAM. (Min.)
Eng. 1784-1869 Brighton. B-DNB-T.
ESSEX, WILLIAM B.
Eng. 1822-1852 Birmingham. B-DNB-T.
ESSIG, GEORGE EMERICK.
Am. b. Phila., Pa. 1838; ac. 1890. [No death date.] A12-B-F.
ESTÉ, FLORENCE.
Am. Cinn., O. 1860-1926 Paris. A023-F.
ESTÉBAN. *see* Murillo.
ESTENSE, BALDASSARE [da Reggio].
It. b. Reggio; ac. 1469-1500 Same. C-T-V.
ÉSTIENNE, HENRY D'.
Fr. b. Conques 1872. DBA.
ESTORACH. *see* Casanova y E.
ESTRADA, JOSÉ MARÍA.
Sp. b. Valencia; ac. 1830/60; d. 1873 Madrid. T.
ETCHEVERRY, HUBERT DENIS.
Fr. b. Bayonne 1867. B-DBA-T.
ETEX, ANTOINE. (S)
Fr. Paris 1808-1888 Chaville. B-E-Hs-T.
ÉTIENNE, FRANCIS PAUL.
Fr. b. Dôel 1874. DBA.
ETNIER, STEPHEN MORGAN.
Am. b. York, Pa. 1903; ad. 1934 So. Harpswell, Me. A.
ETTER, DAVID RENT.
Am. Phila., Pa. 1807-1881 Same. F.
ETTINGER, CHURCHILL. (Et)
Am. b. Haworth, N. J. 1903; ad. 1934 New York. M.
ETTL, ALEX J. (S)
Am. b. Fort Lee, N. Y. 1898; ad. 1934 New York. A.
ETTL, JOHN. (S)
Am. b. Budapest, Hun. 1872; ad. 1934 New York. A.
ETTY, [Sir] WILLIAM.
Eng. York 1787-1849 Same. B-Bd-C-DNB-E-T-722-909.
EUGEN, NAPOLEON NICKOLAUS. [Prince]
Swe. b. Drottingsholm 1865; ex. 1935 Belg. T.
EUGENE, FRANK.
Am. ac. 1890 in New York. M
EULBERG, VERONICA APPOLONIA.
Am. b. Portland, Ore. 1905; ad. 1934 Same. A.
EULER, EDWIN REEVES.
Am. ad. 1934 Provincetown, Mass. M.
EUPHRANOR [l'Isthunien]. (S)
Gr. ac. 375-335 B.C. in Corinth. B-E-Hs.
EUPHRONIUS. (Vase Painter)
Gr. (Athenian) early 5th Cent. E.
EUPOMPOS [Founder Sicyon School].
Gr. ac. 370 B.C. in Sicyon. B-E-T.
EURICH, H. (Et)
Eng. ex. 1930 in London. M.
EURICH, RICHARD ERNST.
Eng. b. Bradford 1903; ad. 1934 Ilkley. Wa.
EUSEBIO DA SAN GIORGIO.
It. Perugia 1465/70-1539? B-T.
EUSTON, JACOB HOWARD.
Am. b. Lebanon, Pa. 1892; ad. 1934 Chicago. A.
EUTYCHIDES OF SICYON. (S)
Gr. ac. 318 B.C. in Sicyon in Achaea. B-E-Hs.
EUWER, ANTHONY HENDERSON. (Ill)
Am. b. Allegheny, Pa. 1877; ad. 1934 Portland, Ore. F-W.
EVANS, BERNARD W.
Eng. Birmingham 1848-1922 London. B-T.
EVANS, BLANCHE RUMSEY.
Mrs. Jocelyn H. de Grasse Evans.
Am. b. Bath, N. Y. 1880; ad. 1934 New York. A.
EVANS, DAVID. (S)
Eng. b. Manchester 1893; ad. 1934 Kensington. Wa.
EVANS, DE SCOTT.
Am. Boston, Ind. 1847-1898 at sea. A01-B-C-F-T-15-181.
EVANS, EDGAR SAMUEL.
Am. East Hamburg, N. Y. 1852-1919 Missoula, Mont. A016.
EVANS, EDMUND. (Eg)
Eng. Southwark 1826-1905 Ventnor. DNB.
EVANS, EDWIN.
Am. b. Lehi, Utah 1860; ad. 1915 Salt Lake City, Utah. A12-F.

EVANS, Ethel.
Am. b. 1866; d. 1929. A026.
EVANS, George H.
Am. ad. 1934 New York. M.
EVANS, Grace French.
Am. b. Davenport, Ia.; ad. 1934 Same. A.
EVANS, Grace Lydia.
Am. b. Pittston, Pa. 1877; ad. 1934 Phila., Pa. A.
EVANS, Jessie Benton.
Am. b. Akron, O. 1866; ad. 1934 Chicago. A.
EVANS, Jocelyn.
Am. ex. 1935 New York. M.
EVANS, John William. (Eg)
Am. b. Brooklyn, N. Y. 1855; ad. Same. A-B-F-T-W.
EVANS, Joseph ["Joe"].
Am. New York 1857-1898 Same. A01-B-T.
EVANS, Powys Arthur Lenthall. (Cari)
Eng. b. London 1899; ad. 1934 Same. Wa-873.
EVANS, Ray O. (Ill)
Am. b. Columbus, O. 1887; ad. 1934 Same. F-W.
EVANS, Richard.
Eng. Hereford 1784-1871 Southampton. B-DNB-T.
EVANS, Rudolph. (S)
Am. b. Washington, D. C. 1878; ad. 1934 Paris. A-Cs-F-W-46.
EVANS, Samuel.
Welsh. b. Wales; d. 1835 Droxford, Hants. DNB-T.
EVANS, Samuel T. G.
Eng. Eton 1829-1904 Same. B-T.
EVANS, Virginia Bargar.
Am. b. Moundsville, W. Va.; ad. 1934 Same. A.
EVANS, William. (Eg)
Eng. 1797-1856 London. B-Bd-T.
EVANS, William [Evans of Bath].
Eng. b. Bath; ac. 1893. [No death date.] M.
EVANS, William [Evans of Bristol].
Eng. Bristol 1811-1858 London. B-DNB-T.
EVANS, William [Evans of Elton].
Eng. Elton 1798-1877 Same. B-DNB-T.
EVENEPOEL, Henri Jacques Édourd.
Belg. Nizza 1872-1899 Paris. T.
EVENO, Édouard Jules.
Fr. b. St. Aubin 1884. DBA.
EVERARD, [Mrs.] Bertha [née King].
Eng. b. London; ad. 1934 Same. Wa.
EVERDINGER, Allaert [or Aldert] van.
Dut. Alkmar 1621?-1675 Amsterdam. B-C-E-T-722.
EVERDINGER, César Boetus van.
Dut. Alkmar 1617-1678 Same. B-C-T.
EVERETT, Caroline Mills.
Am. d. 1921 Paris, Fr. A018.
EVERETT, Elizabeth Rinehart.
Am. b. Toledo, O.; ad. 1934 Seattle, Wash. A.
EVERETT, Ethel Walton.
Am. ex. 1933 New York. M.
EVERETT, Florence.
Am. b. Ontario, Can.; ad. 1934 St. Louis, Mo. A.
EVERETT, Fred. (Ill)
Am. ad. 1934 Nyack, N. Y. M.
EVERETT, George Clowes.
Am. Williamsburg, N. Y. 1865-1926 Brooklyn, N. Y. A023.
EVERETT, Herbert Edward. (S)
Am. b. Worcester, Mass.; ad. 1934 Phila., Pa. A.
EVERETT, Joseph Alma Freestone.
Am. b. Salt Lake City, Utah 1884; ad. 1934 Same. A.
EVERETT, Mary.
Mrs. H. G. Everett.
Am. b. Miffinburg, Pa. 1876; ad. 1934 Los Angeles, Calif. A.
EVERETT, Raymond.
Am. b. Englishtown, N. J. 1885; ad. 1934 Austin, Tex. A-F.
EVERETT, Walter H. (Ill)
Am. ad. 1934 New York. M.
EVERGOOD, Philip Howard Francis.
Am. b. New York 1901; ad. 1934 Martinsville, N. J. A.
EVERHART, Adelaide.
Am. b. Charlotte, N. C.; ad. 1934 Decatur, Ala. A.
EVERITT, Allen Edward.
Eng. Birmingham 1824-1882. B-DNB-T.
EVERS, Anton Clemens Albrecht.
Ger. Morizberg 1802-1848 Hanover. C-T.
EVERS, Helen. (Ill)
Am. ad. 1935 Trumble, Conn. M.
EVERS, Ivar Elis.
Am. b. Sweden 1866; ad. 1935 Tillson, N. Y. A12-F.
EVERS, John.
Am. New Town, N. Y. 1797-1884. F-T-2-6.
EVES, Reginald Grenville.
Eng. b. London 1876. DBA-Wa.
EVRARD, Adèle.
Flem. Henegau 1792-1889 Same. B-T.
EWALD, Louis.
Am. b. Minn., Minn. 1891; ad. 1934 Phila., Pa. A.
EWALD, Reinhard.
Ger. b. 1890 in Germany. M.
EWBANK, Johnn Wilson.
Eng. Darlington 1799-1847 Sunderland. B-DNB-T.
EWELL, Hazel Crow.
Am. b. Bird City, Kan. 1888; ad. 1934 Ravinia, Ill. A.
EWERTZ, Henry. (S)
Am. ad. 1934 Ridley Park, Pa. M.
EWING, Edgar.
Am. ad. 1935 Hartington, Neb. M.
EWORTH [or Ewouts], Hans [or Haunce].
Flem. b. Antwerp; ac. 1540/3-1574. B-T.
EXNER, Johan Julius.
Dan. Copenhagen 1825-1910 Same. B-C-DBA-T.
EXSHAW, Charles. (Eg)
Ir. b. Dublin; ex. 1764-1771 London. B-DNB-T.
EYCK. *see* Van Eyck, H. and J.
EYCKEN, Charles van den.
Belg. b. Brussels 1859. T.
EYCKEN, Jean Baptiste van.
Belg. b. Brussels 1809; d. 1853. B-T.

EYDEN [or Eyde], JERIMIAH VAN DER.
Eng. b. Brussels, Belg.; d. 1695/7 England. DNB-T.
EYDEN, WILLIAM T.
Am. Hanover, Ger. 1859-1919 Richmond, Ind. A016-182.
EYES, CHARLES.
Eng. Liverpool 1754-1803. M.
EYNHOUDTS, REMOLDUS [or Rombout].
Flem. Antwerp 1613-1679/80. B-T.
EYRE, JOHN.
Eng. b. Staffordshire; d. 1927 London. B-T.
EYRE, LOUISA. (S)
Am. b. Newport, R. I. 1872; ad. 1934 Phila., Pa. A-B-Cs-F.
EYRE-WALKER, BERNARD. (Et)
Eng. b. Harlow 1886; ad. 1934 Westmoreland, Eng. Wa.
EYSSERIC, JOSEPH MARIS PHILIPPE.
Fr. b. Carpentras 1860. B-DBA.
EYTEL, CARL.
Am. d. 1928 Palm Springs, Calif. M.
EYTINGE, SOL. (Et)
Am. 1833-1905 Bayonne, N. J. A05-B-T.
EZEKIEL, ABRAHAM EZEKIEL. (Eg)
Eng. Exeter 1757-1806 Same. DNB-T.
EZEKIEL, [Sir] MOSES JACOB. (S)
Am. Richmond, Va. 1844-1917 Rome, It. A014-B-DAB-F-Hs-T-Ta-15-46.
FABBRICOTTI, G.
It. ex. 1935 London. M.
FABER, CONRAD [von Creuznach].
[Master of the Holzhausen Portraits.]
Ger. b. Creuznach; ac. 1500-1551/3. T.
FABER, EUGENE.
Am. ex. 1935 Milwaukee, Wis. M.
FABER, HARMAN.
Am. Germany 1832-1913 Phila., Pa. A011.
FABER, JOHAN [The Elder]. (Eg)
Dut. The Hague 1660-1721 Bristol, Eng. B-Bd-DNB-T.
FABER, JOHAN [The Younger]. (Eg)
Dut. Holland 1684-1756 London. B-Bd-DNB-T.
FABER, JOHN.
Am. d. 1906 New York. A06-B.
FABER, LUDWIG E.
Am. Phila., Pa. 1885-1913 Same. A011-B-F.
FABIAN, LYDIA DUNHAM.
Am. b. Charlotte, Mich. 1857; ad. 1934 Chicago, Ill. A.
FABRE, FRANCOIS XAVIER [Baron].
Fr. Montpelier 1766-1837 Same. B-T.
FABRI, A. E.
Fr. ac. 1872 Rome, It. M.
FABRI, RALPH.
Am. b. Budapest, Hun. 1894; ad. 1934 New York. A.
FABRIANO, GENTILE DA. *see* Gentile da F.
FABRITIUS, BARENT [or Bernard].
Dut. ac. 1650-1672 in Leyden. B-T.
FABRITIUS, KAREL.
Dut. Haarlem 1620/4-1654 Delft. B-C-T.
FABRON [or Fabronius], LUIGI.
It. Turin 1885-1905 Pozzuoli. T.
FACCINI [or Facini], PIETRO.
It. Bologna 1562-1602. C-T.
FACHE, RENÉ. (S)
Fr. b. Douai 1816. [No death date.] B-T.
FACKERT, OSCAR WILLIAM.
Am. b. Jersey City, N. J. 1891. A.
FACTOR, PEDRO NICOLAS.
Sp. Valencia 1520-1583. B-T.
FADINO, IL. *see* Alenis, Tomasco di.
FAED, JAMES, JR.
Eng. b. 1848; d. 1921. Y01921.
FAED, JOHN.
Scot. Burley 1819-1902 Same. B-DNB-T.
FAED, THOMAS.
Scot. Hirkudbright 1826-1900 London. B-Bd-C-DNB-E-T.
FAENZA [or Fenzoni], PACE DA.
It. ac. 1477 in Italy. B-T-V.
FAES, PETER VAN DER. *see* Lely, Sir Peter.
FAGAN, BETTY MAUD CHRISTIAN.
Fr. b. Devizes; ac. 1930 Paris. DBA.
FAGAN, LOUIS ALEXANDER. (Et)
It. Naples 1845-1903 Florence. DNB.
FAGEL, LÉON. (S)
Fr. Valenciennes 1851-1913. B-DBA-T.
FAGERBERG, CARL VILHELM. (S)
Swe. b. Stockholm 1878; ad. 1932 Paris. T.
FAGERLIN, FERDINAND JULIUS.
Swe. Stockholm 1825-1907. B-T.
FAGG, KENNETH S.
Am. ad. 1934 Sunnyside, L. I., N. Y. A.
FAGGI, ALFEO. (S)
Am. b. Florence, It. 1885; ad. 1934 Woodstock, N. Y. A-813.
FAGNANI, GIUSEPPE.
Am. Naples, It. 1819-1873 New York. B-F-T.
FAGUNDES, GUIOMAR.
Fr. b. St. Paul, Fr. 1896. DBA.
FAHEY, EDWARD HENRY.
Eng. London 1844-1907. T.
FAHEY, JAMES.
Eng. Paddington 1804-1885 London. B-DNB-T.
FAHNESTOCK, WALLACE WEIR.
Am. b. Harrisburg, Pa. 1877; ad. 1934 Dorset, Vt. A.
FAHRBACH, KARL LUDWIG.
Ger. Heidelberg 1835-1902 Düsseldorf. B-T.
FAIG, [Mrs.] FRANCES WILEY.
Am. ad. 1934 Cinn., O. A-F.
FAILING, FRANCIS.
Am. ad. 1934 Ind., Ind. M.
FAILLE, CARL ARTHUR.
Am. b. Detroit, Mich. 1883; ad. 1934 San Diego, Calif. A.
FAIR, ROBERT.
Am. Ireland 1847-1907 Phila., Pa. A06-B-F.
FAIRBAIRN, IDA M.
Eng. ex. 1934 in London. M.
FAIRBANKS, AVARD TENNYSON. (S)
Am. b. Provo, Utah 1897; ad. 1934 Ann Arbor, Mich. A-Cs-F-W-46.
FAIRBANKS, [Mrs.] FRANCIS J.
Am. b. 1835; d. 1913 Paterson, N. J. A0X1.
FAIRBANKS, FRANK PERLEY.
Am. b. Boston, Mass. 1875; ad. 1934 Rome, It. A-B-F-W.
FAIRBANKS, J. LEO. (P-S)
Am. ad. 1934 Corvalis, Ore. A.

FAIRBANKS, John B.
Am. b. Payson, Utah 1855; ad. 1934 Salt Lake City, Utah. A.
FAIRBOLT, Frederick William. (Eg)
Eng. London 1814-1866 Brompton. B-DNB-T.
FAIRCHILD, Charles Willard. (Ill)
Am. b. Marinette, Wis. 1886; ad. 1934 New York. A.
FAIRCHILD, E. N.
Am. ad. 1935 New York. M.
FAIRCHILD, Louis. (Eg)
Am. b. Farmington, Conn. 1800. [No death date.] F-T-2-3-6-7.
FAIRCHILD, Mary. *see* Low, M. F.
FAIRCHILD, May. (Min)
Mrs. Charles Nelson Fairchild.
Am. b. Boston, Mass.; ad. 1934 Rhinebeck, N. Y. A.
FAIRCLOUGH, W. (Et)
Eng. ex. 1934 London. M.
FAIRFAX, D. R.
Am. ac. 1835 in Phila., Pa. [No death date.] F.
FAIRFIELD, Charles.
Eng. London 1759/61-1804 Brompton. B-DNB-T.
FAIRLAND, Thomas.
Eng. London 1804-1852 Same. B-DNB-T.
FAIRLESS, Thomas Kerr.
Eng. Hexham 1825-1853 Same. DNB-T.
FAIRMAN, David. (Eg)
Am. b. 1782; d. 1915 Phila., Pa. B-F-7-169.
FAIRMAN, Gideon. (Eg)
Am. b. 1774; d. 1827 Phila., Pa. 7-147.
FAIRMAN, James.
Am. Scotland 1825-1904 New York. A05-C-T.
FAIRMAN, Richard. (Eg)
Am. b. 1788; d. 1821 Phila., Pa. F-T-2-7.
FAISTAUER, Antoine [or Anton].
Aus. b. 1887; d. 1930 in Austria. M.
FAITHORNE, William [The Elder]. (Eg)
Eng. London 1616-1691. B-Bd-DNB-T-364-880.
FAITHORNE, William [The Younger]. (Eg)
Eng. London 1656-1701. B-Bd-DNB-T-364-880.
FAIVRE, Jules Abel.
Fr. b. Lyons 1867. B-DBA-T.
FAIVRE, Léon Maxime.
Fr. ac. 1877-1910 in Paris. B-C-T.
FAIVRE-DUFFER, Louis Stanislas.
Fr. Nancy 1818-1897. B-T.
FALAT, Julian [or Julien].
Pol. Galizien 1853-1929. B-DBA-T.
FALCH [or Falk], Jeremias.
Ger. 1609/10-1677. T.
FALCH [or Falk], Johann.
Ger. 1687-1727. B-T.
FALCONE, Aniello [or Oracolo].
It. Naples 1600-1665 Same. B-E-T.
FALCONER, John M.
Am. Scotland 1820-1903 New York. A04-B-T-4-15.
FALCONET, Maurice Étienne. (S)
Fr. Paris 1716-1791 Same. B-E-Hs-T-675.
FALCONET, Pierre Étienne.
Fr. Paris 1741-1791 Same. B-T.
FALCONETTO, Giovanni Maria.
It. Verona 1458/68-1534/40 Padua. T-V.
FALCONNIER, Léon. (S)
Fr. Ancy 1811-1876. B-T.
FALENS, Karel van.
Flem. Antwerp 1683-1733 Paris. C-T-722.
FALERO, Luis.
Sp. Toledo 1851-1896 London. B-T.
FALGUIÈRE, Jean Alexandre Joseph. (S)
Fr. Toulouse 1831-1900 Paris. B-E-Hs-T.
FALILEIEV, Vadim [Dmitrievich].
Rus. b. 1879 in Russia. T.
FALK, Anna Louise.
Am. b. Branford Point, Conn. 1907; ad. 1934 Branford, Conn. A.
FALK, Nat. (Ill.)
Am. ad. 1934 Sunnyside Gardens, N. Y. M.
FALKNER, Mary.
Am. ad. 1935 Long Beach, Calif. M.
FALLER, Louis Clément.
Fr. Halsheim 1819-1901 Paris. B-T.
FALLS, Charles Buckles. (Ill.)
Am. b. Ft. Wayne, Ind. 1874; ad. 1934 New York. A-F-W.
FALLS, De Witt Clinton.
Am. b. New York 1864; ad. 1934 Same. A28-B-F-W.
FALTER, John. (Ill.)
Am. ad. 1934 New York. M.
FANCELLI, Domenico di Alessandro. (S)
Sp. Settignano 1469-1519 Zaragoza. Hs-T.
FANCELLI, Pandolfo. (S)
It. b. Mantua; d. 1526 Pisa. T.
FANCHER, Louis. (Ill.)
Am. b. Minn., Minn. 1884; ad. 1915 New York. A12.
FANELLI, Francesco. (S)
It. b. Florence; ac. 1610-1665. DNB-T.
FANGEL, Maud Tousey. (Ill.)
Mrs. H. G. Fangel.
Am. ad. 1934 New York. A12-M.
FAN K'UAN.
Chinese. ac. 990-1030. E.
FANNER, Alice Maud.
Mrs. Alice Maud Taite.
Eng. b. Surrey; ad. 1929 London. T.
FANNING, Ralph.
Am. b. New York 1889; ad. 1934 Columbus, O. A.
FANNING, William Sanders.
Am. b. Detroit, Mich. 1887; ad. 1934 Same. A.
FANONE, Il. *see* Civerchio, Vincenzo.
FANSHAW, Herbert Valentine.
Can. b. Sheffield, Eng.; ad. 1935 Winnipeg, Man., Can. M.
FANSHAW, Samuel Raymond.
Am. New York 1814-1888 Same. F-T-6.
FANTIN-LATOUR, Ignace Henri Jean Théodore.
Fr. Grenoble 1836-1904 Buré. B-DBA-E-T.
FA PRESTO. *see* Giordana, Luca Fapresto.
FARASYN, Edgard [or Émile].
Belg. b. Antwerp 1858. DBA.
FARBER, [Mrs.] Effie R.
Am. b. Milwaukee, Wis.; ad. 1934 Same. A.

FARDEL, Robert.
Fr. Besançon 1867-1931 Paris. DBA.
FARGE. *see also* La Farge.
FARGE, Henri.
Fr. b. France 1884; ex. 1933 New York. DBA.
FARGEOT, Ferdinand.
Fr. b. Lyons 1880. DBA.
FARINA, Pasquale.
Am. b. Naples, It. 1864; ad. 1934 Phila., Pa. A.
FARINATO, Giovanni Battista II.
It. Verona 1570-1605 Same. B-T.
FARINATO, Paulo.
It. Verona 1522/5-1606. B-C-E-T-722.
FARINGTON, George.
Eng. Leigh 1752-1788 India. B-DNB-T.
FARINGTON, Joseph.
Eng. Leigh 1747-1821. B-DNB-T.
FARIS, Benjamin Howard.
Am. b. St. Clairsville, O. 1862. A28.
FARJEON, Elliot Emanuel.
Am. b. New York; ad. 1934 Pittsburgh, Pa. A.
FARKAS, Étienne.
Fr. ad. 1931 Paris. DBA.
FARLEIGH, John. (Ill.)
Eng. ad. 1935 in London. M.
FARLEY, Frederic.
Am. ex. 1934 Balt., Md. M.
FARLEY, James.
Am. ex. 1934 New York. M.
FARLEY, Richard Blossom.
Am. b. Poultney, Vt. 1875; ad. 1934 Phila., Pa. A-B-F-W.
FARLEY, William.
Eng. ex. 1935 London. M.
FARLOW, Harry.
Am. b. Chicago 1882; ad. 1934 Forest Hills, N. Y. A-F.
FARMER, Brigitta Moran.
Mrs. Thomas P. Farmer.
Am. b. Lyons, N. Y.; ad. 1934 Syracuse, N. Y. A.
FARMER, John. (Eg.)
Am. Half Moon, N. Y. 1798-1859 Detroit, Mich. F-2-7.
FARNAM, Suzanne Silvercruys. (S)
Mrs. Henry W. Farnam.
Am. b. Maeseyck, Belg.; ad. 1934 New Haven, Conn. A.
FARNDON, Walter.
Am. b. England 1876; ad. 1934 Douglaston, L. I., N. Y. A-B-F-W.
FARNESIUS, Abraham. *see* Furnerius, A.
FARNHAM, Jessica Shirley.
Am. b. New Rochelle, N. Y.; ad. 1934 Birmingham, Ala. A.
FARNHAM, Sally James. (S)
Mrs. Paulding Farnham.
Am. b. Ogdensburg, N. Y.; ad. 1934 New York. F-W-46.
FARNSWORTH, Jerry.
Am. b. Dalton, Ga. 1895; ad. 1934 No. Truro, Mass. A-F-W.
FARNSWORTH, [Mrs.] Louise Richards.
Am. b. Salt Lake City, Utah; ex. 1934 New York. M.
FARNUM, Herbert Cyrus.
Am. b. Gloucester, Mass. 1886; ad. 1935 Prov., R. I. A12-F.
FARNY, Henry F.
Am. b. Ribeauville, Fr. 1847-1916 Cinn., O. A014-B-C-F-T-46.
FARQUHARSON, David.
Scot. Perth 1840-1907 Birnam. B-DNB-T.
FARQUHARSON, Joseph.
Scot. Edinburgh 1846-1935 Finzean.
B-T-Wa-Obit. N. Y. papers, 4-16-1935.
FARR, Helen.
Am. ad. 1934 New York. M.
FARRAR, Thomas Charles.
Am. London 1838-1891 New York. B-F-T-15.
FARRÉ, Henri.
Fr. Foix 1871-1934 Chicago.
B-DBA-T-Obit. N. Y. papers, 10-7-1934.
FARRELL, Katherine Levin.
Mrs. Theo. P. Farrell.
Am. b. Phila., Pa.; ad. 1934 Same. A.
FARRELLY, Regina A. (Lith.)
Am. ex. 1935 New York. M.
FARRER, Henry. (Et.)
Am. London 1843-1903 Brooklyn, N. Y.
A04-B-C-DAB-F-T-W2-4-15.
FARRER, Thomas C.
Eng. London 1839-1891 Same. B-C-T.
FARRIER, Robert.
Eng. Chelsea 1796-1879 London. B-DNB-T.
FARRINGTON. *see* Farington.
FARROW, William McKnight.
Am. b. Dayton, O. 1885; ad. 1934 Chicago. A.
FAR-SI, Georges.
Fr. b. Paris 1866. DBA.
FARUFFINI, Federico.
It. Milan 1831-1869 Perugia. B-T.
FASANO, Clara.
Am. ad. 1935 New York. M.
FASOLO, Berardino.
It. Pavia 1489-1526 Genoa. T.
FASOLO, Giovanni Antonio.
It. ac. 1552-1572 in Venice. T.
FASOLO, Lorenzo [da Pavia].
It. b. Pavia; ac. 1490-1518 in Genoa. C-T.
FASSETT, [Mrs.] Cornelia Adele.
Am. Owasco, N. Y. 1831-1898 Wash., D. C.
A01-B-C-F-T-15.
FASSETT, Truman E.
Am. b. Elmira, N. Y. 1885; ad. 1934 Bronxville, N. Y. A.
FATH, René Maurice.
Fr. Paris 1850-1922. B-DBA-T.
FATTORI, Giovanni.
It. Leghorn 1825/8-1908. B-T.
FATTORI, Il. *see* Penni, Gianfrancesco.
FAUCONNIER, Émile Eugène.
Fr. Paris 1857-1920. B-DBA.
FAUGERON, Adolphe.
Fr. b. Paris 1866. B-DBA.
FAUGHT, Elizabeth Jean. (S)
Mrs. Ray Clinton Faught.
Am. b. Richmond, Va. 1883; ad. 1934 Balt., Md. A.

FAULEY, Albert C.
Am. Fultonham, O. 1859-1919 Columbus, O. A016-B.
FAULKNER, Barry. (Mu.)
Am. b. Keene, N. H. 1881; ad. 1934 New York. A-F-T-W.
FAULKNER, Benjamin Rawlinson.
Eng. Manchester 1787-1849 Fulham. B-DNB.
FAULKNER, Herbert Waldron.
Am. b. Stamford, Conn. 1860; ad. 1934 Wash., D. C. A-B-F-T-W.
FAULKNER, John.
Ir. ac. 1852-1890 in London. B-T.
FAULKNER, Joshua Wilson.
Eng. Manchester 1780-1820 London. B-DNB-T.
FAULKNER, Kady B.
Am. b. Syracuse, N. Y. 1901; ad. 1934 Lincoln, Neb. A.
FAUNTLEROY, Martha Lorimer.
Am. b. No. Yakima, Wash. 1910; ad. 1934 Richmond, Va. A.
FAURE, Hélène. (Min.)
Fr. b. Montbrison 1878; d. 1932. DBA.
FAUSETT, Dean.
Am. ex. 1935 New York. M.
FAUSETT, Lynn.
Am. ex. 1934 New York. M.
FAUTRIER, Jean.
Fr. b. Paris 1897. DBA.
FAUVEAU, Félicie de. (S)
Fr. Florence, It. 1799-1886 Paris. B-Hs.
FAUVEL, Georges Henri.
Fr. b. Havre; ac. 1889-1930 in Paris. B-DBA.
FAUVELET, Jean Baptiste.
Fr. Bordeaux 1819-1883 Chartres. B-T.
FAVA, Giangiacomo. *see* Macrino d'Alba.
FAVAI, Gennaro.
It. b. Venice 1879; ac. 1935. DBA.
FAVANNE, Henri Antoine de.
Fr. London 1668-1752 Paris. B-T.
FAVORSKY, Vladimir. (Ill)
Rus. ad. 1935 Moscow. M.
FAVORY, André.
Fr. b. Paris 1889. DBA.
FAVRAY [or Fauray], Antoine de [Chevalier].
Fr. Bagnolet 1706-1791 Malta. B-T-722.
FAVRE, Le. *see* Lefevre.
FAWCETT, George.
Am. ad. 1934 Coral Gables, Fla. M.
FAWCETT, Robert. (Ill.)
Am. ad. 1934 Ridgefield, Conn. M.
FAXON, Charles Edward.
Am. b. 1845; d. 1918 Boston, Mass. A015.
FAXON, William Bailey.
Am. b. Hartford, Conn. 1849; ad. 1934 New York. A-W.
FAY, Clark. (Ill.)
Am. ad. 1934 Oise, France. M.
FAY, Gaston.
Am. ac. 1870. M.
FAY, Nellie.
Am. b. Eureka, Calif. 1870; ad. 1935 San Fran., Calif. A12-F.
FAYDHERBE, Luc [or Lukas]. (S)
Belg. Mechlin 1617-1694/7. Hs-T.
FAYUM [or Fayoum] Paintings.
Painted portraits on Mummy cases found in the Fayoum, Egypt. Graeco-Roman period. 1st and 2nd Cent. A.D. These may be seen in the U. S., at the Metropolitan Museum, N. Y.; the Fogg Museum, Cambridge, Mass., and some other museums. *see also* Encyclopedia Brittanica, 14th Ed.
FEARNLEY, Thomas.
Nor. Norway 1802-1842 Munich, Ger. B-680.
FEARON, Hilda.
Am. d. 1917; ex. Pittsburgh, Pa. M.
FEARY, John.
Eng. 1745/50-1778 London. B-DNB-T.
FÉAU, Amédée.
Fr. b. Paris 1872. DBA.
FEBVRE, Claude le. *see* Lefebvre.
FECHIN, Nicolai Ivanovich.
Am. b. Kazan, Rus. 1881; ad. 1935 Taos, N. M. A.
FECHNER, Johannes [The Younger].
Ger. b. Berlin 1860. B-DBA-T.
FEDARB, Daphne.
Eng. ex. 1935 London. M.
FEDARB, Ernest J.
Eng. ex. 1935 London. M.
FEDDEN, A. Romilly.
Eng. b. 1875. Wa1929.
FEDER, Adolphe [or Aisik or Aisix].
Fr. b. Odessa, Rus. 1886. DBA.
FEDERICO, Tedesco.
Ger. ac. 1400-1424 in Germany. T.
FEDERIGHI, Antonio. *see* Antonio, F.
FEDI, Pio. (S)
It. Viterbo 1815-1892 Florence. B-T.
FEER, Lisette.
Swi. Zurich 1794-1866. B.
FEGDAL, Suzanne.
Fr. b. Paris; ac. 1923-1931. DBA.
FEHDMER, Richard.
Ger. b. Königsberg 1860. T.
FEHR, Henry Charles. (S)
Eng. b. Kent 1867. B-Hs-Wa.
FEHRER, Oscar.
Am. b. New York 1872; ad. 1934 Lyme, Conn. A.
FEI, Paolo di Giovannio. *see* Paoli di G.
FEIGIN, Dorothy Lubell.
Am. b. New York 1903; ad. 1934 Same. A.
FEININGER, Lyonel.
Ger. ex. 1934 Northampton, Mass. DBA.
FEINT, Adrian.
Aust. ac. 1933 in Australia. M.
FEIST, Erika.
Am. ex. 1935 New York. M.
FEITELSON, Lorser.
Am. b. Paris; ac. 1934 Calif. M.
FEKE, Robert.
Am. Oyster Bay, L. I., N. Y. 1705/24-1750/69 Bermuda. B-Bd-F-T-2-4-182-355-669.
FELDMAN, Charles.
Am. b. Lublin, Rus. 1893; ad. 1934 New York. A.
FELDMAN, [Dr.] George.
Am. ad. 1934 New York. M.
FELDMAN, Hilda.
Am. b. Newark, N. J. 1899; ad. 1934 Maplewood, N. J. A.
FELDMAN, Max.
Ger. b. 1869 in Germany. Fa-M.

FÉLIX, Eugène.
Aus. Vienna 1837-1906 Same. B-T.
FÉLIX, Franz. (Ill)
Am. ad. 1935 Monsey, N. Y. M.
FÉLIX, Léon Pierre.
Fr. b. Périgueux 1869. B-DBA.
FELKES, Ruth Kate.
Mrs. W. D. Thomas.
Am. b. St. Louis, Mo. 1889; ad. 1934 Same. A.
FELL, Herbert Granville.
Eng. b. London 1872. Wa.
FELL, Olive. (Et)
Am. ad. 1935 Cody, Wyo. M.
FELLOWES, Frank Wayland.
Am. b. 1833; d. 1900 New Haven, Conn. A020.
FELLOWES, James.
Eng. ac. 1710-1730 in Cambridge, Eng. B-DNB-T.
FELLOWS, Albert P. (Et)
Am. b. Selma, Ala. 1864; ad. 1934 Phila., Pa. A-F-T.
FELON, Joseph. (S)
Fr. Bordeaux 1818-1896. B-T.
FELSZTYNSKI, Stefan.
Pol. b. Cracow 1888. M.
FELTEN, Major. (Ill)
Am. ad. 1934 Darien, Conn. M.
FELTRE, Morto da. [Luzzo].
It. b. Feltre; ac. 1480-1519 in Venice. E-V.
FELTRINI, Andre di Giovanni di Lorenzo.
It. Florence 1477-1548 Same. T-V.
FENDI, Peter. (P-S)
Aus. Vienna 1796-1842 Same. B-T.
FENN, Harry.
Am. Richmond, Eng. 1845-1911 Montclair, N. J. A09-B-F-T-46.
FENNELL, John Greville. (Ill)
Eng. 1807-1885 London. DNB-T.
FENNER, Maude Richmond.
Mrs. Albert Fenner.
Am. b. Bristol, R. I. 1868; ad. 1934 Prov., R. I. A.
FENSKE, Paula.
Am. b. St. Louis, Mo. 1882; ad. 1934 Same. A.
FENTON, Beatrice. (S)
Am. b. Phila., Pa. 1887; ad. 1934 Same. A-Cs-F-W.
FENTON, Carroll Lane. (Ill)
Am. ad. 1935 New York. M.
FENTON, Hallie Champlin.
Am. b. St. Louis, Mo. 1880; ad. 1934 Bronxville, N. Y. A.
FENTON, John William.
Am. b. Conewango Valley, N. Y. 1875; ad. 1934 Westport, Conn. A.
FÉNYES, Adolf.
Hun. b. Kecskemet 1876; ex. 1934 in London. B-T.
FEO, Charles de. *see* De Feo, C.
FÉRAT, Serge [Jastrebzoff].
Rus. b. Moscow 1881; ex. 1934 New York; ad. 1935 Paris. DBA.
FERDINAND, Louis Élle. *see* Élle, F.
FERENCZY, Károly [or Karl].
Hun. 1862-1917 Vienna, Aus. B-T.
FERG, Franz de Paula [or Francis Paul].
Aus. Vienna 1689-1740 London. B-DNB-T-722.
FERGUSON, Alice L. L.
Mrs. H. G. Ferguson.
Am. b. Wash., D. C.; ad. 1934 Same. A.
FERGUSON, [Mrs.] Dorothy H.
Am. b. Alton, Ill. 1896; ad. 1934 Same. A.
FERGUSON, Duncan. (S)
Am. b. Shanghai, China 1901; ad. 1934 Cape Neddick, Me. A-F-2.
FERGUSON, Edward L. (Eg)
Am. Illinois 1859-1915 New York. A012-F.
FERGUSON, Eleanor M.
Am. b. Hartford, Conn. 1876; ad. 1934 Same. A.
FERGUSON, Helen.
Eng. ex. 1935 London. M.
FERGUSON, Henry A.
Am. Glens Falls, N. Y. 1842-1911 New York. A09-C-F-T.
FERGUSON, John Duncan.
Scot. b. Edinburgh 1874; ex. 1932 London. T-825.
FERGUSON, Lillian.
Am. b. Windsor, Can. 1877. A.
FERGUSON, Nancy Maybin.
Am. b. Phila., Pa.; ad. 1934 Same. A-F.
FERGUSON, William Gowe.
Scot. Scotland 1632/3-1695 London. B-T.
FERGUSON, William Hugh.
Am. b. Reading, Pa. 1905; ad. 1934 Same. A-F.
FERNALD, Helen Elizabeth.
Am. b. Balt., Md. 1891; ad. 1934 Bryn Mawr, Pa. A.
FERNÁNDEZ, Antonio Arias.
Sp. Madrid 1620?-1684. M.
FERNÁNDEZ, Francisco.
Sp. Madrid 1605-1646. B-T.
FERNÁNDEZ [or Hernández], Gregorio. (S)
Sp. ac. 1576-1635 in Vallaloid. Hs-T.
FERNÁNDEZ, Vasco [Grão Vasco].
Por. 1541?-1594? B-T-Wi.
FERNÁNDEZ DE NAVARRETE, Juán.
Sp. Logroño 1526-1579 Toledo. T.
FERNÁNDEZ DEL MORAL, Lesines. *see* Moral, L. F.
FERNÁNDEZ Y GONZALES, Domingo.
Sp. ac. 1553-1558 in Vallaloid. B-T.
FERNARD-TROCHAIN, Jean.
Fr. b. Rueil 1879. DBA.
FERNBACH, Agnes. (Et)
Am. ad. 1935 New York. M.
FERNE, Hortence T.
Am. b. New York; ad. 1934 Phila., Pa. A.
FERNELEY, John E.
Eng. 1781-1860 Melton, Eng. B-DNB-T.
FERNOW, Bernice Pauahi Andrews. (Min)
Mrs. B. E. Fernow, Jr.
Am. b. Jersey City, N. J. 1881; ad. 1934 Clemson College, S. C. A-F.
FERRABOSCO. *see* Forabosco.
FERRAGLIO, Ludovico G. (S)
Am. ac. 1933. M.
FERRARI, Defendente di.
It. Chivasso 1481-1546. B-T.

FERRARI, Febo. (S)
Am. b. Pallanza, It. 1865; ad. 1934 Short Beach, Conn. A-Cs-F.
FERRARI, Gaudenzio.
It. Valduggia 1470/80-1546/9 Milan. B-Bd-E-T-722.
FERRARI, Giuseppe.
It. Rome 1773-1864. B-T.
FERRARI, Luca [da Reggio].
It. Reggio 1605-1654 Padua. C-T.
FERRARIO, Carlo. (S)
Swi. 1833-1907 Milan, It. B-T.
FERRARIS, Arthur von.
Hun. b. Vienna 1864; ad. 1935 Same. B-DBA-T.
FERRARY, Désire Maurice. (S)
Fr. Embrun 1852-1904. B-T.
FERRAZZI, Ferruccio.
It. b. 1891; ad. 1935 Rome; ex. 1934 Pittsburgh, Pa. M.
FERRER, Bassa. *see* Bassa F.
FERRER, Vera L. (Min.)
Am. b. New York 1895; ad. 1934 Little Neck, L. I., N. Y. A.
FERRETA, Ercole. (S)
It. 1610-1686 Rome. B-Hs-T.
FERRETTI DA IMOLA, Giovanni Domenico.
It. Florence 1692-1769. B-T.
FERRI, Ciro.
It. Rome 1634-1689. B-C-E-T.
FERRIER, Gabriel Joseph Marie Augustin.
Fr. Nimes 1847-1914 Paris. B-C-DBA-T.
FERRIS, Bernice Branson. (Ill.)
Mrs. Warren Wesley Ferris.
Am. b. Astoria, Ill.; ad. 1934 Alexandria, Va. A.
FERRIS, Edythe.
Mrs. Raymond H. Ferris.
Am. b. Riverton, N. J. 1897; ad. 1934 Phila., Pa. A-F.
FERRIS, Jean Léon Gérome.
Am. Phila., Pa. 1863-1930 Same. A027-B-DAB-F-T-W16.
FERRIS, Stephen James.
Am. Plattsburg, N. Y. 1835-1915 Phila., Pa. A012-B-C-F-T-40-45.
FERRIS, Warren Wesley.
Am. b. Rochester, N. Y. 1890; ad. 1934 Alexandria, Va. A.
FERRISS, Hugh. (Ill.)
Am. b. St. Louis, Mo. 1889; ad. 1934 New York. A-F.
FERRUCCI [or Ferruzzi] Family.
It. ac. 15-18th Cent. in Italy. T.
FERRUCCI, Francesco [or Ceddo del Tadda].
It. Fiesole 1497/1517-1585. B-T-V.
FERRUZZI, Roberto.
It. b. Sebenico 1854. T.
FERRY, Frances.
Am. ad. 1935 New York. M.
FERRY, [Mrs.] Isabelle H.
Am. b. Williamsburg, Mass.; ad. 1934 Easthampton, Mass. A.
FERRY, Jules Jean.
Fr. b. Bordeaux 1844; ac. 1905 Paris. C-T.
FERSTADT, Louis Goodman.
Am. b. Russia 1900; ad. 1934 New York. A.
FERY, Lucie Louise.
Fr. Paris 1855-1922 Charleston, S. C. M.
FESELEN [or Feselein], Melchior.
Ger. b. Passau; ac. 1521-1538 in Ingolstadt. C-T.
FESZTY [or Feszti], Árpád.
Hun. 1856-1914 Lovrana. B-T.
FETHERSTON, Edith.
Am. ex. 1933 New York. M.
FETI [or Fetti], Domenico.
It. Rome 1589-1624 Venice. B-C-T-722.
FEUCHÈRE, Jean Jacques. (S)
Fr. Paris 1807-1852. B-T.
FEUERBACH, Anselm.
Ger. Spire 1829-1850 Venice, It. B-C-E-T-670-671.
FEUERSTEIN, Martin.
Ger. b. Barr 1856; ac. 1920 in Munich. B-T.
FEULLE, Stanford.
Am. ex. 1934 Minn., Minn. M.
FEVOLA, Félix Pascal. (S)
Fr. b. Poissy 1882. B-DBA.
FEYEN, Jacques Eugène.
Fr. 1815-1908. B-T.
FEYEN-PERRIN, François Nicolas Auguste.
Fr. Nancy 1826-1888 Paris. B-C-T.
FIACCO, Orlando. *see* Flacco, O.
FIALETTI, Odoardo.
It. Bologna 1573-1638 Venice. B-T.
FIAMBERTI [da Campione], Tommaso. (S)
It. ac. 1480-1524/5 in Cesena. T.
FIAMMIMGO, Il. *see* Duquesnoy, François. *see* Honthorst, Gérald van.
FIASELLA, Domenico.
It. Sarzana 1589-1669 Genoa. B-T.
FICHEL, Benjamin Eugène.
Fr. Paris 1826-1895 Same. B-T.
FICQUET [or Fiquet], Étienne. (Eg)
Fr. Paris 1719-1794. B-T-880.
FICTOOR. *see* Victoor, Jan.
FIDLER, Harry.
Eng. b. Teffont, Eng.; ac. 1930. DBA-Wa1929.
FIELD, Charlotte E.
Am. b. 1838; d. 1920 Brooklyn, N. Y. A017.
FIELD, Edward Loyal.
Am. Galesburg, Ill. 1856-1914 New York. A0X1-B-F.
FIELD, Hamilton Easter.
Am. Brooklyn, N. Y. 1873-1922 Same. A019-B-F.
FIELD, [Mrs.] Herman H.
Am. Stoughton, Mass. 1864-1931 Chicago. A028-F.
FIELD, Jason.
Am. ad. 1934 Los Angeles, Calif. M.
FIELD, [Mrs.] Louis Blogett.
Am. b. Boston, Mass.; ad. 1934 Wellesley, Mass. A.
FIELD, Marriott.
Eng. ac. 1850. M.
FIELD, [Mrs.] Mary.
Am. b. Stoughton, Mass. 1864; ad. 1915 Brooklyn, N. Y. A12-F.
FIELD, Robert.
Am. b. England; ac. 1793-1819 Jamaica, West Indies. B-F-T-2-6-7-40-45-171-179-182-184.
FIELD, Walter.
Eng. Hampstead 1837-1901 Same. B-DNB-T.

FIELDING, ANTHONY VANDYKE COPLEY.
Eng. 1787-1855 Worthing, Eng. B-Bd-DNB-E-T.
FIELDING, NEWTON SMITH.
Eng. 1799-1856 London. B-DNB-T.
FIELDING, THALES.
Eng. London 1793-1837 Same. B-DNB-T.
FIELDING, THEODORE HARRY ADOLPHUS. (Eg)
Eng. 1781-1851 Croydon. B-DNB-T.
FIELDING, THOMAS. (Eg)
Br. b. 1758; d. 1790. DNB-T.
FIELDS, MITCHELL. (S)
Am. b. Rumania 1900; ad. 1934 New York. A.
FIELIUS. *see* Tilius.
FIENE, ERNEST.
Am. b. Elberfeld, Ger. 1894; ad. 1934 Southbury, Conn. A-779.
FIENE, PAUL. (S)
Am. ex. 1934 New York. M.
FIERO, ÉMILIE. (S)
Am. b. U. S.; ad. 1930 Paris, Fr. A12-DBA.
FIESINGER, GABRIEL. (Eg)
Ger. Offenburg 1723-1807 London. T.
FIESOLE, GIOVANNI DA. *see* Angelico, Fra.
FIESOLE, MINO DA GIOVANNI. (S)
It. Poppi 1431-1484 Fiesole. E-Hs-V.
FIGARI, JUÁN CARLOS.
Uruguayan. Montevideo 1894-1927 Paris. DBA.
FIGARI, PEDRO.
Uruguayan. b. Montevideo 1861. DBA.
FIGINO, AMBROGIO GIOVANNI.
It. Milan 1548-1608 Same. B-T.
FIGURA, HANS. (Et)
Aus. ex. 1927 New York. M.
FILASTRE-DUMONT, GÉRARD.
Fr. Cussac 1891-1933 Same. DBA.
FILDES, [Sir] SAMUEL LUKE.
Eng. Liverpool 1844-1927 London. B-C-E-T.
FILEMYR, JOSEPH J.
Am. b. Phila., Pa.; ac. 1934 Same. M.
FILIPEPI, SANDRO. *see* Botticello.
FILIPPO DA VERONA.
It. ac. 1509-1515 in Verona. T.
FILLEUL, PAUL.
Fr. b. Paris; ad. 1926 Same. DBA.
FILLIAN, JOHN. (Eg)
Br. ac. 1658-1680. B-DNB-T.
FILLIARD, ERNST.
Fr. Chambéry 1868-1933. B-DBA.
FILOSINI.
It. ac. 1870. M.
FINCH, FRANCIS OLIVER.
Eng. London 1802-1862. B-DNB-T.
FINCH, [Miss] R.
Eng. ac. 1795 London. T.
FINCK, FURMAN.
Am. ex. 1933 New York. M.
FINDEN, WILLIAM. (Eg)
Eng. 1787-1852 London. B-DNB-E-T.
FINDLAY, WILLIAM.
Br. b. 1720; d. 1780. M.
FINI, LÉONOR.
It. ex. 1934 Paris. M.

FINIGUERRA, MASO. (Eg)
[Tommaso di Antonio.]
It. Florence, It. 1426-1464 Same. B-T-V.
FINK, AUGUST.
Bav. b. Munich 1846; d. 1916. B-T.
FINK, BOB.
Am. ad. 1934 Elmsford, N. Y. M.
FINK, DENMAN.
Am. b. Springdale, Pa. 1880; ad. 1934 Haworth, N. J. A-F.
FINK, FREDERICK.
Am. Little Falls, N. Y. 1817-1849. B-Bd-F-T-4.
FINK, LUCILLE.
Am. b. Chicago, Ill. 1910; ad. 1934 Same. A.
FINKELBURG, AUGUSTA.
Am. b. Fountain City, Wis.; ad. 1934 Kimmswick, Mo. A.
FINKLE, MELIK. (S)
Am. ad. 1935 New York. Cs-M.
FINLAYSON, JOHN. (Eg)
Eng. 1730-1776 London. B-T.
FINN, HERBERT JOHN.
Eng. b. London 1861; ex. 1934 Same. Wa.
FINN, JAMES WALL.
Am. d. 1913 in France. A011-B-71.
FINN, JANE E.
Am. ex. 1934 New York. M.
FINN, KATHLEEN MACY.
Am. ad. 1934 Ardsley, N. Y. M.
FINNEMORE, JOSEPH. (Et)
Eng. b. Birmingham 1860; ad. 1935 Northwood, Eng. T-Wa.
FINNEY, SAMUEL. (Min)
Eng. Wilmslow 1719-1798. B-DNB-T.
FINNIE, JOHN.
Scot. Aberdeen 1829-1907 Liverpool, Eng. B-DNB-T.
FINOT, JULES [Baron].
Fr. b. Guéret; ac. 1856-1882 Paris. B-T.
FINSONIUS [or Finson], LOUIS.
Flem. Bruges, Belg. 1580-1632 Arles, Fr. B-T-722.
FINSTERWALD, CORINNE [Mrs. Rowe].
Am. ad. 1934 Hampton, Conn. M.
FINTA, ALEXANDER. (S)
Am. b. Hungary 1881; ad. 1934 New York. A.
FIORDALISI, PETER. (Eg-P)
Am. b. Union City, N. J. 1904; ad. 1934 West New York, N. J. M.
FIORE, AGNOLO ANTELLO DEL. (S)
It. ac. 1645 in Naples. B-T.
FIORE, ANTHONY JOSEPH. (S)
Am. b. New York 1912; ad. 1934 Same. A.
FIORE, JACOBELLO DEL.
It. ac. 1385-1439 in Venice. B-T.
FIORE, NICCOLÒ ANTONIO DEL. *see* Colantonio, N. A.
FIORE, ROSARIO. (S)
Am. ad. 1934 New York. M.
FIORENTINO, PIER FRANCESCO.
It. ac. 1470-1500 in Florence. T-V.
FIORENTINO, ROSSO.
It. Florence 1494-1541. V.
FIORENZO DI LORENZO.
It. Perugia 1440/5-1522/5. B-E-T-V.
FIORI, ERNESTO DE. (S)
It. b. Rome 1884. DBA.

FIORI DA URBINO. *see* Barocci, Federigo.
FIORILLO, JOHANN DOMINICUS.
Ger. Hamburg 1748-1821 Göttingen. B-E-T.
FIORINI, GIOVANNI BATTISTA.
It. b. Bologna; d. 1595 Same. B-T-722.
FIRENZE, ANDREA DA. *see* Andrea da F.
FIRENZE, BERNARDO DA. *see* Daddi, B.
FIRESTONE, ISADORE LOUIS.
Am. b. Austria-Hungary 1894; ad. 1934 New York. A.
FIRK, R. (S)
Pol. b. Warsaw. 798.
FIRLE, WALTHER.
Ger. b. Breslau 1859. B-T.
FIRMIN, ALBERT EDWIN. (S)
Am. b. Mexia, Tex. 1890; ad. 1934 Dallas, Tex. A.
FIRMIN, AMBROISE. (S)
Fr. ac. 1386 in Cambrai. B.
FIRMIN, IRENE.
Am. ad. 1934 Toledo, O. M.
FIRMIN-GIRARD, MARIS FRANÇOIS.
Fr. Poncin 1838-1921. C.
FIRN, EDWARD.
Am. ad. 1935 Cinn., O. M.
FISCHER. *see also* Fisher.
FISCHER, ADAM. (S)
Fr. ad. 1930 in Paris. DBA-798.
FISCHER, ANTON OTTO. (Ill)
Am. b. Munich, Bav. 1882; ad. 1934 Kingston, N. Y. A-F-W.
FISCHER, AUGUST FERDINAND. (S)
Ger. Berlin 1805-1866 Same. B-T.
FISCHER FAMILY
Ger. ac. 18th Cent. in Germany. T.
FISCHER, JOHN GEORGE PAUL.
Ger. Hanover 1786-1875 England. B-DNB-T.
FISCHER, MARTIN.
Am. b. Kiel, Ger. 1879; ad. 1934 Cinn., O. A.
FISCHER, MARY ALLEN SIGSBEE. (Ill)
Mrs. Anton Otto Fischer.
Am. b. New Orleans, La. 1876; ad. 1934 Kingston, N. Y. A-F-W.
FISCUS, CHARLES JOSEPH.
Am. Ind., Ind. 1861-1884. M.
FISH, F. W.
Am. ad. 1934 New York. M.
FISH, GERTRUDE ELOISE. (S)
Am. Roselle Park, N. J. 1908; ad. 1934 Same. A.
FISH, [Mrs.] MARGARET.
Am. ad. 1934 Palestine, Tex. M.
FISHER. *see also* Fischer.
FISHER, ALANSON.
Am. New Haven, Conn. 1807-1884. T.
FISHER, ALEXANDER. (S)
Eng. b. 1864 in England. B-T-798.
FISHER, ALVAN.
Am. Needham, Mass. 1792-1863 Dedham, Mass. B-Bd-DAB-E-F-T-2-4.
FISHER, ANNA S.
Am. b. Cold Brook, N. Y.; ad. 1934 New York. A-F-W.
FISHER, ANNE.
Am. ad. 1935 Weston, Mass. M.
FISHER, EDWARD. (Eg)
Ir. b. Ireland 1730; d. 1785 London. B-Bd-DNB-T.
FISHER, FLAVIUS J.
Am. Wytheville, Va. 1832-1905 Wash., D. C. A05-B-F-T.
FISHER, GEORGE HAROLD. (Mu)
Am. ad. 1934 Detroit, Mich. A.
FISHER, ["Bud"] H. C. (Cart)
Am. b. Illinois 1884; ad. 1934 New York. W.
FISHER, HARRISON. (Ill)
Am. Brooklyn, N. Y. 1875-1934 New York. A-F-W-46-Obit. N. Y. papers, 1-19-1934.
FISHER, HOWELL TRACY. (Min)
Am. ad. 1934 Phila., Pa. M.
FISHER, HUGH ANTOINE. (Et)
Am. b. 1867; d. 1916 Almeda, Calif. A014-F.
FISHER, JONATHAN.
Ir. b. Dublin; d. 1812 Same. B-DNB-T.
FISHER, MARK WIDDINGTON.
Am. Boston, Mass. 1841-1923 London. A020-B.
FISHER, STEFANI MELTON.
Eng. b. London 1861; ad. 1934 Camberley, Surrey. B-T-Wa.
FISHER, [Mrs.] STOWELL LE CAIN.
Am. b. Wellsville, N. Y. 1906; ad. 1934 New York. A.
FISHER, WILLIAM.
Am. ad. 1935 New York. M.
FISHER, WILLIAM MARK.
Am. Boston, Mass. 1841-1923 London. A020-C-F-T-W10-46.
FISHER, W. R.
Am. b. Indiana; ad. 1934 New York. M.
FISHER-PROUT, [Mrs.] MARGARET.
Eng. b. Chelsea 1881; ad. 1934 East Grinstead. Wa.
FISK, LILLIAN.
Am. ex. 1934 in Paris. DBA.
FISK, WILLIAM.
Eng. Thorp-le-Soken 1796-1872 Danbury. B-DNB-T.
FISK, WILLIAM HENRY.
Eng. 1827-1884 Hampstead. B-DNB-T.
FISKE, CHARLES ALBERT.
Am. Alfred, Me. 1837-1915 Greenwich, Conn. A012-B-F.
FISKE, GERTRUDE.
Am. b. Boston, Mass. 1879; ad. 1934 Same. A-F-W.
FIT, JAN. *see* Fyt, Jan.
FITCH, JOHN. (Eg)
Am. So. Windsor, Conn. 1743-1796 Bardstown, Ky. F-2-7.
FITCH, JOHN LEE.
Am. Hartford, Conn. 1836-1895. B-C-F-T-3-15.
FITGER, ARTHUR HEINRICH WILHELM.
Ger. Delmenhorst 1840-1909. B-T.
FITHIAN, FRANK LIVINGSTON. (Ill)
Am. b. 1866; d. 1935 Haddonfield, N. J. Obit., N. Y. papers 4-10-1935.
FITLER, WILLIAM C.
Am. b. Cinn., O.; ac. 1897-1926. B-F-T.
FITLER, [Mrs.] WILLIAM C.
see Hirst, Claude Raguet.
FITSCH, EUGÈNE CAMILLE. (Et)
Am. b. Alsace, Fr. 1892; ad. 1934 New York. A-F.

FITTLER, JAMES. (Eg)
Eng. London 1758-1835 Turnham. B-DNB-T.
FITTON, HEDLEY. (Et)
Eng. Manchester 1858-1929 London. B-T-Wa1929.
FITTON, JAMES.
Eng. b. Oldham 1899; ad. 1934 Dulwich Village. Wa.
FITTS, CLARA ATWOOD. (Ill)
Mrs. F. W. Fitts.
Am. b. Worcester, Mass. 1874; ad. 1934 Roxbury, Mass. A.
FITZ, RUTHERFORD BENJAMIN.
Am. New York 1855-1891 Peconic, L. I., New York. F-T.
FITZ-RANDOLPH, GRACE. (S)
Am. b. New York; d. 1917 Same. A014-B.
FITZER, KARL H.
Am. b. Kansas City, Mo. 1896; ad. 1934 Same. A.
FITZGERALD, HARRINGTON.
Am. Phila., Pa. 1847-1930 Williamstown, Pa. A027-B-F-T-W16.
FITZGERALD, JAMES.
Am. b. Boston, Mass. 1899; ad. 1934 Monterey, Calif. A.
FITZGERALD, JOHN ANSTER.
Eng. London 1819-1906 Same. B-T.
FITZGERALD, MOLLY.
Am. b. Shelton, Conn. 1889; ad. 1934 Woodmont, Conn. A.
FITZGERALD, PITT L.
Am. b. Wash., D. C. 1893; ad. 1934 Columbus, O. A.
FITZGERALD, ZELDA.
Am. ex. 1934 New York. M.
FITZPATRICK, DANIEL ROBERT. (Cart)
Am. b. Superior, Wis. 1891; ad. 1934 Santa Barbara, Calif. W-873.
FITZPATRICK, GRACE MARIE.
Am. b. Brooklyn, N. Y. 1897; ad. 1934 Same. A.
FITZPATRICK, HELENA WAY.
Mrs. W. E. Fitzpatrick.
Am. b. Cape May Court House, N. J. 1889; ad. 1934 Phila., Pa. A.
FITZPATRICK, JOHN KELLY.
Am. b. Wetumpka, Ala. 1888; ad. 1934 Same. A.
FIUMI, CAVILIERE NAPOLEONE GIOVANNI.
Eng. b. London 1898. Wa.
FIVEASH, ROSE CATHERINE.
Aust. b. Adelaide 1854; ad. 1935 No. Adelaide, So. Aust. M.
FJAESTAD, GUSTAF ADOLF.
Swe. b. Stockholm 1868; ex. 1930 Pittsburgh, Pa. D-DBA-T.
FJELDE, PAUL. (S)
Am. b. Minn., Minn. 1892; ad. 1935 New York. A-F-Ta.
FLACCO [or Fiacco], ORLANDO.
It. b. Verona 1530; ac. 1591 Same. C-T.
FLACK, ARTHUR W.
Am. b. San Fran., Calif. 1878; ad. 1926 Rochester, N. Y. A12-F.
FLACK, MARJORIE. (Ill)
Am. ad. 1935 New York. M.
FLAGG, CHARLES NOEL.
Am. Brooklyn, N. Y. 1848-1916 Hartford, Conn. A014-B-F-T.
FLAGG, GEORGE WHITING.
Am. New Haven, Conn. 1816-1897 New York. B-C-DAB-F-T-2-3-4-13-15.
FLAGG, H. PEABODY.
Am. b. Somerville, Mass. 1859 A.
FLAGG, JAMES MONTGOMERY.
Am. b. Pelham Manor, N. Y. 1877; ad. 1935 New York. A-F-W-46-880.
FLAGG, JARED BRADLEY.
Am. New Haven, Conn. 1820-1899 New York. A01-B-C-DAB-F-T-3-4-15.
FLAGG, MONTAGUE.
Am. Hartford, Conn. 1842-1915 New York. A013-F-T.
FLAHERTY, FRANCES.
Ir. ex. 1934 New York. M.
FLAMEN [or Flamand], ALBERT.
Flem. b. Bruges; ac. 1648/74 in Paris. B-T.
FLAMENG, FRANÇOIS.
Fr. Paris 1856-1923 Same. B-C-DBA-T.
FLAMENG, LÉOPOLD. (Eg)
Belg. Brussels 1831-1911 Paris. B-C-DBA-T.
FLAMENG, MARIE AUGUSTE.
Fr. Metz 1843-1893. B-T.
FLAMM, ALBERT.
Ger. Cologne 1823-1906 Düsseldorf. B-DBA-T.
FLANAGAN. *see also* Flannagan.
FLANAGAN, ALBERT E. (Et)
Am. ad. 1935 New York. M.
FLANAGAN, JOHN. (S)
Am. b. Newark, N. J. 1865; ad. 1934 New York. A-B-Cs-F-T-W.
FLANAGAN, JOHN RICHARD. (Ill)
Aust. b. Sydney, N.S.W. 1895; ad. 1934 New York. M.
FLANDES. *see* Juán de Flandes.
FLANDIN, EUGÈNE NAPOLÉON.
Fr. Naples, It. 1809-1876 Paris. B-T.
FLANDRIN, JEAN HIPPOLYTE.
Fr. Lyons 1809-1864 Rome. B-C-E-T.
FLANDRIN, JULES.
Fr. b. Corene 1871. DBA.
FLANDRIN, PAUL HIPPOLYTE.
Fr. Paris 1856-1921. B-DBA-T.
FLANDRIN, PAUL JEAN.
Fr. Lyons 1811-1902 Paris. B-T.
FLANIGEN, JEAN NEVITT.
Am. b. Athens, Ga. 1898; ad. 1934 Same. A.
FLANNAGAN. *see also* Flanagan.
FLANNAGAN, JOHN B. (S)
Am. b. 1898; ex. 1934 New York. M.
FLANNERY, MOIRA.
Am. b. Wynnewood, Pa. 1906; ad. 1934 Haverford, Pa. M.
FLANNERY, VAUGHN.
Am. ad. 1934 New York. M.
FLATMAN, THOMAS.
Eng. London 1633/7-1688. B-Bd-T.
FLATTERS, JEAN JACQUES. (S)
Fr. Crevelt 1786-1845 Paris. B-T.
FLAXMAN, JOHN II. (S)
Eng. York 1755-1826 London. DNB-E-864
FLAXMAN, MARY ANN.
Eng. 1768-1833 London. B-DNB-T.
FLAXMAN, WILLIAM. (S)
Eng. York 1753?-1795? London. B-DNB-T.

FLECK, JOSEPH A.
Am. b. Vienna, Aus. 1892; ad. 1934 Taos, N. M. A.
FLEISCHER, ERNEST PHILIPP.
Ger. b. Breslau 1850; auc. sale New York. 1934. B-T.
FLÉMAEL (or Flémalle), BARTHOLET.
Flem. Liège 1614-1675 Same. C-T-722.
FLÉMAL. *see* FLÉMAEL.
FLÉMALE, MASTER OF. *see* Compin, Robert.
FLEMING, HENRY STUART. (Et)
Am. b. Phila., Pa. 1863. A28-B-F.
FLEMING, JOHN.
Scot. 1792-1845 Glasgow. B-T.
FLEMING, MICHAEL [or Master].
see Michael the Fleming.
FLEMING, RAOUL P.
Am. ex. 1933 in Paris. M.
FLEMING, THOMAS. (Cart)
Am. Phila., Pa. 1853-1931 Maplewood, N. J. A028.
FLEMMING, JEAN ROBINSON.
Mrs. Ralston Flemming.
Am. b. Charleston, S. C. 1874; ad. 1934 Norfolk, Va. A.
FLERI, JOSEPH C. (S)
Am. b. Brooklyn, N. Y. 1899; ad. 1934 New York. A-Cs.
FLERS, CAMILLE.
Fr. Paris 1802-1868 Annet. B-T.
FLETCHER, ANNE.
Am. b. Chicago 1876; ad. 1934 Richmond, Va. A.
FLETCHER, CALVIN.
Am. b. Provo, Utah 1882; ad. 1934 Logan, Utah. A.
FLETCHER, FRANK MORLEY. (Eg)
Am. b. England 1866; ad. 1934 Santa Barbara, Calif. A-W.
FLETCHER, GODFREY BOCKINS.
Am. Watsonville, Calif. 1888-1923 Same. A021-F.
FLETCHER, GRACE.
Am. ac. 1934 [Abroad]. M.
FLETCHER, HENRY. (Eg)
Eng. ac. 1710-1750 London. B-DNB-T.
FLEURY, ALBERT.
Am. b. Havre, Fr. 1848; ad. 1915 Chicago. A12-B-F.
FLEURY, FRANÇOIS ANTOINE LÉON.
Fr. Paris 1804-1858. B-T.
FLEURY, MARCEL.
Fr. b. Vendée 1883. DBA.
FLEURY, PIERRE.
Fr. b. Boulonge 1900. DBA.
FLEURY, ROBERT. *see* Robert-Fleury, J. N.
FLICCIUS [or Flicke], GERHARUS [or Gerlach].
Br. ac. 1546-1554. B-DNB-T.
FLICKEL, PAUL FRANZ.
Ger. Berlin 1852-1903. B-T.
FLIGHT, [Captain] CLAUDE. (Eg)
Eng. b. London 1881; ex. 1934 Brooklyn, N. Y. M-Wa.
FLINCK, GOVERT [or Govaert].
Dut. Clèves 1615-1660 Amsterdam. B-C-E-T-722.
FLINT, ALICE MORLAND.
Am. New Brighton, Pa. 1857-1933 Schenectady, N. Y. A030.
FLINT, RALPH.
Am. b. Boston 1885; ad. 1934 New York. A.
FLINT, SUSAN WILLARD.
Am. b. Cambridge, Mass.; ad. 1934 New York. M.
FLINT, WILLIAM RUSSELL. (Et)
Scot. b. Edinburgh 1880. DBA-Wa-738-820.
FLIPPEN, MARY.
Am. ad. 1935 Nashville, Tenn. M.
FLISHER, EDITH E.
Am. b. Cleveland, O. 1890; ad. 1934 Nashville, Tenn. A.
FLOEGEL, ALFRED E.
Am. b. Leipzig, Ger. 1894; ad. 1934 New York. A.
FLOETHE, RICHARD. (Ill)
Am. ad. 1934 New York. M.
FLOOD, MARY EMMA. (S)
Mrs. T. E. Stebbins.
Am. ad. 1934 Syosset, L. I., N. Y. M.
FLOPPA, VINCENZO. *see* Foppa, V.
FLORA-CARAVIAS, THALIA.
Gr. b. Greece 1875. B-T.
FLOREANI FAMILY.
It. ac. 15th-16th Cents. in Italy. T.
FLORIAN, WALTER.
Am. New York 1878-1909 Same. A07-B-F-T.
FLORIS DE VRIENDT, CORNELIS II. (S)
Flem. Antwerp 1514/8-1572/5. B-Hs.
FLORIS, FRANZ DE VRIENDT.
[Called "The Flemish Raphael"].
Flem. Antwerp 1516-1570 Same. B-C-E-T-722.
FLÖTNER [or Flattner or Fledner], PETER. (S)
Ger. Thurgan 1485-1546 Nürnberg. Hs-T.
FOBES, HARRIET KEITH.
Am. b. Brooklyn, N. Y. 1868; ad. 1934 New York. M.
FOGARTY, FRANK.
Am. b. New York 1887; ad. 1934 Same. A.
FOGARTY, THOMAS. (Ill)
Am. b. New York 1873; ad. 1934 Same. A-F-W.
FOGELBERG, BENEDICT [or Bengt] ERLAND. (S)
Swe. Gothenburg 1786-1854 Trieste, Aus. B-E-Hs-T.
FOGGINI, GIOVANNI BATTISTA. (S)
It. Florence 1652-1725. Hs-T.
FOGGO, GEORGE.
Eng. 1793-1869 London B-DNB-T.
FOGGO, JAMES.
Eng. London 1790-1860 Same. B-DNB-T.
FOGOLINO, MARCELLO.
It. St. Vito 1470-1550. B-T-V.
FOIARD, NINA G. BATCHELOR DE.
Am. b. Frankfort, Ky.; d. 1912 Paris. M.
FOLAWN, THOMAS JEFFERSON.
Am. b. Youngstown, O.; ad. 1934 Boulder, Colo. A.
FOLDSONE, JOHN.
Eng. ex. 1769-1784 London. B-DNB-T.
FOLEY, JOHN HENRY. (S)
Ir. Dublin 1818-1874 Hampstead, Eng. B-DNB-E-Hs-T.

FOLEY, Margaret E. (S)
Am. b. New Hampshire; d. 1877 Meran, Tyrol, Aus. A20-B-F-Hs-T-Ta.
FOLGER, Fred J.
Am. ad. 1934 Toledo, O. M.
FOLIGNO, Niccolò da [Liberatore].
It. Foligno 1430/5-1500/2. B-T-V.
FOLINSBEE, John Fulton.
Am. b. Buffalo, N. Y. 1892; ad. 1934 New Hope, Pa. A-F-W.
FOLLOT, Paul.
Fr. b. Paris 1877. DBA.
FOLSOM, George. (Ill)
Am. 1859-1919 New York. A016.
FOLTZ, Lloyd C. (Et)
Am. ad. 1935 Wichita, Kan. M.
FOLTZ, Philipp von.
Ger. Bingen 1805-1877 Munich. B-T.
FOLWELL, Samuel. (Min)
Am. 1765-1813 Phila., Pa. DAB-F-T-2-6-7-179-786.
FONDILLER, Elizabeth.
Am. ad. 1934 New York. M.
FONGARIO, Bernardino. *see* Fungai (or Fungari), B.
FONNEREAU, Thomas George. (Ill)
Br. b. 1789; d. 1850. DNB.
FONSBERG, Nils.
Swe. Riseberga, Skane. 1842-1934 Swe. M.
FONT, Constantin.
Fr. b. Auch 1890. DBA.
FONT, Francisco E. (Cari)
Porto-Rican. ex. 1934 New York. M.
FONTAINE, Henri.
Fr. b. Lyons 1888. DBA.
FONTAINE, Paul. *see* Mersereau, Paul.
FONTANA, Carlo. (S)
It. Carrara 1634-1714 Rome. T.
FONTANA, Ernesto.
It. b. Lugano 1862; ex. 1900 Rome. B-T.
FONTANA, Giovanni Giuseppe. (S)
It. Carrara 1821-1893 London. B-T.
FONTANA, Lavinia [Zappi].
It. Bologna 1552-1602 Rome. B-C-E-T-722.
FONTANA, Prospero.
It. Bologna 1512-1597 Same. B-E-T-722.
FONTEBASSO, Francesco Salvator.
It. Venice 1709-1769. B-T.
FONTENAY Family.
Fr. ac. 17th Cent. in France. T.
FONTENAY, Jean Baptiste Belin de. *see* Blain [or Belin] de F.
FONVISIN.
Rus. ex. 1935 London. M.
FOOTE, Florence M.
Am. b. Lansdowne, Pa. 1906; ad. 1935 Swarthmore, Pa. M.
FOOTE, Mary Hallock.
Mrs. Arthur De Wint Foote.
Am. b. Milton, N. Y. 1847. B-F-15.
FOOTE, Will Howe.
Am. b. Grand Rapids, Mich. 1874; ad. 1934 Old Lyme, Conn. A-B-F-W-46.
FOPPA, Ambrogio. *see* Caradosso.
FOPPA [or Floppa], Vincenzo.
It. Brescia 1425/30-1515/6 Same. B-Bd-E-T-V-356.
FORABOSCO [or Ferrabosco], Girolamo.
It. Padua 1631?-1675/89 Venice. B-T.
FORAIN, Jean Louis. (Et)
Fr. Reims 1852-1931 Paris. B-DBA-E-T-191-830.
FORBES, Charles F.
Am. b. Geneva, Swi. 1860. B-DBA-T.
FORBES, Edwin.
Am. New York 1839-1895 Brooklyn, N. Y. B-C-DAB-F-T-4-15-46-63.
FORBES, Elizabeth Adela Armstrong.
Mrs. Standhope Alexander Forbes.
Can. Kingston, Ont. 1859-1912. B-T.
FORBES, Helen Katherine.
Am. b. San Fran., Calif. 1891; ad. 1934 Same. A.
FORBES, James.
Scot. b. Scotland 1800; ac. 1857 in London. T.
FORBES, John Colin.
Can. Toronto, Ont. 1846-1925. T.
FORBES, Kenneth K.
Can. b. Toronto, Ont. 1892; ac. 1934 Same. M.
FORBES, Standhope Alexander.
Ir. b. Dublin 1857. B-DBA-T.
FORBES, Vivian.
Eng. b. London 1891; ex. 1935 Same. Wa.
FORBES-ROBERTSON, Eric. (Stage-P)
Scot. 1865-1935; obit. N. Y. papers, 3-11-1935.
FORBIN, Louis Nicolas Philippe Auguste.
Fr. La Roque 1777-1841 Paris. B-T-722.
FORCE, Clara G. (Min)
Am. b. Erie, Pa. 1852; ad. 1934 Pasadena, Calif. A.
FORD, Edward Onslow. (S)
Eng. London 1852-1901 Same. B-DNB-E-Hs-T.
FORD, Elsie Mae.
Am. b. Whitman, Mass.; ad. 1934 New York. A.
FORD, H. J. (Ill)
Am. ad. 1933 New York. M.
FORD, Harriet Mary.
Can. b. Brockville; ac. 1933 Toronto, Ont. Wa-893.
FORD, [Miss] Lauren.
Am. b. New York 1891; ad. 1934 Rye, N. Y. A.
FORD, [Mrs.] L. W. Neilson.
Am. b. Balt., Md.; d. 1931 Same. A028-B-F.
FORD, Michael. (Eg)
Ir. d. 1765 in Dublin. B-DNB-T.
FORD, Ruth Van Sickle.
Am. b. Aurora, Ill. 1898; ad. 1935 Chicago. A.
FORD, Samuel.
Ir. Cork 1805-1828. B-DNB-T.
FOREAU, Louis Henri.
Fr. b. Paris 1866. B-DBA-T.
FORESMAN, Alice Carter. (Min)
Am. b. Darien, Wis.; ad. 1934 Hollywood, Calif. A.
FOREST, Jean Baptiste.
Fr. Paris 1635-1712 Same. C-T-722.
FORESTIER, Adolphe.
Fr. b. 1790; d. 1812. B-T.
FORESTIER, [Sir] Amèdée. (Ill)
Fr. ad. 1930 London. M.
FORESTIER, Antonin Clair. (S)
Fr. Cannes 1865-1912 Paris. T.

FORESTIER, GABRIEL. (S)
Fr. b. Eymet 1889. DBA.
FORESTIER, MARINUS.
Eng. ad. 1934 London. M.
FORINGER, ALONZO EARL. (Mu.)
Am. b. Kaylor, Pa. 1878; ad. 1934 Saddle River, N. J. A.
FORKNER, EDGAR.
Am. b. Richmond, Ind.; ad. 1934 Seattle, Wash. A.
FORLI, ANSUINO. *see* Ansuino da F.
FORLI, PALMEZZANO. *see* Palmezzano da F.
FORLI, MELOZZO. *see* Melozzo da F.
FORMAN, KERR SMITH.
Am. b. Jacksonville, Ill. 1889; ad. 1934 Des Moines, Ia. A.
FORMENT [or Formente], DAMIÁN. (S)
Sp. Valencia 1480-1540 Huesca. B-Hs-T.
FORMILLI, COMMENDATORE C. T. G.
It. ac. 1934 in Italy. M.
FORNARA, CARLO.
It. ac. 1932. M.
FORNEROD, RODOLPHE.
Fr. b. Lausanne 1882. DBA-T.
FORREST, JOHN B. (Eg.)
Am. Scotland 1814?-1870 Hudson Co., N. J. F-T-2-7-40.
FORREST, ROBERT. (S)
Scot. Lanarkshire 1788/9-1852 Edinburgh. B-DNB-T.
FORREST, THEODORE.
Eng. b. Lambert; ac. 1769-1784 in London. B.
FORRESTER, ALFRED HENRY. (Cari.)
[Known as "Crowquill"].
Eng. London 1804-1872. B-DNB-T.
FORSBERG, ELMER A.
Am. b. Gamalakarleby, Finland 1883; ad. 1934 Chicago. A.
FORSBERG, NILS [The Elder]. (Et.)
Swe. b. Riesberga 1842. B-T.
FORSBERG, NILS [The Younger].
Swe. b. Paris 1870. B-DBA.
FÖRSTER, ERNEST JOACHIM.
Ger. Altenburg 1800-1885 Munich. C.
FÖRSTER, FRANÇOIS. (Eg.)
Fr. Locle 1790-1872 Paris. B-E-T.
FÖRSTER, JOHN WYCLIFFE LOWES.
Can. b. Norval, Ont. 1850; ad. 1935 Toronto, Ont. 893.
FÖRSTER, THOMAS. (Et.)
Eng. ac. 1695-1712 in London. DNB-T.
FORSYTH, GORDON MITCHELL.
Scot. b. Aberdeen 1879. Wa.
FORSYTH, WILLIAM.
Am. b. Ohio 1854; d. 1935 Irvington, Ind. A-B-F-W-Obit. Art Digest, 5-15-1935.
FORSYTHE, VICTOR CLYDE.
Am. b. Orange, Calif. 1885; ad. 1934 San Marino, Calif. A.
FORT, [Mrs.] EVELYN CORLETT.
Am. ad. 1935 Rome, It. M.
FORT, JEAN ANTOINE SIMÉON.
Fr. Valence 1793-1861 Paris. B-T.
FORTESQUE, WILLIAM BANKS.
Eng. b. London; d. 1924. Y01925.
FORTESQUE-BRICKDALE, ELEANOR.
Eng. ad. 1929 in London. Wa.
FORTESS, KARL.
Am. ex. 1934 Woodstock, N. Y. M.

FORTI, EDORDO.
It. ac. 19th Cent. in Italy. B.
FORTUNE, [Miss] E. CHARLTON.
Am. b. Calif. 1885; ad. 1934 Monterey, Calif. A.
FORTUNY Y CARBO, MARIANO JOSÉ MARIA BERNARDO.
Sp. Catalonia 1838-1874 Rome, It. B-Bd-C-E-T-128-192.
FORWARD, F. R. (Et.)
Eng. ad. 1932 in Reydon, Eng. M.
FOSBERG, ERNEST GEORGE.
Can. b. Ottawa, Ont. 1874; ad. 1935 Rockcliffe, Ont. B.
FOSDICK, GERTRUDE CHRISTIAN. (S)
Mrs. James William Fosdick.
Am. b. Virginia 1862; ad. 1934 New York. A.
FOSDICK, JAMES WILLIAM. (Mu.)
Am. b. Charlestown, Mass. 1858; ad. 1934 New York. A-B-F-W.
FOSHKO, JOSEF.
Am. b. Russia; ex. 1934 New York. M.
FOSS, HARRIET CAMPBELL.
Am. b. Middletown, Conn. 1860; ad. 1915 Darien, Conn. A12-B-T.
FOSSA-CALDERON, JULIO E.
Fr. b. Valparaiso, Chile; ac. 1930. DBA.
FOSSE, CHARLES DE LA.
Fr. Paris 1636-1716 Same. B-T.
FOSSUM, SIDNEY.
Am. ad. 1935 Minn., Minn. M.
FOSTER, ALAN. (Ill.)
Am. b. Fulton, N. Y. 1892; ad. 1934 New York. A28.
FOSTER, ARTHUR TURNER.
Am. b. Brooklyn, N. Y. 1877; ad. 1934 Los Angeles, Calif. A.
FOSTER, BEN.
Am. North Anson, Me. 1852-1926 New York. A023-B-DAB-F-T-W15-46-757.
FOSTER, BERTHA KNOX.
Am. b. Hymer, Kan. 1896; ad. 1934 Glendale, Calif. A.
FOSTER, CHARLES.
Am. North Anson, Me. 1850-1931. A028-Obit. Art Digest, 8-1-1931.
FOSTER, EDWARD WARD.
Eng. London 1761-1864. B-T.
FOSTER, ELIZABETH JANE ["Betty Foster"].
Am. b. Columbus, Ind. 1910; ad. 1934 Same. A.
FOSTER, ENID.
Am. b. San Fran., Calif. 1896; ad. 1934 Piedmont, Calif. A.
FOSTER, GERALD.
Am. ad. 1934 Westfield, N. J. M.
FOSTER, GILBERT.
Eng. Manchester 1855-1906. B-T.
FOSTER, GRACE.
Am. b. Wolfe City, Tex. 1879; ad. 1934 Greenville, Tex. A.
FOSTER, JEAN MACJANNET.
Am. ex. 1934 in Paris. M.
FOSTER, JOHN. (Et.)
Am. ex. 1934 Provincetown, Mass. M.
FOSTER, JOHN. (Eg.)
Am. Dorcester, Mass. 1648-1681 Boston. F-T-2-7-182-674.

FOSTER, MULFORD B.
Am. ex. 1934 New York. M.
FOSTER, MYLES BIRKET.
Eng. North Shields 1825-1899 Weybridge. B-DNB-E-T-357.
FOSTER, NORMAN. (S)
Am. ad. 1935 New York. M.
FOSTER, O. L.
Am. b. Ogden, Ind. 1878; ad. 1934 Lafayette, Ind. A.
FOSTER, ROBERT. (Ill.)
Am. ad. 1935 New York. M.
FOSTER, THOMAS.
Ir. Dublin 1798-1826 London. B-DNB-T.
FOSTER, WILLET S.
Am. b. Gouverneur, N. Y. 1885; ad. 1934 Riverside, Calif. A.
FOSTER, ["Will"] WILLIAM FREDERICK. (Ill.)
Am. b. Cinn., O. 1882; ad. 1934 Hollywood, Calif. A.
FOUACE, GUILLAUME ROMAIN.
Fr. Réville 1827-1894/5. B-T.
FOUBERT, ÉMILE LOUIS.
Fr. Paris 1848-1911. B-DNB-T.
FOUCHÉ [or Foucher], NICHOLAS.
Fr. 1653-1733 Paris. B-T.
FOUCOU, JEAN JOSEPH.
Fr. Riez 1739-1815 Paris. B-T.
FOUGERAT, ÉMANUEL.
Fr. b. Rennés 1869. B-DBA-T.
FOUGEROUSSE, JEAN LOUIS.
Fr. b. Paris 1879. B-DBA.
FOUGSTEDT, ARVID.
Swe. b. 1888; ex. 1929 Paris. DBA.
FOUJITA [or Fujita], TSUGOUHARU.
Jap. b. Tokio 1886. DBA.
FOULD, CONSUELO.
Fr. b. Cologne, Ger.; ac. 1865-1895. B-DBA-T.
FOULD. *see* Achille-Fould.
FOULON [or Foullon], BENJAMIN.
Fr. Paris 1550-1612 Same. T.
FOUQUERAY, DOMINIQUE CHARLES.
Fr. b. Le Mans 1872; ad. 1934 Paris. B-DBA-T-Wa.
FOUQUET [or Foucquet], JEAN [or Jehan].
Fr. Tours 1415/20-1477/85 Same. B-E-T-358.
FOUQUET, JEUNESSE DE.
[Pseudonym for Jean Fouquet].
(As recorded in Mallett's Library of Reproductions, Hackensack, N. J.)
FOUQUET, LOUIS VINCENT.
Fr. Orleans 1803-1869. B-T.
FOUQUIÈRES, JACQUES [or Joseph].
Flem. Antwerp 1580/90-1659 Paris. B-C-T-722.
FOUQUIÈRES, JEAN ANTOINE VALENTIN.
Fr. Paris 1822-1896. B-T.
FOURDRINIER, PIERRE. (Eg.)
Fr. ac. 1720-1758 in London. B-DNB-T.
FOURIÉ, ALBERT AUGUSTE.
Fr. b. Paris 1854. B-C-DBA-T.
FOURMOIS, THÉODORE.
Belg. Presles 1814-1871 Ixelles. B-T.
FOURNET, JEAN CLAUDE.
Fr. b. Levallois 1878. DBA.
FOURNIER, ALEXIS JEAN.
Am. b. St. Paul, Minn. 1865; ad. 1934 South Bend, Ind. A-B-F-T-W-46.
FOURNIER, CHARLES.
Fr. Salmaise 1803-1854 Birkhead. B-T.
FOURNIER, DANIEL. (Eg.)
Fr. France 1710-1766 Wild Court, Eng. B-DNB-T.
FOURNIER, FÉLICE. (Eg.)
Fr. 1797-1879 Paris. B.
FOURNIER, JEAN.
Fr. 1700-1765 The Hague, Holland. B-T.
FOURNIER, LOUIS ÉDOUARD.
Fr. b. Paris 1857. B-DBA-T.
FOWLER, CARLTON C.
Am. New York 1877-1930 Same. A028.
FOWLER, DANIEL.
Can. b. Down, Kent, Eng. 1810-1894 Canada. B-T.
FOWLER, EVANGELINE.
Am. b. Kingsville, O. 1885; ad. 1934 Birmingham, Mich. A.
FOWLER, FRANK.
Am. b. Brooklyn, N. Y. 1852-1910 New Canaan, Conn. A08-B-C-DAB-F-T-W5-15-46.
FOWLER, GENE. (Ill)
Am. ad. 1934 New York. M.
FOWLER, ROBERT.
Scot. Anstruther 1853/4-1926 New Ferry, Scot. Y01928.
FOWLER, T. T.
Am. ac. 1830-1871 in New Orleans, La. F.
FOWLER, WILLIAM.
Eng. Winterton 1761-1832 Same. B-DNB-T.
FOX, [Mrs.] AGUSTUS HENRY.
see Eckert, Katherine.
FOX, CHARLES. (Eg.)
Eng. Cossey 1794-1849 Leyton, Eng. B-Bd-DNB-T.
FOX, CHARLES JAMES.
Eng. b. 1860; ac. 1907 London. B-T.
FOX, CHARLES LEWIS.
Am. Portland, Me. 1854-1927 Same. A024.
FOX, DANIEL G. (Ill)
Am. ad. 1934 Boston, Mass. A.
FOX, EMANUEL PHILLIPS.
Aust. Melbourne, Victoria 1865-1915. T.
FOX, GILBERT. (Eg)
Am. England 1776-1807? U. S. DAB-F-T-2-7-64.
FOX, HENRY CHARLES.
Eng. ac. 1879-1893 in London. B-T.
FOX, MARGARET M. TAYLOR. (Ill)
Am. b. Phila., Pa. 1857; ad. 1934 Linden, Md. A-F.
FOX, MILTON S.
Am. ex. 1933 Cleveland, O. M.
FOX, SEYMOUR. (S)
Am. b. New York 1900. Cs.
FOY, EDITH GELLENBECK.
Am. b. Cinn., O. 1893; ad. 1934 Same. A.
FOY, FRANCES M.
Am. b. Chicago, Ill. 1890; ad. 1934 Same. A.
FOY, HANS. (Ill)
Am. b. Brooklyn, N. Y. 1892; ad. 1934 Beechurst, L. I., N. Y. A.
FOYATIER, DENIS. (S)
Fr. Bussière 1793-1863 Paris. B-T.
FRA ANGELICO. *see* Angelico.

FRACANZANO, Cesare.
It. 1600-1653/7 France. B-T.
FRACANZANO, Francesco [Ciccio].
It. 1612-1656/7 Naples. B-T.
FRACASSINI [or Fracassi], Cesari.
It. 1828-1868 Rome. B-T.
FRACCAROLI, Innocenzo. (S)
It. Castell Rotto 1805-1882 Milan. B-T.
FRACKER, Ruth Miller.
Am. b. Chicago 1904; ad. 1934 Pasadena, Calif. A.
FRADEL [or Fradelle], Henri Joseph.
Fr. Lille 1778-1865. B-T.
FRAGIACOMO, Pietro.
It. Venice 1856-1922. B-T.
FRAGONARD, Alexander Evariste.
Fr. Grasse 1780-1850 Paris. B-T.
FRAGONARD, Jean Honoré.
Fr. Grasse 1732-1806 Paris.
B-Bd-C-E-T-191-722-847.
FRAGONARD, Marie Anne Gérard. (Min)
Fr. Grasse, 1747-1823. B.
FRAIKEN, Charles Auguste. (S)
Belg. Herenthals 1817-1893 Brussels. Hs-T.
FRAIN, Nellie M. (Ill)
Am. b. Furnessville, Ind. 1887; ad. 1934 Chicago. A.
FRALEY, Laurence K. (S)
Am. b. Portland, Ore. 1897; ad. 1934 Same. A.
FRAME, Walter K.
Am. ad. 1934 White Plains, N. Y. M.
FRAMPTON, Edward Reginald.
Eng. Croyden 1872-1923 Paris. B-T-Y01924.
FRAMPTON, [Sir] George James. (S)
Eng. London 1860-1928.
Hs-Wa1929-Y01929.
FRANC, Desiré Fleury.
Fr. b. Marseilles 1888. DBA.
FRANÇAIS, François Louis.
Fr. Plombieres 1814-1897 Paris. B-C-E-T.
FRANÇAIS, Nicolas.
see Master of the Franciscan Allegories.
FRANCAVILLA. *see* Franqueville, P.
FRANCE, Eurilda Loomis.
Mrs. Jesse Leach Frame.
Am. Pittsburgh, Pa. 1865-1931 New Haven, Conn. A028.
FRANCE, Jesse Leach.
Am. b. Cinn., O. 1862. A20-B-F.
FRANCE, Léonard de.
Flem. Liége 1735-1805 Same. B-T.
FRANCÈS, Mathilde.
Fr. b. St. Pons 1879. DBA.
FRANCESCA, Piero della.
It. Borgo San Sepulcro 1416/20-1492.
B-Bd-C-E-T-359.
FRANCESCHI, Louis Julien [or Jules]. (S)
Fr. Bar-sur-Aube 1828-1893 Paris. B-T.
FRANCESCHI, Piero della. *see* Francesca.
FRANCESCHINI, Baldassare [Volterrano].
It. Volterra 1611-1689 Florence. B-E-T-722.
FRANCESCHINI, Marc Antonio.
It. Bologna 1648-1729 Same. B-C-T.
FRANCESCO di CRISTOFANO.
see Franciabigio.
FRANCESCO di GIORGIO, Martini.
It. Siena 1439-1502 Aufang. T.
FRANCESCO di PIETRO.
see Angelo di Pietro d'Assisi.
FRANCESCO FAMILY.
It. 14-15-16 Cents. in Italy. T.
FRANCHÈRE, Joseph C.
Can. Montreal 1866-1921. M.
FRANCHEVILLE, A. Lenique de. (S)
Fr. ac. 1915 Fa-M.
FRANCHEVILLE, Pierre de. (S)
Fr. Cambrai 1554-1615 Paris. B-T.
FRANCHI, Antonio.
It. Lucca 1634-1709. B-T.
FRANCHI, Rossello di Jacopo.
It. Florence 1376/7-1456. T.
FRANCIA, Il.
[Francesco di Marco di Giacomo Raibolini].
It. Bologna 1448/50-1517/8 Milan.
B-Bd-C-E-T-V-722.
FRANCIA, Francesco [Jacopo Boateri].
It. Bologna 1487?-1557 Same. T.
FRANCIA, François Louis Thomas.
Fr. Calais 1772-1839 Same. B-DNB-T.
FRANCIA, Giacomo di Francesco.
It. Bologna 1486-1557 Same. C-T-722.
FRANCIA, Giovanni Battista.
It. Bologna 1533-1575. T-722.
FRANCIA, Guilio.
It. Bologna 1487-1540. T-722.
FRANCIABIGIO, Mercantonio.
[Francesco di Cristofano].
It. Florence 1482/3-1524/5 Same.
B-C-E-T-V-722.
FRANCIS, Gene.
Am. b. San Fran., Calif.; ad. 1934 Pebble Beach, Calif. M.
FRANCIS, George.
Am. Hartford, Conn. 1790-1873 Same. F-3.
FRANCIS, John. (S)
Eng. Lincolnshire 1780-1861 London.
B-DNB-T.
FRANCIS, William C.
Am. b. Buffalo, N. Y. 1879; ad. 1934 Same. A.
FRANCISCI, Anthony de. *see* De Francissi, A.
FRANCISCO DE HOLLANDA. (Min)
Por. Lisbon 1517-1584 Same. T.
FRANCISCO, John Bond.
Am. Cinn., O. 1863-1931. A-F-W16.
FRANCK, Frans Friedrich.
Ger. Augsburg 1627-1687 Same. C-T.
FRANCK, Gabriel.
Flem. ac. 1605-1639 in Antwerp. E-T.
FRANCK, [Prof.] Philipp.
Ger. b. 1860; ad. 1934 Berlin-Wannsee. T.
FRANCKE FAMILY (Geneology).
Ger. 1540-1717. B-T.
FRANCKEN [or Franck], Ambrosius [The Elder].
Flem. Herenthals 1544-1618 Antwerp.
B-E-T-722.
FRANCKEN [or Franck], Ambrosius [The Younger].
Flem. Antwerp 1581-1632. B-E-T.
FRANCKEN [or Franck], Frans I.
Flem. Antwerp 1542-1616. B-E-T.
FRANCKEN [or Franck], Frans II.
Flem. Antwerp 1581-1642 Same.
B-C-E-T-722.

FRANCKEN [or Franck], FRANS III.
Flem. Antwerp 1607-1667 Same. B-E-T.
FRANCKEN [or Franck], HIERONYMUS I.
Flem. Herenthals 1540-1610 Paris. B-C-E-T.
FRANCKEN [or Franck], HIERONYMUS II.
Flem. Antwerp 1578-1623 Same. B-E-T-722.
FRANCKEN [or Franck], HIERONYMUS III.
Flem. b. Bruges, Holland 1611. B-E-T.
FRANCKEN [or Franck], SÉBASTIAN.
Flem. Antwerp 1578-1647 Same. B-E-T.
FRANCO, GIOVANNI BATTISTA [Il. Semolei].
It. Udine 1498-1561 Venice. B-T-722.
FRANÇOIS, ALEXANDER.
Am. Belgium 1824-1912 Albany, N. Y. A012-B-T.
FRANÇOIS, ALPHONSE. (Eg.)
Fr. Paris 1814-1883. B-T.
FRANÇOIS, BASTIEN [or Sébastien]. (S)
Fr. ac. at Tours; d. 1523. B-Hs.
FRANÇOIS, GUSTAVE [Berrand].
Swi. b. Geneva 1883. DBA.
FRANÇOIS, GUY [or Guide].
Fr. Puy-en-Velay 1578-1650. B-T.
FRANÇOIS, JULES CHARLES REMY. (Eg.)
Fr. Paris 1809-1861 Neuilly. B-T.
FRANCONIA. *see* German, South.
FRANCUCCI, INNOCENZO DI PIETRO.
see Imola, Innocenzo da.
FRANK, ARTHUR.
Am. b. Phila., Pa.; ex. 1935 New York. M.
FRANK, BENA VIRGINIA.
Am. b. Norfolk, Va. 1900; ad. 1934 New York. A.
FRANK, EUGÈNE C.
Am. Germany 1885-1914 Glendale, Calif. A0X1.
FRANK, GERALD A.
Am. b. Chicago 1888; ad. 1934 Same. A.
FRANK, HANS [or Leo].
It. b. 1884 in Italy. T.
FRANK-WILL. [Boggs].
Fr. b. Nanterre 1900. DBA.
FRANKE, ALBERT Z.
Ger. b. Munich 1860. B-T.
FRANKE, PAUL.
Ger. b. 1538; d. 1615. T.
FRANKENSTEIN, GODFREY.
Am. b. 1820; d. 1873. M.
FRANKENSTEIN, JOHN. (S)
Am. 1817-1881 New York. F-T-Ta.
FRANKL, PAUL THEODORE.
Am. ad. 1934 New York. A.
FRANKLIN, DWIGHT.
Am. b. New York 1888; ad. 1934 Same. A-W.
FRANKLIN, EDITH BONNEY. (Min.)
Am. ad. 1934 Phila., Pa. M.
FRANQUE, JEAN PIERRE.
Fr. Buis 1774-1860. B-T.
FRANQUE, JOSEPH.
Fr. Buis 1774-1833. B-T.
FRANQUELIN, JEAN AUGUSTIN.
Fr. Paris 1798-1839 Same. B-C-T.
FRANQUEVILLE, PIERRE [or Pietro]. (S)
Fr. Paris 1553-1615 Same. Hs-T.
FRANQUINET, EUGÈNE.
Am. b. Brussels, Belg. 1875; ad. 1934 Verdugo City, Calif. A.
FRANTZ, MARSHALL. (Ill.)
Am. b. Kiev, Rus. 1890; ad. 1934 New York. A.
FRANZ, CARL JOSEPH.
Ger. Dresden 1829-1875 Same. T.
FRANZ, ETTORE ROESLER.
It. ac. 1875-1889 in Rome. B.
FRANZEN, AUGUST.
Am. b. Norrköping, Swe. 1863; ad. 1934 New York. A-B-F-T-W.
FRANZONI, CARLO. (S)
Am. b. 1780; d. 1850. M.
FRAPPA, JOSÉ.
Fr. St. Étienne 1854-1904. B-T.
FRASCHETTI, VALERIO. (Et.)
It. b. 1910; ad. 1934 Rome; ex. 1935 Chicago. M.
FRASER. *see also* Frazer.
FRASER, ALEXANDER [The Elder].
Scot. Edinburgh 1786-1865 Hornsey, Eng. B-C-DNB-T.
FRASER, ALEXANDER [The Younger].
Scot. Woodcockdale 1827-1899 Wusselburgh. B-C-DNB-T.
FRASER, CHARLES. (Min.)
Am. Charleston, S. C. 1782-1860 Same. B-Bd-C-DAB-F-T-1-2-4-6-15-30-45-65-66-179-701.
FRASER, CLAUDE LOVAT. (Ill.)
Eng. London 1890-1921 Sandgate. DNB-E-360.
FRASER, DOUGLASS.
Am. b. Vallejo, Calif. 1885; ad. 1934 Same. A.
FRASER, JAMES EARLE. (S)
Am. b. Winona, Minn. 1876; ad. 1934 New York. A-B-Cs-F-T-W-1-46-798.
FRASER, JOHN A.
Am. London, Eng. 1838-1898 New York. A01-B-T.
FRASER, LAURA GARDIN. (S)
Mrs. James Earle Fraser.
Am. b. Chicago 1889; ad. 1934 New York. A-Cs-F-W.
FRASER, MALCOLM. (Ill.)
Am. b. Montreal, Can. 1869; ad. 1934 Brookhaven, N. Y. A-B-F-T-W.
FRASER, [Mrs.] MALCOLM.
see Aldrich, Mary Austin.
FRASER, WILLIAM LEWIS. (Ill.)
Am. London 1841-1905 Brookhaven, N. Y. A06-B.
FRATE, IL. *see* Bartolommeo, Fra.
FRATIN, CHRISTOPHE. (S)
Fr. Metz 1810-1864? Raincy. B-T.
FRATREL [or Fratel], JOSEPH.
Fr. Épinal 1730-1783 Mannheim, Ger. B-T.
FRAU, JOSÉ.
Sp. ad. 1935 Madrid; ex. 1934 Pittsburgh, Pa. M.
FRAU, MARGARITA DE.
Sp. ad. 1935 Madrid; ex. 1934 Pittsburgh, Pa. M.
FRAUENDORFER, JOHANNES. (Min.)
Ger. ac. 1454 in Germany. T.
FRAYE, ANDRÉ.
Fr. b. Nantes 1888. DBA.
FRAZEE, JOHN. (S)
[His portrait bust of John Wells at St. Paul's

Church, Broadway, New York, is believed to be the first marble bust carved by a native American.]
Am. Rahway, N. J. 1790-1852 Crompton, N. J. DAB-F-Hs-T-Ta-2-4.

FRAZER, Harland.
Am. ad. 1934 New York. A.

FRAZER, Mable Pearl.
Am. b. Utah 1887; ad. 1934 Salt Lake City, Utah. A.

FRAZER, Oliver.
Am. Kentucky 1808-1864 Lexington, Ky. DAB-F-2-67.

FRAZER, William Miller.
Scot. b. Perth 1864; ad. 1935 Edinburgh. Wa.

FRAZIER, John Robinson.
Am. b. Stonington, Conn. 1889; ad. 1934 Prov., R. I. A.

FRAZIER, Kenneth.
Am. b. Paris 1867; ad. 1934 Garrison, N. Y. A-B-F-T-W.

FRAZIER, Sarah E.
Am. b. Weatherford, Tex. 1908; ad. 1934 Kansas City, Mo. A.

FREDER, Frederick Charles.
Am. b. Monroe, N. Y. 1895; ad. 1934 New York. A.

FRÉDÉRIC, Léon Henri Marie.
Belg. b. Brussels 1856. B-T.

FREDERICK, Austin.
Am. ac. 1855. Fa-M.

FREDERICK, Edmund. (Ill)
Am. b. Phila., Pa. 1870. A28-F.

FREDERICK, Frank Forrest.
Am. b. Methuen, Mass. 1866. A28-B-F.

FREDERICKS, Alfred. (Eg)
Am. ac. 1881-1926. F.

FREDERICKS, Paget J. R. *see* Paget, F. J. R.

FREDERICKSEN, Mary M.
Mrs. Walter Ufer.
Am. b. Copenhagen, Denmark 1869; ad. 1934 Taos, N. M. A.

FREDI, Bartolo. *see* Bartolo di F.

FREDRICK, W. F.
[William Fredrick Fixen].
Am. b. Racine, Wis.; ad. 1934 Los Angeles, Calif. A.

FREE, Karl R.
Am. b. Davenport, Ia. 1903; ad. 1934 New York. A.

FREEBAIRN, Alfred Robert. (Eg.)
Eng. London 1794-1846 Same. DNB-T.

FREEBAIRN, Robert. (Eg.)
Eng. 1765-1808 London. B-T.

FREEBORNE, Zara Malcolm. (S)
Am. Allentown, Pa. 1861-1906 Boston, Mass. A06-B-T.

FREEDLANDER, Arthur R.
Am. b. New York; ad. 1934 Same. A-B.

FREEDMAN, Barnet.
Eng. b. Barbadoes, W. I. 1901; ad. 1935 London. Wa.

FREEDMAN, Maurice.
Am. ad. 1935 New York. M.

FREEDMAN, Sarah.
Am. ex. 1935 New York. M.

FREELAND, Anna C.
Am. b. 1837; d. 1911. F.

FREELON, Allan Randall.
Am. b. Phila., Pa. 1895; ad. 1934 Same. A.

FREEMAN, Charles H.
Am. Camden, N. J. 1859-1918. A016.

FREEMAN, Donald. (Et.)
Am. b. Calif.; ad. 1935 New York. M.

FREEMAN, E. O. (Eg.)
Am. ac. 1850. [No death date]. F-7.

FREEMAN, Florence. (S)
Am. Boston, Mass. 1836-1876 Rome, It. F-T-15.

FREEMAN, George. (Min.)
Am. Spring Hill, Conn. 1787-1868 Hartford, Conn. F-3-6-179.

FREEMAN, James Edward.
Am. Nova Scotia 1808-1884 Rome, It. A9-B-Bd-DAB-F-T-2-4-15.

FREEMAN, Jane.
Am. b. England 1883; ad. 1934 New York. A.

FREEMAN, John.
Eng. ac. 1670-1720 in London. B-DNB-T.

FREEMAN, Margaret. (Ill.)
Am. ad. 1934 New York. A.

FREEMAN, Samuel. (Eg.)
Eng. 1773-1857 London. B-DNB-T.

FREER, Frederick Warren.
Am. Chicago, Ill. 1849-1908 Same. A07-B-C-F-T.

FREER, H. Mortimer.
Am. ad. 1935 Jackson, Mich. M.

FREESE, Johann Oskar Hermann.
Ger. Poméranie 1819-1871 Hasenfelde. B-T.

FREI, Adolph. (Mu)
Am. Germany 1854-1935 Lansdowne, Pa.
Obit. Art Digest, 5-15-1935; Obit. Art News, 5-4-1935.

FRÉLAUT, Jean.
Fr. b. Grenoble 1879; ex. 1933 London. B-DBA.

FRELINGHUYSEN, George Griswold, Jr.
Am. b. Morristown, N. J. 1911; ad. 1934 Same. A.

FRÉMIET, Émmanuel. (S)
Fr. Paris 1824-1911 Same. B-E-Hs-T.

FRÉMIN, René. (S)
Fr. Paris 1672-1744 Same. B-T.

FRÉMINET [or Fréminel], Martin de.
Fr. Paris 1567-1619 Same. B-C-T-722.

FREMONT, Camille Désirée Suzanne.
Fr. b. Châtillon 1876. DBA.

FRENCH, Alice Helm.
Mrs. William M. R. French.
Am. b. Lake Forest, Ill. 1864; ad. 1934 Williamstown, Mass. A.

FRENCH, Annie.
Scot. b. Glasgow; ac. 1865-1915 London. T.

FRENCH, Daniel Chester. (S)
Am. b. Exeter, N. H. 1850; d. 1931. A28-B-Cs-E-F-Hs-T-Ta-W16-15-46-672-779.

FRENCH, David M. (S)
Am. Newmarket, N. H. 1827-1910 Newburyport, Mass. A08-T.

FRENCH, Edwin Davis. (Eg.)
Am. North Attleboro, Mass. 1851-1906 Saranac, N. Y. A06-DAB-F-T-7.

FRENCH, Elizabeth D. L.
Am. b. Plymouth, Pa. 1878; ad. 1934 Kingston, Pa. A.
FRENCH, Frank. (Eg.)
Am. Loudon, N. H. 1850-1933 Reeds Ferry, N. H. A030-B-F-T-W.
FRENCH, Howard B.
Am. b. Fort Thomas, Ky. 1906; ad. 1934 Blairstown, N. J. A.
FRENCH, Jared.
Am. ad. 1935 New York. M.
FRÈRE, Charles Théodore.
Fr. Paris 1815-1888 Same. B-T.
FRÈRE, Pierre Édouard.
Fr. Paris 1819-1886 Écouen. B-C-E-T.
FRESNAYE, Roger de la.
Fr. Le Mans 1885-1925 Grasse. DBA-797.
FRESNOY, Charles Alphonse du.
Fr. Paris 1611-1665 Same. E-T.
FREUDENBERGER, Sigmund.
Swi. Berne 1745-1801 Same. B-T.
FREUND, H. Louis.
Am. b. Clinton, Mo. 1905; ad. 1934 New York. A.
FREY, Edwin F. (S)
Am. Lima, O. 1892; ad. 1934 Columbus, O. A-Cs.
FREY, Eugène H.
Fr. b. Brussels 1864. DBA.
FREY, Wilhelm.
Ger. 1826-1911. T.
FRIANT, Émile.
Fr. Dieuze 1863-1932. B-DBA-T.
FRICK, Adolf. (S)
Ger. Weilburg 1870. B-T.
FRICK, Gottlieb.
Swi. b. Obfelden 1877. B-T.
FRICK, Henri Émile. (Eg.)
Fr. ac. 1900 in Paris. B.
FRICK, Paul de.
Fr. b. Paris 1864. B-DBA-T.
FRICK, [Mrs.] Winifred Marie Louis.
Eng. b. Ramsgate; ad. 1934 London. B-Wa.
FRIDENBURG, [Dr.] Percy. (Pastel Print).
Am. ad. 1934 New York. M.
FRIEDENSON, Arthur.
Eng. b. 1872 in England. B-T.
FRIEDERANG, Maxmillian Franz. (Mu.)
Am. b. 1857; d. 1929 Brooklyn, N. Y. A026.
FRIEDLANDER, Leo. (S)
Am. b. New York 1889; ad. 1934 Same. A-Cs-F-W.
FRIEDMAN, Arnold.
Am. b. New York 1879; ex. 1934 Same. A28.
FRIEDMAN, Martin.
Am. ad. 1935 Brooklyn, N. Y. M.
FRIEDRICH, Caspar David.
Ger. Greifswald 1774-1840 Dresden. B-T.
FRIEDRICH, Otto.
Aus. ac. 1887 in Berlin, Ger. B-T.
FRIEDRICHSEN, Ernestine.
Ger. Danzig 1824-1892. B-T.
FRIEL, Zenith Ivy.
Am. b. Edwardsville, Kan. 1889; ad. 1934 Kansas City, Mo. A.
FRIES, Charles Arthur.
Am. b. Hillsboro, O. 1854; ad. 1934 San Diego, Calif. A-F-T.
FRIES, Christoph. [Pankraz.]
Ger. ac. 1755-1781 in Germany. T.
FRIES, Ernst.
Ger. Heidelberg 1801-1833 Carlsruhe. C-T.
FRIES [or Frieso], Hans.
Swi. Freiburg 1465-1520 Berne. T.
FRIESE, Richard Bernhard Louis.
Ger. b. Gumbinnen 1854; ac. 1886 Hamburg. B-C-T.
FRIESEKE, Frederick Carl.
Am. b. Owosso, Mich. 1874; ad. 1934 New York. A-B-F-T-W-46-757.
FRIESZ, [Achille Émile] Othon.
Fr. b. Havre, Fr. 1879. DBA-797-827.
FRIPP, Alfred Downing.
Eng. Bristol 1822-1895 London. B-T.
FRIPP, Charles Edwin.
Eng. London 1850-1906 Montreal, Can. T.
FRIPP, George Arthur.
Eng. Bristol 1813-1896 London. B-DNB-T.
FRIPP, Thomas W.
Can. b. London, Eng. 1864; d. 1931 Canada. M.
FRISCH, Victor. (S)
Am. b. Vienna, Aus. 1876. Cs-M.
FRISCHKE, Arthur.
Am. b. New York 1893; ad. 1934 Same. A.
FRISHMUTH, Harriet Whitney. (S)
Am. b. Phila., Pa. 1880; ad. 1934 New York. A-Cs-F-W-46.
FRISIUS, Simon Weynouts. *see* Vries, S. de.
FRISM, Barthélemy. (S)
Belg. Tournai 1816-1877 Paris. B-T.
FRISTER Family.
Aus. ac. 18th-19th Cent. in Vienna. T.
FRISTON, Adrian de.
Eng. ex. 1933 in London. M.
FRITH, William Powell.
Eng. Aldfield 1819-1909 St. John's Woods. B-C-DNB-E-T.
FRITZ, Eleanor Virginia.
Mrs. E. B. Fritz.
Am. b. St. Cloud, Minn. 1885; ad. 1934 Fort Worth, Tex. A.
FRITZ, Henry E.
Am. b. Germany 1875; ad. 1934 Pelham, N. Y. A.
FRITZSCH [or Fritsch], Johann Christian Gottfried.
Ger. Hamburg 1720-1802/3. T.
FROEHLICH, Hugo B.
Am. b. Cinn., O. 1862; ad. 1915 Bloomfield, N. J. A12.
FROELICH, Paul.
Am. ad. 1935 New Hope, Pa. M.
FRÖLICH, Finn Haakon. (S)
Am. b. Norway 1868; ad. 1934 Hollywood, Calif. A.
FRÖLICH, Lorens.
Dan. Copenhagen 1820-1908 Same. C-T.
FROMEN, Agnes Valborg. (S)
Am. b. Waldermasvik, Swe. 1868; ad. 1934 Chicago. A-F.
FROMENT, Nicolas.
Fr. ac. 1470-1490 Avignon. B-T-847.

FROMENTIN, EUGÈNE.
Fr. La Rochelle 1820-1876 Paris. B-C-E-T-925.
FROMKES, MAURICE.
Rus.-Am. Russia 1872-1931 Paris. A028-F-W16.
FROMUTH, CHARLES HENRY.
Am. b. Phila., Pa. 1861; ad. 1934 Finistère, Fr. A-B-F-T-W-46.
FRONTIER, JEAN CHARLES.
Fr. Paris 1701-1763 Lyons. B-T.
FRÖSCHL, KARL.
Aus. b. Vienna 1848. B-T.
FROST, ANNA.
Am. b. Brooklyn, N. Y.; ad. 1934 Same. A.
FROST, ARTHUR BURDETT. (Et.)
Am. Phila., Pa. 1851-1928 Pasadena, Calif. A025-B-F-T-W14-361.
FROST, GEORGE.
Eng. Barrow 1754-1821 Ipswich. B-DNB-T.
FROST, GEORGE ALBERT.
Am. b. Boston, Mass. 1843. B-T.
FROST, JOHN.
Am. b. Phila., Pa. 1890; ad. 1934 Haverford, Pa. A-F-W.
FROST, JULIUS H.
Am. b. Newark, N. J. 1867; ad. 1934 Wash., D. C. A.
FROST, ROSAMOND. (S)
Am. ad. 1934 New York. M.
FROST, RUTH STERLING.
Am. ad. 1934 New York. M.
FROST, WILLIAM EDWARD.
Eng. Wandsworth 1810-1877 London. B-C-DNB-E-T.
FROTHINGHAM, JAMES.
Am. Charlestown, Mass. 1786-1864 New York. F-T-2-4-169-182.
FROTHINGHAM, SARAH C. (Min.)
Am. 1821-1861 New York. F-6.
FRUEAUF, ROLAND [The Elder].
Aus. 1440/50-1507 Passau. T.
FRUEAUF, ROLAND [The Younger].
Aus. ac. 1498-1545 in Passau. T.
FRUEH, ALFRED J. (Cari.)
Am. b. 1898; ad. 1935 New York. F-M.
FRUHAUF, ALINE. (Cari.)
Am. ad. 1934 New York. M.
FRUMERIE, AGNÈS DE. (S)
Fr. b. Skoefde 1861. B-DBA.
FRUYTIERS [or Fruitiers], PHILIP.
Flem. 1607/10-1666. B-E-T.
FRY, GEORGIA TIMKEN.
Mrs. John H. Fry.
Am. St. Louis, Mo. 1864-1921 Peking, China. A018-B-F-T.
FRY, GUY EDGAR. (Ill.)
Am. ad. 1934 Phila., Pa. M.
FRY, JOHN HEMMING.
Am. b. Indiana 1860; ad. 1934 New York. A-B-F-T-46-181.
FRY, MARSHALL.
Am. b. Syracuse, N. Y. 1878; ad. 1915 New York. A12-T.
FRY, ROGER ELLIOT.
Eng. London 1866-1934 Same. Wa-825-Obit. Art News, 9-15-1934.
FRY, SHERRY EDMUNDSON. (S)
Am. b. Creston, Ia. 1879; ad. 1934 Roxbury, Conn. A-Cs-F-Hs-T-W-46.
FRY, WILLIAM THOMAS. (Eg.)
Eng. 1789-1843 London. B-DNB-T.
FRYE, THOMAS [or Theodore]. (Eg.)
Ir. Dublin 1710-1762 London. B-DNB-T.
FRYER, LEONARD.
Eng. ac. 1596-1605 in London. B-DNB-T.
FUCHS, ÉMILE. (P-S)
Am. Vienna, Aus. 1866-1929 New York. A026-B-Cs-F-T-W14-218.
FUECHSELL, HERMAN.
Am. Brunswick, Ger. 1833-1915 New York. A012-F-T.
FUERSTENBERG, PAUL W.
Am. ad. 1934 New York. M.
FUERTES, LOUIS AGASSIZ. (Ill.)
Am. Ithaca, N. Y. 1874-1927 Unadilla, N. Y. A024-B-DAB-F-W14.
FUGEL, GEBHARD.
Ger. b. Ravensburg 1863. B-T.
FÜGER [or Fueger] FRIEDRICH HEINRICH.
Ger. Heilbronn 1751-1818 Vienna. B-T.
FUHR, ERNEST. (Ill.)
Am. New York 1874-1933 Westport, Conn. A030-Obit. N. Y. papers, 12-14-1933.
FUHR, XAVER.
Ger. b. 1898 in Germany. M.
FÜHRICH, JOSEPH RITTER VON.
Aus. Bohemia 1800-1876 Vienna. B-C-E-T.
FUICK, MAERTEN.
Dut. ac. 1655 in Holland. M.
FUJITA, BUNZO. (S)
Jap. ac. 1934. M.
FUJITA, JIDO.
Jap.-Am. ad. 1934 Boston, Mass. M.
FUJITA, TSUGONHARU. *see* Foujita, T.
FULDA, ELIZABETH RUNGIUS.
Am. b. Berlin, Ger. 1879; ad. 1934 New York. A.
FULDE, EDWARD B.
Am. b. St. Louis, Mo.; ad. 1915 Neuilly-Sur-Seine, Fr. A12.
FULLER, ANDREW DANIEL, JR.
Am. ad. 1934 Chicago, Ill. M.
FULLER, ARTHUR.
Am. ad. 1934 Westport, Conn. M.
FULLER, CHARLES FRANCIS. (S)
Eng. b. England 1830; d. 1875 Florence, It. B-T.
FULLER, GEORGE.
Am. Deerfield, Mass. 1822-1884 Brookline, Mass. C-DAB-E-F-T-1-15-46-68-69-70-71-748.
FULLER, HENRY BROWN.
Am. Deerfield, Mass. 1867-1934 New Orleans, La. A-B-F-T-W-Obit. N. Y. papers, 7-18-1934; Obit. Art News, 9-15-1934.
FULLER, ISAAC.
Eng. 1606-1672 London. B-DNB-T.
FULLER, LEONARD JOHN.
Eng. b. Dulwich 1891; ad. 1934 Surrey. Wa.
FULLER, LUCIA FAIRCHILD. (Min.)
Mrs. Henry Brown Fuller.
Am. Boston 1872-1924 Madison, Wis. A021-B-F-T-W14-1-46-829.
FULLER, [Mrs.] META WARRICK.
see Warrick, Meta Vaux.

FULLER, Ralph Briggs. (Ill.)
Am. ad. 1934 Leonia, N. J. A.
FULLER, Richard Henry.
Am. Bradford, N. H. 1822-1871 Chelsea, Mass. B-Bd-F-T-15.
FULLER, Sarah E. (Eg.)
Am. b. 1829; d. 1901 Lynbrook, N. Y. A04-B.
FULLER, Spencer.
Am. Deerfield, Mass. 1863-1911 Same. A09-T.
FULLER-LARGENT, Lydia.
Am. b. Calif.; ad. 1934 San Fran., Calif. A.
FULLEYLOVE, John.
Eng. Leicester 1845-1908 London. B-T.
FULLWOOD, Albert Henry.
Eng. b. Birmingham 1864; ad. 1934 London. B-T-Wa.
FÜLOP, Karoly. (P-S)
Hun. b. 1898; ad. 1934 Los Angeles, Calif. M.
FULTON, Cyrus James.
Am. b. Pueblo, Colo. 1873; ad. 1934 Eugène, Ore. A.
FULTON, Dorothy.
Am. b. Uniontown, Pa. 1897; ad. 1934 Bokeelia, Fla. A.
FULTON, George.
Am. ad. 1934 Houston, Tex. M.
FULTON, Robert. [Inventor-P]
Am. Lancaster, Pa. 1765-1815 New York. DAB-F-T-2-4-6-45-72-73-182-673-701.
FUMIANI, Giovanni Antonio.
It. Venice 1643-1710 Same. B-T.
FUNCK, Théodor.
Ger. b. Elberfeld 1867. B-T.
FUNGAI [or Fungari], Bernardino.
It. Siena 1460-1516 Same. B-T-V.
FÜNHOF, Heinrich.
Ger. d. 1484/5 in Hamburg? T.
FUNI, Achille.
It. b. 1890; ad. 1935 Milan. M.
FUNK, Hans [The Elder].
Swi. Zurich 1468/70-1539 Berne. B-T.
FUNK, Hans [The Younger].
Swi. b. Zurich; d. 1562. B-T.
FUNK, Heinrich.
Ger. Herford 1807-1877 Stuttgart. B-T.
FUNK, Joseph T.
Am. b. Shenandoah, Ia. 1901; ad. 1934 Ottumwa, Ia. A.
FUNK, M. Thompson.
Am. ad. 1934 Brooklyn, N. Y. M.
FUNK, Wilhelm Heinrich.
Am. b. Hanover, Ger. 1866; ad. 1915 New York. A12-F-WX1.
FUREDI, Lili.
Am. ad. 1935 New York. M.
FURINI, Filippo.
It. ac. 1600 in Florence. T.
FURINI, Francesco.
It. Florence, It. 1600/4-1646/9 Same. B-C-T-722.
FURLONG, Charles Wellington.
Am. b. Cambridge, Mass. 1874; ad. 1934 Cohasset, Mass. A-B-F.
FURLONG, Thomas.
Am. b. St. Louis, Mo.; ad. 1934 New York. A.
FURNASS, John Mason.
Am. Boston 1763-1804 Dedham, Mass. F-T-2-6-7.
FURNERIUS [or Farnesius], Abraham.
Dut. ac. 1620-1648 in Holland. B-T.
FURNESS, William Henry, Jr.
Am. Phila., Pa. 1827-1867 Cambridge, Mass. F-T-4-15-45.
FURNISS, Harry. (Cari.)
Ir. b. 1854; d. 1925. E-Y01926.
FURSE, Charles Wellington.
Eng. Staines 1868-1904 London. B-DNB-E-T-825.
FURSMAN, Frederick F.
Am. b. El Paso, Ill. 1874; ad. 1934 Sangatuck, Mich. A-F.
FURST, Breading. (S)
Am. b. New York 1918; ex. 1934 Same. M.
FURST, Florence Wilkins.
Mrs. F. E. Furst.
Am. b. Delavan, Wis.; ad. 1934 Freeport, Ill. A.
FURST, Moritz. (Eg.)
Am. Boesing, Hun. 1782; ac. 1834 New York. F-T-2-7.
FUSARI, Louis J.
Am. ad. 1934 Hartford, Conn. M.
FUSELI [or Füssli], Henry (Johann Heinrich).
Eng. Zurich, Swi. 1741-1825 London. B-C-DNB-E-T-722.
FUSINA, Andrea da. (S)
It. ac. 1495 in Milan. B-Hs-T.
FUSSELL, Charles Lewis.
Am. b. 1840; d. 1909. M.
FÜSSLI Family.
Ger. ac. 14th to 19th Cent. in Germany. T.
FÜSSLI, Johann Heinrich. *see* Fuseli, Henry.
FYT [or Fijt], Jan [or Johannes].
Flem. Antwerp 1609/11-1661Same. B-Bd-C-E-T-722.
FYZEE-RAHAMIN, S.
Br.-Indian. ad. 1935 New Delhi, India. M.
GAAL [or Gael], Barent.
Dut. Haarlem 1620-1687/93. B-C-T.
GABA, Lester. (Soap-S)
Am. ad. 1935 New York. M.
GABAIN, Ethel. (Eg)
Mrs. John Copley.
Eng. b. London 1883; ex. 1934 Same. Wa.
GABAY, Esperanza.
•Am. b. New York; ad. 1934 Sheffield, Mass. A.
GABBIANI, Antonio Domenico.
It. Florence 1652-1726 Same. B-C-T.
GABBIANI, Giuseppe.
It. b. Barletta 1862. T.
GABÉ, Nicolas Edward.
Fr. Paris 1814-1865 Same. B-T.
GABL, Alois.
Swi. Wiesen, Ger. 1845-1893 Munich. B-T.
GABO, Pevsner.
Rus. b. Brjansky 1890; ac. 1935 Paris. M.
GABRIEL, Ada Vorhaus.
Am. b. New York 1898; ad. 1934 Same. A.
GABRIEL, Gabrielle.
Am. b. Germantown, Pa. 1904; ad. 1934 Stone Harbor, N. J. A.

GABRIEL, Paul Joseph Constantin.
Dut. Amsterdam 1828-1903 Scheveningen. B-T.
GABRINI, Pietro.
It. b. Rome 1856. B-T.
GABRON, Guiliam [or Willem].
Flem. Antwerp 1619-1678 Same. C-T.
GABY, Charlot. (S)
Fr. ac. 16th Cent. in Tours. B-T.
GADDI, Agnolo [or Angelo].
It. Florence 1333-1396 Same. B-C-E-T-V.
GADDI, Family.
It. ac. 14th Cent. in Italy. T-V.
GADDI, Gaddo [di Zanobi].
It. Florence 1260?-1333? Same. B-C-E-T-V.
GADDI, Giovanni.
It. d. 1383 in Italy. B-T.
GADDI, Taddeo [di Gaddo].
It. Florence 1300?-1366? Same. B-Bd-C-T-V.
GADE, John. (Ill)
Am. b. Tremont, N. Y. 1870; ad. 1934 Floral Park, N. Y. A.
GADSBY, William Hippon.
Eng. 1845-1924 London. B-Y01925.
GAEL. *see* Gaal.
GAELEN, Alexandre van.
Dut. Amsterdam 1670-1728. B-C-T.
GAENSSLEN, Otto Robert.
Am. b. Chicago, Ill. 1876; ad. 1915 Same. A12-B.
GAER, Fay. (S)
Am. b. London 1899; ad. 1934 Berkeley, Calif. A.
GAERTNER, Carl F.
Am. b. Cleveland, O. 1898; ad. 1934 Same. A.
GAETANO, Scipione. *see* Pulzone, G. S.
GAFFRON, Horace.
Eng. ad. 1935 London. M.
GÁG, Wanda Hazel. (Ill)
Am. b. Minn., Minn. 1893; ad. 1934 Milford, N. J. A-F.
GAGE, George William.
Am. b. Lawrence, Mass. 1887; ad. 1934 Brooklyn, N. Y. A.
GAGE, Merrell. (S)
Am. b. Topeka, Kan. 1892; ad. 1934 Santa Monica, Calif. A-Cs.
GAGEN, Robert Ford.
Can. London, Eng. 1848-1926 Canada. M.
GAGINI [or Gaggini], Antonio (Bissone). (S)
It. [Lombard]. 1478-1536. B-Hs-T-V.
GAGINI [or Gaggini], Domenico. (S)
It. [Lombard]; ac. 15th Cent. in Italy. B-Hs-T-V.
GAGLIARDI, Pietro. (S)
It. b. 1818; d. 1890 in Italy. M.
GAGLIARDINI, Julien Gustave.
Fr. Mülhouse 1846/8-1927. B-DBA-T.
GAGNEREAUX, Bénigne.
Fr. Dijon 1756-1795 Florence, It. B-T.
GAGNON, Clarence A.
Can. b. Montreal, Can. 1881; ad. 1934 Paris. A20-B-T.
GAHMAN, Floyd.
Am. b. Elida, O. 1894; ad. 1934 New York. A.
GAHO, Hasimoto.
Jap. J Vol. 1, page 80.
GAILLARD, Claude Ferdinald. (Eg)
Fr. Paris 1834-1887 Same. B-T.
GAILLARD, Robert. (Eg)
Fr. Paris 1722-1785 Same. B-T.
GAINSBOROUGH, Thomas.
Eng. Sudbury 1727-1788 London. B-Bd-C-DNB-E-T-192-362-363,722-725-790-843-844-909-922.
GAISSER, Jakob Emmanuel.
Ger. Augsburg 1825-1899. B-T.
GAISSER, Max.
Bav. b. Munich 1857. B-T.
GAKUTEI, Yashima.
Jap. ac. 1800. J Vol. 2, page 66.
GALAMIS, Demétrios Emmanuel. (Eg)
Gr. b. Athens 1882; ex. 1934 New York. DBA-M.
GALBRUND, Alphonse Louis.
Fr. Paris 1810-1885. B-T.
GALDONE, Paul.
Am. b. Hungary; ad. 1935 Forest Hills, L. I., N. Y. M.
GALE, Edmund Walter. (Cart)
Am. b. Corydon, Ky. 1884; ad. 1934 Los Angeles, Calif. W.
GALE, Walter R. (Ill)
Am. ad. 1934 Balt., Md. A.
GALI FABRA, Francisco de A.
Sp. ad. 1935 Barcelona; ex. 1934 Pittsburgh, Pa. M.
GALL, Della Dayton.
Am. ad. 1934 Buffalo, N. Y. M.
GALLAGHER, Genevieve.
Am. b. Balt., Md. 1899; ad. 1934 Same. A.
GALLAGHER, M. J. (Ill)
Am. ad. 1934 Lansdowne, Pa. M.
GALLAGHER, Sears. (Et)
Am. b. Boston 1869; ad. 1934 West Roxbury, Mass. A-F-T-W.
GALLAIT, Louis.
Belg. Tournai 1810-1887 Brussels. B-C-E-T.
GALLAND, Pierre Victor.
Fr. Geneva, Swi. 1822-1892 Paris. B-T.
GALLARD-LEPINAY, Paul Charles Émmanuel.
Fr. b. Aulnay 1842; ac. 1880. B-T.
GALLAUDET, Edward. (Eg)
Am. Hartford, Conn. 1809-1847 Same. F-2-7.
GALLAUDET, Elisha. (Eg)
Am. New Rochelle, N. Y. 1730-1805 New York. F-T-2-7-147.
GALLAWAY, W. H.
Am. ad. 1934 White Plains, N. Y. M.
GALLE, Cornelis. (Eg)
Flem. 1615-1678 Antwerp. T.
GALLE, Philipp.
Dut. Haarlem 1537-1612 Same. B-T.
GALLEGOS Y ARNOSA, José. (S)
Sp. b. Jérez 1859; ac. 1917 in Madrid. T.
GALLEGOS [or Galecus], Fernando.
Sp. Galicia 1440-1507 Salamanca. T-774.
GALLÉN-KALLELA, Akseli Valdemar.
Fin. b. Pori, Finland 1865; d. 1931. T.
GALLI, Alfredo.
Am. ad. 1934 New Orleans, La. M.

GALLIBERT, GENEVIÈVE.
Fr. b. Paris; ex. 1931 Same. DBA.
GALLISON, HENRY HAMMOND.
Am. Boston 1850-1910 Cambridge, Mass. A09-B-F.
GALLO. *see* San Gallo.
GALLOCHE, LOUIS.
Fr. Paris 1670-1761 Same. B-C-T-722.
GALSWORTHY, FRANK.
Eng. b. London 1863; ad. 1934 Chertsey. Wa.
GALT, ALEXANDER. (S)
Am. Norfolk, Va. 1827-1863 Richmond, Va. F-T.
GALT, CHARLES FRANKLIN.
Am. b. St. Louis, Mo. 1884. A20-F-T.
GAMBARDELLA, SPIRIDIONE.
It. ac. 1842-1868 London. T.
GAMBARELLI, ANTONIO AND BERNARDO.
see Rossellino, A. and B.
GAMBEE, MARTIN H.
Am. ad. 1934 Pawling, N. Y. M.
GAMBLE, EDWIN.
Am. b. Chicago 1876; ad. 1915 Evanston, Ill. A12.
GAMBLE, JOHN MARSHALL.
Am. b. Morristown, N. J. 1863; ad. 1934 Santa Barbara, Calif. A-F.
GAMBLE, ROY C.
Am. b. 1887; ad. 1934 West Detroit, Mich. A-F.
GAMELIN, JACQUES.
Fr. Carcassonne 1738-1803 Same. B-T.
GAMIS, A.
Am. ad. 1934 Pacific Palisades, Calif. M.
GAMLEY, HENRY SNELL. (S)
Scot. Montrose 1865-1928 Edinburgh. T-Wa01929-Y01929.
GAMMELL, ROBERT HALE IVES.
Am. b. Prov., R. I. 1893; ad. 1934 Same. A-F-W14.
GAMPENRIEDER, KARL.
Bav. b. Munich 1860. B-T.
GAMPERT, OTTO.
Swi. b. Ottenbach 1842. B-T.
GANDARA, ANTONIO DE LA.
Fr. Paris 1862-1917 Same. B-DBA-T.
GANDOLA, PAUL MARIO. (S)
Am. b. Besano, It. 1889; ad. 1934 Cleveland, O. A.
GANDY, CURTIS, JR.
Am. ad. 1934 Teaneck, N. J. M.
GANDY, HERBERT.
Eng. ac. 1879 in London. B-T.
GANDY, JAMES.
Br. Exeter 1619-1689 Ireland. B-DNB-T.
GANDY, WILLIAM.
Ir. Kilkenny 1660-1729 Exeter, Eng. DNB-T.
GANESCO, ALEXANDRE.
Fr. b. Brussels, Belg.; ac. 1935 Paris. DBA.
GANGERI, LIO. (S)
It. 1844-1913 Messina. B-T.
GANIERE, GEORGE ÉTIENNE. (S)
Am. b. Chicago 1865; ad. 1934 De Land, Fla. A-F-W.
GANKU, KISHI.
Jap. 1749-1829. J Vol. 2, page 106.
GANNAN, JOHN. (Ill)
Am. ex. 1935 New York. M.
GANNETT, RUTH CHRISMAN. (Ill)
Am. ad. 1934 New York. M.
GANSER, IVAN LAURENCE. (S)
Am. b. Eugene City, Ore. 1906; ad. 1934 Kansas City, Mo. A.
GANSO, ÉMIL.
Am. b. Halberstadt, Ger. 1895; ad. 1934 Woodstock, N. Y. A.
GANTAI, KISHI.
Jap. 1784-1865. J Vol. 2, page 107.
GANZ, HENRY F. W.
Eng. ac. 1891-1906 in England. T.
GARAVAGLIA, GIOVITA. (Eg)
It. Pavia 1790-1835 Florence. B-T.
GARAVILLA, ANGEL.
Sp. ex. 1934 New York. M.
GARAVITO, HUMBERTO.
Guatemalan. b. 1897; ex. 1933 New York. M.
GARBE, LOUIS RICHARD.
Eng. ad. 1934 Burslem. B-Wa-798.
GARBER, DANIEL.
Am. b. North Manchester, Ind. 1880; ad. 1934 Lumberville, Pa. A-B-F-T-W-66-181-757.
GARBIERI, LORENZO [Il. Nepote].
It. Bologna 1580-1654. B-T.
GARBO, RAFFAELLINO DEL.
see Raffaellino del Garbo.
GARCÉS, JOSÉ DE MARTI.
Sp. d. 1802. B.
GARCÍA, [Many Spanish Artists].
Sp. ac. 15th-19th Cent. in Spain. T.
GARCÍA DE MIRANDA, JUÁN.
Sp. Madrid 1677-1749. B-T.
GARDELL, ANNA.
Swe. b. 1853; ac. 1882. M.
GARDELLE FAMILY.
Fr. and Ger. ac. 16th-18th Cent. T.
GARDELLE, THÉODORE. (Min)
Swi. Geneva 1722-1761 London. B-E-T.
GARDET, GEORGES. (S)
Fr. b. Paris 1863. D-DBA-E.
GARDIN, [Mrs.] ALICE TILTON.
Mrs. James Frazer.
Am. b. 1859; ad. 1935 New York. A26-M.
GARDINER, ELIZA DRAPER.
Am. b. Prov., R. I. 1871; ad. 1934 Same. A-F.
GARDINER, WILLIAM NELSON.
Ir. Dublin 1766-1814 London. B-T.
GARDNER [or Gardiner], DANIEL.
Eng. Kendall 1750-1805 London. B-DNB-T.
GARDNER, DONALD. (Ill)
Am. ad. 1934 Bronxville, N. Y. A.
GARDNER, [Mrs.] E. M.
Am. b. Colchester, Conn.; d. 1915 Pitman, N. J. A013.
GARDNER, ELIZABETH JANE.
see Bouguereau, E. J. G.
GARDNER, ELIZABETH RANDOLPH. (S)
Am. ad. 1934 New York. M.
GARDNER, FRED.
Am. b. Syracuse, N. Y. 1880; ad. 1934 Brooklyn, N. Y. A.
GARDNER, GERTRUDE GAZELLE.
Am. b. Fort Dodge, Ia. 1878; ad. 1934 Flushing, L. I., N. Y. A-F.

GARDNER, LOUISE WILLIAMSON.
Am. ad. 1934 Toledo, O. M.
GARDNER, [Mrs.] VIRGINIA N.
Am. ad. 1934 West Hartford, Conn. M.
GARDNER, WALTER.
Am. b. Liverpool, Eng. 1902; ad. 1934 Phila., Pa. A.
GARDNOR, RICHARD [or John].
Eng. 1729-1808 London. B-DNB-T.
GAREMYN [or Gaeremyn], JEAN ANTON.
Flem. Bruges 1712-1799. B-T.
GARESCHE, MARIE R.
Am. b. St. Louis, Mo. 1864; ad. 1934 Same. A.
GARETSON, ALBERT M.
Am. b. Buffalo, N. Y. 1877. A28-F.
GARF, SALOMON.
Dut. b. Amsterdam 1879; ex. 1930 Same. B-T-M.
GARFIELD, MARJORIE S.
Am. ad. 1935 Syracuse, N. Y. M.
GARGALLO, PABLO [or Paul]. (S)
Sp. Aragon 1881-1934 Reus, Sp. DBA-M-798-Obit. N. Y. papers, 12-29-1934.
GARGIULIO, DOMENICO [Micco Spadero].
It. Naples 1612-1679. B-T.
GARIN, LOUIS.
Fr. b. Rennes 1888. DBA.
GARNER, CHARLES S., JR. (Ill)
Am. b. 1890; d. 1933 New Hope, Pa. A030.
GARNER, EDITH MARY. *see* Lee-Hankey, E. M.
GARNER, THOMAS. (Eg)
Eng. Birmingham 1789-1868. B-DNB-T.
GARNERAY, AMBROISE LOUIS.
Fr. Paris 1783-1857 Same. B-T.
GARNEREY, AUGUSTE SIMON.
Fr. Paris 1785-1824 Same. B-T.
GARNEREY, HIPPOLYTE JEAN BAPTISTE.
Fr. Paris 1787-1858 Same. B-T.
GARNEREY, JEAN FRANÇOIS.
Fr. Paris 1755-1837 Same. B-T.
GARNETT, CLAUDE.
Eng. b. Moor Hull; ad. 1935 Kensington, Eng. M.
GARNIER, ALFRED JEAN. (S)
Fr. b. Puiseaux; ac. 1869-1888. B-T.
GARNIER, ÉTIENNE BARTHELÉMY.
Fr. Paris 1759-1849 Same. B-T.
GARNIER, GEOFFREY SNEYD.
Br. b. Wigan 1889; ad. 1934 Penzance. Wa.
GARNIER, JULES ARSÈNE.
Fr. Paris 1847-1889 Same. B-T.
GARNIER, LOUIS HIPPOLYTE. (Eg)
Fr. Paris 1802-1855 Same. T.
GARNIER, MICHEL.
Fr. ac. 1793-1814 in Paris. B-T.
GARNSEY, ELMER ELLSWORTH. (Mu)
Am. b. Holmdel, N. J. 1862; ad. 1934 New York. A-B-F-T-W.
GARNSEY, JULIAN ELLSWORTH. (Mu)
Am. b. New York 1887; ad. 1934 Los Angeles, Calif. A.
GAROFALO IL. BENVENUTO DA TISIO.
It. Ferrara 1481-1559 Same. B-Bd-C-E-T-V.
GAROFINI. *see* Master of the Carnations.
GARRARD, GEORGE. (P-S)
Eng. 1760-1826 Brompton. DNB-T.
GARRARD, MARCUS. *see* Gheerarrts, M.
GARRAWAY, GEORGE HERVEY.
Eng. b. West Indies 1846; ad. 1934 Florence, It. B-T-Wa.
GARRETT, ANNA SHAPLEIGH. (Ill)
Am. ad. 1934 Wilmington, Del. A-F.
GARRETT, CLARA PFEIFER. (S)
Mrs. Edmund A. Garrett.
Am. b. Pittsburgh, Pa. 1882; ad. 1934 Beverly Hills, Calif. A-B-F.
GARRETT, EDMUND HENRY.
Am. Albany, N. Y. 1853-1929 Needham, Mass. A026-B-DAB-F-T-W14-47.
GARRETT, THERESA A. (Et)
Am. b. 1884. A20-F.
GARRIDO, ÉDUARDO LÉON.
Sp. b. Madrid 1856. B-DBA.
GARRIDO, LEANDRO RAMÓN.
Fr. Bayonne 1868-1909 Grasse. B-T.
GARRISON, BENARD.
Br. ac. 1713. Fa.
GARRISON, EVE.
Am. b. Boston, Mass.; ad. 1934 Chicago. A.
GARRISON, JOHN LEWIS.
Am. b. Cinn., O. 1867; ad. 1934 Columbus, O. A.
GARRISON, MARTHA H.
Am. b. Center, Tex. 1874; ad. 1934 Houston, Tex. A.
GARRISON, ROBERT. (S)
Am. b. Fort Dodge, Ia. 1895; ad. 1934 New York. A-W.
GARSIDE, JOHN.
Eng. b. Salford 1887; ad. 1934 London. Wa.
GARSTIN, ELIZABETH WILLIAMS. (S)
Am. b. New Haven, Conn. 1897; ad. 1934 Same. A.
GARSTIN, NORMAN.
Eng. Cornwall 1847-1926. T.
GARTNER, FRANZ [or Fritz].
Ger. b. 1771; d. 1841. T.
GARVEY, EDMUND.
Ir. b. Ireland; ex. 1769-1813 London. B-DNB-T.
GARVEY, WILLIAM.
Am. d. 1925 Hackensack, N. J. A023.
GARY, LOUISA MAGGILL.
Am. b. Balt., Md. 1888; ad. 1934 Catonsville, Md. A.
GASCAR [or Gascard], HENRI.
Fr. Paris 1634/5-1701 Rome. B-DNB-T.
GASH, CHESTER ALAN.
Am. ex. 1934 New York. M.
GASH, WALTER BONNER.
Eng. Lincoln 1869-1928. Wa01929.
GASKELL, GEORGE PERCIVAL. (Et)
Eng. Shipley 1868-1934 London. B-Wa-Obit. Art News, 9-15-1934.
GASKIN, ARTHUR JOSEPH.
Eng. Birmingham 1862-1928. Wa1929.
GASPAR, MIKLOS.
Am. b. Kaba, Hun. 1885; ad. 1934 Chicago. A.
GASPARD, JULES M.
Am. b. Paris 1862; d. 1919 New York. A016.
GASPARD, LÉON.
Am. b. Russia 1882; ad. 1935 Taos, N. Mex. F-W13.

GASPARS [or Jaspars], JAN BAPTIST.
Flem. Antwerp 1620?-1691 London. B-DNB-T.
GASPRE, DUGHET. *see* Poussin, Gaspard.
GASS, MARJORIE EARLE.
Can. b. St. John, N. B. 1889; d. 1928. M.
GASSEL, LUCAS.
Flem. Helmont 1500?-1570 Brussels. C-T.
GASSER, GEORGE.
Ger. b. Borzen 1857. T.
GASSER, HANS.
Ger. 1817-1868 Budapest, Hun. T.
GASSER, JOHANN. (S)
Ger. Graz 1803-1868. T.
GASSIER, JEAN BRUNO.
Fr. Bordeaux 1786-1832 Paris. C-T.
GASSMAN, FRANCES J.
Am. ad. 1935 Birmingham, Ala. M.
GASSNER, MORDI.
Am. b. New York 1899; ad. 1934 Same. A.
GASTALDI, ANDREA.
It. Turin 1810-1889 Same. B-T.
GASTEIGER, ANNA SOPHIE.
Ger. b. 1878; ad. 1934 Munich. T.
GASTEIGER, MATHIAS. (S)
Ger. b. Munich 1871. B-T.
GATCH, LEE.
Am. ex. 1934 in New York. M.
GATCHELL, CHARLES. (Ill)
Am. b. U. S. 1883; d. 1933 Paris. A030.
GATENBY, JOHN WILLIAM, JR.
Am. b. St. Charles, Ill. 1903; ad. 1934 Chicago. A.
GATES, FRANK E.
Am. ad. 1934 Bronxville, N. Y. M.
GATES, MARGARET CASEY.
Mrs. Robert Franklin Gates.
Am. b. Wash., D. C.; ad. 1934 Same. A.
GATES, ROBERT FRANKLIN.
Am. ad. 1934 Wash., D. C. A.
GATES, WENDALL N.
Am. ad. 1934 Cleveland, O. M.
GATEWOOD, EVELYN MULLANEY.
Mrs. J. R. Gatewood.
Am. b. Iowa 1903; ad. 1934 Dallas, Tex. A.
GATHMAN, ELDOR.
Am. ad. 1934 Toledo, O. M.
GATIER, PIERRE.
Fr. b. Toulon 1878. DBA.
GATINE, GEORGES JACQUES [or Jean]. (Eg)
Fr. b. 1773; d. 1824. B-T.
GATINEAU, HENRY.
Eng. 1791-1876 Camberwell. B-DNB-T.
GATLEY, ALFRED. (S)
Eng. Bollington 1816-1863 Rome, It. B-DNB-T.
GATTEAUX, NICOLAS MARIE. (S)
Fr. Paris 1751-1832 Same. B-T.
GATTER, OTTO JULES.
Am. b. Phila., Pa. 1892; d. 1926. A023-F.
GATTI, ANNIBALE.
It. Forli 1828-1909. B-T.
GATTI, BERNARDINO [Sojaro].
It. Pavia 1495-1575 Parma. B-T.
GATTI, SATURNINO DE.
It. San Vittorino 1463-1521. T.
GATTIKER, HERMANN. (Eg)
Swi. b. Enge 1865. B-T.
GATTUSO, PAUL.
Am. ex. 1934 New York. M.

GAUBAULT, ALFRED ÉMILE. (S)
Fr. b. Paris; d. 1895. B-T.
GAUCHEREL, LÉON. (Eg)
Fr. Paris 1816-1886. B-T.
GAUDFROY, ALPHONSE.
Fr. b. Gentilly 1845. B-DBA-T.
GAUDEMARIS, ANATOLE HENRY PIERRE THÉODORE.
Fr. Paris 1853-1908 Massilan. B-T.
GAUDENS. *see* Saint-Gaudens.
GAUDENZI, PIETRO.
It. ad. 1935 Milan; ex. 1934 Pittsburgh, Pa. M.
GAUDEZ, ADRIEN ÉTIENNE. (S)
Fr. b. Lyons 1848. B-T.
GAUDIER-BRZESKA, HENRI. (S)
Fr. b. 1891; d. 1915. 798-825-884.
GAUDIN, FRAY LUIS PASCUAL.
Sp. Catalonia 1566-1621 Scala Dei. C-T.
GAUDIN, MARGUERITE. (Ill)
Am. ad. 1934 Phila., Pa. M.
GAUERMANN, FRIEDRICH.
Aus. 1807-1862 Vienna. B-E-T.
GAUFFIER, LOUIS.
Fr. La Rochelle, 1761-1801 Florence, It. B-C-T.
GAUGAIN, THOMAS. (Eg)
Fr. Abbeville 1748-1808 London. B-DNB-T.
GAUGENGIGL, IGNAZ MARCEL.
Am. Passau, Bav. 1855-1932 Boston, Mass. A029-B-C-F-T-W-15-47.
GAUGUIN, PAUL.
Fr. Paris 1848-1903 Dominica, West Indies. B-DBA-T-192-365-700-783-811-926-931.
GAUJEAN, EUGÈNE. (Eg.)
Fr. Pau 1850-1900 Andrésy. B-T.
GAUL, ARRAH LEE.
Mrs. A. L. G. Brennan.
Am. ad. 1934 Phila., Pa. A.
GAUL, WILLIAM GILBERT.
Am. Jersey City, N. J. 1855-1919 New York. A016-B-DAB-C-E-F-T-W8-1-66-74.
GAULEY, ROBERT DAVID.
Am. b. Ireland 1875; ad. 1934 Winter Park, Fla. A-B-F-T-W.
GAULLI, GIOVANNI BATTISTA [Baciccio].
It. Genoa 1639-1709 Rome. B-C-T-722.
GAULOIS, HÉLÈNE. (S)
Am. ex. 1934 New York. M.
GAULTIER [or Golter], LÉONARD. (Eg.)
Fr. Mayence 1552/61-1628/41. B-T.
GAUMONT, MARCEL ARMAND. (S)
Fr. b. Tours 1880. B-DBA-T.
GAUNT, WILLIAM. (Et.)
Eng. b. Hull 1874; ad. 1934 London. Wa.
GAUSSEN, ADOLPHE LOUIS.
Fr. b. Marseilles 1871. B-DBA-T.
GAUSTA, HERBJORN.
Am. b. Norway 1854; ad. 1935 Minn., Minn. A20-F.
GAUTHEROT, PIERRE.
Fr. Paris 1769-1835 Same. B-T.
GAUTHIER, CHARLES. (S)
Fr. b. 1831; ac. 1882 in Paris. B-T.
GAUTHIER, ZINA.
Fr. b. Russia; ac. 1930 in Paris. DBA-T.
GAUTIER, ÉTIENNE.
Fr. Marseilles 1842-1903 Paris. T.

GAUTIER, Lucien Marcelin. (Eg.)
Fr. b. Aix 1849. B-T.
GAUTIER-DAGOTY, Édouard. (Eg.)
Fr. 1745-1784/5 Milan, It. B-T.
GAUTIER-DAGOTY Family.
Fr. ac. 18th Cent. in France. T.
GAUTIER-DAGOTY, Jacques Fabien. (Eg.)
Fr. Marseilles 1710/7-1781/6 Paris. B-T.
GAVARNI, Paul. (Cari.)
[Hippolyte Guillaume Sulpice]
Fr. Paris 1804-1866 Same.
B-E-T-192-341-854.
GAVARNI, Pierre.
Fr. Paris 1847-1932. B-Y01933.
GAVENCKY, Frank J.
Am. b. Chicago 1888; ad. 1934 Same. A.
GAVIN, Robert.
Scot. Leith 1827-1883 Newhaven, Eng.
B-DNB-T.
GAVIN, [Mrs.] Verona E.
Am. b. Eau Claire, Wis. 1891; ad. Milwaukee, Wis. A.
GAVIT, John E. (Eg.)
Am. b. New York 1817-1874 Stockbridge, Mass. F-7.
GAW, William A.
Am. b. San Fran., Calif. 1895; ad. 1934 Berkeley, Calif. A.
GAWDY [or Gawdie], [Sir] John.
Eng. Norfolk 1639-1699. B-DNB-T.
GAY, Edward B.
Am. Dublin, Ir. 1837-1928 Albany, N. Y.
A025-B-C-F-T-W14-15.
GAY, George Howell.
Am. b. Milwaukee, Wis. 1858; ad. 1915 New York. A20-F.
GAY, Walter.
Am. b. Hingham, Mass. 1856; ad. 1934 Paris.
A-B-C-DBA-F-T-W-15-46.
GAY, Winckworth Allan.
Am. West Hingham, Mass. 1821-1910 Same.
A08-C-DAB-F-T-W6-1-4-15-75.
GAY, Zhenya. (Ill)
Am. ad. 1934 New York. M.
GAYLER, Ruth H.
Am. ad. 1934 White Plains, N. Y. M.
GAYLOR, Samuel Wood.
Am. b. Stamford, Conn. 1883; ad. 1934 Glenwood Landing, L. I., N. Y. A-F.
GAYRAL, Jean Maurice.
Fr. b. Donnazac 1872. DBA.
GAYWOOD, Richard [or Robert]. (Eg.)
Eng. b. 1639; d. 1699. B-DNB-T.
GAZAN, Henry. (Ill.)
Fr. b. Paris 1887. DBA.
GAZZERI, F. (S)
It. ac. 1934 Glendale, Calif. M.
GEAR, Joseph W.
Eng. ac. 1821/52 in London. B-T.
GEARHEART, Frances H. (Eg)
Am. ex. 1935 Wash., D. C. M.
GEARY, Alice Hildegarde.
Am. b. Springfield, Mass. 1897; ad. 1934 Same. A.
GEARY, Fred.
Am. b. Clarence, Mo. 1894; ad. 1934 Kansas City, Mo. A.
GEBERS, Nellie M.
Am. ad. 1935 Lincoln, Iowa. M.
GEBHARDT, Karl.
Ger. Munich 1860-1917. C-T.
GEBHARDT, Karl Franz Édouard von.
Rus. Esthonia 1838-1925. B-C-T.
GEBHARDT, Keith. (S)
Am. ex. 1935 Milwaukee, Wis. M.
GEBHARDT, William Edwin.
Am. b. Franklin, O. 1907; ad. 1934 Miamisburg, O. M.
GEBLER, Friedrich Otto.
Ger. Dresden 1838-1917. B-T.
GECK, Francis Joseph.
Am. b. Detroit, Mich. 1900; ad. 1934 Boulder, Colo. A.
GEDDES, Andrew.
Scot. Edinburgh 1783-1844 London.
B-C-DNB-E-T.
GEDDES, Norman Bel. (Scenic Artist)
Am. b. Adrian, Mich. 1893; ad. 1934 New York. M.
GEE, Yun.
Chinese. b. Canton 1906; ad. 1934 New York.
A.
GEEFS, Guillaume [or Willem]. (S)
Belg. Antwerp 1805-1883 Brussels. Hs-T.
GEEL, Johannes Franciscus van. (S)
Belg. Mechlin 1756-1830 Antwerp. B-Hs-T.
GEEL, Joost van.
Dut. Rotterdam 1631-1698 Same. C.
GEER, Grace Woodbridge.
Am. b. Boston 1854; ad. 1934 Same. A-B-F.
GEERAERTS, Marcus. *see* Gheeraerts, M.
GEERLINGS, Gerald K. (Et.)
Am. b. Milwaukee, Wis. 1897; ad. 1935 New Canaan, Conn. A28.
GEERTGEN [or Gérard], tot Sint Jans.
Dut. ac. 1465-1493 in Leyden. B-T.
GEERTZ, Julius.
Ger. Hamburg 1837-1902. B-C-T.
GEEST, Wybrand Simonsz de [The Elder].
Dut. Leuwarden 1590/2-1659. B-T.
GEGERFELT, Vilhelm.
Swe. b. Gothenburg 1844. B-T.
GEHRING, Louis H.
Am. ad. 1934 New York. A.
GEIAMI.
Jap. Kyoto 1431-1509. T.
GEIFLER, Peter Carl. (Cari.)
Ger. Leipzig 1802-1872. T.
GEIGER, Nicolas. (S)
Bav. b. Laningen 1849. B-DBA-T.
GEIGER, Peter Johann Nepomuk.
Aus. Vienna 1805-1880. T.
GEIGER, Willy.
Ger. b. Landshut 1878. T.
GEIKIE, Walter.
Scot. Edinburgh 1795-1837. B-DNB-E-T.
GEISLER, Frederic.
Am. ad. 1935 Cleveland, O. M.
GEISS, Moritz. (S)
Ger. Berlin 1805-1875 Same. Ms-T.
GEISSBUHLER, Arnold. (S)
Fr. ad. 1934 Paris. M.
GEISSER, Karl. (S)
Swi. ac. 1919. 366.
GEISSLER [Willi], Wilhelm.
Ger. b. Berlin 1848. B-T.

GEISZEL, John H. (Ill.)
Am. b. Akron, Colo.; ad. 1934 Phila., Pa. A.
GEKKO, Ogata.
Jap. ac. 1910. J., Vol. 2, page 113.
GELDER, Arent [or Aert] de.
Dut. Dordrecht 1645-1727 Same. B-T.
GELDER, Nicholas van.
Dut. Leyden 1620/5-1675/7. B-T.
GELDORP, George.
Flem. b. Antwerp; ac. 1611-1666 London. B-DNB-T.
GELERT, Johannes Sophus.
Am. Prussia 1852-1923 New York. A021-B-F-T-Ta-W13.
GELHAY, Édouard.
Fr. b. Braisne 1856. C-T.
GÉLIBERT, Gaston.
Fr. b. 1850; d. 1931. DBA.
GÉLIBERT, Jules Bertrand.
Fr. 1833/4-1916. B-DBA-T.
GÉLIBERT, Paul Jean Pierre.
Fr. Laforce 1802-1883. B-T.
GÉLINET, Marcel.
Fr. b. Marseilles; ac. 1934 Paris. DBA.
GELLÉE [or Gelée], Claude Lorrain.
see Claude Gellée, Le Lorrain.
GELLENBECK, Ann P.
Am. b. Shakopee, Minn.; ad. 1934 Tacoma, Wash. A.
GELLER, Todros. (S)
Am. b. Vinnitza, Rus. 1889; ad. 1934 Chicago. A.
GELLERT, Emery.
Am. b. Budapest, Hun. 1889; ad. 1934 Hollywood, Calif. A.
GELLERT, Hugo. (Ill.)
Am. b. Budapest, Hun. 1892; ad. 1934 White Plains, N. Y. A.
GELLERT, Robert. (Ill.)
Am. ad. 1934 New York. M.
GELLES, Karl. (S)
Aus. ac. 1913 in Vienna. T.
GELLI, Odoardo.
It. b. Savona 1852. B-T.
GELLNER, [Mrs.] Alma.
Am. ad. 1934 Weehawken, N. J. M.
GELMAN, Aaron.
Am. ex. 1935 New York. M.
GELSAVAGE, John.
Am. ad. 1934 Detroit, Mich. M.
GEMBERLING, Grace Thorp.
Am. b. Phila., Pa. 1903; ad. 1934 Same. A.
GEMINI [or Geminus], Thomas. (Eg.)
It. ac. 1540-1570 in London. B-DNB-T.
GEMITO, Vincenzo. (S)
It. b. 1852 in Italy. Hs-T.
GENDALL, John.
Eng. Exeter 1790-1865 Same. B-DNB-T.
GENDROT, Felix Albert. (S)
Am. b. Cambridge, Mass. 1866; ad. 1934 Roxbury, Mass. A.
GENELLI, Giovanni Buonaventura.
Ger. Berlin 1798-1868 Weimar. B-C-E-T.
GENGA, Girolamo.
It. Urbino 1476?-1551 Same. B-E-T-V.
GENIN, John.
Am. France 1830-1895 New Orleans, La. F-144-183.
GENIN, Lucien.
Fr. ad. 1930 Paris. DBA.
GENIN [or Guenine], Robert.
Rus. b. 1884; ex. 1932 Chicago. M.
GENISSON, Jules Victor.
Belg. St. Omer, Fr. 1805-1860 Louvain, Belg. B-T.
GENNARELLI, Amédéo. (S)
Fr. b. Naples, It.; ac. 1913-1930 Paris. DBA.
GENNARI, Benedetto [The Elder].
It. b. Cento; ac. 1585-1610. B-T.
GENNARI, Benedetto [The Younger].
It. Cento 1633-1715 Bologna. B-T.
GENOD, Michel Philibert.
Fr. Lyons 1795/6-1862 Same. B-T.
GENOELS, Abraham [Archimedes].
Flem. Antwerp 1640-1723 Same. C-T-722.
GENOVESE Il Prete. *see* Strozzi, Bernardo.
GENTH, Lillian Mathilde.
Am. b. Phila., Pa. 1876; ad. 1934 New York. A-B-F-T-W-46.
GENTHE, Arnold.
Am. b. Berlin, Ger. 1869; ad. 1934 New York. A.
GENTIL, François. (S)
Fr. Troyes 1510-1588 Same. B-Hs-T.
GENTILE DA FABRIANO.
It. Fabriano 1360/70-1427/50 Rome. B-E-T-V.
GENTILE, Luigi. *see* Primo, Luigi.
GENTILESCHI, Artemisa Lomi [Schiatessi].
It. Pisa 1590/7-1642/51 England. B-DNB-E-T-722-829.
GENTILESCHI, Orazio Lomi de.
It. Pisa 1562/5-1646/7 England. B-C-DNB-E-T-722.
GENTLE, Edward. (Ill.)
Am. ad. 1934 Chicago. A.
GENTRY, Carl Rees.
Am. b. New Florence, Mo. 1888; ad. 1934 Columbia, Mo. A.
GENTRY, Karl Wilhelm.
Ger. 1822-1890 Berlin. B-T.
GENZMER, Berthold.
Ger. b. 1858; ac. in Berlin. B-T.
GEOFFROY, Jean Jules Henri.
Fr. Marennes 1853-1924 Paris. B-DBA-T.
GEORG, Johann. *see* Bremer.
GEORGE, Dorothy Hills.
Am. b. Manchester, N. H.; ad. 1934 Boston, Mass. A.
GEORGE, Eric.
Eng. b. Streatham 1881. Wa.
GEORGE, [Sir] Ernest.
Eng. 1839-1922 London. B-T.
GEORGE, H. Margaret.
Am. ad. 1933 Newton Center, Mass. M.
GEORGE, Richard F. (S)
Am. San Fran., Calif. 1865-1912 Brooklyn, N. Y. A0X.
GEORGE, Vesper Lincoln.
Am. Boston, Mass. 1865-1934 Same. A-B-F-W-Obit. N. Y. papers, 5-11-1934.
GEORGI, Edwin A. (Ill.)
Am. ad. 1934 New York. M.
GEORGI, Walter.
Ger. b. Leipzig 1871. B-T.

GEORIMS DE GEND. [Jorge Gyorgy.]
Flem. ac. 1466-1515. B-T.

GÉRADIN, AUGUSTE.
Fr. b. Mülhouse 1849. B-T.

GERADIN, FRANK.
Am. b. 1856. M.

GERAIGERY, RICHARD.
Am. ad. 1934 Brooklyn, N. Y. M.

GERALD, ELIZABETH BART.
Am. ad. 1935 New York. M.

GÉRARD, FERNAND LE GOUT.
see Le Gout-Gerard, F.

GÉRARD, FRANÇOIS PASCAL SIMON.
Fr. Rome, It. 1770-1837 Paris. B-C-E-T-722.

GÉRARD, JEAN IGNACE ISIDORE.
see Grandville, Gérard.

GÉRARD, MARGUÉRITE.
Fr. Grasse 1761-1837. B-T.

GÉRARD, THÉODORE.
Belg. Ghent 1829-1902 Laeken. B-T.

GÉRARD VAN HAARLEM. *see* Geertgen, Jans.

GÉRARDS, MARCUS. *see* Gheeraerts.

GERAT, SERGE.
Rus. or Fr. b. Moscow, Rus. 1881. Fa.

GERBAULT, HENRY.
Fr. Châtenay 1863-1930 Roscoff. B-DBA-T.

GERBIER D'OUVILLY, [Sir] BALTHASAR.
Eng. Middelburg 1592-1667 London. B-DNB-T.

GERBINO, ROSARIO.
Am. ad. 1935 New York. M.

GERDES, AUGUSTUS M.
Am. ad. 1934 New Canaan, Conn. M.

GERE, CHARLES MARCH.
Eng. b. Leamington 1869; ex. 1934 London. B-Wa.

GERE, MARGARET.
Eng. b. 1878. M.

GERE, NELLIE HUNTINGTON.
Am. b. Norwich, Conn. 1859; ad. 1934 Los Angeles, Calif. A-B.

GERHAERT, NICOLAUS VON LEYDEN. (S)
Dut. ac. 1462-1487 in Leyden. Hs-T.

GERHARD, GEORGE.
Am. Germany 1830-1902 New York. A04-B-T.

GERHARDT, KARL. (S)
Am. b. Boston 1853; ad. 1915 New Orleans, La. A12-F-Ta.

GÉRICAULT, JEAN LOUIS ANDRÉ THÉODORE.
Fr. Rouen 1791-1824 Paris. B-Bd-C-E-T-722-820.

GÉRINES [or Gérnes], JACQUES DE. (S)
Flem. ac. 1392-1463 in Brussels. B-Hs-T.

GERINI, NICCOLÒ DE PIETRO.
see Niccolò di Pietro.

GERLACH, ALBERT ANTHONY.
Am. b. Chicago 1884; ad. 1934 Portland, Ore. A.

GERLACH, GUSTAVE. (S)
Am. ac. 1900. F-Ta.

GERNEZ, PAUL ÉLIE.
Fr. b. Valenciennes 1888. DBA-Wa.

GEROLAMO. *see* Girolamo.

GÉRÔME, JEAN LÉON. (P-S)
Fr. Vesoul 1824-1904 Paris. B-Bd-C-E-T-710-927.

GERRARD, A. HUBERT. (S)
Ger. 1545-1620 Munich. Hs-798.

GERRARD, CHARLES ROBERT.
Eng. b. Antwerp, Belg. 1892; ad. 1934 London. Wa.

GERRER, ROBERT GREGORY.
Am. b. Alsace, Fr. 1867; ad. 1934 Shawnee, Okla. A-F.

GERRIT VAN HAARLEM.
see Geertgen tot Sint Jans.

GERRY, SAMUEL LANCASTER.
Am. Boston 1813-1891 Roxbury, Mass. C-F-T-4-6-15.

GERSHOY, EUGÈNIE. (S)
Am. b. Rus. 1902; ad. 1934 Woodstock, N. Y. A.

GERSHWIN, GEORGE. (Composer-P)
Am. b. Brooklyn, N. Y. 1898; ad. 1935 New York. W.

GERSTLE, MIRIAM ALICE.
Am. b. San Fran., Calif. 1898; ad. 1934 London. A.

GERSTLE, WILLIAM LEWIS.
Am. b. San Fran., Calif. 1868; ad. 1934 Same. A.

GERTLER, MARK.
Eng. b. London 1892; ex. 1933 Pittsburgh, Pa. Wa-825.

GERTNER, JOHAN VILHELM.
Dan. Nyboder 1818-1871 Copenhagen. B-T.

GERTNER, PETER.
Ger. ac. 1527. M.

GERUNG, MATTHIAS.
Ger. Nördlingen 1500-1568/70 Laningen. T.

GERVAIS, CHARLES. *see* Jervas, Charles.

GERVAIS, PAUL JEAN LOUIS.
Fr. b. Toulouse 1859. B-DBA-T.

GERVASI, FRANK.
Am. ad. 1934 Sunnyside, L. I., N. Y. M.

GERVEX, HENRI.
Fr. Paris 1852-1929. B-C-DBA-E-T.

GESELSCHAP, ÉDUARD.
Dut. Amsterdam 1814-1878 Düsseldorf, Ger. C-T.

GESELSCHAP, FRIEDRICH.
Prussian. Wesel 1835-1898 Rome, It. C-T.

GESSEN, KANO [Genzui].
Jap. Sakura 1721-1809 Tamada. T.

GESSEN, SOGA.
Jap. ac. 1750. J., Vol. 1, page 97.

GESSI, FRANCESCO GIOVANNI.
It. Bologna 1588-1649 Same. B-T-722.

GESSNER, ABRAHAM.
Swi. Zurich 1552-1613. B-T.

GESSNER, JOHANN KONRAD.
Swi. Zurich 1764-1826 Same. B-T.

GESSNER, SALOMON.
Swi. Zurich 1730-1788. B-T-367.

GEST, JOSEPH HENRY.
Am. b. Cinn., O. 1859. A24-B-F.

GEST, MARGARET RALSTON.
Am. b. Phila., Pa. 1900; ad. 1934 Same. A.

GETCHELL, EDITH LORING. (Et.)
Am. b. Bristol, Pa.; ad. 1935 Worcester, Mass. A20-F.

GETTIER, G. WILMER.
Am. b. Balt., Md. 1877; ad. Same. A.
GETZ, ARTHUR.
Am. ex. 1934 Montclair, N. J. M.
GEUBELS. *see* Guebels.
GEUSLAIN [or Gueslin], CHARLES ÉTIENNE.
Fr. Paris 1685-1765 Same. B-T.
GEYER, GEORG.
Aus. b. Vienna 1823; ac. 1888. B-T.
GEYER, JOHANN.
Ger. Augsburg 1807-1875 Same. B-T.
GHARIS, CHARLES MASON TUDOR.
Am. b. Dallas, Tex. 1910; ad. 1934 Same. A.
GHEERAERTS, MARCUS [The Elder].
Flem. Bruges 1516-1590 London. B-DNB-T.
GHEERAERTS, MARCUS [The Younger].
Flem. Bruges 1561-1635 London. B-T.
GHENDT, ÉMMANUEL JEAN NEPOMUCÉNE. (Eg.)
Fr. St. Nicolas 1738-1815 Paris. B-T.
GHENT, JUSTUS DE. *see* Justus of Ghent.
GHENT, PETER.
Welsh. b. Wales 1857; d. 1911 Liverpool, Eng. B-T.
GHERARDI, CRISTOFANO [Doceno].
It. Borgo San Sepolcro 1500-1556. B-T.
GHERARDO DEL FORA. (Min)
It. ac. 1445-1497 in Florence. T-V.
GHERARDO DELLE NOTTI.
see Honthorst, Gerard van.
GHERARDO, FIORENTINO.
It. 1407/32-1494/8. B-T.
GHERARDO, GIOVANNI DI.
It. ac. 1445-1497 in Florence. T-V.
GHERASSIMOFF, SERGUEY.
Rus. ad. 1929 in Russia. M.
GHERINGH, ANTHONIS GÜNTHER.
Flem. Allemagne 1620-1667 Antwerp. B-T.
GHERWEN [or Gerwen], REYNIER VAN.
Dut. ac. 1652-1661 in Holland. B-T.
GHEYN [or Geyn], JACOB DE [The Elder].
Flem. Antwerp 1530/2-1582 Utrecht, Holland. B-T.
GHEYN [or Geyn], JACOB DE [The Younger].
Flem. Antwerp 1565-1629. B-T.
GHEZZI. *see also* Domenico di Bartolo.
GHEZZI, GIUSEPPE.
It. Rieti 1634-1721 Rome. B-T.
GHEZZI, PIER LEONE.
It. Rome 1674-1755 Same. B-T.
GHIBERTI, BONACCORSO.
It. Florence 1451-1516 Same. T-V.
GHIBERTI, LORENZO DI CIONE. (S)
It. Florence 1378-1455/6. B-E-Hs-T-V.
GHIBERTI, VITTORIO I. (S)
It. Florence 1416-1496. Hs-V.
GHIGLIA, OSCAR.
It. b. Leghorn 1876; ad. 1934 Florence. T.
GHILIONI, PIETRO. (S)
It. b. Barga; ad. 1934 Grant Park, S. I., N. Y. M.
GHIRLANDAJO, BENEDETTO.
It. Florence 1458-1497 Same. T-V.
GHIRLANDAJO, DAVID.
It. Florence 1452-1525 Same. T-V.
GHIRLANDAJO, DOMENICO BIGORDI.
[Called the "Maker of Garlands".]
It. Florence 1449-1494 Same.
B-Bd-C-E-T-V-78-722.
GHIRLANDAJO, RIDOLFO BIGORDI.
It. Florence 1483-1560/1.
B-Bd-C-E-T-V-78-722.
GHISLANDI, FRA VITTORIO [Paolotto].
It. Bergamo 1655-1743 Venice. B-T.
GHISONI, FERMO DI STEFANO.
It. Caravaggio 1505-1575 Mantua. T-V.
GHOSN, ASSAD THOMAS.
Am. b. Mt. Lebanon, Syria 1880; ad. 1934 Richmond, Va. A.
GHUY, ANTOINE MARCENAY DE. (Et.)
Fr. b. 1722; d. 1811. M.
GIACOMANTONIO, ARCHIMEDES A. (S)
Am. b. N. J. 1918; ad. 1935 Jersey City, N. J. M.
GIACOMELLI, HECTOR.
Fr. Paris 1822-1904 Menton. B-T.
GIACOMETTI, ALBERTO. (S)
It. ex. 1934 New York. M.
GIACOMETTI, AUGUSTO.
Swi. b. Stampa 1877. B-T-681.
GIACOMETTI, FÉLIX HENRI.
Fr. Quingey 1828-1909 Besançon. B-T.
GIACOMETTI, GIOVANNI.
It. Stampa 1868-1933. B-T.
GIAMBONO, MICHELE DI TADDEO.
It. b. Venice; ac. 1420-1462. T.
GIAMMARTINI, ACHILLE. (S)
Am. Pittsburgh 1861-1929 Atlanta, Ga.
A026.
GIAMPIETRINO. *see* Pedrini, G.
GIANFRANCESCO DEI MAINERI.
see Maineri.
GIAQUINTO, CORRADO.
It. Molfetta 1693/9-1765 Naples. T.
GIAUME, ALEXANDER.
Fr. b. Villefranche-sur-Mer 1909. DBA.
GIAUME, JEAN.
Fr. b. Villefranche-sur-Mer 1904. DBA.
GIBB, ROBERT [The Elder].
Scot. Dundee 1801-1837. B-DNB-T.
GIBB, ROBERT [The Younger].
Scot. Laurieston 1845-1932. B-T-Y01933.
GIBBINGS, ROBERT JOHN. (Eg.)
Ir. b. Cork 1889; ex. 1934 London. Wa.
GIBBONS, GRINLING. (Carver)
Eng. London 1648-1721 Same.
B-DNB-Hs-T-368-864.
GIBBS, GEORGE. (Ill.)
Am. b. New Orleans, La. 1870; ad. 1934 Phila., Pa. A-B-F-W.
GIBBS, ROBERT.
Scot. b. 1846; d. 1932. M.
GIBRAN, KAHLIL.
Syrian. d. 1934 New York. M.
GIBSON, CHARLES DANA. (Ill.)
Am. b. Roxbury, Mass. 1867; ad. 1935 New York. A-B-E-F-T-W-46.
GIBSON, CORA PURVIANCE.
Am. b. Phila., Pa. 1904; ad. 1934 Same. A.
GIBSON, JOHN. (S)
Eng. Conway 1790-1866 Rome, It.
B-E-Hs-T.
GIBSON, LYDIA.
Am. b. New York 1891; ad. 1934 Croton, N. Y. A.
GIBSON, PATRICK [or Peter].
Scot. Edinburgh 1782?-1829 Dollar.
B-DNB-T.

GIDDENS, PHILIP H. (Et)
Am. ad. 1935 New York. M..
GIBSON, RICHARD. (Min.)
Eng. 1615-1690 London. B-DNB-T.
GIBSON, SOLOMON. (S)
Eng. ac. in Liverpool; d. 1866 Paris. DNB-T.
GIBSON, SUSAN PENELOPE. (Min.)
Eng. 1652-1700 London. B-DNB-T.
GIBSON, THOMAS.
Eng. 1680?-1751 London. B-DNB-T.
GIBSON, WILLIAM. (Min.)
Eng. 1644-1702 Richmond, Eng. B-DNB-T.
GIBSON, WILLIAM ALFRED.
Scot. b. Glasgow 1866. B-Wa1929.
GIBSON, WILLIAM HAMILTON.
Am. Newtown, Conn. 1850-1896 Wash., D. C. DAB-E-F-76-77.
GIDDENS, PHILIP H. (Et.)
Am. ad. 1935 New York. M.
GIDEON, SAMUEL EDWARD.
Am. b. Louisville, Ky. 1875; ad. 1934 Austin, Tex. A-F.
GIEBERICH, OSCAR H.
Am. b. New York, N. Y. 1886; ad. 1934 Brooklyn, N. Y. A.
GIERYMISKI, MAXIMILIAN [Maks].
Pol. Warsaw 1846-1874 Reichenhall. B-T.
GIES, JOSEPH W.
Am. b. Detroit, Mich.; ac. 1926. A20-B-F-T-46.
GIESBERT, EDMUND.
Am. b. Neuwied, Ger. 1893; ad. 1934 New York. A.
GIFFART, PIERRE. (Eg.)
Fr. Paris 1638-1723 Same. B-T.
GIFFEN, LILIAN.
Am. b. New Orleans, La.; ad. 1934 Balt., Md. A-F.
GIFFORD, FRANCIS ELIOT.
Mrs. Robert Swan Gifford.
Am. b. New Bedford, Mass. 1844. A14-C-F-W13-15.
GIFFORD, GEORGE. (Eg.)
Br. ac. 1640 in London. B-DNB-T.
GIFFORD, REBECCA.
Am. ad. 1934 New Canaan, Conn. M.
GIFFORD, ROBERT GREGORY.
Am. b. West Medford, Mass. 1895; ad. 1934 Duxbury, Mass. A.
GIFFORD, ROBERT SWAIN.
Am. Island of Naushon, Mass. 1840-1905 New York. A05-B-C-DAB-E-T-1-4-22-39-46.
GIFFORD, SANFORD ROBINSON.
Am. Greenfield, Mass. 1873-1880 New York. B-Bd-C-DAB-E-F-T-1-4-15-22-39-219.
GIGER, VERA M.
Mrs. Walter Giger.
Am. b. 1895 Brooklyn, N. Y.; ad. 1934 Milwaukee, Wis. A.
GIGLI, GIOVANNI BATTISTA.
It. Pistoie 1713-1750. B-T.
GIGOUX, JEAN FRANÇOIS.
Fr. Besançon 1806-1894. B-T.
GIGOUX, REGIS.
Fr. Lyons 1816-1882. B-F-T-4-15.
GIHON, ALBERT DAKIN.
Am. b. Portsmouth, N. H. 1866; ad. 1934 Paris. A-F-T-W.
GIHON, CLARENCE MONTFORD.
Am. Phila., Pa. 1871-1929 Paris. A026.
GIL, JOSÉ.
Sp. Valencia 1759-1828 Barcelona. T.
GIL, JOSÉ PEDRO. (Eg)
Sp. b. Paris 1892. DBA.
GILBERT, ALBERT THOMAS JARVIS. (Ill)
Eng. b. London; d. 1927. Wa01929.
GILBERT, [Sir] ALFRED. (S)
[Called "Modern Cellini".]
Eng. London 1854-1934 Same.
B-E-Hs-T-Wa-Obit. N. Y. papers, 11-5-1934, also Obit. Apollo, 12-1934.
GILBERT, ARTHUR HILL.
Am. b. Chicago 1894; ad. 1934 Monterey, Calif. A-F.
GILBERT, CAROLINE.
Am. b. Pardeeville, Wis. 1864; ad. 1934 St. Paul, Minn. A.
GILBERT, CHARLES ALLAN.
Am. Hartford, Conn. 1873-1929 New York. A026-B-F-T-W14.
GILBERT, CHARLES W.
Aust. b. 1869; d. 1925. Y01926.
GILBERT, DOROTHY.
Am. ad. 1935 Woodstock, N. Y. M.
GILBERT, FRANÇOIS AMBROISE GERMAIN. (S)
Fr. b. Choisy-le-Roi 1816; d. 1891. B-T.
GILBERT, GROVE SHELDON.
Am. Clinton, N. Y. 1805-1885 Rochester, N. Y. F.
GILBERT, ISOLDE THERESE.
Am. ad. 1934 Boston, Mass. M.
GILBERT, JAMES J.
Am. ex. 1935 Lawrence, Kan. M.
GILBERT, [Sir] JOHN. (Ill)
Eng. Blackheath 1817-1897 London. B-Bd-C-DNB-E-T.
GILBERT, JOHN GRAHAM.
see Graham-Gilbert, John.
GILBERT, JOSEPH FRANCIS.
Eng. 1792-1855 Portsmouth. B-DNB-T.
GILBERT, PIERRE JULIEN.
Fr. Brest 1783-1860. B-T.
GILBERT, RENÉ JOSEPH.
Fr. Paris 1857/8-1914 Same. B-C-T.
GILBERT, ROBERT.
Am. ad. 1934 Santa Ana, Calif. M.
GILBERT, VICTOR GABRIEL.
Fr. b. Paris 1847. B-DBA-T.
GILBERTSON, WARREN ANTHONY. (S)
Am. b. Watertown, Wis. 1910; ad. 1934 Chicago. A.
GILCHRIST, EMMA S.
Am. d. 1929 Charleston, S. C. A28.
GILCHRIST, WILLIAM WALLACE, JR.
Am. 1879-1926 Brunswick, Me. A024.
GILDER, HELENA DE KAY.
Mrs. R. Watson Gilder.
Am. b. 1846; d. 1916 New York. A013-F-T-15.
GILDER, ROBERT FLETCHER.
Am. b. Flushing, L. I., N. Y. 1856; ad. 1934 Omaha, Neb. A-F.
GILDERSLEEVE, BEATRICE.
Mrs. C. C. Gildersleeve.
Am. b. San Fran., Calif. 1899; ad. 1934 Felton, Calif. A.

GILE, Selden Connor.
Am. b. Stow, Me. 1877; ad. 1934 Belvedere, Calif. A.
GILERMAN, Diana.
Am. ad. 1934 New York. M.
GILES, Ellen.
Am. b. 1874 U. S.; d. 1914 Rome, It. A0X1.
GILES, Howard Everett.
Am. b. Brooklyn, N. Y. 1876; ad. 1934 New York. A-B-F-W.
GILES, James William.
Scot. Glasgow 1801-1870 Aberdeen. B-DNB-T.
GILES, John.
Aust. b. Glanville, Aust. 1885. M.
GILFILLAN, John Alexander.
Scot. b. Glasgow 1793; d. Melbourne, Aust. B-T.
GILKISON, Grace. (Ill)
Am. ad. 1935 So. Norwalk, Conn. M.
GILL, André. *see* Gosset de Guines.
GILL, Colin Unwin.
Eng. b. Kent 1892; ad. 1934 London. Wa.
GILL, De Lancey.
Am. b. Chester, S. C. 1859; ad. 1935 Alexandria, Va. M.
GILL, Edmund.
Eng. Clerkenwell 1820-1894 Hackbridge. B-T.
GILL, Eric [Arthur Eric Rowton]. (S)
Eng. b. Brighton 1882. Wa-369-825-864-884.
GILL, Harry Pelling.
Eng. b. London; d. 1916. M.
GILL, Paul Ludwig.
Am. b. New York 1894; ad. 1934 Wynnewood, Pa. A-F.
GILL, S. Leslie.
Am. b. Valley Falls, R. I. 1908; ad. 1934 Prov., R. I. A.
GILL, [Mrs.] Sue May Westcott.
Am. b. Sabinal, Tex.; ad. 1934 Wynnewood, Pa. A.
GILL, S. T.
Aust. d. 1890 Melbourne, Aust. B-T.
GILLAM, Bernhard. (Cart)
Am. England 1856-1896 Canajoharie, N. Y. DAB-78-79.
GILLAM, William Charles Frederick. (Et)
Am. ad. 1934 Burlingame, Calif. A.
GILLARD, Émile.
Fr. b. Paris 1866. DBA.
GILLÉE, Claude. *see* Claude.
GILLER, William. (Eg)
Eng. b. 1805; d. 1868. T.
GILLESPIE, John.
Am. b. Malta, O. 1901; ad. 1934 McConnellsville, O. A.
GILLESPIE, Sallie Meredith.
Am. ad. 1934 Fort Worth, Tex. M.
GILLET, Edward Frank. (Ill)
Eng. Suffolk 1874-1927. Wa01929.
GILLETTE, Lester A.
Am. b. Columbus, O. 1855; ad. Gloucester, Mass. A.
GILLIAM, Marguerite Hubbard.
Am. b. Boulder, Colo.; ad. 1934 Same. A.
GILLIARD, Eugène.
Fr. Paris 1861-1921. B-DBA-T.
GILLICK, Ernest George. (S)
Eng. b. Nottingham; ac. 1900. B.
GILLIES, Margaret.
Eng. London 1803-1887 Kent, Eng. B-DNB-T.
GILLMORE, Edwina S. (S)
Am. ad. 1934 Great Neck, L. I., N. Y. M.
GILLOT, Claude.
Fr. Langres 1673-1722 Paris. B-C-E-T-722.
GILLRAY, James. (Cari)
Eng. 1757-1815 London. B-DNB-E-T.
GILMAN, Harold.
Eng. Somerset 1876-1919 Canada. 825.
GILMAN, John Ward ["G. J. W."]. (Eg)
Am. Exeter, Mass. 1741-1823 Same. 7-147.
GILMORE, Ada.
Am. ad. 1934 Provincetown, Mass. M.
GILPIN, Blanche Reed. (Min)
Am. ad. 1934 Moorestown, N. J. M.
GILPIN, Charles Armour.
Am. b. Cumberland, Md. 1867; ad. 1934 Phila., Pa. A-F
GILPIN, Sawrey.
Eng. Carlisle 1733-1807 Brompton. B-DNB-T-722.
GILPIN, William Sawrey.
Eng. 1762-1843 Yorkshire. B-DNB-T.
GILSOUL, Victor Olivier.
Belg. b. Brussels 1867. B-DBA-T.
GILSTRAP, W. H.
Am. b. Illinois 1840; d. 1914 Tacoma, Wash. A012.
GIMBER, Stephen H. (Eg)
Am. England 1810-1862 Phila., Pa. F-T-2-6-7.
GIMBREDE, Joseph Napoleon. (Eg)
Am. b. West Point, N. Y. 1820. [No death date.] F-7-40.
GIMBREDE, Thomas. (Eg)
Am. France 1781-1832 West Point, N. Y. F-T-2-6-7-40.
GIMEL, Georges.
Fr. b. Domène 1898. B-DBA-T.
GIMENO, Patricio.
Am. b. Arequipa, Peru, S. A. 1865; ad. 1934 Norman, Okla. A.
GIMIGNANI [or Gemignani], Giacinto.
It. Pistoja 1611-1681 Same. C-T.
GIMOND, Marcel Antoine. (S)
Fr. b. Tournon 1894. DBA.
GINCANO, John. (Ill)
Am. ad. 1933 New York. M.
GINDELE, Mathias.
Am. b. 1851; d. 1930 Cinn., O. A027.
GINER, Balbino.
Sp. ad. 1934 Rome, It. M.
GINER, Carlos G. de los Rios.
Sp. b. Madrid 1874. T.
GINER Y VIDAL, Carlos.
Sp. b. Valencia 1834. [No death date.] B-T.
GINNETT, Louis. (Mu)
Eng. ad. 1934 Ditchling, Eng. Wa.
GINNER, Charles.
Eng. b. Cannes, Fr. 1878; ad. 1934 Hampstead. Wa-825.
GINSBURG, Jacob.
Am. ad. 1935 Brooklyn, N. Y. M.

GINTHER, MARY PEMBERTON.
Mrs. M. P. G. Heyler.
Am. b. Phila., Pa.; ad. 1934 Buckingham, Pa. A-W.
GINTHER, WALTER KARL.
Am. b. Winona, Minn. 1894; ad. 1934 Same. A.
GINZEL, JAKOB.
Ger. Reichberg 1792-1862. T.
GIOCONDO, FRA GIOVANNI.
It. Verona 1433-1515 Rome. T-V.
GIOIA, FRANK DI.
Am. b. Italy; ex. 1935 New York. M.
GIOJA, ÉDOUARDO.
It. b. Rome 1862; ac. 1926. T.
GIOLFINO, NICCOLÒ. II.
It. Verona 1476-1555. T.
GIONFRIDDA, JOSEPH M.
Am. b. Canicattini Bagni, It. 1907; ad. 1934 Hartford, Conn. A.
GIORDANO, LUCA FAPRESTO [Fa Presto].
It. Naples 1632-1705 Same. B-Bd-C-E-T-722-897.
GIORDANO DI PALMA, LÉON JEAN.
Fr. b. Marseilles 1886. DBA.
GIORGIO DA CASTELFRANCO.
It. 1478-1510 Venice. T-722.
GIORGIO, EUSEBIO DI SAN.
see Eusebio da Giorgio.
GIORGIO, FRANCESCO DI. (P-S)
It. Siena 1439-1502 Same. Hs-T-V-78.
GIORGIONE IL. [Giorgio Barbarelli].
It. Castelfranco 1477/8-1510/1 Venice. B-Bd-C-E-T-V-370-371-722.
GIOTTINO [Giotto di Maestro Stefano].
It. ac. 1368-1400 in Florence. T.
GIOTTINO, TOMMASO [Masco di Banco].
It. ac. 1324-1357 in Florence. V.
GIOTTO DI BONDONE [Ambrogitto]. (P-S)
It. Colle 1266/7-1336/7 Florence. B-Bd-C-E-T-V-372-373-374-375-770-784-790-806-878.
GIOVANE, PALMA. *see* Palma, G.
GIOVANNI, ANTONIO DA BRESCIA.
It. b. 1470; d. 1520 in Italy. T.
GIOVANNI, BARTOLOMMEO DI.
It. ac. 1480-1500 in Florence. T-V.
GIOVANNI, DARIO DI. *see* Dario di G.
GIOVANNI, JACOBI. *see* Giovanni da Milano.
GIOVANNI, M.
Am. ad. 1934 Phila., Pa. M.
GIOVANNI, MATTEO. *see* Matteo di G.
GIOVANNI, VENEZIANO.
It. ac. 14th Cent. in Italy. M.
GIOVANNI DA BOLOGNA. *see* Bologna, G.
GIOVANNI DA FIESOLE. *see* Angelico, Fra G.
GIOVANNI DA GIUSTO. *see* Menabuoi.
GIOVANNI DA MILANO [Jacobi].
It. Florence 1300-1369/70 Rome. B-T.
GIOVANNI DA UDINE.
It. Udine 1487-1564 Rome. C.
GIOVANNI DA VERONA, FRA.
It. Verona 1457-1525 Same. T.
GIOVANNI DAL PONTE [da San Stefano].
It. b. 1385; d. 1437/40 in Italy. M.
GIOVANNI DE BOCCATIS. *see* Boccatis, G.
GIOVANNI DEL BIONDO [dei Landini?].
It. Florence 1356-1392. T-V.
GIOVANNI DELL' OPERA. *see* Bandini.
GIOVANNI DI AGOSTINO. *see* Agostino, G.
GIOVANNI DI FRANCESCO.
see Master of the Carrand Triptych.
GIOVANNI DI GUALTIERI. *see* Gualtieri, G.
GIOVANNI DI PAOLO, DI GRAZIA.
It. Siena 1402/3-1482/3 Same. B-T-78-770-905.
GIOVANNI DI PAOLO, DA VENEZIA. (S)
It. ac. 1342-1345 in Italy. B-T.
GIOVANNI DI PIETRO. *see* Spagna.
GIRALDON, ADOLPHE PAUL.
Fr. Marseilles 1855-1933. DBA-T.
GIRALTE, FRANCISCO. (S)
Sp. b. Valladolid; ac. 1549-1561. B-T.
GIRARD VAN HAARLEM.
see Geertgen tot Sint Jans.
GIRARD, MARIE FRANÇOIS FIRMIN.
see Firmin-Girard, M. F.
GIRARD-MOND, EDMOND ÉMILE.
Fr. b. Paris 1892. DBA.
GIRARD-RABACHE, HÈLÉNE.
Fr. b. Paris 1888. DBA.
GIRARDET, BERTHE. (S)
Fr. b. Marseilles 1867. B-DBA-T-829.
GIRARDET, ÉDOUARD HENRI.
Swi. Locie, Swi. 1819-1880 Versailles, Fr. B-T.
GIRARDET, EUGÈNE ALEXIS.
Fr. Paris 1853-1908. B-T.
GIRARDET, JEAN.
Fr. Nancy 1709-1778 Paris. B-T.
GIRARDET, JULES.
Fr. b. Paris 1856. B-DBA-T.
GIRARDET, KARL.
Swi. Locle, Swi. 1813-1871 Paris. B-T.
GIRARDET, LÉON.
Fr. Versailles 1857-1895. B-T.
GIRARDET, PAUL. (Eg.)
Fr. Neuchâtel 1821-1893 Paris. B-T.
GIRARDIN, FRANK J.
Am. b. Louisville, Ky. 1856; ad. 1934 Los Angeles, Calif. A-B-F-T.
GIRARDON, FRANÇOIS. (S)
Fr. Troyes 1628-1715 Paris. B-E-Hs-T.
GIRAUD, GEORGES.
Fr. b. Rennes 1882. DBA.
GIRAUD, JEAN BAPTISTE. (S)
Fr. Aix 1752-1830 Bouleaux. B-T.
GIRAUD, PIERRE FRANÇOIS EUGÈNE.
Fr. Paris 1806-1881. B-T.
GIRAUD, PIERRE FRANÇOIS GRÉGOIRE. (S)
Fr. 1783-1836. B-Hs-T.
GIRAUD, VICTOR JULIEN.
Fr. Paris 1835/40-1871. B-T.
GIRAULT, EUGÈNE. (S)
Fr. b. Toulon 1886. DBA.
GIRIEUD, PIERRE PAUL.
Fr. b. Marseilles 1874/5. DBA.
GIRLANDAIO. *see* Ghirlandajo.
GIRODET DE ROUSSY-TRIOSAN, ANNE LOUIS.
Fr. Montargis 1767-1824 Paris. B-C-E-T-722.
GIRODON, ANNE JOSEPH ALPHONSE [Pralong].
Fr. Ardèche 1812-1898. B-T.
GIROLAMO DI BENVENUTO DEL GUSTA.
It. Siena 1470-1524. T.
GIROLAMO DI BERNARDINO DA UDINE.
It. b. Udine; ac. 1490-1512. T.

GIROLAMO DA CREMONA.
It. ac. 1467-1483 in Padua. T.
GIROLAMO, GENZA. *see* Genza, G.
GIROLAMO DAI LIBRI. *see* Libri, G.
GIROLAMO DA SANTA CROCE. *see* Santa Croce, G.
GIRON, CHARLES.
Swi. b. Geneva 1850; d. 1914. B-DBA-T.
GIRSH, FREDERICK.
Am. Germany 1821-1895 Mt. Vernon, N. Y. F-T-7.
GIRTIN, THOMAS ["Tom"].
Eng. Southwark 1775-1802 London. B-DNB-E-T-722-844-909.
GISBERT, ANTONIO.
Sp. b. Alcoy; ac. 1859-1880. B-T.
GISCH, WILLIAM S.
Am. ad. 1934 Cleveland, O. A.
GISLEBERTUS. (S)
Fr. ac. 1150 in Autun, Fr. B-T.
GIULIANO, BARTOLOMEO.
It. Suse 1825-1909. B-T.
GIULIO, ROMANO [Pippi].
[Giulio di Pietro de Giannuzzi.]
It. Rome 1492/9-1546 Mantua. B-C-E-T-V-722.
GIULIO DA URBINO.
It. ac. 1535-1547 in Siena. B-T-V.
GIUNTA, PISANO.
[Earliest Italian painter whose name is found inscribed upon an extant work.]
It. ac. 1180/1202-1236/58 in Pisa. B-E-T-V.
GIUSTI. *see* Juste.
GIUSTI-AMMIANI, GIOVANNI BATTISTA. (S)
It. ac. 17th Cent. in Italy. B-Hs-T.
GIUSTO, ANDREA DI.
see Andrea di Giusto (Manzini).
GIUSTO DA GIOVANNI. *see* Menabuoi.
GIUSTO DA GUANTO. *see* Justus of Ghent.
GIVEN, EBEN. (Ill.)
Am. ad. 1934 New York. M.
GLACKENS, IRA.
Am. ex. 1935 New York. M.
GLACKENS, LENNA. (Et)
Am. ex. 1935 New York. M.
GLACKENS, LOUIS. (Cart.)
Am. Phlia., Pa. 1866-1933 New York. A030.
GLACKENS, WILLIAM J.
Am. b. Phila., Pa. 1870; ad. 1935 New York. A-B-E-F-T-W-1-46-51-105-172-376-700-701-779.
GLAIZE, LÉON PIERRE PAUL.
Fr. b. Paris 1842. B-C-DBA-T.
GLAMAN, [Mrs.] EUGENIE FISH.
Am. b. St. Joseph, Mo. 1873; ad. 1934 Chicago. A-F.
GLASER, JOSEPHINE.
Am. b. New York 1901; ad. 1934 Same. A.
GLASHAN. *see* McGlashan.
GLASS, [Mrs.] BERTHA WALKER.
Am. ad. 1934 San Fran., Calif. M.
GLASS, JAMES W.
Am. b. 1825; d. 1857 New York. B-Bd-C-F-T-4-15.
GLASS, SARAH KRAMER.
Am. b. Troy, O. 1885; ad. 1934 East Gloucester., Mass. A.
GLASSER, LOUIS EUGÈNE.
Fr. b. Belfort 1897. DBA.
GLASSFORD, PELHAM D.
Am. ac. 1933 Wash., D. C. M.
GLASSON, LANCELOT MYLES.
Eng. b. London 1894; ad. 1934 Same. Wa.
GLATZ, OZKÁR.
Hun. Budapest 1872; ex. 1934 London. B-T.
GLAUBER [Polydore], JAN.
Dut. Utrecht 1646-1726 Schoonhoven. B-T-722.
GLAUKIAS OF ALGINA. (S)
Gr. [Doric]; ac. 490-460 B.C. B-Hs-T.
GLAZEBROOK, HUGH DE TWENEBROKES.
Eng. b. London; ac. 1900. B-DBA.
GLEADAH, J.
Br. ac. 1828. M.
GLEASON, DUNCAN.
Am. b. Watsonville, Calif. 1881; ad. 1934 Hollywood, Calif. A.
GLEESON, CHARLES K. (Et.)
Am. b. St. Louis, Mo. 1878; ad. 1934 Kirkwood, Mo. A-W.
GLEESON, JOSEPH MICHAEL.
Am. b. Dracut, Mass. 1861; ad. 1915 New York. B-F.
GLEHN, WILFRED GABRIEL VON.
Ger. b. London 1870. B-DBA-T.
GLEICHEN, VICTOR [Prince of Hohenloe].
Ger. Wurtemburg, Ger. 1833-1891 London. T.
GLEIZES, ALBERT LÉON.
Fr. b. Paris 1881; ad. 1935 Same. DBA-797.
GLEMAKER, PAUL.
Am. ex. 1934 Minn., Minn. M.
GLENDENNING, ALFRED A.
Eng. b. London; ac. 1861-1903 Same. B-T.
GLENNY, ALICE RUSSELL.
Mrs. John Glenny.
Am. b. Detroit, Mich. 1858; ad. 1915 Buffalo, N. Y. A12-F.
GLENNY, ANNA. (S)
Am. b. 1888; ad. 1934 Buffalo, N. Y. M.
GLEYRE, MARC CHARLES GABRIEL.
Swi. Shevilly 1806-1874. B-C-E-T.
GLICENATEIN, ENOCH HENRYK. (S)
Am. b. Turka, Pol. 1870; ex. 1934 New York. B-Cs-T.
GLICKMAN, MAURICE.
Am. ad. 1934 New York. M.
GLINDONI, HENRY GILLARD.
Eng. 1852-1913 London. B-T.
GLINES, [Mrs.] ELLEN.
Am. ad. 1934 San Juan, P. R. M.
GLINK, FRANZ XAVIER.
Bav. Burgau 1795-1873 Munich. C-T.
GLINSKY, VINCENT.
Am. ad. 1935 New York. M.
GLINTENKAMP, H. ["Glint"]. (Ill)
Am. b. Augusta, N. J.; ad. 1934 Armenia, N. Y. A.
GLISENTI, ACHILLE.
It. b. Brescia; ac. 1906. B-T.
GLOCKENDON, ALBRECHT [The Younger].
Ger. ac. 1547-1568 in Nüremberg. B-T.
GLOCKENDON, GEORGE [or Jorg] [The Elder].
Ger. ac. 1484-1514 in Nüremberg. B-T.

GLOVER, George. (Eg)
Eng. ac. 1625-1650 in London. B-DNB-T.
GLOVER, John.
Eng. Houghton 1767-1849 Tasmania. B-DNB-T-377-515.
GLOVER, Moses.
Eng. ac. 1620-1640 in London. DNB-T.
GLUCK, Louis Théodore Eugène.
Fr. Altkirch 1820-1898 Paris. B-T.
GLUCKLICH, Simon.
Ger. b. Munich; ac. 1903. B-T.
GLUCKMAN, Grigory [or Gregori].
Rus. b. Moscow 1898. DBA.
GLYCON OF ATHENS. (S) Gr. Hs-T.
GOBBO, Il. *see* Solario, Andrea.
GOBELIN, Jehan.
[Founder of the Gobelin family, tapestry makers].
Fr. d. Paris 1476. E.
GOBELL, Gerrit Henderich.
Dut. Raalte 1786-1833 Deventer. B-T.
GOBERT Family.
Fr. ac. 17-18th Cent. in France. T.
GOBERT, Pierre.
Fr. Fontainebleau 1662-1744 Paris. B-T.
GOBLE, Warwick.
Eng. ad. 1934 Merstham, Eng. M.
GOBO, Georges.
Am. b. San Fran., Calif. 1876; ad. 1927 Paris. DBA.
GOBRECHT, Christian. (Eg)
Am. Hanover, Pa. 1785-1844 Phila., Pa. DAB-F-T-2-7-40-80-81.
GODBOULD, Samuel Berry.
Eng. ac. 1842-1875 in London. T.
GODBY, James. (Eg)
Eng. ac. 1790-1820 in London. B-DNB-T.
GODDARD, E.
Am. ac. 1837/40 in Rhode Island. M.
GODDARD, George Bouverie.
Eng. Salisbury 1832-1886 London. B-DNB-T.
GODDARD, John. (Eg)
Eng. ac. 1645-1671 in London. B-DNB-T.
GODDARD, Ralph Bartlett. (S)
Am. b. Meadville, Pa. 1861; ad. 1934 New York. A-B-F-T-W.
GODDARD, Virginia W. (Et)
Am. ad. 1934 New York. M.
GODEBSKI, Cyprien. (S)
Pol. b. Mery-sur-Cher 1835; d. 1909 Paris. B-DBA-T.
GODEFROID. *see* Godefroy.
GODEFROY, Adrien Pierre François. (Eg)
Fr. Paris 1777-1865. B.
GODEFROY, Jean. (Eg)
Fr. London 1771-1839 Paris. B-T.
GODEFROY, Maria Eléonore.
Fr. Paris 1778-1849 Same. B-T.
GODEFROY, Maximilian.
Am. b. France; ac. 1890-1913 U. S. DAB-T-2-82-83.
GODEFROY, Richard Bernard. (Eg)
Eng. London 1728-1794. B-Bd-DNB-T.
GODEMAN, [or Godemannus]. (Min)
[Monk of Hyde Abbey].
Fr.-Br. d. 984 A.D. B-T.
GODFREY, Paul.
Eng. ex. 1934 in London. M.
GODINEAU, Louis Jacques.
Belg. Eeclov 1811-1873. B-T.
GODWARD, John William.
Eng. Wimbledon 1861-1922. Y01923.
GODWIN, Abraham. (Eg)
Am. Paterson, N. J. 1763-1835 Same. F-2-7-184.
GODWIN, Frances Bryant. (S)
Am. b. Newport, R. I. 1892; ad. 1935 Roslyn, L. I., N. Y. Cs.
GODWIN, Frank. (Ill)
Am. b. Wash., D. C. 1889; ad. 1934 Greenwich, Conn. A.
GODWIN, Karl. (Ill)
Am. b. Canada 1893; ad. 1934 New York. A.
GOEHLER [or Göhler], Hermann.
Ger. b. 1874 in Carlsruhe, Ger. T.
GOELLER, Charles L.
Am. ex. 1934 New York. M.
GOENEUTTE, Norbert.
Fr. Paris 1854-1894. B-T.
GOEPP. *see* Guyon.
GOEREE, Jan.
Dut. Middelburg 1670-1731 Amsterdam. T.
GOERG, Édouard Joseph.
Fr. b. Sydney, Aust. 1893; ad. 1934 Paris. DBA-797.
GOES, Hugo [or Hughe] van der.
Flem. Goes, Zeeland 1440-1482 Brussels, Belg. B-Bd-C-E-T-722.
GOETHALS, Raymond Eugène.
Fr. Bordeaux 1804-1864 Paris. B-T.
GOETHE, Joe. (S)
Am. ad. 1935 Washington, D. C. M.
GOETHE, Johann Wolfgang von.
Ger. b. 1750; d. 1832 in Germany. T.
GOETSCH, Gustav F.
Am. b. Minn., Minn. 1877; ad. 1934 St. Louis, Mo. A-F.
GOETZE, Otto. (Et)
Ger. ac. 20th Cent. in Berlin. B-T.
GOFF, Lloyd.
Am. ex. 1935 New York. M.
GOFF, Robert Charles.
Eng. London 1837-1922. T.
GOFF, Sudduth.
Am. Eminence, Ky. 1887; ad. 1934 Chicago. A-F.
GOGH. *see* Van Gogh.
GOHL, Edward Heinrich.
Am. b. Harrisburg, Pa. 1862; ad. 1915 Auburn, N. Y. A12-B-F.
GOLD, Ferdinand. (Eg)
Aus. b. Vienna 1882. B-T.
GOLDBECK, Walter Dean.
Am. St. Louis, Mo. 1882-1925 New York. A22-F.
GOLDBERG, Reuben Lucius. (Cart)
Am. b. San Fran., Calif. 1883; ad. 1934 New York. A-F-W.
GOLDE, R. P. (S)
Am. b. Germany; ad. 1915 New York. A12-B.
GOLDEN, Charles O.
Am. b. Newlon, W. Va. 1899; ad. 1934 Bushkill, Pa. M.
GOLDING, Cecil.
Am. ad. 1935 New York. M.
GOLDING, Richard. (Eg)
Eng. London 1785-1865 Same. DNB-T.

GOLDOBIN, Peter Ivanov.
Rus. ac. 1751/2 in Russia. Fa.
GOLDOBIN, Simon.
Rus. ac. 1751/2 in Russia. Fa.
GOLDSBOROUGH, [Mrs.] Nannie Cox.
Am. d. 1923 Easton, Md. A021.
GOLDSCHMIDT, Hermann.
Ger. Frankfort 1802-1866 Fontainebleau, Fr. B-E-T.
GOLDSTEIN, Joseph.
Am. ad. 1934 Brooklyn, N. Y. M.
GOLDSTEIN, Stanley.
Am. ad. 1934 New York. M.
GOLDSWORTHY, Emelia M.
Am. b. Platteville, Wis. 1869; ad. 1935 Kalamazoo, Mich. A12-F.
GOLDTHWAITE, Anne.
Am. b. Montgomery, Ala.; ad. 1934 New York. A-F-W.
GOLINKIN, Joseph Webster. (Et)
Am. b. Chicago 1896; ad. 1934 New York. A.
GOLTON, Glenn.
Am. b. Milton, Kan. 1897; ad. 1934 Wichita, Kan. M.
GOLTZ, Alexander Demetrius.
Hun. b. Püspok, Hun. 1857. B-T.
GOLTZ, Walter.
Am. b. Buffalo, N. Y. 1875; ad. 1934 Woodstock, N. Y. A-F.
GOLTZIUS, Hendrik. (Eg)
Dut. Mulbracht 1558-1617 Haarlem. B-C-E-T-722.
GOLTZIUS, Hubrecht [or Hubert]. (Eg)
Ger. Wurtzburg 1526-1583 Bruges, Belg. B-T.
GOLZ, Julius, Jr.
Am. b. Camden, N. J. 1878; ad. 1915 Same. A12.
GOMEZ, Sébastian.
[Mulatto servant of Murillo].
Sp. 1646-1682 Sèville. B-T.
GOMON, Eugène. (S)
Fr. b. Paris 1814; ac. 1868 Same. [No death date]. B.
GOMON [or Gaumont], Maria.
Rus. ac. 1820 Leningrad [No death date]. T.
GONÇALVES, Nuno.
Por. ac. 1450-1471 in Portugal. T.
GONCOURT, Jules Huot de. (Eg)
Fr. Paris 1830-1870. B-T.
GONSER, Maude Kershaw.
Am. b. Latty, O. 1901; ad. 1934 Fort Wayne, Ind. A.
GONTCHAROVA, Nathalie.
Rus. b. Moscow 1881; ex. 1935 New York. DBA.
GONZALES, Boyer, Sr.
Am. Houston, Tex. 1867-1934 Woodstock, N. Y. A-F-M-T-Obit. N. Y. papers, 2-16-1934; also Obit. Art Digest 3-1-1934.
GONZALES, Boyer, Jr.
Am. ad. 1934 Woodstock, N. Y. M.
GONZALES, Juán. (S)
Sp. ac. 1562 in Sèville. B-T.
GONZALES, Juán Antonio.
Sp. b. Chiclana, Sp. 1842. B-T.
GONZALES, Juanita. (S)
Am. ad. 1932 New York. M.
GONZALES, Xavier.
Am. b. Spain 1899; ad. 1935 San Antonio, Tex. M.
GONZALES Y SERRANO, Bartholomé.
Sp. Valladolid 1564-1627 Madrid. B-T.
GOOCH, Thelma. (Ill)
Am. ad. 1934 New York. M.
GOOD, Bernard Stafford.
Am. b. England 1893; ad. 1934 Wilmington, Del. A.
GOOD, George W.
Am. ad. 1935 New York. M.
GOOD, Minetta.
Am. b. New York; ad. 1934 Same. A.
GOOD, Thomas Sword.
Eng. Berwick 1789-1872 London. DNB-T.
GOODALL, Albert Gallatin. (Eg)
Am. Montgomery, Ala. 1826-1887 New York. F-7.
GOODALL, Edward. (Eg)
Eng. Leeds 1795-1870 London. B-DNB-T.
GOODALL, Edward Alfred.
Eng. London 1819-1908 Same. B-T.
GOODALL, Frederick.
Eng. London 1822-1904 Same. B-C-DNB-T.
GOODALL, Frederick Trevelyan.
Eng. London 1848-1871 Capri. DNB-T.
GOODALL, Howard.
Eng. London 1850-1874 Cairo, Egypt. DNB-T.
GOODALL, Walter.
Eng. London 1830-1889 Clapham. B-DNB-T.
GOODE, Louise. *see* Jopling-Rowe [Mrs.].
GOODELL, William Newport.
Am. b. Germantown, Pa. 1908; ad. 1934 Same. A.
GOODELMAN, Aaron J.
Am. b. Russia 1890; ad. 1934 Bronx, N. Y. A-F.
GOODEN, Stephen. (Ill)
Eng. b. 1892; ad. 1934 London. Wa.
GOODHUE, [Mrs.] Alice Fuller. (Min)
Am. b. New York 1900; ad. 1934 Garden City, L. I., N. Y. A.
GOODHUE, Harry Wright.
Am. b. 1905; d. 1932 Boston, Mass. A029.
GOODMAN, Anne Bedford.
Mrs. John S. Goodman.
Am. b. Ionia, Mich. 1896; ad. 1934 Detroit, Mich. A.
GOODMAN, Arthur Jule.
Am. b. Hartford, Conn.; d. 1926 Cleveland, O. A023
GOODMAN, Bertram.
Am. b. New York 1904; ad. 1934 Same. A.
GOODMAN, Charles. (Eg)
Am. Phila., Pa. 1790-1835 Same. DAB-F-T-2-7-12-40-81-84.
GOODMAN, [Mrs.] Julia [née Salaman]
Eng. London 1812-1906 Brighton. DNB.
GOODMAN, Maude [Mrs. Seane].
Eng. ac. 1874-1901 London. B-T.
GOODMAN, Robert Gwelo.
Br. b. So. Africa; ad. 1934 Cape Town, S. A. Wa.
GOODMAN, Walter.
Am. b. London 1838; ad. 1870 U. S. [No death date]. F-T.

GOODNOW, Marjorie.
Mrs. David F. Goodnow.
Am. ad. 1934 Pelham Manor, N. Y. M.
GOODRICH, [Mrs.] Alice D. (S)
Am. b. 1881; d. 1920 Brooklyn, N. Y. A017.
GOODRICH, James Harry.
Am. b. Colon, Mich. 1878; ad. 1934 Nashville, Tenn. A.
GOODRICH, M. A. Brandt.
Am. ad. 1935 Brooklyn, N. Y. M.
GOODRIDGE, Elinor.
Am. ad. 1934 Boston, Mass. M.
GOODRIDGE [or Goodbridge], Sarah. (Min)
Am. Templeton, Mass. 1788-1853 Boston. DAB-F-T-2-6-30-66-85-179.
GOODWIN, Albert.
Eng. London 1845-1933 Same. B-T-Wa1929-Y01933.
GOODWIN, Alice Hathaway Hapgood.
Mrs. Harold Goodwin, Jr.
Am. b. Hartford, Conn. 1893; ad. 1934 Wyncote, Pa. A.
GOODWIN, Arthur Clifton.
Am. b. Portsmouth, N. H. 1866. A20-F-T-W14
GOODWIN, Frances M. (S)
Am. b. Newcastle, Ind.; d. 1929 Same. A027-F-T-W14-181.
GOODWIN, Gilberta Daniels.
Am. b. Burlington, Vt. 1888; ad. 1934 Princeton, N. J. A.
GOODWIN, Harry.
Eng. b. Maidstone; d. 1925. B-Y01926.
GOODWIN, Helen M. (Min)
Am. b. Newcastle, Ind.; ad. 1934 Same. A-B.
GOODWIN, Jean.
Am. ad. 1934 Santa Ana, Calif. M.
GOODYEAR, Joseph. (Eg)
Eng. Birmingham 1797/9-1839 London. DNB-T.
GOOKINS, James R.
Am. Terre Haute, Ind. 1840-1906 Chicago. M.
GOOL, Jan Van.
Dut. The Hague 1690/1-1763/5 Same. C-T.
GOOSEN, Jan van.
Dut. ac. 1668 in Haarlem [No death date]. T.
GOOSENS, Josse.
Ger. b. Aachen 1876; ac. Düsseldorf. T.
GOOSSENS, John.
Am. b. Norway, Mich. 1887; ad. 1934 Chicago. A.
GORBATOFF, Constantin.
Rus. b. 1876 in Russia. M.
GORBUTT, John Detwiller.
Am. b. Troy, Kan. 1904; ad. 1934 Topeka, Kan. A.
GORDIGIANI, Michele.
It. Florence 1830-1909. B-T.
GORDON, Boris Bernhard.
Am. ad. 1935 Los Angeles, Calif. M.
GORDON, Elizabeth Stith.
Am. b. Balt., Md. 1898; ad. 1934 Same. A.
GORDON, Emeline H.
Mrs. Beirne Gordon.
Am. b. Boston 1877; ad. 1934 Same. A.
GORDON, Frederick Charles.
Am. Canada 1856-1924 Orange, N. J. A021-F-T.
GORDON, Hilda May.
Br. ex. 1932 London. M.
GORDON, John S.
Can. b. Brantford, Ont.; ad. 1935 Hamilton, Ont. M.
GORDON, [Sir] John Watson.
Scot. Edinburgh 1788-1864 Same. B-DNB-E-T.
GORDON, Léon.
Am. b. Borisov, Rus. 1889; ad. 1934 New York. A-F-W.
GORDON, Witold. (Mu)
Am. ad. 1934 New York. M.
GORE, Spencer Frederick.
Eng. 1878-1914 London. B-T-825.
GORE, Thomas H.
Am. b. Balt., Md. 1863; ad. 1934 Covington, Ky. A.
GORE, William Henry.
Eng. ac. 1909 in London. B-T.
GORGUET, Auguste François Marie.
Fr. 1862-1927 Paris. B-DBA-T.
GORHAM, Sidney.
Am. b. Plattsburg, N. Y. 1870. B.
GORSKI, Stanislas.
Am. Poland 1854-1923 New York. A020.
GORSLINE, Douglas.
Am. ad. 1935 Rochester, N. Y. M.
GORSON, Aaron Henry ["Harry"]
Am. Lithuania 1872-1933 New York. A030-F.
GORTER, Arnold Marc.
Dut. b. Almelo 1866. B-DBA-T.
GORYNSKA, Wiktoria. (Eg)
Pol. ac. 1926 in Poland. M.
GOS, Albert.
Swi. b. Geneva 1852. B-T.
GOSEN, Philipp Theodor. (S)
Ger. b. Augsburg 1873. B-T.
GOSHORN, John Thomas.
Am. b. Independence, Ia. 1870; ad. 1915 Chicago. A12-F.
GOSHUN, Matsumura.
Jap. ac. 19th Cent. J Vol. 2, page 74.
GOSS, John. (Ill)
Am. b. Lewiston, Me. 1886; ad. 1934 Boston. A-F.
GOSSAERT, Jan [or Van]. *see* Mabuse, Jan. G.
GOSSE, Laura Sylvia.
Eng. b. London 1881. Wa.
GOSSE, Nicolas Louis François.
Fr. Paris 1787-1878 Soncourt. B-T.
GOSSELIN, Charles.
Fr. Paris 1834-1892 Same. B-Bd-T.
GOSSELIN, Ferdinand Jules Albert.
Fr. b. Paris 1863. B-DBA-T.
GOSSELIN, Lucien H. (S)
Am. b. Whitefield, N. H. 1883; ad. 1934 Manchester, N. H. A-F.
GOSSET DE GUINES, Louis Alexander. (Cari)
[Same as Gill, André].
Fr. Paris 1840-1885 Same. T.
GOSSET, Isaac. (S in Wax)
Eng. London 1713-1799 Kensington. DNB-T.
GOSSET, Mathew. (S in Wax)
Br. 1683-1744. DNB-T.
GOSSETT, Lee Roy. (Cart)
Am. b. Iowa 1877; d. 1926 Chicago. A023.

GOTCH, Thomas Cooper.
Eng. Kettering 1854-1931 London. B-T-Wa1929.
GOTH, Imre.
Hun. ex. 1935 Birmingham, Eng. M.
GOTH, Marie.
Am. b. Ind., Ind.; ad. 1934 Same. A.
GOTHARD, William Harry.
Am. ad. 1935 Cinn., O. M.
GOTLIEB. *see also* Gottlieb.
GOTLIEB, Jules. (Ill)
Am. ad. 1934 New York. M.
GOTÓ Family.
Jap. ac. 15th-17th Cent. J-T.
GOTT, Joseph [or John]. (S)
Br. 1785-1860 Rome, It. DNB-T.
GOTTHOLD, Florence Wolf.
Mrs. Frederick Gotthold.
Am. Uhrichville, O. 1858-1930. A12-F.
GOTTLIEB, Adolph.
Am. ex. 1934 New York. M.
GOTTLIEB, Harry.
Am. b. Rumania 1895; ad. 1934 Woodstock, N. Y. A.
GOTTLIEB, Léopold.
Pol.-Ger. Drohobycz 1883-1934. DBA-T.
GOTTLOB, Fernand Louis. (Et)
Fr. ac. 1893-1930 in Paris. B-DBA.
GOTTO, Basil. (S)
Eng. b. London 1866. B-T-Wa.
GOTTSCHALK, Albert.
Dan. Stegel 1866-1906. B-T.
GOTTSCHALCK, Oscar H. von.
Am. ad. 1934 Hackensack, N. J. M.
GOTTWALD, Frederic Clark.
Am. b. 1860; ad. 1934 Cleveland, O. A.
GOTZSCHE, Kai. (Ill)
Am. b. Copenhagen, Den. 1886; ad. 1934 Elmhurst, L. I., N. Y. A.
GOUBAUD, Innocent Louis.
Fr. Rome, It. 1780-1847 Brussels, Belg. B-T.
GOUBIE, Jean Richard.
Fr. Paris 1842-1899 Same. B-T.
GOUDREAUX [or Goudréau], Pierre Louis.
Fr. ac. 1506-1551 in Paris. T.
GOUDT, Hendrick de.
Dut. Utrecht 1578-1630. B-T.
GOUDY, Frederic W. (Type Designs)
Am. b. Bloomington, Ill. 1865; ad. 1934 Marlboro, N. Y. A.
GOUJON, Jean. (S)
Fr. Rouen 1520-1572 Paris. B-E-Hs-T.
GOULD, Allan.
Am. ex. 1933 New York. M.
GOULD, [Sir] Francis Carruthers. (Cari)
Eng. Bairnstaple 1844-1925. E.
GOULD, J. J. (Ill)
Am. ad. 1932 Phila., Pa. M.
GOULD, Northam Robinson.
Am. b. Brooklyn, N. Y.; ad. 1934 East Hampton, Conn. A.
GOULD, Thomas Ridgeway. (S)
Am. Boston 1818-1881 Florence, It. B-Bd-DAB-F-Hs-T-Ta-4-15-35-86.
GOULD, Walter.
Am. b. Phila., Pa. 1829 [No death date]. C-F-T-15.
GOULDEN, Richard Reginald. (S)
Eng. Dover 1877-1932 London. B-Y01933-798-Obit. Studio, 5-1933, page 315.
GOULDSMITH, Edmund.
Eng. b. Bristol 1852; ad. 1929 Bath. B-T-Wa1929.
GOULINAT, Jean Gabriel.
Fr. b. Tours 1883; ex. 1930 London. B-DBA.
GOUNOD, François Louis.
Fr. Paris 1758-1822 Same. B-T.
GOUPIL, Jules Adolphe.
Fr. Paris 1839-1883 Same. B-C-T.
GOUPIL, Léon Lucien.
Fr. Paris 1834-1890/1. B-T.
GOUPY, Joseph.
Eng. d. 1763 London. DNB-T.
GOUPY, Lewis [or Louis].
Eng. b. 1700; d. 1747 London. DNB-T.
GOURDEL, Pierre. (S)
Fr. d. 1892 Paris. B-T.
GOURMONT, Jean de I. (Eg)
Fr. ac. 1506-1551 in Paris. T.
GOURMONT, Jean de II. (Eg)
Fr. ac. 1560-1590 in Paris. B-T.
GOURSAT, Georges. *see* "Sem".
GOVAERTS, Abraham.
Flem. b. 1589; d. 1626 Antwerp. B-T-903.
GOVAERTS, Jan Baptiste.
Flem. ac. 1713-1746 in Antwerp. B-T-903.
GOVARDHAN.
Per. Ancient Artist in Persia. M.
GOW, Andrew Carrick.
Eng. London 1848-1920 Same. B-C-T.
GOW, Lucien M.
Eng. ad. 1935 London. M.
GOW, Mary L.
Mrs. Sydney Prior Hall.
Eng. ac. 1869-1927 London. B-T.
GOWER, [Sir] Ronald. (S)
Eng. b. London; ac. 1886. B-Hs.
GOYA, Francisco José de [y Lucientes].
[Called "The Hogarth of Spain"].
Sp. Aragon 1746-1828 Bordeaux, Fr. B-Bd-C-E-T-191-192-378-379-380-748-790-823-830-947-955-956.
GOYEN [or Goijen], Jan Josephsz van.
Dut. Leyden 1596-1656 The Hague. B-Bd-C-E-T-722.
GOZARE, Léon.
Fr. ex. 1935 in Paris. DBA.
GOZLAN, Léon Duval.
Fr. b. Paris 1853. DBA.
GOZZOLI, Benozzo [di Lese].
It. Florence 1420/4-1498 Pisa. B-Bd-C-E-T-V-381-722-729.
GRAAF [or Grave], Josua de.
Dut. ac. 1660-1712 The Hague. B-T.
GRAAT, Barend.
Dut. Amsterdam 1628-1709 Same. B-T.
GRABACH, John R.
Am. b. Newark, N. J. 1866; ad. 1934 Irvington, N. J. A-F.
GRABAR, Igor.
Rus. b. 1871; ad. 1934 Moscow. DBA-M.
GRACE, James Edward.
Eng. ac. 1871-1893 in London. B-T.
GRACE, [Mrs.] Mary [née Hodgkins].
Eng. d. 1786? in London. DNB-T.
GRADA, Raffaele de.
It. ad. 1934 Milan, It.; ex. 1933 Pittsburgh, Pa. M.

GRADY, JAMES.
Am. b. Columbus, O. 1907; ad. 1934 Orrville, O. M.
GRAEB, KARL GEORG ANTON.
Ger. Berlin 1816-1884 Same. B-T.
GRAEF, ROBERT A. (Ill)
Am. ad. 1934 New York. M.
GRAF, CARL C.
Am. b. 1890; ad. 1934 Ind., Ind. A-F.
GRAF [or Graef], GUSTAV.
Ger. Königsberg 1821-1899. B-T.
GRAF, HERMANN.
Ger. b. Frankfort 1873. T.
GRAF, LUDWIG FERDINAND.
Aus. b. Vienna 1868. B-T.
GRAF, PAUL HENRI (S)
Fr. b. Boulogne 1872. B-DBA.
GRAF, URS [or Ursus]. (Eg)
Swi. Soleure 1485-1527/8 Basel. B-T.
GRAFF, ANTOINE [or Anton].
Ger. Winterthur, Swi. 1736-1813 Dresden. B-C-T-801.
GRAFF, JOHAN ANDREAS.
Ger. Nüremberg 1637-1701 Same. B-T.
GRAFLY, CHARLES ALLAN. (S)
Am. Phila., Pa. 1862-1929 Same. A026-B-Cs-F-Hs-T-W14-18-46.
GRAFSTROM, RUTH SIGRID. (Ill)
Am. ad. 1934 New York. M.
GRAFTON, ROBERT WADSWORTH.
Am. b. Chicago, Ill. 1876; ad. 1934 Michigan City, Ind. A-B-F-W-181-183
GRAHAM, CECILIA B. (S)
Am. b. Calif.; ac. 1928. Cs.
GRAHAM, ELIZABETH SUTHERLAND.
Am. b. New York; ad. 1934 Brooklyn, N. Y. A.
GRAHAM, GEORGE. (Eg)
Am. ac. 1813 in Phila., Pa. [No death date]. B-F-T-2-7-147.
GRAHAM, GEORGE.
Eng. b. Leeds 1882; ex. 1934 in London. Wa.
GRAHAM, JAMES L.
Can. b. Belleville, Ont. 1890; ad. 1935 Montreal. M.
GRAHAM, JOHN [The Elder].
Eng. London 1706-1776 The Hague, Holland. B-DNB-T.
GRAHAM, JOHN [The Younger].
Scot. 1754-1817 Edinburgh. B-DNB-T.
GRAHAM, JOHN D.
Am. b. Kiev, Rus. 1890; ad. 1934 New York. A-DBA.
GRAHAM, MARGARET NOWELL.
Mrs. J. L. Graham.
Am. b. Lowell, Mass.; ad. 1934 Winston-Salem, N. C. A.
GRAHAM, PETER.
Scot. Edinburgh 1836-1921 London. B-C-T.
GRAHAM, RALPH W.
Am. b. 1901; ad. 1934 Chicago. M.
GRAHAM, ROBERT ALEXANDER.
Am. b. Brooklyn, N. Y. 1873; ad. 1934 Denver, Colo. A-F.
GRAHAM, THOMAS ALEXANDER FERGUSON.
Scot. Kirkwall 1840-1906 Edinburgh. B-DNB-T.
GRAHAM, WILLIAM.
Am. New York 1832-1911 Buffalo, N. Y. F-T-15.
GRAHAM, GILBERT JOHN.
Scot. Glasgow 1794-1866 Yorkhill. B-DNB-T.
GRAILLON, PIERRE ADRIEN. (S)
Fr. Dieppe 1809-1872 Same. B-T.
GRAMATKY, HARDIE.
Am. b. Dallas, Tex. 1907; ad. 1934 Wilmar, Calif. A.
GRAN, DANIEL.
Aus. Vienna 1694-1757 St. Pölten. B-C-T.
GRANACCI, IL. FRANCESCO.
It. Florence 1477-1543 Same. B-C-T-V-722.
GRANADA, NINA.
Am. ad. 1934 New York. M.
GRANAHAN, DAVID MILTON.
Am. b. Litchfield, Minn. 1909; ad. 1934 Minn., Minn. M.
GRANDGÉRARD, LUCIEN HENRI.
Fr. b. Nancy 1880. DBA.
GRANDI, GIULIO CESARE.
It. Ferrara 1462/3-1531 Same. B-C-T-V.
GRANDIN, ELIZABETH.
Am. b. Hamden, N. Y.; ad. 1934 New York. A.
GRANDON, CHARLES.
Fr. 1691-1762 Lyons. B-T.
GRANDSIRE, PIERRE EUGÈNE.
Fr. Orlèans 1825-1905 Paris. B-T.
GRANDVILLE, [Gerard] JEAN IGNACE ISADORE. (Cari)
Fr. Nancy 1803-1847. B-E-T.
GRANDY, WINIFRED MILTON. (S)
Am. b. Preston, Conn. 1899; ad. 1934 New Haven, Conn. A.
GRANER Y ARRUFI, LUIS.
Am. Barcelona, Sp. 1867-1929 Same. A027-B-F-T-144-183.
GRANET, FRANÇOIS MARIUS.
Fr. Aix 1775/7-1849 Same. B-C-E-F-722.
GRANGE, CORNELIUS.
Am. England 1895-1933 Elmhurst, Ill. A030.
GRANGE, ROBERT.
Fr. ex. 1935 Paris. M.
GRANGER, CAROLINE GIBBONS.
Mrs. Percival H. Granger.
Am. ad. 1935 Phila., Pa. M.
GRANGER, PAUL ÉDOURD ROSSET.
see Rosset-Granger, P. E.
GRANT, ANGUS.
Eng. ac. 1929. M.
GRANT, BLANCHE C.
Am. Leavenworth, Kan.; ad. 1934 Taos, N. M. A.
GRANT, KATHERINE HARLEY.
Am. b. Pittsburgh, Pa. 1897; ad. 1934 Phila., Pa. A.
GRANT, CHARLES HENRY.
Am. b. Oswego, N. Y. 1866; ad. 1934 San Fran., Calif. A-F-W.
GRANT, CLEMENT ROLLINS.
Am. Freeport, Me. 1849-1893 Boston. B-F-T-15.
GRANT, DOUGLAS M.
Am. b. Oakland, Calif. 1894; ad. 1934 Manhasset, L. I., N. Y. A.

GRANT, DUNCAN JAMES CORROWR.
Eng. b. Inverness 1885. E-Wa-825.
GRANT, [Sir] FRANCIS.
Scot. Edinburgh 1803-1878 London. B-C-DNB-E-T.
GRANT, FREDERIC M.
Am. b. Sibley, Ia. 1886; ad. 1934 Chicago. A-F.
GRANT, GORDON.
Am. b. San Fran., Calif. 1875; ad. 1934 New York. A-F-W.
GRANT, JAMES A.
Eng. b. Liverpool 1887; ad. 1934 London. Wa.
GRANT, J. JEFFREY. (P-S)
Am. b. 1883; ad. 1934 Chicago. A-F.
GRANT, LAWRENCE W.
Am. b. Cleveland, O. 1886; ad. 1934 Provincetown, Mass. A.
GRANT, MARY. (S)
Scot. Kilgraston 1831-1908 London. B-T.
GRANT, VERNON. (Ill)
Am. ad. 1934 Phila., Pa. M.
GRANT, WILLIAM JONES.
Eng. London 1829-1866 Same. DNB-T.
GRANVILLE, MARY [Deland].
Eng. 1700-1788. B.
GRANVILLE-SMITH, WALTER.
Am. b. So. Granville, N. Y. 1870; ad. 1935 New York. A-B-F-W.
GRASS, PHILIPPE. (S)
Fr. Wolxheim 1801-1876 Strasburg. B-T.
GRASSER, ERASMUS. (S)
Bav. Oberpfalz 1450-1526 Munich. B-Hs-T.
GRASSET, EUGÈNE SAMUEL.
Swi. Lausanne 1845-1917 Paris. B-DBA-T.
GRASSI [or Grassy], JOSEPH.
Ger. Vienna, Aus. 1755/8-1838 Dresden. T.
GRASSIN, ALEXANDER MARIE.
Fr. b. Courcival 1883. DBA.
GRATE, ERIK. (S)
Swe. b. Stockholm 1896. DBA.
GRATELOUP, JEAN BAPTISTE DE. (Eg)
Fr. Dax 1735-1817. B-T.
GRATELOUP, JEAN PIERRE SILVESTRE DE. (Eg)
Fr. Dax 1782-1862 Bordeaux. T.
GRAU-SALA, EMILI.
Sp. ad. 1934 Barcelona; ex. 1933 Pittsburgh, Pa. M.
GRAUER, NATALIE EYNON.
Mrs. William C. Grauer.
Am. b. Wilmington, Del. 1894; ad. 1934 Cleveland, O. A.
GRAUER, WILLIAM C.
Am. b. Phila., Pa. 1896; ad. 1934 Cleveland, O. A.
GRAVATT, SARA HOFFECKER.
Am. b. Phila., Pa. 1898; ad. 1934 Charleston, W. Va. A.
GRAVE, JOSUA DE. *see* Graaf, Josua de.
GRAVELOT, HUBERT FRANÇOIS. (Ill)
Fr. Paris 1699-1733 Same. B-DNB-T-803.
GRAVES, ABBOTT FULLER.
Am. b. Weymouth, Mass. 1859; ad. 1934 Kennebunkport, Me. A-B-F-T-W.
GRAVES, ELIZABETH EVANS.
Am. b. Fort Brady, Mich. 1895; ad. 1934 Wash., D. C. A.
GRAVES, H. TEMPEST. (Ill)
Am. b. New York 1884; ad. 1934 Same. M.
GRAVES, MAITLAND E.
Am. b. New York 1902; ad. 1934 Same. A.
GRAVES, MARY DE BERNIERE.
Am. b. Chapel Hill, N. C.; ad. 1934 Same. A.
GRAVES, ROBERT. (Eg)
Eng. London 1798-1873 Same. DNB-T.
GRAVESANDE, CHARLES STORM VAN. (Et)
Dut. b. Brenda, Holland 1841. B-T.
GRAY, CHARLES ALDEN.
Am. Iowa 1857-1933 St. Louis, Mo. A030-F.
GRAY, FREDERICK G.
Am. b. St. Louis, Mo.; ad. 1915 Same. A12-B.
GRAY, GEORGE.
Br. b. Newcastle, Eng. 1758; d. 1819 Pudding Chare, Eng. DNB-T.
GRAY, HAROLD LINCOLN. (Cart)
Am. b. Kankakee, Ill. 1894; ad. 1934 New York. M.
GRAY, HAROLD TYNG.
Am. b. So. Orange, N. J. 1879; ad. 1934 Greenwich, Conn. A.
GRAY; HENRY PETERS
Am. New York 1819-1877 Same. B-Bd-C-DAB-F-T-1-4-15.
GRAY, JOSEPH. (Et)
Scot. b. So. Shields 1890. Wa.
GRAY, KATHRYN.
Am. b. Kan. 1917; d. 1931 Kansas City, Kan. A028-F.
GRAY, M. MAY.
Am. ad. 1934 Phila., Pa. M.
GRAY, MARIE CHILTON.
Am. b. Phila., Pa. 1888; ad. 1915 Ind., Ind. A12.
GRAY, MARY.
Am. ad. 1934 New York. A-F.
GRAY, NORA NEILSON. *see* Neilson-Gray, N.
GRAY, PAUL MARY. (Eg)
Ir. Dublin 1842-1866 Brighton, Eng. B-T.
GRAY, PERCY
Am. b. San Fran., Calif. 1869; ad. 1934 Monterey, Calif. A-F.
GRAY, UNA.
Am. ac. 1930. M.
GRAY, WILLIAM FRANCIS.
Am. b. Phila., Pa. 1866; ad. 1934 Same. A.
GRAYSON, CLIFFORD PREVOST.
Am. b. Phila., Pa. 1857; ad. 1934 Old Lyme, Conn. A-B-C-F-T-W-46.
GRAYSON, STANLEY CLARE.
Eng. b. Aylesbury 1898; ad. 1934 London. Wa.
GRAZIANI, ERCOLE [The Younger].
It. Bologna 1688-1765. B-T.
GREACEN, EDMUND WILLIAM.
Am. b. New York 1877; ad. 1934 Same. A-F-T-W.
GREASON, WILLIAM.
Am. b. St. Mary's, Ont. 1884; ad. 1934 East Detroit, Mich. A.
GREATBACH, WILLIAM. (Eg)
Eng. b. 1802; ac. 1865 London [No death date]. T.
GREATHEAD, JOHN.
Am. ad. 1934 Vallejo, Calif. M.

GREATOREX, ELIZA. (Et)
Am. Ireland 1820-1897 Paris. C-F-T-15-46.
GREATOREX, ELIZABETH ELEANOR
Am. b. New York 1854. F.
GREATOREX, KATE [Kathleen Honora].
Am. b. Hoboken, N. J. 1851. A12-B-F-W10.
GREAVES, GEORGE EDMUND.
Am. b. 1860; d. 1926 Minn., Minn. A023.
GREAVES, HARRY E.
Am. Bryn Mawr, Pa. 1854-1919 Phila., Pa. A017-B-T.
GREAVES, WALTER.
Eng. Chelsea 1841-1930. M-Obit. Art News, 12-1930.
GREAVES [or Greves], WILLIAM A.
Am. Watertown, N. Y. 1847-1900. F.
GREBBER, ADRIAN CLAESZ.
Dut. 1576-1661 Haarlem. B-T.
GREBBER, PIETER FRANSZ.
Dut. Haarlem 1600-1652/3. C-T.
GREBEL, ALPHONSE. (P-S)
Fr. b. Hirson 1885. DBA.
GRECHETTO, IL. *see* Castigilione, Giovanni Benedetto.
GRECO, EL [Domenico Theotocopuli]. (P-S)
Sp. Candia, Crete 1545/8-1614 Toledo; Sp. B-Bd-C-E-T-60-88-191-382-383-700-722-748-823 [Spanish name: Domenikos Theotocopulos].
GREEK ARTISTS [Ancient].
see books 712-714-785-792-877.
GREEN. *see also* Greene.
GREEN, ALICE LEORA.
Am. Shawnee, Okla. 1903; ad. Same. A.
GREEN, BENJAMIN. (Eg)
Eng. Halesowen 1736-1800 London. B-DNB-T.
GREEN, BENJAMIN RICHARD.
Eng. London 1808-1876 Same. DNB-T.
GREEN, BERNARD I.
Am. b. Swerzen, Rus. 1887. A-F.
GREEN, BERT. (Cart)
Am. b. England 1885; ad. 1934 Manhasset, L. I., N. Y. W.
GREEN, CHARLES.
Eng. 1840-1898 Hampstead. B-T.
GREEN, CORNELIA ELIZABETH.
Am. 1872-1901. M.
GREEN, EDITH JACKSON.
Am. b. Tarrytown, N. Y. 1876; ad. 1934 Prov., R. I. A.
GREEN, ELIZABETH SHIPPEN.
see Elliott, [Mrs.] Huger.
GREEN, [Mrs.] ERIK.
Am. ad. 1934 Prov., R. I. M.
GREEN, FLORENCE TOPPING.
Mrs. Howard Green.
Am. b. London 1882; ad. 1934 Long Branch, N. J. M.
GREEN, FRANK RUSSELL.
Am. b. Chicago 1856; ad. 1934 New York. A-B-F-T-W14.
GREEN, HAROLD ABBOTT.
Am. b. Montreal, Can. 1883; ad. 1934 Hartford, Conn. A.
GREEN, HIRAM HOWARD.
Am. Paris, N. Y. 1865-1930 Canada. A028-F.
GREEN. JAMES.
Eng. Leytonstone 1771-1834 Bath. B-DNB-T.
GREEN, JOHN. (Eg)
Eng. Hales Owen 1729-1757 Oxford. DNB-T.
GREEN, KENNETH.
Eng. b. 1916; ex. 1934 New York. M.
GREEN, MARY.
Am. ad. 1934 New York. M.
GREEN, MILDRED C.
Am. b. Paris, N. Y.; ad. 1934 Buffalo, N. Y. A.
GREEN, ROBERT R.
Am. b. 1910; ad. 1935 Rome, It. M.
GREEN, RUPERT. (Eg)
Eng. London 1768-1804 Same. DNB-T.
GREEN, VALENTINE. (Eg)
Eng. Hales Owen 1739-1813 London. B-Bd-DNB-E-T-880.
GREEN, WILLIAM. (Eg)
Eng. Manchester 1760/1-1823 Ambleside. DNB-T.
GREEN, WILLIAM BRADFORD.
Am. b. Binghamton, N. Y. 1871; ad. 1934 Hartford, Conn. A.
GREENAMYER, [Mrs.] LEAH J.
Am. ad. 1934 Youngstown, O. A.
GREENAWALT, FRANK F.
Am. ad. 1934 Wash., D. C. A.
GREENAWAY, KATE [or Catherine].
Eng. London 1846-1901 Hampstead. B-DNB-E-T-272-928.
GREENBAUM, DOROTHEA. (Clay-S).
Am. b. Brooklyn, N. Y. 1893; ad. 1935 New York. M.
GREENBERG, MAURICE. (Ill)
Am. b. Milwaukee, Wis. 1893; ad. 1934 Chicago. A-F.
GREENBERG, MORRIS. (Ill)
Am. ad. 1935 Brooklyn, N. Y. A-F.
GREENBURG, SAMUEL.
Am. b. Uman, Ukraine 1905; ad. 1934 Chicago. A.
GREENBURY, ROBERT [or Richard].
Br. ac. 1616-1670. DNB-T.
GREENE. *see also* Green.
GREENE, ALBERT VAN NESSE.
Am. b. Jamaica, L. I., N. Y. 1887; ad. 1934 Phila., Pa. A-F.
GREENE, ANNE BOSWORTH.
Am. b. England 1878; ad. 1934 So. Woodstock, Vt. W.
GREENE, E. D. E.
Am. ac. 1858; d. 1879 New York. F.
GREENE, ELMER W., JR.
Am. b. Somerville, Mass. 1906; ad. 1934 Watertown, Mass. A.
GREENE, FRED STEWART.
Am. b. No. Stonington, Conn. 1876; ad. 1934 Westerly, R. I. A.
GREENE, J. BARRY.
Am. ad. 1935 New York. M.
GREENE, KENNETH E.
Am. b. Buffalo, N. Y. 1902; ad. 1934 Fairlawn, N. J. A.
GREENE, MATTHEW.
Am. ad. 1934 New York. M.
GREENE, THOMAS G.
Can. b. Toronto; ad. 1935 Same. M.
GREENFIELD, E. J. FORREST.
Am. b. London 1866; ad. 1934 Point Pleasant, N. J. A.

GREENGRAS, W. E. (Eg)
Eng. b. 1892; ad. 1934 Essex, Eng. M.
GREENHAM, ROBERT DUCKWORTH.
Eng. b. Streatham 1906; ad. 1934 St. Johns Wood. Wa.
GREENHILL, JOHN.
Eng. Salisbury 1644/9-1676 London. B-DNB-T-702.
GREENLEAF, HELEN. (S)
Am. b. Riverside, Ill. 1885; ad. 1915 Wallingford, Conn. A12.
GREENLEAF, RAY. (Ill)
Am. ad. 1934 New York. A.
GREENMAN, EDWIN. (Eg)
Eng. ex. 1934 London. M.
GREENMAN, [Mrs.] FRANCES CRANMER.
Am. b. Aberdeen, S. D. 1890; ad. 1934 New York. A-F.
GREENOUGH, HENRY.
Am. Newburyport, Mass. 1807-1883 Boston. DAB.
GREENOUGH, HORATIO. (S)
Am. Boston 1805-1852 Somerville, Mass. DAB-E-F-Hs-T-Ta-2-4-15-35-58.
GREENOUGH, JOHN.
Am. U. S. 1801-1852 Paris. F-T-2.
GREENOUGH, RICHARD SALTONSTALL. (S)
Am. Boston 1819-1904 Rome, It. A05-B-DAB-F-T-Ta-4-15-26-87.
GREENSTEIN, BENJAMIN. (S)
Am. ac. 1933. M.
GREENWALT, MARY. (Ill)
Am. ad. 1935 New York. M.
GREENWOOD, ETHAN ALLEN.
Am. Hubbardstown, Mass. 1779-1856 Same. E-T-2.
GREENWOOD, [Mrs.] GERTRUDE B. (S)
Am. ad. 1935 Lawrence, Kan. Cs.
GREENWOOD, JOHN.
Am. Boston 1727-1792 London. B-Bd-DNB-F-T-2-7-182.
GREENWOOD, JOSEPH H.
Am. Spencer, Mass. 1857-1927 Worcester, Mass. A024-F.
GREENWOOD, MARION.
Am. ex. 1932 New York. M.
GREENWOOD, MAY.
Am. ad. 1934 Boston, Mass. M.
GREENWOOD, ORLANDO.
Eng. ad. 1934 London. Wa.
GREENWOOD, WILLIAM RUSSELL.
Am. b. Oxford, Ind. 1906; ad. 1934 Lafayette, Ind. A.
GREER, BLANCHE.
Am. b. Eldora, Ia. 1884; ad. 1934 Summit, N. J. A.
GREGG, LEWIS C. (Cart)
Am. b. Atlanta, Ga. 1880; ad. 1934 Same. A.
GRÉGOIRE, GASPARD.
Fr. Aix 1751-1846 Paris. B-T.
GREGORI, CARLO. (Eg)
It. Florence 1719-1759 Same. B-T.
GREGORI, LUIGI.
It. Bologna 1819-1883 Florence. B-F-T.
GREGORY, ANGELA. (S)
Am. b. New Orleans, La. 1903; ad. 1934 Same. A-Cs.
GREGORY, CHARLES.
Eng. b. Surrey 1850; ac. 1897 London. B-T.
GREGORY, CHRISTINE. (S)
Eng. ad. 1934 London. Wa.
GREGORY, EDWARD JOHN.
Eng. b. 1850; d. 1909 London. B-C-DNB-E-T.
GREGORY, FRANK. (Ill)
Am. ad. 1934 San Fran., Calif. M.
GREGORY, FRANK M.
Am. b. Mansfield, Pa. 1848 F.
GREGORY, JAMES ELIOT.
Am. New York 1854-1915 Same. A012-C-DAB-F-T-W8.
GREGORY, JOHN. (S)
Am. b. London 1879; ad. 1934 New York. A-Cs-F-T-W.
GREGORY, JULIUS.
Am. ad. 1934 New York. M.
GREGORY, KATHERINE V. R. (S)
Mrs. John Gregory.
Am. b. Colo. Springs, Colo. 1897; ad. 1934 New York. A.
GREGORY, WAYLANDE DE SANTIS. (S)
Am. b. Baxter Springs, Kan. 1905; ad. 1934 Metuchen, N. J. A.
GREGORY, [Mrs.] W. B.
Am. ad. 1935 New Orleans, La. M.
GREGSON, MARIE EVANGELINE.
Am. b. New York 1888; ad. 1934 Auburndale, N. Y. A.
GREIFFENHAGEN, MAURICE WILLIAM.
Eng. London 1862-1932. B-T-Wa1929.
GREIG, JOHN.
Eng. b. 1803; d. 1853. DNB-T.
GREIMS, [Mrs.] HERBERT SPENCER.
Am. b. New York; d. 1927 Same. A024-F.
GREINER, OTTO. (Et)
Ger. b. Leipzig 1869. B-T.
GREITZER, JACK J.
Am. b. New York 1910; ad. 1934 Cleveland, O. A.
GRELAT, RENÉ JEAN JULES AUGUSTE.
Fr. St. Jean 1874-1929 Boulogne. DBA.
GRELL, LOUIS FREDERICK. (Mu)
Am. b. Council Bluffs, Ia. 1887; ad. 1934 Chicago. A.
GRENET, EDWARD.
Am. b. San Antonio, Tex. 1857. B.
GRENET, MÁLAGA. (Ill)
Am. ad. 1934 Paris. M.
GRENHAGEN, LORADO MERTON.
Am. b. Orihula, Wis. A.
GRENOUILLOUX, JANE.
Fr. b. Paris 1873. B.
GRENWIS, MARTINA D.
Am. ex. 1933 Cleveland, O. M.
GRASSE, JOHN ALEXANDER ["Jack Grease"].
Eng. London 1740/1-1794 Same. DNB-T.
GRETHE, CARLOS. (Eg)
Por. b. Montevideo, Uruguay 1864; d. 1913. B-T.
GRETTA, J. CLEMENS. (Ill)
Am. ad. 1934 New York. M.
GREUSE, JEAN BAPTISTE.
Fr. Tournus 1725/6-1805 Paris. B-Bd-C-E-T-722.
GREVE, CHERRY.
Am. b. Cinn., O. 1903; ad. 1934 Same. A.
GRÉVEDON, PIERRE LOUIS HENRI.
Fr. Paris 1776-1860 Same. C-T.

GREVENBROECK, Orazio Martinus.
Dut. ac. 1646-1670 The Hague. B-T.
GRIBBLE, Bernard Finegan.
Eng. b. So. Kensington 1873; ad. Parkstone, Eng. B-T-Wa.
GRIBBLE, Vivien. (Eg)
Mrs. Douglas Jones.
Eng. d. 1932. Y01933.
GRIBBON, C. E.
Eng. ex. 1934 London. M.
GRIBELIN, Simon II. (Eg)
Eng. Blois 1661-1733 London. DNB-T.
GRICCI, Giuseppe. (S)
It. ac. 1770-1788 in Leghorn. T.
GRIDEL, Joseph Émile.
Fr. Baccarat 1839-1902 Paris. C-T.
GRIDLEY, Enoch G. (Eg)
Am. ac. 1803/18 in Phila., Pa. F-T-2-7-147.
GRIDLEY, Josephine B.
Am. b. Phila., Pa. 1888; ad. 1934 Larchmont, N. Y. A.
GRIEF. *see* Gryeff.
GRIEG. *see* Greig.
GRIEN. *see* Baldung, Hans.
GRIER, Edmund Wyly.
Can. b. Melbourne, Aust. 1862; ad. 1935 Ontario, Can. M.
GRIERSON, Charles MacIver.
Ir. b. Queenstown 1864; ad. 1934 London. B-T-Wa.
GRIESBACH, David. (S)
Am. b. Evans City, Pa.; ac. 1929. Cs.
GRIEVE, Thomas. (Ill)
Br. b. 1799; d. 1882. DNB.
GRIFF. *see* Gryeff.
GRIFFEN, Davenport.
Am. b. Millbrook, N. Y. 1894; ad. 1934 Chicago. A.
GRIFFIER, Jan [The Elder].
Dut. Amsterdam 1645-1718 London. B-C-DNB-T-722.
GRIFFIER, Jan [The Younger].
Eng. d. 1750? in London. DNB-T.
GRIFFIER, Robert.
Dut. London 1688-1760? Amsterdam. C-DNB-T.
GRIFFIN, Barton B.
Am. ac. 1934 Suffern, N. Y. M.
GRIFFIN, Julia. (S)
Am. ac. 1874. M.
GRIFFIN, Walter.
Am. b. Portland, Me. 1861; d. 1935 Stroudwater, Me. A-F-T-W-Obit. Art Digest 6-1-1935.
GRIFFIN, Worth Dickman.
Am. b. Sheridan, Ind. 1893; ad. 1934 Pullman, Wash. A.
GRIFFITH, Beatrice Fox. (S)
Mrs. Charles F. Griffith.
Am. b. Cheshire, Eng. 1890; ad. 1934 Ardmore, Pa. A.
GRIFFITH, Conway.
Am. d. 1924 Laguna Beach, Calif. A021-F.
GRIFFITH, Julia Sulzer.
Am. b. Chicago; ad. 1934 Same. A.
GRIFFITH, Lillian.
Am. b. Phila., Pa. 1889; ad. 1934 Azusa, Calif. A.
GRIFFITH, Louis Oscar. (Et)
Am. b. Greencastle, Ind. 1875; ad. 1934 Nashville, Ind. A-B-F-T-181.
GRIFFITH, Moses. (Eg)
Br. Llein 1749-1809. B-DNB-T.
GRIFFITH, Rosa B.
Am. b. Merom, Ind. 1868-1927 Terre Haute, Ind. A024.
GRIFFITH, William Alexander.
Am. b. Lawrence, Kan. 1866; ad. 1934 Laguna Beach, Calif. A.
GRIFFITHS, James.
Can. England 1814-1896 Canada. M.
GRIGGORIEV, Boris.
Rus. b. Russia 1886; ad. 1935 Paris. DBA-T.
GRIGGS, Frederick Landseer Maur.
Eng. b. 1876; ad. 1934 Campden. T-Wa-830.
GRIGGS, H. T. Brock. (Et)
Eng. ad. 1934 London. M.
GRIGNION [or Grignon], Charles [The Elder]. (Eg)
Eng. London 1717-1810 Same. DNB-T.
GRIGNION, Charles [The Younger].
Eng. London 1754-1804 Leghorn, It. DNB-T.
GRIGNION, Reynolds. (Eg)
Eng. d. Chelsea 1787. DNB-T.
GRIGNOLA, John. (S)
Am. Italy 1861-1912 New York. M.
GRIGNON. *see* Grignion.
GRIGORESCU, Nicolae Jon.
Rumanian. Bukarest, Pitarou 1838-1907 Câmpina. B-T.
GRIGWARE, Edward T.
Am. b. Caseville, Mich. 1889; ad. 1934 Oak Park, Ill. A-F.
GRILL, Oswald.
Aus. b. Vienna 1878. T.
GRILLANDAJO. *see* Ghirlandajo.
GRIMALDI, Giovanni Francesco.
It. Bologna 1606-1680 Rome. B-E-T-722.
GRIMALDI, William. (Min)
Eng. Middlesex 1751-1830 London. B-DNB-T-722.
GRIMES, Frances. (S)
Am. b. Braceville, O. 1869; ad. 1934 New York. A-Cs-F-W.
GRIMES, John.
Am. Lexington, Ky. 1799-1837. F.
GRIMES, Thayer.
Am. ad. 1934 Westport, Conn. M.
GRIMM, Ludwig Émil.
Ger. Hanau 1790-1863 Cassel. T.
GRIMM, Samuel Hieronymus.
Swi. Burgdorf 1733-1794 London. B-DNB-T.
GRIMM, Stanley A.
Eng. b. London 1891; ad. 1934 Same. Wa.
GRIMMER [or Grimer], Abel.
Flem. Antwerp 1570/3-1619/40. B-T.
GRIMMER, Hans [or Johannes].
Ger. ac. 1570 in Metz. C-T.
GRIMMER [or Grimer], Jacob.
Flem. Antwerp 1525/6-1589/90. B-T.
GRIMMOND, William.
Eng. b. Manchester 1884; ad. 1934 Hampstead. Wa.
GRIMOU [or Grimoux], Alexis [Jean].
Fr. Argenteuil 1678-1733 Paris. B-T-722.
GRIMSON, [Mrs.] Samuel Bonaries.
see Hoffman, Malvina.

GRINAGER, ALEXANDER.
Am. b. Minn.; ad. 1934 Ossining, N. Y. A.
GRINLING, ANTHONY GIBBONS. (Carver)
Eng. b. Stanhope 1896; ad. 1934 London. M.
GRINNELL, G. VICTOR.
Am. ad. 1934 Mystic, Conn. A.
GRIS, JUÁN.
Sp. Madrid 1887-1927 Boulonge, Fr. DBA-797.
GRISCOM, LLOYD CARPENTER.
Am. b. Riverton, N. J. 1872; ad. 1934 New York. A.
GRISELLI, ITALO. (S)
It. ac. 1930 in Florence. M.
GRISET, ERNEST HENRY. (Ill)
Fr. France 1844-1907 England. B-T-880.
GRISEZ, E. A.
Am. b. La Porte, Ind.; ad. 1934 Same. A.
GRISHINA, [Madame] N. (Ill)
Am. b. Rus.; ad. 1934 Los Angeles, Calif. M.
GRISON, FRANÇOIS ADOLPHE.
Fr. Bordeaux 1845-1914 Genf. B-T.
GRISONI, GIUSEPPE.
It. Mons, Belg. 1699-1769 Rome, It. B-DNB-T.
GRISWOLD, CASIMER CLAYTON.
Am. Delaware, O. 1834-1918 Poughkeepsie, N. Y. A015-B-C-F-T-4-15.
GRISWOLD, VIRGINIA A.
Am. ad. 1935 Brooklyn, N. Y. M.
GRIVAZ, EUGÈNE.
Fr. Geneva, Swi. 1852-1915 France. B-T.
GRIVEAU, GEORGES.
Fr. b. Paris 1863. B-DBA.
GRIZZELL, IDA CRAWLEY.
Am. ac. 1930 Augusta, Ga. M.
GROB, KONRAD.
Swi. Zurich 1828-1904 Munich, Ger. T.
GROBE, GERMAN.
Ger. b. Hanau 1857. B-T.
GROBON, JEAN MICHEL.
Fr. Lyons 1770-1853 Same. B-T.
GROENING, S. A.
Am. ad. 1934 New Orleans, La. M.
GROGAN, NATHANIEL.
Ir. b. Cork; d. 1807. B-DNB.
GROLL, ALBERT LOREY.
Am. b. New York 1866; ad. 1934 Same. A-B-F-W-46.
GROLLERON, JEANNE PAULINE.
Fr. b. Paris; ac. 1930. DBA.
GROLLERON, PAUL LOUIS NARCISSE.
Fr. Seignelay 1848-1901 Paris. C-T.
GROMAIRE, MARCEL.
Fr. b. Noyelles 1892; ad. 1934 Paris. DBA-797.
GROMBECKI, HENRYK.
Pol. b. 1883; ad. 1934 Warsaw. M.
GRONGE, HELEN. (S)
Eng. ex. 1933 London. M.
GRONLAND, THEUDE.
Ger. Altona 1817-1876 Berlin. B-T.
GRONSVELD [or Gronsvelt], JOHANNES.
Dut. ac. 1660-1728 The Hague. B-T.
GROOM, EMILY.
Am. b. Wayland, Mass. 1876; ad. 1934 Milwaukee, Wis. A-F.
GROOMBRIDGE, WILLIAM.
Eng. ac. 1770-1790 London. B-DNB-T-2.
GROOME, ESTHER M.
Am. d. 1929 Phila., Pa. A027-F.
GROOMS, REGINALD L.
Am. b. Cinn., O. 1900; ad. 1934 Same. A.
GROOT, ADÉLAÏDE MILTON DE.
Am. b. New York; ex. 1934 Same. DBA-M.
GROPPER, WILLIAM.
Am. b. New York 1897; ad. Croton, N. Y. A.
GROS, [Baron] ANTOINE JEAN.
Fr. Paris 1771-1835 Same. B-C-E-T-722.
GROS, LUCIEN ALPHONSE.
Fr. Wesserling, Fr. 1845-1913. B-T.
GROSCH, CLARA.
Ger. ac. 19th Cent. in Darmstadt. B-T.
GROSS, ANTHONY. (Et)
Eng. b. Dulwich, Eng. 1905; ex. 1934 London. Wa.
GROSS, CHAIM. (S)
Am. ad. 1935 New York. M.
GROSS, JULIET WHITE.
Mrs. John Lewis Gross.
Am. b. Phila., Pa. 1882; ad. 1934 Same. A-F.
GROSS, MILT. (Cart)
Am. b. New York 1895; ad. 1934 Same. W.
GROSS, OSKAR.
Am. b. Vienna, Aus. 1871; ad. 1934 Chicago. A-B-T.
GROSS, PETER ALFRED.
Am. Schnecksville, Pa. 1849-1914 Chicago. A0X1-B-T.
GROSS, SYDNEY.
Am. b. Phila., Pa. 1897; ad. 1934 Same. A.
GROSSE, FRANZ THEODOR.
Ger. Dresden 1829-1891 Same. C-T.
GROSSE, HARRIET ESTELLA.
Mrs. D. T. Grosse.
Am. b. 1863; d. 1914 Brooklyn, N. Y. A012.
GROSSHAUS, FRITZ. (S)
Ger. ex. 1935 New York. M.
GROSSMAN, EDWIN BOOTH.
Am. b. Boston, Mass. 1887; ad. 1934 New York. A.
GROSSMAN, JOSEPH.
Am. ad. 1935 Phila., Pa. M.
GROSSMAN, MILTON H. (S)
Am. b. British Columbia, Can. 1908; ad. 1934 Buffalo, N. Y. A.
GROSSMAN, RUDOLF.
Ger. b. Fribourg, Swi. 1882. DBA.
GROSSNER, MAURICE.
Am. ad. 1935 New York. M.
GROSSO, ALFONSO.
Sp. b. Sèville; ex. 1934 Pittsburgh, Pa. DBA.
GROSVENOR, THELMA CUDLIPP. (Ill)
Am. b. Richmond, Va. 1891; ad. 1934 New York. A-F.
GROSZ, GEORGES. (Cari)
Am. b. Berlin, Ger. 1893; ad. 1934 New York. DBA-T-700-783.
GROTENRATH, RUTH.
Am. ex. 1935 Milwaukee, Wis. M.
GROTH, JOHN. (Et)
Am. ad. 1935 Chicago, Ill. M.
GROTHE, JEAN.
Ger. b. in Holland 1865. T.
GROTTGER, ARTHUR.
Pol. b. 1837; d. 1867 in Poland. T.

GROUX, Charles Cornelis Auguste de.
Flem. Comines 1825-1870 Brussels. B-T.
GROUX, Henry Jules Charles Corneille de.
Fr. Brussels 1867-1930 Marseilles. B-DBA-T.
GROVER, Oliver Dennett.
Am. Earlville, Ill. 1861-1927 Chicago. A024-B-F-T-W14-46-757.
GROVES, [Mrs.] Dorothy Lyon.
Am. b. Coudersport, Pa.; ad. 1934 New Haven, Conn. A.
GROVES, [Mrs.] Hannah Cutler.
Am. b. Camden, N. J. 1868; ad. 1934 Phila., Pa. A.
GROZER, Joseph. (Eg)
Eng. 1755-1799 London. B-DNB-T.
GRUAMONS. (S)
It. (Tuscan); ac. 1880 in Pisa. Hs-T.
GRUBACS, Carlo.
It. ac. 1840-1870 Venice. T.
GRUBE, L.
Am. ac. 1860. M.
GRUELLE, Justin C.
Am. b. Ind., Ind. 1889; ad. 1915 Norwalk, Conn. A12.
GRUELLE, Richard Buckner.
Am. Cynthiana, Ky. 1851-1914 Ind., Ind. A012-B-F-T-181.
GRUET, Jean Paul.
Am. ex. 1934 New York. M.
GRUETZNER, Édouard.
see Grützner, Édouard.
GRUGER, Frederick Roderigo. (Ill)
Am. b. Phila., Pa. 1871; ad. 1934 New York. F-W.
GRUMIEAU, Émile Jacques.
Am. b. Hainaut, Belg. 1897; ad. 1934 Chicago. A.
GRUMIEAUX, Louis P.
Am. b. 1872; ex. 1934 Chicago. M.
GRÜN, Baldung. *see* Baldung, Hans.
GRÜN, Jules Alexandre.
Fr. b. Paris 1868. B-DBA.
GRÜN, Maurice.
Fr. b. Russia 1860. B-DBA.
GRUNDMAN, Émil Otto.
Ger. Meissen 1848-1890 Dresden. B-T-15.
GRUNER, Elioth.
Aust. ac. 1933. M.
GRÜNEWALD, Gustavus.
Ger. Gnadau 1805-1878. F-T-2.
GRÜNEWALD, Isaac (or Isack).
Swe. b. Stockholm 1890; ad. 1935 Same. DBA-T.
GRÜNEWALD, Matthais.
Ger. Frankfort 1470/80-1530. B-E-T-134-384-722-801.
GRÜNWALD, Samuel.
Am. ad. 1934 New York. M.
GRÜNWALD, Béla Iványi.
Hun. ex. 1934 London. M.
GRUPPE, Charles Paul.
Am. b. Pictou, Can. 1860; ad. 1934 New York. A-B-F-T-W-46.
GRUPPE, Émile Albert.
Am. b. Rochester, N. Y. 1896; ad. 1934 E. Gloucester, Mass. A-F.
GRUPPE, Karl Heinrich. (S)
Am. b. Rochester, N. Y. 1893; ad. 1934 New York. A-Cs-F.
GRUST, Theodor.
Ger. b. Munich 1859. B-T.
GRÜTZNER, Édouard.
Ger. b. Grosskarlovitz 1846; d. 1925. B-C-T.
GRYEFF [or Grif], Adriaen de.
Flem. Antwerp 1670-1715 Brussels. B-C-T-722.
GSCHWIND, William E. (S)
Am. ad. 1934 Toledo, O. M.
GUACCIAMANNI, Vittore.
It. b. Ravenna; ac. 1880-1900. B-T.
GUALA, Pier Francesco. *see* Trino, F.
GUALDO, Matteo da.
It. [Umbrian] b. Gualdo; ac. 1468. B-T.
GUALTIERI. *see also* Cimabue.
GUALTIERI [or Gualtiero] Family.
It. ac. 16-17 Cent. in Padua. T.
GUALTIERI, di Giovanni da Pisa.
It. ac. 1389-1411 Pisa. T.
GUARDAHASSI, Guerrino.
It. b. Rome 1841. B-T.
GUARDI, Andrea. (S)
It. ac. 1452 in Florence. T.
GUARDI, Francesco de.
It. Venice 1712-1793 Same. B-Bd-C-E-T.
GUARDI, Giocomo.
It. Venice 1764-1835 Same. T.
GUARDIA, Gabriel.
Sp. [Catalan]; b. Manresa 1501. T.
GUARIENTO [or Guerriero] da Padova.
It. ac. 1338-1370 in Padua. E.
GUARINI [or Guarino], Francesco.
It. St. Agata 1611-1654. T.
GUARNERIO, Pietro. (S)
It. b. 1842; d. 1881 Milan. B-T.
GUASPRE. *see* Poussin, Gaspard.
GUASTALLA, Pierre.
Fr. b. St. Cloud 1891. DBA.
GUBITZ, Frederich Wilhelm. (Eg)
Ger. Leipzig 1786-1870 Berlin. B-T.
GUCHT, Benjamin van der.
Eng. b. London; d. 1794 Chiswick. DNB-T.
GUCHT, Gerard van der. (Eg)
Eng. London 1696-1776 Same. DNB-T.
GUCHT, John van der. (Eg)
Eng. London 1697-1776 Same. DNB-T.
GUCHT, Michael van der. (Eg)
Flem. Antwerp 1660-1725 London. DNB-T.
GUCK, Edna. (S)
Am. ex. 1935 New York. M.
GUDE, Hans Fredrik.
Nor. Christiania 1825-1903 Berlin, Ger. B-C-T.
GUDEBROD, Louis Albert. (S)
Am. b. Middletown, Conn. 1872; ad. 1934 Meriden, Conn. A-B-F-T-Ta-W.
GUDEWERDT [or Guthwerdt] Family.
Dut. ac. 17th Cent. in Holland. T.
GUDIN, Jean Antoine Théodore.
Fr. Paris 1802-1880 Boulogne. C-T.
GUE, David John.
Am. Farmington, N. Y. 1836-1917 Brooklyn. N. Y. A014-B-F-T

GUEBELS, Jacob [or Jacques].
Flem. ac. 1590. T.
GUELDRY, Ferdinand Joseph.
Fr. b. Paris 1858. B-DBA.
GUÉNOT, Auguste. (S)
Fr. b. Toulouse 1882. DBA.
GÜENTHER [or Ginter or Günder], Franz Ignaz. (S)
Ger. b. 1725; d. 1775 Munich. T.
GUENTHER, Lambert.
Am. ad. 1934 New York. M.
GUENTHER, Rafael Yela. (S)
Mex. ad. 1934 Mexico City, Mex. M.
GUENTHER, Sue Cory.
Am. ad. 1934 New York. M.
GUERARD, Henri Charles.
Fr. Paris 1845-1897. B-T.
GUERCINO, Giovanni Francesco Barbieri.
It. Cento 1591-1666 Bologna.
B-Bd-C-E-T-722-803.
GUÉRIN, Charles François Prosper.
Fr. b. Sens 1875. B-DBA.
GUÉRIN, Christophe. (Eg)
Fr. Strasbourg 1758-1831 Same. B-T.
GUÉRIN, Jean Baptiste Paulin.
Fr. Toulon 1783-1855 Paris. B-E-T.
GUÉRIN, Jean Urbain. (Min)
Fr. b. 1760; d. 1836. T.
GUÉRIN, Joseph.
Am. ad. 1934 New York. M.
GUÉRIN, Jules.
Am. b. St. Louis, Mo. 1866; ad. 1934 New York. A-B-F-T-W-46.
GUÉRIN, Pierre Narcisse [Baron].
Fr. Paris 1774-1833 Rome, It. B-C-T-722.
GUERIOT, René.
Fr. b. Paris; ad. 1928 Same. DBA.
GUERMACHEFF, Michel.
Rus. b. Kharkov 1867; ex. 1934 London.
B-DBA.
GUERNIER Family.
Fr. ac. 16-18 Cent. in France. T.
GUERNIER, Louis. (Min)
Fr. Paris 1614-1659 Same. B-T.
GUERNIER, Louis [or Lewis] du. (Eg)
Fr. Paris 1677-1716 London. B-T.
GUERNSEY, Eleanor Louise. (S)
Am. b. Terre Haute, Ind. 1878; ad. 1935 Decatur, Ill. A12-F.
GUERRA, Antoine Minor.
Fr. Perpignan 1666-1711 Same. B-T.
GUERRA, Jean François Antoine Andal.
Fr. Perpignan 1634-1705 Same. B-T.
GUERRIERO. *see* Guariento.
GUERRINI, Giovanni.
It. b. Bagnara 1887; ad. 1934 Rome. M.
GUESLAIN [or Gueslin]. *see* Genslain.
GUESNET, Louis Félix.
Fr. b. 1843 in France. B.
GUEST, George. (S)
Am. b. Buckinghamshire, Eng.; ad. 1915 Boston, Mass. A12.
GUÉTAL, Laurent.
Aust. ac. 1886 Vienna. C.
GUFFENS, Godefroi Egide.
Belg. Hasselt 1823-1901 Schaerbeck. B-C-T.
GUGGENHEIMER, Richard.
Am. ad. 1935 New York. M.
GUGLER, Frida.
Am. b. Milwaukee, Wis.; ad. 1934 New York. A.
GUGLIELMI, Luigi. (S)
It. b. Rome 1834. [No death date.] B-T.
GUGLIELMO, Fra. (S)
It. Pisa 1238?-1312. T.
GUGLIEMO, Victor. (S)
Am. b. Italy; ad. 1926 San Fran., Calif. F.
GUIARD, Labille. *see* Labille-Guiard.
GUIAUD, Jacques.
Fr. Chambord 1811-1875 Paris. B-T.
GUIBAL, Barthélmy. (S)
Fr. Nimes 1699-1757 Lunéville. B-T.
GUIBAL, Nicolas.
Fr. Lunéville 1725-1784 Stuttgart, Ger. B-T.
GUICHARD, Joseph Benoit.
Fr. Lyons 1806-1880 Same. B-T.
GUIDI, Tommaso di Giovanni. *see* Massaccio.
GUIDO DI PALMERUCCIO.
It. Gubbio 1280-1345 Same. B-T.
GUIDO DI PETRO DA MUGELLO.
see Angelico, Fra., Giovanni.
GUIDO, Reni. *see* Reni, Guido.
GUIDO DA SIENA.
[First dated painting (1221)].
It. ac. 1221-1281? in Siena. B-C-T-V.
GUIGLIA, Nadja F.
Am. ac. 1934 [Abroad]. M.
GUIGOU, Paul Camille.
Fr. Villars 1834-1871. Fa-M.
GUIGUET, François Joseph.
Fr. b. in Corbelin 1860. B-DBA-T.
GUILBRAU, Honoré. (Eg)
Mrs. E. V. Cooke.
Am. b. Baton Rouge, La. 1907; ad. 1934 Cleveland Heights, O. M.
GUILD, [Mrs.] Emma Cadwalader. (S)
Am. b. Zanesville, O. 1843. B-T.
GUILD, Frank S.
Am. d. 1929 Phila., Pa. A26.
GUILD, Laurelle Van Arsdale. (Ill)
Am. b. New York 1898; ad. 1934 Same. A.
GUILLAIN, Nicolas. (S)
Fr. b. Cambrai; d. 1639 in Paris. B-Hs.
GUILLAIN, Simon I. (S)
Fr. Paris 1581-1658 Same. B-Hs-T.
GUILLAUME, Albert.
Fr. b. Paris 1873. B-DBA.
GUILLAUME, Jean Baptiste Claude Eugène. (S)
Fr. Martbard 1822-1905 Rome, It.
B-E-Hs-T.
GUILLAUME, Louis Matthieu Didier.
Fr. b. Nantes; ac. 1837 in Paris. B.
GUILLAUME, Paul.
Fr. ex. 1934 in London. M.
GUILLAUMET, Gustave Achille.
Fr. Paris 1840-1887 Same. B-C-T.
GUILLAUMIN, Jean Baptiste Armand.
Fr. Paris 1841-1827. B-DBA-T.
GUILLEMET, Jean Baptiste Antoine.
Fr. Chantilly 1842-1918 Paris. B-C-DBA-T.
GUILLEMIN, Alesandre Marie. (P-S)
Fr. Paris 1817-1880. B-T.
GUILLEMINOT, Armand.
Fr. b. Paris; ac. 1838-1852 Same. B-T.

GUILLEMOT, Alexandre Charles.
Fr. 1786-1831 Paris. B-T.
GUILLERMIN, Jean Baptiste. (S)
Fr. Paris 1622-1699. B-T.
GUILLON, Adolphe Irénée [or René].
Fr. Paris 1829-1896. B-T.
GUILLOT, [Mrs.] Ann.
Am. b. Kentucky 1875; ad. 1935 Dallas, Tex. A.
GUILLOUX, Alphonse Eugène. (S)
Fr. b. Rouen 1852. B-DBA-T.
GUINDRAND [or Gaindrand], Antoine.
Fr. Lyons 1801-1843 Same. B-T.
GUINHALD, Bernard Schauffler de.
Fr. b. Calais 1885. DBA.
GUINIER, Henri Jules.
Fr. Paris 1867/8-1927 Neuilly. B-DBA-T.
GUINZBURG, Frederic Victor. (S)
Am. b. New York 1897; ad. 1934 Same. A-F.
GUION, Molly.
Am. ad. 1934 New Rochelle, N. Y. M.
GUIPON, Léon.
Am. France 1872-1910 New York. A08-T.
GUIRAND DE SCEVOLA, Lucien Victor.
Fr. b. Sète 1871. B-DBA.
GUIT, Roger.
Fr. b. Gironde 1899. DBA.
GUITERREZ. *see* Solana, J. G.
GUJARIN, M.
Rus. b. 1886; ad. 1935 Leningrad. M.
GULBRANSSON, Olaf. (Cari)
Swe. b. Oslo 1873; ad. 1934 Munich, Ger. B-T-873.
GULDBERG, Christian August.
Am. b. Madagascar 1879; ad. 1934 Montclair, N. J. A.
GULDBURG, [Mrs.] Ragna Haigh.
Am. ad. 1934 Birmingham, Ala. M.
GULICH, John Percival. (Cari)
Eng. Wimbledon 1865-1899. B-T.
GULLAGER, Christian. (S)
Am. Copenhagen, Denmark 1762-1826 Boston, Mass. F-T-2-184-786.
GULLAND, Elizabeth. (Eg)
Eng. ac. 1886-1910 London; d. 1935 New York. M-T.
GULLIVER, Mary.
Am. b. Norwich, Conn. 1860; ad. 1934 Eustis, Fla. A-F.
GUMERY, Charles Alphonse Achille. (S)
Fr. Paris 1827-1871 Same. B-T.
GUMMO, Blanchard Stanley.
Am. b. Lock Haven, Pa. 1906; ad. 1934 Same. A.
GUNDLACH, Helen Fuchs.
Am. b. Buffalo, N. Y. 1890; ad. 1934 Ebenezer, N. Y. A.
GUNN, Archie. (Ill)
Am. England 1863-1930 New York. A027.
GUNN, Edwin H.
Am. ad. 1934 New York. M.
GUNN, Herbert James.
Scot. b. Glasgow 1893; ex. 1934 London. Wa.
GUNST, Pieter Stevens van. (Eg)
Dut. 1659-1724 Amsterdam. T.
GUNTER, Charlotte G. Frietsch.
Am. b. Wisconsin 1896; ad. 1934 Spotswood, N. J. A.
GÜNTHER, Erwin Carl Willem.
Ger. b. Hamburg 1864. T.
GÜNTHER [or Gindter], Matthäus.
Ger. Bisenberg 1705-1788/91 Augsburg. B-T.
GUNTRUM, Emilie Ida.
Am. b. Brooklyn, N. Y.; ad. 1934 Elizabeth, N. J. A.
GURNEE, Marie Belle.
Am. d. 1915 Brooklyn, N. Y. A012.
GURR, Lena.
Am. ex. 1935 New York. M.
GUSCIME, Lloyd C.
Am. ad. 1934 Syosset, L. I., N. Y. M.
GUSSOW, Bernard.
Am. b. Russia 1881; ad. 1934 New York. A-F.
GUSSOW, Karl.
Ger. Havelburg 1843-1907 Berlin. B-C-T.
GUSTIN, Paul Morgan.
Am. b. Fort Vancouver, Wash. 1886; ad. 1934 Seattle, Wash. A.
GUTENSOHN, Bruno.
Ger. b. 1895; ad. 1935 Munich. M.
GÜTERSLOH, Albert.
Aus. ex. 1930 in Vienna. M.
GUTH, Jean Baptiste.
Fr. b. Paris; ac. 1921 Same. B-T.
GUTHERZ [or Guthers], Carl. (Mu)
Am. b. Swi. 1844; d. 1907 Wash., D. C. A06-B-F-T-15-46.
GUTHRIE, Gale.
Am. ex. 1933 in Paris. M.
GUTHRIE, James. (Ill)
Scot. b. Glasgow 1874; ad. 1934 Same. Wa.
GUTHRIE, [Sir] James.
Scot. Edinburgh 1859-1930. B-E-Y01931-385-825.
GUTHRIE, J. Gordon.
Am. ad. 1934 Dobbs Ferry, N. Y. M.
GUTHRIE, Robin Craig. (Et.)
Eng. b. Harting 1902; ad. 1934 Brighton. Wa.
GUTMAN, Amy H.
Am. ac. 1934 [Abroad]. M.
GUTMANN, Bernhard.
Am. b. Hamburg, Ger. 1869; ad. 1934 Norwalk, Conn. A-B-F.
GUTTRIDGE, Eleanor.
Am. b. Poughkeepsie, N. Y. 1901; ad. 1934 Berkeley, Calif. A.
GUY, Francis.
Am. Burton, Eng. 1760-1820 Brooklyn, N. Y. F-T-2.
GUY, Jean Baptiste Louis.
Fr. Lyons 1824-1888 Same. B-T.
GUY, Seymour Joseph.
Am. Greenwich, Eng. 1824-1910 New York. A09-B-C-DAB-F-T-1-15-89.
GUYDO, Henri.
Fr. b. Teilleul; ac. 1931 Paris. DBA.
GUYON, Maximilienne (Goepp).
Fr. Paris 1868-1903. B-T.
GUYOT, Antoine Patrice.
Fr. b. Paris 1787. [No death date.] B-T.
GUYOT, George Lucien. (P-S)
Fr. b. Paris 1885. B-DBA-T.
GUYOT, Laurent L. (Eg.)
Fr. Paris 1756-1806. B-T.

GUYS, Constantin [Ernest Adolphe Hyacinthe].
Fr. Flessingue 1805-1892 Paris. B-T-386-387-820.
GUYSI, Alice Viola.
Am. b. Cincinnati, O.; ad. 1934 Birmingham, Mich. A.
GUZZARDI, Giuseppe.
It. ac. 1875-1914 in Florence. B-T.
GUZZARDI, Leonardo.
It. ac. 1800 in Italy. T.
GWYNNE-JONES, Allan.
Eng. b. London 1892; ad. 1934 Same. Wa.
GYER, E. H., Jr.
Am. b. Tacoma, Wash. 1900. A.
GYNGELL, A. E.
Eng. b. 1886; ad. 1935 Johannesburg, Transvaal, So. Africa. M.
GYOKUDÓ, Kawai.
Jap. ac. 1933 in Tokyo. J., Vol. 2, page 113.
GYOKUSHÓ, Kawabata.
Jap. b. Kyoto 1842. T.
GYOTEI, Mano.
Jap. ex. 1930 in Tokyo. M.
GYSIS, Nikolaus.
Gr. Isle of Tinos 1842-1901 Munich, Ger. C-T.
GZARGY. *see* Geargius.
HAAG, Carl.
Eng. Erlangen, Ger. 1820-1915 London. B-E-T-6.
HAAG, Charles Oscar. (S)
Am. b. Norrkoping, Swe. 1867; ad. 1934 Winnetka, Ill. A-F.
HAAG, Tethart Philip Christian.
Ger. Cassel 1737/40-1812 The Hague, Holland. B-T.
HAANEN, Cécil von.
Aus. b. Vienna 1844; ac. 1886 Same. B-C-T.
HAANSBERGEN [or Haensbergen], Johannes van.
Dut. Utrecht 1642-1705 The Hague. B-T.
HAAPANEN, John Nichols.
Am. b. Nyantic, Conn. 1891; ad. 1934 Boothbay Harbor, Me. A.
HAARLEM, Cornelis van. *see* Cornelis van H.
HAARLEM, Gérard (or Geeraert).
see Geertgen, tot Sint Jans.
HAAS. *see also* De Haas.
HAAS, Helen. (S)
Am. ad. 1934 New York. M.
HAAS, Johannes Hubertus Leonardus de.
Dut. Kedel 1832-1880 Brussels, Belg. B-T.
HABERMANN, Hugo von.
Ger. Dillingen 1849. B-T.
HABERSTROH, Alex. (Ill.)
Am. ad. 1934 New York. M.
HABICH, Ludwig. (S)
Ger. b. Darmstadt 1872. T.
HABICHT, J.
Am. ad. 1934 Cincinnati, O. M.
HACK, Gwendolyn Dunley Kelley. (Min.)
Mrs. Charles Wesley Hack.
Am. b. Columbus, O. 1877. A20-F.
HACK, Robert.
Am. ad. 1934 Richmond Hill, N. Y. M.
HACKAERT (or Hackert), Jan (or Joan).
Dut. Amsterdam 1629/36-1699/1700 Same. B-C-T-722.
HACKER, Arthur.
Eng. London 1858-1919 Same. B-T.
HACKERT, Jacob Philipp.
Ger. Prenzlau 1737-1807 Florence, It. B-T.
HACKETT Grace Edith.
Am. b. Boston, Mass. 1874; ad. 1934 Roxbury, Mass. A.
HACKL, Gabriel von.
Ger. b. Marburg 1843. B-T.
HACKMAN, F. J.
Eng. ex. 1934 London. M.
HADDON, Arthur Trevor.
Br. b. 1864; ad. 1934 London. B-Wa.
HADEN, [Sir] Francis Seymour. (Et.)
Eng. London 1818-1910 Abresford. B-DNB-E-T-880.
HADER, Bertha. (Ill.)
Am. ad. 1935 New York, N. Y. M.
HADER, Elmer. (Ill.)
Am. ad. 1935 New York, N. Y. M.
HADFIELD, Marie Louisa Cecilia. *see* Cosway, M. L. C.
HADLEY, George.
Am. England 1876-1922 Brooklyn, N. Y. A019.
HADLEY, Paul.
Am. b. Indianapolis, Ind.; ad. 1934 Same. A.
HAECHT, Tobias von. *see* Verhaegt, T.
HAENEL, Will M.
Am. b. Chicago, Ill. 1885; ad. 1934 Same. A.
HAENIGSEN, Harry. (Ill)
Am. ad. 1935 New York. M.
HAENISCH, Aloys. (Et.)
Aus. b. 1866 in Austria. M.
HAESLER, Gladys Jessie.
Mrs. Paul Haesler.
Am. b. Grand Rapids, Mich.; ad. 1934 Brooklyn, N. Y. A.
HAFEN, John.
Am. b. Scherzingen, Swi. 1856; d. 1910 Provo, Utah. A08-B-T.
HAFEN, Virgil O.
Am. b. Springville, Utah 1889; ad. 1934 Same. M.
HAFNER, Charles Andrew. (S)
Am. b. Omaha, Neb. 1888; ad. 1934 New York. A-Cs.
HAGBORG, Vilhelm Nickolaus August.
Swe. Gothenburg 1852-1921. B-T.
HAGEDORN, Karl.
Ger. b. Berlin 1889; ad. 1934 London. Wa.
HAGEL, Alfred.
Ger. b. 1885 in Germany. T.
HAGELAIDES. *see* Ageladas.
HAGELSTEIN, Thomann von [Jacob Ernest].
Ger. Lindau 1588-1653 Same. B.
HAGEMANS, Maurice.
Belg. b. Liége 1852. B-T.
HAGEMEISTER, Karl.
Ger. b. 1848; ac. 1888 in Berlin. B-T.
HAGEN, Johan C. van der. (Marine-P)
Dut. The Hague 1676-1745 Dublin, Ir. B-T.
HAGEN [or Verhaege], Joris van der.
Dut. 1615/20-1669 The Hague. B-C-T.
HAGEN, Louise.
Am. ex. 1935 New York. M.
HAGEN, Theodor Joseph.
Ger. Düsseldorf 1842-1919 Weimar. C-T.

HAGENBORN, MAX.
Am. b. Stuttgart, Ger. 1870; ad. 1934 Sharon, Mass. A.
HAGER, LUTHER GEORGE. (Ill.)
Am. b. Terre Haute, Ind. 1885; ad. 1934 Seattle, Wash. F-W.
HAGGIN, BEN ALI.
Am. b. New York 1882; ad. 1934 Same. A-F-T-W-46.
HAGHE, LOUIS. (Eg.)
Eng. Tournai, Belg. 1806-1885 London. B-C-DNB-T.
HAGN, LUDWIG KARL HEINRICH VON.
Ger. Munich 1819-1898 Same. C-T.
HAGUE, J. EDWARD HOMERVILLE. (P-S)
Eng. b. Cookham 1885; ex. 1935 London. M-T.
HAGUE, JOSHUA ANDERSON.
Eng. Manchester 1850-1916 Deganwy, Wales. B-T.
HAGUE, MAURICE STEWART.
Am. b. Richmond, O. 1862; ad. 1934 Columbus, O. A-F-W.
HAGUE, MORTON. (S)
Am. b. Brooklyn, N. Y. 1894; ad. 1934 Chicago. A.
HAHERER, CHARLES WINSTON. (Et.)
Am. b. Louisville, Ky. 1905; ad. 1934 Chicago. M.
HAHN, EMANUEL. (S)
Can. b. Germany 1881; ad. 1935 Toronto, Can. M.
HAHN, HERMANN. (S)
Ger. b. Rentlingen 1868; ac. 1935 B-Hs-T.
HAHN, [Mrs.] NANCY COONSMAN. (S)
Am. b. St. Louis, Mo. 1892; ad. 1934 Same. A.
HAHNEL, ERNEST JULIUS. (S)
Ger. Dresden 1811-1891 Same. B-Hs-T.
HAHS, PHILIP B.
Am. Reading, Pa. 1853-1882 Phila., Pa. F.
HAI-SOU, LIU. (Et)
Chinese. ad. 1935 Shanghai. M.
HAID, JOHANN GOTTFRIED. (Eg.)
Ger. Augsburg 1710-1776 Vienna, Aus. B-T.
HAIDT, JOHN VALENTINE.
Am. Germany 1700-1780 Bethlehem, Pa. F.
HAIG [or Hägg], AXEL HERMAN. (Eg.)
Swe. Götland 1835-1921 Southsea, Eng. T.
HAIG, [Mrs.] MABEL GEORGE.
Am. b. Blue Earth, Minn. 1884; ad. 1934 Whittier, Calif. A.
HAIGH-WOOD, CHARLES HAIGH.
Eng. b. Bury 1856; d. 1927. Wa01929.
HAILMAN, JOHANNA K. WOODWILL.
Mrs. James D. Hailman.
Am. b. Pittsburgh, Pa. 1871; ad. 1934 Same. A.
HAINCELIN DE HAGUENOT, JEAN.
Fr. ac. 1403-1448. B-T.
HAINES, BOWEN AYLESWORTH.
Am. b. Canada 1858. A28.
HAINES, FREDERICK STANLEY.
Can. b. Meaford, Can. 1879; ad. 1934 Toronto, Ont. M.
HAINES, MARIE BRUNER. (Mu.)
Am. b. Cincinnati, O. 1885; ac. 1934 College Station, Tex. A.
HAINES, RICHARD.
Am. ex. 1935 Minneapolis, Minn. M.
HAINES, WILLIAM.
Eng. Bedhampton 1778-1848 Brixton; ac. 1800 Phila., Pa. B-DNB-F-T-2-7-45.
HAINES, WILLIAM HENRY.
Eng. London 1812-1884. B-T.
HAITÉ, GEORGE CHARLES.
Eng. Bexley 1855-1924. B-T.
HAKE, OTTO E.
Am. b. Ger. 1876; ad. 1934 Chicago. A.
HAKEWILL FAMILY.
Br. ac. 18th and 19th centuries. DNB-T.
HAKUYER, KATSUNO (Bonseki Art).
Jap. ac. 1928 in Tokyo. M.
HALBERG, CHARLES EDWARD.
Am. b. Gothenberg, Swe. 1855; ad. 1934 Austin, Ill. A.
HALBIG, JOHANN VON. (S)
Ger. Dönnersdorf 1814-1882 Munich. B-T.
HALE, EDWARD MATTHEW.
Eng. Hastings 1852-1924. B-Y01925.
HALE, ELLEN DAY.
Am. b. Worcester, Mass. 1855; ad. 1934 Wash., D. C. A-B-F-T-W16-15.
HALE, GARDNER. (Mu.)
Am. Chicago 1894-1931 Santa Maria, Calif. A028-W16-200.
HALE, GIRARD.
Am. b. New York; ad. 1915 Paris. A12.
HALE, JOHN.
Eng. ac. 1666. M.
HALE, LILIAN WESTCOTT.
Mrs. Philip Leslie Hale.
Am. b. Hartford, Conn. 1881; ad. 1934 Dedham, Mass. A-B-F-T-W.
HALE, MARY POWELL HELME.
Mrs. William Hale.
Am. b. Kingston, R. I. 1862; ad. 1934 Gloucester, Mass. A.
HALE, PHILIP LESLIE.
Am. Boston, Mass. 1865-1931 Same. A028-B-DAB-F-T-W16.
HALE, SUSAN.
Am. Boston, Mass. 1834-1910 Matunuck, R. I. A08-B-F-T-15.
HALE, WALTER. (Ill.)
Am. Chicago, Ill. 1869-1917 New York. A015-T.
HALE, WILLIAM MATTHEW.
Eng. Claverton 1837-1929 London. B-T.
HALEY, JOHN.
Am. ad. 1935 Oakland, Calif. M.
HALFNIGHT, RICHARD WILLIAM.
Eng. b. Sunderland; ac. 1878-1907. B-T.
HALFORD, CONSTANCE.
Eng. ac. 1892-1911 in London. B-T.
HALFPENNY [or Alpenny], JOSEPH SAMUEL.
Ir. Bishopsthorpe 1787-1858. B-T.
HALICKA, ALICIA [Mrs. Marcousis].
Pol. b. Cracow 1895; ad. 1934 Paris. DBA-797.
HALKETT, FRANÇOIS JOSEPH CLEMENT.
Belg. ac. 1886 in Brussels. C-T.
HALL, ANNE [or Ann]. (Min.)
Am. Pomfret, Conn. 1792-1863 New York. F-T-2-6-179.

HALL, Arnold. (Ill.)
Am. b. Binghamton, N. Y. 1901; ad. 1934. Same. A.
HALL, Arthur William. (Et.)
Am. b. Bowie, Tex. 1889; ad. 1935 Howard, Kan. A28.
HALL, Charles. (Eg.)
Eng. 1720?-1783 London. DNB-T.
HALL, Christopher.
Eng. ac. 1929 in London. M.
HALL, Clifford.
Eng. ac. 1932 in London. M.
HALL, Edna Clarke. (Et.)
Eng. ad. 1934 Sussex, Eng. M.
HALL, [Mrs.] Frances Devereux Jones.
Am. b. New Orleans, La.; ad. 1934 Phila., Pa. A.
HALL, Frederick.
Eng. b. Stillington 1860; ad. 1934 Newburg, Eng. B-Wa.
HALL, Frederick Garrison. (Et.)
Am. b. Baltimore, Md. 1879; ad. 1934 New York. A-F.
HALL, George Henry.
Am. Manchester, N. H. 1825-1913 New York. AOXI-B-C-DAB-F-T-W14-4-11-15.
HALL, George Lothian.
Eng. ac. 1856-1878 in London. B-T.
HALL, Harvey.
Eng. b. Newmarket; ac. 1838-1886 in London. B-T-Ya1883.
HALL, Helen Jameson.
Mrs. Arnold Hall.
Am. b. Summit, N. J. 1902; ad. 1934 New York. A.
HALL, Henry Bryan, Jr. (Eg.)
Am. b. London; ac. 1900 New York. F-T-7-45.
HALL, Henry Bryan, Sr. (Eg.)
Am. London 1808-1884 Morrisonia, N. Y. DAB-F-T-6-7-40-45-55.
HALL, James.
Am. b. Boston, Mass. 1869; d. 1917. A014-B.
HALL, James.
Scot. b. Scotland 1797; d. 1854 Ashiestel, Scot. DNB-T.
HALL, John. (Eg.)
Eng. Colchester 1739-1797 London. DNB-T.
HALL, John H. (Eg.)
Am. ac. 1826-1840 in Calif. B-Bd-F.
HALL, Lindsay Bernard.
Eng. b. Liverpool 1859; ac. 1892 Melbourne, Aust. B.
HALL, Mable R.
Am. ad. 1934 Phila., Pa. M.
HALL, Margaret Bernardine.
Eng. Liverpool 1863-1910 London. B.
HALL, Mary Lewis.
Am. ad. 1935 Washington, D. C. M.
HALL, [Mrs.] Norma Bassett.
Am. b. Halsey, Ore. 1889; ad. 1934 Howard, Kan. A28.
HALL, Oliver.
Eng. b. Tulse Hill 1869; ad. 1934 Sutton. B-T-Wa.
HALL, Parker L.
Am. b. Denver, Colo. 1898; ad. 1934 Berkeley, Calif. A.
HALL, Peter. (Eg.)
Am. Birmingham, Eng. 1828-1895 Brooklyn, N. Y. F-7.
HALL, Pierre Adolphe.
Swe. Boras 1739-1793 Liége, Belg. B-T.
HALL, Sydney Prior.
Eng. b. Newmarket, Eng. 1842. B-T.
HALL, Thomas.
Am. b. Sweden 1883; ad. 1934 Chicago. A.
HALL, Thomas Victor.
Am. b. Rising Sun, Ind. 1879; ad. 1934 Peekskill, N. Y. A.
HALL, Weeks.
Am. ad. 1934 New Iberia, La. M.
HALL, William Stanley.
Am. b. New York 1889; ad. 1934 Same. A.
HALLADAY, Milton R. (Ill.)
Am. ad. 1934 Providence, R. I. A.
HALLAERT, Charles.
Am. ad. 1934 New York. M.
HALLÉ, Charles Edward.
Eng. b. England 1846; d. 1919 London. T-Y01920.
HALLÉ, Claude Guy.
Fr. Paris 1652-1736 Same. B-C-T.
HALLÉ, Noël.
Fr. Paris 1711-1781 Same. B-C-T.
HALLER, Heinrich Friedrich. (S)
Ger. ac. 1693-1720 in Madgeburg, Ger. T.
HALLER, Hermann. (S)
Swi. b. 1880 in Zurich. Hs-388.
HALLETT, Hendricks A.
Am. Charlestown, Mass. 1847-1921 Boston. A018-F.
HALLIDAY, Edward Irvine.
Eng. b. Liverpool 1902; ad. 1934 London. M.
HALLIDAY, Laura.
Am. b. Cincinnati, O.; ad. 1915 College Hill, O. A12.
HALLIDAY, Mary Hughitt.
Am. b. Cairo, Ill. 1866; ad. 1934 Santa Monica, Calif. A.
HALLIDAY, Michael Frederick.
Eng. ac. 1853 in London; d. 1869. B-Bd.
HALLMAN, Henry Theodore.
Am. b. Milford Square, Pa. 1904; ad. 1934 Souderton, Pa. A.
HALLO, Charles Jean.
Fr. b. Lille, Fr. 1882. B-DBA.
HALLOCK, Ruth Mary.
Am. b. Erie, Pa. 1876; ad. 1934 New York. A.
HALLOWELL, George Hawley.
Am. Boston, Mass. 1871-1926. A023-F-T-46.
HALLOWELL, Robert. (Ill.)
Am. b. Denver, Colo. 1886; ad. 1934 New York. A-F.
HALLS, John James.
Eng. ac. 1791-1834 in London. B-DNB-T.
HALLSTHAMMAR, Carl. (S)
Am. b. 1897; ad. 1934 Chicago, Ill. M.
HALLSTRÖM, Eric.
Swe. b. 1893; ex. 1934 Paris. DBA.
HALLSTRÖM, Gunnar August.
Swe. b. Stockholm 1875. T.

HALM, George Robert.
Am. b. Ogdensburg, N. Y. 1850; d. 1899. A01.
HALMI, Artur Louis [or Lajos].
Hun. b. Budapest 1866; ac. 1891-1900 Paris. B-T.
HALPEN [or Halpin], John Edmund.
Ir. ac. 1780 in Dublin. DNB-T.
HALPEN [or Halpin], Patrick. (Eg.)
Ir. ac. 1750-1790 in Dublin. DNB-T.
HALPERT, Samuel.
Am. Russia 1884-1930 Detroit, Mich. A027-B-F-T.
HALPIN, Frederick W. (Eg.)
Am. England 1805-1880 Jersey City, N. J. B-Bd-F-T-7-40.
HALS, Dirk [or Thierry].
Dut. Haarlem 1591-1656. B-C-T.
HALS, Frans [The Elder].
Dut. Antwerp, Belg. 1580/4-1666 Haarlem. B-Bd-C-E-T-128-389-390-722-790-902-929-930.
HALS, Frans [The Younger.].
Dut. Haarlem 1617/23-1669? B-Bd-C-E-T-128-389-390-790-902-929-930.
HALS, Nicolaas Claes Fransz.
Dut. Haarlem 1628-1686. B-T.
HALSALL, William Formsby.
Am. England 1841-1919 Provincetown, Mass. A017-B-F-T-15-47.
HALSE, Emmeline. (S)
Eng. ac. 1878-1929 in London. B-T-Wa1929.
HALSWELLE, Keeley.
Eng. Richmond 1832-1891 Paris. B-DNB-T.
HALTON, Minnie Hollis.
Am. b. Belton, Tex.; ad. 1934 Austin, Tex. A.
HAMACHER [or Hammacher], Willy.
Ger. Breslau 1865-1909. B-T.
HAMANN, Charles F. (S)
Am. ac. 1926. F.
HAMBOURG, André.
Fr. b. Paris 1909. DBA.
HAMBRIDGE, Jay.
[Discoverer of Dynamic Symmetry.]
Am. Canada 1867-1924 New York. A021-F.
HAMDY BEY, Osman Edhem. (Statesman-P)
Turkish. Constantinople 1842-1910 Stamboul. B-T.
HAMEEL, Alart [or Alaert]. (Eg.)
Flem. Bois-le-Duc, Fr. 1449-1509 Same. B-T.
HAMEL, Eugène.
Can. b. Canada 1845; d. 1932 Same. M.
HAMEN, y Léon, Juan van der.
Sp. Madrid 1596-1632. B-T.
HAMERTON, Philip Gilbert. (Author-P)
Eng. Laneside 1834-1894 Boulogne, Fr. B-DNB-E-T.
HAMERTON, Robert Jacob.
Eng. ac. 1831-1858 in London. B-T.
HAMILTON, Blanche.
Am. ad. 1935 West Barrington, R. I. M.
HAMILTON, Carl Wilhelm.
Aus. Brussels, Belg. 1668-1754 Augsburg, Ger. B-T.
HAMILTON, [Mrs.] Clara Langhlin.
Am. b. Belle Center, O. 1872; ad. 1934 Kokomo, Ind. A.
HAMILTON, David Osborne.
Am. b. Detroit, Mich. 1893. A28.
HAMILTON, Edgar Scudder.
Am. San Antonio, Tex. 1869-1903 Sullivan Co., N. Y. A04-B-T.
HAMILTON, [Mrs.] Ethel Heaven.
Am. b. Mexico 1871; ad. 1934 New York. A.
HAMILTON, Everett. (S)
Am. b. Phila., Pa.; ad. 1927 Paris. DNB.
HAMILTON, Ferdinand Philipp.
Flem. Brussels, Belg. 1664-1750 Vienna, Aus. B-DNB-T.
HAMILTON, Frans de.
Flem. ac. 1661-1695 in Germany. B-T.
HAMILTON, Gavin.
Eng. Lamark 1730-1797 Rome, It. B-DNB-T.
HAMILTON, George.
Am. ex. 1935 Seattle, Wash. M.
HAMILTON, Hamilton.
Am. Oxford 1847-1928 Norwalk, Conn. A025-B-C-F-T-W14.
HAMILTON, Helen.
Am. ad. 1934 [Silvermine, P.O.], Norwalk, Conn. M.
HAMILTON, Hildegarde.
Mrs. L. H. Ryland.
Am. b. Syracuse, N. Y. 1906; ad. 1934 Lexington, Va. A.
HAMILTON, Hugh Douglas.
Ir. Dublin 1734?-1806 Same. B-DNB-T.
HAMILTON, James.
Am. b. Ireland 1819; d. 1878 Phila., Pa. B-Bd-F-T-4-15.
HAMILTON, James.
Eng. b. England 1640; d. 1720 Brussels, Belg. B-DNB.
HAMILTON, James Whitelaw.
Scot. Glasgow 1860-1932. A20-B-T-Wa1929-Y01933.
HAMILTON, John.
Ir. b. Dublin; ac. 1765-1786 in London. DNB-T.
HAMILTON, John B. (P-S)
Am. ex. 1934 in New York. M.
HAMILTON, John McLure.
Am. b. Phila., Pa. 1853; ad. 1934 Jamaica, W. Indies. A-B-C-F-T-W14-1-15.
HAMILTON, Johann Georg von.
Flem. Brussels 1662-1736 Vienna, Aus. B-DNB-T.
HAMILTON, Letitia Marion.
Ir. b. Dublin; ad. 1934 Same. Wa.
HAMILTON, Mary R.
Can. b. Cubross, Can.; ac. 19th Cent. in Paris. B.
HAMILTON, Norah. (Et)
Am. b. Fort Wayne, Ind. 1873. A28-F.
HAMILTON, Robert.
Am. b. Ireland; ad. 1934 New York. A.
HAMILTON, Thomas M.
Am. ex. 1934 Cincinnati, O. M.
HAMILTON, Wilbur Dean.
Am. b. Summerfield, Pa. 1864; ad. 1934 Boston, Mass. A20-B-F-T-W17.
HAMILTON, William.
Eng. Chelsea 1751-1801 London. B-DNB-T.
HAMLIN, Genevieve Karr. (S)
Am. b. New York 1896; ad. 1934 Same. A-Cs-F.

HAMLIN, PAUL.
Am. ad. 1934 No. Baltimore, O. M.
HAMLIN, WILLIAM. (Eg)
Am. Prov., R. I. 1772-1869 Same.
DAB-F-T-2-7-55-90.
HAMM, PHINEAS ELDRIDGE. (Eg)
Am. Phila., Pa. 1779-1861 Same. F-T-2-7.
HAMMAN, ÉDOUARD JEAN CONRAD.
Belg. Ostend 1819-1888 Paris. B-T.
HAMMAN, ÉDOUARD MICHEL FERDINAND.
Fr. b. Paris; ac. 1880 Same. B-T.
HAMMARGREN, F. E. (S)
Am. b. Orebro, Swe. 1892; ad. 1934 Leonia, N. J. A.
HAMME, P. ALEXIS VAN.
Belg. Brussels 1818-1875 Same. B-T.
HAMMELL, ELIZABETH LANSDELL. (Ill)
Mrs. Will Hammell.
Am. ad. 1934 New York. M.
HAMMELL, WILL. (Ill)
[Mr. and Mrs. Hammell known as "The Hammells".]
Am. ad. 1934 New York. M.
HAMMER, CHRISTIAN GOTTLOB.
Ger. Dresden 1775/9-1864 Same. B-T.
HAMMER, EDMUND GUIDO.
Ger. Dresden 1821-1898 Same. C-T.
HAMMER, FERNAND. (S)
Fr. ex. 1934 New York. M.
HAMMER, JOHN. (Ill)
Am. ad. 1934 New York. M.
HAMMER, TRYGVE. (S)
Am. b. Arendal, Nor. 1878; ad. 1934 Douglaston, L. I., N. Y. A-Cs-F-46-701.
HAMMER, VIKTOR.
Aus. b. Vienna 1882; ad. 1934 Florence, It. T.
HAMMER, WILLIAM.
Dan. Copenhagen 1821-1889 Same. B-T.
HAMMER, WOLF. (Eg)
Ger. ac. 1480 in Munich. T.
HAMMERSHÖI, VILHELM.
Dan. Copenhagen 1864-1916. B-T.
HAMMERSLEY, JAMES ASTBURY.
Eng. Burslem 1815-1869 Manchester.
DNB-T.
HAMMERSMITH, PAUL. (Et)
Am. b. Naperville, Ill. 1857; ad. 1934 Milwaukee, Wis. A-F.
HAMMITT, CLAWSON SHAKESPEARE.
Am. Wilmington, Del. 1857-1927 Same.
A025-F-T.
HAMMOND, ARTHUR J.
Am. b. Vernon, Conn. 1875; ad. 1934 Rockport, Mass. A.
HAMMOND, GERTRUDE DEMAIN.
Eng. ex. 1934 in London. T.
HAMMOND, JANE NYE. (S)
Am. New York 1857-1901 Prov., R. I.
A04.
HAMMOND, JOHN.
Can. b. Montreal, Can. 1843; ad. 1935 Sackville, N. B. B.
HAMMOND, NATALIE HAYS.
Am. b. Lakewood, N. J. 1905; ad. 1934 New York. A.
HAMMOND, RICHARD HENRY.
Am. b. Cincinnati, O. 1854; ad. 1915 Same.
A12-F.
HAMNETT, NINA.
Eng. b. 1890; ad. 1932 Paris, Fr. M.
HAMON, JEAN LOUIS. (Vase-P)
Fr. St. Loup 1821-1874 St. Raphäel, Fr.
B-C-E-T.
HAMPTON, HERBERT. (S)
Eng. Hoddesdon, 1863-1929.
Wa1929-Y01930.
HAMZA, JOHANN.
Ger. b. Teltsch, Ger. 1850. B-T.
HAN, HUANG.
Chinese. ac. 8th century. E.
HAN KAN.
Chinese. ac. 8th century; d. 780? E.
HANAK, ANTON. (S)
Rus. Brno 1875-1934 Vienna.
T-Obit. Art News, 2-3-1934.
HANATSCHEK, HERMANN.
Am. ac. in New York 1923. M.
HANAU, JEAN.
Fr. b. Paris 1899. DBA.
HANCOCK, CHARLES.
Eng. ac. 1819-1868 in London. B-T.
HANCOCK, JOSEPH LANE.
Am. b. Chicago, Ill. 1864; d. 1925. A12-F.
HANCOCK, WALKER. (S)
Am. b. St. Louis, Mo. 1901; ad. 1934 New York. A-Cs-F.
HAND, MOLLY WILLIAMS.
Am. b. Keene, N. H. 1892; ad. 1934 Roselle, N. J. A.
HAND, THOMAS.
Eng. ac. 1790-1804 in London. B-T.
HANDFORTH, THOMAS SCOFIELD. (Et)
Am. b. Tacoma, Wash. 1897; ad. 1934 Peiping, China. A.
HANDLER, HUGO.
Ger. b. Frankfort 1861. B-T.
HANDLEY, [Mrs.] HESTER MERWIN. (Mu)
Am. ex. 1935 New York. M.
HANDLEY-READ, EDWARD HARRY.
Eng. b. London 1870; ad. 1934 Salisbury.
Wa.
HANEDOES, LOUWRENS.
Flem. Woudrichem 1822-1905 Kraaiveld.
B-T.
HANEY, IRENE W.
Am. b. Pittsburgh, Pa. 1890; ad. 1934 Same.
A.
HANEY, JAMES PARTON.
Am. New York 1869-1923 Same. A20-F.
HANICOTTE, AUGUSTIN.
Fr. b. Béthune 1870. B-DBA.
HANKEY, EDITH MARY LEE.
Eng. b. 1881 in England. M.
HANKEY, WILLIAM LEE.
Eng. b. Chester 1869. B-T.
HANKINS, CORNELIUS.
Am. ad. 1935 Nashville, Tenn. M.
HANLEY, HARRIET CLARK. (S)
Am. b. St. Louis, Mo.; ad. 1934 Minneapolis, Minn. A.
HANLEY, SARAH E.
Am. ad. 1934 Oyster Bay, L. I., N. Y. M.
HANLON, LOUIS.
Am. ad. 1934 Phila., Pa. A.
HANNA, THOMAS KING.
Am. b. Kansas City, Mo. 1872; ad. 1934 Caldwell, N. J. A-B-F-T.

HANNAFORD, Alice Ide. (S)
Mrs. Foster Hannaford.
Am. b. Balt., Md. 1888; ad. 1934 Winnetka, Ill. A.
HANNAFORD, Mark V.
Am. ad. 1934 Toledo, O. M.
HANNAH, William M.
Am. Brooklyn, N. Y. 1855-1927 Prov., R. I. A025.
HANNAUX, Émmanuel. (S)
Fr. Metz 1855/60-1934. B-T-DBA.
HANNELL, Hazel Johnson.
Am. b. La Grange, Ill. 1895; ad. 1934 Chicago. A.
HANNELL, V. M. S.
Am. b. Negaunee, Mich. 1896; ad. 1934 Chicago. A.
HANNEMAN, Adrian.
Dut. The Hague 1600/11-1671 Same. B-T.
HANNER, Hanns.
Ger. b. St. Goar 1883. T.
HANNES, Harold G.
Am. ad. 1934 Toledo, O. M.
HANNOTIN, Simone. (S)
Fr. b. Paris 1906. DBA.
HANOTEAU, Hector Charles Auguste.
Fr. Decize 1823-1890. B-C-T.
HANRIOT, Jules Armand.
Fr. Metz 1855-1930 Paris. DBA.
HANS OF GMUND. (S)
Ger. (Swabian); ac. 1470-1480. Hs.
HANS MALER ZU SCHWAZ. *see* Maler.
HANSELAERE, Pieter van.
Flem. Ghent 1786-1862 Same. B-T.
HANSEN, Armin Carl.
Am. b. San Fran., Calif. 1886; ad. 1934 Monterey, Calif. A-F-W.
HANSEN, Carl Christian Constantin.
Dan. Rome, It. 1804-1880 Copenhagen. B-C-T.
HANSEN, Einar.
Am. ad. 1934 Pasadena, Calif. M.
HANSEN, Hans Nicolaj.
Dan. Copenhagen 1853-1923. B-T.
HANSEN, Oscar J. W. (S)
Am. b. 1892; ad. 1934 Chicago. M.
HANSEN, Sonia Aimee.
Dan. b. Copenhagen 1901. DBA.
HANSEN-JACOBSEN Niels. (S)
Dan. b. Jutland 1861. T-798.
HANSI, Jacques Waltz.
Fr. b. Colmar 1873. DBA.
HANSON, Albert J.
Aus. ac. 19th century in Austria. B-T.
HANSON, Nils Edwin. (S)
Am. ad. 1934 Cleveland, O. M.
HAPGOOD, Dorothy Alden.
Am. b. Hartford, Conn. 1892; ad. 1934 Same. A.
HAPPERSBURGER, Frank. (S)
Am. b. San Fran., Calif. 1859. F-T-Ta.
HAQUETTE, Georges Jean Maria.
Fr. Paris 1854-1906. B-DBA-T.
HARA, Katsmo.
Jap. ac. 1929 in Paris. DBA.
HARBESON, Georgiana Brown.
Mrs. John F. Harbeson.
Am. b. New Haven, Conn. 1894; ad. 1934 New York. A.
HARBURGER, Edmund.
Ger. Eichstadt 1846-1906 Munich. B-T.
HARCOURT, George.
Scot. b. Dumbarton 1868/9; ac. 1929 London. B-T-Wa1929.
HARCOURT, George E. (Ill)
Am. b. Detroit, Mich. 1897; ad. Same. A.
HARCOURT, [Earl of], George Simon.
Eng. 1736-1809 London. B-T.
HARCOURT, Millicent Gifford.
Am. ad. 1934 Larchmont, N. Y. M.
HARDCASTLE, Ephraism.
see Pyne, William Henry.
HARDENBUGH, Elizabeth Rutgers.
Am. b. New Brunswick, N. J.; ad. 1934 Williamstown, Mass. A-F.
HARDENBUGH, Gerard Rutgers. (Ill)
Am. b. 1855; d. 1915 Bay Head, N. J. A012.
HARDER, Heinrich.
Ger. b. 1858; ac. 1930 Berlin. T.
HARDIE, Charles Martin. (Eg)
Scot. Edinburgh 1858-1916. B-T.
HARDIE, Martin. (Eg)
Eng. b. London 1875; ad. 1934 Same. Wa.
HARDIE, Robert Gordon.
Am. Brattleboro, Vt. 1854-1904 Same. A05-B-F-T.
HARDIMÉ [or Hardumé], Pieter.
Flem. Antwerp 1677-1758 The Hague, Holland. B-T.
HARDIMÉ, Simon.
Flem. Antwerp 1672-1737 London. B-DNB-T.
HARDIN, Adlai S. (S)
Am. b. Minneapolis, Minn. 1901; ad. 1934 New York. M.
HARDIN, Ernest R.
Am. ad. 1935 Austin, Tex. M.
HARDING, Chester.
Am. Conway, Mass. 1792-1866 Boston. B-Bd-C-DAB-F-T-1-2-4-15-46-391.
HARDING, [General] Chester.
Am. b. Enterprise, Miss. 1866; ad. 1934 New Orleans, La. A.
HARDING, [Mrs.] Dorothy Sturgis. (Ill)
Am. b. Boston 1891; ad. 1934 Portsmouth, N. H. M.
HARDING, George. (Mu)
Am. b. Phila., Pa. 1882; ad. 1934 Same. A-F-T-W-46.
HARDING, George Perfect.
Eng. ex. 1840-1853 London. B-DNB-T.
HARDING, James Duffield.
Eng. Deptford 1798-1863 Barnes. B-DNB-E-T.
HARDING, Nelson. (Cart)
Am. b. New York 1879; ad. 1935 Brooklyn, N. Y. W.
HARDING, Sylvester.
Eng. New Castle 1745-1809 London. B-DNB-T.
HARDRICK, Alice R.
Mrs. Melbourne Havelock Hardrick.
Am. b. Chicago, Ill.; ad. 1934 Annisquam, Mass. A.
HARDRICK, John W.
Am. b. Indianapolis, Ind. 1891; ad. 1934 Same. A.

HARDRICK, Melbourne Havelock.
Am. Digby, Can. 1857-1916 Belmont, Mass. A014-B-F-T.
HARDUMÉ, Pieter. *see* Hardimé, P.
HARDY, Anna E.
Am. b. Bangor, Me. 1839; ad. 1915 So. Orrington, Me. [No death date.] A12-B-F.
HARDY, Bernhardt Caspar.
Ger. Cologne 1726-1819 Same. B-T.
HARDY, [Mrs.] Beulah Greenough.
Am. b. Providence, R. I. 1874; ad. 1934 Phila., Pa. A.
HARDY, Charles. (Ill)
Am. London 1888-1935 Utica, N. Y. A-Obit. N. Y. papers 8-13-1935.
HARDY, Dudley.
Eng. b. 1867; d. 1922 in England. B-T.
HARDY, Frederick Daniel.
Eng. Windsor 1826-1911. B-T.
HARDY, Heywood.
Eng. Bristol 1843-1932 London. B-T.
HARDY, James, Jr.
Eng. Bristol 1832-1889. B-T.
HARDY, Jeremiah Pearson.
Am. Pelham, N. H. 1800-1888 Bangor, Me. F.
HARDY, Thomas.
Eng. ac. 1778-1801 in London. B-T.
HARDY, Thomas Bush.
Eng. Sheffield 1842-1897. B-T.
HARDY, Walter Manley.
Am. b. Brewer, Me. 1877; ad. 1915 Same. A12-B-F.
HARE, Channing.
Am. ad. 1935 New York. M.
HARE, J. Knowles. (Ill)
Am. b. Montclair, N. J. 1884; ad. 1934 New York. A-F.
HARE, Jeannette R. (S)
Am. b. Antwerp, Belg. 1898; ad. 1934 Forest Hills, L. I., N. Y. A-Cs.
HARE, Thomas Leman.
Eng. b. London 1872; ex. 1934 Same. Wa.
HARER, Frederick William. (Et)
Am. b. Blossburg, Pa. 1880; ad. 1934 Uhlerstown, Pa. A-F.
HAREUX, Ernest Victor.
Fr. Paris 1847-1909 Grenoble. B-T.
HARGENS, Charles. (Ill)
Am. ad. 1934 Phila., Pa. M.
HARGRAVE, J. (Eg)
Eng. ac. 1693-1710 in England. T.
HARGREAVES, Thomas. (Min)
Eng. Liverpool 1775-1846 Same. B-DNB-T.
HARINGH [or Haaring], Daniel.
Flem. 1636-1706/9 The Hague, Holland. B-T.
HARITONOFF, Nicholai.
Rus. b. Leningrad 1881; ad. 1935 New York. M.
HARKAVY, Minna.
Am. ex. 1935 New York. M.
HARLAMOFF [or Charlmoff], Alexis Alexejewitsch.
Rus. b. Ssaratoff 1849; ac. 1912 Paris. B-T.
HARLAN, Grace Paul.
Am. b. Seattle, Wash. 1908; ad. 1934 Omaha, Neb. A.
HARLAND, Mary.
Am. b. Yorkshire, Eng. 1863; ad. 1934 Santa Monica, Calif. A.
HARLEY, Charles Richard. (S)
Am. b. Phila., Pa. 1864. A20-B-F-Ta-W14.
HARLEY, George.
Eng. 1791-1871 London. B-DNB-T.
HARLEY, Primrose.
Eng. b. London 1908; ad. 1934 Same. M.
HARLFINGER, Richard.
Ger. b. Vienna, Aus. 1873. T.
HARLOS, Stella.
Am. b. Milwaukee, Wis. 1901; ad. 1934 Same. A.
HARLOW, George Henry.
Eng. London 1787-1819 Same. B-Bd-C-DNB-T-722.
HARLOW, Harry Merrick Sutton.
Am. b. Haverhill, Mass. 1882; ad. 1934 Portsmouth, N. H. A-F-T.
HARMAR, [Miss] Fairlie.
Eng. b. Weymouth; ad. 1935 London; ex. 1934 Pittsburgh, Pa. Wa.
HARMER, Alexander F.
Am. Newark, N. J. 1857-1925 Santa Barbara, Calif. A022.
HARMES, Elmer Esmond.
Am. b. Milwaukee, Wis. 1902; ad. 1934 Minn., Minn. A.
HARNETT, William M.
Am. b. Phila., Pa. 1851. B-C-F-T.
HARNEY, Charles Y. (S)
Am. d. 1912 New York. M.
HARNEY, Paul E.
Am. New Orleans, La. 1850-1915 St. Louis, Mo. A12.
HARNISCH, Albert E. (S)
Am. b. Phila., Pa. 1843. B-F-T-Ta-15.
HARNLY, Perkins.
Am. b. Ogalalla, Neb. 1901; ex. 1934 New York. M.
HARNONCOURT, René. *see* D'Harnoncourt, R.
HAROLD, Alexander.
Can. b. Scotland; d. Montreal, Can. M.
HAROOTIAN, Koren der.
Am. b. Armenia; ac. 1932, U. S. M.
HARPER, F. R.
Am. b. Illinois 1876; ad. 1934 Glencoe, Ill. A.
HARPER, George Coburn. (Et)
Am. b. Leetonia, O. 1887; ad. 1934 Northville, Mich. A.
HARPER, Lillie Hyde. (S)
Am. ad. 1934 New York. A.
HARPER, Marian Dunlap. (Min)
Am. ad. 1934 Glencoe, Ill. A-F.
HARPER, Thomas. (Min)
Eng. ac. 1817-1856 in London. B-T.
HARPER, William A.
Am. Canada 1873-1910 Mexico. A08-46.
HARPER, William St. John.
Am. Rhinebeck, N. Y. 1851-1910 New York. A09-B-F-T.
HARPIGNIES, Henry Joseph.
Fr. Valenciennes 1819-1916 Paris. B-Bd-C-DBA-E-T-847.
HARRACH, [Count] Ferdinand von.
Ger. Selesia 1832-1915 Berlin. C-T.

HARRADEN, Richard. (Eg)
Eng. London 1756-1838 Cambridge. DNB-T.
HARRADEN, Richard Bankes. (Eg)
Eng. England 1778-1862 Cambridge. DNB-T.
HARRINGTON, Charles.
Eng. ad. 1934 Brighton, Eng. Wa.
HARRINGTON, George.
Am. 1832-1911 Springfield, Mass. A09.
HARRIS, Alexandrina Robertson. (Min)
Am. b. Aberdeen, Scot. 1866; ad. 1934 Brooklyn, N. Y. A-F.
HARRIS, Belle C. (S)
Am. ad. 1934 New York. M.
HARRIS, Betty. (S)
Am. ad. 1935 Madison, Wis. M.
HARRIS, Charles Gordon.
Am. b. Prov., R. I. 1891; ad. 1934 No. Prov., R. I. A.
HARRIS, C. Hartman
Am. d. 1909 Boston, Mass. A07.
HARRIS, Charles X.
Am. b. Foxcroft, Me. 1865. A28-B-F-T.
HARRIS, George Albert.
Am. b. San Fran., Calif. 1913; ad. 1934 Same. A.
HARRIS, George Edgerly.
Am. b. Milford, Del. 1898; ad. 1934 New York. A.
HARRIS, Jaffrey.
Am. ad. 1935 Bronxville, N. Y. M.
HARRIS, John I.
Eng. ac. 1802-1834 London. DNB-T.
HARRIS, Lawren S.
Can. b. Brantford, Ont.; ad. 1935 Toronto, Ont. M.
HARRIS, Louis.
Am. b. St. Louis, Mo. 1902; ad. 1934 New York. M.
HARRIS, Margaret A.
Am. ad. 1934 Norwich, Conn. M.
HARRIS, Marion D.
Am. b. Phila., Pa. 1904; ad. 1934 Wilmington, Del. A.
HARRIS, Philip Spooner.
Am. Heath, Mass. 1824-1884 Brooklyn, N. Y. M.
HARRIS, Robert.
Can. Vale of Conway, No. Wales 1849-1919 Montreal, Can. B-T.
HARRIS, Samuel. (Eg)
Am. Boston, Mass. 1783-1810. F-T-2-7.
HARRIS, William Laurel. (Mu)
Am. New York 1870-1924 Lake George, N. Y. A021-B-F-T-W13.
HARRISBURGER, Elizabeth. (Eg)
Am. ex. 1935 Seattle, Wash. M.
HARRISON, Bernard.
Fr. b. London; ad. 1930 Paris. B-DBA-T.
HARRISON, Dorothy.
Am. ad. 1934 Brooklyn, N. Y. M.
HARRISON, Gabriel.
Am. Phila., Pa. 1881-1902 Boston, Mass. A04-B-T.
HARRISON, George Henry.
Eng. Liverpool 1816-1846 Paris. B-DNB-T.
HARRISON, Henry.
Am. Nottingham, Eng. 1844-1923 Jersey City, N. J. A020-F.
HARRISON, James.
Am. ad. 1935 Memphis, Tenn. M.
HARRISON, J. C.
Eng. ex. 1934 London. M.
HARRISON, Lowell Birge.
Am. Phila., Pa. 1854-1929 Woodstock, N. Y. A026-B-C-DAB-F-T-W14-1-46-60-92.
HARRISON, Mary P. Rosnter.
Eng. Liverpool 1788-1875 London. B-DNB-T.
HARRISON, Richard G., Sr. (Eg)
Am. ac. 1814-1845 in Phila., Pa. F-T-2-7.
HARRISON, Richard G., Jr.
Am. ac. 1860-1865 in Phila., Pa. F-T-7.
HARRISON, Thomas Alexander.
Am. Phila., Pa. 1853-1930 Paris. A027-B-C-E-F-T-W14-1.
HARRISON, William Frederick.
Eng. England 1815-1880 Goodnick, Aust. B-DNB-T.
HARRISS, Belle C. (S)
Am. b. Brenham, Tex.; ad. 1934 New York. A.
HARRITON, Abraham.
Am. b. Bucharest, Rumania 1893; ad. 1934 Sunnyside, L. I., N. Y. A.
HARSANYI, Charles.
Am. ad. 1934 Jackson Heights, N. Y. M.
HARSHBUGER, [Mrs.] Florence E. Smith.
Am. b. Freetown, N. Y. 1863; ad. 1915 Syracuse, N. Y. A12-B.
HARSHE, Robert Bartholow.
Am. b. Salisbury, Mo. 1879; ad. 1935 Chicago. A-F-W.
HART, George Overbury ["Pop"].
Am. Cairo, Ill. 1868-1933 New York. A030-F-W-Obit. N. Y. papers, 9-9-1933.
HART, James McDougal.
Am. Scotland 1828-1901 Brooklyn, N. Y. A04-B-C-DAB-F-T-1-3-4-15.
HART, James Turpin.
Eng. Nottingham 1835-1899. T.
HART, Joel Tanner. (S)
Am. Winchester, Ky. 1810-1877 Florence, It. B-Bd-DAB-F-Hs-T-Ta-4-15-58-67-93-94-95.
HART, John Francis. (Cart)
Am. b. Phila., Pa. 1867; ad. 1934 Same. A28-F-W.
HART, Joseph H.
Am. 1858-1916 New York. A013.
HART, Letitia Bennet.
Am. b. New York 1867; ad. 1934 Brooklyn, N. Y. A-B-F-T-W.
HART, Mary E.
Am. d. 1899. A02.
HART, Mary Theresa.
Am. Brooklyn, N. Y. 1872-1921 Lakeville, Conn. A018-B-T.
HART, Robert Gorsuch.
Am. d. 1906 in Mexico. A06-B-T.
HART, Solomon Alexander.
Eng. Plymouth 1806-1881 London. B-DNB-T.
HART, William Howard.
Am. b. Fishkill, N. Y. 1863; ad. 1934 New York. A.
HART, William M.
Am. Paisley Scot. 1823-1894 Mt. Vernon, N. Y. B-C-DAB-E-F-T-1-4-15-22-51.

HARTIG, HANS.
Ger. b. Carvin 1873; ac. 1920 Berlin. T.
HARTING, GEORGE W. (Ill)
Am. b. Little Falls, Minn. 1877. A28.
HARTL, LÉON.
Am. b. Paris; ad. 1935 New York. M.
HARTLAND, HENRY ALBERT.
Ir. Cork 1840-1893 Waterloo, Eng. B-T.
HARTLEY, ALFRED.
Eng. b. Pelham 1855. B-DBA-Wa.
HARTLEY, GEORGE INNESS.
Am. ad. 1934 Southampton, L. I., N. Y. M.
HARTLEY, JOAN. (S)
Am. ad. 1934 New York. M.
HARTLEY, JONATHAN SCOTT. (S)
Am. Albany, N. Y. 1845-1912 New York. A0X-B-DAB-E-F-T-Ta-W7-15.
HARTLEY, MARSDEN.
Am. b. Lewiston, Me. 1878; ad. 1934 Aix-en-Provence, Fr. A-F.
HARTLEY, RACHEL.
[Granddaughter of George Inness, Sr.]
Am. b. New York 1884; ad. 1934 Southampton, N. Y. A.
HARTMAN. *see also* Hartmann.
HARTMAN, BERTRAM.
Am. b. Junction City, Kan. 1882; ad. 1934 New York. A-F.
HARTMAN, ELSA. (Et)
Am. ad. 1934 New York. M.
HARTMAN, ROSELLA.
Am. ad. 1934 Woodstock, N. Y. M.
HARTMAN, SYDNEY K.
Am. Germany 1863-1929 New York. A12-F.
HARTMANN, CARL CHRISTIAN ERNEST. (S)
Dan. Copenhagen 1837-1901 Same. T.
HARTMANN, CHRISTIAN FERDINAND.
Ger. Stuttgart 1774-1852 Dresden. B-T.
HARTMANN, GEORG.
Am. ad. 1934 New York. M.
HARTMANN, ISABEL. (Min)
Am. ad. 1934 Wortendyke, N. J. M.
HARTMANN, JOHANN JACOB.
Ger. Kuttenburg 1680-1728/45 Prague, Czec. B-T.
HARTMANN, KARL.
Ger. b. Heilbronn 1861. T.
HARTMANN, SADAKICHI.
Am. ad. 1935 Hollywood, Calif. M.
HARTRATH, LUCILE.
Am. b. Boston, Mass.; ad. 1934 Chicago. A-B-F-W.
HARTRICK, ARCHIBALD STANDISH.
Scot. b. Madras, India 1864; ad. 1920 London. T.
HARTSHORNE, HOWARD MORTON.
Am. b. New York; ad. 1915 Same. A12-B.
HARTSON, WALTER C.
Am. b. Wyoming, Ia. 1866; ad. 1915 New York. A12-B-F.
HARTUNG, HEINRICH.
Ger. Coblenz 1851-1919. B-T.
HARTWELL, ALONZO. (Eg)
Am. Littleton, Mass. 1805-1873 Waltham, Mass. F-2-45.
HARTWELL, CHARLES LEONARD. (S)
Eng. b. Blackheath 1873; ad. 1934 London. Wa-798.
HARTWELL, GEORGE KENNETH.
Am. b. Fitchburg, Mass. 1891; ad. 1934 New York. A-F.
HARTWICH, HERMAN.
Am. New York 1853-1926. A12-B-F-W9.
HARUNOBU, SUZUKI.
Jap. 1703-1770. J., Vol. 2, page 35.
HARUSHIGÉ [Shiba Kokan]. .
Jap. 1747-1818. J., Vol. 2, page 43.
HARVEY, ALICE [Mrs. Ramsey]. (Ill)
Am. b. Chicago 1894; ad. 1934 Westport, Conn. W.
HARVEY, CHARLES Y. (S)
Am. 1869-1912 New York. A0X.
HARVEY, ELI. (S)
Am. b. Ogden, O. 1860; ad. 1934 Alhambra, Calif. A-B-F-T-W.
HARVEY, GEORGE.
Am. ac. 1835-1840 in Washington, D. C. F.
HARVEY, [Sir] GEORGE.
Scot. St. Ninian 1806-1876 Edinburgh. B-C-DNB-E-T.
HARVEY, HAROLD LE ROY.
Am. b. Balt., Md. 1899; ad. 1934 Same. A.
HARVEY, HERBERT JOHNSON. (Et)
Eng. London 1884-1928. Wa01929.
HARVEY, JAMES. (Eg)
Eng. ac. 1855 in London. Auc. Sale 1934 New York. B-T.
HARVEY, PAUL.
Am. b. Chicago, Ill.; ad. 1934 New York. A.
HARVEY, ROBERT.
Am. b. Dublin, Ir. 1868; ad. 1934 New York. A.
HARVEY, WILLIAM. (Eg)
Eng. Newcastle 1796-1866 Richmond. B-DNB-T.
HARWOOD, BURT.
Am. b. Iowa 1897; d. 1923. A12-F.
HARWOOD, JAMES T.
Am. b. Lehi, Utah 1860; ad. 1934 Salt Lake City, Utah. A-DBA.
HARWOOD, SABRA B. (S)
Am. b. Brookline, Mass. 1895; ad. 1934 Boston. A.
HASAN. *see also* Hassan.
HASAN, ABOUL.
Persian. ac. 1628 in Delhi, India. M.
HASAN AL-KASHANI. (Metals)
Persian. ac. 1066/7 in Persia. M.
HASBROUCK, DU BOIS FENELON.
Am. b. Pine Hill, N. Y. 1860; ad. 1934 Stamford, N. Y. B-M.
HASCH, KARL.
Aus. Vienna 1835-1897. B-T.
HASEGAWA, KIYOSHI. (Et)
Jap. b. Yokohama 1891; ex. 1934 Chicago; ad. 1935 Paris. DBA.
HASELTINE. *see also* Hazeltine.
HASELTINE, CHARLES FIELD.
Am. Phila., Pa. 1840-1915 Same. A013-B.
HASELTINE, ELIZABETH. (S)
Mrs. Frederick C. Hibbard.
Am. b. Portland, Ore. 1894; ad. 1934 Chicago. A.
HASELTINE, HERBERT. (S)
Am. b. Rome, It. 1877; ad. 1934 Paris, Fr. A-B-Cs-T.

HASELTINE, James Henry. (S)
Am. Phila., Pa. 1833-1907 Rome, It. B-DAB-F-Hs-T-15.
HASELTINE, William Stanley.
Am. Phila., Pa. 1835-1900 Rome, It. A02-B-Cs-F-T-4-15.
HASEMANN, Wilhelm Gustav Friedrich.
Ger. Mühlberg 1850-1913. B-T.
HASENCLEVER, Johann [or Joseph Peter].
Ger. Remscheid 1810-1853 Düsseldorf. B-C-T-722.
HASENPFLUG, Karl Georg Adolph.
Ger. Berlin 1802-1858 Halberstadt. B-T.
HASIMOTO, Gaho.
Jap. ac. 1900-1929 in Paris. DBA.
HASIMOTO, [Mrs.] Michi.
Jap.-Am. b. Japan 1890; ad. 1934 Los Angeles, Calif. A.
HASKELL, Ernest.
Am. Woodstock, Conn. 1876-1925 Maine. A022-B-DAB-F-T-55-96.
HASKELL, Ida C.
Am. Calif. 1861-1932 Brookhaven, L. I., N. Y. A029-B.
HASLEHUST, Ernest William.
Eng. b. Essex 1866; ex. 1934 London. Wa.
HASLER, William N.
Am. b. Wash., D. C. 1865; ad. 1935 Caldwell, N. J. A12-B-F.
HASSALL, John. (Ill)
Eng. b. 1868; ex. 1934 London. B-Wa.
HASSAM, Childe.
Am. Boston, Mass. 1859; ad. 1935 New York. A-B-E-F-T-W-1-5-46-47-71-220-701-757.
HASSAN, Ali Khan Vaziree. (P-S)
Persian. b. Teheran, Per.; ad. 1934 New York. M.
HASSELBERG, Karl Peter. (S)
Swe. b. 1850; d. 1894 in Sweden. B-T.
HASSELBUSCH, Louis.
Am. b. Phila., Pa. 1863; ad. 1934 Same. A-B.
HASSELL, Edward.
Eng. d. 1852 in Lancaster. B-DNB-T.
HASSELL, John.
Eng. ac. 1809-1825 in London. DNB-T.
HASSELLS [or Hassel], Warner [or Werner].
Eng. ac. 1680-1710 in London. DNB-T.
HASSELMAN, Anna.
Am. b. Indianapolis, Ind. 1873; ad. 1934 Same. A-W.
HASSELRIIS, Malthe M. (Ill)
Am. ad. 1934 Forest Hills, L. I., N. Y. M.
HASTINGS, Donald. (S)
Eng. b. New York 1900; ad. 1935 London. M.
HASTINGS, Edward.
Eng. ac. 1804-1827 in London. T.
HASTINGS, Émile.
Am. ex. 1934 Minneapolis, Minn. M.
HASTINGS, Marion Keith.
Am. b. Geneva, N. Y. 1894; ad. 1934 Seattle, Wash. A.
HASTINGS, Thomas. (Et)
Eng. ac. 1813-1831 in Liverpool. DNB-T.
HASTINGS, William Granville. (S)
Am. England 1868-1902 Mt. Vernon, N. Y. A04.

HASWELL, Ernest Bruce. (S)
Am. b. Kentucky 1887; ad. 1934 Cinn., O. A-F.
HATCH, Emily Nicolas.
Am. b. Newport, R. I.; ad. 1934 New York. A-F-W.
HATCH, George W. (Eg)
Am. New York 1805-1867 Dobbs Ferry, N. Y. B-Bd-F-T-2-7.
HATCH, Lorenzo James.
Am. Hartford, N. Y. 1857-1914 New York. A0X1-F-7.
HATFIELD, Dalzell.
Am. b. Pittsburgh, Pa. 1893; ad. 1934 Los Angeles, Calif. A.
HATFIELD, Joseph Henry.
Am. Kingston, Can. 1863-1928. A026.
HATFIELD, Karl Leroy.
Am. b. Jacksonville, Ill. 1886; ad. 1934 El Paso, Tex. A.
HATFIELD, Thomas F.
Am. d. 1925 Hoboken, N. J. A022.
HATTON, Clara Anna.
Am. b. Bunker Hill, Kan. 1901; ad. 1934 Lawrence, Kan. A.
HATTORF, Alvin Frederick.
Am. b. Newport News, Va. 1899; ad. 1934 Richmond, Va. A.
HAUBER, Joseph.
Ger. Geratsrted 1766-1834 Munich. B-T.
HAUBISEN, Christopher.
Am. 1830-1913 St. Louis. A0X1.
HAUDEBOURT-LESCOT, Antoinette Cécile Hortense.
Fr. Paris 1784-1845 Same. B-C-T.
HAUENSTEIN, Oskar. (Mu)
Am. b. Vienna, Aus. 1883; ad. 1934 New York. A.
HAUER [or Haven], Jean Jacques.
Fr. Algesheim 1751-1829 Paris. B-T.
HAUG, Robert von.
Ger. Stuttgart 1857-1922. B-T.
HAUGHTON, Benjamin.
Ent. Dawlish 1865-1924. B-Y01925.
HAUGHTON, Moses [The Elder.] (Enamel-P)
Eng. Wednesbury 1734-1804 Asbrasted. B-DNB-T.
HAUGHTON, Moses [The Younger]. (Min)
Eng. Wednesbury 1772-1848 Same. B-DNB-T.
HAUGSETH, A. J.
Am. b. 1884; ad. 1934 Chicago. M.
HAUPERS, Clement B. (Et)
Am. ad. 1934 St. Paul, Minn. A.
HAUPT, Erik Guide.
Am. b. Cassel, Ger. 1891; ad. 1934 New York. A-F.
HAUSBUCHMEISTER [Ger. 15th Cent.].
see Master of the Amsterdam Cabinet.
HAUSER, Alonzo.
Am. b. La Crosse, Wis. 1909; ad. 1934 New York. M.
HAUSER, John.
Am. 1858-1918 Clifton, O. A0X1.
HAUSER, Joseph S.
Am. ad. 1934 New York. M.
HAUSHALTER, George M.
Am. b. Portland, Me. 1862; ad. 1934 New Hope, Pa. A.

HAUSMANN, Elias Gottlob.
Ger. 1695-1774 Leipzig. T.
HAUSMANN, George E.
Am. b. St. Louis, Mo.; ad. 1934 New York. A.
HAUSNER, Clara.
Am. ex. New York 1935. M.
HAUTOT, Rachel Lucy Ludivine. (S)
Fr. b. Fermanville 1882. DBA.
HAVELL, Daniell. (Eg)
Eng. ac. 1812-1826 in London. B-DNB-T.
HAVELL, Robert [The Elder]. (Eg)
[Published Audubon's Birds of America].
Eng. ac. 1800-1840 in London. DNB-T-7.
HAVELL, Robert [The Younger]. (Eg)
Am. Reading, Eng. 1793-1878 Tarrytown, N. Y. B-Bd-DAB-DNB-F-T-7-97-98.
HAVELL, William.
Eng. Reading 1782-1857 London. DNB-T.
HAVEMEYER, Helen M.
Am. ex. 1935 New York. M.
HAVEN, Franklin de. *see* De Haven.
HAVENS, James D. (Eg)
Am. b. Rochester, N. Y. 1900; ad. 1935 Fairport, N. Y. M.
HAVERMAN, Hendrik Johannes.
Dut. b. Amsterdam 1857. B-T.
HAVERMAN, Margareta.
Dut. b. Breda; ac. 1722-1795 Paris. B-Bd-T.
HAVERS, Alice Mary.
Mrs. Frederick Morgan.
Eng. Norfolk 1850-1890 London. B-T.
HAVERTY, Joseph Patrick.
Ir. Galway 1794-1864 Dublin. DNB-T.
HAVET, Henri Charles Julien.
Fr. b. Paris; ac. 1890. B-T.
HAVILAND, Francis. (Min)
Eng. 1869/70-1912. M.
HAWEIS, Stephen.
Am. b. London; ac. 1925 N. Y. A22-F-T.
HAWKER, Thomas.
Eng. b. 1642; d. 1722 Windsor. DNB-T.
HAWKIN, John. (S)
Belg. ac. 1367 in Liége. M.
HAWKINS, Arthur, Jr. (Ill)
Am. ad. 1934 New York. M.
HAWKINS, Benjamin. (S)
Am. b. St. Louis, Mo. 1896; ad. 1934 New York. A-Cs
HAWKINS, Cornelius Haly.
Am. b. Tupelo, Miss. 1861. F-183.
HAWKINS, Edward Mack Curtis.
Am. b. New York 1877; ad. 1934 Ithaca, N. Y. A.
HAWKINS, [Mrs.] Grace Milner.
Am. b. Bloomington, Wis. 1869; ad. 1934 Madison, Wis. A.
HAWKINS, Mary Palmer.
Mrs. Edward Mack Curtis Hawkins.
Am. b. London 1879; ad. 1934 Ithaca, N. Y. A.
HAWKS, Rachel Marshall. (S)
Mrs. Arthur W. Hawks.
Am. b. Port Deposit, Md. 1879; ad. 1934 Ruxton, Md. A-Cs-F-T.
HAWKSLEY, Arthur.
Eng. Nottingham 1842-1920 B-M.
HAWKSLEY, Dorothy W.
Eng. b. London 1884; ad. 1934 Same. M.
HAWLEY, Carl T.
Am. b. Montrose, Pa. 1885; ad. 1934 Syracuse, N. Y. A-F.
HAWLEY, Helen Holt.
Am. ad. 1935 Scarsdale, N. Y. M.
HAWLEY, James J. (S)
Am. b. 1871; d. 1899. A02.
HAWLEY, Margaret Foote. (Min)
Am. b. Guilford, Conn. 1880; ad. 1934 New York. A-F-T-46.
HAWLEY, Sarah E.
Am. ad. 1934 Oyster Bay, L. I., N. Y. M.
HAWLY-LEVER. *see* Lever, Richard Hawley.
HAWORTH, Charles S.
Eng. b. 1884; d. 1917 in England. Y01918.
HAWORTH, Peter.
Can. ad. 1935 Toronto, Ont. M.
HAWTHORN, Elmir.
Eng. ex. 1934 London. M.
HAWTHORN, Wilfrid Charles.
Eng. b. Kettering 1877. Wa.
HAWTHORNE, Charles Webster.
Am. Maine 1872-1930 Baltimore, Md. A027-B-DAB-F-T-W16-1-46-757.
HAWTHORNE, Edith G.
Am. b. Copenhagen, Denmark 1874; ad. 1934 San Fran., Calif. A.
HAWTHORNE, Edwin.
Eng. ad. 1934 London. M.
HAWTHORNE, Marion Campbell.
Mrs. Charles Webster Hawthorne.
Am. b. Joliet, Ill.; ad. 1934 New York. A-F.
HAY, [Mrs.] Genevieve Lee.
Am. Cleveland, O. 1881-1918 Flemington, N. J. A016.
HAY, George.
Scot. Leith 1831-1912. B-T.
HAY, James Hamilton.
Eng. Birkenhead 1874-1916 Cheshire. T.
HAY, Peter Alexander.
Scot. b. Edinburgh; ex. 1934 London. DBA-T.
HAY, Stuart. (Ill)
Am. ad. 1934 New York. M.
HAYDEN, Charles Henry.
Am. b. Plymouth, Mass. 1856-1901 Belmont, Mass. A04-B-DAB-F-T-99.
HAYDEN, Edward Parker.
Am. d. Haydenville, Mass. 1922. A019-F.
HAYDEN, Ella Frances.
Am. b. Boston, Mass. 1860; ad. 1934 Prov., R. I. A.
HAYDEN, Hayden. (Ill)
Am. ad. 1934 New York. M.
HAYDEN, Henri.
Pol. b. Warsaw 1883. DBA.
HAYDEN, Palmer.
Am. b. Virginia; ad. 1934 New York. M.
HAYDEN, Sara S.
Am. b. Chicago, Ill.; ac. 1931. A28.
HAYDON, Benjamin Robert.
Eng. Plymouth 1786-1846 London. B-DNB-C-E-T-392-722.
HAYES, Claude.
Eng. ac. 1873-1890 in London. B-T.
HAYES, Edwin.
Eng. Bristol 1819-1904 London. DNB-T.
HAYES, Eleanor.
Am. ex. 1935 Boston, Mass. M.

HAYES, Frederick William.
Welsh. Cardiff, Wales 1848-1918. B-T.
HAYES, John.
Eng. 1786-1866 London. B-DNB-T.
HAYES, Katharine Williams.
Am. b. Wash., D. C. 1889; ad. 1934 Wallingford, Pa. A.
HAYES, Lee.
Am. b. Platteville, Wis. 1854; ad. 1915 Butte, Mont. A12.
HAYES, Michael Angelo.
Ir. Waterford 1820-1877 Dublin. B-DNB-T.
HAYES, William. (Eg)
Eng. ac. 1773-1799 in England. B-DNB-T.
HAYEZ, Francesco.
It. Venice 1791-1882 Milan. B-T.
HAYLEY [or Haly], Robert. (Chalk)
Ir. ac. 1765-1770 in Dublin. B-DNB-T.
HAYLEY, Thomas Alfonso. (S)
Eng. ac. 1780-1800 Felpham, Sussex, Eng. DNB-T.
HAYLS [or Hales], John.
Eng. d. 1679 in London. DNB-T.
HAYMAN, Francis.
Eng. Exeter 1708-1776 London. B-DNB-T.
HAYNES, Caroline Coventry.
Am. b. New York; ad. 1934 Highlands, N. J. A12-M.
HAYNES, John. (Eg)
Eng. ac. 1730-1750 in York. DNB-T.
HAYNES, Joseph [or John]. (Eg)
Eng. Shrewsbury, 1760-1829 Chester. B-DNB-T.
HAYNES-WILLIAMS, John.
see Williams, J. H.
HAYNESWORTH, William. (Eg)
Eng. ac. 1659 in London. B-DNB-T.
HAYS, Austin. (S)
Am. New York 1869-1915 White Mountains. A012-F-T.
HAYS, George A.
Am. b. Greenville, N. H. 1854; ad. 1934 Prov., R. I. A.
HAYS, William Jacob, Jr.
Am. Catskill, N. Y. 1872-1934 Milbrook, N. Y. A-F-T-W-Obit. N. Y. papers, 10-1-1934.
HAYS, William Jacob, Sr.
Am. New York 1830-1875 Same. Bd-C-DAB-F-T-4-15.
HAYTER, Charles. (Min)
Eng. 1761-1835 London. B-DNB-T.
HAYTER, Charles Healy.
Am. b. 1813; d. 1894. M.
HAYTER, [Sir] George.
Eng. London 1792-1871 Same. B-DNB-E-T.
HAYTER, Stanley William.
Eng. b. London 1901; ad. 1934 Paris. Wa.
HAYTHE, Ethel C.
Am. ad. 1934 Lynchburg, Va. M.
HAYTLEY [or Hately], Edward.
Eng. ac. 1746-1762 in London. B-DNB-T.
HAYWARD, Alfred. (Cart)
Am. b. Camden, N. J. 1893; ad. 1934 Phila., Pa. A-F.
HAYWARD, Alfred Frederick William.
Can. b. Ontario 1856; ad. 1934 London, Eng. Wa.
HAYWARD, Alfred Robert.
Eng. b. London 1875; ad. 1934 Chelsea. Wa.
HAYWARD, Beatrice Burt. (Min)
Mrs. Caleb Anthony Hayward, Jr.
Am. b. New Bedford, Mass. 1893; ad. 1934 Same. A.
HAYWARD, F. Howard.
Am. b. Romeo, Mich. 1867; ad. 1915 Mt. Clemens, Mich. A12.
HAYWARD, Gerald Sinclair. (Min)
Am. 1845-1926 New York. A023.
HAYWARD, Joshua Henshaw.
Eng. ac. 1798-1820 London. T.
HAYWARD, Mary Carolyn.
Am. b. Phila., Pa. 1898; ad. 1934 Same. A.
HAZARD, Arthur Merton.
Am. No. Brightwater, Mass. 1872-1930 France. A028-F-T.
HAZELL, Frank.
Am. b. Hamilton, Ont., Can. 1883; ad. 1934 New York. A.
HAZELTINE, Florence.
Am. b. Jamestown, N. Y. 1889; ad. 1934 St. Louis, Mo. A.
HAZELTINE, Isaac Brewster.
Am. b. Boston, Mass. 1875; ad. 1934 New York. A.
HAZELTINE, Mary Brewster.
Am. b. Milton, Mass.; ad. 1934 Boston. A-F-T-W.
HAZEN, Bessie Ella.
Am. b. Waterford, N. B., Can. 1862; ad. 1934 Los Angeles, Calif. A-F
HAZEN, Wilhelmina.
Mrs. B. F. Ledford.
Am. b. Murphy's Gulch, Calif. 1877; ad. 1934 Los Angeles, Calif. A
HAZELHURST, Thomas. (Min)
Eng. ac. 1760-1818 in Liverpool. B-DNB-T.
HAZLITT, John.
Eng. b. Wem, Eng. 1767/9; d. 1837 Stockport, Eng. B-F-T-2-4-6-45.
HAZON DE SAINT-FIRMIN, Jane d'.
Fr. b. Paris 1874. B-DBA.
HAZZARD, Sara. (Min)
Am. b. Jamestown, N. Y.; ad. 1934 Same. A.
HEAD, Cecil.
Am. b. Lebanon, Ind. 1906; ad. 1934 Indianapolis, Ind. M.
HEAD, Guy.
Eng. Carlisle 1753-1800 London. DNB-T.
HEADE, Martin Johnson.
Am. b. Bucks Co., Pa.; ac. 1855-1872, Phila., Pa. B-C-F-T-15.
HEALD, Cress.
Am. ex. 1934 Yonkers, N. Y. M.
HEALD, Lawrence.
Am. b. Canada; ad. 1934 Santa Monica, Calif. M.
HEALY, A. K. D.
Am. ad. 1934 Middlebury, Vt. M.
HEALY, George Peter Alexander.
Am. Boston, Mass. 1808/13-1894 Chicago. B-C-DAB-E-F-T-1-2-4-15-100-101-144-182-183-221.
HEANEY, Charles Edward. (Ill)
Am. ad. 1934 Portland, Ore. A.
HEANLEY, Mildred.
Br. ex. 1934 London. M.
HEAPHY, Thomas [The Elder].
Eng. London 1775-1835. B-Bd-DNB-T.

HEAPHY, THOMAS FRANK [The Younger].
Eng. 1813-1873 London. B-Bd-DNB-T.
HEAPS, BELLE G.
Am. ad. 1935 Houston, Tex. M.
HEARNE, THOMAS.
Eng. Brinkworth 1744-1817 London. B-DNB-T.
HEASLIP, WILLIAM. (Et)
Am. b. Toronto, Can. 1898; ad. 1934 New York. M.
HEATH, CHARLES [The Elder]. (Eg)
Eng. 1785-1848 London. Bd-DNB-T.
HEATH, EDDA MAXWELL.
Am. b. Brooklyn, N. Y.; ad. 1934 Carmel, Calif. A.
HEATH, GRACE COMSTOCK.
Am. b. Ithaca, Mich. 1897; ad. 1934 Milwaukee, Wis. A.
HEATH, HOWARD P.
Am. b. Boulder, Colo 1879; ad. 1934 Norwalk, Conn. A.
HEATH, JAMES. (Eg)
Eng. London 1757-1834 Same. DNB-T.
HEATON, AUGUSTUS GOODYEAR.
Am. Phila., Pa. 1844-1930 Wash., D. C. A027-F-T-W16.
HEATON, CLEMENT. (Glass-P)
Eng. Bradford 1824-1882 London. DNB-T.
HEBER, CARL AUGUSTUS. (S)
Am. b. Stuttgart 1874; ad. 1934 New York. A-F-T-W.
HÉBERT, ERNEST AUGUSTE ANTOINE.
Fr. Grenoble 1817-1908 La Touche. B-C-T.
HÉBERT, HENRI. (S)
Can. b. Montreal, Can. 1884; ad. 1934 Same. B-DBA.
HÉBERT [or Herbert] LOUIS PHILIPPE. (Carver)
Can. b. Sainte Sophie d'Halifax, Que. 1850-1917. B-M.
HEBERT, MARIAN. (Et)
Am. ad. 1935 Santa Barbara, Calif. M.
HEBRAD, ERNEST GERMAINE.
Fr. b. Thiais 1889; ac. 1917. DBA.
HECHT, JOSEPH. (Et)
Ger. ex. 1934 London. M.
HECHT, VICTOR DAVID.
Am. b. Paris 1873; ac. U. S. ad. unknown. A-F.
HECHT, ZOLTAN.
Am. ex. 1935 New York. M.
HECK. *see also* Hecke. *see* Hecken.
HECK [or Hecken], ABRAHAM VAN DER.
Belg. ac. 1636-1655 The Hague, Holland. B-T.
HECK, CLAES NICOLAS DIRKSZ VAN DER.
Dut. ac. 1604-1648 in Holland. B-T.
HECK, WILHELM ÉMIL ROBERT.
Ger. Stuttgart 1831-1889 Same. B-T.
HECKE, JAN VAN DEN.
Belg. Oudenarde 1620-1684 Antwerp. B-T.
HECKEL, ERICH.
Ger. b. Doebeln, Saxony 1883; ad. 1934 Berlin. DBA-393.
HECKENDORF, FRANZ.
Ger. b. 1888 in Germany. T.
HECKER, FRANZ.
Ger. b. 1870 in Germany. T.
HECKMAN, ALBERT WILLIAM. (Et)
Am. b. Meadville, Pa. 1893; ad. 1934 Woodstock, N. Y. A-F.
HECKOUT, GERHARDT. *see* Eeckhout, G.
HECYLCES. (S)
Gr. ac. 550 B.C. in Sparta. M.
HEDA, GERRIT WILLEMSZ.
Dut. ac. 1642-1702 in Holland. B-T.
HEDA, WILLEM CLAASZ.
Dut. Haarlem 1594?-1678/82. B-E-T-722.
HÉDIN, SVEN ANDERS. (Ill)
Swe. b. Stockholm 1865; ad. 1934 Same. M.
HEDGES, DON.
Am. ex. 1934 New Hope, Pa. M.
HEDLEY, RALPH.
Eng. Newcastle 1851-1913. B-T.
HEDOUIN, PIERRE EDMOND ALEXANDRE.
Fr. Boulogne 1820-1889 Paris. B-T.
HEEM, CORNELIS DE.
Dut. Leyden 1631-1695 Antwerp, Belg. B-T.
HEEM, JAN DAVIDSZ VAN.
Dut. Utrecht 1606?-1683/4 Antwerp, Belg. B-C-E-T-722.
HEEMSKERK, EGBERT VAN [The Elder].
Dut. Haarlem 1610-1680 London. B-DNB-T-722.
HEEMSKERK, EGBERT VAN [The Younger].
Dut. Haarlem 1634/45-1704 London. B-T.
HEEMSKERK, MARTEN JACOBSZ. [Veen]
Dut. Heemskerk 1498-1574 Haarlem. B-C-E-T-V-722.
HEERE, LUCAS DE [or Minheere].
Flem. Ghent 1534-1584 Paris. B-Bd-T.
HEEREMANSZ, FRANS [or Thomas].
Dut. b. Haarlem; ac. 1670-1697. B-T.
HEERMAN, NORBERT.
Am. b. Frankfort, Ger. 1891; ad. 1934 Woodstock, N. Y. A-F.
HEFFER, EDWARD A.
Eng. ac. 1862-1885 in Liverpool. B-T.
HEFFNER, KARL.
Ger. b. Nüremberg 1849. B-T.
HEGEDÜS, LÁSZLÓ [or Ladislas].
Hun. Szentes 1870-1911 Budapest. B-T.
HEGER, HEINRICH.
Ger. Hadersleben 1832-1888 Munich. B-T.
HEGESIAS [or Hegias], I. (S)
Gr. ac. 480 B.C. in Athens. B-T.
HEGI, FRANZ. (Eg)
Swi. Lausanne, 1774-1850 Zurich. B-T.
HEGWALDER [or Hegwald]. (S)
Swe. ac. 1090-1130. T-824.
HEICHERT, OTTO.
Ger. b. Halberstadt 1868. B-T.
HEIDE, BEATRICE.
Am. ad. 1934 Feldston, N. Y. M.
HEIDECK. *see* Heydeck.
HEIDNER, JANE D.
Am. ex. 1933 Paris. M.
HEIL, CHARLES ÉMILE.
Am. b. Boston 1870; ad. 1934 Roslindale, Mass. A-B-F-T-W.
HEIL, DANIEL VAN.
Flem. Brussels 1604-1662? B-T.
HEIL, ELIZABETH.
Am. b. Columbus, O. 1877; ad. 1915 Seattle, Wash. A12.

HEILBUTH, FERDINAND.
Fr. Hamburg, Ger. 1826-1889 Paris. B-T.
HEIM, FRANÇOIS JOSEPH.
Fr. Belfort 1787-1865 Paris. B-E-T.
HEIN, FRANZ. (Et)
Ger. b. Altona 1863. B-T.
HEINE, FRIEDRICH WILHELM.
Am. Germany 1845-1921 Milwaukee, Wis. A018-T.
HEINE, PETER BERNARD WILHELM.
Ger. Dresden 1827-1885. B-T.
HEINEMANN, ERNEST. (Eg)
Am. Germany 1848-1912 Fort Wadsworth, N. Y. A0X-B-DAB-T-W7-52.
HEINIGKE, OTTO. (Mu)
Am. Brooklyn, N. Y. 1851-1915 Bay Ridge, N. Y. A012-46.
HEINS, D.
Ger. b. Allemagne; ac. 1725-1779. B-T.
HEINS, JOHN THEODORE.
Eng. Munich, Ger. 1732-1771 Chelsea, Eng. B-DNB-T.
HEINSIUS, JEAN [or Johann] JULES ERNEST.
Ger. Weimar 1740-1812 Orléans, Fr. B-T.
HEINTZ, MARION.
Am. b. Buffalo, N. Y. 1900; ad. 1934 Same. A.
HEINTZELMAN, ARTHUR WILLIAM. (Et)
Am. b. Newark, N. J. 1892; ad. 1935 New York. A28-DBA-F-W.
HEINZ, CHARLES LLOYD.
Am. b. Shelbyville, Ind. 1885; ad. 1934 Same. A.
HEINZ [or Heintz], JOSEPH [The Elder].
Swi. Basel 1564/5-1609 Prague, Czec. B-C-T.
HEINZ [or Heintz], JOSEPH [The Younger].
Ger. 1590/1600-1678. B-C-T.
HEINZE, ADOLPH.
Am. b. Chicago, Ill. 1887; ad. 1934 Same. A.
HEINZMANN, KARL FRIEDRICH.
Ger. Stuttgart 1795-1846 Munich. B-T.
HEINZMANN, S. L. J.
see Jameson, S. L. J.
HEISE, WILHELM.
Ger. b. Wiesbaden 1892. DBA.
HEITER, MICHAEL M.
Am. b. New York 1883; ad. 1934 Scarsdale, N. Y. A.
HEITKAMP, CHARLES P.
Am. Brooklyn, N. Y. 1852-1933 Same. A030.
HEITLAND, WILMOT EMERTON. (Ill)
Am. B. Superior, Wis. 1893; ad. 1934 Darien, Conn. A-F-W.
HEKKING, WILLEM.
Dut. Amsterdam 1796-1862. B-T.
HEKKING, WILLIAM M.
Am. b. Chelsea, Mass. 1885; ad. 1934 Buffalo, N. Y. A.
HELBECK, [Mrs.] DEWEES COCHRAN.
Am. b. Dallas, Tex. 1892; ad. 1934 Holicong, Pa. M.
HELBIG, [Mrs.] MARGARET A.
Am. b. Leesville, Va. 1884; ad. 1934 Lynchburg, Va. A.
HELCK, CLARENCE PETER. (Ill)
Am. b. 1897; ad. 1935 New York. F-M.
HELD, ALMA M.
Am. b. Iowa 1898; ad. 1934 Waterloo, Ia. A.
HELD, JOHN, JR. (Cari)
Am. b. Salt Lake City, Utah 1889; ad. 1935 Westport, Conn. A.
HELDNER, KNUTE.
Am. b. Sweden 1886; ad. 1935 New Orleans, La. M.
HÉLION, JEAN.
Fr. b. Couterne 1904; ad. 1934 Paris. DBA-M.
HELLAWELL, JOHN. (Eg)
Am. Yorkshire, Eng. 1837-1919 Brooklyn, N. Y. A016.
HELLÉ, ANDRÉ. (Ill)
Fr. ac. 1905-1930 Paris. DBA.
HELLEBRANTH. *see* de Hellebrandt.
HELLEMONT, MATHYS VAN.
see Helmont, M.
HELLER, BESSIE PEIRCE. (Mu)
Am. b. St. Paul, Minn.; ad. 1934 New Hope, Pa. A.
HELLER, EUGENIE M.
Am. ad. 1934 New York. A.
HELLER, HELEN WEST.
Am. b. Rushville, Ill.; ad. 1934 Brooklyn, N. Y. A.
HELLEU, PAUL CÉSAR.
Fr. Varmes 1859-1927 Paris. B-DBA-T-Y01928.
HELLGREWE, RUDOLF.
Ger. b. 1860 in Germany. T.
HELLMAN, BERTHA LOUISE.
Am. b. La Grange, Tex. 1900; ad. 1934 Houston, Tex. A.
HELLMER, EDWARD VON. (S)
Aus. b. Vienna 1850. T-798.
HELLQVIST, KARL GUSTAF.
Swe. Kungsor 1851-1890 Munich, Ger. B-T.
HELLRATH, ÉMIL.
Ger. b. Düsseldorf 1838; ad. 1901 Munich [No death date]. B-T.
HELLWAG, RUDOLF.
Ger. b. 1867 in Germany. T.
HELLYER, THOMAS. (Eg)
Eng. ac. 1800 in London. M.
HELM, KATHERINE.
Am. ac. 1928. Fa-M.
HELMICK, HOWARD.
Am. Zanesville, O. 1845-1907 Wash., D. C. A06-B-F.
HELMONT [or Hellemont], GASPAR VAN.
Flem. Antwerp 1656 [No death date]. B-T.
HELMONT [or Hellemont], MATHYS VAN.
Flem. Antwerp 1623-1674 Brussels. B-C-T.
HELOK, C. PETER.
Am. b. New York 1893; ad. 1934 Yonkers, N. Y. A.
HELSBY, ALFREDO.
Br. b. Chile, S. A.; ac. 1931. M.
HELST, BARTHOLOMEUS VAN DER.
[Reported to have painted the first recorded portrait. He was styled the "Van Dyck of Holland."]
Dut. Haarlem 1611/13-1670 Amsterdam. B-Bd-C-E-T-722.
HELST, LODEWYK VAN DER.
Dut. Amsterdam 1642/5-1680 Same. B-T.
HELT-STOCKADE [or Stocade], NICOLAS DE.
Dut. Nimègue 1614-1669 Amsterdam. B-T.

HELWIG, ARTHUR LOUIS.
Am. b. Cinn., O. 1900; ad. 1934 Same. M.
HEMARD, JOSEPH.
Fr. b. Mureaux, Fr. 1880. DBA.
HEMENWAY, ALICE S.
Am. ad. 1935 Tampa, Fla. M.
HEMENWAY, LOUIS JORDAN.
Am. ad. 1935 Alexandria, La. M.
HEMESSEN, JAN SANDERS VAN.
[Master of the Brunswick Monogram].
Flem. Antwerp 1500/4-1566 Haarlem, Holland. B-C-T-394-722.
HEMESSEN, KATHERINA VAN.
Flem. b. Antwerp 1527/8; ac. 1548 Amsterdam, Holland. T.
HEMING, ARTHUR. (Ill)
Am. b. Ontario, Can. 1870; ad. 1935 Toronto. A28-B-F-T-W12.
HEMINGWAY, GRACE HALL.
Am. b. Chicago 1872; ad. 1934 Oak Park, Ill. A.
HEMLING. *see* Memling.
HEMMICK, ALICE BARNEY.
Mrs. Christian Hemmick.
Am. b. Cinn., O.; ac. 1915; ad. 1915 Wash., D. C. A12.
HEMMINGS, ROBERT.
Am b. Boston, Mass.; ad. 1915 Paris. A12.
HEMPSTEAD, JOSEPH LESLIE.
Am. b. Brooklyn, N. Y. 1884; ad. 1934 Chicago. A.
HEMY, CHARLES NAPIER.
Eng. Newcastle 1841-1917 Falmouth. B-E-T.
HENDERSON, A. ELIZABETH. (Min)
Am. b. Ashland, Ky. 1873; ad. 1915 New York. A12-F.
HENDERSON, ALAN KEITH.
Eng. b. 1883; ad. 1934 London. Wa-Y1929.
HENDERSON, ANDREW.
Scot. 1783-1835 Glasgow. DNB-T.
HENDERSON, CHARLES COOPER.
Eng. 1803-1877 London. B-DNB-T.
HENDERSON, EVELYN.
Am. b. Cape Ann, Mass.; ad. 1934 Mill Valley, Calif. A.
HENDERSON, HARRY V. K.
Am. b. Poughkeepsie, N. Y. 1883; ad. 1934 New York. A.
HENDERSON, HELEN WESTON.
Am. b. Phila., Pa. 1874; ad. 1934 Same. F-W.
HENDERSON, JAMES.
Scot. b. Glasgow; ad. 1934 Qu'Appelle Valley, Sask., Can. M.
HENDERSON, [Mrs.] JENNIE H. REID.
Am. d. 1921 in London. A018.
HENDERSON, JOSEPH.
Scot. Perthshire 1832-1908 Glasgow. B-DNB-T.
HENDERSON, MARTHA.
Am. ad. 1934 Birmingham, Ala. M.
HENDERSON, WILLIAM PENHALLOW. (Mu)
Am. b. Bedford, Mass. 1877; ad. 1934 Santa Fé, N. Mex. A-F-T-W.
HENDLEY, JOHN WALTER. (S)
Am. Virginia 1827-1899. A01.
HENDRICKS, BESSIE.
Am. Cinn., O. 1865-1929 Indianapolis, Ind. A026.
HENDRICKS, EMMA STOCKMAN.
Mrs. H. G. Hendricks.
Am. b. Calif. 1869; ad. 1934 Tucumcari, N. M. A.
HENDRICKS, [Mrs.] H. G.
Am. ad. 1935 Amarillo, Tex. M.
HENDRICKSEN, RALF.
Am. ad. 1935 Chicago, Ill. M.
HENDRICKSON, DAVID.
Am. ad. 1935 New Hope, Pa. M.
HENDRIE, MARION.
Am. ad. 1934 Denver, Col. M.
HENDRIKS, FREDERIK HENDRIK.
Dut. Arnheim 1808-1865 Same. B-T.
HENDRIKS, WYBRAND.
Dut. Amsterdam 1744-1831 Haarlem. B-T.
HENDSCHEL, ALBERT LOUIS ULRICH.
Ger. Frankfort 1834-1883. B-C-T.
HENIUS, [Mrs.] LILLIAN GRACE.
Am. 1879-1925 Pittsburgh, Pa. A023.
HENKE [or Henka], BURNARD ALBERT.
Am. b. Cologne, Ger. 1888; ad. 1934 Pasadena, Calif. A.
HENKORA, LEO AUGUSTA.
Am. b. Vienna, Aus. 1893; ad. 1934 Minneapolis, Minn. A.
HENNEBERG, RUDOLPH FRIEDRICH AUGUST.
Ger. Brunswick 1825-1876 Same. B-T.
HENNEBICQ, ANDRÉ.
Flem. Tournai 1836-1904 St. Gilles. B-T.
HENNERMAN, VALENTINE.
Am. Belgium 1861-1930 Bangor, Me. A028.
HANNEQUIN, PHILIPPE AUGUSTE.
Fr. Lyons 1763-1833 Leuze, Belg. B-C-E-T.
HENNER, JEAN JACQUES.
Fr. Bernviller 1829-1905 Paris. B-Bd-C-E-T.
HENNÈS, GERMAINE.
Fr. ac. 1931 in Paris. DBA.
HENNESSEY, FRANK.
Can. ad. 1935 Ottawa, Can. M.
HENNESSEY, WILLIAM JOHN.
Am. Thomastown, Ir. 1839-1917 London. A016-B-C-DAB-F-T-W10-4-15
HENNIKER, A. L.
Ger. ac. 1896 in Germany. M.
HENNING, ALBIN. (Ill)
Am. St. Paul, Minn. 1886; ad. 1934 Woodstock, Conn. M.
HENNING, CHRISTOPH DANIEL.
Ger. b. Nüremberg 1734 [No death date]. B-T.
HENNING, GERHARD. (S)
Swe. b. 1880; ac. 1930 Paris. DBA-798.
HENNING, WILLIAM EDWIN.
Am. b. Cedar Rapids, Ia. 1911; ad. 1935 Same. M.
HENNINGER, JOSEPH MORGAN.
Am. b. 1906; ad. 1934 Indianapolis, Ind. A.
HENNINGS, ERNEST MARTIN.
Am. b. Pennsgrove, N. J. 1886; ad. 1934 Taos, N. M. A-F-W.
HENNINGS, JOHANN FRIEDRICH.
Ger. Bremen 1838-1899 Munich. B-T.
HENOCH, S. STELLA.
Am. b. Sedalia, Mo.; ad. 1934 New York. A.
HENRI, ROBERT.
Am. b. Cinn., O. 1865; d. 1929 New York. A026-DAB-E-F-T-W14-1-46-71-102-103-104-105-138-172-395-701-757-779.

HENRI, [Mrs.] ROBERT.
see Organ, Marjorie.
HENRI-DÉZIRÉ. *see* Déziré, H.
HENRI-MARTIN, JEAN GUILLAUME.
Fr. b. Toulon 1860; ad. 1934 Paris. DBA.
HENRI-MATISSE. *see* Matisse, H.
HENRIET, CHARLES FRÉDERIC.
Fr. b. Chateau-Thierry 1826 [No death date]. B-T.
HENRIET [or Henriette] FAMILY.
Fr. ac. 16th Cent. at. Châlons, Fr. T.
HENRION, ARMAND FRANÇOIS JOSEPH.
Fr. b. Liége, Belg. 1875. DBA.
HENRIQUEL-DUPONT, LOUIS PIERRE.
Fr. Paris 1797-1892 Same. B-T-880.
HENRIQUES, ETHEL QUIXANO.
Eng. ad. 1934 London. Wa.
HENRY, ALBERT P. (S)
Am. Versailles, Ky. 1836-1872. F.
HENRY, CHARLES TRUMBO.
Am. b. Niagara Falls, N. Y. 1902; ad. 1934 New York. M.
HENRY, [Miss] COAH.
Am. b. Hamilton, Mo.; ad 1934 Kansas City, Mo. A.
HENRY, EDWARD LAMSON.
Am. Charleston, S. C. 1841-1919 Ellenville, N. Y. A016-B-C-DAB-E-F-T-W10-1-15-104-105.
HENRY, EVERETT.
Am. ex. 1933 New York. M.
HENRY, GEORGE.
Scot. b. Ayrshire 1859; ad. 1929 Chelsea, Eng. B-T-Wa-1929.
HENRY, HOWARD [Forrest].
Am. b. Nashville, Tenn. 1901; ad. 1934 Same. A.
HENRY, PAUL.
Eng. ex. 1934 London. M.
HENRY, PAUL EDMUND.
Ir. b. Belfast; ac. 1874-1904 Paris. B-T.
HENRY, QUIDABON.
Am. b. Connersville, Ind. 1907; ad. 1934 Same. A.
HENSCHE, HENRY.
Am. b. Chicago 1901; ad. 1934 Provincetown, Mass. A-F.
HENSEL, MAURICE HENRI.
Fr. b. Paris 1890. DBA.
HENSEL, WILHELM.
Ger. Trebbin 1794-1861 Berlin. B-T.
HENSELER, ERNEST.
Ger. b. Wepritz 1852. B-DBA-T.
HENSHAW, ANNE BIGELOW.
Am. b. Prov., R. I.; ad. 1934 Newport, R. I. A.
HENSHAW, FREDERICK HENRY.
Eng. Birmingham 1807-1891. B-T.
HENSHAW, GLENN COOPER.
Am. b. Windfall, Ind. 1881; ad. 1934 New York. A28-M.
HENSLEY [Miss].
Br. ex. 1934 London. M.
HENTSCHEL, KONRAD. (S)
Ger. Munich 1872-1907 Same. T.
HEPBURN, CORNELIA. *see* Cushman, C.
HEPBURN-EDMUNDS, NELLIE MARY. (Min)
Eng. b. West Norwood; ac. 1930. B-DBA-T-Wa1929.
HEPPENER, JOHANNES JACOBUS.
Dut. The Hague 1826-1898 Same. B-T.
HEPWORTH, BARBARA. *see* Skeaping, [Mrs.] J. B.
HERAIN, FRANÇOIS DE. (S)
Fr. b. Paris 1877. DBA-T.
HERBERT. *see also* Hebert.
HERBERT, ALFRED.
Eng. ex. 1847-1861 in London. B-DNB-T.
HERBERT, BARBARA. (S)
Am. b. New York; ac. 1931. DBA.
HERBERT, CYRIL WISEMAN.
Eng. London 1847-1882 Same. B-DNB-T.
HERBERT, FRANCIS H.
Am. Richmondale, O. 1864-1918 Columbus, O. A015.
HERBERT, HAROLD.
Aust. ac. 1933 in Australia. M.
HERBERT, JAMES DOWLING.
Ir. Dublin 1762/3-1837 Isle of Jersey. T.
HERBERT, JAMES DRUMMOND.
Am. b. New York 1896; ad. 1934 Same. A.
HERBERT, JOHN ROGERS.
Eng. Maldon 1810-1890 London. B-DNB-T.
HERBIG, OTTO.
Ger. b. 1889; ad. 1935 Berlin; ex. 1934 Pittsburgh, Pa. M.
HERBIN, AUGUSTE.
Fr. b. Quiévy 1882; ex. 1932 Chicago, Ill. DBA.
HERBST [or Herbster], HANS.
Ger. Strasburg 1468-1550 Basel, Swi. T.
HERDLE, GEORGE LINTON.
Am. Rochester, N. Y. 1868-1922 Same. A019-F.
HERDMAN, ROBERT.
Scot. Rattray 1829-1888 Edinburgh. B-DNB-T.
HERDMAN, ROBERT DUDDINGSTOWE.
Scot. Edinburgh 1863-1922. T-Y01923.
HERDMAN, WILLIAM GAWIN.
Eng. Liverpool 1805-1882 Same. B-DNB-T.
HÉREAU, JULES.
Fr. Paris 1839-1879 Same. B-T.
HERFORD, OLIVER. (Author-Ill)
Am. Sheffield, Eng. 1863-1935 New York. W-Obit. N. Y. Papers 6-6-1935.
HERGENRODER, ÉMILE.
Am. d. 1925 Baltimore, Md. A022.
HERGESHEIMER, ELLA SOPHONISBA.
Am. b. Allentown, Pa. 1873; ad. 1935 Nashville, Tenn. A.
HERING, ADOLPH ÉMIL.
Ger. b. Bosem 1863. B-T.
HERING, ELSIE WARD. (S)
Mrs. Henry Hering.
Am. Fayette, Mo. 1872-1920 New York. A20-F.
HERING, ÉMIL.
Am. New York 1872-1916 Ridgewood, N. J. A014.
HERING, GEORGE EDWARDS.
Eng. London 1805/6-1879 Same. B-DNB-T.
HERING, HARRY.
Am. b. New York 1887; ad. 1934 Same. A.
HERING, HENRY. (S)
Am. b. New York 1874; ad. 1934 Same. A-Cs-F-T-W.

HERING, Loy.
Ger. b. 1484/5; d. 1554 in Germany. T.
HERKIMER, Herman Gustave.
Am. b. Cleveland, O. 1863; ad. 1915 Auburn, Calif. A12-B-T.
HERKOMER, [Sir] Hubert von.
Eng. b. Waal, Bav. 1849; d. 1914 Devon, Eng. B-Bd-C-DNB-E-T.
HERLE, Wilhelm von.
Ger. Herle 1320-1378. B-T-722.
HERLIN, Auguste Joseph.
Fr. Lille 1815-1900 Same. B-T.
HERLIN [or Hörlen], Friedrich [or Fritz].
Ger. Rothenburg 1435/49-1499/1500 Nördlingen. B-E-T.
HERLIN, Robert.
Am. ad. 1934 Montclair, N. J. M.
HERMAN, Harold.
Am. ad. 1935 New York. M.
HERMAN, Leonora Owsley.
Am. b. Chicago 1893; ad. 1934 Phila., Pa. A.
HERMANN, Frank S.
Am. b. New York 1866; ex. 1935 Same. M.
HERMANN, Max.
Am. b. Dresden 1879; ad. 1934 Brooklyn, N. Y. A.
HERMANN-PAUL.
Fr. b. Paris 1865. B-DBA.
HERMANNS, Heinrich.
Ger. b. Düsseldorf 1862. B-T.
HERMANS, Charles.
Belg. b. Brussels 1839 [No death date]. B-T.
HERMES, Gertrude Anna Bertha. (S)
Mrs. Hughes-Stanton.
Eng. b. Bromley 1901; ad. 1934 London. Wa-Y1929.
HERMITTE, Léon Augustin.
see L'Hermitte, L. A.
HERNÁNDEZ, Daniel.
Peruvian. b. Lima 1856; ac. 1910 Paris. B-T.
HERNÁNDEZ, Gregorio.
see Fernández, G.
HERNÁNDEZ, Matéo. (S)
Sp. b. Béjar 1888; ad. 1934 Paris. DBA-T.
HERNDL, Marie.
Am. d. 1912; Milwaukee, Wis. A0X.
HEROLD, Don. (Ill)
Am. b. Bloomfield, Ind. 1889; ad. 1934 Los Angeles, Calif. F-W.
HERP, William [or Guilliam] van.
Flem. Antwerp 1614-1676/7 Same. B-C-T.
HERPST, Martha.
Am. ad. 1934 Titusville, Pa. M
HERR, Laetitia Neff.
Am. b. Lancaster, Pa. 1881; ad. 1915 New York. A12.
HERRAN, Saturnino.
Mex. ac. 1923 in Mexico. M.
HERRERA, Francisco de [The Elder].
Sp. Séville 1576-1656 Madrid. B-C-E-T-722.
HERRERA, Francisco [The Younger].
Sp. Séville 1612/22-1685 Madrid. B-C-E-T-722.
HERREYNS [or Herryens], Willem Jacob.
Flem. Antwerp 1743-1827 Same. B-T-722.
HERRICK, Henry W. (Min)
Am. ac. 1843 in Nashville, Tenn. [No death date]. F-6.
HERRICK, Hugh M.
Am. b. Rocky Ford, Colo. 1890; ad. 1934 Los Angeles, Calif. A.
HERRICK, Margaret Cox.
Am. b. San Fran., Calif. 1865; ad. 1934 Piedmont, Calif. A-F.
HERRING, Frank Stanley.
Am. ad. 1934 New York. M.
HERRING, Harry. (Et)
Am. ex. 1935 Seattle, Wash. M.
HERRING, James.
Am. London 1794-1867 Paris. B-Bd-DAB-F-7-2-11-45.
HERRING, James Vernon.
Am. b. Clio, S. C. 1887; ad. 1934 Wash., D. C. A.
HERRING, John Frederick, Sr.
Eng. Surrey 1795-1865 Tunbridge Wells. B-Bd-C-DNB-T-396.
HERRMANN, Curt.
Ger. Merseburg 1854-1929. B-T.
HERRMANN, Eva. (Cari)
Am. b. Munich, Ger. 1904; ad. 1935 Ste. Trinide, Fr. M.
HERRMANN, Fernande Luise.
Am. b. San Fran., Calif.; ad. 1934 Same. A.
HERRMANN, Hans Johann Émil Rudolf.
Ger. b. Berlin 1858. B-T.
HERRMANN, Léon Charles.
Fr. Havre 1838-1907. B-T.
HERRON, [Miss] Jason. (S)
Am. b. Denver, Colo.; ad. 1934 Los Angeles, Calif. M.
HERSCHEL, [Mrs.] Arthur H. [S. Frances].
Am. b. Boston; ad. 1934 Montclair, N. J. A.
HERSCHER, Ernest Marie.
Fr. b. Paris 1870. DBA.
HERSENT, Louis.
Fr. Paris 1777-1860 Same. B-E-T-722.
HERSHEY, Samuel Franklin.
Am. b. Peru, Ind. 1904; ad. 1934 Rockport, Mass. A.
HERSLOFF, Laura.
Am. ex. 1934 New York. M.
HERTER, Adele.
Mrs. Albert Herter.
Am. b. New York 1869; ad. 1934 Santa Barbara, Calif. A-B.
HERTER, Albert. (Mu)
Am. b. New York 1871; ad. 1934 Santa Barbara, Calif. A-B-F-T-W-46.
HERTER, Christine.
Am. b. Irvington, N. Y. 1890; ad. 1934 Hot Springs, Va. A.
HERTER, Everit A.
Am. d. 1918 in France. A015.
HERTERICH, Johann Casper.
Ger. Ausbach 1843-1905. B-T.
HERTERICH, Ludwig.
Ger. b. Ausbach 1856. B-T.
HERTERVIK [or Hertervig], Lars.
Nor. Tysvaer 1830-1902 Stavanger. T.
HERTHEL, Alice.
Am. b. St. Louis, Mo.; ad. 1934 Same. A.
HERVÉ, Gabriel.
Fr. b. Bonnes 1868. B-DBA.
HERVÉ, Jules.
Fr. b. Langres 1887. DBA.

HERVEY-SMITH. *see* Smith, H.
HERVIER, AUGUSTE. (Min)
Am. ac. 1827-1858. F-6.
HERVIER, LOUIS ADOLPHE. (Eg)
Fr. Paris 1818/21-1879. B-T-880.
HERVIEUE, AUGUSTINE JEAN.
Fr. b. Paris 1794; ac. 1819-1858. B-F.
HERVIEUE, LOUISE JEANNE AIMÉE.
Fr. b. Alençon; ac. 1910-1931. DBA.
HERZBERG, ROBERT A.
Am. b. Germany 1886; ad. 1934 Detroit, Mich. A.
HERZEL, PAUL. (S)
Am. b. Germany 1876; ad. 1934 Brooklyn, N. Y. A-Cs-F.
HERZOG, HERMANN.
Am. b. Bremen, Ger. 1832; came to U. S. 1876; d. 1932 Phila., Pa. A29-B-T-Y01933.
HERZOG, LEWIS E.
Am. b. Phila., Pa. 1868; ad. 1934 New York. A.
HESDIN, JACQUEMART DE.
Fr. ac. 1380-1413. T.
HESS, ANTON HEINRICH. (S)
Ger. Munich 1838-1909. Hs-T.
HESS, HEINRICH MARIA VON.
Ger. Düsseldorf 1798-1863 Munich. B-C-E-T-722.
HESS, KARL.
Ger. Düsseldorf 1801-1874. B-C-E-T.
HESS, PETER HEINRICH LAMBERT VON.
Ger. Düsseldorf 1792-1871 Munich. B-E-T.
HESS, SARA M.
Am. n. Troy Grove, Ill. 1880; ad. 1934 Hillsdale, N. J. A.
HESSE, ALEXANDRE JEAN BAPTISTE.
Fr. Paris 1806-1879. B-T.
HESSE, HENRI JOSEPH.
Fr. Paris 1781-1849 Same. B-T.
HESSE, NICOLAS AUGUSTE.
Fr. Paris 1795-1869 Same. B-T.
HESSELBOM, JOHANN OTTO.
Swe. Aninskogs 1848-1913. T.
HESSELIUS, GUSTAVUS.
[Regarded as the earliest painter in America.] *see* Harper's Magazine March 1898; *see also* Pa. Magazine of Hist. and Biog., April 1905.
Am. b. Folkarna, Sweden 1682; d. 1775 Phila., Pa. DAB-F-Fa-T-2-182.
HESSELIUS, JOHN. [Son of Hesselius, G.]
Am. Phila., Pa. 1728-1778 Annapolis, Md. DAB-F-Fa-T-2-182.
HESSELTINE, FRANCIS S.
Am. 1833-1916 Boston, Mass. A013.
HESTER, EDWARD GILBERT. (Eg)
Eng. b. Cheswick; d. 1903 St. Albans. B-T.
HESTER, WALLACE. (Eg)
Eng. ac. 1905 in London. B.
HESTHAL, WILLIAM.
Am. ex. 1935 San Fran., Calif. M.
HETHERINGTON, WALTER.
Eng. b. Liverpool; ac. 1927 in Paris. DBA.
HETSCH, PHILIPP FRIEDRICH VON.
Ger. Stuttgart 1758-1838 Same. C-T.
HETZEL, GEORGE.
Am. Alsace, Fr. 1826-1906 Pittsburgh, Pa. F-T.
HEUBACH, WALTER.
Ger. b. Leicester, Eng. 1865; ac. 1911 Munich, Ger. T.
HEUDEBERT, RAYMONDE.
Fr. b. Paris; ac. 1931 Same. DBA.
HEUERMANN, MAGDA.
Am. b. Galesburg, Ill. 1868; ad. 1934 Oak Park, Ill. A-B-F-T.
HEUPEL, LUDWIG WILHELM.
Bav. b. Siegen 1864. B-T.
HEUSCH, JACOB DE.
Dut. Utrecht 1657-1701 Amsterdam. B-C-E-T.
HEUSCH, WILLEM [or Guilliam] DE.
Dut. Utrecht 1638-1692 Same. B-E-T-722.
HEUSS, FRANZ ÉDOUARD VON.
Ger. Oggersheim 1808-1880 Rodenheim. B-T.
HEUSSEN, NICOLAES VAN.
Flem. ac. 1599-1631. T.
HEUSTIS, LOUISE LYONS.
Am. b. Mobile, Ala.; ad. 1934 New York. A-B-829.
HEUSTON, FRANK ZELL.
Am. b. La Crosse, Wis. 1880; ad. 1934 New York. A.
HEUVEL, THÉODORE BERNARD.
Belg. b. Eeclov 1817; ad. 1840-1858 [No death date]. B-T.
HEUZÉ, EDMOND AMÉDÉE.
Fr. b. Paris 1884. DBA.
HEWARD, HAROLD CORNELIUS.
Eng. b. Southsea 1881. Wa1929-Y1928.
HEWIT, FORREST.
Eng. b. Salford 1870; ad. 1934 Wilmslow. Wa.
HEWITT, EDWIN H.
Am. b. Red Wing, Minn. 1874; ad. 1934 Excelsior, Minn. A.
HEWITT, WILLIAM KEESEY.
Am. Phila., Pa. 1817-1893. F.
HEWLETT, JAMES.
Eng. Bath 1789-1836 Isleworth. B-DNB-T.
HEWLETT, JAMES MONROE. (Mu)
Am. b. Lawrence, N. Y. 1868; ad. 1934 Same. A-F.
HEWTON, RANDOLPH S.
Can. b. Megantic, Que.; ad. 1935 Glen Miller, Ont. M.
HEY, PAUL.
Ger. b. 1867 in Germany. M.
HEYDE, C. L.
Am. ac. 1850-1859 in Brooklyn, N. Y. M.
HEYDECK, JOHANNES.
Ger. Königsberg 1835-1910. B-T.
HEYDECK [or Heideck], KARL WILHELM VON.
Ger. Saaralben 1788-1861 Munich. B-T.
HEYDEL, PAUL.
Ger. b. Dresden 1854. B-T.
HEYDEN, AUGUST JACOB THÉODOR VON.
Ger. Breslau 1827-1897 Berlin. C-T.
HEYDEN, JAN VAN DER.
Dut. Gorkum 1637-1712 Amsterdam. B-C-E-T-722.
HEYDEN, MATTHAUS.
see Verheyden, M.
HEYDEN, PIETER VAN DER.
see Verheyden, P.
HEYDT, EDNA.
Am. ad. 1934 Union City, N. J. M.
HEYENEMAN, ANNE. (Ill)
Am. ad. 1934 San Fran., Calif. M.

HEYER, William. (Ill)
Am. ad. 1934 New York. M.
HEYERMANS, Jean Arnould.
Belg. b. Rotterdam 1837; ac. 1900 Antwerp [No death date]. B-T.
HEYL, Philipp Heinrich George.
Ger. b. Frankfort 1864. T.
HEYLIGERS, Gustave A. F.
Belg. ac. 1860 in Antwerp. B-T.
HEYMAN, Charles.
Fr. Paris 1881-1915. DBA.
HEYMANS, Adriaan Joseph.
Flem. Antwerp 1839-1921. B-DBA-T.
HEYNEMAN, [Mrs.] Amy Josephine.
Am. b. San Diego, Calif. 1903; ad. 1934 San Fran., Calif. M.
HEYSEN, Hans.
Ger. b. Hamburg 1876; ad. 1933 Sydney, Aust. B-T.
HEYSER, Friedrich.
Ger. b. Gnoien 1857. B-T.
HEYWARD, Katherine Bayard.
Am. b. Lexington, Va. 1886. A28.
HIATT, [Mrs.] Bertha.
Am. ad. 1935 Jackson, Miss. M.
HIBBARD, Aldro Thompson.
Am. b. Falmouth, Mass. 1886; ad. 1934 Rockport, Mass. A-F-T-W.
HIBBARD, Frederick Cleveland. (S)
Am. b. Canton, Mo. 1881; ad. 1934 Chicago. A-F-T-Ta-W.
HIBBARD, Mary P.
Am. ad. 1934 New York. M.
HIBBEN, Helene. (S)
Am. b. Indianapolis, Ind. 1882; ad. 1934 Same. A.
HIBBEN, Thomas. (Ill)
Am. ad. 1933 Phila., Pa. M.
HICHERT, Otto.
Ger. b. Halberstadt 1868. B-T.
HICKEL [or Hickl], Carl Anton.
Ger. 1745-1798 Hamburg. B-T.
HICKEL [or Hickl], Josef.
Aus. 1736-1807 Vienna. C-T.
HICKEY, John. (S)
Ir. Dublin 1756-1795 London. DNB-T.
HICKEY, Thomas.
Ir. Dublin 1741-1824 Madras, India. B-DNB-T.
HICKOK, Conde Wilson.
Am. b. Batavia, Ill.; ad. 1934 Berwyn, Ill. A.
HICKOX, Ann Lenhard.
Am. b. Phoenixville, Pa. 1893; ad. 1934 Weekapaug, R. I. A.
HICKS, Arnold L. (Ill)
Am. ad. 1934 New York. M.
HICKS, Edward.
Am. b. 1780; d. 1849. M.
HICKS, Elizabeth.
Am. b. New York 1886; ad. 1934 Tolland, Conn. A.
HICKS, George Elgar.
Eng. Lymington 1824-1914 London. B-T.
HICKS, Herbert.
Am. b. Columbus, O. 1894; ad. 1934 Clarendon, Va. A.
HICKS, Morley.
Am. b. Picton, Ont. Can. 1877; ad. 1934 Milwaukee, Wis. A.
HICKS, Philip Trueman.
Am. b. Boston 1906; ad. 1934 Same. A.
HICKS, Thomas.
Am. Newton, Pa. 1823-1890 Trenton Falls, N. Y. B-C-DAB-F-T-3-4-15.
HICKSON, Wilma. (Ill)
Am. ad. 1935 New York. M.
HIDALGO DE CAVIEDES, Hipolito.
Sp. ad. 1935 Madrid; ex. 1934 Pittsburgh, Pa. M.
HIDALGO, Félix Resurrection.
Am. Manila, Phil. Is. 1857-1915 Paris. A012-B-T.
HIDALGO, Luis. (Wax-S)
Sp. ad. 1934 Mexico City, Mex. M.
HIDDEMAN, Friedrich Peter.
Ger. Düsseldorf 1826-1892 Same. B-T.
HIGDON, Helen.
Am. b. Decatur, Ala.; ad. 1934 Birmingham, Ala. A.
HIGGINS, A. Earle.
Am. ad. 1934 Hempstead, L. I., N. Y. M.
HIGGINS, Eugène.
Am. b. Kansas City, Mo. 1874; ad. 1934 New York. A-B-F-T-W-46-892.
HIGGINS, Frank Wilfrid.
Eng. b. Chester 1893; ad. 1934 London. Wa.
HIGGINS, Irene M.
Am. ad. 1934 Boston, Mass. M.
HIGGINS, Reginald Edward.
Eng. b. London 1877; ad. 1934 Same. Wa.
HIGGINS, William Victor.
Am. b. Shelbyville, Ind. 1884; ad. 1934 Taos, N. M. A-F-T-W-46.
HIGHAM, Thomas. (Eg)
Eng. 1795-1844 London. DNB-T.
HIGHMORE, Anthony. (Et)
Br. b. 1719; d. 1799. DNB-T.
HIGHMORE, Joseph.
Eng. London 1692-1780 Canterbury. B-DNB-T.
HIGHMORE, Thomas.
Br. d. 1720. DNB-T.
HIGHWOOD, Charles.
Am. ac. 1850 in New York. F.
HILAIRE, Jean Baptiste.
Fr. b. 1753; d. 1822. B-T.
HILBERT, George Stéphane. (S)
Fr. b. Algeria; ac. 1933 in Paris. DBA.
HILDEBRAND, Adolph Ernest Robert. (S)
Ger. b. Marburg 1847. B-DBA-Hs-T-813.
HILDEBRAND, Ernest.
Ger. Falkenberg 1833-1893. B-T.
HILDEBRAND, Ott. (S)
Ger. Metz 1874-1928. T.
HILDEBRANDT, [Mrs.] Cornelia Ellis.
Am. Eau Claire, Wis.; ad. 1934 New York. A-F.
HILDEBRANDT, Éduard.
Ger. Danzig 1818-1868 Berlin. B-C-E-T.
HILDEBRANDT, Ferdinand Théodor.
Ger. Stettin 1804-1874 Düsseldorf. B-C-E-T.
HILDER, Howard.
Am. b. London 1866; d. 1935 Cocoanut Grove, Fla. A-W-Obit. N. Y. papers, 7-1-1935.
HILDER, J. J.
Aust. ac. 1933 in Australia. M.

HILDERBRANDT, Grace Brooks. (Min)
Am. ad. 1934 Baltimore, Md. M.
HILDERBRANDT, Howard Logan.
Am. b. Allegheny, Pa. 1872; ad. 1934 New York. A-B-F-T-W.
HILDRETH, Susan W.
Am. b. Cambridge, Mass.; ad. 1934 Same. A.
HILER, Hilaire. (Mu)
Am. b. St. Paul, Minn. 1900; ad. 1935 New York. M.
HILES, Bartram.
[Had no hands; held brush in his mouth.]
Eng. 1872-1927. M.
HILGENDORF, Fred C.
Am. b. Milwaukee, Wis. 1888; ad. 1934 Same. A.
HILL, Abby Williams.
Mrs. F. R. Hill.
Am. b. Grinnell, Ia. 1861; ad. 1934 Tacoma, Wash. A.
HILL, Adrian Keith Graham.
Eng. b. Charlton 1896; ad. 1934 London. Wa.
HILL, Arthur Turnbull.
Am. New York 1868-1929 East Hampton, N. Y. A027-B-F-T-W.
HILL, Carl Frederick.
Swe. Lund 1849-1911 Same. T.
HILL, [Lady] Caroline Emily Gray.
Eng. b. 1843; d. 1924. M.
HILL, Carrie L.
Am. b. Tuscaloosa, Co. Ala.; ad. 1934 Birmingham, Ala. A.
HILL, Clara. (S)
Am. b. Mass.; d. 1935 Wash., D. C. A-Obit. N. Y. papers, 7-9-1935.
HILL, David Octavius.
Scot. Perth 1802-1870 Edinburgh. B-T.
HILL, George Snow.
Am. b. Munising, Mich. 1898; ad. 1934 St. Petersburg, Fla. A.
HILL, George William. (S)
Can. Shifton, Que. 1861-1934. M.
HILL, Howard.
Am. ad. 1860 New York. [Currier & Ives painter.] M.
HILL, James. (Eg)
Am. ac. 1803 Charleston, Mass. [No death date.] F-T-2-7-147.
HILL, James Jerome.
Am. b. St. Paul, Minn. 1905; ad. 1934 Same. A.
HILL, John. (Eg)
Am. London 1770-1850 Nyack, N. Y. B-Bd-DAB-F-T-2-7-55-106-107.
HILL, John William.
Am. b. England 1812; d. 1897 Nyack, N. Y. F-T-2-7.
HILL, Mabel Betsey. (Ill)
Am. b. Cambridge, Mass. 1877; ad. 1934 New York. A.
HILL, Pamelia E. (Min)
Am. b. Framingham, Mass. 1803; d. 1860. F-T-2-6.
HILL, Pearl L.
Am. b. Lock Haven, Pa. 1884. F.
HILL, Polly Knipp. (Et)
Am. b. Ithaca, N. Y. 1900; ad. 1934 St. Petersburg, Fla. A.
HILL, Raven. (Cart)
Eng. ac. 1915 in England. M.
HILL, Raymond.
Am. ad. 1934 Seattle, Wash. M.
HILL, Robert Jerome.
Am. b. Austin, Tex.; ad. 1934 Dallas, Tex. A-F.
HILL, Samuel. (Eg)
Am. ad. 1789-1803. F-T-2-7-147.
HILL, Thomas.
Am. Birmingham, Eng. 1829-1908 Raymond, Calif. A07-B-C-DAB-F-T-W4-15-39.
HILLAIRET, Anatole Eugène.
Fr. b. Chay; d. 1928 in France. DBA.
HILLARD, William H.
Am. d. 1905 Wash., D. C. A05.
HILLBORM, Hendrik.
Am. b. Sweden 1863; ad. 1934 Wallingford, Conn. A.
HILLEGAERT [or Hilligaard], Pauwels van [The Elder].
Dut. Amsterdam 1595/6-1640 Same. B-Bd-T.
HILLEMACHER, Eugène Ernst.
Fr. Paris 1818-1887. B-T.
HILLER, Joseph, Jr. (Eg)
Am. Salem, Mass. 1777-1795 at sea. F-T-2-7-147-169.
HILLER, Joseph, Sr. (Eg)
Am. Boston 1748-1814 Lancaster, Pa. 2-7-169.
HILLER, Lejaren A. (Ill)
Am. b. Milwaukee, Wis. 1880. A28.
HILLER, Williams.
Ger. b. 1884; ex. 1930 New York. M.
HILLERBRANDT, Johann Heinrich.
Ger. b. Hamburg 1804. [No death date.] T.
HILLESTRÖM, Per [The Elder].
Swe. Roslagen 1732-1816 Stockholm. B-T.
HILLIARD, F. John.
Am. b. Burlington, Vt. 1886; ad. 1934 Boston. A.
HILLIARD, Lawrence. (Min)
Eng. b. 1581/2; d. 1640 England. B-E-T.
HILLIARD, Nicolas. (Min)
[First English miniature painter.]
Eng. b. 1537; d. 1619 England. B-Bd-DNB-E-T.
HILLIARD, William Henry.
Am. Auburn, N. Y. 1836-1905 Wash., D. C. A05-B-C-F-T-15.
HILLINGFORD, Robert Alexander.
Eng. 1828-1893 London. B-T.
HILLS, Anna A.
Am. b. Ravenna, O.; d. 1930. A027.
HILLS, John W.
Am. ad. 1934 Colchester, Conn. M.
HILLS, Laura Combs. (Min)
Am. b. Newburyport, Mass. 1859; ad. 1934 Boston. A-B-F-T-W-1-46-829.
HILLS, Metta V.
Mrs. Elijah C. Hills.
Am. b. Orleans, N. Y. 1873; ad. 1934 Berkeley, Calif. A.
HILLS, Robert.
Eng. Islington 1769-1844 London. DNB-T.
HILLYER, William.
Am. ac. 1834-1861 Phila., Pa. F-2-6.

HILTON, ANNA L.
Am. b. Atlanta, Ga.; ad. 1935 New York. M.
HILTON, HAROLD.
Am. ad. 1934 Jacksonville, Fla. M.
HILTON, ROY.
Am. b. Boston, Mass. 1891; ad. 1935 Pittsburgh, Pa. M.
HILTON, WILLIAM [The Elder].
Eng. Nottingham 1752-1822 London. B-Bd-DNB-E-T.
HILTON, WILLIAM [THE YOUNGER].
Eng. Lincoln 1786-1839 London. B-Bd-DNB-E-T.
HIMONA, NICOLAS.
Rus. b. Russia; ac. 1929 in London. Wa1929.
HINCHLIFF, JOHN ELLEY. (S)
Eng. 1777-1867 London. B-DNB-T.
HINCHLIFF, JOHN JAMES. (Eg)
Eng. 1805-1875 Walton. B-DNB-T.
HINCHLIFFE, GEORGE FREDERICK.
Br. b. Allara, Queensland, Aust. 1896; ad. 1934 Liverpool, Eng. Wa.
HINCHLIFFE, RICHARD GEORGE.
Eng. b. Manchester 1868; ad. 1934 Liverpool. Wa.
HINCHMAN, JOHN HERBERT.
Am. b. Detroit, Mich. 1884; ad. 1934 Laguna Beach, Calif. A.
HINCHMAN, MARGARETTA S.
Am. b. Phila., Pa.; ad. 1934 Same. A.
HINCKLEY, ROBERT.
Am. b. Boston, Mass. 1853; ad. 1934 Belhaven, Del. F-T-W.
HINCKLEY, THOMAS HEWES.
Am. b. Milton, Mass. 1813; d. 1896. C-F-T-4-15.
HINCKS, WILLIAM.
Br. ac. 1791 in England. M.
HIND, ARTHUR MAYGER. (Et)
Eng. b. Burton 1880; ad. 1934 London. Wa.
HINE, CHARLES.
Am. Bethany, Conn. 1827-1871 New Haven, Conn. F-3.
HINE, ELEANOR.
Am. b. 1907; ad. 1934 Westport, Conn. M.
HINE, HARRY T.
Eng. b. London 1845. B-Wa1929-T.
HINE, HENRY GEORGE.
Eng. Brighton 1811-1895. B-DNB-T.
HINES, DONALD.
Am. ad. 1935 New Rochelle, N. Y. M.
HINKELMAN, EDNA WEBB.
Mrs. Edward Hinkelman.
Am. b. Cohoes, N. Y. 1892; ad. 1934 Navesink, N. J. A.
HINKLE, CLARENCE K.
Am. n. Auburn, Calif. 1880; ad. 1934 Laguna Beach, Calif. A28.
HINKLE, LUCILLE BERNICE.
Am. b. Kansas City, Mo. 1895; ad. 1934 Fullerton, Calif. A.
HINSDALE, RICHARD L.
Am. b. Hartford, Conn. 1825. [No death date.] F.
HINSHELWOOD, ROBERT. (Eg)
Am. b. Edinburgh 1812; ac. 1850 New York. [No death date.] F-T-7-40-147.
HINTERMEISTER, HENRY. (Ill)
Am. b. New York 1897; ad. 1934 Brooklyn, N. Y. A.
HINTON, CHARLES LOUIS. (P-S)
Am. b. Ithaca, N. Y. 1869; ad. 1934 Bronxville, N. Y. A-B-F-T-W.
HINTON, [Mrs.] HOWARD. (S)
Am. b. 1834; d. 1921 New York. A019.
HIOLLE, ERNEST EUGÈNE. (S)
Fr. Paris 1833-1887. B-T.
HIRAMÓTO, MASAJI.
Jap.-Am. b. Fukui, Jap. 1888; ad. 1934 New York. A-W16.
HIRAYAMA, KWANTEI. (S)
Jap. b. Tokio; ac. 1900 Paris. B.
HIRE [or Hyre], LAURENT DE LA.
see La Hire.
HIRONAO, SUMIYOSHI.
Jap. 1780-1828. J., Vol. 1, page 77.
HIROSHI, YOSHIDA.
Jap. b. 1876 in Japan. M.
HIROSHIGÉ II [Hironobu].
Jap. ac. 1860-1896 in Yeddo. E.
HIROSHIGÉ, MOTONAGA [or Utagawa].
Jap. 1797-1858 Yeddo. B-E-J-T.
HIRSCH, AUGUSTE ALEXANDRE.
Fr. Lyons 1833-1912. B-T.
HIRSCH, JOSEPH.
Am. b. Phila., Pa. 1910; ad. 1934 Same. A.
HIRSCH, PETER.
Ger. ex. 1934 Scarsdale, N. Y. M.
HIRSCH, STEFAN.
Am. b. Nüremberg, Ger. 1899; ad. 1934 Brooklyn, N. Y. A-1-779.
HIRSCH, WILLARD.
Am. ad. 1935 New York. M.
HIRSCHBERG, ALICE KERR-NELSON.
Mrs. Carl Hirschberg.
Am. b. England 1852; ad. 1930 Buffalo, N. Y. A12-B.
HIRSCHBERG, CARL.
Am. Germany 1854-1923 Danbury, Conn. A020-B-F-T.
HIRSCHFELD, ÉMILE BENEDICKTOFF.
Rus. b. Odessa; ac. 1892-1910. B-T.
HIRSCHMANN, JOHANN BAPTIST.
Ger. b. 1770; d. 1821 in Germany. B-T.
HIRSCHVOGEL [or Hirssfogel], AUGUSTIN.
Ger. Nüremberg 1503-1553 Vienna, Aus. B-T.
HIRSHBURG, RAY.
Am. ad. 1934 Richmond, Ind. M.
HIRST, CLAUDE RAGUFT.
Mrs. W. C. Fitler.
Am. b. Cinn., O.; ad. 1934 New York. A.
HIRST, NORMAN. (Eg)
Eng. b. Liverpool 1862; ad. 1934 Seaford. B-T-Wa.
HIRT, HEINRICH.
Ger. Frankfort 1727-1796. B-T.
HIRT, JOHANN CHRISTIAN. (S)
Ger. Furth 1836-1897 Munich. B-T.
HIRT, SAMUEL.
Ger. b. 1727. [No death date.] B-T.
HIRT, WILHELM FRIEDRICH.
Ger. Frankfort 1721-1772 Same. B-T.
HIRZEL, SUSETTE [Ott].
Swi. Zurich 1769-1858 Same. T.

HIS, René Charles Edmond.
Fr. b. Colombes 1877. B-DBA.
HISCOX, George Dunkerton.
Eng. North Wooton 1840-1901. Bd-DNB-T.
HITCHCOCK, Cecil Jay. *see* Jay, Cecil.
HITCHCOCK, David Howard.
Am. b. Honolulu, Hawaii 1861; ad. 1934 Same. A.
HITCHCOCK, George.
Am. Prov., R. I. 1850-1913 Holland. A0X1-B-E-F-T-46.
HITCHCOCK, Helen Marshall.
Am. b. Hartford, Conn. 1902; ad. 1934 Same. A.
HITCHCOCK, Lucius Wolcott.
Am. b. West Williamsfield, O. 1868; ad. 1934 New Rochelle, N. Y. A-B-T-W-46.
HITCHENS, Sydney Ivon.
Eng. b. London 1893; ad. 1935 Same. Wa.
HITE, George H.
Am. ac. 1839-1861 in New York. F-6.
HITE, Marcia S.
Mrs. Allen R. Hite.
Am. ad. 1935 Louisville, Ky. M.
HITTELL, Charles J.
Am. b. San Fran., Calif. 1861; ad. 1915 Same. A12-F-T-W12.
HITTELL, Margaret A.
Am. b. Victor, Iowa 1886; ad. 1915 Chicago. A12-F.
HJERLOW, Rangvald Amandus.
Nor. b. Christiania; ac. 1889 in Paris. B-T.
HJORTH, Bror. (S)
Swe. b. 1894; ex. 1930 Paris. DBA.
HLADIKOVA-BERNKOPFOVA, Jeanne.
Jap. ac. 1930 in Paris. DBA.
HOADLEY, Sarah.
Br. ac. 1700-1743. DNB-T.
HOARD, Margaret. (S)
Am. b. Iowa; ad. 1934 Mt. Vernon, N. Y. A-F-T.
HOARE, Prince [The Younger]. (Author-P)
Eng. Bath 1755-1834 Brighton. B-DNB-T.
HOARE, William ["Hoare of Bath"].
Br. b. Eye 1706; d. 1792 Bath. B-Bd-DNB-T.
HOBART, Clark. (Et)
Am. b. Illinois; ad. 1935 San Fran., Calif. A20-F.
HOBART, Gladys Marie.
Am. b. Santa Cruz, Calif. 1892; ad. 1934 San Fran., Calif. A.
HOBBEMA, Meindert [Minder-Hout].
Dut. Amsterdam 1638?-1709 Same. B-Bd-C-E-T-722.
HOBBS, Morris Henry.
Am. ad. 1934 Chicago. M.
HOBDAY, William Armfield.
Eng. Birmingham 1771-1831. B-DNB.
HOBDY, Ann.
Am. ex. 1934 New York. M.
HOBLEY, Edward George.
Eng. Brightwell 1866-1916 Penrith. B-T.
HOBSON, Henry E.
Eng. ac. 1857-1866 in Bath. B-T.
HOCHARD, Gaston.
Fr. b. Orléans; ac. 1905 in Rouen. B-T.
HOCHECKER, Franz.
Ger. Frankfort 1730-1782. B-T.
HOCHMANN, Franz Gusta.
Ger. b. Dresden 1861. B-T.
HOCKER. *see* Hoecker.
HODÉ, Pierre.
Fr. b. Rouen 1889. DBA.
HODEBERT, Léon Auguste César.
Fr. ac. 1877-1900 in Paris. B-T.
HODER, Paul.
Ger. ac. 1889 in Germany. M.
HODGE, Albert H. (S)
Eng. Campden Hill 1876-1918 London. B-Y01919.
HODGE, [Mrs.] Helen.
Am. b. Topeka, Kan.; ad. 1934 Same. A.
HODGE, Lydia Herrick. (S)
Am. b. Valparaiso, Ind. 1889; ad. 1934 Eugène, Ore. A-Cs.
HODGE, Margaret Magill.
Am. b. Wash., D. C.; ad. 1915 Same. A12.
HOGES, Charles Howard. (Eg)
Eng. London 1764-1837 Amsterdam, Holland. B-DNB-T.
HODGES, C. M.
Eng. b. 1858; d. 1916. M.
HODGES, George Schuyler.
Am. b. Pontiac, Mich. 1864; ad. 1915 Same. A12-B.
HODGES, Harold. (S)
Am. ad. 1934 Hagerstown. Md. M.
HODGES, William.
Eng. London 1744-1797 Brixam. DNB-T.
HODGES, William C.
Am. b. 1856; d. 1914 Phila., Pa. A0X1.
HODGES, William Merritt. (Et)
Eng. ad. 1934 Birmingham. Wa.
HODGETTS, Thomas. (Eg)
Eng. ac. 1801; d. 1846 London. B-T.
HODGIN, Marston Dean.
Am. Cambridge, O. 1903; ad. 1934 Oxford, O. A.
HODGKINS, Frances.
Eng. ex. 1935 London. M.
HODGSON, Edward.
Ir. Dublin 1719-1794 London. DNB-T.
HODGSON, John Evan.
Eng. London 1831-1895 Same. B-Bd-C-DNB-T-15.
HODGSON, William.
Am. 1830-1914 Grand Rapids, Mich. A0X1.
HODLER, Ferdinand.
Swi. Gurzelen 1853-1918 Geneva. B-E-DBA-T-397-715.
HOEBER, Arthur.
Am. New York 1854-1915 Nutley, N. J. A012-B-F-T.
HOECKE, Jan van den.
Flem. Antwerp 1611-1651 Brussels. B-C-T-722.
HOECKER, Hazel.
Am. ac. 1933. M.
HOECKER, Paul.
Ger. Oberlanganau 1854-1910 Munich. B-DBA-T.
HOECKGEEST. *see* Honckgeest.
HOECKNER, Carl.
Am. b. Munich, Ger. 1883; ad. 1934 Chicago. A.
HOEFNAGEL, Jacob.
Ger. Frankfort 1575-1629 Munich. B-T.

HOEFNAGEL, Joris [or Georg]. (Eg)
Flem. Antwerp 1542/5-1600 Vienna, Aus. B-E-T.
HOEGGER, Augustus.
Am. b. Switzerland 1848; d. 1908 Phila., Pa. A07-B.
HOEHN, Werner.
Am. ad. 1934 New Orleans, La. M.
HOELSCHER, May B.
Am. b. Aurora, Ill. 1884; ad. 1934 Same. A.
HOERMAN, Carl.
Am. b. Babenhausen, Bav. 1885; ad. 1934 Highland Park, Ill. A.
HOEROLDT, Johann Gregor.
Ger. Jena 1696-1775 Meissen. M.
HOERTZ, Fred.
Am. ac. 1918 in New York. M.
HOESSLIN [or Hosslin], George von.
Aus. b. 1851 in Austria. M.
HOET, Gérard.
Dut. Bommel 1648-1733 The Hague. B-C-T.
HÖETGER, Bernhard. (S)
Ger. b. 1874 in Germany. Hs-398.
HOFER, André.
Swi. b. Autum; ac. 1912-1930. DBA.
HOFER, Gottfried.
Aus. b. Bozen 1858. B-T.
HOFER, Karl.
Ger. b. Carlsruhe 1878; ad. 1934 Berlin, Schöneberg. B-DBA-T.
HOFF, Charlotte M.
Am. b. Akron, O.; ad. 1934 Same. A.
HOFF, Guy. (Ill)
Am. ad. 1934 New York. M.
HOFF, Inez Chatfield.
Am. ad. 1935 Astoria, L. I., N. Y. M.
HOFF, Karl.
Ger. Mannhéim 1838-1890 Carlsruhe. B-C-T.
HOFF, Rayner. (S)
Aust. ac. 1933 in Australia. M.
HOFF, Sidney. (Cart)
Am. ad. 1934 Chicago, Ill. M.
HOFFBAUER, Charles.
Fr.-Am. b. Paris 1875; ad. 1934 Same. A-B-DBA-F-T.
HOFFLER, Othmar.
Am. ad. 1934 Chicago. M.
HOFFMAN. *see also* Hoffmann.
see also Hofman and Hofmann.
HOFFMAN, Belle.
Am. Garretsville, O. 1889; ad. 1934 New York. A.
HOFFMAN, Frank B. (Ill)
Am. ad. 1934 New York. M.
HOFFMAN, Grace Le Grand.
Am. b. Syracuse, N. Y. 1890; ad. 1934 New Rochelle, N. Y. A.
HOFFMAN, Gustave Adolph.
Am. b. Brandenburg, Ger. 1869; ad. 1934 Rockville, Conn. A-F-T.
HOFFMAN, Harry Leslie.
Am. b. Cressona, Pa. 1880; ad. 1934 Old Lyme, Conn. A-W.
HOFFMAN, Helen.
Am. b. St. Paul, Minn. 1900; ad. 1934 New York. M.
HOFFMAN, Irwin D.
Am. b. Boston, Mass. 1901; ex. 1935 New York. M.
HOFFMAN, Malvina. (S)
Mrs. Samuel B. Grimson.
Am. b. New York 1887; ad. 1934 Same. A-Cs-E-F-T-W-339-408.
HOFFMAN, Maximilian.
Am. b. Germany 1887-1922 U. S. A020-F.
HOFFMAN, Murray.
Am. ex. 1932 New York. M.
HOFFMAN, Polly.
Mrs. Luther Hoffman.
Am. b. Bryan, Tex. 1890; ad. 1934 Wichita Falls, Tex. A.
HOFFMAN, Samuel.
Ger. Zurich, Swi. 1591/2-1648 Frankfort, Ger. M.
HOFFMAN, Seth.
Am. ad. 1935 New York. M.
HOFFMAN, Tekla.
Am. ex. 1935 New York. M.
HOFFMANN, Arnold.
Am. b. Russia 1886; ad. 1934 New York. A.
HOFFMANN, Hans.
Am. b. Saxony 1893; ad. 1934 Gloucester, Mass. A28.
HOFFMANN, Hans [or Johann].
Ger. Nüremburg 1545-1600 Vienna, Aus. B-T.
HOFFMANN, Johann Michael Heinrich.
Ger. Frankfort 1824-1895 Same. B-T.
HOFFMANN, Margareta. (S)
Am. ad. 1935 Cleveland, O. M.
HOFLAND, Thomas Christopher.
Br. b. 1777; d. 1843. DNB.
HOFMAN, Hans O. (Ill)
Am. b. Germany 1893; ac. U. S.; ad. unknown. A.
HOFMANN, Ludwig von.
Ger. b. Dresden 1861. T.
HOFMANN, Vlastinil.
Pol. b. Crakow 1881; ad. 1930 Paris. DBA.
HOFFMASTER, Maud Miller.
Am. b. Manistee, Mich. 1886; ad. 1934 Traverse City, Mich. A.
HOFNER, Johann Baptist.
Ger. b. Aresing 1832; ac. 1863 Munich. [No death date.] B-T.
HOFSTETTER, W. A.
Am. b. Phila., Pa. 1884; ad. 1934 Glenside, Pa. A-F.
HOFTRUP, Julius Lars.
Am. b. Sweden 1874; ad. 1934 Elmira, N. Y. A-F.
HOGAN, Inez. (Ill)
Am. ad. 1934 New York. M.
HOGAN, John. (S)
Ir. 1800-1858 Dublin. DNB-T.
HOGARTH, William. (Eg-P)
Eng. London 1697-1764 Same. B-Bd-C-DNB-E-T-191-364-400-401-707-722-790-909-922-924.
HOGENBERG Family.
Flem. ac. 16-17 Cent. in Belgium. T.
HOGENBURG [or Hoogenbergh], Franz. (Eg)
Ger. b. Mechlin; d. 1590 in Cologne. B-DNB-T.
HOGENBURG, Johann Nicolas.
Flem. b. 1500; d. 1544. B-T.
HOGENBURG [or Hoogenburgh], Remigius. (Eg)
Flem. b. Mechlin; d. 1580? B-DNB-T.

HOGGATT, William.
Eng. b. Lancaster 1879; ex. 1934 London. Wa.
HÖGGER, Andreas Renatus.
Swi. St. Gallen 1808-1854 Same. T.
HOGNER, Nils.
Am. ad. 1934 Taos, N. M. M.
HOGUE, Alexandre.
Am. b. Memphis, Mo. 1898; ad. 1934 Dallas, Tex. A.
HOGUE, Kate L.
Am. ad. 1934 Youngstown, O. M.
HOGUET, Charles.
Ger. b. Berlin 1821; d. 1870 Same. B-C-T.
HOHENSTEINER, John.
Am. b. Wurttemberg, Ger. 1901; ad. 1934 Brooklyn, N. Y. A.
HOHMANN, Hans.
Am. ad. 1934 New York. M.
HOIN, Clarence Jean Baptiste.
Fr. Dijon 1750-1817 Same. B-T.
HOITSU, Sakai.
Jap. b. 1761; d. 1828. J., Vol. 2, page 14.
HOKEAH, Jack.
Am. Indian; ex. 1932 New York. 411.
HOKINSON, Helen E. (Ill)
Am. ad. 1935 New York. M.
HOKKEI, Tatoya.
Jap. Tokio 1780-1850. B-J., Vol. 2, page 65.
HOKUBA, Teisai.
Jap. ac. 1800 in Japan. J., Vol. 2, page 65.
HOKUSAI, Katsushika.
Jap. Honjo 1760-1849 Yeddo. B-E-J-T.
HOLANDA, Antonio de. (Min)
Por. ac. 1495-1540 in Lisbon. B.
HOLANDA, Francisco de. (Min)
Por. Lisbon 1515-1584. B.
HOLBEIN, Ambrosius [or Prosy].
Ger. Augsburg, 1494/5-1526. B-T.
HOLBEIN, Hans [The Elder].
Ger. Augsburg 1460/70-1524 Isenheim. B-Bd-C-E-T-402-403-722-917.
HOLBEIN [or Olpeius], Hans [The Younger].
Ger. Augsburg 1497/8-1543 London. B-Bd-C-DNB-E-T-402-404-722-917.
HOLBEIN, Sigismund.
Ger. Augsburg 1465/70-1540 Berne, Swi. B-T.
HOLBERG, Ludwig O.
Am. b. Norway 1878; ad. 1915 Milwaukee, Wis. A12.
HOLBERG, Richard A.
Am. Milwaukee, Wis. 1889; ad. 1934 Rockport, Mass. A.
HOLBERG, [Mrs.] Ruth Langland.
Am. b. Milwaukee, Wis. 1891; ad. 1934 Rockport, Mass. A.
HOLBURTON, Wakeman.
Am. New York 1839-1898. A01-B-T.
HOLDEN, Cora Millet.
Am. b. Alexandria, Va. 1895; ad. 1934 Cleveland, O. A-F.
HOLDEN, Luella Stewart.
Mrs. Hendrick S. Holden.
Am. d. 1931 Syracuse, N. Y. A028.
HOLDEN, Ray. (Ill)
Am. ad. 1935 Somers, Conn. M.
HOLDER, Alfred.
Am. ad. 1934 Toledo, O. M.
HOLDER, Peggy. (S)
Am. ac. 1928-1933 in Paris. DBA.
HOLDING, Edgar Thomas.
Eng. b. Horncastle 1876; ex. 1934 in London. Wa.
HOLE, Henry Fulke Plantagenet Woolicombe. (Eg)
Eng. d. 1820 in Liverpool. DNB-T.
HOLE [or Holle], William. (Eg)
[Earliest English engraver of music on copper plates.]
Eng. ac. 1600-1630 London. DNB-T.
HOLE, William Brassey.
Eng. Salisbury 1846-1917. B-T.
HOLFIELD, Hippolyte Dominique.
Fr. Paris 1794-1872 Same. B-T.
HOLGATE, Edwin Headley.
Can. b. Allandale, Ont.; ad. 1935 Montreal. M.
HOLIDAY, Gilbert Joseph.
Eng. b. London 1879; ad. 1934 Same. Wa.
HOLIDAY, Henry.
Eng. 1839-1927 London. B-Y01928.
HOLL, Francis [The Elder]. (Eg)
Eng. London 1815-1884 Milford, Eng. DNB-T.
HOLL, Frank [Francis Montague].
Eng. London 1845-1888 Madrid, Sp. B-C-DNB-E-T.
HOLL, William [The Elder]. (Eg)
Eng. 1771-1838 London. DNB-T.
HOLL, William [The Younger]. (Eg)
Eng. Plaistow 1807-1871 London. DNB-T.
HOLLAND, Francis Raymond.
Am. Pittsburgh, Pa. 1886-1934 New York. A-Obit. N. Y. papers, 4-22-1934. Obit. Art News, 4-28-1934.
HOLLAND, James.
Eng. Burslem 1800-1870 London. B-DNB-T.
HOLLAND, John Joseph.
Am. b. London 1776; ac. 1797 Phila., Pa. [No death date.] F-T-2.
HOLLAND, [Sir] Nathaniel Dance.
see Dance, Sir N.
HOLLAR, Wenzel [or Wenceslaus], von Prachma. (Eg)
Eng. b. Prague, Czec. 1607-1677 London. B-DNB-E-T-364.
HOLLERITH, Lucia Beverley.
Am. b. Wash., D. C. 1891; ad. 1934 Same. A.
HOLLIDAY, Carroll.
Am. ad. 1934 New Canaan, Conn. M.
HOLLINGSWORTH, George.
Am. Milton, Mass. 1813-1882 Same. F.
HOLLINGSWORTH, Ruth.
Eng. b. London; ad. 1934 Holbrook, Eng. Wa-Y1928.
HOLLINGSWORTH, Will. (Ill)
Am. ad. 1934 New York. M.
HOLLINS, Peter. (S)
Eng. Birmingham 1800-1866. DNB-T.
HOLLIS, George. (Eg)
Eng. Oxford 1792/3-1842 Walworth, Eng. B-T.
HOLLIS, Thomas. (Eg)
Eng. 1818-1843 Walworth, Eng. B.
HOLLISTER, Antoinette B. (S)
Am. b. Chicago, Ill. 1873; ad. 1934 Greenwich, Conn. A-Cs-T.

HOLLOS, AUGUST A.
Am. ad. 1934 Toledo, O. M.
HOLLOWAY, CHARLES EDWARD.
Eng. Christchurch 1838-1897. B-T.
HOLLOWAY, EDGAR J.
Eng. ex. 1934 London. M.
HOLLOWAY, EDWARD STRATTAN. (Ill)
Am. b. Ashland, N. Y.; ad. 1934 Phila., Pa. A-F-W.
HOLLOWAY, IDA HOLTERHOFF.
Mrs. George C. Holloway.
Am. b. Cinn., O.; ad. 1934 Same. A.
HOLLOWAY, JAMES. (Eg)
Eng. London 1748-1827 Norwich, Eng. M.
HOLLOWAY, THOMAS. (Eg)
Eng. London 1748-1827 Cottishal. B-DNB-T.
HOLLYER, SAMUEL. (Eg)
Am. London 1826-1919 New York. A016-DAB-F-T-Y01921-7-55.
HOLM, MILTON W.
Am. ad. 1935 Rochester, N. Y. M.
HOLM, VICTOR SOPHUS JOACHIM. (S)
Am. b. Copenhagen, Den. 1876; ad. 1934 St. Louis, Mo. A-B-Cs-F-T-W.
HOLMAN, BILL. (Ill)
Am. ad. 1935 New York. M.
HOLMAN, FRANCIS.
Eng. ac. 1760-1790 in London. DNB-T.
HOLMAN, FRANK.
Am. b. Attleboro, Mass. 1865. B-T.
HOLMAN, LOUIS ARTHUR. (Ill)
Am. b. Summerside, P.E.I. Can. 1866; ad. 1934 Boston. F-W.
HOLMAN-HUNT, WILLIAM.
see Hunt, W. H.
HOLMBERG, AUGUST JOHANN.
Ger. Munich 1851-1911. B-T.
HOLMBOE, THOROLF.
Nor. b. Christiania 1866. B-T.
HOLME, JOHN FRANCIS [or Frank]. (Ill)
Am. Corinth, W. Va. 1868-1904 Denver, Colo. A05-B.
HOLME, LUCY D.
Am. b. New Jersey; ad. 1915 Phila., Pa. A12.
HOLMES, [Sir] CHARLES JOHN.
Eng. b. Preston 1868; ad. 1934 London. B-T-Wa-825.
HOLMES, GEORGE AUGUSTUS.
Eng. Chelsea 1852-1909. B-T.
HOLMES, FRANK G.
Am. ad. 1934 Trenton, N. J. M.
HOLMES, GRAHAM.
Am. ad. 1934 Trenton, N. J. M.
HOLMES, HARRIET MORTON. (Et)
Am. ac. 20th century. M.
HOLMES, JAMES.
Eng. Burslem 1777-1860. DNB-T.
HOLMES, [Mrs.] KATE OSGOOD.
Am. d. 1925 Washington, D. C. A022.
HOLMES, KENNETH.
Eng. b. Skipton 1902; ad. 1934 London. Wa.
HOLMES, MARJORIE DAINGERFIELD. (S)
Am. b. New York; ad. 1934 Same. A.
HOLMES, RALPH.
Am. b. La Grange, Ill. 1876; ad. 1934 Hollywood, Calif. A.
HOLMES, RIA MITCHELL.
Am. ad. 1934 New York. M.
HOLMES, ROBERT.
Can. Cannington, Ont. 1861-1930 Toronto, Ont. 893-Y01931.
HOLMES, WILLIAM H.
Am. b. Ohio 1860; ad. 1932 Wash., D. C. M.
HOLMES, WILLIAM HENRY.
Am. b. Harrison Co. O. 1846; d. 1933. A28-B-F-T-W-Obit. Art News, 5-6-1933.
HOLMGREN, R. JOHN.
Am. b. St. Paul, Minn. 1897; ad. 1934 New York. A.
HOLMSTEDT, PETER L.
Am. b. Cinn., O.; ad. 1934 San Antonio, Tex. M.
HOLSLAG, EDWARD J. (Mu)
Am. Buffalo, N. Y. 1870-1925 De Kalb, Ill. A022-F-T.
HOLSMAN, ELIZABETH TUTTLE.
Am. b. Brownville, Neb. 1873; ad. 1934 Chicago. A-F-T.
HOLST, JOHANN GUSTAF VON.
Swe. b. Stockholm 1841; ac. 1888 Munich, Ger. B-T.
HOLST, LAURITS BERNARD.
Dan. Bogense 1848-1934 Bournemouth, Eng. T-Obit. N. Y. papers, 7-20-1934.
HOLST, THEODORE VON.
Eng. London 1810-1844 Same. DNB-T.
HOLSTEYN, CORNELIS.
Dut. Haarlem 1618-1658 Amsterdam. B-T.
HOLT, MAUDE S.
Mrs. Winfield Scott Holt.
Am. b. Carbondale, Ill. 1866; ad. 1934 Little Rock, Ark. A.
HOLT, PERCY WILLIAM.
Am. b. Mobile, Ala.; ad. 1934 Galveston, Tex. A.
HOLT, WINIFRED. (S)
Mrs. Rufus Graves Mather.
Am. b. New York; ad. 1915 Same. A12-W14.
HOLTON, LEONARD T. (Ill)
Am. b. Phila., Pa. 1900; ad. 1934 New York. A.
HOLTZBECHER, HANS.
Ger. b. Berlin 1864. B-T.
HOLTZMAN, IRVING.
Am. b. Russia; ad. 1934 Bronx, N. Y. M.
HOLTZMANN, KARL FRIEDRICH.
Ger. Dresden 1740-1811 Same. B-T.
HOLWORTHY, JAMES.
Eng. 1781-1841 London. DNB-T.
HOLY, ADRIEN.
Fr. b. St. Imier; ac. 1935. DBA.
HOLY, KINSHIP.
see Master of the Holy Kinship.
HOLYROYD, [Sir] CHARLES.
Eng. Leeds 1861-1917 Weybridge. B-DNB-E-T.
HÖLZEL, ADOLF RICHARD.
Ger. b. Stuttgart 1853. T.
HOLZER, J. A. (Mu)
Am. b. Berne, Swi. 1858; ad. 1935 New York. A12-B-F.
HOLZHAUER, ÉMIL.
Am. b. Germany 1887; ad. 1934 New York. A.

HOLZHAUSEN, Fritz Freiherr von.
Ger. b. 1857; d. 1923. T.
HOM, George.
Ger. Frankfort 1838-1911 Berlin. B-T.
HOMBERG, Louis Marie.
Fr. b. Paris; d. 1926. DBA.
HOME, Gordon.
Eng. ad. 1935 Epsom, Eng. T.
HOME, Robert.
Eng. London 1752-1836 Calcutta, India. B-DNB-T.
HOME, Robert.
Scot. Edinburgh 1865; ad. 1934 Fife, Scot. Wa.
HOMER, Winslow.
Am. Boston 1836-1910 Scarboro, Mass. A08-B-C-DAB-E-F-T-1-4-5-15-22-32-35-46-51-69-70-71-96-104-105-108-109-127-128-138-172-405-691-697-701-702-748-762-779-807-826.
HOMMEL, Konrad.
Bav. b. Mainz, Ger. 1883; ex. 1933 Pittsburgh, Pa. T.
HONDECOETER Family.
Dut. ac. 15-16 centuries in Holland. T.
HONDECOETER, Gillis [or Jelis] Claesz d'.
Dut. ac. 1602-1638 in Amsterdam. B-T.
HONDECOETER, Gizsbert Gillis d'.
Dut. Utrecht 1604-1653 Same. B-T.
HONDECOETER [or Eondekoeter], Melchior d'.
Dut. Utrecht 1636-1695 Amsterdam. B-Bd-C-E-T-722.
HONDIUS [or de Hondt], Abraham Danielsz.
Dut. Rotterdam 1630/8-1691/5 London. B-Bd-C-DNB-T-722.
HONDIUS, Gerritt.
Am. ad. 1935 Riverdale, N. Y. M.
HONDIUS [or Hond], Hendrik [The Elder].
Dut. Duffel 1573-1662. B-T.
HONDIUS [or Hond], Hendrik [The Younger].
Dut. Amsterdam 1597-1658 London. B-T.
HONDIUS, Jodocus [Joos, or Josse de Hondt].
Dut. Ghent 1563-1611 Amsterdam. DNB-T.
HONDIUS [or Hond], Willem.
Dut. The Hague 1597-1652/8 Danzig, Ger. B-T.
HONE, Horace. (Min)
Eng. b. 1756; d. 1825 in England. B-DNB-T.
HONE, John Camilus. (Min)
Ir. b. 1759; d. 1836 Dublin. B-DNB-T.
HONE, Nathaniel [The Elder].
Ir. Dublin, 1718-1784 London. B-DNB-T.
HONE, Nathaniel [The Younger].
Ir. Dublin 1831-1917 Same. B-DNB-E-T.
HONEL, Jean Pierre Louis Laurent.
Fr. b. 1735; d. 1813 in France. M.
HONG, Anna Helga.
Am. b. Monono Co. Ia. 1894; ad. 1934 Altadena, Calif. A.
HONIG, George H.
Am. b. Rockport, Ind. 1881; ad. 1934 Evanston, Ind. A-F-W-181.
HONORÉ [or Honoratus], Maitre. (Min)
Fr. ac. 1288-1318 in Amiens and Paris. T.
HONORÉ, Paul.
Am. b. Pennsylvania 1885; ad. 1934 Detroit, Mich. A-F-W.
HONTHORST, Gérard van Fiammingo.
Dut. Utrecht 1590-1656 Same. B-C-E-T-722.
HONTHORST, Willem [or Guglielmo] van.
Dut. Utrecht 1594-1666 Same. B-T.
HOOCH [or Hoogh], Charles Cornelisz de.
Dut. ac. 1627-1638 in Utrecht. B-T.
HOOCH [or Hoogh], Horatius de.
Dut. ac. 1652-1692? in Utrecht. B-T.
HOOCH [or Hoogh], Pieter de.
Dut. Rotterdam 1629/32-1677/83 Amsterdam. B-Bd-C-E-T-722.
HOOCH [or Hoogh], Romeyn de.
Dut. Amsterdam 1645/6-1708 Haarlem. B-T.
HOOD, George Washington. (Ill)
Am. ad. 1934 Weehawken, N. J. A.
HOOG, Barnard de.
Dut. b. Holland 1867. B-T.
HOOGENBERG. *see* Hogenberg.
HOOGH or HOOGHE. *see* Hooch.
HOOGHLAND, William. (Eg)
Am. ac. 1815-1841 New York. F-T-2-7-40-147.
HOOGSTAETEN, Jan [or Hans] van.
Dut. The Hague 1629/31-1654 Vienna, Aus. B-T.
HOOGSTRATEN, Dirk van.
Flem. Antwerp 1595/6-1640. B-T.
HOOGSTRATEN, Jan [or Hans].
Flem. 1568-1605 Antwerp. B-T.
HOOGSTRATEN, Samuel Dirksz van.
Dut. Dordrecht 1627-1678 Same. B-C-E-T-722.
HOOK, James Clarke.
Eng. London 1819-1907 Churt, Eng. B-C-DNB-E-T.
HOOK, Rosalie.
Am. ad. 1935 New York. M.
HOOKER, Helen M.
Am. ad. 1935 Greenwich, Conn. M.
HOOKER, Margaret Huntington. (Ill)
Am. b. Rochester, N. Y. 1869; ad. 1915 Same. A12-F-W9.
HOOKER, William. (Eg)
Am. ac. 1804-1846 in New York. DAB-F-T-2-7-169.
HOOL, Johannes Baptista van. (S)
Belg. Antwerp 1769-1837. Hs-T.
HOOPER, [Mrs.] Annie Blakeslee.
Am. b. Calif.; ac. 1931 in New York. A28-B.
HOOPER, Edward. (Eg)
Am. London, Eng. 1829-1870 Brooklyn, N. Y. F.
HOOPER, Elizabeth.
Am. b. Balt., Md. 1901; ad. 1934 Same. A.
HOOPER, John Horace.
Eng. ac. 1870-1891 in London. B-T.
HOOPER, Luther.
Eng. 1849-1932 London. B-Y01933.
HOOPER, Rosa. (Min)
Am. b. San Fran., Calif. 1876; ad. 1934 New York. A.
HOOPER, Will Phillip.
Am. b. Biddeford, Me.; ad. 1934 Forest Hills, N. Y. A-F.
HOOPES, Elizabeth.
Am. ad. 1935 New York. M.

HOOPES, [Mrs.] HENRIETTA.
Am. ex. 1934 in Paris. M.
HOOPLE, WILLIAM CLIFFORD. (Ill)
Am. b. Brooklyn, N. Y. 1893; ad. 1934 New York. A.
HOORN, JORDANUS.
Dut. Amersfoort 1753-1833 Same. B-T.
HOOVEN, HERBERT NELSON.
Am. b. Hazelton, Pa. 1898; ad. 1934 Athens, O. A.
HOOVER, CHARLES.
Am. b. Wash., D. C. 1897; ad. 1934 Same. A.
HOOVER, [Mrs.] JAY F.
Am. ad. 1934 Buffalo, N. Y. M.
HOOVER, [Mrs.] LOUISE ROCHON.
Am. b. Wash., D. C. 1898; ad. 1934 Same. A.
HOOVER, MARY AUGUSTA.
Am. ad. 1935 New York. M.
HOPE, JAMES.
Am. Abbotsford, Scot. 1818-1892 New York. F.
HOPE, LEONA.
Am. b. Meadville, Pa. 1873; ad. 1915 Madison, Wis. A12.
HOPE, ROBERT.
Scot. b. Edinburgh 1869; ad. 1934 Same. Wa.
HOPE, THELMA PADDOCK.
Am. b. La Porte, Ind. 1898; ad. 1934 Beverly Hills, Calif. A.
HOPE, THOMAS H.
Am. b. England; d. 1926 Devon, Conn. A023.
HOPE, THOMAS W.
Am. ac. 1839-1845 in New York. F-2-6.
HOPE, WILLIAM.
Can. b. Montreal, Que. 1863; d. 1931. Y01932.
HOPE-PINKER, HENRY RICHARD. (S)
Eng. 1850-1927 London. B-Y01928-T.
HOPFER, DANIEL [The Elder].
Ger. 1470-1536 Augsburg. B-T.
HOPFER [or Hopffer], HIERONYMUS.
Ger. ac. 1520-1550 in Augsburg, Ger. B-T.
HOPKIN, ROBERT.
Am. Glasgow, Scot. 1832-1909 Detroit, Mich. A07-B-F-T-46.
HOPKINS, ANNA MARY. (Min)
Am. ad. 1934 Lansdowne, Pa. M.
HOPKINS, ARTHUR.
Eng. 1848-1930 London. B-Wa1929-Y01931.
HOPKINS, CHARLES BENJAMIN.
Am. b. Toledo, O. 1882; ad. 1934 Marysville, Calif. A.
HOPKINS, EDNA BOIES.
Mrs. James R. Hopkins.
Am. b. Hudson, Mich. 1878; ad. 1933 Paris, Fr. A28-F-T-W-46.
HOPKINS, ELEANOR F.
Am. ad. 1935 New York. M.
HOPKINS, FRANCES ANN.
Eng. b. 1856; d. 1919 in England. Y01920.
HOPKINS, GEORGE EDWARD.
Am. b. Covington, Ky. 1855; ad. 1915 Raleigh, N. C. A12-B.
HOPKINS, JAMES R.
Am. b. Ohio 1878; ad. 1934 Columbus, O. A-B-F-T-W.
HOPKINS, MARK. (S)
Am. b. Williamstown, Mass. 1881; d. 1935 Pau, France.
A28-B-Obit. N. Y. papers, 6-26-1935.
HOPKINSON, CHARLES SYDNEY.
Am. b. Cambridge, Mass. 1869; ad. 1935 Boston. A-B-F-T-W-1.
HOPPE [or Hoeppe], FERDINAND BERNHARDT.
Dut. b. Cleves, Ger. 1841. B-T.
HOPPER, EDWARD.
Am. b. Nyack, N. Y. 1882; ad. 1935 New York. A-F-105-406-701-779-835.
HOPPER, HUMPHREY. (S)
Eng. ex. 1799-1834 in London. B-DNB-T.
HOPPIN, AUGUSTUS. (Ill)
Am. Prov., R. I. 1828-1896 Flushing, L. I., N. Y. B-DAB-F-4-15-55-110.
HOPPIN, THOMAS FREDERICK. (Et)
Am. b. Prov., R. I. 1816. [No death date.] B-F-T-4-7.
HOPPNER, JOHN.
Eng. London 1758-1810 Same.
B-Bd-DNB-E-T-722-723.
HOPSON, WILLIAM FOWLER. (Eg)
Am. b. Watertown, Conn. 1849; d. 1935 New Haven, Conn.
A28-B-F-T-W-Obit. N. Y. papers, 2-14-1935.
HOPWOOD, HENRY SILKSTONE.
Eng. Markfield, Eng. 1860-1914 Edinburgh, Scot. B-T.
HOPWOOD, WILLIAM. (Eg)
Br. b. 1784; d. 1853. DNB-T.
HÖRBERG, PEHR.
Swe. Småland 1746-1816. B-T.
HORCHERT, JOSEPH A. (S)
Am. b. Hechingen, Ger. 1874; ad. 1934 St. Louis, Mo. A.
HORCZICKA, FRANZ.
Ger. Prague, Czec. 1776-1856 Same. C-T.
HORD, DONAL. (S)
Am. b. Wisconsin 1902; ad. 1934 Santa Barbara, Calif. A-Cs.
HORDYK, GERARD.
Dut. b. The Hague; ad. 1935 Scarsdale, N. Y. M.
HOREAU, HECTOR.
Fr. b. 1801; d. 1872 in France. M.
HOREBOUT. *see* Hornebolt.
HOREMANS, JAN JOSEPH [The Elder].
Flem. Antwerp 1682-1759 Same. B-C-T.
HOREMANS, JAN JOSEPH [The Younger].
Flem. Antwerp 1714-1790/1 Same. B-C-T.
HOREMANS, PIETER JACOB.
Flem. Antwerp 1700-1776 Munich, Ger. B-T.
HORN, MILTON. (S)
Am. b. Russia 1905; ad. 1934 New York. A.
HORNBOSTEL, RUTH. (S)
Am. ex. 1933 in Paris. M.
HORNBROOK, T. L.
Eng. ac. 1836-1864 in London. T.
HORNBY, LESTER GEORGE. (Et)
Am. b. Lowell, Mass. 1882; ad. 1934 Paris. A28-F-T-W-46.
HORNE, LAURA TREVITTE.
Am. b. Dalton, Ga. 1891; ad. 1934 New York. A.

HORNEBOLT [or Hoorenbault], GERARD.
Eng. Ghent, Belg. 1480?-1550 London. B-DNB-T.
HORNEBOLT [or Hoorenbault], LUCAS.
Eng. ac. 1534-1544 in London. DNB-T.
HORNEBOLT, SUSANNA. (Min)
Mrs. Parker.
Eng. b. 1503; d. 1545 Worcester, Eng. B-T.
HORNEL, EDWARD ATKINSON.
Aust. b. Victoria, Aust. 1864. B-T.
HORNEMAN, CHRISTIAN.
Dan. Copenhagen 1765-1844 Same. B-T.
HOROWITZ, FRANK.
Am. b. Odessa, Rus. 1889; ad. 1934 New York. A.
HORSBURGH, JOHN. (Eg)
Scot. Edinburgh 1791-1869 Same. DNB-T.
HORSCHELT, THEODOR.
Ger. Munich 1829-1871 Same. C-T.
HORSFALL, CAROLYN SARAH.
Am. b. Hartford, Conn. 1901; ad. 1934 Same. A.
HORSFALL, ROBERT BRUCE.
Am. b. Clinton, Ia. 1869; ad. 1934 Wash., D. C. F-T-W.
HORSLEY, JOHN CALLCOTT.
Eng. London 1817-1903 Kensington. B-C-DNB-E-T.
HORST, ÉMIL CARL WILHELM.
Ger. Hamburg 1854-1910. T.
HORST, GERRIT WILLEMSZ.
Dut. b. 1612; d. 1667. B-T.
HORST, NICOLAUS VAN DER.
Flem. Antwerp 1598-1646 Brussels. B-T.
HORTER, CHARLES ORSON.
Am. b. Hayward, Calif. 1896; ad. 1935 Oakland, Calif. M.
HORTER, EARL. (Ill)
Am. b. 1881; ad. 1934 Phila., Pa. A-F.
HORTON, DOROTHY E.
Mrs. T. J. Stewart.
Am. b. Poplar Bluff, Mo. 1898; ad. 1934 Erie, Pa. A.
HORTON, ELIZABETH SUMMER.
Am. b. Boston, Mass. 1902; ad. 1934 Brookline, Mass. A.
HORTON, HARRIET HUTCHINSON.
Am. d. 1922 St. Paul, Minn. A019-F-T.
HORTON, WILLIAM SAMUEL.
Am. b. Grand Rapids, Mich. 1865; ad. 1934 Paris, Fr. A-B-F-T-W-46.
HORVATH, FERDINAND HUSZTI.
Am. ad. 1934 New York. A.
HOSEMANN, FREDERICK WILHELM THÉODOR.
Ger. Brandenburg 1807-1875 Berlin. B-C-T.
HOSFORD, HARRY LINDLEY.
Am. b. Terre Haute, Ind. 1877; ad. 1935 St. Paul, Minn. W.
HOSIASSON, PHILIPPE.
Fr. b. Odessa, Rus. 1898; ad. 1934 Paris. DBA.
HOSKIN, ROBERT. (Eg)
Am. b. Brooklyn, N. Y. 1842; ad. 1883 Paris. F-8-185.
HOSKINS, GAYLE PORTER. (Ill)
Am. b. Brazil, Ind. 1887; ad. 1934 Wilmington, Del. A.
HOSKINS, JOHN [The Elder]. (Min)
Eng. ac. 1620-1664; d. in London. B-Bd-DNB-E-T.
HOSKINS, JOHN [The Younger]. (Min)
Eng. ac. 1686-1700 in London. B-Bd-E-T.
HOSMER, HARRIET GOODHUE. (S)
Am. Watertown, Mass. 1830-1908 Same. A07-B-DAB-E-F-Hs-T-Ta-15-46-111-932.
HOSSLIN. *see* Hoesslin.
HOTCHKIS, ISABEL.
Scot. b. Scotland; ad. 1934 Liverpool, Eng. Wa.
HOTCHKISS, T. H.
Am. b. 1857 [Deceased]. M.
HOTCHKISS, WALES.
Am. b. Bethany, Conn. 1826. [No death date.] F-3-4.
HOTTINGER, WILLIAM A. (Ill)
Am. ad. 1934 Chicago, Ill. A.
HOTVEDT, CLARENCE ARNOLD.
Am. b. Eau Claire, Wis. 1900; ad. 1934 Wichita, Kan. A.
HOUASSE [or Ouasse], MICHELE ANGE.
Fr. Paris 1680-1730 Arpajon. B-C-T.
HOUASSE [or Ouasse], RENÉ ANTOINE.
Fr. Paris 1644/5-1710 Same. B-T.
HOUBRAKEN, ARNOLD.
Dut. Dordrecht 1660-1719 Amsterdam. B-C-T-722.
HOUBRAKEN, JACOBUS.
Dut. Dordrecht 1698-1780 Amsterdam. B-E-T.
HOUCKGEEST, GERARD JORISZ.
Dut. The Hague 1600-1661. B-T.
HOUDON, JEAN ANTOINE. (S)
Fr. Versailles 1741-1828 Paris. B-E-F-Hs-T-2-182-191-407-786.
HOUEL, JEAN PIERRE LOUIS LAURENT.
Fr. Rouen 1735-1813 Paris. B-T.
HOUGH, RUTH BEVERLY.
Am. b. Crescent, Ia. 1899; ad. 1934 Council Bluffs, Ia. A.
HOUGH, WALTER.
Am. Morgantown, W. Va. 1859; ad. 1934 Wash., D. C. A.
HOUGHTON, ARTHUR BOYD. (Ill-Min.)
Eng. 1836-1875 Hampstead. B-DNB-T-880.
HOUGHTON, MAY P.
Am. b. Tuscaloosa, Ala. 1878. M.
HOULAHAN, KATHLEEN.
Am. b. Winnipeg, Can. 1887; ad. 1934 Seattle, Wash. A.
HOURDEBAIGHT, [Miss].
Am. ex. 1935 New York. M.
HOUSE, JAMES, JR. (S)
Am. b. Benton Harbor, Mich. 1902; ad. 1934 Phila., Pa. A.
HOUSER, IVAN. (S)
Am. b. Pendleton, Ore. 1901; ad. 1934 Keystone, S. D. M.
HOUSER, LOWELL.
Am. ad. 1935 Ames, Iowa. M.
HOUSH, CARTER.
Am. b. 1887; d. 1928. A028.
HOUSSIN, ÉDOUARD CHARLES MARIE. (S)
Fr. Douai 1847-1917 Paris. B-DNB-T.
HOUSTON, CAROLINE A. (Min)
Am. b. Brooklyn, N. Y. 1871. B-T.

HOUSTON, Frances C.
Mrs. William C. Houston.
Am. Hudson, Mich. 1867-1906 Windsor, Vt. A06-B-F-46.
HOUSTON, George.
Scot. b. Dalry, Scot. 1869. B-Wa1929.
HOUSTON, Grace.
Am. b. Marysville, O.; ad. 1934 Indiana, Pa. A.
HOUSTON, H. H. (Eg)
Am. b. Ireland; ac. 1798 in Phila., Pa. F-T-2-7-40-147.
HOUSTON, John Adam.
Scot. Galles 1813-1884 London. B-T.
HOUSTON, Nora.
Am. ad. 1934 Richmond, Va. A.
HOUSTON, Richard. (Eg)
Ir. Dublin 1721-1775 London. B-DNB-T.
HOUSTON, Robert.
Scot. b. Kilbirnie 1891; ad. 1934 Glasgow, Scot. Wa.
HOVE, Bartholomeus Johannes van.
Dut. The Hague 1790-1880 Same. B-T.
HOVE, Edward Thedov van.
Flem. b. Bruges, Belg. 1852. B-T.
HOVE, Hubertus van.
Dut. The Hague 1814-1865 Antwerp, Belg. B-T.
HOVELL, Joseph. (S)
Am. b. Kiev, Rus. 1897; ad. 1934 New York. M.
HOVENDEN, Martha. (S)
Am. b. Plymouth Meeting, Pa. 1884; ac. 1934 Same. A.
HOVENDEN, Thomas.
Am. Cork, Ir. 1840-1895 Plymouth Meeting, Pa. B-C-E-F-T-1-15-46.
HOVER, [Mrs.] Lillian Sooy.
Am. b. Colorado Springs, Colo. 1889; ad. 1934 New York. A.
HOW, Julia Beatrice.
Eng. b. England 1867; d. 1932 in Paris. B-T-Wa1929-Y01933-828.
HOW, Kenneth G.
Am. ad. 1934 Coral Gables, Fla. M.
HOWARD, Cecil de Blaquiere. (S)
Am. b. Canada 1888; ex. 1934 New York. Cs-F.
HOWARD, Clara Frances. (Min)
Am. b. Poughkeepsie, N. Y. 1866; ad. 1934 Same. A.
HOWARD, Eloise.
Am. b. Pine Village, Ore. 1889; ad. 1934 Woodstock, N. Y. A-F.
HOWARD, Ethel Lucile.
Am. b. Bellow Falls, Vt.; ad. 1934 Wilmington, Del. A.
HOWARD, E. Sterling.
Eng. ac. 1834-1870 in Sheffield, Eng. B-T.
HOWARD, Florence.
Am. d. 1914 in Colorado Springs, Colo. A0X1.
HOWARD, Francis. (Eg)
Eng. 1759-1797 Lambeth. DNB-T.
HOWARD, Francis.
Eng. b. 1874; ac. 1929 London. B-Wa.
HOWARD, Frank.
Eng. London 1805?-1866 Liverpool. DNB-T.
HOWARD, George James.
Eng. London 1843-1911 Surrey. DNB.
HOWARD, Henry.
Eng. London 1769-1847 Oxford, Eng. B-Bd-C-DNB-T-722.
HOWARD, [Miss] Howell.
Am. ex. 1935 Dayton, O. M.
HOWARD, Hugh.
Ir. Dublin 1675-1737 London. DNB-T.
HOWARD, Hugh Huntington.
Am. Cherry Valley, O. 1860-1927 Cleveland, O. A024-B.
HOWARD, Loretta Hines.
Am. b. Chicago, Ill. 1905; ad. 1934 Dayton, O. A.
HOWARD, Marion.
Am. b. Roxbury, Mass. 1883; ad. 1915 Boston. A12-F.
HOWARD, Oscar F. (Ill)
Am. ad. 1934 New York. M.
HOWARTH, Albany E.
Eng. b. 1872; ad. 1934 Watford, Eng. T-Wa.
HOWE, Arthur Virgil.
Am. b. 1860; d. 1925 Troy, N. Y. A022-F.
HOWE, George. (Ill)
Am. ad. 1935 New York. M.
HOWE, Gurdon S.
Am. ad. 1935 New York. M.
HOWE, James.
Scot. Stirling 1780-1836 Edinburgh. DNB-T.
HOWE, William Henry.
Am. Ravenna, O. 1846-1929 Bronxville, N. Y. A026-B-DAB-F-T-W14-46.
HOWELL, Alfred. (S)
Can. b. Oldbury, Eng.; ad. 1935 Toronto, Ont. Can. M.
HOWELL, Edward A.
Am. Phoenixville, Pa. 1848-1924 Reading, Pa. M.
HOWELL, Felicie Waldo.
Am. b. Honolulu, Hawaii 1897; ad. 1934 New York. A-F.
HOWELLS, Alice Imogen.
Am. b. Pittsburgh, Pa.; ad. 1934 East Orange, N. J. A.
HOWELLS, Mildred. (Ill)
Am. b. Cambridge, Mass. 1872; ad. 1934 York Harbor, Me. W.
HOWES, John. (Min)
Eng. ac. 1772-1793 in London. DNB-T.
HOWISON [or Howieson], William. (Eg)
[First engraver elected to membership in the Scot. Acad. of Edinburgh.]
Scot. Edinburgh 1798-1850 Same. DNB-T.
HOWITT, John Newton.
Am. b. White Plains, N. Y. 1885; ad. 1934 Same. A.
HOWITT, Samuel. (Et)
Eng. 1765-1822 London. B-DNB-T.
HOWLAND, Alfred Cornelius.
Am. Walpole, N. H. 1838-1909 Pasadena, Calif. A07-B-C-DAB-F-T-15-112.
HOWLAND, [Mrs.] Anna Goodhart.
Am. b. Atchison, Kan. 1871; ad. 1934 Wash., D. C. A.
HOWLAND, Edith. (S)
Am. b. Auburn, N. Y.; ad. 1934 Catskill, N. Y. A-Cs-F.
HOWLAND, George.
Am. New York 1865-1928 France. A025-B-F-T.

HOWLAND, Isabella.
Am. b. Brookline, Mass. 1895; ad. 1934 Woodstock, N. Y. A.
HOWLETT, Bartholomeo. (Eg)
Eng. Louth 1767-1827 Newington, Eng. DNB-T.
HOWORTH, Louise.
Am. ad. 1935 Meridian, Miss. M.
HOWS, John Augustus.
Am. New York 1832-1874 Same. B-Bd-F-15.
HOXIE, Vinnie Ream. (S)
[First woman to execute sculpture for the U. S. Government.]
Mrs. Richard L. Hoxie.
Am. Madison, Wis. 1847-1914 Wash., D. C. A012-DAB-F-Ta-W8-26-113.
HOYDEN, Nishijama.
Jap. 1803-1867 Osaka. J., Vol. 2, page 104.
HOYSTRADT, Emily.
Am. ad. 1935 Kingston, N. Y. M.
HOYT, Andrew J.
Am. 1847-1919 Phila., Pa. A016.
HOYT, Edith.
Am. b. West Point, N. Y. 1890; ad. 1934 Wash., D. C. A.
HOYT, Henry E.
Am. d. 1906 Germantown, Pa. A06.
HOYT, Henry Martyn.
Am. Rosemont, Pa. 1887-1920 New York. A017.
HOYT, Hettie J.
Am. b. Harvard, Ill.; ad. 1934 Stamford, Conn. A.
HOYT, Margaret Howard Yeaton.
Am. b. Balt., Md. 1885; ad. 1934 Lexington, Va. A.
HOYTEMS [or Hoytemo], Th. van.
Dut. b. The Hague; ac. 19th Cent. B-T.
HSIA KÜEI.
Chinese. ac. 12th Cent. E.
HSI-CHIN CHU-SHIL.
Chinese. Sung Dynasty [960-1280]. M.
HSIEH HO.
Chinese. ac. 6th Cent. E.
HSÜ HSI.
Chinese. ac. 900-960. E.
HUANG CH'UAN.
Chinese. ac. 900-960. E.
HUANG KUNG-WANG.
Chinese. Yuan Period [1260-1368]. E.
HUAS, Pierre Adolfe.
Fr. La Rochelle 1838-1900 Paris. B-T.
HUBACHER, Hermann.
Swi. b. Biel 1885. T-682.
HUBBARD, Charles Daniel.
Am. b. Newark, N. J. 1876; ad. 1934 Guilford, Conn. A.
HUBBARD, Eric Hesketh.
Eng. b. London 1892; ad. 1934 Same. Wa.
HUBBARD, Florence T.
Am. ad. 1934 Jackson Heights, N. Y. M.
HUBBARD, Frank McKinney ["Kin"]. (Cari)
Am. Bellefontaine, O. 1868-1930 Indianapolis, Ind. DAB-W14-114.
HUBBARD, Hesketh.
Eng. b. London 1892; ad. 1934 Same. Wa.
HUBBARD, Mary Wilson.
Am. b. Springfield, Mass. 1871; ad. 1934 New York. A.
HUBBARD, Platt.
Am. b. Columbus, O. 1889; ad. 1934 Old Lyme, Conn. A.
HUBBARD, Richard William.
Am. Middletown, Conn. 1817-1888 Bronxville, N. Y. C-DAB-F-T-2-3-4-15-115.
HUBBARD, Whitney Myron.
Am. Middletown, Conn. 1875; ad. 1934 Greenport, N. Y. A.
HUBBARD, William James.
Am. England 1807-1862 Richmond, Va. F-T-2.
HUBBELL, Henry Salem.
Am. b. Paolo, Kan. 1870; ad. 1934 Miami, Fla. A-B-F-T-W-46.
HUBER, C. Rudolf.
Aus. b. Schleinz 1839; d. 1898. B-T.
HUBER, Ernst.
Aus. b. Vienna 1895; ad. 1935 Same; ex. 1934 Pittsburgh, Pa. M-T.
HUBER, Johann Rudolf [The Elder].
Swi. 1668-1748 Geneva. Bd-T.
HUBER, Johann Rudolf [The Younger].
Swi. Geneva 1722-1786. B-C-T.
HUBER, Leo.
Am. b. Switzerland; ad. 1935 Jamaica, L. I., N. Y. M.
HUBER, Léon Charles.
Fr. Paris 1858-1928 Same. B-DBA-T.
HUBER, Wilhelm.
Swi. Zurich 1788-1879. B-T.
HUBER, Wolfgang [or Wolf].
Ger. b. 1490; d. 1553. B-T-803.
HUBERLAND, Jeannette.
Fr. b. Aubergenville 1904. DBA.
HUBERT, Jean Baptiste Louis.
Fr. b. Paris 1801. [No death date.] B-T.
HUBERT-ROBERT, Marius.
see also Robert, Hubert.
Fr. b. Paris; ac. 1929 Same. DBA.
HÜBNER [or Hüebner], Bartholomé. (Eg)
Ger. Augsburg 1727-1755. B-T.
HÜBNER [or Hüebner], Karl Wilhelm.
Ger. Königsberg 1814-1879 Düsseldorf. B-C-T.
HÜBNER, Rudolph Jules Benno.
Ger. Ols 1806-1882 Loschnitz. B-C-T.
HÜBNER, Ulrich.
Ger. b. Berlin 1872. B-T.
HUCHTENBURG [or Hughtenburg], Jan van.
Dut. Haarlem 1646-1733 Amsterdam. B-C-E-T-722.
HUDSON, Charles Bradford.
Am. b. Ontario, Can. 1865; ac. 1934 Pacific Grove, Calif. A.
HUDSON, Charles William.
Am. b. Boston 1871; ad. 1934 Same. A.
HUDSON, Edith Frazier.
Am. b. Centralia, Ill.; ad. 1934 Dallas, Tex. A.
HUDSON, Elmer Forrest.
Am. b. Boston 1862; ad. 1934 Monhegan Island, Me. A.
HUDSON, Eric.
Am. b. Boston; d. 1932 Rockport, Mass. A029-F-906.

HUDSON, [Mrs.] HENRIETTA. (Ill)
Am. b. Hudson City, N. J. 1862; ad. 1934 Bolton Landing, N. Y. A.
HUDSON, HENRY. (Eg)
Eng. ac. 1784-1800 in London. DNB-T.
HUDSON, HENRY JOHN.
Eng. ac. 1881 in London. B-T.
HUDSON, JERRY.
Am. ex. 1934 Minneapolis, Minn. M.
HUDSON, MABEL RUTH.
Am. ad. 1934 New York. M.
HUDSON, N.
Eng. ac. 1782. Fa-M.
HUDSON, THOMAS.
Eng. Devonshire 1701-1779 Twickenham, Eng. B-C-DNB-T.
HUDSPETH, ROBERT NORMAN. (S)
Am. Canada 1862; ad. 1934 Concord, Mass. A-F.
HUÉ, CHARLES DÉSIRÉ.
Fr. b. Meaux; ac. 19th Cent. B-T.
HUÉ, JEAN FRANÇOIS.
Fr. St. Arnould 1751-1823 Paris. B-C-T.
HUEBNER. *see* Hubner.
HUERTA, JUÁN DE LA. (S)
Sp. ac. 1437-1462 in Spain. Hs-T.
HUET, CHRISTOPE [not Charles].
Fr. ac. 1735-1759 in Paris. B-T.
HUET, JEAN BAPTISTE.
Fr. Paris 1745-1811 Same. B-C-T-722-900.
HUET, PAUL.
Fr. Paris 1803-1869 Same. B-T.
HUEY, ALICE.
Am. ad. 1935 St. Paul, Minn. M.
HUEY, FLORENCE GREENE.
Mrs. J. Wistar Huey.
Am. b. Phila., Pa.; ad. 1934 Ruxton, Md. A.
HUEZ, JEAN BAPTISTE CYPRIEN D'. (S)
Fr. Arras 1728-1793 Paris. B-T.
HUF, KARL PHILIP.
Am. b. Phila., Pa. 1887; ad. 1934 Same. A.
HUFF, WILLIAM GORDON. (S)
Am. b. Fresno, Calif. 1903; ad. 1934 Berkeley, Calif. A-Cs.
HUFFINGTON, JOHN C.
Am. Brooklyn, N. Y. 1864-1929 Darien, Conn. A026.
HUFNAGEL, JORIS.
see Hoefnagel, Joris [or Georg].
HUGENHOLTZ, [Miss] ARINA.
Dut. Haarlem 1849-1934 Lauren. M.
HUGER, EMILY HAMILTON.
Am. b. New Orleans, La. 1881; ad. 1934 Lafayette, La. A.
HUGFORD, IGNAZIO ENRICO.
Eng. Pisa, It. 1703-1778 Florence, It. B-DNB-T.
HUGGINS, WILLIAM JAMES.
Eng. Liverpool 1820-1884 Christleton, Eng. B-DNB-T.
HUGGINS, WILLIAM JOHN.
Eng. 1781-1845 London. B-DNB-T.
HUGGLER, ARNOLD. (S)
Swi. b. Brienz 1894. DBA.
HUGHES, ARTHUR.
Eng. London 1832-1915 Kew Green. B-DNB-T.
HUGHES, ARTHUR FOORD.
Eng. b. 1878; d. 1914. T.
HUGHES, DAISY M.
Am. b. Los Angeles, Calif. 1883; ad. 1934 Same. A-DBA-F.
HUGHES, DONALD.
Eng. b. Clifton 1881; ad. 1935 Same. Wa.
HUGHES, EDWARD.
Eng. Pentonville 1832-1908 London. DNB.
HUGHES, EDWARD ROBERT.
Eng. b. 1851; d. 1914. B-T.
HUGHES, [Mrs.] ELEANOR.
Aust. b. New Zealand 1882; ad. 1934 Cornwall, Eng. Wa1929.
HUGHES, ELFRIDA THARLE.
Am. ad. 1935 London. M.
HUGHES, [Dr.] FREDERICK J.
Am. ad. 1934 Plainfield, N. J. M.
HUGHES, GEORGE.
Am. Albany, N. Y. 1863-1932 Same. A029.
HUGHES, GEORGE.
Eng. ac. 1813-1858 in England. B-T.
HUGHES, HUGH.
Welsh. b. Wales 1790?; d. 1863 Great Malvern. DNB-T.
HUGHES, JOHN. (S)
Ir. b. Dublin 1849. B-T.
HUGHES, JOHN.
Welsh. b. Wales 1790; d. 1857 London. DNB-T.
HUGHES, [Miss] MYRA K. (Et)
Ir. d. 1918 London. M.
HUGHES, PHILIPPA.
Am. ad. 1934 Provincetown, Mass. M.
HUGHES, ROBERT BALL. (S)
Am. London 1806-1868 Boston, Mass. DAB-DNB-F-Hs-Ta-2-15-116-117-118-119.
HUGHES, ROY V.
Am. b. Elmira, N. Y. 1879; ad. 1934 Pittsburgh, Pa. A.
HUGHES, WILLIAM. (Eg)
Eng. Liverpool 1793-1825 Lambeth. DNB-T.
HUGHES-MARTIN, [Mrs.] AGNES.
Am. Ireland 1898-1930 Boston. A028.
HUGHES-STANTON, BLAIR ROWLANDS. (Eg)
Eng. b. London 1902; ad. 1935 Same. Wa.
HUGHES-STANTON, GERTRUDE.
see Hermes, Gertrude Anna Bertha.
HUGHES-STANTON, [Sir] HERBERT EDWIN PELHAM.
Eng. b. Chelsea 1870. B-DBA-T.
HUGHTENBURGH, JAN VAN.
see Huchtenburg, Jan van.
HUGO, GEORGES VICTOR.
Fr. b. 1867; d. 1925. M.
HUGO, JEAN.
Fr. b. Paris 1894; ex. 1933 New York. DBA-M.
HUGUES DE BEAUMONT.
see Beaumont, Hugues de.
HUGUET, JAIME [or Jaume].
Sp. ac. 1448-1487 in Spain. 409.
HUGUET, VICTOR PIERRE.
Fr. b. Lude 1835; d. 1902. B-T.
HUGUET-VERGOS. *see* Vergos, Jaime II.
HUILLARD, ESTHER.
Fr. b. Sedan; ac. 20th Cent. B-T.
HUI TSUNG.
Chinese. b. 1082; d. 1135. E.
HUKAN, KAROL. (S)
Pol. b. Crakow 1888. T-798.

HULBERT, Charles Allen.
Am. b. Mackinaw Island, Mich.; ad. 1934 So. Egremont, Mass. A.
HULBERT, Katherine Allmond.
Mrs. Charles Allen Hulbert.
Am. b. Sacramento Valley, Calif.; ad. 1934 So. Egremont, Mass. A.
HULK, John F.
Dut. b. Haarlem, Holland 1855. B-T.
HULL, Lester Theodore.
Am. b. Chicago, Ill. 1890; ad. 1934 Same. A.
HULL, [Mrs.] Marie Atkinson.
Am. b. Summit, Miss. 1890; ad. 1934 Jackson, Miss. A-F.
HULL, William.
Br. Graffham 1820-1880 Rydal. DNB-T.
HULLMANDEL, Charles Joseph. (Eg)
Eng. London 1789-1850. DNB-T.
HULME, Frederick Edward.
Eng. Hanley 1841-1909 Kew, Eng. DNB.
HULME, Frederick William.
Eng. Swinton 1816-1884 London. B-DNB-T.
HULME, James Sanford.
Am. ad. 1934 New York. M.
HULSBERG, Henry. (Eg)
Dut. b. Amsterdam; d. 1729 in London. B-DNB-T.
HUMBERT, Jacques Charles Ferdinand.
Fr. b. Paris 1842; d. 1934 B-C-DBA-T.
HUMBOLT, Émile Joseph.
Fr. b. Joinville 1862; d. 1931. B-DBA-T.
HUMES, Ralph Hamilton. (S)
Am. b. Phila., Pa. 1902; ad. 1934 Shrewsbury, N. J. A.
HUMFELD, Marion Aiken.
Am. ad. 1935 So. Car.; ex. 1935 New York. M.
HUMMERSTONE, Philip. (Ill)
Am. b. New York 1905; ad. 1934 Long Island City, N. Y. M.
HUMPHREY, David W.
Am. b. Elkhorn, Wis. 1872; ad. 1915 Chicago. A12-F.
HUMPHREY, Ozias.
Eng. Honiton 1742-1810 London. B-Bd-DNB-E-T-410.
HUMPHREY, Walter Beach. (Ill)
Am. ad. 1934 New Rochelle, N. Y. A.
HUMPHREY, William. (Eg)
Eng. 1740-1810? London. DNB-T.
HUMPHREYS, Albert.
Am. b. Cinn., O.; ad. 1926 New York. A12-F.
HUMPHREYS, [Mrs.] Beatrice Jackson.
Am. b. London 1905; ad. 1934 Paris. M.
HUMPHREYS, David.
Am. b. Morristown, N. J.; ad. 1934 Paris, Fr. A-DBA.
HUMPHREYS, Henry Nöel. (Ill)
Eng. Birmingham 1810-1879 London. DNB-T.
HUMPHREYS, Malcolm.
Am. b. Morristown, N. J. 1894; ad. 1934 Same. A-DBA.
HUMPHREYS, Marie Champney.
Mrs. John Sanford Humphreys.
Am. Deerfield, Mass. 1867-1906 New Rochelle, N. Y. A06-B-F-T-46.
HUMPHREYS, Philip Callon.
Eng. ad. 1933 London. M.
HUMPHREYS, Sallie Thompson.
Am. ad. 1934 Delaware, O. A29.
HUMPHREYS, William. (Eg)
Ir. Dublin 1793-1865 Genoa, It. B-Bd-DNB-F-T-2-7.
HUMPHREYS-JOHNSTON, John.
see Johnston, J. H.
HUMPHRIES, Charles H. (S)
Am. b. England 1867; ad. 1934 New York. A-F-W.
HUNDLEIGH, William T.
Am. Central, Ky. 1848-1916 Georgetown, Ky. A014.
HÜNERWADEL, Arnold. (S)
Swiss. b. Lenzburg 1877. T.
HUNGERFORD, Marian.
Am. ad. 1935 New Britain, Conn. M.
HUNLEY, Katherine J.
Am. b. Beacon, Ia. 1883; ad. 1934 Redlands, Calif. A.
HUNNER, Isabella Stevens.
Am. b. Balt., Md. 1903; ad. 1934 Same. A.
HUNT, Alfred William.
Eng. Liverpool 1830-1896 London. B-Bd-DNB-E-T.
HUNT, Andrew.
Eng. Erdington 1790-1861 Liverpool. B-DNB-T.
HUNT, Cecil Arthur.
Eng. b. Torquay 1873; ad. 1934 London. Wa.
HUNT, Charles. (Eg)
Br. b. 1803; d. 1877. B-T-97-735-880.
HUNT, Charles D.
Am. Detroit, Mich. 1840-1914 Brooklyn, N. Y. A0X1-T.
HUNT, Clyde Du Vernet. (S)
Am. b. Glasgow, Scot. 1861; ac. 1930 Paris. DBA-F-W15.
HUNT, Dorothy H. W.
Am. ad. 1934 Prov., R. I. M.
HUNT, Esther.
Am. b. Nebraska 1885; ad. 1934 New York. A.
HUNT, E. Aubrey.
Am. Weymouth, Mass. 1855-1922 England. A020-B-T.
HUNT, Eugenia Howard.
Am. ad. 1934 Houston, Tex. M.
HUNT, George. (Eg)
Eng. ac. 1820/45 in London. T-97-735-880.
HUNT, Leigh. (Et)
Am. b. Galena, Ill. 1858. A28-B-F.
HUNT, Lynn Bogue. (Ill)
Am. ac. in New York 1931. A28.
HUNT, [Mrs.] Mabelle Alcott.
Am. b. New York 1898; ad. 1934 Savannah, Ga. A.
HUNT, Samuel Valentine. (Eg)
Am. England 1803-1893 Bay Ridge, L. I., N. Y. F-T-7-40.
HUNT, Thomas.
Eng. Skipton 1854-1929. B-Wa1929-Y01930.
HUNT, Thomas L.
Am. ad. 1934 Laguna Beach, Calif. M.

HUNT, Una Clarke.
Mrs. Arthur P. Hunt.
Am. b. Cinn., O. 1876; ad. 1934 Pasaconaway, N. H. A.
HUNT, Walter.
Eng. b. Wandsworth 1861. B-T.
HUNT, William Harvey.
Am. b. Indiana; ex. 1935 Chicago, Ill. M.
HUNT, William Henry.
Eng. London 1790-1864 Same. B-DNB-E-T.
HUNT, William Holman.
Eng. London 1827-1910 Same. B-Bd-C-DBA-DNB-E-T-922.
HUNT, William Morris.
Am. Brattleboro, Vt. 1824-1879 Wethersfield, N. H. B-Bd-C-DAB-E-F-T-1-4-46-48-51-120-121-122-701.
HÜNTEN, Franz.
Ger. b. Hamburg 1822; ac. 1870 [No death date]. C.
HUNTER, Colin.
Scot. Glasgow 1841-1904 London. B-C-DNB-T.
HUNTER, David C. (S)
Am. England 1846-1927 New York. A024.
HUNTER, Frances Tipton. (Ill)
Am. ad. 1935 Philadelphia, Pa. M.
HUNTER, Isabel.
Am. b. San Fran., Calif.; ad. 1934 Alameda, Calif. A.
HUNTER, John Kelso.
Scot. Dumkeith 1802-1873 Glasgow. DNB-T.
HUNTER, Lizbeth Clifton.
Am. b. Gilroy, Calif. 1868; ad. 1934 New York. A.
HUNTER, Pearl.
Am. ad. 1934 Toledo, O. M.
HUNTER, Robert.
Ir. b. Dublin; ac. 1750-1780. B-DNB-T.
HUNTER-YOUNG. *see* Young-Hunter.
HUNTINGTON, Anna Vaughn Hyatt. (S)
Mrs. Archer M. Huntington.
Am. b. Cambridge, Mass. 1876; ad. 1935 New York. A-B-Cs-E-F-Hs-T-Ta-W-46-932.
HUNTINGTON, Clara. (S)
Am. b. Oneonta, N. Y. 1878; ad. 1934 Los Gatos, Calif. A-Cs.
HUNTINGTON, Daniel P.
Am. New York 1816-1906 Same. A06-B-C-DAB-E-F-T-W4-1-3-4-6-15-45-124-182.
HUNTINGTON, Daniel Riggs.
Am. b. Newark, N. J. 1871; ad. 1934 Seattle, Wash. A.
HUNTINGTON, Elizabeth H. T.
Am. ex. 1935 New York. M.
HUNTINGTON, John W.
Am. ad. 1934 New York. M.
HUNTINGTON, Margaret Wendell.
Am. ad. 1934 New York. A.
HUNTINGTON, Robert Leslie. (S)
Am. b. Yonkers, N. Y. 1890; ad. 1935 Same. Cs.
HUNTLEY, [Mrs.] Samantha Littlefield.
Am. b. Watervliet, N. Y.; ad. 1934 Kinderhook, N. Y. A-F.
HUNTOON, Mary [Hull]. (Et)
Am. ad. 1934 Topeka, Kan. A.
HUOT, Charles Édouard.
Can. Quebec 1855-1930. B-T.
HUQUIER, James Gabriel.
Fr. Paris 1725-1805 England. B-DNB.
HURD, Clement.
Am. ex. 1935 New York. M.
HURD, Eleanor Hammond.
Am. b. Kalamazoo, Mich.; ad. 1934 Balt., Md. A.
HURD, Nathaniel. (Eg)
Am. Boston, Mass. 1730-1777 Same. B-Bd-F-T-7-40.
HURD, Peter.
Am. b. Roswell, N. M. 1904; ad. 1934 Same. A.
HURDIS, James Henry.
Eng. Southampton 1800-1857 Same. DNB-T.
HUREL, Suzanne.
Fr. b. Mortagne 1876. B-DBA.
HURET, Grégoire.
Fr. Lyons 1606-1670 Paris. B-T.
HURLESTON, Richard.
Eng. ac. 1764-1780 in London. DNB-T.
HURLEY, Edward Timothy. (Et)
Am. b. Cinn., O. 1869; ad. 1934 Same. A-B-F-T-W.
HURLEY, Helen Q.
Am. ad. 1934 Brooklyn, N. Y. M.
HURLEY, Irene Bishop. (Min)
Mrs. E. T. Hurley.
Am. Colorado Springs, Colo. 1881-1925 Cinn., O. A12-T.
HURLSTONE, Frederick Yeates.
Eng. London 1800-1869 Same. B-DNB-E-T.
HURRY, [Mrs.] Lucy Washington.
Am. b. Hagerstown, Md. 1884; ad. 1934 Hempstead, L. I., N. Y. A-F.
HURST, [Mrs.] Clara Scott.
Am. b. Kirwin, Kan. 1889; ad. 1934 Same. A.
HURST, Earl Oliver. (Ill)
Am. ex. 1935 New York. M.
HURST, Hal ["Holl"]. (Min)
Eng. ac. 1929 in London. B-T-Wa1929.
HURT, Louis Bosworth.
Scot. d. 1929 in Ivonbrook, Scot. B-Wa1929.
HURTT, Arthur R.
Am. b. Wisconsin 1861; ad. 1934 Los Angeles, Calif. A-F.
HUSE, Marion.
Am. b. Lynn, Mass. 1896; ad. 1934 Springfield, Mass. A.
HUSON, Thomas.
Br. Liverpool, Eng. 1844-1920 Bala, Wales. B-T.
HUSSA, Theodore Frederick.
Am. b. East Orange, 1909; ad. 1934 Montclair, N. J. A.
HUSSEY, Giles.
Eng. Warnhull 1710-1788 Beeston. B-DNB-T.
HUSSEY, Philip.
Ir. Cork 1713-1782/3 Same. DNB-T.
HUSSMANN, Albert Heinrich. (S)
Ger. b. Lüdingworth 1874; ac. 1925 Berlin. B-T-798.
HUSSON, Honoré Jean Aristide. (S)
Fr. Paris 1803-1864 Bellevue. B-T.
HUSSON, Jeanne Elizabeth [Chaudet].
Fr. Paris 1767-1832 Same. B-T.
HUSTED, Mary Irving.
Am. b. Brooklyn, N. Y.; ad. 1934 Boston, Mass. W.

HUTAF, August William.
Am. Hoboken, N. J. 1879; ad. 1934 Woodcliff, N. Y. A.
HUTCHENS, Frank Townsend.
Am. b. Canandaigua, N. Y. 1869; ad. 1934 Norwalk, Conn. A-B-F-T-W-46.
HUTCHINS, Charles Bowman.
Am. b. Seattle, Wash. 1889; ad. 1934 Boulder, Colo. A.
HUTCHINS, Frederic Loudon.
Am. b. Seattle, Wash. 1896; ad. 1934 Boulder, Colo. A.
HUTCHINS, [Mrs.] Maude Phelps. (S)
Am. b. New York 1889; ad. 1934 Chicago. A.
HUTCHINS, Will.
Am. b. Coldchester, Conn. 1878; ad. 1934 Wash., D. C. W.
HUTCHINSON, Allen. (S)
Eng. ac. 1886 in London. B-Hs.
HUTCHINSON, David.
Am. ad. 1934 Yonkers, N. Y. M.
HUTCHINSON, [Mrs.] Ellen Wales.
Am. b. East Hartford, Conn. 1868; ad. 1934 New Haven, Conn. A.
HUTCHINSON, Frederick W.
Am. b. Montreal, Can.; ad. 1934 New York. A.
HUTCHINSON, Mary Elizabeth.
Am. b. Melrose, Mass. 1907; ad. 1934 New York. A.
HUTCHINSON, Robert Gemmell.
Scot. ac. 1879-1929 in Edinburgh. B-T-Wa1929.
HUTIN, Charles François.
Fr. Paris 1715-1776 Dresden, Ger. C-T.
HUTSON, Charles Woodward.
Am. b. McPhersonville, S. C. 1840; ad. 1934 New Orleans, La. A-F.
HUTSON, Ethel.
Am. b. Baton Rouge, La. 1872; ad. 1935 New Orleans, La. A-F.
HUTSON, Victoria Ebbels. (Eg)
Am. b. Hasbrouck Heights, N. J. 1900; ad. 1935 New York. A28-M.
HUTT, Henry. (Ill)
Am. b. Chicago, Ill. 1875. F-W13.
HUTTBUG, Charles E.
Am. b. Sweden 1874; ad. 1934 Biloxi, Miss. A.
HUTTON, [Mrs.] Dorothy Wackerman.
Am. b. Cleveland, O. 1899. A28.
HUTTON, Phillip.
Eng. ex. 1934 London. M.
HUTTY, Alfred Heber.
Am. b. Grand Haven, Mich. 1877; ad. Charleston, S. C. 1934 A-F-W-46.
HUVEY, Louis.
Fr. b. St. Étienne, 1868. B-DBA-T.
HUYCK, Laura Talmadge.
Am. ex. 1935 New York. M.
HUYS, Modest.
Belg. b. Olsene 1875. B-DBA.
HUYSMANS, Constantine Cornelius.
Dut. b. Breda 1810 [No death date]. B-T.
HUYSMANS, Cornelis II.
Flem. Antwerp 1648-1727 Mechlin. B-C-E-T-722.
HUYSMANS [or Houseman], Jacob.
Flem. Antwerp 1633-1696 London. B-DNB-E-T.
HUYSMANS, Jan Baptist.
Flem. Antwerp 1654-1716 Same. T.
HUYSMANS, Jan Baptist.
Belg. b. Antwerp 1826 [No death date]. T.
HUYSSING [or Hysing], Hans.
Swe. Stockholm 1678-1752/3 London. DNB-T.
HUYSUM, Jacob [or James] van.
Dut. Amsterdam 1687-1746 London. DNB-T.
HUYSUM, Jan Van.
Dut. Amsterdam 1682-1749 Same. B-C-E-T-722.
HUYSUM, Justus van [The Elder].
Dut. Amsterdam 1659-1716 Same. B-T.
HUYSUM, Justus van [The Younger].
Dut. Amsterdam 1685-1707 Same. T.
HWANG-HO.
Chinese. ac. Sung Dynasty [960-1280]. E.
HWEI-tsung. [Emperor]
Chinese. ac. Sung Dynasty [960-1280]. E.
HYAM, Myer.
Chinese. Modern. M.
HYAMS, William.
Eng. b. Portsmouth 1878; ad. 1934 Brighton. M.
HYATT, Anna Vaughn.
see Huntington, A. H.
HYDE, Della Mae.
Am. b. Oakland, Md.; ad. 1934 Wash., D. C. A.
HYDE, Emily Griffin.
Am. Indiana 1859-1919 Spiceland, Ind. A017.
HYDE, Helen.
Am. Lima, N. Y. 1868-1919 Pasadena, Calif. A016-B-F-T-46-829.
HYDE, John. (Et)
Am. England 1846-1927 New York. A024.
HYDE, Russell Taber.
Am. b. Waltham, Mass. 1886; ad. 1934 Same. A.
HYDE, William Henry.
Am. b. New York 1858; ad. 1934 Same. A-B-F-T-W.
HYDEN, Ethel.
Am. ad. 1934 Riverside, Conn. M.
HYDEN, Seymour. *see* Haden, Seymour.
HYETT, Will J.
Am. b. Cheltenham, Eng. 1876; ad. 1934 Pittsburgh, Pa. A-F-T.
HYNAIS, Vojtech Adalbert.
Czec. b. Vienna, Aus. 1854. B-DBA.
HYND, Frederic Stuart.
Am. b. Cleveland, O. 1905; ad. 1934 Bloomfield, Conn. A.
HYNEMAN, Herman N.
Am. Phila., Pa. 1859-1907 Same. A07-B-T.
HYRE. *see* La Hire.
IACOVLEFF, Alexandras.
Rus. b. Leningrad 1887; ex. 1934 Pittsburgh, Pa. DBA.
IAMS, John Howard.
Am. b. Washington, Pa. 1897; ad. 1934 Same. A.
IAN, Mac Iver.
Am. ex. 1934 New York. M.

IANNELLI, ALFONSO. (S)
Am. b. Andretta, It. 1888; ad. 1934 Park Ridge, Ill. A.
IBBETSON, JOHN.
Eng. ac. 1812 London [No death date]. B.
IBBETSON, JULIUS CAESAR.
Eng. Fulneck 1759-1817 Masham, Eng. B-DNB-T.
IBELS, HENRI GABRIEL.
Fr. b. Paris 1867. B-DNB-T.
IBI, SINIBALDO.
It. Gubbio 1475-1550. B-T.
IBLING, MIRIAM.
Am. ex. 1934 Minneapolis, Minn. M.
ICART, LOUIS.
Fr. b. 1888; ex. 1922 New York. DBA-M.
ICKES, PAUL A. (Ill)
Am. b. Laclede, Mo. 1895; ad. 1934 Bronxville, N. Y. A.
IDE, ALICE STEELE.
see Hannford, [Mrs.] Foster.
IDRAC, JEAN ANTOINE MARCEL. (S)
Fr. Toulouse 1849-1885. B-T.
IGLER, GUSTAV.
Hun. b. Oedenburg 1842. B-T.
IGOUNET DE VILLERS, CHARLES ANDRÉ.
Fr. b. Paris 1881. DBA.
IGUEL, CHARLES FRANÇOIS MARIE. (S)
Fr. Paris 1827-1898 Geneva, Swi. B-T.
IHLEFELD, HENRY.
Am. Germany 1859-1932 Mt. Vernon, N. Y. A029-B.
IHRIG, CLARA LOUISE.
Am. b. Pittsburgh, Pa. 1893; ad. 1934 Same. A.
IJKENS. *see* Ykens.
ILKKA, ELIAS. (S)
Fin. b. Jalasjarvi, Finland 1889. DBA.
ILLAVA, KARL. (S)
Am. ad. 1934 Bronxville, N. Y. A.
ILLIAN, GEORGE JOHN.
Am. Milwaukee, Wis. 1894-1932 New York. A029.
ILLIDGE, THOMAS HENRY.
Eng. Birmingham 1799-1851 London. B-DNB-T.
ILLITSCH, ALEXANDER. (S)
Aus. b. Vienna 1860. T.
ILLMAN, PHILIP.
Am. ad. 1934 New York. M.
ILLMAN, THOMAS. (Eg)
Am. b. England; ac. 1824-1866 New York. F-2-7.
ILLNER, WALTHER.
Ger. b. Leipzig 1874. T.
ILSLEY, FREDERICK JULIAN.
Am. b. Portland, Me. 1855; d. 1933 Same. A.
IMBERT, JOSEPH GABRIEL.
Fr. b. Marseilles 1666; d. 1749 Villeneuve. B-T.
IMFELD, FRED M.
Am. d. 1927 Cincinnati, O. A024.
IMLER, EDGAR.
Am. b. St. Clairsville, Pa. 1894; ad. 1934 New York. A.
IMMENKAMP, WILHELM.
Ger. b. Essen 1870. T.
IMOLA, INNOCENZA DA [Francucci].
It. Imola 1494-1550 Bologna. B-T-V-722.
INCE, ADA.
Eng. ex. 1934 in London. M.
INCE, CHARLES.
Eng. b. London 1875. Wa.
INCE, EVELYN GRACE.
Br. b. India; ad. 1934 Letchworth, Eng. Wa.
INCE, JOSEPH MURRAY.
Belg. Presteign 1806-1857 Same. B-DNB-T.
INCHBOLD, JOHN WILLIAM.
Eng. Leeds 1830-1888 Same. B-Bd-DNB-T.
INCHBOLD, STANLEY.
Eng. b. London 1856. B-Wa1929.
INDACO, FRANCESCO DELL .
It. b. 1492; d. 1560. B-V.
INDACO, JACOPO DELL'.
It. b. 1476; d. 1554. B-V.
INDIA [Hindu] ARTISTS.
see books 690-777-851 [*also* State Gallery, Baroda, India and Government Art Gallery, Calcutta, India].
INDIAN [American] ARTISTS.
see book no. 411 [*also* Exposition of Indian Tribal Arts, New York].
INDONI, FILIPPO.
It. ac. 1870-1884 in Rome. B-T.
INDUNO, DOMENICO.
It. Milan 1815-1878 Same. B-T.
INDUNO, GIROLAMO.
It. Milan 1827-1891 Same. B-T.
INGALLS, MABLE S.
Am. ad. 1934 New York. M.
INGALLS, W.
Am. ac. 1842 Washington, D. C. [No death date]. M.
INGANNATI, CAMILLO.
It. b. 1871 in Italy. M.
INGEGNO, ANDREA DI LUIGI.
It. ac. 1484-1516 in Italy. T-V-722.
INGELS, FRANK LEE. (S)
Am. b. Tamora, Neb. 1886; ad. 1934 Los Angeles, Calif. A.
INGEN. *see* Van Ingen, Henry.
INGERLE, RUDOLPH F.
Am. b. Vienna, Aus. 1879; ad. 1934 Chicago. A.
INGERSOLL, EMMA KIPLING HESS.
Mrs. D. W. Ingersoll.
Am. b. Chicago 1878; ac. 1934 Chestertown, Md. A.
INGHAM, CHARLES CROMWELL.
Am. Dublin, Ir. 1796-1863 New York. B-Bd-C-DNB-E-F-T-1-2-4-6-15-182.
INGHAM-SMITH, [Mrs.] ELIZABETH.
Am. b. Easton, Pa.; ad. 1934 No. Shirley, Mass. A.
INGLES, JORGE [Master George].
Sp. ac. 1455 in Spain. B-T-774.
INGLIS, ANTOINETTE CLARK.
Am. b. Cortland, N. Y.; ad. 1934 Cambridge, Mass. A.
INGLIS, JOHN J.
Am. b. Dublin, Ir. 1867; ad. 1934 Rochester, N. Y. A.
INGRAHAM, [Mrs.] ELLEN M. (Min)
Am. New Haven, Conn. 1832-1917 Indianapolis, Ind. M.
INGRAM, JOHN. (Eg)
Eng. London 1721-1771? B-DNB-T.

INGRES, JEAN AUGUSTE DOMINIQUE.
Fr. Montauban, 1780-1867 Paris.
B-Bd-C-E-T-191-192-412-820-847-870.
INJALBERT, JEAN ANTONIN. (S)
Fr. Béziers 1845-1933. B-DNB-T.
INMAN, F. TEMPEST. (Ill)
Am. ad. 1935 New York. M.
INMAN, HENRY.
Am. Utica, N. Y. 1802-1846 New York.
B-Bd-C-DAB-E-F-1-2-4-6-15-45-46-51-53-144-179-182-183.
INMAN, JOHN O'BRIEN.
Am. New York 1828-1896 Same. B-F-4-6.
INNES, JAMES DICKSON [or Dixon].
Eng. Llanelly 1887-1914 Swanley, Eng. T.
INNESS, GEORGE, JR.
Am. Paris 1853-1926 Cragsmoor, N. Y.
A023-B-C-F-W14-15-46.
INNESS, GEORGE, SR.
Am. Newburgh, N. Y. 1825-1894 Bridge of Allan, Scot. B-Bd-C-DAB-E-F-T-1-4-5-15-46-58-71-105-126-127-128-129-144-183-192-413-701-748.
INNOCENTI, BATTISTA DEGLI.
see Naldini, Battista di Matteo.
INNOCENTI, CAMILLO GIOVANNI.
It. ac. 1902 in Italy. B-T.
INNOCENZIA DA IMOLA. *see* Imola.
INSKIPP, JAMES.
Eng. 1790-1868 Godalming. B-DNB-T.
INSLEY, ALBERT.
Am. b. Orange, N. J. 1842. B-M.
INUKAI, KYOHEI.
Jap.-Am. b. Japan; ad. 1934 New York. A-F.
INURRIA, LAINOSA MATEO. (S)
Sp. b. 1867; d. 1924 in Spain. B-T.
INVERARITY, ROBERT BRUCE. (Ill)
Am. b. Seattle, Wash. 1909; ad. 1934 Vancouver, B. C., Can. A.
INVERNIZZI, PROSPER.
It. b. Milan 1875; ad. 1935 New York. M.
I'ONS, F.
Br. Islington, Eng. 1802-1889 Grahamstown, So. Africa. M.
IPPU, MORI.
Jap. ac. 1860 in Japan. J. vol. 2, page 98.
IPSEN, ERNEST LUDWIG.
Am. b. Malden, Mass. 1869; ad. 1934 So. Dartmouth, Mass. A-F-W.
IRELAND, BERYL. (Min)
Ad. 1934 Ann Arbor, Mich. M.
IRELAND, LEROY.
Am. b. Phila., Pa. 1889; ad. 1934 New York. A-F.
IRELAND, WILLIAM ADDISON. (Ill)
Am. Chillicothe, O. 1880-1935 Columbus, O.
A-Obit. N. Y. papers, 5-30-1935.
IRIATE [or Iriarte], IGNACIO DE.
Sp. Azcoitia 1620/1-1685 Sèville. B-T.
IRISH, MARGARET HOLMES.
Am. b. Blenheim, Can. 1878; ad. 1934 Webstre Groves, Mo. A.
IRVIN, REA. (Ill)
Am. b. San Fran., Calif. 1881; ad. 1934 Spuyten Duyvil, N. Y. A.
IRVINE, JAMES.
Scot. Menmuir 1833-1889 Monstrose. DNB-T.
IRVINE, WILSON HENRY.
Am. b. Byron, Ill. 1869; ad. 1934 Lyme, Conn. A-B-F-W.

IRVING, ANNA DUER.
Am. ad. 1934 New York. M.
IRVING, JAY. (Cart)
Am. ad. 1934 Chicago, Ill. M.
IRVING, JOHN BEAUFAIN.
Am. Charleston, S. C. 1826-1877 New York.
B-Bd-C-DAB-F-T-15-35.
IRWIN, BENONI.
Am. Newmarket, Can. 1840-1896 So. Coventry, Conn. F.
IRWIN, WILLIAM HYDE.
Am. b. San Fran., Calif. 1903; ad. 1934 Brookdale, Calif. A.
ISAAC, APA.
Egyptian. ac. 893 A.D. in Ptepouhar, Egypt. [*see* Morgan Library, New York].
ISAACKSEN [or Isaacsz], ISAAC.
Dut. Amsterdam 1599-1665 Same. T.
ISABEY, JEAN BAPTISTE.
Fr. Nancy 1767-1855 Paris.
B-Bd-C-E-T-414-722.
ISABEY, LOUIS GABRIEL EUGÈNE.
Fr. Paris 1803-1886 Same. B-Bd-C-T.
ISACOVEFF, ALEXANDRE.
Rus. b. Russia; ad. 1935 Boston, Mass. M.
ISAKSON, KARL OSCAR.
Swe. Stockholm 1878-1922 Copenhagen.
DBA-T.
ISENBART, MARIS VICTOR ÉMILE.
Fr. b. Besançon 1846; d. 1921. B-DBA-T.
ISENBRANT, ADRIAEN.
Flem. b. 1485?; d. 1551 Bruges, Belg. B-T.
ISENMANN, CASPAR.
Ger. ac. 1436-1472? in Colmar. B-T.
ISERMAN, HAINO. (S)
Am. b. 1829; d. 1899 Chicago, Ill. A01.
ISHAM, SAMUEL. [Artist and Historian of Artists].
Am. New York 1855-1914 Easthampton, N. Y.
A0X1-B-DAB-F-W8-1-46.
ISHII, KOWHOO.
Jap. ac. 1929 in Japan. J. vol. 1, page 88.
ISIGONOS [or Isigone]. (S)
Gr. ac. 236 B.C. B-Hs.
ISKANTOR.
Am. b. Russia 1906; ad. 1934 New York. A.
ISRAELS, ISAAC [or Izack].
Dut. b. Amsterdam, Holland 1865. B-T.
ISRAELS, JOZEF [or Joseph].
Dut. Gröningen 1824-1911 The Hague.
B-Bd-C-E-T-474-480.
ITALIAN PAINTERS.
see new source book, Pittori Italiani Dell Ottocento; by A. M. Comanducci. Milan, It. 1934.
ITARU, TANABE.
Jap. b. 1886 in Japan. M.
ITASSE, ADOLPHE. (S)
Fr. Loumarin 1830-1893 Paris. B-T.
ITCHO, HANABUSA [Fujiwara].
Jap. 1652-1724 Yeddo. J. vol. 1, page 143.
ITTENBACH, FRANZ.
Ger. Königswinter 1813-1879 Düsseldorf.
B-T.
IVANOFF, ALEXANDER ANDREEVITCH.
Rus. Leningrad 1806-1858 Same. B-T.
IVANOFF, EUGÈNE.
Am. ex. 1935 San Fran., Calif. M.

IVANOFF, S. V.
Rus. b. Moscow 1854. B-T.
IVERD, Eugène.
Am. b. St. Paul, Minn. 1893; ad. 1934 Erie, Pa. A.
IVES, Chauncy Bradley. (S)
Am. b. Hamden, Conn. 1812; d. 1894. B-DAB-F-Hs-Ta-3-4-15-26.
IVES, [Mrs.] Elsie.
Am. d. 1915 Detroit, Mich. A013.
IVES, Halsey Cooley.
Am. Montour Falls, N. Y. 1847-1911 London. A09-B-DAB-F-46-130.
IVES, James Merritt.
Am. New York 1824-1895 Rye, N. Y. DAB-54-131-132-133.
IVES, Neil McDowell.
Am. ad. 1935 Woodstock, N. Y. M.
IVES, Percy.
Am. Detroit, Mich. 1864-1928 Same. A025-B-F-W14-46.
IVES, Reginald Grenville.
Eng. ad. 1935 in London. M.
IVES, Sarah Noble. (Ill)
Am. b. Grosse Isle, Mich.; d. Port Huron, Mich. W16.
IVEY, Elizabeth Hall.
Mrs. A. Lynn Ivey.
Am. b. Thomson, Ga.; ad. 1934 Richmond, Va. A.
IVONE, Arthur. (S)
Am. b. Naples, It. 1894; ad. 1934 Cinn., O. A.
IVY, Gregory D.
Am. ex. 1935 New York. M.
IWAI, Takahito.
Jap. ex. 1926 in London. M.
IWILL, Marie Joseph Léon Clavel.
Fr. Paris 1850-1923. B-F-T.
IYKENS. *see* Ykens.
IZOR, Estelle Peele.
Am. ac. 1926 in Indianapolis, Ind. A12-F.
JAACOPO DE SANDRO.
[Pier Francesco di Jacone].
It. ac. 1500 in Florence; d. 1553. B-T-V.
JACCACI, August Florian. (Mu)
Fr. France 1856-1930 Same. A027.
JACK, Richard.
Eng. b. Sunderland 1866; ad. 1934 Montreal, Can. B-Wa.
JACKEL, Heinrich.
Ger. ac. 1850 in Berlin. M.
JACKMAN, W. G. (Eg)
Am. b. England; ac. 1841 in New York [No death date]. F-7.
JACKSON, Alexander Young. D. 4/6/74
Can. b. Montreal 1883; ad. 1935 Toronto. M.
JACKSON, Annie Hulbert.
Am. b. Minneapolis, Minn. 1877; ad. 1934 Brookline, Mass. A.
JACKSON, Charles Akermann.
Am. b. Jamaica Plain, Mass. 1857; ad. 1935 Boston. A12-F-WX1.
JACKSON, Elizabeth Lesley.
Am. b. Rochester, Minn.; ad. 1934 Wash., D. C. W.
JACKSON, Everett Gee.
Am. b. Mexia, Tex. 1900; ad. 1934 San Diego, Calif. A.
JACKSON, E. M. (Ill)
Am. ad. 1934 Douglaston, L. I., N. Y. M.
JACKSON, F. Hamilton.
Eng. b. 1848; d. 1923 in England. B-Y01924.
JACKSON, Francis Earnest. (Eg)
Eng. b. 1873; ac. 1935 London. B-T.
JACKSON, Frank Henry.
Am. b. England 1864; ac. 1915 Boston, Mass. A12-B.
JACKSON, Frederick William.
Eng. Middleton 1859-1918. B-T.
JACKSON, George. (Min)
Eng. ac. 1810-1839 in England. B-T.
JACKSON, Gilbert.
Eng. ac. 1622-1642 London. B-T.
JACKSON, Hazel Brill. (S)
Am. b. Phila., Pa. 1894; ad. 1934 Rome, It. A-Cs-F.
JACKSON, Howard Merritt.
Am. b. San Bernardino, Calif. 1906; ad. 1934 Carmel, Calif. A.
JACKSON, John.
Eng. Lastingham 1778-1831 London. B-DNB-T-722.
JACKSON, John. (Eg)
Eng. Ovingham 1801-1848 London. DNB-T-722.
JACKSON, John Adams. (S)
Am. Bath, Me. 1825-1879 Italy. B-Bd-DAB-F-Hs-Ta-4-6-15.
JACKSON, John Baptist. (Eg)
Eng. 1701-1780 Battersea, Eng. B-DNB-T.
JACKSON, John Edwin.
Am. b. Eagleville, Tenn. 1876; ad. 1934 New York. A28-B-F-W.
JACKSON, John Richardson. (Eg)
Eng. Portsmouth 1819-1877 Southsea, Eng. B-DNB-T.
JACKSON, Lee.
Am. ex. 1935 New York. M.
JACKSON, [Miss] Lesley.
Am. b. Rochester, Minn.; ad. 1934 Wash., D. C. A-F.
JACKSON, Martin Jacob.
Am. b. Newburgh, N. Y. 1871; ad. 1934 Los Angeles, Calif. A-F.
JACKSON, Mason. (Eg)
Eng. Ovingham 1819-1903 London. DNB-E-T.
JACKSON, [Mrs.] May Howard. (S)
Am. Phila., Pa. 1877-1931 Wash., D. C. A029.
JACKSON, Muriel Bloomfield. (Eg)
Eng. b. London 1901; ad. 1935 Same. Wa.
JACKSON, Nathaniel L'Hommedieu. (Min)
Am. ad. 1934 So. Orange, N. J. M.
JACKSON, Robert Fuller.
Am. b. Minneapolis, Minn. 1875; ad. 1934 Brookline, Mass. A.
JACKSON, Samuel.
Eng. Bristol 1794-1869 Clifton, Eng. B-DNB-T.
JACKSON, Samuel Phillips.
Eng. Bristol 1830-1904 Same. B-DNB-T.
JACKSON, Thomas G.
Eng. b. 1835; ac. 1896 in London [No death date]. B-T.
JACOB, Alexandre.
Fr. b. Paris 1876. B-DBA-T.

JACOB, CHARLES. (S)
Fr. b. Sedan 1897. DBA.
JACOB, JULIUS.
Ger. Berlin 1811-1882 Same. B-T.
JACOB, MAX CYPRIEN.
Fr. b. Quimper 1876. DBA.
JACOBBER [or Jacob Ber], MOISE.
Fr. 1786-1863 Paris. T.
JACOBÉ, JOHANN. (Eg)
Aus. Vienna 1733-1797 Same. B-T.
JACOBELLO DE BONOMO.
It. b. 1384; ac. 1401-1439 in Venice, It. B-T.
JACOBELLO DEL FIORE.
see Fiore, J.
JACOBI, GIOVANNI.
see Giovanni da Milano.
JACOBI, OTTO REINHOLD.
Can. Königsberg, Prussia 1812-1901 Canada. B-T.
JACOBI, RUDOLPH.
Ger. b. Mühlhausen 1889; ad. 1935 Westport, Conn. M.
JACOBIDES, GEORGES.
Gr. b. Mityléne, Greece 1853. B-T.
JACOBS. *see also* Jacobsz.
JACOBS, ISABEL M.
Am. b. Phila., Pa.; ad. 1934 Same. A.
JACOBS, LEONEBEL.
Am. b. Tacoma, Wash.; ad. 1935 New York. A-W.
JACOBS, LOUISE.
Ir. ex. 1935 London, Eng. M.
JACOBS, MAX.
Am. ad. 1935 New York. M.
JACOBS, MICHEL.
Am. b. Montreal, Can. 1877; ad. 1934 New York. A-F-W.
JACOBS, WILLIAM LEROY. (Ill)
Am. Cleveland, O. 1869-1917 New York. A015.
JACOBSEN, AUGUST.
Dan. b. Copenhagen 1868. B-T.
JACOBSEN, NORMAN.
Am. b. Cokeville, Wyo. 1884. F-WX1.
JACOBSEN, SOPHUS.
Nor. Christiania 1833-1912. B-T.
JACOBSON, A. DREXLER.
Am. ad. 1934 Norwalk, Conn. M.
JACOBSON, OSCAR BROUSSE.
Am. b. Westervik, Swe. 1882; ad. 1934 Norman, Okla. A-F-W.
JACOBSSON, EDWARD GUSTAVE.
Am. ad. 1934 Chicago. M.
JACOBSZ [or Jacobs], ALBRECHT MICHAEL.
Belg. Antwerp 1812-1879 Same. B-T.
JACOBSZ [or Jacobs], HUYBRECHT GRIMANIE.
Dut. Delft 1562-1631 Same. B-T.
JACOBSZ [or Jacobsen], JURIAEN.
Ger. Hamburg 1625-1685. B-T.
JACOBUS. (Eg)
Ger. ac. 1480 in Germany. Bd.
JACOBY, HAZEL.
Am. ad. 1934 Toledo, O. M.
JACOMART, JAINE BACO.
Sp. b. 1413; d. 1461/4 in Spain. B-T.
JACOMB-HOOD, GEORGE PERCY.
Eng. Redhill 1857 [Deceased]. Wa1929.
JACOMIN, ALFRED LOUIS VIGNY.
Fr. b. Paris 1842. B-T.

JACONE [Jacopo].
see Jacopo di Giovanni.
JACOPI, BERNARDINO. *see* Butimone.
JACOPO DEL CASENTINO LANDINI.
It. b. 1278; d. 1358 in Italy. V.
JACOPO DI CIONE. *see* Cione, J.
JACOPO DI GIOVANNI DI FRANCESCO.
It. ac. 1525-1553 in Florence. T-V.
JACOPO DELLA QUERCIA. *see* Quercia, J.
JACOPO DE SANDRO. [Pier Francesco di Jacone].
It. ac. 1500 in Florence; d. 1553. B-T-V.
JACOPO DA VALENTIA.
see Calenza [or Valencia], Jacopo da.
JACOVACCI, FRANCESCO.
It. b. Rome 1838; d. 1908. B-T.
JACOVLEFF, ALEXANDRE.
Rus. b. Leningrad, Rus. 1887; ad. 1935 Boston, Mass. M.
JACQUAND, CLAUDIUS [or Claude].
Fr. Lyons 1804-1878 Paris. B-C-T.
JACQUE, CHARLES ÉMILE.
[Last survivor of the Barbizon Fontainebleau painters.]
Fr. Paris 1813-1894 Same. B-Bd-C-T-843-880.
JACQUEMART, JULES FERDINAND. (Et)
Fr. Paris 1837-1880 Nice. B-T.
JACQUEMART, NÉLIE BARBE HYACINTHE.
Fr. Paris 1841-1912 Same. C-T.
JACQUEMIN, ANDRÉ.
Fr. b. Épinal 1904; ac. 1930 in Paris. DBA.
JACQUEMOT, CHARLES.
Fr. b. Tours 1879. DBA.
JACQUES, [Prof.] ÉMIL.
Am. b. Moorslede, Flanders, Belg. 1894; ad. 1935 South Bend, Ind. A.
JACQUES, NICOLAS.
Fr. Jarville 1780-1844 Paris. B-T.
JACQUES, PIERRE [Angouléme]. (S)
Fr. Reims 1516/20-1596 Same. B-T.
JACQUET, ACHILLÉ.
Fr. Courbévoie 1846-1908 Paris. B-T.
JACQUET, DÉSIRÉ ALBERT. (S)
Fr. b. Paris 1873. B-DBA.
JACQUET, GUSTAVE JEAN.
Fr. Paris 1846-1909 Same. B-T.
JACQUET, JULES. (Eg)
Fr. Paris 1841-1913. B-DBA-T.
JACQUET, MAURICE.
Fr. b. Paris 1877. B-DBA.
JACQUIER, HENRI.
Fr. St. Étienne 1878-1921. B-T.
JACQUIN FAMILY.
Fr. ac. 17-18th Cent. in France. T.
JACQUOT, CHARLES. (S)
Fr. b. Bains 1865. B-DBA-T.
JACQUOT, GEORGES. (S)
Fr. Nancy 1794-1874 Paris. B-T.
JADIN, LOUIS GODEFROY.
Fr. Paris 1805-1882 Same. B-T.
JAECKEL, [Prof.] WILLI.
Ger. b. Breslau 1888; ad. 1935 Berlin; ex. 1934 Pittsburgh, Pa. DBA-T.
JAEGER, AUGUST.
Fr. [Alsatian]. b. 1881. M.
JAEGER [or Jäger], HANS.
Ger. b. Zschopan 1887. T.

JAEGERS, Albert. (S)
Am. Elberfeld, Ger. 1865-1925 Suffern, N. Y. A022-B-F.

JAEGERS, Augustine. (S)
Am. b. Barmen, Ger. 1878; ad. 1934 Long Island City, N. Y. A-Cs-F-W.

JAGGER, Charles. (Min)
Eng. Bath 1770-1827 Same. B-T.

JAGGER, Charles Sargeant. (S)
Eng. Yorkshire 1885-1934 London. T-798-Obit. N. Y. papers, 11-16-1934. Obit. Studio, London, 1-1935. Obit. Art Digest, 12-1-1934.

JAHN Family.
Ger. ac. 17-19th Cent. in Germany. T.

JAKOBIDES. *see* Jacobides.

JAKOVLEV, Alexander Jewjenzewitsch.
Rus. b. 1887; ad. 1935 Moscow. M-T.

JAKOVLEV, P. F.
Rus. b. Moscow 1883; ex. 1933 New York. B-M.

JALABERT, Charles François.
Fr. Nimes 1819-1901. B-T.

JALEY, Jean Louis Nicolas. (S)
Fr. Paris 1802-1866 Neuilly. B-T.

JALIFIE, Félix Émile.
Fr. b. Marseilles 1882. DBA.

JAMAR, S. Corinne. (Min)
Am. b. Elkton, Md. 1876; ad. 1934 Same. A.

JAMBOR, Louis.
Am. b. Nagyvarad, Hun. 1884; ad. 1934 New York. A.

JAMES, Alexander R.
Am. b. Cambridge, Mass. 1890; ad. 1934 Dublin, N. H. A-F.

JAMES, Alice Archer Sewall.
Mrs. John H. James.
Am. b. Glendale, O. 1870; ad. 1934 Urbano, O. A12-B-F-W.

JAMES, Austin. (S)
Am. b. Phila., Pa. 1855; ad. 1934 Pasadena, Calif. A-Cs.

JAMES, Bess.
Am. b. Big Springs, Tex. 1897; ad. 1934 Monroe, La. A.

JAMES, Clifford R.
Eng. ad. 1934 Fortfield, Eng. Wa.

JAMES, Francis Edward.
Eng. Sussex 1849-1920. B-T.

JAMES, Frederick.
Am. 1845-1907 Peru, Que., Canada. A06-B.

JAMES, George Watson, Jr.
Am. b. Richmond, Va. 1887; ad. 1934 Same. A.

JAMES, George.
Eng. London 1683-1735. DNB.

JAMES, George.
Eng. b. London; d. 1795 in Boulogne, Fr. B-DNB-T.

JAMES, John Wells.
Am. b. Brooklyn, N. Y. 1873; ad. 1934 Same. A.

JAMES, Mary.
Am. ex. 1935 Boston, Mass. M.

JAMES, R. F. (Ill)
Am. ad. 1934 Mt. Vernon, N. Y. M.

JAMES, Roy Walter.
Am. b. Gardena, Calif. 1897; ad. 1934 Covina, Calif. A.

JAMES, Stephan. (Eg)
Am. ex. 1935 Seattle, Wash. M.

JAMES, Victor.
Am. ad. 1934 Ridgefield, Conn. M.

JAMES, [Sir] Walter John [Northborne].
Eng. b. London 1869. T-Wa1929.

JAMES, Will [Not William].
Am. b. Great Falls, Mont. 1892; ad. 1934 Pryor, Mont. A.

JAMES, William.
Am. b. Cambridge, Mass. 1882; ad. 1934 Same. A-W.

JAMES, William.
Eng. ac. 1760-1771 in London. B-DNB-T.

JAMESON. *see also* Jamieson.

JAMESON, Arthur Edward. (Ill)
Am. b. England 1872; ad. 1934 New York. A.

JAMESON, Cecil.
Eng. ad. 1934 London, Eng. M.

JAMESON, Kenneth Thomas.
Am. b. Bakersfield, Calif. 1900; ad. 1934 Manhattan Beach, Calif. M.

JAMESON, Middleton.
Scot. b. Edinburgh; d. 1919. B-Y01920.

JAMESON, Minor Story.
Am. b. New York 1873; ad. 1934 Chevy Chase, Md. A.

JAMESON, Samilla Love.
Mrs. S. L. J. Heinzmann.
Am. b. Indianapolis, Ind. 1881; ad. 1934 Prince Bay, N. Y. A-F.

JAMESONE, George.
Scot. Aberdeen 1586/8-1644 Edinburgh. B-Bd-E-T.

JAMET, Henri Pierre.
Fr. b. Gien 1858. B-DBA.

JAMIESON, Alexander.
Scot. b. Glasgow 1873; ad. 1934 Redditch, Eng. T-Wa.

JAMIESON, Bernice Evelyn.
Am. b. Prov., R. I. 1898; ad. 1934 Cranston, R. I. A.

JAMIESON, Cecelia Viets Dakin Hamilton.
Am. Nova Scotia 1837-1909 Roxbury, Mass. DAB-W5.

JAMIESON, Robert Kirkland.
Eng. b. Lanark 1881; ad. 1934 London. Wa.

JAMOIS, Edmond Victor.
Fr. b. Lille 1876. B-DBA.

JAMONTT, Bronislaw.
Pol. b. 1886; ad. 1935 Vilno, Pol.; ex. 1934 Pittsburgh, Pa. M.

JANEL, Émil. (S)
Swe. b. Orsa 1897; ad. 1934 San Fran., Calif. M.

JANENSCH, Gerhard. (S)
Ger. b. Zamborst 1860; ac. 1924 Berlin. B-T.

JANET, Ange Louis [Janet Lange].
Fr. Paris 1815-1872 Same. B-T.

JANIN, Jean.
Fr. b. Geneva, Swi. 1899. DBA.

JANIN, Louise.
Fr. ac. 1931 in Paris. DBA.

JANINET, Jean François. (Eg)
Fr. Paris 1752-1814 Same. B-T-900.

JANK, Angelo. (Ill)
Ger. b. Munich 1868. T.

JANNECK, Franz Christoph.
Aus. Gratz 1703-1761 Vienna. B-T.
JANNELLA, Ottaviano. (Min)
It. Asoli 1635-1661 Same. T.
JANNI, Pino.
Am. ad. 1935 New York. M.
JANNIOT, Alfred Auguste. (S)
Fr. b. Paris 1889. B-DBA.
JANNOT, Anne François Louis.
Fr. Lyons 1814-1892 Same. B-T.
JANNOT, René Louis.
Fr. ac. 1925 in Paris. DBA.
JANOWSKI, Ludomir.
Pol. b. 1862 in Poland-Russia. T.
JANOWSKY, Béla. (S)
Am. b. Budapest, Hun. 1900; ad. 1935 New York. A-Cs.
JANSEN, Richard.
Am. ad. 1935 New York. M.
JANSON, Andrew R.
Am. b. New York 1900; ad. 1934 Same. A.
JANSON, Dorothy Plymouth. (Ill)
Am. b. Jersey City, N. J.; ad. 1934 Los Angeles, Calif. A.
JANSSEN, Geraert [or Gérard]. (S)
Dut.-Eng. ac. 1616 in England. DNB.
JANSSEN, Gerhard.
Ger. Calcar 1863-1931 Düsseldorf. B-T.
JANSSEN, Karl. (S)
Ger. b. Düsseldorf 1853/5. B-T.
JANSSEN, Peter Johann Theodor.
Ger. Düsseldorf 1844-1908. B-T.
JANSSENS, Hieronymus ["Den Danser"].
Flem. Antwerp 1624-1693. B-T.
JANSSENS, Pieter [Elinga].
Dut. Haarlem 1612-1672 Amsterdam. B-T.
JANSSENS [or Jonson] VAN CEULEN, Cornelius.
Flem. London 1593/4-1662/4 Utrecht, Holland. B-Bd-DNB-E-T.
JANSSENS van NUYSSEN, Abraham.
Flem. Antwerp, Belg. 1567/75-1632 Same. B-E-T-722.
JANSSENS, Victor Honoré.
Flem. Brussels, Belg. 1664-1739 Same. B-C-E-T-722.
JANSSON, Alfred.
Am. Sweden 1863-1931 Chicago, Ill. A028-B-F.
JANSSON, Arthur August.
Am. b. White Mills, Pa. 1890; ad. 1934 New York. A.
JANSSON, Eugène Frederick.
Swe. Stockholm 1862-1915 Same. DBA-T.
JANTSCHA, Laurenz.
Aus. b. 1742; d. 1812 in Austria. M.
JANVIER, Catherine Ann.
Mrs. Thomas Allibone Janvier.
Am. Phila., Pa. 1841-1922 Merion, Pa. DAB-W12-135.
JAPANESE ARTISTS.
see books J-769-914. [*Also consult* Imperial School of Art and National Fine Art Association. Tokio, Jap.]
JAPY, Louis Aimé.
Fr. Berne, Swi. 1850-1916. B-T.
JAQUES, Bertha Evelyn. (Et)
Mrs. W. K. Jaques.
Am. b. Covington, O. 1863. A28-B-F.
JAQUES, Francis Lee.
Am. b. Genesco, Ill. 1887; ad. 1934 New York. A.
JÁRAY, Sandor. (S)
Ger. b. Temesvár 1870; ac. 1911 Berlin. B-T.
JARDIN, Karel du.
Dut. Amsterdam 1622/5-1678 Venice, It. B-Bd-C-T-722.
JARDINES, José Maria.
Fr. b. Cadix 1862. DBA.
JAROCKI, Wladyslaw.
Pol. b. Podhajezyski 1879; ex. 1933 Pittsburgh, Pa. DBA.
JAROSZ, Romain.
Fr. b. Rawa 1889; d. 1932 Paris. DBA.
JARVIS, Charles Wesley.
Am. b. New York 1821; d. 1862 Newark, N. J. 6.
JARVIS, John Wesley.
Am. South Shields, Eng. 1780-1839 New York. B-Bd-C-DAB-E-F-1-2-4-6-7-45-144-182-183.
JARVIS [or Jervais], Thomas. (Glass-P)
Ir. b. Dublin; d. 1799 Windsor, Eng. B-DNB-T.
JARVIS, W. Frederick.
Am. b. Monroe Co., O.; ad. 1934 Dallas, Tex. A.
JASINSKI, Félix Stanislas. (Eg)
Pol.-Fr. b. Zabkow, Pol. 1862; d. Puteaux, Fr. T.
JASPERS, Jan Baptist. *see* Gaspars, J. B.
JAUDIN, Henri Laurent.
Fr. b. Paris 1851; d. 1929 Lavallois-Perret. DBA.
JAUSSELY, Léon.
Fr. Toulouse 1875-1933. DBA.
JAWLENSKY, Alexej von.
Ger. b. 1867. T.
JAY, Cecil. (Min)
Mrs. George Hitchcock.
Am. ac. 1915 New York. A12-F.
JAY, William Samuel.
Eng. 1843-1933 London. B-T. Obit. London Morning Post.
JAZET, Jean Pierre Marie.
Fr. Paris 1788-1871 Yerres. B-T-900.
JAZET, Paul Léon.
Fr. b. Paris 1848. B-T.
JEAKES, Joseph. (Eg)
Eng. ac. 1796-1815 London. B-T.
JEAN-AMAN. *see* Aman-Jean.
JEAN, Antoine. *see* Gros.
JEAN DE BOTTON.
Fr. b. 1898; ac. 1930 Paris. DBA.
JEAN, Paul. (Min)
Eng. Jersey 1755-1802 London. B-T.
JEAN, Philip. (Min)
Eng. St. Quen 1755-1802 Hempstead. DNB-T.
JEAN-BOUCHER. *see* Boucher, Jean Marie.
JEANFIL, Henri Jacques.
Am. b. No. Tonawanda, N. Y. 1909; ad. 1934 Buffalo, N. Y. A.
JEANNERET, Charles Édouard.
Swi. b. La Chaux-de-Fonds 1887. T.
JEANNERET, Édouard.
Fr. Joux-Perret 1846-1916 Geneva, Swi. DBA-797.

JEANNIN, GEORGES.
Fr. Paris 1841-1925. B-DBA-T.
JEANNIOT, PIERRE GEORGES.
Fr. Geneva, Swi. 1848-1934 Paris. B-DBA-M-T-Obit. N. Y. papers, 1-4-1934. Obit. Art Digest, 1-15-1934.
JEANRON, PHILIPPE AUGUSTE.
Fr. Boulogne 1807-1877 Comborn. B-T.
JEANROT, ÉTIENNE.
Fr. Vermenton 1699-1789 Versailles. B-C-T-722.
JEANVONS, THOMAS. (Eg)
Welch. b. Wales 1816; d. 1867 Welshpool, Wales. B-DNB-T.
JEFFERSON, JOSEPH. (Actor-P)
Am. b. Phila., Pa. 1829; d. 1905. A05-B-DAB-E-F-710.
JEFFERYS, CHARLES WILLIAM.
Can. b. Rochester, Eng. 1869; ad. 1934 Toronto, Can. M.
JEFFERYS, JAMES.
Eng. Maidstone 1757-1784 London. DNB-T.
JEFFERYS, MARCEL.
Belg. Milan, It. 1872-1924 Brussels, Belg. B-T.
JEFFREYS, LEE.
Am. b. New York 1901; ad. 1934 Utica, N. Y. A.
JEGART, RUDOLF. (S)
Am. ad. 1935 Madison, Wis. M.
JEGERLEHNER, HANS.
Swi. b. Berne 1906. DBA.
JEGHER [or Jegers], JAN CHRISTOFFEL.
Ger. Allemagne 1596-1652/3 Antwerp, Belg. B-Bd-T.
JEHAN DE BOULLOGNE.
see Bologna, Giov. Valentin.
JEHNER [or Jenner], ISAAC. (Eg)
Eng. Westminster 1750-1806? B-DNB-T.
JEHU, JOHN M. (S)
Am. ad. 1915 New York. A12.
JEKYLL, GERTRUDE. (Ill)
Am. ad. 1934 New York. M.
JEMNE, [Mrs.] ELSA LAUBACH.
Am. St. Paul, Minn. 1888; ad. 1934 Same. A-F.
JENCKES, JOSEPH. (Eg)
Am. Colbrooke, Eng. 1602-1683 Saugus, Mass. F-7.
JÊN JÊN-FA.
Chinese. Yuan Period (1260-1368). E.
JENKINS, BURRIS, JR. (Cart)
Am. ad. 1935 New York. M.
JENKINS, FRANK LYNN.
see Lynn-Jenkins, F.
JENKINS, [Mrs.] HANNAH TEMPEST.
Am. b. Phila., Pa.; ad. 1934 Los Angeles, Calif. A.
JENKINS, JOHN ELIOT.
Am. b. Onaga, Kan. 1868; ad. 1934 Amarillo, Tex. A.
JENKINS, JOSEPH JOHN. (Eg)
Eng. London 1811-1885 Same. B-DNB-T.
JENKINS, [Mrs.] MARTHA E.
Am. b. Charleston, Ill.; d. 1923. A020.
JENKINS, MATTIE MAUD.
Am. b. So. Abington, Mass. 1867; ad. 1934 Whitman, Mass. A.
JENKINS, THOMAS.
Eng. Devonshire 1720-1798 Yarmouth. DNB-T.
JENKS, ALBERT.
Am. New York 1824-1901 Los Angeles, Calif. A04-B.
JENKS, JO. (S)
Am. b. 1904; ad. 1934 New York. M.
JENKS, [Mrs.] PHOEBE A. PICKERING HOYT.
Am. Portsmouth, N. H. 1847-1907 Boston. A06-B-F-15-47-829.
JENNER, THOMAS. (Eg)
Eng. ac. 1631-1656 in England. DNB.
JENNEWEIN, CARL PAUL. (S)
Am. b. Stuttgart, Ger. 1890; ad. 1934 Bronx, N. Y. A-Cs-F-W.
JENNEY, EDGAR WHITFIELD.
Am. b. New Bedford, Mass. 1869; ad. 1934 Nantucket, Mass. A.
JENNINGS, [Mrs.] DOROTHY.
Am. b. St. Louis 1894; ad. Same. A.
JENNINGS, LOUISE B.
Mrs. H. S. Jennings.
Am. b. Tecumseh, Mich. 1870; ad. 1934 Balt., Md. A.
JENNINGS, RIXFORD U.
Am. ad. 1934 East Aurora, N. Y. M.
JENNYS, J. WILLIAM.
Am. ac. 1800 in Phila., Pa. [No death date]. F.
JENNYS, RICHARD, JR. (Eg)
Am. ac. 1774-1832 in Boston. F-2-7.
JENSEN, CHRISTIAN ALBRECHT.
Dan. Bredsted 1792-1870 Copenhagen. B-T.
JENSEN, GEORGE.
Am. ad. 1934 Toledo, O. M.
JENSEN, HOLGER W.
Am. b. Denmark 1880; ad. 1934 Dixon, Ill. A-F.
JENSEN, JOHAN LAURENTS.
Dan. Gjentofte 1800-1856. B-T.
JENSON, THOMAS M.
Am. Denmark 1831-1916 Brooklyn, N. Y. A013-F.
JEPSON, GEORGE.
Am. Leeds, Eng. 1844-1917-U. S. A014.
JEPSON, [Mrs.] W. R.
see Wiles, Gladys.
JERACE, VINCENZO L. (S)
It. b. Polistena, It. 1862. T.
JERICHAU, JENS ADOLF. (S)
Dan. Copenhagen 1816-1883. B-Hs-T.
JERICHAU-BAUMANN, ANNA MARIA ELIZABETH.
Dan. Warsaw, Pol. 1817/9-1881 Copenhagen. B-C-T.
JERNBERG, OLOF AUGUST ANDREAS.
Swe. b. 1826; d. 1896 in Sweden. B-T.
JEROME, MILDRED.
Am. ad. 1934 New York. M.
JEROME DE SANCTIS. (Eg)
It. ac. 1487-1506 in Italy. M-Met. Mus. N. Y. Bul. 3-1934.
JERRY, SYLVESTER.
Am. b. Milwaukee, Wis. 1904; ad. 1934 Kalamazoo, Mich. A.
JERVAIS. *see* Jarvis.
JERVAS [or Jervis], CHARLES.
It. Ireland 1675-1739 London. B-DNB-T.

JESPERS, OSCAR. (S)
Belg. b. Brussels; ac. 1910. B.
JESSEL, ROBERT WILLIAM ALBERT.
Eng. b. London 1899; ad. 1934 Same. M.
JESSEN, AGNES.
Am. ex. 1935 Milwaukee, Wis. M.
JESSUP, JOSEPHINE.
[First woman member Nat. Acad.].
Am. b. 1858; d. 1933 Norwalk, Conn. A030.
JESTER, RALPH. (S)
Am. ad. 1934 New York. M.
JETTEL, EUGÈNE.
Aus. Johnsdorf 1845-1901 Trieste. B-T.
JEUNE. *see* Le Jeune.
JEWETT, CHARLES A. (Eg)
Am. Lancaster, Mass. 1816-1878 New York. F-7.
JEWETT, FREDERIC STILES.
Am. Simsbury, Conn. 1819-1864 Cleveland, O. F.
JEWETT, MAUDE SHERWOOD. (S)
Mrs. Edward H. Jewett.
Am. b. Englewood, N. J. 1873; ad. 1934 Easthampton, N. Y. A-Cs-F.
JEWETT, WILLIAM.
Am. East Haddam, Conn. 1795-1873 Jersey City, N. J. B-Bd-DAB-F-1-2-3-4-182.
JEWETT, WILLIAM S.
Am. South Dover, N. Y. 1812-1873. B-F.
JEWITT, THOMAS ORLANDO SHELDON. (Eg)
Eng. Derbyshire 1799-1869 London. DNB-T.
JEX, GARNET W.
Am. ad. 1934 Washington, D. C. A.
JIMÉNEZ Y ARANDA, JOSÉ.
Sp. Sèville 1837-1903. B-T.
JIMÉNEZ Y ARANDA, LUIS.
Sp. b. Sèville 1845. B-T.
JIMÉNEZ, MIGUEL.
Sp. ac. 1466-1497 in Spain. M.
JIPPO, ARAKI.
Jap. b. Nagasaki 1872; ad. 1933 Tokyo. J. vol. 1, page 88.
JIRAK, IVAN.
Am. b. Allegheny, Pa. 1893; ad. 1934 Pittsburgh, Pa. A.
JIROUCH, FRANK L. (S)
Am. b. Cleveland, O. 1878; ad. 1934 Same. A-Cs-DBA-F.
JOANES [or Juánes], JUÁN DE VICENTE MACIP.
Sp. Valencia 1500-1579 Same. B-E-T-722.
JOANNON, ÉTIENNE ALBERT EUGÈNE.
Fr. b. Lyons 1857. B-T.
JOANOWITCH, PAUL.
Aus. b. Vienna 1859. B-T.
JOANSSON, RUTH.
Am. b. Chicago, Ill. 1912; ad. 1934 Same. A.
JOB, ALICE E.
Am. b. Alton, Ill.; ad. 1934 New York. A.
JOBIN, LOUIS. (Carver)
Can. b. 1843; d. 1928 Quebec, Can. M—*see* Art Digest 1-15-1934.
JOCELYN, NATHANIEL. (Eg)
Am. New Haven, Conn. 1796-1881 Same. DAB-F-1-2-3-4-6-7-136-137-179.
JOCELYN, SIMEON S. (Eg)
Am. New Haven, Conn. 1799-1878 Tarrytown, N. Y. F-2-7.
JOCHINSEN, MARION.
Am. ex. 1935 New York. M.
JODE, GERHARD DE. (Eg)
Flem. Nimègue 1509-1591 Antwerp. B-T.
JOCKMUS, HARRY.
Ger. Harburg 1855-1915. B-T.
JODE [or Oude], PEETER DE [The Elder]. (Eg)
Flem. Antwerp 1570-1634 Same. B-T.
JODE [or Oude], PEETER DE [The Younger]. (Eg)
Flem. Antwerp 1606-1674 England? T.
JOEST. *see* Joost.
JOFFE, MARK S.
Am. ex. 1935 New York. M.
JOHANNOT, ALFRED.
Fr. Offenbach, Ger. 1800-1837 Paris. B-T-722.
JOHANNOT, TONY.
Fr. Offenbach, Ger. 1803-1852 Paris. B-T-722.
JOHANSEN, ANDERS D.
Am. b. Denmark; ad. 1935 Brooklyn, N. Y. A.
JOHANSEN, JOHN CHRISTEN.
Am. b. Copenhagen, Denmark 1876; ad. 1934 New York. A28-B-F-W-46-757.
JOHANSEN, [Mrs.] JOHN CHRISTEN.
see MacLane, Myrtle Jean.
JOHANSEN, MARGARET.
Am. ad. 1935 New York. M.
JOHANSEN, VIGGO.
Dan. b. Copenhagen 1851. B-T.
JOHANSSON, JOHAN ALBIN.
Swe. b. Lund. 1879; ex. 1930 Paris, Fr. DBA-T.
JOHANSSON-THOR, ÉMIL NILS.
Swe. b. 1889; ad. 1935 Stockholm. DBA-T.
JOHN, AUGUSTUS EDWIN.
Welsh. b. Tenby, Wales 1878; ad. 1934 Chelsea, Eng. B-E-T-Wa-415-416-825-871.
JOHN, GRACE SPAULDING.
Am. b. Battle Creek, Mich. 1890; ad. 1934 Houston, Tex. A.
JOHN, GWEN. [Sister A. E. John].
Welsh. ad. 1934 Chelsea, Eng. Wa-825.
JOHN, [Mrs.] MARGARET SAWYER.
Am. b. Marion Co., Ill. 1871; ad. 1934 Corvallis, Ore. A.
JOHN, [Sir] WILLIAM GOSCOMBE. (S)
Welsh. b. Cardiff 1860; ad. 1934 London. B-Hs-Wa.
JOHN THE BAPTIST.
see Master of John the Baptist.
JOHN, AMBROSE BODWEN.
Eng. Plymouth 1776-1858 Same. B-DNB-T.
JOHNSON. *see also* Johnston.
JOHNSON, [Mrs.] ADELAIDE. (S)
Am. b. Plymouth, Ill.; ad. 1934 Wash., D. C. A-Cs-F-W.
JOHNSON, ARTHUR. (Cari)
Am. b. Cinn., O. 1874; ad. 1934 Berlin, Ger. T-873.
JOHNSON, ARTHUR CLARK.
Am. b. Hyde Park, Mass. 1897; ad. 1934 Same. A.
JOHNSON, BELLE.
Am. ad. 1935 New York. M.

JOHNSON, B. PAULINE.
Am. b. Everett, Wash.; ad. 1934 Ellensburg, Wash. A.
JOHNSON, BURT W. (S)
Am. Flint, O. 1890-1927 Claremont, Calif. A024-F-W14.
JOHNSON, C. EVERETT.
Am. b. California 1866. A28.
JOHNSON, CHARLES EDWARD.
Eng. Stockport 1832/6-1913 London. B-T.
JOHNSON, CLARENCE R.
Am. b. Maxtown, O. 1894; ad. 1934 Lumberville, Pa. A.
JOHNSON, CLIFTON. (Ill)
Am. b. Hadley, Mass. 1865; ad. 1934 Same. A12-W.
JOHNSON, [Miss] CONTENT.
Am. b. Bloomington, Ill.; ad. 1934 New York. A.
JOHNSON, CORDELIA.
Am. b. Omaha, Neb. 1871; ad. 1934 Same. A.
JOHNSON, CORNELIUS.
see Janssens, Van Ceulen.
JOHNSON, CORNELIUS W.
Am. b. Texas 1905; ad. 1934 Chicago, Ill. M.
JOHNSON, CYRUS.
Eng. 1848-1925 London. B-Y01926.
JOHNSON, DAVID.
Am. New York 1827-1908 Walden, N. Y. A07-B-C-F-15.
JOHNSON, DONALD M. (S)
Am. ad. 1934 East Orange, N. J. M.
JOHNSON, DORIS ISABEL.
Am. b. Prov., R. I. 1910; ad. 1934 Trenton, N. J. M.
JOHNSON, EDWIN BOYD.
Am. b. 1904; ex. 1934 Chicago. M.
JOHNSON, EDYTH A. B. (Min)
Am. b. Portsmouth, N. H. 1880. A.
JOHNSON, ELENA MIX.
Mrs. Alexander L. P. Johnson.
Am. b. Nogales, Ariz. 1889; ad. 1934 Wash., D. C. A.
JOHNSON, ERNEST BOROUGH.
see Borough-Johnson, E.
JOHNSON, FRANCIS NORTON.
[Inventor of registering human voice in motion pictures.]
Am. b. 1878; d. 1931 Paris. A028.
JOHNSON, FRANK EDWARD.
Am. b. Norwich, Conn. 1873; ad. 1934 Same. A.
JOHNSON, FRANK TENNEY.
Am. b. Big Grove, Ia. 1874; ad. 1935 Alhambra, Calif. A.
JOHNSON, GRACE MOTT. (S)
Am. b. New York 1882; ad. 1935 Pleastville, N. Y. A-Cs-F.
JOHNSON, HARRY JOHN.
Eng. Birmingham 1826-1884 St. John's Wood. B-DNB-T.
JOHNSON, HARRY L. (Min)
Am. ad. 1934 Swarthmore, Pa. A-F.
JOHNSON, HELEN LESSING.
Mrs. Frank Edgar Johnson.
Am. b. Poughkeepsie, N. Y. 1865; ad. 1934 Yonkers, N. Y. A.
JOHNSON, HELEN SEWELL.
Am. ad. 1934 Washington, D. C. A.
JOHNSON [or Johnston], HENRIETTA.
[First woman painter in America].
Am. ac. 1711-1728/9 in Charleston, S. C. DAB-F-2-45-141 [*see* So. Car. Hist. and Gen. Magazine, Vol. 26].
JOHNSON, HERBERT. (Ill)
Am. b. Sutton, Neb. 1878; ad. 1934 Phila., Pa. A28-F-W.
JOHNSON, HORACE CHAUNCEY.
Am. b. Oxford, Conn. 1820/4. [No death date.] B-F-3-15.
JOHNSON, IRENE CHARLESWORTH. (S)
Am. b. Gering, Neb. 1888; ad. 1934 Nashville, Tenn. A
JOHNSON, IVAR. (S)
Swe. ad. 1934 Stockholm. DBA.
JOHNSON, JAMES. (Eg-Pub)
Eng. ac. 1750-1811 in London. B-DNB-T.
JOHNSON, JEANNE PAYNE.
Mrs. Louis C. Johnson.
Am. b. Danville, O. 1887; ad. 1934 Brooklyn, N. Y. A.
JOHNSON, [Mrs.] JESAMINE INGLEE.
Am. b. Delphi, Ind. 1874; ad. 1934 Connersville, Ind. A.
JOHNSON, JOHN.
Am. ex. 1935 New York. M.
JOHNSON, JONATHAN EASTMAN.
Am. Lovell, Me. 1824-1906 New York. A06-B-C-DAB-E-F-1-4-15-51-138.
JOHNSON, J. THEODORE.
Am. b. Oregon, Ill. 1902; ad. 1934 Chicago. A.
JOHNSON, LAWRENCE. (Eg)
Eng. ac. 1603 in London. B-DNB-T.
JOHNSON, MALVIN GRAY.
Am. b. Greensboro, N. C. 1896; d. 1934 New York. A.
JOHNSON, MAMIE. [C. Irwin.]
Am. b. Saline Co., Kan. 1879; ad. 1934 Tescott, Kan. A.
JOHNSON, MARGARET. (Ill)
Am. b. Boston 1860; ac. 1915 Mt. Vernon, N. Y. A20-W14.
JOHNSON, [Mrs.] MARIANNE FLOWERS.
Am. ad. 1935 Memphis, Tenn. M.
JOHNSON, MARJORIE REMY. (S)
Am. b. 1894; d. 1925 Indianapolis, Ind. A022.
JOHNSON, MARSHALL.
Am. b. Boston, Mass.; ad. 1915 Same. A12-F-46.
JOHNSON, MARTIN.
Br. d. 1868. DNB-T.
JOHNSON, MERLE DE VORE. (Ill)
Am. b. Oregon City, Ore. 1874; ad. 1934 New York. A28-W.
JOHNSON, ROBERT. (Eg)
Eng. Shotley 1770-1796 Kenmore. B-DNB-T.
JOHNSON, SAMUEL FROST.
Am. b. New York 1835. [No death date.] C-F.
JOHNSON, SARGENT CLAUDE. (S)
Am. b. Boston 1899; ad. 1934 Berkeley, Calif. A.
JOHNSON, SEWELL.
Am. b. 1906; ac. 1931. M.

JOHNSON, SIGFRIED.
Am. ad. 1934 New York. M.
JOHNSON, THEODORE WOOLSEY.
Am. b. Phila., Pa. 1874; ad. 1934 Annapolis, Md. A.
JOHNSON, THOMAS. (Eg)
Am. London b. 1844; d. 1904; ac. 1878 U. S. F.
JOHNSON, THOMAS.
Eng. Boston, Eng. 1708-1767 Same. B-T.
JOHNSON, TOM LOFTIN.
Am. b. Denver, Colo. 1900; ad. 1934 New York. A.
JOHNSON, WALTER CLAUDE.
Eng. Sidmouth 1848-1928. Wa01929.
JOHNSON, WILLIAM H.
Am. b. Florence, S. C. 1901; ad. 1934 Denmark. A.
JOHNSON, WILLIAM MARTIN. (Ill)
Am. b. Boston, Mass. 1862; ad. 1934 Flushing, L. I., N. Y. W.
JOHNSON, W. NÖEL.
Eng. b. Bowdon; ac. 1892 Manchester. M.
JOHNSON, W. T. (Eg)
Am. ac. 1850. F-7.
JOHNSSON, IVAR. (S)
Swe. b. Stockholm 1885; ex. 1933 World's Fair, Chicago. DBA.
JOHNSTON, ALEXANDER.
Scot. Edinburgh 1815-1891 London. B-DNB-T.
JOHNSTON, ARNRID BANNIZA.
Eng. b. Sweden 1895; ad. 1930 London. Wa1929.
JOHNSTON, DAVID CLAYPOOLE. (Eg)
[Called "The American Cruikshank"].
Am. Phila., Pa. 1797-1867 Dorchester, Mass. DAB-F-2-7-12-45-55-139-140.
JOHNSTON, FRANCIS HANS.
Can. b. Toronto, Ont.; ad. 1935 Same. M.
JOHNSTON, HENRIETTA. *see* Johnson, H.
JOHNSTON, INA W.
Am. ad. 1934 Brooklyn, N. Y. M.
JOHNSTON, JOHN.
Am. Boston 1752-1818 Same. F-2-45.
JOHNSTON, JOHN BERNARD.
Am. Boston 1847-1886 Same. F.
JOHNSTON, JOHN HUMPHREYS.
Am. b. New York 1857; ad. 1915 Paris. A12-B-F-WX1-46.
JOHNSTON, LOWELL.
Am. ad. 1935 Detroit, Mich. M.
JOHNSTON, MARY G.
Am. b. Evansville, Ind. 1872; ad. 1934 Pewee Valley, Ky. A.
JOHNSTON, [Mrs.] MARY VIRGINIA DEL CASTILLO.
Am. b. Puerto Principe, Cuba 1865; ad. 1934 San Fran., Calif. A.
JOHNSTON, REUBEN LE GRANDE.
Am. Alexandria, Va. 1850-1918 Riverdale, Md. A015-B.
JOHNSTON, ROBERT E. (Ill)
Am. b. Toronto, Can. 1885; d. 1933 Leonia, N. J. A-Obit. N. Y. papers, 11-29-1933.
JOHNSTON, RUTH.
Am. b. Sparta, Ga. 1864; ad. 1934 Balt., Md. A.
JOHNSTON, SCOTT.
Am. Sac City, Ia. 1903; ad. 1934 Chicago. A.
JOHNSTON, THOMAS. (Eg)
Am. Boston 1708?-1767/9 Same. DAB-F-2-7-142.
JOHNSTON, WILLIAM M.
Am. New York 1821/4-1907 Brooklyn, N. Y. A06-B.
JOHNSTONE, GEORGE WHITTON.
Scot. Glamis 1849-1901 Edinburgh. B-T.
JOHNSTONE, HENRY JAMES.
Eng. Birmingham 1835-1907 London. B-T.
JOHNSTONE, JOHN YOUNG.
Can. b. Montreal 1887; d. 1930. M.
JOHNSTONE, WILL. (Ill)
Am. ex. 1933 New York. A28.
JOHNSTONE, WILLIAM BORTHWICK.
Scot. Edinburgh 1804-1868 Same. B-DNB-T.
JOINER, HARVEY.
Am. Charlestown, Ind. 1852-1932 Louisville, Ky. A029-B-Obit. Art Digest, 7-1-1932.
JOLIN, EINAR.
Swe. b. Stockholm 1880; ad. 1935 Same; ex. 1934 Pittsburgh, Pa. DBA.
JOLIVET, HENRI.
Dr. b. Djion; d. 1825 in London. B-T.
JOLLAIN, NICOLAS RENÉ [The Younger].
Fr. Paris 1732/3-1804. B-T.
JOLLAIN [or Joullain], PIERRE.
Fr. Paris 1720-1766. B-T.
JOLLIVET, PIERRE JULES.
Fr. Paris 1794-1871 Same. B-T.
JOLVERT, BARON.
Fr. b. 1803; d. 1871 in France. M.
JONAS, LE ROY F.
Am. b. Wassau, Wis. 1897; ad. 1934 Same. A.
JONAS, LOUIS PAUL. (S)
Am. b. Budapest, Hun. 1894; ad. 1934 New Rochelle, N. Y. A.
JONAS, LUCIEN HECTOR.
Fr. b. Anzin, Fr. 1880. B-DBA-T.
JONAS, RUTH. (P-S)
Am. ex. 1930 New York. Fa.
JONCIÈRES, LÉONCE JOSEPH V DE.
Fr. b. Dompiérre 1871. B-DBA.
JONES, ADRIAN. (S)
Eng. b. Ludlow, Eng. 1845. B-Hs-Wa1929.
JONES, [Mrs.] AGNES BLACKWELL.
Am. ad. 1934 Montclair, N. J. M.
JONES, ALBERTUS E.
Am. b. So. Windsor, Conn. 1882; ad. 1934 Same. A-F.
JONES, ALFRED. (Eg)
Am. Liverpool, Eng. 1819-1900 New York. A020-B-F-7-15-40.
JONES, ANNIE WEAVER.
Am. ac. 1915 in Chicago. A12-B.
JONES, ARTHUR S. H.
Am. ad. 1934 Pittsfield, Mass. M.
JONES, BAYARD. (Ill)
Am. b. Rome, Ga. 1869; ad. 1915 Merrick, L. I., N. Y. A12-F.
JONES, BURNE. *see* Burne-Jones.
JONES, CHARLOTTE. (Min)
Eng. 1768-1847 London. B-DNB-T.
JONES, [Mrs.] CORA ELLIS.
Am. Aurora, Ill. 1875-1932 Birmingham, Ala. A029.

JONES, Dorothy B.
Am. b. 1908; ad. 1934 So. Windsor, Conn. A.

JONES, Elberta Mohler.
Am. b. Kansas City, Mo. 1896; ad. 1934 Hollywood, Calif. A.

JONES, Elizabeth Sparhawk.
see Sparhawk-Jones, E.

JONES, Ernest E.
Am. b. Penn Yan, N. Y. 1885; ad. 1915 Same. A12.

JONES, E. T.
Eng. b. Leeds; ad. 1929 Same. M.

JONES, Eugene Arthur.
Am. b. Brooklyn, N. Y.; ad. 1934 Same. A.

JONES, Fitzedward. (Eg)
Am. ac. 1854 Cinn., O. [No death date.] F-7.

JONES, Francis Coates.
Am. Balt., Md. 1857-1932 New York. A029-B-W.

JONES, George.
Eng. London 1786-1869 Same. B-DNB-T.

JONES, Grace Church ["Jonzi"].
Am. b. West Falls, N. Y.; ad. 1934 Denver, Colo. A-F.

JONES, Gwynne. *see* Gwynne-Jones.

JONES, Henry Bozeman.
Am. b. Phila., Pa. 1889; ad. 1934 Same. A.

JONES, Hugh Bolton.
Am. Balt., Md. 1848-1927 New York. A024-B-C-F-W14-1-15-46-89.

JONES, Hugh Griffith.
Can. b. Randolph, Wis. 1872; ad. 1935 Montreal, Can. M.

JONES, Inigo [or Ignace]. (Eg)
Eng. London 1573-1652 Same. DNB-T.

JONES, Isaac A.
Am. ad. 1934 New York. W.

JONES, James Pope.
Am. b. Crewe, Va. 1890; ad. 1934 Richmond, Va. A.

JONES, Jessie Barrows.
Am. ad. 1934 Cleveland, O. A.

JONES, Joe.
Am. b. St. Louis, Mo. 1909; ad. 1934 Same. A.

JONES, John. (Eg)
Eng. b. 1740; d. 1797. B-DNB-T.

JONES, John Edward. (S)
Ir. Dublin 1806-1862 Same. B-DNB-Hs-T.

JONES, Leon Foster.
Am. b. Manchester, N. H. 1871; ad. 1934 Port Jefferson, L. I., N. Y. A-F.

JONES, Lloyd R.
Am. b. 1890; ad. 1934 Des Plaines, Ia. M.

JONES, Louis Edward.
Am. b. Rushville, Pa. 1878; ad. 1934 Woodstock, N. Y. A.

JONES, Marion.
Aust. b. Victoria, Aust.; ad. 1934 Chelsea, Eng. Wa.

JONES, Martha Miles.
Am. b. Denison, Ia. 1870; ad. 1934 La Jolla, Calif. A.

JONES, Mary Elizabeth.
Am. b. Scranton, Pa. 1903; ad. 1934 Same. A.

JONES, Mary Klauder. (S)
Am. ad. 1934 Palma, Mallorca Island [Spain]. M.

JONES, Maud Raphael.
Eng. b. Bradford, Eng.; ac. 1930. T.

JONES, Nell Choate.
Am. b. Hawkinsville, Ga.; ad. 1934 Brooklyn, N. Y. A.

JONES, Paul.
Am. b. Harrodsburg, Ky. 1860; ad. 1934 Cinn., O. A.

JONES, Prescott M.
Am. ad. 1934 Boston, Mass. M.

JONES, Rachel Rand.
Am. b. New Haven, Conn. 1905; ad. 1934 Same. A.

JONES, Reginald.
Eng. b. Kent; ac. 1880-1904 in Canada. B-T.

JONES, Richard.
Eng. b. Reading 1767; d. 1840. DNB-T.

JONES, Ruth Gertrude.
Am. ad. 1934 Schenectady, N. Y. M.

JONES, Seth C.
Am. Rochester, N. Y. 1853-1930 Same. A028-F.

JONES, Sidney.
Am. b. Montreal, Can. 1875; ad. 1934 New York. A.

JONES, Susan.
Am. b. Phila., Pa. 1897; ad. 1934 Same. A.

JONES, Sydney Robert. (Et)
Eng. b. Birmingham 1881; ad. 1934 London. Wa.

JONES, Thomas.
Welsh. b. Wales 1743; d. 1803 Same. DNB-T.

JONES, [Sir] Thomas Alfred.
Irish. b. Dublin 1823; d. 1893 Same. B-T.

JONES, Thomas D. (S)
Am. b. 1808; d. 1881 Cinn., O. B-F.

JONES, Thomas Hampson.
Eng. Liverpool 1846-1916 Birkenhead. T.

JONES, Thomas Hudson. (S)
Am. b. Buffalo, N. Y. 1892; ad. 1934 New York. A.

JONES, William R. (Eg)
Am. ac. 1810-1824. F-2-7.

JONGERS, Alphonse.
Am. b. France 1872; ad. 1915 New York. A-B-F-W14.

JONGH [or Jonge], Ludolf de.
Dut. Overschie 1616-1679 Hillegesberg. B-C-T.

JONGH, Tinus de.
Dut. ex. 1934 London. M.

JONGHE, Gustave Léonhard de.
Belg. Courtrai 1828/9-1893 Antwerp. B-T-15.

JONGHE, Jan Baptiste de.
Fr. Courtrai 1785-1844 Brussels, Belg. C-T.

JONGKIND, Johann Barthold.
Dut. Latrop, Holland 1819-1891 France. B-C-T.

JONSON, Jon Magnus. (S)
Am. b. Upham, N. D. 1893; ad. 1934 Frankfort, Ind. A.

JONSON, Raymond.
Am. b. Chariton, Ia. 1891; ad. 1934 Santa Feé, N. M. A-F.

JONSON, Van Ceulen.
see Janssens, Van C.
JÖNSSEN, Anders. (S)
Swe. b. Sweden 1883; ad. 1930 Paris. DBA.
JÖNSSON, Einar. (S)
Icelandic. b. Iceland 1874; ac. 1930. T-798.
JONVAL, Fernand.
Fr. ac. 1907; d. 1928 Paris. DBA.
JONZEN, Basil.
Nat.? ex. 1934 London, Eng. M.
JOOST [or Joest or Jooesten], Jan.
Dut. b. 1460; d. 1519 Haarlem. B-C-T.
JOPLING, Joseph Middleton.
Eng. London 1831-1884 Chelsea. B-T.
JOPLING-ROWE, Mrs. [née Louise Goode].
Eng. b. Manchester 1843; d. 1933. 829.
JOR, Chu H.
Am. ad. 1935 New York. M.
JORDAENS, Hans I [The Elder].
Flem. Antwerp 1539-1604/13 Delft, Holland. B-T.
JORDAENS, Hans II.
Flem. Antwerp 1581-1653 Same. B-T.
JORDAENS, Hans III [Lelong].
Flem. Antwerp 1584-1642/4. B-T.
JORDAENS, Hans IV [Pollepel].
Dut. Delft 1616-1681 The Hague. B-Bd-T.
JORDAENS, Jakob [or Jacques].
Flem. Antwerp 1593-1678 Same. B-Bd-C-E-T-449-722-935.
JORDAN, Charles.
Am. ac. 1815-1820 in Connecticut. M.
JORDAN, David Wilson.
Am. b. Harrisburg, Pa. 1859; ad. 1934 New York A-B.
JORDAN, Ésteban. (S)
Sp. Valladolid 1534-1600. B-T.
JORDAN, F. Elmer. (S)
Am. b. Bedford, Ind. 1884; ad. 1934 Detroit, Mich. A.
JORDAN, Henry. (Eg)
Am. b. England; ac. 1836 U. S. [No death date.] F-7.
JORDAN, James Blount.
Am. b. Nashville, Tenn. 1904; ad. 1934 Same. A.
JORDAN, Lena E.
Am. ad. 1934 Springfield, Mass. M.
JORDAN, Mildred C. (Min)
Am. b. Portland, Me.; ad. 1935 New Haven, Conn. A12-F.
JORDAN, Rudolph.
Ger. Berlin 1810-1887 Düsseldorf. B-C-T.
JORGE. *see Inglés.*
JORGENSEN, Jorgen.
Am. b. Denmark 1871; ad. 1934 Maplewood, N. J. A.
JORIN, Jean. (S)
Swi. b. Basel, Swi. 1888. DBA.
JORIS, Pio.
It. b. Rome 1843; d. 1921 Same. B-C-T.
JORISZ, David [or Jan]. (Eg)
Flem. b. Bruges 1501; d. 1556 Basel, Swi. B-T.
JOSEPH, George Francis.
Ir. Dublin 1764-1846 Cambridge, Eng. B-DNB-T.
JOSEPH, Julian.
Am. ex. 1934 Mystic, Conn. M.
JOSEPH, Samuel. (S)
Eng. ac. 1811-1850 in London. B-DNB-T.
JOSEPH, Sydney.
Am. ad. 1934 San Fran., Calif. M.
JOSEPHI, Isaac A. (Min)
Am. b. New York; ad. 1934 Same. A-B-W-46.
JOSEPHSON, Ernest.
Swe. Stockholm 1851-1906 Same. T.
JOSEY, Richard. (Eg)
Eng. b. 1840/1; d. 1906 London. B-T.
JOSI, Christian. (Eg)
Dut. b. Utrecht; d. 1828 London. B-DNB-T.
JOSIMOVICH, George.
Am. b. Mitrovica, Srem, Yugoslavia 1894; ad. 1934 Chicago. A.
JOSLYN, Florence Brown.
Am. b. Michigan; ad. 1934 Okla. City, Okla. A.
JOSSELYN, Christine S.
Am. ex. 1935 New York. M.
JOSSET, Raoul Jean. (S)
Am. b. Tours, Fr. 1898; ad. 1934 Chicago. A.
JOU, Louis.
Fr. b. Gracia, Barcelona, Sp. 1882; ad. 1930 Paris. DBA.
JOUAS, Charles.
Fr. b. Paris 1866; ad. 1930 Same. B-DBA.
JOUBERT, Andrée.
Fr. ad. 1935 Paris. DBA.
JOUBERT, Léon.
Fr. b. Quimper; ac. 1884-1900 in France. B-T.
JOUCLARD, Adrienne Lucie.
Fr. b. Orville 1882; ex. 1934 Warsaw, Pol. B-DBA-T.
JOUETT, Matthew Harris.
Am. Harrodsburg, Ky. 1787-1827 Louisville, Ky. B-Bd-C-DAB-F-2-4-6-67-144-183.
JOUFFROY, François. (S)
Fr. Dijon 1806-1882 Laval. B-Hs-T.
JOULLAIN, François. (Eg)
Fr. Paris 1697-1779 Same. B-T.
JOULLIN, Amédée.
Am. San Fran., Calif. 1862-1917 Same. A014-B-F.
JOULLIN, Lucile.
Mrs. Lucile J. Benjamin.
Am. Geneseo, Ill. 1876-1924 San Fran., Calif. A20-F.
JOURDAIN, Francis.
Fr. b. Paris 1876; ad. 1930 Same. B-DBA-T.
JOURDAIN, Henri.
Fr. b. Paris 1864; d. 1931. B-DBA.
JOURDAIN, Joseph Roger.
Fr. b. Louviers 1845; d. 1918. B-T.
JOURDAN, Adolphe.
Fr. b. Nimes 1825; d. 1889. B-T.
JOURNEAY, Helen. (S)
Am. ad. 1935 Odenton, Md. M.
JOURNOT, Louis Isidore. (Eg)
Fr. b. Port-Marly 1867. B-DBA.
JOUSSET, Léon.
Fr. b. Montereau 1877. DBA.
JOUVE, Paul Pierre. (Ill)
Fr. b. Marlotte 1880. B-DBA.
JOUVENAL, Jacques. (S)
Fr. b. 1829; d. 1905 in France. M.
JOUVENET, Jean Baptiste [Le Grand].
Fr. Rouen 1644-1717 Paris. B-C-E-T-722-897.

JOUVET-MAGRON, Dominique.
Fr. ad. 1930 Paris. T.
JOWETT, Matthew Harris.
Eng. b. 1787; d. 1827 in England. M.
JOY, Albert Bruce. (S)
Ir. Dublin 1842-1924. B-T.
JOY, George Williams.
Ir. Dublin 1844-1925 Woodside, Scot. T-Y01926.
JOY, John Cantiloe.
Eng. 1806-1867 Chichester. B-DNB-T.
JOY, Robert.
Am. ex. 1934 Houston, Tex. M.
JOY, Sue.
Am. ad. 1934 Nashville, Tenn. M.
JOY, Thomas Musgrave.
Eng. Boughton 1812-1866. B-DNB-T.
JOY, William.
Eng. 1803-1867 Chichester. B-DNB-T.
JOYEUX, Pierre. (S)
Fr. b. Angouleme 1881; ac. 1930 Paris. DBA.
JÓZSA [or Józsa], Karl.
Hun. b. Budapest 1872. T.
JOZAN, Saintin François.
Fr. b. Paris 1797; ac. 1831-1859 Same. B-T.
JU-PEÓN.
Chinese. ad. 1935 Nankin, China; ex.1934 Milan, It. M.
JUÁN de BORGONA.
see Borgona, J.
JUÁN de BURGOS.
Sp. ac. 1450 in Sèville. B-T.
JUÁN, Flamenco.
Sp. ac. 1496-1519 in Spain. T.
JUÁN de FLANDES.
Flem. b. 1470? d. 1519? Palencia. T.
JUÁN, Pedro [or Pere]. (S)
Sp. ac. 1400-1445 in Zaragoza. T.
JUÁN de SEGOVIA.
Sp. ac. 1498 in Spain. T.
JUÁN de SÈVILLA [Escalante].
Sp. Granada 1643-1695 Same. T-722.
JUÁN de SIGÜENZA. (S)
Sp. ac. 15th-16th Cent. in Guadalajara, Sp. T.
JUÁNES, Juán de.
see Joanes, Juán de Vicente.
JUCH, Ernest. (Cari)
Aus. b. Gotha, Ger. 1838; d. 1909 Vienna, Aus. T.
JUDSON, Alice.
Am. b. Beacon, N. Y.; ad. 1934 New York. A-F.
JUDSON, Almira.
Am. b. Milwaukee, Wis.; ad. 1934 San Fran., Calif. A.
JUDSON, C. Chapel.
Am. b. Detroit, Mich. 1864; ad. 1934 Carmel, Calif. M.
JUDSON, Jane Berry. (Eg)
Am. ex. 1935 Syracuse, N. Y. M.
JUDSON, [Mrs.] Minnie Lee.
Am. b. Milford, Conn. 1865; ad. 1934 Stratford, Conn. A.
JUDSON, Sylvia Shaw. (S)
Am. b. Chicago, Ill. 1897; ad. 1934 Same. A.
JUDSON, William Lees.
Am. Manchester, Eng. 1852-1928 Los Angeles, Calif. A026-B-F-W14.
JUEL, Jens.
Dan. Gamborg 1745-1802 Copenhagen. B-T.
JUENGLING, Frederick. (Eg)
Am. Leipzig, Ger. 1846-1889 New York. DAB-F-8-55-145-185.
JUERGENS, Alfred.
Am. b. Chicago, Ill. 1866; d. 1934 Same. A-B-F-W-Obit. N. Y. papers, 4-20-1934.
JUERGENS, Charles.
Am. Cinn., O. 1875-1919 Same. A12.
JUKES, Francis.
Eng. b. Martley 1745; d. 1812. B-DNB-T.
JULIEN, Bernard Romain.
Fr. b. Bayonne 1802; d. 1871 Same. B-T.
JULIEN, Jean.
Fr. b. Marseilles 1888; ac. 1930. DBA.
JULIEN, Octave Henri.
French-Canadian; b. 1852; d. 1908. M.
JULIEN, Pierre. (S)
Fr. b. St. Paulien 1731; d. 1804 Paris. B-T.
JULIEN Simon [Julien L'Apostat].
Fr. b. Toulon 1735; d. 1800 Paris. B-T.
JULIO, E. B. D. Fabino.
Am. b. St. Helena 1843; d. 1879 Georgia. F-144-183.
JULIUS, Oscar.
Am. b. Boston, Mass. 1883; ad. 1934 Malverne, L. I., N. Y. A.
JULIUS, Victor.
Am. b. Boston, Mass. 1882; ad. 1934 Red Bank, N. J. A.
JULLIEN, Anthelmé Joseph Claude.
Fr. Lyons 1840-1867 Same. B-T.
JUNCKER, Justus.
Ger. Mainz 1703-1767 Frankfort. T.
JUNCKER, Zacharias. (S)
Ger. b. 1578/80; d. 1657 in Germany. T.
JUNE, John. (Eg)
Eng. ac. 1740-1770 in London. B-DNB-T.
JUNG, Charles Frédéric.
Fr. b. Lyons 1865; ac. 1930. DBA.
JUNG, George. (Mu)
Aus. ac. 1934 in Austria. M.
JUNGBLUT, J.
Ger. ac. 1842 in Düsseldorf. B-T.
JUNGE, Carl Stephen.
Am. b. Stockton, Calif. 1880; ad. 1934 Oak Park, Ill. A-F-W.
JUNGHANNS, Julius Paul.
Ger. b. Vienna, Aus. 1867. B-T.
JUNGMANN, Nico W. [or Nicolaus].
Dut. b. 1872 in Holland. B-T.
JUNGNICKEL, Ludwig-Heinrich.
Aus. ad. 1935 Vienna; ex. 1934 Pittsburgh, Pa. M.
JUNI [or Jony], Juán de. (S)
Sp. Joigny 1507-1577 Valladolid. B-Hs-T.
JUNKER, Bruno.
Am. ad. 1935 New York. M.
JUNKER, Leo Helmholz.
Am. b. Chicago, Ill. 1882; ad. 1934 Pelham, N. Y. A.

JUNKIN, Marion M.
Am. b. Chuiu, Korea 1905; ad. 1934 Lexington, Va. A.
JUNYER, Joan.
Sp. b. 1904; ad. 1935 Paris; ex. 1934 Pittsburgh, Pa. M.
JURECKA, Cyril. (S)
Am. b. Moravia, Czec; ad. 1934 Claremont, Calif. A.
JURRES, Johannes Hendrik.
Dut. b. Leeuwarden 1875; ac. 1930. DBA.
JUSTE, Antoine. (S)
It. Florence 1479-1519 Tours, Fr. B-Hs-T.
JUSTE Family.
It. ac. 16th Cent. in Italy and France. T.
JUSTE, Jean. (S)
It. Florence 1485-1549 Tours, Fr. B-Hs-T.
JUSTICE, Martin. (Ill)
Am. ad. 1934 Los Angeles, Calif. A.
JUSTIS, Lyle. (Ill)
Am. ac. 1931 in Phila., Pa. M.
JUSTUS OF GHENT [Wassenhoven].
Flem. b. Ghent 1410; d. 1475. B-E-T.
JUSTUS OF PADUA.
see Menabuoi, Giusto di Giovanni de.
JUSTUS, Roy Braxton. (Cart)
Am. b. Avon, S. D. 1901; ad. 1934 Sioux City, Ia. M.
JUSTYNE, Percy William. (Ill)
Eng. b. Rochester, Eng. 1812; d. 1883. DNB-T.
JUSZKO, Jeno. (S)
Am. b. Hungary 1880; ad. 1935 New York. A-Cs-F.
JUTA, Jan. (Mu)
Br. ac. 1934 So. Africa. M.
JUTSUM, Henry.
Eng. London 1816-1869 St. Johns' Wood. B-Bd-DNB-T.
JUTTNER, Franz.
Ger. b. Friedenau; ac. 1909 in Berlin. B-T.
JUTZ, Karl.
Ger. Windschlag, Baden 1838; d. 1916. B-T.
JUVENEL [or Juvenell], Nikolas.
Flem. Pays-Bas 1540-1597 Nüremberg, Ger. B-T.
JUVENEL, Paul.
Ger. Nüremberg 1574/9-1643. B-T.
JUVENET. *see* Jouvnet.
JUVIN, Juliette.
Fr. b. Paris 1896; ad. 1930 Same. DBA.
KABOTIE, Fred.
Indian (American); ex. 1932 New York. 411.
KACHINSKY, Alexander.
Am. b. Russia 1888; ad. 1934 White Plains, N. Y. A.
KADULIN, Vladimir.
Am. ex. 1935 New York. M.
KAELIN, Charles Salis.
Am. Cinn., O. 1858-1929 Rockport, Mass. A026-B-F-W14.
KAEMMERER [or Kammerer], Frédérick Hendrik.
Dut. The Hague 1839-1902 Paris. B-C-T.
KAENDLER, Johann Joachim. (S)
Prus. b. Firshbach, Prussia 1705. [No death date.] M.
KAEP, Louis J.
Am. b. Dubuque, Iowa 1903; ad. 1934 Chicago. A.
KAER, Isider. (Eg)
Hun. *see* Studio, London, 5-1934, page 280.
KAESBACH, Rudolf. (S)
Ger. b. Munich 1873. T.
KAESELAU, Charles Anton.
Am. b. Stockholm, Swe. 1889; ad. 1934 Provincetown, Mass. A.
KAGER, Johan Matthias.
Ger. Munich 1566-1634 Augsburg. B-T.
KAGY, Sheffield Harold.
Am. b. Cleveland, O. 1907; ad. 1934 Same. A.
KAHAN, S. B. (S)
Am. ex. 1935 Brooklyn, N. Y. M.
KAHILL, Joseph B.
Am. b. Alexandria, Egypt 1882; ad. 1934 Portland, Me. A.
KAHLE, [Mrs.] Julie.
Am. ad. 1934 New York. A.
KAHN, Isaac.
Am. b. Cinn., O. 1882; ad. 1934 Same. A.
KAHN, Julia S.
Am. b. Cinn., O. 1875; ad. 1934 New York. A.
KAINER, Jacob.
Am. ex. 1935 New York. M.
KAINER, Ludwig. (Ill)
Ger. b. Munich 1885; ac. 1934. T.
KAINZ, Martin.
Am. b. Dachan, Bav. 1899; ad. 1935 Tuckahoe, N. Y. A.
KAISER, Charles. (Ill)
Am. b. Buffalo, N. Y. 1893; ad. 1934 Bronxville, N. Y. A.
KAISER, Richard.
Ger. b. Magdeburg 1868; ad. 1930 Munich. B-T.
KAJIWARA, Takuma.
Jap.-Am. b. Japan 1876; ad. 1934 St. Louis, Mo. A-F.
KAKUZO, Sano. *see* Goto.
KALAMIS [or Calamis]. (S)
Greek. (Ionian); ac. 460-445 B.C. B-E-Hs.
KALBECK, Marie Wautner.
Aus. ex. 1935 Vienna. M.
KALCKREUTH, Karl Walter Léopold.
Ger. Carlsruhe 1855-1928. B-E-T.
KALCKREUTH, [Count] Stanislaus von.
Prus. b. Kozmin, Pozen 1820; d. 1894 Munich. C-T.
KALDENBACH, Martin [Hesse]. (Eg)
Ger. b. 1470; d. 1518 Frankfort. T.
KALDENBERG, Frederic Robert. (S)
Am. New York 1855-1923 Same. A020-F-Ta.
KALEY, Winifred.
Am. ex. 1934 New York. M.
KALF [or Kalff], Willem.
Dut. Amsterdam 1621/2-1693 Same. B-C-T-722.
KALFA, Bohumil. (S)
Czec. b. Nová Paka, Czec. 1878; ac. 1930. T-798.
KALIDE, Theodor. (S)
Ger. Königshütte 1801-1863 Gleiwitz. T.
KALISH, Max. (S)
Pol.-Am. b. Poland 1891; ad. 1935 New York. A-Cs.

KALKAR [or Calcar], HANS VON.
Ger. Kalkar 1510-1546 Naples, It. C-T.
KALLMEYER, MINNIE.
Can. b. Detroit, Mich.; ad. 1935 Toronto, Ont. Can. M.
KALLMORGEN, FRIEDRICH.
Ger. b. Altona 1856; d. 1924. B-T.
KALLOS, ARPAD.
Am. b. Hungary 1882. [Address unknown.] A.
KALLSTENIUS, GOTTFRIED.
Swe. b. Vestarvick 1861; ac. 1930. B-DBA-T.
KÁLMAN, PÉTER.
Hun. b. Budapest 1877; ac. 1930. T.
KALMÁR DE KÖVESHÁZA, ELIZA. (Eg)
Aus. b. Vienna 1876; ac. 1930. T.
KALMENOFF, MATTHEW.
Am. b. New York 1905; ad. 1934 Same. A.
KALMIKOFF, IVAN LÉONIDOVITCH.
Rus. b. Russia 1866; ac. 1930. B-T.
KALPAR, NICHOLAS.
Hun. b. 1886; d. 1935 Budapest. Obit. N. Y. papers, 4-13-1935.
KALRAET [or Kalraat], ABRAHAM VON.
Dut. b. Dordrecht 1643; d. 1669/1721. B-Bd-T.
KALRAET, BAREND VAN.
Dut. b. Dordrecht, 1649/50; d. 1721 Same. B-T.
KALTENBACH, LUCILE.
Am. b. Durban, So. Africa; ad. 1934 Chicago, Ill. A.
KALTENMOSER, KASPAR.
Ger. b. 1806; d. 1867 Munich. B-T.
KALTENMOSER, MAX.
Ger. b. Munich 1842; d. 1887 Same. B-T.
KALTWASSER, GEORGE A.
Am. d. 1917 Brooklyn, N. Y. A014.
KALVODA, ALOIS.
Ger. b. 1875 in Germany. M.
KAMBLI [or Kambly], HEINRICH FRIEDRICH. (S)
Ger. Potsdam 1750-1801 Same. T.
KAMENSKY, PAWEL PAWLOWITSCH. (S)
Rus. b. 1858 in Russia. T.
KAMENSKY, THEODORE [or Feodor]. (S)
Am. Leningrad, Rus. 1836-1913 Florida. A12-B-Hs-T.
KAMIENSKI, ANTOINE. (Eg)
Pol. b. Vilno 1861; ad. 1916 Warsaw. B-T.
KAMKÉ, GEORGE LUCIEN LOUIS.
Fr. b. Paris 1889; ad. 1930 Same. DBA.
KAMMERER, FRÉDÉRIC HENDRIK.
see Kaemmerer, F. H.
KAMMERER, MARIA DE.
Hun. b. Hungary; ad. 1934 New York. M.
KAMOCKI, STANISLAW.
Pol. b. Warsaw 1875; ac. 1930. T.
KAMPF, ARTHUR.
Ger. b. Aix-la-Chapelle 1864. B-T.
KAMPF, [Mrs.] MELISSA Q.
Am. b. Phila., Pa. 1867; ad. 1934 Norfolk, Va. A.
KAMPHUYSEN, GOVERT DIRSKSZ.
see Camphuysen, G. D.
KAMPMANN, GUSTAVE.
Ger. Grötzingen 1859-1917. B-T.

KANACHOS [of Sikyon]. (S)
Gr. ac. 500-465 B.C. Hs-T.
KANAOKA, KOSÉ.
Jap. ac. 928-987. J., Vol. 1, page 33.
KANAREK.
Pol. ex. 1933 New York. M.
KANDINSKY, WASSILY.
Rus. b. Moscow 1866; ex. 1935 Oakland, Calif. B-T-417.
KANDLER, JOHANN JOACHIM. (S)
Ger. Fischbach 1706-1775 Munich. T.
KANE, JOHN.
Am. b. West Colder, Scot. 1860; d. 1934 Pittsburgh, Pa. M-Obit. N. Y. papers, 8-11-1934.
KANE, PAUL.
Can. Toronto, Ont. 1810-1883 Same; ac. 1844 U. S. M.
KANEKE, EGON VAN.
Ger. b. Luckenwalde 1881; ex. 1930 Berlin. T.
KANO FAMILY.
Jap. ac. 15th-18th Cent. in Japan. J-T.
KANO TO-UN [Masunobu].
Jap. b. 1624; d. 1694. J., Vol. 1, page 140.
KANOLDT, ALEXANDER.
Ger. b. Carlsruhe 1881. T.
KANOLDT, EDMUND.
Ger. Grossrudestedt 1839-1907 Carlsruhe. B-T.
KANTHAROS [of Sikyon]. (S)
Gr. 500-490 B.C. T.
KANTOR, JOSEPH.
Am. b. Russia 1904; ad. 1934 Stone Ridge, N. Y. A.
KANTOR, MORRIS.
Am. b. Russia 1896; ad. 1934 New York. A-F-701-779.
KANZ, CARL CHRISTIAN. (Min)
Ger. Plauen 1758-1818. B-T.
KAO CHI-FENG.
Chinese. ad. 1935 Canton, China. M.
KAO CHIEN-FU.
Chinese. ad. 1935 Canton, China. M.
KAPFENBERGER, JOSEPH. (S)
Am. ad. 1934 New York. M.
KAPP, EDMUND XAVIER. (Cari)
Eng. b. London 1890; ad. 1934 Same. Wa-873.
KAPPEL, PHILIP. (Et)
Am. b. Hartford, Conn. 1901; ad. 1935 Sarasota, Fla. A28-W.
KAPPES, ALFRED.
Am. b. New York 1850; d. 1894. B-C.
KAPPES, KARL.
Am. b. Zanesville, O. 1861; ad. 1934 Toledo. A-F.
KAPPSTEIN, CARL FREDRICH.
Ger. b. Berlin 1869. B-T.
KARANINA, ERICA.
Am. ad. 1934 Boston, Mass. M.
KARASICK, [Mrs.] MARY K.
Am. ad. 1934 Mt. Vernon, N. Y. M.
KARASZ, ILONKA. (Et)
Am. b. Budapest, Hun. 1896; ad. 1935 Brewster, N. Y. A28-F.
KARAZIN, NICHOLAS N.
Rus. Charkoff 1842-1908 Gatschina. B-T.

KARFOIL, Bernard.
Am. b. Budapest, Hun. 1866; ad. 1934 New York. A-F-T-418-700-779.
KARFUNKLE, David.
Am. b. Vienna, Aus.; ad. 1935 New York. A12-F.
KARGER, Karl.
Aus. Vienna 1848-1913 Same. C-T.
KARL, J. (Ill)
Am. ad. 1934 New York. M.
KARL, [Mrs.] Mable Fairfax. (S)
Am. b. Glendale, Ore. 1901; ad. 1935 Houston, Tex. A.
KARLOVZKY, Berci [Bertalan].
Hun. b. 1858; ac. 1912 Budapest, Hun. B-T.
KAROLIS, Adolfo de.
It. b. Montefiore 1874. T.
KAROLY. *see* Kotasz, Charles.
KAROLY, Andrew.
Am. b. Hungary 1896; ad. 1935 New York. M.
KARP, Leon.
Am. b. Brooklyn, N. Y. 1903; ad. 1934 Ambler, Pa. A.
KARPINSKI, Alfonse.
Pol. b. Poland 1875. Fa.
KARRAS, Spiros John.
Am. b. Kollerion Ellis, Gr. 1897; ad. 1934 Pasadena, Calif. A.
KARS [or Karpelès], Georges.
Fr. b. Prague, Czec. 1882. DBA-T.
KARST, John. (Eg)
Am. Bingen, Ger. 1836-1922 De Bruce, N. Y. A019-F.
KASE, Paul George.
Am. b. Reading, Pa. 1895. A28-F.
KASIMER, Luigi. (Et)
Ger. b. 1881; ad. 1934 Paris. DBA.
KASPARIDES, Éduard.
Ger. b. Markt-Kronau 1858. B-T.
KASSLER, [Mrs.] Bennett. (S)
Am. b. Tacoma, Wash. 1895; ad. 1935 Denver, Colo. M.
KASSLER, Charles Moffat II. (Mu)
Am. b. Denver, Colo. 1897; ad. 1934 Los Angeles. DBA-F.
KAT, Anne-Pierre de.
Belg. ex. Brooklyn, N. Y. 1930. M.
KAT, William.
Am. b. Holland 1891; ad. 1934 New York. A.
KATCHADOURIAN, Sarkis. (Mu)
Per. b. Tabris, Persia 1886; ad. 1934 Paris. M.
KATCHAMAKOFF, Atanas. (S)
Am. b. Leskovetz, Bulgaria 1898; ad. 1935 Los Angeles, Calif. A.
KATE, Herman Frederick Carel ten.
see Ten Kate, H. F. C.
KATES, Herbert S. (Et)
Am. b. New York 1894; ad. 1934 Same. A.
KATHARIN, Calvin.
Am. ad. 1934 Akron, O. M.
KATO, Kentaro.
Jap.-Am. b. Japan 1889; d. 1926 New York. A023.
KATOAKA, Genjiro.
Jap.-Am. b. Ariti, Jap. 1867; ad. 1935 Tokyo, Jap. A12-F.
KATSUGAWA Family. (Jap) T.
KATZ, Amy.
Am. ex. 1935 New York. M.
KATZ, Ethel.
Am. ad. 1934 Boston, Mass. M.
KATZ, Leo.
Am. ad. 1934 Los Angeles, Calif. M.
KATZMAN, Evgeny Alexsandiovich.
Rus. b. 1890; ex. 1934 Phila., Pa. M.
KAUFFER, E. McKnight. (Posters)
Am.-Eng. b. U. S.; ad. 1934 London. Wa-825.
KAUFFMAN and KAUFFMANN.
see also Kaufman and Kaufmann.
KAUFFMAN, Jean François.
Fr. b. 1720; ac. 1750 in Paris. B-T.
KAUFFMAN, Marie Anna Angelica Catharina.
Swiss. b. Coire 1741-1807 Rome, It. B-Bd-C-DNB-E-T-722-829.
KAUFFMANN, Camille Andrene.
Am. b. Chicago, Ill. 1905; ad. 1934 Same. A.
KAUFFMANN, Hermann.
Ger. Hamburg 1808-1889 Same. C-T.
KAUFFMANN, Hugo Wilhelm.
Ger. Hamburg 1844-1915. B-T.
KAUFFMANN, Isidore.
Aus. b. Arad 1853; d. 1921. B-T.
KAUFMAN and KAUFMANN.
see also Kauffman and Kauffmann.
KAUFMAN, Edwin.
Am. ad. 1935 Cleveland, O. M.
KAUFMAN, John François.
Am. b. Switzerland 1870. [Ad. unknown.] A-F.
KAUFMANN, Ferdinand.
Am. b. Oberhausen, Ger. 1864; ad. 1934 Pasadena, Calif. A.
KAUFMANN, Hugo. (S)
Ger. b. Schotten 1868. B-C-T.
KAUFMANN, Wilhelm.
Ger. ad. 1932 Salzburg, Ger. M.
KAULA, Lee Lufkin.
Mrs. William Jurian Kaula.
Am. b. Erie, Pa.; ad. 1934 Boston, Mass. A-B.
KAULA, William Jurian.
Am. b. Boston, Mass. 1871; ad. 1934 Same. A-B-F.
KAULBACH, Friedrich August von.
Ger. Hanover 1850-1920 Munich. B-C-T.
KAULBACH, Hermann.
Ger. Munich 1846-1910. B-C-T.
KAULBACH, Wilhelm von.
Ger. Arolsen, Westphalia 1805-1874 Munich. B-C-E-T.
KAUS, Max.
Ger. b. Berlin 1891; ex. 1934 Pittsburgh, Pa. DBA.
KAUTSKY, Theodore.
Am. ad. 1935 New York. M.
KAUW, Albrecht.
Ger.-Swi. b. Strasburg, Ger. 1621; d. 1681 Berne, Swi. B-T.
KAVEL, Martin.
see Martin-Kavel, François.
KAVLI, Arne Texnes.
Nor. b. Bergen 1878. T.

KAWAMURA, Gozo. (S)
Jap.-Am. b. Japan 1886; ad. 1934 New York. A.
KAY, Gertrude Alice. (Ill)
Am. b. Alliance, O. 1884; ad. 1934 Same. A-F-W.
KAY, James.
Scot. b. Lamlash 1858; ac. 1928. B-Wa1929.
KAY, John. (Cari)
Scot. Dalkeith 1742-1826/30 Edinburgh. B-DNB-E-T.
KAY, [Mrs.] Katherine.
Scot. b. Glasgow; ad. 1934 London. Wa.
KAY, Willem. *see* Key, Willem.
KAYN, Hilde B.
Am. ad. 1934 Brooklyn, N. Y. M.
KAY-SCOTT, Cyril.
Am. b. Richmond, Va. 1879; ad. 1935 New York. A.
KAYSER, Charles Edmond.
Fr. b. Paris 1882; ad. 1930 Same. DBA-T.
KAYSER [or Kaiser], Victor. (S)
Ger. ac. 1516-1547 in Augsburg, Ger. T.
KAYSER-EICHBERG, Carl.
Ger. ac. 1910 in Berlin. B-T.
KAZE, Henrietta. (S)
Am. ex. 1934 New York. M.
KAZUMA, Oda.
Jap. ad. 1935 Osaka, Jap.; ex. 1934 New York. M.
KAZWINI.
Per. ac. 14th Cent. in Persia. M.
KAZYMIR IN RACZYI.
Fr. ac. 15th Cent. in France. T.
KEALING, Ruth Elizabeth.
Am. b. Indianapolis, Ind. 1890; ad. 1934 Same. A.
KEAN, Michael. (Min)
Ir. b. Dublin; d. 1823 in London. B-DNB-T.
KEANE, Theodore J.
Am. b. San Fran., Calif. 1880; ad. 1934 Chicago, Ill. A-F.
KEANE, Virginia.
Mrs. C. A. Bryce.
Am. ad. 1934 Richmond, Va. M.
KEARFOTT, Robert Ryland. (P-S)
Am. b. Martinsville, Va. 1890; ad. 1934 Mamaroneck, N. Y. M.
KEARNE [or Kerne], Andreas [or Andrew]. (S)
Br. b. Holland; ac. 1627-1650 in London. DNB-T.
KEARNEY, Francis. (Eg)
Am. Perth Amboy, N. J. 1785-1837 Same. DAB-F-2-6-7-12-40-56-146-147.
KEARNEY, William Henry.
Eng. b. 1800; d. 1858 London. B-DNB-T.
KEASBEY, Henry Turner.
Am. b. Phila., Pa. 1882; ad. 1934 New York. A.
KEAST, Susette Schulty.
Am. Phila., Pa. 1892-1932 West Chester, Pa. A029-F.
KEATE, George. (P-and Author)
Eng. Trowbridge 1729-1797 London. B-DNB-T.
KEATING, George. (Eg)
Ir. Ireland 1762-1842 London. B-DNB-T.
KEATING, John.
Ir. b. Limerick 1889; ex. 1934 New York. Wa.
KEATING, Mary A.
Am. ad. 1935 San Antonio, Tex. M.
KECK, Charles. (S)
Am. b. New York 1875; ad. 1934 Same. A-F-W.
KEDJIERSKI, Apolonjusz.
Pol. b. 1851. M-T.
KEELAN, Ofelie Ellen.
Am. ad. 1935 Rome, It. M.
KEELER, Burton.
Am. b. Phila., Pa. 1886; ad. 1934 Scarsdale, N. Y. M.
KEELER, Charles Buller.
Am. b. Cedar Rapids, Ia. 1882; ad. 1934 Glendora, Calif. A-W.
KEELER, Dorothy Jola. (Min)
Am. ad. 1934 Westboro, Mass. M.
KEELER, Rolston [Louis Bertrand].
Am. b. New York 1882; ad. 1925 Same. A12-F.
KEELING, William Knight.
Eng. Manchester 1807-1886 Barton, Eng. B-DNB-T.
KEENE, Charles Samuel. (Cart)
Eng. Hornsey 1823-1891 London. B-DNB-E-T-803-880.
KEENER, Anna Elizabeth.
Am. b. Flagler, Colo. 1895; ad. 1934 Dalhart, Tex. A-F.
KEENEY, Anna. (S)
Am. b. Falls City, Ore. 1898; ad. 1934 Eugene, Ore. A-Cs.
KEEP, Helen Elizabeth.
Am. b. Troy, N. Y.; ad. 1934 East Detroit, Mich. A.
KEERINCX [or Keirincx], Alexandre.
Flem. Antwerp 1600-1652 Amsterdam, Holland. B-C-T-722.
KEFFER, Frances.
Am. b. Des Moines, Ia. 1881; ad. 1934 Hillsdale, N. J. A-F.
KEGLER, August.
Ger. ac. 1878 in Berlin. B-T.
KEHM, W. Bimel.
Am. ad. 1935 New York. M.
KEIBUN, Matsumura.
Jap. b. 1770; d. 1843 in Japan. J., Vol. 2, page 103.
KEINKE, Karl.
see Corcas, Vittorio Matteo.
KEION, Sumiyoshi Family.
Jap. ac. 13th Cent. in Japan. J-T.
KEIRINCK [or Kierings], Alexander.
see Keerincx, Alexandre.
KEISTER, Roy C.
Am. b. Germantown, O. 1886; ad. 1934 Chicago. A.
KEITH, Dora Wheeler.
Am. b. Jamaica, L. I., N. Y. 1857; ad. 1934 New York. A-B-F-W15.
KEITH, Elisha Boudinot.
Am. b. 1892; d. 1918. A016.
KEITH, Elizabeth. (Eg)
Scot. b. Macduff 1887; ad. 1934 Tokyo, Jap. Wa.

KEITH, WILLIAM.
Am. Old Meldrum, Scot. 1839-1911 Berkeley, Calif.
A09-B-DNB-F-W6-46-144-148-183-757.
KELEN, EMERIC. (Cari)
Hun. b. Györ, Hungary 1896. 873.
KELLER, ALBERT VON.
Swi.-Ger. Gais, Swi. 1844/5-1920 Munich, Ger. B-C-E-T.
KELLER, ARTHUR IGNATIUS.
Am. New York 1866-1924 Riverdale, N. Y.
A022-B-DAB-F-W13-46.
KELLER, CHARLES FREDERICK. (Et)
Am. Milwaukee, Wis. 1852-1928 New York. A025.
KELLER, CLYDE LEON.
Am. b. Salem, Ore. 1872; ad. Portland, Ore. A-F.
KELLER, DEANE.
Am. b. New Haven, Conn. 1901; ad. 1934 Same. A.
KELLER, EDGAR MARTIN.
Am. Crescent City, Calif. 1868-1932 Los Angeles, Calif. A029.
KELLER, ELIZABETTA.
Swi. ex. 1933 Milan, It. M.
KELLER, FERDINAND.
Ger. Carlsruhe 1842-1922 Baden-Baden. B-C-T.
KELLER, GEORGE A. (S)
Am. ex. 1935 Davenport, Ia. M.
KELLER, GOTTFRIED.
Swi. Zürich 1819-1890 Same. T.
KELLER, HEINRICH. (S)
Swi. Zürich 1771-1832 Rome, It. T.
KELLER, HENRY GEORGE.
Am. b. Cleveland, O. 1870; ad. 1934 Same. A-F.
KELLER, JOSEPH F.
Am. ex. 1935 New York. M.
KELLER, REAMER. (Cari)
Am. ad. 1935 New York. M.
KELLERHOVEN, MORITZ.
Ger. Altenrath 1758-1830 Munich. B-T.
KELLEY. *see also* Kelly.
KELLEY, MAY MCCLURE.
Mrs. William Fitch Kelley.
Am. ad. 1934 Wash., D. C. A.
KELLEY, SUE E.
Am. b. Calif.; ad. 1934 Riverside, Calif. A.
KELLNER, CHARLES HARRY.
Am. b. Kasa, Czec. 1890; ad. 1934 Chicago. A.
KELLO, [Mrs.] ESTHER [or Hester]. (Min)
Eng. b. Dieppe, Fr. 1571; d. 1624. DNB-T.
KELLOGG, EDMUND PHILO.
Am. b. Chicago, Ill. 1879; ad. 1934 Same. A.
KELLOGG, JANET REID.
Am. b. Merrill, Wis. 1894; ad. 1934 Yonkers, N. Y. A.
KELLOGG, JARVIS GRIGGS. (Eg)
Am. Tolland, Conn. 1805-1873 Hartford, Conn. F-2-7.
KELLOGG, MINOR KILBOURNE.
Am. b. Cinn., O.; ac. 1839-1879. F-4-6.
KELLY. *see also* Kelley.
KELLY, ANNIE D.
Am. d. 1933 in Wash., D. C. A030.
KELLY, CLAY.
Am. b. Jeffersonville, Ind. 1874; ad. 1934 Chicago. A.
KELLY, EDNA. (S)
Am. b. Bolivar, N. Y. 1890; ad. 1934 Long Beach, Calif. A.
KELLY, GERALD FESTUS.
Eng. b. London 1879; ad. 1934 Same. Wa.
KELLY, GRACE VERONICA.
Am. b. Cleveland, O. 1884; ad. 1934 Same. A.
KELLY, JAMES EDWARD. (S)
Am. New York 1855-1933 Same.
A030-F-Ta-W-46-Obit. Art Digest, 6-1-1933.
KELLY, JOHN. (Et)
Am. b. San Fran., Calif.; ad. 1935 Honolulu, Hawaii; ex. 1934 New York. M.
KELLY, JULIA READING.
Am. b. New York 1873; ad. 1935 Same. A-F.
KELLY, LEON.
Am. b. Phila., Pa. 1901; ad. 1934 Same. A.
KELLY, LOUISE.
Mrs. Edward P. Kelly.
Am. b. Waukon, Ia.; ad. 1934 Minn., Minn. A.
KELLY, MARY LOUISE.
Mrs. J. C. Kelly.
Am. b. Shellmound, Tenn. 1874; ad. 1934 So. Pittsburg, Tenn. M.
KELLY, MICHAEL F.
Am. ad. 1934 Katonah, N. Y. M.
KELLY, REDDING J.
Am. ad. 1935 New York. M.
KELLY, ROBERT TALBOT.
Eng. b. Birkenhead 1861; ad. 1934 London. B-T-Wa.
KELLY, THOMAS. (Eg)
Am. Ireland 1795?-1841? New York. F-2-7-40.
KELPE, KARL.
Am. b. 1898; ad. 1934 Chicago, Ill. M.
KELS, FRANZ.
Ger. b. Derendorf 1828; d. 1893. B-T.
KELS, HANS [or Dauher, Hans]. (S)
Ger. Augsburg 1480/5-1559.
T-[*See* Morgan Library, N. Y.].
KELSEY, RICHMOND IRWIN.
Am. ad. 1934 Santa Barbara, Calif. A.
KEMBLE, EDWARD WINDSOR. (Cari)
Am. b. Sacramento, Calif. 1861-1933 Ridgefield, Conn. A030-F-W-46.
KEMEYS, EDWARD. (S-of Animals)
Am. Savannah, Ga. 1843-1907 Wash., D. C.
A06-B-DAB-F-Hs-Ta-W4-15-46.
KEMEYS, [Mrs.] LAURA S. (S)
Am. b. Cumberland Co. N. J.; ad. 1915 Wash., D. C. A12.
KEMM, ROBERT F.
Eng. ac. 1874-1885 in London. T.
KEMMELMEYER, F.
[Made life portraits of George Washington.]
Ger. ac. 1790-1810 in Maryland. 786.
KEMMER, JOHANN.
Dut. 1495-1554 Lübeck, Ger. T.
KEMP, OLIVER.
Am. b. Trenton, N. J. 1887; ad. 1934 Detroit, Mich. A.

KEMP-WELCH, LUCY ELIZABETH.
Eng. b. Bournemouth 1869; ad. 1934 Bushey, Herts, Eng. B-DBA-Wa.
KEMP-WELCH, MARGARET.
Eng. ad. 1934 London. M.
KEMPER, RUBY WEBB.
Am. b. Cinn., O. 1883; ad. 1934 Milford, O. A.
KEMPF, TUD.
Am. ad. 1934 Chicago. A.
KEMPNER, PEDRO [Petrus van de Velde].
Flem. b. Brussels 1502/3; d. 1580/8 Same. B-T-722.
KEMPSON, [Mrs.] JULIE HART.
Am. Pittsfield, Mass. 1835-1913 Trenton, N. J. AOX1.
KEMPTON, ELMIRA.
Am. b. Richmond, Ind. 1892; ad. 1934 Same. A.
KENAR, ANTONI. (S)
Pol. ac. 1932 Poland. M.
KENDALL, BEATRICE.
Am. b. New York 1902; ad. 1934 Hot Springs, Va. A.
KENDALL, [Mrs.] MARGARET STICKNEY. (Min)
Am. b. Staten Island, N. Y. 1871; ad. 1934 Simsbury, Conn. A-B-F-W-46.
KENDALL, [Mrs.] MARIE BOENING.
Am. b. Mt. Morris, N. Y. 1885; ad. 1934 Redondo, Calif. A.
KENDALL, WILLIAM SERGEANT. (P-S)
Am. b. Spuyten Duyvil, N. Y. 1869; ad. 1934 Hot Springs, Va. A-B-F-W-46.
KENDERDINE, AUGUSTUS F.
Can. b. Manchester, Eng.; ad. 1935 Saskatoon, Sask., Can. M.
KENDRICK, CHARLES. (Ill)
Am. d. 1914 Brooklyn, N. Y. AOX1.
KENDRICK, EMMA ELEONORA. (Min)
Eng. b. 1788; d. 1871 London. DNB-T.
KENJI.
Jap. ac. 1932 in Japan. M.
KENNARD, [Mrs.] EVA H.
Am. ad. 1934 Coral Gables, Fla. M.
KENNEDY, CHARLES NAPIER.
Eng. London 1852-1898 St. Ives. B-T.
KENNEDY, EDWARD SHERARD.
Eng. ac. 1862-1910 in London. B.
KENNEDY, FAY.
Am. ex. 1934 New York. M.
KENNEDY, LAWRENCE.
Am. b. Pittsburgh, Pa. 1880; ad. 1934 Hinsdale, Ill. A.
KENNEDY, WILLIAM DENHOLM.
Eng. Dumpins 1813-1865 London. B-DNB-T.
KENNEL, LOUIS.
Am. b. North Bergen, N. J. 1886; ad. 1934 Union City, N. J. A.
KENNICOTT, [Dr.] R. H.
Am. ad. 1934 Los Angeles. M.
KENNINGTON, ERIC HENRY.
Eng. b. 1888; ad. 1934 London. Wa.
KENNINGTON, THOMAS BENJAMIN.
Eng. b. Great Grimsby 1856; d. 1916 London. B-T.
KENNION, CHARLES JOHN.
Eng. 1789-1853 London. B-DNB-T.
KENNION, EDWARD.
Eng. Liverpool 1743/4-1809. B-DNB-T.
KENSETT, JOHN FREDERICK.
Am. Cheshire, Conn. 1816-1872 New York. B-Bd-C-DAB-E-F-1-3-4-7-15-26-38.
KENSETT, THOMAS. (Eg)
Am. Hampton Court, Eng. 1786-1829 Hampton, Conn. F-2-7.
KENT, ADA HOWE.
Am. b. Rochester, N. Y.; ac. 1926. A12-F.
KENT, ADALINE. (S)
Am. ex. 1935 New York. M.
KENT, NORMAN. (Eg)
Am. ad. 1935 Geneva, N. Y. M.
KENT, ROCKWELL ["Hogarth, Jr."].
Am. b. Tarrytown, N. Y. 1882; ad. 1935 New York. A-E-F-T-W-1-46-419-779-936.
KENT, WILLIAM. (P-S)
Eng. Yorkshire 1684/5-1758 London. B-Bd-DNB-T.
KENWORTHY, DAVID.
Eng. ex. 1934 London. M.
KENWORTHY, MILDRED TERESE. (Min)
Am. ad. 1934 Long Beach, Calif. M.
KENYON, HENRY R.
Am. ad. 1934 Ipswich, Mass. A-F.
KEPHISODORUS, I. (S)
Gr. ac. 372-369 B.C. Hs-T.
KEPPLER, JOSEPH. (Cari)
Am. Vienna, Aus. 1838-1894 New York. DAB-55-78-149.
KERCKHOVE, ERNEST VAN DEN.
Belg. Brussels 1840-1879. B-T.
KERHOFF, D.
Dut. Amsterdam 1766-1821 Same. B-T.
KERIGAN, [Mrs.] MILDRED ANDERSON POST.
Am. Wayne, Pa. 1892-1921. A018.
KERKAN, EARL CAVIS.
Am. ad. 1935 New York. M.
KERN FAMILY.
Ger. ac. 16-18th Cent. in Germany. T.
KERNAN, JOSEPH F.
Am. b. Brookline, Mass. 1878; ad. 1934 New York. A.
KERNS, MAUDE I.
Am. b. Portland, Ore. 1876; ad. 1934 Eugene, Ore. A.
KERR, [Mrs.] BLANCHE WEYBURN.
Am. b. Rockford, Ill. 1872; ad. Oak Park, Ill. A.
KERR, EDWARD T.
Am. b. 1862; d. 1907 New York. A06-B.
KERR, GEORGE. (Ill)
Am. ad. 1934 New York. A.
KERR, JAMES WILFRID.
Am. b. New York 1897; ad. 1934 Same. A.
KERR-LAWSON, JAMES.
Eng. b. Fife, Scot. 1864; ad. 1934 London. Wa.
KERRY, WILLIAM LOUIS.
Eng. Liverpool 1818-1893 Waterloo, Eng. B-T.
KERSCHENSTEINER, JOSEF.
Ger. b. Augsburg 1864. T.
KERSEBOOM, FREDERICK.
Eng. Solingen, Ger. 1632-1690 London. B-DNB-T.
KERVILY, [Count] GEORGES LE SERREC DE.
Fr. ex. 1935 San Fran., Calif. M.
KERWIN, MARY CATHERINE. (Min)
Am. ad. 1934 Los Angeles, Calif. M.

KESLER, Clara Elise.
Am. b. Minn., Minn. 1910; ad. 1934 So. Minn., Minn. A.
KESSEL, Ferdinand van.
Flem. Antwerp 1648-1696 Bréda. C-T.
KESSEL, Johan van I.
Flem. Antwerp 1626-1679 Same. B-C-T-722.
KESSEL, Johan van II.
Flem. Antwerp 1654-1708 Madrid, Sp. B-T.
KESSEL, Johan van III.
Dut. Amsterdam 1641/2-1680 Same. B-T.
KESZTHELYI, Alexander S.
Am. b. Hungary 1874; ad. 1915 Los Angeles, Calif. A12.
KETCHAM, Austin.
Am. b. Richmond Hill, L. I., N. Y. 1898; ad. 1934 Kansas City, Mo. A.
KETCHAM, Susan M.
Am. b. Indianapolis, Ind.; ad. 1935 New York. A12-F.
KETEL, Cornelis.
Dut. Gouda 1548-1616 Amsterdam. C-DNB-T.
KETTEN, Maurice Prosper Fiorino. (Cart)
Am. b. 1875; ad. 1934 New York. W.
KETTERER, Gustav.
Am. b. Germany 1870; ad. 1934 Phila., Pa. A-F.
KETTIG, Dorothy.
Am. ad. 1934 New York. M.
KETTLE, [Sir] Rupert A.
Eng. b. 1817; d. 1894. B-T.
KETTLE, Tilly.
Eng. b. London 1735; d. 1786. B-DNB-T.
KEULEN, van. *see* Ceulen, van.
KEULÉYAN, Jean Lafon.
Fr. b. Paris 1886. DBA.
KEVER, Jacob Simon Hendrik.
[Also called "Monogramist, I. K."]
Dut. Laren 1854-1922 Amsterdam. B-T.
KEY [or Keyen], Adrian Thomas [The Younger].
Flem. ac. 1558-1589 in Antwerp. B-T.
KEY, John Ross.
Am. Balt., Md. 1832-1920 Same. A017-B-F-15.
KEY, Mable.
Am. Paris 1874-1926 Chicago. A023.
KEY, Rae.
Mrs. Edmund Key, Jr.
Am. b. Marshall, Tex.; ad. 1934 Same. A.
KEY [or Kay], Willem.
Flem. Bréda 1515/20-1568 Antwerp. B-T.
KEYNES, J. Maynard.
Eng. ex. 1935 London. M.
KEYS, Samuel. (China P)
Eng. b. 1771; d. 1850 Derby. DNB-T.
KEYSE, Thomas.
Eng. b. 1722; d. 1800 Bermondsey, Eng. B-DNB-T.
KEYSER, Ephraim. (S)
Am. b. Balt., Md. 1850; ad. 1934 Same. A-B-Cs-F-Hs-Ta-W.
KEYSER, Ernest Wise. (S)
Am. b. Balt., Md. 1875; ad. 1934 New York. A-B-W.
KEYSER, Hendrik de. (S)
Dut. Utrecht 1565-1621 Amsterdam. B-Hs-T.
KEYSER, Nicaise [or Nicasius] de.
Flem. Santvliet 1813-1887 Antwerp. B-C-T.
KEYSER, Pieter de.
Dut. Amsterdam 1595-1676 Same. Hs-T.
KEYSER, [Miss] Ragnhild.
Nor. b. Norway; ad. 1935 Paris. M.
KEYSER, Thomas de [or Theodore Dirk].
Dut. Amsterdam 1596/7-1667 Same. B-C-E-T-722.
KEYSER, Willem de [The Younger]. (S)
Flem. Antwerp 1647-1692 London. B-DNB-Hs-T.
KHNOPFF, Fernand Edmond Jean Marie. (S)
Belg. Grembergen 1858-1921. B-E-T-798.
KIBBEY, Ilah Marian.
Am. b. Geneva, O.; ad. 1934 Kansas City, Mo. A.
KICK [or Kik], Cornelis.
Dut. Amsterdam 1635-1675. B-Bd-T.
KICK [or Kuck], Symon van.
Dut. Delft 1603-1652 Amsterdam. B-Bd-T.
KIDD, Harry.
Am. b. Detroit, Mich. 1899; ad. 1935 El Paso, Tex. M.
KIDD, Velma Enslen.
Am. b. Birmingham, Ala. 1912; ad. 1934 Same. A.
KIDD, William.
Scot. Edinburgh 1796-1863. B-DNB-T.
KIDDIER, William.
Eng. 1859-1934 Nottingham. M-Wa-Obit. Art News, 3-17-1934.
KIERINCKS [or Keirinck], Alexander.
see Keerinck, A.
KIESEL [or Kisel], Comad.
Ger. Düsseldorf 1846-1921. B-T.
KIESSLING, Johann Paul Adolf.
Ger. Breslau 1836-1919. B-T.
KIFFER, Charles.
Fr. b. Paris 1902. DBA.
KIHN, Wilfred Langdon.
Am. b. Brooklyn, N. Y. 1898; ad. 1934 East Haddam, Conn. A-F.
KIKOINE, Michel.
Rus. b. Russia 1892; ac. 1929 in Paris. DBA.
KILBERT, Robert P.
Am. ad. 1934 Chicago. A.
KILBURN, William.
Ir. Dublin 1745-1818 Wallington. DNB-T.
KILBURNE, George Goodwin.
Eng. b. 1839; d. 1924. B-T-Y01925.
KILYENYI, Julio. (S-Med)
Am. b. Hungary 1885; ad. 1934 New York. A-Cs-F.
KILGOUR, A. Wilkie.
Can. Kirkcaldy, Scot. 1868-1930 Montreal, Can. M.
KILHAM, Aline.
Am. ad. 1934 Boston, Mass. M.
KILHAM, Jane Houston.
Am. b. 1870; d. 1930 Boston, Mass. A028.
KILHAM, Walter H.
Am. b. Beverley, Mass. 1868; ad. 1934 Boston. A.
KILIAN [or Kilien], Lukas.
Ger. Augsburg 1579-1637 Same. B-T.

KILIAN, PHILIPP. (Eg)
Ger. b. 1628; d. 1693. B-T.
KILIAN, PHILIPP ANDREAS.
Ger. Augsburg 1714-1759 Same. B-T.
KILIAN, WOLFGANG.
Ger. Augsburg 1581-1622 Same. B-T.
KILLAM, WALTER MILTON.
Am. b. Prov., R. I. 1907; ad. 1934 Woodstock, N. Y. M.
KILLIGREW, ANNE. (Poet and P)
Eng. London 1660-1685. B-DNB-T.
KILPATRICK, AARON EDWARD.
Am. b. St. Thomas, Can. 1872; ad. 1934 Eagle Rock, Calif. A-F-W.
KILPATRICK, DE REID GALLATIN.
Am. b. Uniontown, Pa. 1884; ad. 1934 Same. A.
KILPATRICK, ELLEN.
Am. ad. 1934 Baltimore, Md. M.
KILPATRICK, MARY.
Am. ad. 1934 Baltimore, Md. M.
KILPIN, LEGH MULHALL.
Can. Ryde in Isle of Wight 1853-1919 Montreal, Can. M.
KILVERT, B. CORY.
Am. b. Ontario, Can.; ad. 1934 Nyack, N. Y. M.
KIMBALL, ALONZO MYRON.
Am. Green Bay, Wis. 1874-1923 Evanston, Ill. A020-B-T.
KIMBALL, CHARLES FREDERICK. (Et)
Am. b. 1836; d. 1907. M.
KIMBALL, DOROTHY LONG.
Am. ad. 1934 Glen Ridge, N. J. M.
KIMBALL, E. WYATT.
Am. d. 1927 Cambridge, Mass. A024.
KIMBALL, HARRIET STOCKTON.
Am. ad. 1934 Buffalo, N. Y. M.
KIMBALL, ISABEL MOORE. (S)
Am. b. Wentworth, Ia.; ad. 1934 Brooklyn, N. Y. A-F.
KIMBALL, KATHARINE. (Et)
Am. b. Fitzwilliam, N. H.; ad. 1934 London. A28-F-W.
KIMBALL, LEWIS.
Am. ad. 1935 New York. M.
KIMBALL, MAULSBY, JR.
Am. b. 1904; ad. 1934 Phila., Pa. A.
KIMBEL, RICHARD M.
Am. b. New York; ad. 1934 Same. A.
KIMBERLY, CARA DRAPER.
Mrs. Samuel A. Kimberly.
Am. b. St. Louis, Mo.; ad. 1934 Wash., D. C. A.
KIMBERLY, DENISON.
Am. Guilford, Conn. 1814-1863. F-2-3-7.
KIMBROUGH, FRANK RICHMOND. (Ill)
Am. b. Tenn.; d. 1902 England. A04.
KIMMEL, LU.
Am. b. Brooklyn, N. Y.; ad. 1934 Same. A.
KIMPTON, AMY L.
Am. ad. 1934 Toledo, O. M.
KINDLER, ALBERT [or Alfred].
Ger. Allensbach 1833-1876 Méran, Swi. B-T.
KINDLER, ALICE RIDDLE.
Mrs. Hans Kindler.
Am. b. Germantown, Pa. 1892; ad. 1934 Balt., Md. A-F.
KINDLUND, ANNA BELLE WING. (Min)
Mrs. James Candie Kindlund.
Am. b. Buffalo, N. Y. 1876; d. 1922. A20.
KING, ALBERT F.
Am. b. Pittsburgh, Pa. 1854; ad. 1934 Same. A-F.
KING, CECIL.
Eng. b. 1881; ex. 1934 London. Wa.
KING, CHARLES B. (Et)
Am. b. Angel Island, Calif. 1869; ad. 1935 Detroit, Mich. A12-F.
KING, CHARLES BIRD.
Am. Newport, R. I. 1785-1862 Wash., D. C. B-Bd-F-2-4.
KING, CLARENCE V.
Am. ad. 1934 New York. M.
KING, CLINTON BLAIR.
Am. b. Fort Worth, Tex. 1901; ad. 1934 Same. A.
KING, DANIEL. (Eg)
Eng. b. Chester; d. 1664 London. B-DNB-T.
KING, ELEANOR.
Am. b. Marlow, Okla. 1909; ad. 1934 Pensacola, Fla. A.
KING, ELIZABETH A. [Bessie].
Am. b. 1855; ad. 1934 Atlanta, Ga. A.
KING, EMMA B. (Poet and P)
Am. Indianapolis, Ind. 1858-1933 Same. A030.
KING, FRANCIS SCOTT. (Eg)
Am. Auburn, Me. 1850-1913 Newark, N. J. A12-B-F-8-185.
KING, FRANK O. (Cart)
Am. b. Cashton, Wis. 1883; ad. 1934 Kissimmee, Fla. W.
KING, FREDERIC LEONARD.
Am. b. New York 1879; ad. 1934 Rockport, Mass. A.
KING, GERTRUDE.
Mrs. L. H. Colville.
Am. b. Newark, N. J.; ad. 1934 Mendhan, N. J. A.
KING, [Mrs.] GILLIS.
Am. b. Dewville, Tex. 1904; ad. 1934 Austin, Tex. A.
KING, HAMILTON.
Am. b. Lewiston, Me. 1871; ad. 1934 East Hampton, N. Y. A-B.
KING, HAYNES.
Eng. b. Barbadoes 1831; d. 1904 London. B-T.
KING, HENRIETTA M. (Ill)
Am. ac. 1934 New York. M.
KING, JAMES S. (Et)
Am. New York 1852-1925 Montclair, N. J. A022-B-F-7.
KING, [Mrs.] JESSIE MARION. (Et)
Scot. ad. 1934 Kirkcudbright, Scot. T-Wa.
KING, JOHN.
Eng. Dartmouth 1788-1847 Same. B-DNB-T.
KING, JOHN CROOKSHANKS. (S)
Am. Ayrshire, Scot. 1806-1882 Boston, Mass. F-T-Ta.
KING, JOHN M.
Am. b. Richmond, Ind. 1897; ad. 1935 Dayton, O. A.
KING, JOSIAH BROWN.
Am. b. 1831. [No death date.]
KING, LOUISE HOWLAND [Mrs. Kenyon Cox]. *see* Cox, Louise [Howland King].

KING, Marian Permelia. (S)
Am. b. Ashtabula, O. 1894; ad. 1934 Same. A-F.
KING, Paul.
Am. b. Buffalo 1867; ad. 1934 Stoney Brook, N. Y. A-F.
KING, Roy E. (S)
Am. ad. 1935 New York. M.
KING, Ruth. (Ill)
Am. b. Chicago, Ill.; ad. 1934 New York. M.
KING, Samuel.
Am. Newport, R. I. 1749-1819 Same. F-2-6-179.
KING, Thomas.
Eng. d. 1769 in London. B-DNB-T.
KING, William Berdan.
Am. Paterson, N. J. 1880-1927 Same. A024.
KING, William Gunning. (Et)
Eng. b. Kensington 1859; ad. 1934 Petersfield. B-T-Wa.
KING, Wyncie. (Ill)
Am. b. Covington, Ga. 1884; ad. 1934 Bryn Mawr, Pa. A28-W.
KING, Yeend. *see* Yeend-King.
KINGS, William Joseph.
Eng. b. Astley 1857. [Deceased.] Wa1929.
KINGSBURY, Alison Mason.
Mrs. Morris Bishop.
Am. b. Durham, N. H. 1898; ad. 1934 Ithaca, N. Y. A.
KINGSBURY, Edna A.
Am. b. Xenia, O. 1888; ad. 1934 Indianapolis, Ind. A.
KINGSBURY, Edward Reynolds.
Am. b. Boston, Mass.; ad. 1934 Oquinquit, Me. A.
KINGSBURY, Henry. (Eg)
Eng. ac. 1750-1791 in London. B-T.
KINGSLEY, Elbridge. (Eg)
Am. Carthage, O. 1842-1918 Brooklyn, N. Y. A015-DAB-F-W9-150-151.
KININGER, Vincenz Georg.
Ger. Regensburg 1767-1851 Vienna, Aus. T.
KINIRY, Dorcas Campbell.
Mrs. Ralph Kiniry.
Am. ad. 1934 Claremont, N. H. M.
KINKHEAD, Charles Edwin.
Am. ad. 1935 Altoona, Pa. M.
KINNEY, Charlotte Conkright.
Am. b. Ionia, Mich.; ad. 1934 Baldwin City, Kan. W.
KINNEY, Margaret West. (Ill)
Mrs. Troy Kinney.
Am. b. Peoria, Ill. 1872; ad. 1935 Falls Village, Conn. A-F-W-46.
KINNEY, Troy. (Et)
Am. b. Kansas City, Mo. 1871; ad. 1935 Falls Village, Conn. A28-F-W-46.
KINSELLA, James.
Am. New York 1857-1923 Same. A020-F.
KINSELLA, Katharine.
Am. ex. 1929 New York. M.
KINSEY, Helen Fairchild.
Am. b. Phila., Pa. 1877; ad. 1934 Same. A.
KINSMAN-WATERS, Ray.
Am. b. Columbus, O. 1887; ad. 1934 Same. A.
KINSON [or Kinsoen], Franciscus Josephus.
Flem. Bruges 1770/1-1839 Same. B-T.
KIORBOE, Carl Frederik.
Swe. Christianofeld, Swe. 1799-1876 Dijon, Fr. B-T.
KIOSAI, Sho-Fu.
Jap. b. 1831; d. 1889. M.
KIP, Johannes. (Eg)
Dut. Amsterdam 1652/3-1722 London. B-DNB-T.
KIPRENSKY, Orest Adamovitch.
Rus. Horporia, Rus. 1783-1836 Rome, It. B-C-T.
KIRALFY, Verona Arnold.
Am. b. New York 1893; ad. 1934 Pittsburgh, Pa. A.
KIRBERG, Otto.
Ger. b. Elberfeld 1850. B-T.
KIRBY, John Joshua.
Eng. Suffolk 1716-1772/4 Kew, Eng. B-T.
KIRBY, John Kynnersley.
Eng. b. Nottinghamshire; ac. 1933 in London. Wa.
KIRBY, Rollin. (Cart)
Am. b. Galva, Ill. 1875; ad. 1934 Westport, Conn. W.
KIRCHBACH, Frank.
Ger. b. London 1859. B-T.
KIRCHMAYER, John. (S-Carver)
Am. b. Bavaria 1860-1930, Mass. DAB-M.
KIRCHNER, Albert Émil.
Ger. Leipzig 1813-1885 Munich. B-T.
KIRCHNER, Ernest Ludwig.
Ger. b. Aschaffenburg 1880. T.
KIRCHNER, Friedrich.
Ger. b. 1748; d. 1789. M.
KIRCHNER, Johann Gottlob. (S)
Ger. b. Merseburg 1706; ac. 1741 in Munich, Ger. T.
KIRCHNER, Raphael.
Am. b. Vienna, Aus.; d. 1917 New York. A015-F.
KIRIN, F.
Jugo-Slav. ac. 1929. M.
KIRK, Elizabeth.
Am. b. Waterbury, Conn. 1866; ad. 1934 Same. A.
KIRK, Eve.
Eng. ad. 1934 London. M.
KIRK, Frank C.
Am. b. Russia 1889; ad. 1934 New York. A.
KIRK, John. (Med)
Eng. b. 1724?; d. 1778? London. DNB-T.
KIRK, Maria Louise.
Am. b. Phila., Pa.; ac. 1894 Same. F.
KIRK, Thomas.
Eng. b. 1765?; d. 1797. DNB-T.
KIRK, Thomas. (S)
Ir. Cork 1777-1845 Dublin. B-DNB-Hs-T.
KIRKALL, Elisha [or Edward]. (Eg)
Eng. Sheffield 1682?-1742 London. B-DNB-T.
KIRKBRIDE, Earle Rosslyn. (Ill)
Am. b. Pittsburgh, Pa. 1891; ad. 1935 Newtown, Pa. A-M.
KIRKHAM, [Mrs.] Charlotte Burt.
Am. b. East Saginaw, Mich.; ad. 1934 Springfield, Mass. A.

KIRKLAND, Forrest.
Am. b. Mist, Ark. 1892; ad. 1934 Dallas, Tex. A.

KIRKLAND, Vance H.
Am. b. Convoy, O. 1904; ad. 1934 Denver, Colo. A.

KIRKPATRICK, Ethel.
Eng. ad. 1934 Harrow, Eng. T-Wa.

KIRKPATRICK, Frank Le Brun.
Am. Phila., Pa. 1853-1917 Same. A05-F.

KIRKPATRICK, Ida Marion.
Eng. b. Jersey 1866; ad. 1934 Harrow, Eng. T-Wa.

KIRKPATRICK, William Arber Brown. (Ill)
Am. b. England 1880; ad. 1934 Waldoboro, Me. A.

KIRKUP, Mary A.
Am. b. Fort Atkinson, Ia.; ad. 1934 Larchmont, N. Y. A.

KIRKUP, Seymour Stocker.
Eng. London 1788-1880 Leghorn, It. B-Bd-DNB-T.

KIRMSE, Marguerite. (Et)
Am. b. England 1885; ad. 1934 New York. A.

KIRSCH, Agatha Beatrice.
Am. b. Creston, Iowa 1879; ad. 1934 Seattle, Wash. A.

KIRSCH, Frederick Dwight.
Am. b. Lincoln, Neb. 1899; ad. 1934 Same. A.

KIRSH, Harriette.
Am. ex. 1934 New York. M.

KISEL. *see* Kiesel.

KISELEWSKI, Joseph A. (S)
Am. b. Browerville, Minn. 1901; ad. 1934 New York. A.

KISER, Virginia Lee.
Am. b. Roanoke Co. Va. 1874; ad. 1934 Columbus, O. A.

KISH, Maurice.
Am. ad. 1935 Brooklyn, N. Y.; ex. 1935 Wash., D. C. M.

KISLING, Moïse [or Maurice].
Pol.-Fr. b. Crakow, Pol. 1891; ad. Paris; ex. 1934 Pittsburgh, Pa. DNB-T-123-797.

KISS, Adolphe.
Hun. ac. 1933. M.

KISS, August Karl Edward. (S)
Ger. Paprotzan 1802-1865 Berlin. B-Hs-T.

KISSACK, R. A.
Am. b. St. Louis, Mo. 1878; ad. 1934 New York. A.

KISSEL, Eleanor.
Am. ad. 1935 Taos, New Mexico. M.

KISSLING, Richard. (S)
Swi. Wolfwyl 1848-1919 Zurich. T.

KITAGAWA, Tamiji.
Jap. b. Japan 1894; ex. 1930 New York. M.

KITAYAMA, Kangen.
Jap. ac. 1800 in Japan. J., Vol. 2, page 83.

KITCHELL, Joseph Gray.
Am. b. Cinn., O. 1862; ad. 1934 Hollywood, Calif. F-W.

KITCHINGMAN, John.
Eng. b. 1740? d. 1781 London. B-DNB-T.

KITSON, Henry Hudson. (S)
Am. b. Huddersfeld, Eng. 1865; ad. 1934 Boston, Mass. A-B-F-W.

KITSON, Samuel James. (S)
Am. b. England 1848; d. 1906 New York. A06-B-F-Ta.

KITSON, Theo. Alice Ruggles. (S)
Mrs. Henry Hudson Kitson.
Am. Brookline, Mass. 1876-1932 Boston. A029-B-F-W.

KITT, Ferdinand.
Aus. ad. 1935 Vienna, Aus.; ex. 1934 Pittsburgh, Pa. M.

KITT, Katherine Florence.
Am. b. Chico, Calif. 1876; ad. 1934 Tucson, Ariz. A.

KITTELSEN, Theodor.
Nor. Kragerö 1857-1914 Oslo. T-683.

KITTENSTEYN, Cornelis van.
Dut. b. Delft; ac. 1600-1638 in Holland. B-T.

KITTON, Frederick George. (Eg)
Eng. Norwich 1856-1904 St. Albans. DNB.

KITTS, Jessie de Lancey.
Mrs. L. T. Kitts.
Am. b. Knoxville, Tenn. 1869; ad. 1934 San Fran., Calif. A.

KIU YING.
Chinese. ac. 15th Cent. in China. E.

KIYOHIRO, Torii.
Jap. ac. 1755 in Japan. J., Vol. 2, page 35.

KIYOKATA, Kaburaki.
Jap. ac. 1932. M.

KIYOMASU, Torii.
Jap. ac. 1785 in Japan. M.

KIYOMITSU, Torii.
Jap. b. 1735; d. 1785. J., Vol. 2, page 34.

KIYONAGA, Torii.
Jap. Uruga 1742-1815 Tokyo. B-J-T.

KIYONASU, Torii.
Jap. b. 1679; d. 1762. J., Vol. 2, page 33.

KIYONOBU, Torii.
Jap. b. 1664; d. 1729. J., Vol. 2, page 31.

KIYOTSUNE.
Jap. ac. 1758-1774 in Japan. B.

KIZER, Charlotte Elizabeth.
Am. b. Lincoln, Neb. 1901; ad. 1934 Same. A.

KJARVAL, Joh S.
Icelandic. ac. 1928 in Iceland. Fa.

KLAGMAN, Jean Baptiste Jules. (S)
Fr. Paris 1810-1867 Same. B-T.

KLAGSTAD, Arnold.
Am. b. Marinette, Wis. 1898; ad. 1934 Minn., Minn. M.

KLAGSTAD, August.
Am. b. Modum, Nor. 1866; ad. 1934 Minn., Minn. A-F.

KLAMAR, Jozef Juraj.
Am. ad. 1934 Cleveland, O. M.

KLAPKA, Jerome J.
Am. b. Czec. 1888; ad. 1934 Chicago. A.

KLAR, Walter Hughes.
Am. b. Westfield, Mass. 1882; ad. 1934 Springfield, Mass. A.

KLASSTORNER, Samuel. (S)
Am. b. Russia 1895; ad. 1934 Chicago. A.

KLAUBER, Alice.
Am. b. San Diego, Calif. 1871; ad. 1934 Same. A.

KLAW, ALONZO.
Am. b. Louisville, Ky. 1885; ad. 1934 Carmel, N. Y. A.
KLEARCHOS [of Rhegion]. (S)
Greek. (Doric); ac. 500-465 B.C. Hs-T.
KLEBE, ELFREDA D.
Am. b. New Haven, Conn. 1884; ad. 1934 Same. A.
KLEE, HERMANN.
Aus. ac. 1853 in Vienna. B-T.
KLEE, PAUL.
Swi.-Ger. b. Berne 1879. DBA-T-420-421-775-904.
KLEEHAAS, THODOR.
Ger. b. Germersheim 1854. B-T.
KLEEN, TYRA DE [or Tyrakleen].
Swe. ac. 1900-1930 in Stockholm. T.
KLEIBER, HANS. (Et)
Am. b. Cologne, Ger. 1887; ad. 1934 Dayton, Wyo. A28.
KLEIMINGER, A. F.
Am. b. Chicago 1865; ad. 1934 Same. A.
KLEIN, BENJAMIN.
Am. b. Hungary 1898; ad. 1934 Long Island City, N. Y. A.
KLEIN FAMILY.
Ger. ac. 16-19th Cent. in Germany. T.
KLEIN, ISIDORE.
Am. b. Russia 1897; ad. 1935 New York. A28-F.
KLEIN, JOHANN ADAM.
Ger. Nüremberg 1792-1875 Munich. B-C-T.
KLEIN, KARL.
Czec. b. Nymburk 1898; ac. 1929 Paris. DBA.
KLEIN, KARL AUGUST VON.
Ger. b. Ulm 1794; d. 1870. T-803.
KLEIN, MICHAEL.
Am. ad. 1935 New York. M.
KLEIN-OR, VICTOR CHARLES ALBER.
Fr. b. Paris 1871. DBA.
KLEINERT, HERMONIE.
Am. ex. 1934 Woodstock, N. Y. M.
KLEINSCHMIDT, PAUL.
Ger. b. Pomerany 1883; ad. 1935 Schwaben, Ger. DBA-T.
KLEITSCH, JOSEPH.
Am. b. Banad, Hun.; ad. 1934 Laguna Beach, Calif. A.
KLEMM, WALTHER.
Aus. b. 1883 in Austria. Ms.
KLEMMER, FRANZ.
Ger. b. Fischenich 1879; ac. Munich. T.
KLEMPNER, EARNEST S.
Am. b. Vienna, Aus.; ad. 1934 Evanston, Ill. A.
KLEPPER, FRANK L.
Am. b. Plano, Tex. 1890; ad. 1934 Dallas, Tex. A-F.
KLEPPER, MAX FRANCIS.
Am. b. Zeitz, Ger. 1861; d. 1907 Brooklyn, N. Y. A06-B-F.
KLETT, WALTER CHARLES. (Ill)
Am. b. St. Louis, Mo. 1897; ad. 1934 New York. A.
KLEVER, JULIUS SERGIUS VON.
Rus. b. Dorpat, Rus. 1850; d. 1924 Leningrad. B-T.
KLEY, HEINRICH.
Ger. b. Carlsruhe, Ger. 1863. B-T.
KLIMSCH, ERNEST. (S)
Ger. ac. 1934 in Berlin. M.
KLIMSCH, EUGEN JOH GEORGE.
Ger. Frankfort, 1839-1896 Same. B-T.
KLIMSCH FAMILY.
Ger. ac. 19-20th Cent. in Germany. T.
KLIMT, GUSTAV.
[Founder of modern painting in Austria.]
Aus. b. Vienna 1862; d. 1918 Same. B-T-422.
KLINE, HIBBARD V. B.
Am. ad. 1935 Syracuse, N. Y. M.
KLINE, WILLIAM FAIR. (Mu)
Am. Columbia, S. C. 1870-1931 New York. A028-B-F-W16-Obit. Art Digest, 9-1-1931.
KLINGER, MAX. (S)
Ger. Plagwitz 1857-1920 Naumburg. B-DBA-E-Hs-T-798.
KLINGHOFFER, CLARA.
Dut. b. Lemberg; ad. 1935 Haarlem, Holland; ex. 1934 Pittsburgh, Pa. DBA-Wa-Y1928.
KLINGSON, TRISTAN [Léon Leclère].
Fr. b. La Chapelle 1874. B-DBA.
KLINGSTEDT [or Klingstet], KARL GUSTAV. (Min)
Fr. b. Riga, Rus. 1657; d. 1734 Paris. T.
KLINKENBERG, JOHANN KAREL CHRISTIAN.
Dut. b. The Hague 1852; d. 1924. B-T.
KLINKERT, WALTER. (Et)
Ger. b. Berlin 1901; ex. 1930 Same. DBA.
KLITGAARD, GEORGINA.
Mrs. Kaj Klitgaard.
Am. b. Spuyten Duyvil, N. Y. 1893; ad. 1934 Bearsville, N. Y. A.
KLJAKOVIC, JOSA.
Yugo-Slavian. b. 1890. M.
KLÖCKER VON EHRENSTRAHL, DAVID.
Ger. Hamburg, Ger. 1620-1698 Stockholm, Swe. C.
KLODT, [Baron] M. K. VON J.
Rus. 1832-1902. B-M.
KLOEBER, AUGUST CARL FRIEDRICH VON.
Ger. Breslau 1793-1864 Berlin. C-T.
KLOMBECK, J. B.
Dut. ac. 1865-1875 in Holland. T.
KLOMP [or Clomp], ALBERT JANSZ.
Dut. Amsterdam 1618-1688 Same. B-C-T.
KLOPPER, ZANWILL DAVID.
Am. b. Russia 1870; ac. 1926 in Chicago, Ill. A12-F.
KLOSS, GENE. (Et)
Am. ad. 1935 Oakland, Calif. M.
KLOTZ [or Kloss or Kletz], VALENTINUS.
Dut. ac. 1712 in Amsterdam. T.
KLOUIS, BERNARD.
Am. ad. 1934 New York. M.
KLOUS, ROSE M.
Mrs. Isidore P. Klous.
Am. b. Leningrad, Rus. 1889; ad. 1934 New York. A.
KLUKOWSKI, JOSEPH. (S)
Pol. ac. 1934 in London. M.
KLUMPKE, ANNA ELIZABETH.
Am. b. San Fran., Calif. 1856; ad. 1934 Thomery, Fr. A-B-DBA-F-829.
KLUTH, ROBERT.
Am. Mecklenburg, Ger. 1854-1921 Brooklyn, N. Y. A018-F.

KLUTTS, Ethel Lindsay.
Am. d. 1935 Gadsden, Ala.
Obit. Art Digest, 5-15-1935-M.
KNAP, Joseph Day. (Et)
Am. b. 1875. M.
KNAPP, C. W.
Am. Phila., Pa. 1822-1900 Same. A02.
KNAPP, George Kasson.
Am. b. 1833; d. 1910 Syracuse, N. Y. A08.
KNAPP, Grace Le Duc.
Mrs. C. C. Knapp.
Am. b. Minn. 1874; ad. 1934 Pasadena, Calif. A.
KNAPP, Willi.
Am. b. Germany 1901; ad. 1934 Milwaukee, Wis. A.
KNAPPE, Karl.
Ger. b. Munich 1884. T-684.
KNAPTON, George.
Eng. b. London 1698; d. 1778 Kensington, Eng. B-DNB-T.
KNATHS, Otto Karl.
Am. b. Eau Clair, Wis. 1891; ad. 1934 Provincetown, Mass. A-W.
KNAUBER, Alma Jordan.
Am. b. Cinn., O. 1893; ad. 1934 Same. A-F.
KNAUS, Ludwig [or Louis].
[Foremost genre painter in Germany.]
Ger. Wiesbaden 1829-1910 Berlin. B-C-DBA-T.
KNEASS, William. (Eg)
Am. Lancaster, Pa. 1781-1840 Phila., Pa. F-2-7.
KNECHT, [Mrs.] Fern [Elizabeth] Edie.
Am. b. Du Bois, Neb.; ad. 1934 Little Rock, Ark. A.
KNELL, William Adolphus.
Eng. d. 1875 in London. B-DNB-T.
KNELLER, [Sir] Godfrey [Gottfried Kniller].
Dut.-Eng. Lübeck, Ger. 1646-1723 Twickenham, Eng. B-Bd-C-DNB-E-T-702-722-803.
KNELLER [or Kniller], John Zacharias.
Dut.-Eng. Lübeck 1644-1702 England. B-DNB-T.
KNIGHT, Augusta.
Am. b. Augusta, Ill.; ad. 1934 Omaha, Neb. A.
KNIGHT, Benjamin Thackston ["Tack"]. (Cart)
Am. b. Dillsboro, N. C. 1895; ad. 1934 Chicago. W.
KNIGHT, Charles. (Eg)
Eng. b. 1743; d. 1826 London. B-DNB-T.
KNIGHT, Charles K. (Ill)
Am. ad. 1935 New York. M.
KNIGHT, Charles Parsons.
Eng. Bristol 1829-1897 Tiverton, Eng. B-T.
KNIGHT, Charles Robert.
Am. b. Brooklyn, N. Y. 1874; ad. 1934 New York. A-F-W.
KNIGHT, Clayton. (Ill)
Am. b. Rochester, N. Y. 1891; ad. 1934 New York. M.
KNIGHT, Daniel Ridgway.
Am. Phila., Pa. 1839-1924 Paris, Fr. A021-B-C-DAB-E-F-T-W12-15-46-143.
KNIGHT, E. H. (Eg)
Am. Brooklyn, N. Y. 1853-1896 Same. F.
KNIGHT, Edward Loxton.
Eng. b. Long Eaton 1905; ad. 1935 Same. Wa.
KNIGHT, Frederic.
Am. b. Phila., Pa. 1898; ad. 1934 Bearsville, N. Y. A.
KNIGHT, Harold.
Eng. b. Nottingham 1874; ad. 1934 London. B-T-Wa-825.
KNIGHT, H. H. (Ill)
Am. ad. 1934 New York. M.
KNIGHT, Horace J. (Ill)
Am. ad. 1935 New York. M.
KNIGHT, John Bavenstock.
Eng. Langton 1785-1859 Dorset, Eng. B-DNB.
KNIGHT, John Prescott.
Eng. Stafford 1803-1881 London. B-DNB-T.
KNIGHT, John William Buxton.
Eng. Sevenoaks 1842-1908 Same. B-E-T.
KNIGHT, Joseph.
Eng. Manchester 1837-1909 Tywyn, Eng. B-DNB-T.
KNIGHT, Katherine Sturges. (Ill)
Am. ad. 1934 Roslyn, L. I., N. Y. A.
KNIGHT, [Dame] Laura.
Eng. b. Long Eaton 1877. B-T-Wa-825.
KNIGHT, Louis Aston.
Am. b. Paris 1873; ad. 1934 Same. A-B-DBA-F-T-W.
KNIGHT, Mary Anne. (Min)
Eng. London 1776-1831 St. John's Wood, Eng. Bd-DNB.
KNIGHT, William.
Eng. b. Leicester 1871; ad. 1934 Same. Wa.
KNIGHT, William Henry.
Eng. b. Birmingham 1859. Wa1929.
KNIGHT, William Henry.
Eng. Newbury 1823-1863 London. B-DNB-T.
KNILLE, Otto.
Ger. Osnabruck 1832-1898 Berlin. B-C-T.
KNILLER. *see* Kneller.
KNIPE, Emilie Benson. (Ill)
Am. b. Phila., Pa. 1870; ad. 1934 New York. W.
KNOBLOCH, Josef Rolf.
Ger. b. 1891; ac. 1934 in Munich. T.
KNOLL, Konrad Ritter von. (S)
Ger. Bergzabern 1829-1899 Munich. Hs-T.
KNOLLER, Martin.
Ger. Steinach, Ger. 1725-1804 Milan, It. B-T.
KNOPF, Herman.
Aus. b. Vienna 1870. B-T.
KNOPF, Nellie Augusta.
Am. b. Chicago, Ill. 1875; ad. 1934 Jacksonville, Ind. A.
KNOPFF, Fernand.
Belg. b. Termonde, Belg. 1858. DBA.
KNOPP, [Mlle.] Giutou.
Fr. ex. 1935 Paris. M.
KNÖRLEIN, Rudolf.
Aus. ad. 1934 Vienna. M.
KNÖRR, Charles Émile.
Ger. b. Soultzem 1890. DBA.
KNOTT, Franklin Price.
Am. b. 1854; d. 1930 Santa Barbara, Calif. A027.

KNOTT, John Francis. (Cart)
Am. b. Austria 1878; ad. 1934 Dallas, Tex. W.
KNOWLES, Davidson.
Eng. ac. 1879-1909 in London. B-T.
KNOWLES, [Mrs.] Elizabeth A. McGillvray.
Am. Ottawa, Can. 1866-1929 Riverton, N. H. A026-F.
KNOWLES, Farquar McGillvray.
Am. Syracuse, N. Y. 1859-1932 Toronto, Ont., Can. A029-F.
KNOWLES, George Sheridan.
Eng. b. 1863; ac. 1929 in London. B-T-Wa1929.
KNOWLTON, Helen Mary.
Am. Worcester, Mass. 1832-1918. B-F-15.
KNOX, Archibald.
Eng. d. 1933 Isle of Man, Eng. Obit. Studio, 5-1933, page 324.
KNOX, [Mrs.] Clara Thomson.
Am. b. Andover, Mass. 1882; ad. 1934 New Haven, Conn. A.
KNOX, Grace M.
Am. ad. 1934 Schenectady, N. Y. M.
KNOX, James.
Am. b. Glasgow, Scot. 1866; ad. 1934 Brooklyn, N. Y. A-F.
KNOX, Susan Ricker.
Am. b. Portsmouth, N. H.; ad. 1934 New York. A-F-46.
KNUDSEN, Henri Jacob.
see Brockman, H. J.
KNUDSON, Helen Eliza.
Am. b. Farmingdale, Ill.; ad. 1934 Springfield, Ill. A.
KNÜPFER, Benès [or Benedict].
Czec. b. Friedstein 1848. B-T.
KNÜPFER [or Knipper], Nicolaus.
Ger. Leipzig 1603-1660 Utrecht, Holland. T.
KNUTESEN, Edwin B.
Am. b. La Crosse, Wis. 1901; ad. 1934 New Orleans, La. A.
KNYFF, Leonard [or Leendert].
Dut. Haarlem 1650-1721 London. B-DNB-T.
KNYFF [or Knyf], Wouter.
Dut. b. Wezel 1607; d. 1693. B-T.
KOBAK, Evelyn.
Am. ad. 1935 New York. M.
KOBBE, Marie Olga.
Am. b. New Brighton, S. I., N. Y. 1870; ad. 1934 New York. A.
KOBELL, Ferdinand.
Ger. Mannheim 1740-1799 Munich. B-T.
KOBELL, Franz.
Ger. Mannheim 1749-1822 Munich. B-T.
KOBELL, Hendrik [or Heinrich].
Dut. Rotterdam 1751-1782 Same. B-T.
KOBELL, Jan I.
Dut. Rotterdam 1756-1833 Same. B-T.
KOBELL, Jan II [or Johan Baptiste].
Dut. Delftshaven 1778-1814 Amsterdam. B-T.
KOBELL, Jan III.
Dut. Rotterdam 1800-1838 Same. B-T.
KOBELL, Wilhelm Alexander Wolfgang von.
Ger. Mannheim 1766-1855 Munich. B-T.
KOBER, Leo.
Am. b. 1878; d. 1931 New York. A028.
KOBERGER, Anton [or Anthoni].
Ger. b. Nürmberg 1440; d. 1513. T.
KOBO, Daishi Kikai.
Jap. b. 774; d. 835 in Japan. J. Vol. 1, page 31.
KOBUN. (S)
Jap. ac. 1300 in Japan. Hs.
KOCH [or Kock], Eliza.
Fr. b. Leghorn, It.; ac. 19-20th Cent. B-T.
KOCH, Georg.
Ger. b. Cassel 1819; d. 1889.
KOCH, Helen C.
Am. b. Cinn., O. 1895; ad. 1934 Same. A.
KOCH, Herman.
Ger. b. Dömitz, Ger. 1856. B-T.
KOCH, John.
Am. b. Toledo, O. 1910; ad. 1934 Ann Arbor, Mich. A.
KOCH, Joseph Anton.
Ger. Obergibeln, Ger. 1768-1839 Rome, It. B-C-T.
KOCH, Pyke.
Dut. b. 1901 in Holland. Fa-M.
KOCSIS, Ann.
Am. ad. 1934 New York. M.
KOECHLIN, Daniel Jules Camille.
Fr. b. Mülhouse, Ger. 1845. B-T.
KOEDYCK, Isaac.
Dut. Leyden 1616/7-1668/77 Amsterdam. B-T.
KOEHLER, Paul R.
Am. New York 1875-1909 Colorado Springs, Colo. A07.
KOEHLER [or Kohler], Robert.
Am. Hamburg, Ger. 1850-1917 Minn., Minn. A014-B-DAB-F-W9-152.
KOEK-KOEK, Barend Cornelis.
Dut. Middelburg 1803-1862 Cleves, Ger. B-C-T.
KOEK-KOEK, Hermanns W.
Dut. Middelburg 1815-1882 Haarlem. B-T.
KOEK-KOEK, Marinus Adrianus.
Dut. Middelburg 1807-1862 Cleves, Ger. B-T.
KOEK-KOEK, Willem.
Dut. b. Amsterdam 1839; d. 1895. B-T.
KOELLE, Fritz. (S)
Ger. b. Augsburg 1895; ac. 1930 Munich. T.
KOEN, Irma René.
Am. b. Rock Island, Ill.; ad. 1934 Same. A.
KOENIGER, Walter.
Am. b. Germany 1881; ad. 1934 New York. A.
KOEPERSHOEK, Martin Johannes.
Dut. b. Rotterdam 1880; ad. 1934 Same. M.
KOEPNICK, Robert. (S)
Am. ex. 1935 Cincinnati, O. M.
KOEPPEL, Reinhold.
Ger. b. Oschersleben, Ger. 1887. T.
KOEPPING, Carl.
Ger. b. Dresden 1848. B-T.
KOERBECKE, Johann.
Ger. ac. 1446-1491 in Münster, Ger. T.
KOERNER, Ernest Karl Eugen.
Ger. b. Stibbe 1846; ac. 1891. B-T.
KOERNER, W. H. D. (Ill)
Am. ad. 1935 New York. M.
KOESTER, Alexander Max.
Ger. b. 1864 in Germany. B-T.

KOFFERMANS [or Coffermaker], MARCELLIS.
Flem. ac. 1549-1579 in Antwerp. B-Bd-T.
KOFRÁNCK, LADISLAV. (S)
Rus. (Modern). *see* book 798.
KOHL, PIERRE ERNEST.
Swi. b. Monaco, Swi. 1897. DBA.
KÖHLER, ALBERT.
Ger. b. 1883 in Germany. T.
KÖHLER [or Koehler], CHRISTIAN.
Ger. Werben, Ger. 1809-1860 Montpelier, Fr. B-T.
KOHLER, ROSE.
Am. b. Chicago, Ill.; ad. 1934 New York. A.
KÖHLHOFF, WILHELM.
Ger. b. 1893 in Germany. T.
KOHLMANN, RENA TUCKER.
see Magee, R. T. K.
KOHN, IRMA.
Am. b. Rock Island, Ill.; ad. 1926 Same. A12-F.
KO-I, KANO [Sadanobu].
Jap. Ashikaga 1566-1636. J. Vol. 1, page 132.
KOIRANSKY, ALESANDER.
Am. b. Moscow, Rus. 1884; ad. 1934 Seattle, Wash. A.
KOJANOGU, SÉI.
Jap. b. 1896. Fa.
KOKAM, SHIBA. Japanese. J. Vol. 2, page 43.
KOKARSKI [or Kucharski], ALEXANDER.
Fr. Warsaw, Pol. 1741-1819 Paris. T.
KOKOSCHKA, OSKAR.
Aus. b. Poechlarn, Aus. 1886; ex. 1933 Pittsburgh, Pa. DBA-M-775.
KOKU-SAI.
Jap. b. 1760; d. 1849 in Japan. M.
KOLB, ALOIS.
Ger. b. 1875 in Germany. T.
KOLBE, CARL WILHELM [The Elder].
Ger. Berlin 1757-1835 Dresden. B-T.
KOLBE, CARL WILHELM [The Younger].
Ger. Berlin 1781-1853 Same. B-T.
KOLBE, GEORG. (S)
Ger. b. Waldheim 1877. B-DBA-T-424-798-813.
KOLDE, FREDERICK WILLIAM.
Am. ad. 1934 Cinn., O. M.
KOLIG, ANTON.
Aus. b. Neutitschein 1886, Aus.; ac. 1934. T.
KOLITZ, LOUIS.
Ger. Tilsitt 1845-1914. B-T.
KOLLER, E. LEONARD. (S)
Am. b. Hanover, Pa. 1877; ad. 1934 Scranton, Pa. A.
KOLLER, GUILLAUME.
Belg. Vienna, Aus. 1829-1885 Brussels. T.
KOLLER, JOHANN JACOB.
Swi. Zurich 1746-1806 Amsterdam, Holland. B-T.
KOLLER, JOHANN RUDOLPH.
Swi. Zurich 1828-1905. B-T.
KOLLMAN, KARL IWANOWITSCH.
Rus. Russia 1788-1846. T.
KOLLOCK, MARY.
Am. Norfolk, Va. 1840-1911 New York. A09-B-F-15.
KOLLORSZ, RICHARD F.
Am ex. 1935 Los Angeles, Calif. M.
KOLLWITZ, KÄTHE [née Schmidt].
Ger. b. Königsberg 1867. T-423.
KOLOTES, I. (S)
Greek. ac. 440 B.C. at Paros. Hs-T.
KOLOTES, II. (S)
Greek. ac. 1st Cent. B.C. T.
KOLOZSVÁR, MARTIN AND GEORGE [Brothers].
Hun. ac. 1373 in Prague. T.
KOLSKI, GAN. (Et)
Am. Poland 1899-1932 New York. A029.
KOLTZ, VALENTINIUS. *see* Klotz, V.
KOMJÁTI, JULIUS. (Et)
Hun. ex. 1934 New York. M.
KOMURO, DAVID.
Jap. ad. 1935 New York. M.
KONARSKA, JANINA [or Johann]. (Eg)
Pol. ac. 18th Cent. Warsaw. T.
KÖNIG, HUGO.
Ger. Dresden 1856-1909. B-T.
KONINCK [or Koningh], JACOB, I.
Dut. Amsterdam 1616-1708 Denmark. B-T.
KONINCK [or Koningh], PHILIP DE.
Dut. Amsterdam 1619-1688 Same. B-C-E-T-722.
KONINCK [or Koningh], SALOMON DE.
Dut. Amsterdam 1609-1668 Same. B-C-T.
KONINGH, CORNELIS. (Eg)
Dut. Haarlem 1610-1671. B-T.
KONODY, PAULINE EVELYN.
Eng. b. London; ex. 1934 Same. Wa.
KONTCHALOVSKY, PETER [or Pierre].
Rus. b. 1881; ad. 1935 Moscow; ex. 1934 Pittsburgh, Pa. DBA.
KONTI, ISADORE. (S)
Am. b. Vienna, Aus. 1862; ad. 1934 Yonkers, N. Y. A-B-Cs-F-W.
KONYNENBURG, WILLEM VAN.
Dut. b. The Hague 1868; ex. 1930 Pittsburgh, Pa. B-T.
KOOPMAN, AUGUSTUS.
Am. Charlotte, N. C. 1869-1914 Étaples, Fr. AOX1-B-DBA-F-W7-46.
KOOPMAN, JOHN R.
Am. b. Falmouth, Mich. 1881; ad. 1934 Denville, N. J. A-F.
KOORT, JAN. (S)
Estonia. b. Tartu 1883. E.
KOPECKI [or Kupetsky], JEAN.
Aus. b. Hungary 1666; d. 1740 Austria. B-T.
KOPF, MAXIM.
Fr. ac. 1926 in Vienna, Aus. DBA.
KOPIETZ, ESMUND M.
Am. b. Everest, Kan. 1900; ad. 1934 Minn., Minn. A.
KOPMAN, BENJAMIN D.
Am. b. Russia 1887; ex. 1935 New York. A18-DBA-F-M.
KOPPAY, JOSEF [or Zozsi].
Hun. b. Hungary 1857. B-T.
KOPPE, RICHARD.
Am. ad. 1935 St. Paul, Minn. M.
KOPTA, EMRY. (S)
Am. ad. 1934 Phoenix, Ariz. M.
KORB, RUSSELL.
Am. ex. 1935 New York. M.
KORBEL, MARIO JOSEPH. (S)
Am. b. Osik, Czec. 1882; ad. 1934 New York. A-Cs-F-W.

KORDA, Vincent.
Hun. b. 1897; ex. 1934 London. DBA.
KORENZ, Samuel.
Am. ad. 1934 Chicago. M.
KŌRIN, Ogata Nichijin.
Jap. b. 1655/7; d. 1716 Kyoto.
E-J. Vol. 1, page 76.
KORIUSAI, Isoda [Shobei].
Jap. b. 1710; d. 1780. B-J. Vol. 2, page 43.
KORNHAUSER, David E.
Am. ad. 1926 Phila., Pa. A20-F.
KORNHAUSER, Mary Parker.
Am. ad. 1933 Phila., Pa. M.
KÖRÖSFOR [or Kriesch], Aladar.
Aus. b. 1863 in Austria. T.
KOROVINE, Konstantine A.
Rus. b. Moscow 1861; ac. 1900 Paris. DBA.
KORTHEUER, Francis Dayrell.
Am. b. New York 1906; ad. 1934 Same. A.
KORTRIGHT, Reginald Guy.
Eng. b. Clifton 1877; ad. 1934 London. Wa.
KORYBUT, Kasimir.
Mrs. Wanda Korybut.
Am. ad. 1934 New York. M.
KORYBUT, Wanda.
Am. b. Russia; ad. 1934 New York. M.
KORYUSAI.
Jap. ex. 1933 New York. M.
KORZYBSKA, Mira Edgerly.
[Countess Alfred de Korzybska].
Am. b. Aurora, Ill. 1879; ad. 1934 Warsaw, Pol. A-46.
KOSA, Emil, Jr.
Am. ad. 1935 Los Angeles, Calif. M.
KOSCIUSZKO, Taddé [or Thaddeus].
Pol. Poland 1746-1817 Switzerland. B-T.
KOSHIRO, Onchi. (Eg)
Jap. ex. 1934 Chicago; ad. 1935 Tokyo. M.
KOSICKI, [Mrs.] Catherine Watha.
Am. b. 1890; ad. 1934 Detroit, Mich. A.
KOSSAK, Juljusz [or Jules] Fortunat.
Pol. b. Wisniez 1824; d. 1899 Crakow. T.
KOSSAK, Wojciech.
Pol. b. Paris 1857; ac. 1922 Warsaw, Pol. B-T.
KOSSIAKOFF, Georges.
Rus. b. 1872; ad. 1934 Leningrad. T.
KOST, Frederick W.
Am. New York 1865-1923 Brookhaven, N. Y. A020-F.
KOSTELLOW, Alexander J.
Am. b. Persia 1897; ad. 1934 Pittsburgh, Pa. A.
KOSTER, Everhardus.
Dut. The Hague 1817-1892. B-T.
KOSZTA, József.
Hun. b. Budapest 1864. B-T.
KOTARBINSKI, Mieczyslaw.
Pol. b. 1890; ad. 1934 Warsaw. T.
KOTASZ [Karoly], Charles.
Hun. b. Budapest 1872. DBA-T.
KOTCH, George.
Am. ad. 1934 Carmel, Calif. M.
KOTEI, Fukui.
Jap. ac. 1907 in Japan. J. Vol. 2, page 105.
KOTSCHENREITER, Hugo.
Ger. Hof 1854-1908 Munich. B-T.
KOTSIS [or Kotzelne], Alexandre de.
Pol. Loudviow 1835-1877. B-C-T.
KOTTEK, Edna.
Am. ex. 1934 New York. M.
KOTZ, Daniel.
Am. b. So. Bend, Ind. 1848-1933 Park Ridge, N. J. A030.
KOUSTODYEFF, Boris Mikhailowitch.
Rus. b. 1880; d. 1928. M.
KOUZNETZOFF, Paul V.
Rus. b. 1878; ad. 1935 Moscow; ex. 1934 Pittsburgh, Pa. B-DBA-T.
KOWALSKY, Léopold François.
Fr. b. Paris 1856. B-DBA.
KOWALSKY, Paul.
Rus. Kiev 1843-1903. B-T.
KOWALSKI-WIERNSZ, Alfred von.
Pol. Poland 1849-1915 Munich, Ger. B-T.
KOWNATSKI, Hans.
Am. b. Königsberg, Ger. 1866; ad. 1934 Peconic, N. Y. A.
KOZAKIEVITCH [or Kozakievicz], Anton.
Pol. b. Crakow 1841. B-T.
KOZLOW, Sigmund.
Am. ad. 1934 Woodside, L. I., N. Y. M.
KRACHKOVSKY, Ivan.
Rus. 1854-1913. M.
KRAEMER, Alfred.
Am. ex. 1935 New York. M.
KRAFFT [or Kraft], Adam. (S)
Ger. Nüremberg 1450-1507/9. E-Hs-T.
KRAFFT, Carl R.
Am. b. Reading, O. 1884; ad. 1934 Oak Park, Ill. A-F-W.
KRAFFT Family.
Ger. ac. 15-19th Cent. in Germany. T.
KRAFFT, Johann Peter.
Ger. Hanau, Ger. 1780-1856 Vienna, Aus. T.
KRAHE, Johann Lambert.
Ger. Düsseldorf 1712/30-1790. B-T.
KRALY, Tone [or Anton].
Jugl.-Slav. b. Zagorica 1900. T-798.
KRAMER, Edward Adam.
Am. b. New York 1866; ad. 1934 Same. M.
KRAMER, Johann Victor.
Aus. b. Vienna 1862. B.
KRAMER, Reuben Robert. (S)
Am. b. 1910; ad. 1934 Balt., Md. M.
KRAMER, Scheire B.
Am. ac. 1898 in New York. F.
KRAMSKOI, Ivan Nikolaevitch.
Rus. b. 1837; d. 1887 Leningrad. B-T.
KRAMSTYK, Romain.
Am. b. Warsaw, Pol. 1885; ac. 1911-1931 Paris. DBA.
KRASNOW, Peter.
Am. ad. 1934 Los Angeles, Calif. M.
KRATINA, Joseph M. (S)
Am. b. Prague, Czec. 1872; ad. 1934 Brooklyn, N. Y. A.
KRATINA, Lydia. (Et)
Am. b. Prague, Czec.; ad. 1934 New York. M.
KRATKÉ, Charles Louis.
Fr. b. Paris 1848. B-T.
KRATOCHVIL, Stephen.
Am. b. Czec. 1876; ad. 1934 Cleveland, O. A.
KRATSCHKOWSKI, Joseph E.
Rus. b. 1854 in Russia. B-T.

KRATZENSTEIN-STUB, CHRISTIAN GOTTLIEB.
Dan. Copenhagen 1783-1816. B-T.
KRATZMANN, GUSTAV PHILIPP.
Hun. Kratzau 1812-1902 Teplitz. T.
KRAUS, ADOLPH F. (S)
Am. Germany 1850-1901 Danvers, Mass. A04.
KRAUS, AUGUST F. J. (S)
Ger. Ruhrort 1868-1934 Berlin. T-Obit. N. Y. papers, 2-10-1934.
KRAUS, ÉTIENNE.
Ger. b. Bemsberg; ac. 19th Cent. in Germany. B.
KRAUS FAMILY.
Ger. ac. 16-19th centuries in Germany. T.
KRAUS, FRIEDRICH.
Prus. b. Krottingen 1826; ac. 1852-1880 in Germany. C.
KRAUS, GEORG MELCHIOR JOHANN.
Ger. Frankfort 1727/37-1806 Weimar. B-T.
KRAUS, ROBERT ADOLF. (S)
Am. Germany 1850-1901 Denver, Colo. F.
KRAUSE, ERIK HANS.
Am. b. Halle, Ger. 1899; ad. 1934 Rochester, N. Y. A.
KRAUSE, MAX REINHOLD. (S)
Ger. Filehne 1875-1920 Berlin. T.
KRAUSS [or Kruse], FRANÇOIS.
Ger. Softingen 1705/6-1754 Venice, It. B-T.
KRAUSZ [or Krauss], SIMON ANDREAS.
Dut. The Hague 1760-1825 Same. B-T.
KRAUSZ, WILHELM VIKTOR.
Aus. b. Vienna 1878. B-T.
KRAUTH, CHARLES PHILIP.
Am. b. Pittsburgh, Pa. 1893; ad. 1934 Pine Knot, Calif. A.
KRAWTSCHENKO, ALEXEJ. (Eg)
Rus. b. 1889; ad. 1935 Moscow. T.
KRAWIEC, HARRIET B.
Am. b. Chicago, Ill. 1894; ad. 1934 Same. A.
KRAWIEC, WALTER.
Am. b. 1889; ad. 1935 Chicago, Ill. M.
KRAY, WILHELM.
Ger. Berlin 1830-1889 Munich. B-T.
KRAY, HUGO.
Ger. b. 1885; d. 1919. T.
KREHBIEL, ALBERT H.
Am. b. Chicago, Ill.; ad. 1934 Same. A.
KREHBIEL, DULAH EVANS.
Mrs. Albert H. Krehbiel.
Am. ad. 1934 Chicago. A.
KREIDOLF, ERNEST.
Swi. b. Tägerwilen 1863. B-T.
KREINDLER, DORIS BARSKY.
Am. b. Passaic, N. J. 1901; ad. 1934 Brooklyn, N. Y. A.
KRELING, AUGUST VON. (S)
Ger. Osnabrück 1819-1876 Munich. B-C-T.
KRÉMÈGNE, PINCHUS [Paul].
Rus. b. Vilno 1890. DBA.
KREMELBERG, MARY.
Mrs. Frederick Gibson.
Am. ad. 1934 Baltimore, Md. A.
KREMER, PETRUS.
Flem. Antwerp 1801-1888 Same. B-T.
KREMLICKA, RUDOLF.
Czec. ex. 1931 Pittsburgh, Pa. [Deceased.] M.
KREMP, LAURA AMELIA MILLER.
Mrs. L. Dixon Miller Kremp.
Am. b. Wilmington, Del. 1856; ad. 1934 Reading, Pa. A.
KRENN, EDMUND FRÉDÉRIC ARTHUR.
Aus. Vienna 1846-1902 Zurich, Swi. B-T.
KRESILAS. (S)
Gr. (Cretan); ac. 480-410 B.C. Hs-T.
KRESTIN, LAZAR.
Aus. b. Kowno 1868; ac. in Vienna. T.
KRETZINGER, CLARA JOSEPHINE.
Am. b. Chicago, Ill. 1883; ad. 1934 Same. A-B-DBA.
KRETZSCHAMER, BERNHARD.
Ger. b. Dresden 1889. DBA-T.
KRETZSCHAMER, JOHANN HERMANN.
Ger. Prussia 1811-1890 Berlin. B-T.
KREUGER, NILS EDWARD.
Ger. b. Kalmar 1858; d. 1930. B-DBA-T.
KREUL, JOHANN FREDERICH KARL.
Ger. Ausbach 1804-1876 Munich. B-T.
KREUTZBERG, MARGUERITE G.
Am. b. Elgin, Ill. 1880; ad. 1934 Bethlehem, Pa. A.
KREYDER, JOSEPH ALEXIS.
Fr. b. Andlau 1839; d. 1912. B-T.
KREYMBORG, DOROTHY.
Am. ad. 1935 Petersham, Mass. M.
KRIDER, ALDEN.
Am. b. Newton, Kan. 1908; ad. 1934 Same. A.
KRIEGHOFF, CORNELIUS.
Can. b. Düsseldorf, Ger. 1812; d. 1872 Canada. M-*see* Art Digest, 2-1-1934.
KRIEGHOFF, WILLIAM G.
Am. Phila., Pa. 1876-1930 Ardmore, Pa. A027-F.
KRIER, ÉTIENNE AUGUSTE.
Fr. b. Marne 1875. B-DBA.
KRIER-LAMBRETTE, MARCELLE FRANÇOIS.
Fr. b. Limoges 1899. DBA.
KRIMMEL, JOHN LEWIS.
Am. Wurtemberg, Ger. 1787-1821 Phila., Pa. Bd-F-2-6.
KRINGS, HUGO.
Ger. Düsseldorf 1878-1924. B-T.
KRIZMAN, TOMISLAV.
Jugo-Slavian. b. 1883. T.
KRODEL, MATTHIAS [The Elder].
Ger. ac. 1570-1605 in Germany. B-T.
KRODEL, WOLFGANG.
Ger. ac. 1528-1561 in Germany. B-T.
KROENER, CHRISTIAN JOHANN.
see Kroner, J. C.
KROGER, FLORENCE.
Am. ad. 1935 New York. M.
KROHG [or Krogh], CHRISTIAN.
Nor. Christiania 1852-1925 Same. B-E-T.
KROHG, PER LASSON.
Nor. b. Oslo 1889; ad. 1935 Same; ex. 1934 Pittsburgh, Pa. DBA-T.
KROLL, ANNE.
Am. ex. 1935 New York. M.
KROLL, LEON.
Am. b. New York 1884; ad. 1935 Same. A-F-W-779.
KROMER, ADELAIDE.
Am. b. Elgin, Ill. 1892; ad. 1934 Los Angeles, Calif. A.

KRON, Paul.
Fr. b. Besançon 1870. DBA.
KRONBERG, Louis.
Am. b. Boston, Mass. 1872; ad. 1935 Same. A-B-DBA-F-W.
KRONBERGER, Karl.
Aus. b. Freystadt 1841. B-T.
KRONENGOLD, A. (Ill)
Am. ad. 1935 New York. M.
KRÖNER, Johann Christian.
Ger. Kinteln 1838-1911 Berlin. B-DBA-T.
KROP, Hildo. (S)
Dut. b. Steenwijk, Holland 1884. T.
KROTH, Richard.
Am. ad. 1935 New York. M.
KRÖYER, Peter Séverin.
Dan. Stavenger 1851/5-1909 Copenhagen. B-C-DBA-T.
KRUELL, Gustav. (Eg)
Am. Düsseldorf, Ger. 1843-1907 San Luis Obispo, Calif. A06-B-DAB-F-W-8-55-153-185.
KRUETZFELDT, Pauline W.
Am. ad. 1934 Fort Plains, N. Y. M.
KRÜG, Édouard.
Fr. Drubec 1833-1899. B-T.
KRÜG [or Krüger], Ludwig [or Lukas]. (Eg)
Ger. Nüremberg 1449/50-1535. B-T.
KRÜGER, Franz. (S)
Ger. Berlin 1849. C-DBA-T.
KRÜGER, Franz [Pferdekrüger].
Ger. Radegast 1797-1857 Berlin. B-C-T.
KRUMHAAR, Ritter von.
Am. ac. 1900 in Wash., D. C. M.
KRUMHOLZ, Ferdinand.
Aus. Stof 1810-1878 Berne, Swi. B-T.
KRUMPPER, Adam. (S)
Ger. Weilheim 1540-1625. T.
KRUMPPER, Hans. (S)
Ger. Weilheim 1570-1634 Munich. Hs-T.
KRUPKA, Joseph. (S)
Am. b. Bohemia 1880; ad. 1915 New York. A12.
KRUSE, Albert. (Ill)
Am. ad. 1935 Wilmington, Del. M.
KRUSE, Alexander Z. (Et)
Am. ad. 1934 Brooklyn, N. Y. A.
KRUSE, Max [or Karl]. (S)
Ger. b. Berlin 1854. T.
KRUSEMAN, Cornelis.
Dut. Amsterdam 1797-1857 Lisse, Holland. B-T.
KRUSEMAN, Frederik Marianus.
Dut. b. Haarlem 1817. [No death date.] B.
KRUSEMAN, Jan Adam.
Dut. Haarlem 1804-1862 Same. B-T.
KRUSEMAN VAN ELTEN, Heinrich Dirk. *see* Van Elten, K.
KRUSEMARK, Max.
Ger. Berlin 1852-1905 Breslau. B-T.
KRUSKOFF, Bruno.
Ger. b. 1892; ad. 1935 in Germany. M.
KRUSZ [or Krauss], Simon Andreas.
Dut. The Hague 1760-1825 Same. B-T.
KRUZE. *see* Kruse.
KRYMOFF, Nickolaj Petrowtsch.
Rus. b. Moscow 1884. B-T.
KRYZANOWSKI, Konrad.
Pol. Ukraine 1872-1922/7 Kiev, Rus. T.
KRYZANOWSKY, Roman.
Am. Rus. 1885-1929 Detroit, Mich. A026.
KU-K'AI-CHI.
Chinese. ac. 4th Cent. in China. E.
KU SHU-SEN.
Chinese. ad. 1935 Shanghai, China. M.
KUAN YIN. Chinese. M.
KUBIN, Alfred.
Czec. b. Germany 1877; ac. 1930 in Paris. DBA-T.
KUBINYI, Kalman [Matyas Bela]. (Ill)
Am. ad. 1934 Cleveland, O. A.
KÜBLER, Werner [or Werli] [The Elder].
Swi. Schaffhausen 1555-1586. B-T.
KÜBLER, Werner [or Werli] [The Younger].
Swi. Schaffhausen 1582-1621. B-T.
KUCHARSKI, P.
Pol. ac. 1780 in Paris. B-T.
KÜCHLER, Albert.
Dan. Copenhagen 1803-1886 Rome, It. C-T.
KUCK, Cornelis. *see* Kick, C.
KUDER, René.
Fr. b. 1882 in France. DBA.
KUEHL [or Kühl], Göttbardt Johann.
Ger. Munich 1850/1-1915 Dresden. B-T.
KUEHNE, Max.
Am. b. New York 1880; ad. 1934 Same. A.
KUEMMEL, Cornelia A.
Am. b. Glasgow, Mo.; ad. 1934 Same. A.
KUFELD, Yankel.
Am. ex. 1934 New York. M.
KÜGELGEN, Franz Gerhard von.
Ger. Bacharach 1772-1820. B-T.
KUGHLER, Francis William Vandever.
Am. b. New York 1901; ad. 1934 Same. A.
KÜHL. *see* Kuehl.
KÜHLES, August.
Ger. ac. 1909 in Berlin. B-T.
KUHLMAN, G. Edward.
Am. b. Woodville, O. 1882; ad. 1934 Oil City, Pa. A.
KUHLMAN, Isabel.
Am. ad. 1934 Toledo, O. M.
KUHN, Charles.
Am. ex. 1934 New York. M.
KUHN, Harry Philip.
Am. b. Zurich, Swi. 1862; ad. 1934 Paterson, N. J. A.
KUHN, Walt.
Am. b. New York 1880; ad. 1934 Same. A-F.
KUHNERT, Wilhelm Karl.
Ger. Oppeln 1865-1926. B-T.
KU K'AI-chich.
Chinese. ac. 4th Cent. E.
KULISIEWICZ, Tadeusz. (Eg)
Pol. ac. 20th Cent. in Poland. M.
KULMBACH [or Culmbach], Hans von [Suess].
Ger. Kulmbach 1476/80-1522 Nüremberg. B-C-T.
KUMME, Walter Herman.
Am. b. Phila., Pa. 1895; ad. 1934 New York. A.
KUNA, Henryk. (S)
Pol. b. Warsaw 1885. T.

KUNG CHI.
Chinese. Northern Sung Period (960-1127). M.
KUNG HSIEN.
Chinese. ac. 1698 Nanking, China. T.
KUNHARDT, BOROTHY. (Ill)
Am. ad. 1935 New York. M.
KUNISADA, UTAGAWA.
Jap. b. 1786; d. 1864. B-J-T.
KUNIYASU.
Jap. ac. 1820 in Japan. M.
KUNIYOSHI, KATHERINE SCHMIDT.
Am. b. Xenia, O. 1898; ad. 1934 Brooklyn, N. Y. A28-W.
KUNIYOSHI, UTAGAWA.
Jap. 1798-1861 Tokio. J-T.
KUNIYOSHI, YASUO.
Jap.-Am. b. Okayama 1893; ad. 1934 Brooklyn, N. Y. A-F-T-700-779.
KUNKEL, MARY TREAT.
Am. ad. 1934 New Hope, Pa. M.
KUNKLER, ANDRÉ LAURENT.
Swi. b. Rolle 1898. DBA.
KUNTZ, KARL.
Ger. Mannheim 1770-1830 Carlsruhe. B-T.
KUNTZE, EDWARD J. (S)
Am. Prussia 1826-1870 New York. B-F-15.
KUNZ [and Kuntz] FAMILY.
Ger. ac. 14-19 Cent. in Germany. T.
KUNZ, JOHANN FRITZ.
Swi. b. Einsiedeln 1868. B-T.
KUNZ, LUDWIG ADAM.
Aus. b. Vienna 1857. B-T.
KUNZE, WILLIAM LUTHER.
Am. b. New York 1907; ad. 1934 Hillsdale, N. J. M.
KUO JO-HSU [or Kuo Hsi].
Chinese. b. 1020; d. 1090. E-T.
KUPETZKY, JOANNES [The Elder].
Hun. Possing 1667-1740 Nüremberg, Ger. B-C-T-425.
KUPFERMAN, MURRAY.
Am. b. Brooklyn, N. Y. 1897; ad. 1935 Same. A.
KUPKA, FRANTISEK [or Franz].
Czec. b. Opocno 1871. B-E-DBA-T.
KUROWSKI, JÓSEF SZYMON.
Pol. Crakow 1809-1851 Same. T.
KURTZ, BENJAMIN TURNER. (S)
Am. b. Balt., Md. 1899; ad. 1934 Same. A-Cs.
KURTZ, JULIA WILDER.
Am. b. Harrodsburg, Ky.; ad. 1934 Buffalo, N. Y. A.
KURTZ, KARL.
Ger. b. Stuttgart 1817; d. 1887 Germany. B-T.
KURTZ, WILBUR G.
Am. b. Oakland, Ill. 1882; ad. Atlanta, Ga. A.
KURTZ, WILLIAM.
Am. b. 1833; d. 1904 Far Rockaway, L. I., N. Y. A05-F.
KURTZWORTH, HARRY MUIR.
Am. b. Detroit, Mich. 1887; ad. 1934 Los Angeles, Calif. A.
KURZ, LOUIS.
Am. b. Austria 1834; d. 1921 Chicago, Ill. A018.
KURZBAUER, ÉDUARD.
Ger. b. Semberg 1840; d. 1879 Munich. B-C-T.
KURZWELLY, KONRAD MÜLLER.
Ger. b. 1855; d. 1914. M.
KÜSTNER, KARL.
Ger. b. Hesse 1861. B-T.
KUTZER, ERNST. (Ill)
Am. ad. 1933 New York. M.
KUWASSEG, CHARLES EUPHRASIE.
Fr. b. Draveil 1833; d. 1904 Paris. B-T.
KUWASSEG, CHARLES JOSEPH.
Fr. Trieste, Aus. 1802-1877 Nanterre, Fr. B-T.
KUYCK, FRANS PIETER LODEWIJK VAN.
Belg. b. Antwerp 1852/4; d. 1915. B-T.
KUYCK, JEAN LOUIS VAN.
Belg. b. Antwerp 1821; d. 1871. B-T.
KUYPER, JACQUES.
Dut. b. Amsterdam 1761; d. 1808. B-T.
KUZNETZOV, PAVEL WARFOLOMEJEWITSCH.
Rus. b. Ssaratow 1878; ad. 1935 Moscow. T.
KVAPIL, CHARLES.
Belg. b. Antwerp 1884; ac. 1930 Same. DBA.
KYHN, PETER VILHELM CARL.
Dan. b. Copenhagen 1819; d. 1903 Same. B-C-T.
KYLBERG, PETER VILHELM CARL.
Dan. Copenhagen 1819-1903 Same. T.
KYLE, JOSEPH. (P-S)
Am. b. Ohio 1815; d. 1863 New York. B-F.
KYMLI, F. P.
Ger. ac. 1772-1787 in Germany. B-T.
KYOSAL, KAWANABÉ [To-iku].
Jap. b. Koga 1831; d. 1889. E-J. Vol. 1, page 147.
KYTE, FRANCIS [Milvius]. (Eg)
Eng. ac. 1710-1745 in London. B-DNB-T.
LAAR, JAN HENDRIK VAN DE.
Dut. Rotterdam 1807-1874. B-C-T.
LAAR [or Laer], PIETER JACOBEZ [Bamboccio].
Dut. Haarlem 1592/5-1642. B-C-E-T-722.
LABAT, FERNAND.
Fr. b. Beautiran; 1889. DBA.
LABAUDT, LUCIEN.
Am. b. Paris 1880; ad. 1934 San Mateo, Calif. A.
LABBÉ, NICOLAS.
Fr. b. Clerval; d. 1637 Paris. B.
LA BERGE, AUGUSTE CHARLES DE.
see Berge, A. C. de la.
LABILLE-GUIARD, ADÉLAIDE [Vertus].
Fr. Paris 1749-1803. T-756.
LA BOITEAUX, MARY [Mrs. Isaac].
Am. ad. 1934 Bryn Manor, Pa. M.
LABORDE, CHAS. [or Charles]. (Ill)
Argentinian. b. Buenos-Aires 1886. DBA.
LABORDE, LÉON EMMANUEL JOSEPH SIMON.
Fr. Paris 1807-1869 Fontenay. B-T.
LABOUCHÈRE, PIERRE ANTOINE.
Fr. Nantes 1807-1873 Paris. B-T.
LABOURÉ, CLAUDIUS PIERRE.
Fr. b. Lyons 1888. DBA.
LABOUREUR, JEAN ÉMILE. (Et)
Fr. b. Nantes 1887; ex. 1934 Minn., Minn. B-DBA-T.
LABROUSSE, JEANNE A.
Fr. ac. 1796 in Paris. T.

LA BRUCE, [Mrs.] FLORA MACDONALD.
Am. b. New York; ad. 1934 Charleston, S. C. A.
LABRUZZI, CARLO.
It. Rome 1765-1830. B-T.
LA CAVÉ [or Le Cavé]. P.
Eng. ac. 1769-1810 in London. B-T.
LACAZE, JULIEN.
Fr. b. Paris 1886. DBA.
LACEY, BERTHA J.
Am. b. Perrysville, Ind. 1878; ad. 1934 Same. A.
LACEY, EDWARD HILL. (S)
Eng. b. Bradford 1892; ad. 1934 London. M.
LACHAISE, EUGÈNE A.
Am. b. New York; d. 1925 Paris. A022.
LACHAISE, GASTON. (S)
Am. b. Paris 1882; ad. 1934 New York. A-F-W-701-813.
LA CHANCE, GEORGE.
Am. b. Utica, N. Y. 1888; ad. 1934 Toledo, O. A.
LACHENMEYER, PAUL N. (S)
Am. ac. 1926. F-Ta.
LACHENWITZ, SIGMUND.
Ger. Neuss 1820-1868 Düsseldorf. B-T.
LACHER, [Mrs.] GISELLA LOEFFLER.
Am. b. Vienna, Aus. 1900; ad. 1934 Kirkland, Mo. A.
LACHMAN, HARRY B.
Am. b. LaSalle, Ill. 1886. A-F-W15-46.
LACK, MARTYN. (Eg)
Eng. ac. 1934. M.
LACOSTI, CHARLES.
Fr. b. Floirac 1870. DBA-T.
LACRETELLE, JEAN EDOUARD.
Fr. Forbach 1817-1900 Paris. T.
LACROIX, GASPARD JEAN.
Fr. Turin, It. 1810-1878 Paris. B-T.
LA CROIX [de Marseille], CHARLES FRANÇOIS.
Fr. b. Marseilles; d. 1782 Berlin, Ger. T.
LACY, LUCILE LAND.
Am. b. Temple, Tex. 1901; ad. 1935 Same. M.
LADANYI, EMORY.
Am. b. Kecskemet, Hun. 1902; ad. 1935 New York. M.
LADBROOKE, HENRY.
Eng. 1800-1870. DNB.
LADBROOKE, JOHN BERNEY.
Eng. Norwich 1803-1879 Same. B-DNB.
LADBROOKE, ROBERT.
Eng. Norwich 1768/70-1842 Same. Bd-DNB-T.
LADD, ANNA.
Eng. London 1746-1770 Same. B-T.
LADD, ANNA COLEMAN. (S)
Mrs. Margaret Ladd.
Am. b. Bryn Mawr, Pa. 1878; ad. 1934 Boston. A-Cs-F-W-46.
LADD, LAURA D. STROUD.
Mrs. Westray Ladd.
Am. b. Phila., Pa. 1863; ad. 1934 Same. A.
LADUREAU, PIERRE.
Fr. b. Dunkerque 1882. DBA.
LADURNER, ADOLPHE.
Rus. Moscow 1789-1855/6. B-T.
LAER, ALEXANDER T. VAN.
see Van Laer.
LAER, PIETER VAN.
see Laar, Pieter van.
LAERMANS, EUGÈNE JULES JOSEPH.
Belg. b. Brussels 1864. B-DBA-E-T.
LAESSLE, ALBERT. (S)
Am. b. Phila., Pa. 1877; ad. 1934 Same. A-Cs-F-W.
LA FAGE, NICHOLAS RAYMOND DE. (Eg)
Fr. Lisle 1656-1684 Lyons. B-T-722.
LA FARGE, BANCEL.
Am. ad. 1934 Mt. Carmel, Conn. A-F-T-W.
LA FARGE, CHRISTOPHER. (Ill)
Am. ac. 1934. M.
LA FARGE, JOHN. (Author-P)
Am. New York 1836-1910 Prov., R. I. A09-B-C-DAB-E-T-1-4-5-46-127-128-155-156-701-748.
LA FARGE, MABLE HOOPER.
Mrs. Bancel La Farge.
Am. b. Cambridge, Mass. 1875; ad. Mt. Carmel, Conn. A.
LA FARGE, OLIVER H. P.
Am. ex. 1934 New York. M.
LA FARGE, THOMAS SERGEANT.
Am. b. Paris 1904; ad. 1934 New York. A.
LA FAVOR, WILL. (S)
Am. b. Frankfort, N. Y. 1861. A12-F-Ta.
LAFFITTE, LOUIS.
Fr. Paris 1770-1828 Same. B-T.
LA FLEUR, ABEL.
Fr. b. Rodez 1875. DBA.
LAFON, FRANÇOIS.
Fr. ac. 1875-1890 in Paris. B-T.
LAFON, JACQUES ÉMILE.
Fr. Périgneux 1817-1886. B-T.
LA FOND, SIMEON DANIEL.
Swi. Berne 1763-1831 Same. B-T.
LAFOSSE, CHARLES DE.
Fr. Paris 1636/40-1716 Same. B-C-E-T-722.
LAFRENSEN, NICOLAS.
see Lavreince, Nicolas.
LA FRESNAYE. *see* Fresnaye.
LAGAË, JULES. (S)
Belg. b. Roeselare 1862. Hs-T.
LAGANA, FILIPPO. (S)
Am. b. Italy 1896; ad. 1934 Darien, Conn. A.
LA GANDARA, ANTONIO DE.
see Gandara, Antonio de la.
LAGAR, CELSO.
Sp. b. Cindad 1891. DBA.
LAGARDE, PIERRE.
Fr. Paris 1853-1910. B-T.
LA GATTA, JOHN. (Ill)
Am. b. Naples, It. 1894; ad. 1934 Port Washington, N. Y. A.
LAGLENNE, JEAN FRANCIS.
Fr. b. Paris 1898; ex. 1934 London. DBA-797.
LAGNEAU, NICOLAS.
Fr. 1590-1666. B-T.
LAGRENÉE, JEAN JACQUES [The Younger].
Fr. Paris 1739/40-1821 Same. B-C-T-722.
LAGRENÉE, LOUIS JEAN FRANÇOIS.
Fr. Paris 1724/5-1805 Same. B-C-E-T-722.
LAGUERRE, JOHN [or Jack]. (Actor-P)
Eng. b. London; d. 1748 Same. B-DNB-T.

LAGUERRE, Louis [The Elder].
Fr. Paris 1663-1721 London. B-DBA-T.
LA GUILLERMIE, Frédéric Auguste.
Fr. b. Paris 1841. B-DBA-T.
LAGUT, Irène.
Fr. b. Paris 1893. DBA-T.
LAGYE, Victor.
Belg. Ghent 1825-1896 Antwerp. B-T.
LAHAYE, Alexis Marie.
Fr. ac. 1876-1900 in Paris. B-T.
LAHEY, Francis Vida.
Aust. b. Brisbane, Queensland 1882. M.
LAHEY, Richard Francis.
Am. b. Jersey City, N. J. 1893; ad. 1934 Palisades, N. Y. A-F.
LA HIRE [or La Hyre], Laurent de.
Fr. Paris 1606/16-1656/8 Same. B-C-E-T-722.
LAHM, [Mrs.] Renée.
Am. ad. 1934 Stamford, Conn. M.
L'HOTE, André.
Fr. b. 1885; ex. 1932 Chicago. M.
LAHR, Florence G.
Mrs. Walter L. Lahr.
Am. b. Medaryville, Ind. 1898; ad. 1934 Chicago. A.
LAHUERTA, Genero.
Sp. ad. 1934 Valencia. M.
LA HYRE. *see* La Hire.
LAIDLAW, [Mrs.] Jennie L.
Am. b. Milwaukee, Wis. 1861; ad. 1934 New York. A.
LAIGHTON, Margaret.
Mrs. Edw. W. Forbes.
Am. ad. 1935 Cambridge, Mass. M.
LAING, Frank.
Scot. b. Tayport 1862. B-T.
LAING, James G.
Scot. Aberdeen 1852-1915. T.
LAIRESSE, Gérard de.
Flem. Liége, Belg. 1640/1-1711 Amsterdam, Holland. B-C-T-722.
LAIRESSE, Jan Gérard de.
Dut. Liége 1641-1711 Amsterdam. B-T.
LAITTRE, Eleanor de.
Am. ad. 1935 Wayzata, Minn. M.
LAJARRIGE, Louis.
Fr. Chamboulève 1873-1933. DBA.
LAJOS, Brucke. *see* Brucke-Lajos.
LAJOUE, Jacques de.
Fr. Paris 1687-1761 Same. B-T.
LAKE, Florence Thorne.
Aust. b. Adelaide, So. Aust. 1873. M.
LAKEY, Emily Jane.
Mrs. Charles D. Lakey.
Am. Quincy, N. Y. 1837-1896 Cranford, N. J. F.
LAKHOVSKY, Arnold.
Rus. b. Kiev 1885; ex. 1935 New York. DBA-M.
LALAING, Jacques de. (S)
Belg. London 1858-1917. B-T-798.
LALANNE, Maxime François Antoine. (Et)
Fr. Bordeaux 1827-1886 Nogent. B-T.
LALAU, Maurice George Elie.
Fr. b. Paris 1881; ac. 1932 Same. DBA.
LALAURIE, Marcel.
Fr. b. Arcachon 1885. DBA.
LALAUZE, Adolphe.
Fr. 1838-1905 Milly. T.
LALIBERTÉ, Alfred. (S)
Can. b. Quebec 1872; ad. 1935 Montreal. B-DBA.
LALINE, Suzanne.
Fr. ex. 1935 Paris. M.
LALIQUE, René. (S)
Fr. b. Marne 1860; ad. 1934 Paris. B-DBA-T.
LALLENAND, George.
Fr. Nancy 1560-1648 Paris. B-T.
LALLEMAND, Jean Baptiste [Le Romain].
Fr. Dijon 1710-1803/5 Paris. B-T.
LALLEMAND, Louis.
Belg. b. Marbehan 1891. DBA.
LALONDE, Joseph Wilfred.
Am. b. Minn., Minn. 1897; ad. 1934 New York. A.
LALONE, Robert.
Fr. Paris 1884-1929. DBA.
LALYRE [or Lalire], Adolphe.
Fr. b. Rouvres 1850. B-DBA-T.
LALYRE [or Lalire], N.
Fr. b. 1887. M.
LAMAR, Julian.
Am. b. Augusta, Ga. 1893; ad. 1934 New York. A.
LA MARE-RICHART, Florent de.
Fr. Bayeux 1630-1718 Versailles. T.
LAMB, Adrian.
Am. b. New York 1901; ad. 1934 Same. A.
LAMB, Charles Rollinson. (Mu)
Am. b. New York; ad. 1934 Same. A-F.
LAMB, Charles Vincent.
Ir. b. Armagh 1893. Wa.
LAMB, Ella Condie. (Mu.)
Mrs. Charles R. Lamb.
Am. b. New York; ad. 1934 Creskill, N. J. A-F-W-46.
LAMB, F. Mortimer.
Am. b. Middleboro, Mass. 1861; ad. 1934 Stoughton, Mass. A-F.
LAMB, Frederick Stymetz. (Mu.)
Am. New York 1863-1928 Brooklyn, N. Y. A025-F-W14-46.
LAMB, Henry.
Br. b. Aust. 1885; ex. 1934 London, Wa-825.
LAMB, Joseph.
Am. England 1833-1898 U. S. A01.
LAMB, Kate B.
Am. ad. 1934 Toledo, O. M.
LAMBDEN, Herman.
Am. b. New Rochelle, N. Y. 1859; d. 1935 Same. A-Obit. New York papers, 5-15-1935.
LAMBDIN, George Cochran.
Am. Phila., Pa. 1830-1896 Germantown, Pa. B-C-F-4-6-15.
LAMBDIN, James Reid.
Am. Pittsburgh, Pa. 1807-1889 Phila., Pa. DAB-F-T-2-6-45-66-157.
LAMBDIN, R. L. (Ill)
Am. ad. 1935 New York. M.
LAMBEAUX, Jef. (S)
[Joseph Marie Thomas].
Belg. Antwerp 1852-1908. B-E-Hs-T.
LAMBERT, Albert Antoine.
Fr. b. Paris 1854. B-DBA-T.

LAMBERT, Antoine Eugène.
Fr. Dijon 1824-1902 Paris. B-T.
LAMBERT, Bradford.
Am. ex. 1935 New York. M.
LAMBERT, Clem.
Eng. 1854-1924. Y01925.
LAMBERT, Fernand Alexis.
Fr. b. Lyons 1868. DBA.
LAMBERT, George.
Eng. Kent 1710-1765. B-DNB-T.
LAMBERT, George Washington. (P-S)
Aust. Leningrad, Rus. 1873-1930 Sydney, N. S. W. Aust. B-T-Y01931.
LAMBERT, Gertrude A.
Am. b. So. Bethlehem, Pa. 1885; ad. 1934 New York. A-F.
LAMBERT, John.
Am. Phila., Pa. 1861-1907 Jenkintown, Pa. A07.
LAMBERT, Louis Eugène.
Fr. Paris 1825-1900 Same. B-T.
LAMBERT, Martin.
Fr. Paris 1630-1699 Same. B-T.
LAMBERT, Maurice. (S)
Eng. b. Paris 1901; ad. 1934 London. Wa-798.
LAMBERT, Maurice Walter Edmund de.
Fr. b. Paris 1873; ac. 1932 Same. DBA.
LAMBERTI, Nicolò di Piero. (S)
It. Florence 1393-1451 Venice. B-T-V.
LAMBERTINI, Michele di Matteo.
It. ac. 1440-1469 in Bologna. B-T.
LAMBINET, Émile Charles.
Fr. Versailles 1815-1878 Bougival. B-T.
LAMBORN, Peter Spendelowe. (Eg)
Eng. London 1722-1774 Cambridge. DNB-T.
LAMBRECHTS, Jan Baptiste.
Flem. Antwerp 1680-1750. B-T.
LAMEN, Christoph Jacobesz van der.
Flem. Brussels 1606/15-1651/2 Antwerp. B-T.
LAMI, Eugène Louis.
Fr. Paris 1800-1890 Same. B-T.
LAMI, Marc.
Fr. ac. 1930. Fa.
LAMI, Stanislas. (S)
Fr. b. Paris 1858. B-DBA-T.
LAMME, Arie.
Dut. 1748-1801 Dordrecht. B-T.
LA MONACA, François. (S)
It. b. Cantanzaro, It. 1882; ad. 1934 Paris. DBA.
LAMONT, Frances Kent. (S)
Mrs. Robert P. Lamont, Jr.
Am. ad. 1934 Denver, Colo. A.
LA MONTAGUE, Walter E.
Am. b. 1839; d. 1915 Detroit, Mich. A012.
LA MORE, Chet Harmon.
Am. b. Wis. 1908; ad. 1934 Madison, Wis. A.
LAMORINIÈRE, Jean Pierre François.
Belg. Antwerp 1828-1911. B-T.
LAMORINIÈRE, Willem.
Belg. ac. 1893. M.
LAMOTHE, Louis.
Fr. Lyons 1822-1869 Paris. B-T.
LAMOTTE, Bernard.
Fr. b. Paris 1903. DBA.
LAMOUR, Charles Jean.
Fr. ac. 1909-1929 in Paris. DBA.
LAMOUR, Jean Baptiste.
Fr. Nancy 1698-1771 Same. T.
LAMOURDEDIEU, Raoul. (S)
Fr. b. Faugueroles 1897. B-DBA-T.
LAMPI, Francesco.
It. Bologna 1783-1852 Warsaw, Pol. B.
LAMPI, Giovanni Battista [The Elder].
It. Rome 1751-1830 Vienna, Aus. B.
LAMPI, Giovanni Battista [The Younger].
It. Trente 1775-1837 Vienna, Aus. B.
LAMPI, Johann Baptist von [The Elder].
Aus. Romeno 1751-1830 Vienna. T.
LAMPI, Johann Baptist von [The Younger].
Aus. Triest 1775-1837 Vienna. T.
LAMY, Aline.
Fr. b. Paris 1862. B-DBA-T.
LAMY, Charles.
Fr. Mortagne 1689/99-1743. B-Bd-T.
LAMY, Pierre Désiré Eugène.
Fr. b. Clermont 1855. B-T.
LANA, Jaime.
Sp. d. Zaragaza 1515. T.
LANA DI MODENA, Lodovico.
It. Ferrara 1597-1646 Modena. B-T.
LANCASTER, [Mrs.] Clara Bracebridge.
Eng. b. Hongkong, China; ad. 1934 London. Wa.
LANCASTER, Hume.
Eng. d. 1850 in Erith. B-DNB-T.
LANCASTER, Percy.
Eng. b. Manchester 1878; ex. 1934 London. T-Wa.
LANCE, George.
Eng. Little Easton 1802-1864 Birkenhead. B-Bd-DNB-T.
LANCHARES, Antonio de.
Spa. Madrid 1586-1658 Same. B-T.
LANCIANI, Rodolfo Amedeo.
It. 1846-1929. M.
LANCON, Auguste André.
Fr. St. Claude 1836-1885. B-T.
LANCON, Edourd Michel.
Fr. ac. 1910. M.
LANCRET, Nicolas.
Fr. Paris 1690-1743 Same. B-Bd-C-E-T-245-722-900.
LANDACRE, Paul H. (Eg)
Am. ad. 1934 Los Angeles, Calif. M.
LANDAU, Emilie.
Rus. b. Odessa; ac. 1931 Paris. B.
LANDAU, Jacob.
Am. b. Phila., Pa. 1917; ad. 1935 Same. M.
LANDEAU, Rémy.
Fr. b. Sèvres 1859. B-DBA.
LANDEAU, Sandor L.
Am. b. Hungary 1864; ac. 1910 U. S. A12-B-F.
LANDECK, Armin. (Eg)
Am. ad. 1935 West Nyack, N. Y. M.
LANDELLE, Charles Zacharie.
Fr. Laval 1821-1908. B-T.
LANDELLS, Ebenezer. (Eg)
Eng. New Castle 1808-1860 London. DNB-T.
LANDELLS, Robert Thomas.
Eng. London 1833-1877 Same. DNB-T.

LANDENBERGER, Christian Adam.
Ger. b. Ebingen 1862. B-T.
LANDER, E. (Ill)
Am. ad. 1934 New York. M.
LANDER, John St. Helier.
Eng. b. Isle of Jersey 1869; ad. 1935 London. B-T-Wa.
LANDER, Louisa. (S)
Am. b. Salem, Mass. 1826; ac. 1853 Washington, D. C. F-W7.
LANDER, Robert Scott.
Scot. Edinburgh 1803-1869 Same. B-T.
LANDI, Gasparo.
It. Plaisance 1756-1830 Rome. B-T.
LANDI, Neroccio di Bartolommeo.
It. Siena 1447-1500? Same. B-Bd-T.
LANDINI, Andréa.
It. b. Florence 1847. B-T.
LANDINI, Jacopo del Casentino.
It. Prato 1310-1390 Same. B-T.
LANDINI, Taddeo. (S)
It. Florence 1517-1594 Rome. B-T.
LANDON, Charles Paul.
Fr. Nonant 1760-1826 Paris. B-E-T.
LANDON, Edward A.
Am. b. Hartford, Conn. 1911; ad. 1934 Springfield, Mass. M.
LANDOWSKI, Paul Maximilien. (S)
Fr. b. Paris 1875. B-DBA-Hs-T-426-798.
LANDSEER, Charles.
Eng. 1799-1879 London. B-C-DNB-T.
LANDSEER, [Sir] Edwin Henry.
Eng. London 1802-1873 Same. B-Bd-C-DNB-E-T.
LANDSERE, Jessica. (Min.)
Eng. London 1810-1880 Folkestone. DNB-T.
LANDSERE, John. (Eg)
Eng. Lincoln 1769-1852 London. DNB-T.
LANDSERE, Thomas. (Eg)
Eng. London 1795-1880 Same. DNB-T.
LANDSHUT. *see* Maire de Landshut.
LANE, Betty.
Am. b. Washington, D. C. 1907; ad. 1934 Falls Church, Va. A.
LANE, Camille.
Fr. b. Brixton, Eng.; ac. 1927 in Paris. DBA.
LANE, John Bryant.
Eng. Helston 1788-1868 London. DNB-T.
LANE, Joseph.
Am. ad. 1935 Chicago. M.
LANE, Katherine Ward. (S)
Am. b. Boston 1899; ad. 1934 Same. A-Cs-DBA.
LANE, Richard James. (Eg)
Eng. Hereford 1800-1872 London. DNB-T.
LANE, Samuel.
Eng. Norfolk 1780-1859 Ipswich. DNB-T.
LANE, Susan Minot.
Am. Cambridge, Mass. 1832-1893 Same. F.
LANE, Theodore.
Eng. Isleworth 1800-1828 London. DNB-T.
LANE, Thomas Henry. (Min.)
Am. Phila., Pa. 1815-1900 Elizabeth, N. J. A04-F.
LANE, William. (Eg)
Eng. 1746-1819 London. B-DNB-T.
LANFANT DE METZ, François Louis.
Fr. Metz 1814-1892 Havre. T.
LANFRANCO, Giovanni di Stefano.
It. Parma 1580/1-1647 Rome. B-C-T-722.
LANG, Annie Traquair.
Am. Phila., Pa. 1885-1918 New York. A016.
LANG, Charles Michael Angelo. (P-S)
Am. Albany, N. Y. 1860-1934 Greenfield Centre, N. Y. A-F-M-W-Obit Art News, 3-31-1934.
LANG, [Mrs.] Florence R.
Mrs. Henry Lang.
Am. ad. 1934 Montclair, N. J. M.
LANG, Hans Kaspar [The Elder].
Swi. Schaffhausen 1571-1645. B-T.
LANG, Heinrich.
Ger. Ratisbonne 1838-1891 Munich. B-T.
LANG, Louis.
Am. Germany 1814-1893 New York. B-C-F-2-15.
LANG, William Anton. (Ill)
Am. ad. 1934 New York. M.
LANGE, Erna.
Am. b. Elizabeth, N. J. 1896; ad. 1934 Same. A.
LANGE, Joseph.
Ger. Wurzburg 1751-1831 Vienna, Aus. B-T.
LANGE, Julius.
Ger. Darmstadt 1817-1878 Munich. B-T.
LANGE, Otto.
Ger. b. Dresden 1879. DBA-T.
LANGEBAHN, August A. (S)
Am. Germany 1831-1915 Buffalo, N. Y. A012.
LANGENBACH, Clara Emma.
Am. b. Ontario, Can. 1871; ad. 1934 Buffalo, N. Y. A.
LANGENBECK, [Mrs.] Elizabeth MacCubbin.
Am. b. Washington, D. C. 1907; ad. Same. A.
LANGENBERG, Gustave C.
Am. b. Germany; d. 1915 New York. A013.
LANGENDYKE, Dirk [or Thierry].
Dut. Rotterdam 1748-1805 Same. T.
LANGERFELDT, Theodore Otto.
Am. b. Ger. 1841; ex. 1876 Phila., Pa. F-T.
LANGHAM, Emily.
Am. b. Shepherd, Tex. 1895; ad. Houston, Tex. A.
LANGHAMMER, Arthur. (Ill)
Ger. Lützen 1854-1901 Dachau. B-T.
LANGHAMMER, Karl.
Ger. b. Berlin 1868. B-T.
LANGHEIM, Friedrich Wilhelm.
Ger. b. 1804; ac. 1828 in Berlin. T.
LANGLEY, Lisa.
Am. b. Chicago 1907; ad. 1934 Phila., Pa. A.
LANGLEY, Sarah.
Mrs. Earl Mendenhall.
Am. b. Texas 1885; ad. 1934 Phila., Pa. A.
LANGLEY, Thomas.
Eng. 1700?-1751 London. B-DNB-T.
LANGLEY, Walter.
Eng. Birmingham 1852-1922 Penzance. B-T-Y01923.
LANGLOIS, Eustache Hyacinthe.
Fr. 1777-1837 Rouen. B-T.
LANGLOIS, Jean Charles.
Fr. Beaumont 1789-1870. B-T.
LANGLOIS, Jérôme Martin.
Fr. Paris 1779-1838 Same. B-T.

LANGMAN, OTTO FREDERICK.
b. New York 1884; ad. 1934 Same. M.
LANGTON, BERNICE FRANCES. (S)
Mrs. Daniel W. Langton.
Am. ad. 1934 New York. A-DBA.
LANGUEREAU, MARIE.
Fr. ac. 1907 in Paris. B.
LANGZETTEL, GEORGE HENRY.
Am. b. Springfield, Mass. 1864; ad. 1934 New Haven, Conn. A.
LANIER, NICHOLAS. (Et)
It. Italy 1588-1665 London. B-DNB-T.
LANING, EDWARD.
Am. b. Petersburgh, Ill. 1906; ad. 1934 New York. A.
LANINO, BERNARDINO.
It. Vercelli 1510/20-1578/83 Milan. B-Bd-T.
LANKES, JULIUS J. (Eg)
Am. b. Buffalo, N. Y. 1884; ad. 1934 Hilton, Va. A28-F-W.
LANKRINK, PROSPER HENRICUS.
Flem. Antwerp 1628-1692 London. B-DNB-T.
LANMAN, CHARLES.
Am. Monroe, Mich. 1819-1895. C-F-3.
LANNO, FRANÇOIS GASPARD ANNE. (S)
Fr. Rénnes 1800-1871 Beaumont. B-T.
LANOUE [or Lanque], FÉLIX HIPPOLYTE.
Fr. Versailles 1812-1872 Same. B-T.
LANOYER. *see* Lansyer.
LANQUE. *see* Lanoue.
LANSIL, WALTER FRANKLIN.
Am. b. Bangor, Me. 1846. A12-B-C-F-15-47.
LANSON, ALFRED DÉSIRÉ. (S)
Fr. Orléans 1851-1896. B-T.
LANSYER, MAURICE EMMANNUEL.
Fr. Vendee 1835-1895 Paris. B-C-T.
LANTARA, SIMON MATHURIN.
Fr. Oncy 1729/45-1778 Paris. B-C-E-T-722.
LANTOINE-NEVEUX. *see* Neveux, L.
LAN YING.
Chinese. b. 1565. T.
LANZ, KARL ALFRED. (S)
Swi. b. 1847; d. 1907 Berne. B-T.
LANZA, JOANNA.
Am. ad. 1934 New York. M.
LANZANI, POLIDORO [or Venezianio].
It. Venice 1515-1565. B-T.
LAP, ENGELBERT. (Eg)
Aust. ac. 1934. M.
LAPARRA, WILLIAM.
Fr. Bordeaux 1873-1920 Paris. B-DBA-T.
LAPINE, ANDRÉ C. G.
Can. b. Shujen, Rus.; ad. 1935 Toronto, Ont., Can. M.
LAPIS, GAETANO.
It. Cagli 1704-1776. B-T.
LAPITO, LOUIS AUGUSTE.
Fr. Joinville 1803-1874 Boulogne. B-T.
LAPLANTE, CHARLES.
Fr. b. Sèvres; d. 1903. B-T.
LAPO [or Lapi], ARNOLFO DI.
It. ac. 1265-1289. T-V.
LAPORTE, GEORGE HENRY.
Ger. Hanover 1789-1873 London. B-DNB-T.
LA PORTE, HENRI HORACE ROLAND DE.
see Roland de la Porte.
LAPORTE, JOHN.
Eng. 1761-1839 London. B-DNB-T.
LAPOSTELET, CHARLES.
Fr. Velars 1824-1890 Domiens. B-T.
LAPPOLI, GIOVANNI ANTONIO.
It. Arezzo 1492-1552 Same. T-V.
LAPRADE, PIERRE.
Fr. Narbonne 1875-1932. DBA.
LAPSHIN, NIKOLAI FYODORVITCH. (Ill)
Rus. ac. 1934 in Russia. M.
LAQUY, WILLEM JOSEPH.
Ger. Bruel 1738-1798 Clève. B-T.
LARCHE [or Laroche], FRANÇOIS RAOUL. (S)
Fr. St. André 1860-1912 Paris. B-DBA-T-798.
LARGILLIÈRE [or Largillièrre], NICHOLAS DE.
Fr. Paris 1656-1746 Same. B-Bd-C-E-T-722.
LARIAR, LAWRENCE. (Cari)
Am. ad. 1935 New York. M.
LARIONOFF, JEAN.
Rus. Tripoli, It. 1884-1919 Moscow. DBA.
LARIONOFF, MICHEL FJODOROWITSCH.
Rus. b. Teraspol; 1881. DBA-T.
LA RIVE-GODEFROY, PIERRE LOUIS DE.
Swi. Geneva 1735-1817 Persingue. B-T.
LARIVIÈRE, CHARLES PHILLIPPE ANGUETTE DE.
Fr. Paris 1798-1876 Same. B-T.
LARIVIÈRE, PIERRE.
Fr. Paris 1883-1932 Same. DBA.
LARKINS, WILLIAM MARTIN. (Et)
Eng. b. London 1901; ad. 1934 Same. B-T-Wa.
LARMESSIN, NICOLAS DE [The Elder].
Fr. Paris 1636/8-1694 Same. B-T.
LARMESSIN, NICOLAS DE IV.
Fr. Paris 1684-1753/5 Same. B-T.
LARNED, MARGARETTE YOUNGLOVE.
Am. ad. 1934 New York. A-F.
LAROCHE, ERNESTO.
Uruguayian. b. Montevideo 1879. DBA.
LARONZE, JEAN.
Fr. b. Genelard 1852. B-DBA-T.
LAROON [or Lauron], MARCELLUS [The Elder]. (Eg)
Dut. The Hague 1653-1702 Richmond, Eng. B-DNB-T-803.
LAROON, JOHN MARCELLUS [The Younger].
Eng. London 1679-1774 Oxford. B-DNB-T-803.
LA ROSE, JEAN BAPTISTE DE.
Fr. Aix 1612-1687 Toulon. B-T.
LARSEN, BENT FRANKLIN.
Am. b. Monroe, Utah 1882; ad. 1934 Provo, Utah. A.
LARSEN, CARL FREDERICK EMMANUEL.
Dan. 1823-1859. B-T.
LARSEN, MAE SYBIL.
Am. b. Chicago; ad. 1934 Same. A.
LARSH, THEODORE. (Min)
Mrs. Francis Dane Chase.
Am. b. Crawsfordsville, Ind.; ad. 1934 New York. A-F.
LARSON, FRANK. (Ill)
Am. ad. 1934 New York. M.
LARSON, FRED T.
Am. b. Chicago 1868; ad. 1934 Same. A.
LARSSON, CARL OLOF.
Swe. Stockholm 1853-1919. B-DBA-T-683.
LARUE, PHILIBERT BENÔIT DE.
Fr. Paris 1718-1763. B-T.

LARWIN, JOHANN.
Ger. b. Vienna, Aus. 1873. T.
LA SALLE, CHARLES. (Ill)
Am. ad. 1934 New York. M.
LASCARI, HILDA KRISTINA. (S)
Am. b. Sweden 1886; ad. 1934 New York. Cs-M.
LASCARI, SALVATORE.
Am. ad. 1935 New York. A22-M.
LASCAUX, ÉLIE.
Fr. b. Limoges 1888; ex. 1934 London. DBA.
LASCELLES, CHARLES.
Eng. b. London 1890; ad. 1934 Bath. Wa.
LASCELLES, FRANK.
Eng. Sibford 1876-1934 Brighton. Wa1929-Obit. N. Y. papers, 5-26-1934.
LASCH, KARL JOHANN.
Ger. Leipzig 1822-1888 Moscow, Rus. C-T.
LASH, LEE.
Am. b. San Fran., Calif. 1864; ad. 1935 New York. M.
LASINIO, [Count] CARLO. (Eg)
It. Trévise 1757-1839 Pisa. B-T.
LASINIO, GIOVANNI PAOLO.
It. 1789/96-1855. B-T.
LASKE, OSKAR.
Ger. b. 1841; ad. 1934 Vienna, Aus. T.
LASKY, BESSIE.
Mrs. Jesse L. Lasky.
Am. b. Boston 1890; ad. 1934 New York. A.
LASNE [or L'Asne], MICHEL.
Fr. Caen 1595/6-1667 Louvre. B-T.
LA SPAGNOLETTO. *see* Ribera.
LASSELL, CHARLES.
Am. ac. 1931 in Westport, Conn. A28.
LASSONDE, OMER THOMAS.
Am. b. Concord, N. H. 1903; ad. 1934 Same. A.
LASTMAN, CLAES PIETERSZ [Nicolas Petri].
Dut. 1586-1625 Amsterdam. T.
LASTMAN, PIETER PIETERSZ.
Dut. Amsterdam 1562/83-1633/49 Haarlem. B-C-T.
LASZCZKA, KONSTANT. (S)
Pol. b. Kalisch 1865. T-798.
LÁSZLÓ, GEORGE.
Am. b. Zalaszentivan, Hun. 1891; ad. 1934 New York. A.
LÁSZLÓ [de Lombo], PHILIPP [or Fülóp] ALEXIUS DE.
Eng. b. Budapest, Hun. 1869; ad. 1934 London. B-DBA-T-Wa-857.
LATHAM, BARBARA.
Mrs. Howard Coak.
Am. b. Walpole, Mass. 1896; ad. 1934 Norwichtown, Conn. A.
LATHAM, JAMES.
Ir. Tipperary 1696-1747 Dublin. B-DNB-T.
LA THANGUE, HENRY HERBERT.
Eng. 1859-1929 Dulwich. B-Y01930-Wa.
LATHROP, DOROTHY PULIS. (Ill)
Am. b. Albany, N. Y. 1891; ad. 1934 Same. A-W.
LATHROP, FRANCIS AUGUSTUS.
Am. 1849-1909 Woodcliffe Lake, N. Y. A08-B-C-DAB-E-F-W5-15-46.
LATHROP, GERTRUDE K. (S)
Am. b. Albany, N. Y. 1896; ad. 1934 Same. A-Cs-F.
LATHROP, IDA PULIS.
Mrs. Cyrus Clark Lathrop.
Am. b. Troy, N. Y. 1859; ad. 1934 Albany, N. Y. A.
LATHROP, WILLIAM LANGSON.
Am b. Warren, Ill. 1859; ad. 1934 New Hope, Pa. A-F-W14.
LATINVILLE, S.
Fr. ac. 1760. Wi.
LA TOMBE [or Stopper], NICOLAAS.
Dut. Amsterdam 1616-1676 Same. B-T.
LA TOUCHE, GASTON.
Fr. St. Cloud 1854-1913. B-DBA-T.
LATOUR, FANTIN. *see* Fantin-Latour.
LA TOUR, GEORGES DUMESNIL DE.
Fr. Lunéville 1600-1652 Same. B-T.
LA TOUR, MAURICE QUENTIN DE.
Fr. Quentin 1704-1788 Same. B-E-T-154-427-428-722-756.
LATROBE, BENJAMIN HENRY.
Am. Yorkshire, Eng. 1764-1820 New Orleans, La. T.
LATTANZIO DA RIMINI.
It. b. Venice; ac. 1495 Same. B-T-V.
LATTIMORE, ELEANOR FRANCES. (Ill)
Am. ad. 1934 Hanover, N. H. M.
LAUBER, JOSEPH. (Mu)
Am. b. Meschede, Westphalia, Ger. 1855; ad. 1934 New York. A-F-46.
LAUDER, JAMES ECKFORD.
Scot. Edinburgh 1811-1869 Same. DNB-T.
LAUDER, ROBERT SCOTT.
Scot. Silvermills 1803-1869 Edinburgh. DNB-T.
LAUDERDALE, URSULA.
Mrs. Edward Seay Lauderdale.
Am. ad. 1934 Dallas, Tex. A.
LAUDIN, JACQUES [The Elder].
Fr. 1627-1695. B-T.
LAUENSTEIN, HEINRICH.
Ger. 1835-1910 Düsseldorf. B-T.
LAUER, CATHERIN GAVIN.
Am. b. Toledo, O. 1907; ad. 1934 Same. A.
LAUFBERGER, FERDINAND JULIUS WILHELM.
Aus. Czec. 1829-1881 Vienna. C-T.
LAUFFER, EMIL JOHANN.
Aus. Hof, Ger. 1837-1909 Prague, Czec. B-T.
LAUFMAN, SIDNEY.
Am. b. Cleveland, O. 1891; ad. 1934 Paris. A-DBA-892.
LAUGÉE, DÉSIRÉ FRANÇOIS.
Fr. Maromme 1823-1896 Paris. B-T.
LAUGÉE, GEORGES.
Fr. b. Montivilliers 1853. B-C-DNB-T.
LAUGHLIN, ALICE.
Am. ex. 1934 New York. M.
LAUGHMAN, LANE.
Am. ad. 1935 New York. M.
LAUNAY, FABRIEN [Viellard].
Fr. Paris 1877-1907 Same. DBA.
LAUNAY, LÉON.
Fr. b. Breste 1890. DBA.
LAUNAY [or Delaunay], NICOLAS DE.
Fr. Paris 1739-1792. T-900.
LAUNITZ, ROBERT EBERHARD SCHMIDT VON.
Am. Riga, Rus. 1806-1870 New York. B-DAB-F-2-15-158.

LAUNOIS, JEAN.
Fr. b. Sables-d'Olonne 1898. DBA.
LAUPHEIMER, ANTON.
Ger. b. Erlbach 1846. B.
LAURANA, FRANCESCO. (S)
Fr. Vrana, It. 1420/5-1502 Avignon, Fr. B-Hs-T.
LAURENCE. *see also* Lawrence.
LAURENCE [or Lawrence], SAMUEL.
Eng. Surrey 1812-1884 London. B-Bd-E-T-45.
LAURENCE, SIDNEY M.
Am. b. Brooklyn, N. Y. 1865. A26-B.
LAURENCIN, MARIE.
Fr. b. Paris 1885. DBA-T-429-700-797.
LAURENS, HENRI. (S)
Fr. b. Paris 1885. DBA-T.
LAURENS, JEAN PAUL.
Fr. Fourquervaux 1838-1921 Paris. B-C-DBA-T.
LAURENS, JEAN PIERRE.
Fr. Paris 1875-1932 Fontenay. B-T-DBA-Y01933.
LAURENS, JULES JOSEPH AUGUSTIN.
Fr. Carpentras, 1825-1901 St. Didier. B-T.
LAURENS, PAUL ALBERT.
Fr. b. Paris 1870. B-DBA-T.
LAURENSON. *see also* Lawrenson.
LAURENSON, EDWARD LOUIS.
Ir. b. Dublin 1868. T-364.
LAURENT [or Lawrence], ANDRÉ. (Eg)
Fr. London 1708-1747 Paris. DNB-T.
LAURENT, ERNEST JOSEPH.
Fr. Paris 1859-1929 Same. B-DBA-T.
LAURENT, JEAN ANTOINE. (Min)
Fr. Baccarat 1763/5-1832 Epinal. B-T.
LAURENT, ROBERT. (S)
Am. b. Conarneau, Fr. 1890; ad. 1934 Brooklyn, N. Y. A-Cs-F-W-813.
LAURENTI, CESARE.
It. b. Venice 1854. B-T.
LAURI, FILIPPO.
It. Rome 1623-1694 Same. B-T.
LAURIE [or Lawrie], ROBERT. (Eg)
Scot. 1755-1836 Broxburn. DNB-T.
LAURIE-WALLACE, JOHN.
Am. b. Garvagh, Ir. 1864; ad. 1934 Omaha, Neb. A.
LAURITZ, PAUL.
Am. b. Larvik, Nor. 1889; ad. 1934 Los Angeles, Calif. A.
LAUROEUS, ALEXANDER.
Dan. Abo, Finland 1783-1823; Rome, It. B-T.
LAUSSUCQ, HENRY L.
Am. ad. 1934 New York. M.
LAUTER, FLORA.
Am. b. New York 1874; ad. 1934 Indianapolis, Ind. A.
LAUTERBURG, MARTIN.
Swi. b. Berne 1891. T.
LAUTERSACK, HANS SEBALD. (Eg)
Ger. Bamberg 1524-1560/3. B-T.
LAUTERSACK, HEINRICH.
Ger. Bamberg 1522-1590 Frankfort. B-T.
LAUTERSACK, PAUL.
Ger. Bamberg 1478-1558? Nüremberg. B-T.
LAUTH, CHARLES FRÉDÉRIC.
Fr. Paris 1865-1922 Same. B-DBA-T.
LAUTREC, HENRI DE TOULOUSE.
see Toulouse-Lautrec, Henri de.
LAUTZ, WILLIAM. (S)
Am. Germany 1838-1915 Buffalo, N. Y. A012.
LAUX, AUGUST.
Am. Bavaria 1853-1921 Brooklyn, N. Y. A018-F.
LAUX, MARIE.
Ger. b. Wiesbaden 1852. T.
LAVALLE, JOHN.
Am. b. Nahant, Mass. 1896; ad. 1934 Boston. A-F.
LAVALLEY, ALEXANDRE CLAUDE LOUIS.
Fr. Paris 1863-1927. DBA.
LAVALLEY, GEORGES HENRI.
Fr. Paris 1869-1902. B-T.
LAVALLEY, JONAS JOSEPH.
Am. Rouses Point, N. Y. 1858-1930 Springfield, Mass. A027.
LAVARRON, LEONIDE C.
Am. New York 1866-1931 Chicago. A028.
LAVERY, [Sir] JOHN.
Ir. b. Belfast, 1856/7. B-E-T-Wa-430-825.
LAVIELLE, EUGÈNE ANTOINE SAMUEL.
Fr. Paris 1820-1889 Same. B-C-T.
LAVIELLE, JACQUES ANDRIEN.
Fr. Paris 1818-1862 Same. B-T.
LAVIGNE, MAURI MAURICETTE.
Fr. b. Paris 1900. DBA.
LAVREINCE [or Lafriensen], NICOLAS. (Min)
Swe. Stockholm, 1737-1807 Same. B-T-900.
LAVRIN, [Mrs.] NORA. (Et)
Eng. ad. 1934 London. M.
LAW, DAVID.
Scot. Edinburgh 1831-1902 Worthing, Eng. B-DNB-T.
LAW, MARGARET MOFFETT.
Am. b. Spartansburg, S. C.; ad. 1934 Same. A-F.
LAW, PAULINE ELIZABETH.
Am. ex. 1935 New York. M.
LAWES-WITTERONGE, [Sir] CHARLES BENNET. (S)
Eng. Teignmouth 1843-1911 London. DNB-E-T.
LAWLESS, CARL.
Am. b. Illinois 1894; ad. 1934 Mystic, Conn. A-F.
LAWLESS, MATTHEW JAMES.
Ir. Dublin 1837-1846 Bayswater. Bd-DNB-T.
LAWMAN, JASPER HOLMAN.
Am. Xenia, O. 1825-1906 Pittsburgh, Pa. A06-B-F-15.
LAWRANCE, MARY [Mrs. Kearse].
Eng. ac. 1794-1830 London. DNB-T.
LAWRENCE. *see also* Laurence.
LAWRENCE, ALFRED KINGSLEY.
Eng. b. Lewes 1893. Wa-825.
LAWRENCE, EDITH MARY. (Eg)
Eng. b. Surrey 1890; ex. 1934 Brooklyn, N. Y. M-Wa.
LAWRENCE, EDNA W.
Am. b. Concord, N. Y. 1898; ad. 1934 Prov., R. I. A.
LAWRENCE, HELEN CHRISTOPHER.
Mrs. Frank Lawrence.
Am. b. Red Oak, Ia. 1895; ad. 1934 Darien, Conn. A.

LAWRENCE, [Mrs.] HELEN H.
Am. ad. 1934 New York. M.
LAWRENCE, JOSEPHINE. (Min)
Am. ad. 1934 Birmingham, Ala. M.
LAWRENCE, ROBERT P.
Am. ad. 1934 White Plains, N. Y. M.
LAWRENCE, [Sir] THOMAS.
Eng. Bristol 1769-1830 London.
B-Bd-C-DNB-E-T-431-722-727-909.
LAWRENCE, T. CROMWELL. (Ill)
Am. Eng. 1867-1905 Brooklyn, N. Y. A06.
LAWRENCE, WILLIAM HURD.
Am. b. Keene, N. H. 1866; ad. 1934 New Dorp, N. Y. A.
LAWRENCE-WETHERILL, MARIA.
Am. b. Phila., Pa. 1892; ad. 1934 New York. A.
LAWRENSON, EDWARD LOUIS.
Ir. b. Dublin 1868. T-Wa1929.
LAWRENSON [or Lawranson], THOMAS.
Ir. b. Dublin; ex. 1760-1777 London. B-DNB-T.
LAWRENSON, WILLIAM.
Br. ex. 1760-1780 London. B-DNB.
LAWRIE, ALEXANDER.
Am. New York 1828-1917 Lafayette, Ind.
A014-B-C-DAB-F-15-45.
LAWRIE, LEE. (S)
Am. b. Bixford, Ger. 1877; ad. 1934 New York. A-F-W.
LAWS, ARTHUR J.
Am. ad. 1934 Cleveland, O. M.
LAWSON, ADELAIDE J.
Am. b. New York 1890; ad. Glenwood Landing, L. I., N. Y. A-F.
LAWSON, ALEXANDER. (Eg)
Am. Scotland 1772/3-1846 Phila., Pa.
F-DAB-2-7-40-147.
LAWSON, CECIL GORDON.
Eng. Wallington 1851-1882 London.
B-C-DNB-E-T.
LAWSON, ERNEST.
Am. b. Calif. 1873; ad. 1934 New York.
A-F-W-46-432.
LAWSON, FREDERICK.
Eng. b. Yeadon 1888; ad. 1934 Redmire. Wa.
LAWSON, GEORGE ANDERSON. (S)
Scot. Edinburgh 1832-1904 Richmond, Eng.
B-DNB-E-Hs-T.
LAWSON, JAMES KERR.
see Kerr-Lawson, James.
LAWSON, JESS M. *see* Lawson-Peacey, Jess M.
LAWSON, [Mrs.] KATHERINE STEWART. (S)
Am. b. Indianapolis 1885; ad. 1934 Westport, Conn. A-Cs-F-181.
LAWSON, KERR. *see* Kerr-Lawson.
LAWSON, MARIE A. (Ill)
Am. ad. 1934 New York. M.
LAWSON, OSCAR A.
Am. Phila., Pa. 1813-1854 Same. F-7-40.
LAWSON, ROBERT. (Et)
Am. b. New York 1892; ad. 1935 Same. M.
LAWSON, THOMAS BAYLEY.
Am. Newburyport, Mass. 1807-1888 Lowell, Mass. F-2-169.
LAWSON-PEACEY, JESS M. (S)
Am. b. Edinburgh, Scot. 1885; ad. 1934 New York. A.

LAY, CHARLES DOWNING.
Am. b. Newburgh, N. Y. 1877; ad. 1934 New York. A.
LAY, DAVID.
Am. ex. 1935 New York. M.
LAY, OLIVE INGRAHAM.
Am. New York 1845-1890. B-C-F-15.
LAYMAN, WALTER.
Am. b. Covington, Ky. 1871. A12.
LAYNG, FRANCIS.
Br. ac. 1930. M.
LAZARO, BASTIANNA.
see Sebastiani, Lazaro Bastianna.
LAZARUS, JACOB H.
Am. New York 1822-1891 Same. F-T.
LAZARUS, MINNIE RACHEL.
Am. Baltimore, Md. 1872-1932 Same. A029.
LAZERGES, JEAN BAPTISTE PAUL.
Fr. Paris 1845-1902 Asnières. B-C-T.
LAZERGES, JEAN RAYMOND HIPPOLYTE.
Fr. Narbonne 1817-1887 Mustapha. B-C-T.
LAZZARI, DONATO D'ANGELO.
[Bramante da Urbino.]
It. Urbino, 1444-1514 Rome. B-T.
LAZZARI, OTTAVIANO. (S)
It. ac. 1613 in Rome. T.
LAZZARI, PILTRO.
Am. ex. 1934 New York. M.
LAZZARINI GREGORIO.
It. Venice 1654/7-1735/40 Same. B-T.
LAZZELL, BLANCHE.
Am. b. Maidsville, W. Va.; ad. 1934 Morganstown, W. Va. A-F.
LE. *see also* specific names.
LEACH, BERNARD HOWELL.
Br. b. Hongkong, China 1887; ad. 1934 St. Ives, Cornwall, Eng. Wa.
LEACH, ETHEL PENNEWILL BROWN.
Am. b. Wilmington, Del.; ad. 1934 Frederica, Del. A.
LEACH, HILTON. *see* Leech, H.
LEACH, LOUIS L. (S)
Am. ad. 1935 Taunton, Mass. M.
LEADER, [Sir] BENJAMIN WILLIAM.
Eng. Worcester 1831-1923 Shere. B-C-E-T.
LEAKE, EUGENE W.
Am. ad. 1935 New York. M.
LEAKE, GERALD.
Am. b. London 1885; ad. 1935 New York. A-F.
LEAKEY, JAMES.
Eng. Exeter, 1775-1865 Same. B-DNB-T.
LEAL, JUAN DE VALDES.
see Valdes-Leal, Juan de.
LEALE, MARION. (Min)
Am. b. New York; ad. 1934 Same. A.
LEAMING, CHARLOTTE.
Am. b. Chicago 1878; ad. 1934 Colorado Springs, Col. A.
LÉANDRÉ, CHARLES LUCIEN. (Cari)
Fr. Champsecret 1862-1934 Paris.
B-DBA-E-T.
LEAR, EDWARD. (Author-P)
Eng. 1812-1888 San Remo, It. B-DNB-E-T.
LEAR, GEORGE.
Am. b. Doylestown, Pa. 1879; ad. 1934 Germantown, Pa. A.

LEARNED, ARTHUR GARFIELD. (Et)
Am. b. Chester, Mass. 1872; ad. 1934 New York. A-F-W.
LEATHERMAN, RUTH ANNE.
Am. b. Muskegon, Mich. 1900; ad. 1934 Hinsdale, Ill. A.
LEAVITT, AGNES.
Am. b. Boston, Mass. 1859. A12.
LEAVITT, DAVID FRANKLIN. (Ill)
Am. b. St. Louis, Mo. 1897; ad. 1934 Same. A.
LEAVITT, EDWARD C.
Am. d. 1904 Providence, R. I. A05.
LEB, WOLFGANG. (S)
Ger. ac. 1500 in Altbayern. T.
LEBARBIER, JEAN JACQUES FRANÇOIS.
Fr. Rouen 1738-1826 Paris. B-C-T-722.
LEBASQUE, HENRI.
Fr. b. Champigné 1865; ad. 1934 Paris. B-DBA-T.
LEBDUSKA, LAWRENCE H.
Am. b. Baltimore, Md. 1894; ad. 1934 Brooklyn, N. Y. A.
LEBEDER, KONSTANTINE.
Rus. b. Russia 1852; ac. 1900 in Paris. B-T.
LEBEDEV, MIKHAIL.
Rus. Russia 1812-1837 Naples, It. B-T.
LEBEDEV, VALDIMER.
Rus. b. Russia 1891. T.
LEBEL, EDMOND.
Fr. Amiens 1834-1908. B-T.
LEBLANC, ALEXANDRE.
Fr. 1793-1866. B-T.
LE BLANC, EMILIE DE HOA.
Am. b. New Orleans, La. 1870; ad. 1934 Same. A.
LE BLANC, MARIE DE HOA.
Am. b. New Orleans, La. 1874; ad. 1934 Same. A.
LE BLANT, JULIEN.
Fr. b. Paris 1851. B-DBA-T.
LE BLON, JACQUES CHRISTOFFEL. (Eg)
Fr. Frankfort, Ger. 1670-1741 Paris. B-DNB-T.
LE BLON, MICHIEL. (Min)
Ger. Frankfort 1587-1656 Amsterdam, Holland. B-T.
LEBOURG, CHARLES ALBERT.
Fr. Montfort, 1849-1928 Rouen. B-DBA-T.
LE BOUTEILLIER, JEAN. (S)
Fr. ac. 14th century in Paris. Hs.
LE BOUTEUX, PIERRE MICHEL
Fr. Paris 1683-1750 Lille. B-T.
LEBROC, JEAN BAPTISTE. (S)
Fr. b. Paris 1825. B-T.
LE BRON, WARREE CARMICHAEL.
Am. b. Elba, Ala. 1910; ad. 1935 Montgomery, Ala. M.
LE BRUN, CHARLES. (P-S)
Fr. Paris 1619-1690 Same. B-Bd-C-E-Hs-T-722.
LEBRUN, FREDERICO.
Am. ad. 1935 New York. M.
LEBRUN, JEAN BAPTISTE PIERRE.
Fr. Paris 1748-1813 Same. B-T.
LEBRUN, RICO. (Ill)
Am. ad. 1934 New York. M.
LEBRUN, VIGÉE. *see* Vigée-Lebrun.
LECAPELAIN, ANDRÉ ABEL.
Fr. b. Paris 1906. DBA.
LECARON.
Fr. ex. 1935 Paris. M.
LE CARPENTIER, CHARLES LOUIS FRANÇOIS.
Fr. Pont-Audemer 1744-1822 Rouen. B-T.
LE CHEVALIER, DE DIEPPE.
Fr. ac. 1742-1763. B.
LE CHEVALIER, GEORGINA.
Fr. b. St. Ouen 1899. DBA.
LE CLAIR, B. (Eg)
Fr. ac. 1791 Paris. T.
LE CLAIRE, VICTOR.
Fr. Paris 1830-1885 Same. B-T.
LE CLEAR, THOMAS.
Am. Owego, N. Y. 1818-1882 Rutherford, N. J. B-Bd-C-DAB-F-4-15-116-159.
LE CLERC, DAVID.
Ger. Berne, Swi. 1680-1738 Frankfort, Ger. B-T.
LE CLERC, JEAN.
Fr. Nancy 1585-1633 Same. B-T.
LE CLERC, SÉBASTIEN [The Elder].
Fr. Metz 1637-1714 Paris. B-T.
LE CLERC, SÉBASTIEN [The Younger].
Fr. Paris 1676-1763 Gobelins. B-T.
LE CLERC, SÉBASTIEN JACQUES.
[Le Clerc des Gobelins.]
Fr. Paris 1734-1785 Same. B-T.
LECOMTE, FÉLIX. (S)
Fr. Paris 1737-1817 Same. B-T.
LECOMTE, HIPPOLYTE.
Fr. Puiseaux 1781-1857 Paris. B-T.
LECOMTE, LOUIS. (S)
Fr. Boulogne 1639-1694. B-T.
LECOMTE, PAUL.
Fr. Paris 1842-1920. B-T.
LECOMTE, PAUL ÉMILE.
Fr. b. Paris 1877. B-DBA-T.
LECOMTE, VICTOR.
Fr. b. Paris 1856; d. Same. B-DBA-T.
LECOMTE DU NOVY, JEAN JULES ANTOINE.
Fr. Paris 1842-1923 Same. B-C-DBA-T.
LE CONTE, SAUVEUR.
Fr. Paris 1659-1694 Same. B-T.
LECOQ DE BOISBAUDRAN, HORACE.
Fr. Paris 1802-1897. B-T.
LE CORBUSIER, CHARLES EDOUARD JEANNERET.
Fr. b. Chaux-de-Fonds, Swi. 1887; ex. 1933 New York. DBA-M-T.
LECOURT, RAYMOND LOUIS.
Fr. b. Havre 1882. DBA.
LECOURTIER, PROSPER. (S)
Fr. b. Grenelle 1850. B-T.
LE COUTEUX, LIONEL ARISTEDE. (S)
Fr. Le Mans 1847-1909 Paris. B-T.
LECURIEUX, JACQUES JOSEPH.
Fr. b. Dijon 1881. B-T.
LEDBETTER, [Mrs.] ALICE MCGEHEE.
Am. ad. 1934 Montgomery, Ala. A.
LEDERER, CHARLES. (Cart)
Am. Lowell, Mass. 1856-1925, Chicago. A023.
LEDERER, ESTELLE MAC GILL.
Am. b. Cleveland, O. 1892; ad. 1934 New Haven, Conn. A.
LEDERER, HUGO. (S)
Ger. b. 1871; ad. 1928 Berlin. T-798.
LEDERER, LUCY.
Am. ad. 1935 State College, Pa. M.

LEDGERWOOD, Ella Ray.
Mrs. H. O. Ledgerwood.
Am. b. Dublin, Tex.; ad. 1934 Fort Worth, Tex. A.
LEDNICKA, Maryla. (S)
Pol. ex. 1934 New York. M.
LEDOCHOWSKI, Napoleon.
Pol. b. Warsaw 1849. M.
LEDOUX, Auguste Louis Charles.
Fr. Paris 1816-1869 Montrouge. B-T.
LEDOUX [or Doux], Jeanne Philiberte.
Fr. Paris 1767-1840 Belleville. B-T.
LEDOUX, Phillippe.
Eng. ad. 1934 London. M.
LE DRU, Hilaire.
Fr. Oppy, 1769-1840 Paris. B-T.
LE DUC, Arthur Conrad.
Am. b. Washington, D. C. 1892; ad. Haddonfield, N. J. A.
LEDUC, Ozias.
Can. b. St. Hilaire; ad. 1935 Same. M.
LEDWARD, Gilbert. (S)
Eng. London 1888; ad. 1934 Kensington. T-Wa.
LEE, Arthur. (S)
Am. b. Trondjhem, Nor. 1881; ad. 1934 New York. A-Cs-F.
LEE, Bertha Stringer.
Am. b. San Fran., Calif. 1873; ad. 1934 Same. A-F.
LEE, Doris Emrick.
Am. b. Aledo, Ill. 1905; ad. 1934 Woodstock, N. Y. A.
LEE, Elizabeth.
Mrs. Allan McKissack.
Am. b. Boston, Mass. 1906; ad. 1934 Same. A.
LEE, Frederick Richard.
Eng. Barnstable 1798-1879 Cape Town, Africa. B-T.
LEE, George.
Am. Brookline, Mass. 1859-1932 Boston. A029.
LEE, Henry Charles.
Am. New York 1864-1930 Paris. A027.
LEE, Henry J.
Am. ad. 1934 Harmon, N. Y. A.
LEE, Homer. (Eg)
Am. Mansfield, O. 1856-1923 New York. A020-B-F-W9-7.
LEE, Josephine Watt.
Am. b. Denver, Col. 1910; ad. 1934 Washington, D. C. A.
LEE, Laura.
Am. ad. 1934 Stoneham, Mass. M.
LEE, Leslie W.
Am. ad. 1934 El Cajon, Calif. M.
LEE, Manning de Vileneuve.
Am. b. Summerville, S. C. 1894; ad. 1934 Phila., Pa. A.
LEE, Percy Myron.
Am. b. Tacoma, Wash. 1903; ad. 1934 New York. A.
LEE, Robert Edmund.
Am. b. San Fran., Calif. 1899; ad. 1934 New York. A.
LEE, [Mrs.] Ruth Hudson.
Am. b. Ellisburg, N. Y. 1885; ad. 1934 Syracuse, N. Y. A.
LEE, Selma. (Et)
Am. ad. 1934 Scarsdale, N. Y. A.
LEE, Sydney.
Eng. b. Manchester 1866; ad. 1934 Kensington. B-T-Wa.
LEE, Thomas Sterling. (S)
Eng. London 1856-1916. B-Hs-T.
LEE, Vivian E.
Am. b. Anderson, Ind.; ad. 1934 Minneapolis, Minn. A.
LEE, William.
Eng. 1809-1865 London. B-DNB-T.
LEE-HANKEY. *see* Hankey.
LEE-ROBINS, Lucy.
Am. b. New York 1865. A12.
LEECH, Hilton.
Am. b. Bridgeport, Conn. 1906; ad. 1934 Sarasota, Fla. A.
LEECH, John. (Cari)
Eng. London 1817-1864 Same. B-DNB-E-T-433.
LEEDY, [Mrs.] Laura A.
Am. b. Bloomington, Ill. 1881; ad. 1934 St. Paul, Minn. A.
LEEKE, Ferdinand.
Ger. b. Burg 1859. B-T.
LEEMPOELS, Joseph [or Jef].
Belg. b. Brussels 1867. B-DBA-T.
LEEMPUT, Remigius [or Remy] van.
Dut. Antwerp, Belg. 1607-1675 London. DNB-T.
LEEMPUTTEN, Corneille van.
Belg. Verchter 1841-1902 Schaerbeek. T.
LEEMPUTTEN, Franz van.
Belg. Verchter 1850-1914. B-T.
LEENHARDT, Michel Maximilien.
Fr. b. Montpelier 1853. B-DBA-T.
LEEPER, Vera Beatrice.
Am. b. Denver, Colo. 1893; ad. 1934 Yorktown Heights, N. Y. A.
LEERMANS, Pieter.
Dut. 1655-1706. B-T.
LEES, Charles.
Scot. Cupar-Fife 1800-1880. B-DNB-T.
LEES, Derwent.
Aust. Brisbane, Queensland 1885-1931. Y01932.
LEES, H. E. Ida.
Eng. d. 1928. Wa01929.
LEES, Harry Hansen. (Ill)
Am. ad. 1934 New York. A.
LEEUW, Cateau de. (Ill)
Am. ex. 1934 New York. M.
LEEUW, Govaert [or Greghetto da Leone].
Dut. Dordrecht 1645-1688 Same. B-T.
LEEUW, Pieter van der.
Dut. Dordrecht 1647-1679/1704 Same. B-T.
LEEUWEN, Gerrit Jan van.
Dut. Arnheim 1756-1825. B-T.
LEEUWEN, Philipp van.
Dut. ac. 1693/7 in Rotterdam. B-T.
LEEWITZ, Alice Conklin.
see Bevin, Alice Conklin.
LE FAGUAYS, Pierre. (S)
Fr. b. Nantes, 1892. DBA.
LE FAUCONNIER, Henri Victor Gabriel.
Fr. b. 1881; ac. 1934 Paris. DBA-T.
LEFÈBVRE, Charles Victor Eugéne.
Fr. Paris 1805-1882. B-T.

LEFÈBVRE, CLAUDE.
Fr. Fontainebleau 1632/6-1675 Paris. (S) B-C-T-722.

LEFÈBVRE, HIPPOLYTE. (S)
Fr. b. Lille 1863. B-DBA-T.

LEFÈBVRE, JULES JOSEPH.
Fr. Tournan 1834/6-1912 Paris. B-Bd-C-DBA-T.

LEFÈBVRE, ROLAND.
Fr. Anjou, 1608-1677 London. B-DNB-T.

LEFÈRE, GEORGE AUGUSTE EUGÈNE. (S)
Fr. b. Calvados 1876; ac. 1934 Paris. DBA.

LEFÈUVRE, ARSÈNE M. (S)
Fr. ac. 1906 in Paris. B-T.

LEFÈVRE, ADOLPHE RENÉ.
Fr. Paris 1834-1868 Same. B-T.

LEFÈVRE, CHARLES.
Fr. b. Paris 1875. B-C-DBA-T.

LEFÈVRE, ROBERT.
Fr. Bayeux 1756-1830 Paris. B-T.

LEFFERTS, WINIFRED EARL.
Am. b. Newtonville, Mass. 1903; ad. 1934 Brooklyn, N. Y. A.

LEFFINGWELL, EDITH.
Am. ad. 1934 Caldwell, N. J. M.

LEFFINGWELL, LUCIA DODGE.
Am. b. Oakland, Calif. 1866; ad. 1934 New York. A.

LEFLER, FRANZ.
Ger. Langenbrück 1831-1898. B-T.

LEFORT, HENRI ÉMILE. (Eg)
Fr. b. Paris 1852. B-DBA-T.

LEFORT, JEAN LOUIS.
Fr. b. Bordeaux 1875. DBA.

LEGA, SILVESTRO.
It. 1826-1895 Florence. B-T.

LEGAT, FRANCIS. (Eg)
Scot. Edinburgh 1755-1809 London. DNB-T.

LEGENDRE, LÉONCE.
Belg. 1831-1893. B-T.

LEGENDRE, NICOLAS. (S)
Fr. Estampes 1619-1671 Paris. B-T.

LÉGER, FERNAND.
Fr. b. Argentine, S. A. 1881. DBA-797.

LE GOUT GÉRARD, FERNAND MARIE EUGÈNE.
Fr. Saint Lô 1856-1924 Paris. DBA-T.

LEGOUX [or Legoust], L. R.
Fr. ac. 1773-1800 in Paris. T.

LEGRAND, AUGUSTE CLAUDE SIMON. (Eg)
Fr. Paris 1765-1808. B-T.

LEGRAND [Edy], EDWARD LÉON LOUIS.
Fr. b. Bordeaux 1892. DBA.

LEGRAND, LOUIS.
Fr. b. Dijon 1863. B-DBA-T.

LEGRAND, RENÉ LOUIS R.
Fr. b. Paris 1847. T.

LEGRAS, AUGUST.
Dut. Amsterdam 1864-1915 Laren. T.

LEGREW, JAMES.
Eng. Caterham 1803-1857 London. DNB-T.

LEGROS, ALPHONSE. (P-S)
Br.-Fr. Dijon, Fr. 1837-1911 London. B-C-DBA-DNB-E-T-830.

LEGROS [or Le Gros], JEAN.
Fr. Paris 1671-1745. T.

LEGROS, PIERRE [The Elder]. (S)
Fr. 1629-1714 Paris. B-T.

LEGROS, PIERRE [The Younger]. (S)
Fr. Paris 1666-1719 Rome, It. B-T.

LE GUAY, CHARLES ETIENNE.
Fr. Sèvres 1762-1840. B-T.

LE GUERCHINO. *see* Guercino.

LEHEUTRE, GUSTAVE. (Et)
Fr. b. Troyes 1861; ex. 1934 U. S. DBA-T.

LEHMAN, CHARLES ERNEST RUDOLPHE HENRI.
Fr. Kiel, Rus. 1814-1882 Paris. B-T.

LEHMAN, GEORGE.
Am. d. 1870 in Phila., Pa. F-2-7.

LEHMAN, IRVING.
Am. ex. 1934 New York. M.

LEHMAN, LÉON.
Fr. b. Altkirch 1873. DBA.

LEHMAN, RUDOLF.
Eng. Hamburg, Ger. 1819-1905 Bushey, Eng. DNB.

LEHMBRUCK, WILHELM VON. (S)
Ger. Meiderich 1881-1919 Berlin. E-Hs-T-813-937.

LEHMER, CAROLINE.
Am. d. 1933 Cincinnati, O. A030.

LEHONGRE, ETIENNE. (S)
Fr. Paris 1628-1690 Same. B-T.

LEHR, ADAM.
Am. 1853-1924 Cleveland, O. M.

LEIBL, WILHELM.
Ger. Cologne 1844-1900. B-C-T-434-849.

LEICH, CHESTER. (Et)
Am. ad. 1934 Leonia, N. J. A.

LEICKERT, CHARLES HENRI JOSEPH.
Belg. Brussels 1818-1908 Mainz, Ger. B-T.

LEIDY, [Mrs.] CARTER R.
Am. d. 1933 Easthampton, Mass. A030.

LEIFCHILD, HENRY STORMOUTH. (S)
Eng. 1823-1884 London. DNB-T.

LEIGH, CLARA MARIA. *see* Pope, C. M.

LEIGH, HOWARD.
Am. b. Cecelia, Ky. 1896; ad. 1934 Chicago. A-W.

LEIGH, JAMES MATTHEWS. (Author-P)
Eng. 1808-1860 London. DNB-T.

LEIGH-JARED.
Eng. 1724-1769 London. DNB-T.

LEIGH, WILLIAM ROBINSON.
Am. b. Berkeley Co. W. Va. 1866; ad. 1934 New York. A-F-W-46.

LEIGHTON, CHARLES BLAIR.
Eng. 1823-1855 London. B-DNB-T.

LEIGHTON, CLARE VERONICA HOPE.
Eng. b. London 1900; ad. 1934 Same. T-Wa.

LEIGHTON, EDMUND BLAIR.
Eng. 1853-1923. B-T.

LEIGHTON, [Sir] FREDERICK. (P-S)
[Baron of Streeton.]
Eng. Scarborough 1880-1896 London. B-Bd-C-DNB-E-Hs-T-938.

LEIGHTON, KATHRYN WOODMAN.
Mrs. Edward Everett Leighton.
Am. b. Plainfield, N. H. 1876; ad. 1934 Los Angeles, Calif. A-W.

LEIGHTON, NICHOLAS WINFIELD SCOTT.
Am. b. Auburn, Me.; d. 1898 Waverly, Mass. A01-F-47.

LEINBERGER, HANS. (S)
Ger. ac. 1516-1530. T.

LEINWEBER, ROBERT ANTON.
Bohemian. Leipa 1845-1921. B-T.

LEIPOLD, KARL.
Ger. b. Duisburg 1864. B-T.
LEISENRING, L. MORRIS.
Am. b. Lutherville, Md. 1875; ad. 1934. Washington, D. C. A.
LEISENRING, MATHILDE MUEDEN.
Mrs. L. Morris Leisenring.
Am. b. Washington, D. C.; ad. 1934 Same. A-F.
LEISTEN, JACOBUS.
Ger. Düsseldorf 1845-1918. B-T.
LEISTIKOW, WALTER.
Ger. Bromberg 1865-1908. B-T.
LEITCH, WILLIAM LEIGHTON.
Scot. Glasgow 1804-1883 London. B-DNB-T.
LEITCH-ROSS, HARRY.
Am. b. Mauritius 1886; ad. 1934 Woodstock, N. Y. A-F-W.
LEITNER, LEANDER.
Am. b. Delphos, O. 1873; ad. 1934 New York. A-F.
LEJEUNE, ADOLPHE FRÉDÉRIC.
Fr. b. Boulogne 1879; ac. 1934 Paris. B-T.
LEJEUNE, EUGÈNE.
Fr. Beaumont 1818-1894. B-T.
LEJEUNE, HENRI PIERRE.
Fr. b. St. Ouen 1881. DBA.
LEJEUNE, HENRY.
Eng. London 1819-1904 Same. C-DNB.
LEJEUNE, JEAN MICHEL MOREAU.
Fr. 1741-1814. M.
LEJEUNE, LOUIS AIMÉ. (S)
Fr. b. 1884. B-DBA-T.
LEJEUNE, LOUIS FRANÇOIS.
Fr. Versailles 1775/6-1848. E-T.
LE KEUX, HENRY. (Eg)
Eng. London 1787-1868 Bocking. DNB-T.
LE KEUX, JOHN. (Eg)
Eng. London 1783-1846 Same. DNB-T.
LE KEUX, JOHN HENRY. (Eg)
Eng. London 1812-1896 Durham. DNB-T.
LELAND, CLARA WALSH.
Mrs. D. R. Leland.
Am. b. Lockport, N. Y. 1869; ad. 1934 Lincoln, Neb. A.
LELAND, HENRY.
Am. Walpole, Mass. 1850-1877 Paris. Bd-C-F-T-15.
LELEU, ALEXANDRE FÉLIX.
Fr. b. Vicoigne 1871. DBA.
LELEU, CHARLOTTE [Moorhouse].
Fr. b. New York 1885; ad. 1934 Paris. DBA.
LELEUX, ARMAND.
Fr. b. Paris 1894. DBA.
LELEUX, ARMAND HUBERT SIMON.
Fr. Paris 1818/20-1885. B-T.
LELIE, ADRIAEN DE.
Dut. Telburg 1755-1820 Amsterdam. B-T.
LELIENBERGH, CORNELIS.
Dut. ac. 1626-1672 The Hague. B-C-T.
LELLA, CARL.
Am. b. Bari, It. 1899; ad. 1934 Colonia, N. J. A.
LELOIR, ALEXANDRE LOUIS.
Fr. Paris 1843-1884 Same. B-C-T.
LELOIR, MAURICE.
Fr. b. Paris 1853. B-DBA-T.
LE LORRAIN, LOUIS JOSEPH.
Fr. Paris 1715-1759 Leningrad, Rus. B-T.
LE LORRAIN, ROBERT. (S)
Fr. Paris 1666-1743 Same. B-T.
LELY, [Sir] PETER [Van der Faes].
Dut.-Eng. Soest 1618-1690 London. B-Bd-C-DNB-E-T-702-722-909.
LEMAIRE, FRANÇOIS. (S)
Fr. ac. 1780 in Le Mans. B-T.
LEMAIRE, HECTOR JOSEPH. (S)
Fr. Lille 1846-1933. B-DBA-T.
LEMAIRE, JEAN [or Pierre] "LEGROS LEMAIRE".
Fr. Dammartin 1597-1659 Gaillon. B-T.
LEMAIRE, MADELEINE JEANE.
Fr. Fréjus, 1845/6-1928 Paris. B-DBA-T.
LEMAIRE, PHILIPPE JOSEPH HENRI. (S)
Fr. Valenciennes 1798-1880 Paris. B-T.
LEMAIRE, PIERRE ["Le petit Lemaire"].
Fr. 1612-1688. T.
LEMAR, MARCEL. (S)
Fr. b. Paris 1892. DBA.
LEMATTE, JACQUES FRANÇOIS FERNARD.
Fr. b. St. Quentin, 1850. B-C-DBA-T.
LEMBKE, HALFORD. (S)
Am. b. Topeka, Kan. 1889; ad. 1934 Seattle, Wash. A.
LE MEILLEUR, GEORGES.
Fr. b. Rouen 1861. B-DNB-T.
LEMENS, BALTHASAR VAN.
Flem. Antwerp, Belg. 1637-1704 Eng. DNB-T.
LEMERCIER, PHILIPPE. *see* Mercier.
LEMET, L. (Eg)
Am. ac. 1804 in Phila., Pa. F-2-7-45-184.
LE MIRE, NÖEL. (Eg)
Fr. Rouen 1724-1801 Paris. B-T.
LEMLY, BESSIE CARY.
Am. b. Jackson, Miss. 1871. A28.
LEMOINE [or Le Moyne], FRANÇOIS.
Fr. Paris 1688-1737 Same. B-C-T-722.
LEMOINE [or Le Moyne], JACQUES.
Fr. b. Dieppe; d. 1588 London. T.
LEMOINE [or Le Moyne], J. ANTOINE MARIE.
Fr. Rouen 1752-1824 Paris. B-T.
LE MOITURIER, PIERRE ANTOINE. (S)
Fr. Avignon 1425-1497 Dijon. B-Hs-T.
LEMON, FRANK. (S)
Am. b. Washington, D. C. 1867. A12.
LEMORDANT, JEAN JULIAN.
Fr. b. St. Malo 1878; ad. 1935 Paris. B-DBA-T.
LEMOS, FRANK B. (Et)
Am. b. Austin, Nev. 1877. A20.
LEMOS, PEDRO J. (Et)
Am. b. Austin, Nev. 1882. A-F.
LEMOT, FRANÇOIS FRÉDÉRIC. (S)
Fr. Lyons 1771/3-1827 Paris. B-Hs-T.
LE MOYNE. *see also* Lemoine.
LE MOYNE, JEAN BAPTISTE [The Younger]. (S)
Fr. Paris 1704-1778 Same. B-Hs-T.
LE MOYNE, JEAN LOUIS. (S)
Fr. Paris 1665-1755 Same. B-T.
LEMPICKA, TAMARA DE.
Pol. b. Warsaw 1902. DBA.
LEMUD, FRANÇOIS JOSEPH AIMÉ DE.
Fr. Thionville, 1817-1887. B-T.
LE NAIN, ANTOINE.
Fr. Laon 1588?-1648 Paris. B-Bd-C-E-T-722-847.

LE NAIN, Louis ["The Roman"].
Fr. Laon 1583/93-1648 Paris.
B-Bd-E-C-T-722-847.
LENAIN, Mathieu.
Fr. Laon 1607?-1677 Paris.
B-Bd-C-E-T-722-847.
LENBACH, Franz von.
Ger. Bavaria 1836-1904 Munich. B-E-T.
LENC, Stanislaw.
Pol. 1862-1920. M.
LENEPVEU, Jules Eugéne.
Fr. Angers 1819-1898 Paris. B-T.
LENEY, William Satchwell. (Eg)
Eng. London 1769-1831 Montreal, Can.
B-Bd-DAB-DNB-F-7-40-55-147-160.
LENFANT, Jean.
Fr. Abbeville 1615-1674 Paris. B-T.
LENFANT, Pierre.
Fr. Anet 1704-1787 Gobelins. B-T.
LENFESTEY, Giffard Hocart.
Eng. b. Faversham 1872; ad. 1934 Acton.
T-Wa.
LĒNG, Mei.
Chinese. ac. 17th century. E.
LENGERICH, Heinrich [Immanuel].
Ger. Stettin 1790-1865 Berlin. C-T.
L'ENGLE, Lucy.
Am. b. New York 1889; ad. 1934 Same. A.
L'ENGLE, William J., Jr.
Am. b. Jacksonville, Fla. 1884; ad. 1934 New York. A-F.
LENHARD, Josef.
Am. ad. 1934 New York. M.
LENK, [Prof.] Franz.
Ger. b. Saxony 1898; ad. 1934 Berlin. M.
LENNARD, E. H.
Br. ac. 1932 in London. M.
LENOIR, Charles Anable.
Fr. b. Chatelaillon 1860. B-DBA-T.
LENOIR, Louis. (S)
Fr. Nancy 1712-1772 Same. B-T.
LENOIR, Marcel [or Marcel-Lenoir].
Fr. Montauban 1872-1931. DBA-T.
LENOIR, Pierre. (S)
Fr. b. 1879. DBA-T.
LE NOIR [or Lenoir], Simon Bernard.
Fr. Paris 1729-1789 Same. B-T.
LENS, Andrew Benjamin. (Min)
Eng. ex. 1765-1770 in London. DNB-T.
LENS, Andries [or Andreas] Cornelis.
Flem. Antwerp, Belg. 1739-1822 Brussels.
B-C-T.
LENS, Bernard [The Elder]. (Enamel-P)
Eng. Holland 1659-1725 London. B-DNB-T.
LENS, Bernard [The Younger]. (Eg)
Eng. London 1659-1725 Knightsbridge.
B-DNB-T.
LENS Family.
Flem.-Eng. ac. 17-19th Centuries. T.
LENSKI, Lois. (Ill)
Mrs. Arthur Covey.
Am. b. Springfield, O. 1893; ad. 1934 Torrington, Conn. A.
LENSON, Michael.
Am. ad. 1935 New York. M.
LENT, Margaret [Mrs. Mulford].
Am. b. Washington, D. C. 1896; ad. 1934 Same. A.
LENTELLI, Leo. (S)
Am. b. Bologna, It. 1879; ad. 1934 New York. A-Cs-F-W.
LENTHE, Gaston Camillo.
Ger. Dresden 1805-1860 Schwerin. C-T.
LENZ, Alfred David. (S)
Am. Fond du Lac, Wis. 1872-1926 Havana, Cuba. A023-F.
LENZ, Oscar.
Am. Providence, R. I. 1874-1912 New York.
A010-F-Ta.
LEOCHARES. (S)
Gr. ac. 372-324 B.C. B-E-Hs.
LÉON, Edouard Henri.
Fr. b. Paris 1873. B-DBA-T.
LÉON Y ESCOSURA, Ignacio de. *see* Escosura.
LÉON [or Leal], Simon.
Sp. Madrid 1610-1687 Same. B-T.
LÉON, Stanislas.
Belg. b. 1860. M.
LEONARD, Beatrice.
Am. b. Marion, Ind. 1889. A28.
LEONARD, George Henry.
Am. b. Boston 1869; ad. 1934 Northampton, Mass. A.
LEONARD, Helen. (Ill)
Am. San Fran., Calif. 1885-1908 Wilmington, Del. A07.
LEONARD, Jack [de Coudres].
Am. b. Chicago 1903; ad. Flushing, N. Y.
A.
LÉONARD, Maurice.
Fr. b. Paris 1899. DBA.
LEONARD, Robert L. (Ill)
Am. ad. 1934 Brooklyn, N. Y. M.
LEONARD, William Jackson.
Am. b. Hinsdale, N. H. 1869. A12-F.
LEONARDO, José [or Juseppe].
Sp. Calatayud 1605/16-1656 Zaragoza.
B-C-T.
LEONARDO DA VINCI. (P-S)
It. Vinci 1452-1519 Cloux, Fr.
B-Bd-C-E-Hs-T-V-192-435-436-437-438-439-722-790-853.
LEONI, Léone [Aretino]. (S)
It. 1509-1592 Milan. B-Hs-T-V.
LEONI [or Léone] Ottavio Mario.
It. Rome 1575/8-1626/30 Same.
B-C-T-722-803.
LEONI, Pompeo [or Pompeyo]. (S)
Sp. b. Pavia; d. 1610. B-Hs-T.
LÉONID.
Fr. ad. 1935 near Mont San Michel. M.
LÉONNEC, Paul Félix. (Cari)
Fr. Brest 1842-1899 Same. T.
LEOPARDI [or Leopardo], Alessandro. (S)
It. Venice, 1447-1552 Same. E-Hs-V-T.
LEOPOLD, Franz Joseph.
Ger. b. 1783; d. 1832 Hanover. T.
LEOPOLD, Joseph Friedrich.
Ger. Augsburg 1668-1726 Same. T.
LÉOPOLD-LÉVY.
Fr. b. Paris 1882. DBA-T.
LEPAGE, Bastien. *see* Bastien-Lepage.
LEPAGE, Paul Hubert.
Fr. b. Frimay 1878. DBA.

LEPAON, JEAN BAPTISTE [Louis].
Fr. Paris 1736/8-1785. B-T.
LEPAULLE, FRANÇOIS GABRIEL GUILLAUME.
Fr. Versailles 1804-1886. B-T.
LEPAUTRE [or Lepaultre], JEAN.
Fr. Paris 1617-1682. B-T.
LEPAUTRE, PIERRE. (S)
Fr. Paris 1660-1744 Same. B-T.
LEPEINTRE, CHARLES.
Fr. Paris 1735-1803. B-T.
LEPÈRE, LOUIS AUGUSTE.
Fr. Paris 1849-1919 Domme. B-DBA-T-880.
LE PETIT. *see also* Petit.
LE PETIT, ALFRED.
Fr. Aumale 1841-1909. DBA-T.
LE PETIT, ALFRED MARIE.
Fr. b. Fallencourt 1876. DBA-T.
LÉPICIÉ, BERNARD FRANÇOIS [The Elder].
Fr. Paris 1698/1700-1755 Same. B-T.
LÉPICIÉ, MICHEL NICOLAS BERNARD.
Fr. Paris 1735-1784 Same. B-C-T-722.
LÉPINE, STANISLAS VICTOR EDOUARD.
Fr. Caen 1835-1892 Paris. B-T.
LEPIPRE [or Le Piper], FRANCIS. (Cari)
Eng. b. Kent; d. 1698 London. B-DNB-T.
LE POITTEVIN, EUGÈNE MODESTE EDMOND.
Fr. Paris 1806-1870 Auteuil. B-C-T.
LE POITTEVIN, LOUIS.
Fr. Neuville, 1849-1909 Same. B-T.
LEPPERT, R. E.
Am. ad. 1934 New York. M.
LEPRIEUR [or Le Prieur], ADRIEN.
Fr. ac. 1715-1728 in France. T.
LEPRIN, MARCEL FRANÇOIS.
Fr. Cannes 1891-1933 Paris. DBA-T.
LE PRINCE, AUGUSTE XAVIER.
Fr. Paris 1799-1826 Nice. C-T-722.
LE PRINCE, G. MARIE.
Am. ad. 1934 New York. M.
LE PRINCE, JEAN BAPTISTE.
Fr. Metz 1733/4-1781 St. Denis. B-C-T-722.
LE PUTTEVIN. *see* Poittevin.
LE QUESNE, FERNARD.
Fr. b. Paris 1856. B-T.
LE RAT, PAUL EDMÉ. (Et)
Fr. Paris 1849-1882. B-T-880.
LERAY, LÉON.
Fr. b. St. Méen-le-Grand 1901. DBA.
LERAY, PRUDENT LOUIS.
Fr. Couëran 1820-1879 Paris. B-T.
LERCH, FRANZ.
Aus. b. 1895 Austria. M.
LERCH, NICOLAS [or Leyden]. (S)
Ger. ac. 1462-1493 Strasburg. B-T.
LERICHE, JOSSE FRANÇOIS JOSEPH. (S)
Flem. Mons, Belg. 1738-1812 Same. B-T.
LERIUS, JOSEPH HENRI FRANÇOIS VAN.
Belg. Antwerp 1823-1876 Mechlin. B-T.
LERMONT, CHARLOTTE KUDLICH.
Mrs. Basil Lermont.
Am. ad. 1934 New York. M.
LEROLLE, HENRI.
Fr. Paris 1848-1929 Same. B-DBA-T.
LEROLLE, PAUL ALEXIS.
Fr. Paris 1874-1932 Same. DBA.
LEROUX, GEORGES PAUL.
Fr. b. Paris 1877. B-DBA-T.
LEROUX, JEAN MARIE. (Eg)
Fr. Paris 1788-1870 Same. B-T.
LEROUX, JULES MARIE AUGUSTE.
Fr. b. Paris 1871; ad. 1934 Same. B-DBA-T.
LEROUX, LOUIS ALEXANDER.
Fr. b. Courbevoie 1847; ac. 1931 Paris. DBA.
LEROUX, LOUIS HECTOR.
Fr. Verdun 1829-1900 Angers. B-Bd-C-T.
LEROUX-REVAULT, LAURA.
Fr. b. Dun-sur-Meuse; ac. 1892-1900 Paris. B-T.
LEROY, JOSEPH.
Fr. 1728-1797 Genoble. B-T.
LEROY, PAUL ALEXANDRE ALFRED.
Fr. b. Paris 1860. B-DBA-T.
LERPINIÈRE, DANIEL. (Eg)
Eng. 1745?-1785 London. B-DNB-T.
LESCORNEL, JOSEPH STANISLAS. (S)
Fr. Langres 1799-1871. B-T.
LESE, BENOZZO DI. *see* Gozzoli.
LE SÉNÉCHAL DE KERDRÉORET, GUSTAVE EDOUARD.
Fr. b. Hannebout 1845/50. B-DBA-T.
LE SIDANER, HENRI EUGÈNE AUGUSTIN.
Fr. b. Port Louis, Mauritius 1862; ad. 1934 Versailles. B-DBA-T-440.
LESIRE [or Lesyre], PAULUS.
Dut. Dordrecht 1611-1655/6. B-T.
LESLIE, [Miss] CECIL. (Et)
Eng. b. 1900; ac. 1934 London. Wa.
LESLIE, CHARLES ROBERT.
Br.-Am. London 1794-1859 Same.
B-Bd-C-DAB-DNB-E-F-T-1-2-4-6-15-45-161-182-722.
LESLIE, FRANK [Henry Carter]. (Eg-Pub.)
Am. Ipswich, Eng. 1821-1880 New York.
DAB-DNB-T-162.
LESLIE, GEORGE DUNLOP.
Eng. London 1835-1921 Same. B-C-T-15.
LESLIE, JEAN GORMAN.
Mrs. Grant Leslie.
Am. b. Omaha, Neb. 1888; ad. 1934 Santa Monica, Calif. A.
LE SOEUR. *see* Le Sueur.
LESPINGOLA, FRANÇOIS. (S)
Fr. Joinville 1644-1705 Paris. B-T.
LESREL, ADOLPHE ALEXANDRE.
Fr. b. 1830/9; ac. 1890 in Paris. B-T.
LESSARD. *see* Delassard.
LESSER-URY. *see* Ury, Lesser.
LESSHAFFT, FRANZ.
Am. b. Berlin, Ger. 1862; ad. 1934 Phila., Pa. A-F.
LESSING, CARL FRIEDRICH.
Ger. Breslau 1808-1880 Carlsruhe. B-C-T.
LESSING, OTHON [or Otto]. (S)
Ger. Düsseldorf 1846-1912 Grünewald.
B-DBA-T.
LESSORE, JULES.
Fr. ac. 1864-1892 in Paris. B-T.
LESSORE, THÉRÈSE.
Eng. ad. 1934 London. M.
LESTANG-PARADE, JOSEPH LÉON ROLLAND DE.
Fr. Aix 1801/2-1887 Paris. B-T.
LE SUEUR, BLAISE NICOLAS.
Fr. Paris 1716-1782. B-T.
LE SUEUR, CHARLES ALEXANDRE.
Am. France 1778-1846 Same; ac. 1816-1837 U. S. DAB-F-2-163-181.

LE SUEUR, EUSTACHE.
Fr. Paris 1616/7-1655 Same. B-C-E-T-722.
LE SUEUR, HERBERT. (S)
Fr. Paris 1580-1670 London. B-DBA-T.
LE SUEUR, MAC.
Am. b. San Antonio, Tex. 1908; ad. 1934 Minneapolis, Minn. M.
LE SUEUR, NICOLAS. (Eg)
Fr. Paris 1690-1764 Same. B-T.
LE SUEUR, PIERRE.
Fr. b. Paris; d. 1786 Bordeaux. B-T.
LETELLIER, JEAN.
Fr. Rouen 1614-1676 Same. B-T.
LETHBRIDGE, RODNEY.
Am. ad. 1934 Woodhaven, N. Y. M.
LETHBRIDGE, WALTER STEPHENS. (Min)
Eng. Charlton 1771/2-1831? Stonehouse. DNB-T.
LETHIÈRE [or Letièrs], GUILLAUME GUILLON.
Fr. St. Anne 1760-1832 Paris. B-C-T-722.
LETIN [or Ninet], JACQUES [Pestin].
Fr. b. Troyes; d. 1662. B-T.
LEU, AUGUST WILHELM.
Ger. Munster 1819-1897 Seelisberg. B-T.
LEU [Leuw or Low], HANS [The Elder].
Swi. Bade 1460-1507/8. B-T.
LEU, HANS [The Younger].
Swi. 1490-1531. B-T.
LEU [or Deleu], THOMAS DE.
Flem. ac. 1576-1614 in Paris. T.
LEUNG, GEORGE.
Am. ad. 1934 Los Angeles, Calif. M.
LEUTZE, EMANUEL.
Am. Wurtemburg, Ger. 1816-1868 Washington, D. C. B-Bd-C-DNB-E-F-T-1-4-15-26-46-51-138-164.
LEUX [or Luycx], FRANZ [Leuxenstein].
Flem. Antwerp, Belg. 1604-1668 Vienna, Aus. B-T.
LEVACHEZ, CHARLES FRANÇOIS GABRIEL. (Eg)
Fr. ac. 1760-1820 in Paris. B-T.
LE VALLEY, WILLIAM.
Am. ex. 1934 Manchester, Vt. M.
LEVASSEUR, JULES GABRIEL. (Eg)
Fr. b. Paris 1823; ac. 1878. B-T.
LE VÉEL, ARMAND. (S)
Fr. 1821-1905 Cherbourg. T.
LÉVEILLÉ, ANDRÉ.
Fr. b. Lille 1880. DBA-T.
LEVER [Richard], HAWLEY.
Am. b. Adelaide, So. Aust. 1876; ad. 1934 New York. A-F-T-W.
LEVERING, ALBERT. (Ill)
Am. Hope, Ind. 1869-1929 New York. A20-F-W14.
LEVEY, H. C.
Am. ex. 1933 in Paris. M.
LEVEY, JEFFREY KING.
Am. b. New York 1908; ad. 1934 Same. A.
LÉVI, BASILE.
Rus. b. Leningrad 1878; ac. 1934 Paris. DBA.
LEVI, GUILLÉN [or Guillém].
Sp. ac. 1380-1406 in Spain. T.
LEVI, JULIAN CLARENCE.
Am. b. New York 1874; ad. 1934 Same. A.
LEVICK, RICHARD.
Am. Phila., Pa. 1864-1917 London. A015.
LÉVIN, ALEXANDER B.
Am. b. Russia 1906; ad. 1934 Chester Springs, Pa. A.
LÉVIN, JOSEPH.
Am. b. Leningrad, Rus. 1894. DBA.
LEVIN, MURRAY. (Ill)
Am. ad. 1934 New York. M.
LEVINSON, A. F.
Am. ad. 1935 Rockport, Mass. M.
LEVITT, JOEL J.
Am. b. Kiev, Rus. 1875; ad. 1934 New York. A.
LEVITZKY, DIMITRI GREGORIEVITCH.
Rus. 1735-1822. B-T.
LEVONE, ALBERT JEAN. (Ill)
Am. b. Rus. 1895; ad. 1934 Phila., Pa. A.
LEVOW, IRVING.
Am. ad. 1935 New York. M.
LEVRAC-TOURNIERES, ROBERT.
Fr. Ifs 1668-1752 Caen. B-C-T-722.
LEVY, ALEXANDER OSCAR.
Am. b. Bonn, Ger. 1881; ad. 1934 Buffalo, N. Y. A.
LEVY, BEATRICE S. (Et)
Am. b. Chicago 1892; ad. 1934 Same. A-F.
LEVY, BERT. (Cari)
Am. 1871-1934 Los Angeles, Calif. M.
LÉVY, ÉMILE.
Fr. Paris 1826-1890 Passy. B-C-T.
LEVY, HENRY L.
Am. b. Hartford, Conn. 1868; ad. 1934 Chicago. A.
LÉVY, HENRI LÉOPOLD.
Fr. Nancy 1840-1904. B-C-T.
LEVY, ISIDORE.
Am. ex. 1935 New York. M.
LEVY, JOAN.
Am. ad. 1934 New York. M.
LEVY, JOSEPHINE. (S)
Am. ex. 1934 Woodstock, N. Y. M.
LÉVY, SIMON.
Fr. b. Strasburg 1886. DBA-T.
LEVY, WILLIAM AUERBACH.
see Auerbach-Levy, William.
LÉVY-BLOCH, LAURENCE RACHEL.
Fr. b. Vesoul 1894. DBA.
LÉVY-DHURMER, LUCIEN.
Fr. b. Alger 1865. B-DBA-T.
LÉVY-ENGELMANN, YVONNE.
Fr. b. Paris 1894. DBA.
LEWANDOWSKI, EDMUND D.
Am. ad. 1935 Milwaukee, Wis. M.
LEWIN, STEPHEN.
Eng. ac. 1890-1908 London. T.
LEWIN-FUNCKE, ARTHUR WILLEM OTTO.
Ger. b. Dresden 1866. T.
LEWINO, WALTER AFFROVILLE.
Eng. b. London 1887; ac. 1932 Paris. DBA.
LEWIS, ALICE L.
Am. b. Providence, R. I. 1872. A28.
LEWIS, A. NEVILLE.
Eng. b. So. Africa 1895; ad. 1934 London. Wa.
LEWIS, ARTHUR ALLEN. (Et)
Am. b. Mobile, Ala. 1873; ad. 1934 Brooklyn, N. Y. A-F-W.

LEWIS, Charles George. (Eg)
Eng. Enfield 1808-1880 Felpham. DNB.
LEWIS, Charles James.
Eng. London 1830-1892 Chelsea. B-DNB-T.
LEWIS, Edmonia. (S)
Am. b. Albany, N. Y. 1845. B-F-Hs-Ta-46.
LEWIS, Edmund Darch.
Am. Phila., Pa. 1835-1910 Same. DAB-F.
LEWIS, Elizabeth.
Mrs. M. H. Lewis.
Am. b. Capitol View, Md. 1908; ad. 1934 Victorville, Calif. A.
LEWIS Family.
Eng. ac. 18-19th centuries in England. T.
LEWIS, Frederick Christian [The Elder]. (Eg)
Eng. London 1779-1856 Enfield. B-DNB-T.
LEWIS, Frederick Christian [The Younger]. [Called the "Indian Lewis".]
Eng. London 1813-1875 Genoa, It. DNB-T.
LEWIS, George Albert.
Am. d. 1915 Phila., Pa. A013.
LEWIS, George Robert.
Eng. London 1782-1871 Hampstead. B-DNB-T.
LEWIS, Gertrude C.
Am. ex. 1935 Jersey City, N. J. M.
LEWIS, H. Emerson.
Am. b. Hutchinson, Kan. 1892; ad. 1934 San Fran., Calif. A.
LEWIS, H. Mostyn.
Eng. ex. 1934 London. M.
LEWIS, Helen Vaughan.
Am. b. New York 1879; ad. 1934 Irvington, N. Y. A.
LEWIS, Henry.
Am. England 1819-1904 Germany. A05.
LEWIS, Herbert Taylor.
Am. b. Chicago 1893; ad. 1934 Rockford, Ill. A.
LEWIS, Jeannette Maxfield. (Et)
Mrs. H. C. Lewis.
Am. b. Oakland, Calif. 1894; ad. 1934 Fresno, Calif. A.
LEWIS, John.
Eng. ac. 1762-1766 in London. T.
LEWIS, John.
Ir. ac. 1750-1757. T.
LEWIS, John Frederick.
Eng. London 1805-1876 Walton. B-Bd-DNB-E-T.
LEWIS, Josephine Miles.
Am. b. New Haven, Conn. 1865; ad. 1934 New York. A.
LEWIS, Lalla Walker. (Eg)
Am. ex. 1935 New Orleans, La. M.
LEWIS, [Mrs.] Laura C.
Am. b. Phila., Pa. 1874; ad. 1934 Same. A.
LEWIS, Martin. (Et)
Am. b. Aust.; ad. 1934 Sandy Hook, Conn. A-441-830.
LEWIS, Monty.
Am. b. Cardiff, Wales 1906; ad. 1934 New York. A.
LEWIS, Morland.
Eng. ad. 1934 London. M.
LEWIS, Neville.
Br. ac. 1934 So. Africa. M.
LEWIS, Percy Wynham. (Et)
Eng. b. 1884; ex. 1932 London. T-Wa1929.
LEWIS, Phillips Frisbie.
Am. Oakland, Calif. 1892-1930 Same. A027.
LEWIS, Reginald Augustus. (S)
Eng. b. Birmingham 1901; ad. 1934 London. Wa.
LEWIS, Richard Jeffreys.
Eng. ac. 1849 in Bristol. M.
LEWIS, Rose K.
Mrs. G. Lewis.
Am. b. New York 1891; ad. 1934 Same. M.
LEWIS, Ross A. (Cart)
Am. ad. 1934 Milwaukee, Wis. M.
LEWIS, Tom E.
Am. b. Los Angeles, Calif. 1909; ad. 1934 Laguna Beach, Calif. A.
LEWISTSKA, Sonia [or Sophie].
Pol. b. Tchenstochowa 1882. DBA.
LEY, Mary Helen.
Am. b. Leadville, Colo. 1886; ad. 1934 Ft. Wayne, Ind. A.
LEYDE, Otto Theodore.
Ger. Wehlau 1835-1897 Edinburgh, Scot. B-T.
LEYDEN, Lucas van.
see Lucas van Leyden.
LEYENDECKER, Frank X. (Ill)
Am. Germany 1877-1924 New Rochelle, N. Y. A021-F-W14.
LEYENDECKER, Joseph Christian. (Ill)
Am. b. Montabour, Ger. 1874; ad. 1934 New Rochelle, N. Y. A-F-W.
LEYLAND, Joseph Bartley. (S)
Can. Halifax, N.S. 1811-1851 Same. DNB-T.
LEYS, [Baron] Jan August Hendrik.
Belg. Antwerp 1815-1869 Same. B-C-E-T.
LEYSTER, Judith Molenaer.
Dut. Haarlem 1600-1660 Heemstedt. B-T.
LEYVA, Diego.
Sp. Haro 1580-1637 Miraflores. B-T.
LHERMITTE, Léon Augustin.
Fr. Mont-St. Pere 1844-1925 Paris. B-Bd-C-DBA-T.
LHÔTE, André.
Fr. b. Bordeaux 1885; ad. 1934 Paris. DBA-T-700-797.
LI CHAO-TAO.
Chinese. ac. 680 A.D. E.
LI CHÊN.
Chinese. ac. 800 A.D. E.
LI CH'ENG.
Chinese. ac. Sung Dynasty (960-1280). E.
LI HSIUNG-tsai.
Chinese. ad. 1935 Canton, China. M.
LI-LIN.
Chinese. ac. 15th century. M.
LI LUNG-MIEN.
Chinese. 1040-1106. E-733.
LI MARZI, Joseph.
Am. b. Chicago 1907; ad. 1934 New York. A.
LI SSU-HSÜN.
Chinese. 651-716. E.
LI T'ANG.
Chinese. ac. 1100. E.
LI TI.
Chinese. ac. Sung Dynasty (960-1280). E.
LIÃNO [or Ligno], Félipe de.
[El Titiano Pequeno.]
Sp. Madrid 1556-1625 Same. B-T.

LIART, MATTHEW. (Eg)
Eng. London 1736-1782? Same. DNB-T.
LIBBY, FRANCIS O.
Am. ad. 1934 Portland, Me. M.
LIBERALE DA VERONA, ANTONIO DI JACOPO.
It. Verona 1445/51-1526/36. T-V.
LIBERATORE, NICCOLÒ DI [Fuligno].
It. [Tuscan] 1430-1502. V.
LIBERI, PIETRO [Libertino].
It. Padua 1605-1687 Venice. B-T-722.
LIBERMANN, ABRAHAM.
Am. ad. 1934 Union City, N. J. M.
LIBERTÉ, JEAN.
Am. ex. 1935 New York. M.
LIBRI, FRANCESCO DAI [The Elder]. (Min)
It. Verona 1452-1502/14 Same. T-V.
LIBRI, GIROLAMO DAI [The Younger]. (Min)
It. Verona 1474-1556 Same. B-Bd-T-V.
LICHTEN, FRANCIS M.
Am. b. Bellefonte, Pa.; ad. 1934 Phila., Pa. A.
LICHTENAUER, JOSEPH MORTIMER.
Am. b. New York 1876; ad. 1934 Westport, Conn. A-F-W.
LICHTENFELS, EDUARD PEITHNER FREIHERR VON.
Aus. Vienna 1833-1913 Berlin, Ger. B-T.
LICHTIN, ROSA.
Mrs. Aaron Lichtin.
Am. b. Russia 1898; ad. 1934 Phila., Pa. A.
LICHTNER, F. SCHOMER.
Am. b. Peoria, Ill. 1905; ad. 1934 Milwaukee, Wis. A.
LICINIO, BERNARDINO.
It. 1489-1565 Venice. B-T-V.
LICINIO, GIOVANNI ANTONIO [Pordenone].
It. ac. 1500 in Murano. T-V.
LIDDELL, [Mrs.] ALBERTA B.
Am. b. Laporte, Ind. 1887; ad. 1934 Same. A.
LIDDELL, KATHERINE FORBES.
Am. b. Montgomery, Ala.; ad. 1934 Provincetown, Mass. A.
LIE, EMIL. (S)
Nor. ad. 1935 Oslo, Norway. M.
LIE, JONAS.
Am. b. Norway 1880; ad. 1935 New York. A-F-W-1-46-105-138-172-779.
LIEB, MICHAEL.
see Munkásky, Michaly de.
LIEBERICH, NICKOLAI IVANOWITSCH. (S)
Rus. b. 1828; d. 1883 Leningrad. Hs-T.
LIEBERMAN, FRANK.
Am. b. Atlanta, Ga. 1910; ad. 1935 New York. M.
LIEBERMANN, ERNEST.
Ger. b. Langemüss 1869. B-T.
LIEBERMANN, FERDINAND. (S)
Ger. b. Sonneberg 1883. T.
LIEBERMANN, MAX.
Ger. Berlin 1847-1935 Same.
B-DBA-E-M-T-775-Obit. N. Y. papers, 2-9-1935.
LIEBL, WILHELM.
Ger. b. 1844. Fa.
LIEDL, CHARLES.
Am. ex. 1932 New York. M.
LIEMAKER, NICOLAES [Roose or Roze].
Flem. Ghent, Belg. 1601-1644 Same. B-C-T.
LIENZ, EGGER. *see* Egger-Lienz.
LIER, ADOLF HEINRICH.
Ger. Herrnhut 1826-1882 Tyrol, Swi. B-T.
LIERNUR, WILLEM ADRIANUS ALEXANDER.
Dut. b. The Hague 1856. B-T.
LIES, JOSEPH HENRI HULBERT.
Belg. Antwerp 1821/2-1865 Same. B-C-T.
LIEVENS [or Livenz], ANDRIES.
Flem. ac. 1644-1680 Antwerp, Belg. B-C-T-422-722.
LIEVENS, DIRK.
Dut. Leyden 1612-1650/1 Niederl, India. T.
LIEVENS [or Lyvyns], JOHANNIS.
Dut. Leyden 1607-1672/4 Amsterdam. B-C-T.
LIEZEN-MAYER, ALEXANDER VAN.
Aus. Raab 1839-1898 Munich, Ger. B-C-T.
LIGGET, JANE STEWART.
Am. b. Atlantic City, N. J. 1893; ad. 1934 Phila., Pa. A.
LIGHT, RUTH.
Am. ad. 1934 Palestine. M.
LIGHTFOOT, PETER. (Ill)
Eng. 1805-1885 Blurton. T-Y01886.
LIGNELL, LOIS INGLEBORG.
Am. b. Duluth, Minn. 1911; ad. 1934 Same. M.
LIGORIO, PIRRO.
It. Naples 1500-1583 Ferrara. T-V.
LIGOZZI, JACOPO.
It. Verona 1543-1627 Same. B-T.
LIJEFORS, BRUNO ANDREAS.
Swe. b. Upsal 1860; ad. 1934 Stockholm. B-DBA-T-403-683.
LILIEN, EPHARAIM MOSE. (Et)
Ger. Drohobyez 1874-1925 Braunschweig. T.
LILLIE, ELLA FILLMORE.
Am. ad. 1935 Cambridge, Mass. M.
LILLY [or Lelly], EDMOND.
Eng. b. Richmond; d. 1716 Norwich. DNB-T.
LIMBACH, RUSSELL T. (Eg)
Am. ad. 1934 Cleveland, O. A.
LIMBORCK, HENDRIK VAN.
Dut. The Hague 1682-1759 Same. B-C-T-722.
LIMBOURG, PAUL [or Polequin de]. (Min)
Fr. ac. 1402/3-1434. B-T.
LIMERICK, JAMES ARTHUR. (Bronze Caster)
Am. Phila., Pa. 1870-1931 Baltimore, Md. A028-F.
LIMMER, EMIL.
Ger. ac. 1880. B-T.
LIMOUSIN, JEAN [or Jehan].
Fr. Limoges 1528-1610. B-T.
LIMOUSIN, LÉONARD [The Elder].
Fr. Limoges 1505-1575/7. B-Bd-E-T-641.
LIMOUSIN, LÉONARD [The Younger].
Fr. Limoges 1550-1625. B-Bd-E-T-641.
LIN LIANG.
Chinese. Ming Dynasty 1368-1644. E.
LINCK. *see* Link.
LINCOLN, AGNES HARRISON.
Am. b. Minneapolis, Minn. 1880; ad. 1934 Same. A.
LINCOLN, JAMES SULLIVAN.
Am. Taunton, Mass. 1811-1888 Providence, R. I. F-2-7.
LINCOLN, NETTA W.
Am. ad. 1934 Bowling Green, O. M.

LIND, Carl Victor. (Et)
Nor. ad. 1935 New York. M.
LIND, Edward G.
Am. b. Kansas City, Mo. 1884; ad. 1934 Same. A.
LINDBERG, Arthur H.
Am. b. Worcester, Mass. 1895; ad. 1934 Lynbrook, N. Y. A.
LINDBERG, Thorsten Harold Frederick.
Am. b. Stockholm, Swe. 1878; ad. 1934 Omaha, Neb. A.
LINDE, Ossip L.
Am. b. Chicago; ad. 1934 Westport, Conn. A-F-46.
LINDEGREN, Amalia.
Swe. Stockholm 1814-1891. B-T.
LINDENMUTH, Arlington N.
Am. ad. 1934 Allentown, Pa. M.
LINDENMUTH, Tod. (Et)
Am. b. Allentown, Pa. 1885; ad. 1934 Provincetown, Mass. A-F-W.
LINDENMUTH, [Mrs.] Tod.
see Warren, Elizabeth Boardman.
LINDENSCHMIT, Wilhelm [The Elder].
Ger. Mayence 1806-1848 Same. B-C-T.
LINDENSCHMIT, Wilhelm [The Younger].
Ger. Munich 1829-1895. B-C-T.
LINDER, C. Bennett.
Am. ad. 1934 New York. F-M.
LINDER [or Linderen], Franz.
Aus. Klagenfurt 1736/8-1802 Vienna. B-T.
LINDER, Henry. (S)
Am. Brooklyn, N. Y. 1854-1910 Same. A08-F-46.
LINDER, Johann Hans.
Belg. Basel, Swi. 1611-1687. T.
LINDER, Moffatt.
Eng. b. Birmingham; ac. 1905. M.
LINDERMANN-FROMMEL, Karl August.
Ger. Alsace, Fr. 1819-1891 Rome, It. C-T.
LINDERUM, Richard.
Ger. b. Dresden 1851. B-T.
LINDHEIM, Ray.
Am. New York 1884-1910 Same. A08.
LINDHOLM, Berndt Ad.
Swe. b. Goteberg 1841. B-T.
LINDIN, Carl Olof Eric.
Am. b. Sweden 1869; ad. Wellesley, Mass. A.
LINDNER, Dalphne.
Eng. b. Cheltenham 1912; ad. 1934 Same. Wa.
LINDNER, Moffat Peter.
Eng. b. Birmingham 1852. B-Wa1929.
LINDNEUX, Robert Ottakar.
Am. b. New York 1891; ad. 1934 Denver, Colo. A.
LINDNIG, [Mrs.] Lillian.
Am. b. New York 1887; ad. 1935 Ossining, N. Y. M.
LINDQUIST, Hilding.
Swe. b. 1891; ad. 1934 Stockholm. DBA.
LINDSAY, Daryl.
Aust. ac. 1933 in London. M.
LINDSAY, Lionel Arthur. (Et)
Aust. b. Creswick, Victoria 1874; ad. 1934 London. T-Wa.
LINDSAY, Norman. (Cart)
Aust. b. Creswick, Victoria 1879; ex. 1925 London. E-T-Wa.
LINDSLEY, [Mrs.] Catherine Conant.
Am. ac. 1870 in Thetford, Vt. M.
LINDSLEY, Emily Earle.
Am. b. New Rochelle, N. Y. 1858; ad. 1934 Larchmont, N. Y. A.
LINDTMAYER, Daniel [The Younger].
Swi. Schaffhouse 1552-1607. B-T.
LINEN, George.
Am. Scotland 1802-1888 New York. F-T.
LINES, Samuel. (Eg)
Eng. Allersby 1778-1863 Birmingham. DNB-T.
LINES, Samuel Restell.
Eng. Birmingham 1804-1833 Same. DNB-T.
LINFORD, Charles.
Am. Pittsburgh, Pa. 1846-1897. F.
LINGAN, Violetta D. P.
Am. b. New York; ad. 1934 Brooklyn, N. Y. A.
LINGE, Jules Dominique.
Fr. b. Paris 1884. DBA.
LINGÉE, Charles Louis. (Eg)
Fr. Paris 1748/51-1819 Same. B-T.
LINGELBACH, Johannes [or James].
Dut. Frankfort, Ger. 1622/5-1674/87 Amsterdam. B-C-T-722.
LINGEN, Penelope. (S)
Am. ac. 1927 in Houston, Tex. A24.
LINGKE, Johann August.
Ger. Zittau 1764/9-1842 Dresden. T.
LINGNER, Otto.
Ger. b. Kolberg 1856. B-T.
LINK, B. Lillian. (S)
Am. b. New York 1880; ad. 1934 Boston. A.
LINK, Carl.
Am. ex. 1935 New York. M.
LINK [or Linck], Konrad Franz. (S)
Ger. Speier 1730-1793 Mannheim. T.
LINN, Bandel. (Cari)
Am. ad. 1935 New York. M.
LINNELL, James Thomas.
Eng. 1826-1905 London. B-C-T-15.
LINNELL, John.
Eng. London 1792-1882 Redhill. B-Bd-C-DNB-E-T-444.
LINNIG, William [The Elder].
Belg. Antwerp 1819-1885 Same. B-T.
LINNIG, William [The Younger].
Belg. Antwerp 1842-1890. B-T.
LINNQUIST, Hilding.
Swe. b. Stockholm 1891; ex. 1929 Paris. DBA-T.
LINS, Adolf.
Ger. Cassel 1856-1927 Düsseldorf. B-T.
LINS, Theodore.
Am. b. New York 1885. A12.
LINSELL, C.
Br. ac. 1801-1830 London. T.
LINSON, Corwin Knapp.
Am. b. Brooklyn, N. Y. 1864; ad. 1934 Atlantic Highlands, N. J. A-F-W.
LINT, Hendrik Frans van.
Flem. Antwerp 1684-1763 Rome, It. T.
LINT, Peter van.
Flem. Antwerp 1609-1690 Same. B-T.
LINTHORST, Johannes [or Jacobus].
Dut. Amsterdam 1745/55-1815 Same. B-T.

LINTON, FRANK B. A.
Am. b. Phila., Pa. 1871; ad. 1934 Same. A.
LINTON, [Sir] JAMES DROMGOLE.
Eng. London 1840-1916. B-C-T.
LINTON, WILLIAM.
Eng. Liverpool 1791-1876 London. B-DNB-T.
LINTON, WILLIAM JAMES. (Poet-Eg)
Am. London 1812-1898 New Haven, Conn. A01-B-Bd-DAB-DNB-E-F-3-8-15-55-185.
LINTOTT, EDWARD BARNARD.
Am. b. London 1875; ad. 1934 New York. A-Wa.
LINYARD, JOSEPH. (S)
Eng. b. Keighley 1897; ad. 1934 Cheshire. Wa.
LION, [Mrs.] FLORA.
Eng. ad. 1934 London. Wa.
LION, HENRY. (S)
Am. b. Fresno, Calif. 1900; ad. 1934 Los Angeles. A.
LION, JAN JOSEF.
Flem. Dinant 1729-1809 Same. B-T.
LIONARDO. *see* Bassano, Leandro.
LIOTARD, JEAN ÉTIENNE.
Swi. 1702-1789. B-Bd-C-E-T.
LIPCHITZ, JACQUES. (S)
Fr. b. Druskieniki 1891. d. 5/29/73 Capri, Italy DBA.
LIPNICKI, FELIKS.
Pol. ac. 19th Cent. in Cracow. T.
LIPPERT, LÉON.
Am. b. Bavaria 1863; ad. 1934 Cinn., O. A.
LIPPI, FILIPPINO.
It. Prato 1457/60-1504/5 Florence. B-Bd-C-E-T-V-722.
LIPPI, FRA FILIPPO DI TOMASO.
It. Florence 1406?-1469 Same. B-Bd-C-E-T-V-722.
LIPPI, LORENZO.
It. Florence 1606-1664 Same. B-E-T.
LIPPINCOTT, MARGARETTE.
Am. Phila., Pa. 1862-1910. A010-F.
LIPPINCOTT, WILLIAM HENRY.
Am. Phila., Pa. 1849-1920 New York. A017-B-C-F-Y01921-15.
LIPPISCH, FRANZ.
Ger. b. Munich 1859. B-T.
LIPPMAN, ROMEYN VAN VLECK.
Am. ad. 1934 Boston, Mass. M.
LIPPO, MEMMI.
see Memmi da Siena, Lippo.
LIPS, JOHANN HEINRICH.
Swi. Kloten 1758-1817. B-T.
LIPSCHITZ, JACQUES. *see* Lipchitz, J.
LIS [or Liss or Lys], JAN [or Pan].
Dut. Hoornen 1570-1629 Venice, It. B-C-T.
LIS [or Liss or Lys], JAN DIRK VAN DER.
Dut. Bréda 1600-1657 Rotterdam. B-C-T.
LISKA, EMANUEL K.
Hun. b. Nicklowitz 1853. B-T.
LISMER, ARTHUR.
Can. b. Sheffield, Eng.; ad. 1935 Toronto, Can. M.
LISS. *see* Lis.
LISSAC [or Pierlis], PIERRE. (Ill)
Fr. b. Limoges 1878. DBA.
LISSANDRINO, IL.
see Magnasco, Allessandro.
LISSE, DIRK VAN DER.
Dut. b. Bréda; d. 1669 The Hague. B-T.
LISSEN. *see* Lis.
LISSIM, SIMON.
Rus. b. Kiev 1900. DBA.
LISSITZKY, EL.
Rus. b. Smolensk 1890. T.
LISTA, STANISLAO. (S)
It. b. Salerna 1824; ac. 1878 Rome, It. B-T.
LISTER-LISTER, WILLIAM.
Aust. b. Sydney, N. S. W. 1859. B-T.
LITAUER, MARY. (Eg)
Pol. ex. 1934 Chicago. M.
LITHGOW, DAVID CUNNINGHAM.
Am. b. Glasgow, Scot. 1868; ad. 1935 Albany, N. Y. Fa-M.
LITLE, ARTHUR. (Ill)
Am. ad. 1934 New York. A.
LITTELL, WILLIAM DOUGHTY. (Eg)
Am. New York 1849-1911 Brooklyn, N. Y. A09.
LITTEN, SIDNEY MACKENZIE. (Et)
Eng. b. 1887; d. 1934 London. T-Wa-Y1928.
LITTLE, [Mrs.] EDITH TADD.
Am. b. Phila., Pa. 1882; ad. 1934 St. Petersburg, Fla. A.
LITTLE, GERTRUDE L.
Am. b. Minn., Minn.; ad. 1934 Los Angeles, Calif. A.
LITTLE, JOHN WESLEY.
Am. Forksville, Pa. 1867-1923 Williamsport, Pa. A020-F-46.
LITTLE, NATHANIEL STANTON. (Ill)
Am. b. Helena, Mont. 1893; ad. 1934 Phila., Pa. A-W.
LITTLE, PHILIP.
Am. b. Swampscott, Mass. 1857; ad. 1934 Salem, Mass. A-F-W.
LITTLE, ROBERT.
Scot. b. Greenock 1854/5; ad. 1934 Hackendon. T-Wa.
LITTLE, TACEY MAY BATES. (Et)
Mrs. Frank Little.
Am. b. Whitehall, Ill. 1879; ad. 1934 So. Orange, N. J. A.
LITTLEFIELD, JOHN HARRISON.
Am. Cicero, N. Y. 1835-1902 Brooklyn, N. Y. M.
LITTLEFIELD, WILLIAM HORACE.
Am. b. Roxbury, Mass. 1902; ad. 1934 Boston. A.
LITTLEJOHN, CYNTHIA PUGH.
Am. b. Assumption Parish, La.; ad. 1934 New Orleans, La. A.
LITTLEJOHNS, JOHN.
Eng. b. Bideford 1874; ad. 1934 London. T-Wa.
LITZINGER, DOROTHEA M.
Am. Penn. 1889-1925 New York. A022-F.
LIÜ HAI-SÜ. (Prof. Acad. Arts.)
Chinese. ad. 1935 Shanghai, China. M.
LIVENS. *see also* Lievens.
LIVENS, HORACE MANN.
Eng. b. Croydon; ad. Springfield, Eng. T-Wa.
LIVERSEEGE, HENRY.
Eng. Manchester 1803-1832 London. DNB-T.

LIVESAY, Richard.
Br. d. 1823? in Southsea, Eng. B-DNB-T.
LIVI, Francesco di Domenico. (Glass-P)
It. b. Gambassi; ac. 1436 Lübeck, Ger. T-V.
LIVINGSTON, Charlotte.
Am. b. New York; ad. 1934 Bronx, N. Y. A.
LIVIZZANI, Girolamo da. *see* Carpi, G. da.
LIX, Frédéric Théodore.
Fr. Strasburg 1830-1897 Paris. B-T.
LIZARS, William Home. (Eg)
Scot. Edinburgh 1788-1859 Jedburgh. DNB-T.
LLANOS, Ferrando de los.
Sp. ac. 1505-1525. T-V.
LLANOS Y VALDÉS, Sebastián de.
Sp. Séville 1602-1668. B-T.
LLEWELLYN, [Sir] William.
Eng. b. Gloucestershire 1860; ad. 1934 London. B-T-Wa.
LLORÉNS, Cristobal [The Elder].
Sp. Bocairente 1550-1620. T.
LLOYD, Benjamin.
Eng. b. Rhayader 1868; ad. 1934 Lambeth. Wa.
LLOYD, Lucile. (Mu)
Am. b. Cinn., O. 1894; ad. 1934 Hollywood, Calif. A.
LLOYD, Mary Wingate.
Mrs. Horatio Gates Lloyd.
Am. b. New York 1868. A12.
LLOYD, Sara A. Worden.
Mrs. Hinton S. Lloyd.
Am. b. Xenia, O.; ad. 1935 Hamilton, N. Y. A12-F.
LLOYD, Stuart.
Eng. ad. 1934 Brighton. T-Wa.
LLOYD, Thomas James ["Tom"].
Eng. b. London 1849; ac. 1910 Same. B-T.
LLOYD, W. Stuart.
Eng. 1875-1913.
LOARTE, Alexandro de.
Sp. z. Toledo; ac. 1626. B-T.
LOBEL-RICHE, Alméry. (Ill)
Fr. b. Geneva, Swi. 1880. DBA.
LOBER, George John. (S)
Am. b. Chicago 1892; ad. 1934 New York. A-Cs-F-W.
LOBLEY, James.
Eng. Hull 1829-1888 Bradford. M.
LOBLEY, John Hodgson.
Eng. b. Huddersfield 1878; ad. 1934 Poole. T-Wa.
LOBRE, Maurice.
Fr. b. Bordeaux 1862. DBA-T.
LOBRICHON, Timoléon Marie.
Fr. Cornod 1831-1914. B-T.
LOCATELLI [or Lucatelli], Andréa.
It. Rome 1660/95-1741 Same. B-T.
LOCATELLI, Giovan Francesco.
It. ac. 1840/61 in Venice. B-T.
LOCHNER, Stéphan of Cologne.
Ger. ac. 1410-1451 Cologne. Bd-T-722-897.
LOCHOFF, Nicola.
Rus. ac. 1933. M.
LOCHOFF, Signore.
It. ac. 1932 in Florence. M.
LOCICERO, Frank Peter.
Am. ad. 1935 New York. M.
LOCK, Anton.
Eng. b. Westminster 1893; ex. 1932 London. M.
LOCKARD, Robert Ivan.
Am. b. Norton, Kan. 1905; ad. 1934 Kansas City, Mo. A.
LOCKE, Alexander S. (Mu)
Am. b. New York 1860; ad. 1934 Brooklyn, N. Y. A.
LOCKE, Charles Wheeler. (Et)
Am. b. Cinn., O. 1899; ad. 1934 Brooklyn, N. Y. A-F.
LOCKE, Lucie Harris.
Mrs. David Roger Locke.
Am. b. Valdosta, Ga. 1904; ad. 1934 Corpus Christi, Tex. A.
LOCKE, W. R.
Am. b. Winchester, Mass. 1883; ac. 1935 Florida. M.
LOCKER, Edward Hawke.
Eng. Kent 1777-1849. DNB-T.
LOCKEY, Rowland.
Eng. ac. 1590-1610 in London. DNB-T.
LOCKHART, [Mrs.] Glada Trenchard.
Am. b. Boone, Ia. 1892; ad. 1934 Calumet, Ill. A.
LOCKHART, William Ewart.
Scot. Anman 1846-1900 London. B-DNB-T.
LOCKIE, Thomas.
Am. ad. 1934 Pontiac, Ill. M.
LOCKINGTON, Walter Percy.
Am. England 1857-1905 Phila., Pa. A05.
LOCKLEY, J. Hodson.
Eng. ex. 1934 London. M.
LOCKMAN, De Witt McCellan.
Am. b. 1870; ad. 1934 New York. A-F-W.
LOCKWOOD, Clinton Benedict.
Am. b. New York 1907; ad. 1934 Same. A.
LOCKWOOD, John Ward.
Am. b. Atchison, Kan. 1894; ad. 1934 Taos, N. M. A.
LOCKWOOD, Robert Wilton.
Am. Wilton, Conn. 1861-1914 Boston. A01-B-DAB-E-F-1.
LODER, Matthaüs.
Aus. Vienna 1781-1828. B-T.
LODGE, William. (Eg)
Eng. Leeds 1640-1689. B-DNB-T.
LOWICK, Agnes.
Am. b. Bergen Point, N. J.; ad. 1934 St. Louis, Mo. A.
LOEB, Dorothy.
Am. b. Bavaria 1887; d. 1934 Provincetown, Mass. A-F.
LOEB, Louis.
Am. Cleveland, O. 1866-1909 Canterbury, N. H. A07-B-DAB-F-1-46.
LOEDERER, Richard A. (Ill)
Am. ad. 1934 New York. A.
LOEFFLER, Gisella.
see Lacher, [Mrs.] Gisella Loeffler.
LOEFFLER, Moritz. (S)
Am. ad. 1934 Bloomfield, N. J. M.
LOERCHER, Elsie A. (S)
Am. ad. 1934 New York. M.
LOEVY, Edouard.
Pol. Warsaw 1857-1910 Paris. DBA-T.
LOEWENGUTH, Frederick M.
Am. b. Rochester, N. Y. 1887; ad. 1934 Same. A.

LÖFFLER, Ludwig.
Ger. Frankfort 1819-1876 Berlin. C-T.
LÖFFTZ, Ludwig von.
Ger. Darmstadt 1845-1910 Munich. T.
LOFTHOUSE, [Mrs.] Mary [née Forster].
Br. 1853-1885. DNB.
LOFTING, Hugh. (Ill)
Am. Maidenhead, Eng. 1886; ad. 1934 New York. A-W.
LOGAN, Robert Fulton. (Et)
Am. b. Lauder, Manitoba, Can. 1889; ad. 1934 Paris. A-F-W.
LOGASA, Charles.
Am. b. Davenport, Ia. 1883; ad. 1934 New York. A-892.
LOGGAN, David. (Eg)
Ger. Danzig 1633-1692 London. B-Bd-DNB-T.
LOGGIE, Helen A. (Et)
Am. ad. 1935 Bellingham, Wash. M.
LOGSDAIL, William.
Eng. b. Lincoln 1859; ac. 1929 Oxford. T-Wa1929.
LOGUINOFF, Tatiana.
Rus. b. Sebastopol 1904. DBA.
LOHMANN, Erika.
Am. b. Hamburg, Ger. 1900; ad. 1934 New York. A.
LOHR, George A.
Am. b. Woodstock, Va. 1898; ad. 1935 Aurora Hills, Va. M.
LOHSE, W. R.
Am. ex. 1934 New York. M.
LOIR, Lugi.
Fr. Goritz 1845-1916 Paris. B-DBA-T.
LOIR, Marianne.
Fr. ac. 1735-1760 in Paris. B-T.
LOIR [or Loyr], Nicolas Pierre.
Fr. Paris 1624-1670 Same. B-T.
LOIS, Jacob.
Dut. Rotterdam 1620-1676 Same. B-T.
LOISEAU, Gustave.
Fr. Paris 1865-1928. DBA.
LOISEAU-BAILLY, Georges. (S)
Fr. b. Sauvigny 1858. B-DBA-T.
LOISEAU-ROUSSEAU, Paul Louis Émile. (S)
Fr. Paris 1861-1927 Same. B-DBA-T.
LOISEL, Robert. (S)
Fr. ac. 1382-1408. B-T.
LOMAX, Conrad Hope.
Eng. b. London 1883; ad. 1934 Same. Wa.
LOMAX, John Arthur.
Eng. b. 1857. M.
LOMAZZO, Giovanni Paolo.
It. Milan 1538-1600. B-C-T.
LOMBARD, Émile Félicien.
Swi. b. Aubigno 1883. DBA.
LOMBARD, Henri Ed. (S)
Fr. Marseilles 1855-1929 Paris. DBA.
LOMBARD, Jean.
Fr. b. Dijon 1895. DBA.
LOMBARD, Lambert [Susterman].
Flem. Liége 1505/6-1566 Same. B-T.
LOMBARDI. *see also Lombardo.*
LOMBARDI, Alfonso. (S)
It. 1497-1537 Lucca. Hs-T-V.
LOMBARDO, Antonio. (S)
It. ac. 17th Cent. in Parma. B-E-Hs-T.
LOMBARDO, Emilio Vincent.
Am. b. Italy 1890. A24.
LOMBARDO, Girolamo [Calamia]. (S)
It. 1822-1880 Venice. B-Hs-T.
LOMBARDO, Girolamo [Ferrarese].
It. Ferrara 1504-1590. T-V.
LOMBARDO, Pietro. (S)
It. Venice 1435-1515. E-Hs-T.
LOMBARDO, Tommaso. (S)
It. ac. 1537-1556 in Venice. Hs-T.
LOMBARDO, Tullio Solari. (S)
It. Venice 1455-1532. E-Hs-T.
LOMBART [or Lombard], Pierre.
Fr. Paris 1612/3-1682 Same. B-DBA-T.
LOMI. *see* Gentileschi.
LOMME, Janin [Jehan le Home]. (S)
Flem. ac. 1415-1445 in Tournai, Belg. B-Hs-T.
LONDON, Frank Marsden.
Am. b. Pittsboro, N. C. 1876; ad. 1934 New York. A.
LONDONER, Amy.
Am. b. Lexington, Mo. 1878; ac. 1926 New York. A24-F.
LONE WOLF. [Blackfeet Tribe.]
Am.-Indian. ex. 1930 New York. 411.
LONERGAN, Arthur B.
Am. ad. 1934 New York. M.
LONERGAN, John.
Am. ex. 1935 New York. M.
LONG, Adelaide Husted.
Mrs. George T. Long.
Am. b. New York; ad. 1934 White Plains, N. Y. A.
LONG, Birch Burdette. (Mu)
Am. b. 1878; d. 1927 New York. A024.
LONG, Edwin Longsden.
Eng. Bath 1829-1891 Hampstead. B-C-DNB-T.
LONG, Ellis Barcroft. (S)
Am. b. Baltimore, Md. 1874. A20-F.
LONG, Essie.
Am. ad. 1934 Indianapolis, Ind. A.
LONG, Frank Weathers.
Am. b. Knoxville, Tenn. 1906; ad. 1934 Chicago. A.
LONG, Marion.
Can. b. Toronto; ad. 1935 Same. M.
LONG, Nat. (Et)
Br. ad. 1935 Willoughby, Aust. M.
LONGACRE, James Barton. (Eg)
Am. Penn. 1794-1869 Phila., Pa. B-DAB-F-2-6-7-40-45-84.
LONGACRE, Lydia Eastwick. (Min)
Am. b. New York 1870; ad. 1934 Same. A.
LONGCHAMPS, Gaston. (P-S)
Fr. b. Paris 1894; ad. 1934 New York. M.
LONGEPIED, Léon Eugène. (S)
Fr. Paris 1849-1888 Same. B-T.
LONGFELLOW, Ernest Wadsworth.
Am. Cambridge, Mass. 1845-1921 Boston. A018-B-C-F-15.
LONGFELLOW, William Pitt Preble.
Am. Portland, Me. 1836-1913 East Gloucester, Mass. M.
LONGHI, Alessandro.
It. Venice 1733-1813. B-T.
LONGHI, Barbara.
It. Ravenna, 1552-1619? B-T.

LONGHI, GIUSSEPPE.
It. Monzo, 1766-1831. B-T.
LONGHI, LUCA [Raphael de Ravenna].
It. Ravenna, 1507-1580. B-T.
LONGHI, PIETRO.
It. Venice, 1702-1785 Same. B-E-T-722.
LONGLEY, STANISLAUS S.
Eng. ex. 1935 London. M.
LONGMAN, [Mary], EVELYN BEATRICE. (S)
Mrs. Nathaniel Horton Batchelder.
Am. b. Winchester, O. 1874; ad. 1934 Windsor, Conn. A-B-Cs-F-W-46.
LONGPRE, PAUL DE.
Am. Lyons, Fr. 1855-1911 Hollywood, Calif. A09.
LONGSTAFF, [Sir] JOHN.
Aust. b. Clunes, Victoria 1862; ac. 1933. B-T.
LONGUET, ALEXANDER MARIE.
Fr. 1805-1850/1 Paris. B-T.
LONGUET, CARL JEAN. (S)
Fr. b. Paris 1904. DBA.
LONSDALE, JAMES.
Eng. Lancaster 1777-1839 London. B-DNB-T.
LONSING, FRANÇOIS JOSEPH.
Flem. Brussels 1739/43-1799 Bordeaux, Fr. B-T.
LONZO, ANTONIO.
It. ac. 1800 in Trieste. B-T.
LOO, CARLE VAN [or Charles André].
Fr. Nice 1705-1765 Paris. B-C-E-T-722.
LOO, CHARLES AMÉDÉE PHILIPPE VAN.
Fr. Turin, It. 1715/19-1795. B-T.
LOO, JACOB VAN.
Dut. Sluys 1614-1670 Paris. B-C-T-722.
LOO, JEAN BAPTISTE VAN.
Fr. Nice 1684-1745 Same. B-C-E-T-722.
LOO, JULES CÉSAR DENIS VAN.
Fr. Paris 1743-1821 Same. B-T.
LOO, LOUIS MICHEL VAN.
Fr. Toulon 1707-1771 Paris. B-T.
LOO, MARTIN.
see Van der Loo, Martin.
LOOKING ELK.
Am.-Indian. ex. 1933 New York. 411.
LOOMIS, ANDREW. (Ill)
Am. b. Syracuse, N. Y. 1892; ad. 1934 Chicago. A.
LOOMIS, CHESTER.
Am. Syracuse, N. Y. 1852-1924 Englewood, N. J. A022-B-F-T-W13.
LOOMIS, HELEN.
Am. b. Andover, Mass.; d. 1920 New York. A017.
LOOMIS, KENNETH BRADLEY.
Am. b. Steubenville, O. 1902; ad. 1934 New York. A.
LOOMIS, MANCHUS C.
Am. b. Dairview, Pa.; ad. 1934 Chicago. A.
LOON, THÉODORE IVAN.
Flem. Brussels 1590-1678. B-T.
LOON, THÉODORE DIRK II VAN.
Flem. Brussels, 1629-1678. B-T.
LOOP, HENRY AUGUSTUS.
Am. Hillsdale, N. Y. 1831-1895 Lake George, N. Y. B-C-DAB-F-3-15.
LOOP, [Mrs.] HENRY AUGUSTUS.
Am. New Haven, Conn. 1840-1909 Saratoga, N. Y. A07-B-15.
LOOP, LEOTA WILLIAMS.
Am. b. Fountain City, Ind. 1893; ad. 1934 Kokomo, Ind. A.
LOOSCHEN, HANS.
Ger. Berlin 1859-1923 Same. B-T.
LOOSE, BASILE DE.
Dut. Zerle 1809-1860. B-C-T.
LOOTEN, JAN [not Jacob].
Dut. Amsterdam 1618-1681 London. B-C-DNB-T.
LOOY, JEAN VAN.
Belg. b. Brussels 1882. DBA.
LOPEZ, ALBERT EGEA.
Am. ex. 1933 New York. M.
LOPEZ, CHARLES ALBERT. (S)
Am. Mexico 1869-1906 New York. A06-B-F-46.
LOPEZ, F. CARLOS.
Am. ad. 1935 Detroit, Mich. M.
LOPEZ, GASPARO DI FIORI.
It. Naples 1650-1732 Florence. B-T.
LÓPEZ Y PORTANA, VINCENTE.
Sp. Valencia 1772-1850 Madrid. B-T.
LOPEZ, RENÉ.
Mex. ad. 1934 Los Angeles, Calif. M.
LORAN, ERLE.
Am. b. Minn., Minn. 1905; ad. 1934 Same. A.
LORCH [or Lorichs], MELCHIOR. (Eg)
Dan. 1527-1583/6 Copenhagen. T.
LÖRCHER, ALFRED. (S)
Ger. ac. 1934 Stuttgart. T.
LORD, AUSTIN WILLARD.
Am. Rolling Stone, Minn. 1860-1922 Silvermine, Conn. A018.
LORD, CAROLINE A.
Am. Cincinnati, O. 1860-1928 Same. A026
LORD, [Miss] ELYSE [or Elise].
Eng. ad. 1934 Kent. Wa-Y1928.
LORD, EVELYN RUMSEY.
Am. b. Brooklyn, N. Y.; ad. 1934 Same. A.
LORD, HARRIET.
Am. b. Orange, N. J. 1879; ad. 1934 New York. A-F.
LORD, PHOEBE GRIFFIN. (Min)
Am. East Haddam, Conn. 1797-1875 Lyme, Conn. F.
LORDON, PIERRE JÉROME.
Fr. Guadeloupe 1780-1838 Paris. B-T.
LORENSEN, CARL. (S)
Am. Denmark 1864-1916 Chicago. A013.
LORENTINO DI ANDREA D'AREZZO [The Elder].
It. ac. 1495-1505. Fa-V.
LORENTINO DI AREZZO, ANGELO DI [The Younger].
It. Arezzo 1430-1506 Same. Fa-V.
LORENTINO DI GIOVANNI, TURA.
It. ac. 1399-1429. Fa-V.
LORENTZEN, CHRISTIAN AUGUST.
Dan. Sonderborg 1749-1828. B-T.
LORENZ, ALCIDE JOSEPH.
Fr. b. Paris 1813. B-T.
LORENZ, RICHARD.
Am. Weimar, Ger. 1858-1915 Milwaukee, Wis. A012-B-F.
LORENZANI, ARTHUR E. (S)
Am. b. Carrara, It. 1885; ad. 1934 New York. A-Cs-F.

LORENZETTI, AMBROZIO.
It. ac. 1323-1348 in Siena. B-T-V-905.
LORENZETTI [or Laurati], PIETRO.
It. ac. 1280-1348 in Siena. B-T-V-905.
LORENZETTI, UGOLINO.
[Master of the Ovile Madonna].
It. ac. 14th Century in Siena. T-V-445.
LORENZINO. *see* Sabbatini, Lorenzo.
LORENZO DI BICCI. *see* Bicci.
LORENZO DI CREDI. *see* Credi.
LORENZO DI FIORENZO. *see* Fiorenzo.
LORENZO DI MARIANO.
It. Siena 1476-1534. M.
LORENZO DON, IL. MONACO.
It. 1370?-1425 Florence. B-T-V.
LORENZO DI NICOLÒ. *see* Gerini.
LORENZO DI PIERO. *see* Piero di Cosimo.
LORENZO, VECCHIETTA. *see* Vecchietta.
LORENZO, VENEZIANO. *see* Veneziano.
LORICH. *see* Lorch.
LORIMER, JOHN HENRY.
Scot. b. Edinburgh 1856. B-DBA-T-Wa.
LORING, FRANCES. (S)
Can. b. Wardner, Idaho; ad. 1935 Toronto, Ont. M.
LORING, FRANCIS WILLIAM.
Am. Boston 1838-1905 Austria. F.
LORING, WILLIAM CUSHING.
Am. b. Newton Center, Mass. 1879; ad. 1934 Boston. A-F-W.
LORME, ANTON DE.
Dut. Rotterdam 1610-1673. C-T.
LORRAIN, CLAUDE LE.
see Claude, Gellee.
LORRAIN, LOUIS JOSEPH.
see Le Lorrain, Louis Joseph.
LORRAIN, ROBERT LE. (S)
Fr. Paris 1666-1743 Same. Hs-T.
LORRAINE, ALMA ROYER.
Am. b. Randolph, O.; ad. 1934 Seattle, Wash. A.
LORRAINE, HELEN. (Ill)
Am. b. Webster Grove, Mo. 1892; ad. 1934 Richmond, Va. A.
LORTA, JEAN PIERRE [or François]. (S)
Fr. Paris 1752-1837 Versailles. B-T.
LORY [or Lori], GABRIEL LUDWIG [The Elder].
Swi. Berne 1763-1840 Altenberg, Ger. B-T.
LORY [or Lori], MATHAIS GABRIEL [The Younger].
Swi. Berne 1784-1846 Same. B-T.
LOS, NAUM MICHEL. (S)
Am. b. Ukraine 1882; ad. 1934 New York. A-Cs.
LOSENKO [or Losenzo], ANTON PAVLOVICH.
Rus. Gluchov, 1737-1773 Leningrad. B-T.
LO SPAGNA. *see* Spagna.
LOSSING, BENSON JOHN. (Ill)
Am. Beekman, N. Y. 1813-1891 Dover Plains, N. Y. DBA-F-45-165-166-185.
LOSSOW, HEMRICH.
Ger. Munich 1843-1897 Schleissheim. B-C-T.
LOTAVE, CARL.
Am. d. 1924 New York. A022-F.
LOTH, JOHANN KARL [or Carlotto].
Ger. Munich 1632-1698 Venice, It. B-C-T.
LOTIRON, ROBERT.
Fr. b. Paris 1886; ex. 1930 Same. DBA-T.
LOTTERHOS, HELEN JAY.
Am. b. McComb, Miss. 1905; ad. 1935 Jackson, Miss. M.
LOTTI, LORENZETTO [Lorenzo di Ludivico]. (S)
It. Florence 1490-1541. T-V.
LOTTO, CARLOTTO. *see* Loth, J. K.
LOTTO, LORENZO.
It. Bergamo 1480?-1554/6 Venice. B-Bd-C-E-T-V-722.
LOTZ, KAROLY.
Hun. Hessen 1833-1904. B-T.
LOUBON, CHARLES JOSEPH ÉMILE.
Fr. Aix 1809-1863 Marseille. B-T.
LOUCHANSKY, JACQUES.
see Loutschansky, Jacques.
LOUD, MARION V.
Am. b. Medford, Mass. 1880; ad. 1934 Detroit, Mich. A.
LOUD, MAY HALLOWELL.
Mrs. Joseph Prince Loud.
Am. b. West Medford, Mass. 1860-1916 Boston. A014.
LOUDAN, W. MOUAT.
Eng. London 1868-1925. T-Wa1924-Y01926.
LOUDERBACK, WALT.
Am. b. Valparaiso, Ind.; ad. 1934 New York. A.
LOUGH, JOHN GRAHAM. (S)
Eng. Hexham 1789-1876 London. T.
LOUGHBOROUGH, MARGARET MCLELLAND.
Am. b. Montgomery Co., Md.; ad. 1934 Washington, D. C. A.
LOUIS, ARISTIDE. (Eg)
Fr. b. Toul; ac. 1839-1853. B-T.
LOUIS, AURELLO.
It. Pisa 1566-1622. B-T.
LOUIS, HUBERT NÖEL. (S)
Fr. b. St. Ouen 1839. B-T.
LOUIS [or Louys], JACOB [or Jan].
Flem. b. Antwerp, Belg. 1595; ac. 1635. T.
LOUKOMSKI [or Lukomski], Georges.
Rus. b. Moscow 1881. DBA-T.
LOUND, THOMAS.
Eng. 1802-1861 Norwich. DNB-T.
LOUP, EUGÈNE.
Fr. b. Rodez 1867. DBA-T.
LOUPPE, MARGUERITE.
Fr. ex. 1934 in Paris. M.
LOUSTAUNAU, LOUIS AUGUSTE GEORGES.
Fr. Paris 1846-1898 Versailles. B-T.
LOUTCHANSKY, JACQUES. (S)
Rus. b. Vinnitza 1876; ac. 1929 in Paris. DBA-T.
LOUTHERBOURG, PHILIP JACQUES DE.
Eng. Fulda, Ger. 1740-1812 London. B-C-DNB-T-722.
LOUTREUIL, MAURICE, ALBERT.
Fr. Montmirail 1885-1925 Paris. DBA-T.
LOUVERINI, PONZIANO.
It. b. Bergamo, 1858. B-T.
LOUVET, HENRI EUGÈNE.
Fr. b. Versailles 1866- B-DBA-T.
LOUYOT [or Loujot], EDMUND.
Ger. b. Metz; ac. 1880 in Berlin. B-T.
LOVE, GEORGE PATERSON.
Am. b. Prov., R. I. 1887; ad. 1934 Same. A.
LOVE, HORACE BEEVOR.
Eng. Norwich 1780-1838. B-T.

LOVE, JOHN WASHINGTON.
Am. 1850-1880. M.
LOVE, NANCY C. JONES.
Mrs. George Paterson Love.
Am. b. Prov., R. I. 1888; ad. 1934 Same. A.
LOVEGROVE, STANLEY D. (Ill)
Am. b. East Orange, N. J. 1881; ad. 1934 Phila., Pa. A.
LOVELAND, JOHN WINTHROP.
Am. b. West Pittston, Pa. 1866; ad. 1934 Washington, D. C. A.
LOVELL, KATHERINE A.
Am. b. New York; ad. 1934 Brooklyn, N. Y. A.
LOVEN, FRANK W.
Am. b. Jersey City, N. J. 1869; ad. 1934 Same. A.
LOVER, SAMUEL.
Ir. Dublin, 1797-1868. B-T.
LOVEROFF, F. NICHOLAS.
Can. b. Tifflis, Rus.; ad. 1934 Toronto, Ont. M.
LOVET-LORSKI, BORIS. (S)
Am. b. Russia 1891; ad. 1934 New York. A20-F-M-T.
LOVETT, WILLIAM.
Am. Boston 1773-1801 Same. F-2-6-169.
LOVINS, HENRY.
Am. b. New York 1883; ad. 1934 Hollywood, Calif. A.
LOW, DAVID. (Cari)
Aust. b. Dunedin, N. Z. 1891; ad. 1935 London. Wa-873.
LOW, MARY FAIRCHILD.
Mrs. Will Hicox Low.
Am. b. New Haven, Conn. 1858; ad. Bronxville, N. Y. A-B-F-W.
LOW, SANFORD [Ballard Dole].
Am. b. Honolulu, Hawaii 1905; ad. New Britain, Conn. A.
LOW, WILL HICOX.
Am. Albany, N. Y. 1853-1932 New York. A029-B-C-E-F-W-66-187.
LOWCAY, ROSE.
Br. b. So. Africa 1889; ad. 1935 So. Aust. M.
LOWCOCK, CHARLES FREDERICK.
Eng. ac. 1878-1917 in London. B-T.
LOWDON, [Mrs.] ELSIE MOTZ.
Am. b. Waco, Tex.; ad. 1934 New York. A.
LOWE, MAURITIUS.
Br. 1746-1793 London. DNB-T.
LOWELL, FREDERICK ELDRIDGE.
Am. Boston 1873-1933 Concord, Mass. A030.
LOWELL, LEMUEL L.
Am. d. 1914 Watertown, N. Y. A011.
LOWELL, MILTON H.
Am. Lamberton, N. Y. 1848-1927 New Rochelle, N. Y. A024.
LOWELL, NAT. (Et)
Am. ad. 1934 New York. M.
LOWELL, ORSON. (Ill)
Am. b. Wyoming, Ia. 1871; ad. 1934 New York. A-F-W.
LOWENGRUND, MARGARET. (Et)
Mrs. Joseph Lilly.
Am. b. Phila., Pa.; ad. 1934 New York. A.
LOWENHEIM, FREDERICK. (Ill)
Am. b. Berlin, Ger.; ac. 1926 New York. A12-F.
LOWENTHAL, JULIA.
Eng. ex. 1934 London. M.
LOWES, SADIE H.
Am. b. Indiana 1870; ad. 1934 Chicago. A.
LOWINSKY, THOMAS ESMOND.
Eng. b. 1892; ad. 1934 London. Wa.
LOWITH, WILHELM.
Aus. b. Vienna 1861. B-T.
LOWREY, ROSALIE.
Am. b. Dayton, O. 1893; ad. 1934 Same. A.
LOWRIE, [Mrs.] AGNES POTTER.
Am. b. 1892; ad. 1934 Cincinnati, O. M.
LOWRY, JOSEPH [or John], WILSON. (Eg)
Eng. 1803-1879. DNB.
LOWRY, LAURENCE STÉPHANE.
Eng. b. Manchester 1887; ad. 1934 Same. DBA-Wa.
LOWRY, STRICKLAND.
Eng. b. Whitehaven; ac. 1779. DNB-T.
LOWRY, WILSON. (Eg)
Eng. Whitehaven 1762-1824 London. DNB-T.
LOYAU, MARCEL FRANÇOIS. (S)
Fr. b. Onzain 1895. DBA-T.
LOYSEN, ARTHUR L.
Am. ad. 1934 Rochester, N. Y. M.
LOZOWICK, LOUIS. (Eg)
Am. b. Russia 1892; ad. 1934 New York. A-DBA.
LÜ CHI.
Chinese. Ming Dynasty (1368-1644). E.
LUARD, JOHN DALBIAC.
Eng. Lincolnshire 1830-1860 Salisbury. B-DNB-T.
LUARD, LOWES D. (Et)
Eng. ad. 1934 London. Wa.
LUBAN, BORIS.
Am. ac. 1932 New York. M.
LUBBERS, ADRIAAN.
Dut. b. Amsterdam 1892. DBA.
LÜBEN, ADOLF.
Ger. Leningrad, Rus. 1837-1905. B-C.
LUBIENIECKI, BOYDAN THEODOR.
Pol. Cracow 1653-1729. B-T.
LUBIENIECKI, CHRISTOFFEL.
Ger. Stettin 1660/1-1724/8 Amsterdam, Holland. B-T.
LUCA DI TOMMÈ.
It. Siena 1330?-1389. T-V.
LUCANTINIO. *see* Ulberti, L. D.
LUCAS, ALBERT DURER.
Eng. Salisbury 1829-1919 London. T-Y01920.
LUCAS, ALBERT PIKE. (P-S)
Am. b. Jersey City, N. J.; ad. 1934 New York. A-F-W-46.
LUCAS, AUGER.
Fr. Paris 1685-1765 Same. B-T.
LUCAS, AUGUST.
Ger. Darmstadt 1801/3-1863 Same. B-T.
LUCAS, DAVID. (Eg)
Br. 1802-1881. Bd-T.
LUCAS, [Mrs.] ELSIE LEONE LEAVEY.
Am. Lexington, Ky. 1872-1932 Wis. A029.
LUCAS, EUGENIO.
Sp. Madrid 1824-1870. T.
LUCAS, HORATIO JOSEPH.
Eng. London 1839-1873. DNB-T.

LUCAS, JEAN WILLIAMS.
Am. b. Hagerstown, Md. 1873; ad. 1934 New York. A.
LUCAS, JOHN.
Eng. London 1807-1874 Same. B-DNB-T.
LUCAS, JOHN SEYMOUR.
Eng. London 1849-1923 Southwold. B-C-E-T.
LUCAS, JOHN TEMPLETON.
Eng. 1836-1880 Whitby. B-DNB-T.
LUCAS, LOUIS DÉSIRÉ.
Fr. b. 1869. DBA.
LUCAS DE MONTIGNY, JEAN ROBERT NICOLAS.
see Montigny, J. R. N. L. de.
LUCAS, RICHARD COCKLE. (S)
Eng. Salisbury 1880-1883 Chilworth. DNB-T.
LUCAS, SAMUEL.
Eng. Hitchin 1805-1870 Same. DNB-T.
LUCAS VAN LEYDEN [Jacobsz].
Dut. 1494? Leyden 1533 Same. B-Bd-C-E-T-V-446-449-722-917.
LUCAS, WILLIAM JAMES.
Eng. b. Cheshire 1888; ad. 1934 Same. Wa.
LUCAS-ROBIQUET, MARIE AIMÉE.
Fr. b. Avranches, 1864. B-DBA-T.
LUCATELLI [or Locatelli], ANDRÉA.
It. Rome 1660-1741 Same. B-T.
LUCCA DI TOMME. *see* Luca di T.
LUCCHESI, ANDRÉA CARLO. (S)
It. b. Italy 1860-1925 London. T-Y01926.
LUCCHESI, GIORGIO.
It. b. Lucca; ac. 1892 in London.
LUCE, [Mrs.] LAURA H.
Am. b. Salem, N. Y. 1845; ad. Titusville, Pa. A.
LUCE, LEONARD E.
Am. b. Ashtabula, O. 1893; ad. 1934 Cleveland. A.
LUCE, [Mrs.] MARIE HUXFORD.
Am. b. Skaneateles, N. Y.; ac. 1915. A12.
LUCE, MAXILILIEN.
Fr. b. Paris 1858. B-DBA-T.
LUCE, MOLLY.
Mrs. Alan Burroughs.
Am. b. Pittsburgh, Pa. 1896; ad. 1934 Belmont, Mass. A.
LUCENTI, GIROLAMO. (S)
It. Carreggio, 1627-1698 Rome. B-T.
LUCHTEMEYER, E. A.
Am. b. St. Louis 1887; ad. 1934 Webster Groves, Mo. A.
LUCIANI, SEBASTINO.
see Sebastiano del Piombo.
LUCIDEL. *see* Neufchatel, Nicolas.
LUCIENTES. *see* Goya y Lucientes.
LUCIONI, LUIGI.
Am. b. Malnate, It. 1900; ad. 1934 New York. A.
LUCK [or Luckx], FRANZ JOSEF.
Belg. Mechlin 1802-1849 Brussels. B-T.
LUCK [or Luckx], JOHANN. (S)
Ger. ac. 1765 in Germany. T.
LÜCKE FAMILY. (S)
Ger. ac. 18th Century in Dresden. T.
LUCKER, PAUL. (S)
Am. ex. 1935 New York. M.
LUCY, CHARLES [The Younger].
Eng. Hereford, 1814-1873 London. B-DNB-T.
LUDBY, MAX.
Eng. b. London 1858; ex. 1934 Same. T.
LUDEKENS, FRED.
Ger. ac. 1934. M.
LUDINS, EUGÈNE DAVID.
Am. b. Rus. 1904; ad. 1934 Woodstock, N. Y. A.
LUDINS, SYLVIA.
Am. ex. 1935 New York. M.
LUDIUS, MARCUS.
It. ac. 63 B.C.-14 A.D. B-T.
LUDLOW, HAL. (Ill)
Eng. b. Newport 1861; ad. 1934 Hanwell. Wa.
LUDOVICI, ALBERT.
Eng. Prague, Czec. 1852-1932. Wa-Y01933.
LUDOVICI, ALICE EMELIE. (Min)
Am. b. Dresden, Ger. 1872; ad. 1934 Pasadena, Calif. A-F-W.
LUDWIG, HEINRICH.
Ger. Hanau 1829-1898 Rome, It. B-T.
LUDWIG, KARL JULIUS EMIL.
Ger. Römhild 1839-1901 Berlin. B-T.
LUGARDON, JEAN LÉONARD.
Fr. Geneva, Swi. 1801-1884. B-T.
LUGO, EMIL.
Ger. Stokach 1840-1902 Munich. B-T.
LÜHRIG, GEORG. (Eg)
Ger. b. Göttingen 1868. T.
LUHRS, HENRY.
Am. ad. 1934 Westport, Conn. M.
LUIGI-LOIR. *see* Loir, Luigi.
LUIGINI, FERDINAND JEAN. (Et)
Fr. b. Orléans 1870; ex. 1934 U. S. B-DBA-T.
LUINI, AURELIO.
It. Luini 1530-1590. B-T-V.
LUINI, BERNARDINO.
It. Luini 1465/75-1531/3. B-Bd-C-E-T-V-722.
LUINI, COSTANZO. (S)
Am. b. Milan, It. 1886; ad. 1934 Elmhurst, N. Y. A.
LUITFRECHT. (S)
Bav. ac. 1150 in Freisung. M.
LUKA, MADELEINE.
Fr. ac. 1931 in Paris. DBA.
LUKEMAN, HENRY AUGUSTUS. (S)
Am. Richmond, Va. 1872-1935 New York. A-B-Cs-E-W-46-798-Obit. N. Y. papers, 4-4-1935.
LUKER, WILLIAM, JR.
Eng. b. London 1867; ad. 1934 Same. T-Wa.
LUKER, WILLIAM, SR.
Eng. ac. 1852-1889 London. T.
LUKITS, THEODORE NICKOLAI.
Am. ad. 1934 Los Angeles, Calif. A.
LUKS, GEORGE BENJAMIN.
Am. Williamsport, Pa. 1867-1933 New York. A030-F-T-W-1-46-71-447-701-779-Obit. N. Y. papers, 10-30-1933.
LUKSCH, RICHARD. (S)
Ger. b. Vienna, Aus. 1872. T-798.
LULING, PETER.
Eng. ex. 1935 London. M.

LUM, [Mrs.] BERTHA BOYNTON. (Eg)
Am. b. Iowa 1934 San Fran., Calif. A-F-W16.

LUMINAIS, EVARISTE VITAL.
Fr. Nantes 1822-1896 Paris. B-C-T.

LUMIS, HARRIET RANDALL.
Mrs. Fred W. Lumis.
Am. b. Salem, O. 1870; ad. 1934 Springfield, Mass. A.

LUMLEY, ARTHUR.
Am. Ireland 1837-1912 Mt. Vernon, N. Y. A010.

LUMSDEN, [Mrs.] CHRISTINE MARIE.
Am. b. Brooklyn, N. Y.; ad. 1934 New York. A-W.

LUMSDEN, ERNEST S.
Scot. b. Dez 1883; ad. 1934 Edinburgh. T-Wa-830.

LUNA, CHARLES DE.
Fr. ac. 1833-1866 in Paris. B-T.

LUND, BELLE JENKS.
Am. b. Alexandria, S. D. 1879; ad. 1934 Hammond, Ind. A.

LUND, FREDRIK CHRISTIAN.
Dan. Copenhagen 1826-1901 Same. C-T.

LUND, HAROLD.
Am. ad. 1934 Brooklyn, N. Y. M.

LUND, HENRIK LOUIS.
Nor. b. Bergen 1879; ad. 1934 Oslo. T.

LUND, JOHAN LUDWIG GEBHARD.
Dan. Kiel, Ger. 1777-1867 Copenhagen. T.

LUND, NIELS MÖLLER.
Ger. Faaborg 1863-1916 London. T.

LUNDBERG, GUSTAF.
Swe. Stockholm 1695-1786 Same. B-T-756.

LUNDBORG, FLORENCE. (Mu)
Am. b. San Fran., Calif.; ad. 1934 New York. A-F-W.

LUNDBYE, JOHAN THOMAS.
Dan. Copenhagen 1818-1848 Bested. C-T.

LUNDEBERG, HELEN.
Am. ad. 1934 Los Angeles, Calif. M.

LUNDENS, GERRIT.
Dut. Amsterdam, 1622-1677. B-T.

LUNDGREN, EGRON SELLIF.
Swe. Stockholm 1816-1875 Same. B-DNB-T.

LUNDGREN, FERDINAND HARVEY.
Am. Hagerstown, Md. 1859-1932 Santa Barbara, Calif. A029-F.

LUNDGREN, MARTIN. (Mu)
Am. b. Sweden 1871; ad. 1934 Chicago. A.

LUNDQUIST, ANDERS.
Swe. Orebro 1803-1853 Stockholm. T.

LUNDQUIST, EINAR.
Am. b. Shovde, Swe. 1901; ad. 1934 Rockford, Ill. A.

LUNDQUIST, JOHN. (S)
Swe. b. 1882; ex. 1929 Paris. DBA.

LUNG, ROWENA CLEMENT.
Am. b. Tacoma, Wash. 1905; ad. 1934 Same. A.

LUNN, H. AUGUSTUS.
Eng. ex. 1934 Kingston. M.

LUNOIS, ALEXANDRE. (Eg)
Fr. Paris 1863-1916. B-DBA-T.

LUNY, THOMAS.
Eng. 1759-1837 Teignmouth. B-DNB-T.

LUPPI, ERMENEGILDO. (S)
It. ac. 19-20th Cent. in Italy. M.

LUPTON, THOMAS GOFF. (Eg)
Eng. London 1791-1873 Same. B-DNB-T.

LUQUIENS, ELIZABETH KOLL.
Am. b. Salem, O. 1878; ad. 1934 New Haven, Conn. A.

LUQUIENS, HUC MAZELET. (Et)
Am. b. Auburndale, Mass. 1881; ad. Honolulu, Hawaii. A.

LURÇAT, JEAN.
Fr. b. Bruyèrs, 1892; ex. 1933 New York. DBA-448.

LUSH, VIVIAN R.
Am. ad. 1935 New York. M.

LUSK, MARIE KOUPAL.
Mrs. Charles D. Lusk.
Am. b. Bohemia 1862; ac. 1915 Wilmette, Ill. A12.

LUST, DORA C.
Am. b. Riga, Rus.; ad. 1934 New York. A.

LUSTIG, SALLY.
Am. ad. 1934 New York. M.

LUSURIER [or Usurier], CATHERINE.
Fr. 1753-1781 Paris. B-T.

LUSY, MARINO M.
Fr. b. Triest, 1880. T.

LÜTHY, JOHANNES.
Swi. 1803-1863. Fa.

LUTI, BENEDETTO.
It. Florence 1666-1724 Rome. B-C-T-722.

LUTTICHUYS, ISAAC.
Dut. London 1616-1673 Amsterdam. B-DNB-T.

LUTTICHUYS, SIMON.
Dut. London 1610-1662/3 Amsterdam. B-DNB-T.

LUTTRELL [or Lutterel], EDWARD. (Eg)
Ir. Dublin, 1650-1710 London. DNB-T.

LUTYENS, [Sir] EDWIN LANDSEER.
Eng. b. London 1869. T.

LÜTZENBERGER FAMILY. (Eg)
Ger. ac. 16th Cent. in Augsburg. T.

LUX, GLADYS MARIE.
Am. b. Chapman, Neb.; ad. 1934 Lincoln, Neb. A.

LUX, GWEN.
Am. ac. 1932 New York. M.

LUX, RICHARD.
Ger. b. Vienna, Aus. 1877. T.

LUX, THEODORE.
Ger. b. Berlin 1910; ad. 1934 Paris-Boulogne, Fr. M.

LUYCX VON LEUXENSTEIN, FRANZ.
see Leux, Franz.

LUYKX, CHRISTIAN [or Kerstraen].
Flem. Antwerp, 1623-1653. B-T.

LUYTEN, JEAN HENRI.
Belg. b. Roermonde 1859. B-T.

LUZANOWSKY-MARINESCO, LYDIA. (S)
Rus. b. Kiev 1899. DBA.

LYALL, AGNES E.
Am. ad. 1934 Summit, N. J. M.

LYALL, LAURA [Laura Muntz].
Can. England 1860-1930 Canada. M.

LYCIUS, [Son of Myron]. (S)
Gr. ac. 450-420 B.C. in Athens. Hs-T.

LYDE, LUCAS VAN.
see Lucas van Leyden.

LYDIS, MARIETTE.
Aus. b. Vienna 1894; ad. 1935 Paris. DBA.

LYFORD, PHILIP. (Ill)
Am. b. Worcester, Mass. 1887; ad. 1934 Hinsdale, Ill. M.
LYMAN, HARRY.
Am. 1856-1933 Chicago. A030.
LYMAN, JOSEPH.
Am. Ravenna, O. 1843-1913 Wallingford, Conn. A011-B-C-F.
LYNCH, ALBERT. (Ill)
Peruvian. b. Lima, Peru 1851; ac. 1930 Paris. B-DBA-T.
LYNCH, ANNA. (Min)
Am. b. Elgin, Ill.; ad. 1934 Chicago. A-F-W.
LYNCH, VIRGINIA.
Am. b. New York; ad. 1934 Same. A.
LYND, J. NORMAN. (Ill)
Am. b. Northwood, O. 1878; ad. 1934 Lynbrook, N. Y. A.
LYNE, RICHARD. [Earliest English artist].
Eng. ac. 1570-1600 in London. B-DNB-T.
LYNN, [Mrs.] KATHERINE EVANS.
Am. Phila., Pa. 1875-1930 Switzerland. A027-F.
LYNN, SAMUEL FERRIS. (S)
Ir. Fethard 1836-1876 Belfast. DNB-T.
LYNN-JENKINS, FRANK. (S)
Am. England 1870-1927 New York. A024-Y01928.
LYON, ARCADIUS.
Am. ad. 1934 Boston, Mass. M.
LYON, CORNEILLE.
see Corneille de Lyon.
LYON, [Mrs.] ELEANOR POWELL.
Am. ad. 1934 New York. M.
LYON, JEANNETTE AGNEW.
Mrs. William T. Lyon.
Am. b. Pittsburgh, Pa. 1862; ad. 1934 Cleveland, O. A.
LYON, ROWLAND.
Am. b. Washington, D. C. 1904; ad. Chevy-Chase, Md. A.
LYS, JAN. *see* Lis, Jan.
LYSIPPUS [or Lysippos]. (S)
Gr. [Argos-Sicyon] ac. 370-324 B.C. B-E-Hs-T-817.
LYSISTRATUS. (S)
Gr. Sicyon; ac. 324 B.C. B-E-T.
LYTTON, NEVILLE.
Br. b. Calcutta, India 1879; ad. 1934 London. DBA-Wa.
LYVERSBERG PASSION. *see* Master of L. P.
MA FEN [Ho-Chung].
Chinese. ac. Sung Dynasty. M-T.
MA PE-WI.
Indian [Am.] b. Zia Pueblo; ad. 1934 Santa Fé, N. M. 411.
MA YÜAN.
Chinese. ac. 12th Century. E.
MAAS. *see* Maes.
MAASEN, MARGARET [Baesemann].
Am. b. Milwaukee, Wis. 1907; ad. 1934 Same. A.
MABIE, GEORGE. (Ill)
Am. ad. 1935 Leonia, N. J. M.
MABIE, HELEN.
Am. ad. 1934 Summit, N. J. M.
MABILLE, JULES LOUIS. (S)
Fr. Valenciennes, 1843-1897. B-T.
MABUSE, JAN GOSSAERT VAN.
[Known also as Jean de Maubeuge].
Flem. Hainault, Belg. 1462/70-1533/41 Antwerp. B-Bd-C-E-T-722.
MAC. *see also* Mc.
MACADAM, FREDA CHURCHWELL.
Am. b. Chester, Pa. 1907; ad. 1934 Wilmington, Del. A.
MAC ARDELL, JAMES. (Eg)
Ir. Dublin 1710?-1765 London. Bd-DNB.
MACARTNEY, CATHERINE NAOMI.
Am. b. Des Moines, Ia.; ad. 1934 Iowa City, Ia. A.
MACAULEY, CHARLES RAYMOND. (Cart)
Am. Canton, O. 1871-1934 New York. W17-Obit. N. Y. papers, 11-25-1934.
MACBETH, NORMAN.
Scot. Aberdeen 1821-1888 London. B-Bd-DNB-T.
MACBETH, ROBERT WALKER. (Et)
Scot. Glasgow 1848-1910 London. B-Bd-C-DNB-T-Y01911.
MAC BRAYNE, FRANCES.
Am. b. Lowell, Mass. 1912; ad. 1934 Belmont, Mass. M.
MAC CALLUM, ANDREW.
Eng. Nottingham 1821-1902 London. B-DNB-T.
MAC CALLUM, HAMILTON.
Scot. Kames 1841-1896. B-DNB-T.
MAC CAMERON, ROBERT LEE.
Am. Chicago 1886-1912 New York. A010-B-DAB-F-W7-46.
MACCARI, CESARE.
It. Siena 1840-1919. B-T.
MAC CARTHY, HAMILTON P. (S)
Can. b. London 1847; ad. 1935 Ottawa, Ont. M.
MAC CHESNEY, CLARA TAGGART.
Am. Brownsville, Calif. 1860-1928 London. A025-F-W15-829.
MACCHIAVELLI, ZENOBIO [or Zanobi] DI.
It. Jacopo di Piero 1418-1479 Florence. B-T-V.
MACCHIETTI [or Maglietti], GIROLAMO [Crocifissajo].
It. Florence 1535/4-1564/1600. B-T.
MAC COLL, DUGALD SUTHERLAND.
Scot. b. Glasgow, 1859. T.
MAC CORD, CHARLES WILLIAM.
Am. Allegheny City, Pa. 1852-1923 Bridgport, Conn. A020-F.
MAC CORD, MARY NICHOLENA.
Am. b. Bridgport, Conn.; ad. 1934 New York. A.
MAC COY, GUY.
Am. ex. 1934 New York. M.
MAC CUISTON, [Miss] JACQUES [Jax]. (S)
Am. b. Texarkana, Tex. 1906; ad. 1934 Dallas, Tex. A.
MAC CULLOCH, HORATIO.
Scot. Glasgow 1805-1867 Edinburgh. B-DNB-E-T.
MAC CURDY, HATTIE.
Can. b. Leipzig, Ger. 1883; ad. 1934 China. M.
MAC DERMOTT, STEWART SINCLAIR. (Et)
Am. b. New York 1889; ad. 1934 Same. A.
MACDONALD, BARBARA. (S)
Eng. ex. 1934 London. M.

MACDONALD, Evan.
Can. ex. 1935 Toronto, Ont. M.
MACDONALD, Frank E.
Am. b. Kansas City, Mo. 1896; ad. Same. A.
MACDONALD, G. Alister. (Et)
Am. ad. 1935 Papete, Tahiti. M.
MAC DONALD, Harold L.
Am. b. Manitowoc, Wis. 1861. A12-F.
MAC DONALD, James. (Ill)
Am. ad. 1934 New York. M.
MAC DONALD, James E. H.
Can. b. Durham, Eng. 1873; d. 1932 Canada. M.
MAC DONALD, James Wilson Alexander. (S)
Am. Steubenville, O. 1824-1908 Yonkers, N. Y. A07-DAB-F-Ta-4-15-46-167-168.
MAC DONALD, James W. G.
Scot. b. Thurso; ad. 1935 Vancouver, B. C., Can. M.
MAC DONALD, John Blake.
Scot. Boharm 1829-1901 Edinburgh. B-DNB-T.
MAC DONALD, Lawrence. (S)
Scot. Perthshire 1799-1878 Rome, It. DNB-E.
MAC DONALD, Manley E.
Can. b. Port Anne, Ont.; ac. 1933. M.
MAC DONALD, Saint Claire. (Min)
Am. ad. 1934 New York. M.
MAC DONALL, Augus Peter.
Am. St. Louis, Mo. 1876-1927 Westport, Conn. A20-F-W14.
MAC DOUGALL, John A. (Min)
Am. b. New York 1843; ac. 1915 Same. A12-F-6.
MAC DOUGALL, Robert Bruce.
Am. d. 1931 Long Beach, N. Y. A028.
MAC DOWELL, Patrick (S)
Ir. Belfast 1799-1870 London. DNB-T.
MAC DOWELL, Susan Hannah.
Am. b. Phila., Pa. 1851. F-15.
MACEDO. *see* Clovio.
MACFARLAN, Christina.
Am. b. Phila., Pa.; ad. 1926 Same. A12-F.
MAC FARLANE, David H.
Can. ad. 1935 Montreal, Can. M.
MAC GILLIVRAY, James Pittendrigh. (S)
Scot. b. Inverurie 1856; ad. 1929 Edinburgh. Wa1929.
MAC GILVARY, Norwood Hodge.
Am. b. Bangkok, Siam 1874; ad. 1934 Pittsburgh, Pa. A-F-W.
MAC GINNIS, Henry R.
Am. b. Martinsville, Ind. 1875; ad. 1934 Trenton, N. J. A.
MAC GOWAN, Clara.
Am. b. Montreal, Can. 1895; ad. 1934 Chicago. A.
MAC GREGOR, Donald.
Am. b. Phila., Pa.; ac. 1915. A12.
MAC GREGOR, Robert.
Scot. Edinburgh 1848-1922. B-T.
MAC GREGOR, Sarah Newlin. (Min)
Mrs. Donald Mac Gregor.
Am. b. Penn.; ad. 1934 Princeton, N. J. A.
MAC GREGOR, William Yorke.
Scot. Finnart 1885-1923. B-Y01924-825.
MAC GUINESS, W. Bingham.
Ir. ac. 1914 in Dublin. M.
MAC GURRIN, Buckley.
Am. b. Kalamazoo, Mich. 1896; ad. 1934 Hollywood, Calif. M.
MACHADO, Cyrillo Volkmar.
Port. Lisbon 1748-1823. M.
MACHANIC, Ethel.
Am. b. Burlington, Vt. 1908; ad. 1934 Boston. A.
MACHARD, Jules Louis.
Fr. Sampars 1839-1900 Bellevue. B-T.
MACHEREN, Philip van.
Dut. Middelburg 1632-1699 Amsterdam. B-T.
MACHIAVELLI. *see* Macchiavelli.
MACHIN, [Mrs.] George Keeler.
Am. Ohio 1841-1917 Asbury Park, N. J. A014.
MACHO, Victorio. (S)
Sp. b. Palencia 1885; ac. 1930 Madrid. T.
MACHY, Pierre Antonie de.
see Demachy, Pierre Antoine.
MAC IAN [or M'Ian], Robert Ronald.
Scot. Edinburgh 1803-1856 London. DNB-T.
MAC INTOSH, Frank. (Ill)
Am. ac. 1934 New York. M.
MAC INTOSH, Marian T.
Am. b. Belfast, Ir.; ad. 1934 Princeton, N. J. A.
MAC INTOSH, William W. (S)
Am. b. Phila., Pa.; ac. 1915 Same. A12.
MACIP, Vincente Juanes.
see Joanes, Juan de.
MACK, Frank.
Am. ad. 1935 Atlanta, Ga. M.
MACKALL, R. Mc Gill.
Am. b. Balt., Md. 1889; ad. 1934 Same. A.
MACKAY, Edwin Murray.
Am. Sebewaing, Mich. 1869-1926 Detroit. A023-F.
MACKAY, Frances I. (S)
Am. b. Balt., Md. 1906. Cs.
MACKAY, William Andrew. (Mu)
Am. b. Phila., Pa. 1878; ad. 1934 New York. A-F.
MACKE, August.
Ger. Meschede 1887-1914 in War. E-T.
MACKENNAL, [Sir] Bertram. (S)
Aust. Melbourne, Victoria 1863-1931. Yo1932-798.
MACKENZIE, Catherine.
Am. ad. 1935 Portland, Ore. M.
MAC KENZIE, Frederick.
Scot. Edinburgh 1787-1854 London. B-DNB-T.
MAC KENZIE, J. Hamilton.
Scot. d. 1926. M.
MAC KENZIE, Roderick D.
Am. b. London 1865; ad. 1934 Mobile, Ala. A.
MAC KENZIE, R. Tait. (S)
Can. b. Almonte, Ont.; ad. 1935 Same. M.
MAC KENZIE, Samuel.
Scot. Cromarty 1785-1847 Edinburgh. DNB-T.
MACKESSON, John.
Am. ad. 1935 Paris, Fr. M.
MACKIE, Charles H.
Scot. Aldershot 1862-1920. B-T.

MAC KILLOP, WILLIAM.
Am. b. Phila., Pa.; ad. 1934 New York. A.
MAC KINLAY, MARY.
Eng. ad. 1934 Bushey. M.
MAC KINLAY, MIGUEL.
Aust. b. Guadalajura, Sp. 1895; ad. 1934 Essex, Eng. Wa.
MAC KINNON, ARCHIBALD ANGUS. (Et)
Am. d. 1918 East Orange, N. J. A016.
MACKINNON, [Miss] SINE.
Ir. b. Down 1901; ad. 1934 Paris. Wa.
MAC KINTOSH, CHARLES RENÉ.
Scot. 1868-1928. M.
MAC KNIGHT, DODGE.
Am. b. Prov., R. I. 1860; ad. 1934 East Sandwich, Mass. A-F-W-224.
MAC KUBIN, FLORENCE.
Am. Florence, It. 1861-1918 Balt., Md. A015-DAB-F-W10.
MACKY, CONSTANCE L.
Aust. ad. 1934 San Fran., Calif. M.
MACKY, E. SPENCER.
Am. ad. 1934 San Fran., Calif. M.
MAC LANE [Myrtle], JEAN.
Mrs. John C. Johansen.
Am. b. Chicago 1878; ad. 1934 New York. A-F-W-46.
MAC LAUGHLAN, DONALD SHAW. (Et)
Am. b. Boston 1876; ad. 1935 New York. A12-B-F-46.
MACLEAN, ALEXANDER.
Eng. b. London 1877; ad. 1934 Same. Wa-Y1928.
MACLEAN, THOMAS NELSON. (S)
Eng. Deptford 1845-1894 London. B-Hs-T.
MAC LEAN, WILLIAM.
Am. ad. 1934 New York. M.
MAC LEAN, WILLIAM LACY.
Am. Ohio 1860-1930 Maryland. A027.
MAC LEARY, BONNIE. (S)
Am. b. San Antonio, Tex. 1892; ad. 1934 New York. A-Cs-W.
MAC LEAY, KENNETH [The Younger]. (Min)
Scot. Oban 1802-1878 Edinburgh. B-DNB-T.
MAC LEISH, NORMAN HILLIARD.
Am. b. Glencoe, Ill. 1890; ad. 1934 Same. A.
MAC LELLAN, CHARLES A.
Am. b. Trenton, Ont., Can. 1885; ad. 1934 Wilmington, Del. A.
MAC LENNAN, EUNICE CASHION.
Am. b. Marquand, Mo. 1888; ad. 1934 Santa Barbara, Calif. A.
MAC LEOD, ALEXANDER S.
Am. b. Canada 1888; ex. 1934 New York. A28-F.
MAC LEOD, [Miss] YAN. (S)
Am. ad. 1935 Paris, Fr. M.
MAC LEOD, LOUISA ELIZABETH GARDEN.
Am. b. England; ad. 1934 Los Angeles, Calif. W.
MACLEOD, WILLIAM DOUGLAS. (Et)
Scot. b. Clarkston 1892; ad. 1934 Glasgow. Wa.
MACLET, ÉLISÉE.
Fr. b. Paris 1881. DBA.
MACLISE, DANIEL.
Ir. Cork 1806-1870 London. B-Bd-C-DNB-E-T.
MAC MASTER, WILLIAM E.
Am. b. Ballston, N. Y. 1823. C-Fa-T.
MAC MONNIES, FREDERICK WILLIAM. (S-P)
Am. b. Brooklyn, N. Y. 1863; ad. 1934 New York. A-B-E-F-Hs-W-46.
MAC MONNIES, MARY FAIRCHILD.
see Low, [Mrs.] Will H.
MAC MORRIS, LE ROY DANIEL.
Am. b. Sedalia, Mo. 1893; ad. 1934 New York. A.
MAC MULLEN, MARY SHAW.
Eng. ex. 1934 in London. M.
MAC NAUGHTON, MARY HUNTER.
Am. ad. 1934 Palestine, Tex. A.
MAC NEE, [Sir] DANIEL.
Scot. Fintry 1806-1882 Edinburgh. B-C-DNB-E-T.
MAC NEIL, CAROL BROOKS. (S)
Mrs. Hermon Atkins Mac Neil.
Am. b. Chicago 1871; ad. 1934 College Point, L. I., N. Y. A-B-Cs-F-W-46.
MAC NEIL, HERMON ATKINS. (S)
Am. b. Everett, Mass. 1866; ad. 1934 College Point, L. I., N. Y. A-B-Cs-E-F-W-46.
MAC NUTT, JOSEPH SCOTT.
Am. b. Russell, Wyo. 1885; ad. 1934 St. Louis, Mo. A.
MACOMBER, MARY LIZZIE.
Am. Fall River, Mass. 1861-1916 Boston. A013-DAB-F-46-104-829.
MACOMBER, STEPHEN.
Am. ad. 1934 Westerly, R. I. A.
MACONACHY, HENRY DARNELL.
Am. ac. 1930. M.
MAC PHERSON, JOHN HAVARD.
Am. b. Phila., Pa. 1894; ad. 1935 Bushkill, Pa. M.
MAC PHERSON, MARGARET CAMPBELL.
Scot. b. St. Johns, N. F.; ac. 1898-1914 Paris. T.
MAC PHERSON, MARGARET ROSE.
Mrs. W. G. Preston.
Am. b. Adelaide, So. Aust. 1877. M
MAC PHERSON, MARIE RAUCHFUSS.
Am. b. Cinn., O. 1879; ad. 1934 Same. A12-M.
MAC PHERSON, ORISON. (Ill)
Am. ad. 1933 Phila., Pa. M.
MAC RAE, ELMER LIVINGSTON.
Am. b. New York 1875; ad. 1934 Cos Cob, Conn. A-F-W
MAC RAE, EMMA FORDYCE.
Mrs. Homer Swift.
Am. b. Vienna, Aus. 1887; ad. 1934 New York. A-W
MACRINO, D'ALBA [Giangiacomo Fava].
It. Vercelli 1470?-1528? Alba. T-V.
MACRUM, GEORGE HERBERT.
Am. b. Pittsburgh, Pa. 1888; ad. 1934 New York. A-F-W.
MACSOUD, NICOLAS S.
Am. b. Zahle, Mt. Lebanon, Syria 1884; ad. 1934 Brooklyn, N. Y. A.
MAC TAGGART, WILLIAM R.
Scot. Campbeltown, 1835-1910 Edinburgh. B-T.

MACTEY, Nathan. (Ill)
Am. ad. 1934 New York. M.
MAC VEAGH, Louis Thoron.
Am. b. Lenox, Mass.; ad. 1934 New York. A.
MAC WHIRTER, John A.
Scot. Edinburgh 1839-1911 London. B-C-DNB-T.
MAC WHITE, Paula.
Mrs. Michael Mac White.
Dan.-Ir. b. Hillerod, Denmark; ad. 1934 Wash., D. C. M.
MACY, Harriet.
Am. b. Des Moines, Ia.; ad. 1934 Same. A.
MACY, Madeleine.
Am. ad. 1935 New York. M.
MACY, William Starbuck.
Am. New Bedford, Mass. 1853-1916. C-F-15.
MA DAN, Fred B.
Am. ad. 1934 Brooklyn, N. Y. M.
MADDOX, Willis.
Eng. Bath 1813-1853 Constantinople, Turkey. DNB-T.
MADEIRA, [Mrs.] Clara N.
Am. b. Phila., Pa.; d. 1929 Same. A029.
MADELINE, Paul.
Fr. Paris 1864-1921. B-DBA.
MADER, George.
Swi. Steinach 1824-1881 Bad-Gastein. B-T.
MADER, Joseph.
Bav. ac. 1927 in Prien, Bav. M.
MADERNO, Stefano. (S)
It. Bissone 1576-1636 Rome. Hs-T.
MADOU, Jean Baptiste.
Belg. Brussels 1796-1877 Same. B-C-E-T.
MADRASSI, Lucien [or Luca]. (S)
Fr. b. Paris; ad. 1934 Same. DBA-T.
MADRAZO Y KUNT, Don Fredrigo de.
Sp. Rome, It. 1815-1894 Madrid. B-E-T.
MADRAZO, Raymundo de.
Sp. Rome, It. 1841-1920 Versailles, Fr. B-C-DBA-T.
MADROZO Y AGUDO, José.
Sp. Santander 1781-1859. B-T.
MADROZO Y GARRETA, Ricardo de.
Sp. Madrid 1852-1917. B-T.
MADSEN, Otto.
Am. b. Germany 1882; ac. 1926 Kansas City, Mo. A20-F.
MAELESKIRCHER, Gabriel.
Ger. ac. 1455-1496 Munich. T.
MAELLO SALVADOR, Mariano.
Sp. Valencia 1739-1819 Madrid. B-T.
MAENE, Edward. (S)
Am. 1852-1931 Phila., Pa. A028.
MAERINO D'Alba [Fava].
see Macrino D'Alba.
MAES [or Maas], Aert van.
Dut. ac. 1640 in Amsterdam. T.
MAES [or Maas], Dirk [or Thedorus].
Dut. Haarlem 1656-1715/17 The Hague. B-C-T.
MAES [or Maas], Godefried.
Flem. Antwerp, Belg. 1649-1700/10. B-C-T.
MAES, Jan Baptiste Lodewyck [Canini].
Flem. Ghent, Belg. 1794-1856 Rome, It. B-T.
MAES [or Maas], Nicolaes.
Dut. Dordrecht 1632-1693 Amsterdam. B-Bd-C-E-T-722-941.
MAES, Peter. (Eg)
Flem. ac. 1572-1591 in Cologne, Ger. T.
MAESCH, Ferdinand.
Am. b. Mühlhausen, Ger. 1865; ad. 1934 Yonkers, N. Y. A.
MAESTRO. *see* Master.
MAETERLINCK, Louis.
Belg. b. Ghent, Belg. 1846. B-T-449.
MAFAI, Marco.
It. b. 1902 in Italy. M.
MAGANZA, Allessandro.
It. Venice 1556-1630 Same. B-T.
MAGANZA Family.
It. ac. 16-17th Cent. in Venice. T.
MAGAUD, Antoine Jean Baptiste Dominique.
Fr. Marseilles 1817-1899 Same. B-T.
MAGEE, James C.
Am. Brooklyn, N. Y. 1846-1924 Phila., Pa. A021-F.
MAGEE, Rena Tucker Kohlman.
Mrs. Franklin Magee.
Am. b. Indianapolis, Ind. 1880; ad. 1934 New York. A-W.
MAGER, Charles A. (Cart.)
Am. b. Newark, N. J. 1878; ad. 1934 So. Orange, N. J. A.
MAGGS, J. C.
Br. ac. 1819. Fa-M.
MAGIE, Gertrude. (Et)
Am. b. Trenton, N. J. 1862; ad. 1934 Princeton, N. J. A.
MAGNASCO, Alessandro [Lissandrino].
It. Genoa 1681-1749 Same. B-T.
MAGNE DE LA CROIX, Louis Auguste Paul.
Fr. b. Paris 1875; ad. 1931 Same. DBA.
MAGNE, Désiré Alfred.
Fr. b. Luisgnan 1885. B-DBA-T.
MAGNIER [or Maniére], Laurent. (S)
Fr. Paris 1618-1700. B-T.
MAGNIER, Philippe. (S)
Fr. Paris 1647-1715 Same. B-T.
MAGNUS, Eduard.
Ger. Berlin 1799-1872 Same. B-C-T.
MAGNUSSEN, Christian Karl.
Ger. Bredstedt, 1821/4-1896. B-T.
MAGNUSSON, Kristjan H.
Am. b. Isafjord, Iceland 1903; ad. 1934 Winchester, Mass. A.
MAGONIGLE, Edith Marion. (Mu)
Mrs. H. Van Buren Magonigle.
Am. b. Brooklyn, N. Y. 1887; ad. 1934 New York. A-W.
MAGONIGLE, H. Van Buren. (S)
Am. b. Bergen Heights, N. J. 1867; ad. 1934 New York. A.
MAGRATH, Edmund.
Am. ad. 1934 East Orange, N. J. M.
MAGRATH, William.
Am. Cork, Ir. 1838-1918 New York. A12-C-F-15.
MAHARANA, Giridhari. (S)
Br.-India. ac. 1930 in Orissa, India. M.
MAHÉ, Edouard.
Fr. b. Rennes 1905. DBA.
MAHIER, Edith.
Am. b. Baton Rouge, La. 1892; ad. 1934 Norman, Okla. A.

MAHL, CLARA. (Et)
Am. ex. 1934 New York. M.
MAHLER, REBECCA.
Am. b. New York 1871; ad. 1935 Same. A12-M.
MAHON, JOSEPHINE.
Am. b. Caldwell, N. J. 1881; ad. 1934 Same. A.
MAHONEY, CYRIL. (Mu)
Eng. b. London 1903; ac. 1930 Same. M.
MAHONEY, JAMES OWEN.
Am. b. Dallas, Tex. 1907; ad. 1934 Same. M.
MAHONEY, JOHN H.
Am. Wales 1855-1919 Indianapolis, Ind. A20-F-181.
MAHONY, FELIX.
Am. b. New York; ad. 1934 Wash., D. C. A.
MAIANO [or Majano], BENEDETTO DA. (S)
It. Florence, 1442-1497. Hs-V-450.
MAIANO, GUILIANO DA.
It. ac. 1599-1652 in Turin. T-V.
MAIER-KRIEG, EUGEN. (P-S)
Am. b. Ger.; ad. 1934 Los Angeles, Calif. M.
MAIGNON, ALBERT PIERRE RENÉ.
Fr. Beaumont, 1845-1908. B-C-T.
MAILLART, DIOGÈNE ULYSEE NAPOLÉON.
Fr. 1840-1926 Paris. B-C-DBA-T.
MAILLART, ÉMILE.
Fr. ac. 1884-1893 in Paris. B-T.
MAILLAUD, FERNAND.
Fr. b. Mouhet 1863. B-DBA-T.
MAILLET, JACQUES LÉONARD. (S)
Fr. Paris 1823-1895 Same. B-T.
MAILLOL, ARISTIDE JOSEPH BONAVENTURE. (S)
Fr. b. Banyuls 1861; ac. 1934 Paris. B-DBA-Hs-T-700-798-813-884.
MAILLOL, GASPARD.
Fr. b. Barcelona, Sp. 1880. DBA-T.
MAILLOS, ANDRÉ JEAN MARIE.
Fr. b. Paris 1871. DBA.
MAILLOT, THÉODORE PIERRE NICOLAS.
Fr. Paris 1826-1888 Passy. B-T.
MAIN, WILLIAM. (Eg)
Am. b. New York; d. 1876. F-2-7.
MAINARDI, SEBASTIANO DE BARTOLO.
It. San Gimignano, 1460-1513/5 Florence. B-T-V.
MAINDRON, ÉTIENNE HIPPOLYTE. (S)
Fr. Champtoceaux, 1801-1884. B-T.
MAINDS, ALLAN DOUGLASS.
Scot. b. Helensburg 1881; ad. 1934 Ponteland. Wa.
MAINERI, BARTOLOMEO.
It. ac. 1461-1477 in Reggio. B-T.
MAINERI, GIOVANNI BATTISTA.
It. b. Genoa, 1600-1657. B-T.
MAINERI, GIOVANNI FRANCESCO.
It. ac. 1486-1504/5 Parma. B-T.
MAINERI, JACOPINO.
It. ac. 1461-1467 in Reggio. B-T.
MAINGAUD, MARTIN.
Fr. ac. 1699 in Paris. B-T.
MAINO. *see* Mayno.
MAINSSIEUX, LUCIEN.
Fr. b. Voiron 1885. DBA.
MAIO, SALVATORE DE.
Am. ad. 1934 New Haven, Conn. M.
MAIR [or Mayr], ALEXANDER. [Monagramist A.M.].
Ger. Augsburg 1559-1620. B-T.
MAIR VON LANDSHUT, NICOLAUS ALEXANDER.
Ger. ac. 1492-1514 in Landshut. B-T.
MAIRE, JEAN BAPTISTE. (S)
Fr. Besançon, 1789-1859. B-T.
MAISON, PIERRE EUGÈNE JULES.
Fr. Aube 1814-1879 Paris. B-T.
MAISON, RUDOLF. (S)
Ger. Regensburg 1854-1904 Munich. B-Hs-T.
MAISTRE, LE ROY LIVINGSTONE DE.
Aust. b. Sydney, N. S. W. 1898; ad. 1935 London, Eng. M.
MAITANI, LORENZO. (S)
It. Milan 1275-1330 Orvieto. Hs-T.
MAITLAND, LOUIS GILL.
Eng. 1854-1928. M.
MAÎTRE. *see* Master.
MAIUS [or Magius]. (Illuminator)
Sp. ac. 926 near Leon, Spain. M.
MAJANO, BENEDETTO DA. *see* Maiano.
MAJOLI, EZIO OLIO.
It. ex. 1934 New York. M.
MAJOR, CHARLOTTE RUTH.
Am. ad. 1934 Milwaukee, Wis. A.
MAJOR, ERNEST L.
Am. b. Wash., D. C. 1864; ad. 1934 Boston. A-F.
MAJOR, HENRY. (Cari)
Am. ad. 1935 New York. M.
MAJOR, JAMES PARSONS. (Eg)
Am. England 1818-1900 Somerville, N. J. F-2-7.
MAJOR, THOMAS. (Eg)
Eng. 1720-1799 London. B-DNB-T.
MAJORELLE, JACQUES.
Fr. b. Nancy; ac. 1935 Paris. DBA.
MAKART, HANS.
Aus. Salzburg 1840-1884 Vienna. B-C-E-T.
MAKIELSKI, BRONISLAU A.
Am. b. So. Bend, Ind. 1901; ad. 1934 Detroit, Mich. A.
MAKIELSKI, LEON A.
Am. b. Morris Run, Pa. 1885; ad. 1934 Detroit, Mich. A.
MAKO, B.
Am. b. Budapest 1890; ad. 1934 Los Angeles, Calif. M.
MAKOVSKY, CONSTANTIN EGOROVITCH.
Rus. Moscow 1839-1915 Leningard. B-DBA-T.
MAKOVSKY, VALDIMIR EGOROVITCH.
Rus. b. Moscow 1846; d. 1920. B-T.
MAKOWSKY, TADÉ JOSEPH.
Pol. Cracow 1882-1932 Paris. DBA.
MALACAN, JEAN BAPTISTE. (S)
Fr. b. Béziers, 1875. B-DBA.
MALANCA, JOSÉ.
Peruvian. ex. 1929 New York. M.
MALARDOT, CHARLES ANDRÉ. (Eg)
Fr. b. Metz, 1817. T.
MALATHIER, ANDRÉ.
Fr. d. 1852 Paris. T.

MALBONE, Edward Greene. (Min)
Am. Newport, R. I. 1777-1807 Savannah, Ga. B-Bd-C-DAB-F-1-2-3-4-6-30-45-66-179-182-184.
MALCHIN, Karl Wilhelm Christian.
Ger. Kröpelin 1838-1923 Schwerin. C-T.
MALCOM [or Malcolm], James Peller. (Eg)
Am. Phila., Pa. 1767-1815 London. B-Bd-DAB-DNB-F-2-7-40-84.
MALCOM, Thalia Westcott.
Mrs. Donald Malcom.
Am. b. New York 1885; ad. 1934 Paris. A-F.
MALCZEWSKI, Jacek Hyacinth.
Pol. Radom 1854-1929. B-T.
MALCZEWSKI, Rafel.
Pol. b. 1892; ad. 1934 Zakopane. M.
MALDARELLI, Oronzio. (S)
Am. b. Naples, It. 1892; ad. 1934 New York. Cs-M.
MALDURA, Cesare C.
Am. Rome, It. 1853-1907 New York. A06.
MALER ZU SCHWAZ, Hanz.
[Master of the Welzer Portraits].
Aust. Tyrolese, 1488-1529? M-T.
MALESPINA, Louis Ferdinand.
Fr. b. Nancy 1874. B-DBA-T.
MALET, Guy Warre.
Eng. b. Southsea 1900; ad. 1934 London. Wa.
MALET, Joseph Frédéric Antonin. (S)
Fr. b. Millau 1873. B-DBA-T.
MALHOA, José.
Por. b. Caldas 1860. B-T.
MALI, Christian Friedrich.
It. 1832-1906 Munich, Ger. B-T.
MALIAVINE, Philippe.
Rus. b. Samara, 1869. B-DBA-T.
MALICOAT, Philip C.
Am. b. Indianapolis, Ind. 1908; ad. 1934 Provincetown, Mass. A.
MALIN, Violet Stevenson.
Am. ad. 1934 Youngstown, O. M.
MALINOWSKI, A. (S)
Rus. b. Russia; ac. 1933 Copenhagen, Denmark. M.
MALJUTIN, Ssergej Wassiljevitsch.
Rus. b. Moscow 1859. B-T.
MALKNECHT, Dominque. (S)
Fr. Tyrol, Swi. 1793-1878 Paris. B-T.
MALLEBRANCHE, Louis Claude.
Fr. Caen 1790-1838 Same. B-T.
MALLET, Antoine. (S)
Fr. b. Clermont 1865. DBA.
MALLET, Beatrice. (Ill)
Eng. b. Long Eaton; ac. 1929 in Paris. DBA.
MALLET, Jean Baptiste.
Fr. Grasse 1753-1835 Paris. B-T-900.
MALLET, Joseph Xavier.
Fr. Theil 1827. B-T.
MALLET, Pierre Louis Nicolas. (S)
Fr. b. Granquevilly; ac. 1848 Paris. B-T.
MALLET-VEAL, [Mrs.] Diana.
Eng. b. Woodford, Essex 1883; ad. 1934 South Rhodesia, Africa. M.
MALLETTE-PROUST, Alice.
Fr. b. Paris 1869. DBA.
MALLIA, René.
Fr. Paris 1885-1931. DBA.
MALLISON, Euphame Clason.
Am. b. Balt., Md. 1895; ad. 1934 University, Va. A.
MALLORY, Frances. (S)
Am. ad. 1934 Memphis, Tenn. M.
MALMSTRÖM, Johann August.
Swe. 1829-1901 Stockholm. B-T.
MALO, Vincent.
Flem. Cambray 1600-1650/6 Ghent, Belg. B-T.
MALONE, Robert James. (Cari)
Am. b. Birmingham, Ala. 1892; ad. 1934 St. James, L. I., N. Y. A.
MALONEY, Louise B.
Am. b. Cleveland, O. 1887; ad. 1935 Amsterdam, Holland. Fa-M.
MALOUEL [or Maelwael], Jean.
Flem. ac. 1396-1419 Paris. B-T.
MALSBARY, Charlotte.
Am. ex. 1935 New York. M.
MALTESE, Il, Francesco.
It. 1635-1680. T.
MALTON, James.
Eng. 1748-1803 London. B-DNB-T.
MALTON, Thomas [The Younger].
Br. London 1748-1804 Dublin. B-DNB-T.
MALYAVIN. *see* Maliavine.
MAMBOUR, Auguste.
Fr. b. Liége 1896. T-797.
MAMMERI, Si Azouaou.
Algerian. ac. 20th century. DBA-M.
MAN [or Maan], Cornelis Willems de.
Dut. Delft 1621-1706 Same. B-T.
MANATT, William Whitney. (S)
Am. b. Granville, O. 1875; ad. 1915 Berkeley, Calif. A12.
MANBERT, Barton.
Am. b. Jamestown, N. Y.; ad. 1934 Glendale, Calif. A.
MANBY, Thomas.
Eng. ac. 1670-1690 in London. B-DNB-T.
MANCEAUX, Hughes. (Ill)
Fr. b. Beauvais 1895. DBA.
MANCHON, Raphaël.
Fr. b. Dozule 1886. DBA.
MANCINI, Antonio.
It. Naples 1852-1930. B-M-T-191.
MANDEL, Johann August Eduard. (Eg)
Ger. Berlin 1810-1882 Same. B-T.
MANDER, Karel van I.
Flem. Meulebeke 1548-1606 Amsterdam, Holland. B-C-E-T-451.
MANDER, Karel van II.
Flem. Courtrai, Fr. 1579-1623 Delft, Holland. B-C-T-451.
MANDER, Karel van III.
Dut. Delft 1600-1672 Copenhagen, Denmark. B-T-451.
MANDLER, Ernest.
Czec. b. Humpolec 1886. T.
MANDYN, van Haarlem, Jan.
Dut. Haarlem 1500-1560. B-T.
MANÉ, Paul. (S)
Fr. b. Montevideo, Uruguay; ad. 1929 Paris. DBA.
MANÉ-KATZ.
Rus. b. Kremtchong 1894. DBA.
MÁNES, Anton.
Czec. 1784-1843 Prague. B-T.

MÁNES, Joseph.
Czec. Prague 1820-1871 Same. B-T.
MÁNES, Paolo. (S)
Sp. b. La Plata, Argentine; ac. 1931 Paris. DBA.
MANESSE, Georges Henri.
Fr. b. Rouen 1854. B-DBA-T.
MANET, Edouard.
Fr. Paris 1832-1883 Same. B-Bd-C-E-DBA-T-191-452-453-469-700-790-820-880-947.
MANETTI.
It. b. Tuscany; ex. 1934 London. M.
MANETTI Family.
It. ac. 16-17th Cent. in Siena. T.
MANETTI, Rutilio.
It. 1571-1637. T-722.
MANFREDI. *see* Bartolo. *see* Bartolomeo.
MANFREDINO, D'Aberto da Pistoia.
It. ac. 1280-1293 Pistoia. T.
MANGIN, Marcel Paul Maurice Stéphane.
Fr. b. Cherbourg; ac. 1875-1914 in Paris. B-T.
MANGLARD, Adrien.
Fr. Lyons 1695-1760 Rome. B-T.
MANGOLD, Burkhard.
Swi. b. Basel 1873. B-T.
MANGRAVITE, Pepino.
Am. b. Lipari, It. 1896; ad. 1934 Rye, N. Y. A-F-DBA.
MANGUIN, Henri Charles.
Fr. b. Paris 1874. DBA-T.
MANIEVITCH, Abraham.
Am. b. Russia 1883; ad. 1934 Bronx, N. Y. A.
MANIGAULT, Edward Middleton.
Am. Canada 1887-1922 San Fran., Calif. A019-F.
MANKOVSKY, Constantin.
Pol. Krakow 1861-1897. B-T.
MANLEY, Edna. (S)
Eng. ex. 1933 in London. M.
MANLEY, Thomas R. (Et)
Am. b. Buffalo, N. Y. 1853; ad. 1934 Upper Montclair, N. J. A-F.
MANLY, C. Macdonald.
Can. Surrey, Eng. 1855-1924 Canada. M.
MANN, Alexander.
Scot. Glasgow 1853-1908 London. B-T.
MANN, Cathleen.
Br. ad. 1935 in London. M.
MANN, Harrington.
Scot. b. Glasgow 1864; ad. 1934 London. B-T-Wa-868.
MANN, James Scrimgeon.
Scot. b. Dundee 1883; ex. 1934 London. Wa.
MANN, Joshua Hargrave Sams.
Eng. ac. 1849-1884 in London. T.
MANN, Parker.
Am. Rochester, N. Y. 1852-1918 Princeton, N. J. A016-F.
MANNEN, Paul William.
Am. b. Topeka, Kan. 1906; ad. Lawrence, Kan. A.
MANNEHIM, Jean.
Am. b. Kreuznach, Ger. 1863; ad. 1934 Pasadena, Calif. A-F-W.
MANNI, Gionnicola di Paolo.
It. ac. 1493-1544 in Perouse. B-T-722.
MANNIN, James.
Ir. ac. 1746-1779 in Dublin. B-DNB-T.
MANNING, Rosalie H. (S)
Am. b. Boston; ac. 1933. Cs.
MANNING, Samuel [The Elder]. (S)
Br. d. 1847. DNB.
MANNING, Samuel [The Younger]. (S)
Br. ac. 1846. DNB.
MANNING, William Westley.
Eng. b. 1868; ad. 1934 London. T-W.
MANNING-SANDERS, Joan.
Eng. ac. 1931. 454.
MANOIR, Irving K.
Am. b. Chicago 1891; ad. 1934 Same. A-F.
MANOLO, Manuel Martinez Hugue. (S)
Sp. b. Havana, Cuba 1876; ad. 1934 Paris. DNB-T.
MANOR, Florence. (S)
Am. b. Santa Cruz, Calif. 1881; ad. 1915 San Fran., Calif. A12.
MANOZZI, Giovanni.
It. San Giovanni 1590-1636. B-C-T-722.
MANSFIELD, Blanche McManus.
see McManus, B.
MANSFIELD, Louise Buckingham. (Ill)
Am. b. Le Roy, N. Y. 1876; ad. 1934 Brooklyn, N. Y. A-F.
MANSHIP, Paul. (S)
Am. b. St. Paul, Minn. 1885; ad. 1935 New York. A-Cs-E-F-DBA-Hs-Ta-W-66-71-172-455-693-721-768-779-798-809-813.
MANSION, L. [The Elder]. (S)
Fr. ac. 1785-1834 in Paris. B-T.
MANSON, George.
Scot. Edinburgh 1850-1876. B-DNB-E-T.
MANSON, James Bolivar.
Eng. b. London 1879; ad. 1934 Same. Wa.
MANSUETI, Giovanni di Niccolò.
It. Venice 1485-1527 Same. B-T-722.
MANSUR, Abu'l Kasun [Firdansi].
Per. Shadab 934-1020 Tus. M.
MANTEGAZZA, Antonio. (S)
It. [Milanese]; d. 1495. Hs.
MANTEGAZZA, Cristoforo. (S)
It. [Milanese]; d. 1482. Hs.
MANTEGNA, Andrea.
It. Padua 1431-1506 Mantua. B-Bd-C-E-T-V-456-722-917-923.
MANTELL, Ann.
Am. ex. 1935 New York. M.
MANTON, G. Greenville. (Ill)
Eng. 1855-1932. Y01933.
MANUEL, Bossini.
Am. b. Pieve di Teco, It. 1890; ad. 1934 New York. A.
MANUEL, Hans Rudolph.
Swi. Erlach 1525-1572 Basel. B-T.
MANUEL, Margaret. (Et)
Am. b. Hawick, Scot.; ad. 1935 Lake Grove, L. I., N. Y. A28-M.
MANUEL-DEUTSCH, Nicolaus.
Swi. ac. 1484-1531 in Berne. B-C-T-722.
MANUILOV, Giorgi.
Am. b. Rus.; ad. 1934 Stamford, Conn. M.
MANY, Alexis B.
Am. b. Indianapolis, Ind. 1879; ad. 1934 Wash., D. C. A-F.

MANYOKI [or Mangoki], ADAM DE.
Hun. Szokolya 1673-1741 Warsaw, Pol. B-T.
MANZINI. *see* Andrea di Guisto.
MANZUOLI, TOMMASO D'ANTONIO.
It. San Friano 1536-1575. B-T.
MAO I.
Chinese. ac. Sung Dynasty [960-1280]. E.
MAPES, JAMES JAY. (Min)
Am. New York 1806-1866 Same. F-2-6.
MARACHETTI, CHARLES. (S)
It. 1805-1868. M.
MARAFFI, LUIGI. (S)
Am. b. Aversa, It. 1891; ad. 1934 Phila., Pa. A.
MARAINI, ANTONIO. (S)
It. b. Rome 1886; ac. 1930 Florence. T.
MARAIS, ADOLPHE CHARLES.
Fr. b. Honfleur 1856. B-T.
MARAIS, J. B. (Eg)
Fr. b. 1768; ac. 1800 in Paris. B.
MARAIS-MILTON. *see* Milton, M.
MARAK, JULIUS EDUARD.
Czec. 1835-1899 Prague. B-T.
MARANS, MOISSAYE. (S)
Am. ad. 1935 Brooklyn, N. Y. M.
MARATTA [or Maratti], CARLO.
It. Carnerano 1625-1713 Rome. B-Bd-C-T-722.
MARATTA, HARDESTY GILMORE.
Am. Chicago 1864-1924. A022.
MARBLE, JOHN NELSON.
Am. Woodstock, Vt. 1855-1918 Same. A015-F.
MARC, FRANZ.
Ger. Munich 1880-1916 in War. E-457.
MARCANTONIO. *see* Raimondi, M.
MARCEL-BERONNEAU, PIERRE AMÉDEÉ.
Fr. b. Bordeaux 1869. DBA-T.
MARCELLIS VAN SCHRIECK. *see* Marsens, von S.
MARCERON-MAILLE, JEANNE.
Fr. b. Brive 1871. B-DBA-T.
MARCETTE, ALEXANDRE.
Belg. b. Spa 1853; ac. 1930 Paris. B-T.
MARCH, ELSIE. (S)
Eng. b. Hull; ad. 1934 Kent. Wa.
MARCH [or Marc], ESTÉBAN [Batailles].
Sp. Valencia 1590?-1660 Same. B-C-T.
MARCH [or Marc], MIGUEL.
Sp. Valencia 1633-1670 Same. B-C-T.
MARCH, SYDNEY. (S)
Eng. b. Hull; ad. 1935 Kent. T.
MARCH, VERNON. (S)
Eng. Hull 1891-1930. M.
MARCHAL, CHARLES FRANÇOIS.
Fr. Paris 1825-1877 Same. B-T.
MARCHAND, ANDRÉ.
Fr. b. Paris 1877. B-DBA-T.
MARCHAND [or Marchant], FRANÇOIS. (S)
Fr. ac. 1541-1553 in Orléans. B-T.
MARCHAND, JACQUES. (Eg)
Fr. b. 1769 Paris; ac. 1831 Same. B-T.
MARCHAND, JEAN HIPPOLYTE.
Fr. b. Paris 1883. E-DBA-T.
MARCHANT, EDWARD DALTON.
Am. Edgartown, Mass. 1806-1887 Asbury Park, N. J. F-2-6.
MARCHANT, NATHANIEL. (Med)
Eng. Hamburg, Ger. 1739-1816 London. DNB-T.
MARCHÉ, ERNEST GASTON.
Fr. b. Nemours 1864. DBA-T.
MARCHESI, ANDREA. *see* Mosca, Simone.
MARCHESI DA COTIGNOLA, GIROLAMO.
It. Cotignola 1480-1550 Naples. B-T-V-722.
MARCHETTI, GIROLAMO. *see* Marchesi.
MARCHI, DOMENICO [Tempesta].
It. Florence 1652-1718/37. B-T.
MARCHI, GIUSEPPE FILIPPO LIBERATI. (Eg)
It. Rome 1735?-1808 London. B-DNB-T.
MARCHIG, GIANNINO.
It. b. Triest 1888; ad. 1934 Florence. T-M.
MARCHIONE, D'AREZZO. (S)
It. ac. 1207-1216 in Arezzo. B-T.
MARCILLAT, GUILLAUME PIERRE DE.
Fr. Verdun 1467/75-1529/37 Arezzo, It. B-T.
MARCIUS-SIMONS, PINCKNEY.
Am. New York 1867-1909 Germany A07.
MARCKE DE LUMMEN, ÉMILE.
Fr. Sèvres 1827-1890 Hyers. B-T.
MARCKS, GERHARD. (S)
Ger. b. Berlin 1889; ex. 1935 Same. DBA-T.
MARCO. *see* Marko.
MARCO DA OGGIONE. *see* Oggione.
MARCONI [or Marcone], ROCCO.
It. b. Trévise; d. 1529 in Venice. B-T-722.
MARCOUSIS, LOUIS CASIMIR LADISLAS.
Pol. b. Warsaw 1882; ac. 1934 in Paris. DBA-T-797.
MARCUARD, ROBERT SAMUEL. (Eg)
Eng. 1751-1792? B-DNB-T.
MARCUS, PETER. (Et)
Am. New York 1889-1934 Stonington, Conn. A-F-Obit. N. Y. papers, 6-9-1934.
MARCUS, SEYMOUR.
Am. ad. 1934 New York. M.
MARE, ANDRÉ.
Fr. b. Argentine 1885; ac. 1929 Paris. DBA-T.
MARE, JOHN.
Am. ac. 1761-1768 New York. F.
MARE, JOHN DE. (Eg)
Am. b. Belgium; ac. 1850-1861 New York. F.
MARÉCHAL, RODOLPHE.
Fr. ac. 1920 Paris; d. 1927. DBA.
MARÉCHAL, VICTOR.
Fr. b. Paris 1879. DBA.
MARÉES, HANS VON.
Ger. Elberfeld 1837-1887 Rome, It. B-E-T-458.
MAREK, MAX. (Eg)
Am. ad. 1935 New York. M.
MAREMBERT, JEAN.
Fr. b. 1900; ac. 1934 Paris. DBA.
MARGARITONE [or Margarito], DA AREZZO [Magano].
It. Arezzo 1216-1293. B-T.
MARGESON, GEORGE T.
Am. ac. 1910-1920 in Boston. M.
MARGETSON, WILLIAM HENRY.
Eng. b. 1861; ex. 1934 London. T-Wa.
MARGOLIES [or Margo], BORIS. (Mu)
Rus. b. Wololskisek 1902; ad. 1935 Brooklyn, N. Y. M.
MARGOLIES, SAMUEL.
Am. ad. 1934 Hollis, L. I., N. Y. M.

MARGULIES, Joseph. (Et)
Am. b. Austria 1896; ad. 1934 New York. A.
MARIA BERGLER, Ettore de.
It. b. Naples 1851. B-T.
MARIAGE, Louis François ["Eguairam"].
Fr. ac. 1785-1811 in Paris. T.
MARIANO. *see* Bronzino.
MARIANO, Lorenzo di. (S)
It. 1476-1534. Hs.
MARIANO, Pellegino. *see* Pellegino.
MARIANO-ANDREU.
Sp. b. Barcelona 1888; ex. 1933 Pittsburgh, Pa. DBA-M.
MARIE, Adrien Emmanuel.
Fr. Neuilly, 1848-1891. B-T.
MARIE, Marin.
Fr. b. Fougerolles 1901; ad. 1934 Granville. M.
MARIE-TERESA, [Sister].
Am. b. Stillwater, Minn. 1877; ad. 1934 St. Paul, Minn. A-F.
MARIEN, Edmund.
Am. ad. 1935 New York. M.
MARIENTREU, R. Schneider von.
Aus. ac. 1933. M.
MARIESCHI, Jacopo [or Giacomo].
It. Venice 1711-1791. B-T.
MARIESCHI, Michele.
It. Venice 1696-1743 Same. B-T.
MARIETTE, Pierre Jean. (Ill)
Fr. Paris 1694-1774 Same. B-T.
MARIL, Herman.
Am. b. Balt., Md. 1908; ad. 1934 Same. A.
MARILHAT, Prosper Georges Antoine. [Called "The Egyptian."]
Fr. Vertaizon 1811-1847 Thiers. B-T-722.
MARILLIER, Clément Pierre. (Eg)
Fr. Dijon 1740-1808 Beaulieu. T.
MARIN, John.
Am. b. Rutherford, N. J. 1875; ad. 1934 Cliffside, N. J. A-F-46-105-459-700-701-779-809.
MARIN, Joseph Charles. (S)
Fr. Paris 1759-1834 Same. B-T.
MARIN, Louis. *see* Bonnet, L. M.
MARINELLI, Vincenzo.
It. 1820-1892 Naples. T.
MARINI, Antonio. (Eg)
It. Prato 1788-1861 Florence. T.
MARINI, Marino. (S)
It. ac. 1932 in Milan. M.
MARINI, Michele di Luca. (S)
It. b. Fiesole 1459. T-V.
MARINKO, George J.
Am. b. Derby, Conn. 1908; ad. Waterbury, Conn. A.
MARINSKY, Harry. (P-S)
Am. b. London 1909; ad. 1934 New York. M.
MARINUS, van Roymerswaele.
Dut. Seeland 1497-1567? B-T.
MARIOTTO, Bernardo di.
see Bernardino di M.
MARIOTTO di NARDO, Florent.
It. ac. 1394-1424 in Florence. T-V.
MARIS, Jacobus [or Jacob].
Dut. The Hague 1837-1899 Carlsbad, Ger. B-E-T-474.
MARIS, Matthys [or Matthew].
Dut. The Hague 1839-1917 London. B-T-474.
MARIS, Simon.
Dut. b. The Hague 1873. T.
MARIS, Willem.
Dut. The Hague 1844-1910. B-T.
MARK, Louis.
Am. b. Hungary 1867; ad. 1935 New York. F.
MARKELBACH, Alexandre.
Belg. Antwerp 1824-1906. B-T.
MARKHAM, Charles C.
Am. 1837-1907. M.
MARKHAM, Kyra.
Am. ad. 1935 Maplewood, N. J. M.
MARKHAM, Marion E.
Am. b. Syracuse, N. Y. 1875; ad. 1935 New York. F.
MARKIEVICZ, Kasimir Dunin.
Rus. b. Kiev 1874. T.
MARKLE, Alvan, Jr.
Am. b. Hazelton, Pa. 1899; ad. 1934 Same. A.
MARKÓ, Andrea.
Aus. Vienna 1831-1895. B-T.
MARKÓ, Karl [or Károly, The Elder].
Hun. Budapest 1791-1860 Florence, It. B-C-T.
MARKÓ, Karl [or Károly, The Younger].
Hun. Budapest 1822-1891 Moscow, Rus. B-T.
MARKOE, Francis Hartman.
Am. b. New York 1884; ad. 1934 Same. A.
MARKS, Henry Stacy.
Eng. London 1829-1898 Same. B-C-DNB-T.
MARKS, Isaac. (S)
Am. b. Lithuania 1859; ad. 1934 Harvey, Ill. A.
MARKS, Stella Lewis. (Min)
Mrs. Montague Marks.
Am. b. Melbourne, Aust. 1892; ad. 1934 New York. A.
MARKS, William. (Ill)
Am. d. 1906 Calumet, Mich. A06-F.
MARLATT, H. Irving.
Am. b. Woodhull, N. Y.; d. 1929 Mt. Vernon, N. Y. A026.
MARLET, Jean Henri. (Cari)
Fr. Autun 1770/1-1846/7 Paris. B-T.
MARLOW, Henry. (S)
Am. Liverpool, Eng. 1838-1911 New Rochelle, N. Y. A010.
MARLOW, William.
Eng. Southwark 1740-1813 Twickenham. B-DNB-T.
MARMION, Simon.
Fr. Valenciennes 1425-1489 Same. B-T.
MARNE, Jean Louis de.
see Demarne, J. L.
MAROCHETTI, Carlo [Baron]. (S)
It. Turin 1805-1867 London. B-DNB-E-T.
MARON, Anton von.
Aus. Vienna 1733-1808 Rome, It. B-T.
MAROÑIEZ, Georges Philibert Charles.
Fr. b. Douai 1865; d. 1933. B-DBA-T.
MARÓTI, Géza. (S)
Hun. b. Vörösvar 1875. T.

MARPLES, George. (Et)
Eng. ac. 1934 Liverpool. Wa.
MARQUE, Albert. (S)
Fr. b. Nanterre 1872. DBA-685.
MARQUES, Adolfo. (Carver)
Por. ad. 1935 Oporto, Portugal. M.
MARQUESTE, Laurent Honoré. (S)
Fr. Toulouse 1848-1920 Paris. B-E-DBA-T.
MARQUET, Aimé Benôit.
Fr. Lyons 1797-1865 Paris. B-T-827.
MARQUET, Pierre Albert.
Fr. b. Bordeaux 1875; ex. 1934 Chicago. DBA-T-827.
MARR, Carl.
Am. b. Milwaukee, Wis. 1858; ad. 1934 Munich, Ger. A-B-E-F.
MARREL [or Marellus], Jacob.
Dut. Utrecht 1614-1681/5 Frankfort, Ger. B-T.
MARRET, Henri Justin.
Fr. b. Paris 1878. B-DBA-T.
MARRIOTT, Frederick.
Eng. b. Stoke-on-Trent 1860. B-T-Wa1929.
MARRIOTT, Richard W.
Eng. ex. 1935 London. M.
MARRON, [Mrs.] Eugenie.
Am. ad. 1934 Glen Rock, N. J. M.
MARS, Ethel. (Eg)
Am. b. Springfield, Ill. 1876; ad. 1934 France. A.
MARS, Irma Bratton. (Ill)
Mrs. Reginald Degge Mars.
Am. b. Newton, Ia. 1901; ad. 1934 Des Plaines, Ill. A.
MARS, P. L.
Am. ad. 1934 New Orleans, La. M.
MARS, Reginald Degge. (Ill)
Am. b. Petersburg, Ill. 1901; ad. 1934 Des Plaines, Ill. A.
MARSAL, Edouard Antoine.
Fr. b. Montpellier 1845. B-T.
MARSCHALL, Rudolph. (S)
Aus. b. Vienna 1873. B-T.
MARSCHNER, Arthur A.
Am. b. Detroit, Mich. 1884; ad. 1934 Same. A.
MARSDEN, Edith Frances.
Am. b. Utica, N. Y.; ad. 1934 Springfield, Mass. A.
MARSDEN, Ruth G.
Am. b. Pittsfield, Mass. 1898; ad. 1934 Springfield, Mass. A.
MARSEILLE LA CROIX.
see La Croix, Charles F.
MARSENS [or Marcellis], van Shrieck, Otto.
Dut. Nimègue 1619-1678 Amsterdam. B-C-T-722.
MARSH, Anne Steele.
Am. ad. 1935 Essex Fells, N. J. M.
MARSH, Alice Randall. (Min)
Mrs. Fred Dana Marsh.
Am. b. Coldwater, Mich.; ac. 1930. A20-F-66.
MARSH, Charles Howard.
Am. b. Magnolia, Ia. 1885; ad. 1934 Orlando, Fla. A-F.
MARSH, Florence.
Mrs. Harold Dickson Marsh.
Am. ad. 1934 Portland, Ore. A.
MARSH, Fred Dana.
Am. b. Chicago 1872; ad. 1934 Ormond, Fla. A-F-W.
MARSH, Harold Dickson.
Am. b. Portland, Ore. 1889; ad. 1934 Same. A.
MARSH, James.
Am. ac. 1860-1865. Fa.
MARSH, [Mrs.] Lucile Patterson. (Ill)
Am. b. Rapid City, S. D. 1890; ad. 1934 New York. A28-M.
MARSH, Mary E.
Mrs. Conrad Buff.
Am. b. Cinn., O.; ad. 1934 Eagle Rock, Calif. A.
MARSH, Reginald.
Am. b. Paris, 1898; ad. 1934 New York. A-M.
MARSHALL ["Ben"], Benjamin.
Eng. 1767-1835 London. B-DNB-T.
MARSHALL, Charles.
Eng. London 1806-1890 Same. B-DNB-T.
MARSHALL, Clark S.
Am. b. 1882. M.
MARSHALL, Edward. (S)
Eng. 1578-1675. DNB-T.
MARSHALL, Frank Howard.
Am. b. England 1866; ad. 1934 Carmel, Calif. A-F.
MARSHALL, Frank W. (Ill)
Am. b. Prov., R. I. 1866; d. 1930 Same. A027-F.
MARSHALL, George.
Scot. d. 1732. B-T.
MARSHALL, Helen.
Eng. ex. 1934 in London. M.
MARSHALL, Herbert Menzies.
Eng. Leeds 1841-1913 London. B-T.
MARSHALL, Joshua. (S)
Eng. 1629-1678. DNB-T.
MARSHALL, Margaret J. (Ill)
Am. b. Phila., Pa. 1895; ad. 1934 Same. A.
MARSHALL, [Mrs.] Mary E.
Am. b. Plainfield, N. J.; ad. 1934 Phila., Pa. A.
MARSHALL, Mary Chiswell.
Am. b. Markham, Va.; ad. 1934 Columbia, S. C. A.
MARSHALL, Thomas Falcon.
Eng. Liverpool 1818-1878 London. B-DNB-T.
MARSHALL, Thomas W.
Am. ac. 1850-1874 New York. F-15.
MARSHALL, William. (Eg)
Eng. ac. 1630-1650 London. B-DNB-T.
MARSHALL, William Calder. (S)
Scot. Edinburgh 1813-1894 London. B-DNB-E-T.
MARSHALL, William Edgar. (Eg)
Am. New York 1837-1906 Same. A06-DAB-F-4-7-40-55-160-172.
MARSIGLIA, Gerlando.
Am. Italy 1792-1850 New York. F-2.
MARSILI, Emilio. (S)
It. b. Venice 1841. B-T.
MARSTRAND, Vilhelm Nikolaj.
Dan. Copenhagen 1810-1873 Same. B-C-T.
MARSY, Gaspard. (S)
Fr. Cambrai 1624-1681 Paris. B-T.

MARTENS, H.
Eng. ac. 1828-1845 in London. T.
MARTENS, THEODOR.
Ger. Wismar 1822-1884 Portici, It. C-T.
MARTENS, WILLY [or Willem].
Dut. b. Java 1856. B-T.
MARTIAL, ARMAND. (S)
Fr. b. Paris 1884. B-DBA-T.
MARTIN, ANTON MARIUS.
Fr. b. Arles 1869. DBA.
MARTIN, ARTHUR EDWARD.
Eng. d. 1932. Y01933.
MARTIN, BASIL EDWIN.
Am. b. England 1903; ad. 1934 New York. A.
MARTIN, CHARLES.
Eng. 1820-1906 London. B-T.
MARTIN, CHARLES J.
Am. b. Mansfield, Eng. 1886; ad. 1934 Bronxville, N. Y. M.
MARTIN, CHARLES MARIE FÉLIX (S)
Fr. Neuilly 1844-1916 Paris. B-T.
MARTIN, CLAUDE RENÉ.
Fr. b. Paris 1885. DBA.
MARTIN, DAVID.
Scot. Anstruther 1737-1798 Edinburgh. B-DNB-T.
MARTIN, ELIAS.
Swe. Stockholm 1739-1818 Same. B-DNB-T.
MARTIN, FRANCIS THOMAS BECKETT.
Am. b. Omaha, Neb. 1904; ad. 1934 Same. A.
MARTIN, FRITZ.
Bav. b. Leipzig, Ger. 1859; ac. 1892 Munich, Ger. B-T.
MARTIN, HOMER DODGE.
Am. Albany, N. Y. 1836-1897 St. Paul, Minn. C-DAB-E-F-T-1-15-46-70-104-127-173-174-225-701-748.
MARTIN, HENRI JEAN GUILLAUME.
see Henri-Martin, J. G.
MARTIN, JEAN BAPTISTE [The Elder].
Fr. Paris 1659-1735 Same. B-T-722.
MARTIN, JEAN BAPTISTE [The Younger].
Fr. Paris 1700-1741 Same. B-T-722.
MARTIN, JOHN.
Eng. Hexham 1789-1854 Douglas. B-C-DNB-E-T-722.
MARTIN, JOHN BRECKENRIDGE.
Am. b. London, Ky. 1857; ad. 1934 Dallas, Tex. A.
MARTIN, JOHN D.
Am. 1797-1857. M.
MARTIN, JOHN FREDERICK. (Eg)
Swe. Stockholm 1845-1808 Same. B-DNB-T.
MARTIN, KEITH MORROW.
Am. b. Lincoln, Neb. 1911; ad. 1935 New York. M.
MARTIN VON KLAUSENBURG.
see Kolozvár, M.
MARTIN, MARIA AUGUSTE. (S)
Fr. Dunleroi 1828-1910 Paris. B-T.
MARTIN, MARIE JOSEPH PIERRE. (S)
Fr. b. Neufchâteau 1890. DBA.
MARTIN, MILO. (S)
Swi. b. Morges 1893. DBA.
MARTIN, PIERRE DENIS [The Younger]
Fr. Paris 1672/3-1742 Same. B-T.
MARTIN, THOMAS MOWER.
Can. London, Eng. 1839-1934 Toronto, Ont. M-Obit. N. Y. papers, 3-17-1934.
MARTIN, TOM. (Ill)
Am. ad. 1934 New York. M.
MARTIN, WILLIAM.
Eng. ac. 1765-1821 in London. DNB-T.
MARTIN, WILLIAM ALISON.
Eng. ac. 1929 in Liverpool. Wa1929.
MARTIN, WILLIAM A. K.
Am. Phila., Pa. 1817-1867 Same. F.
MARTIN-FERRIÈRS, JACK.
Fr. b. 1893; ac. 1929 in Paris. DBA.
MARTIN-KAVEL, FRANÇOIS.
Fr. ac. 1881 in Paris. DBA.
MARTIN-SAUVAIGO, CHARLES.
Fr. b. Nice 1881. DBA.
MARTINEAU, ROBERT BRAITHWAITE.
Eng. London 1826-1869 Same. T.
MARTINET, ACHILLE LOUIS.
Fr. Paris 1806-1877 Same. B-T.
MARTINET, MARJORIE D'ORSI.
Am. b. Balt., Md. 1886; ac. 1934 Same. A.
MARTINETTI, ANGELO.
It. ac. 1875 in Rome. T.
MARTINEZ, ALFREDO RAMOZ.
Mex. ad. 1934 Los Angeles, Calif. M.
MARTINEZ, JOSÉ II.
Sp. Saragosse 1612-1682 Same. B-T.
MARTINEZ, JOSÉ PINOZO.
Sp. b. Rome, It. 1879; ac. 1933 Madrid. B-T.
MARTINEZ, JUAN MAZO.
see Mazo, Juan Bautista de.
MARTINEZ, JULIAN.
Indian (Am.) ad. 1934 Santa Fé, N. M. A-411.
MARTINEZ, RAMOS.
Mex. ex. 1935 Chicago. M.
MARTINEZ, SEBASTIAN.
Sp. Jaen 1602-1667 Madrid. B-C-T.
MARTINEZ, XAVIER [Orozco].
Am. b. Guadalajara, Mex. 1874; ad. 1934 Piedmont, Calif. A-F-W.
MARTINI, BERNARDINO [Zenale].
see Zenale, B.
MARTINI, HERBERT E.
Am. b. Brooklyn, N. Y. 1888; ad. 1934 Long Island City, N. Y. A.
MARTINI, JOSEPH DE.
Am. ex. 1932 New York. M.
MARTINI [or Memmi], SIMONE.
It. Siena 1283?-1344/5 Avignon. B-Bd-C-E-T-V-905.
MARTINI, STANISLAO. (S)
Am. 1837-1915 Boston, Mass. M.
MARTINO, ANTONIO PIETRO.
Am. b. Phila., Pa. 1902; ad. 1934 Same. A.
MARTINO DI BARTOLOMMEO DI BIAGIO.
It. ac. 1387-1434 Siena. T-V.
MARTINO DI BATTISTA. *see* Pellegrino.
MARTINO, GIOVANNI.
It. b. Naples 1870; ad. 1935 Phila., Pa. M-T.
MARTINO, MICHEL. (S)
Am. b. Caserta, It. 1889; ad. 1934 New Haven, Conn. A-F.
MARTINO DA UDINE.
see Pelligrino da San Daniele.

MARTINO DA VERONA.
It. d. 1412 Verona. T.
MARTINY, PHILIP. (S)
Am. France 1856-1927 New York.
A024-F-Hs-T-Ta-W14-19-104-167-175.
MARTIS, OTTAVIANO DI MARTINO DE.
see Nelli, Ottaviano di Martino de.
MARTORELL, BERNARDO [or Benito].
Sp. ac. 1433-1454 Barcelona. T.
MARTOZEN [or Martsen], JAN [or Jacob].
Dut. Haarlem 1609?-1647. B-T.
MARTY, ANDRÉ EDOUARD.
Fr. b. Paris 1882. DBA.
MARTY, EDOUARD.
Fr. Pleaux 1851-1913 Paris. T.
MARTY, LOUIS EDOUARD.
Fr. b. Paris 1871. DBA.
MARUSSIG, ANTON.
Aus. Gratz 1868-1925 Same. B-T.
MARUSSIG, GUIDO.
It. b. Trieste 1885. DBA-T.
MARUSSIG, PIETRO.
It. b. Trieste 1879; ad. 1934 Milan. M-T.
MARVAL, JACQUELINE.
Fr. b. Paris; d. 1932 Same. DBA.
MARVILLE, JEAN DE. (S)
Fr. d. 1389, Champmol. Hs.
MARX, MAURICE ROGER. (S)
Fr. b. Fontainebleau 1872. DBA.
MARX, SAMUEL A.
Am. b. 1885; ex. 1934 Chicago. M.
MARYON, HERBERT.
Eng. ad. 1934 New Castle. M-798.
MARZÁL DE SAS, ANDRÉS.
Sp. ac. 1393-1410 Valencia. T.
MARZIALE, MARCO.
It. Venice 1492-1507 Same. B-T.
MARZOCCHI DE BELLUCCI, NUMA.
Fr. b. Paris; ad. 1922 Same. B-DBA-T.
MARZOLO, LEO AURELIO.
Am. b. Martinez, Calif. 1887; ad. 1934 Chicago. A.
MAS Y FONDERILA, ARCADIO.
Sp. b. Barcelona 1850. T.
MASACCIO, MASO DI BARTOLOMMEO.
It. ac. 1445-1462. V.
MASACCIO, TOMMASO GUIDI.
It. Valdarno 1401/2-1428/9 Rome.
B-Bd-C-E-T-V-460-722.
MASANOBU, KANO.
Jap. Idzu 1453-1490 Kyoto. J-T.
MASANOBU, KITAO.
Jap. 1761-1816 Tokio. J-T.
MASANOBU, OKUMURA.
Jap. Baio 1668-1768 Tokio. J-T.
MASAYOSHI, SANKO.
Jap. 1761-1824 Tokio. T.
MASCAGNI, DONATO [Arsenio].
It. Florence 1579-1636 Same. T.
MASCRÉ, OSCAR LOUIS. (S)
Belg. Péronne, Fr. 1865-1929. DBA-Y01930.
MASE, CAROLYN CAMPBELL.
Am. b. Mattawan, N. Y.; ad. 1934 Utica, N. Y. A-F.
MASEGNE, JACOBELLO. (S)
It. ac. 1392 in Bologna. Hs-T.
MASEGNE, PIER PAOLO.
It. ac. 1392 in Bologna. Hs-T.
MASEREEL, FRANS.
Belg. b. Flanders 1889. DBA-T-10.
MASLEY, ALEXANDER SAMUEL.
Am. ad. 1934 Minn., Minn. A.
MASLINE, CAMILLE. (Ill)
Am. b. Greenwich, Conn. 1906; ad. 1935 New York. M.
MASO DA SAN FRIANO.
see Manzuoli, Tomasso d'Antonio.
MASO DI BIANCO.
It. ac. 1320-1346 Florence. T.
MASOLINO, TOMMASO DI CHRISTOFORE.
It. Panicale 1383?-1440 Florence.
E-T-460-722.
MASON, ARNOLD.
Eng. ad. 1934 Balearic Islands. M.
MASON, C. D. (S)
Am. France 1830-1915 Mineola, N. Y.
A012.
MASON, FRANK H. (Ill)
Eng. b. 1876; ad. 1934 London. Wa.
MASON, GEORGE CHAMPLIN.
Am. 1820-1894. Fa-M.
MASON, GEORGE HEMMING.
Eng. Wetley 1818-1872 London.
B-Bd-C-DNB-E-T.
MASON, JAMES. (Eg)
Eng. 1710-1780 London. B-DNB-T.
MASON, MARY STODDARD. (S)
Am. b. Jackson, Tenn.; ad. 1935 Elmsford, N. Y. F-W15.
MASON, MARY STUART TOWNSEND.
Mrs. William Clarke Mason.
Am. b. Zanesville, O. 1886; ad. 1934 Phila., Pa. A-F-W15.
MASON, MAUD MARY.
Am. b. Russellville, Ky. 1867; ad. 1934 New Canaan, Conn. A-F-W.
MASON, MURIEL.
Am. ex. 1935 New York. M.
MASON, NÖEL. (Eg)
Fr. Paris 1858-1889. B-T.
MASON, ROBERT LINDSAY. (Ill)
Am. b. Knoxville, Tenn. 1874. A28.
MASON, ROY MARTELL.
Am. b. Gilbert Mills, N. Y. 1886; ad. 1934 Batavia, N. Y. A-W.
MASON, WILLIAM ALBERT.
Am. Cambridge, Mass. 1855-1923 Phila., Pa.
A022-F.
MASQUERIER, JOHN JAMES.
Eng. Chelsea 1778-1855 Brighton. B-DNB-T.
M•ASSACCIO. *see* Masaccio.
MASSAGUER, CONRADO. (Cari)
Cuban. ex. 1934 New York. M.
MASSANI, POMPEO.
It. Florence 1850-1920 Same. B-T.
MASSARI, LUCIO.
It. Bologna 1569-1623/5. B-T.
MASSAU, EDMUND.
Ger. b. Düsseldorf 1860. B-T.
MASSAU [or Masseau], PIERRE FÉLIX. (S)
Fr. b. Lyons; ac. 1907 Paris. B.
MASSÉ, JEAN BAPTISTE.
Fr. Paris 1687-1767 Same. B-T.
MASSEGNE. *see* Masegne.
MASSES, BERTRAM. *see* Bertram-Masses.
MASSEY, STANLEY A.
Am. b. Delaware 1877. M.

MASSLOFF-TARDIEU, Pala Massimila de.
Fr. ac. 1931 in Paris. DBA.
MASSON, Alphonse Charles.
Fr. Paris 1814-1898. B-T.
MASSON, André.
Fr. b. in Belagny 1896; ex. 1935 New York. DBA-M.
MASSON, Antoine. (Eg)
Fr. Laury 1636-1700 Paris. B-Bd-T.
MASSON [or Massou], Benoît. (S)
Fr. Richelieu 1627-1684 Paris. B-T.
MASSON, François. (S)
Fr. 1745-1807 Paris. B-T.
MASSON, Madeleine. (Eg)
Fr. 1646-1713. B-T.
MASSON, Margaret. (Ill)
Am. b. Peterboro, Ont. Can.; ad. 1934 Penacook, N. H. A.
MASSONE, Giovanni.
It. ac. 1490 in Piedmont. B-T.
MASSOU. *see* Masson.
MASSYS [or Matsys], Cornelis.
Flem. Antwerp, Belg. 1510/2-1580/1 Same. B-Bd-C-T.
MASSYS [or Matsys], Jan II.
Flem. Antwerp, Belg. 1509/11-1575/80 Same. B-C-T.
MASSYS [or Matsys], Quentin.
Flem. Louvain, Belg. 1460/6-1530 Antwerp, Belg. B-Bd-C-E-T-722-903.
MAST, Herman van der.
Dut. Brielle 1550-1604 Delft. B-T.
MAST, Josephine.
Am. b. New York; ad. 1934 Brooklyn, N. Y. A.
MASTENBROEK, Johan Hendrik van.
Dut. b. Rotterdam 1875. B-DBA-T.
MASTER [Extensive card indexes listing the Masters who signed their works by symbols may be consulted at The Metropolitan Museum of Art. Frick Art Reference Library and The Pierpont Morgan Library, New York].
MASTER, A. F.
It. ac. 15th Cent.
MASTER, A. D. [Altar of St. Jerome.]
Ger. ac. 1511. Bd.
MASTER ALFONSO.
Sp. ac. 1473. Book No. 774.
MASTER ANDRÉ.
It. ac. 1410-1425 Venice.
MASTER BERTRAM OF MINDEN.
Ger. ac. 1367-1387.
MASTER B. X. G.
MASTER E. S.
Ger. ac. 1450-1470. Bd.
MASTER FLEMISH.
see Master of Antwerp.
MASTER 4 [School of Lucas Cranach].
Ger. ac. 1560.
MASTER FROM HOOGSTRAATEN. M.
MASTER F. V. B. [or Bocholt].
Ger. ac. 1455-1480. B-Bd.
MASTER, G. A., with the Calthorp. (Eg)
It. ac. 16th Cent. Bd.
MASTER G. Z.
Swi. ac. 16th Cent.
MASTER H. E.
see Beccafuni, Domenico di Pace.
MASTER H. H.
So. Ger. (Franconian); ac. 15th Cent.
MASTER I. A. M. [Zwolle].
Ger. ac. 1485 in Allemagne. B-Bd.
MASTER I. B.
Br. ac. 1821. Bd.
MASTER I. E.
It.
MASTER, J. S. [Jonas Silber].
Dut. ac. 1652.
MASTER L. CZ.
Ger. ac. 1492. Bd.
MASTER MATTHEW. (S)
Sp. ac. 1183. Hs.
MASTER MICHAEL THE FLEMING [Zittoz].
Ger. ac. 1481-1492.
MASTER M. Z. *see* Zasinger Matthaus.
MASTER N. A. R. [Reichs].
Dut. ac. 1528.
MASTER N. H.
Dut.
MASTER N. K.
Dut. ac. 18th Cent.
MASTER OF AIX ANNUNCIATION.
Fr. ac. 14th Cent.
MASTER OF ALBÁTARECH.
Sp. (Catalan) 14th-15th Cent.
MASTER OF ALKMAAR.
Dut. ac. 1504.
MASTER OF ANTWERP.
Flem. ac. 1518.
MASTER OF AUGSBURG.
Ger. ac. 1430.
MASTER OF BALAAM. (Eg)
Fr. ac. 15th Cent. Bd.
MASTER OF B. M.
Ger. ac. 1480. Bd.
MASTER OF CALVARY.
Flem. ac. 15th Cent.
MASTER OF CAPPENBERG.
[Victor Dünwege.]
Ger. early 16th Cent. in Westphalia. B-Bd.
MASTER OF CATHERINE VAN CLEEF.
Dut. ac. 15th Cent. in Utrecht.
MASTER OF COLOGNE.
Ger. ac. 15th Cent. B.
MASTER OF 1515.
It. ac. 1515-1520. Bd.
MASTER OF 1518.
Flem.
MASTER OF FLÉMALLE. *see also* Campin, Robert.
[or Master of the Merode Altarpiece.]
Flem. 1375?-1444.
MASTER OF FRANKFURT.
Flem. ac. 1493-1520. B-Bd-C.
MASTER OF LIESBORN.
Ger. ac. 1465-1520 in Westphalia. B-C.
MASTER OF MARIENLEBENS.
Ger. ac. 1463-1480.
MASTER OF MESSKIRCH.
Ger. ac. 1520-1550 in Haute-Sovabe. B.
MASTER OF MOULINS.
[Identified as Jean Perréal.]
Fr. Lyons 1455-1530 Paris. B-T.
MASTER OF OULTREMONT.
see Mostaert, Jan.

MASTER OF PANZANO.
[or Pieve of Panzano.]
It.
MASTER OF PARADISE.
Port. ac. 1525.
MASTER OF RIBAUCOURT.
Flem. ac. 17th Cent.
MASTER OF ST. BARTHOLOMÉ.
Ger. ac. 1470-1510. B-Bd.
MASTER OF ST. CHRISTOPHER.
Ger. ac. 1440-1460.
MASTER OF ST. ERASMUS. (Eg)
Ger. Lower Rhine; ac. 1450. Bd.
MASTER OF ST. GEORGE.
Sp. (Catalan); ac. 1435. Book Nos. 719-774.
MASTER OF ST. GUDULE.
Flem. ac. 1485.
MASTER OF ST. JOHN THE BAPTIST.
Ger. ac. 15th Cent.
MASTER OF ST. PAUL.
It.
MASTER OF ST. SÉVERIN.
Ger. ac. 1500-1515. B-Bd.
MASTER OF ST. VERONICA.
see Master Wilhelm of Cologne.
MASTER OF SALZBURG. (S)
Ger. ac. 1500.
MASTER OF SAN IDELFONSO.
Sp. ac. 1500.
MASTER OF SEGOVIA.
Sp. ac. 1460.
MASTER OF SIGMARINGEN.
Ger. ac. 16th Cent. C.
MASTER OF THE ABBEY OF AFFLIGHEM.
Dut. ac. 1465-1538. B.
MASTER OF THE AEVEAIDE.
Fr. ac. 1525-1530.
MASTER OF THE AIX LA CHAPELLE VIRGIN.
Ger. ac. 1493.
MASTER OF THE AMSTERDAM CABINET.
[or Master of the House Book.]
Ger. Swabia 1430-1505 Mayence. B-Bd.
MASTER OF THE ANGERER PORTRAITS.
Ger. ac. 1519.
MASTER OF THE BAMBINO VISPO.
It. (Tuscan) b. 1423?
MASTER OF THE BANDROLLES [or 1464].
Swi. Ger. ac. 1461-1467. Bd.
MASTER OF THE BEARDED SAINTS.
Ger. ac. 1500.
MASTER OF THE BEAU CHRIST.
Nor. ac. 13th Cent.
MASTER OF THE BERLIN PASSION.
Ger. Bd.
MASTER OF THE BOCCACCIO. (Eg)
Dut. ac. 1476. Bd.
MASTER OF THE BRUNSWICK DIPTYCH.
Dut. ac. 1490.
MASTER OF THE CADUCEUS.
see Barbari, Jacopo de.
MASTER OF THE CARNATION [or Pink].
It. late 15th Cent. in Verona.
MASTER OF THE CARRAND TRIPTYCH.
[or Giovanni di Francesco.]
It. (Florentine) ac. 1460.
MASTER OF THE CASTELLO NATIVITY.
It. (Florentine) late 15th Cent.

MASTER OF THE CODEX OF ST. GEORGE.
It. ac. 14th Cent. in Siena.
MASTER OF THE CRAB [or Monogramist N. H.].
Dut. Bd.
MASTER OF THE DARMSTADT PASSION.
Ger. ac. 15th Cent.
MASTER OF THE DEATH OF MARY.
see Cleves, Joos van [The Elder].
MASTER OF THE DEATH OF THE VIRGIN.
see Cleves, Joos van [The Elder].
MASTER OF THE DIE.
It. ac. 1532. Bd.
MASTER OF THE DOMINICAN EFFIGIES.
It. ac. 1350-1360 in Florence.
MASTER OF THE FIGDOR DEPOSITION.
Dut. ac. 15th Cent.
MASTER OF THE FOGG PIETA.
It. ac. 14th Cent.
MASTER OF THE FORTIES. (Portraits)
Flem. ac. 1540-1551.
MASTER OF THE FRANCISCAN ALLEGORIES.
It. ac. 14th Cent.
MASTER OF THE GARDENS OF LOVE.
Ger. ac. 15th Cent. Bd.
MASTER OF THE GLORIFICATION OF MARY.
Ger. Second half 15th Cent. in Cologne. Bd.
MASTER OF THE GOTHIC BUILDINGS.
It. ac. 16th Cent. in Florence.
MASTER OF THE HALF-FIGURES.
Flem. ac. 1510-1530.
MASTER OF THE HAPSBURGS.
Ger. ac. 1500.
MASTER OF THE HOLY BLOOD CHAPEL.
["Maitre du Saint Sang."]
Flem. b. Bruges; ac. 1500-1525.
MASTER OF THE HOLY KINSHIP.
["Meister der Heiligen Sippe."]
Ger. ac. 1485-1515 in Cologne. Bd.
MASTER OF THE HOLZHAUSEN FAMILY PORTRAITS. *see* Faber, Conrad.
MASTER OF THE HOURS OF THE MARÉCHAL BOUCICAULT.
Fr. ac. 1400 in Paris.
MASTER OF THE HOUSE BOAT.
see Master of the Amsterdam Cabinet.
MASTER OF THE INNOCENT CORONATION.
[or Master of the Straus Madonna.]
It. ac. 1420-1480 Florence.
MASTER OF THE KEY. (Eg)
Ger. ac. 1557-1572. Bd.
MASTER OF THE KRAINBURG ALTAR.
Aus. ac. 15th Cent.
MASTER OF THE LARGER VIENNA PASSION.
[or Master of the Grand Passion.]
Ger. ac. 1456-1460 in Cologne. B.
MASTER OF THE LAST SUPPER.
Flem. ac. 16th Cent. Fa.
MASTER OF THE LATTICE BACKGROUND.
Ger.
MASTER OF THE LEGEND OF THE MAGDALEN.
Flem. ac. 1510-1520. B.

MASTER OF THE LEGEND OF ST. CATHERINE.
Flem. ac. 1450.
MASTER OF THE LEGEND OF ST. GEORGE.
Ger. ac. 1450-1465 in Cologne. B-Bd.
MASTER OF THE LEGEND OF ST. LUCIA.
Flem. ac. 1475-1480.
MASTER OF THE LEGEND OF ST. URSULA.
Flem. ac. 1470-1501 in Bruges. B-Bd.
MASTER OF THE LEIPZIG CABINET.
see Ort, Arnold van der.
MASTER OF THE LIFE OF THE VIRGIN.
Ger. ac. 1460-1480. B-Bd.
Nor. ac. 13th Cent. B-Bd.
MASTER OF THE LITTLE PASSION.
Ger. ac. 14th Cent. in Cologne. B.
MASTER OF THE LYVERSBERG [or Lipporger] PASSION.
Ger. ac. 1463-1480. B-Bd-C.
MASTER OF THE MADONNA OF GHENT.
Flem. ac. 1500.
MASTER OF THE MANSI MAGDALEN.
Flem. ac. 16th Cent.
MASTER OF THE MASS OF ST. GREGORY.
Ger. ac. 16th Cent.
MASTER OF THE MERODE ALTARPIECE.
see Master of Flémalle.
MASTER OF THE MIDDLE RHINE. (School of)
Ger. ac. 1410.
MASTER OF THE MOUSETRAP.
Ger.
MASTER OF THE NETHERLANDS. (School of)
Dut. ac. 1460.
MASTER OF THE NÜREMBERG ALTAR.
Ger. ac. 1440-1500.
MASTER OF THE ORLÉANS TRIPTYCH.
Fr. ac. 16th Cent.
MASTER OF THE OVILE MADONNA.
see Lorenzetti, Ugolino.
MASTER OF THE PEARL OF BRABANT.
Flem. ac. 15th Cent.
MASTER OF THE PEN DRAWINGS.
Swi. ac. 1457-1483.
MASTER OF THE PLAYING CARDS.
Swi. ac. 1445. Bd.
MASTER OF THE ST. NICHOLAS FRESCOES.
[Stefano Fiorentino or da Ponte Vecchio.]
It. 1301-1350. Fa.
MASTER OF THE SAN MINIATO ALTARPIECE.
It. (Tuscan) ac. 1460-1470.
MASTER OF THE SEVEN SORROWS OF MARY.
Flem. ac. 15-16th Cent.
MASTER OF THE SHUTTLE.
see Master I. A. M. of Zwolle.
MASTER OF THE SIGNS OF ST. ANTHONY.
Dut. ac. 1533-1559 in Amsterdam. Bd.
MASTER OF THE STAR.
see Vellert, Dirick Jacobszoon.
MASTER OF THE UNICORN.
see Duvet, Jean.
MASTER OF THE UNRULY CHILDREN. (S)
It. (Florence) ac. 15th Cent. Fa.
MASTER OF THE UTRECHT VIRGIN. (S)
Dut. ac. late 10th Cent. M.
MASTER OF THE VALOIS REVELS.
Dut. ac. 16th Cent.
MASTER OF THE VITUS LEGEND.
Franconian. ac. 1470.
MASTER OF THE WELZER PORTRAITS.
see Maler Zu Schwaz.
MASTER OF THE WHITE VESTMENTS.
Fr. ac. 16th Cent. in Rouen.
MASTER PAOLO, VEREZIANO.
It. ac. 1333-1362 in Venice. B-T.
MASTER PARIS [or Paris Master].
It. (Florentine). ac. 1450-1470.
MASTER P. W. (Eg)
Ger. ac. 15th Cent. in Cologne. Bd.
MASTER R. R. WITH THE ANCHOR. (Eg)
Ger. Lower Rhine; ac. 15th Cent. Bd.
MASTER S. [W. C. B.].
Dut. ac. 18th Cent. Bd.
MASTER SCHWEIZER.
Ger. ac. 16th Cent.
MASTER SECERES.
Sp. ac. 1468-1479 in Valencia.
MASTER 1368. *see* Pietro di Niccolò.
MASTER T. Z. W.
Ger. ac. 1490-1510.
MASTER UNBEKANNTER.
Ger. ac. 1490.
MASTER VIRGO INTER VIRGINES.
Dut. Delft or Gouda 1450-1510. B.
MASTER W. A. [With the Key.]
Dut. Bd.
MASTER W OF THE GABLE. (Eg)
Dut. ac. 15th Cent. Bd.
MASTER W. B.
Ger. ac. 1480.
MASTER W.C.I.E.F.
Ger. ac. 1586.
MASTER W. H.
So. Ger. ac. 15th Cent. Bd.
MASTER WILHELM OF COLOGNE.
Ger. d. 1378 in Cologne.
MASTER WILLIAM OF VERONA. (S)
Ger. ac. 1140 in Verona.
MASTER WILTEN.
see Master of the Life of the Virgin.
MASTER WITH THE GESTICKTEN LAUB.
Ger. M.
MASTER WITH THE NAME OF JESUS. (Eg)
It. ac. 1556-1572 in Rome. Bd.
MASTER WITH THE PARROT.
Flem. ac. 16th Cent. Bd.
MASTER WITH THE PINK.
[*see also* Master of the Carnation.]
Swi. ac. 1490-1501 in Berne.
Swi. ac. 1480-1500 in Zurich.
MASTERS, FRANK B. (Ill)
Am. b. Watertown, Mass. 1873. A28.
MASTON, RAYMOND T.
Am. ad. 1934 Rochester, N. Y. M.
MASTRO-VALERIO, ALLESANDRO. (Et)
Am. b. Italy; ad. 1934 Ann Arbor, Mich. M.
MASURE, JULES.
Fr. b. Braisne 1819; ac. 1900 in Paris. B-T.
MATAHEI, ISAWA [Ukiyo].
Jap. Stawi 1578-1650 Yeddo. J-T.
MATAHEI OF OTSU.
Jap. ac. 1700-1735. J.

MATANIA, Fortunino.
Eng. b. Naples, It. 1861; ex. 1934 London. Wa.
MATEJKO, Jan B. Aloysius.
Pol. Krakow 1838-1893 Same. B-C-T.
MATEN, Nancy.
Am. ac. 1840. M.
MATHAM, Théodorus [or Dierik].
Dut. Haarlem 1606-1660 The Hague. B-T-803.
MATHER, Brown. *see* Brown, M.
MATHEU, Cornelis.
Dut. ac. 1637-1653 Antwerp, Belg. T.
MATHEWS. *see also* Matthews.
MATHEWS, Arthur Frank.
Am. b. Wisconsin 1860; ac. San Fran., Calif. A-F-W.
MATHEWS, Ferdinand Schuyler. (Ill)
Am. b. New Brighton, N. Y. 1854; ad. 1934 Cambridge, Mass. A-F-W.
MATHEWS, Lucia Kleinhaus.
Mrs. Arthur F. Mathews.
Am. b. San Fran., Calif. 1882. A28.
MATHEWS, Morrison.
Eng. ac. 1932 in London. M.
MATHEWSON, Frank Convers.
Am. b. Barrington, R. I. 1862; ac. 1934 Prov., R. I. A-F.
MATHEWSON, George Bowen.
Am. 1804-1877. Fa.
MATHEWSON, Thomas.
Am. b. 1815? d. 1862 East Greenwich, R. I. M.
MATHEY, Paul.
Fr. b. Paris 1844. B-T.
MATHIAS [or Mathieu], Gabriel.
Eng. 1725-1804 Acton. B-T.
MATHIESEN, Marie Lokke.
Mrs. Finn Mathiesen.
Am. b. Christiania, Nor. 1877; ad. 1915 Chicago. A12.
MATHIEU, Hubert. (Ill)
Am. b. Brookings, S. D. 1897; ad. 1934 New York. A.
MATHIEU, Lambert Joseph.
Belg. Bure, 1804-1861 Louvain. C-T.
MATHIEU-MEUNIER, Mathieu Rolland. (S)
Fr. Paris 1824-1896 Same. B-T.
MATHUS, Henry.
Am. b. Boston 1870; ad. 1934 Cranston, R. I. A.
MATIFAS, Louis Rémy.
Fr. Amiens 1846-1896 Paris. B-T.
MATIGNON, Albert [or Alfred].
Fr. b. Sallé 1869. B-DBA-T.
MATIGNON, Albert [or Alfred].
Fr. b. Salle 1869. B-T.
MATISSE, Henri.
Fr. b. Le Cateau 1869; ad. 1935 Paris. DBA-E-T-461-700-783-811-827-847-904.
MATOUT, Louis.
Fr. Renwez 1811-1888 Paris. B-T.
MATSCH, H. V. (Eg)
Am. ad. 1935 New York. M.
MATSCHAT, [Mrs.] Cecile Hulse.
Am. ad. 1934 Brooklyn, N. Y. M.
MATSYS. *see* Massys.
MATTE, Nicolas Augustin. (S)
Fr. Paris 1781-1837. B-T.

MATTEI, Antonio.
Am. ex. 1934 New York. M.
MATTEI, Virgilio P.
Am. b. Ponce, Porto Rico 1898; ad. 1934 Same. A.
MATTEINO. *see* Matteo di Giovanni.
MATTEIS, Paolo de.
It. Cilento 1662-1728 Naples. B-T.
MATTEO DA GIOVANNI.
It. Siena 1430/5-1495 Same. B-T-78.
MATTEO DA GUILA.
see Guila da Matteo.
MATTEO DA SIENA.
see Matteo da Giovanni.
MATTERN, J. J.
Am. ad. 1934 Virginia. M.
MATTERN, Karl.
Am. b. Durkheim, Ger. 1892; ad. 1934 Lawrence, Kan. A.
MATTESON, Barton van Voorhis. (Ill)
Am. ad. 1934 New York. A.
MATTESON, Tomkins Harrison.
Am. Peterboro, N. Y. 1813-1884. B-Bd-C-F-4-15.
MATTHEWS, Anna Lou. (S)
Am. b. Chicago; ad. 1934 Green Bay, Wis. A.
MATTHEWS, [Mrs.] Elizabeth St. John. (S)
Am. Phila., Pa. 1876-1911 New York. A09.
MATTHEWS, George Bagby.
Am. b. Tappahanock, Va. 1857; ad. 1935 Wash., D. C. F.
MATTHEWS, Marmaduke.
Can. England 1837-1913 Canada. M.
MATTHEWS, Richard George. (Et)
Can. b. Montreal 1870; ad. 1934 London. Wa.
MATTHEWS, William F.
Am. b. St. Louis 1878; ad. 1934 Brooklyn, N. Y. A.
MATTHIAS, Martha.
Am. b. Los Angeles, Calif. 1903; ad. 1934 Same. A.
MATTHYS [or Matthysens], Abraham.
Flem. Antwerp, Belg. 1581-1649. B-T.
MATTISON, Donald M.
Am. b. Beloit, Wis. 1905; ad. 1934 Indianapolis, Ind. A.
MATTON, Ida. (S)
Swe. b. Gèfle 1863; ac. 1934 Paris. DBA-T-829.
MATTOS, Francesco de.
Por. ac. 1565/84 in Lisbon. T.
MATTSON, Henry Elis.
Am. b. Sweden 1887; ad. 1934 Woodstock, N. Y. A.
MATTYASOVSZKY-ZSOLNAY, László.
Hun. b. 1892; ex. 1934 in London. M.
MATULKA, Jan.
Am. b. Prague, Czec. 1890; ad. 1934 New York. A.
MATURINO DA FIRENZE.
It. ac. in Rome. T-V.
MATVEIFF, Fédor Michailovitsch.
Rus. Leningrad 1758-1826 Rome, It. B-T.
MATZAL, Leopold Charles.
Am. b. Vienna, Aus. 1890; ad. 1934 Newark, N. J. A.

MATZEN, Herman N. (S)
Am. b. Loitkjerkeby, Denmark 1861; ad. 1934 Cleveland, O. A-F-Ta-W.
MATZINGER, Philip Frederick.
Am. b. Tiffin, O.; ad. 1934 Oakland, Calif. A.
MATZKE, Albert.
Am. b. Indianapolis, Ind. 1882; ad. 1935 New York. A12-F.
MAUBERT, Jacques [or James].
Eng. d. 1746 in London. B-T.
MAUCH, Carl.
Am. Germany 1854-1913 Chicago. A011.
MAUCH [or Moch], Daniel.
Ger. b. 1504/10 Ulm. T.
MAUCH, Max. (S)
Am. Vienna, Aus. 1864-1905 Chicago. A05-F-Ta.
MAUFRA, Maxime Émile Louis.
Fr. Nantes 1862-1918 Poncé. B-DBA-T.
MAULBERTSCH, Franz Anton.
Aus. Langenargen 1724-1796 Vienna. B-T.
MAULL, Margaret Howell. (Ill)
Am. b. Whitford, Pa. 1897; ad. 1934 Phila., Pa. A.
MAUNSBACH, Eric.
Am. b. Sweden 1890; ad. 1934 New York. A.
MAUNY, Jacques.
Fr. b. Paris 1893; ex. 1933 New York. DBA-T.
MAURER, Adam C.
Am. b. Phila., Pa.; ex. 1935 New York. M.
MAURER, Alfred Henry.
Am. New York 1868-1932 Same. A029-F.
MAURER, Charles G.
Am. Lorraine, Fr. 1844-1931 Phila., Pa. A028.
MAURER [or Murer], Christopher.
Swi. Zurich 1558-1614 Winterthur. B-T.
MAURER, Jakob Samuel.
Swi. Berne 1745-1828. T.
MAURER, Louis.
Am. Biebrich, Ger. 1832-1932 New York. A029.
MAURER, S. A. (Ill)
Am. ad. 1934 New York. M.
MAURIER, George Louis Pamella Busson du. (Ill)
Fr. Paris 1831/4-1896 London. B-DNB-E-T-272.
MAURI-LAVIGNE. *see* Lavigne, M.
MAURIN, Nicolas Eustache. (Eg)
Fr. Perpignan 1799-1850 Paris. T.
MAURONER, Fabio.
It. b. 1884; ex. 1925 New York. Fa-M.
MAURY, Cornelia Field.
Am. b. New Orleans, La. 1866; ad. 1934 St. Louis, Mo. A-F.
MAURY, Matthew Fontaine. (S)
Am. ac. 1931. M.
MAUVE, Anton.
Dut. Zaandam 1838-1888 Arnheim, Ger. B-E-T-474-880.
MAUZAISSE, Jean Baptiste.
Fr. Corbeil 1784-1844 Paris. B-T.
MAVERICK, Peter. (Eg)
Am. New York 1780-1831 Same. DAB-F-2-7-12-40-55-184.
MAVERICK, Peter Rushton. (Eg)
Am. New York 1775-1811 Same. B-E-2-7-40-184.
MAVERICK, Samuel. (Eg)
Am. ac. 1805-1847 in New York. F-2-7.
MAVRO, Maria.
Rus. b. Odessa 1889. DBA.
MAVROGORDATO, Alex. J.
Eng. ad. 1934 London. Wa.
MAVROGORDATO, Julia. (Eg)
Eng. ex. 1935 London. M.
MAX, Gabriel Cornelius von.
Aus. Prague 1840-1915 Munich, Ger. B-Bd-C-T.
MAX, Joseph Calasanza. (S)
Aus. b. 1804; d. 1855 in Prague. T.
MAXENCE, Edgard Henri Marie.
Fr. b. Nantes 1871. B-DBA-T.
MAXEY, H. Holderread.
Am. b. Des Moines, Ia. 1907; ad. 1934 New York. A.
MAXIME, Chevalier.
see Stanzioni, Massimo.
MAXWELL, Coralie de Long. (S)
Am. b. Ohio 1878; ad. 1934 Cleveland, O. A-Cs.
MAXWELL, John Alan. (Ill)
Am. ad. 1934 New York. M.
MAXWELL, Marian D.
Am. ad. 1934 Toledo, O. M.
MAXWELL, Perriton. (Ill)
Am. ad. 1934 New York. M.
MAY, Beulah. (S)
Am. b. Hiawatha, Kan. 1883; ad. 1934 Santa Ana, Calif. A.
MAY, Charles C. (Et)
Am. ad. 1935 New York. M.
MAY, [Mrs.] C. B. K.
Br. b. Hondurus 1876; ad. 1929 London. Wa1929.
MAY, Edward Harrison.
Am. b. England 1824; ac. New York 1850; d. 1887 Paris. C-F-15.
MAY, [Mrs.] Florence Lister Land.
Am. b. Louisiana; ad. 1915 New York. A12.
MAY, George Oswald.
Ger. Offenbach 1738-1816 Frankfort. T.
MAY, H. Mabel.
Can. b. Montreal; ad. 1935 Westmount, P. Q., Can. M.
MAY, Philip William ["Phil May"]. (Cari)
Eng. Worthley 1864-1903 London. B-DNB-E-T-462.
MAY, Thomas. (Cart)
Am. Detroit, Mich. 1860-1928 Same. A025.
MAYA ARTISTS. *see* book No. 794.
MAYER, Bela.
Am. b. Hungary 1888; ad. 1934 New York. A.
MAYER, Casper. (S)
Am. Bavaria 1871-1931 New York. A029-F-Ta.
MAYER, Christian.
Aus. Vienna 1812-1870 Same. B-T.
MAYER, Constant.
Am. Besancon, Fr. 1832-1911 Paris. A029-B-DAB-F-1-15-89.
MAYER, Frank Blackwell.
Am. Balt., Md. 1827-1899. C-F-15.

MAYER, Fred A. (Ill)
Am. ad. 1935 New York. M.
MAYER, Hendrik Martin.
Am. b. Nashua, N. H. 1908; ad. 1934 Indianapolis, Ind. M.
MAYER, [Mrs.] Hendrik Martin.
Am. ad. 1934 Indianapolis, Ind. M.
MAYER, Henry ["Hy"]. (Cari)
Am. b. Germany 1868; ad. 1934 Norwalk, Conn. A28-17.
MAYER, Leo.
Ger. b. 1902; ad. 1935 Frankfort, Ger. M.
MAYER, Liezen.
see Liezen-Mayer, Alexander.
MAYER, Louis. (S)
Am. b. Milwaukee, Wis. 1869; ad. 1934 Hopewell, N. Y. A-Cs-F.
MAYER, Marie François Constance.
Fr. Paris 1775-1821 Same. B-T.
MAYER, Milton.
Am. ad. 1934 New Rochelle, N. Y. M.
MAYFIELD, Robert Bledsoe. (Et)
Am. b. Carlinville, Ill. 1869; ad. 1934 New Orleans, La. A28-F.
MAYHEW, Nell Brooker.
Am. b. Astoria, Ill. 1875. A28.
MAYNARD, George Willoughby.
Am. Wash., D. C. 1843-1923 New York. A20-C-DAB-F-W12-15-46-176.
MAYNARD, Richard Field.
Am. b. Chicago 1875; ad. 1934 New York. A-F-W.
MAYNARD, Robert Ashwin. (Eg)
Eng. b. London 1888; ad. 1934 Middlesex. Wa.
MAYNO, Fray Juan Bautista.
Sp. Toledo 1569-1649 Madrid. B-T.
MAYO, Eileen. (Eg)
Eng. ex. 1934 Brooklyn, N. Y. M.
MAYOR, [Mrs.] Harriet Hyatt.
Am. b. Salem, Mass. 1868; ad. 1934 Princeton, N. J. A-Cs-F.
MAYR, Carl [or Mayr-Grager].
Aus. b. Graz, 1850. B.
MAYR, Christian.
Am. b. Ger.; ac. 1840-1850 in New York. F.
MAYR, Heinrich von.
Ger. Nüremburg, 1806-1871 Munich. B-T.
MAZE, Paul Lucien.
Fr. b. Havre 1887; ad. 1935 London. M.
MAZELIN, Charles Firmin.
Fr. b. Elbeuf 1882. B-DBA-T.
MAZEROLLE, Alexis Joseph.
Fr. Paris 1826-1889. B-T.
MAZO, Juan Bautista Martinez del.
Sp. Madrid 1606-1667 Same. B-C-T-722-823.
MAZUR, Wladyslaw. (S)
Am. b. at Sea 1871; ad. 1935 Cinn., O. A12-F.
MAZZANOVICH, Lawrence.
Am. b. Calif. 1872; ad. 1934 Tryon, N. C. A-F-W-757.
MAZZEI, Corrado Alberto. (S)
It. b. Carrara 1885. DBA.
MAZZOLA [or Mazzuola], Filippo [Erbette].
It. Parma 1460?-1505. B-Bd-T.
MAZZOLA [or Mazzuola], Francesco.
see Parmigianino.
MAZZOLA-BEDOLI, Girolamo.
It. Parma 1500?-1569. B-T.
MAZZOLINO, Lodovico.
It. Ferrara 1470-1530. B-T.
MAZZOLONI, Giuseppe.
It. b. Rome 1868. M.
MAZZONI, Guido [Il. Monamino]. (S)
It. Modena 1450-1518. B-Hs-T.
MAZZONI-ZARINI, Emilio. (Et)
It. b. Florence 1869; ad. 1935 Same. M.
MAZZUOLI, Giuseppe. (S)
It. Volterra 1644-1725 Rome. T.
Mc. *see also* Mac.
McADAMS, Gladys.
Am. ad. 1934 Lexington, Ky. M.
McALPIN, Madeleine.
Am. ad. 1935 Morristown, N. J. M.
McARDELL, James. (Eg)
Ir. Dublin 1728/9-1765 London. T.
McARTHUR, Betty.
Am. b. Miss. 1865; ad. 1935 McHenry, Miss. M.
McAULIFFE, James J.
Am. St. Johns, N. F. 1848-1921 New Bedford, Mass. A018-F.
McAUSLAN, Helen.
Am. b. Prov., R. I.; ad. 1934 New York. A.
McBEY, James. (Et)
Scot. b. Newburgh 1883; ad. 1934 London. T-Wa-472-830.
McBRIDE, Edward J. (Cart)
Am. b. St. Louis 1889; ad. 1934 New York. A.
McBURNEY, James E.
Am. b. Lore City, O. 1868; ad. 1934 Chicago. A.
McCALL, Virginia Armitage.
Am. b. Phila., Pa. 1906; ad. 1934 Haverford, Pa. A.
McCANNELL, Otway.
Br. ex. 1934 London. M.
McCARTAN, Edward. (S)
Am. b. Albany, N. Y. 1879; ad. 1935 San Fran., Calif. A-Cs-F-W-191.
McCARTER, Henry. (Ill)
Am. b. Norristown, Pa. 1866; ad. 1934 Phila., Pa. A-F-W-46.
McCARTHY, Elizabeth White.
Am. b. Lansdowne, Pa. 1891; ad. 1934 Phila., Pa. A.
McCARTHY, Helen K.
Am. Poland, O. 1884-1927. A026-F.
McCARTHY, John O'Toole.
Am. Ireland 1843-1923 Wash., D. C. A020.
McCARTNEY, Edith.
Am. ac. 1933 Wash., D. C. M.
McCAUSLIN, William C. (P-S)
Am. Steubenville, O. 1860-1929 Wash., D. C. M.
McCAY, Winsor. (Cart.)
Am. b. Spring Lake, Mich.; d. 1934 Brooklyn, N. Y. Obit. N. Y. papers, 7-27-1934.
McCHESNEY, Clara T. (P-S)
Am. b. Bronsville, Calif.; ac. 1907. M.
McCLAIN, Helen Charleton.
Am. b. Toronto, Can. 1887; ad. 1934 Same. A.
McCLEAN, Avis L.
Am. ad. 1934 New York. M.

McCLEAN, Clara.
Am. b. Washington, Ia. 1889; ad. 1934 Cleveland, O. A.
McCLEAN, Roberta Fisk.
Am. b. Russellville, Ky. 1882; ad. 1934 Same. A.
McCLELLAN, Mary.
Am. Phila., Pa. 1860-1929. A026.
McCLINTOCK, Mary Howard.
Eng. b. Surrey 1888; ad. 1934 Same. Wa.
McCLOSKEY, Martha.
Am. ad. 1934 East Palestine, O. M.
McCLUNG, Florence White.
Am. b. St. Louis, Mo. 1896; ad. 1934 Dallas, Texas. A.
McCLURE, Caroline Summer. (S)
Mrs. G. G. McClure.
Am. b. St. Louis, Mo.; ad. 1934 New York. A.
McCLURE, Maud Quimby. (S)
Am. b. Mt. Morris, Ill. 1884. A12.
McCOLL, Mary A.
Am. b. Forrest, Ont., Can.; ad. 1934 St. Louis. A.
McCOMAS, Francis John. (Mu)
Am. b. Fingal, Tasmania 1874; ad. 1934 Pebble Beach, Calif. A-F-W14.
McCOMB, Maris Louise. (Ill)
Am. b. Louisville, Ky.; ad. 1934 Kew Gardens, L. I., N. Y. A.
McCONAHA, Lawrence.
Am. b. Centerville, Ind. 1894; ad. 1934 Richmond, Ind. A.
McCONOMY, Nancy.
Am. b. Phila., Pa. 1903; ad. 1934 Same. A.
McCORD, George Herbert.
Am. New York 1848-1909 Same. A07-C-F-15.
McCORMACK, Nancy Cox.
Am. ad. 1935 New York. M.
McCORMICK, Amy Irwin.
Mrs. Robert R. McCormick.
Am. b. Fort Riley, Kan. 1880. A.
McCORMICK, Howard. (Ill)
Am. b. Indiana 1875; ad. 1934 Leonia, N. J. A-F-W-181.
McCORMICK, Katherine Hood.
Am. b. Phila., Pa. 1882; ad. 1934 Same. A.
McCOSH, David John.
Am. b. Cedar Rapids, Ia. 1903; ad. 1934 Same. A.
McCOUCH, Gordon Mallet.
Am. b. Phila., Pa. 1885; ad. 1934 Porto di Ronco, Swi. A.
Mc. CRADY, John.
Am. ad. 1934 Oxford, Miss. M.
McCRAIG, [Mrs.] Flora Thomas.
Am. b. Royalton, N. Y.; d. 1933 Flintridge, Calif. A030.
McCREA, Harold W.
Can. b. Peterboro, Ont.; ad. 1935 Toronto. M.
McCREA, Samuel Harkness.
Am. b. Palatine, Ill. 1867; ad. 1934 Darien, Conn. A.
McCREARY, Caroline.
Am. ex. 1935 Pittsburgh, Pa. M.
McCREERY, Franc Root.
Am. b. Dodge City, Kan.; ad. 1934 Buffalo, N. Y, A.
McCREERY, James Lindsay. (Ill-S)
Am. b. Berkeley, Calif.; ad. 1934 Same. M.
McCROSSAN, Mary.
Br. ad. 1934 St. Ives, Cornwall. Wa.
McCUBBIN, Frederick.
Aust. b. Melbourne 1855. M.
McCULLOUGH, [Mrs.] Max.
Am. b. Elmwood Plantation, Ark.; ad. 1934 Eastland, Tex. A.
McCURDY, Caroline G.
Am. ad. 1934 Nassau, Bahamas. M.
McCUTCHEON, John Tinney. (Cari)
Am. b. South Raub, Ind. 1870; ad. 1934 Chicago. A28-F-W-181.
McDAVID, Mittie Owen.
Am. b. Birmingham, Ala.; ad. 1934 Same. A.
McDERMITT, W. T.
Am. ad. 1934 Los Angeles, Calif. M.
McDONALD, [Mrs.] Ann Heebner.
Am. b. Phila., Pa.; ad. 1934 Same. A.
McDONALD, Harriett D.
Am. ad. 1934 Lexington, Ky. M.
McDONALD, William Purcell.
Am. b. Cinn., O. 1863. A28.
McDONNELL, John.
Am. b. Chicopee, Mass. 1880; ad. 1934 Chicago. A.
McDOWELL, Patrick. (S)
Ir. 1799-1870. B-Hs-T.
McENTEE, Jervis.
Am. Rondout, N. Y. 1828-1891 Same. B-C-DAB-E-F-1-4-15-22-104.
McEVOY, Arthur Ambrose.
Eng. Wiltshire 1878-1927 London. T-825-947.
McEWAN, Thomas.
Scot. Busby 1861-1914 Glasgow. T.
McEWEN, Katherine.
Am. b. Nottingham, Eng. 1875; ad. 1934 Dragoon, Ariz. A.
McEWEN, Walter.
Am. b. Chicago 1860; ad. 1934 Paris. A-F-W-46.
McFADDEN, Florence Glyn-Wells. (Eg)
Am. b. London, Eng.; ad. 1934 San Antonio, Tex. A.
McFALL, Jay Vaughn. (Ill)
Am. Sandusky, O. 1878-1912 Detroit, Mich. A010.
McFEE, Henry Lee.
Am. b. St. Louis 1886; ad. 1934 Woodstock, N. Y. A-F-473-701-779.
McGAVOCK, Bessie Dawson.
Am. ad. 1935 Columbia, Tenn. M.
McGEHEE, Helen Mahood.
Am. b. Lynchburg, Va.; ad. 1934 Jackson, Miss. A.
McGILL, [Mrs.] Lena.
Am. ad. 1934 Fort Worth, Tex. M.
McGILLIVRAY, Florence Helena.
Cam. b. Whitby, Ont. 1864; ad. 1934 Same. A.
McGRATH, Beatrice Willard. (S)
Am. b. Dodge City, Kan. 1896; ad. 1934 New Haven, Conn. A.
McGRATH, John.
Am. b. Ireland 1880; ad. 1934 Balt., Md. A.
McGRATH, William J.
Am. ex. 1935 New York. M.

McHENRY, James.
Br. b. East Indies; ac. 1840-1886 in London. M.
McHUGH, Arline B.
Am. b. Owensboro, Ky. 1891; ad. 1934 Larchmont, N. Y. A.
McHUGH, John Paul.
Am. b. Holyoke, Mass. 1895; ad. 1934 New Canaan, Conn. A.
McILHENNY, Charles Morgan.
Am. Phila., Pa. 1858-1904. F.
McINNES, Robert.
Scot. Edinburgh 1801-1886 Stirling. B-T.
McINNES, William Beckwith.
Aust. b. St. Kilda, Victoria 1889; ad. 1934 Victoria. Wa.
McINTEE, William H.
Am. Almont, Mich. 1857-1917 Detroit, Mich. A015.
McINTIRE, Katherine Angela.
Am. b. Richmond, Va. 1880; ad. 1934 New York. F-M.
McINTIRE, Samuel. (Carver)
Am. Salem, Mass. 1757-1811 Same. DAB-F-T-169-170.
McINTOCH, Frank. (Ill)
Am. ad. 1934 New York. M.
McINTOSH, Joseph H. (S)
Am. ad. 1934 New York. M.
McINTOSH, Pleasant R.
Am. b. New Salisbury, Ind. 1897; ad. 1934 Peoria, Ill. A.
McKAGUE, Yvonne.
Can. b. Toronto, Ont.; ad. 1935 Same. M.
McKAY, D. (Cart)
Am. ad. 1934 Chicago. M.
McKEAN, Hugh.
Am. ad. 1935 Rollins College, Fla. M.
McKEE, Donald. (Ill)
Am. b. Ind., Ind. 1883; ad. 1934 Westport, Conn. A.
McKEE, John Dukes. (Ill)
Am. b. Kokomo, Ind. 1899; ad. 1934 Chicago. A.
McKEE, Katherine.
Am. ad. 1934 Cleveland, O. M.
McKELL, James C.
Am. ad. 1935 Penfield, Pa. M.
McKELLAR, Archibald.
Am. Scot. 1844-1901 Bridgeport, Conn. A04.
McKENZIE, Robert Tait. (S)
Am. b. Almonte, Ont., Can. 1867; ad. 1934 Phila., Pa. A-Cs-F-W-46.
McKENZIE, Vinnorma Shaw.
Am. b. Downs, Kan. 1891; ad. 1934 Huron, Mich. A.
McKERMAN, Frank.
Am. b. Phila., Pa. 1861; ad. 1934 Ridley Park, Pa. A.
McKESSON, John Alexander.
Am. b. Wisconsin 1880. DBA.
McKEWAN, David Hall.
Scot. 1816/7-1873. B-DNB-T.
McKEY, Edward Michael.
Am. 1877-1918. A015.
McKIERNAN, John. (Mu)
Am. ad. 1934 New York. M.
McKILLOP, William.
Am. ad. 1934 New York. M.
McKINNIE, Mirian.
Am. ad. 1935 Edwardsville, Ill. M.
McKINNEY, Earl B. (Et)
Am. b. Ohio 1881; ad. 1935 New York. M.
McKINNEY, [Mrs.] Katie Cable.
Am. b. Shenandoah, Ia. 1903; ad. 1934 Bolivar, Mo. A.
McKINNEY, Roland Joseph.
Am. b. Niagara Falls, N. Y. 1898; ad. 1934 Balt., Md. A-W.
McKINSTRY, Grace E.
Am. b. Fredonia, N. Y.; ad. 1934 New York. A-F-W.
McKNIGHT, Eliza.
Am. ad. 1934 New York. M.
McKNIGHT, [Mrs.] J. R.
Am. ad. 1934 New Orleans, La. M.
McKNIGHT, Robert Johnson. (S)
Am. ad. 1935 Bayside, L. I., N. Y. M.
McLACHLAN, Thomas Hope.
Eng. Darlington 1845-1897. B-DNB-T.
McLAIN, Mary.
Am. ad. 1934 New York. M.
McLAUGHLIN, Charles J.
Am. b. Covington, Ky. 1888; ad. 1934 Same. A-F.
McLAUGHLIN, Mary Louise.
Am. b. Cinn., O.; ad. 1934 Same. A-W.
McLAUGHLIN, [Miss] Willie C.
Am. ad. 1934 Birmingham, Ala. M.
McLAWS, Virginia Randall.
Am. b. Augusta, Ga. 1872; ad. 1934 Sweet Brair, Va. A.
McLEAN, [Mrs.] Grace.
Am. b. Jasper Co., Ia. 1885; ad. 1934 Los Angeles, Calif. A.
McLEAN, James Augustus.
Am. b. Lincolnton, N. C. 1904; ad. 1934 Raleigh, N. C. A.
McLEAN, Ruth S. (Min.)
Am. ad. 1934 Larchmont, N. Y. M.
McLEISH, Norman.
Am. ad. 1935 Chicago. M.
McLELLAN, Ralph.
Am. b. San Marcos, Tex. 1884; ad. 1934 Phila., Pa. A-F.
McLENGAN, Harry Richardson.
Am. b. Milwaukee, Wis. 1899; ad. 1934 Same. A.
McLENNAN, Teana.
Am. ex. 1934 New York. M.
McLEOD, Ronald. (Ill)
Am. ad. 1934 New York. M.
McMANUS, Blanche. (Ill)
Mrs. Francis Miltoun Mansfield.
Am. b. East Felician, La. 1870; ad. 1934 Paris. A28-W16-829.
McMANUS, George. (Cart.)
Am. b. St. Louis 1884; ad. 1934 Hollywood, Calif. A28-W.
McMANUS, James Goodwin.
Am. b. Hartford, Conn. 1882; ad. 1934 Same. A-F.
McMEEN, Irene.
Am. b. Pittsburgh, Pa. 1904; ad. 1934 New York. A.
McMEIN, Neysa Moran.
Mrs. John G. Baragwanath.
Am. b. Quincy, Ill. 1890; ad. 1934 New York. A-F-W.

McMILLAN, Duncan.
Am. ad. 1934 Boston, Mass. M.
McMILLAN, [Mrs.] Laura Brown.
Am. b. Malone, N. Y.; ad. 1934 Kokomo, Ind. A.
McMILLAN, Mary.
Am. b. Ilion, N. Y. 1895; ad. 1934 Syracuse, N. Y. A.
McMILLAN, William. (S)
Scot. b. Aberdeen 1887; ad. 1934 Chelsea, Eng. Wa.
McMORRIS, Le Roy D.
Am. b. Sedalia, Mo. 1893. A20.
McMULLEN, E. Ormond.
Am. ad. 1934 New York. M.
McMURTRIE, Edith.
Am. b. Phila., Pa.; ad. 1934 Same. A.
McNAB, Allan. (Eg)
Eng. b. Southampton 1901; ad. 1934 London. Wa.
McNAB, Robert Allan.
Eng. Preston 1865; ad. 1934 London. Wa.
McNAIR, William.
Am. ad. 1934 New York. M.
McNALLY, M. T.
Aust. b. Victoria 1874; ac. 1933. M.
McNAMEE, Dorothy.
Am. b. Erie, Pa. 1880. A12.
McNEELY, Perry.
Am. b. Kansas 1886; ad. 1934 Los Angeles, Calif. M.
McNEELY, Stephen Thomas. (S)
Am. b. East Orange, N. J. 1909; ad. 1934 New York. A.
McNERNEY, Eugene.
Am. ad. 1934 Westport, Conn. M.
McNESS, Leora.
Am. b. Tallahassee, Fla. 1903; ad. 1935 Kingsville, Tex. M.
McNICOLL, Helen G.
Can. Toronto, Ont. 1879-1915. M.
McNITT, Frank.
Am. ad. 1934 Palmer, Mass. M.
McNULTY, Harold.
Am. ad. 1934 Norwalk, Conn. M.
McNULTY, William Charles. (Et)
Am. b. Ogden, Utah 1889; ad. 1935 New York. A28-F-M.
McPHERSON, J. C.
Am. ex. 1934 New York. M.
McQUAID, Mary Cameron.
Am. b. Jacksonville, Fla. 1886; ad. 1934 New York. A28.
McQUOID, Winston.
Br. ex. 1934 in London. M.
McRAE, Emma.
Am. ex. 1935 New York. M.
McRAE, John C. (Eg)
Am. ac. 1855-1880 in New York. F-7.
McRICKARD, James P.
Am. b. 1872; ad. 1934 Bayside, L. I., N. Y. A-F.
McTAGGART, William.
Scot. Campbelltown 1835-1910. B-T-825.
McVEY, Leroy.
Am. ex. 1935 Kansas City, Mo. M.
McVEY, William M. (S)
Am. b. Boston 1905; ad. 1934 Cleveland, O. A.
McWHINNEY, Harold.
Am. ad. 1934 Eaton, O. M.
McWHIRTER, John.
Scot. Edinburgh 1839-1911. T.
McWILLIAMS, [Mrs.] Anna Walbridge.
Am. ad. 1934 Ogunquit, Me. M.
MEAD, Bradford B.
Am. ex. 1934 Manchester, Vt. M.
MEAD, Larkin Goldsmith. (S)
Am. Chesterfield, N. H. 1835-1910 Florence, It. A09-DAB-F-Ta-4-15-26.
MEAD, Roderick Fletcher.
Am. b. So. Orange, N. J. 1900; ad. 1934 New York. A.
MEADOWS, Joseph Kenny.
Eng. 1790-1874. B-DNB-T.
MEAGHER, Marion T.
Am. b. New York; ad. 1934 Same. A.
MEAKIN, Louis Henry.
Am. New Castle, Eng. 1853-1917 Boston. A014-F.
MEANS, Elliott Anderson. (S)
Am. b. Stamford, Conn. 1905; ad. 1934 New York. A.
MEANS, Glenn.
Am. ad. 1935 North Haven, Conn. M.
MEARNS, Peter.
Am. ex. 1934 Woodstock, N. Y. M.
MEARS, Helen Farnsworth. (S)
Am. Oshkosh, Wis. 1876-1916 New York. A013-DAB-F-26-46-175.
MEARS, Henrietta Dunn.
Am. b. Milwaukee, Wis.; ad. 1934 St. Paul, Minn. A.
MECARINO [or Mecharino].
see Beccafumi, Domenico.
MECHAU, Frank, Jr.
Am. b. Denver, Colo. 1904; ad. 1935 Colorado Springs, Colo. M.
MECHAU, Jakob Wilhelm.
Ger. Leipzig 1745-1808 Dresden. B-T.
MECHTROVITCH. *see* Městrović.
MECKENEM, Israel von. (Eg)
Ger. 1450-1503/17 Bocholt. B-T.
MECKLEM, Austin M.
Am. b. Colfax, Wash. 1894; ad. Woodstock, N. Y. A.
MECKLEM, Hannah. (S)
Mrs. Austin M. Mecklem.
Am. ad. 1934 Woodstock, N. Y. M.
MECUCCIO. *see* Beccafumi, Domenico.
MÉDARD, Eugène.
Fr. Paris 1849-1887 Same. B-C-T.
MEDARY, Annie Hampton. (Min)
Am. b. Groton, Conn. 1903; ad. 1934 Taunton, Mass. A.
MEDGYÈS, Ladislas.
Hun. b. Budapest 1892. DBA-T.
MEDIAEVAL ART.
see books Nos. 720-789.
MEDICI. *see* Pietro da Medici.
MEDINA, John.
Scot. 1721-1796 Edinburgh. B-DNB.
MEDINA, [Sir] John Baptist.
Scot. Brussels, Belg. 1659-1710 Edinburgh. B-DNB-T.
MEDLAND, Thomas. (Eg)
Br. d. 1833. B-DNB-T.

MEDLEY, Robert.
Eng. ex. 1934 London. M.
MEDLEY, Samuel.
Eng. Liverpool 1769-1857 Chatham. DNB-T.
MEDWORTH, Frank Charles.
Eng. b. London 1892; ad. 1934 Same. Wa.
MEE, Anne [née Foldsone]. (Min)
Eng. 1775?-1851. B-DNB-T.
MEEKER, Joseph Rusling.
Am. b. Newark, N. J. 1827. C-F-T.
MEEKER, Ruth.
Am. ad. 1934 Cinn., O. M.
MEEL. *see* Miel, Jan.
MEER, Barend [or Bernardus] van der.
Dut. b. Haarlem 1659?; ac. 1689. C.
MEER, Jan van der.
see Vermeer, Johannes.
MEER [of Delft], Johannes van der.
Dut. 1632-1675 Delft. B-T-722.
MEER [of Utrecht], Johannes van der.
Dut. 1630/5-1688 Utrecht. B-T.
MEERE, Gerard van der.
see Meire, Gerard van der.
MEERHOUT, Johan.
Dut. ac. 1661-1677 in Amsterdam. B-T.
MEERT, Joseph.
Am. ad. 1935 New York. M.
MEERTE [or Meert], Peter.
Flem. Brussels, Belg. 1619-1669. B-T.
MEESER, Lillian B.
Mrs. Spencer B. Meeser.
Am. b. Ridley Park, Pa. 1864; ad. 1934 Same. A.
MEGAN [or Meganet], Renier.
Flem. Brussels, Belg. 1637-1690. B-T.
MEGAREY, John.
Am. d. 1845. M.
MEGARGEE, Edwin.
Am. ad. 1934 New York. M.
MEGARGEE, Lon. (Eg)
Am. ad. 1934 Phoenix, Ariz. M.
MÈGEE, Violette.
Fr. b. Algeria 1889. DBA.
MEGLINGER, Johann Kasper.
Swi. Lucerne 1595-1670 Same. T.
MÉGRET, Louis Nicolas Adolphe. (S)
Fr. Paris 1829-1911 Same. B-T.
MEHEUT, Mathurin.
Fr. b. Lamballe 1882; ac. 1930 Paris. T.
MEHOFFER, Joseph.
Pol. b. Galicia 1869. B-T.
MEHUS, Lieven [or Livio].
Flem. Oudenarde 1630-1691 Florence, It. C-T.
MEI YUAN CHANG.
Chinese. Sung Dynasty. M.
MEIER. *see* Meyer.
MEIÈRE, Hildreth. (Min)
Am. b. New York; ad. 1934 Same. A-W.
MEIERHANS, Joseph.
Am. b. Ober Lunkhofen Aargau, Swi. 1890; ad. 1934 Perkasie, Pa. A.
MEIFREN Y ROIG, Eliséo.
Sp. b. Barcelona 1857. B-T.
MEILINGER, Lothar Rudolf.
Ger. b. Munich 1887. T.
MEINSHAUSEN, George F. F.
Am. b. Hanover, Ger. 1855; ad. 1935 Norwood, O. A28-F.
MEIRE, Gerard van der.
Dut. Ghent, Belg. 1450-1512 Same. B-T-722.
MEISSNER, Adolf Ernest.
Ger. Dresden 1837-1902 Munich. B-T.
MEISSNER, Leo John. (Eg)
Am. b. Detroit, Mich. 1895; ad. 1935 New York. A28-M.
MEISSONIER, Jean Charles.
Fr. Paris 1852-1917. B-T.
MEISSONIER, Jean Louis Ernest.
Fr. Lyons 1815-1891 Paris. B-Bd-C-E-T-710-942.
MEISSONIER, Justin Aurèle.
Fr. Turin, It. 1693/5-1750 Paris. B-T.
MEISTER. *see* Master.
MEIT [or Meijet], Conrad. (S)
Ger. ac. 1500-1544 in Worms. Hs-T.
MEIXNER, Ludwig.
Bav. Munich 1828-1885 Same. B-T.
MELANTHIUS [or Melanthus].
Gr. Sicyon; ac. 4th Century B.C. B-F-T.
MELBYE, Daniel Herman Anton.
Dan. Copenhagen 1818-1875 Paris. B-C-T.
MELCHER, Betsy Flagg. (Min)
Am. ad. 1935 Dongen Hills, S. I., N. Y. M.
MELCHERS, Corinne.
Am. ad. 1935 Falmouth, Va. M.
MELCHERS [Julius], Gari.
Am. Detroit, Mich. 1860-1932 Falmouth, Va. A029-B-DAB-E-F-T-W-1-46-105-177-178, 693-779.
MELCHIOR, Heinrich Anton. (S)
It. ac. 1760-1796 in Berlin, Ger. B-T.
MELCHIOR, Johann Peter. (S)
Ger. Lintorf 1742-1825 Nymphenburg. T.
MELCHIOR, Wilhelm.
Ger. 1813-1860 Munich. C-T.
MELDOLLA, Andrea. *see* Schianone.
MELDRUM, Max.
Aust. ac. 1890. M.
MELER, S. F. van.
Dut. ac. 1850. M.
MELIDA Y ALINARI ENRIQUE.
Spa. Madrid 1834-1892 Paris. B-T.
MELIK, Soss Efrem.
Am. b. Baku, Rus. 1912; ad. 1934 New York. A.
MELIN, Joseph Urbain.
Fr. Paris 1814-1886. B-T.
MÉLINGUE, Etienne Lucien.
Fr. Paris 1844-1889 Aix-les-Bains. B-T.
MÉLINGUE, Georges Gaston Théodore.
Fr. b. Paris 1840. B.
MELIODON, Jules André. (S)
Am. b. Paris 1867; ad. 1934 Phila., Pa. A-B-F.
MELIORE, Toscano.
It. ac. 1271 in Florence. T.
MELLAN, Claude.
Fr. Abbeville 1598-1688 Paris. B-T-803-880.
MELLÉ, Léon August.
Fr. Paris 1816-1889 Same. T.
MELLEN, Frank.
Am. d. 1925 in Greenwich, Conn. A023.
MELLING, Anton Ignaz.
Ger. Carlsruhe 1763-1831 Paris. B-T.

MELLON, Eleanor M. (S)
Am. b. Narberth, Pa. 1894; ad. 1934 New York. A-B-F.
MELONE, Ferrari Altobello.
It. ac. 1497-1517 in Cremona. T.
MELOSH, [Mrs.] Mildred E.
Am. b. Jersey City, N. J. 1901; ad. 1934 New York. A.
MELOY, Henry.
Am. ex. 1934 Woodstock, N. Y. M.
MELOZZO DA FORLI [Ambrosi].
It. Forli 1438?-1494 Same. E-T-722.
MELTON, Catherine Parker.
Am. b. Nashville, Tenn.; ad. 1934 Wash., D. C. A.
MELTSNER, Paul R.
Am. b. 1905; ad. 1934 New York. M.
MELTZER, Arthur.
Am. b. Minn., Minn. 1893; ad. 1934 Langhorne, Pa. A-F.
MELVILL, [Mrs.] Antonia.
Am. b. Berlin, Ger. 1875; ad. 1934 Los Angeles, Calif. A-F.
MELVILLE, Arthur.
Scot. b. East Linton 1855-1904 Witley, Eng. B-DNB-E-T.
MELVILLE, Frank [or Francis]. (Et)
Am. Brooklyn, N. Y. 1832-1916 N. H. A013.
MELZER, Moritz.
Ger. b. Albendorf 1877. T.
MELZI [or Melzo], Francesco.
It. Milan 1492/3-1568/70 Same. B-T.
MEMLING [or Memlinc], Hans [or Jean].
Flem. Memling 1430/5-1494 Bruges, Belg. B-Bd-C-E-T-191-475-722.
MEMMI DA SIENA, Lippo.
It. d. 1356/7 Siena. 905.
MEMMI, Simone. *see* Martini, S.
MEMO, Vagaggini.
It. b. Santa Flora 1892. M.
MENA Y MEDRANO, Pedro. (S)
Sp. Granada 1628-1693 Malaga. E-Hs-T.
MENABUOI, Giusto di Giovanni de. [or Padovano or Justus of Padua.]
It. d. 1393 in Padua. B-C-T.
MÉNAGEOT, François Guillaume.
Fr. London 1744-1816 Paris. B-T-722.
MÉNARD AMÉDÉE RENÉ.
Fr. Nantes 1806-1879 Same. B-T.
MÉNARD, Marie Auguste Émile René.
Fr. Paris 1862-1930 Same. B-T.
MENASCO. *see* Magnasco.
MENCONI, Frank G. (S)
Am. Tuscany, It. 1884-1928 Union City, N. J. A025.
MENDELSOHN, Mirian.
Am. ex. 1935 New York. M.
MENDENHALL, Emma.
Am. b. Cinn., O. 1873; ad. 1934 Same. A.
MENDES DA COSTA.
Dut. b. 1863. M.
MENDEZ, Leopoldo. (Eg)
Mex. b. Mexico City 1903; ad. 1934 Same. M.
MENDOLOWITZ, Daniel.
Am. ex. 1935 Santa Cruz, Calif. M.
MÈNE, Pierre Jules. (S)
Fr. Paris 1810-1879 Same. B-T.
MENELAUS. [Pupil of Stephanus.]
Gr. ac. 5th Cent. B.C. Hs-T.
MENESES OSORIO, Francisco.
Sp. Sèville 1630?-1705? Same. B-C-T.
MENG, John.
Am. Phila., Pa. 1794-1854 West Indies. F-T.
MENGARINI, Fausta Vittoria. (S)
Am. b. Rome, It. 1893; ad. 1934 New York. A.
MENGELBURG, Egidius.
Ger. Cologne 1770-1849 Same. B-T.
MENGELBURG, Otto.
Ger. Cologne 1817/8-1890 Düsseldorf. B-T.
MENGHINI, Niccolò. (S)
It. Rome 1610-1655. T.
MENGS, Anton Raphael.
Ger. Aussig 1728-1779 Rome, It. B-Bd-C-E-T-722-801.
MENGS, Ismael Israel.
Dan. Copenhagen 1688-1764 Dresden, Ger. B-T.
MENINSKY, Bernard.
Rus. b. Russia 1891; ad. 1934 London. Wa-825.
MENKES, Zygmunt.
Pol. b. Lemberg 1896; ac. 1934 Paris. DBA-797.
MENN, Barthelemy.
Swi. Geneva 1815-1893 Same. B-T.
MENPES, Mortimer.
Aust. b. Australia 1860; ad. 1929 London. T-Wa1929.
MENTE, Charles.
Am. New York 1857-1933 Congers, N. Y. A030-Obit. N. Y. papers, 12-9-1933.
MENTEL, Lillian A.
Am. b. Cinn., O. 1882; ad. 1934 Same. A.
MENZEL, Adolph Friedrich Erdmann von.
Ger. Breslau 1815-1905 Berlin. B-C-E-T.
MENZEL, Herman.
Am. b. 1904; ex. 1933 Chicago. M.
MENZIO, Francesco.
It. ac. 1927. M.
MENZLER, Wilhelm.
Ger. b. Cassel 1846; ad. 1890 Munich. B-T.
MENZLER-PEYTON, Bertha S.
Mrs. Alfred Conway Peyton.
Am. b. Chicago 1874; ad. 1934 Gloucester, Mass. A-F-W.
MERCADANTE, Lorenzo. (S)
Flem. ac. 1464-1467 in Sèville, Sp. Hs-T.
MERCER, Andrew. (Min. and Poet)
Eng. 1775-1842. B-DNB.
MERCER, Geneva. (S)
Am. b. Jefferson, Ala. 1889; ad. 1934 Demopolis, Ala. A.
MERCHI, Gaetano. (S)
It. Brescia 1747-1823. T.
MERCIÉ, Marius Jean Antonin. (S)
Fr. Toulouse 1845-1916 Paris. B-DBA-E-Hs-T.
MERCIER, Michel Louis Victor. (S)
Fr. Meulan 1810-1894. B-T.
MERCIER, Philippe le.
Fr. Berlin, Ger. 1689-1760 London. B-DNB-T.

MERCK, JACOB FRANSZ VAN DER.
Dut. Gravandeel 1610-1664 Leyden. B-T.
MERCKE, EVELYN SCALES.
Am. ad. 1934 Phila., Pa. M.
MEREDITH, DOROTHY L.
Am. b. Milwaukee, Wis. 1906; ad. 1934 Same. A.
MEREDITH, SOPHIE D'OUSELEY.
Eng. b. Waterford; ad. 1934 Keynsham, Scot. Wa.
MEREDITH-WILLIAMS, [Mrs.] ALICE. (S)
Eng. b. Liverpool; ad. 1934 Edinburgh, Scot. Wa-798.
MEREDITH-WILLIAMS, MORRIS.
Scot. b. Cowbridge; ad. 1934 Devon. Wa.
MERENCINAO-PUCHOL, FRANCISCO.
Sp. b. Valencia 1885. DBA.
MERIAN, MARIA SIBYLLA.
Ger. Frankfort 1647-1717 Amsterdam, Holland. B-C-T.
MERIAN, MATTHAÜS [The Elder]. (Eg)
Ger. Basel, Swi. 1593/5-1650/1 Schwalbach. B-C-E-T.
MERIAN, MATTHAÜS [The Younger]. (Eg)
Ger. Basel, Swi. 1621-1687 Frankfort. B-C-T.
MERIDA, CARLOS.
Guatemalan; ex. 1932 New York. M.
MÉRIMÉE, JEAN FRANÇOIS LEONOR.
Fr. Broglie 1757-1836 Paris. B-T.
MÉRIMÉE, PROSPER.
Fr. Paris 1803-1870 Cannes. B-T.
MERINGTON, RUTH.
Am. b. London; ad. 1935 Newark, N. J. A12-F.
MERKE, H. (Eg)
Swi. b. Zurich; ac. 1800-1820 London. T.
MERKLER, EDWARD D.
Am. ad. 1935 Lawrence, L. I., N. Y. M.
MERLE, HUGUES.
Fr. St. Marcellin 1823-1881 Paris. B-T.
MERLIN, DANIEL.
Fr. 1861-1933 Paris. DBA.
MERODE, KARL FREIHERR VON.
Ger. Mödling 1853-1909 Vienna, Aus. B-T.
MERRELS, [Mrs.] GRAY PRICE. (Min)
Am. b. Topeka, Kan. 1884; ad. 1934 Hartford, Conn. A.
MERRILD, KNUD.
Am. b. Jutland, Denmark 1894; ad. 1934 Los Angeles, Calif. A.
MERRILL, FRANK THAYER.
Am. b. Boston 1848. F-W10-47.
MERRILL, HIRAM CAMPBELL.
Am. b. Boston 1866. A28-F.
MERRILL, KATHERINE. (Et)
Am. b. Milwaukee, Wis. 1876; ad. 1934 New York. A-F-W.
MERRILL, MARION. (Ill)
Am. ad. 1934 New York. M.
MERRIMAM, HELEN BIGELOW.
Mrs. Daniel Merriman.
Am. b. Boston 1844; ad. 1934 Same. A-F.
MERROTT, ANNA LEA.
Mrs. Henry Merritt.
Am. Phila., Pa. 1844-1930 London. A027-B-DAB-F-WX1-46.
MERSEREAU, PAUL ["Paul Fontaine"].
Am. b. Dallas, Tex. 1868; ad. 1934 Shreveport, La. A.
MERSON, LUC OLIVIER.
Fr. Paris 1846-1920 Same. B-DBA-T.
MERTENS, FRANCIS WILLIAMS.
Am. ad. 1934 New York. M.
MERTON, OWEN.
Am. Christchurch, New Zealand 1885-1930 London. A028-F.
MERUVIA, ARTURO RECUE.
Sp. b. Bolivia, S. A.; ex. 1934 London. M.
MERWIN, [Mrs.] ANTOINETTE DE FOREST.
Am. b. Cleveland, O. 1861; ad. 1934 Pasadena, Calif. A.
MERYMAN, RICHARD SUMMER.
Am. b. Boston 1882; ad. 1934 Wash., D. C. A.
MÉRYON, CHARLES. (Et)
Fr. Paris 1821-1868 St. Maurice. B-Bd-E-T-647-830-880.
MESDACH [or Mesdag], SALOMON.
Dut. ac. 1617-1738 in Middelbourg. B-T.
MESDAG, HENDRIK WILLEM.
Dut. Groningen 1831-1915 The Hague. B-C-DBA-T.
MESENS, JEANNE HENDRIX.
Belg. ad. 1911 Brussels. DBA.
MESGRIGNY, FRANK DE.
Fr. Paris 1836-1884 Same. B-T.
MESLÉ, JOSEPH PAUL.
Fr. St. Servan 1885-1927. B-T.
MESPLÈS, PAUL EUGÈNE.
Fr. b. Paris 1849. B-T.
MESS, GEORGE JOSEPH.
Am. b. Cinn., O.; ad. 1934 Ind., Ind. A.
MESS, GORDON BENJAMIN.
Am. b. Cinn., O.; ad. 1934 Ind., Ind. A.
MESSEL, OLIVER.
Eng. ac. 1933 in London. M.
MESSER, EDMUND CLARENCE.
Am. Skowhegan, Me. 1842-1919 Menomonie, Wis. A016.
MESSER, JEANETTE.
Am. d. 1917 Wash., D. C. A016.
MESSERSCHMIDT, FRANZ XAVIER. (S)
["Hogarth of Sculpture."]
Aus. Geisingen, Ger. 1736-1783 Vienna. Hs-T.
MESSINA, ANTONELLO.
see Antonello da Messina.
MESSINA, FRANCESCO. (S)
It. ac. 1901. Fa-M.
MESSMER [or Mesner], JOHANN GEORGE.
Aus. 1715-1798 Saulgau. T.
MESSYS [or Metsys]. *see* Massys.
MĚSTROVIĆ, IVAN.
Jug. Slav; b. Otavice 1883; ac. 1934 Zagreb. DBA-E-Hs-T-Wa-798-813-844.
METCALF, ELIAB.
Am. Franklin, Mass. 1785-1834 New York. F-2-6-144-183-184.
METCALF, JACK. (S)
Am. ad. 1935 New York. M.
METCALF, WILLARD LEROY.
Am. Lowell, Mass. 1858-1925 New York. A022-B-E-F-T-W13-1-46-71-105-757.

METCALFE, PERCY. (Med)
[Designed the 1935 Silver Jubilee Medals.]
Eng. ad. 1935 London. M.
METEYARD, THOMAS BUFORD.
Am. Rock Island, Ill. 1865-1928 Swi. A025-F-W14.
METHFOSSEL, HERMAN. (Ill)
Am. Stapleton, N. Y. 1873-1912 Great Kills, N. Y. A010.
METHVEN, CATHCART WILLIAM.
Scot. Edinburgh 1849-1926 Durban, Natal. M.
METHVEN, H. WALLACE.
Am. b. Phila., Pa. 1875; ad. 1934 Paris. A.
METSU, GABRIEL.
Dut. Leyden 1629/30-1667 Amsterdam. B-Bd-C-E-T-722.
METSYS. *see* Massys.
METTLING, LOUIS.
Fr. Dijon 1847-1904 Neuilly. B-T.
METZINGER, JEAN.
Fr. b. Nantes 1883. DBA-T-797.
METZLER. *see* Peyton, M.
METZMACHER, ÉMILE PIERRE.
Fr. ac. 1863-1889 in Paris. B-T.
METZNER, FRANZ. (S)
Aus. Pilsen 1870-1919 Berlin, Ger. Hs-T-798.
METZU, GABRIEL. *see* Metsu, G.
MEULEN, ADAM FRANZ VAN DER.
Flem. Brussels 1631/4-1690 Paris. B-C-E-T-722.
MEULEN, FRANÇOIS PIETER TER.
Dut. b. 1843. B-T.
MEUNIER, CONSTANTIN ÉMILE. (S)
Belg. Ellerbeck 1831-1905 Brussels. B-E-Hs-T-18-798.
MEUNIER, EDMUND JOSEPH CHARLES.
Fr. b. Colombes; ac. 1878 in Paris. B.
MEURER, ALBERT J. T.
Am. b. Louisville, Ky. 1887; ad. 1934 Wash., D. C. A.
MEURER, CHARLES A.
Am. b. Germany 1865; ad. 1934 Terrace Park, O. A.
MEURISSE, JOSEF.
Ger. b. Aachen 1868. T.
MEURON, ALBERT DE.
Swi. Neuchâtel 1823-1897 Same. B-T.
MEURON, MAXIMILIEN DE.
Swi. Corcelles 1785-1868 Neuchâtel. B-T.
MEURS, HARMEN. (Et)
Dut. ex. 1934 in London. M.
MEUSER, CASPAR. (S)
Ger. b. Dresden 1593? T.
MEUX, GWENDOLYN D.
Am. ad. 1934 Boulder, Colo. A.
MEVES, AUGUSTUS. (Min)
Eng. d. London 1818. T.
MEWHINNEY, [Mrs.] ELLA K.
Am. b. Nelsonville, Tex. 1891; ad. 1934 Holland, Tex. A.
MEXICAN ARTISTS.
see books Nos. 791-794; *also consult* Palacio de Bellas Artes, Mexico City.
MEYENBERG, JOHN C. (S)
Am. b. Tell City, Ind. 1860. A-F-181.
MEYER, ALVIN WILLIAM. (S)
Am. b. Bartlett, Ill. 1892; ad. 1934 New York. A-F.
MEYER, AUGUST EDWARD NICOLAUS [or Claus].
Ger. Linden 1856-1919 Düsseldorf. B-T.
MEYER, CHRISTIAN.
Am. Germany 1838-1907 Brooklyn, N. Y. A06-F.
MEYER, ENNO.
Am. b. Cinn., O. 1874. A12-F.
MEYER, ERNEST.
Am. ex. 1935 Brooklyn, N. Y. M.
MEYER, FELICIA.
Am. ad. 1935 Dorset, Vt. M.
MEYER, GEORGE.
Am. Chicago 1896-1930 Indiana. A028.
MEYER, HANS.
Ger. Berlin 1846-1919 Same. B-T.
MEYER, HENRY HOPPNER. (Eg)
Eng. 1782-1847 London. B-DNB-F-2-6-7.
MEYER, HERBERT.
Am. b. New York 1882; ad. 1934 Dorset, Vt. A-F.
MEYER [or Meier], JERIMIAH. (Min)
Eng. Tubingen 1735-1789 Kew. B-DNB.
MEYER, JOHANN GEORGE.
Ger. Bremen 1813-1886. B-C-T.
MEYER, LIEZEN. *see* Liezen-Meyer.
MEYER, PAUL AUBERLIN.
Am. b. Cleveland, O. 1910; ad. 1934 Same. A.
MEYER-EBERHARDT. *see* Eberhardt, Meyer.
MEYERHEIM, EDWARD FRANZ.
Ger. Berlin 1838-1880 Marburg. B-C-T.
MEYERHEIM, FRIEDRICH EDOUARD.
Ger. Danzig 1808-1879 Berlin. B-C-T.
MEYERHEIM, PAUL FRIEDRICH.
Ger. Berlin 1842-1915 Same. B-C-T.
MEYERHEIM, ROBERT GUSTAV.
Ger. Danzig 1847-1920. T.
MEYEROWITZ, WILLIAM.
Am. b. Russia 1889; ad. 1934 New York. A-F-W.
MEYERS, HARRY MOORE. (Ill)
Am. b. New Orleans, La. 1886; ad. 1934 New York. M.
MEYERS, JEROME.
Am. ad. 1934 New York. M.
MEYERSAHM, [Mrs.] EXENE REED.
Am. b. Northville, Mich.; ad. 1934 Prov., R. I. A.
MEYLAN, PAUL JULIEN. (Ill)
Am. b. Canton of Vaud, Swi. 1882; ad. 1934 Redding, Conn. A-W.
MEYNER, WALTER.
Am. b. Phila., Pa. 1867; ad. 1934 New York. A.
MEYNIER, CHARLES.
Fr. Paris 1768-1832 Same. B-T.
MEYROWITZ, JENNEY DELONG RICE.
see Rice-Meyrowitz, J. D.
MEYTENS [or Mytens], MARTIN VAN [The Elder].
Swe. Stockholm 1648-1736. T.
MEYTENS [or Mytens], MARTIN VAN [The Younger].
Swe. Stockholm 1695-1770 Vienna, Aus. B-T.

MEYVIS, Almé Leon.
Am. b. St. Gilles-Waas, Belg. 1877; ad. 1934 East Rochester, N. Y. A.
MEZEROVA, Julie W.
Czec. b. Upice 1893. DBA.
MEZQUITA, José Maria López.
Sp. b. Granada 1883. B-M.
MI FEI.
Chinese. Kiangsu 1051-1107. E-T.
MICARINO. *see* Beccafumi.
MICHAEL [Master], The Fleming.
Ger. ac. 1481-1492. Fa-M.
MICHAELANGELO. *see* Michelangelo.
MICHAILOFF, Grigoij Karpowitsch.
Rus. 1814-1867 Leningrad. B-T.
MICHALAK, Antoni.
Pol. b. 1902; ad. 1935 Dolny, Pol. M.
MICHALAK, Ludwig.
Pol. b. Temesvár 1859; ad. 1934 Kazimerz Dolny. B-T.
MICHALLON, Achille Etna.
Fr. Paris 1796-1922 Same. B-C-T-722.
MICHALOWSKI, Peter [or Piotr].
Pol. Krakow 1801-1855 Same. B-T.
MICHARINO. *see* Beccafumi.
MICHAU, Théobald.
Flem. Tournai, Belg. 1676-1765 Antwerp. B-T-722.
MICHEL, Claude. *see* Clodion.
MICHEL, Émile François.
Fr. Metz 1828-1909 Paris. B-T.
MICHEL, Ernest Barthélemy.
Fr. Montpelier 1833-1902 Same. B-T.
MICHEL, Georges.
Fr. Paris 1763-1843 Same. B-T.
MICHEL, Henri François.
Fr. Paris 1846-1925. T.
MICHELANGELO, Buonarroti. (P-S)
It. Caprese 1475-1564 Rome. B-Bd-C-E-Hs-T-V-463-464-465-466-710-790-898.
MICHELANGELO DA SIENA.
It. ac. 1470 in Siena. T-V.
MICHELE DI MATTEO DA BOLOGNA.
see Lambertini, Michele di Matteo.
MICHELINO, Domenico di.
It. 1417-1491. T.
MICHELOZZO DI BARTOLOMMEO. (S)
It. Florence 1396-1472 St. Marco. E-Hs-T-V.
MICHETTI, Francesco Paolo.
It. Chieti 1851-1929 Naples. B-T.
MICHIE, James Coutts.
Scot. Marywell 1861-1919 Edinburgh. T.
MICHIELI [or Micheli], Parrasio.
It. 1516-1578 Venice. T.
MICHNICK, David. (S)
Am. b. Ukraine 1892. Cs.
MICKLE, Alfred E.
Can. b. Guelph, Ont.; ad. 1935 Toronto. M.
MICON. (P-S)
Gr. ac. 460 B.C. B-E.
MIDDIMAN, Samuel. (Eg)
Eng. 1750-1831 London. B-DNB-T.
MIDDLETON, James Godsell.
Eng. 1826-1872 London. B-T.
MIDDLETON, John.
Eng. Norwich 1827-1856 Same. DNB-T.
MIDDLETON, Stanley Grant.
Am. b. Brooklyn, N. Y. 1852; ad. 1934 New York. A-F-W-T.
MIDDLETON, Thomas.
Am. Fanclure, S. C. 1797-1863 Charleston, S. C. F-T-2-7.
MIDGLEY, Waldo.
Am. b. Salt Lake City, Utah; ac. 1933 New York. M.
MIDJO, [Prof.] Christian.
Am. b. Trondheim, Nor. 1882; ad. 1934 Ithaca, N. Y. M.
MIDLER, V.
Rus. ex. 1934 Phila., Pa. M.
MIDY, Arthur.
Fr. b. St. Quentin 1877. DBA-T.
MIEL, Jan [Jean or Bike or Jamieli].
Flem. Antwerp 1599-1644 Turin, It. B-C-T-722.
MIELATZ, Charles Frederick William. (Et)
Am. Germany 1864-1919 New York. A016-F-46.
MIELICH. *see* Müelich.
MIELZINER, Leo.
Am. b. New York 1869; d. 1935 No. Truro, Mass. Obit. N. Y. papers, 8-12-1935. A-F-W.
MIEREVELD, Michel Janszoon van.
Dut. Delft 1567-1641 Same. B-Bd-C-E-T.
MIERIS, Frans van [The Elder].
Dut. Leyden 1635-1681 Same. B-C-E-T-722.
MIERIS, Frans van [The Younger].
Dut. Leyden 1689-1763 Same. B-C-T.
MIERIS, Willem van.
Dut. Leyden 1662-1747 Same. B-C-E-T-722.
MIERISCH, Dorothea.
Am. ad. 1935 Califon, N. J. M.
MIESCHANINOFF, Oscar.
Rus. b. Vitebsk 1886. DBA-T.
MIESSE, Jacob.
Am. b. Reading, Pa. 1845. M.
MIFFLIN, Lloyd.
Am. 1846-1921 Norwood, Pa. A018.
MIGNARD, Nicolas [d'Avignon].
Fr. Troyes 1606-1668 Paris. B-C-T.
MIGNARD, Pierre [Le Romain].
Fr. Troyes 1610/2-1695 Paris. B-C-E-722.
MIGNON [or Minjon], Abraham.
Ger. Frankfort 1640-1679? Wetzlar. B-C-E-T-722.
MIGNOT, Louis Remy.
Am. Charleston, S. C. 1831-1870 Brighton, Eng. B-DAB-F-T-3-4-11-15-35.
MIJANTO. *see* Miyanato.
MIJTENS. *see* Mytens.
MIKELL, Minnie.
Mrs. Alexander B. Mikell.
Am. b. Charleston, S. C. 1891; ad. 1934 James Island, S. C. A.
MIKKIADES OF CHIOS. (S)
Gr. ac. first half of 6th Cent. Hs-T.
MIKOUN, Mika. (S)
Pol. ac. 1933. M.
MILAM, [Mrs.] Annie Nelson.
Am. b. Homer, La. 1870; ad. 1934 Ennis, Tex. A.
MILANO, Ambrogino da.
see Ambrogino da Milano.
MILANO, Giovanni. *see* Giovanni da Milano.

MILATZ, F. A.
Dut. Haarlem 1763-1808 Same. B-T.
MILBANK, MARJORIE ROBBINS.
Mrs. Albert G. Milbank.
Am. Boston 1875-1933 Lloyd Harbor, N. Y. A28-Obit. N. Y. papers, 10-12-1933.
MILBANKE, MARK RICHARD.
Eng. London 1875-1927 Same. T-Y01929.
MILBOURN, JOHN.
Eng. ac. 1773-1790 in London. DNB-T.
MILBURN, OLIVER.
Am. Toronto, Can. 1883-1934 Los Angeles, Calif. A.
MILEHAM, [Mrs.] CHRISTOPHER J.
see Durkee, Helen Winslow.
MILES, EDWARD. (Min)
Am. England 1752-1828 Phila., Pa. B-DAB-DNB-F-T-2-6-30-45-179.
MILES, EMILY WINTHROP. (S)
Mrs. C. L. Miles.
Am. b. New York; ex. 1935 Same. Cs.
MILES, GEORGE FRANCIS [or Frank].
Eng. Bingham 1852-1891. B-DNB-T.
MILES, HAROLD W.
Am. b. Des Moines, Ia. 1887; ad. 1934 Hollywood, Calif. A.
MILES, LOU.
Am. ex. 1934 New York. M.
MILESI, ALESSANDRO.
It. b. Venice 1856. B-T.
MILHAU, [Miss] ZELLA DE. (Et)
Am. b. New York; ad. 1934 Southampton, L. I., N. Y. M.
MILHOMME, FRANÇOISE DOMINQUE AIMÉ. (S)
Fr. Valenciennes 1758-1823 Paris. B-T.
MILICH, ADOLPH.
Czec. b. Poland 1886. DNB.
MILIGAN, MARTHA. (S)
Am. ad. 1935 Cleveland, O. M.
MILIONE, LOUIS. (S)
Am. b. Padua, It. 1884; ad. 1934 Phila., Pa. A-F.
MILLAIS, [Sir] JOHN EVERETT.
Eng. Southampton 1829-1896 London. B-Bd-C-DNB-E-T-467-922.
MILLÁN, PEDRO. (S)
Sp. ac. 1500-1526 in Sèville. Hs-T.
MILLAR, ADDISON THOMAS.
Am. Warren, O. 1860-1913 So. Norwalk, Conn. A011-F-T.
MILLARD, C. E. (Ill)
Am. ad. 1934 New York. A.
MILLARD, CHARLES S.
Br. 1837-1917. B-T.
MILLARD, ELIZABETH BOYNTON.
Am. b. Chicago; ad. 1934 Highland Park, Ill. A.
MILLARD, ERNEST JEAN MARIE.
Fr. b. Paris 1872. DBA.
MILLARD, PATRICK FERGUSON.
Eng. b. Aspatria 1902; ad. 1934 London. Wa.
MILLER, ALFRED JACOB.
Am. Balt., Md. 1810-1874 Same. B-Bd-C-F-T-4-15.
MILLER, ANNA HAZZARD.
Mrs. Edward J. Miller.
Am. b. Minnesota 1863; ad. 1934 Okla. City, Okla. A.
MILLER, BARSE.
Am. b. New York 1904; ad. 1934 Los Angeles, Calif. A.
MILLER, BENJAMIN. (Eg)
Am. b. Cinn., O.; ad. 1934 Same. A.
MILLER, BURR CHURCHILL. (S)
Am. b. Wilkesbarre, Pa. 1904; ad. 1934 Paris. A-F.
MILLER, CHARLES HENRY.
Am. New York 1842-1922 Same. A019-B-C-DAB-F-T-1-15-22-89.
MILLER, CORA E.
Am. b. Jenkintown, Pa.; ad. 1934 Phila., Pa. A.
MILLER, DELLE.
Am. b. Independence, Kan.; d. 1932 Kansas City, Mo. A030.
MILLER, D. ROY.
Am. b. Mechanicsburg, Pa. 1891; ad. 1934 Chester Springs, Pa. A.
MILLER, EARLE.
Am. b. Phila., Pa. 1907; ad. 1934 Same. A.
MILLER, EDGAR. (S)
Am. b. 1899; ex. 1933 Chicago. M.
MILLER, ELEAZER HUTCHINSON.
Am. Shepherdstown, W. Va. 1831-1921 Wash., D. C. A018-F-T.
MILLER, [Mrs.] EVYLENA NUNN.
Am. b. Mayfield, Kan. 1888; ad. 1934 Los Angeles, Calif. A28.
MILLER, FELIX MARTIN. (S)
Eng. ac. 1842-1880 London. T.
MILLER, FRANCIS.
Am. Columbus, O. 1855-1930 New York. A027.
MILLER, FRANK L.
Am. ad. 1934 Memphis, Tenn. M.
MILLER, GEORGE WASHINGTON. (S)
Am. ex. 1933 Paris. 786.
MILLER, HARRIETTE G. (P-S)
Am. b. Cleveland, O.; ad. 1934 Arlington, Vt. A.
MILLER, HELEN ADELE LERCH. (S)
Am. ex. 1934 Chicago. M.
MILLER, HELENA W.
Am. d. 1929 New York. A027.
MILLER, HESTER.
Am. ac. 1933 in New York. A27.
MILLER, IRIS MARIE ANDREWS.
Mrs. William N. Miller.
Am. b. Ada, O. 1881; ad. 1934 Detroit, Mich. A-T.
MILLER, ISABELLE LAZARUS.
Am. b. Phila., Pa. 1907; ad. 1934 Same. A.
MILLER, JOHN.
see Müller, Johann Sebastian.
MILLER, JOHN FREDERICK. (Et)
Eng. ac. 1785 in London. DNB.
MILLER, JOSEPH MAXWELL. (S)
Am. Balt., Md. 1877-1933 Same. A030-B-F-T-W.
MILLER, KATE RENO.
Am. Illinois 1874-1929 Norwood, O. A027-F.
MILLER, KENNETH HAYES.
Am. b. Kenwood, N. Y. 1876; ad. 1934 New York. A-B-F-T-W-1-468-701.

MILLER, Leslie William.
Am. b. Brattleboro, Vt. 1848; ad. 1915 Phila., Pa. A12-W15.
MILLER, Lilian May.
Am. ad. 1934 Higham Center, Mass. A.
MILLER, Marguerite Cuttino.
Am. b. Charleston, S. C. 1895; ad. 1934 Same. A.
MILLER, Maud Albeva.
Am. b. Skyland, Calif. 1883; ad. 1934 Oakland, Calif. A.
MILLER, Mildred Bunting.
Am. b. Phila., Pa. 1892; ad. 1934 Chester Springs, Pa. A.
MILLER, Minnie M.
Am. ad. 1934 Germantown, Pa. A.
MILLER, Oscar.
Am. b. New York 1867; ad. 1934 Bristol, R. I. A.
MILLER, Philip.
Am. b. Milwaukee, Wis. 1898; ad. 1934 Same. A.
MILLER, Ralph Willett.
Eng. 1762-1799. Wi.
MILLER, Richard Emil.
Am. b. St. Louis 1875; ad. 1934 Provincetown, Mass. A-B-F-T-W-1-46.
MILLER, Ruth. *see* Fracker, R. M.
MILLER, [Mrs.] Susan Barse.
Am. b. Adrian, Mich.; ad. 1934 Gloucester, Mass. A.
MILLER, Suzanne.
Am. b. Cortlandt, N. Y.; ad. 1934 Boston. A.
MILLER, Viola.
Am. b. St. Louis 1890; ad. 1915 Paris. A12.
MILLER, William.
Eng. 1740?-1810 London. B-DNB-T.
MILLER, William. (Eg)
Scot. Edinburgh 1796-1882 Sheffield, Eng. B-DNB-E-T.
MILLER, William Henry.
Am. Phila., Pa. 1854-1928 Same. A026-F-T.
MILLER, William Ongley.
Eng. b. Sussex 1883; ad. 1934 Kent. Wa.
MILLER, William R. (Eg)
Am. New York 1850-1923. A020-F-T.
MILLER, Winfried von.
Ger. Munich 1853/4-1925 Same. B-T.
MILLÈS, Carl. (S)
Swe. b. Lagga 1875. B-Hs-T-470-683-798-849.
MILLÈS, Ruth Anna Marie. (S)
Swe. b. Wallentuna 1873. B-T.
MILLESON, Royal Hill.
Am. b. Batavia, O. 1849; ad. 1935 Chicago, Ill. A18-F-T.
MILLET, Aimé. (S)
Fr. Paris 1819-1891 Same. B-T.
MILLET, Clarence.
Am. b. Hahnville, La. 1897; ad. 1934 New Orleans, La. A.
MILLET, Francis Davis.
Am. Mattapoisett, Mass. 1846-1912. A010-B-C-DAB-E-F-T-1-15-46-71-180.
MILLET, Jean François.
Fr. Gréville 1814-1875 Barbizon. B-Bd-C-E-T 710-820-843-870-943-944.
MILLET [or Mile], Jean François [The Elder]. [Called Françisque I.]
Fr. Antwerp, Belg. 1642-1679/80 Paris. B-E-T-722.
MILLET [or Mile], Jean François [The Younger].
[Called Françisque II.]
Fr. Paris 1666-1723 Same. B-C-E-T.
MILLET, Joseph François.
Fr. La Fère 1697-1777 Versailles. B-T.
MILLET, Louis J. (Mu)
Am. b. New York; d. 1923 Chicago. A020-F.
MILLET, Pierre. (S)
Fr. Gréville 1833-1914 Same. T.
MILLETT, G. Van.
Am. b. Kansas City, Mo. 1864; ad. 1934 Same. A-T.
MILLIER, Arthur. (Et)
Am. b. England 1893. A28.
MILLIÈRE, Maurice. (Eg)
Fr. b. Havre 1871; ad. 1934 Paris. DBA.
MILLIGAN, Gladys.
Am. ad. 1935 Wash., D. C. M.
MILLINGTON, James Heath.
Ir. Cork 1799-1872 London. DNB-T.
MILLMORE, Joseph. (S)
Am. Ireland 1852-1886 Geneva, Swi. F-Ta.
MILLMORE, Martin. (S)
Am. Ireland 1844-1883 Roxbury, Mass. DAB-F-Hs-T-Ta-4-15-26.
MILLNER, Karl.
Ger. Munich 1825-1895 Same. B-T.
MILLS, Alfred. (Et)
Eng. 1776-1833 Walworth. B-DNB-T.
MILLS, Clark. (S)
Am. Onondaga, N. Y. 1815-1883 Wash., D. C. F-T.
MILLS, George. (Med)
Eng. 1792/3-1824 Birmingham. DNB-T.
MILLS, J. Harrison.
Am. 1841-1916 Buffalo, N. Y. A014.
MILLS, Theodore Augustus. (S)
Am. Charleston, S. C. 1839-1916 Pittsburgh, Pa. A014-F-T.
MILLS, Thomas Henry.
Am. b. Hartford, Conn. 1877; ad. 1934 Gloucester, Mass. A-F.
MILNE, David B.
Am. b. Paisley, Can. 1882; ad. 1935 Boston Corners, N. Y. A12-F-T.
MILNE, J. Maclauchlan.
Scot. ad. 1934 Dundee. Wa.
MILNER, T. Stuart.
Eng. ad. 1935 Essex, Eng. M.
MILNOR, James Wilson. (Eg)
Am. ad. 1934 Montclair, N. J. M.
MILSOM, Eva Grace.
Am. b. Buffalo, N. Y. 1868; ad. 1934 Angola, N. Y. A.
MILTON, John.
Eng. ac. 1767-1774 London. DNB-T.
MILTON, John. (Med)
Eng. d. 1805 in London. DNB-T.
MILTON, Thomas. (Eg)
Eng. 1743-1827 Bristol. B-DNB-T.
MILTON, Victor Marias.
Fr. b. Puteaux 1872. DBA.
MILWARD, [Mrs.] Marguerite. (S)
Eng. ex. 1933 London and Paris. M.

MINARDI, TOMMASCO.
It. Faenza 1787-1871 Rome. B-T.
MINAZZOLI, EDWARD A. (S)
Am. b. Momo, It. 1887; ad. 1934 Paris. A.
MINCHO [or Myocho].
Jap. 1352-1431 Kyoto. T.
MIND, GOTTFRIED [Katzenrafael].
Swi. Berne 1768-1814 Same. B-T.
MINDERHOUT, HENDRIK VON.
Flem. Rotterdam 1632-1696 Antwerp. B-C-T.
MINELLA, CARLO BONATTO.
It. Frassineto 1855-1878. T.
MINELLA, PIETRO DI TOMMASO.
It. Siena 1391-1458. T.
MINELLI, GIOVANNI. *see* Bardi, G. A. M.
MINER, EDWARD HERBERT.
Am. b. Sheridan, N. Y. 1882; ad. 1934 Westbury, N. Y. A.
MINER, FRED R.
Am. b. New London, Conn. 1876. A.
MINER, GEORGIA WATSON.
Mrs. Lewis H. Miner.
Am. b. Springfield, Ill. 1876; ad. 1934 Same. A.
MINGLE, JOSEPH F.
Am. Phila., Pa. 1839-1903 Same. A04-T.
MINGORANCE, JUAN.
Sp. ex. 1935 New York. M.
MINGOZZI [or Mengozzi], GIROLAMO.
It. Ferrara 1688-1776 Verona. B-T.
MINGUILLÓN, JULIA.
Sp. ad. 1934 Madrid; ex. 1934 Pittsburgh, Pa. M.
MINIFIE, H. GORDON.
Am. ex. 1933 in Paris. M.
MINIO, TIZIANO.
It. ac. 1517-1552 in Padua. T.
MINNE, GEORGE. (S)
Belg. b. Ghent 1866. B-Hs-T-471.
MINNIGERODE, MARIETTA.
Am. ac. 1893. M.
MINO DA GIOVANNI. *see* Fiesole, M. da G.
MINO DEL REAME [Regno]. (S)
It. ad. 1463-1490 Rome. T-V.
MINO DI SIMONE SENESE.
It. ac. 1284-1321 in Siena. T.
MINOR, ANNE B. ROGERS.
Mrs. George Maynard Minor.
Am. b. East Lyme, Conn. 1864; ad. 1934 Waterford, Conn. A.
MINOR, ROBERT CRANNELL.
Am. New York 1840-1904 Waterford, Conn. A05-C-DAB-E-F-T-W3-15-46.
MINOTT, JOSEPH OTIS.
Am. b. Orange, N. J.; d. 1909 Paris. A07-T.
MINOZZI, BERNARDINO.
It. Bologna 1699-1769 Same. B-T.
MINTCHINE, ABRAHAM.
Rus. Kiev 1898-1931 La Garde, Fr. DBA.
MINTROP, THEODOR.
Ger. Werden 1814-1870 Düsseldorf. C-T.
MINTZ, HARRY.
Am. ad. 1934 Chicago. M.
MINTZ, MARY.
Am. b. Morristown, N. J. 1906; ad. 1935 Same. M.
MIR SAJYID ALI. (Min)
Per. ac. 1550 in Persia. M-T.
MIRACOVICI, PAUL.
Rumanian. ex. 1935 Bucharest. M.
MIRAK.
Per. ac. 1524-1550 in Persia. M.
MIRALHETI, JEAN.
Fr. Montpellier 1394-1457 Nice. B-T.
MIRANDA.
see Careno de Mirando.
see Garcia de Miranda.
MIRANDA Y CASELLAS, FERNANDO. (S)
Am. Valencia, Sp. 1842-1925 New York. F-T-Ta.
MIRANDA, SEBASTIAN. (S)
Sp. b. Oviedo. M.
MIRANDE, HENRY. (Eg)
Fr. b. Nice 1877. DBA.
MIRANDO, FERNANDO. (S)
Am. ac. 1925. F-Ta.
MIRBEL, LIZINKA AIMÉE ZOÉ. (Min)
Fr. Cherbourg 1796-1849 Paris. B-T-722.
MIRÓ, JOÁN.
Sp. b. Barcelona 1893; ad. 1935 Paris. DBA-T.
MIROU [or Miron], ANTHONIE.
Flem. Antwerp, Belg. 1570-1653 Same.
MISH, CHARLOTTE ROBERTA.
Am. b. Lebanon, Pa. 1903; ad. 1934 Portland, Ore. A.
MITAN, JAMES. (Eg)
Eng. London 1776-1822 Same. B-DNB-T.
MITAN, SAMUEL. (Eg)
Eng. 1786-1843 London. DNB-T.
MITCHELL, ALFRED R.
Am. b. York, Pa. 1888; ad. 1934 San Diego, Calif. A-F.
MITCHELL, ARTHUR.
Am. b. Gillespie, Ill. 1864; ad. 1934 St. Louis, Mo. A-T.
MITCHELL, BRUCE.
Am. ad. 1935 Upper Montclair, N. J. M.
MITCHELL, CHARLES D. (Ill)
Am. ad. 1934 Phila., Pa. M.
MITCHELL, [Mrs.] ELEANOR B.
Am. b. Pittsburgh, Pa. 1872. A18.
MITCHELL, FRANCES BUHOLZ.
Am. ad. 1934 Minn., Minn. M.
MITCHELL, GEORGE B.
Am. b. East Bridgewater, Mass. 1874; ad. 1934 Rutherford, N. J. A.
MITCHELL, [Mrs.] GLADYS VINSON.
Am. b. Albuquerque, N. M. 1894. A18.
MITCHELL, GLEN.
Am. b. New Richmond, Ind. 1894; ad. 1934 Minn., Minn. A.
MITCHELL, GUERNSEY. (S)
Am. d. 1921 Rochester, N. Y. A018.
MITCHELL, HARVEY.
Am. ac. 1830 in Charleston, S. C. F.
MITCHELL, JOHN AMES. (Et)
Am. New York 1845-1918 Ridgfield, Conn. A015-T-46.
MITCHELL, JOHN CAMPBELL.
Scot. Campbeltown 1862-1922 Edinburgh. B-T-Y01923.
MITCHELL, LAURA M. D. (Min)
Am. b. Halifax, N. S.; ad. 1934 Alhambra, Calif. A.

MITCHELL, Neil Reed.
Am. New York 1860-1934 New Haven, Conn. M-Obit. N. Y. papers, 1-29-1934.
MITCHELL, Robert. (Eg)
Eng. 1820-1873 Bromley, Eng. B-DNB-T.
MITCHELL, Thomas.
Eng. ac. 1735-1790 in London. B-DNB-T.
MITCHELL, Thomas John.
Am. b. Rochester, N. Y. 1875; ad. 1934 Same. A.
MITCHELL, Thomas W.
Can. b. Clarksburg; ad. 1935 Toronto, Ont. M.
MITIUS, Louis.
Am. b. 1842; d. 1911 Cinn., O. A010.
MITSUNAGA, Kasuga [Fujiwara].
Jap. ac. 1168-1173 in Kyoto. J-T.
MITSUNOBU, Haseawa [Tosa].
Jap. 1433/4-1525 Kyoto. J-T.
MITSUOKI, Tosa [Josho].
Jap. Sakai 1616/7-1691 Kyoto. J-T.
MIX, Florence.
Am. Hartford, Conn. 1881-1922 Glenwood, N. Y. A019-F-T.
MIYANOTO, Kaname.
Jap.-Am. ad. 1935 New York. M.
MIYAZAKI, Schiro.
Jap.-Am. b. Japan 1910; ad. 1934 Seattle, Wash. A.
MIZEN, Frederic. (Ill)
Am. ad. 1934 Chicago. M.
MNESIKLES. (S)
Gr. ac. 5th century B.C. T.
MOBERG, Donna.
Am. ad. 1935 Minn., Minn. M.
MOCETTO, Girolamo. (Eg)
It. Murano 1458-1531 Venice. B-T-722.
MOCHI [or Mocchi], Francesco. (S)
It. Florence 1580-1654 Rome. T.
MOCHI, Ugo. (Ill)
It. b. Florence, It. 1889; ad. 1935 New Rochelle, N. Y. M.
MOCHIDZUKI, Giokusen.
Jap. ac. 1800 in Japan. J., Vol. 2, page 109.
MOCK, George Andrew.
Am. b. Muncie, Ind. 1886; ad. 1934 Same. A.
MOCK, Gladys Amy.
Am. b. New York; ad. 1934 Same. A.
MODENA, Barnaba. *see* Barnaba da M.
MODENA, Nicoletto Rosex da. (Eg)
It. 1450-1516 Italy. T.
MODENA, Tommaso da.
It. 1325-1376 Italy. M.
MODERNO [Riccio]. *see* Briosco, Andrea.
MODERSOHN, Otto.
Ger. b. Soest 1865. B-T.
MODERSOHN-BECKER, Paula.
Ger. Dresden 1876-1907 Worpswede. T-477.
MODIGLIANI, Amedeo. (P-S)
It. Leghorn 1884-1920 Paris. B-DBA-T-478-700-783-797.
MODRA, Theodore P.
Am. Poland 1873-1930 Los Angeles, Calif. A028.
MODRAKOWSKA, Eleanor A.
Am. b. College Point, L. I., N. Y.; ad. 1934 New York. M.
MOE, Louis. (Ill)
Am. ad. 1934 New York. M.
MOELLER, Elizabeth Anna.
Am. b. Davenport, Ia. 1906; ad. 1934 Mt. Carmel, Ill. A.
MOELLER, Gustave.
Am. Wisconsin 1881-1931 Milwaukee, Wis. A028-F.
MOELLER, Henry Nicholas.
Am. b. New York 1883; ad. 1934 Same. A.
MOELLER, Louis Charles.
Am. New York 1855-1930 Weehawken, N. J. A028-F-W16.
MOELLER, Selma. (Min)
Am. b. New York 1880; ad. 1934 Same. A.
MOER, Jean Baptiste van.
Belg. Brussels 1819-1884. B.
MOERENHOUT, Joseph Jodocus.
Belg. Eeckeren 1801-1874 Antwerp. B-T.
MOESSEL, Julius.
Am. b. Germany 1872; ad. 1934 Same. A.
MOEYAERT [or Moijart], Claesz Cornelisz.
Dut. Amsterdam 1600-1669. B-T.
MOFFETT, Ross E.
Am. b. Clearfield, Ia. 1888; ad. 1934 Provincetown, Mass. A-F-T-W.
MOFFITT, John M. (S)
Am. Eng. 1837-1887 New York. F-T.
MOGALLI, Cosmus. (Eg)
It. 1667-1730. T.
MOGFORD, Thomas.
Eng. Exeter 1808-1868 Guernsey. DNB-T.
MOHAN, Jenny C.
Am. ad. 1934 Birmingham, Ala. M.
MOHLTE, John Alfred.
Am. b. Gothenburg, Swe. 1865; ad. 1934 Brooklyn, N. Y. A12-M.
MOHN, Sigvard M.
Am. b. Northfield, Minn. 1891; ad. 1934 Brooklyn, N. Y. A.
MOHN, Viktor Paul.
Ger. Meissen 1842-1911 Berlin. B-T.
MOHR, Alex.
Ger. ex. 1935 Athens, Gr. M.
MOHR, Olga.
Am. ad. 1935 Cinn., O. M.
MOIGNIEZ, Jules. (S)
Fr. Senlis 1835-1894 St. Martin. B-T.
MOILAN, Otto E.
Am. b. Finland; ad. 1934 Kansas City, Mo. A.
MOIN.
Per. ac. 17th Century in Persia. M.
MOINE, Antoin Marie. (S)
Fr. St. Etienne 1796-1849 Paris. B-Hs-T.
MOINE. *see also* Lemoine.
MOINE, Antonin Marie. (S)
Fr. St. Etienne 1796-1849 Paris. B-Hs-T.
MOIRA, Gerald Edward. (Mu)
Eng. b. London 1867. T.
MOISE, Theodore Sydney.
Am. Charleston, S. C. 1806-1883 La. F-T-144-183.
MOITTE, Jean Guillaume. (S)
Fr. Paris 1746-1810 Same. B-T.
MOITTE, Pierre Etienne.
Fr. Paris 1722-1780 Same. B-T.
MOKUAN [or Mo-An].
Jap. ac. 14th century in Japan. T.
MOKUBEI.
Jap. Nagoya 1767-1833 Kyoto. T.

MOL, PIETER VAN.
Flem. Antwerp 1599-1650 Paris. B-C-T-722.
MOL, WOUTERUS.
Dut. Haarlem 1785/6-1857/8. T.
MOLA, PIER FRANCESCO.
It. Coldre 1612/20-1666/8 Rome. B-C-T-722.
MOLARSKY, ABRAM.
Am. b. Kiev, Rus. 1883; ad. 1934 Nutley, N. J. A-F.
MOLARSKY, MAURICE.
Am. b. Kiev, Rus. 1885; ad. 1934 Phila., Pa. A-F-T.
MOLE, HILMA.
Am. b. Croyden, Utah 1901; ad. 1934 Ogden, Utah. A.
MOLENAER, CORNELIS [Strabo].
Flem. Antwerp 1540-1591 Same. B-C-T.
MOLENAER, JAN MIENSE.
Dut. Haarlem 1605/10-1668 Same. B-Bd-C-T.
MOLENAER, JUDITH. *see* Leyster, J. M.
MOLENAER, KLAES-NICOLAES.
Dut. Haarlem 1620?-1676 Same. B-C-T.
MOLIN, BENÔIT HERMOGASTE.
Fr. Chambéry 1810-1894. B-T.
MOLIN, C. GUNNAR.
Am. b. Stockholm, Swe.; ad. 1934 Brooklyn, N. Y. A.
MOLINA, ALFONSO.
Aragonese; ac. 1487? Aragon, Sp. M.
MOLINA, VALENTINO.
Am. b. Savannah, Ga. 1880. M.
MOLINARI, ALEXANDER.
Ger. Berlin 1772-1831 Dresden. B-T.
MOLINARI, ANTONIO.
It. Venice 1655-1727. B-T.
MOLINARY, ANDREW.
Am. Gibraltar 1847-1915 New Orleans, La. A012-T-144-183.
MOLINARY, MARIE SEEBOLD.
Mrs. Andiés Molinary.
Am. b. New Orleans, La. 1876; ad. 1934 Same. A-T.
MOLITOR [or Müller], JOHANN PETER.
Ger. Coblentz 1702-1756 Krakow, Pol. B-T.
MOLK [or Mölck], JOSEF ADAM RITTER VON.
Aus. Vienna 1714-1794 Same. T.
MOLL, AAGE [Peter Marinus].
Am. b. Ribe, Denmark; ad. 1934 Hartford, Conn. A.
MOLL, CARL.
Aus. b. Vienna 1861. B-T.
MOLL, OSKAR.
Ger. b. Brieg 1875. T.
MÖLLER [or Miller], ANTON.
Ger. Königsberg 1563-1611 Danzig. B-T-803.
MÖLLER, OLAF.
Am. ac. 1933. M.
MÖLLERSBERG, NILS. (S)
Swe. b. Ekestad 1892. DBA.
MOLNAR, C. PAOLO.
Hun. b. Budapest 1894. T.
MOLS, ROBERT CHARLES GUSTAVE LAURENS.
Belg. Antwerp 1848-1903 Same. B-T.
MOLYN, PIETER DE [The Elder].
Dut. London 1595-1661 Haarlem. B-C-T.
MOLYN, PIETER DE [The Younger].
[Called Il. Cavaliere Tempesta.]
Dut. Haarlem 1637-1701 Milan, It. C-T-722.
MOLYNEUX, EDWARD FRANK. (Ill)
Am. b. London 1896; ad. 1934 New York. A.
MOMMER, PAUL.
Am. b. Luxemberg, Fr. 1899; ad. 1934 New York. M-892.
MOMMERS, HENDRIK.
Dut. Haarlem 1623-1693 Amsterdam. B-C-T.
MOMPER, FRANÇOIS [or Franz] DE.
Flem. Antwerp 1603-1660 Same. B-C-T.
MOMPER, JODOCUS [or Joost] DE [The Younger].
Flem. Antwerp 1564-1635 Same. B-C-T-722.
MOMPOU, D. JOSÉ.
Sp. ad. 1934 Barcelona, Sp. M.
MONACO, IL. *see* Lorenzo, M.
MONAGHAN, GERTRUDE. (Mu)
Am. b. West Chester, Pa. 1887; ad. 1934 Phila., Pa. A.
MONAMY, PETER.
Eng. Jersey 1670?-1749 Westminster. B-Bd-DNB-T.
MONCASSIN, HENRY RAPHAËL. (S)
Fr. b. Toulouse 1883. DBA-T.
MONCAYO, ISABEL.
Am. ex. 1934 New York. M.
MONCEL, ALPHONSE EMMANUEL. (S)
Fr. ac. 1933 in Paris. B-T-798.
MONCHABLON, JEAN FERDINAND.
Fr. Châtillon 1855-1904 Same. B-T.
MONCORNET, BALTHASAR.
Fr. Rouen 1630-1668/70 Paris. B-T.
MONCURE, LISA VANCE.
Am. b. Gallipolis, O. 1886; ad. 1935 Wash., D. C. M.
MOND, FRANK. *see* Du Mond.
MONDINEU, JEAN ETIENNE.
Fr. b. Paris 1872. B-T.
MONDRIAAN [or Mondrian], PIETER CORNELIS.
Dut. b. Amersfoort 1872; ad. 1934 Paris. DBA-T.
MONDZAIN, SIMON.
Pol. b. Poland 1890. DBA.
MONE [or Monet], JEAN [or Jehan]. (S)
Flem. ac. 1524-1548 in Antwerp. Hs-T-479.
MONET, CLAUDE JEAN.
Fr. Paris 1840-1926 Giverny. B-DBA-E-T-192-820-947.
MONFALCONE, EUGENE D.
Am. b. Italy; d. 1922 Richmond, Va. A019-T.
MONGAY-MUNOZ, DINA.
Fr. b. Buenos Aires, Argentine, S. A. 1910. DBA.
MONGIN, ANTOINE PIERRE.
Fr. Paris 1761-1827 Versailles. B-T.
MONGINOT, CHARLES.
Fr. Aube 1825-1900 Deauville. B-T.
MONI, LOUIS DE [The Younger].
Dut. Breda 1698-1771 Leyden. C-T-722.
MONK, WILLIAM. (Eg)
Eng. b. Chester 1863; ad. 1934 London. B-T-Wa.
MONKS, EDWARD E. (Ill)
Am. ad. 1934 New York. A.

MONKS, John Austin Sands.
Am. Cold Springs, N. Y. 1850-1917 Chicago. A014-F-T-46.
MONKS, R. H.
Am. ac. 20th Century. M.
MONNET, Charles.
Fr. Paris 1732-1808 Same. B-T.
MONNICKENDAM, Jacques.
Dut. b. Amsterdam; ad. 1934 New York. M.
MONNICKENDAM, Martin.
Dut. b. Amsterdam 1874. T.
MONNIER, France X. (S)
Am. Belfort, Fr. 1831-1912 Detroit, Mich. A010.
MONNIER, Henri Bonaventure. (Ill)
Fr. Paris 1799-1877 Same. B-T-480.
MONNIER, [Mrs.] Maud Nottingham.
Am. Abbotts, N. Y. 1876-1932 Hartford, Conn. A030.
MONNINGTON, Walter Thomas.
Eng. b. London 1903; ad. 1934. Same. Wa.
MONNOT. *see also* Monot.
MONNOT, Maurice Louis.
Fr. b. Paris 1869. DBA.
MONNOYER, Antoine.
Fr. Paris 1670-1847 St. Germain. DBA-T.
MONNOYER, Jean Baptiste.
Fr. Lille 1634-1699 London. B-C-DNB-T-722
MONOGRAMMISTS. [*see also* Masters.]
Note: For data regarding Monogrammists consult following books.
"Dictionaire des Monogrammes, Marques, Figurées, Lettres, Initials, Noms, Abrégés, Etc." by François Brulliot, Munich, Ger. 1832.
"Die Monogrammisten" [5 Vols.] by Dr. G. K. Nagler, Munich, Ger. 1879.
"Dictionaire Encyclopédique Marques et Monogrammes" [2 Vols.] by Ris-Parquot, Paris, 1895.
MONOT. *see also* Monnot.
MONOT [or Monnot], Martin Claude. (S)
Fr. Paris 1733-1803 Same. B-T.
MONOT [or Monnot], Pierre Etienne. (S)
Fr. Doubs 1657-1733 Rome. B-T.
MONRAD, Margaret. (S)
Am. b. New Zealand 1879; ad. 1934 New Haven, Conn. A.
MONRO, Henry.
Eng. London 1791-1814. B-T.
MONRO, J. C. (Eg)
Eng. ac. 1866-1889 in London. T.
MONRO, Thomas.
Eng. London 1759-1833. T.
MONSALDY [or Monsaldi], Antoine Maxime. (Ill)
Fr. Paris 1768-1816. B-T.
MONSIAU, Nicolas André.
Fr. Paris 1754-1837 Same. T.
MONSORNO, Johann Maria. (Min)
Aus. 1768-1836 Vienna. T.
MONT, Deodat. *see* Delmont, D.
MONT, James, Sr. (S)
Turkish. ad. 1934 Constantinople, Turkey. M.
MONTAGNA, Bartolommeo.
It. 1450/60-1523 Vicenza. B-C-T-722.
MONTAGNA, Benedetto. (Eg)
It. Vicenza 1481-1558. B-T.
MONTAGNANA, Jacopo da.
It. Padua 1440/3-1499. B-T.
MONTAGNÉ, Agricol Louis.
Fr. b. Avignon 1879. DBA-T.
MONTAGNÉ, Émile Pierre de la.
Belg. b. Antwerp 1873. DBA.
MONTAGNE, James L.
Am. ex. 1935 New York. M.
MONTAGNÉ, Pierre Marius [or Marie]. (S)
Toulon, 1828-1879 Same. B-T.
MONTAGNY [or Montagni], Etienne.
Fr. St. Etienne 1816-1895. B-T.
MONTAGUE, Harriotte Lee Taliaferro.
Mrs. Jeffry Montague.
Am. ac. 1926. F-T.
MONTALBA, Clara.
Eng. Cheltenham 1842-1929 Venice, It. B-T-Wa-15.
MONTALBA, Henrietta Skerrett. (S)
Eng. England 1856-1893 Venice, It. DNB-T.
MONTALD, Constant.
Belg. b. Ghent 1862. DBA-T.
MONTANA, Pietro. (S)
Am. b. Alcamo, It. 1890; ad. 1934 New York. A-Cs-F.
MONTANARI, Giuseppe.
It. b. Osimo; ad. 1934 Varese. T.
MONTAÑÉS, Juan Martinez. (S)
Sp. Alcala 1568-1649 Sèville. B-Hs-E-T.
MONTANINI, Pietro [Perugino].
It. Perugia 1626-1689. B-T.
MONTE DEL FLORA [Giovanni].
It. Florence 1448-1529. T.
MONTELATICI, Francesco [Cecco Bravo].
It. Florence 1600-1661 Innsbruck, Aus. B-T.
MONTELUPO, Baccio da. (S)
It. Florence 1469-1535? Luccà. T-V.
MONTELUPO, Raffaello da. (S)
It. 1505?-1566/7 Orvieto. Hs-T-V.
MONTEMAZZO, Antonio.
Ger. Treviso, It. 1841-1898 Munich, Ger. B-T.
MONTEN, Heinrich Maria Dietrich.
Ger. Düsseldorf 1799-1843 Munich. B-C-T.
MONTENARD, Frédéric.
Fr. Paris 1849-1926 Besse. B-T.
MONTENEGRO, Roberto.
Mex. b. Mexico 1885. T.
MONTEPULCIANO, Pietro.
see Pietro di Domenico da M.
MONTERDE, Juan de.
Aragonese. ac. 1461-1466 Aragon, Sp. M.
MONTESINOS Y RAMIRO, Rafael.
Sp. Valencia 1811-1877 Same. T.
MONTEVERDE, Guilio. (S)
It. Bistagno 1837-1917 Rome. B-T-Y01918.
MONTÉZIN, Pierre Eugène.
Fr. b. Paris 1874. B-DBA-T.
MONTFOORT, Antoine van Blocklandt.
Dut. 1532-1583. M.
MONTFORT, Antoine Alphonse.
Fr. Paris 1802-1884 Same. B-T.
MONTFORD, Paul Raphael. (S)
Eng. b. London 1868; ad. 1935 Melbourne, Aust. T.
MONTGOMERY, Alfred.
Am. b. 1857; d. 1922 Los Angeles, Calif. A019-F-T.

MONTGOMERY, Carrie Lewis.
Am. b. Montevallo, Ala. 1865; ad. 1934 Birmingham, Ala. A.
MONTGOMERY, Roselle Mercier.
Am. ad. 1935 Hartford, Conn. M.
MONTI, Cesare.
It. ad. 1934 Milan; ex. 1934 Pittsburgh, Pa. M.
MONTI, Francesco Brescianino.
It. Brescia 1646-1712 Parma. B-T.
MONTI, Gaetano Matteo. (S)
It. Ravenna 1776-1847 Milan. B-T.
MONTI, Giovanni Battista.
It. Genoa 1610-1657 Same. B-T.
MONTI, Maurice.
It. b. 1895; ac. 1934 in Italy. DBA.
MONTI, Niccolò [or Nicolas].
It. b. Pistoja, 1780. B-T.
MONTI, Raffaelo. (S)
It. Milan, 1818-1881 London. B-T.
MONTICELLI, Adolphe Joseph Thomas.
Fr. Marseille 1824-1886 Same. B-C-T-191.
MONTIGNY, Jean Robert Nicolas Lucas de. (S)
Fr. Rouen, 1747-1810 Paris. T.
MONTIGNY, Jules Léon.
Belg. Brussels 1847-1899 Tervueren. B-T.
MONTOLIN, Valentin.
Sp. ac. 1439-1469 Tarragona. T.
MONTORFANO, Giovanni Donato da.
Fr. ac. 1495 in Milan, It. B-T.
MONTORSOLI, Fra Giovanni Agnolo. (S)
It. 1500/7-1563 Florence. Hs-T-V.
MONTPETIÂT, Armand Vincent de.
Fr. Macon 1713-1800 Paris. B-T.
MONTRICHARD, Raymond Desmus.
Am. b. Berkeley, Calif. 1887; ad. 1934 Los Angeles. A.
MONTURIAL, Enrique Pascuel de.
Sp. Barcelona 1878-1934 New York.
M-Obit. N. Y. papers, 4-22-1934.
MONTZAIGLE, Edgard de.
Fr. b. Angouléme, 1867. B-T.
MONVAERNI.
Fr. Late 15th century in France. T.
MONVEL. *see* Boutet De Monvel.
MONVOISIN, Pierre Raymond Jacques.
Fr. Bordeaux, 1794-1870 Cologne, Ger. B-C-T.
MOODY, Helen Newington.
see Wills, H. N.
MOON, Carl.
Am. b. Wilmington, O. 1879; ad. 1934 Pasadena, Calif. A-W.
MOONEY, Edward Ludlow.
Am. New York 1813-1887 Same. C-F-T-2-15.
MOOR. *see also* Moro.
MOOR, Karel Van [The Elder].
Dut. Leyden 1656-1738 Warmond. B-C-T-722.
MOORE, Albert Joseph.
Eng. York, 1841-1893 London. B-Bd-C-DNB-E-T.
MOORE, Anita.
Am. b. Cleveland, O. 1900; ad. 1934 Chichaska, Okla. A.
MOORE, Arthur W.
Am. Nottingham, Eng. 1840-1913 Rochester, N. Y. A011.
MOORE, Benson Bond.
Am. b. Wash., D. C. 1882; ad. 1934 New York. A-F-T-W.
MOORE, Bessie.
Am. ex. 1934 New York. M.
MOORE, Bethuel C.
Am. b. Barbourville, Ky. 1902. A.
MOORE, Bruse. (S)
Am. b. Bern, Kan. 1905; ad. 1934 Wichita, Kan. A.
MOORE, Cecil Gresham.
Am. b. Kingston, Ont., Can. 1880; ad. 1934 Rochester, N. Y. A.
MOORE, Charles Herbert.
Am. New York 1840-1930 England. A027-DAB-F-T-W16.
MOORE, Edwin.
Eng. Birmingham 1813-1893 York. B-DNB-T.
MOORE, Frank. (Et)
Eng. b. Watford 1876; ad. 1934 Kent. Wa.
MOORE, Frank Montague.
Am. b. England 1877; ad. 1934 Pasadena, Calif. A.
MOORE, George Belton.
Eng. 1805/6-1875. B-DNB-T.
MOORE, Guernsey. (Ill)
Am. Phila., Pa. 1874-1925 Same. A022.
MOORE, Harry Humphrey.
Am. New York 1844-1926 Paris. A023-B-C-F-T-15.
MOORE, Henry.
Eng. York 1831-1896 Margate. B-Bd-C-DNB-E-T-855.
MOORE, Henry Spencer. (P-S)
Eng. b. Castleford, 1898; ad. 1934 London. Wa-798.
MOORE, John D.
Aust. b. Sydney, N. S. W.; ex. 1935 London. M.
MOORE, John Francis. (S)
Eng. Hanover, Ger.; d. 1809 London. DNB-T.
MOORE, Joseph. (Med)
Eng. Birmingham 1817-1892 Same. DNB-T.
MOORE, Katherine Naomi.
Am. d. 1915 Dobbs Ferry, N. Y. A012.
MOORE, [Mrs.] Lou Wall. (S)
Am. ac. 1904-1925 Chicago. F-Ta.
MOORE, Martha. (S)
Mrs. Charles H. Rathbone, Jr.
Am. b. New Britain, Conn. 1902; ad. 1934 New York. A.
MOORE, Mary E. (S).
Am. b. Taunton, Mass.; ad. 1934 Cambridge, Mass. M.
MOORE, Mary V.
Am. ad. 1934 Memphis, Tenn. M.
MOORE, Nelson Augustus.
Am. Kensington, Conn. 1824-1902 New York. F-M.
MOORE, Samuel. (Eg)
Eng. ac. 1680-1720 in London. DNB-T.
MOORE, Thomas Sturge. (Eg)
Eng. b. Hampshire 1870. T-364.
MOORE, William.
Eng. York 1790-1851 Birmingham. B-Bd-DNB-T.
MOOREPACK, Carton. (Et)
Am. b. New York 1887. T.

MOORMANS, Franz.
Dut. Rotterdam, 1831-1873. B.
MOR, Antonis. *see* Moro, Antonio.
MORA, Domingo. (S)
Am. d. 1911 in New York. F-Ta.
MORA, Francis Luis.
Am. b. Montevideo, Uruguay 1874; ad. 1934 Gaylordsville, Conn. A-F-T-W-46.
MORA, José. (S)
Sp. Bassa, 1638/42-1724/5 Granada. E-T.
MORA, Joseph Jacinto. (S)
Am. b. Montevideo, Uruguay 1876; ad. 1934 Carmel, Calif. A-Cs-F-Ta-W.
MORAHAN, Eugene. (S)
Am. b. Brooklyn, N. Y. 1869; ad. 1934 Santa Monica, Calif. A-Cs-F.
MORAL, Lesmes Fernández del. (S)
Sp. ac. 1600 in Vallalodid. Hs-T.
MORÁLES [El Divino], Luis de.
Sp. Badajoz 1509?-1586 Same. B-T-722-774.
MORALT, Willy.
Ger. b. Munich, 1884. T.
MORAN, Edward.
Am. Bolton, Eng. 1829-1901 New York. A04-B-Bd-C-DAB-E-F-T-1-4-15-22-46-226.
MORAN, [Edward] Percy.
Am. Phila., Pa. 1862-1935 New York. A-M-T-W-Obit. N. Y. papers, 3-6-1935.
MORAN, [John] Léon.
Am. b. Phila., Pa. 1864; ad. 1934 Plainfield, N. J. A-F-T-W.
MORAN, Mary Nimmo. (Et)
Mrs. Thomas Moran.
Am. Strathaven, Scot. 1842-1899 U. S. A01-F-T-46.
MORAN, Paul Nimmo.
Am. d. 1907 Los Angeles, Calif. A06-T.
MORAN, Peter.
Am. Bolton, Eng. 1841-1914 Phila., Pa. A012-C-DAB-F-T-W8-15-22-40-46-55.
MORAN, Thomas.
Am. Bolton, Eng. 1837-1926 Santa Barbara, Calif. A023-C-DAB-E-F-T-W14-1-26-55.
MORANDI, Giorgio.
It. ad. 1934 Bologna. M.
MORANDI, Giovanni Maria.
It. Florence, 1622-1717 Rome. B-T.
MORANDINI, Francesco. [Il Poppi.]
It. Poppi, 1544-1597 Florence. B-T.
MORANDO, Paolo Cavazzola.
see Cavazzola, P. M.
MORANZONE. *see* Caterino.
MORAS, Walter.
Ger. ac. 1876-1910 in Berlin. B-T.
MORAZZONE, Pier Francesco.
It. 1571-1626 Italy. T.
MORBIDUCCI, Publio. (Eg)
It. b. 1889; ad. 1935 Rome, It. M.
MORCOM, J. Herbert. (S)
Eng. b. Wrexham, 1871. T-Wa1924.
MORE, [Sir] Anthony. *see* Moro, Antonio.
MORE, Hermon.
Am. b. Medford, Mass. 1889; ad. 1934 New York. A.
MORE, Jacob.
Scot. Edinburgh, 1740-1793 Rome, It. B-DNB-T.
MORE, John.
Eng. 1453-1538. T.
MOREAU, Adrien. [Louis.]
Fr. Troyes, 1843-1906 Paris. B-C-T.
MOREAU, Auguste. (S)
Fr. b. Dijon, 1861. B-T.
MOREAU, Charles.
Fr. b. Loiret 1830. B-T.
MOREAU, Chocarne.
see Chocarne-Moreau, Paul.
MOREAU, Gaston Auguste.
Fr. b. Paris 1885. DBA.
MOREAU, Gustave.
Fr. Paris 1826-1898 Same. B-C-E-T.
MOREAU, Jean.
Fr. ex. 1934 in Paris. M.
MOREAU, Jean Michel [The Younger].
Fr. Paris 1741-1814 Same. B-T.
MOREAU, Louis Gabriel [The Elder].
Fr. Paris 1740-1806 Same. B-T-481.
MOREAU, Luc-Albert. (Ill)
Fr. b. Paris 1882; ex. 1933 Pittsburgh, Pa. DBA-T.
MOREAU-NÉLATON, Adolphe Etienne.
Fr. Paris 1859-1927 Same. B-T.
MOREAU-VAUTHIER, Gabriel Jean Paul. (S)
Fr. b. Paris 1871; ex. 1930 London. DBA-T.
MOREELSE, Paulus.
Dut. Utrecht 1571-1638 Same. B-C-T-722.
MOREL, Jacques. (S)
Fr. Lyons, 1417-1459 Angers. T.
MOREL, Jean Baptiste.
Flem. Antwerp, 1662-1732/4 Liége. B-T.
MOREL-FATIO, Antonie Léon.
Fr. Rouen, 1810-1871 Paris. B-T.
MORELL, Imogene Robinson.
Am. ac. Wash., D. C.; d. 1908. M.
MORELLI, Domenico.
It. Naples, 1826-1901 Same. B-T.
MORENO Y CARBONERO, José.
Sp. b. Malaga 1861. B-T.
MORET [or Morret], Henri.
Fr. Cherbourg, 1856-1913 Paris. B-T.
MORET [or Morret], Jean Baptiste. (Eg)
Fr. ac. 1790-1820 in Paris. T.
MORETTI, Antonio.
It. ac. 18th century in Italy. M.
MORETTI, Giuseppe. (S)
Am. b. Siena, It. 1859. A20-F-W15.
MORETTO DA BRECIA.
[Allessandro Bonvicino.]
It. Brescia 1498-1554/5 Same. B-Bd-C-E-T-V-722.
MOREY, Bertha Graves.
Am. b. Ottumwa, Ia. 1881; ad. 1934 Same. A.
MORGAN. *see also* De Morgan.
MORGAN, Alexander Converse.
Am. Sandusky, O. 1849-1933 New York. A-M.
MORGAN, Alfred Kedington.
Eng. So. Kensington 1868-1928 Rugby. Wa01929.
MORGAN, [Mrs.] Alice Mary [née Havers].
Br. 1850-1890. DNB.
MORGAN, Arthur C. (S)
Am. b. Louisiana; ad. 1934 Shreveport, La. A.
MORGAN, Caroline.
Am. ad. 1934 Toledo, O. M.

MORGAN, [Mrs.] CHARLOTTE E. BODWELL.
Am. b. Lakewood, Calif.; ad. 1934 Carmel, Calif. A.
MORGAN, EMMYLOU.
Mrs. Ralph Depew Morgan.
Am. Albany, N. Y. 1891-1932 Buffalo, N. Y. A029.
MORGAN, FRANKLIN TOWNSEND. (Et)
Am. b. Brooklyn, N. Y. 1883; ad. 1934 Moylan, Pa. A-F.
MORGAN, FREDERICK.
Eng. ac. 1856-1927 in London. B-T-Y01928.
MORGAN, GEORGIA WESTON.
Am. b. Virginia; ad. 1934 Lynchburg, Va. A.
MORGAN, HERBERT.
Am. ad. 1934 New York. M.
MORGAN, HERBERT A.
Am. New York 1857-1917. A015.
MORGAN, JOHN.
Eng. London 1823-1885 Hastings. B-T.
MORGAN, JOSEPH. (Ill)
Am. ad. 1933 New York. M.
MORGAN, LOUIS.
Am. 1814-1852. F-T.
MORGAN, LYNN THOMAS. (Et)
Am. b. Richmond, Ind. 1889; ad. 1934 New York. A.
MORGAN, M. DE NEALE.
Am. b. San Fran.; ad. 1934 Carmel, Calif. A.
MORGAN ["Matt"], MATTHEW SOMERVILLE. (Cart)
Am. London 1839-1890 New York. DAB-F-T-15-55.
MORGAN, SYLVANNUS. (Heraldic-P)
Eng. 1620-1693. DNB-T.
MORGAN, THEODORE J.
Am. b. Cinn., O. 1872; ad. 1934 Wash., D. C. A.
MORGAN, WALLACE. (Ill)
Am. b. New York; ad. 1934 Same. A-F.
MORGAN, WILLIAM.
Am. London 1826-1900 New York. A04-F-T-15.
MORGAN, WILLIAM JAMES.
Ir. Cork 1856-1925. T-Y01926.
MORGANTI FAMILY.
It. ac. 16-17th Cent. in Italy. T.
MORGARI, LUIGI.
It. b. Turin 1857. B-T.
MORGENSTERN, CHRISTIAN ERNEST BERNHARD.
Ger. Hamburg 1805-1867 Munich. B-C-T.
MORGENSTERN, JOHANN CHRISTOPH.
Ger. Altenburg 1697-1767 Rudolstadt. T.
MORGENSTERN, JOHANN LUDWIG ERNEST.
Ger. Rudolstadt 1738-1819 Frankfort. B-T.
MORGHEN, RAFAELLO SANZIO. (Eg)
It. Naples 1788-1833 Florence. B-E-T-880.
MORI, KWANSAI.
Jap. 1814-1894 Japan. J., Vol. 2, page 98.
MORI, NENO.
It. ad. 1935 Venice; ex. 1934 Pittsburgh, Pa. M.
MORIER, PIERRE DAVID.
Swi. Berne 1705/36-1770/2 London. B-Bd-E-T.
MORIGI. *see* Caravaggio.
MORIKAGE, KUSUMI.
Jap. Kyoto 1630-1700 Tokyo. J-T.
MORIN, JEAN.
Fr. Paris 1609-1650 Same. B-T.
MORIN, VITALIS.
Fr. b. Cholet 1876. B-T.
MORIN-JEAN, ALEXIS JOSEPH.
Fr. b. Paris 1877. DBA.
MORISON, DOUGLAS.
Eng. Tottenham 1810-1847 London. B-DNB-T.
MORISOT, BERTHE MARIE PAULINE.
Fr. Bruges, Belg. 1841-1895 Paris. B-T-71-482.
MORISSE, BERNHARD. (S)
Ger. b. Olde 1883. T.
MORISSET, FRANÇOIS HENRI.
Fr. b. Paris 1870. B-T.
MORITZ, LOUIS.
Dut. The Hague 1773-1850 Amsterdam. B-C-T.
MORJAERT, CHRISTIAN LODEWIJK.
Dut. ac. 1639 in Holland. M.
MORLAND, GEORGE.
Eng. London 1763-1804 Same. B-Bd-C-DNB-E-T-483-484-722-722-909.
MORLAND, GEORGE HENRY.
Eng. d. 1789 in London. B-DNB.
MORLAND, HENRY ROBERT.
Eng. London 1730?-1797 Same. B-Bd-C-DNB-T.
MORLAND, JAMES SMITH.
Eng. d. 1921 in Liverpool. T-Y01922.
MORLEY, HARRY. (Eg)
Eng. b. Leicester 1881; ad. 1935 London. T-Wa.
MORLEY, HENRY.
Eng. b. Nottingham 1869. T-Wa1929.
MORLEY, HUBERT. (Et)
Am. ad. 1935 Chicago. M.
MORLEY, ROBERT.
Eng. b. London 1857; ad. 1934 Langford. T-Wa.
MORLEY, RUTH KILLICK. (S)
Am. b. London 1888; ad. 1934 New York. A.
MORLON, PAUL ÉMILE ANTHONY.
Fr. b. Sully; ac. 1868-1905 in Paris. B-T.
MORLON, PIERRE ALEXANDRE. (S)
Fr. b. Mâcon 1878. DBA-T.
MORLOT, ALPHONSE ALEXIS.
Fr. Isôme 1838-1918. B-T.
MORNER, CARL GUSTAF HJALMAR.
Swe. Stockholm 1794-1837 Paris. B-T.
MORO [or Mor], ANTONIO.
Dut. Utrecht 1512/9-1575/7 Antwerp, Belg. B-Bd-C-E-T-722-945.
MORO, GIAMBATTISTA D'ANGELO.
It. Verona 1530?-1560. B-T-722.
MORO, IL. *see* Torbido, Francesco.
MORO, PAUL.
Am. ad. 1934 New York. M.
MORONE, DOMENICO [Pelacane].
It. Verona 1442-1517. B-T-V.
MERONE, GIOVANNI FRANCESCO.
It. Verona 1471-1529 Same. B-C-T-V.
MORONI, ANTONIO.
It. b. Bergano; ac. 1623-1664. T.
MORONI, GIOVANNI BATTISTA.
It. Bondo 1510/25-1578 Brescia. B-E-T-78-722-782-806.
MORONOBU, HISHIGAWA.
Jap. 1625-1694. T-J., Vol. 2, page 20.

MOROT, AIMÉ NICOLAS.
Fr. Nancy 1850-1913 Dinard. B-C-DBA-T.
MOROZZI, DANTE. (S)
It. ac. 1932. M.
MORRELL, IMOGENE ROBINSON.
Am. b. Attleboro, Mass.; d. 1908 Wash., D. C. C-F-T-15.
MORREN, GEORGE.
Belg. b. Cawpine 1868.
MORRET. *see* Moret.
MORRICE, JAMES WILSON.
Can. Montreal 1874-1924 Tunis, Egypt. T.
MORRILL, GRACE.
Am. ad. 1935 Ogunquit, Me. M.
MORRIS, ADELAIDE.
Am. b. Brooklyn, N. Y. 1898; ad. 1934 Same. A.
MORRIS, [Mrs.] BETH K. (Ill)
Am. ad. 1934 New York. M.
MORRIS, CEDRIC.
Welsh. b. Wales 1889; ex. 1934 Pittsburgh, Pa. T-Wa.
MORRIS, DUDLEY.
Am. b. New York 1912; ad. 1935 Burlington, Vt. M.
MORRIS, EDMUND MONTAGUE.
Can. Perth, Ont. 1871-1913. M.
MORRIS, ELLWOOD.
Am. b. Richmond, Ind. 1848; ad. 1934 Same. A.
MORRIS, FLORENCE.
Am. b. Nevada, Mo. 1876; ad. 1934 Roswell, N. M. A.
MORRIS, GEORGE FORD.
Am. ex. 1933 New York. M.
MORRIS, JOHN C.
Eng. ac. 1851-1864. T.
MORRIS, KATHLEEN MOIR.
Can. b. Montreal; ad. 1935 Same. M.
MORRIS, LOUISE. (Mu)
Am. ad. 1934 Cleveland, O. M.
MORRIS, NATHALIE.
Am. b. Phila., Pa.; ac. 1915 Same. A12.
MORRIS, PAUL WINTERS. (S)
Am. Du Quion, Ill. 1865-1916 New York. A014-F-T.
MORRIS, PHILIP RICHARD.
Eng. Devonport 1836-1902 London. B-C-DNB-T.
MORRIS, ROBERT C.
Am. b. Anderson, Ind. 1896; ad. 1934 Same. A.
MORRIS, THOMAS. (Eg)
Eng. 1750-1800 London. B-DNB-T.
MORRIS, VIRGINIA LEIGH. (S)
Am. b. Norfolk, Va. 1899; ad. 1934 Same. A.
MORRIS, WILLIAM. (P and Poet)
Eng. 1834-1896 London. B-DNB-T.
MORRIS, WILLIAM BRIGHT.
Eng. b. Salford, Eng. 1844; ac. 1900. B-Bd-T-485.
MORRIS, WILLIAM CHARLES. (Cart)
Am. b. Salt Lake City, Utah 1874; ad. 1934 Grand View, N. Y. W.
MORRISON, DAVID HERRON.
Am. Rawalpindi, Punjab, India 1885-1934 New York. A-M-Obit. N. Y. papers, 9-4-1934.
MORRISON, KENNETH MACIVER.
Eng. b. Claygate; ad. 1934 London. Wa.
MORRISON, MARY COPLES. (S)
Am. b. Petersburg, Va. 1908; ad. 1934 Wash., D. C. A.
MORRISON, OLIVIA BROWN.
Am. ad. 1934 Houston, Tex. M.
MORRISON, ROBERT EDWARD.
Eng. b. Isle of Man 1852-1925 Liverpool. B-T-Y01926.
MORRISON, ZAIDEE LINCOLN.
Am. b. Showhegan, Me.; ad. 1934 New York. A-F.
MORRO, FRANCESCO.
It. Genoa 1759-1845 Rome. T.
MORROW, ALBERT.
It. Belfast 1863-1927. T-Y01928-Wa01929.
MORROW, CHARLOTTE.
Am. ad. 1935 Cleveland, O. M.
MORROW, JULIE.
Mrs. Cornelius Wortendyke de Forest.
Am. b. New York; ad. 1934 Cinn., O. A.
MORSE, ANNA G.
Am. ad. 1934 New York. A29.
MORSE, ANNE GODDARD.
Am. b. Prov., R. I. 1855; ad. 1934 Same. A.
MORSE, EDWARD LIND.
Am. Poughkeepsie, N. Y. 1857-1923 Pittsfield, Mass. A020-F-T.
MORSE, IRENE MILNER.
Mrs. Norman K. Morse.
Am. b. Phila., Pa. 1894; ad. 1934 Same. A.
MORSE, JEAN HOWE.
Am. b. Derby, Can. 1876; ad. 1934 Englewood, N. J. A.
MORSE, MARY MINNS.
Am. b. Dorchester, Mass. 1859; ad. 1935 Boston. A12-F-T.
MORSE, NATHANIEL. (Eg)
Am. Dedham, Mass. 1676-1748 Boston. F-T-2-7.
MORSE, PAULINE HESTIA.
Am. Marlborough, Mass.; ad. 1934 Worcester, Mass. A.
MORSE, SAMUEL FINLEY BREEZE.
[Inventor of Telegraphy.]
Am. Charlestown, Mass. 1791-1872 New York. Bd-C-DAB-F-T-1-2-3-6-136-144-182-183-486-487-701-748-840-946.
MORSE, VERNON JAY.
Am. b. Benton Harbor, Mich. 1898; ad. 1934 Pasadena, Calif. A.
MORSE-BROWN, SYDNEY.
Eng. b. India 1903; ad. 1934 London. Wa.
MORSE-RUMMEL, FRANK.
Ger. b. Berlin 1884. DBA.
MORTELLITO, DOMENICO.
Am. ex. 1935 New York. M.
MORTEN, THOMAS.
Eng. Uxbridge 1836-1866 Freitod. DNB-T.
MORTIER, ROBERT.
Fr. b. Nice 1877. DBA-T.
MORTIMER, JOHN HAMILTON.
Eng. Eastbourne 1741-1779 London. B-DNB-T-722.
MORTIMER, NORMAN J. (S)
Am. b. San Fran., Calif. 1901; ad. 1934 New Hope, Pa. A.
MORTIMER, STANLEY.
Am. New York 1853-1932 Same. A029.

MORTLOCK, Ethel.
Eng. b. Cambridge; d. 1928. T-Y01929.
MORTO DA FELTRE, Pietro Luzzi.
It. Feltre 1467-1522. B-C-T-V.
MORTON, Andrew.
Eng. Newcastle 1802-1845 London. B-DNB-T.
MORTON, Christina.
Mrs. Benjamin A. Morton.
Am. b. Dardanelle, Ark.; ad. 1934 New York. A-F.
MORTON, John Ludlow.
Am. New York 1792-1871 Same. F-T.
MORTON, Thomas Corsan.
Scot. b. Glasgow 1859. T-Wa1929.
MORZENTI, Natale.
It. ac. 1926 in Venice. T.
MORZETTI, Giovanni.
It. 1650 in Naples. T.
MOSCA, Francesco [Il. Moschino]. (S)
It. Settignano 1540?-1578 Pisa. T-V.
MOSCA, Simone [Marchesi]. (S)
It. Settignano 1492-1553 Orvieto. T-V.
MOSCHCOVITZ, Paul.
Am. b. Giralt, Hun. 1876; ad. 1934 New York. A-F-W.
MOSCHELES, Felix Stone.
Eng. London 1833-1917 Tunbridge Wells. T.
MOSCHER [or Mosker], Jacob van.
Dut. ac. 1593-1623 in Haarlem. T.
MOSCHINO. *see* Mosca.
MOSCOS, Joannes.
Gr. ac. 1645. T.
MOSE, Carl C. (S)
Am. b. Copenhagen, Denmark 1903; ad. 1934 Minn., Minn. A.
MOSELEY, Helen E.
Am. Grand Rapids, Mich. 1883-1928 Boston. A025-F.
MOSER, Ernst Christian. (Eg)
Aus. Graz 1815-1867 Same. B-T.
MOSER Family.
Ger. ac. 18-19th Cent. in Germany. T.
MOSER, George Michael.
Swi. Shaffhouse 1704/7-1783 London. B-T.
MOSER, James Henry.
Am. Canada 1854-1913 Wash., D. C. AOX1-F-T.
MOSER, Joseph.
Eng. London 1748-1819 Same. DNB-T.
MOSER, Lucas.
Ger. ac. Souahe 1431. B-T.
MOSER, [Mrs.] Mary Lloyd.
Eng. 1744-1819 London. DNB-T.
MOSER, Oswald.
Eng. b. London 1874. Wa1929.
MOSES, Henry.
Eng. London 1782?-1870 Cowley. B-DNB-T.
MOSES, Thomas G.
Am. Liverpool, Eng. 1856-1934 Oak Park, Ill. A-F-M.
MOSKOVITZ, Ira. (Et)
Am. b. Poland; ad. 1935 New York. M.
MOSKOVITZ, S. (Et)
Am. b. Poland; ad. 1935 New York. M.
MOSLER, Gustave Henry.
Am. Munich, Ger. 1875-1906 N. Y. State. A06.
MOSLER, Henry.
Am. New York 1841-1920. A017-B-E-DAB-F-T-46-138.
MOSLEY, Charles. (Eg)
Eng. 1720-1770 London. B-DNB-T.
MOSMAN, Melzar Hunt. (S)
Am. b. 1845; d. 1926 Chicopee, Mass. A023.
MOSMAN, Warren Towle. (S)
Am. ad. 1935 Minn., Minn. M.
MOSNIER [or Monnier], Jean.
Fr. Blois 1600-1656 Same. B-T.
MOSNIER, Jean Laurent. (Min)
Fr. Paris 1743/4-1808 Leningrad, Rus. B-T.
MOSS, Charles E.
Can. U. S. 1860-1901 Canada. M.
MOSS, Elizabeth Campbell.
Br. ex. 1935 London. M.
MOSSES, Alexander.
Eng. Liverpool 1793-1837 Same. B-DNB-T.
MOSSOP, William. (Med)
Ir. Dublin 1751-1805 Same. DNB-T.
MESSOP, William Stephen. (Med)
Ir. Dublin 1788-1827 Same. DNB-T.
MOST, August Ludwig.
Ger. Stettin 1807-1883 Same. B-T.
MOSTAERT, Gillis [Sinapius].
Flem. Hulst 1525/34-1598 Antwerp. B-T.
MOSTAERT, Jan [Sinapius].
Dut. Haarlem 1475-1555/6 Same. B-T.
MOTCHALOV.
Rus. ex. 1935 London. M.
MOSTYN, Tom Edwin.
Eng. Liverpool 1864-1930. B-T-Y01931.
MOTE, Alden.
Am. West Milton, O. 1840-1917 Richmond, Ind. A014-F-T-181.
MOTELEY, Georges Jules.
Fr. Caen 1865-1923/4. B-T.
MOTLEY, Archibald John, Jr.
Am. b. New Orleans, La. 1891; ad. 1934 Chicago. A.
MOTLEY, Eleanor W.
Mrs. Thomas Motley.
Am. b. Boston 1847; ad. 1934 Same. A.
MOTONOBU, Kano.
Jap. 1476-1559. J-T.
MOTT-SMITH, May [Mrs. Small]. (S)
Am. b. Honolulu, Hawaii 1879; ad. 1934 New York. A.
MOTTA, Raffaellino da Reggio.
It. Reggio 1550-1578. B-T.
MOTTE, Henri Paul.
Fr. Paris 1846-1922 Same. B-T.
MOTTE, Jeanie Gallup.
Mrs. Henry Mottet.
Am. Prov., R. I. 1864-1934 New York. A-F-M-T-W-Obit. N. Y. papers, 11-1-1934.
MOTTER, Mabel J.
Am. ad. 1934 Toledo, O. M.
MOTTEZ, Victor Louis.
Fr. b. Lille 1809-1897 Brèvres. B-T.
MOTTO, Joseph C. (S)
Am. b. Cleveland, O. 1892; ad. 1934 Same. A.
MOTTRAM, Charles. (Eg)
Eng. 1807-1876. B-DNB-T.
MOTZ, [Mrs.] Ray Estep.
Am. Whitsett, Pa. 1875-1930 Pittsburgh, Pa. A028.

MOUCHERON, Frederik de [The Elder].
Dut. Emblen 1633/7-1686 Amsterdam.
B-C-T.
MOUCHERON, Isaac de [Ordonantie].
Dut. Amsterdam 1667-1744 Same. B-C-T.
MOUCHET, François Nicolas.
Fr. Gray 1750-1814 Same. B-T.
MOUCHOT, Louis Claude.
Fr. Paris 1830-1891. B-T.
MOUCHOT, Ludovic [Louis Hippolyte].
Fr. Poland 1846-1893 Paris. B-T.
MOUCHY, Louis Philippe. (S)
Fr. Paris 1734-1801 Same. B-T.
MOUILLERON, Adolphe.
Fr. Paris 1820-1881. B-T.
MOUILLOT, Marcel.
Fr. b. Paris 1889. DBA.
MOULEN. *see* Meulen.
MOULINET, Antoine Edouard Joseph.
Fr. Cloyes 1833-1891 Chartres. B-T.
MOULINS. *see* Master of the Moulins.
MOULTHROP, Reuben.
Am. b. 1763; d. 1814 East Haven, Conn.
F-T-2.
MOULTON, [Mrs.] Sue Buckingham.
Am. b. Hartford, Conn. 1873; ad. 1934 Phila., Pa. A.
MOUNT, Henry Smith.
Am. Setauket, N. Y. 1802-1841 Stoney Brook, N. Y. F-2.
MOUNT, Rita.
Can. b. Montreal, Can.; ad. 1935 Same. M.
MOUNT, Shepard Alonzo.
Am. Setauket, N. Y. 1804-1868 Stony Brook, N. Y. B-Bd-F-T-2-15.
MOUNT, William Sidney.
Am. Setauket, N. Y. 1807-1869 Same.
Bd-C-DAB-E-F-T-1-2-4-10-15.
MOUNTFORT, Arnold.
Am. b. Eng. 1873; ad. 1926 New York.
F-T.
MOUNTFORT, Julia Ann.
Am. b. Coaticooke, Can. 1892; ad. 1934 Damariscotta, Me. A.
MOUSETRAP. *see* Master of the Mousetrap.
MOUSSET, Pierre Joseph.
Fr. b. Paris; d. 1894 Same. B-T.
MOUTTE, Jean Joseph Marie Alphonse.
Fr. Marseille 1840-1913 Same. B-T.
MOWAT, H. J. (Ill)
Am. ad. 1934 New York. A28.
MOWBRAY, Harry Siddons. (Mu)
Am. Alexandria, Egypt 1858-1928 Wash., Conn. A025-DAB-E-F-T-W14-1-46-176-191.
MOWBRAY-CLARKE, John Frederick. (S)
Am. b. Jamaica, West Indies 1869; ad. 1934 Pomona, N. Y. A-F-T-W.
MOYA, Pedro de.
Sp. Granada 1610-1674 Same. B-T-722.
MOYAERT [or Moeyaert], Claes Cornelisz.
Dut. Amsterdam 1592/3-1655 Same. B-C-T.
MOYNE. *see* Lemoyne.
MOYNIHAN, Frederick. (S)
Am. Eng. 1843-1910 New York. A08-F-Ta.
MOZIER, Joseph. (S)
Am. Burlington, Vt. 1812-1890 Faids, Swi.
DAB-F-Hs-Ta-4-15-26-52.
MOZIN, Charles Louis.
Fr. Paris 1806-1862 Trouville. B-C-T.
MUCCIO [or Muzio], Giovanni Francesco.
It. Bologna 1620-1665. B-T.
MUCHA, Alphonse Marie.
Aus. b. Monrovia, Liberia, Africa 1860. B-T.
MU-CH'I [A Zen Artist-Priest].
Chinese. ac. 13th Century. M.
MÜCKE, Karl Anton Heinrich.
Ger. Breslau 1806-1891 Düsseldorf. B-C-T.
MUDO, Juan Fernandez Navarrete.
see Navarrette, J. F.
MUELICH [or MIELICH], Hans. (Min)
Ger. Munich 1516-1573 Same. B-T.
MUELLER. *see also* Müller.
MUELLER, Alexander.
Am. b. Milwaukee, Wis. 1872; ad. 1934 San Marino, Calif. A.
MUELLER, Arion. (Et)
Am. ad. 1935 New York. M.
MUELLER, Carl. (Ill)
Am. ad. 1934 Westport, Conn. A.
MUELLER, John Charles. (Ill)
Am. b. Cinn., O. 1889; ad. 1934 Norwood, O.
A.
MUELLER, Louis F.
Am. b. Ind., Ind. 1886; ad. 1934 Same. A.
MUELLER, Michael J.
Am. Durand, Wis. 1893-1931 Bend, Ore.
A028.
MUELLER, Peter Paul.
Ger. b. Berlin 1853; ac. 1891 Same. B-T.
MUENCH, Julian Rhodes.
Am. ac. 1932. M.
MUENDEL, George F.
Am. b. West Hoboken, N. J. 1871; ad. 1934 Rowayton, Conn. A.
MUENIER, Jules Alexis.
Fr. b. Vesoul 1863; ad. 1934 Paris.
B-DBA-T.
MUENTER, Gabriele.
Ger. ac. 1933. M.
MUGNON, Alexander.
Am. ex. 1935 New York. M.
MUGUET, Georges. (S)
Fr. b. Moissy 1903; ad. 1934 Paris. DBA.
MUH KI.
Chinese. ac. Sung Dynasty [960-1280]. E.
MUHLHOPER, Elizabeth.
Am. b. Maryland; ad. 1934 Wash., D. C. A.
MÜHLIG, Theodor Hugo.
Ger. Dresden 1854-1929 Düsseldorf. B-T.
MUHRMAN, Henry.
Am. Cinn., O. 1854-1916. A12-B-C.
MUHSAM, F. H.
Ger. ex. 1935 London. M.
MUIR, William H. (S)
Am. ad. 1934 Pelham, N. Y. M.
MUIRHEAD, David.
Scot. Edinburgh 1867-1930.
Wa1929-Y01931-818.
MUIRHEAD, John.
Scot. Edinburgh 1863-1927.
Wa01929-Y01928.
MULERTT, Carel Eugène.
Am. b. Brunswick, Ger. 1869; ad. 1915 Holland. A12.
MULFORD, Stockton. (Ill)
Am. ad. 1934 New York. M.

MULHAUPT, FREDERICK JOHN.
Am. b. Rockford, Mo. 1871; ad. 1934 Gloucester, Mass. A-W.

MULHOLLAND, CHARLES. (Ill)
Am. ad. 1934 New York. M.

MULIER [or Molier], PIETER [The Elder].
Dut. Haarlem 1615-1670 Same. B-C-T.

MULIER, PIETER [or Pietro Muller], [The Younger].
Dut. Haarlem 1637-1701 Milan, It. B-C-T.

MULINARI, STEFANO. (Eg)
It. Florence 1741-1790/5. B-T.

MULLER, BUELL.
Mrs. James Bernard Muller.
Am. b. Chicago 1901; ad. 1934 Highland Park, Ill. M.

MULLEN, RICHARD. (Eg)
Am. Germany 1849-1915 Brooklyn, N. Y. A013-F-T.

MULLEN, VERNE.
Am. ad. 1934 Oak Park, Ill. M.

MÜLLER. *see also* Mueller.

MÜLLER. *see also* Cranach, Lucas.

MÜLLER, ADAM.
Dan. Copenhagen 1811-1844. B.

MÜLLER, ALFRED.
Fr. b. Paris 1882; ad. 1934 Same. B-DBA.

MÜLLER, ANDREAS JOHANN JACOB HEINRICH.
Ger. Cassel 1811-1890 Düsseldorf. B-T.

MÜLLER, ANTON.
Aus. Vienna 1853-1897 Same. B-T.

MÜLLER, BERNHARD.
Ger. b. Essen, 1880. T.

MULLER, CHARLES [or Carlo]. (S)
Swi. ac. 1849 in Paris. B-T.

MULLER, CHARLES LOUIS LUCAS.
Fr. Paris 1815-1892 Same. B-C-T.

MULLER, EDMUND G.
Eng. Bristol 1816-1888. M.

MÜLLER, EDUARD.
Ger. Mülhouse 1828-1895 Paris. B-T.

MÜLLER, FRANZ HUBERT.
Ger. Bonn 1784-1835 Darmstadt. B-T.

MÜLLER, FRIEDRICK [Teufel Müller].
Ger. Kreuznach 1749-1825 Rome, It. B-T.

MÜLLER, GEORGE.
Ger. b. Munich 1880. T.

MÜLLER, GERARD.
Dut. Amsterdam 1861-1923. T.

MÜLLER, HANS. (S)
Aus. b. Vienna 1873. B-T.

MULLER, HELEN CHANCE.
Mrs. Eugene Muller.
Am. b. Phila., Pa.; ad. 1934 Merion, Pa. M.

MÜLLER, HERMAN. (Eg)
Dut. ac. 1550-1596 in Amsterdam. B.

MÜLLER, JAN HARMENSZ.
Dut. Amsterdam 1571-1628. B.

MÜLLER, JOHANN GEORGE.
Swi. Mosnang 1822-1849 Vienna, Aus.

MÜLLER, JOHANN GOTTHARD VON.
Ger. 1747-1830 Stuttgart. B-T.

MÜLLER, JOHANN JACOB.
Ger. Riga, Rus. 1765-1831 Stuttgart, Ger. B-T.

MÜLLER, JOHANN SEBASTIAN. (Eg)
Ger. Nüremberg 1715?-1790? England. B-DNB.

MÜLLER, KARL.
Ger. Darmstadt 1818-1893 Düsseldorf. B-T.

MÜLLER, LEOPOLD KARL.
Ger. Dresden 1834-1892 Vienna, Aus. B-T.

MÜLLER, MICHAEL.
Ger. ac. 1607 in Munich. T.

MÜLLER, MORITZ [Steinla].
Ger. Hildesheim 1791-1858 Dresden. B.

MÜLLER, MORTEN.
Nor. Holmestrand 1828-1911 Düsseldorf, Ger. B-T.

MULLER, [Mrs.] OLGA POPOFF. (S)
Am. b. New York 1883; ad. 1934 Flushing, L. I., N. Y. A.

MÜLLER, OTTO.
Ger. Liebau 1874-1930 Breslau. T.

MÜLLER, RICHARD.
Ger. Bohemia 1874-1930 Dresden. B-T.

MÜLLER, ROBERT.
Ger. Göttingen 1815-1854 Same. B-T.

MÜLLER, VICTOR.
Ger. Frankfort 1829-1871 Munich. B-T.

MULLER, WILLIAM JAMES [or John].
Eng. Bristol 1812-1845 Same. B-DNB-E-T-722.

MÜLLER, YVES EDGARD.
Fr. b. Vitrey 1876; ac. 1930 Paris. B-T.

MÜLLER-BRESLAU, GEORGE.
Ger. Breslau 1856-1911. B.

MÜLLER-KURZWELLY, KONRAD ALEXANDER.
Ger. Chemnitz 1855-1914 Berlin. B-T.

MÜLLER-LANDECK. *see* Landeck.

MÜLLER-LINGKE. *see* Lingke, Müller.

MÜLLER-SAMERBERG. *see* Samerberg.

MULLER-URI, HILDEGARDE.
Am. b. New York 1894; ad. 1934 St. Augustine, Fla. A.

MULLER-URY, ADOLPH.
Am. b. Airolo, Ticino, Swi. 1868; ad. 1934 New York. A-F-W.

MULLIGAN, CHARLES J. (S)
Am. Ireland 1866-1916 Chicago. A13-DAB-F-Ta.

MULLIKINS, MARY AUGUSTA.
Am. b. Springfield, O. 1874; ad. 1934 Tientsin, China. A.

MULLIN, CHARLES EDWARD.
Am. b. Chicago 1885; ad. 1934 Orland Park, Ill. A.

MULLINEUX, MARY.
Am. b. Germantown, Pa.; ad. 1934 Same. A.

MULLINS, EDWIN ROSCOE. (S)
Eng. London 1848/9-1907 Suffolk. B-DNB-Hs-T.

MULLINS, GEORGE.
Ir. b. Dublin; ac. 1756-1775 London. DNB-T.

MULREADY, WILLIAM.
Ir. Ennis 1786-1863 London. B-Bd-C-DNB-E-T.

MULRONEY, REGINA WINIFRED. (S)
Am. b. New York 1895; ad. 1934 Same. A-Cs.

MULTSCHER, Hans. (S)
Ger. 1400-1467 Ulm. B-T-856.
MULVANY, George Francis.
Ir. Dublin 1809-1869 Same. DNB-T.
MULVANY, John.
Am. Ireland 1844-1906 New York. A06-F-T.
MULVANY, Thomas James.
Ir. Dublin 1779-1845. B-Bd-DNB-T.
MUMFORD, Alice Turner.
see Culin, Alice Mumford.
MUMFORD, Robert T.
Eng. ex. 1934 in London. M.
MUMMA, Lilian F.
Am. ad. 1935 Waynesboro, Pa. M.
MUMMERT, Sallie Blythe.
Am. b. Cisco, Tex.; ad. 1934 Fort Worth, Tex. A.
MUNCASTER, Claude.
Eng. b. West Chillington 1903; ad. 1934 Pentworth. Wa.
MUNCH, Edvard.
Nor. b. Loeiten 1863; ad. 1934 Oslo. B-E-T-904.
MUNCH, Jacob Edvard.
Nor. b. 1776; d. 1839 Christiania. B.
MUNCY, Percy W.
Am. ad. 1935 New York. M.
MUNDHENK, August. (S)
Am. b. 1848; d. 1933 Cinn., O. A019.
MUNDY, Ethel Frances. (Wax-S)
Am. b. Syracuse, N. Y.; ad. 1934 Same. A-F-W.
MUNDY, Louise Easterday.
Am. b. Nokomis, Ill.; ad. 1934 Lincoln, Neb. A.
MUNGER, Anne Wells.
Mrs. W. L. C. Munger.
Am. b. Springfield, Mass. 1862; ad. 1934 Pass Christian, Miss. A.
MUNGER, Caroline.
Am. Guilford, Conn. 1808-1892 Madison, Conn. F-6.
MUNGER, George.
Am. Guilford, Conn. 1781-1825 New Haven, Conn. F-T-2-3-6-7.
MUNGER, Gilbert.
Am. Madison, Conn. 1836-1903 Wash., D. C. A04-B-T.
MUNIER, Émile.
Fr. Paris 1810-1885. B-T.
MUNKÁCSY, Mihály de [Michael Lieb].
Hun. Munkacs, Hun. 1844-1900 Bonn, Ger. B-Bd-C-E-T.
MUNN, George Frederick.
Am. Utica, N. Y. 1852-1907 New York. A06-B-F-227.
MUNN, Marguerite Campbell.
Am. b. Wash., D. C. 1862; ad. 1934 University, Va. A-F.
MUNN, Paul Sandly.
Eng. Greenwich 1773-1845 Margate. B-DNB-T.
MUNNINGS, Alfred J.
Eng. b. Mendham 1878; ad. 1934 London. B-T-Wa-825.
MUNNS, John Bernard.
Eng. b. Birmingham; ad. 1934 Same. Wa.
MŨNOZ Y CUESTA, Domingo.
Sp. Madrid 1850-1912 Same. T.
MŨNOZ, Sébastian.
Sp. Segovia 1654-1690 Madrid. B-T.
MŨNOZ-DEGAIN, Antonio.
Sp. Valencia 1843-1924 Malaga. B-T.
MUNRO, Alexander. (S)
Scot. Inverness 1825-1871 Cannes, Fr. B-DNB-T.
MUNRO, Jean.
Can. ad. 1930 Montreal. M.
MUNRO, Norma Leslie.
Am. b. New York 1884; ad. 1915 Same. A12.
MUNROE, Faustina. *see* Degener.
MUNROE, Katherine.
Am. ex. 1935 Wash., D. C. M.
MUNROE, Marjorie.
Am. b. New York 1891; ad. 1934 Same. A-F.
MUNROE, Sally C.
Mrs. Vernon Munroe.
Am. b. New York 1881; ad. 1934 Same. A.
MUNROE, Sarah Sewell.
Am. b. Brooklyn, N. Y.; ad. 1934 Wash., D. C. A.
MUNSCH, Joseph.
Aus. Linz 1832-1896 Munich, Ger. B-T.
MUNSELL, Albert Henry.
Am. Boston 1858-1918 Brookline, Mass. A015-F-T.
MUNSELL, Richard.
Am. ex. 1935 Los Angeles, Calif. M.
MUNSELL, William A. O.
Am. b. Cold Water, O. 1866; ad. San Marino, Calif. A-F-T.
MUNSON, Lucius.
Am. New Haven, Conn. 1796-1823 West Indies. F-T-2-3.
MUNSON, Samuel B. (Eg)
Am. Conn. 1806-1880 Cinn., O. F-2-7.
MÜNSTERMAN, Ludwig. (S)
Ger. 1570/80-1637/9 Oldenburg. Hs-T.
MUNTHE, Alf.
Swe. b. Stockholm 1892. T.
MUNTHE, Gerhard Peter Vilhelm.
Nor. Elverum 1849-1929 Same. B-T.
MUNTHE, Ludwig.
Nor. Sogn 1841-1896 Düsseldorf, Ger. B-T.
MUNTZ, Elizabeth. (S)
Eng. ad. 1932 London. Wa1929.
MÜNTZ, John Henry.
Ger. Mülhausen 1727-1798 Cassel. DNB-T.
MÜNZER, Adolf Franz Theodor.
Ger. b. Pless 1870. B.
MUNZIG, George Chickering.
Am. Boston 1859-1908 New York. A07-F-T-15.
MURA [or Muro], Francesco de.
It. Naples 1698-1782 Same. B-T.
MURA, Frank.
Am. b. Ramspach, Alsace 1861; ad. 1930 London. A12-T.
MURANO, Nadalino da.
It. ac. 1558. B.
MURANT [or Meuron], Emanuel.
Dut. Amsterdam 1622-1700 Leeuwarden. B-T.
MURÁNYI, Gyula Julius.
Hun. b. Budapest 1881. T.

MURATORI, DOMENICO MARIA.
It. Vendrana 1661-1749 Rome. B-T.
MURAYAMA, HASHINE.
Jap. b. Yonezawa 1879; ad. 1934 Wash., D. C. M.
MURDOCK, DORA LOUISE.
Am. New Haven, Conn. 1857-1933 Balt., Md. A030-T.
MURDOCK, EDWIN F.
Am. b. Wash., D. C.; ad. 1934 New Rochelle, N. Y. M.
MURDOCK, FLORENCE.
Am. ad. 1934 Cinn., O. A.
MURDOCK, ROWLAND R. (Ill)
Am. d. 1917 in Pittsburgh, Pa. A014.
MURER [or Maurer], CHRISTOPH.
Swi. Zurich 1558-1614 Winterthur. B-T.
MURER, EUGÈNE.
Fr. Moulins 1845-1906 Auvers. T.
MURILLO, BARTHOLOMÉ ESTÉBAN.
Sp. Séville 1618-1682 Same. B-Bd-C-E-T-488-722-774-823.
MURPHY, ADA CHIFFORD.
Mrs. J. Francis Murphy.
Am. ad. 1934 Arkville, N. Y. A-F.
MURPHY, ALICE HAROLD.
Am. b. Springfield, Mass.; ad. 1934 New York. A.
MURPHY, CECIL TREMAYNE [née Buller]. (Eg)
Can. b. Montreal 1888; ad. 1935 New York. M.
MURPHY, CHRISTOPHER, JR.
Am. b. Savannah, Ga. 1902; ad. 1934 Same. A.
MURPHY, DENIS BROWNELL. (Min)
Ir. b. Dublin; d. 1842 London. B-DNB-T.
MURPHY, DIANA. (Ill)
Eng. ad. 1934 London. M.
MURPHY, HENRY CRUSE, JR.
Am. Brooklyn, N. Y. 1886-1931 Greenwich, Conn. A028.
MURPHY, HERMANN DUDLEY.
Am. b. Marlboro, Mass. 1867; ad. 1934 Lexington, Mass. A-F-T-W.
MURPHY, JAMES EDWARD, JR. (Cart.)
Am. b. Chicago 1892; ad. 1934 New York. W.
MURPHY, JOHN. (Eg)
Ir. Ireland 1748-1820 London. B-DNB-T.
MURPHY, JOHN FRANCIS.
Am. Oswego, N. Y. 1853-1921 New York. A018-B-C-DAB-E-F-T-46-61-71-104-228-757.
MURPHY, J. LEO.
Am. ad. 1935 Cinn., O. M.
MURPHY, M. LOIS. (Et)
Am. ad. 1934 Brooklyn, N. Y. A.
MURPHY, MICHAEL THOMAS. (S)
Am. b. Ireland 1867; ad. 1926 Chicago. A20-F-T-W14.
MURPHY, NELLY LITTLEHALE.
Mrs. Hermann Dudley Murphy.
Am. b. Stockton, Calif. 1867; ad. 1934 Lexington, Mass. A.
MURPHY, WILLIAM D.
Am. b. Alabama 1834. F-T.
MURRAY, CHARLES OLIVER.
Eng. Denholm 1842-1923 London. B-T.
MURRAY, [Sir] DAVID.
Scot. Glasgow 1849-1933 London. B-E-T-Wa.
MURRAY, EDWARD.
Am. b. Mass. 1902. DBA.
MURRAY, ELIZABETH [Heaphy].
Mrs. Henry John Murray.
Eng. London 1815-1822 San Remo, It. B-T.
MURRAY, ELLA I. (S)
Am. ad. 1934 Plainfield, N. J. M.
MURRAY, GRACE H.
Mrs. Archibold Gordon Murray.
Am. b. New York 1872; ad. 1934 Same. A-T.
MURRAY, GRAHAM.
Scot. ad. 1934 Cambuslang. M.
MURRAY, HESTER M.
Am. b. 1904; ex. 1934 Chicago. M.
MURRAY, JACK. (Ill)
Am. ad. 1934 New York. M.
MURRAY, SAMUEL. (S)
Am. b. Phila., Pa. 1870; ad. 1934 Same. A-F-T-Ta-W.
MURRAY, THOMAS.
Scot. Scotland 1666-1734 London. B-T.
MURRAY, WILLIAM STAITE.
Eng. b. London 1881; ad. 1934 Same. T-Wa.
MUSASHI, MIYOMOTO [Nitten].
Jap. 1582-1645 Japan. J., Vol. 1, page 100.
MUSGRAVE, ARTHUR FRANKLYN. (Mu)
Am. b. Brighton, Eng. 1880; ad. 1934 Cambridge, Mass. A-F.
MUSGRAVE, EDITH.
Am. b. New York 1887; ad. 1934 Mt. Vernon, N. Y. A.
MUSGRAVE, HELEN GREENE.
Am. b. Cinn., O. 1890; ad. 1934 Cambridge, Mass. A.
MUSI [or Mussi], AGOSTINO VENEZIANO.
It. Venice 1490-1540 Rome. B-T.
MUSICK, WILLIAM EARL.
Am. b. Brashear, Mo. 1896; ad. 1934 Chicago. A.
MUSIN, AUGUSTE HENRI.
Belg. b. Ostend 1852. B-T.
MUSIN, FRANÇOIS ETIENNE.
Belg. Ostend 1820-1888 Brussels. B-T.
MUSS, ARNOLT GUSTAV.
Am. b. 1858; d. 1927 Avon, Mass. A024.
MUSS [or Musso], CHARLES. (Enamel-P)
Eng. Newcastle 1779-1824. B-DNB-T.
MUSSCHER, MICHIEL VAN.
Dut. Rotterdam 1645-1705 Amsterdam. B-C-T-722.
MUSSELMAN-CARR, MYRA V. (S)
Am. b. Georgetown, Ky. 1880; ad. 1934 Woodstock, N. Y. A.
MUSSULMAN ARTISTS.
see book No. 800.
MUTER, MARIE MELA.
Pol. b. Warsaw 1876; ad. 1934 Paris. DBA-T.
MUTH, ALICE LOLITA HELEN.
Am. b. Cinn., O. 1887. A.
MUTRIE, ANNIE FERAY.
Eng. Manchester 1826-1893 Brighton. B-DNB-T.
MUTRIE, MARTHA DARLEY.
Eng. Manchester 1824-1885 London. DNB-T.
MUZIANO, GIROLAMO [Bressano].
It. Brescia 1528/30-1592 Rome. B-C-E-T-722.
MUZZIOLI, GIOVANNI.
It. Modena 1854-1894 Same. B-E-T.

MYER, Hyam.
Eng. ex. 1935 London. M.
MEYERS, Annie M.
Am. b. Warsaw, N. Y. 1858; ad. 1934 Castile, N. Y. A.
MYERS, Datus E.
Am. b. Jefferson, Ore. 1879; ad. 1934 Santa Fé, N. M. A.
MYERS, Emmet Edwin.
Am. b. Edinburgh, O. 1868; ad. 1934 Huntington, W. Va. A.
MYERS, Ethel. (S)
Mrs. Jerome Myers.
Am. b. Brooklyn, N. Y. 1881; ad. 1934 New York. A.
MYERS, Frank Harmon.
Am. Cleves, O. 1899; ad. 1934 Cinn., O. A.
MYERS, Jennie Chace.
Am. b. Avon, N. Y. 1861; ad. 1934 Castile, N. Y. A.
MYERS, Jerome.
Am. b. Petersburg, Va. 1867; ad. 1934 New York. A-F-T-W-46.
MYERS, Lloyd Burton.
Am. b. Sterling, Ill. 1892; ad. 1934 Los Angeles, Calif. A.
MYERS, [Mrs.] Mary Shepherd Lukens.
Am. b. Conshohocken, Pa. 1878; ad. 1934 Same. A.
MYIN, Maria Jacola [Ommeganck].
Flem. 1760-1849. T.
MYLNE, Alexander. (S)
Scot. 1613-1643 Edinburgh. DNB-T.
MYLNE [or Myln] Family.
Scot. ac. 16-19th centuries. T.
MYN, Francis von der.
Dut. Düsseldorf, Ger. 1719-1783 London. B-T.
MYN, George van der.
Dut. London 1723/8-1763 Amsterdam. B-T.
MYN, Hendrick Aarnout.
Flem. Antwerp, Belg. 1760-1826. B-T.
MYN, Herman van der.
Dut. Amsterdam 1684-1741 London. B-DNB-T.
MYNSHEEREN, François. (S)
Flem. ac. 1535-1565 in Mechlin. B-T.
MYOTAKU, Takeda.
Jap. Mino 1308-1388 Kyoto. T.
MYR, Louis Marcel.
Fr. ad. 1929 Paris. Fa.
MYRICK, Katherine S. (Min)
Mrs. H. M. Myrick.
Am. ad. 1934 Pelham Manor, N. Y. A.
MYRON OF ELENTHERAE. (S)
Gr. b. Borotia; ac. 492-430 B.C. in Athens. E-Hs-T-817-855.
MYSLBEK, Josef Vaeslav. (S)
Czec. Prague 1848-1922 Same. B-E-T-798.
MYTENS, Aert [or Carl] Izack.
Flem. Brussels 1541-1602 Rome. B-T.
MYTENS, Daniel [The Elder].
Dut. Delft 1590-1658 The Hague. B-Bd-DNB-T-702.
MYTENS, Daniel [The Younger].
Dut. The Hague 1644-1688 Same. B-T.
MYTENS, Isaac.
Dut. 1602-1665/6 The Hague. B-T.
MYTENS, Jan [or Johannes].
Dut. The Hague 1614-1670 Same. B-C-T.
MYTENS, Martimus I.
Dut. The Hague 1648-1736 Stockholm, Swe. B-T.
MYTENS, Martimus II.
Swe. Stockholm 1695-1770 Vienna, Aus. B-T.
MYTS, Johannes.
Dut. ac. 1645. Fa-Wi.

NABERT, Wilhelm Julius August.
Ger. 1799-1846 Munich. B-T.
NACHTMANN, Franz Xaver.
Ger. Obermans 1799-1846 Munich. B-T.
NADELMAN, Elie. (S)
Am. b. Warsaw, Pol. 1885; ad. 1934 Riverdale, N. Y. A-Cs-F-T-46.
NADLER, Robert.
Aus. b. 1858. B.
NADORP, Franz.
Ger. Anholt 1794-1876 Rome, It. B-T.
NADZOV, Alexis. (S)
Chilean, b. Valparaiso, Chile 1907. DBA.
NAEGELE, Charles Frederick.
Am. b. Knoxville, Tenn. 1857; ad. 1934 Marietta, Ga. A-F-T-W.
NAEKE [or Nacke], Gustav Heinrich.
Ger. Frauenstein 1786-1835 Dresden. B-T.
NAFTEL, Paul Jacob.
Eng. Gurnsey 1817-1891 London. B-DNB-T.
NAGHARU, Odo.
Jap. 1862-1752 Edo, Japan. T.
NAGAI, Thomas.
Am. ad. 1935 New York. M.
NAGATAKA.
Jap. ac. 1273-1288 in Kyoto. T.
NAGEL, Eva M.
Am. b. Chicago 1880; ad. 1915 Phila., Pa. A12.
NAGEL [or Naghel], Jan.
Dut. ac. 1600-1616 in Haarlem. B-T.
NAGLE, Edward Pierce.
Am. b. Revere, Mass. 1893; ad. 1934 Charlottesville, Va. A.
NAGLER, Edith Kröger.
Am. b. New York 1895; ad. 1934 Spuyten Duyvil, N. Y. A-F.
NAGLER, Fred. (Et)
Am. b. West Springfield, Mass. 1891; ad. 1934 New York. A-F.
NAGY, Sigismond de.
Rumanian. b. Ungarn 1872. T.
NAHL, Charles [or Karl].
Am. Cassel, Ger. 1819-1878 Brooklyn, N. Y. B-T.
NAHL, Johann August [The Elder]. (S)
Ger. Berlin 1710-1785 Cassel. B-T.
NAHL, Johann August [The Younger].
Ger. Clanne 1752-1825 Cassel. B-T.
NAHL, Perham W.
Am. b. San Fran. 1869; d. 1935 Berkeley, Calif. A-Obit. Art Digest, 5-15-1935.
NAIGEON, Jean Claude.
Fr. Dijon 1753-1832 Same. B-T.
NAIGEON, Jean Guillaume Elzidor.
Fr. Paris 1797-1867 Same. C-T.
NAIN. *see* Le Nain.
NAISH, William. (Min)
Eng. b. Axbridge; ex. 1783-1800 in London. B-DNB-T.

NAIVEU [or Neveu], MATHYS.
Dut. Leyden 1647-1721 Amsterdam. B-T.
NAIWINX, HERMAN.
Dut. 1624-1651 Hamburg, Ger. T.
NAKAMIZO, FUGI.
Jap.-Am. b. Japan 1895; ad. 1934 New York. A.
NAKAMURA, KANZI.
Jap.-Am. Japan 1887-1932 Boston, Mass. A029-Y01933.
NAKIAN, REUBEN. (S)
Am. b. College Point, L. I., N. Y. 1897; ad. 1935 New York. A.
NALDINI, BATTISTA DI MATTEO.
It. Florence 1537?-1590/8 Same. B-C-T.
NANDA LAL BOSE.
Hindu. India. M.
NANGAKU, WATANABÉ.
Jap. ac. 1800 in Japan. J., Vol. 2, page 15.
NANKAI, GION.
Jap. 1677-1751 Tokyo. T.
NANKIVELL, EDITH.
Am. ad. 1934 New York. M.
NANKIVELL, FRANK ARTHUR.
Am. b. Maldon, Aust. 1869; ad. 1934 New York. A-F-W.
NANNI DI BACCIO, BIGIO.
It. ac. 1540-1568 in Florence. T-V.
NANNI DI BANCO. *see* Banco, N. di.
NANNI [or Nani], GIOVANNI DA UDINE.
It. Udine 1487-1564 Rome. B-T-V.
NAN-RIÛ [or Shin-Ki].
Jap. ac. 5th Cent. in Japan. M.
NANTEUIL, CHARLES FRANÇOIS LEBOEUF. (S)
Fr. Paris 1792-1865 Same. B-T.
NANTEUIL, ROBERT. (Eg)
Fr. Reims 1623/5-1678 Paris. B-E-T-880.
NANTEUIL-LEBOEUF, CÉLESTIN FRANÇOIS.
Fr. Rome, It. 1813-1873 Marlotte, Fr. B-T.
NAONOBU, KANO.
Jap. Kyoto 1607-1650 Tokyo. J-T.
NAPIER, CHARLES.
Scot. b. Edinburgh 1889; ad. 1934 Same. Wa.
NAPOLI, MICHELE DE.
It. Terlizzi 1808-1892. B-T.
NAPOLITANO, FRANCESCO.
It. ac. 1500 in Milan. B.
NAPOLITANO, P. G.
Am. ad. 1934 Los Angeles, Calif. M.
NAPPENBACH, HENRY ["Nap"]. (Ill)
Am. Bavaria 1862-1931 New York. A028.
NARAY, AURELIO.
Hun. b. Budapest 1883. T.
NARBETH, WILLIAM ARTHUR. (Et)
Eng. b. Eltham 1893; ad. 1934 Seaford. Wa.
NARBONNE, EUGÈNE.
Fr. b. Trouillon 1885; ex. 1933 Pittsburgh, Pa. DBA.
NARBERT, EGOR.
Rus. 1886-1920 Kiev. T.
NARCISCO [or Narcisse]. *see* Diaz de la Pena.
NARDEAUX, HENRI.
Fr. ac. 1883-1850 Paris. B.
NARDI, ANGELO.
It. Florence 1601-1660 Madrid. B-T.
NARDO [or Leonardo], DI CIONE.
It. ac. 1345-1366. T-V.
NARDO, MARIOTTO DI. *see* Mariotto, di N.
NARKISSOS. *see* Dionysos. (S)
NÄSBJORN. (S)
Swe. ac. 1030 in Stockholm. 824.
NASH, ANNE TAYLOR.
Am. b. Pittsboro, N. C. 1884; ad. 1934 Charleston, S. C. A.
NASH, FREDERICK.
Eng. Lambeth 1782-1856 Brighton. B-DNB-T.
NASH, JOHN NORTHCOTE.
Eng. b. London 1893; ad. 1934 Bucks. T-Wa-825.
NASH, JOSEPH. (Eg)
Eng. Marlow 1809-1878 Bayswater. B-DNB-T.
NASH, PAUL. (Eg)
Eng. b. London 1889; ad. 1934 Same. E-T-Wa-825.
NASH, WILLARD AYER.
Am. b. Phila., Pa. 1898; ad. 1934 Santa Fé, N. M. A-F.
NASINI, GIUSEPPE NICCOLÒ.
It. Siena 1657/64-1736 Same. B-T.
NASMYTH, ALEXANDER.
Scot. Edinburgh 1758-1840 Same. B-Bd-DNB-E-T.
NASMYTH, PATRICK [or Peter].
Scot. Edinburgh 1787-1831 London. B-Bd-E-T-722.
NASON, GERTRUDE.
Am. b. Boston, Mass. 1890; ad. 1934 New York. A.
NASON, PIETER.
Dut. Amsterdam 1612-1688/91 The Hague. B-C-T.
NASON, THOMAS WILLOUGHBY. (Et)
Am. b. Lowell, Mass. 1889; ad. 1934 Reading, Mass. A28.
NASSARO, MATTEO DAL.
It. ac. 1515-1548 in Verona. T-V.
NAST, THOMAS. (Cari)
Am. Landau, Bav. 1840-1902 Quayaquil Equador. A04-B-Bd-DAB-E-F-T-4-9-15-46-162-764.
NATOIRE, CHARLES JOSEPH.
Fr. Nimes 1700-1777 Castel. B-C-T-722.
NATSUO.
Jap. Kyoto 1827-1898 Tokyo. T.
NATTER, JOHN LORENZ. (Med)
Br. Biberach, Ger. 1705-1763 Leningrad, Rus. DNB-T.
NATTIER, JEAN BAPTISTE.
Fr. Paris 1686-1726 Same. B-T.
NATTIER, JEAN MARC.
Fr. Paris 1685-1766 Same. B-Bd-C-E-T-489-722.
NATTINI, OPIZIO AMOS.
It. 1757-1800 Rome. T.
NATUS, ANTHONY.
Dut. 1636-1660 Amsterdam. B-T.
NAUDE, HUGO.
Br. ac. 1934 So. Africa. M.
NAUDET, THOMAS CHARLES.
Fr. Paris 1773-1810 Same. T.
NAUDIN, BERNARD.
Fr. b. 1876; ad. 1934 Paris. B-DBA-T.
NAUEN, HEINRICH.
Ger. b. Krefeld 1880. T.
NAJOK, GUSTAV.
Ger. b. Götzendorf 1861. B-T.

NAUKYDES I. (S)
Gr. ac. 423-420 B.C. in Argos. B-T.
NAUKYDES II. (S)
Gr. ac. 400 B.C. in Argos. T.
NAUMAN, FRED ROBERT.
Am. b. St. Louis, Mo. 1892; ad. 1934 Glendale, Mo. A.
NAUMANN, FRIEDRICH GOTTHARD.
Ger. Blasewitz 1750-1815/21 Ansbach. B-T.
NAUPIN, CHIN.
Chinese. ac. 1731. J., Vol. 2, page 73.
NAUWINX [or Naiwink], HERMAN.
Dut. Schonhoven 1619-1651/4 Hamburg, Ger. B-T.
NAVARRE, HENRI EDOUARD. (S)
Fr. b. Paris 1885. DBA.
NAVARRETE, JUAN FERNÁNDEZ [El Mudo].
Sp. Logrono 1526-1579 Madrid. C-E-T-722.
NAVARETTE Y FOS, RICARDO.
Sp. Alcoy 1834-1910 Madrid. B-T.
NAVE, ROYSTON.
Am. b. La Grange, Tex. 1876; ad. 1935 New York. A28-F.
NAVEZ, FRANÇOIS JOSEPH.
Belg. Charleroi 1787-1869 Brussels. B-C-T.
NAVIASKY, PHILIP.
Eng. b. Leeds 1894; ad. 1934 Same. T-Wa.
NAVLET, VICTOR.
Fr. 1819-1886 Paris. B-T.
NAVONE, GIUSEPPE. (S)
It. ac. 1934 in Rome. M.
NAVOSOV, V. I. (Ill)
Rus. Moscow 1870-1917. M.
NAYLOR, [Miss] MARIE J. [or I].
Eng. ac. 1883-1912 in London. B-T.
NAZARI [or Nazzari], BARTOLOMMEO.
It. Bergamo 1699-1758 Milan. B-T.
NAZON, FRANÇOIS HENRI.
Fr. Réalmont 1821-1902 Montauban. B-T.
NEAFIE, EDITH S.
Am. ad. 1934 New York. M.
NEAGLE, JAMES. (Eg)
Am. London 1760?-1822 Phila., Pa. DNB-F-T-2-7.
NEAGLE, JOHN.
Am. Boston, Mass. 1796-1865 Phila., Pa. B-Bd-C-DAB-F-T-1-2-4-7-15-40-229-701-838.
NEAGOE, ANN.
Am. b. 1894; ex. 1935 New York. DBA.
NEAL, DAVID DALHOFF.
Am. Lowell, Mass. 1838-1915 Munich, Ger. A012-B-C-DAB-E-F-T-W8-1-15-39.
NEAL, GRACE PRUDEN. (S)
Am. b. St. Paul, Minn. 1876; ad. 1934 New York. A-Cs-F-T.
NEALE, GEORGE HALL.
Eng. ad. 1934 Liverpool. Wa.
NEALE, JOHN PRESTON.
Eng. 1780-1847 Tattingstone. B-T.
NEALE, [Mrs.] MAUD HALL.
Eng. b. Waterloo; ad. 1934 Liverpool. Wa.
NEALE, THOMAS. (Eg)
Eng. ac. 1657 Paris; ac. 1678-1699 London. B-DNB-T.
NEALKES.
Gr. ac. 250 B.C. in Sicyon. T.
NEANDROSS, SIGUARD. (S)
Am. b. Stavanger, Nor. 1871; ad. 1934 Ridgefield, N. J. A-T-46.
NEATBY, WILLIAM JAMES.
Eng. Barnsley 1860-1910 High Wycombe. T.
NEATE, MARGARET.
Eng. ex. 1934 London. M.
NEAVE, [Sir] RICHARD DIGBY.
Eng. 1793-1868. T.
NEBBIA, CESARE.
It. Orvieto 1536-1614 Same. B-T.
NEBEL, BERTHOLD. (S)
Am. b. Basle, Swi. 1889; ad. 1934 New York. A-Cs.
NECK, JOHAN VAN.
Dut. Naarden 1635-1714 Amsterdam. B-C-T.
NÉE, FRANÇOIS DENIS. (Eg)
Fr. Paris 1732-1817 Same. B-T.
NEEDHAM, ALFRED CARTER.
Am. b. Beechville, Can. 1872; ad. 1934 Boston. A.
NEEDHAM, CHARLES AUSTIN.
Am. Buffalo, N. Y. 1844-1923. A020-B-F-T.
NEEDHAM, RAY CLAY.
Am. b. Owasso, Mich. 1893; ad. 1934 Richmond, Ind. A.
NEEFFS, PIETER [The Elder].
Flem. Antwerp 1579-1656/61 Same. B-C-T-722.
NEEFFS, PIETER [The Younger].
Flem. Antwerp 1620-1675 Same. B-C-T-722.
NEEL, ALICE.
Am. ex. 1935 New York. M.
NEEL, FRANK. (Min)
Am. Toledo, Ohio 1874-1933 Same. A030.
NEELD, CLARENCE ELLSWORTH.
Am. b. New Albany, Ind. 1875; ad. 1934 Glen Ellyn, Ill. A.
NEER, AERNOUT [or Aert] VAN DER.
Dut. Amsterdam 1603/4-1677 Same. B-Bd-C-E-T-722.
NEER, EGLON HENDRIK VAN DER.
Dut. Amsterdam 1634/5-1703 Düsseldorf, Ger. B-C-T-722.
NEES. *see* Nes, Jan van.
NEFF, TIMOTHÉ ANDREVITCH.
Rus. Estland 1805-1877 Leningrad. T.
NEGKER [or Necker], JOST DE. (Eg)
Flem. Antwerp 1485-1544 Augsburg, Ger. B-T.
NEGOE, ANNE.
Mrs. Peter Negoe.
Am. b. Rumania; ad. 1934 France. M.
NEGRETTI, GIACOMO.
see Palma Il. Giovane, Jacopo.
NEGRO ARTISTS. *see* book No. 254; *consult* Harmon Foundation, New York.
NEGULESCO, JEAN.
Rumanian; ac. 1931. M.
NEHER, BERNARD [The Elder].
Ger. 1743-1801 Biberach. T.
NEHR, BERNARD [The Younger].
Ger. Biberach 1806-1868 Stuttgart. B-C-T.
NEHER, FRED. (Cart)
Am. ad. 1935 New York. M.
NEHER, MICHAEL.
Ger. Munich 1798-1876 Same. B-C-T.
NEHLIG, VICTOR.
Am. Paris 1830-1909 New York. C-F-T-4-15.
NEIDE, EMIL.
Ger. b. Königsberg 1843. T.

NEILL, FRANCES ISABLE.
Am. b. Warren, Pa.; ad. 1934 New York. A.
NEILLOT, LOUIS.
Fr. b. Vichy 1898. DBA.
NEILSEN, M. P. (S)
Am. ac. 1915 Westbury, N. Y. A12.
NEILSON, HENRY IVAN.
Can. Cap Rouge, Que. 1865-1931. M.
NEILSON, RAYMOND PERRY RODGERS. PORTPTR
Am. b. New York 1881; ad. 1934 Same. A-W.
NEILSON-GRAY, NORAH.
Scot. b. Helensburgh; ad. 1929 Glasgow. T-Wa1929.
NEITHARDT [or Göthardt], MATHIAS. [Monogramist, M. N.]
Ger. Würzburg 1460-1528 Halle. T.
NELAN, CHARLES. (Cart)
Am. Akron, O. 1854-1904 Cave Spring, Ga. A05.
NELKE, DORA K.
Am. ad. 1934 Phila., Pa. M.
NELL, [Miss] TONY.
Am. b. Wash., D. C.; ad. 1934 New York. A.
NELLI, OTTAVIANO DI MARTINO DE.
It. 1370/5-1445/50 Urbino. B-T.
NELLIUS, MARTIMUS.
Dut. ac. 1670-1706 in Leyden. B-T.
NELSON, BRUCE.
Am. b. San Jose, Calif. 1888. M.
NELSON, CARL GUSTAF SIMON.
Am. b. Horby, Swe. 1898; ad. 1934 New York. A.
NELSON, DAN.
Am. ad. 1934 Greencastle, Pa. M.
NELSON, GAIL.
Am. ad. 1935 Wash., D. C. M.
NELSON, G. PATRICK. (Ill)
Am. ad. 1934 New York. M.
NELSON, GEORGE LAURENCE.
Am. b. New Rochelle, N. Y. 1887; ad. 1934 New York. A-T.
NELSON, HAROLD. (Bookplates)
Eng. b. Dorchester 1871; ad. 1934 London. Wa.
NELSON, JOHN. (S)
Eng. 1726-1812 Shrewsbury. DNB-T.
NELSON, MARGARET.
Am. b. Sweden 1901; ad. 1934 West Hartford, Conn. A.
NELSON, WILLIAM HENRY DE BEAUVOIR.
Am. London 1861-1920 New York. A017-T-Y01921.
NEMENOW, GUERTA.
Ger. b. Berlin 1908. DBA.
NEPO, ERNEST.
Ger. b. Dauba 1895. T.
NERI DI BICCI. *see* Bicci.
NERI, DARIO. (Eg)
It. ad. 1932 Rome. M.
NERBY [or Nehrlich], FRIEDRICH CHRISTIAN.
Ger. Erfurt 1807-1878 Venice, It. B-C-T.
NEROCCIO DI BARTOLOMEO. *see* Landi, N.
NERONI, BARTOLOMMEO [Riccio].
It. Siena 1500?-1571/3. B-T.
NERRMANN, FRANK.
Am. ex. 1935 New York. M.
NES [or Nees, or Nis], JAN [or Johan] VAN.
Dut. ac. 1618-1650 in Delft. B-T.
NESBIT [or Nesbitt], CHARLTON. (Eg)
Eng. Durham 1775-1838 London. DNB-T.
NESBITT, SIDNEY.
Eng. ac. 1872-1878 in London. B.
NESEMANN, ENNO.
Am. b. Marysville, Calif. 1861; ad. 1934 Berkeley, Calif. A.
NESFIELD, WILLIAM ANDREWS.
Eng. 1793-1881 London. B-DNB-T.
NESIOTES. (S)
Gr. ac. 478 B.C. in Athens. E-Hs-T.
NESMITH, J. H. (Eg)
Am. ac. 1805-1828 New Haven, Conn. F-2-7.
NESMITH, HOWARD MACCOMBER.
Am. Brooklyn, N. Y. 1859-1935 Roslyn, L. I., N. Y. M-Obit. N. Y. papers, 4-18-1935.
NESS, ALBERT KENNETH.
Am. b. St. Ignace, Mich. 1903; ad. 1934 Chicago. A.
NESSLER, ROSA.
Am. ad. 1934 New York. M.
NESTEROFF, MICHAIL VASSILVITCH.
Rus. b. Ufa 1862. B-T.
NESTLER, [Mrs.] MABLE BALLOU.
Am. ad. 1934 So. Norwalk, Conn. M.
NESTOR, BERNARD D.
Am. b. Minnesota 1903; ad. 1934 Seattle, Wash. A.
NESTOR DE LA TORRE, MARTÍN FERÁNDEZ.
Sp. b. Las Palmas 1869. DBA-T.
NESTOR [or Deneter], LAURENTIUS DE.
Ger. Elbing 1600-1638. T.
NETSCHER, CASPER [or Gaspar].
Dut. Heidelberg, Ger. 1639-1684 The Hague. B-Bd-C-E-T-722.
NETSCHER, CONSTANTINE.
Dut. The Hague 1668-1723 Same. B-T.
NETSCHER, THEODORUS.
Dut. Bordeaux, Fr. 1661-1732 Hulst. B-C-T.
NETTLESHIP, JOHN TRIVETT.
Eng. Kettering 1841-1902 London. B-DNB-T.
NETTLETON, WALTER.
Am. b. New Haven, Conn. 1861; ad. 1934 Stockbridge, Mass. A-B-T-Wa.
NETZER, HUBERT. (S)
Ger. b. Isny 1865; ad. 1931 Munich. T.
NEUBAUER, FREDERICK AUGUST.
Am. b. Cinn., O. 1855; ad. 1915 Same. A12-F-T.
NEUBERGER, DANIEL.
Ger. 1600-1660 Vienna, Aus. T.
NEUBERT, LOUIS [or Ludwig].
Ger. Leipzig 1846-1892 Sonnenstein. B-T.
NEUFCHATEL, NICOLAS [Lucidel].
Flem. Bergen 1525/7-1590 Nüremberg, Ger. B-T.
NEUFELD, DIETRICH HENRY.
Am. b. So. Russia 1906; ad. 1934 Dayton, O. M.
NEUHAUS, EUGEN.
Am. b. Barmen, Ger. 1879; ad. 1934 Berkeley, Calif. A-F-W.
NEUHAUS, FRITZ KARL AUGUST.
Ger. b. Elberfeld 1852. B-T.

NEUHAUSER, Marguerite Phillips.
Mrs. Roy L. Neuhauser.
Am. b. No. Arlington, Va.; ad. 1934 Wash., D. C. A.
NEUHYS, Albert.
Dut. Utrecht 1844-1914 Laren. B-T.
NEUMANN, Gilbert Franz.
Am. b. San Antonio, Tex. 1906; ad. 1934 Same. A.
NEUMANN, Max.
Ger. b. Königsberg 1885. T.
NEUMANN, Robert von.
Am. b. Rostock, Ger. 1888; ad. 1934 Milwaukee, Wis. M.
NEUREUTHER, Eugen Napoleon.
Ger. Munich 1806-1882 Same. B-C-T.
NEUVILLE, Alphonse Marie de.
Fr. St. Omer 1835-1885 Paris. B-Bd-C-E-T.
NEVE, Cornelius.
Eng. Antwerp, Belg. 1612-1678 London. DNB-T.
NEVE [or Neue], Frans de.
Flem. Antwerp 1606-1681 Brussels. B-T.
NEVEUX, Lantoine.
Ger. b. Stenay 1892. DBA.
NEVILLE, Kate Young.
Am. b. Camden, Ala. 1876; ad. 1934 Montgomery, Ala. M.
NEVIN, Blanche. (S)
Am. Phila., Pa. 1838-1925 Lancaster, Pa. A022-F-Hs-T-15.
NEVIN, John D.
Am. b. Easton, Pa. 1880; ad. 1934 New Hope, Pa. M.
NEVIN, [Mrs.] Josephine Welles. (S)
Am. b. Chicago; d. 1929 Saranac Lake, N. Y. A027-Ta.
NEVINSON, Christopher Richard Wynne.
Aust. b. London 1889; ad. 1934 Same. T-Wa-825.
NEW, Edmund Hort. (Ill)
Eng. Eversham 1871-1931 Oxford. T-Wa1929.
NEWBERRY, Francis H.
Scot. b. Membury; ad. 1934 Glasgow. T-Wa.
NEWBERRY, Rosamond S.
Mrs. John Strong Newberry.
Am. b. Winchester, Mass. 1888; ad. 1934 Boston. M.
NEWBURY, A. E.
Aust. b. Melbourne, Victoria, 1891. M.
NEWBY, [Mrs.] Ruby Warren.
Am. b. Goff, Kan. 1886; ad. 1934 Sarasota, Fla. A.
NEWCOMB, Marie Guise.
Am. b. Newark, N. J. 1865. T-46.
NEWCOMBE, George W.
Am. Eng. 1799-1845 New York. F-T-2-6.
NEWCOMBE, Warren.
Am. b. Waltham, Mass. 1894; ad. 1934 Brentwood Heights, Calif. A.
NEWELL, Clifton.
Am. ex. 1935 New York. M.
NEWELL, George Glenn.
Am. b. Berrian Co., Mich. 1870; ad. 1934 Dover Plains, N. Y. A-F-T-W-46.
NEWELL, Hugh.
Am. b. Belfast, Ir. 1830. A20-F-T-15.
NEWELL, James Michael. (Mu)
Am. b. Carnegie, Pa. 1900; ad. 1934 New York. A.
NEWELL, Peter Sheaf Hersey.
Am. Illinois 1862-1924 Little Neck, N. Y. A021-DAB-F-46.
NEWENHAM, Frederick.
Ir. Cork 1807-1859 London. B-DNB-T.
NEWHALL, Harriott B.
Am. b. Topeka, Kan. 1874; ad. 1934 Provincetown, Mass. M.
NEWHOUSE, C. B.
Br. ac. 1820. M-Wi.
NEWKING, Natalie.
Am. b. N. Y. 1904; ad. 1934 Hollywood, Calif. M.
NEWLAND, Harry.
Am. b. Erie, Pa. 1877; ad. 1934 New Bedford, Mass. A28-F-T-W.
NEWLIN, John North.
Am. ad. 1934 Dover Plains, N. Y. M.
NEWMAN, Allen George. (S)
Am. b. N. Y. 1875; ad. 1934 Kingston, N. Y. A-Cs-F-T-W.
NEWMAN, Anna Mary.
Am. d. 1930 Richmond, Ind. A028.
NEWMAN, Carl.
Am. b. Phila., Pa. 1858; ad. 1915 Same. A12-F-T.
NEWMAN, Clara G.
Am. b. Brownville, Neb. 1870; ad. 1934 Richmond, Ind. A.
NEWMAN, Elias.
Am. b. Poland 1903; ad. 1934 Brooklyn, N. Y. A.
NEWMAN, Harry W.
Am. b. London, Eng. 1873; ad. 1934 New York. A.
NEWMAN, Henry Roderick.
Am. Easton, N. Y. 1843?-1918 Florence, It. A015-B-DAB-F-T-15.
NEWMAN, Hugo R. B.
Am. ex. 1934 New York. M.
NEWMAN, Joseph.
Am. b. New York 1890; ad. 1934 Brooklyn, N. Y. A.
NEWMAN, Philip Henry.
Eng. London 1840-1927 Same. T-Y01928.
NEWMAN, Robert Loftin.
Am. Richmond, Va. 1827-1912 New York. A010-DAB-F-T-32-104-892.
NEWMAN, Willie Betty.
Mrs. J. W. Newman.
Am. b. Murfreesboro, Tenn. 1864; ad. 1934 Nashville, Tenn. A-B-F-T-W14.
NEWSAM, Albert. (Eg)
Am. Steubenville, O. 1809-1864 Wilmington, Del. F-T-2-6-7.
NEWTON, Alice.
Am. ex. 1934 New York. M.
NEWTON, Alfred Pizzey.
Eng. Rayleigh 1830-1883 Liverpool. B-DNB-T.
NEWTON, Algernon.
Eng. b. Hampstead 1880; ad. 1934 Same. T-Wa.
NEWTON, Ann Mary.
Eng. Rome, It. 1832-1866 London. DNB-T.
NEWTON, Edith. (Eg)
Am. ad. 1935 New Milford, Conn. M.

NEWTON, Eric.
Eng. ad. 1934 Manchester. M.
NEWTON, Francis.
Am. b. Lake George, N. Y. 1873; ad. 1934 East Hampton, L. I., N. Y. A-T.
NEWTON, Francis Milner.
Eng. London 1720-1794 Taunton. DNB-T.
NEWTON, Gilbert Stuart.
Br.-Am. Halifax, N. S. 1794-1835 London. B-Bd-C-DNB-F-T-1-2-4-45.
NEWTON, Harry Groll.
Am. b. Indiana 1891; ad. 1935 Austin, Tex. M.
NEWTON, Helen F.
Am. b. Woodbridge, Conn. 1878; ad. 1934 Westfield, Conn. A.
NEWTON, Herbert H.
Eng. b. London 1881; ad. 1934 Same. T-Wa.
NEWTON, Josephine Pitkin.
Mrs. R. C. Newton.
Am. ad. 1934 Scarsdale, N. Y. A.
NEWTON, Lilias Torrance.
Can. b. Montreal; ad. 1935 Same. M.
NEWTON, Parker.
Am. b. New York; d. 1928 France. A025.
NEWTON, Richard. (Cari)
Eng. ac. 1777-1798 in London. B-DNB-T.
NEWTON, Richard, Jr.
Am. ex. 1934 East Hampton, L. I., N. Y. A18.
NEWTON, [Sir] William John. (Min)
Eng. London 1785-1869 Same. B-Bd-DNB-T.
NEY, Elizabeth. (S)
Am. Westphalia, Ger. 1833-1907 Austin, Tex. A06-DAB-F-46.
NEY, Lloyd Raymond.
Am. b. Friedenburg, Pa. 1893; ad. 1934 New Hope, Pa. A.
NEYLAND, Harry.
Am. b. McKean, Pa.; ad. 1934 So. Dartmouth, Mass. A.
NEYLAND, Watson.
Am. b. Liberty, Tex. 1898; ad. 1934 Same. A.
NEYT, B.
Belg. ac. 1844-1875 Brussels. T.
NEYTS [or Nyts], Aegidius Gillis.
Flem. Ghent, Belg. 1623-1687 Antwerp. B-T.
NGAN, Hwui.
Chinese. ac. 13th Cent. in China. M.
NGUYEN PHAN CHAUH.
Jap. ac. 1932 in Paris. M.
NICCOLÒ DI ANDRAE.
see Andrae di N.
NICCOLÒ DELL' ARCA. *see* Arca.
NICCOLÒ D'AREZZO [or Selli]. (S)
It. Arezzo 1350-1417 Bologne. B-Hs-T.
NICCOLÒ DA BARI. *see* Bari.
NICCOLÒ DA BOLOGNA.
It. ac. 1410 in Bologna. M.
NICCOLÒ DA FOLIGNO.
see Foligno, N.
NICCOLÒ DI BUONACCORSO.
see Buonaccorso di N.
NICCOLÒ DI LORENZO.
see Lorenzo di N.
NICCOLÒ PERICOLI. *see* Tribolo.
NICCOLÒ DI PIERO LAMBERTI [Il. Pela]. (S)
It. d. 1451 in Florence. Hs-T-V.
NICCOLÒ DI PIETRO, Gerini.
It. ac. 1368-1415 Florence. B-T-V.
NICCOLÒ DI TOMMASO.
see Tommaso di N.
NICE, Eugéne.
Am. Italy 1840-1911 New York. A010.
NICHOLAS [or Nicolau], Francés.
Sp. b. 1400; d. 1468 Léon. T.
NICHOLAS, Hilda Rix.
Aust. ac. 1933. M.
NICHOLAS, Prince.
Gr. ad. 1935 Athens, Gr. M.
NICHOLL, Andrew.
Ir. Belfast 1804-1886 London. B-T.
NICHOLLS, Bertram.
Eng. b. Didsbury 1883; ad. 1934 Steyning, Sussex. T-Wa-825.
NICHOLLS, Burr H.
Am. Lockport, N. Y. 1848-1915 Stamford, Conn. A012-F-T.
NICHOLLS, Josephine Lewis.
Mrs. Burr H. Nicholls.
Am. b. Hamilton, Ont., Can. 1865; ad. 1934 Buffalo, N. Y. A.
NICHOLLS, [Mrs.] Rhoda Holmes.
Am. Coventry, Eng. 1854-1930 Stamford, Conn. A027-DAB-F-T-W16-46-829.
NICHOLS, [Dr.] Carroll Leja.
Am. ad. 1934 Brooklyn, N. Y. M.
NICHOLS, Dale.
Am. ad. 1935 Chicago. M.
NICHOLS, Edith L.
Am. b. Brooklyn, N. Y.; ad. 1934 Same. A.
NICHOLS, Edward W.
Am. New Hampshire 1819-1871 Peekskill, N. Y. F-3.
NICHOLS, Frederick B. (Eg)
Am. Bridgeport, Conn. 1824-1906 Same. F-T.
NICHOLS, Harley De Will. (Ill)
Am. b. Barton, Wash., 1859; ad. 1934 Brooklyn, N. Y. A-F.
NICHOLS, Henry Hobart.
Am. b. Wash., D. C. 1869; ad. 1934 Bronxville, N. Y. A-F-T-W.
NICHOLS, John Fountain.
Am. b. Chicago 1912; ad. 1934 Same. M.
NICHOLS, John W.
Am. b. Keokuk, Iowa 1881; ad. 1935 New York. A28-F.
NICHOLS, Melvin N. (Min)
Am. ad. 1934 So. Amboy, N. J. M.
NICHOLS, Spencer Baird.
Am. b. Wash., D. C. 1875; ad. 1934 Kent, Conn. A-F-T-W.
NICHOLSON, Alfred.
Eng. Whitby 1788-1833 London. DNB-T.
NICHOLSON, Alice B.
Am. b. Milwaukee, Wis. 1898; ad. 1915 Same. A12.
NICHOLSON, Delos Charles.
Am. b. Edgerton, Wis. 1885; ad. 1934 Webster Groves, Mo. A.
NICHOLSON, [Sir] Francis.
Eng. Yorkshire 1753-1844 London. B-DNB-T.

NICHOLSON, George.
Eng. 1795?-1839? DNB.
NICHOLSON, George. (Eg)
Eng. ex. 1934 Brooklyn, N. Y. M.
NICHOLSON, George.
Eng. 1787-1878. DNB.
NICHOLSON, George W.
Am. b. 1832; d. 1911 Hammonton, N. J. A010-T.
NICHOLSON, Isaac. (Eg)
Eng. Melmerby 1789-1848. B-DNB-T.
NICHOLSON, [Mrs.] Isabel Ledcreigh.
Am. b. St. Louis, 1890; ad. 1934 Pebble Beach, Calif. A.
NICHOLSON, Peter Walker.
Scot. Cupar 1856-1885 Nigg. B-Bd-T.
NICHOLSON, Reginald P.
Br. ac. 1928 London. M.
NICHOLSON, William.
Scot. New Castle, Eng. 1781-1844 Edinburgh, Scot. B-DNB-E-T.
NICHOLSON, William.
Eng. b. Newark-on-Trent 1872; ex. 1934 London. T-Wa-818-825.
NICHOLSON, [Mrs.] Winifred.
Eng. b. Oxford; ad. 1934 London. Wa.
NICHT, Edward William.
Am. b. Auburn, N. Y. 1872; ad. 1934 Syracuse, N. Y. A.
NICIAS [Son of Nicomedez].
Gr. Attic; ad. 348-308 B.C. in Athens. B-E.
NICKAM, Charles W.
Am. Dayton, O. 1844-1913 Ind., Ind. A011-181.
NICKELE, Isaak Van.
Dut. 1660-1703 Haarlem. B-C-T.
NICKERSON, Jenny Ruth. (S)
Am. b. Appleton, Wis. 1905; ad. 1934 New York. A.
NICKODAMUS.
Gr. ac. 400 B.C. in Arkadien. T.
NICKOLAUS VON HAGENAU. (S)
Ger. b. 1445. T.
NICKOMACHOS.
Gr. ac. 4th century B.C. T.
NICKOLAUS, Gerhaert von Leyden. (S)
Ger. ac. 1462-1473 Vienna, Aus. T.
NICODEMUS, Chester Roland. (S)
Am. b. Barberton, O. 1901; ad. 1934 Columbus, O. A.
NICOL, Erskine.
Scot. Leith 1825-1904 Feltham. B-DNB-C-T.
NICOL, John Watson.
Scot. Edinburgh 1856-1926. T.
NICOLA D'APULIA.
see Pisano, Nicola.
NICOLAIDES, Kimon. (Mu)
Am. b. Wash., D. C. 1892; ad. 1934 New York. A.
NICOLAU, Pedro.
Sp. ac. 1390-1412 in Valencia. T.
NICOLAUS, [Master]. (S)
Ger. ac. 1140 in Verona, It. T.
NICOLÁS. *see* Nicholas.
NICOLET, Gabriel Émile Edouard.
Swi. Pores, Swi. 1856-1921 Villefranche, Fr. B-T.
NICOLETTO DA MODENA, Rosez.
see Modena, N. R. da.
NICOLINI, Giovanni. (S)
It. b. Palermo 1872. T-798.
NICOLL, Archibald F.
Br. ad. 1932 Christchurch, N. Z., Aust. M.
NICOLL, James Craig.
Am. New York 1846-1918 Norwalk, Conn. A015-B-C-DAB-F-T-W9-Y01919-15-55.
NICOLLE, Jean.
Fr. Louviers 1614-1650 Same. B-T.
NICOLOSI, Joseph. (S)
Am. b. Italy 1893; ad. 1934 New York. A-Cs-F.
NICOMACHUS.
Gr. ac. 400 B.C. in Thebes. B-E.
NICOT, Louis Henri. (S)
Fr. b. Rennes 1878. DBA-T.
NICZKY, Edourd.
Ger. Cassel 1850-1919 Munich. B-T.
NIEDECKER, George Mann. (Mu)
Am. b. Milwaukee, Wis. 1878; ad. 1934 Same. A.
NIEDERHAUSERN, Auguste de. (S)
Swi. Vevey 1863-1913 Munich, Ger. B-T.
NIEDERLANDISCHER.
see Master Niederlandischer.
NIEHAUS, Charles Henry. (S)
Am. b. Cinn., O. 1855; d. 1935 Clifside Park, N. J. Obit. N. Y. papers, 6-20-1935. A-Cs-E-F-Hs-T-Ta-W-46.
NIELSEN, Amaldus Clarin.
Nor. b. Mandal 1838; ad. 1869 Christiania. B-T.
NIELSEN, Anne Marie Carl. (S)
Dan. b. Copenhagen 1863. B-T.
NIELSEN, Ejnar August.
Dan. b. Copenhagen 1872. B-T.
NIELSEN, Kai. (S)
Dan. 1882-1924 Copenhagen. B-T-798.
NIELSEN, Peter.
Am. b. Denmark; ad. 1934 Eagle Rock, Calif. M.
NIEMANN, Edmund John.
Eng. London 1813-1876 Brixton. B-DNB-T.
NIEMEYER, John Henry.
Am. Bremen, Ger. 1839-1932 New Haven, Conn. A029-DAB-F-T-W-15-181.
NIEPER, Ludwig.
Ger. Brunswick 1826-1906 Dresden. B-T.
NIEPOLD, Frank.
Am. Frederick, Mo. 1890; ad. 1934 Wash., D. C. A-F.
NIEULANDT, Adriaen van.
Flem. Antwerp 1592/3-1634 Amsterdam. B-T.
NIEULANDT, Jacob van.
Dut. Amsterdam 1592/3-1634 Same. B-T.
NIEULANDT, William Van II.
Flem. Antwerp 1584-1635 Amsterdam. B-C-T.
NIEUWEKAMP, Wijnand Otto Jan. (Et)
Dut. b. Amsterdam 1874. T.
NIEUWERKERKE, Alfred Émile O'Hara. (S)
Fr. Paris 1811-1892. B-T.
NIGG, Joseph.
Aus. Vienna 1782-1863 Same. B-T.
NIGHTINGALE, Frederick C.
Br. ac. 1865-1885. B.
NIGRO, Gaspar.
It. ac. 1516-1538 in Venice. M.

NIJLAND, Dirk.
Dut. b. Dördrecht 1881. T.
NIKERATOS.
Gr. ac. 200 B.C. in Athens. T.
NIKIAS.
Gr. ac. second half 4th Cent. B.C. T.
NIKITIN, Ivan Nicolaievitch.
Rus. 1690-1741 Leningrad. T.
NIKITIN, Roman Nicolaievitch.
Rus. Moscow 1689-1752/4 Same. T.
NIKKELEN [or Nickelen], Isaak van.
Dut. 1640-1703 Haarlem. T.
NIKOLAUS. *see* Nickolaus.
NIKONOV, Nicolas.
Rus. ad. 1934 Moscow. M.
NIKUTOWSHI, Johann Arthur Severin.
Ger. Königsberg 1830-1888 Düsseldorf. B-T.
NILES, Rosamond.
Am. b. Portsmouth, N. H.; ad. 1934 Old Lyme, Conn. A.
NILLET, Germain David. (S)
Fr. 1861-1932. M.
NILOUSS, Pierre.
Rus. b. 1869. B.
NILSEN, Margit. (S)
Am. ad. 1934 New York. M.
NILSON, Friedrich Christian.
Ger. Augsburg 1811-1879 Munich. B-T.
NILSON, Johann Esaias. (Min)
Ger. Augsburg 1721-1788. B-T.
NILSSON, Axel.
Swe. b. Gotland 1887. T.
NILSSON, Vera.
Swe. b. Jönköping 1888. T.
NIMMO, Louise Everett. (P-S)
Mrs. Ray E. Nimmo.
Am. b. Des Moines, Ia.; ad. 1934 Los Angeles, Calif. A.
NIMS, Jeremiah.
Am. b. 1814; d. 1842 Kingston, Jamaica, West Indies. M.
NINET DE L'ESTAIN, Jacques.
see Letin.
NINHAM, Henry.
Eng. Norwich 1793-1874 Same. B-T.
NINI, Giovanni [or Jean] Battista.
It. Urbino 1717-1786 Chaumont, Fr. B-T.
NINSEI.
Jap. 1584-1656. T.
NIQUET, Claude [The Elder]. (Eg)
Fr. 1770-1831. B-T.
NISART [or Nisard], Pedro.
Sp. ac. 1468-1470. T.
NISBET, [Mrs.] C. Bacheler.
Am. b. East Hartford, Conn. 1902; ad. 1934 Devon, Eng. A.
NISBET, Hume.
Scot. 1850-1923. Y01924.
NISBET, Robert Buchan.
Scot. Edinburgh 1857; ad. 1934 Same. B-T-Wa.
NISBET, Robert Hogg.
Am. b. Prov., R. I. 1879; ad. 1934 So. Kent, Conn. A-F-T-W.
NISENSON, Samuel. (Ill)
Am. ad. 1934 New York. M.
NISON, Margaret Lawson. (S)
Am. ad. 1934 New York. M.
NISS, Thevald Simeon.
Dan. Assens 1842-1905 Seeland. B-C-T.

NISSL, Rudolf.
Ger. b. 1870; ad. 1930 Munich. B-T.
NISWONGER, [Mrs.] Ilse V. (S)
Am. b. Metz, Ger. 1900; ad. 1934 Passaic, N. J. Cs-M.
NITEN, Miyamoto.
Jap. Kokura 1582/4-1645 Kumamoto. T.
NI-TSAN.
Chinese. ac. 1371-1374. E-T.
NITTIS, Giuseppe de.
It. Barletta 1845/6-1884 St. Germain, Fr. B-T.
NITZSCHE, Elsie Koenig.
Am. b. Phila., Pa. 1880; ad. 1934 Same. A-F-T-W.
NIVELON, Anne Baptiste.
Fr. ac. 1750-1764. T.
NIVELT, Roger.
Fr. b. Paris 1899. DBA.
NIVET, Émile Ernest. (S)
Fr. b. Levroux; ac. 1905-1911. B-T.
NIVINSKI, Ignati.
Rus. b. Moscow 1881. T.
NIXON, James. (Min)
Eng. 1741?-1812 Tiverton. B-DNB-T.
NIXON, Job. (Et)
Eng. b. Stoke 1891; ad. 1934 Cornwall. T-Wa.
NIXON, John. (Cari)
Eng. 1760-1818 London. B-DNB-T.
NIXON, Robert.
Eng. Foots Cray 1759-1837. B-DNB-T.
NIXON, Samuel. (S)
Eng. 1803-1854 London. DNB-T.
NOACK, August.
Ger. Darmstadt 1822-1905 Same. B-T.
NOAKOWSKI, Stanislaw.
Pol. Nieszawa 1867-1928 Warsaw. T.
NO-AMI, Nakao.
Jap. ac. 1436-1484. J-T.
NOBLE, George. (Eg)
Eng. ac. 1795-1806. B-DNB-T.
NOBLE, James Campbell.
Scot. Edinburgh 1846-1913 Ledaig. B-T.
NOBLE, John.
Am. Wichita, Kan. 1874-1934 New York. A-F-M-T-W-46-Obit. N. Y. papers, 7-7-1934.
NOBLE, John Sargeant.
Eng. 1848-1896. B-T.
NOBLE, Mamie Jones.
Mrs. J. V. Jones.
Am. b. Auburn, Tex. 1875; ad. 1934 Corsicana, Tex. A.
NOBLE, Matthew. (S)
Eng. Hackness 1818-1876 London. B-DNB-Hs-T.
NOBLE, Robert.
Scot. Edinburgh 1857-1917 East Linton. B-T.
NOBLE, Thomas Satterwhite.
Am. Lexington, Ky. 1835-1907 New York. A06-T-4.
NOBLE, William Bonneau.
Eng. London 1780-1831 Same. B-DNB-T.
NOBLE, William Clark. (P-S)
Am. b. Gardiner, Me. 1858; ad. 1934 Wash., D. C. A-F-T-W.
NOBORU, Haegawa.
Jap. ac. 1932 in Japan. M.

NOBUIYE, Myochin.
Jap. ac. 1486-1564 in Japan. T.
NOBUZANÉ, Fujiware.
Jap. 1176-1265. J-T.
NOCI, Arturo.
Am. b. Rome, It. 1874; ad. 1934 New York. A.
NOCQ, Henri Eugène. (S)
Fr. b. Paris 1868. B-T.
NOCRET [or Naucret], Jean [The Elder].
Fr. Nancy 1615/8-1672 Paris. B-T.
NOCRET [or Naucret], Jean Charles [The Younger].
Fr. Paris 1647/8-1691/19. B-T.
NODDER, Frederick P. (Eg)
Eng. ac. 1786-1800 in London. B-DNB-T.
NOÉ, Amédeé Charles Henri ["Chan"].
Fr. Paris 1819-1879 Same. B-T-880.
NOËL, Alexandre Jean.
Fr. Brie 1752-1834 Paris. B-T.
NOËL, Alexis Nicolas.
Fr. Clinchy 1792-1871. B-T.
NOËL, Alphonse Léon. (Eg)
Fr. Paris 1807-1884 Same. B-T.
NÖEL, Amelia.
Eng. ac. 1795-1805 in London. T.
NÖEL, Jules Achille.
Fr. Quimper 1813-1881 Alger. B-T.
NÖEL, "Tony" [Edmé Anthony Paul]. (S)
Fr. Paris 1845-1909. B-T.
NÖEL, Peter Paul Joseph.
Belg. Waulsort 1789-1822 Sosoye. B-T.
NOGALES SEVILLIA, José.
Sp. b. Malaga 1860. T.
NOGARI, Giuseppe.
It. Venice 1699-1763 Same. B-T.
NOGARI, Paris [Il. Romano].
It. Rome 1531/6-1596 Same. B-T.
NOGUCHI, Isamu. (S)
Am. b. Los Angeles, Calif. 1904; ad. 1934 New York. A-F.
NOGUÉS, Xavier.
Sp. b. Barcelona 1874. T.
NOHEIMER, Mathias J.
Am. ad. 1934 Cinn., O. M.
NOIZEUX, Henri.
Fr. b. Paris 1871. DBA.
NOLAN, Daniel.
Am. b. 1862; d. 1920 Boston. A017.
NOLDE [or Hansen], Emile.
Dut. b. Nolde 1867; ex. 1933 Pittsburgh, Pa. T-775.
NOLE. *see* Colyns de Nole.
NOLF, John Thomas.
Am. b. Allentown, Pa. 1871; ad. 1934 Dixon, Ill. A.
NOLLEKENS, Joseph. (S)
Eng. London 1737-1823 Same. B-DNB-E-Hs-T.
NOLLEKENS, Joseph Frans. (S)
[Called "Old Nollekens."]
Flem. Antwerp 1702-1748 London. B-DNB-Hs-T.
NOLLI, Carlo.
It. b. Como; d. 1770 Naples. B-T.
NOLPE, Pieter.
Dut. Amsterdam 1613/4-1652/3 Same. B-C-T.
NOMELLINI, Plinio.
It. b. Leghorn 1866. T.
NOMURA, Kenjiro.
Jap.-Am. b. Japan 1869; ad. 1934 Seattle, Wash. A.
NONCLERCQ, Élie.
Fr. b. Paris 1847. B-T.
NONELL Y MONTURIOL, Isidore.
Sp. Barcelona 1873-1911 Same. T.
NONNENBRUCH, Max.
Ger. Viersen 1857-1922 Munich. B-T.
NONNENMACHER, Marcus. (S)
Ger. 1653-1720 Prague, Czec. T.
NONNOTTE, Donat [or Donatien].
Fr. Besançon 1708-1785 Lyons. B-T.
NONO, Luigi.
It. Fusina 1850-1918 Venice. B-T.
NOOMS, Reynier. *see* Zeeman.
NOORDE, Cornelis van.
[Monogramist C. V. N.]
Dut. Haarlem 1731-1795. B-T.
NORDT [or Noort], Jan van.
Dut. Amsterdam 1620-1676. B-T.
NOORT [or Cort], Adam van [The Elder].
Dut. Antwerp, Belg. 1562-1641 Ende. B-C-T-722.
NOORT [or Cort], Lambert van.
Dut. Amersfoort 1520-1570/1 Antwerp, Belg. B-C-T.
NOORT [or Nordt], Pieter van.
Dut. b. Leyden 1592 [or 1602]; ac. 1626-1648. T.
NOQUET, Paul Ange. (S)
Belg. Brussels 1877-1905 L. I., N. Y. T.
NORBLIN DE LA GOURDAINE, Jean Pierre.
Fr. Misy 1745-1830 Paris. B-T.
NORBURY, Richard.
Eng. Macclesfield 1815-1886 Liverpool. B-Bd-T.
NORCROSS, Eleanor.
Am. d. 1923 in Fitchburg, Mass. A020.
NORCROSS, Emily D.
Am. b. 1849; d. 1909 Cambridge, Mass. A07.
NORDBERG, C. Albert.
Am. b. Chicago 1895; ad. 1934 Same. A.
NORDBLAD, Gösta.
Swe. ad. 1934 Stockholm. M.
NORDELL, Carl J.
Am. b. Copenhagen, Denmark 1885; ad. 1934 New York. A-F-T-W.
NORDELL, E. Parker ["Polly Nordell"].
Mrs. Carl J. Nordell.
Am. b. Gardner, Mass.; ad. 1934 Boston. A.
NORDENBERG, Bengt.
Swe. Blekinge 1822-1902 Düsseldorf, Ger. B-T.
NORDFELDT, Bror Julius Olsson.
Am. b. Tulstorg, Swe. 1878; ad. 1934 Santa Fé, N. M. A-F-T-W-46.
NORDGREN, Anna.
Fin. Mariestad 1847-1916 Stockholm, Swe. B-T.
NORDGREN, Axel Wilhelm.
Swe. Stockholm 1828-1888 Düsseldorf, Ger. B-T.
NORDHAUSEN, August Henry.
Am. b. Hoboken, N. Y. 1901; ad. 1934 New York. A.

NORDMARK, Olle. (Mu)
Swe. ex. 1934 New York. M.
NORDQUIST, Clyde.
Am. No. Dak. 1904-1931 Ann Arbor, Mich. A028.
NORDSTRÖM, Carl Harold.
Am. b. Chelsea, Mass. 1876; ad. 1934 Ipswich, Mass. A.
NORDSTRÖM, Karl Frederik.
Swe. Hoga 1855-1923 Drottningholm. B-DBA-T.
NORGATE, Edward. (Heraldic-P)
Eng. b. Cambridge; d. 1650 in London. D-DNB-T.
NORIMB, Christoph Albrecht. (Pen Work)
Ger. ac. 1766. M.
NORLING, Ernest Ralph.
Am. b. Pasco, Wash. 1892; ad. 1934 Seattle, Wash. A.
NORMAN, [Mrs.] Da Loria.
Am. b. Leavenworth, Kan. 1872; ad. 1934 Lyme, Conn. A.
NORMAN, John. (Eg)
Am. Eng. 1748-1817 Boston, Mass. DAB-F-T-2-7-55.
NORMAN, Viola. (S)
Am. b. 1889; ex. 1933 in Chicago. [Deceased.] M.
NORMAND, Ernest.
Fr. London 1857-1923 Paris. B-T.
NORMANN, Eilert Adelsteen.
Nor. Bodoe 1848-1918 Christiania. B-T.
NORMANOFF, Peter.
Rus. ac. 1832. T.
NORRIS, S. Walter.
Am. b. Phila., Pa. 1868; ad. 1934 Same. A-F.
NORRIS, W. J. (Ill)
Am. b. Chicago 1869; ad. 1934 Columbus, O. A.
NORRISS, Bess.
see Tait, [Mrs.] Bess Norriss.
NORSTAD, Magnus.
Am. b. Nor. 1884; ad. 1934 Valhalla, N. Y. A.
NORTH, Earl W.
Am. ad. 1934 Toledo, O. M.
NORTH, John William.
Eng. London 1842-1924 Taunton. B-T.
NORTH, Lois. (Eg)
Am. b. New Haven, Conn. 1908; ad. 1934 Orange, Conn. A.
NORTH, Marianne.
Eng. Hastings 1830-1890 Gloucester. B-DNB-T.
NORTH, Robert.
Am. ad. 1935 East Aurora, N. Y. M.
NORTHBOURNE, [Sir] Walter John James. (Et)
Eng. London 1869-1932. Wa1929-Y01933.
NORTHCOTE, James.
Am. Hammerston, Eng. 1822-1904 Brooklyn, N. Y. A05-T.
NORTHCOTE, Stafford Mantle. (Eg)
Am. b. Brooklyn, N. Y. 1869; ad. 1934 Same. A-F-T-W.
NORTHCOTE, Thomas James. (Author-P)
Eng. Plymouth 1746-1831 London. B-C-DNB-E-T-490-722.
NORTON, Christopher. (Eg)
Eng. ac. 1740-1760. B-DNB-T.
NORTON, Clara Mamie.
Am. b. Burlington, Conn.; ad. 1934 Bristol, Conn. A.
NORTON, Elizabeth.
Am. b. Chicago 1887; ad. 1934 Palo Alto, Calif. A.
NORTON, Helen Gaylord.
Am. b. Portsmouth, O. 1882; ad. 1934 Riverside, Calif. A.
NORTON, John Warner. (Mu)
Am. Lockport, Ill. 1876-1934 Charleston, S. C. A-M-W-Obit. N. Y. papers, 1-8-1934.
NORTON, S. Mary.
Am. d. 1922 Nutley, N. J. A019.
NORTON, William Edward.
Am. Boston 1843-1916 New York. A013-B-DAB-F-T-W8-15-169.
NORWELL, Graham Noble.
Can. b. Edinburgh, Scot. 1901; ad. 1935 Montreal, Can. M.
NORWID, Cypryan Kamil.
Pol. Warsaw 1821-1883 Paris. B-T.
NOSKE, Hugo.
Aus. b. Vienna 1886. T-Wa1926.
NOSSITER, Dorrie.
Eng. ad. 1935 London. M.
NOSWORTHY, Florence England. (Ill)
Mrs. William Alfred Nosworthy.
Am. b. Milwaukee, Wis.; ad. 1934 Hampton, Conn. A.
NOTER, David Émile Joseph de.
Belg. Ghent 1825-1900 Brussels. B-C-T.
NOTER, Pieter François de.
Flem. Waelhem 1779-1843 Ghent, Belg. C-T.
NOTERMAN, Emmanuel.
Belg. Oudenarde 1808-1863 Antwerp. B-T.
NOTKE, Bernt. (S)
Swe. Lübeck, Ger. 1440-1509 Stockholm. T-824.
NOTKER [Monk of St. Gall].
Swi. d. 976 St. Gall. B-T.
NOTMAN, Howard.
Am. b. Brooklyn, N. Y. 1881; ad. 1934 Staten Island, N. Y. A-F.
NOTTE, Emilio.
It. b. 1891; ad. 1930 Naples. T.
NOTTINGHAM, Mary Elizabeth.
Am. b. Salisbury, N. C. 1907; ad. 1934 Culpeper, Va. M.
NOTZ, Johannes.
Swi. Oberstrass 1802-1862 Zurich. T.
NOUAILHER [or Noylier], Colin. (Enamels)
Fr. ac. 1514-1531. T.
NOURSE, Elizabeth.
Am. b. Cinn., O. 1860; ad. 1934 Paris. A-B-F-T-W-46.
NOUTS, Michiel.
Dut. b. Delft 1628; ac. 1656 Amsterdam. B-T.
NOUVIAIRE, François.
Fr. Stenay 1805-1837. B-T.
NOUY, Jean Lecomte du.
see Le Comte du Nouy.
NOVAK. *see* Nowak.
NOVANI, Guilio C. (S)
Am. b. Italy 1889; ad. 1926 New York. A20-Cs-F.
NOVELLI, Antonio.
It. 1600-1662 Florence. B-T.

NOVELLI, Francesco [The Elder].
It. Venice 1764-1836 Same. B-T.
NOVELLI, James. (S)
Am. b. Italy 1885. Cs-T.
NOVELLI, Pietro [Monrealese].
It. Montreal 1603-1677 Palermo. B-T.
NOVELLI, Pietro Antonio.
It. Venice 1729-1804 Same. B-T.
NOVELLI, Rudolfo.
Am. b. Italy 1879; ad. 1934 Bronx, N. Y. A.
NOVELLI, Sebastiano.
It. Venice 1853-1916 Perugia. T.
NOVEMBER, Sara D.
Am. ad. 1934 Richmond, Va. M.
NOVA, Stefano.
It. b. Cavarzere 1862. T.
NOWAK [or Novak], Ernest.
Aus. Troppau 1853-1919 Vienna. B-T.
NOWAK, Willi.
Ger. b. 1886; ad. 1930 Prague, Czec. T.
NOWELL, Arthur Trevethin.
Welsh. b. Garndiffith 1861/2; ad. 1934 London. B-T-Wa.
NOWOTNOWA, Janina. (Eg)
Pol. ex. 1934 Chicago; ad. 1935 Lwów, Poland. M.
NOWOTTNY, Vincent.
Am. Cinn., O. 1854-1908 Alderson, W. Va. A07-T.
NOYES, Bertha.
Am. b. Wash., D. C.; ad. 1934 Same. A-F.
NOYES, George Loftus.
Am. b. Canada 1864; ad. 1934 Boston. A-F-W.
NOYES, Henriette.
Am. ad. 1935 New York. M.
NOZAL, Alexandre.
Fr. Paris 1852-1913 Same. B-T.
NUCCI, Allegretto. *see* Nuzi, A.
NUCCI, Avancino.
It. Castello 1552-1629 Rome. B-T.
NUDERSCHER, Frank.
Am. b. St. Louis, Mo. 1880; ad. 1934 New York. A-T.
NUECKEL [or Nükel], Otto.
Ger. b. Cologne 1888. T.
NUHFER, Olive Harriett.
Am. b. Pittsburgh, Pa. 1907; ad. 1934 Norman, Okla. A.
NÚÑEZ, Juan.
Sp. ac. 1480-1525 in Sèville. T-774.
NÚÑEZ DE VILLAVICENCIO, Pedro.
Sp. Sèville 1635-1700 Same. B-T.
NUNN, Frederic.
Am. b. Phila., Pa. 1879; ad. 1934 Cape May Court House, N. J. A-T.
NURA. *see* Ulreich, Nura Woodson.
NÜREMBERG. *see* Master, N.
NURICK, Irving. (Ill)
Am. b. New York 1896; ad. 1934 Same. A28-M.
NUSBAUM, Esther Commons.
Am. ex. 1934 in Chicago. M.
NUSE, Roy Cleveland.
Am. b. Springfield, O. 1885; ad. 1934 Rushland, Pa. A-F-W.
NUSSBAUM, Rut. (Et)
Ger. ex. 1934 London. M.
NUSSDORF, Joseph. (Ill)
Am. ad. 1932 Phila., Pa. M.
NUTT, Elizabeth Styring.
Can. b. Isle of Man; ad. 1935 Halifax, N. S. M.
NUTTER, William. (Eg)
Eng. 1754-1802 Somerstown. B-DNB-T.
NUTTING, Joseph. (Eg)
Eng. 1660-1722 London. Bd-DNB-T.
NUVOLONE, Carlo Francesco [Il. Panfilo].
It. Cremona 1608-1661/5. B-C-T.
NUVOLONE, Giuseppe [Panfilo].
It. Milan 1619-1703 Same. B-C-T.
NUYEN, Wynand Jan Joseph.
Dut. The Hague 1813-1839 Same. C-T.
NUYTTENS, Joseph Pierre.
Am. b. Antwerp, Belg. 1885; ad. 1934 New York. A-F-T-W.
NUZI, Alegretto.
It. ac. 1345-1385 in Cancello, It. B-T.
NUZI, Mario [da Fiori].
It. 1603/5-1673 Rome. B-T.
NYE, Edgar Hewitt.
Am. b. Richmond, Va. 1879; ad. 1934 Wash., D. C. A-W.
NYE, Robert T.
Am. ad. 1934 Bellevue, O. M.
NYFERGALT [or Niewergold], Nikolaus.
Ger. ac. 1475-1505 in Worms. T.
NYHOLM, Arvid Frederick.
Am. Stockholm, Swe. 1866-1927 Chicago. A024-F-T.
NYMEGEN, Dionys van.
Dut. Rotterdam 1705-1789 Same. B-T.
NYMEGEN, Elias van.
Dut. 1667-1755 Rotterdam. B-T.
NYPORT [or Nieupoort], Justus van.
Dut. Utrecht 1625-1691/2 Ostereich. B-T.
NYS, Carl [or Charles].
Belg. b. Antwerp 1858. B-T.
NYS, Pieter.
Dut. Amsterdam 1624/5-1681 Same. B-T.
NYTS, Aegidius Gillis. *see* Neyts, A. G.

OAKES, John Wright.
Eng. Middewich 1820-1887 London. B-DNB-T.
OAKES, Maud.
Am. ad. 1934 New Canaan, Conn. M.
OAKES, Wilbur L.
Am. b. Cleveland, O. 1876; ad. 1934 Same. A.
OAKEY, Maria R. [Dewing].
Am. b. New York 1845. A20-B-F-15.
OAKLEY, George.
Am. b. 1793; d. 1869 New York. B-F-T.
OAKLEY, Octavius.
Eng. 1800-1867 Bayswater. B-Bd-DNB-T.
OAKLEY, Thornton. (Ill)
Am. b. Pittsburgh, Pa. 1881; ad. 1934 Villa Nova, Pa. A-F-T-W.
OAKLEY, Violet. (Mu)
Am. b. New York 1874; ad. 1934 Phila., Pa. A-F-T-W-46.
OAKMAN, John. (Eg)
Eng. Slendon 1748?-1793. B-Bd-DNB-T.
OBERHARDT, William. (Et)
Am. b. Guttenberg, N. J. 1882; ad. 1934 New York. A-F-T-W.

OBERKAMPF DE DABRUN, Roger Louis.
Fr. b. Lyons 1887. DBA.
OBERLÄNDER, Adam Adolf. (Cari)
Ger. Regensburg 1845-1923 Munich. B-E-T.
OBERLÉ, Jean.
Fr. ac. 1930 in Paris. M.
OBERTEUFFER, George.
Am. b. Phila., Pa. 1878; ad. 1934 New York. A-F-T.
OBERTEUFFER, Henriette Amiard.
Mrs. George Oberteuffer.
Am. b. Havre, Fr. 1878; ad. 1934 New York. A.
OBERTEUFFER, Karl Amiard.
Am. b. Paris 1908; ad. 1934 New York. A.
O'BRIEN, [Mrs.] Catherine C.
Am. b. New York; ad. 1934 Same. A.
O'BRIEN, Daniel J.
Am. b. Belvidere, Ill.; ad. 1934 Chicago. A.
O'BRIEN, Lucius R.
Can. Bairie, Ont. 1832-1899 Toronto, Ont. T.
O'BRIEN, Nell Pomeroy.
Mrs. John A. O'Brien.
Am. ad. 1934 New Orleans, La. M.
O'BRIEN, Seumas. (S)
Am. b. Ireland 1880; ad. 1934 Glen Ridge, N. J. F-W.
O'BRIEN, Smith.
Am. b. Cork, Ir.; ad. 1934 San Fran., Calif. A.
O'BRIEN, Thomas. (S)
Am. Ireland 1834-1904 Galveston, Tex. A05.
O'BRIEN, William Dermod.
Ir. b. Limerick 1865; ad. 1934 Dublin. T-Wa.
OBRIG, Clara.
Am. d. 1930 in New York. A028.
OBRISSET [or O'Brisset], John. (Carver)
Eng. ac. 1705-1728. T.
O'CALLAHAN, Kevin B. (Eg)
Am. ad. 1935 Buffalo, N. Y. M.
OCHS, Johann Rudolph. (Med)
Swi. Berne 1673-1749 London. DNB-T.
OCHS [or Ocks], John Ralph. (Med)
Swi. Berne 1705-1788 London. DNB-T.
OCHTERVELT, Jacobus.
Dut. Rotterdam 1634/5-1708/10 Amsterdam. B-T-722.
OCHTMAN, Dorothy.
Am. b. Riverside, Conn. 1892; ad. 1934 Cos Cob, Conn. A-F-W.
OCHTMAN, Leonard.
Am. Zonnemaire, Holland 1854-1934 Cos Cob, Conn. A-B-E-F-T-W-1-46-
Obit. N. Y. papers, 10-28-1934.
OCHTMAN, Miria Fonda.
Mrs. Leonard Ochtman.
Am. Laconia, N. H. 1862-1924 Cos Cob, Conn. A021-F.
OCKERT, Erich.
Ger. b. 1889. M.
O'CONNOR, Andrew, Jr. (S)
Am. b. Worcester, Mass. 1874; ad. 1934 Paris. A20-B-DBA-T-W-46-71.
O'CONNOR, Andrew, Sr. (S)
Am. b. Lanark, Scot. 1846-1924 Holden, Mass. A022-T.
O'CONNOR, Henry M.
Am. b. Brookline, Mass. 1891; ad. 1934 Cambridge, Mass. A.
O'CONNOR, James Arthur.
Ir. Dublin 1791-1841 London. B-DNB-T.
O'CONNOR, John.
Ir. County Derry 1830-1889 Yately. B-DNB-T.
OCTAVIEN, François.
Fr. Rome, It. 1695-1736/40 Paris. B-T.
OCTOBRE, Aimé Jérémie Delphin. (S)
Fr. b. Vienna, Aus. 1868; ad. 1934 Paris. B-DBA-T-798.
OCTOBRE, Daniel.
It. b. Paris 1903; ad. 1934 Same. DBA.
ODAZZI [or Odosi], Giovanni.
It. Rome 1663-1731 Milan. B-T.
ODBERT.
[Abbot of the Monastery of St. Bertin.]
Flem. ac. 1008 in St. Omer, Fr. M.
ODDI, Mauro.
It. Parma 1639-1702/3. B-T.
ODDIE, Walter M.
Am. New York 1805-1865 Same. B-2.
ODELL, [Mrs.] Lansing.
Am. ad. 1934 Norwalk, Conn. M.
ODERIGO, Lorenzo d'Andrea.
see Credi, Lorenzo di [Barducci].
ODERISI [or Oderigi], da Gubbio.
It. Gubbio 1240-1299 Bologna. B-T.
ODEVAERE, Joseph Dionisius.
Belg. Bruges 1778-1830 Brussels. B-C-T.
ODIER, Edouard Alexandre.
Fr. Hamburg, Ger. 1800-1887 Paris. B-T.
ODIOT, Jean Baptiste Claude. (Metal Ware)
Fr. 1763-1850. T.
ODLE, Alan Elsden. (Et)
Eng. ad. 1934 London. Wa.
O'DOHERTY, William James. (S)
Ir. Dublin 1835-1868 Berlin, Ger. DNB-T
ODOM, Minnie Rae.
Am. b. Alabama; ad. 1934 Parrish, Ala. A.
O'DONNELL, Agnes.
Am. ad. 1934 New York. M.
O'DONOVAN, William Rudolph. (P-S)
Am. b. Virginia 1844-1920 New York. A017-B-DAB-E-F-T-W10-15-104.
OEHLER, Bernice Olivia.
Am. b. Lake Mills, Wis.; ad. 1934 Same. A.
OEHLER, Helen Gasper.
Am. b. Ottawa, Ill. 1893; ad. 1934 Ridgewood, N. J. M
OEHME, Ernest Erwin.
Ger. Dresden 1831-1907 Same. B-C-T
OEHME, Karl Friedrich.
Ger. Berlin 1731-1801 Frankfort. T.
OEHMICHEN, Hugo.
Ger. b. Borsdorf 1843. B-T.
OELENHAINZ, August Friedrich.
Ger. Edingen 1747-1804 Pfalzburg. B-T.
OENICKE, Clara Wilhelmine.
Ger. Berlin 1818-1899 Same. C-T.
OËR, Theobald Reinhold.
Ger. Nottbeck 1807-1885 Coswig. B-T.
OERTEL, Johannes Adam Simon.
Am. Furth, Ger. 1823-1909 Vienna, Va. DAB-F-T-7-26-230
OESER, Adam Friedrich.
Ger. Presburg 1717-1799 Leipzig. B-T.

OESTERLEY, KARL AUGUST HEINRICH FERDINAND.
Ger. Göttingen 1839-1930 Altona. B-T.
OESTERLEY, KARL WILHELM FRIEDRICH.
Ger. Göttingen 1805-1891 Hanover. B-T.
OESTERMANN, MILDRED CAROLINE. (Et)
Am. ad. 1934 San Fran., Calif. A.
OFFERMANS, TONY LODEWIJK GEORGE.
Dut. The Hague 1854-1911 Lauren. B-T.
OGBORNE, DAVID.
Eng. ac. 1740-1764 in Chelmsford. DNB-T.
OGBORNE, JOHN. (Eg)
Eng. Chelmsford 1725-1795 London. B-DNB-T.
OGDEN, HENRY ALEXANDER. (Ill)
Am. b. Phila., Pa. 1856; ad. 1934 New York. A-W.
OGÉ, PIERRE MARIE. (S)
Fr. Plérin 1817-1867 St. Brienc. B-T.
OGÉ, PIERRE MARIE FRANÇOIS. (S)
Fr. St. Brienc 1849-1912 Paris. B-T.
OGER, ALBERT LOUIS.
Fr. b. 1886. DBA.
OGGIONO, MARCO DE.
It. Oggiono 1470/5-1540/9. B-Bd-T.
OGILVIE, CLINTON.
Am. New York 1838-1900 Same. A04-B-F-T-15.
OGLESBY, MARGARET.
Am. 1849-1914 New York. A012.
OGNABENE, ANDREA DI JACOPO. (Metal Ware)
It. [Pistoian]; ac. 1287-1316. T.
OGUNJAMI, SUZANNA.
Am. ex. 1934 New York. M.
O'HARA, DOROTHY WARREN. (S)
Am. b. Malta Bend, Mo.; ad. 1934 Darien, Conn. A-W.
O'HARA, ELIOT.
Am. Waltham, Mass. 1890; ad. 1934 Wash., D. C. A.
O'HIGGINS, PAUL ESTEBAN.
Am. b. San Fran., Calif. 1904; ad. 1934 Mexico. A.
OHLSEN, DORA. (S)
Aust. ac. 1933. M.
OHMACHT [or Omacht], LANDOLIN. (S)
Fr. Rottweil 1760-1834 Strasburg. B-T.
OJETTI, UGO.
It. b. 1871. M.
O'KEEFE, GEORGIA.
Am. b. Sun Prairie, Wis. 1887; ad. 1934 New York. A-F-701.
O'KEEFE, JOHN. (Min)
Ir. Dublin 1747-1833 Southampton, Eng. B-T.
O'KEEFE, NEIL. (Ill)
Am. ad. 1934 New York. M.
O'KELLY, ALOYSIUS.
Am. b. Dublin, Ir. 1850; ad. 1935 New York. A12-F-T.
O'KELLY, STEPHEN J.
Am. b. Dublin, Ir. 1850; d. 1898 New York. A01.
OKEY, SAMUEL. (Eg)
Eng. ac. 1770 London; ac. 1773-1780 Newport, R. I. B-DNB-F-T-2-7-147.
OKYO FAMILY.
Jap. ac. 18th century. T.
OKYO, MARUYAMA.
Jap. Anatamura 1733-1795 Kyoto. J-T.
OLDACH, JULIUS.
Ger. Hamburg 1804-1830 Munich. B-T.
OLDE, HANS [or Johann] WILHELM.
Ger. Süderau 1855-1917 Cassel. B-T.
OLDFIELD, J. EDWIN.
Eng. ac. 1825-1854 in London. B-T.
OLDFIELD, OTIS.
Am. b. Sacramento, Calif. 1890; ad. 1935 San Fran., Calif. M.
OLDS, ELIZABETH.
Am. b. Minn., Minn. 1897; ad. 1934 Omaha, Neb. A.
O'LEARY, ANGELA.
Am. Prov., R. I. 1879-1921 Same. A018-T.
OLEFFE, AUGUSTE.
Belg. ac. 1867 in St. Josse. T.
OLESEN, OLAF.
Am. ad. 1934 New York. M.
OLESZCZYNSKI, ANTON.
Pol. Krasnystaw 1794-1879 Paris. B-T.
OLEY, MOSES.
Am. ad. 1935 New York. M.
OLINSKY, IVAN GREGOREWITCH.
Am. Russia 1878; ad. 1934 New York. A-F-T-W.
OLINSKY, TOSCA.
Am. b. Florence, It. 1909; ad. 1934 New York. M.
OLIPHANT, FRANCIS WILSON.
Eng. Newcastle 1818-1859 Rome, It. DNB-T.
OLIS, JAN.
Dut. Gorkum 1610-1655? Amsterdam. B-T.
OLIVA, ALEXANDRE JOSEPH. (S)
Fr. Saillagouse 1823-1890 Paris. B-T.
OLIVE, JEAN BAPTISTE JOSEPH.
Fr. b. Marseille 1848. B-DBA-T.
OLIVEIRA-BERNARES, IGNACIO DE.
Por. Lisbon 1695-1781 Same. B-T.
OLIVER, ARCHER JAMES.
Eng. 1774-1842 London. B-DNB-T.
OLIVER, [Mrs.] ANNIE PETREE [Mrs. V. G.]
Am. b. Russellville, Ala. 1893; ad. 1935 Birmingham, Ala. M.
OLIVER, ELIZABETH PAXTON.
Mrs. Herbert Oliver.
Am. ad. 1934 Atlanta, Ga. M.
OLIVER, EMMA SOPHIA.
Eng. London 1819-1885. DNB-T.
OLIVER, FREDERICK W.
Am. b. New York 1876; ad. 1934 Boston, Mass. A.
OLIVER, ISAAC. (Min)
Eng. Rouen, Fr. 1556?-1617 London. B-Bd-C-DNB-E-T.
OLIVER, JEAN NUTTING. (Min)
Am. b. Lynn, Mass.; ad. 1934 Boston. A-F-W.
OLIVER, LOUISE.
Am. b. Rialto, Calif. 1912; ad. 1934 Los Angeles, Calif. A.
OLIVER, MYRON ANGELO.
Am. b. Fulton, Kan. 1891; ad. 1934 Monterey, Calif. A.
OLIVER, PETER. (Min)
Eng. London 1594-1648 Isleworth. B-Bd-C-DNB-E.

OLIVER, William.
Eng. 1805-1853 Halstead. B-DNB-T-722.
OLIVER, [Mrs.] William [Elburne].
Eng. London 1819-1885. B-T.
OLIVERIO, Alessandro.
It. ac. 1500-1539. B-T.
OLIVETTI, Salvatore.
It. Turin 1833-1902 Paris. T.
OLIVIÉ, Jean Baptiste Joseph.
Fr. b. 1848. M.
OLIVIÉ, Léon.
Fr. Narbonne 1832/3-1901 Étretat. B-T.
OLIVIÉ-BON, Léon.
Fr. Paris 1863-1901 Same. B-T.
OLIVIER, Heinrich.
Ger. Dessau; 1783-1848 Berlin. T.
OLIVIER, Herbert Arnould.
Eng. b. Battle 1861. T-Wa1929.
OLIVIER, Johann Heinrich Ferdinand van.
Ger. Dessau 1785-1841 Munich. B-T.
OLIVIER, Woldemar Friedrick.
Ger. Dessau 1791-1859 Same. B-T.
OLIVIERI, Maffeo. (S)
It. Brescia 1484-1534. T.
OLLIVIER [or Olivier], Michel Barthélmy.
Fr. Marseille 1712-1784 Paris. B-T.
OLMÜTZ, Wenzel [or Jacob] von. (Eg)
Ger. ac. 1480-1500 in Germany. B-M.
OLNEY, Daniel G. (S)
Am. ad. 1935 Wash., D. C. M.
OLRIK, Ole Hendrick Benedikt.
Dan. Copenhagen 1830-1890 Same. B-T.
OLSEN, Harry Emil.
Am. b. Brooklyn, N. Y. 1887; ad. 1934 Same. A-F.
OLSON, Albert Byron.
Am. b. Montrose, Colo. 1885; ad. 1934 Denver, Colo. A-F.
OLSON, Carl Gustaf Theodore.
Am. b. Sweden 1875; ad. 1934 Belmont, Mass. A.
OLSON, J. Olaf.
Am. b. Buffalo, Minn. 1894; ad. 1934 New York. A-F.
OLSSON, Albert Julius.
Eng. b. London 1864; ad. 1934 Same. B-T-Wa.
OLSTOWSKI, Franciszek. (S)
Am. b. Zaborowo, Pol. 1901; ad. 1934 Matawan, N. J. A.
OLYPHANT, Donald.
Am. ad. 1935 Pine City, N. Y. M.
O'MALLEY, Power.
Am. b. County Waterford, Ir. 1870; ad. 1934 Scarborough, N. Y. A.
OMMEGANCK, Balthasar Pauwet.
Belg. Antwerp 1775-1826 Same. B-C-T-722.
OMODEO. *see* Amadeo.
ONATAS. (S)
Gr. (Aegina); ac. 490-460 B.C. B-E-Hs-T.
ONDERDONK, Julian.
Am. San Antonio, Tex. 1882-1922 Same. A019-F.
ONDERDONK, Percy.
Am. b. 1878; d. 1927 Port Chester, N. Y. A024.
ONDERDONK, Robert Jenkins.
Am. Balt., Md. 1853-1917 San Antonio, Tex. A014-F-T.
O'NEIL, George Bernard.
Ir. Dublin 1828-1917 London. B-T.
O'NEIL, Henry.
Ir. Clonmel 1798-1880 Dublin. B-T.
O'NEIL, Henry Nelson.
Eng. Leningrad, Rus. 1817-1880 London. DNB-T.
O'NEIL, Rose Cecil. (Ill)
Am. ad. 1934 Saugatuck, Conn. M.
O'NEILL, Raymond.
Am. ex. 1934 New York. M.
ONGHERS [or Ongers], Oswald.
Flem. Mechlin 1628-1706 Wurzburg, Ger. B-T.
ONOFRI, Vincenzo. (S)
It. ac. 1503-1524. T.
ONTHON-FRIESZ, Achille Émile.
Fr. b. 1879. DBA.
OOST, Jakob van [The Elder].
Flem. Bruges 1600-1671 Same. B-Bd-C-T-722.
OOST, Jakob van [The Younger].
Flem. Bruges 1639-1713. B-Bd-C-T-722.
OOSTERWYCK [or Osterwick], Maria van.
Dut. Noodrop 1630-1693 Witdam. B-C-T.
OOSTSANEN, Jacob Cornelisz van.
[*see also* Cornelisz, Jacob van A.]
Dut. Ostsanen 1468/70-1533 Amsterdam. B-T-657.
OPENKOFF, George Willem [Witzel].
Dut. Fulda 1807-1873 The Hague. B-T.
OPERA, Giovanni dell'. *see* Bandini, G.
OPERTI, Albert Jasper Ludwig.
Am. Turin, It. 1852-1927 New York. A026-F-T-W14.
OPIE, Edward.
Eng. St. Agnes 1810-1894. B-T.
OPIE, John.
Eng. St. Agnes 1761-1807 London. B-Bd-C-DNB-E-T-722.
OPITZ, Georg Emanuel.
Ger. Prague 1775-1841 Leipzig. B-T.
OPLER, Hazal Maybel.
Am. b. Buffalo, N. Y. 1910; ad. 1934 Same. A.
OPPENHEIM, Moritz Daniel.
Ger. Hanau 1799-1882 Frankfort. B-C-T.
OPPENHEIMER, Charles.
Eng. b. Manchester 1875; ad. 1934 Scotland. Wa.
OPPENHEIMER, Max.
Ger. b. Vienna, Aus. 1885. T.
OPPENHEIMER, Selma L.
Am. ex. 1935 Balt., Md. M.
OPPENORT [or Oppenord], Gilles Marie.
Fr. Paris 1672-1742 Same. B-T.
OPPER, Frederick Burr. (Cart)
Am. b. Madison, O. 1857; ad. 1934 New Rochelle, N. Y. A28-F-W.
OPPER, Laura.
Am. d. 1924 N. Y. A021-F-T.
OPPI, Ubaldo.
It. b. Bologna 1889. T.
OPPLER, Ernest.
Ger. Hanover 1867-1929 Berlin. B-T.
OPPO, Cipriano Efisio.
It. b. Rome 1890. T.
OPSOMER, Isadore.
Belg. b. Lier 1878; ad. 1934 Antwerp. T.

OPSTAL [or Obstal], Gérard van. (S)
Flem. Brussels 1595/7-1668 Paris. B-T.
OPSTAL, Kasper Jacob van [The Younger].
Flem. Antwerp 1654-1717 Same. B-C-T.
ORAM, Edward.
Eng. ac. 1770-1800 in London. DNB-T.
ORAM, William ["Old Oram"].
Eng. ac. 1730-1777 in London. B-DNB-T.
ORANGE, Maurice Henri.
Fr. Granville 1868-1916 Ende. B-T.
ORAZI [or Orazu], Andrea Antonio.
It. Rome 1630-1690. B-T.
ORAZIO DI JACOPO.
It. ac. 1430-1445 in Bologna. B-T.
ORCAGNA, Andrea di Cione. (S)
It. Florence 1308?-1368/9 Same.
B-C-E-Hs-T-V.
ORCAGNA, Jacopo di Cione.
It. ac. 1386-1408 in Florence. T-V.
ORCAGNA, Nardo di Cione.
It. d. 1364/6 in Florence. T-V.
ORCHARDSON, Charles M. Quiller.
Scot. 1873-1917. B-Y01918.
ORCHARDSON, [Sir] William Quiller.
Scot. Edinburgh 1832-1910 London.
B-C-DNB-E-T.
ORD, Joseph Biays.
Am. Phila., Pa. 1805-1865 Same. F-T.
ORDBROUN, Joyce.
Br. ac. 1934 South Africa. M.
ORDE, Gertrude Cederstrom.
Am. b. St. Louis, Mo. 1902; ad. 1934 Chicago. A.
ORDÓÑEZ, Bartolomé. (S)
Sp. d. 1520 Carrara. B-Hs-T.
ORDWAY, Alfred.
Am. 1819-1897 Boston. A01-F-T.
ORDWAY, [Mrs.] Frances Hunt Troop.
Am. New York 1860-1933 East Hampton, N. Y. A030.
ORELLI, Giuseppe Antonio Felice.
It. Locarno 1700-1770/4 Bergamo. B-T.
ORFELIN, Zacharias. (Eg)
Serbian. Vukovar, Serbia 1726-1785. T.
ORGAN, Marjorie. (Cari)
Mrs. Robert Henri.
Am. b. N. Y. 1886; ad. 1934 Same. A.
ORGAZ, Rodriguez.
Am. ex. 1935 New York. M.
ORIENT, Joseph.
Hun. Burbach 1677-1737 Vienna, Aus. B-T.
ORIENTAL Artists.
see books Nos. 731-732-733-734-767-769-888-914-919-934.
ORLANDI [or Orlando], Bernardo.
It. ac. 1611-1618 in Turin. B-T.
ORLANDI [or Orlando], Deodato.
It. ac. 1288-1337 in Florence. B.
ORLÉANS, Antoine Philippe de.
Fr. Paris 1775-1807 London. T.
ORLÉANS, Marie Amelie Françoise. (S)
Fr. 1865-1909. B-T.
ORLEY, Bernard [or Barend] van.
Flem. Brussels 1485/93-1542 Same.
B-Bd-C-E-T-722.
ORLEY, Jan van.
Flem. Brussels 1665-1735 Same. B-T-722.
ORLEY, Richard van.
Flem. Brussels 1652/63-1732/8 Same. B-T.
ORLIK, Emil.
Ger. Prague 1870-1932. T-Y01933.
ORLOFF [or Orlowa], Chana. (S)
Rus. b. Ukraine 1888. DBA-T-798.
ORLOFF, Gregory.
Am. b. Russia 1890; ad. 1934 Chicago. A.
ORLOWSKI, Alexander Ossipovitch. (Cari)
Pol. Warsaw 1777-1832 Leningrad, Rus. B-T.
ORLOWSKI, Vladimir Donatowitsch.
Rus. b. 1842; d. 1914 Leningrad. B-T.
ORMANNI, Antonio da Siena. (S)
It. Siena 1457-1519 Same. T.
ORME, Daniel.
Eng. London 1766?-1832? B-DNB-T.
ORME, Lydia Gardner.
Mrs. James Orme.
Am. ad. 1934 New York. M.
ORMEA, Willem.
Dut. ac. 1638-1665 in Amsterdam. B-T.
ORMOND, M. Georgia. (S)
Am. ad. 1934 Toledo, O. A12-M.
ORMSBY, Waterman Lilly. (Eg)
Am. Hampton, Conn. 1809-1883 Brooklyn, N. Y. DAB-F-T-2-7-912.
OROVIDA. *see* Pissaro, O. C.
OROZCO, José Clemente.
Mex. b. Jalisco, Mex. 1883.
T-200-491-783-791.
ORPEN, [Sir] William Nevenham Montague.
Ir. Dublin 1878-1931 London.
B-E-T-Wa1929-492-818-825-947.
ORR, Alfred Everitt [or Edward].
Am. b. New York 1886; ex. 1933 Paris.
F-M.
ORR, Carey Cassius. (Cart.)
Am. b. Ada, O. 1890; ad. 1934 Wilmette, Ill.
W.
ORR, Eleanor Mason. (Min)
Mrs. James Hunter Orr.
Am. b. Newton Center, Mass. 1902; ad. 1934 Same. A.
ORR, Elliott.
Am. b. Flushing, L. I., N. Y. 1904; ad. 1934 New York. A-892.
ORR, Frances Morris.
Am. b. Springfield, Mo. 1880; ad. 1934 Sewickley, Pa. A.
ORR, John William. (Eg)
Am. Ireland 1815-1887 Jersey City, N. J.
F-T.
ORR, Louis. (Et)
Am. b. Hartford, Conn. 1879; ad. 1934 Paris.
A-F-T-W.
ORR, Monroe Scott.
Scot. b. Irvine 1874; ad. 1934 Glasgow.
T-Wa.
ORR, Steward.
Scot. b. Glasgow 1872; ad. 1929 Same.
Wa1929.
ORRENTE, Pedro.
Sp. Monte Alegre 1560-1644 Toledo. B-C-T.
ORROCK, James.
Scot. Edinburgh 1829-1913 London. B-T.
ORSAY, Alfred Guillaume Gabriel.
Fr. Paris 1798-1852 Same. B-T.
ORSEL, André Jacques Victor.
Fr. Oullins 1795-1850 Paris. B-T-722.
ORSI, Achille D'. (S)
It. Naples 1845-1929 Same. B-T.

ORSI, BENEDETTO.
It. b. Pescia; d. 1680 Same. B-T.
ORSI, BERNARDINO.
It. Reggio 1450-1532. B-T.
ORSI, CARLO.
Ir. ac. 1881-1896 in Florence. B-T.
ORSI, LELIO DA NOVELLARA.
It. Novellara 1511-1587 Same. B-T.
ORSINI, BALDASSARRE.
It. Perugia 1732-1810 Same. T.
ORSOLINI, CARLO. (Eg)
It. Venice 1710/24-1780. B-T.
ORT [or Hort or Aart], ARNOLD VAN DER. [Master of the Leipzig Cabinet.]
Flem. ac. 1520-1540 in Antwerp. B-T.
ORTELIUS [or Oertel], ABRAHAM. (Cartographer.)
Flem. Antwerp 1527-1598 Same. B-T.
ORTH, BENJAMIN HEINRICH.
Ger. Carlsruhe 1803-1875 Same. B-T.
ORTH, JACOB.
Ger. Carlsruhe 1775/80-1861 Mainz. T.
ORTH, JOHN WILLIAM.
Am. b. Marktsteft, Ger. 1889; ad. 1934 Kansas City, Mo. A.
ORTIZ, PABLO.
Sp. ac. 1489 in Avila. B-T.
ORTIZ-ECHAGÜE, ANTONIO.
Sp. b. Guadalajara 1883; ad. 1933 Madrid. T.
ORTLIEB, FRIEDRICH.
Ger. Stuttgart 1839-1909 Munich. B-T.
ORTLIP, AIMEE E.
Mrs. H. Willard Ortlip.
Am. b. Phila., Pa. 1888; ad. 1934 Fort Lee, N. J. A.
ORTLIP, H. WILLARD.
Am. b. Norristown, Pa. 1886; ad. 1934 Fort Lee, N. J. A.
ORTMANS, FRANÇOIS AUGUSTE.
Fr. Paris 1827-1884 Fontainebleau. B-T.
ORTMAYER, CONSTANCE. (S)
Am. ad. 1934 New York. M.
ORTO, UBERTO DELL'.
It. Milan 1848-1895. B-T.
ORTOLANO. *see* Benvenuti, G. B.
ORTONEDA, MATEO.
Sp. ac. 1417-1425 Tarragona. T.
ORWIG, LOUISE.
Am. b. Miffinburg, Pa.; ad. 1934 Des Moines, Ia. A.
OS, GEORGIUS JACOBUS JOHANNES VAN.
Dut. The Hague 1782-1861 Paris. B-C-T.
OS, JAN VAN.
Dut. Middelharmus 1744-1808 The Hague. B-C-T.
OS, PIETER GERARDUS VAN.
Dut. The Hague 1776-1839 Same. B-T.
OSBERT, ALPHONSE.
Fr. b. Paris 1857. B-DBA-T.
OSBORN, EMILY MARY.
Eng. b. London 1834. B-T.
OSBORN, FRANK C.
Am. b. Altamont, N. Y. 1887; ad. 1934 New York. A.
OSBORN, LUE.
Am. ad. 1935 New York. M.
OSBORN, WILLIAM PATTEN.
Am. b. New York 1902; ad. 1934 Tarrytown, N. Y. A.
OSBORNE, LILLIE. (S)
Mrs. Lithgow Osborne.
Am. b. Aalholm, Denmark 1887; ad. 1934 Auburn, N. Y. A.
OSBORNE, MALCOLM.
Eng. b. Frome 1880; ad. 1934 London. T-Wa-830.
OSBORNE, WALTER FREDERICK.
Ir. Dublin 1859-1903 Same. B-DNB-T.
OSCROFT, SAMUEL WILLIAM.
Eng. Nottingham 1834-1924. B-T.
OSGOOD, CHARLES.
Am. Salem, Mass. 1809-1890. F-T-2-169.
OSGOOD, JULIA.
Am. d. 1908 New York. A07.
OSGOOD, RUTH.
Am. b. Minn., Minn.; ad. 1934 Wash., D. C. A.
OSGOOD, SAMUEL S.
Am. Boston 1808-1885 Calif. F-T-2-3.
OSGOOD, VIRGINIA M.
Am. b. Calif. 1907; ad. 1934 Los Angeles. A.
O'SHAUGHNESSY, THOMAS A.
Am. ad. 1934 Chicago. A.
O'SHEA, JOHN.
Am. ad. 1934 Carmel Highlands, Calif. M.
OSHIVER, HARRY J.
Am. b. Moscow, Rus. 1888; ad. 1934 Phila., Pa. A.
OSK, ROSELLE HELLENBERG.
Am. ad. 1934 New York. A.
OSLÉ SÁENZ DE MEDRANO, LUCIANO. (S)
Sp. b. Barcelona 1880. T.
OSLÉ SÁENZ DE MEDRANO, MIGUEL. (S)
Sp. b. Barcelona 1879. T.
OSMAN, HAMDY. *see* Hamdy, Osman [Bey].
OSMOND, EDWARD.
Eng. b. Suffolk 1900; ad. 1934 London. Wa.
OSNIS, BENEDICT A.
Am. b. Russia 1872; ad. 1935 Phila., Pa. A12-F.
OSORIO, FRANCISCO. *see* Menesses.
OSSENBECK, JAN JOSIAS.
Dut. Rotterdam 1624/7-1674/8 Vienna, Aus. B-T.
OSSLUND, JONAS HELMER.
Swe. b. Tuna 1866. T.
OSTADE, ADRIAN JANZOON VAN.
Dut. Haarlem 1610-1685 Same. B-Bd-C-E-T-722.
OSTADE, ISAAC VAN.
Dut. Haarlem 1621-1649 Same. B-Bd-C-E-T-722.
OSTENDORFER, MICHAËL. (P-S)
Ger. 1490-1559 Regensburg. B-T.
OSTERHOUDT, DANIEL VAN.
Dut. Tiel 1786-1850 Cassel, Ger. B-T.
OSTERMAN, BERNHARD.
Swe. b. Suderwannie 1870. DBA.
OSTERMAN, K. EMIL.
Swe. b. 1870. B.
OSTERWALD, GEORG.
Ger. Rinteln 1803-1884 Cologne. B-T.
OSTHAUS, EDMUND HENRY.
Am. Hildesheim, Ger. 1858-1928 Marianna, Fla. A025-F-T-W14-46.
OSTMAN, LEMPI.
Am. ad. 1934 New York. M.

OSTRANDER, William Chesebourgh.
Am. b. New York 1858; ad. 1934 Same. A.
OSTRIAN, Florence.
Am. ex. 1935 New York. M.
OSTROM, Anna Sherwood.
Am. Stonington, Conn. 1866-1907 Brooklyn, N. Y. A06.
OSTROM, Cora Chambers.
Am. b. Harrison, Ark. 1871; ad. 1934 Eagle Pass, Tex. A.
OSTROUMOWA-LEBEDEWA, Anna Petrowna.
Rus. b. Leningrad 1871. T.
OSTROWSKY, Abbo.
Am. b. Russia 1889; ad. 1934 New York. A-W.
OSTROWSKY, Sam.
Am. b. Russia 1885; ad. 1934 Chicago. A-F.
OSTROWSKY, Stanislaw.
Pol. b. Warsaw 1879. T.
OSWALD, Fritz.
Swi. b. Zurich 1879. B.
OTAKE, Kikuha.
Jap. ac. 1900 in Paris. B.
OTIS, Amy. (Min)
Am. b. Sherwood, N. Y.; ad. 1934 Norton, Mass. A-F-46.
OTIS, Bass.
[Made first Lithograph in America in 1819.]
Am. Bridgewater, Mass. 1784-1861 Phila., Pa. DAB-F-T-2-6-7.
OTIS, George Demont.
Am. b. 1877; ad. 1934 Burbank, Calif. A.
OTIS, Samuel Davis. (Ill)
Am. ad. 1934 Norwalk, Conn. A.
OTMAN, J. (Ill)
Am. ad. 1934 New York. M.
O'TOOLE, Cathal.
Am. ad. 1934 Long Island City, N. Y. M.
OTT, Peter Paul [or "Peterpaul"]. (S)
Am. b. Pilsen, Czec. 1895; ad. 1934 Evanston, Ill. A-Cs-T.
OTT, Ralph Chesley.
Am. Springfield, Mo. 1875-1931. A28-T.
OTT, Hirzel Susette. *see* Hirzel, S.
OTTAVIANO DA FAENZA.
It. ac. 14th Century in Italy. T-V.
OTTENFELD, Rudolf Otto Ritter von.
It. Verona 1856-1913 Prague, Czec. T.
OTTER, Thomas.
Am. ac. 1860 in Phila., Pa. F-T.
OTTESEN, Otto Didrik.
Dan. Broager 1816-1892 Copenhagen. B-C-T.
OTTINO [or Ottini], Pasqualotto.
It. 1570/80-1630 Verona. B-T.
OTTLEY, William Young. (Eg)
Eng. Berkshire 1771-1836 London. B-DNB-T.
OTTMANN, Henri.
Fr. Ancenis 1877-1927 Paris. B-DBA-T.
OTTO, Carl [or Karl].
Ger. Osterode 1830-1902 Munich. B-T.
OTTO, Heinrich. (Eg)
Aus. Vienna 1832-1902. B-T.
OTTONE [or Ottoni], Lorenzo.
It. Rome 1648-1736 Same. T.
OUANG TSE-YUN.
Chinese. b. Suchow 1897. DBA.
OUASSE, Michel Ange.
see Houasse, M. A.
OUDENAARDE. *see* Audenaerde.
OUDENDYK, Evert.
Dut. ac. 1640-1646 in Haarlem. B-T.
OUDENROGGE, Johannes Dircksz.
Dut. Leyden 1622-1653 Haarlem. B-T.
OUDIN, Dorothy Savage.
Mrs. Charles F. Oudin.
Am. b. Balt., Md. 1898; ad. 1934 Cooperstown, N. Y. A.
OUDINÉ, Eugène André. (S)
Fr. Paris 1810-1887 Same. B-E-T.
OUDOT, Rolland.
Fr. b. Paris 1897; ex. 1934 Pittsburgh, Pa. T-797.
OUDRY, Jacques Charles.
Fr. Paris 1720-1778 Lausanne. B-T.
OUDRY, Jean Baptiste.
Fr. Paris 1686-1755 Beauvais. B-Bd-C-T-722.
OULESS, Walter William.
Eng. b. St. Helier 1848. B-C-T-Wa1929.
OURDAN, Joseph Prosper. (Eg)
Am. New York 1828-1881 Wash., D. C. F-7.
OURDAN, Joseph James Prosper. (Eg)
Am. Marseilles, Fr. 1803-1874 Wash., D. C. F-T-7.
OURDAN, Vincent Le Comte. (Eg)
Am. b. Brooklyn, N. Y. 1855; ad. 1882 Wash., D. C. F-7.
OUREN, Karl.
Am. b. Fredrikshald, Nor. 1882; ad. 1934 Chicago. A-F.
OURLAE, Jean Nicolas.
Am. New Orleans, La. 1789-1821 Paris. F.
OUSHIN, N. (Ill)
Rus. ad. 1929 Leningrad. M.
OUTBANK, Nahum B.
Am. ac. 1856-1879 in Boston. F.
OUTCAULT, Richard Felton. (Cart)
Am. Lancaster, O. 1863-1928 Flushing, L. I., N. Y. A025-DAB-F-T-W14-Obit. N. Y. papers, 9-26-1928.
OUTIN, Pierre.
Fr. Moulins 1840-1899 Paris. B-T.
OUVRIÉ, Pierre Justin.
Fr. Paris 1806-1879 Rouen. B-T.
OUWATER, Aelbert van.
Dut. ac. 1430-1460 in Haarlem. B-Bd-T.
OVENS, Jurriaen [or Jürgen].
Dut. 1623-1678. B-T-493.
OVERBECK, Fritz.
Ger. Bremen 1869-1909 Bröcken. B-T.
OVERBECK, Johann Friedrick.
Ger. Lübeck 1789-1869 Rome, It. B-C-E-T-722.
OVERBECK, Margarete.
Am. ex. 1935 New York. M.
OVEREND, William Heysham.
Am. London 1851-1898 U. S. A5-T-Y01899.
OVIATT, Anna P.
Am. Cleveland, O. 1863-1930. M.
OVRYN, Benjamin S.
Am. b. Russia 1892; ad. 1934 Brooklyn, N. Y. A.
OWEN, Edward Pryce. (Et)
Eng. 1788-1863 Cheltenham. DNB-T.

OWEN, Esther S. D.
Mrs. Charles H. Owen.
Am. Boston 1843-1927 Hartford, Conn. A025.
OWEN, Frank Edward. (Ill)
Am. b. Clarksville, Tex. 1907; ad. 1934 New York. M.
OWEN, Frederick L. (Et)
Am. b. Prince Edward Island, Can.; ad. 1935 New York. M.
OWEN, Robert Emmett.
Am. b. No. Adams, Mass. 1878; ad. 1934 New York. A.
OWEN, Samuel.
Eng. 1768/9-1857 Sunbury. B-DNB-T.
OWEN, [Sir] William.
Eng. Ludlow 1769-1825 London. B-DNB-T.
OWENS, Charles. (Ill)
Am. ad. 1934 Los Angeles, Calif. M.
OYENS, David.
Flem. Amsterdam 1842-1902 Brussels. B-T.
OZANNE, Jeanne Françoise. (Eg)
Fr. Brest 1735-1795 Paris. B-T.
OZANNE, Marie Jeanne. (Eg)
Fr. Brest 1734/6-1786 Paris. B-T.
OZANNE, Nicolas Marie.
Fr. Brest 1728-1811 Paris. B-T.
OZANNE, Pierre.
Fr. Brest 1737-1813 Same. B-T.
OZENFANT, Amédée. (S)
Fr. b. St. Quentin 1886. DBA-T-797.
OZERSKY, J. W. (S)
Am. b. Russia 1890; ex. 1926 New York. Cs-Fa.
OZIER, Kenneth H.
Am. b. Cinn., O. 1905; ad. 1934 Same. A.
OZUI, Maruyama.
Jap. 1766-1829 Kyoto. T.
OZUNJAMI, Suzanna.
Am. ex. 1934 New York. M.

PAÁL, Laszló [Ladislaus].
Hun. Zám 1846-1879 Charenton, Fr. B-T.
PABST, Camille Alfred.
Fr. Heiteren 1821-1898 Paris. B-T.
PACCHIA, Girolamo del.
It. Siena 1477-1533. B-E-T.
PACCHIAROTTO, Jacopo [or Giacomo].
It. Siena 1474-1540? Viterbo. B-Bd-E-T.
PACE, Michael Angelo [di Campidoglio].
It. ac. 1610-1670. B-T.
PACH, Magda F.
Mrs. Walter Pach.
Am. b. Dresden, Ger. 1884; ad. 1935 New York. M.
PACH, Walter.
Am. b. New York 1883; ad. 1935 Same. A-F-T-W-701.
PACHECO, Francisco.
Sp. Sèville 1564/71-1654 Same. B-C-E-T-722.
PACHER, Friedrich.
Ger. Brixen 1435/40-1508. T.
PACHER, Michael. (S)
Swi. Bruneck 1435-1498 Salzburg, Ger. B-Hs-T-494.
PACICCO. *see* Rosa, Francesco di.
PACINO DI BONAGUIDA.
see Bonaguida, P. di.
PACK, Faithful Christopher.
Eng. Norwich 1759-1840 London. B-T.
PACKARD, Alton. (Cart)
Am. Taunton, Mass. 1870-1929 Okla. City, Okla. A026-W14.
PACKARD, Mable. (Min)
Am. b. Iowa; ad. 1934 So. Pasadena, Calif. A.
PACKER, Francis Herman. (S)
Am. b. 1873; ad. 1934 Rockville Center, L. I., N. Y. A-F-W.
PACKMAN, Frank G.
Am. b. England 1896; ad. 1934 Detroit, Mich. A.
PACZKA, Franz [or Ferencz].
Hun. Monor 1856-1925 Berlin, Ger. B-T.
PADDOCK, Ethel Louise.
Am. b. New York 1887; ad. 1934 Same. A.
PADDOCK, Josephine.
Am. ad. 1935 New York. A12-F-M.
PADDOCK, Willard Dryden. (P-S)
Am. b. Brooklyn, N. Y. 1873; ad. 1934 So. Kent, Conn. A-F-Cs-W.
PADELFORD, Morgan.
Am. b. Seattle, Wash. 1902; ad. 1934 Same. A.
PADER, Hilaire.
Fr. Toulouse 1607-1677 Same. B-T.
PADOVANINO, Alessandro [Varotari].
It. Padua 1590-1650 Venice. B-C-722.
PADOVANO, Il. *see* Menabuoi.
PADUA, Justus of. *see* Menabuoi.
PADWICK, Philip Hugh.
Eng. b. Horsham 1876; ad. 1934 Fittleworth. Wa.
PAEFF, Bashka. (S)
Am. b. Minsk, Rus. 1893; ad. 1934 Boston. A-Cs-F-W-46.
PAELINCK, Joseph.
Belg. Oostacker 1781-1839 Brussels. B-C-T.
PAEONIUS [or Paionios]. (S)
Gr. ac. 5th Cent. B.C. in Olympia. E-Hs-T.
PAERELS, Willen.
Flem. b. Delft 1878; ad. 1934 Brussels, Belg. T.
PAESCHKE, Paul.
Ger. Berlin 1875-1920. T.
PAEZ, Joseph.
Mex. ac. 17th Century. M.
PAGANELLI, Niccolò.
It. Florence 1538-1620 Rome. B-T.
PAGANI, Gregorio [Goro].
It. Florence 1558-1605 Same. B-T.
PAGANI, Vincenzo.
It. Monterubbiano 1490/6-1568. B-T.
PAGE, Charles.
Eng. ex. 1932 in London. M.
PAGE, Katherine Stuart.
Am. b. Cambridge, Md.; ad. 1934 Wash., D. C. A.
PAGE, Marie Danforth.
Mrs. Calvin G. Page.
Am. b. Boston 1890; ad. 1934 Same. A-F-W.
PAGE, Walter Gilman.
Am. b. Boston 1862-1934 Nantucket, Mass. A-F-M-T-W-46-Obit. N. Y. papers, 3-27-1934.
PAGE, William.
Am. Albany, N. Y. 1811-1885 Tottenville, S. I., N. Y. B-Bd-DAB-C-E-F-T-1-2-3-4-7-15.

PAGES, JULES EUGENE.
Am. b. San Fran., Calif. 1867; ad. 1934 Paris. A-B-F-T.
PAGET, SIDNEY EDWARD.
Eng. London 1860-1908 Same. B-DNB-T.
PAGET ["Wal"], WALTER STANLEY. (Ill)
Eng. 1863-1935 Brownsgrove. M-Obit. N. Y. papers, 1-31-1935.
PAGET-FREDERICKS, JOSEPH ROUS.
Am. b. San Fran., Calif. 1903; ad. 1934 Berkeley, Calif. A.
PAGGI [or Pagi], GIOVANNI BAPTISTA.
It. Genoa 1554-1627 Same. B-C-T.
PAGLIA, FRANCESCO.
It. Brescia 1636-1713 Same. B-T.
PAGLIACENTTI, RAFFAELLO. (S)
It. Guilianuova 1839-1900 Same. B-T.
PAGLIANO, ELENTERIO.
It. 1826-1903 Milan. B-T.
PAGNEST, AMABLE LOUIS CLAUDE.
Fr. Paris 1790-1819 Same. B-T-722.
PAGNO DI LAPO PORTIGIANI.
It. Fiesole 1408-1470 Florence. T.
PAGON, KATHERINE DUNN.
Mrs. William Watters.
Am. b. Phila., Pa. 1892; ad. 1934 Balt., Md. A-F.
PAGUETTE, M. (S)
Am. ad. 1934 New York. M.
PAHNKE, SERGE.
Swi. b. Zurich 1875. B-T.
PAIL, EDOUARD.
Fr. b. Corbigny 1851. B-T.
PAILLARD HENRI PIERRE.
Fr. Paris 1844-1912 Same. B-T.
PAILLET, ANTOINE.
Fr. Paris 1626-1701. B-T.
PAILLET, FERNAND.
Fr. Niort 1850-1918 Paris. DBA-T.
PAILLOT DE MONTABERT, JACQUES NICOLAS.
Fr. Troyes 1771-1849 St. Martin. B-T.
PAILLOU, PETER.
Eng. ac. 1763-1805 in London. T.
PAIN, LOUISE CAROLYN. (S)
Am. b. Chicago 1908; ad. 1934 Same. A.
PAIN, ROBERT TUCKER.
Eng. ac. 1863-1877 in London. B-T.
PAINE. *see also* Payne.
PAINE, JAMES.
Eng. ac. 1761-1829 in London. B-DNB-T.
PAINE, MAY.
Am. b. Charleston, S. C. 1873; ad. 1934 Same. A.
PAINE, RICHARD G. (S)
Am. b. Charleston, S. C. 1875; ad. 1935 East Falls Church, Va. A12-F-T.
PAINE, ROBERT. (S)
Am. ad. 1915 West Hoboken, N. J. A12.
PAIONIOS. (S)
Gr. ac. 5th Cent. B.C. in Olympia. Hs-T.
PAJOU, AUGUSTIN. (S)
Fr. Paris 1730-1809 Same. B-E-Hs-T-495.
PAJOU, JACQUES AUGUSTIN CATHÉRINE.
Fr. Paris 1766-1829 Same. B-T.
PAL, JAVOR.
Hun. ex. 1895 in Paris. M.
PALADINI, LITTERIO.
It. Messina 1691-1743 Same. B-T.
PALADINO, IL. *see* Zabraelli, Adriano.
PALADINO [or Paladini], FILIPPO DI BENEDETTO.
It. Florence 1544-1614 Mazzarino. B-T.
PALAGI, PELAGIO.
It. Bologna 1775-1860 Turin. B-T.
PALAMEDESZ, ANTHONIE [Stevaerts].
Dut. Delft 1600/1-1673 Amsterdam. B-C-T-722.
PALAMEDESZ, PALAMADES I.
Dut. Delft 1607-1638 Same. B-C-T.
PALAMEDESZ, PALAMADES II.
Dut. Delft 1633-1705 Same. B-C-T.
PALAVICINI, PERA [or Petrus]. (S)
Pol. b. 1888; ad. 1931 in Belgrade, Servia. T-798.
PALAZZI, BERNARDINO.
It. ad. 1935 Milan; ex. 1934 Pittsburgh, Pa. M.
PALAZZO, ANTHONY.
Am. ex. 1935 New York. M.
PALEALOGUE, ION.
Am. ad. 1934 New York. M.
PALENCIA, JUAN DE. (S)
Sp. ac. 1469 in Sèville. T.
PALFREY, SARA H.
Am. ac. 19th Century. M.
PALISSY, BERNARD.
Fr. Saintes 1510-1588/90 Paris. B-T.
PALIZZI, FILIPPO.
It. Vasto 1818-1899 Naples. B-T.
PALIZZI, GIUSEPPE.
It. Lanciano 1810/3-1887/9 Paris. B.
PALLADAY, THÉODORE.
Rumanian. b. Jassy; ac. 1900 in Paris. B-T.
PALLADIO, ANDREA.
It. Cartona 1518-1580 Venice. B-T.
PALLAZZO [or Palazzi], ANTHONY.
It. ex. 1934 New York. M.
PALLIERE [or Pailliere], JEAN LÉON.
Fr. b. Rio de Janeiro, Brazil 1823. B-T.
PALLISER, HERBERT WILLIAM. (S)
Eng. b. New York 1883; ad. 1934 London. Wa.
PALM, GUSTAV WILHELM.
Swe. Christiania, Nor. 1810-1890 Stockholm. B-T.
PALM, TORSTEN.
Swe. b. Vaxholm 1885. T.
PALMA, ANTONIO.
It. Serina 1510/5-1575 Venice. B-T.
PALMA, FELICE.
It. Massa Carrara 1583-1625 Same. T.
PALMA IL. GIOVANE, JACOPO [Negretti].
It. Venice 1544-1628 Same. B-C-T-722.
PALMA IL. VECCHIO, JACOPO [or Giacomo].
It. Bergamo 1480?-1528 Venice. B-Bd-C-E-T-V-614-722.
PALMAROLI Y GÓNZALEZ VINCENTE.
Sp. Madrid 1834/5-1896 Same. B-C-T.
PALME, EINAR.
Swe. ad. 1935 Stockholm; ex. 1934 New York. M.
PALMEDO, LILLIAN GAERTNER.
Mrs. Harold B. Palmedo.
Am. b. New York 1906; ad. 1934 Same. A.
PALMEGGIANI. *see* Palmezzano.
PALMER, ADELAIDE.
Am. b. Orford, N. H.; ad. 1931 Same. A28.

PALMER, Alfred Field.
Br. ac. 1903. B.
PALMER, Allen. (Ill)
Am. ad. 1935 New York. M.
PALMER, Edith.
Eng. Bath 1770-1834. B-T.
PALMER, Erastus Dow. (S)
Am. Pompey, N. Y. 1817-1904 Albany, N. Y. A05-DAB-E-F-Hs-T-Ta-15.
PALMER, [Mrs.] Fanny Frances.
Am. b. Eng. 1812. Came U. S. 1840; d. 1876 New York. F-T.
PALMER, [Mrs.] Fredrikke Schjoth.
Am. b. Norway 1860; ad. 1915 New Haven, Conn. A12-F.
PALMER, Harry Sutton.
Eng. Plymouth 1854-1933 Cheswick. B-T-Wa1929-Obit. Art Digest, 9-1-1933.
PALMER, Hattie Virginia Young.
Mrs. C. F. Palmer.
Am. b. Ripley, O. 1910; ad. 1934 Houston, Tex. A.
PALMER, Herbert Sidney.
Can. b. Toronto, Ont. 1881; ad. 1935 Same. M.
PALMER, Herman.
Am. b. 1894; ex. 1935 New York. M.
PALMER, James Lynwood.
Eng. b. Linwood; ad. 1934 Heston. Wa.
PALMER, [Mrs.] Jessie A.
Am. b. Lawrence, Tex. 1882; ad. 1934 Dallas, Tex. A.
PALMER, Lemuel. (Ill)
Am. b. Portland, Me. 1893; ad. 1934 Springfield, Mass. A.
PALMER, Margaret Longyear. (S)
Am. b. Detroit, Mich. 1897; ad. 1934 Same. A.
PALMER, Myron T.
Am. ad. 1934 Toledo, O. M.
PALMER, Pauline.
Mrs. Albert E. Palmer.
Am. b. McHenry, Ill.; ad. 1934 Chicago. A-F-T-W.
PALMER, Samuel.
Eng. London 1805-1881 Reigate. B-DNB-E-T-496.
PALMER, Solveig.
Am. ex. 1934 New York. M.
PALMER, Sutton.
Eng. Plymouth 1854-1933. T-Wa1929.
PALMER, Walter Launt.
Am. b. Albany, N. Y. 1854-1932 Same. A029-B-C-DAB-F-W16-T-Y01933-1-15-46.
PALMER, William.
Ir. Limerick 1763-1790 Bruff. T.
PALMER, William C. (Et)
Am. ex. 1934 New York. M.
PALMERUCCI, Guiduccio [or Guido].
It. Gubbio 1280-1345 Same. B.
PALMEZZANO, Marco di Antonio.
It. Forli 1456/9-1539 Same. B-Bd-C-T.
PALMIÉ, Charles J.
Ger. Aschersleben 1863-1911 Munich. T.
PALMIERI, Pietro Giacomo.
It. Parma 1737/40-1804 Turin. B-T.
PALMYRENE. (S)
Roman. ac. 3rd Cent. A.D. in Rome. M.
PALOMINO DE CASTRO Y VELASCO, Acislo Antonio.
Sp. Bujalance 1653-1726 Madrid. B-E-T.
PALOWETSKI, Charles E.
Am. b. New York 1885; ad. 1915 Paris. A12.
PALTHE, Jan.
Dut. Deventer 1719-1769 Leyden. B-T.
PALUMBO, Alphonse.
Am. b. Raito, It. 1892; ad. 1934 New York. A.
PAMPALONI. Luigi. (S)
It. Florence 1791-1847 Same. Hs-T.
PAMPHILUS.
Gr. ac. 4th Cent. B.C. in Amphipolis, Turkey. B-E-T.
PAN. *see* Lis, Pan [or Jan].
PANABAKER, Frank S.
Am. ad. 1934 Burlington, Ont. Can. M.
PANAENUS [Brother of Phedias].
Gr. Middle 5th Cent. B.C. in Athens. E-T.
PANCOAST, Henry Boller, Jr.
Am. b. Phila., Pa. 1876; ad. 1935 Same. A12-F-T.
PANCOAST, Morris Hall.
Am. b. Salem, N. J. 1877; ad. 1934 New York. A.
PANDOLFI, Alessandro.
It. b. 1887; ad. 1930 in Turin. T.
PANDOLFI, Giangiacomo.
It. b. Pesaro; d. 1630. B-T.
PANETTI, Domenico.
It. Ferrara 1460-1513. B-T.
PANFILO, Il.
see Nuvolone, Carlo Francesco.
PANICALE. *see* Masolino.
PANINI. *see* Pannini.
PANKE, Edith.
Am. ad. 1934 New York. M.
PANKIEWICZ, Józef.
Pol. b. Lublin 1866. B-T.
PANKOK, Bernard.
Ger. b. Münster 1872. B-T.
PANKRAZ. *see* Fries.
PANN, Abel.
Rus. b. Kreslawka 1883; ex. 1935 London. T.
PANNEELS, Willem.
Flem. ac. 1600-1632 in Antwerp. B-T.
PANNEMAKER, Erasmus de. (Tapestry)
Flem. ac. 1644-1690 in Brussels. T.
PANNEMAKER, Franz de. (Tapestry)
Flem. ac. 1684-1700 in Lille, Fr. T.
PANNEMAKER, Wilhelm.
Ger. ac. 1548-1561. T.
PANNINI, Giovanni Paolo.
It. Piacenza 1691/5-1765/8 Rome. B-C-T-722.
PANSING, Fred.
Am. ac. 1818. M.
PANTOJA DE LA CRUZ, Juan.
Sp. Madrid 1551-1608/9 Same. B-T-722.
PANTON, Lawrence A. C.
Can. b. Egremont, Eng.; ad. 1935 Toronto, Ont. M.
PANZA, Federico.
It. Milan 1633/43-1703 Same. B-T.
PAOLETTO, Antonio Ermolao.
It. 1834-1912 Venice. B-T.
PAOLETTI [Fra Vittore], Ghislandi.
see Ghislandi, Fra Vittore.

PAOLETTI, Rodolfo.
It. b. Venice 1866. T.
PAOLINO DA PISTOJA, Fra [Signoraccio].
It. Pistoja 1490-1547 Same. B-T.
PAOLO, Bartolommeo. *see* Bartolommeo di P.
PAOLO, C. S. (S)
Am. ex. 1935 New York. M.
PAOLO, Giovanni. *see* Giovanni di P.
PAOLO DI GIOVANNI FEI [Frederici].
It. ac. 1372-1410 Siena. T-78-783.
PAOLO DI STEFANO. *see* Stefano, P. di.
PAOLO, Veneziano. *see* Master Paolo.
PAOLOTTO, Fra. *see* Ghislandi.
PAON, Jean Baptiste. *see* Lepaon, J. B.
PAPA, Simone I [Vecchio].
It. Naples 1430-1488. B-T.
PAPA, Simone II [Giovine].
It. Naples 1506-1566/7 Same. B-T.
PAPACELLO [or Paparello], Bernabei Tomaso.
It. Cortona 1500-1559 Same. B-T.
PAPASIAN, Jack Charles. (S)
Am. b. Olympia, Gr. 1878; ad. 1934 New York. A.
PAPAZOFF, Georges.
Bulgarian. b. Jamloli 1894; ex. 1934 New York. T.
PAPE, Abraham de.
Dut. Leyden 1620/5-1666 Same. B-T.
PAPE, Alice Monroe.
Am. b. Boston; d. 1911 Manchester, Mass. A09-F-T.
PAPE, Eric.
Am. b. San Fran., Calif. 1870; ad. 1934 New York. A-F-T-W-46.
PAPE, Fredrick Georg William.
Ger. Rendsburg 1859-1920 Stockholm, Swe. B-T.
PAPE, Martin Didier.
Fr. Limoges 1574-1609. B.
PAPE, William. (Ill)
Ger. 1859-1920 Stockholm, Swe. T.
PAPENHOVEN, Alexander van. (S)
Flem. Antwerp, Belg. 1668-1757/9. B-T.
PAPÉTY, Dominique Louis Ferréol.
Fr. Marseilles 1815-1849 Same. B-T-722.
PAPIAS.
Gr. ac. 4th century B.C. T.
PAPILLON, Jean Baptiste Michel. (Eg)
Fr. Paris 1720-1766 Same. B-T.
PAPILLON, Jean Michel. (Eg)
Fr. Paris 1698-1776 Same. B-T.
PAPOTTI, N. Cantalamessa. (S)
It. ac. 1858-1873 in Italy. M.
PAPPAS, John L.
Am. b. Florina, Gr. 1898; ad. 1934 Detroit, Mich. A-T.
PAPPELENDAM. *see* Van Pappelendan.
PAPPERITZ, Friedrich Georg.
Ger. Dresden 1846-1918 Munich. B-T.
PAPPERITZ, Gustav Friedrich.
Ger. Dresden 1813-1861 Same. B-T.
PAPPRILL, H. A. (Eg)
Eng. ac. 1846. M.
PAPWORTH, Edgar George. (S)
Eng. London 1809-1866 Same. DNB-T.
PAPWORTH, John Buonarotti.
Eng. London 1775-1847 Little Paxton. DNB-T.
PARACCA, Giovanni Antonio [Valsoldo]. (S)
It. ac. 1572-1642 in Rome. T.
PARADISE, John.
Am. New Jersey 1783-1833 Springfield, N. J. F-T.
PARADISE, John Wesley. (Eg)
Am. New Jersey 1809-1862 New York. F-T-2-7-40.
PARADISE, Phil.
Am. ad. 1934 So. Pasadena, Calif. M.
PARAMINO, John Francis. (S)
Am. b. Boston 1889; ad. 1934 Same. A-T-W.
PARANT, Louis Bertin.
Fr. Mers 1768-1851 Paris. B-T.
PARAYRE, Henri Ernest. (S)
Fr. b. Toulouse 1883. T-687-813.
PARCELL, Malcolm Stevens.
Am. b. Claysville, Pa. 1896; ad. 1934 Wash, Pa. A-F-T-W.
PARDI, Justin Anthony.
Am. b. Castelli, It. 1898; ad. 1934 Phila., Pa. A.
PARDUCCI, Rudolph. (S)
Am. ac. 1932. M.
PAREJA, Juan de.
Sp. Sèville 1606/10-1670 Madrid. B-C-E-T-722.
PARENT, Léandre. (Carver)
Fr.-Can. ac. 1800-1860/5 Quebec, Can. M.
PARENT, Léon.
Fr. b. 1869; ac. 1932 Paris. T.
PARENT, Roger.
Fr. b. Paris 1881. T.
PARENTINO [or Parenzano], Bernardo.
It. Paenzo 1437-1531 Vicenza. B-T.
PARET Y ALCÁZAR, Luis.
Sp. Madrid 1746-1799 Same. B-T.
PARIGI, Guilio. (Eg)
It. d. 1635 in Florence. B-T.
PARIS BORDONE. *see* Bordone, P.
PARIS, Camille Adrien.
Fr. Paris 1834-1901 Barbizon. B-T.
PARIS, Jean. *see* Perréal, Jean.
PARIS, Jehan de. *see* Master of the Moulins.
PARIS, Mathew [or Mathieu].
Eng. ac. 1217-1259. B-T.
PARIS, Pierre Adrien.
Fr. Besançon 1745-1819 Same. B-T.
PARIS, Walter.
Am. London 1842-1906 Wash., D. C. A06-B-DAB-F-T-41.
PARIS, William Francklyn. (Mu)
Am. b. New York; ad. 1934 Same. A-F-T.
PARIS-MASTER. *see* Master Paris.
PARISIANI, Napoleone.
It. b. Çamerimo 1854. T.
PARK, Henry.
Eng. Bath 1816-1871 Bristol. B-T.
PARK, Madeleine. (S)
Mrs. Harold H. Park.
Am. b. Mt. Kisco, N. Y. 1891; ad. 1934 Katonah, N. Y. A.
PARK, Patric. (S)
Scot. Glasgow 1811-1855 Warrington, Eng. B-DNB-T.

PARK, Richard Hamilton. (S)
Am. b. New York 1832; ac. 1890 Florence, It. [No death date.] T.
PARK, Stuart.
Scot. b. Kidderminster 1862. B-T.
PARK, Thomas. (Eg)
Eng. ac. 1759-1834 London. B-T.
PARKE, Jessie Burns.
Am. b. Paterson, N. J. 1889; ad. 1934 Arlington Heights, Mass. A.
PARKE, Nathaniel Ross.
Am. b. Williamsport, Pa. 1904; ad. 1934 West Hartford, Conn. A.
PARKER, [Mrs.] Agnes Miller. (Eg)
Scot. b. Ayrshire 1895; ex. 1934 London. Wa.
PARKER, Al. (Ill)
Am. ad. 1934 New York. M.
PARKER, Arvilla. (Ill)
Am. ad. 1935 San Fran., Calif. M.
PARKER, Brynhild.
Eng. ex. 1932 in London. M.
PARKER, Charles H. (Eg)
Am. Salem, Mass. 1793/5-1819 Phila., Pa. F-2-7-169.
PARKER, Cora.
Am. b. Kentucky; ad. 1934 Coral Gables, Fla. A.
PARKER, Cushman.
Am. b. Boston 1881; ad. 1934 Onset, Mass. A.
PARKER, Dana. (Cart)
Am. b. 1891; d. 1933 Port Wash., N. Y. A030.
PARKER, Edgar.
Am. b. Framingham, Mass. 1840. F-T-46.
PARKER, Emma Alice.
Am. Gardner, Mass. 1876; ad. 1935 Prov., R. I. A12-F-T.
PARKER, George. (Eg)
Am. b. England; d. 1868 New York. F-T-2-7-40.
PARKER, George Waller.
Am. b. New York 1888; ad. 1934 Same. A.
PARKER, Harold. (S)
Aust. b. Aust. 1873; ad. 1934 London. T-Wa.
PARKER, Harry Henley. (Mu)
Am. Phila., Pa. 1869-1917 Same. A014-F-T.
PARKER, Henry Perlee.
Eng. Devonport 1795-1873 London. DNB-T.
PARKER, James. (Eg)
Eng. 1750-1805 London. B-DNB-T.
PARKER, John.
Eng. 1730?-1765? London. B-DNB-T.
PARKER, John.
Eng. ac. 1762-1776 in London. B-DNB-T.
PARKER, John.
Eng. Birmingham 1830-1916 London. T.
PARKER, John Adams.
Am. b. New York 1827. C-F-T.
PARKER, John Clay.
Am. ad. 1934 New Orleans, La. M.
PARKER, John F.
Am. b. New York 1884. A20-F-T.
PARKER, Lawton S.
Am. b. Fairfield, Mich. 1868; ad. 1934 France. A-B-F-T-W15-46.
PARKER, Lester Shepard.
Am. Worcester, Mass. 1860-1925 Rochester, Minn. A023.
PARKER, [Miss] Miller. (Eg)
Eng. ex 1935 London. M.
PARKER, Mordaunt.
Eng. ad. 1934 Kobe, Jap. M.
PARKER, Paul.
Am. b. La Grange, Ill. 1905; ad. 1934 Chicago. A.
PARKER, Richard Henry.
Eng. Dewsbury 1881-1930. Wa1929.
PARKER, Sarah Leffingwell Horton.
Am. b. Albany, N. Y. 1889; ad. 1934 Milford, Mass. M.
PARKER, Stephen Hills.
Am. d. 1925 Florence, It. A022.
PARKER, Sybil C.
Eng. b. 1860; ac. 1893 London. T.
PARKER, Thomas C.
Am. b. Holyoke, Mass. 1904. M.
PARKER, David.
Eng. Hales Owen 1763-1833 Shrewsbury. B-T.
PARKHURST, Anita [Mrs. Willcox].
Am. b. Chicago 1892; ad. 1934 New York. A.
PARKHURST, Burleigh.
Am. ad. 1934 Ogunquit, Me. M.
PARKHURST, Henry Landon.
Am. Oswego, N. Y. 1867-1921 New York. A018-T.
PARKHURST, Thomas Shrewsbury.
Am. Manchester, Eng. 1853-1923 Calif. A020-F-T.
PARKINSON, Thomas.
Eng. ac. 1769-1789 in London. B-DNB-T.
PARKINSON, William Edward. (S)
Eng. Chester 1871-1927. WaO1929
PARKINSON, Henry Spurrier.
Eng. Bristol 1814-1864. T.
PARLER VON GMÜND, Heinrich.
Ger. ac. 1385. T.
PARLIN, Florence W.
Am. ad. 1935 Rochester, Minn. M.
PARMASEN. *see* Parmigianino, Francesco.
PARMENTIER, Jacques [or James].
Fr. Paris 1658-1730 London. B-DNB-T.
PARMIGIANINO, Francesco [Mazzola].
It. Parma 1503/5-1540 Maggiore. B-C-E-T-V-722.
PARMIGIANINO, Michele [Rocca].
It. 1671-1751/7. T.
PARNELL, Eileen. (S)
Mrs. Gustav Bohland.
Am. b. Ireland 1902; ad. 1934 New York. Cs.
PARODI [or Parrodi], Domenico.
It. Genoa 1668-1740 Same. B-T.
PARODI [or Parrodi], Filippo.
It. Genoa, It. 1630-1702 Same. B-T.
PAROLINI, Giacomo Filippo.
It. Ferrara 1663-1733 Same. B-T.
PARR, Harry. (S)
Eng. b. Wolstanton 1882; ad. 1934 Chelsea. Wa.
PARR, Nathaniel. (Eg)
Eng. ac. 1730-1760 in London. B-DNB-T.

PARR, Remi [or Remigius]. (Eg)
Eng. Rochester 1723-1750/60. B-DNB-T.
PARR, Russell C.
Am. Evansville, Wis. 1895; ad. 1934 Wash., D. C. A.
PARRHASIUS [of Ephesus].
Gr. (Attic) ac. 390-350 B.C. B-E-T.
PARRIS, Edmund Thomas.
Eng. London 1793-1873 Same. B-DNB-T.
PARRISH, Clara Weaver.
Mrs. William P. Parrish.
Am. b. Selma, Ala.; d. 1925 New York. A022-F-T-W13.
PARRISH, Maxfield. (Ill)
Am. b. Phila., Pa. 1870; ad. 1934 Windsor, Vt. A-B-F-W-46.
PARRISH, Stephen. (Et)
Am. b. Phila., Pa. 1846; ad. 1934 Windsor, Vt. A-F-T-W-46.
PARROCEL, Charles.
Fr. Paris 1688-1752 Same. B-C-T-722.
PARROCEL, Etienne.
Fr. Avignon 1696-1773/6 Rome, It. B-T.
PARROCEL, Jean Joseph.
Fr. Paris 1690-1704 St. Malo. B-C-T-722.
PARROCEL, Joseph [Batailles].
Fr. Brignoles 1646-1704 Paris. B-C-T-722.
PARROCEL, Pierre.
Fr. Avignon 1670-1739 Paris. B-T.
PARROTT, William Samuel.
Am. Missouri 1844-1915 Goldendale, Wash. A12-F-T.
PARRY, Charles James [The Elder].
Eng. Manchester 1824-1894 London. DNB-T.
PARRY, David Henry [The Elder].
Eng. Manchester 1793-1826 London. DNB-T.
PARRY, Joseph.
Eng. Liverpool 1744-1826 Manchester. B-Bd-DNB-T.
PARRY, Thomas Gambier.
Eng. London 1816-1888 Highnam. B-Bd-DNB-T.
PARRY, William.
Eng. London 1742?-1791 Same. B-Bd-DNB-T.
PARS, Henry. (Et)
Eng. 1734-1806 London. B-DNB-T.
PARS, William.
Eng. London 1742-1782 Rome, It. B-Bd-DNB-T-884.
PARSHALL, De Witt.
Am. b. Buffalo, N. Y. 1864; ad. 1934 Santa Barbara, Calif. A-F-T-W.
PARSONS, Alfred Wilde.
Eng. ac. 1900-1933 Bristol. B-T.
PARSONS, Alfred William.
Eng. Beckington 1847-1920 Broadway. B-DNB-T.
PARSONS, Charles.
Am. Eng. 1821-1910 New York. C-F-T-15.
PARSONS, David T. (S)
Am. ex. 1934 Manchester, Vt. M.
PARSONS, [Mrs.] Edith Barretto Stevens. (S)
Am. b. Houston, Va. 1878; ad. 1934 New York. A-Cs-F-T.
PARSONS, Edith Gilman. (S)
Am. ad. 1934 New York. M.
PARSONS, Francis.
Eng. ac. 1763-1804 in London. B-DNB-T.
PARSONS, James Herbert.
Am. d. 1905 New Brighton, N. Y. A06.
PARSONS, Lloyd.
Am. ad. 1935 New York. M.
PARSONS, Margaret H.
Am. ad. 1935 New York. M.
PARSONS, Sheldon.
Am. b. New York 1868; ad. Santa Fé, N. M. M.
PARSONS, Theophilus.
Am. b. New York 1876; ad. 1934 Wash. D. C. A.
PARTEE, McCullough.
Am. ad. 1934 Nashville, Tenn. A.
PARTIKEL, Alfred.
Ger. b. Goldap 1888; ad. 1930 Berlin. T.
PARTINGTON, Richard Lantry.
Am. Stockport, Eng. 1868-1929 Phila., Pa. A026-T.
PARTON, Arthur.
Am. Hudson, N. Y. 1842-1914 Yonkers, N. Y. A011-B-C-DAB-F-T-15-46.
PARTON, Ernest.
Am. b. Hudson, N. Y. 1845; d. in London. A20-B-C-F-T-W9-15.
PARTON. Henry Woodbridge.
Am. Hudson, N. Y. 1858-1933 New York. A030-F-T-W.
PARTON, Hulda.
Mrs. Daniel Day Walter, Jr.
Am. b. Hudson, N. Y.; ad. 1915 Yonkers, N. Y. A12.
PARTRIDGE, Charlotte Russell.
Am. b. Minn.; ad. 1934 Milwaukee, Wis. A.
PARTRIDGE, John.
Scot. Glasgow 1790-1872 London. B-DNB-T.
PARTRIDGE, [Sir] John Bernard. (Ill)
Eng. b. London 1861; ad. 1934 Same. E-T-Wa.
PARTRIDGE, Roi. (Et)
Am. b. Centralia, Wash. 1888; ad. 1935 Mills College, P. O. Calif. A28-F-T-W.
PARTRIDGE, William H.
Am. b. Wheeling, Va. 1858; ad. 1934 Wellesley Hills, Mass. A.
PARTRIDGE, William Ordway. (S)
Am. Paris 1861-1930 New York. A027-DAB-E-F-Hs-T-Ta-W15-46.
PARZINGER, Tommi. (Ill)
Am. ad. 1934 New York. M.
PASAVANT, Frederick Joseph.
Am. Brandon, Vt. 1887-1919 New York. A016.
PASCAL, Francois Michel.
Fr. Paris 1810-1882 Same. B-T.
PASCAL, Paul.
Fr. Toulouse 1832-1903 Quebec, Can. DBA-T.
PASCALIS, Louise.
Fr. b. Paris 1893. DBA.
PASCH FAMILY.
Swe. ac. 18th century in Stockholm. T.
PASCH, Lorenz [or Lorens].
Swe. Stockholm 1733-1805 Same. B-T.
PASCH, Ulrika [or Ulla] Fredrika.
Swe. Stockholm 1735-1796 Same. B-T.
PASCH, Albert. (S)
Swi. b. Geneva 1873. DBA.

PASCIN, JULES [Julius Pincas].
Am. Bulgaria 1885-1930 Paris.
A027-DBA-F-T-497-797.
PASIAS.
Gr. ac. 3rd century B.C. T.
PASINELLI, LORENZO.
It. Bologna 1629-1700 Same. B-T-722.
PASINI, ALBERTO.
It. Basseto 1826-1899 Cavoretto. B-C-T.
PASITELES. (S)
Gr. [Neo-Attic] ac. 102-44 B.C. E-Hs-T.
PASQUIER, PIERRE. (Min)
Fr. Villefranche 1731-1806 Paris. B-T.
PASS [or Passe], WILLIAM. (Eg)
Eng. Cologne, Ger. 1598?-1637? London.
DNB-T.
PASSAGE, MARIE CHARLES DU. (S)
Fr. b. Somme; ac. 1865-1885 Paris. B.
PASSAGLIA, AUGUSTO. (S)
It. Lucca 1838-1918 Florence. B-T.
PASSAROTTI, BARTOLOMMEO.
It. Bologna 1529-1592 Same. B-C-T-V-722.
PASSAROTTI, TIBURZIO.
It. Bologna 1555/7-1612 Same. B-T.
PASSE, CRISPIN DE [The Elder]. (Eg)
Dut. Zeeland 1564/5-1637 Utrecht. B-T.
PASSE, CRISPIN DE [The Younger]. (Eg)
Dut. Cologne 1593/8-1670 Amsterdam. B-T.
PASSE FAMILY.
Ger. ac. 16-17th centuries in Germany. T.
PASSE [or Pass], SIMON DE. (Eg)
Dut. Utrecht 1590/5-1647 Copenhagen, Denmark. B-DNB-T.
PASSEROTTI. *see* Passarotti.
PASSIGNANO, DOMENICO DA CAVALIERE.
It. Passignano 1550-1638 Florence. C-T-722.
PASSINI, LUDWIG JOHANN.
Aus. Vienna 1832-1903 Venice, It. B-C-T.
PASSOS, JOHN DOS. (Ill)
b. Russia; ac. 1934. M.
PASTELOT, JEAN AMABLE AMÉDÉE.
Fr. ac. 1846-1870 in Paris B-T.
PASTERNACKI, VETOLD H.
Am. b. Detroit, Mich. 1897; ad. 1934 Same.
A.
PASTERNACK [or Pasternanc], LÉONIDE.
Rus. b. Odessa 1862. B-T.
PASTEUR, LOUIS.
Fr. Dôle 1822-1895 Garches. T.
PASTI [or Bastia], MATTEO DI ANDREA DE. (S)
It. ac. 1446-1467 in Verona. B-Hs-T.
PASTORINI, BENEDETTO [or Benedict]. (Eg)
It. b. Italy 1746; ac. 1775-1803 London. T.
PASTORINI, GIOVANNI MICHELE DE.
It. Siena 1508-1592 Florence. B-T.
PASTURE, ROGER DE LA.
see Weyden, Roger van der.
PATA, CHERUBINO [or Cherubin].
Fr. ac. 1868-1884 in Paris. B-T.
PATAKY, TIBOR.
Am. b. Budapest, Hun. 1901; ad. 1934 Orlando, Fla. M.
PATANAZZI, ALFONZO.
It. ac. 1580-1616 in Italy. B-T.
PATCH, THOMAS. (Eg)
Eng. Devonshire 1700-1772 Florence, It.
B-DNB-T.
PATEL, PIERRE [The Elder].
Fr. Picardie 1605?-1676 Paris. B-C-T-722.
PATEL, PIERE ANTOINE [The Younger].
Fr. Paris 1648-1707 Same. B-C-T.
PATENIER [or Patinir], HENRI DE.
Flem. ac. 1535 in Antwerp. B-T.
PATENIER, JOACHIM. *see* Patinir, J.
PATER, ANTOINE JOSEPH. (S)
Fr. Valenciennes 1670-1747 Same. B-T.
PATER, JEAN BAPTISTE JOSEPH.
Fr. Valenciennes 1695-1736 Paris.
B-Bd-C-T-722.
PATERINA, CARLOTTA.
It. ac. 1930. M.
PATERS, JOHN.
ex. 1934 New York. M.
PATERSON. *see also* Patterson.
PATERSON, ALEXANDER NESBIT.
Scot. b. Glasgow 1862. T.
PATERSON, EMILY MURRAY.
Scot. Edinburgh; d. 1934 London.
T-Wa-Obit. N. Y. papers, 7-24-1934.
PATERSON, JAMES.
Scot. Glasgow 1854-1932 Edinburgh.
B-T-Wa1929-Y01933.
PATERSON, JOHN FORD.
Aust. ac. 1890-1900 in Victoria, So. Aust.
B-T.
PATIGIAN, HAIG. (S)
Am. b. Armenia 1876; ad. 1934 San Fran., Calif. A-Cs-F-T-W.
PATINIR, JOACHIM DE.
Flem. Dinant, Belg. 1475/80-1524 Antwerp.
B-T-662-722.
PATKÓ, KÁROLY [or Karl].
Hun. b. Budapest 1895. T.
PATLAGEAN, NUMA GRIGORIEVITCH. (S)
Rus. b. Russia 1888. M.
PATOCCHI, ALDO. (Eg)
Swi. b. Swi. 1907; ex. 1934 Chicago; ad. 1935 Ticino, Swi. M.
PATON [or Patton], DAVID.
Scot. ac. 1668-1693 in Edinburgh.
Bd-DNB-T.
PATON, FRANK. (Ill)
Eng. London 1856-1909. T.
PATON, HUGH. (Et)
Scot. Glasgow 1853-1927 Manchester, Eng.
T-WaO1929.
PATON, [Sir] JOSEPH NÖEL.
Scot. Dumfermline 1821-1901 Edinburgh.
B-Bd-C-DNB-E-T.
PATON, RICHARD.
Eng. London 1717-1791 Same. B-Bd-DNB-T.
PATON, WALLER HUGH.
Scot. Dumfermline 1828-1895 Edinburgh.
B-Bd-DNB-T.
PATRAS, LAMBERT. (S)
Ger. ac. 1112 in Germany. Hs-T.
PATRICK, JAMES MCINTOSH.
Scot. b. Dundee 1907; ad. 1934 Same.
T-Wa.
PATRICK, JOHN DOUGLAS.
Am. b. Hopewell, Pa. 1863. B-T.
PATROIS, ISIDORE.
Fr. Noyers 1815-1884 Paris. B-T.
PATROKLES I.
Gr. ac. 5th Cent. B.C. in Sicyon. T.
PATRU, LOUIS.
Swi. Champel 1871-1905. B-T.

PATRY, EDWARD.
Eng. b. London 1856; ad. 1934 Sussex, Eng. B-T-Wa.
PATTE, PIERRE. (Eg)
Fr. Paris 1723-1812 Nantes. B-T.
PATTEE, ELSIE DODGE. (Min)
Am. b. Chelsea, Mass. 1876; ad. 1934 New York. A-F-T-W.
PATTEIN, CÉSAR.
Nor. b. Steenvoorde; ad. 1882-1914 Paris. B-T.
PATTEN, GEORGE.
Eng. London 1801-1865 Winchmore Hill. B-DNB-T.
PATTEN, MARION.
Am. ad. 1935 Brookline, Mass. M.
PATTERSON, AMBROSE.
Am. b. Daylesford, Victoria, Aust.; ad. 1934 Seattle, Wash. A-F-T.
PATTERSON, A. DICKSON.
Can. b. Picton, Can. 1854; d. 1930. M.
PATTERSON, CATHERINE NORRIS. (Min)
Am. b. Phila., Pa.; ad. 1934 Same. F-T-W.
PATTERSON, CHARLES ROBERT.
Am. b. England 1878; ad. 1934 New York. A-F-T.
PATTERSON, CHARLES W.
Am. b. Belle Vernon, Pa. 1870; ad. 1934 Pittsburgh, Pa. A.
PATTERSON, GEORGE MALCOLM. (Et)
Eng. b. Twickenham 1873; ad. 1935 St. Andrews, Fife. Wa.
PATTERSON, HENRY STUART.
Am. b. East Orange, N. J. 1874; ad. 1934 Suffern, N. Y. A.
PATTERSON, HOWARD ASHMAN.
Am. b. Phila., Pa. 1891; ad. 1934 Santa Fé, N. M. A.
PATTERSON, JAMES S. (Eg)
Am. 1832-1916 Hackensack, N. J. A013-T.
PATTERSON, LAWRENCE A. (Ill)
Am. ad. 1934 Los Angeles, Calif. M.
PATTERSON, MARGARET JORDAN.
Am. b. Soerabaija, Java; ad. 1934 Boston. A-F-T.
PATTERSON, NELLIE.
Am. b. Statesville, N. C.; ad. 1934 Wash., D. C. A.
PATTERSON, REBECCA BURD PEALE.
Am. b. Phila., Pa.; ad. 1934 Same. A-F-T.
PATTERSON, RUSSELL. (Ill)
Am. b. Omaha, Neb. 1896; ad. 1934 New York. A.
PATTERSON, VIOLA.
Mrs. Ambroise Patterson.
Am. b. Seattle, Wash. 1898; ad. 1934 Same. A.
PATTISON, CARRIE A.
Am. ad. 1935 Indiana, Pa. M.
PATTISON, HELEN SEARLE.
Mrs. James William Pattison.
Am. b. Burlington, Vt.; d. 1884 Jacksonville, Ill. 829.
PATTISON, JAMES WILLIAM.
Am. Boston 1844-1915 Asheville, N. C. A012-DAB-F-T-W8.
PATTISON, ROBERT J.
Am. New York 1838-1903 Brooklyn, N. Y. A04.
PATTON, ALICE CORSON.
Am. ac. 1915 in Phila., Pa. A12.
PATTON, KATHERINE.
Am. b. Phila., Pa.; ad. 1934 Same. A-F-T-W.
PATTON, ROY EDWIN.
Am. b. Springfield, O. 1878; ad. 1934 Erie, Pa. A.
PATTY, WILLIAM ARTHUR.
Am. b. New Hartford, Conn. 1889; ad. 1934 New York. A.
PATZIG, EDNA.
Am. b. Le Mars, Ia.; ad. 1934 Iowa City, Ia. A.
PAUDISS [or Bauditz], CHRISTOPH.
Dut. Basse-Saxe 1618-1666/7 Freising. B-C-T.
PAUL, [Miss] FLORENCE.
Eng. ex. 1935 London. M.
PAUL, HERMANN [René Georges]. (Eg)
Fr. b. Paris 1864; ac. 1932 Same. T.
PAUL, JEREMIAH.
Am. ac. 1791-1820 in Phila., Pa. F-T-2.
PAUL, J. S.
Eng. ac. 1760 in London. B-T.
PAUL, JOSEPH E.
Am. ad. 1935 Rockville Center, L. I., N. Y. M.
PAUL, RICHARD.
Ger. Breslau 1853-1900 Munich. B-T.
PAUL, VERONESE.
see Veronese, Paolo Caliari.
PAULDING, JOHN. (S)
Am. b. Dark Co., O. 1870; d. 1935 Chicago. A-Obit. N. Y. papers, 4-16-1935.
PAULÉMILE, PISSARRO BENJAMIN.
Fr. b. 1884 in France. DBA.
PAULI, GEORG VILHELM.
Swe. b. Rochlitz 1855. B-T.
PAULI, RICHARD.
Am. Chicago 1855-1892 New Jersey. M.
PAULEY, F.
Am. ad. 1935 Milwaukee, Wis. M.
PAULL, GRACE A. (Ill)
Am. b. Cold Brook, N. Y. 1898; ad. 1935 New York. M.
PAULLIN, TELFORD.
Am. Le Mars, Ia. 1885-1933 New York. A030.
PAULSEN, ANTON.
Ger. ac. 1718-1748 in Leipzig. T.
PAULSEN, FRITZ.
Ger. Schwerin 1838-1898 Berlin. B-C-T.
PAULSEN, JULIUS.
Dan. b. Odense 1860. B-T.
PAULUS, FRANCIS PETRUS. (Et)
Am. Detroit, Mich. 1862-1933 Same. A030-F-T-W-46.
PAULUS, PIERRE.
Flem. b. Châtelet 1881; ad. 1934 Brussels. T.
PAULYN [or Paulin], HORATIUS.
Dut. Amsterdam 1640/5-1686? B-T.
PAUNZEN, ARTHUR.
Ger. b. Vienna, Aus. 1890. T.
PAUPION, EDUARD JÉRÔNE.
Fr. Dyon 1854-1912 Orchamps. B-T.
PAUQUET, JEAN LOUIS CHARLES.
Fr. Paris 1759-1824. B-T.

PAUS, HERBERT. (Ill)
Am. ad. 1934 Mamaroneck, N. Y. M.
PAUSANIAS.
Gr. ac. 369 B.C. T.
PAUSER, SERGIUS.
Aus. b. Vienna 1896; ad. 1934 Same. T.
PAUSIAS.
Gr. ac. 4th Cent. B.C. in Sicyon. E-T.
PAUSINGER, CLEMENS VON.
Ger. b. Salzburg 1855. B-T.
PAUSINGER, FRANZ XAVER CAN.
Ger. Wurzbach 1839-1915 Same. B-T.
PAUTROT, JULES. (S)
Fr. b. 1831; ac. 1875 Paris. B-T.
PAUTSCH, FRYDERYK.
Pol. b. Delatyn 1877. T.
PAUWELS, FERDINAND WILHELM.
Belg. Eckeren 1830-1904 Dresden, Ger. B-C-T.
PAVIE, JEAN.
Fr. d. 1928 in Toulouse. T.
PAVLOFF, NICOLAS.
Am. b. Russia 1872; ex. 1934 New York. M.
PAVÓN, JOSÉ M.
Mex. b. Mexico 1902; ex. 1931 Chicago. M.
PAVONA, FRANCESCO.
It. Udine 1682-1777 Venice. T.
PAWLA, FREDERICK ALEXANDER.
Am. b. England 1877; ad. 1934 Santa Barbara, Calif. A.
PAWLOVNA, MARIE [Grand Duchess].
Rus. 1854-1912. M.
PAXON, EDGAR SAMUEL.
Am. b. East Hamburg, N. Y. 1852; ad. 1915 Missoula, Mont. A12-F-T.
PAXSON, ETHEL.
Mrs. Clement Esmond.
Am. b. Meriden, Conn. 1885; ad. 1934 Kew Gardens, L. I., N. Y. A-F-T.
PAXSON, MARTHA.
Am. b. Phila., Pa. 1875; ad. 1915 Same. A12.
PAXTON, [Mrs.] ELIZABETH OKIE.
Am. b. Prov., R. I.; ad. 1934 Newton Center, Mass. A.
PAXTON, JOHN.
Scot. d. 1780 in Bombay, India. B-DNB-T.
PAXTON, WILLIAM MCGREGOR.
Am. b. Balt., Md. 1869; ad. 1934 Boston. A-F-T-W-46.
PAYNE, CHARLES HENRY.
Am. Newburyport, Mass. 1850-1916 Chicago. A013.
PAYNE, EDGAR ALWIN.
Am. b. Washburn, Mo. 1882; ad. 1934 New York. A-F-T-W.
PAYNE, ELSIE PALMER.
Mrs. Edgar Alwin Payne.
Am. b. San Antonio, Tex. 1884; ad. 1934 Beverly Hills, Calif. A.
PAYNE, EMMA LANE.
Am. b. Canada 1874; ad. 1934 Euclid, O. A.
PAYNE, GEORGE. (Ill)
Am. ad. 1934 East Orange, N. J. A.
PAYNE [or Paine], JOHN. (Eg)
Eng. b. 1608; d. 1648 in London. B-Bd-DNB-T.
PAYNE, WILLIAM.
Eng. Plymouth 1760-1813 London. B-Bd-DNB-T.
PAYNE, WYNDHAM. (Ill)
Eng. ad. 1934 London. M.
PAYOR, EUGENE.
Am. ex. 1935 New York. M.
PAZZI [or Protopazzi], ANTOINE. (Cari)
Gr. b. Mytilène, Gr. 1897. DBA.
PAZZI, ENRICO. (S)
It. Ravenna 1819-1899 Florence. B-T.
PEABODY, AMELIA. (S)
Am. b. Marble Head Neck, Mass. 1890; ad. 1934 Boston. A-Cs-F.
PEABODY, HELEN L.
Am. b. New York 1879; ad. 1934 Same. A.
PEABODY, JULIAN.
Am. ac. 1920; d. 1934 at sea. M.
PEABODY, MARIAN LAWRENCE. (S)
Am. b. Boston, Mass. 1875; ad. 1934 Same. A-Cs.
PEABODY, RUTH. (S)
Am. b. Highland Park, Ill.; ad. 1934 Laguna Beach, Calif. A.
PEACHAM, HENRY.
Eng. North Mimms 1576-1650 London. B-Bd-DNB-T.
PEACOCK, JEAN ELEANOR.
Mrs. William C. King.
Am. b. Norfolk, Va. 1900; ad. 1934 Richmond, Va. A.
PEACOCK, RALPH.
Eng. b. London 1868; ad. 1934 Same. B-T-Wa.
PEAKE [or Peak], JAMES. (Eg)
Eng. London 1729-1782 Same. B-DNB-T.
PEAKE [or Peak], ROBERT, SR.
Eng. ac. 1580-1782 London. B-DNB-T.
PEALE, ANNA CLAYPOOLE. (Min)
Am. Phila., Pa. 1791-1878 Same. DAB-F-T-2-6-30-66-84-179.
PEALE, CHARLES WILLSON.
Am. Chestertown, Md. 1741-1827 Phila., Pa. DAB-B-Bd-C-E-F-T-1-2-4-6-7-30-45-46-138-160-179-182-188-189-231-701-786.
PEALE, JAMES.
Am. Annapolis, Md. 1749-1831 Phila., Pa. DAB-F-T-2-4-6-66-179-182-231-786-839.
PEALE, MARIA.
Am. ac. 1810-1840. F.
PEALE, RAPHAELLE [or Raphael].
Am. Annapolis, Md. 1774-1825 Phila., Pa. DAB-F-T-2-6-66-84-138-179-184.
PEALE, REMBRANDT.
Am. Bucks Co., Pa. 1778-1860 Phila., Pa. B-Bd-C-DAB-E-F-T-2-4-6-15-53-138-182-185-231-786.
PEALE, RUBENS.
Am. ac. 1784-1864 in Phila., Pa. T.
PEALE, SARAH MIRIAM.
Am. Phila., Pa. 1800-1885 Same. DAB-F-T-2-6-15-30.
PEALE, TITIAN RAMSAY.
Am. Phila., Pa. 1800-1885 Same. F.
PEARCE, CHARLES MARESCO.
Eng. b. London 1874; ad. 1934 Chelsea. T-Wa.
PEARCE, CHARLES SPRAGUE.
Am. Boston, Mass. 1851-1914 Paris. A0X1-B-C-DAB-E-F-T-W6-1-15-46.
PEARCE, GLENN STUART.
Am. b. Erie, Pa. 1909; ad. 1934 Same. A.

PEARCE, STEPHEN.
Eng. London 1819-1904 Same. B-DNB-T.
PEARMAN, KATHERINE K.
Mrs. Arthur Pearman.
Am. b. Beloit, Wis. 1893; ad. 1934 Rockford, Ill. A.
PEARS, CHARLES.
Eng. b. London 1873; ad. 1934 Same. T-Wa.
PEARSALL, RICHARD MONTAGUE STACK. (Et)
Ir. b. Dublin 1891; ad. 1934 London. Wa.
PEARSON, EDWIN. (S)
Am. b. Yuma, Colo. 1889; ad. 1934 New York. A.
PEARSON, EGLINGTON MARGARET. (Glass-P)
Eng. ac. 1800-1823 in London. B-DNB.
PEARSON, JAMES. (Glass-P)
Ir. Dublin 1750-1805 London. B-DNB-T.
PEARSON, JOSEPH O.
Am. d. 1917 Little Falls, N. Y.. A014.
PEARSON, JOSEPH THURMAN, JR.
Am. b. Phila., Pa. 1876; ad. 1934 Huntington, Pa. A-F-T-W.
PEARSON, MARGARET STUBER.
Am. b. Phila., Pa.; ad. 1934 Boston. A-F.
PEARSON, RALPH M. (Et)
Am. b. Angus, Ia. 1883; ad. 1934 New York. A28-F-T-W.
PEART, CHARLES. (S)
Eng. ac. 1778-1798 in London. B-DNB-T.
PEASE, JOSEPH IVES. (Eg)
Am. Norfolk, Conn. 1809-1883 Salisbury, Conn. DAB-F-T-2-3-7-40-45-55.
PEASE, LUTE.
Am. b. Winnemucca, Nev. 1869; ad. 1935 Newark, N. J. M.
PEAT, FERN BISEL. (Ill)
Mrs. Frank E. Peat
Am. b. Erie, Pa. 1893; ad. 1934 New York. M.
PEBBLES, FRANCIS MARION.
Am. Weathersfield, N. Y. 1839-1928 Almeda, Calif. A026-T.
PECHSTEIN, MAX HERMANN.
Ger. b. Zwickau 1881. T-498-775.
PECHT, AUGUST FRIEDRICH.
Ger. Constance, Swi. 1814-1903 Munich, Ger. B-C-T.
PECK, ANNE MERRIMAN. (Ill)
Mrs. Frank E. Fite.
Am. ad. 1934 Croton, N. Y. A.
PECK, CHARLES.
Am. 1827-1900. M.
PECK, CLARA ELSENE. (Ill)
Am. ad. 1934 Edgewater, N. J. A.
PECK, GRACE BROWNELL.
Am. Moodus, Conn. 1861-1931 Bristol, Conn. A028.
PECK, HENRY JARVIS.
Am. b. Galesbury, Ill. 1880; ad. 1934 Prov., R. I. A.
PECK, JOSEPH ALANSON.
Am. Augusta, Me. 1874-1933 New York. A-M.
PECK, LAWRENCE F. (Et)
Am. ad. 1935 New York. M.
PECK, ORRIN.
Am. b. N. Y. State 1860-1921 Los Angeles, Calif. A018-B-F-T.
PECKER, ALEC MAURICE. (Et)
Eng. b. 1893; ad. 1934 London. Wa.
PECKHAM, MARY C.
Mrs. F. H. Peckham.
Am. b. Prov., R. I. 1861; ad. 1934 Same. A.
PECKITT, WILLIAM. (Glass-P)
Eng. Carlton 1731-1795 York. B-DNB-T.
PECORI, DOMENICO.
It. 1480-1527 Arezzo. B-T-V.
PECORINI [Comtessa], MARGARET B.
Am. b. Phila., Pa. 1879; ad. 1934 New York. A.
PÉCRUS, CHARLES FRANÇOIS.
Fr. b. Limoges 1826; ad. 1905 Paris. B-T.
PECZARSKI, FELIKS.
Pol. Warsaw 1804-1862. T.
PEDDER, JOHN.
Eng. Liverpool 1850-1929. T-Wa1929-Y01930.
PEDDLE, CAROLINE C.
see Ball, [Mrs.] Caroline Peddle.
PEDERSON, OLE.
Dan. Farnum 1856-1898 Copenhagen. T.
PEDERSEN, VIGGO CHRISTIAN FREDERIK.
Dan. Copenhagen 1854-1926 Roskilde. B-T.
PEDONI [or Pedone], GIOVANNI GASPARE. (S)
It. ac. 1499-1520 in Cremona. T-V.
PEDOUE, ANTONIO.
Argentine. b. 1899 Cordoba, Arg. M.
PEDRINI, GIANPETRINO [Ricci].
It. ac. 1520-1540 in Milan. B-T.
PEDRO DE CÓRDOBA.
see Córdoba, Pedro de.
PEDROSO, PASTOR ARGUDIN Y.
Cuban. ex. 1935 New York. M.
PEDULLI, FEDERIGO.
It. b. 1860; ac. 1932 Florence. B-T.
PEE [or Peene or Penen], JAN VAN.
Flem. Amsterdam 1640/50-1710 Antwerp. B-T.
PEE, THEODOR VAN.
Dut. Amsterdam 1688-1746 The Hague. B-T.
PEEBLES, ROY B.
Am. b. Adams, Mass. 1899; ad. 1934 Same. A.
PEEL, JAMES.
Eng. Newcastle 1811-1906 Reading. B-DNB-T.
PEEL, PAUL.
Can. London, Can. 1861-1892 Paris. B-DNB-T-893.
PEELE, JOHN THOMAS.
Br.-Am. Peterbourgh, Eng. 1822-1897 London. C-F-T-15.
PEERDT, ERNEST CARL FRIEDRICH.
Ger. Tecklenburg 1852-1932 Düsseldorf. B-T.
PEETERS [or Pietersz], BONAVENTURA [The Elder].
Flem. Antwerp 1614-1652 Hoboken, Belg. B-C-T-722.
PEETERS, GILLIS [The Elder].
Flem. Antwerp 1612-1653 Same. T.
PEETERS [or Pieters], JAN [The Elder].
Flem. Antwerp 1624-1680 Same. B-C-T.
PEETERS [or Pieters], JAN III.
Flem. Antwerp 1667-1727 England. B-DNB-T.

PEETS, ORVILLE HOUGHTON.
Am. b. Cleveland, O. 1884; ad. 1934 Woodstock, N. Y. A-T.
PEGRAM, A. BETRAM. (S)
Eng. ac. 20th Cent. B-M.
PEGRAM, FRED. (Ill)
Eng. b. London 1870. B-T.
PEGRAM, HENRY ALFRED. (S)
Eng. b. London 1862; ad. 1934 Same. B-Hs-Wa-T.
PEIFFER-WATENPHUL, MAX.
see Watenphul, M. P.
PEIRCE. *see also* Pierce.
PEIRCE, ALZIRA.
Am. b. New York 1908; ad. 1934 Bangor, Me. A.
PEIRCE, D. S.
Am. ac. 1860. M.
PEIRCE, H. WINTHROP.
Am. b. Boston 1850; ad. 1934 West Newbury, Mass. A-F-T.
PEIRCE, [Mrs.] SYLVIA MARGARET STIASTNY.
Am. b. Lincoln, Neb. 1906; ad. 1934 Same. A.
PEIRCE, THOMAS MITCHELL.
Am. b. Grand Rapids, Mich. 1864. F-T-W15.
PEIRCE, WALDO.
Am. b. Bangor, Me. 1884; ad. 1934 Same. A-F.
PEIRSEN, H.
Am. ac. 1865. M.
PEIXOTTO, ERNEST CLIFFORD. (Ill)
Am. b. San Fran., Calif. 1869; ad. 1934 New York. A-B-F-T-W-46.
PEIXOTTO, GEORGE.
b. Cleveland, O.; ad. 1934 Crestwood, N. Y. A-F-T.
PEIXOTTO, MARY H.
Mrs. Ernest Clifford Peixotto.
Am. b. San Fran., Calif.; ad. 1934 New York. A-F.
PEKÁRY, ISTVÁN.
Hun. b. Budapest 1905; ex. 1933 New York. T.
PEKENINO, MICHELE. (Eg)
Am. ac. 1820. A-2-7-147.
PELACANE. *see* Morone, Domenico.
PELEZ, FERNAND EMMANUEL.
Fr. Paris 1843-1913 Same. B-T.
PELHAM, HENRY.
Am. Boston, Mass. 1749-1806 Ireland. B-DAB-DNB-F-T-2-6-7.
PELHAM, JAMES [The Elder]. (Min)
Eng. London 1800-1874 Liverpool. B-Bd-T.
PELHAM, JAMES [The Younger].
Eng. Essex 1840-1906 Liverpool. B-Bd-T.
PELHAM, PETER. (Eg)
[First Artist resident in New England.]
Am. London 1684-1751 Boston, Mass. B-DAB-DNB-F-T-1-2-7-182-499.
PELIKAN, ALFRED GEORGE.
Am. b. Breslau, Silesia 1893; ad. 1934 Milwaukee, Wis. A.
PELL, ELLA FERRIS.
Am. b. St. Louis, Mo. 1846; ad. 1935 Beacon, N. Y. A12-F-T.
PELL, YACK.
Am. b. Russia 1899; ad. 1935 New York. M.
PELLAR, HANS.
Ger. b. Vienna, Aus. 1886. T.
PELLEGRINI, ALFRED HEINRICH.
Swi. b. Basel 1881. B-T.
PELLEGRINI, CARLO. (Cari)
It. Capua 1838-1889 London. B-DNB-T.
PELLEGRINI, DOMENICO.
It. Bassano 1759-1840 Rome. B-T.
PELLEGRINI, ERNEST G. (S)
Am. b. Verona, It. 1889; ad. 1934 Boston, Mass. A.
PELLEGRINI, GIOVANNI ANTONIO.
It. Venice 1675-1741 Same. B-T.
PELLEGRINO. *see also* Pellegrini.
PELLEGRINO DI MARIANO, ROSSINI.
It. ac. 1449-1492 in Milan. B-T-V.
PELLEGRINO, MODÈNE DE.
It. 1465-1523. T-722.
PELLEW, JOHN C.
Am. b. Penzance, Cornwall, Eng. 1903; ad. 1934 Astoria, L. I., N. Y. M.
PELLICCIAIO, GIACOMO DI MINO DEL.
It. ac. 1362-1398 in Siena. B-T.
PELLIGRINO DA SAN DANIELE.
[Real name Martino da Udine.]
It. Udine? 1460/70-1547. T-V.
PELLIPARIO, NICOLÒ.
It. ac. 1525-1542 in Urbino. T.
PELOSO, FRATINO N.
Am. ad. 1934 Bronx, N. Y. M.
PÉLOUSE, LÉON GERMAIN.
Fr. 1838-1891 Pierrelaye, Seine-et-Oise. B-C-T.
PELTIER [or Pelletier], PIERRE JACQUES.
Fr. b. Clermont-Ferrand 1867; ad. 1934 Paris. B-DBA.
PELTON, AGNES.
Am. b. Stuttgart, Ger. 1881; ad. 1934 Cathedral City, Calif. A-F-T.
PELTON, OLIVER. (Eg)
Am. Portland, Conn. 1799-1882 East Hartford, Conn. F-T-2-7-40.
PEMBROOKE, THEODORE KENYON.
Am. b. Elizabeth, N. J.; d. 1917 New York. A014.
PENA, NARCISO VIRGILIO.
see Diaz De La Pena.
PEÑAFLOR, DOMINGO.
Sp. ac. 1329-1335 in Spain. M.
PENAGINI, SIRO.
It. ad. 1934 Lesa, It. M.
PENCZ [or Penz], GEORGE. (Eg)
Ger. Nüremberg 1500?-1550 Breslau, Silesia. B-C-T.
PENDLETON, WILLIAM LARNED MARCY.
Am. b. Paris 1865; ad. 1934 Bethel, Conn. A.
PENE, GUY. *see* Du Bois.
PENFIELD, EDWARD. (Ill)
Am. Brooklyn, N. Y. 1866-1925 Beacon, N. Y. A022-DAB-F-T-W13-55.
PENFOLD, FRANK C.
Am. b. Buffalo, N. Y. 1849; ad. 1915 Same. A12-B-F-46.
PENIĆ, DUJAM. (S)
Fr. b. Split 1890. T.
PÉNICAUD, JEAN I.
Fr. ac. 1520-1530 in Limoges. B-T.
PÉNICAUD, JEAN II.
Fr. ac. 1534-1549 in Limoges. B-T.

PÉNICAUD, Jean III.
Fr. ac. 16th Cent. in Limoges. B-T.
PÉNICAUD, Lèonard [or Nardon]
Fr. Limoges 1470?-1542/3. B-T.
PÉNICAUD, Pierre.
Fr. Limoges 1515?-1590. B-T.
PENLEY, Aaron Edwin.
Eng. 1807-1870 Lewisham. B-DNB-T.
PENMAN, Edith.
Am. London 1860-1929 New York. A026-F.
PENN, William Charles.
Eng. b. London 1877; ad. 1934 Birkhead. T-Wa.
PENNACCHI, Gerolamo da Treviso.
It. Treviso 1497-1544 Bologna. B-T.
PENNACCHI, Pietro Maria.
It. Treviso 1464-1528 Same. B-C-T.
PENNE, Charles Olivier de.
Fr. Paris 1831-1897 Marlotte. B-T.
PENNELL, Joseph. (Et)
Am. Phila., Pa. 1860-1926 Brooklyn, N. Y. A023-B-DAB-E-F-T-W13-17-46-63-186-500-779-830-880.
PENNEY, Frederick D.
Am. ad. 1934 Los Angeles, Calif. M.
PENNY, James J.
Am. ex. 1935 New York. M.
PENNI, Gianfrancesco. [Il. Fattore.]
It. Florence 1488?-1528 Naples. B-C-E-T-V-722.
PENNI, Luca [Romano].
It. Florence 1500-1556 Paris. B-C-T.
PENNI, Robert M.
Am. b. Scotland; d. Albany, N. Y. M.
PENNIMAN, Helen.
Am. b. New York 1882; ac. 1926 Balt., Md. A22-F-T.
PENNIMAN, Leonora Naylor.
Am. b. Minn., Minn. 1884; ad. 1934 Santa Cruz, Calif. A.
PENNING, Tomas. (S)
Am. ex. 1934 Woodstock, N. Y. M.
PENNINGTON, Harper.
Am. Newport, R. I. 1854-1920 Balt., Md. A017-F-T.
PENNOYER, Albert Sheldon.
Am. b. Oakland, Calif. 1888; ad. 1934 New York. A-F-T-W.
PENNY, Edward.
Eng. Knutsford 1714-1791 London. B-DNB-T.
PENOT, Albert Joseph.
Fr. ac. 1910 in Paris. B-T.
PENROSE, James Doyle.
Eng. Michelstrom 1864-1932 London. T-Y01933.
PENT, Rose M.
Mrs. Howard Franklin Pent.
Am. b. St. Louis, Mo.; ad. 1934 Jenkintown, Pa. A.
PENTLARGE, Georgiana.
Am. ad. 1934 Montclair, N. J. M.
PENZ, Ludwig. (S)
Ger. Weiler 1876-1918 Schwaz. T.
PENZYNA, Gustave.
Pol. b. Poland 1882. DBA.
PEOLI, Juan Jorge.
Sp. ac. 1847 in Madrid. T.

PEPERS, Pierre [or Pieter]. (S)
Flem. Bruges 1730/1-1785 Same. B-T.
PEPLOE, Fitzgerald Cornwall.
Am. England 1861-1906 Purchase, N. Y. A06.
PEPLOE, S. J.
Scot. b. Edinburgh 1871; ad. 1934 Same. T-Wa-825.
PEPPER, Charles Hovey.
Am. b. Waterville, Me. 1864; ad. 1934 Brookline, Mass. A-F-T-W.
PEPPER, George Douglas.
Can. b. Ottawa, Ont. 1903; ad. 1935 Toronto, Ont. M.
PEPPERCORN, Arthur Douglas.
Eng. London 1847-1926. B-T.
PEPYN [or Pepin], Marten.
Flem. Antwerp 1575-1642/3 Same. B-C-T-722.
PÉQUIN, Charles Étienne.
Fr. b. Nantes 1879. B-DBA-T.
PÉRAC, Étienne du. *see* Duperac, E.
PERAN, Marjorie.
Am. ex. 1935 Santa Cruz, Calif. M.
PERANDA, Santo.
It. Venice 1566-1638 Same. T.
PÉRARD, Victor Semon. (Et)
Am. b. Paris 1870; ad. 1934 New York. A28-F-T-W.
PÉRAUX, Lionel.
Fr. b. Nantes 1871. DBA-T.
PERBOYRE, Paul Emile Léon.
Fr. b. Colmar; ac. 1881-1914 in Paris. B-T.
PERCY, Arthur C.
Swe. b. Oland 1886. T.
PERCY, Isabelle Clark. (Ill)
Mrs. George Parsons West.
Am. b. Alameda, Calif. 1882; ad. 1934 Sausalito, Calif. A-T.
PERCY, Samuel. (Wax-P)
Ir. b. Dublin; d. 1820 in London. T.
PERCY, Sidney Richard Williams.
Welsh. Wales 1821?-1886 Sutton, Eng. B-Bd-DNB-T.
PERDRIAT, Hélène Marie Marguerite.
Fr. b. La Rochelle 1894. DBA.
PEREDA [or Perea], Antonio.
Sp. Valladolid 1608/11-1678 Madrid. B-C-T.
PEREDA, Raimando. (S)
Swi. Lugano 1840-1915 Same. B-T.
PEREIRA, [Miss] I. Rice.
Am. b. Boston 1905; ad. 1934 New York. A.
PEREIRA, Manuel. (S)
Por. Porto 1574-1667 Madrid, Sp. T.
PEREIRA [or Perea], Vasco.
Por. Evora 1535-1609 Sèville, Sp. T.
PERELLE [or Perrelle], Gabriel.
Fr. Vernon 1602/3-1677 Paris. B-T.
PERELLE, Nicolas.
Fr. Paris 1631-1695 Orléans. B-T.
PERELLI, Achille. (S)
Fr. d. 1889. B-T.
PERELMA, Ossip [or Joseph].
Rus.-Am. b. Shabelsk, Rus. 1876; came to U. S. 1917. M.
PEREPLETCHIKOFF, V. V.
Rus. b. 1863; ad. 1930 Moscow. B-T.

PERERA, Gino. (S)
Am. b. Siena, It. 1872; ad. 1934 Boston, Mass. A.
PERESINOTTI, Antonio.
It. Bologna 1708-1778 Leningrad, Rus. T.
PERET, Marcelle.
Am. ad. 1934 New Orleans, La. M.
PERETTI, Achille.
Am. b. Italy; d. 1923 Chicago. A020-T-183.
PERETTI, Bernard.
It. ac. 1665 in Italy. T.
PÉREZ, Alonzo.
Sp. b. 1858. B-T.
PÉREZ, Alonzo de Hebrera.
Sp. ac. 1660/72 in Sèville. B-T.
PÉREZ, Andres.
Sp. Sèville 1660-1727. B-T.
PÉREZ, Bartolomé.
Sp. Madrid 1634-1693. B-T.
PÉREZ, Gonzalo.
Sp. ac. 1405-1423 in Sèville and Valencia. B-T.
PÉREZ, Ignacio. (Pen-Work)
Sp. ac. 1599 in Madrid. M.
PÉREZ DE ALLECIO, Matteo Pietro.
Sp. Rome, It. 1547-1600 Same. B-T.
PÉREZ DE BURGOS, Pedro.
Sp. ac. 1332 in Spain. M.
PÉREZ DE VILLAMAYOR, Júan.
Sp. ac. 1847-1883. T.
PÉREZ-BOSCH, Lila.
Argentine. b. Buenos Aires; ad. 1934 Paris. DBA.
PÉREZ-RUBIO, Antonio.
Sp. Madrid 1822-1888 Same. B-T.
PÉREZ-RUBIO, Timoteo.
Sp. ad. 1934 Madrid. M.
PERFILIEFF, Vladimir.
Am. b. Russia 1895; ad. 1934 Phila., Pa. A.
PERGER, Sigmund Ferdinand Ritter van.
Ger. Vienna, Aus. 1778-1841 Same. B-T.
PERI, Lászlo [or Ladislaus]. (S)
Hun. b. Budapest 1889; ex. 1933 London. M-T.
PERICOLI, Niccolò. *see* Tribolo, Il.
PERIGAL, Arthur [The Elder].
Scot. 1784?-1847 Edinburgh. B-DNB-T.
PERIGAL, Arthur [The Younger].
Scot. 1816-1884 Edinburgh. B-DNB-T.
PÉRIGNON, Alexis Joseph.
Fr. Paris 1806-1882 Same. B-T.
PÉRIGNON, Alexis Nicolas [The Elder].
Fr. Nancy 1725/6-1782 Paris. B-T.
PÉRIGNON, Alexis Nicolas [The Younger].
Fr. Paris 1785-1864 St. Denis. B-T.
PÉRIN, Henri Alphonse.
Fr. Paris 1798-1874 Same. B-T.
PÉRIN-SALLREUX, Lié Louis.
Fr. Reims 1753-1817 Same. B-T.
PERINE, George Edward. (Eg)
Am. So. Orange, N. J. 1837-1885 Brooklyn, N. Y. F-T-7.
PERINO DEL VAGA. *see* Buonaccorti, P.
PERKARY, Stephen.
Hun. b. Budapest 1905; ex. 1935 Brooklyn, N. Y. M.
PERKINS, Charles Callahan.
Am. Boston, Mass. 1823-1886. B-Bd-E-F-T-15.
PERKINS, Christopher.
Eng. b. Peterbourgh 1891; ad. 1934 St. Aubin. Wa.
PERKINS, Edna.
Am. ad. 1935 New York. M.
PERKINS, Harley.
Am. ad. 1934 Boston, Mass. A.
PERKINS, John Ure.
Am. b. Wash., D. C. 1875; ad. 1915 Same. A12-F-T.
PERKINS, Lucy Fitch. (Ill)
Mrs. Dwight H. Perkins.
Am. b. Maples, Ind. 1865; ad. 1934 Evanston, Ind. A28-W.
PERKINS, Mary Smyth.
see Taylor, M. S. P.
PERKINS, Philip.
Am. ad. 1935 Nashville, Tenn. M.
PERKS, Paul.
Ger. b. Görlitz 1879. T.
PEARL, Margaret Anneke.
Am. b. Duluth, Minn. 1887; ad. 1934 Monterey Park, Calif. A.
PERLMUTTER, Izsak.
Hun. Budapest 1866-1932 Same. B-T.
PERLMUTTER, Paul.
Am. ad. 1934 Toledo, O. M.
PERMAN, Louise E. [Mrs. Torrance].
Scot. d. 1921 in Paris. T-Y01922.
PERMEKE, Constant.
Belg. b. Antwerp 1886. T.
PERNET, Jean Henry Alexandre.
Fr. ac. 1763-1779 in Paris. B-T.
PERNOT, François Alexandre.
Fr. Vassy 1793-1865 Same. B-T.
PEROFF [or Perow], Vassili Grigorwitsch.
Rus. Tobolsk 1833-1882 Moscow. B-T.
PEROMSER, Balthasar. (S)
Ger. Kammer 1651-1732 Dresden. B-Hs-M-T.
PERONI, Giuseppe.
It. Parma 1700-1776 Same. B-T.
PEROT, Annie Lovering.
Am. b. Phila., Pa. 1854. F-T.
PEROUX, Joseph Nicolaus.
Ger. Ludwigsburg 1771-1849 Frankfort. B-T.
PERPER, Marc.
Am. ex. 1934 New York. M.
PERRACHE, Michel. (S)
Fr. Lyons 1686-1750 Same. B-T.
PERRAUD, Jean Joseph. (S)
Fr. Monay 1819-1876 Paris. B-Hs-T.
PERRAULT, Claude.
Fr. Paris 1613-1688 Same. T.
PERRAULT, Henri Paul.
Fr. Versailles 1867-1932. DBA-T.
PERRAULT, Léon Jean Basile.
Fr. Poictiers 1832-1908 Royan. B-C-T.
PERRE, Henri.
Can. Alsace. Fr. 1828-1890 Montreal, Can. M.
PERRE, Nicolas van der.
Flem. ac. 1569-1595 in Antwerp. B-T.

PERRÉAL, JEHAN [Jean de Paris].
see Master of Moulins.
PERRET, AIMÉ.
Fr. Lyons 1847-1927 Paris. B-T.
PERRET [or Peret], PEDRO [or Petrus]. (Eg)
Flem. Antwerp 1555-1639 Madrid, Sp. B-T.
PERRETT, A. LOUISE.
Am. b. Chicago; ad. 1934 Oak Hill, Ill. A.
PERRETT, GALEN JOSEPH.
Am. b. Chicago 1875; ad. 1934 Rockport, Mass. A-T.
PERREY, JULIEN AUGUSTE.
Fr. b. Champigny 1871. DBA.
PERREY, LÉON AUGUSTE. (S)
Fr. Paris 1841-1900 Same. B-T.
PERREY, LOUIS JUSTIN MAURICE.
Fr. b. Gray 1856. B-T.
PERRICHON, JULES LÉON. (Eg)
Fr. b. Paris 1866. DBA-T.
PERRIE, BERTHA EVERSFIELD.
Am. Wash., D. C. 1868-1921 Gloucester, Mass. A018-T.
PERRIER, ALEXANDRE.
Swi. b. in Geneva 1862. B-T.
PERRIER, FRANÇOIS BOURGUIGNON.
Fr. Mâcon 1590-1650 Paris. B-C-T-722.
PERRIGARD, HAL ROSS.
Can. b. Montreal; ad. 1935 Same. M.
PERRIN, ÉMILE CÉSAR VICTOR.
Fr. Rouen 1810/4-1884 Paris. B-T.
PERRIN, FLYEN. *see* Flyen-Perrin.
PERRIN, JACQUES. (S)
Fr. Lyons 1847-1915 Paris. B-T.
PERRIN, JEAN CHARLES NICAISE.
Fr. Paris 1754-1831 Same. B-T.
PERRIN, OLIVIER STANISLAS.
Fr. 1761-1832 Quimper. B-T.
PERRINE, VAN DEARING.
Am. b. Garnet, Kan. 1869; ad. 1934 Maplewood, N. J. A-F-T-W-1.
PERRING, CORNELIA S.
Am. Bloomington, Ind. 1840-1923 Louisville, Ky. M.
PERRISSIN, JEAN [or Jacques].
Fr. Lyons 1536/8-1611/18 Same. B-T.
PERRONEAU, JEAN BAPTISTE.
Fr. Paris 1715-1783 Amsterdam, Holland. B-Bd-T-756.
PERROT, ADOLPHE ANTOINE.
Fr. Nimes 1818-1887 Same. B-T.
PERRY, ALFRED.
Eng. ac. 1847-1881 in London. B-T.
PERRY, CLARA FAIRFIELD.
Mrs. Walter Scott Perry.
Am. b. Brooklyn, N. Y.; ad. 1934 Same. A-T.
PERRY, CLARA GREENLEAD.
Am. b. Long Branch, N. J. 1871; ad. 1934 Wash., D. C. A.
PERRY, EDITH DEAN WEIR. (Min)
Mrs. James De Wolf Perry.
Am. b. New Haven, Conn. 1875; ad. 1934 Prov., R. I. A-T.
PERRY, EMILIE S. (S)
Am. New Ipswich, N. H. 1873-1929 Ann Arbor, Mich. A027-T.
PERRY, ENOCH WOOD.
Am. Boston 1831-1915 New York. A013-C-DAB-F-T-W8-15-144-183.
PERRY, FRANCIS. (Eg)
Eng. d. 1765 in London. B-DNB-T.
PERRY, JAMES RAYMOND.
Am. b. Northfield, Mass. 1863; ad. 1934 Chicago. A.
PERRY, JOHN D.
Am. b. Swanton, Vt. 1845. F-T-15.
PERRY, LILLA CABOT.
Mrs. Thomas S. Perry.
Am. b. Boston; d. 1933 in Hancock, N. H. A030-F-T-W14.
PERRY, MAEBLE CLAIRE. (S)
Am. b. Idaho 1902; ad. 1934 Evanston, Ill. A.
PERRY, OSWALD. (S)
Am. ac. 1925 in Cinn., O. F-Ta.
PERRY, RAYMOND K.
Am. b. Sterling, Ill. 1886; ad. 1934 New York. A.
PERRY, RAYMOND W.
Am. b. Natick, Mass. 1883; ad. 1934 Prov., R. I. A.
PERRY, ROLAND HINTON. (S)
Am. b. New York 1870; ad. 1934 Same. A-F-T-Ta-W-Obit. Art News, 9-15-1934.
PERRY, WALTER SCOTT.
Am. Stoneham, Mass. 1856-1934. A28-M-T.
PERSEUS.
Gr. ac. 300 B.C. B-T.
PERSÉUS, EDWARD.
Swe. Lund 1841-1890 Stockholm. B-T.
PERSEVAL, MICHEL NICOLAS.
Fr. Chamery 1745-1837 Reims. B-T.
PERSHING, LOUISE. (Mu)
Am. ad. 1934 Dormont, Pa. M.
PERSIAN ARTISTS. *see* books 780-808; *also consult* Amer. Inst. for Persian Art, New York.
PERSICO, LUIGI. (S)
It. Naples 1791-1860 Marseilles, Fr. T.
PERSON, NICKOLAUS. (Eg)
Ger. ac. 1680-1710 in Mainz. B-T.
PERSONS, GERALDINE.
Am. ad. 1934 Worcester, Mass. M.
PERSYN, REGNIER [Narcisse].
Dut. Alkmaar 1615-1668 Gouda. B-T.
PÉRU, JEAN BAPTISTE II. (S)
Fr. Avignon 1707-1790. B-T.
PERUGIA, BARTOLOMEO CAPORALI.
It. ac. 1472-1499 [Umbrian]. M.
PERUGINI, CHARLES EDWARD.
Eng. Naples, It. 1839-1919 London. B-T.
PERUGINI, KATE [née Dickens].
Eng. London 1839-1929 Same. T-Y01930.
PERUGINO, PIETRO DI CHRISTOFORO VANNUCCI.
It. Castello 1446-1523 Fontignano. B-Bd-C-E-T-V-501-502-722.
PERUVIAN ARTISTS. *see* book no. 698.
PERUZZI, BALDASSARE DA SIENA.
It. Siena 1481-1536 Rome. B-C-E-T-V-722.
PERUZZI, GIOVANNI.
It. Pesaro 1629-1694 Milan. B-T.
PERUZZINI, DOMENICO.
It. ac. 1640-1661 in Pesaro. B-T.
PERVUSHA.
Rus. ac. 17th century in Russia. M.

PESARESE, IL.
see Cantarini, Simon de Pesaro.
PESCHECK, CARL JUSTUS LUDWIG.
Ger. Zittau 1803-1847 Dresden. B-T.
PESCHEL, KARL GOTTLIEB.
Ger. Dresden 1798-1879 Same. B-C-T.
PESELLINO, FRANCESCO DI STEFANO.
It. Florence 1422?-1457 Same. T-V-722.
PESELLO, GUILIANO.
It. 1367-1446 Florence. T-V
PESKE, GÉZA.
Hun. Kelecsény 1859; ac. 1930 in Budapest. B-T.
PESNE, ANTOINE.
Fr. Paris 1683-1757 Berlin. B-C-T.
PESTINIEN [or Pestivien], JEHAN DE.
Fr. Paris 1380-1463 Dijon. B-T.
PESZKA, JOSEPH.
Pol. Cracow 1767-1831 Same. B-T.
PETEL [or Betle], GEORG.
Ger. Augsburg 1590-1633/4. T.
PETER, EMANUEL THOMAS. (Min)
Ger. Jägerndorf 1799-1873 Vienna, Aus. B-T.
PETER, ROBERT CHARLES. (Et)
Eng. b. London 1888. Wa.
PETER, VICTOR. (S)
Fr. Paris 1840-1918 Same. B-T.
PETER, WENCESLAUS [or Wenzel].
Aus. Carlsbad 1742/5-1829 Rome, It. B-T.
PETER, HISPANUS ["Peter of Spain"].
Sp. ac. 13th century in Spain. M.
PETERS. *see also* Peeters.
PETERS, ANNA.
Ger. Mannheim 1843-1926 Sonnenberg. B-T.
PETERS, ANTO DE [or Johann].
Ger. Cologne 1723-1795 Same. B-T.
PETERS, CARL WILLIAM.
Am. b. Rochester, N. Y. 1897; ad. 1934 Fairport, N. Y. A.
PETERS, CHARLES ROLLO.
Am. b. San Fran., Calif. 1862. A20-F-T-W14.
PETERS, CHRISTIAN CARL. (S)
Dan. Dalover 1822-1899 Espergärde. B-T.
PETERS, CURTIS ARNOUX, JR. *see* Arno, Peter.
PETERS, DEWITT CLINTON.
Am. b. Balt., Md. 1865; ad. 1934 New York. A-B-T.
PETERS, JEAN ANTOINE DE.
Fr. b. 1740; d. 1787 in St. Luc. B.
PETERS, JULIA V.
Am. ad. 1934 Toledo, O. M.
PETERS, [Rev.] MATTHEW WILLIAM.
Ir. Dublin 1742-1814 Kent, Eng. B-DNB-T.
PETERS, PIETER FRANCIS.
Dut. Nymwegen 1818-1903 Stuttgart, Ger. T.
PETERS, WILLIAM OTTO.
Nor. b. Christiania 1851. B-T.
PETERSEN, ANNA SOFIE.
Dan. Copenhagen 1845-1910 Same. T.
PETERSEN, AXEL. (S)
Nor. ac. in Goteberg. 798.
PETERSEN, CHRISTIAN. (S)
Am. b. Denmark 1855; ad. 1934 Belvidere, Ill. A.
PETERSEN, EDVARD FREDERIK.
Nor. Copenhagen, Denmark 1841-1911 Same. T.
PETERSEN, EUGEN H.
Am. b. Bluefields, Nicaragua 1894; ac. 1934 Manhasset, N. Y. A.
PETERSEN, HANS RITTEN VON.
Ger. Husum 1850-1914 Munich. B-T.
PETERSEN, HEINRICH LUDWIG.
Ger. Altona 1806-1874 Nürnberg. B-T.
PETERSEN, HJALMAR ELIF EMANUEL.
Nor. Christiania 1852-1928 Lysaker. B-T.
PETERSEN, JOHAN ERIK CHRISTIAN.
Am. Copenhagen, Denmark 1839-1874 Boston, Mass. B-F-T.
PETERSEN, MARTIN.
Am. b. Denmark 1870; ad. 1934 New York. A.
PETERSHAM, MAUD. (Ill)
Am. ad. 1934 Woodstock, N. Y. M.
PETERSHAM, MISKA. (Ill)
Am. ad. 1934 Woodstock, N. Y. M.
PETERSHAM [or Petrezselyem], MIHÁLY. (Ill)
Am. b. Hungary 1888; ad. 1934 New York. T.
PETERSON, ELNA.
Am. ad. 1935 So. Minn , Minn. M.
PETERSON, ELSA KIRPAL. (S)
Mrs. R. M. Tower Peterson.
Am. b. New York 1891; ad. 1934 Flushing, L. I., N. Y. A.
PETERSON, JANE.
Mrs. M. Bernard Philipp.
Am. b. Elgin, Ill.; ad. 1934 New York. A-F-T-W.
PETERSON, MARGARET. (Ill)
Am. ad. 1935 Berkeley, Calif. M.
PETERSON, OSWALD.
Eng. ex. 1935 London. M.
PETERZANO [or Preterzono], SIMONE.
It. ac. 1573-1595 in Milan. B-T.
PETHER, ABRAHAM ["Old Pether"].
Eng. Chichester 1756-1812 Southampton. B-DNB-T.
PETHER, SEBASTIAN.
Eng. 1790-1844 Battersea. B-DNB-T.
PETHER, WILLIAM. (Eg)
Eng. Carlisle 1731-1795 London. B-Bd-DNB-T.
PETHERICK, HORACE WILLIAM.
Eng. b. 1839; d. 1919 London. T-Y01920.
PETICOLAS. *see also* Petticolas.
PETICOLAS, SHERRY. (S)
Am. b. Waterloo, Ia. 1904; ad. 1934 Los Angeles, Calif. M.
PETIT, ALEXANDER [or Le Petit].
Dut. ac. 1676 at the Hague. B-T.
PETIT, EUGÈNE.
Fr. Paris 1839-1886 Same. B-T.
PETIT, JEAN CLAUDE. (S)
Fr. Besançon 1819-1903 Paris. B-T.
PETIT, JEAN LOUIS.
Fr. Paris 1795-1876 Same. B-T.
PETIT, LÉONIE JUSTIN ALEXANDRE.
Fr. Taden 1839-1884 Paris. B-T.
PETITI, FILIBERTO.
It. Turin 1845-1924 Rome. B-T.
PETITJEAN, EDMOND MARIE.
Fr. Neufchâteau 1844-1925. B-T.

PETITOT, ENNEMOND ALEXANDRE.
Fr. Lyons 1727-1801 Parma, It. B-T.
PETITOT, JEAN. (Enamel)
Fr.-Swi. Geneva, Swi. 1607/8-1691 Vevey, Fr. B-Bd-E-T.
PETITOT, JEAN LOUIS. (Enamel)
Fr. Paris 1652/3-1730 London. B-E-T.
PETITOT, LOUIS MESSIDOR LEBON. (S)
Fr. Paris 1794-1862 Same. B-T.
PETITOT, PIERRE. (S)
Fr. Langres 1751/60-1840 Paris. B-T.
PÉTRE, CHARLES. (S)
Fr. Metz 1828-1907 Bourges. B-T.
PETREZSELYEM [Pseudonym].
see Petersham, Michály.
PETRI, PIETRO ANTONIO DA.
It. Premia 1663/71-1716 Rome. B.
PETRIE, GRAHAM.
Eng. b. London 1859; ad. 1934 Same. Wa.
PETRINA, CARLOTTA. (Ill)
Am. b. Kingston, N. Y. 1901; ad. 1934 Roslyn, L. I., N. Y. A.
PETRINA, JOHN. (Ill)
Am. b. Venice, It. 1893; d. 1935 Evanston, Wyo. A-Obit. N. Y. papers, 6-16-1935.
PETRINI [or Pietrini], GIUSEPPE ANTONIO.
It. Carona 1677-1758 Same. B-T.
PETROV-VODKIN, KUZMA.
Rus. b. Ssartov 1878. T.
PETROVIC, MILAN V.
Am. b. Pancevo, Serbia 1893; ad. 1934 Cinn., O. A.
PETROVITS, MILAN.
Am. b. Vienna, Aus. 1892; ad. 1934 Verona, Pa. A.
PETRUCCIOLI DA OVIETO, COLA DI.
It. ac. 1372-1385 in Italy. T.
PETRY, VICTOR. (Ill)
Am. b. Phila., Pa. 1903; ad. 1934 Douglaston, L. I., N. Y. A.
PETTENKOFEN. AUGUST XAVER CARL RITTER VAN.
Aus. Vienna 1822-1889 Same. B-E-T.
PETTER, ANTON.
Aus. Vienna 1781-1858 Same. B-T.
PETTER, FRANZ XAVER [The Elder].
Aus. Vienna 1791-1866 Same. B-T.
PETTICOLAS, EDWARD F.
Am. ac. 1805-1834 in Richmond, Va. F-T-2-4-6.
PETTICOLAS, PHILIP A. (Min)
Am. Italy 1760-1843 Richmond, Va. F-T-2-6-786.
PETTIE, JOHN.
Scot. Edinburgh 1839-1893 Hastings, Eng. B-Bd-C-DNB-E-T.
PETTINGILL, LILLIAN ANNIN.
Mrs. C. K. Pettingill.
Am. b. Le Roy, N. Y. 1871; ad. 1934 La Crosse, Wis. A.
PETTITT, EDWIN ARNOLD.
Eng. Birmingham 1840-1912 London. B-T-Y01913.
PETTITT, GEORGE W.
Eng. d. 1910. T.
PETTRICH, FERDINAND FRIEDRICH AUGUST. (S)
Ger. Dresden 1798-1872 Rome, It. T.
PETTY, GEORGE. (Cart.)
Am. ad. 1934 Chicago. M.
PETTY, JESSIE W.
Am. b. Navasota, Tex.; ad. 1934 San Antonio, Tex. A.
PETTY, ROBERT.
Eng. London 1740-1789 Holland. B-Bd-T.
PÉTUA LÉON JUAN.
Fr. Besançon 1846-1921 Zurich, Swi. B-T.
PETZHOLDT, ERNEST CHRISTIAN FREDERIK.
Dan. Copenhagen 1805-1838 Patras, Gr. B-T.
PETZL, JOSEPH.
Bav. Munich, Ger. 1803-1871 Same. B-T.
PEUGNIEZ, PAULINE.
Fr. ac. 1931. M.
PEVSNER, ANTOINE.
Fr. b. Orel, Rus. 1882; ad. 1935 Paris. DBA.
PEW, GERTRUDE L. (Min)
Mrs. Frederic G. Robinson.
Am. b. Niles, O. 1876; ad. 1934 New York. A-F.
PEW, SUSAN MARGARET.
Am. ex. 1933 New York. M.
PEYER [or Beyer], JAKOB.
Swi. Graz, Aus. 1728-1803 Same. B-T.
PEYNOT, ÉMILE EDMOND. (S)
Fr. b. Villeneuve 1850; ad. 1896 Paris. B-DBA-T.
PEYRAUD, ELIZABETH K.
Mrs. Frank C. Peyraud.
Am. b. Carbondale, Ill.; ad. 1934 Highland Park, Ill. A.
PEYRAUD, FRANK CHARLES.
Am. b. Bulle, Swi. 1858; ad. 1934 Highland Park, Ill. A-F-T-W-757.
PEYRE, RAPHAEL CHARLES. (S)
Fr. b. Paris 1872. B-DBA-T.
PEYROL, FRANÇOIS AUGUSTE HIPPOLYTE. (S)
Fr. Paris 1856-1929 Neuilly. B-DBA-T.
PEYROL-BONHEUR, JULIETTE.
see Bonheur, Juliette.
PEYRON, JEAN FRANÇOIS PIERRE.
Fr. Aix 1744-1814 Paris. B-C-T-722.
PEYSON, PIERRE FRÉDÉRIC.
Fr. Montpelier 1807-1877 Same. B-T.
PEYTON, ALFRED CONWAY.
Am. b. Dera Doon, Br. India 1875; ad. 1934 Gloucester, Mass. A.
PEYTON, [Mrs.] ALFRED CONWAY.
see Menzler-Peyton, Bertha.
PEZ, AIMÉ.
Belg. Tournai 1808-1849. B-T.
PEZANT, AYMAR [or Aimard Alexandre].
Fr. b. Bayeux 1846; ad. 1914 Paris. B-T.
PEZOUS, JEAN.
Fr. Toulon 1815-1885 Paris. B-T.
PEZZATI, PETER.
Am. b. Boston, Mass. 1902; ad. 1934 Same. A.
PFANNSCHMIDT, CARL GOTTFRIED.
Ger. b. 1819; d. 1887 Berlin. B-T.
PFANNSCHMIDT, ERNEST CHRISTIAN.
Ger. b. Berlin 1868. B-T.
PFANSTILL, JOHAN LUDWIG.
Aus. b. Vienna; d. 1665 Frankfort, Ger. B-T.
PFAU [or Pfauw], ABRAHAM.
Swi. Winterthur 1637-1691 Same. B-T.

PFEIFER, HERMAN.
Am. b. Milwaukee, Wis. 1879; ad. 1934 New York. A.
PFEIFFER, FRANÇOIS JOSEPH.
Fr. Aix 1741-1807 Brussels, Belg. B-T.
PFEIFFER, FRITZ.
Am. b. Adams Co. Pa., 1889; ad. 1934 Provincetown, Mass. A.
PFEIFFER, HEINRICH.
Am. b. Hanover, Pa. 1874; ad. 1934 Provincetown, Mass. A-F.
PFEIFFER, HOMER.
Am. ad. 1935 Hadlyme, Conn. M.
PFENNING, MASTER.
Ger. ac. 1449 in Germany. B-T.
PFENNINGER, ELIZABETH.
Swi. Zurich 1772-1837 Paris. B-T.
PFENNINGER, HEINRICH.
Swi. Zurich 1749-1851. B-T.
PFERDEKRÜGER, FRANZ. *see* Krüger, Franz.
PFISTER, ANTOINE.
Swi. Lucerne 1720-1790 Freiburg, Ger. B-T.
PFISTER, JEAN JACQUES.
Am. b. Switzerland 1878; ad. 1934 Winter Park, Fla. A.
PFLANMER, PAUL GOTTLIEB, 2ND.
Am. b. Phila., Pa. 1907; ad. 1934 Same. A.
PFLÜG, JOHANN BAPTIST.
Ger. Biberaeh 1785-1865 Same. B-T.
PFLÜGER, LOUIS.
Swi. Lausanne 1847-1893 Same. B-T.
PFORR, FRANZ.
Ger. Frankfort 1788-1812 Albano, It. B-T.
PFORR, JOHANN GEORG.
Ger. Ulfen 1745-1798 Frankfort. B-T.
PFRÜNDT [or Pfründ], GEORG.
Ger. Flachslanden 1603-1663 Durlach. B-T.
PFYFFER, NICKLAUS.
Swi. Lucerne 1836-1908 Same. B-T.
PHEIDIAS [or Phidias]. (S)
[Greatest of Greek sculptors.]
Gr. Athens 496/88 B.C.-432/1 B.C. Same. B-E-Hs-T-710-792-817.
PHELAN, HAROLD LEE.
Am. b. New York 1881; ad. 1934 Same. F-T.
PHELIPS, [Mrs.] EMILY BANCROFT.
Am. b. England 1869; ad. 1934 Kimmswick, Mo. A.
PHELPS, EDITH CATLIN.
Mrs. Stowe Phelps.
Am. b. New York 1879; ad. 1934 Santa Barbara, Calif. A-F-T.
PHELPS, HELEN WATSON.
Am. b. Attleboro, Mass. 1859; ad. 1934 New York. A-F-T-W.
PHELPS, WILLIAM PRESTON.
Am. b. New Hampshire; ac. 1880 in New York. C-F-T-15.
PHIDIAS. *see* Pheidias.
PHILBRICK, ALLEN E. (Mu)
Am. b. Utica, N. Y. 1879; ad. 1934 Chicago. A-T.
PHILBRICK, OTIS.
Am. b. Mattapan, Mass. 1888; ad. 1934 Winchester, Mass. A-F-T.
PHILIP, FREDERICK WILLIAM.
Am. Brooklyn, N. Y. 1814-1841 Same. T.
PHILIP, JOHN BIRINE. (S)
Eng. London 1824-1875 Same. DNB-E-T.
PHILIPON, CHARLES. (Cari)
Fr. Lyons 1800-1862 Paris. B-T.
PHILIPP, ROBERT.
Am. b. New York 1895; ad. 1935 Same. A-M.
PHILIPPE, MAITRE [Master].
Flem. ac. 1520-1527 in Brussels. B-T.
PHILIPPOTEAUX, FÉLIX EMMANUEL HENRI.
Fr. Paris 1815-1884 Same. B-C-T.
PHILIPPOTEAUX, PAUL DOMMIQUE.
Fr. b. Paris 1846; ac. 1889 Same. B-T.
PHILIPS, J.
Eng. ac. 1838 in London. T.
PHILISKOS.
Gr. ac. 2nd Cent. B.C. in Rhodes, Gr. T.
PHILLIBROWNE, THOMAS.
Eng. b. London; ac. 1834-1860. F-7.
PHILLIMORE, LUCY H.
Am. ad. 1934 London. M.
PHILLIP, JOHN.
Scot. Aberdeen 1817-1867 London. C-DNB-T.
PHILLIPS, BERT GEER.
Am. b. Hudson, N. Y. 1868; ad. 1934 Taos, N. M. A-T-W.
PHILLIPS, CHARLES.
Eng. 1708-1747. B-DNB-T.
PHILLIPS, CHARLES. (Eg)
Eng. b. 1737; ad. 1766/83 in London. DNB-T.
PHILLIPS, CLAIRE DOONER.
Am. b. Los Angeles, Calif. 1887; ad. 1934 Prescott, Ariz. A.
PHILLIPS, CLARENCE COLES. (Ill)
Am. Springfield, O. 1880-1927 New Rochelle, N. Y. A024.
PHILLIPS, C. DOROTHEA.
Am. ad. 1934 Paterson, N. J. M.
PHILLIPS, GILES FIRMAN.
Eng. b. 1780; d. 1867 London. DNB-T.
PHILLIPS, HARRIET SOPHIA.
Am. Delta, N. Y. 1849-1928 New York. A025.
PHILLIPS, HENRY WYNDHAM.
Br. 1820-1868. DNB-T.
PHILLIPS, HOLMEAD.
Am. b. Shippensburg, Pa. 1889; ad. 1934 New York. A-F.
PHILLIPS, J. CAMPBELL.
Am. b. New York 1873; ad. 1934 Same. A-F-T-W.
PHILLIPS, J. S.
Br. ac. 1821/42. T.
PHILLIPS, JOSEPHINE NEALL. (Min)
Am. ad. 1934 So. Orange, N. J. M.
PHILLIPS, MARJORIE.
Mrs. Duncan Phillips.
Am. b. Bourbon, Ind. 1895; ad. 1934 Wash., D. C. A-T.
PHILLIPS, MARTHA.
Mrs. J. Campbell Phillips.
Am. b. Stockholm, Swe.; ad. 1934 New York. M.
PHILLIPS, NATHANIEL GEORGE.
Eng. Manchester 1795-1831 Liverpool. B-DNB-T.

PHILLIPS, Thomas.
Eng. Dudley 1770-1845 London. B-Bd-DNB-E-T-722.
PHILLIPS, Walter Joseph. (Eg)
Am. b. Barton, Eng. 1884; ad. 1935 Winnipeg, Can. A28-T.
PHILLIPS, Willer Elmer.
Am. b. Bogard, Mo. 1907; ad. 1934 Brooklyn, N. Y. A.
PHILLIPS, Winifred E.
Am. ad. 1934 Milwaukee, Wis. A.
PHILOXENOS.
Gr. ac. 3rd century B.C. B-T.
PHILPOT, Glyn Warren.
Eng. b. London 1884; ad. 1934 Same. B-T-Wa-825.
PHIROSMANASCHVILLE, Niko.
Rus. East Georgia, Rus. 1859-1918. M.
PHIZ. *see* Browne, Halbot Knight.
PHOCAS, Suzanne.
Fr. ad. 1934 Montrouge, Fr. M.
PHOENIX, Frank.
Am. d. Glendale, Calif. 1924. A022.
PHOENIX, Lauros Monroe. (Mu)
Am. b. Chicago 1885; ad. 1934 New York. A.
PIAGGIO, Teramo.
It. Zoagli 1480-1572 Genoa. B-T.
PIAZZA, Albertino da Lodi [Toccagni].
It. Lodi 1450?-1529. B-T.
PIAZZA, Calisto da Lodi.
It. Lodi 1500-1561. B-T.
PIAZZA, Paolo [Cosimo].
It. Castelfranco 1577-1663 Venice. B-T.
PIAZZETTA, Giacomo.
It. Treviso 1640-1705 Venice. T.
PIAZZETTA, Giovanni Battista.
It. Pietrarossa 1682-1754 Venice. B-C-T-722.
PIAZZONI, Gottardo F. P.
Am. b. Intragna, Swi. 1872; ad. 1934 San Fran., Calif. A-W.
PIBWORTH, Charles James. (S)
Eng. b. Bristol 1878; ad. 1929 Chelsea. T-Wa1929.
PICABIA, Francis.
Cuban. b. Paris 1878; ex. 1934 New York. B-T-797.
PICARD, Edmond.
Fr. Besnaçon 1861-1889 Jura. B-T.
PICARD, Hughes.
Fr. Isère 1841-1900 Paris. B-T.
PICARD [or Picart], Jean [Le Roux]. (S)
Fr. ac. 1536-1594 in Fontainebleau. T-V.
PICARD, Louis.
Fr. b. Paris 1861. B-DBA-T.
PICARD, [Miss] Maxime. (Ill)
Am. ad. 1934 Staten Island, N. Y. M.
PICARDO, Júan.
Sp. ac. 1507-1558 in Vallalodid. B-T.
PICART [or Picard], Bernard.
Fr. Paris 1673-1733 Amsterdam, Holland. B-T.
PICART, Charles.
Eng. London 1780-1837. B-T.
PICART LE DOUX, Charles Alexandre. (Ill)
Fr. b. 1881 in Paris. DBA-T.
PICART, Étienne [or Stephanus le Romain].
Fr. Paris 1631/2-1721 Amsterdam, Holland. B-T.
PICASSO, Matteo.
It. b. 1800; d. 1866 in Genoa? B-T.
PICASSO, Pablo Ruiz [or Ruys].
Sp. b. Malaga 1881; ad. 1935 Paris. d MOUGINS, FRANCE 4/9/73
B-DBA-E-T-503-504-700-783-797-827-847-867-904.
PICAUD, Charles Louis. (S)
Fr. b. Lyons; d. 1919 Roanne. B-T.
PICAULT, Emile Louis. (S)
Fr. ac. 1863-1909 in Paris. B-T.
PICAULT, Pierre. (Eg)
Fr. Blois 1680-1711 Paris. B-T.
PICCARD, Louis Rodolphe. (Min)
Swi. Payerne 1807-1888 Lausanne. B-T.
PICCHI, Giorgio.
It. 1550-1599 Rome. B-T.
PICCINELLI, Andrea da [Brescianino].
It. Siena 1485?-1525 Florence. T-V.
PICCINELLI, Raffelo dei Bresciannie.
It. ac. 1507-1545 in Florence. B-T-V.
PICCINI, Gaetano. (Eg)
It. Venice 1617-1669. B-T.
PICCININO, Lucio.
It. ac. 1550-1589 in Milan. T.
PICCIRILLI, Attilio. (S)
Am. b. Massa, It. 1866; ad. 1934 New York. A-Cs-F-T-W-46.
PICCIRILLI, Bruno. (S)
Am. b. New York 1903; ad. 1935 Same. Cs.
PICCIRILLI, Furio. (S)
Am. b. Massa, It. 1868; ad. 1934 New York. A-Cs-F-W.
PICCIRILLI, Giuseppe. (S)
Am. Rome, It. 1843-1910 New York. A08-T.
PICCIRILLI, Horace. (S)
Am. b. Massa, It. 1872; ad. 1934 New York. A-Cs.
PICCOLI, Girolamo. (S)
Am. b. Palermo, Sicily 1902; ad. 1934 New York. A.
PICCOLPASSO, Capriano. (Potter)
It. Castel Durante 1524-1579 Same. T.
PICCONE, Angelo.
It. ad. 1346 in Savona. T.
PICELLER, Bernardin.
It. Reschong 1775-1853 Perugia. T.
PICHAT, Olivier.
Fr. Paris 1857-1912 Same. B-T.
PICHIO [or Picq], Ernest Louis.
Fr. Paris 1840-1893 Same. B-T.
PICHLER, Johann Anton.
It. Naples 1734-1791 Rome. B-T.
PICHLER, Johann Peter.
Ger. Bozen 1775-1806/7 Vienna, Aus. B-T.
PICHLER, Joseph van.
Ger. Kötschach 1730-1808 Vienna, Aus. T.
PICHON, Pierre Auguste.
Fr. Sorèze 1805-1900 Paris. B-T.
PICHOT, Gironés Ramón Antonio.
Sp. Barcelona 1872-1925 Paris. T.
PICKARD, Louise.
Eng. Hull 1865-1928. T-Wa01929.
PICKEN, Andrew. (Et)
Eng. b. 1815; d. 1845 London. DNB-T.

PICKEN, GEORGE ALEXANDER. (Et)
Am. b. New York 1898; ad. 1934 Hawthorne, N. Y. d. 1971 PITTSFIELD, MASS. A.
PICKENOY, NICOLAES ELIASZ.
see Picquenoy, N. E.
PICKERING, GEORGE.
Eng. Yorkshire 1794-1857 Chester. B-DNB-T.
PICKERING, HENRY.
Eng. ac. 1767-1790 in Liverpool. B-T.
PICKERING, J. L.
Eng. Wakefield 1845-1912 London. B-T.
PICKERING, SIMEON HORACE.
Am. b. Salt Lake City, Utah 1894; ad. 1934 New York. A.
PICKERSGILL, FREDERICK RICHARDS.
Eng. London 1820-1900 Isle of Wight. B-Bd-DNB-T.
PICKERSGILL, HENRY HALL.
Eng. London 1812-1861 Same. B-Bd-DNB-T.
PICKERSGILL, HENRY WILLIAM.
Eng. London 1782-1875 Same. B-Bd-C-DNB-T.
PICKETT, JOSEPH.
Am. New Hope, Pa. 1848-1918. M.
PICKHARDT, CARL E., JR.
Am. ad. 1935 West Newton, Mass. M.
PICKNELL, GEORGE W.
Am. b. Springfield, Vt. 1864; ad. 1934 Norwalk, Conn. A.
PICKNELL, WILLIAM LAMB.
Am. Windham, Vt. 1854-1897 Marblehead, Mass. B-Bd-C-DAB-E-F-T-15-46.
PICOT, FRANÇOIS EDOUARD.
Fr. Paris 1786-1868 Same. B-T.
PICOT, VICTOR MARIE. (Eg)
Fr. Abbeville 1744-1802 Amiens. B-T.
PICOU, HENRI PIERRE.
Fr. Nantes 1824-1895 Same. B-T.
PICOU [or Picquot], ROBERT.
Fr. Tours 1593-1671 Paris. B-T.
PICQ, ERNEST LOUIS. *see* Pichio, E. L.
PICQUÉ, CHARLES [or Karel].
Flem. Deynse 1799-1869 Brussels. B-T.
PICQUENOY, NICOLAES ELIASZ.
Dut. b. 1590/1-1653/6 Amsterdam. B-T.
PICQUOT, THOMAS.
Fr. ac. 1636 in Paris. B-T.
PIDDING, HENRY JAMES.
Eng. Cornwall 1797-1864 Greenwich. B-DNB-T.
PIDGEON, HENRY CLARK.
Eng. b. 1807; d. 1880 London. B-DNB-T.
PIDOLL DE QUINTENBACH, KARL VON.
Ger. Vienna, Aus. 1847-1901 Rome, It. B-T.
PIECHOWSKI, WOJCIECH ADALBERT.
Rus. Nosarzew 1849-1911 Kutno. B-T.
PIECK, ANTON.
Dut. b. Holland 1895. T.
PIEN, CHING-CHAO [or Luan].
Chinese. T'Ang Dynasty (618-906). T.
PIEN, WEI CH'I.
Chinese. ac. 1729-1750 in Kiangsu. E-T.
PIEN, WÈN YÜ.
Chinese. 1600-1672 China. T.
PIENEMAN, JAN WILLEM.
Dut. Abcoude 1779-1853 Amsterdam. B-C-T.
PIENEMAN, NIKOLAAS.
Dut. Amersfoort 1810-1860 Amsterdam. B-C-T.
PIÉNKOWSKI, IGNACY.
Pol. b. Dolobawa 1877. T.
PIÉPAPE, CHARLES JEAN BAPTISTE DE.
Fr. Besançon 1810-1867 Paris. B-T.
PIER, FRANCESCO FIORENTINO.
see Fiorentino, F.
PIER, FRANCESCO DA PARIA. *see* Sacchi di Pari.
PIERCE. *see also* Peirce.
PIERCE, ANNA HARRIET.
Am. b. So. Britain, Conn. 1880; ad. 1934 New Haven, Conn. A-T.
PIERCE, CHARLES FRANKLIN.
Am. Sharon, N. H. 1844-1920 Brookline, Mass. A017-F-T.
PIERCE, EDWARD [The Elder].
Eng. ac. 1640-1658 in London. B-T.
PIERCE, EDWARD [The Younger].
Eng. d. 1695 in Oxford. B-DNB-T.
PIERCE, ERNEST.
Eng. ex. 1934 in London. M.
PIERCE, GLENN M. (Ill)
Am. ad. 1934 Brooklyn, N. Y. A.
PIERCE, HENRY H., JR. (Et)
Am. b. New York 1908; ad. 1935 Same. M.
PIERCE, MARTHA.
Am. b. New Cumberland, W. Va. 1873; ad. 1934 Wayne, Neb. A.
PIERCE, WILLIAM H. C.
Am. b. Hamilton Co., N. Y.; ad. 1934 San Diego, Calif. A.
PIERDON, FRANÇOIS.
Fr. St. Gerard 1821-1904 Paris. B-T.
PIERI, ANTONIO DE [Toppo].
It. ac. 1738 in Venice. B-T.
PIERI, STEFANO [Rossi].
It. Florence 1542-1629 Same. B-T.
PIERINI, ANDREA.
It. Florence 1798-1858 Same. B-T.
PIERNEEF, J. H. (Mu)
Br. ac. 1934 South Africa. M.
PIERO DI COSIMO [or Lorenzo].
It. Florence 1462-1521? Same. B-E-T-V-722.
PIERO DELLA FRANCESCA.
see Francesca, P.
PIERO DI GIOVANNI TEDESCO.
see Tedesco, P. di G.
PIERO DI NICCOLÒ. *see* Niccolò, P. di.
PIERRE [Called le Verrier].
Fr. ac. 1499 in Troyes. B-T.
PIERRE, CLAUDE [or Klaudius]. (Min)
Ger. Mainz 1803-1854 Vienna, Aus. T.
PIERRE, DIEUDONNÉ.
Fr. Nancy 1807-1838 Same. B-T.
PIERRE, GUSTAV RENÉ.
Fr. b. Verdun 1875; ac. Paris. B-DBA-T.
PIERRE, JEAN BAPTISTE MARIE.
Fr. Paris 1713-1789 Same. B-C-T.
PIERREY, LOUIS MAURICE.
Fr. Alger 1854-1912 Paris. B-T.
PIERSEN, ALDEN.
Am. Balt., Md. 1874-1921 New York. A018.
PIERSON, CHRISTOFFEL.
Dut. The Hague 1631-1714 Gouda. B-T.
PIERSON, [Mrs.] ELIZABETH G.
Am. ad. 1934 New York. M.

PIETERS, Evart [or Toert].
Dut. Amsterdam 1856-1932. B-T.
PIETERSZ. *see also* Peeters.
PIETERSZ [or Pieterszen], Aert.
Dut. Amsterdam 1550-1612 Same. B-T.
PIETERSZ, Bertus.
Am. b. Amsterdam, Holland 1869; ad. 1934 Springfield, Mass. A.
PIETERSZ, Roelof.
Dut. ac. 1517 in Utrecht. T.
PIETRASANTA, Cecchino Francesco da.
It. ac. 1587 in Rome. T.
PIETRO BARATTA. *see* Baratta, P.
PIETRO, Cagnaccio di S.
It. b. Desenzano 1899; ad. 1932 Rome. M.
PIETRO, Cartaino di Sciarrino. (S)
Am. Palermo, Sicily 1886-1918 Pelham, N. Y. A016.
PIETRO DA CORTONA, Berrettini.
see Berretini, P. da C.
PIETRO DA CORTONA, da Urbano.
see Cortona, U. da.
PIETRO DI COSIMO. *see* Piero di C.
PIETRO DI DOMENICO DA MONTPULCIANO.
It. 1457-1506. T.
PIETRO DI DOMENICO DI PIETRO.
It. Siena 1457-1501 Same. T.
PIETRO, Giovanni di. *see* Spagna, Lo.
PIETRO DI GIOVANNI DI AMBROGIO.
It. ac. 1428-1438 in Siena. T.
PIETRO DI GIOVANNI TEDESCO.
see Tedesco.
PIETRO DI MEDICI.
It. Florence 1567-1648. T.
PIETRO DI NICCOLÒ [Gerini].
see Nicolò di P.
PIETRO DI NICCOLÒ D'AREZZO.
see Lamberti, P. di N.
PIETRO DA PETRI.
It. 1674-1716. M.
PIETRO POLO MASSEGNE.
see Massegne, P. P.
PIETRO DA RIMINI.
It. ac. 1328. T.
PIETRO DE SALIBA [or Risaliba].
It. ac. 1500 in Genoa. T.
PIETRO SANO [or Ansano] DI MENICO.
It. Siena 1406-1481. B-78.
PIETRO DI SENNO.
It. 1845-1904. M.
PIETSCHMANN, Ernest Max.
Ger. b. Dresden 1865. B-T.
PIETTE, Ludovic [Monfoucault].
Fr. Niort 1826-1877 Paris. DBA-T.
PIETZ, Adam. (Med)
Am. b. Offenbach, Ger. 1873; ad. 1934 Phila., Pa. A-F-T.
PIFFARD, Jeanne. (S)
Fr. ad. 1934 Paris. DBA.
PIGAL, Edmé Jean.
Fr. Paris 1798-1872 Sens. B-T.
PIGALLE, Jean Baptiste. (S)
Fr. Paris 1714-1785 Same. B-E-Hs-T.
PIGGOT, Robert. (Eg)
Am. New York 1795-1887 Sykesville, Md. T-2-7-40.
PIGLHEIN, Elimar Ulrich Bruno.
Ger. Hamburg 1848-1894 Munich. B-T.
PIGUENIT, Charles.
[First Australian born Artist.]
Aust. ac. 1880 in Sidney, N.S.W. M.
PIKOV. (Eg)
Rus. ex. 1935 London. M.
PILACORTE, Giovanni Antonio.
It. Lugano 1484-1531 Friaul. T.
PILHS, Hans.
Aus. ex. 1935 Vienna, Aus. M.
PILICHOWSKI, Léopold.
Pol. Zadzim 1869-1933 London. B-T.
PILKINGTON, C. A.
Eng. ac. 1819 in Boston, Mass. M.
PILKINGTON, Flora.
Eng. ad. 1934 London. Wa.
PILKINGTON, G. W.
Br. ac. 1934 South Africa. M.
PILLARS, Charles Adrian. (S)
Am. b. Rantoul, Ill. 1870; ad. 1934 Sarasota, Fla. A-F-T-W.
PILLATI Family.
Pol. ac. 19th century in Poland. T.
PILLE, Charles Henri.
Fr. Essonnes 1844-1897 Paris. B-C-T.
PILLEMERT, Jean Baptiste.
Fr. Lyons 1727-1808 Same. B-DNB-T.
PILO, Karl Gustav.
Swe. Rutuna 1712-1792 Stockholm. B-T-683.
PILON [or Pillon], Germain. (S)
Fr. Paris 1535-1590 Same. B-Hs-T-603.
PILOT, Robert W.
Can. b. St. Johns, N. F.; ad. 1935 Montreal. M.
PILOTELLE, Georges Labadie. (Et)
Fr. Portiers 1844-1918 London. B-T.
PILOTY, Ferdinand [The Elder].
Ger. Hamburg 1786-1844 Munich. B-C-T.
PILOTY, Ferdinand [The Younger].
Ger. Munich 1828-1895 Same. T.
PILOTY, Karl Theodor von.
Ger. Munich 1826-1886 Ambach. B-C-E-T.
PILS, Isidore Alexandre Augustin.
Fr. Paris 1813/5-1875 Douarnenez. B-C-T.
PILSBURY, Wilmot.
Eng. Dorking 1840-1908 London. B-T.
PILTZ, Otto.
Ger. Allstedt 1846-1910 Munich. B-T.
PILZ, Joseph.
Ger. Raitz 1712-1796 Olmütz. T.
PIM, William Paul. (Cart)
Am. b. Freeport, Pa. 1885; ad. 1934 Birmingham, Ala. W.
PIMENOV, Iuri Iwanowitsch.
Rus. b. Moscow 1903; ad. 1934 Same. T.
PIMENOV, Nikolai Stepanowitsch. (S)
Rus. 1812-1864 Leningrad. B-T.
PIMENOV, Stephen Stepanowitsch. (S)
Rus. 1784-1833 Leningrad. T.
PIMONENKO, Nikolai Korniliewitsch.
Rus. Kiev 1862-1912 Same. T.
PINA, Alfredo. (S)
It. b. Milan 1883; ad. 1934 Paris. T.
PINAZO-MARTINEZ, José. *see* Martinez, J. P.
PINCELLOTTI, Bartolomeo.
It. ac. 1730-1740 in Rome. T.
PINCHART, Émile Auguste.
Fr. b. Cambrai 1842; ad. 1930 Paris. B-T.
PINCHON, S. R.
Fr. ex. 1934 Paris. M.

PINCK, Ferdynand.
Pol. 1761-1797. T.
PINCK [or Bink or Pink], Franciszek.
Pol. Vienna, Aus. 1733/4-1798 Warsaw. T.
PINE, John. (Eg)
Eng. London 1690-1756 Same. DNB-T.
PINE, Robert Edge.
Br.-Am. London 1730-1788 Phila., Pa. B-Bd-DAB-DNB-E-T-2-4-6-45-179-182-786.
PINE, Theodore E.
Am. d. 1905 in Ogdensburg, Pa. A05.
PINEANT [or Pinault], Nicolas. (S)
Fr. Paris 1684-1754 Same. B-T.
PINEAU [or Pineaut], Jean Baptiste. (S)
Fr. Paris 1652/4-1699 Same. B-T.
PINELLI, Bartolommeo. (S)
It. Rome 1781-1835 Same. B-T.
PINELLI, Jean Paul Innocent de.
Swi. b. Geneva 1823; ad. 1878 Paris. B-T.
PINGO, John. (Med)
Eng. ac. 1768-1786 in London. DNB.
PINGO, Lewis. (Med)
Eng. Italy 1743-1830 London. DNB-T.
PINGO, Thomas. (Med)
Eng. Italy 1692-1776 England. DNB-T.
PINGRET, Edouard Henri Théophile.
Fr. St. Quentin 1788-1875 Same. B-T.
PINHAS, Juda [or Leo]. (Min)
Ger. Ansbach 1727-1793 Same. T.
PINHAS, Saloman [or Leo]. (Min)
Ger. Bayreuth 1759-1837 Cassel. T.
PINHEY, John C.
Can. Canada 1860-1912. M.
PINCHON, S. R.
Fr. ex. 1934 in Paris. M.
PINI, Giuseppe.
It. b. Parma 1696. T.
PINI [or Pino], Paolo.
It. ac. 1534-1565 in Venice. T.
PINKAS, Soběslau.
Aus. Prague, Czec. 1827-1901 Same. T.
PINKER, Henry Richard Hope.
see Hope-Pinker, H. R.
PINNAZIO, Jan Simonsz. *see* Pynas, J. S.
PINNER, Erma.
Ger. b. Frankfort 1893. T.
PINNER, Philip.
Am. b. San Fran., Calif. 1910; ad. 1934 Same. A.
PINO, José Moya del.
Am. b. Spain 1891; ad. 1934 San Fran., Calif. M.
PINO, Marco dal.
It. Siena 1525-1587/8 Naples. T.
PINTA, Amable Louis.
Fr. Evry 1820-1888 Andelys. B-T.
PINTNER, Dora.
Am. b. Hooley Hill, Eng.; ad. 1934 Cambridge, Mass. A.
PINTO, Angelo.
Am. ad. 1934 Phila., Pa. M.
PINTO, Biagio.
Am. ad. 1934 Phila., Pa. M.
PINTO, Salavatore.
Am. ad. 1934 Phila., Pa. M.
PINTURICCHIL [Bernardino di Biogio].
It. Perugia 1454-1513 Siena. B-Bd-C-E-T-V-505-722.

PINWELL, George John. (Ill)
Eng. Wycombe 1842-1875 London. B-Bd-DNB-E-T-803-880.
PIÒ, Angelo Gabriello.
It. Bologna 1690-1770. T.
PIOLA, Domenico [The Elder].
It. Genoa 1628-1703. B-C-T.
PIOLA, Paolo Gerolamo.
It. Genoa 1666-1724. T.
PIOLA, Pellegro.
It. Genoa 1617-1640. T.
PIOMBO, Sebastiano. *see* Sebastiano del P.
PIOT, Antoine.
Fr. ac. 1870 in Paris. B.
PIOT, Étienne Adolphe.
Fr. b. Dijon; ad. 1850-1910 in Paris. B-T.
PIOT, René.
Fr. Paris 1869-1934. DBA-T.
PIOTROWSKI, Antoni.
Pol. Kunów 1853-1924 Warsaw. T.
PIOTROWSKI, Maksymiljan Antoni.
Pol. Bromberg, Ger. 1813-1875 Königsberg, Ger. T.
PIPER, Natt.
Am. b. Pueblo, Colo. 1886; ad. 1934 Long Beach, Calif. A.
PIPPEL, Otto Eduard.
Ger. b. Lodz 1878; ac. 1929. T.
PIPPI, Giulio. *see* Guilo, Romano.
PIPPICH, Karl.
Aus. Vienna 1862-1932 Same. B-T.
PIQUER DUART, José III.
Sp. Valencia 1806-1871 Madrid. T.
PIRANDELLO, Fausto.
It. b. Rome 1899; ex. 1935 San Fran., Calif. M.
PIRANESI, Francesco. (Eg)
It. Rome 1758/9-1810 Same. B-T.
PIRANESI, Giovanni Battista. (Eg)
It. Venice 1720-1778 Rome. B-Bd-E-T.
PIRCHAN, Emil [The Elder].
Aus. b. St. Katharein 1844-1928 Vienna. B-T.
PIRIE, George.
Scot. b. Campbeltown 1866; ad. 1934 Torrance. T-Wa.
PIRONI, Girolamo.
It. ac. 1530-1550 in Padua. T.
PIROTA [or Pirotti] Family.
It. ac. 16th Cent. in Faenza. T.
PISA, Giovanna da. (S)
It. ac. 15th Cent. in Padua. Hs-T.
PISANELLO [or Pisano], Antonio.
It. Pisa 1395-1455/6 Rome. B-T-506.
PISANO, Andrea. (S)
It. Pontedera 1270/3-1348/9 Orvieto. B-E-Hs-T-V.
PISANO, Giovanni. (S)
It. Pisa 1250?-1330? Siena. E-Hs-T-V-507.
PISANO, Niccolò. (S)
It. Pisa 1206?-1278/80 Perugia. E-Hs-T-V-508.
PISANO, Niccolò.
It. ac. 1484-1538. B-T-V.
PISANO, Nino. (S)
It. ac. 1349-1368 in Pisa. T-V.
PISANO, Tomaso.
It. ac. 1363-1371 in Pisa. T-V.
PISANO [or Pisanello], Vittore. (Med)
It. Verona 1380-1456 Rome. B-Bd-E-T-V.

PISBOLICA, Jacopo.
It. ac. 1540-1572 in Venice. T-V.
PISENTI Family.
It. ac. 16th Cent. in Cremona. T.
PISIS, Filippo de. (P-Poet)
It. b. Ferrara 1896; ad. 1935 Paris. DBA-T.
PISSARRO [or Pisarro], Camille Jacob.
Fr. St. Thomas, W. Indies 1830/1-1903 Paris. B-DBA-E-T-847.
PISSARRO, Lucien.
Eng. b. Paris 1863; ad. 1934 London. T-Wa.
PISSARRO, [Miss] Orovida Camile.
Eng. b. Epping 1893; ad. 1934 London. T-Wa-847.
PISTON. (S)
Gr. ac. 300 B.C. T.
PISTORIUS, Eduard Karl Gustav.
Ger. Berlin 1796-1862 Carlsbad. C-T.
PISTOXENOS. (Vase Painter.)
Gr. ac. 500 B.C. T.
PISTRUCCI, Benedetto. (Med)
It. Rome 1784-1855 England. DNB-T.
PITATI, Bonifazio de.
see Veronese, B. di P.
PITAU [or Pitault], Nicolas [The Elder].
Flem. Antwerp 1632-1671 Paris. T.
PITCHFORTH, Roland Vivian. (Et)
Eng. b. Wakefield 1895; ad. 1934 Chelsea. Wa.
PITKIN, Caroline W.
Am. b. New York 1858; ad. 1934 Same. A.
PITLOO, Anton Sminck.
Ger. Arnheim 1791-1837 Naples, It. T.
PITMAN, Sophia L.
Am. b. Prov., R. I.; ad. 1934 Same. A.
PITOCCHI, Matteo de.
It. d. 1700 in Florence. T.
PITSCH, Émile Jean.
see Du Marboré, P. E. J.
PITSCHMANN, Joseph Franz.
Aus. Triest 1758-1834 Vienna. T.
PITTARA, Carlo.
It. Turin 1836-1890. T.
PITTERI, Giovanni Marco Alvise. (Eg.)
It. Venice 1702-1786 Same. B-T.
PITTMAN, Hobson. (Eg)
Am. b. Tarboro, N. C. 1898; ad. 1934 Manoa, Pa. A.
PITTONI, Giovanni Battista [The Elder].
It. Venice 1520?-1583? T.
PITTONI, Giovanni Battista [The Younger].
It. Venice 1687-1767 Same. B-T.
PITTS, Fred L.
Am. b. Maryland 1842; ac. 1915 Phila., Pa. A12.
PITTS, Lendall. (Et)
Am. b. Detroit, Mich. 1875. A20-46.
PITTS, William. (S)
Eng. London 1790-1840 Same. B-Hs-T.
PITZ, Henry C. (Ill)
Am. b. Phila., Pa. 1895; ad. 1934 Drexel Hill, Pa. A.
PITZ, Karl Kaspar.
Ger. 1756-1795. T.
PIWARSKI, Jan Feliks.
Pol. b. 1795; d. 1859 in Warsaw. T.
PIXELL, Maria.
Eng. ac. 1793-1805 in London. T.
PIXIS, Theodor.
Ger. 1831-1907. B-C-T.
PIZZELLA, Edmund.
It. b. Naples 1868; ad. 1935 New York. B-T.
PIZZI, Angelo. (S)
It. Milan 1775-1819 Venice. T.
PIZZOLI, Gioacchino.
It. Bologna 1651-1731/3 Same. T.
PIZZOLO, Niccolò.
It. ac. 1421-1453 in Padua. C-T-V.
PLAAS [or Plas], Pieter David van der.
Dut. Amsterdam 1647-1704 Same. B-Bd-T.
PLACE, Francis. (Eg)
Eng. Yorkshire 1647-1728 York. B-Bd-DNB-T.
PLACE, [Mrs.] Vera Clark.
Am. b. Minn., Minn. 1890; ad. 1934 Same. A.
PLACENTINUS. (S)
It. ac. 1228. T.
PLACHT, Richard. (Med)
Ger. b. 1880. T.
PLAES, David van der.
see Plaas, P. D. van der.
PLAGEMANN, Carl Gustaf.
Swe. Sweden 1805-1868 Rome, It. T.
PLAISTED, Zelpha M.
Am. b. Maine; ac. 1915 in Boston, Mass. A12.
PLAISTRIDGE, Philip. (Et)
Am. ad. 1934 Winchester, N. H. A.
PLAMONDON, Ant.
Can. 1804-1895 Montreal. M.
PLANCKH, Victor.
Czec. ex. 1935 New York. M.
PLANELLA Family.
Sp. ac. 18-19th Cent. in Barcelona. T.
PLANES, Luis Antonio.
Sp. Valencia 1742-1821 Same. T.
PLANET, Marie François Xavier Louis.
Fr. Toulouse 1814-1875 Paris. T.
PLANK, Joseph.
Swi. Tyrol 1815-1901 Vienna, Aus. T.
PLANQUETTE, Félix.
Fr. b. Arras 1873; ad. 1934 Paris. B-DBA-T.
PLANTEY, Robert Gilles.
Fr. b. Bordeaux 1881. DBA.
PLANTIN, Christoph.
Flem. Antwerp 1514/20-1559. T.
PLAS. *see* Plaas.
PLASCHKE, Paul Albert. (Cart)
Am. b. Berlin, Ger. 1878; ad. 1934 New Albany, Ind. A-T-W.
PLASENCIA Y MAESTRO, Carl.
Sp. Guadalajara 1846-1890 Madrid. T.
PLASSAU, Antoine Émile.
Fr. Bordeaux 1817-1903 Paris. B-C-T.
PLASSMAN, Ernest. (S)
Am. Sondern, Westphalia, Ger. 1823-1877 New York. F-T-1-15.
PLATH, Karl.
Am. b. Chicago; ad. 1934 Same. A.
PLATNER, Ernest Zacharias.
Ger. Leipzig 1773-1855 Paris. T.
PLATT, Alethea Hill.
Am. b. 1861; d. 1932 White Plains, N. Y. A029-F-T-46.

PLATT, Charles Adams.
Am. New York 1861-1933 Cornish, N. H. A03-B-DAB-F-T.
PLATT, Eleanor.
Am. b. 1910; ad. 1935 New York. M.
PLATT Family.
Eng. ac. 18th-19th Cent. in London. DNB-T.
PLATT, John Edgar.
Eng. b. Leek 1886; ad. 1934 Leicester. T-Wa.
PLATT, John Gerald.
Eng. b. Balton 1892; ad. 1934 Twickenham. Wa.
PLATT, Mary Cheney.
Am. ad. 1934 New York. M.
PLATT, Richard N.
Am. ad. 1934 New Canaan, Conn. M.
PLATTE-MONTAGNE, Matthieux.
Flem. Antwerp 1608-1660 Paris. B-T.
PLATTE-MONTAGNE, Nicolas de.
Fr. Paris 1631-1706 Same. B-T.
PLATTENBERG Family.
Flem. ac. 17th Cent. in Antwerp and Paris. T.
PLATTNER, Albert.
Swi. Innsbruck 1869-1919 Same. T.
PLATTNER, Christian.
Swi. Innsbruck 1869-1921 Same. T.
PLATTNER, Franz.
Swi. Zirl 1823-1887 Innsbruck. T.
PLATTNER, Hans.
Ger. ac. 1531-1562 in Nürnberg. T.
PLATZ, Ernest Heinrich.
Ger. b. Carlsruhe 1867; ac. 1894 Munich. T.
PLATZER, Ignaz Franz [The Elder].
Ger. Pilsen 1717-1787 Prague, Czec. T.
PLATZER, Ignaz Michael [The Younger].
Ger. Prague, Czec. 1757-1826 Same. T.
PLATZER, Johann Nepomuk.
Ger. Prague, Czec. 1745-1780. T.
PLATZER [or Plazier], Johann George.
Aus. Epau 1702/4-1761 St. Michel, Fr. B-C-T.
PLATZER [or Plazer], Joseph.
Aus. Prague, Czec. 1751-1806 Vienna. B-T.
PLAVCAN, Joseph Michael.
Am. b. Braddock, Pa. 1908; ad. 1934 Erie, Pa. A.
PLÉ, Henri Honoré. (S)
Fr. Paris 1853-1922 Same. B-T.
PLEADWELL, Amy Margaret.
Am. b. Taunton, Mass. 1875; ad. 1934 Boston. A.
PLEISSNER, Ogden M.
Am. b. Brooklyn, N. Y. 1905; ad. 1934 Same. A.
PLESSIS, H. E. du.
Fr. ex. 1935 London. M.
PLETSCH, Oskar. (Ill)
Ger. Berlin 1830-1888 Dresden. T.
PLEUER, Hermann.
Ger. b. 1863; d. 1911 Stuttgart. T.
PLEUTHNER, Walter C.
Am. b. Buffalo, N. Y. 1885; ad. 1934 Scarsdale, N. Y. A.
PLEYDENWURFF, Hans.
Ger. ac. 1432-1472 in Nürnberg. T.
PLEYDENWURFF, Wilhelm.
Ger. ac. 1482-1494 in Nürnberg. T.
PLIERSCH [or Plesch], Jan Boguniel.
Pol. Warsaw 1730/2-1817 Same. T.
PLIERSCH, Johann Georg.
Pol. 1704-1774 Warsaw. T.
PLIMER, Andrew. (Min)
Eng. Wellington 1763-1827 Brighton. B-Bd-DNB-E-T.
PLIMER, Nathaniel. (Min)
Eng. Wellington 1751-1822. B-Bd-DNB-E-T.
PLIMSOLL, Fanny Grace.
Eng. b. London. [Dates not known.] M.
PLOCKHORST, Bernhard.
Ger. Brunswick 1825-1907 Berlin. B-C-T.
PLOCKROS-IRMINGER, Ingeburg.
Dan. b. Copenhagen 1872. T.
PLOETZ, Hans Henrik.
Dan. Rellingen 1748-1830 Copenhagen. T.
PLONCZYNSKA, Aleksander.
Pol. Cracow 1820-1858 Same. T.
PLONSKI, Michal.
Pol. Warsaw 1778-1812 Same. T.
PLONTKE, Paul.
Ger. Breslau 1884-1930 Berlin. T.
PLOOS VAN AMSTEL, Jacob Cornelis. (Eg)
Dut. Weesp 1726-1798 Amsterdam. B-T.
PLOTT, John. (Min)
Eng. Winchester 1732-1803 Stoke. B-DNB-T.
PLOWMAN, George Taylor. (Et)
Am. Le Sueur, Minn. 1869-1932 Cambridge, Mass. A029-DAB-F-T-W16-46.
PLUBEL, Georges.
Fr. b. Bar-sur-Aube 1867. DBA.
PLÜDDEMANN, Hermann Freihold.
Ger. Kolberg 1809-1868 Dresden. T.
PLUM, Poul August.
Dan. Copenhagen 1815-1876 Fredensberg. T.
PLUMB, Henry Grant.
Am. Sherburne, N. Y. 1847-1930 New York. A027-B-C-F-T.
PLUMENTHAL [or Blumenthal], Anton.
Ger. ac. 1571-1604. T.
PLUMIER, Edmond [or Théodore Aimond].
Flem. Liège 1694-1733 Same. B-T.
PLUMIER, Pierre Denis.
Flem. Antwerp 1688-1721 London. T.
PLUMMER, Elmer.
Am. ad. 1934 Los Angeles, Calif. M.
PLUMMER, Ethel McClellan.
Mrs. Norman Jacobsen.
Am. b. Brooklyn, N. Y. 1888; ad. 1934 New York. A-F-T.
PLUYM, Karel van der.
Dut. Leyden 1620/5-1672 Same. B-T.
PLUYS, Léopold.
Ger. ac. 1840 in Munich. B-T.
PNEUMAN, Mildred Young.
Mrs. Fred A. Pneuman.
Am. b. Oskaloosa, Ia. 1899; ad. 1934 Gary, Ind. A.
PÒ, Giacomo del.
It. Rome 1652-1726 Naples. B-T.
PÒ, Pietro del.
It. Palermo 1610-1692 Naples. B-T.
POCABELLO, Martin.
Ger. ac. 1607-1630 in Graz, Aus. T.
POCCETTI, Bernardino.
It. Florence 1548-1612 Same. T-722.

POCCI, Franz Graf von. (Eg)
Ger. Munich 1807-1876 Same. T.
POCHITONOFF, Iwan Pawlowitsch.
Rus. Russia 1850-1923 Liège. B-T.
POCHMAN, Traugott Leberecht.
Ger. Dresden 1762-1830 Same. B-T.
POCHWALSKI, Kasimer.
Pol. b. Cracow 1855. B-T.
POCK, Johann Jacob.
Swi. Constance 1604-1651 Vienna, Aus. T.
POCK [or Poch], Johann Giovanni. (Min)
It. Starno 1780-1842 Milan. T.
POCK [or Poch], Tobias.
Swi. Constance 1609-1682 Vienna, Aus. B-T.
POCOCK, Anna [Mrs. Airy].
Eng. b. London 1882; ad. 1934 Playford. Wa.
POCOCK, Geoffrey Buckingham.
Eng. b. London 1879; ad. 1934 Playford. T-Wa.
POCOCK, Henry Childe.
Eng. Sussex 1854-1934 London. T-Wa.
POCOCK, Isaac.
Eng. Bristol 1782-1835 Maidenhead. B-DNB-T.
POCOCK, Julia. (Min)
Eng. ac. 1871-1903 in London. T.
POCOCK [or Poocock], Lewis.
Eng. 1808-1882. DNB.
POCOCK, Lilian Josephine.
Eng. b. London; ad. 1934 Same. Wa.
POCOCK, Nicolas.
Eng. Bristol 1740-1821 Maidenhead. B-DNB-T.
PODESTÀ, Giovanni Andrea.
It. ac. 1650-1674 in Genoa. T.
PODESTÀ, Paul G.
Argentine. b. Buenos Aires, Arg. 1899. DBA.
PODESTI, Francesco.
It. Ancona 1800-1895. T.
PODGÓRSKI, Stanislaw Jan.
Pol. b. Kalusz 1882. T.
PODKOWINSKI, Wladyslaw.
Pol. Warsaw 1866-1895 Same. T.
PODOSKI, Janusz.
Pol. b. Losice 1898. T.
PODOSKI, Wiktor.
Pol. b. Ukraine 1901; ad. 1927 Paris. T.
PODRYSKI, Misha.
Am. ad. 1935 New York. M.
POE, Hugh M.
Am. b. Dallas, Tex. 1902; ad. 1934 Ind., Ind. A-T.
POEDERBUSSE. *see* Pourbus.
POEL, Adriaen Lievensz van der.
Dut. Delft 1626-1685/6 Leyden. B-T.
POEL, Egbert Lievensz van der.
Dut. Delft 1621-1664 Rotterdam. B-C-T-722.
POELENBURG, Cornelis van.
Dut. Utrecht 1586-1667 Same. B-Bd-C-T-722.
POETZELBERGER, Robert.
Aus. Vienna 1856-1930. B-T.
POGANY ["Willy"], William Andrew. (Mu)
Am. b. Hungary 1882; ad. 1935 New York. A-F-T-W.
POGGENBEEK, Georges Jan Hendrick.
Dut. Amsterdam 1853-1903 Same. B-T.
POGGINI, Domenico. (S)
It. Florence 1550-1590 Rome. T.
POGGINI, Gianpaolo. (Med)
It. Florence 1518-1552 Madrid, Sp. T.
POGGIO, del. *see* Giovanni di Paolo.
POGLIAGHI, Lodovic.
It. b. Milan 1857. T.
POHL, Hugo.
Am. b. Detroit, Mich. 1878; ad. 1934 San Antonio, Tex. A.
POHL, J.
Br. b. Cape Colony, So. Africa 1878. M.
POHLE, Friedrich Léon.
Ger. Leipzig 1841-1908 Dresden. B-C-T.
POILLEUX-SAINT ANGE, Georges Louis.
Fr. ac. 1879-1901 in Paris. B-T.
POIDEVIN, Eugéne Modeste Edmond.
see Le Poittevin, E. M. E.
POILLEVÉ Family.
Fr. ac. 16-17th Cent. in France. T.
POILLY, Edouard François.
Fr. Abbeville 1811-1879 Boulogne. T.
POILLY, François de [The Elder].
Fr. Abbeville 1622-1693 Paris. T.
POILLY, François de [The Younger].
Fr. Paris 1671-1741 Same. B-T.
POILLY, Nicolas Jean Baptiste de. (Eg)
Fr. ac. 1758 in paris. [No death date.] B-T.
POINCY, Paul.
Am. New Orleans, La. 1833-1909 Same. F-T-144.
POINT, Armand.
Fr. Algiers 1861-1932 Naples, It. B-DBA-T.
POINTELIN, Auguste Emmanuel.
Fr. Arbois 1839-1933 Paris. B-DBA-T-Obit. Rev. de Art Bull.
POINTER, Auguste L. (S)
Am. b. Durango, Colo. 1898; ad. 1934 New York. A-Cs.
POIRIER, Claude. (S)
Fr. Paris 1656-1729 Varsy. B-T.
POIRSON, Maurice.
Fr. Paris 1850-1882. B-T.
POISSON, Pierre Marie. (S)
Fr. b. Niort 1876; ad. 1934 Paris. DBA-T.
POITEVIN, Auguste.
Fr. La Fère 1819-1873 Paris. B-T.
POITEVIN, Pierre Jean.
Fr. b. Chatellerault 1889. DBA.
POITREAU, Etienne.
Fr. Corbigny 1693-1767 Paris. T.
POKITONOV, Ivan.
Rus. b. Cherson 1851; d. 1924? Brussels, Belg. B.
POKORJENEUSHY, Pietro.
Rus. ac. 1840 in Wologda. T.
POL [or Paul], Christian van.
Dut. Berkeurode 1752-1813 Paris. B-T.
POLA, Hendrik.
Dut. 1676-1748 The Hague. T.
POLACK, Hans Johannes.
see Pollack, Jan.
POLAK, Martin Theophilus.
Pol. ac. 1600-1639 in Trient. T.
POLÁSEK, Albin. (S)
Am. Frenstat, Czec. 1879; ad. 1934 Chicago, Ill. A-Cs-F-Hs-T-W-46.

POLAZZO, Francesco.
It. Venice 1683-1753 Same. T.
POLEJOWSKI, Maciej.
Pol. ac. 1766-1776. T.
POLELONEMA, Otis.
Indian (American). ex. 1932 New York. 411.
POLENOFF [or Poljenowa], Hélène. [or Jélèna.]
Rus. 1850-1898 Moscow. T.
POLENOFF, Wassilj Dmit.
Rus. Leningrad 1844-1927. B-T.
POLIDORE DA CARAVAGGIO.
It. b. 1495; d. 1543 in Mantua. V.
POLIDORO DE RENZI DA LANCIANO.
It. Venice 1515-1565 Same. B-T.
POLITZER, Irving. (Book Jackets)
Am. ad. 1935 New York. M.
POLK, Charles Peale.
Am. Maryland 1767-1822 Phila., Pa. F-T-2-786.
POLK, George.
Am. ac. 19th century. F-T.
POLK, Mary Alys.
Am. b. Greenwood, Ind. 1902; ad. 1934 Ind., Ind. A.
POLKINGHORN, George.
Am. b. Leadville, Colo. 1898; ad. 1934 Los Angeles, Calif. A.
POLL, Hugo.
Hun. Budapest 1867-1931 Same. B-T.
POLLACK [or Polack], Jan.
Ger. b. 1483; d. 1519 in Munich. T.
POLLACK [or Pollak], Max. (Et)
Bohemian. b. Prague, Czec. 1886; ad. 1934 Vienna, Aus. M.
POLLAK, Rita.
Am. ex. 1934 New York. M.
POLLAK, Theresa.
Am. b. Richmond, Va. 1899; ad. 1934 Same. A.
POLLAIUOLLO, Antonio di Jacopo [Benci]. (P-S)
It. Florence 1433-1498 Rome. B-Bd-C-E-Hs-T-V-509-722.
POLLAJUOLO, Piero di Jacopo.
It. Florence 1443-1496 Rome. B-E-T-V.
POLLARD, James.
Eng. London 1797-1859 Same. T-735.
POLLARD [or Pollar or Pollart], Robert. (Eg)
Eng. Newcastle 1775-1838 London. B-DNB-T.
POLLASTRINI, Enrico.
It. Leghorn 1817-1876 Florence. B-T.
POLLEN, John Hungerford.
Eng. London 1820-1902 Same. B-DNB-T.
POLLEPEL. *see* Jordaens, Hans IV.
POLLET, Joseph.
Am. b. 1879; ad. 1934 Saugerties, N. Y. A.
POLLET, Joseph Michel Ange. (S)
Fr. Palermo, It. 1814-1870 Paris. B-T.
POLLET, Victor Florence.
Fr. Paris 1810-1822 Mayenne, It. B-T.
POLLEY, Frederick. (Et)
Am. b. Union City, Ind. 1875; ad. 1934 Ind., Ind. A-E-T.
POLLIA, Joseph P. (S)
Am. b. Italy 1893; ad. 1935 New York. A28-Cs.
POLLACK, Courtenay Edward Maxwell. (S)
Eng. b. Birmingham 1877; ad. 1934 London. T-Wa.
POLLOCK, Charles.
Am. ad. 1935 New York. M.
POLO, Diego.
Sp. Burgos 1560-1600 Madrid. T.
POLOWETSKI, Charles Ezekiel.
Am. b. Russia 1884; ad. 1934 New York. A.
POLTAWSKI, Adam. (Ill)
Pol. b. Warsaw 1881. T.
POLYDOROS [or Polygnotus]. (S)
Gr. [Region]; ac. 484-460 B.C. B-E-Hs-T.
POLYKLEITOS [or Polyclitus] I. (S)
Gr. [Doric]; ac. 450-420 B.C. in Argos. E-Hs-T-817.
POLYKLEITOS [or Polyclitus] II. (S)
Gr. ac. 390-340 B.C. in Argos. T.
POLZONE, Gaetano Scipione. *see* Pulzone.
POMARANCIO, Antonio.
It. ac. 1623-1644. T.
POMARANCIO, Niccolò.
It. Pomarance 1517-1596. T.
POMEDELLI, Giovanni Maria. (Med)
It. Villafranca 1478/9-1537. T.
POMEROY, Elsie Lower.
Am. b. New Castle, Pa. 1882; ad. 1934 Riverside, Calif. A.
POMEROY, Frederick William. (S)
Eng. London 1857-1924 Clintonville. B-Hs-T-Y01925.
POMEROY, [Mrs.] Laura Skeel. (S)
Am. New York 1833-1911 Same. A09.
POMI, Alessandro.
It. b. Venice 1890; ad. 1934 Same. M-T.
POMPADOUR, Jeanne Antoinette.
Fr. Paris 1721-1764 Versailles. B-T.
POMPE [or Pomp], Gerrit.
Dut. ac. 1671-1691 in Rotterdam. B-T.
POMPE, Walthier.
Flem. 1703-1777 Antwerp. T.
POMPEO DI ANSELMO.
It. ac. 1489-1541 in Perugia. T.
POMPON, François. (S)
Fr. Saulieu 1855-1933 Paris. B-DBA-T-510.
PONCE, Jacquio. (S)
It. ac. 1527-1566 in Rome. T.
PONCE, Nicolas. (Eg)
Fr. Paris 1746-1831 Same. T.
PONCE-CAMUS, Marie Nicolas.
Fr. Paris 1778-1839. B-T.
PONCET, François Marie.
Fr. b. Lyons; ac. 1754-1792 in Paris. T.
PONCET, Jean.
Fr. ac. 1429-1452. T.
PONCET, Jean Baptiste.
Fr. St. Laurent 1827-1901 Lyons. T.
PONCET, Marcel.
Dut. 1603-1658 Holland. M.
PONCHIN, Antoine.
Fr. Marseilles 1872-1934 Paris. DBA-T.
PONCHINO, Giovanni Battista.
It. Bozzato 1500-1570. T-V-722.
POND, Arthur. (Eg)
Eng. London 1701/5-1758. B-DNB-T.
POND, Emma McHenry.
Am. b. San Fran., Calif.; ad. 1934 Berkeley, Calif. A.

PONGIALIS, CONSTANTINE.
Am. b. 1894; ad. 1934 Chicago. M.
PONS-ARMAN [or Arnau], FRANCISCO.
Sp. b. Valencia 1886. T.
PONSAN, EDOUARD BERNARD DEBAT.
see Debat-Ponson, E. B.
PONSART, JEAN NICOLAS. (Eg)
Fr. Malmedy 1788-1870 Same. T.
PONSCARME, FRANÇOIS JOSEPH HUBERT. (S)
Fr. Belmont 1827-1903 Paris. T.
PONSEN, TUNIS.
Am. b. Holland 1891; ad. 1934 Chicago. A.
PONSON, LUC RAPHAËL.
Fr. Solliès-Pont 1835-1904 Marseilles. B-T.
PONT, CHARLES ERNEST. (Ill)
Am. ad. 1934 Elmhurst, L. I., N. Y. A.
PONTE, GIOVANNI DAL [Stefano].
It. Florence 1385-1437. T-V.
PONTE, JACOPO DA. *see* Bassano, J.
PONTE, LEANDRO. *see* Bassano, L.
PONTELLI, BACCIO [Bartolomeo di Fino].
It. Florence 1450-1492 Urbino. T-V.
PONTIUS, PAUL [or Du Pont].
Flem. Antwerp 1603-1658 Same. B-T.
PONTORMO, IL. *see* Carrucci, Jacopo.
PONZ Y PIQUER, ANTONIO.
Sp. Bechí 1725-1792 Madrid. T.
PONZANO, ANTONIO.
Ger. ac. 1565-1602 in Munich. T.
PONZANO Y GASCÓN, PONCIANO.
Sp. Zargoza 1813-1877 Madrid. T.
PONZONE, MATTEO.
It. 1580/90-1664 Venice. T.
POOL, JURIAEN II.
Dut. Amsterdam 1665/6-1745. B-T.
POOL, MATTHYS.
Dut. Amsterdam 1670-1730/2. B-T.
POOLE, ABRAM.
Am. b. Chicago 1883; ad. 1934 New York. A-T-W.
POOLE, BERT.
Am. b. Brockton, Mass. 1853; ad. 1934 East Milton, Mass. A-F-T.
POOLE, BURNELL.
Am. b. 1884; d. 1933 Englewood, N. J. A030.
POOLE, EARL LINCOLN. (Ill)
Am. b. Haddonfield, N. J. 1891; ad. 1934 West Reading, Pa. A-T.
POOLE, FREDERICK VICTOR. (Ill)
Am. b. Southampton, Eng.; ad. 1934 Chicago. A-F-T.
POOLE, HENRY. (S)
Eng. London 1873-1928 Same. T-Wa01929.
POOLE, HORATIO NELSON. (Ill)
Am. b. Haddonfield, N. J. 1885; ad. 1934 San Fran., Calif. A.
POOLE, PAUL FALCONER.
Eng. Bristol 1807-1879 London. B-C-E-T.
POOLEY, OLE.
Eng. ex. 1934 London. M.
POOR, HENRY VARNUM.
Am. b. Chapman, Kan. 1888; ad. 1934 New City, N. Y. A-T-W.
POOR, HENRY WARREN.
Am. b. Boston, Mass. 1863; ad. 1915 Medford, Mass. A12-F-T.
POORE, HENRY RANKIN.
Am. b. Newark, N. J. 1859; ad. 1934 Orange, N. J. A-C-F-T-W.
POORTENAAR, JAN C.
Dut. b. Amsterdam 1886; ac. 1933. T.
POORTER, WILLEM DE.
Dut. 1608-1648 Haarlem. B-C-T.
POOST. *see* Post.
POPE, ALEXANDER.
Am. Boston 1849-1924 Hingham, Mass. A021-F-T-46.
POPE, ALEXANDER. (Poet-P)
Eng. London 1688-1744 Twickenham. B-DNB-T.
POPE, ALEXANDER. (Actor-Min)
Ir. Cork 1763-1835 London. B-DNB-T.
POPE, ARTHUR.
Am. b. Cleveland, O. 1880; ad. 1934 Cambridge, Mass. M.
POPE, CLARA MARIA [Leigh].
Eng. ex. 1796-1838 in London. B-DNB-T.
POPE, GUSTAV.
Eng. ac. 1852-1895 in London. T.
POPE, JOHN.
Am. b. 1821; d. 1881 New York. T.
POPE, [Mrs.] MARION HOLDEN.
Am. b. San Fran., Calif.; ad. 1934 Sacramento, Calif. A.
POPE, WILLIAM FREDERICK. (S)
Am. Fitchburg, Mass. 1865-1906 Boston. A06-F-T.
POPE-STEVENS, JUSTIN.
Ir. d. 1771 in Dublin. T.
POPELIN, CLAUDIUS MARCEL.
Fr. Paris 1825-1892 Same. T.
POPELIN, GUSTAVE LÉON ANTOINE MARIE.
Fr. ac. 1880-1900 in Paris. B-T.
POPHAM, JAMES KIDWELL.
Eng. b. Kent 1884; ex. 1934 London. Wa.
POPINEAU, FRANÇOIS ÉMILE. (S)
Fr. b. St. Amand 1887. DBA-T.
POPOFF, ALEXANDER.
Rus. 1876-1910 Russia. M.
POPOFF, ALEXANDER ANDREJEWITSCH.
Rus. 1852-1896 Odessa. B-T.
POPOFF, CONSTANTIN. (Mu)
Rus. b. Russia 1897. DBA.
POPOV. *see* Popoff.
POPOWSKI, STEFAN.
Pol. b. Warsaw 1870. T.
POPP, BARBARA [or Babette].
Ger. Amberg 1802-1870 Regensberg. T.
POPP, HEINRICH.
Ger. Nürnberg 1637-1682 Same. T.
POPP, OSKAR.
Ger. b. Leipzig 1875. T.
POPPE, GEORG.
Ger. b. Frankfort 1883. T.
PÖPPELMAN, JOHANN DAVID.
Ger. Dresden 1729/31-1813 Same. T.
PÖPPELMAN, PETER. (S)
Ger. b. Harsewinkel 1866. B-T.
PORAY, STAN POCIECHA.
Am. b. Cracow, Pol. 1888; ad. 1934 Hollywood, Calif. A.
PORBUS. *see* Pourbus.
PORCELLIS [or Persellis], JAN [The Elder].
Dut. Ghent 1580/5-1632 Leyden. B-T.
PORCELLIS [or Parcellis], JULIUS.
Dut. Rotterdam 1609-1645 Leyden. B-T.

PORDENONE, IL. [Giovanni Antonio Licinio da].
It. Pordenone 1483/4-1538/9 Ferrara. C-E-T-V-722.
PORPORA, PAOLO.
It. b. Naples; d. 1673 Rome. T.
PORPORATI, CARLO ANTONIO.
It. Turin 1741-1816 Same. T.
PORRAS [or Porres], JUAN.
Sp. ac. 1592-1637 in Madrid. T.
PORRI, DANIELE DA PARMA.
It. Parma 1500-1577 Rome. T-V.
PORRI, FILIPPO.
It. Ferrara 1610-1680 Same. T.
PORRO, GIROLAMO.
It. b. Padua; ac. 1574-1604 in Rome. T.
PORTA, ANDREA DA MILAN.
It. Milan 1656-1723. T.
PORTA, ANDREA DA VERONA.
It. Verona 1720-1805. T.
PORTA, ANTONIO DELLA [Tamagnino].
It. ac. 1491-1520 in Lombard. T.
PORTA, BARTOLOMMEO [Baccio] DELLA.
see Bartolommeo di Pagholo.
PORTA, CARLO ANDREA.
It. Gubbio 1809-1890 Same. T.
PORTA, FERDINANDO.
It. Milan 1689-1767 Same. T.
PORTA, GIACOMO DELLA. (S)
It. Rome 1537-1604. B-Hs-T.
PORTA, GIOVANNI BATTISTA DELLA.
It. Milan 1542?-1597 Rome. T-V.
PORTA, GIOVANNI GIACOMO DELLA. (S)
It. b. 1485; d. 1555 Genoa. T-V.
PORTA, GIUSEPPI. *see* Salviati, G. P.
PORTA, GUGHIELMO DELLA. (S)
It. ac. 1531-1557 in Rome. Hs-T-V.
PORTA, NICOLA.
It. Bari 1710-1784. T.
PORTA, TEODORA DELLA.
It. Rome 1567-1638 Same. T-V.
PORTAEL, JEAN FRANÇOIS.
Belg. Brussels 1818-1895 Same. B-C-E-T.
PORTAIL, JACQUES ANDRÉ.
Fr. Brest 1695-1759 Versailles. B-Bd-T.
PORTE, LEANDRO. *see* Bassano, L.
PORTELLI, CARLO.
It. ac. 1545-1574 in Florence. T-V.
PORTER, BENJAMIN CURTIS.
Am. Melrose, Mass. 1845-1908 New York. A07-B-C-DAB-E-F-T-W5-1-15.
PORTER, BRUSE. (Mu)
Am. b. San Fran., Calif. 1865; ad. 1934 Same. A-F-T-W.
PORTER, CHARLES ETHEN.
Am. Hartford, Conn. 1850-1923. A020-3.
PORTER, DORIS LUCILE.
Am. b. Portsmouth, Va. 1898; ad. 1934 Same. A.
PORTER, ELMER JOHNSON.
Am. b. Richmond, Ind. 1907; ad. 1934 Same. A.
PORTER, FAIRFIELD.
Am. ad. 1935 New York. M.
PORTER, FREDERICK JAMES.
Aust. b. Auckland, N. Z. 1883; ex. 1934 London. Wa-825.
PORTER, JAMES A.
Am. b. Balt., Md. 1905; ad. 1934 Wash., D. C. A.
PORTER, JAMES TANK. (S)
Am. b. Tientsin, China 1883; ad. 1934 New York. A-F-T.
PORTER, [Mrs.] JEAN MACDONALD. (Ill)
Am. ad. 1934 Long Island City, N. Y. M.
PORTER, JOHN S. (Min)
Am. ac. 1833 in Boston. F-T-2-6.
PORTER, LOVE.
Am. ad. 1934 New York. M.
PORTER, MARY KING. (Min)
Am. b. Batavia, Ill. 1865; ad. 1934 Wash., D. C. A-F-T.
PORTER, RAYMOND AVERILL. (S)
Am. b. Hermon, N. Y. 1883; ad. 1934 Boston. A-F-T.
PORTER, [Sir] ROBERT KER.
Eng. Durham 1777-1842 Leningrad, Rus. B-DNB-T.
PORTER, WILLIAM A.
Am. England 1842-1909 Phila., Pa. A8.
PORTH, HANS HEINRICH. (Eg)
Ger. Wilhelmsburg 1796-1882 Hamburg. T.
PORTIELJE, EDOUARD ANTOINE.
Belg. b. 1861 Antwerp. B-T.
PORTIELJE, GÉRARD [or Geeraard].
Belg. b. Antwerp 1856. B-T.
PORTIELJE, JON FREDERIK PIETER.
Dut. Amsterdam 1829-1895 Same. B-T.
PORTMAN, CHRISTIAAN JULIUS LODEWYCK.
Dut. Amsterdam 1799-1895 Beverwÿk. C-T.
PORTMAN, LODEWYK GOTTLIEB. (Eg)
Ger. Darmstadt 1772-1813. B-T.
PORTNOFF, ALEXANDER. (S)
Am. b. Russia 1887; ad. 1934 Phila., Pa. A-Cs-F.
PORTO FAMILY.
It. ac. 1420-1545 in Modena. T.
PORTORMO. *see* Carrucci, Jacopo.
POSCH, LEONHARD.
Ger. b. 1750; d. 1831 Berlin. T.
POSE, EDUARD WILHELM.
Ger. Düsseldorf 1812-1878 Frankfort. C-T.
POSSESSE, ALBIN FRANÇOIS DE. (S)
Fr. b. Paris 1888. DBA.
POSSIN, RUDOLF.
Ger. b. in Magdeburg 1861. T.
POSSOZ, [Miss] MILY.
Belg. b. Lisbon, Por. 1896; ad. 1934 New York. M.
POST, CHARLES JOHNSON. (Ill)
Am. b. New York 1873; ad. 1935 Bayside, L. I., N. Y. A12-F-M.
POST, FRANK. (Et)
Am. ad. 1934 Phila., Pa. M.
POST, FRANZ JANSZ.
Dut. Leyden 1612-1680 Haarlem. B-T.
POST, HERMANN. (Ill)
Am. ad. 1934 New York. M.
POST, MARY AUDUBON.
Am. b. New York; d. 1929 Same. A026-F-T.
POST, WILLIAM MERRITT.
Am. b. Brooklyn, N. Y. 1856-1935 New York. A-F-T-W-Obit. N. Y. papers, 3-23-1935.
POSTELLE, GERMAIN.
Fr. ac. 1833-1847 in Paris. B-T.
POSTEMPSKI, ROMAN.
Pol. Ukraine 1808-1878 Rome, It. T.

POSTGATE, MARGARET J. (S)
Am. b. Chicago; ad. 1934 Brooklyn, N. Y. A-Cs.

POSTIGLIONE, SALVATORE.
It. Naples 1861-1906 Same. T.

POSTL [or Postel], KARL.
Ger. Bechin 1769-1836 Prague, Czec. T.

POT, HENDRIK GERRITSZ.
Dut. Haarlem 1585-1657 Amsterdam. B-Bd-T-722.

POTÉMONT, ADOLPHE THÉODORE JULES MARTIAL.
Fr. Paris 1828-1883 Same. B-T.

POTERATE FAMILY.
Fr. ac. 17-18th Cent. in Rouen. T.

POTERLET, HIPPOLYTE.
Fr. Epernay 1804-1835 Paris. B-T.

POTHAST, BERNARD.
Dut. b. Hal, Belg. 1882. M.

POTHOVEN, HENDRIK.
Dut. Amsterdam 1725-1795 The Hague. B-T.

POTT, CONSTANCE MARY.
Eng. b. London 1862. T.

POTT, LASLETT JOHN.
Eng. Newark 1837-1898 London. B-T-15.

POTTER, AGNES SQUIRE.
Am. b. London 1892; ad. 1934 Chicago. A.

POTTER, BARTHA HERBERT.
Mrs. Edward Potter, Jr.
Am. b. Nashville, Tenn. 1895; ad. 1934 Same. A.

POTTER, EDNA. (Ill)
Am. ad. 1934 New York. M.

POTTER, EDWARD CLARK. (S)
Am. New London, Conn. 1857-1923 Same. A020-DAB-F-T-Ta-46.

POTTER, FRANK. (Et)
Eng. ad. 1934 London. Wa.

POTTER, FRANK HUDDLESTONE.
Eng. London 1845-1887 Same. B-Bd-T.

POTTER, FULLER JR.
Am. ex. 1935 New York. M.

POTTER, HARRY SPAFFORD. (Ill)
Am. b. Detroit, Mich. 1870; ad. 1934 New York. A-F-T.

POTTER, JOHN BRIGGS.
Am. b. Lansing, Mich. 1864; ad. 1934 Boston, Mass. M.

POTTER, LOUIS MCCLELLAN. (S)
Am. Troy, N. Y. 1873-1912 Seattle, Wash. A010-DAB-F-T-Ta-W7-46.

POTTER, MARTHA JULIA.
Am. b. Essex, Conn. 1864; ad. 1934 New Haven, Conn. A-F-T.

POTTER, MARY KNIGHT.
Am. b. Boston; ac. 1926 Same. A12-F.

POTTER, MATHILDE.
Am. b. Phila., Pa. 1880; ad. 1934 Santa Barbara, Calif. A.

POTTER, NATHAN DUMONT. (S)
Am. Enfield, Mass. 1893-1934 Old Lynne, Conn.
A-F-M-T-Obit. Art Digest, 12-15-1934.

POTTER, PAUL [or Paulus].
Dut. Enkhuysen 1625-1654 Amsterdam. B-Bd-C-E-T-722.

POTTER, PIETER SIMMONSZ.
Dut. Enkhuysen 1579-1652 Amsterdam. B-T.

POTTER, WILLIAM J.
Am. b. Bellefonte, Pa. 1883; ad. 1934 Greenwich, Conn. A-F-T-W.

POTTGIETER, DIETRICH.
Ger. ac. 1645-1690 in Cologne. T.

POTTHAST. *see also* Pothast.

POTTHAST, EDWARD HENRY.
Am. Cinn., O. 1857-1927 New York. A024-F-T-W14-46.

POTTS, WILLIAM SHERMAN.
Am. Milburn, N. J. 1876-1930 Stonington, Conn. A027-F-T.

POTUYL, HENDRIK.
Dut. ac. 17th century in Holland. T.

POUCHER, EMILY ROLLINSON.
Am. ad. 1934 Scarsdale, N. Y. M.

POUCKE, CHARLES FRANÇOIS VAN. (S)
Flem. Dixmuiden 1740-1809 Ghent. T.

POUGIALIS, CONSTANTINE.
Am. b. Greece 1894; ad. 1935 Chicago. M.

POULSEN, RICHARD AXEL. (S)
Dan. b. Copenhagen 1887. T.

POULTIÈR, JEAN BAPTISTE. (S)
Fr. Abbeville 1683-1719 Paris. T.

POUNCY, BENJAMIN THOMAS. (Eg)
Eng. d. 1799 in London. B-DNB-T.

POUPARD, JAMES. (Eg)
Am. ac. 1772-1814. F-2-7-147.

POUPELET, JANE. (S)
Fr. Dordogne 1878-1932 Paris. B-DBA-T.

POURBUS, FRANS I [The Elder].
Flem. Bruges, Belg. 1545-1581 Antwerp. B-Bd-C-T-722.

POURBUS, FRANS II [The Younger].
Flem. Antwerp 1568/70-1622 Paris. B-Bd-C-T-722.

POURBUS, PIETER JANSZ [The Elder].
Flem. Gonda, Belg. 1510-1584 Bruges. B-Bd-C-T-722.

POUSETTE-DART, NATHANIEL J. (Author-P)
Am. b. St. Paul, Minn. 1886; ad. 1934 Valhalla, N. Y. A-F-T.
[*see also* Index of Authors.]

POUSSIN, GASPARD. *see* Doughet, G.
[Note: Nicolas Poussin was his brother-in-law and he assumed his name.]

POUSSIN, NICOLAS.
Fr. Villeres, Normandy 1593/4-1665 Rome, It. B-Bd-C-E-T-512-722-783.

POVEDA Y JUÁN, VICENTE.
It. b. Petrell [Valencia] 1857; ad. 1895 Berlin, Ger. B-T.

POWELL, ARTHUR JAMES EMERY.
Am. b. Vanwert, O. 1864; ad. 1934 Dover Plains, N. Y. A-F-T-W.

POWELL, CAROLINE AMELIA. (Eg)
Am. b. Dublin, Ir. 1852. A28-F-T-W16-829.

POWELL, DOANE. (Masks-S)
Am. ad. 1934 New York. M.

POWELL, JENNETTE M.
Am. b. Kingston, Can.; ad. 1934 Norton, Mass. A.

POWELL, JOHN I.
Eng. ac. 1770-1785 in London. B-DNB-T.

POWELL, JOHN II.
Eng. ac. 1796-1833 London. B-Bd-DNB-T.

POWELL, LESLIE.
Am. ad. 1935 New York. M.

POWELL, LUCIEN WHITING.
Am. Virginia 1846-1930 Wash., D. C. A027-DAB-F-T-W16.
POWELL, MOILA.
Eng. ex. 1934 London. M.
POWELL, WILLIAM HENRY.
Am. Ohio 1824-1879 New York. Bd-C-F-T-4-15-46-513.
POWER, CYRIL EDWARD. (Eg)
Eng. b. London; ex. 1934 Brooklyn, N. Y. Wa.
POWER, JOHN WARDELL.
Aust. b. Sydney, N.S.W. 1881. DBA.
POWERS, HIRAM. (S)
Am. Woodstock, Vt. 1805-1873 Florence, It. B-C-DBA-E-F-Hs-T-Ta-4-15-26-52.
POWERS, JOHN M. (Ill)
Am. ad. 1934 New York. A.
POWERS, LONGWORTH. (S)
[Son of Hiram Powers.]
Am. d. Florence, It. 1904. A05-F-Hs.
POWERS, MARION.
Mrs. W. A. B. Kirkpatrick.
Am. b. London; ad. 1934 Waldoboro, Me. A-F-T.
POWERS, [Mrs.] MARY SWIFT.
Am. b. Leeds, Mass. 1885; ad. 1934 Manchester, Vt. M.
POWERS, PRESTON. (S)
[Son of Hiram Powers.]
Am. b. Florence, Italy 1843. A23-F-Hs-T-15.
POWERS, T. E. (Cart)
Am. ad. 1934 New York. M.
POWLE, GEORGE. (Et)
Eng. ac. 1764-1771 in London. B-Bd-DNB-T.
POWOLNY, MICHAEL. (S)
Ger. b. Judeburg 1871; ad. 1933 Vienna, Aus. T.
POWRIE, ROBERT. (S)
Am. 1843-1922. A022.
POYEGE.
Indian (American). ex. 1933 New York. 411.
POYET, JEAN. (Min)
Fr. ac. 1483-1497 in Tours. T.
POYNTER, [Sir] EDWARD JOHN.
Eng. Paris 1836-1919 London. B-Bd-C-DNB-E-T.
POZZI, ENNIO.
It. ad. 1934 Florence. M.
POZZI FAMILY.
Ger. ac. 18-19th centuries in Germany. T.
POZZI, STEFANO.
It. Rome 1707-1768. T.
POZZO, PADRE ANDREAS.
It. Trente 1642-1709 Vienna. B.
POZZOSERRATO. *see* Toeput.
PRACHNER FAMILY. (S)
Ger. ac. 18th century in Germany. T.
PRADELLES, HIPPOLYTE.
Ger. b. Strasburg 1824; ac. 1866 in Bordeaux, Fr. B-T.
PRADIER, CHARLES SIMON.
Fr. Geneva, Swi. 1783-1847 Mornex, Fr. B-T.
PRADIER, JEAN JACQUES [or James]. (S)
Fr. Geneva, Swi. 1790-1852 Bougival, Fr. B-E-Hs-T.
PRADILLA Y ORTIZ, FRANCESCO.
Sp. Saragossa 1848-1921 Madrid. B-E-T.
PRADO, BLAS DEL [or De Prado].
Sp. Toledo 1540/5-1595/60 Madrid. B-T.
PRAGA, ALFRED. (Min)
Eng. ac. 1928 in South Kensington. M.
PRAGER, BLANCHE.
Am. ad. 1934 New York. M.
PRAHAR, RENEE. (S)
Am. b. New York 1880; ad. 1934 Same. A-F.
PRAMPOLINI, ENRICO.
It. b. Modena 1895; ad. 1934 Paris. DBA-T.
PRANG, LOUIS. (Eg)
Am. Germany 1823-1909 Los Angeles, Calif. A07-T.
PRANISCHNDCKOFF, HILLARION.
Rus. Moscow 1839/40-1894 Same. B.
PRASUHN, JOHN G. (S)
Am. b. Versailles, O. 1877; ad. 1934 Ind., Ind. A.
PRATERE [or Praetere], EDMUND JOSEPH.
Belg. Courtrai 1826-1888 Brussels. B-T.
PRATI, EUGENIO.
It. Trentino 1842-1907. T.
PRATO, FRANCESCO ORTENSI DI GIROLAMO DAL. (Med)
It. Caravaggio 1512-1562 Florence. T.
PRATT, BELLA LYON. (S)
Am. Norwich, Conn. 1867-1917 Boston. A014-B-DAB-F-Hs-T-Ta-W9-19-46-768.
PRATT, CHARLES HYDE.
Am. ad. 1935 Winter Park, Fla. M.
PRATT, HENRY CHEEVES.
Am. Oxford, N. H. 1803-1880 Wakefield, Mass. F-T-2-25.
PRATT, JONATHAN.
Eng. Northampton 1835-1911. B-T.
PRATT, JOSEPH BISHOP. (Eg)
Eng. London 1854-1910 Same. DNB-T-Y01911.
PRATT, JULIA D.
Am. b. No. Collins, N. Y.; ad. Buffalo, N. Y. A.
PRATT, LORUS.
Am. Salt Lake City, Utah 1856-1924. A021.
PRATT, MATTHEW.
Am. Phila., Pa. 1734-1805 Same. B-Bd-DAB-C-T-1-2-4-6-182-839.
PRATT, PHILIP HENRY.
Am. b. Kansas City, Mo. 1888; ad. 1934 Brooklyn, N. Y. A.
PRATT, ROBERT M.
Am. Binghamton, N. Y. 1811-1888 New York. F-T-6.
PRATT, [Mrs.] ROSALIND CLARK.
Am. b. 1857; d. 1932 Branford, Conn. A029.
PRATT, V. CHAFFLIN. (S)
Am. ex. 1934 Seattle, Wash. M.
PRATT, WILLIAM.
Scot. b. Glasgow 1855; ad. 1934 Same. B-T-Wa.
PRAX, VALENTINE HENRIETTE.
Fr. b. Bone, Algeria 1899. DBA.
PRAXIAS II. (S)
Gr. ac. 4th Cent. B.C. in Athens. E-Hs-T.

PRAXITELES [of Athens] II. (S)
[Considered the greatest of Attic sculptors.]
Gr. ac. 390?-332? B.C. E-Hs-T-817.
PRÉAULT, ANTOINE AUGUSTE. (S)
Fr. Paris 1809-1879 Same. B-Hs-T.
PREBOSTE, FRANCISCO.
Sp. Toledo 1554-1610? T.
PRECHT, BURCHARDT [The Elder]. (S)
Ger. Bremen 1651-1731 Stockholm, Swe. T.
PRECHT, CHRISTIAN [The Elder]. (S)
Ger. ac. 1663-1703 in Hamburg. T.
PRECIADO DE LA VEGA, FRANCISCO.
Sp. b. Sèville; ac. 1733-1789 Rome, It. T.
PREDA [or Pietra], CARLO.
It. ac. 1700 in Milan. T.
PREDA Y SALGARDO, ANTONIO.
Sp. 1606/8-1678. M.
PREDIS, CRISTOFORO DE. (Min)
It. ac. 1471-1486 in Milan. T.
PREDIS, GIOVANNI AMBROGIO DE.
It. Milan 1455-1522. B-T-78-783.
PREETORIUS, EMIL.
Ger. b. Mainz 1883. T.
PREISLER FAMILY.
Ger. ac. 17-18th Cent. in Nürnberg. T.
PRELL, HERMANN.
Ger. Leipzig 1854-1922 Dresden. B-T.
PRELLER, FRIEDRICH [Johann Christian Ernest].
Ger. Eisenach 1804-1878 Weimar. B-C-E-T.
PRELLWITZ, EDITH MITCHELL.
Mrs. Henry Prellwitz.
Am. b. So. Orange, N. J. 1865; ad. 1934 Peconic, L. I., N. Y. A-F-W-46.
PRELLWITZ, HENRY.
Am. b. New York 1865; ad. 1934 Peconic, L. I., N. Y. A-F-T-W-46.
PRENCIPIPE, UMBERTO.
It. b. Naples 1879. T.
PRENDERGAST, CHARLES E. (S)
Am. b. Boston 1868; ad. 1934 New York. A-F.
PRENDERGAST, MAURICE BRAZIL.
Am. Boston 1859-1924 New York. A021-DAB-F-T-W13-1-172-514-701-779.
PRENNER, ANTON JOSEPH.
Ger. Wallerstein 1683-1761 Vienna, Aus. T.
PRENTIS, EDWARD.
Eng. Monmouth 1797-1854 London. DNB-T.
PRENTZEL, HANS.
Ger. b. in Rothenberg 1880. T.
PREPELICZAY, SAMU [or Samuel].
Hun. Budapest 1794-1859 Arad. T.
PRESCIUTTI FAMILY.
It. ac. 15-16th century in Italy. T.
PRESCOTT, CHARLES BARROW CLARKE.
Eng. b. Wilmslow 1870; d. 1932. Wa1929-Y01933.
PRESCOTT, KATHERINE T. (S)
Mrs. Harry L. Prescott.
Am. b. Biddeford, Me.; ad. 1935 New York. A12-F-W9.
PRESSOIR, ESTHER ESTELLE.
Am. b. Phila., Pa.; ac. 1934 New York. A.
PRESTEL, JOHANN ERDMANN GOTTLIEB.
Ger. Frankfort 1804-1885 Mainz. T.
PRESTEL, JOHANN THEOPHIL [Amadeus].
Ger. Grünenbach 1739-1808 Frankfort. B-T.
PRESTEL, MARIA CATHERINA.
Ger. Nürnberg 1747-1794 London. B-T.
PRESTINARI FAMILY.
It. ac. 16th century in Milan. T.
PRESTON, ALICE BOLAM. (Ill)
Am. b. Malden, Mass. 1888; ad. 1934 Beverly Farms, Mass. A.
PRESTON, JAMES MOORE. (Ill)
Am. ad. 1934 New York. M.
PRESTON, [Mrs.] JESSIE GOODWIN.
Am. b. East Hartford, Conn. 1880; ad. 1934 Same. A.
PRESTON, MARGARET.
Aust. ad. 1933 Sydney, N.S.W. M.
PRESTON, MARY WILSON. (Ill)
Mrs. James Moore Preston.
Am. b. New York 1873; ad. 1934 Same. A12-F-W-46.
PRESTON, THOMAS [or Captain Preston].
Eng. d. 1785 in London. B-T.
PRETI, CAVALIÈRE MATTIA. *see* Calabrese, Il.
PREU, JORGE. *see* Breu, Jorg.
PREUDHOMME. *see also* Prudhomme.
PREUDHOMME, JEAN.
Swi. Neuchâtel 1732-1795 Same. T.
PREUSSL, C. C.
Am. b. 1894; ex. 1934 Chicago. M.
PREVITALI, ANDREA [Cordelliaghi].
It. Brembate 1470-1528 Bergamo. B-Bd-T.
PREVITALI, GAETANO.
It. Ferrara 1852-1920 Lavagna. B-T.
PRÉVOST, ALEXANDRE CÉLESTE GABRIEL.
Fr. ac. 1850-1886 in Paris. B-T.
PRÉVOST, BENOIT LOUIS.
Fr. Paris 1735-1804/9. B-T.
PRÉVOST, JACQUES.
Fr. ac. 1530-1580 in Rome, It. T.
PRÉVOST [or Provost], JEAN [or Jan].
Flem. Mons 1460/5-1529 Bruges. B-T-662.
PRÉVOST, JEAN LOUIS.
Fr. Nointel 1760-1810. B-T.
PREWITT, WILLIAM.
Eng. b. Suffolk; ac. 1735 in London. Bd-T.
PREYER, ÉMILIE.
Ger. Düsseldorf 1849-1930 Same. B-T.
PREYER, JOHANN WILHELM.
Ger. Rheydt 1803-1889 Düsseldorf. B-C-T.
PRIAMO DI PIETRO.
It. ac. 1438-1467 in Siena. T.
PRIBISLAVIC, IVAN. (S)
Rus. b Russia; ac. 1441-1471 in Venice, It. T.
PRICE, ANNA G.
Am. b. New York; ad. 1934 Forest Hills, L. I., N. Y. A.
PRICE, CHESTER B. (Ill)
Am. b. Kansas City, Mo. 1885; ad. 1935 New York. A28-M-W.
PRICE, EDITH BALLINGER.
Am. ad. 1934 Newport, R. I. A.
PRICE, EUGENIA. (Min)
Am. Beaumont, Tex. 1865-1923 Los Angeles, Calif. A020-F-T.
PRICE, GARRET.
Am. ex. 1934 Mystic, Conn. M.
PRICE, [Mrs.] HATTIE LONGSTREET. (Ill)
Am. ad. 1934 Phila., Pa. M.
PRICE, HELEN F.
Am. ad. 1935 Johnstown, Pa. M.

PRICE, Hilda M. (Ill)
Eng. ad. 1934 London. M.
PRICE, Joshu. (Glass-P)
Eng. ac. 1715-1740 in Oxford. B-DNB-T.
PRICE, Julius Mendes.
Eng. b. 1857; d. 1924 London. T-Y01925.
PRICE, Luxor. (Ill)
Am. ac. 1934 New York. M.
PRICE, Mary Elizabeth.
Am. b. Martinsburg, W. Va.; ad. 1934 New Hope, Pa. A-F-T.
PRICE, Margaret Evans.
Am. b. Chicago 1888; ad. 1934 East Aurora, N. Y. A-F-W.
PRICE, Norman Mills.
Am. b. Canada 1877; ad. 1931 New York. A28.
PRICE, Ricard.
Eng. Bristol 1820-1865. T.
PRICE, Samuel Woodson.
Am. b. Nicholsonville, Ky. 1828; ad. 1915 St. Louis, Mo. A12-F.
PRICE, William [The Elder]. (Glass-P)
Eng. ac. 1700-1722 in York. B-DNB-T.
PRICE, William [The Younger]. (Glass-P)
Eng. b. York; d. 1765 in London. B-DNB-T.
PRICE, William Henry.
Am. ad. 1934 Pasadena, Calif. M.
PRICE, William Lake.
Eng. b. 1810; d. 1891 in London. B-T.
PRICKE [or Pryke], Robert. (Eg)
Eng. ac. 1669-1698 in London. DNB-T.
PRIEST, Alfred.
Eng. Harborne 1874-1929 Chelsea. Wa1929-Y01930.
PRIEST, Alfred. (Eg)
Eng. Norwich 1810-1850 Same. T.
PRIESTMAN, Arnold.
Eng. Bradford 1854-1925. B-T-Y01926.
PRIESTMAN, Bertram.
Eng. b. Bradford 1868; ad. 1934 London. B-T-Wa.
PRIEUR, Barthélemy. (S)
Fr. ac. 1570-1611 Paris. B-Hs-T.
PRIEUR [or Le Prieur], Pierre. (Min)
Fr. ac. 1640-1676 in Paris. B-Bd-E-T.
PRIMATICCIO, Francesco. (P-S)
It. Bologna 1504-1570 Paris. B-C-Hs-T-V-722.
PRIMO [or Primont], Luigi [Gentile].
Flem. Brussels 1606-1669 Rome, It. B-T.
PRINCE, William Meade. (Ill)
Am. b. Roanoke, Va. 1893; ad. 1934 New York. A.
PRINCEHORN, Betz. (Ill)
Am. ad. 1934 New York. M.
PRINCETEAU, René Pierre Charles. (S)
Fr. Libourne 1844-1914 Same. B-T.
PRINDEVILLE, Mary.
Am. b. 1876; ac. Buffalo, N. Y. M.
PRINET, René François Xavier.
Fr. b. Vitry-le-François 1861. B-T.
PRINS, Johannes Hulbert [or Hendric].
Dut. The Hague 1757-1806 Utrecht. B-T.
PRINSEP, Valentine Cameron.
Eng. Calcutta, India 1836-1904 London. B-C-DNB-E-T.
PRINZHOFER, August.
Ger. St. Veit 1817-1885 Kapfenberg. T.
PRIOR, Charles M.
Am. b. New York 1865; ad. 1934 Same. A-T.
PRIOR, Edward Schroeder.
Eng. b. Greenwich 1852; d. 1932. T-Wa1929.
PRIOR, Laurits Terpager Malling.
Dan. Stege 1840-1879 Copenhagen. T.
PRIOR, Melton.
Eng. London 1845-1910 Chelsea. DNB-T.
PRIOR, Ruby Adair.
Am. b. Pescadero, Calif. 1899; ad. 1934 San Mateo, Calif. A.
PRIOR, Thomas Abiel. (Eg)
Eng. b. England 1809; d. 1886 Calais, Fr. DNB-T-Y01887.
PRIORE, Niccolò del.
It. ac. 1470-1501 in Perugia. T.
PRIOU, Louis.
Fr. b. Toulouse 1845. B-T.
PRITCHARD, J. Ambrose.
Am. Boston, Mass. 1858-1905 Same. A05-F-T.
PRITCHETT, Edward.
Eng. ac. 1828-1864 in London. B-T.
PRITCHETT, Eunice Clay.
Am. b. Keeling, Va. 1897; ad. 1934 Danville, Va. A.
PRITCHETT, Robert Taylor. (Ill)
Eng. b. 1828; d. 1907 in Burghfield. B-DNB-T.
PRIVAT, Gilbert Auguste. (S)
Fr. b. Toulouse 1892. DBA-T.
PROBENER, Michael.
Ger. ac. 1680-1701 in Berlin. T.
PROBERT, Sidney W.
Am. Paterson, N. J. 1865-1919 Same. A017.
PROBST Family.
Ger. ac. 18th century in Germany. T.
PROBST, Karl.
Aus. b. Vienna, Aus. 1854. B-T.
PROBST, Thorwald A.
Am. b. Warrensburg, Mo. 1886; ad. 1934 Los Angeles, Calif. A.
PROCACCINI, Andrea.
It. Rome 1671-1734 San Ildefonso, It. B-T.
PROCACCINI, Camillo.
It. Bologna 1546-1629 Milan. B-C-T-722.
PROCACCINI, Ercole [The Elder].
It. Bologna 1515-1595 Milan. B-T.
PROCACCINI, Ercole [The Younger].
It. Milan 1596-1676 Same. B-T.
PROCACCINI, Guilio Cesare.
It. Bologna 1570-1625/6 Milan. B-C-T-722-803.
PROCTOR, Alexander Phimister. (S)
Am. b. Bosanquit, Ont. Can. 1862; ad. 1934 Wilton, Conn. A-B-Cs-E-F-Hs-T-W-46.
PROCTOR, Dod.
Mrs. Ernest Proctor.
Eng. ad. 1934 London. Wa-825.
PROCTOR, Ernest.
Eng. b. Northumberland; ad. 1934 London. Wa.
PROCTOR, G. MacGregor. (S)
Am. b. 1912; ad. 1935 Rome, It. M.
PROCTOR, Thea.
Aust. ad. 1933 Sydney, N.S.W. M.
PROCTOR, Thomas. (S)
Eng. Settle 1753-1794 London. B-DNB-T.

PROHASKA, Raymond. (Ill)
Am. ad. 1934 New York. M.
PROKOFJEFF, Iwan Prok. (S)
Rus. Leningrad 1758-1828 Same. T.
PROKOP, Philipp Jakob.
Czec. Ronsberg 1740-1814 Vienna, Aus. T.
PRÖLSS, Friedrich.
Ger. b. Dresden 1855. B.
PRON, Louis Hector.
Fr. Sézanne 1817-1902 Troyes. B-T.
PRONASZKO, Andrzej.
Pol. b. 1889 in Poland. T.
PRONASZKO, Zbigniew. (S)
Pol. b. Zychlin 1885. T.
PRONCK [or Pronk], Cornelis.
Dut. Amsterdam 1691-1759 Same. T.
PROPHET, Nancy Elizabeth. (S)
Am. b. Ortic Center, R. I. 1890; ad. 1934 Paris. A.
PROSPERO DA PIAZZOLA.
It. Piazzola 1445/50-1521/4 Padua. T.
PROSZOWSKI, Jan Chryzostom.
Pol. b. 1599; d. 1666 in Cracow. T.
PROSZYNSKI, Henri. (S)
Fr. b. in Pau 1887. DBA.
PROTAIS, Paul Alexander.
Fr. Paris 1826-1890 Same. B-C-T.
PROTOGENES.
Gr. ac. 330-300 B.C. in Rhodes. B-E-T.
PRÖTZNER [or Bretzner], Josef.
Ger. b. Erding; ac. 1752-1761 in Munich. T.
PROU, René.
Fr. b. Nantes 1887. DBA.
PROUT, Fisher. *see* Fisher-Prout.
PROUT, John Skinner.
Eng. Plymouth 1806-1876 London. B-DNB-T.
PROUT, Samuel.
Eng. Plymouth 1783-1852 London. B-C-DNB-E-T-515.
PROUVÉ, Émile Victor.
Fr. b. Nancy 1858. DBA-T.
PROVAGLI [or Provaglia], Allessandro.
It. b. Bologna; d. 1636 in Modena. T.
PROVENZALE [or Provenzali], Marcello.
It. Cento 1577-1639 Rome. T.
PROVIS, Alfred.
Eng. ac. 1843-1906 in London. C-T.
PROVOST. *see* Prévost.
PROW, [Mrs.] Hallie Pace.
Am. b. Salem, Ind. 1869; ad. 1934 Bloomington, Ill. A.
PRUCKER [or Prugger], Nickolaus.
Ger. Trudering 1620-1694 Munich. T.
PRUDENTI, Bernardino.
It. ac. 1631-1694 in Venice. T.
PRUD'HOMME, Jean.
Fr. Berlin, Ger. 1686-1726 Wilton, Eng. B-T.
PRUD'HOMME, John Francis Eugène. (Eg)
Am. St. Thomas, W. I. 1800-1892 Georgetown, D. C. DAB-F-T-2-7-40.
PRUD'HON, Pierre [or Paul].
Fr. Cluny 1758-1823 Paris. B-Bd-C-E-T-192-722-847.
PRUNA, Pedro [Pablo].
Sp. b. 1904; ad. 1934 Vaucluse, Fr. M.
PRUNAIRE, Léon Alphonse Alfred. (Eg)
Fr. ac. 1867-1900 in Paris. B-T-880.
PRUNATI, Michelangelo.
It. Verona 1690-1756 Same. T.
PRUNATI, Santo.
It. Verona 1652-1728 Same. T.
PRUNIER, Gaston.
Fr. Havre 1863-1927. B-T.
PRUSHECK, Harvey Gregory.
Am. b. Sodrazica, Yugoslavia 1887; ad. 1934 Cleveland, O. A.
PRUSZKOWSKI, Tadeusz.
Pol. b. Borucice 1889; ad. 1934 Warsaw. T.
PRUSZKOWSKI, Witold.
Pol. Ukraine 1846-1896 Budapest, Hun. B-T.
PRUSZYNSKI, Andizej. (S)
Pol. Warsaw 1836-1895 Same. T.
PRYDE, James.
Scot. b. Edinburgh 1869; ad. 1934 London. B-T-Wa-825.
PRYOR, [Mrs.] Joseph W.
Am. b. Lexington, Ky.; ad. 1934 Same. M.
PRYSE, Gerald Spence.
Welsh. b. Wales 1864. T.
PSALMAIER Family.
Ger. ac. 17th century in Berlin. T.
PSENNER, Anton.
Ger. Bozen 1791/3-1866 Same. T.
PSTROKONSKI, Stanislaw.
Pol. b. Kalisz 1871; ad. 1933 Paris. T.
PU JU.
Chinese. ad. 1935 Pekin, China. M.
PUCCINELLI, Angelo di.
It. ac. 1350-1399 in Lucca. T.
PUCCINELLI, Antonio.
It. Castelfranco 1822-1897 Florence. T.
PUCCINELLI, [Mrs.] Dorothy Wagner.
Am. b. San Antonio, Tex. 1901; ad. 1934 San Fran., Calif. A.
PUCCINI, Biagio.
It. Rome 1675-1721 Same. T.
PUCCINI, Mario.
It. Leghorn 1869-1920 Florence. T.
PUCCIO DI SIMONE.
It. ac. 1320-1358 in Florence. T.
PUCELLE, Jehan. (Min)
Fr. ac. 1319-1343 in Paris. T.
PUCHINGER, Erwin.
Aus. b. Vienna 1876. T.
PUECH, Denys [or Denis], Pierre. (S)
Fr. b. Gavernac 1854. B-T.
PUELLACHER, Joseph Anton.
Swi. Telfs [Tyrol] 1737-1799 Same. T.
PUELLACHER, Leopold.
Swi. Telfs [Tyrol] 1776-1842 Same. T.
PUGA, Antonio.
• Sp. ac. 1650-1660 in Madrid. B-T.
PUGET, François.
Fr. Toulon 1651-1707 Marseilles. B-T.
PUGET [or Pujet], Pierre. (S)
Fr. Marseilles 1622-1694 Same. B-E-Hs-T-517.
PUGET-PUSZET, Baron Ludwik du. (S)
Pol. b. Cracow 1877. T.
PUGH, Herbert.
Ir. ac. 1758-1788 in London. DNB-T.
PUGH, Mabel.
Am. b. Morrisville, N. C. 1891; ad. 1934 New York. A.
PUGHE, [Miss] Buddig Anwylini.
Welsh. b. Wales 1857; ad. 1934 Same. T-Wa.

PUGIN, AUGUSTUS CHARLES.
Eng. Normandie 1769-1832 London. B-DNB-T-515.
PUGLIESCHI [or Puglicochi], ANTONIO.
It. Florence 1660-1732. T.
PUGLIESE, ANTHONY. (Et)
Am. ad. 1934 Brooklyn, N. Y. M.
PUGLIESE-LEVI, CLEMENTE.
It. b. Vercelli 1855; ac. 1921 Turin. T.
PUHLMANN, JOHANN GOTTLIEB.
Ger. Potsdam 1751-1826 Same. B-T.
PUHONNY, IVO.
Ger. b. Baden-Baden 1876. T.
PUHONNY, VICTOR.
Ger. Prague, Czec. 1838-1909 Baden-Baden. T.
PUIFORCAT, JEAN. (S)
Fr. b. Paris 1897. DBA.
PUIGAUDEAU, FERDINAND DE.
It. 1864/6-1930. DBA-T.
PUJOL, ALEX DENIS [Abel de].
Fr. Valenciennes 1785-1861 Paris. B-T-722.
PUJOS, ANDRÉ.
Fr. Toulouse 1738-1788 Paris. B-T.
PULAERE [or Pullier], FÉLIX.
Fr. ac. 1507-1528 in Cambria. T.
PULAERE [or Pullaire], PIERRE VAN. (S)
Fr. ac. 1498-1511 in Cambria. T.
PULFREY, DOROTHY LING.
Am. b. Prov., R. I. 1901; ad. 1934 Sheffield, Eng. A.
PULIGO, DOMENICO UBALDINI.
It. Florence 1475-1527 Same. B-T-V.
PULINCKX, LOUIS.
Flem. b. Antwerp, Belg. 1843; ac. 1900 Paris. T.
PULINX, HENDRIK [The Elder]. (S)
Flem. Bruges, Belg. 1698-1781 Same. T.
PULINX, HENDRIK [The Younger]. (S)
Flem. ac. 1751-1787 in Belgium. T.
PULLINCKS. *see* Pulinx.
PULLINGER, HERBERT. (Ill)
Am. b. Phila., Pa. 1878; ad. 1935 Same. A28-F-M-T.
PULZONE, SCIPIONE [or Gaetano].
It. Gaeta 1550/62-1598/1600 Rome. B-T.
PUNT, JAN.
Dut. Amsterdam 1711-1779 Same. T.
PUPILER [or Popelier], ANTONI.
Flem. ac. 1550-1567 in Antwerp, Belg. T.
PURCELL, RICHARD [Corbutt]. (Eg)
Ir. Dublin 1736-1766 London. B-DBA-T.
PURDIE, EVELYN. (Min)
Am. b. Smyrna, Asia Minor 1859; ad. 1934 Cambridge, Mass. A-F-T.
PURDY, ALBERT J.
Am. b. 1835; d. 1909 Ithaca, N. Y. A07-T.
PURDY, EARL.
Am. ad. 1934 New York. A.
PURDY, MAUD H. (Min)
Am. b. Phila., Pa. 1874; ad. 1934 Brooklyn, N. Y. A.
PUREFOY, HESLOPE. (Min)
Am. b. Chapel Hill, N. C. 1884; ad. 1934 Asheville, N. C. A.
PURKISS, MYRTON.
Am. ad. 1934 Los Angeles, Calif. M.
PURKYNE, KAREL. (Ill)
Ger. Breslau 1834-1868 Prague, Czec. T.
PURRMANN, HANS.
Ger. b. Speyer 1880; ad. 1934 Berlin. T.
PURSSELL, MARIE LOUISE.
Am. ad. 1934 New York. M.
PURTSCHERT FAMILY.
Ger. ac. 18th century in Germany. T.
PURVES, AUSTIN, JR.
Am. b. Phila., Pa. 1900; ad. 1934 New York. A.
PURVITIS, VILHELMS.
Rus. b. Jürgensburg 1872. T.
PURY, EDMOND JEAN DE [Baron].
Swi. Neuchâtel 1845-1911 Lausanne. B-T.
PUSHMAN, HOVSEP T.
Am. b. Diarbaker, Armenia 1877; ad. 1935 New York. A-F.
PUSTEANI, FRIEDRICH VON.
Ger. Prague, Czec. 1849-1917 Munich, Ger. T.
PUSTERLA, ATTILIO. (Mu)
Am. b. Milan, It. 1862; ad. 1934 New York. T.
PUTER [or Putter], PIETER DE.
Dut. The Hague 1600-1695 Beverwijk. B-T.
PUTHUFF, HANSON DUVALL.
Am. b. Waverly, Mo. 1875; ad. 1934 La Crescenta, Calif. A-F-W.
PUTMAN, ARTHUR. (S)
Am. Waveland, Miss. 1873-1930 Paris. A027-DAB-F-T-W16-701.
PUTNAM, BRENDA. (S)
Am. b. Minn., Minn. 1890; ad. 1935 New York. A-Cs-F.
PUTNAM, SARAH G.
Am. b. Nashua, N. H.; ac. 1900. B.
PUTNAM, STEPHEN GREELEY. (Eg)
Am. b. Nashua, N. H. 1852; ad. 1934 College Point, L. I., N. Y. A28-B-F-T-W.
PÜTT [or Pütte], HANS VAN. (Med)
Ger. b. 1592; d. 1653 in Cassel. T.
PUTTI, GIOVANNI. (S)
It. Bologna 1771-1847 Same. T.
PUTTI, MASSIMILIANO. (S)
It. Bologna 1809-1890 Same. T.
PUTTINATI, ALESSANDRO. (S)
It. Verona 1801-1872 Milan. T.
PUTTINATI, FRANCESCO. (Med)
It. Verona 1775-1848 Milan. T.
PUTTINI, PIETRO. (S)
It. ac. 1743-1793 in Verona. T.
PÜTTNER, WALTER.
Ger. b. Leipzig 1872; ad. 1933 Munich. T.
PUTZ, LEO.
Ger. b. Meran 1869; ad. 1933 Rio de Janeiro, Brazil. B-T.
PUVIS DE CHAVANNES, PIERRE CECILE.
Fr. Lyons 1824-1898 Paris. B-Bd-C-E-T-192-518.
PUY, DU. *see* Du Puy.
PUY, JEAN.
Fr. b. Lyons 1876; ad. 1934 Paris. DBA-T.
PUYENBROEK, PIERRE.
Ger. Löwen 1804-1884 Brussels, Belg. B-T.
PUYL, LOUIS FRANÇOIS GÉRARD.
Dut. Utrecht 1750-1824. B-T.
PUYROCHE-WAGNER, ELISE. *see* Wagner, E. P.

PYALL, H. C.
Eng. ac. 1810-1833 London. T.
PYE, CHARLES. (Eg)
Eng. Birmingham 1777-1864. B-DNB-T.
PYE, FRED.
Am. b. Yorkshire, Eng. 1882; ad. 1934 Cinn., O. A.
PYE, JOHN [The Elder]. (Eg)
Eng. b. 1745; ac. 1774 in London. B-DNB-T.
PYE, JOHN [The Younger]. (Eg)
Eng. Birmingham 1782-1874 London. B-DNB-T.
PYKE-NOTT, JAMES.
Eng. ex. 1934 London. M.
PYLE, CLIFFORD COLTON.
Am. b. Missouri 1894; ad. 1934 Oakland, Calif. A.
PYLE, ELLEN B. T.
Am. ad. 1934 New York. M.
PYLE, HOWARD.
Am. Wilmington, Del. 1853-1911 Florence, It. A010-B-DAB-E-F-T-46-232.
PYLE, WALTER. (Ill)
Am. ad. 1934 Greenville, Del. M.
PYLES, V. E. (Ill)
Am. ad. 1934 New York. M.
PYNACKER [or Pynaker], ADAM.
Dut. Delft 1622-1673 Amsterdam. B-C-T-722.
PYNACKER, ADRIAEN.
Dut. ac. 1679-1707 in Delft. T.
PYNAS [or Pinas], JACOB SYMONSZ.
Dut. Delft 1590-1648 Same. B-T.
PYNAS [or Pinas], JAN SYMONSZ.
Dut. Haarlem 1583/4-1631 Amsterdam. B-T.
PYNE, CHARLES CLAUDE.
Eng. b. 1802; d. 1878 in Guilford. B-Bd-T.
PYNE, JAMES BAKER.
Eng. Bristol 1800-1870. B-DNB-T.
PYNE, THOMAS.
Eng. b. Fulham 1843; ac. 1874-1893 in London. B-T-Y1928.
PYNE, WILLIAM HENRY.
["Ephrarim Hardcastle".]
Eng. London 1769-1843 Same. B-DNB-T.
PYREICUS.
Gr. ac. 320 B.C. B-T.
PYRGOTELES, GIOVANNI GIORGIO LASCARIS.
Gr. ac. 1480-1531 in Italy. T.
PYROMACHOS [or Phyromachos]. (S)
Gr. [Pergamon] ac. 156 B.C. Hs-T.
PYTHAGORAS. (S) [*see also* Polydoros.]
Gr. [Doric] b. Samos; ac. 480-448 B.C. in Region, Gr. E-Hs-T.
PYTHEOS. (Architect)
Gr. ac. 350 B.C. in Athens. T.
PYTHOKRITOS. (S)
Gr. ac. 2nd Cent. B.C. in Rhodes, Gr. T.

QARA, HISSARI [or Hissar] AHMED.
Turkish. d. 1555/6 in Turkey. T.
QÂSIM.
Hindu. ac. 1556-1605 in India. T.
QĀSIM, ALI. (Min)
Per. ac. 1488-1522 in Persia. T.
QUADAL [or Chwátal], MARTIN FERDINAND.
Ger. b. 1736; d. 1811 Leningrad, Rus. B-T.
QUADRELLI, EMILIO. (S)
It. Milan 1863-1925 Same. B-T.
QUADRI [or Quadro], BERNARDINI.
Ger. 1648-1721 Bayreuth. T
QUADRI, FRANCESCO. (S)
It. ac. 1708-1720. T.
QUADRIO [or Quadria] FAMILY.
Ger. ac. 17-18th Cent. in Germany and Italy. T.
QUADRONE, GIOVANNI BATTISTA.
It. Mondovi 1844-1898 Turin. T.
QUAGLIA, FERDINANDO [Paul F. Louis].
It. Plaisance 1780-1853 Paris. B-T.
QUAGLIATA, GIOVANNI ANDREA.
It. Messina 1600-1660. T.
QUAGLIATA, GIOVANNI BATTISTA.
It. Messina 1603-1673. T.
QUAGLIO, DOMENICO [The Younger].
Ger. Munich 1786-1837. B-T.
QUAGLIO [or Quaglia or Qualio] FAMILY.
Ger. ac. 17-20th Cent. in Germany. T.
QUANCHI, LEON WILLIAM.
Am. b. New York 1892; ad. 1934 Maywood, N. J. A-F.
QUANI, LUIGI [The Younger].
It. Ravenna 1643-1717 Bologna. B-T.
QUARANTE, LUCIEN NICOLAS.
Fr. Metz 1860-1902 Paris. B-T.
QUARNSTRÖM, CARL GUSTAF.
Swe. Stockholm 1810-1867 Same. T.
QUARTARARO, RICCARDO.
It. ac. 1485-1501 in Naples. T.
QUARTLEY, ARTHUR.
Am. Paris 1839-1886 New York. B-C-DAB-F-T-11-15-39.
QUARTLEY, FREDERICK WILLIAM. (Eg)
Am. Bath, Eng. 1808-1874 New York. F-T.
QUARTON. *see* Charonton.
QUAST, PEETER JANSZ.
Dut. The Hague 1606-1647 Amsterdam. B-C-T.
QUATAL [or Quartal], ANTON.
Ger. ac. 1736 in Berlin. T.
QUATTRINI, ENRICO. (S)
It. b. Rome 1863. T.
QUEBOORN [or Queborne], CHRISPYN VAN DEN.
Dut. The Hague 1604-1652 Same. T.
QUEBORN [or Queeborne], CHRISTIAN VAN DEN.
Flem. Antwerp 1515-1578 Same. T.
QUECQ, JACQUES EDOUARD.
Fr. Cambrai 1796-1863 St. Geneviève. B-T.
QUEIROLO, FRANCESCO. (S)
It. Genoa 1704-1762 Naples. T.
QUELLIN [or Quellinus], ARTUS I. (S)
Flem. Antwerp 1609-1700 Same. B-Hs-T-722.
QUELLIN [or Quellinus], ARTUS II. (S)
Flem. St. Trond 1625-1700 Antwerp. B-T.
QUELLIN [or Quellinus], ARTUS III. (S)
Flem. Antwerp 1653-1686 London. T.
QUELLIN [or Quellinus], ERASMUS I. (S)
Flem. Liège 1584-1639/40 Antwerp. B-T.
QUELLIN [or Quellinus], ERASMUS II.
Flem. Antwerp 1607-1678 Same. B-C-T.
QUELLIN [or Quellinus], HUBERTUS.
Flem. Antwerp 1619?-1687 Same. B-T.

QUELLIN [or Quellinus], JAN ERASMUS.
Flem. Antwerp 1634-1715 Mechlin, Belg. B-T.
QUELLINUS, THOMAS. (S)
Flem. Antwerp 1661-1709/10 Same. B-T.
QUELVÉE, FRANÇOIS ALBERT.
Fr. b. Evreux 1884; ad. 1934 Paris. DBA-T.
QUENNEVILLE, [Mlle.] CHAUTAL.
Fr. ex. 1930 in London. M.
QUENTIN, NICOLAS.
Ger. ac. 1482-1525 in Lüttich. B-T.
QUERCIA, JACOPO DELLA. (S)
It. 1367-1438. Hs-T-V.
QUERENA, LATTANZIO.
It. Bergamo 1768-1853 Venice. T.
QUERENA, LUIGI.
It. ac. 1854-1879 in Venice. T.
QUERFURTH, AUGUSTUS.
Ger. Wolfenbüttel 1696-1761 Vienna, Aus. B-C-T.
QUERFURT FAMILY.
Ger. ac. 18th Cent. in Hamburg. T.
QUEROL Y SUBIRATS, AUGUSTIN. (S)
Sp. Tortosa 1863-1909 Madrid. B-Hs-T.
QUESNAL, FRANÇOIS.
Fr. Edinburgh, Scot. 1544-1619 Paris. B-T.
QUEST, CHARLES F.
Am. b. Troy, N. Y. 1904; ad. 1934 St. Louis, Mo. A.
QUEST, DOROTHY JOHNSON.
Am. b. St. Louis, Mo. 1909; ad. 1934 Same. T.
QUETIN [or Quantin], PHILIPPE.
Fr. Dijon 1600-1636 Same. T.
QUEVERDO, FRANÇOIS MARIE ISIDORE.
Fr. Josselin 1748-1797 Paris. B-T.
QUIDOR, JOHN.
Am. Tappan, N. Y. 1800-1881 Jersey City, N. J. AX1-DAB-F-T-2.
QUIGNON, FERNAND JUST.
Fr. b. Paris 1854. B-DBA-T.
QUILLARD [or Quilliard], PIERRE ANTOINE.
Fr. Paris 1701-1733 Lisbon, Por. B-T.
QUILLIVIC, RENÉ.
Fr. b. Finistère 1879; ad. 1934 Paris. B-T.
QUIMBY, FREDERICK G.
Am. Sandwich, N. H. 1863-1923 Arlington, Mass. M.
QUINCKHARDT [or Quinchard], JAN MAURITS.
Dut. Rees 1688-1772 Amsterdam. B-T.
QUINCY, EDMUND.
Am. b. Biarritz, Fr. 1903; ad. 1934 Boston. A.
QUINLAN, MARJORIE.
Am. ex. 1934 New York. M.
QUINLAN, WILL J. (Et)
Am. b. Brooklyn, N. Y. 1877; ad. 1934 Yonkers, N. Y. A-F-T.
QUINN, EDMOND THOMAS. (S)
Am. Phila., Pa. 1868-1929 New York. A027-Cs-DAB-F-T-Ta-W14-18-46.
QUINN, JAMES PETER.
Aust. b. Melbourne 1871; ad. 1934 London. T-Wa.
QUINSAC, PAUL FRANÇOIS.
Fr. b. Bordeaux 1858; ac. 1903 Paris. B-T.
QUINTANILLA, LUIS. (Et)
Sp. ex. 1934 New York. M.
QUINTERO, BALTASAR.
Sp. ac. 1606-1638 in Sèville. T.
QUINTINIE, LÉON VICTOR DE LA.
Fr. b. Paris 1875. DBA.
QUINTON, ALFRED ROBERT.
Eng. b. London 1853; ac. 1928 Same. T-Wa1929.
QUINTON, CLÉMENT.
Fr. b. Paris 1851; ac. 1914 Same. B-T.
QUINTON, [Mrs.] WILLIAM WARREN.
see Sage, Cornelia Bentley.
QUINZIO, GIOVANNI.
It. Genoa 1832-1918 Same. T.
QUINZIO, TULLIO SALVATORE.
It. Genoa 1858-1918 Same. T.
QUIQUEREZ-BEAUJEN, FERDINAND VON.
It. b. Italy 1845; d. 1893 in Agram, Hun. T.
QUIRICO, GIOVANNI.
It. ac. 1467-1503 in Tortona. T.
QUIRIZIO DI GIOVANNI DA MURANO.
It. ac. 1461-1478 in Venice. T.
QUIRK, FRANCIS J.
Am. b. Pawtucket, R. I. 1907; ad. 1934 Same. A.
QUIRÓS, CESÁREO BERNALDO DE.
Sp. b. Argentine 1881; ad. 1934 Paris. DBA.
QUIRÓS, LORENZO.
Sp. Santos, Brazil 1717-1789 Sèville. B-T.
QUIRT, WALTER W.
Am. b. Iron River, Mich. 1902; ad. 1934 Milwaukee, Wis. A.
QUISTGAARD, HARALD ERIC EINAR. (S)
Dan. b. Copenhagen 1887; ad. 1934 Paris. T.
QUISTGAARD, JOHANN WALDEMAR.
Am. b. Denmark 1877; ad. 1934 Paris. A-F-T.
QUITER, HERMAN HENDRIK [The Elder].
Dut. Holland 1628-1708 Cassel, Ger. B-T.
QUITER, HERMAN HENDRIK [The Younger].
Ger. b. Bonn; d. 1731? Brunswick. B-T.
QUITER, MAGNUS DE.
Ger. Cassel 1694-1744 Same. T.
QUITTEINER, ANDREAS PHILIPP.
Aus. ac. 1694-1729 in Prague, Czec. T.
QUITTNER FAMILY.
Aus. ac. 19th Cent. in Budapest, Hun. T.
QUITTNER, RUDOLF.
Aus. Troppau 1872-1910 Paris. B-T.
QUIZET, LÉON ALPHONSE.
Fr. b. Paris 1885; ex. 1934 London. DBA-T.
QUOST, ERNEST.
Fr. b. Avallon 1843/4. B-T.

RAAB, [Mrs.] ADA.
Am. ad. 1934 New York. M.
RAAB, GEORGE.
Am. b. Sheboygan, Wis. 1866; ad. 1934 Decatur, Ill. A-F-T.
RAAB, GEORGE.
Aus. Vienna 1821-1885 Same. T.
RAAB, IGNAZ JOSEF.
Aus. Nechanitz 1715-1787 Prague, Czec. T.
RAABE, ALFRED.
Am. b. 1872; d. 1913 New York. A0X1.
RAABE [or Rabe], CARL JOSEF.
Ger. Wartenberg 1750-1846 Breslau. B-T.

RAADSIG, Johan Peter.
Dan. Copenhagen 1806-1882 Same. T.
RABANUS, Maurus.
Ger. Mainz 776-856 Same. T.
RABE, Edmund Friedrich Theodor.
Ger. Berlin 1815-1902. C-T.
RABEL, Daniel.
Fr. Paris 1578-1637 Same. B-T.
RABEL, Jean. (S)
Fr. Beauvais 1545-1602 Paris. T.
RABENSTEINER, Hans.
Ger. Villanders 1849-1930 Munich. T.
RABER, Virgil.
Ger. Sterzing 1475-1552 Dez. T.
RABES, Max Friedrich.
Ger. b. Pozen 1868; ac. 1930 Berlin. T.
RABES, Pierre.
Fr. Havre 1619-1684 Paris. T.
RABON, Johannes.
Dan. b. Copenhagen 1721? ac. 1778 in Haarlem. T.
RACHETTE, Antoine Jacques Dominique. (S)
Rus. Valencay 1744-1809 Leningrad. T.
RACHOTES, [Miss] Matene.
Am. b. Boston 1905; ad. 1934 Same. A.
RACKHAM, Arthur. (Ill)
Eng. London 1867; ad. 1934 Same. B-T-Wa-272.
RACZYŃSKI, Aleksander.
Pol. Lemberg 1822-1889 Same. T.
RADBOURNE, William H.
Am. Brooklyn, N. Y. 1838-1914 Orleans, N. Y. A0X1-T.
RADCLYFFE, Edward. (Eg)
Eng. Birmingham 1809-1863 Camden. B-DNB.
RADCLYFFE Family.
Eng. 18-19th Cent. in Birmingham. Bd-DNB-T.
RADCLYFFE, William [The Elder]. (Eg)
Eng. Birmingham 1796-1855 Same. B-Bd-DNB-T.
RADCLYFFE, William [The Younger].
Eng. Birmingham 1813-1846 London. B-Bd-DNB-T.
RADEMAKER, Abraham.
Dut. Lisse 1675-1735 Haarlem. B-T.
RADEMAKER, Gerrit [or Gérard].
Dut. Amsterdam 1672-1711. B-T.
RADENKOVITCH, Yovan.
Yugo-Slav. ex. 1935 New York. M.
RADER, Elaine Myers.
Am. ad. 1934 Wichita, Kan. A.
RADER, Isaac.
Am. Brooklyn, N. Y. 1906; ad. 1934 Detroit, Mich. A.
RÄDERSCHEIDT, Anton.
Ger. b. 1892. M.
RADITZ, Lazar.
Am. b. Dvinsk, Rus. 1887. Came to U. S. 1908; ad. 1934 Phila., Pa. A-F-T-W.
RADITZ, Violetta.
Am. ad. 1934 Phila., Pa. M.
RADL, Anton.
Ger. Vienna, Aus. 1774-1852 Frankfort. B-T.
RADNITZKY, Karl. (Med)
Aus. Vienna 1818-1901 Same. T.
RADOS, Luigi. (Eg)
It. Parma 1773-1840. B-T.
RADWÁNSKI, Andrzej.
Pol. b. 1709; d. 1762 in Cracow. T.
RADZIWILL, Anton Heinrich.
Pol. Wilnö 1775-1833 Berlin, Ger. T.
RADZIWILL, Franz.
Ger. b. Oldenberg 1895. T.
RAE, Henrietta.
Mrs. Ernest Normand.
Br. b. 1859; d. 1928 London. B-T-Y01929.
RAE, John. (Ill)
Am. b. Jersey City, N. J. 1882; ad. 1934 Caldwell, N. J. A-F-T-W.
RAEBEN, Norman.
Am. ad. 1934 New York. M.
RAEBURN, [Sir] Henry.
Scot. Stockbridge 1756-1823 Same. B-Bd-C-DNB-E-T-192-519-722-812.
RAEMAEKERS [or Reemaekers], Louis. (Cari)
Dut. b. Roermond 1869. B-E-T-873.
RAES Family.
Ger. ac. 17th Cent. in Germany. T.
RAFFAELLI, Giacomo.
It. Rome 1753-1836 Same. T.
RAFAELE DAL COLLE.
see Della Colle, Raffaellino.
RAFFAELLI, Jean François.
Fr. Paris 1850-1924 Same. B-DBA-T.
RAFFAELLINO DI BORGO SAN SEPOLORO.
see Della Colle, R.
RAFFAELLINO DEL GARBO.
It. 1466/76-1524 Florence. B-C-T.
RAFFAELLINO DA REGGIO.
see Motta, R. da R.
RAFFAELLO DA MONTELUPO.
see Montelupo, R. da.
RAFFAELLO, Sanzio. *see* Raphael, S.
RAFFALT Family.
Ger. ac. 19th Cent. in Germany. T.
RAFFET, Denis Auguste Marie. (Et)
Fr. Paris 1804-1860 Genoa, It. B-E-T-722.
RAGAN, Leslie.
Am. ad. 1934 New York. M.
RAGGI, Antonio [Lombardo]. (S)
It. Vico Morcote 1624-1686 Rome. T.
RAGGI, Mario. (S)
Eng. Carrara, It. 1821-1907 Farnam, Eng. DNB-T.
RAGGI, Nicolas Bernard. (S)
Fr. Carrara, It. 1790-1862 Paris. B-T.
RAGGI, Pietro Paolo.
It. Genoa 1646-1724 Bergamo. T.
RAGGIO, Giuseppe.
It. Chiavari 1823-1916 Rome. T.
RAGIS [or Ragel or Raxis], Gaspar.
Sp. ac. 1596-1609 in Sèville. T.
RAGOGLIA [or Raglia], Michele.
It. b. Palermo; ac. 1632-1686 in Naples. T.
RAGNENET [Father and Son].
Fr. ac. 1750-1777 in Paris. B-T.
RAHL, Karl.
Aus. Vienna 1812-1865 Same. C-T.
RAHL, Karl Heinrich.
Aus. b. 1779; d. 1843 in Vienna. T.
RAHMING, Norris.
Am. b. New York 1886; ad. 1934 Cleveland, O. A.
RAIBOLINI. *see* Francia, Il. Francesco.
RAIKEN, Leo.
Am. ex. 1934 Woods Hole, Mass. M.

RAILTON, HERBERT. (Ill)
Eng. Pleasington 1858-1910 London. DNB-T.
RAIMBACH, ABRAHAM. (Eg)
Eng. London 1776-1843 Greenwich. B-DNB-E-T.
RAIMBACH, DAVID WILKIE.
Eng. London 1820-1895. B.
RAIMONDI, CARLO. (Eg)
It. 1809-1883. B-T.
RAIMONDI, MARC ANTONIO. (Eg)
It. Bologna 1480/8-1527/34 Same. B-Bd-E-T-V-880-917-923-880.
RAIN, CHARLES WHEDON.
Am. b. Knoxville, Tenn. 1911; ad. 1935 New York. M.
RAINALDI, CARLO. (S)
It. Rome 1611-1691 Same. B-T.
RAINALDI FAMILY.
It. ac. 16th-17th Cent. in Rome. T.
RAINALDICTUS OF SPOLETO [or Raindaldo].
It. ac. 13th Cent. in Spoleto. T.
RAINALTER FAMILY.
Ger. ac. 18th-19th Cent. in Germany. T.
RAINES, MINNIE L.
Am. ad. 1935 Memphis, Tenn. M.
RAINEY, WILLIAM.
Eng. b. London 1852; ad. 1929 Same. B-T-Wa1929.
RAINGO-PELOUSE, GERMAIN FRANCK ERNEST.
Fr. b. Paris 1893. DBA.
RAISHO, NAKAJIMA.
Jap. d. 1876 in Japan. J., Vol. 2, page 95.
RAJECKA, ANNA. (Min)
Pol. Warsaw 1760-1832 Paris. T.
RAJON, PAUL ADOLPHE. (Eg)
Fr. Dijon 1843-1888 Auvers. B-T.
RAKEMANN, CARL. (Mu)
Am. b. Wash., D. C. 1878; ad. 1934 No. Chevy Chase, Md. A-F-T-W.
RAKU FAMILY.
Jap. ac. 16th-18th Cent. in Japan. T.
RALEIGH, HENRY PATRICK. (Ill)
Am. b. Portland, Ore. 1880; ad. 1934 New York. A28-F-W-T.
RALLI, THÉODORE JACQUES.
Fr. Constantinople, Turkey 1852-1909 Lausanne, Swi. B-T.
RALPH, GEORGE KEITH.
Eng. ex. 1778-1811 in London. DNB-T.
RALPH, LESTER.
Am. New York 1877-1927 Same. A024.
RÂM.
Hindu. ac. 1556-1605 India. T.
RAM, JOHANNES DE.
Dut. Amsterdam 1647/8-1696 Same. T.
RAMA, CAMILLO.
It. ac. 1610-1622 in Brescia. T.
RAMACCIOTTI, GIOVANNI BATTISTA.
It. Siena 1628-1671. T.
RAMAGE, JOHN. (Min)
Ir.-Am. Dublin 1748-1802 Montreal, Can.; came to U. S. 1775. DAB-F-T-2-701-786.
RAMASANOFF, NIKOLAI ALEXANDROWITSCH.
Rus. 1818-1867 Moscow. T.
RAMAUGÉ, ROBERTO.
Fr. b. Buenos Aires, Argentine 1890. DBA.
RAMAZZANI, ERCOLE.
It. Arcevia 1530-1598 Same. T.
RAMBERG, ARTHUR GEORG VON.
Aus. Vienna 1819-1875 Munich, Ger. B-C-T.
RAMBOUX, JOHANN HEINRICH.
Ger. Trèves 1790-1866 Cologne. B-T.
RAMBUSCH, FRODE C. W.
Am. Denmark 1860-1924 Brooklyn, N. Y. A022.
RAMELLI, FELICE. (Min)
It. Asti 1666-1741 Rome. T.
RAMENGHI, BARTOLOMEO [The Elder].
see Bagnacavallo, Il.
RAMENGLI, GIOVANNI BATTISTA.
It. Contarini 1521-1601 Bagnacavallo. T-V.
RAMER, NAT.
Am. ad. 1935 New York. M.
RAMEY, CLAUDE. (S)
Fr. Dijon 1754-1838 Paris. B-T.
RAMEY, ÉTIENNE JULES. (S)
Fr. Paris 1796-1852 Same. B-T.
RAMEY, HENRY.
Fr. b. La Fère 1890. DBA.
RAMÍFREZ, ANDRÉS.
Sp. ac. 1532-1567 in Sèville. T.
RAMIFREZ, JERÓNIMO.
Sp. ac. 1600 in Sèville. T.
RAMIFREZ, JÚAN.
Sp. ac. 1515-1554 in Sèville. T.
RAMIFREZ-IBÁÑEZ, MANUEL.
Sp. Arjona 1856-1925 Madrid. T.
RAMMELMAYER, ADAM. (S)
Aus. Vienna 1808/10-1850 Same. T.
RAMO DI PAGANELLO [Ramus]. (S)
It. ac. 1281-1320? in Siena. T.
RAMOS Y ALBERTOS, FRANCISCO JAVIER.
Sp. Madrid 1744-1817 Same. T.
RAMSAY, ALLAN.
Scot. Edinburgh 1713-1784 Dover, Eng. Bd-DNB-E-T-722.
RAMSAY, DAVID.
Scot. ac. 1613-1653 in Edinburgh. DNB-T.
RAMSAY, DAVID.
Scot. b. Ayr 1869; ad. 1934 Greenock. Wa.
RAMSAY, JAMES.
Eng. 1786-1854 Newcastle. B-DNB-T.
RAMSAY, MILNE.
Am. Phila., Pa. 1847-1915 Same. A012-C-F-T-15.
RAMSDELL, FRED WINTHROP.
Am. b. 1865; d. 1915 Manistee, Mich. A012-F-T.
RAMSEY, [Mrs.] ALICE HARVEY. *see* Harvey, Alice.
RAMSEY, EDITH. (S)
Am. ad. 1934 Brooklyn, N. Y. M.
RAMSEY, L. A.
Am. b. Bridgeport, Ill. 1873; ad. 1934 Salt Lake City, Utah. A-F.
RAMUS, CHARLES FREDERICK.
Am. ad. 1934 Cleveland, O. A.
RAMUS, JOSEPH MARIUS. (S)
Fr. Aix 1805-1888 Nogent. B-T.
RANC, JEAN.
Fr. Montpelier 1674-1735 Madrid, Sp. T.
RANCOULET, ERNEST. (S)
Fr. b. Bordeaux; ac. 1876. B.

RAND, Ellen G. Emmet.
Mrs. William Blanchard Rand.
Am. b. San Fran., Calif. 1876; ad. 1934 Salisbury, Conn. A-B-T.
RAND, Henry Asbury.
Am. b. Phila., Pa. 1886; ad. 1934 Holicong, Pa. A-F.
RAND, Margaret Arnold.
Am. Dedham, Mass. 1868-1930 Cambridge, Mass. A028-F.
RANDALL, Asa Grant.
Am. b. Waterboro, Me. 1869; ad. 1934 Prov., R. I. A-F.
RANDALL, D. Ernest.
Am. b. Rush Co., Ind. 1877; ad. 1935 San Fran., Calif. A12-F.
RANDALL, Paul A.
Am. b. Warsaw, Ind. 1879-1933 Indiana. A030.
RANDANINI, Carlo.
It. d. 1884 Rome. B-T.
RANDLE, Frederick W.
Eng. b. London 1847; d. Liverpool. Bd.
RANDOLPH, Lee F.
Am. b. Ravenna, O. 1880; ad. 1934 San Fran., Calif. A-F-W.
RANGER, Henry Ward.
Am. Syracuse, N. Y. 1858-1916 New York. A014-B-E-F-T-1-46.
RANKEN, William Bruse Ellis.
Scot. b. Edinburgh 1881; ad. 1934 Eversley. T-Wa.
RANKLEY, Alfred.
Eng. 1819-1872 London. B-DNB-T.
RANNELLES, Will.
Am. b. Caldwell, O. 1892; ad. 1934 Columbus, O. A.
RANNEY, Glenn.
Am. ex. 1934 Minn., Minn. M.
RANNEY, William S.
Am. Middletown, Conn. 1813-1857 West Hoboken, N. J. F-4.
RANSHÜ, Dan.
Jap. ex. 1930 in Tokyo. M.
RANSON, Caroline L. Ormes.
Am. Newark, O. 1838-1910 Wash., D. C. F.
RANSON, Thomas Frazer. (Eg)
Eng. Sunderland 1784-1828. B-DNB-T.
RANSONNETTE, Pierre Nicolas.
Fr. Paris 1745-1810 Same. B-T.
RANTVIC, Bernard [Flammengo]. (Min)
Flem. ac. 1573-1596 in Siena, It. B-T.
RÄNTZ Family.
Ger. ac. 17-18th Cent. in Bayreuth and Berlin. T.
RANVIER, Joseph Victor.
Fr. Lyons 1832-1896 Châtillon. B-T.
RANZONI, Gustav.
Aus. Unter-Nalb 1826-1900 Vienna. B-T.
RAON, Jean. (S)
Fr. Paris 1630-1707 Same. B-T.
RAOUX, Jean.
Fr. Montpelier 1677-1734 Paris. B-C-E-T-722.
RAPHAEL, Joaquin.
Por. Porto 1783-1864 Lisbon. B-T.
RAPHAEL, Joseph.
Am. b. Jackson, Calif. 1872; ad. 1934 San Fran., Calif. A-B-F.
RAPHAEL, Sanzio.
[or Raffaello Santi, or Sanzio da Urbino.]
It. Urbino 1483-1520 Rome. B-Bd-C-E-V-192-520-521-522-523-722-898.
RAPHAEL, William.
Can. Prussia 1833-1914 Montreal, Can. M.
RAPHAEL-SCHWARTZ. (P-S)
Rus. b. Kiev 1884. DBA.
RAPHON [or Raphun], Hans [or Johan].
Ger. b. Tinbeck; d. 1512 Dez. B-T.
RAPIN, Aimée.
Swi. b. Payerne 1869. T-829.
RAPIN, Alexandre.
Fr. Noroy 1840-1889 Paris. B-C-T.
RAPP, George. (Ill)
Am. ad. 1934 Phila., Pa. M.
RAPPAPORT, Dario.
Am. ad. 1934 Hollywood, Calif. M.
RAPPAPORT, Judith.
Am. ad. 1935 East Rockaway, L. I., N. Y. M.
RAPPARD, Clara de.
Swi. Berne 1862-1912 Same. B-T.
RASARIO, Ada. *see* Cecere.
RASCH, Heinrich.
Ger. Norburg 1840-1913 Koburg. B-T.
RASCHEN, Carl Martin.
Am. b. 1882; ad. 1934 Rochester, N. Y. A.
RASCOVICH, Roberto.
Am. Dalmatia, Aus. 1857-1904 Chicago. M.
RASER, J. Heyl.
Am. Mobile, Ala. 1824-1901 Williamsport, Pa. M.
RASINELLI, Roberto.
It. b. Rome; ac. 1877 in Naples. B.
RASKIN, Joseph.
Am. ad. 1935 New York. M.
RASKIN, Saul. (Et)
Am. ad. 1934 New York. A.
RASMUSSEN, Carl.
Dan. Isle of Aerö 1841-1893 Copenhagen. B-C-T.
RASPAY, Jean Pierre [The Younger].
Fr. Avignon 1748-1825 Same. B-T.
RASSENFOSSE, André Louis Armand.
Belg. Liège 1862-1934 Brussels. B-DBA-T.
RASTIELLI, Bartolomeo Carlo. (S)
It. Florence 1675?-1744 Leningrad, Rus. T.
RATGEB, Jerg.
Ger. 1480-1526. T.
RATHBONE, Charles H., Jr.
Am. b. New York 1902; ad. 1934 Same. A.
RATHBONE, Harold Steward.
Eng. b. 1858; ac. 1889-1929 in Liverpool. B.
RATHBONE, John.
Eng. Cheshire 1750-1807 London. B-DNB-T.
RATHBONE, Richard Adams.
Am. b. Parkersburg, Va. 1902; ad. 1934 New Haven, Conn. A.
RATHBUN, Seward Hume.
Am. b. Wash. 1886; ad. 1934 Same. A.
RATHSACK, Svend.
Swe. b. Copenhagen 1885. T.
RATLIFF, Blanche Cooley.
Mrs. Walter B. Ratliff.
Am. b. Smithville, Tex. 1896; ad. 1934 Atlanta, Ga. A.

RATTER, JANES. (Carver)
Br. 1820-1855. DNB.
RATTI, CARLO GIUSEPPE.
It. Savona 1737-1795 Genoa. T.
RATTI, GIOVANNI AGOSTINO.
It. Savona 1699-1775 Genoa. T.
RATTNER, ABRAHAM.
Am. ex. 1934 New York. M.
RATTY, ALBERT.
Belg. ex. 1934 New York. M.
RATZKA, ARTHUR LUDWIG.
Am. b. Andrejova, Hun. 1869; ad. 1934 New York. A.
RAU, KARL EMIL.
Ger. b. Dresden 1858. B-T.
RAU, LEOPOLD. (S)
Ger. Nüremberg 1847-1880 Rome, It. B-T.
RAU, WILLIAM.
Am. b. New York 1874; ad. 1934 Same. A.
RAUBER, WILHELM KARL.
Ger. b. Marienwerder 1849. B.
RAUCH, CHARLES.
Fr. Strasbourg 1791-1857 Nancy. B-T.
RAUCH, CHRISTIAN DANIEL. (S)
Ger. Arolsen 1777-1857 Dresden. B-E-Hs-T.
RAUCH, JOHANN NEPOMUK.
Aus. Vienna 1804-1847 Rome, It. B-T.
RAUCHIMILLER [or Rauchmüller], MATTHIAS. (S)
Ger. Baden-Baden 1645-1686 Vienna, Aus. T.
RAUGHT, JOHN WILLARD.
Am. Dunmore, Pa. 1857-1931 Same. A030.
RAUH, MAX.
Ger. ad. 1934 Munich; ex. 1934 Pittsburgh, Pa. M.
RAUH, STEPHAN.
Ger. Nürnberg 1822-1860 Dresden. T.
RAUL, HARRY LEWIS. (S)
Am. b. Easton, Pa. 1883; ad. 1934 Orange, N. J. A-Cs-F-W.
RAUL, JOSEPHINE GESNER.
Mrs. Harry Lewis Raul.
Am. b. Linden, N. J.; ad. 1934 Orange, N. J. A.
RAULSTON, MARION CHURCHILL.
Am. b. Great Falls, Mont. 1883; ad. 1934 Los Angeles, Calif. A.
RAUNACHER [or Rannacher], JOHANN BAPT. JAKOB.
Ger. Kärnten 1705-1757 Graz. T.
RAUPP, KARL.
Ger. Därmstadt 1837-1918 Munich. B-C-T.
RAURICH Y PETRE, NICOLÁS.
Sp. b. Barcelona 1872. T.
RAUSCHER, FRANZ ANTON.
Ger. b. Germany 1731. T.
RAUSCHNER, JOHN CHRISTIAN. (Wax)
Am. b. Germany 1760; ac. 1807 Boston, Mass. M-T.
RAVANNE, LÉON GUSTAVE.
Fr. Meulen 1854-1904 Mureaux. B-T.
RAVAUX, RENÉ HENRI.
Fr. b. Paris; ac. 1910 Same. B-T.
RAVÉ, JEAN.
Fr. Montpelier 1674-1735 Madrid, Sp. B.
RAVEL, EDOUARD JOHN.
Swi. Versoix 1847-1920 Geneva. B-T.
RAVEN, JOHN SAMUEL.
Eng. Suffolk 1829-1877 Harlech. B-DNB-T.
RAVEN-HILL, LEONARD. (Cart)
Eng. b. 1867; ad. 1934 London. E-T-Wa.
RAVENAUGH, AURELIUS O.
Am. Zanesville, O. 1840-1908 Louisville, Ky. M.
RAVENEL, PAMELA VINTON. (Min)
Am. ad. 1934 St. Mary's, Ga. M.
RAVENET, SIMON FRANÇOIS. (Eg)
Fr. Paris 1710-1774 London. B-DNB-T.
RAVENSCROFT, ELLEN.
Am. b. Jackson, Miss.; ad. 1934 New York. A.
RAVERAT, [Mrs.] GWENDOLEN. (Eg)
Eng. b. 1885; ad. 1934 Harlton. T-Wa.
RAVERAT, VINCENT NICOLAS.
Fr. St. Jean 1801-1865 Paris. B-T.
RAVESON, SHERMAN H.
Am. ad. 1935 New York. M.
RAVESTEYN, ARNOLD [or Arent].
Dut. 1625-1690 The Hague. B-T.
RAVESTEYN, JAN ANTHONISZ VAN, I.
Dut. 1572?-1657 The Hague. B-C-T-722.
RAVESTEYN, JAN ANTHONISZ VAN, II.
Dut. 1580-1669 The Hague. B-T.
RAVESTEYN, NICOLAS VAN, II.
Dut. Zalt-Bommel 1661-1750. B-T.
RAVIER, FRANÇOIS AUGUSTE.
Fr. Lyons 1814-1895 Morestel. B-T.
RAVILIOUS, ERIC WILLIAM. (Mu)
Eng. b. London 1903; ad. 1934 Same. Wa-825.
RAVLIN, GRACE.
Am. b. Kaneville, Ill. 1885; ad. 1934 New York. A-F-W14.
RAVY, JEAN. (S)
Fr. ac. 1318-1346 Paris. Hs-T.
RAWDON, FREEMAN. (Eg)
Am. b. Tolland, Conn. 1804 F-2-7-147.
RAWLE, SAMUEL. (Eg)
Eng. 1771-1860. B-DNB-T.
RAWLINS, THOMAS. (Med)
Eng. 1620?-1670 London. DNB-T.
RAWLINSON, ELAINE.
Am. ad. 1934 New York. M.
RAWSON, ALBERT LEIGHTON. (Ill)
Am. Chester, Vt. 1829-1902 New York. A04.
RAWSON, CARL WENDELL.
Am. b. Des Moines, Ia. 1884; ad. 1934 Minn., Minn. A-W.
RAY, RICHARD ARCHIBALD. (S)
Eng. b. London 1884; ad. 1934 Sunderland. Wa.
RAYMOND, ELIZABETH.
Am. b. New Orleans, La. 1904; ad. 1934 Same. A.
RAYMOND, FRANK WILLOUGHBY. (Et)
Am. b. Dubuque, Ia. 1881; ad. 1934 Chicago. A.
RAYMOND, GRACE RUSSELL.
Am. b. Mt. Vernon, O. 1877; ad. 1934 Winfield, Kan. A.
RAYMOND, JEAN. (S)
Am. ad. 1935 New York. M.
RAYMOND [or Resmont], PIERRE. (Enamel)
Fr. 1513-1584. B.

RAYNAUD, AUGUSTE.
Fr. b. Lyons; ac. 1877 in Paris. B.
RAYNAUD, LOUIS.
Am. b. New Orleans, La. 1905; ad. 1934 Same. A.
RAYNER, LOUIS J.
Eng. ac. 1852-1886 in London. B.
RAYNER, SAMUEL A.
Eng. ac. 1841-1872 in Brighton. B-DNB-T.
RAYNES, SIDNEY.
Am. b. Melrose, Mass. 1907; ad. 1934 Rockport, Mass. A.
RAYNESS, GERARD MATHIASSEN.
Am. b. Slater, Ia. 1898; ad. 1934 Ames, Ia. A.
RAYNESS, VELMA WALLACE.
Am. b. Davenport, Ia. 1896; ad. 1934 Ames, Ia. A.
RAYSKI, LOUIS FERDINAND VON.
Ger. Pegau 1807-1890 Dresden. B-T.
REA, BETTY. (S)
Eng. ex. 1933 London. M.
REA, DOROTHY [Mrs. Gardner].
Am. ad. 1934 Brook Haven, L. I., N. Y. M.
REA, JAMES.
Am. b. Forsythe, Mont. 1910; ad. 1935 St. Paul, Minn. M.
REA, JOHN LOWRA. (S)
Am. b. Beekmantown, N. Y. 1882; ad. 1934 Plattsburg, N. Y. A-Cs-F.
REA, WILLIAM CECIL.
Eng. b. London 1860. Wa1929.
READ, ADELE VON HELMOLD.
Am. b. Phila., Pa.; ad. 1934 Same. A.
READ, CATHERINE.
Scot. b. 1723 Scot.; ac. 1760-1778 in London. B-DNB-T.
READ, DAVID CHARLES.
Eng. Salisbury 1790-1851 London. B-DNB-T.
READ, EDWARD HARRY HANDLEY.
see Handley-Read, E. H.
READ, ELMER JOSEPH.
Am. b. Howard, N. Y. 1862; ad. 1934 Palmyra, N. Y. A.
READ, HENRY.
Am. b. Twickenham, Eng. 1851; ad. 1934 Denver, Col. A12-F-M.
READ, HOPE. (Et)
Eng. ex. 1934 in London. M.
READ, NICOLAS. (S)
Eng. d. 1787 in London. B-DNB-T.
READ, RICHARD. (Eg)
Eng. b. 1745?; d. 1790? Birmingham. B-DNB-T.
READ, SAMUEL.
Eng. Neadham 1815/6-1882/3 Sidmouth. B-DNB-T.
READ, THOMAS BUCHANAN.
Am. Chester Co., Pa. 1822-1872 New York. B-Bd-DAB-F-T-4-46.
READ, WILLIAM.
Am. England 1607-1679 Norwich, Conn. F. [Painted the first known portrait in U. S.]
READER, WILLIAM.
Eng. b. Maidstone; ac. 1680 in London. B-DNB-T.
READING, BURNET [or Benjamin]. (Eg)
Eng. b. Colchester; ac. 1776-1882 in London. B-DNB-T.
READIO, WILFRED A. (Eg)
Am. b. Florence, Mass. 1895; ad. 1934 Pittsburgh, Pa. A.
REAL DEL SARTE, MAXIME. (S)
Fr. b. Paris 1888. DBA-T.
REAM, CARDUCIUS PLANTAGENET.
Am. Lancaster, O. 1837-1917 Chicago. A014-F.
REAM, VINNIE [Mrs. Hoxie]. (S)
Am. b. Madison, Wis. 1847. F-Hs-Ta-15.
REASER, WILBUR AARON.
Am. b. Hicksville, O. 1860; ad. 1934 New York. A-F-W.
REATU, JACQUES.
Fr. Arles 1760-1833 Same. B-T.
REAUGH, FRANK.
Am. b. Jacksonville, Ill. 1860; ad. 1934 Oak Cliff, Tex. A-F.
REAVIS, ESMA JACOBS.
Am. b. Corinth, Miss. 1900; ad. 1934 Greenville, Tex. A.
REBAY, HILLA. [Baroness von Ehienwiesen.]
Am. b. Strasbourg, Alsace 1895; ad. 1935 New York. A.
REBECCA, BIAGIO.
It. Italy 1735-1808 London. B-DNB-T.
REBECK, STEVEN AUGUSTUS. (S)
Am. b. Cleveland, O. 1891; ad. 1934 Same. A-Cs-F.
REBELL, JOSEPH.
Aus. Vienna 1787-1828 Dresden, Ger. B-T.
REBISSO, LOUIS T. (S)
Am. Genoa, It. 1837-1899 U. S. A01-F-Hs-Ta.
REBOUET-ALBOY, ALFRED MARIE.
Fr. Paris 1841-1875. B-T.
REBOUL, JEAN BAPTISTE.
Fr. Chateauneuf 1810-1882 Beaucaire. B-T.
RECCA, GEORGE.
Am. ad. 1935 New York. M.
RECCHI, GIOVANNI PAOLO.
It. Como 1600-1683? T.
RECCHIA, RICHARD H. (S)
Am. b. Quincy, Mass. 1885; ad. 1934 Rockport, Mass. A-Cs-F.
RECCO, GIUSEPPE [Il Cavalière].
It. Naples 1634-1695 Madrid, Sp. B-C-T.
RECKHARD, GARDNER ARNOLD.
Am. Poughkeepsie, N. Y. 1858-1908 Same. A07.
RECKITT, FRANCIS WILLIAM.
Br. 1860-1932. Y01933.
RECKLESS, STANLEY LAWRENCE.
Am. b. Phila., Pa 1892; ad. 1934 New Hope, Pa. A.
RECKNAGEL, OTTO.
Ger. Eisfeld 1845-1926 Munich. B-T.
RECLAM, JEAN FRÉDÉRIC.
Ger. Madgeburg 1734-1774 Berlin. T.
RECTOR, ANNE. (Glass-P)
Am. ex. 1934 New York. M.
REDDING, JOHN Y.
Am. ad. 1934 Augusta, Ga. M.
REDELL, RAYMOND.
Am. ad. 1935 Milwaukee, Wis. M.
REDFERN, JAMES FRANK. (S)
Eng. Hartington 1838-1876 Hampstead. DNB-Hs-T.

REDFIELD, Edward Willis.
Am. b. Bridgeville, Del. 1869; ad. 1935 Center Bridge, Pa. A-B-F-W-46.
REDFIELD, Heloise Guillou. (Min)
Am. b. Phila., Pa. 1883; ad. 1934 Barnstable, Mass. A-F-46.
REDGRAVE, Richard.
Eng. Pimlico 1804-1888 London. B-Bd-DNB-E-T.
REDGRAVE, Samuel. (Eg)
Eng. London 1802-1876 Same. B.
REDI, Tommaso.
It. Florence 1665-1726 Same. B-T.
REDMAN, Harry Newton.
Am. b. Mt. Carmel, Ill. 1869; ad. 1934 Boston, Mass. A.
REDMOND, Charles C.
Am. Solon, Me. 1850-1889 Salem, Mass. M.
REDMOND, Frieda Voelter.
Am. b. Thun, Swi.; ac. 1893-1915 New York. A12.
REDMOND, Granville.
Am. b. Phila., Pa. 1871; ad. 1934 Los Angeles, Calif. A-F-W.
REDMOND, John J.
Am. b. Salem, Mass.; ac. 1891-1915 New York. A12.
REDMOND, Thomas. (Min)
Eng. Brecon 1745?-1785 Bath. B-DNB-T.
REDON, Odilon.
Fr. Bordeaux 1840-1916 Paris. B-DBA-T-192-524.
REDOUTÉ, Pierre Joseph.
Fr. St. Hubert 1759-1840 Paris. B-T.
REECE, Dora.
Am. Philipsburg, Pa.; ad. 1934 Phila., Pa. A.
REED, Abner. (Eg)
Am. East Windsor, Conn. 1771-1866 Toledo, O. F-2-7.
REED, Doel.
Am. b. Logansport, Ind. 1895; ad. 1934 Stillwater, Okla. A.
REED, Earl Howell. (Et)
Am. Geneva, Ill. 1863-1931 Chicago. A028-DAB-F-W16-46.
REED, Gardner.
Am. ad. 1934 New Orleans, La. M.
REED, Grace Adelaide.
Am. b. Boston 1874; ad. 1934 Same. A.
REED, James.
Am. ad. 1934 Brooklyn, N. Y. M.
REED, Joseph Charles.
Eng. b. 1822; d. 1877 in London. D-DNB-T.
REED, Lillian R.
Am. b. Phila., Pa.; ad. 1934 Same. A.
REED, Mary Williams ["Kate Carew"]. (Cari)
Am. b. San Fran., Calif. 1872; ad. 1934 London, Eng. W.
REED, Merle A. (Ill)
Am. ad. 1935 New York. M.
REED, Warren B.
Am. ad. 1934 New Orleans, La. M.
REEDER, Dickson.
Am. ad. 1935 Fort Worth, Tex. M.
REEMAEKERS. *see* Raemaekers.
REESBROECK, Jacob van.
Flem. Antwerp 1620-1704 Hoogstraten, Holland. B-T.
REEVE, R. G. (Eg)
Eng. ac. 1810-1837 London. T.
REEVES, Joseph Mason.
Am. b. Wash., D. C. 1898; ad. 1934 Los Angeles, Calif. M.
REEVES, Ruth.
Am. ad. 1934 New York. M.
REEVS, George M.
Am. b. Yonkers, N. Y.; ad. 1935 New York. A12-F.
REFINGER [or Reffinger], Ludwig.
Ger. Munich 1510/5-1548/9 Same. T.
RÉGAMEY, Félix Élie.
Fr. Paris 1844-1907 Antibes. B-T.
RÉGAMEY, Frédéric. (Eg)
Fr. Paris 1849-1925 Dez. B-T.
RÉGAMEY, Guillaume Urbain.
Fr. Paris 1837-1875 London. B-T.
REGEMORTER, Ignatius Josephus van.
Flem. Antwerp 1785-1873 Same. B-T.
REGEMORTER, Petrus Johann van.
Flem. Antwerp 1755-1830 Same. B-T.
REGENSBURG, Mary Pollak.
Am. ad. 1934 New York. M.
REGESTER, Charlotte.
Am. b. Balt., Md.; ad. 1934 New York. A.
REGGIANINI, Tirtorio [or Vittorio].
It. b. Modena 1858. B-T.
REGNAUDIN, Thomas. (S)
Fr. Moulins 1622-1706 Paris. B-T.
REGNAULT, Alexandre Georges Henri.
Fr. Paris 1843-1871 in battle. B-Bd-E-C-T.
REGNAULT, Guillaume. (S)
Fr. Nantes 1450-1531/3. B-Hs-T.
REGNAULT, Hippolythe Armand. (Eg)
Fr. ac. 1906 in Paris. B.
REGNAULT, Jean Baptiste [Baron].
Fr. Paris 1754-1829 Same. B-C-E-T-722.
REGNAULT, Nicolas François.
Fr. Paris 1746-1810. B-T-900.
REGNAULT-DELANDE, François Léandre.
Fr. Paris 1762-1824 Same. B-T.
RÉGNIER, Jacques Auguste.
Fr. Paris 1787-1860 Same. B-T.
RÉGNIER, Nicolas [Niccolò Renieri].
Flem. Maubeuge 1590-1667 Venice, It. B-T.
REGT, P. de.
Dut. b. Holland 1877. T.
REHBEINTZ, Markus Théodor.
Ger. Borstel 1791-1861 Kiel. T.
REHBERG, Frédéric.
Ger. Hanover 1758-1835 Munich. B-T.
REHFOUS, Alfred.
Swi. Geneva 1860-1912 Saillon. B-T.
REHN, Frank Knox Morton.
Am. Phila., Pa. 1848-1914 Magnolia, Mass. A0X1-B-C-DAB-F.
REICH, Jacques. (Et)
Am. Hungary 1852-1923 Dunraven, N. Y. A020-C-F.
REICHARD, Ernest Heinr. (S)
Ger. b. Gera; d. 1764 Berlin. T.
REICHENBACH, [Count] Woldemar von.
Ger. Walddorf 1846-1914 Dresden. B-T.

REICHERT, KARL.
Ger. Vienna, Aus. 1836-1918 Graz, Ger. T.
REICHERT, KARL FRIEDRICH.
Ger. b. Magdeburg; d. 1881 Berlin. B-T.
REICHL, ERNEST. (Ill)
Am. ad. 1934 New York. M.
REICHLE [or Reichel], HANS. (S)
Ger. Schongau 1570-1642 Berlin. T.
REICHLICH, MARX.
Ger. ac. 1494-1508 Salzburg. T.
REICHMANN, GEORG FRIEDRICH.
Ger. Münden 1798-1853 Hanover. B-T.
REICHMANN, [Mrs.] JOSEPHINE LEMOS.
Am. b. Louisville, Ky. 1864; ad. 1934 Chicago. A-F.
REID, ALBERT TURNER. (Ill)
Am. b. Concordia, Kan. 1873; ad. 1935 New York. A28-F.
REID, ALEXANDER.
Scot. Kirkcudbright 1747-1823. B-DNB-T.
REID, ARCHIBALD DAVID.
Scot. Aberdeen 1844-1908 Same. B-DNB-T.
REID, AURELIA WHEELER.
Am. b. Beekman, N. Y.; ad. 1934 San Pedro, Calif. A.
REID, CELIA CREGOR. (Eg)
Am. ad. 1934 St. Augustine, Fla. M.
REID, FLORA MAC DONALD.
Eng. b. London; ac. 1895-1929 Same. B-T-Wa1929.
REID, [Sir] GEORGE.
Scot. Aberdeen 1841-1913 Oakhill. B-E-T.
REID, GEORGE AGNEW.
Can. b. Wingham, Ont. 1860; ac. 1933 Montreal. M-T.
REID, GEORGE OGLIVY.
Scot. Leith 1851-1928 Edinburgh. B-T-Y01929.
REID, JAMES. (Ill)
Am. ad. 1934 Trevose, Pa. M.
REID, JEAN ARNOT. (Min)
Am. b. Brooklyn, N. Y. 1882; ad. 1934 New York. A.
REID, JOHN ROBERTSON.
Scot. Edinburgh 1851-1926. B-T.
REID, LORNA FYFE.
Can. b. London, Ont. 1887; ad. 1935 Toronto. M.
REID, MARIE CHRISTINE WESTFELDT.
Am. b. New York; ad. 1934 Same. A-F.
REID, MARY HIESTER.
Am.-Can. Reading, Pa. 1854-1921 Toronto, Ont. M.
REID, NINA MARGARET.
Eng. b. Hove 1891; ad. 1934 Surrey. Wa.
REID, N. WINDER.
Eng. ex. 1934 in London. M.
REID, OLIVER RICHARD.
Am. b. Eaton, Ga. 1898; ad. 1934 New York. A.
REID, PEGGY.
Am. b. Liverpool, Eng. 1910; ad. 1934 Westford, N. Y. A.
REID, ROBERT.
Am. Stockbridge, Mass. 1862-1929 Clifton Springs, N. Y. A027-B-DAB-E-F-T-W14-1-46-176.
REID, ROBERT O. (Ill)
Am. ad. 1935 New York. M.
REID, ROBERT PAYTON.
Scot. b. Edinburgh 1859; ad. 1934 Same. Wa.
REID, STEPHEN.
Scot. Aberdeen 1873; ad. 1934 London. T-Wa.
REIFFEL, CHARLES.
Am. b. Ind., Ind. 1862; ad. 1934 East San Diego, Calif. A-F-W-181.
REIFFENSTEIN, JOHANN FRIEDRICH.
Rus. Ragnit 1719-1793 Rome, It. T.
REIFFENSTUEL FAMILY.
Ger. ac. 16-17 Cent. in Germany. T.
REIGENBACH.
Ger. ac. 1800 in Germany. T.
REILLY, FRANK J.
Am. ad. 1935 New York. M.
REIMANS, RICHARD.
Dut. b. Amsterdam 1882; ad. 1934 Paris. DBA-T.
REIN, SURICA SINGER.
Am. ex. 1934 Brooklyn, N. Y. M.
REINA, SALVATORE. (S)
Am. b. Girgenti, It. 1898; ad. 1934 New York. A.
REINAGLE, GEORGE PHILIP.
Eng. b. 1802; d. 1835 in London. B-DNB-T.
REINAGLE, HUGH.
Am. Phila., Pa. 1790-1834 New Orleans, La. F-2.
REINAGLE, PHILIP.
Eng. b. 1749; d. 1833 Chelsea. B-DNB-T-722.
REINAGLE, RAMSAY RICHARD.
Eng. b. 1775; d. 1862 in Chelsea. B-DNB-T.
REINDEL, EDNA.
Am. b. Detroit, Mich.; ad. 1934 New York. A.
REINDEL, WILLIAM GEORGE.
Am. ad. 1934 Euclid, Ohio. A.
REINER, WENZEL LORENZ.
Czec. Prague 1686/9-1742 Same. T.
REINERT, FRED F.
Am. ad. 1934 Brooklyn, N. Y. M.
REINHARD, ALBERT GRANTLEY.
Am. b. 1854; d. 1926 Brielle, N. J. A023.
REINHARDT [or Reinhard], JOSEPH.
Swi. 1749-1824 Lucerne. B-T.
REINHART, BENJAMIN FRANKLIN.
Am. Waynesboro, Pa. 1829-1885 Phila., Pa. C-DAB-F-15-22-144-183.
REINHART, CHARLES STANLEY.
Am. Pittsburgh, Pa. 1844-1896 New York. Bd-C-DAB-E-F-15-46-55.
REINHART, HANS [The Elder]. (Med)
Ger. d. 1581 Leipzig. T.
REINHART, HANS [The Younger]. (Med)
Ger. d. 1622 Leipzig. T.
REINHART, JOHANN CHRISTIAN.
Ger. Hofe 1761-1847 Rome, It. B-C-E-T.
REINHOLD, FREDERICH PHILIPP.
Aus. Gera 1779-1840 Vienna. T.
REINHOLD, HEINRICH.
Aus. Gera 1790/90-1825 Albano, It. B-T.
REINHOLD, JOHANN FRIEDRICH. (S)
Ger. b. 1744; d. 1807 Gera, Aus. T.
REINICKE, PAUL RENÉ.
Ger. Strenz 1860-1926 Wildsteig. B-T.
REINICKE, PETER. (S)
Ger. Danzig 1715-1768 Munich. T.

REINIGER, Otto [The Younger].
Ger. b. Stuttgart 1863-1909 Same. B-T.
REISAPFEL, Berthold.
Am. b. Chicago 1911; ad. 1934 Same. A.
REISMAN, Philip.
Am. ad. 1934 New York. A.
REISNER, Irma Victoria.
Mrs. Ferdinand Betzlmann.
Am. b. Budapest, Hun. 1889; ad. 1934 Wilmette, Ill. A.
REISS, Fritz Winold.
Am. b. Germany; ad. 1934 New York. A-F.
REISS, Henriette.
Am. ad. 1934 New York. M.
REISS, Lionel S. (Et)
Am. b. Austria 1894; ex. 1933 New York. A-28.
REITLINGER, Gerald Roberts.
Eng. b. London 1900; ad. 1934 Same. Wa.
REITZEL, Marques E.
Am. b. Fulton, Ind. 1896; ad. 1934 Rockford, Ill. A.
REJCHAU [or Reichau or Rejhau] Family.
Pol. ac. 18-20th Cent. in Poland. T.
RELYEA, Charles M. (Ill)
Am. b. Albany, N. Y. 1863; d. 1932. A029-F-W7.
REM [or Rems], Gaspar.
Flem. Antwerp 1542-1615/7 Venice, It. B-T.
REMBERT, [Mrs.] Catherine Phillips.
Am. ad. 1934 Columbia, S. C. A.
REMBRANDT, Hermanszoon Van Rijn. (P-Eg) [or Harmensz Van Ryn.]
Dut. Leyden 1606-1669 Amsterdam. B-Bd-C-E-T-128-192-525-526-527-528-529-530-710-722-748-830-862-880-902-903-917.
REMBSKI, Stanislav.
Am. b. Sochaczew, Pol. 1896; ad. 1934 New York. A.
REMEEUS, David.
Flem. Antwerp, Belg. 1559-1626. B-T.
REMEEUS, Gillis.
Flem. 1605/22-1669/72 Antwerp, Belg. B-T.
REMINGTON, Elizabeth H.
Am. b. 1825; d. 1917 Flushing, L. I., N. Y. A014.
REMINGTON, Frederic. (P-S)
Am. Canton, N. Y. 1861-1909 Ridgefield, Conn. A08-B-DAB-E-F-T-46-71.
REMISOFF, Nicolai.
Am. b. 1887; ad. 1935 Wayne, Ill. M.
RÉMOND, Jean Charles Joseph.
Fr. Paris 1795-1875 Same. B-T.
RÉMOND, Joan [or Jean].
Fr. Nancy 1872-1913 Paris. B-DBA-T.
REMY, August.
Ger. Pasewalk 1800/1-1872 Berlin. B-T.
REMY, Louis Jean Marie.
Fr. Paris 1792-1869/72 Same. B-T.
RENALDICTUS DA SPOLETO.
[Rainaldo di Ranuccio da Spoleto.]
It. ac. 13th Cent. in Italy. T.
RENAN, Cornélis Ary.
Fr. Paris 1855/8-1900 Same. B-T.
RENARD, Émile.
Fr. Sèvres 1850-1930 Paris. B-T.
RENARD, François Xavier.
Fr. b. Paris; ac. 1864-1870 Same. B.
RENARD, Marcel. (S)
Fr. b. Lyons, 1893. DBA.
RENARD, Nicolas. (S)
Fr. Nancy 1654-1720 Same. B-T.
RENARD DE SAINT ANDRÉ, Simon.
Fr. Paris 1613/4-1677 Same. B-T.
RENAUD, Charles Alexandre.
Fr. Spoix 1756-1834 Vienna, Aus. B-T.
RENAUD, Francis. (S)
Fr. b. St. Brieuc 1887. DBA.
RENAUDOT, Paul.
Fr. Rome, It. 1871-1920 Paris. B-T.
RENDERS, Maurice. (Min)
Fr. b. Paris 1877. DBA.
RENÉ DUC D'ANJOU. [King of Naples.]
Fr. Angers 1408-1480 Aix. B-T.
RENEFER, Jean Constant Raymond.
Fr. b. Bétheny 1879. DBA.
RENESSE, Constantin Adrien.
Flem. Eindhoven 1626-1680 Same. B-T.
RENEVIEV, Julien.
Swi. Lausanne 1847-1907 Vevey. B-T.
RENI, Guido [Le Guide].
It. Bologna 1575-1642 Same. B-Bd-C-E-T-722-867.
RENICKE, Paul René.
Ger. Strenznaundorf 1860-1926 Wildsteig. B-T.
RENIER, Adriaen. (Illuminator)
Flem. d. 1519 in Belgium. B-T.
RENIER, Joseph E. (S)
Am. b. Union Hill, N. J. 1887; ad. 1934 Same. A.
RENIERI, Niccolò.
see Régnier, Nicolas.
RENNER, Otto Hermann.
Am. b. San Fran., Calif. 1881; ad. 1934 Paso Robles, Calif. A.
RENNIE, Frank. (Ill)
Am. ad. 1934 New York. M.
RENNIE, George. (S)
Eng. 1802-1860 London. DNB-T.
RENNIE, Nicolas.
Fr. Paris 1808-1859. B-T.
RENOIR, Antoine.
Fr. Paris 1731-1806 Same. B-T.
RENOIR, Pierre Auguste. (P-S)
Fr. Limoges 1841-1919 Cagnes. B-E-DBA-T-191-192-516-531-532-533-534-700-827-847-947.
RENOUARD, Charles Paul.
Fr. Churcheverny 1845-1924 Paris. B-T.
RENOUARD, George. (Et)
Am. b. Rochester, N. Y. 1885; ad. 1935 New York. M.
RENOUF, Émile.
Fr. Paris 1845-1894 Havre. B-C-T.
RENOUX, Charles Caius.
Fr. Paris 1795-1846 Same. B-T.
RENWICK, Christian.
Am. Eastham, Mass. 1726. F-2-233.
RENWICK, William Whetten. (P-S)
Am. Lenox, Mass. 1864-1933 Short Hills, N. J. A030.
RENZAN, Aoki [Ganku].
Jap. d. 1859 in Japan. J., Vol. 2, page 108.
REPIN, Ilja Jefimovich.
Rus. Leningrad 1844-1930 Knokkala. B-E-T.
REPPERT-BISMARCK, Jack von.
Ger. b. 1861; ex. 1931 New York. M.

RESCHI, Pandolfo.
Pol. Danzig, Ger. 1643-1699 Florence, It. B-T.
RESLER, George Earl. (Et)
Am. b. Waseca, Minn. 1882; ad. 1934 St. Paul, Minn. A-F.
RESLFELD [or Reselfeld], Johann Karl von.
Swi. Schwaz 1658-1735 Stift Garsten. T.
RESTOUT, Jean [The Younger].
Fr. Rouen 1692-1768 Paris. B-C-E-T-722.
RESTOUT, Jean Bernard.
Fr. Paris 1732-1797 Same. C-T.
RETHEL, Alfred. (Eg)
Ger. Aix 1816-1859 Düsseldorf. B-C-E-T-722.
RETTI Family.
Ger. ac. 18th Cent. in Germany. T.
RETTIG, John.
Am. b. Cinn., O.; d. 1932. A029.
RETTIG, Martin.
Am. b. Cinn., O.; ac. 1931. A28-F.
RETZ, Philip.
Am. b. Berlin, Ger. 1902; ad. 1934 New York. A.
RETZSCH, Friedrich Moritz August.
Am. Germany 1779-1857 New Dresden, N. Y. B-F-T-2.
REUSSING, William. (Ill)
Am. b. Somerville, N. J. 1902; ad. 1934 New York. M.
REUTERDAHL, Henry.
Am. Malbö, Swe. 1871-1925 Wash., D. C. A023-DAB-F-W13-46.
REUTERN, Gerarhdt Wilhelm von. [or Gerhard Christophorovitch.]
Rus. Russia 1794-1865 Frankfort, Ger. B-T.
REUVEN [or Ruyven], Pieter Jansz.
Dut. Delft 1651-1716 Same. B.
REUWICH [or Rewich], Erhart. (Eg)
Dut. b. Utrecht; ac. 1483. M.
REVEL, Gabriel.
Fr. Château-Thierry 1643-1712 Dijon. B-T.
REVERDY, Georges [or Cesare Riverdino].
It. ac. 1529-1561 in Padua. B-T.
REVERE, Marriette Winn.
Am. ad. 1934 Westfield, N. J. M.
REVERE, [Colonel] Paul. (Eg)
Am. Boston, Mass. 1735-1818 Same. F-2-7-40-535-536-537-880.
REVET, Nicolas.
Eng. Suffolk 1720-1804 London. B-T.
REVIER DE HUY. (S)
Flem. ac. 1140 in Liége. M.
REVOIL, Pierre Henri.
Fr. Lyons 1776-1842 Paris. B-T.
REVOLD, Axel.
Nor. b. Alesund 1887; ad. 1934 Lysaker, near Oslo. T.
REY, Augustin Adolphe.
Fr. b. Milan, It. 1864; ac. 1925 Paris. B-T.
REYL-HAMISCH, Herbert von.
Aus. b. Vienna 1898; ad. 1934 Same. T.
REYMOND, Carlos.
Fr. b. Paris 1884; ad. 1935 Same. DBA-T.
REYMOND, Pierre. *see* Raymond, P.
REYMOND-SUFFREN, Nanette.
Fr. b. Monaco 1895. DBA.
REYNARD, Grant T. (Et)
Am. b. Grand Island, Neb. 1887; ad. 1935 Leonia, N. J. A.
REYNAUD, François Maurice.
Fr. Marseilles 1825-1909 Paris. B-T.
REYNERSON, June.
Am. b. Mound City, Kan. 1891; ad. 1934 Terre Haute, Ind. A.
REYNOLDS, Frances.
Eng. Plympton 1729-1807 London. B-DNB-T.
REYNOLDS, Frank. (Ill)
Eng. b. London 1876; ad. 1934 Same. T-Wa.
REYNOLDS, Frederick Thomas. (Et)
Am. b. London 1882; ad. 1934 New York. A-F.
REYNOLDS, Harry Reuben.
Am. b. Centerburg, O. 1898; ad. 1934 Logan, Utah. A.
REYNOLDS, James. (Ill)
Am. ex. 1933 New York. M.
REYNOLDS, [Sir] Joshua.
Eng. Plympton 1723-1792 London. B-Bd-C-DNB-E-T-191-192-538-539-540-710-722-790-863-904-909-922.
REYNOLDS, Lawrence. (Cari)
Am. ad. 1935 New York. M.
REYNOLDS, Richard.
Am. England 1827-1918 Cinn., O. A015.
REYNOLDS, Samuel William [The Elder]. (Eg)
Eng. London 1773-1835 Bayswater. B-Bd-DNB-T.
REYNOLDS, Samuel William [The Younger].
Eng. London 1794-1872 Sussex. B-DNB-T.
REYNOLDS, Wellington Jarrard.
Am. b. Chicago 1866; ad. 1934 Same. A-F-W.
REYNOLDS-STEPHENS, [Sir] William. (S)
Eng. b. Detroit, Mich. 1862; ad. 1934 London. T-Wa-798.
REYNTJENS, Heinrich Engelbert.
Dut. Amsterdam 1817-1859 Same. B-T.
REZENDE [or Resende], Garcia de.
Por. Evora 1470?-1554. T.
REZNIKOFF, Misha.
Am. ad. 1935 New York. M.
RHEAD, Louis John. (Ill)
Am. Etruria, Eng. 1857-1926 Amityville, L. I., N. Y. A023-F-W14.
RHEAM, Henry Meynell.
Eng. Birkenhead 1859-1921. B-T.
RHEES, Morgan L.
Am. ac. 1888. M.
RHETT, Antoinette Francesca.
Mrs. Arthur Rhett.
Am. b. Balt., Md. 1886; ad. 1934 Charleston, S. C. A29.
RHETT, Hannah Mc Cord.
Am. b. Columbia, S. C. 1871; ad. 1935 Brevard, S. C. A28.
RHEYDAMS, Henry (Tapestry).
Belg. ac. 1629 in Brussels. M.
RHIND, John Massey. (S)
Am. b. Edinburgh, Scot. 1860; ad. 1934 New York. A-Cs-F-Hs-46.
RHIND, William Birnie. (S)
Scot. Edinburgh 1853-1933. B-T-Wa1929.
RHINELANDER, Olive Francis (Illuminator).
Am. ad. 1935 Sharon, Conn. M.

RHOADS, HARRY D. (Eg)
Am. ad. 1935 Stow, O. M.
RHOADS, KATHERINE.
Am. b. Richmond, Va. 1895; ad. 1934 Same. A.
RHODES, CHARLES WARD.
Am. d. 1905 Buffalo, N. Y. A06.
RHODES, HELEN N.
Am. b. Milwaukee, Wis.; ad. 1934 Seattle, Wash. A.
RHODES, JOHN N.
Eng. Leeds 1809-1842 Same. B-DNB-T.
RHODES, RICHARD. (Eg)
Eng. 1765-1838 Camdentown. DNB-T.
RHOECUS [or Rhoikos], (S)
Gr. ac. 575 B.C. in Samos. E-Hs-T.
RHOMBERG, HANNO.
Ger. Munich 1820-1869 Walchsee. B-C-T.
RHOMBERG, JOSEPH ANTON.
Ger. Dornbirn 1786-1853/5 Munich. C-T.
RHOME, LILY B. P. (Min)
Am. b. Phila., Pa. 1874; ad. 1934 Asbury Park, N. J. A.
RIBAK, LOUIS.
Am. b. Poland 1902; ad. 1934 New York. A.
RIBALTA, FRANCESCO DE.
Sp. Castellon 1551-1628 Valencia. B-T-722.
RIBALTA, JÚAN DE.
Sp. Madrid 1596-1628 Valencia. B-T.
RIBALTA, RUDOLF.
Aus. Vienna 1848-1904 Same. B-T.
RIBAUCOURT. *see* Master of R.
RIBCOWSKY, DEY DE.
Am. b. Bulgaria 1880; ad. 1935 Los Angeles, Calif. A20-F.
RIBEANCOURT, JULES.
Fr. d. 1932. B.
RIBERA, JUSÈPE [or Giuseppe].
[Called also Lo Spagnoletto.]
Sp. Jatiba 1588/90-1652/6 Naples, It. B-Bd-C-E-T-191-542-722-823.
RIBERA Y FERNANDEZ, JÚAN ANTONIO.
Sp. Madrid 1779-1860 Same. B-T.
RIBOT, AUGUSTIN THÉODULE.
Fr. Breteuil 1823-1891 Colombes. B-C-E-T-543.
RICARD, LOUIS GUSTAVE [or Gaston].
Fr. Marseilles 1823-1872 Paris. B-E-T.
RICCA, GASPANO.
Am. ad. 1935 New York. M.
RICCI and RICCIO. *see also* Rizi.
RICCI, ARTHURO.
It. b. Florence 1854. B-T.
RICCI, CAMILLO.
It. Ferrara 1580-1618 Same. C-T.
RICCI, FRANCESCO.
Sp. Madrid 1608-1685. T.
RICCI, GIAN PIETRO. *see* Gianpietrinio.
RICCI, MARCO.
It. Belluno 1676/9-1729 Venice. B-C-T-722.
RICCI, PIO.
It. d. 1919 Florence. B-T.
RICCI [or Rizzi], SEBASTIANO [or Bastiano].
It. Belluno 1659-1734 Venice. B-C-T-722.
RICCI, STEFANO. (S)
It. Florence 1765-1837 Same. Hs-T.
RICCI, ULYSSES A. (S)
Am. ad. 1934 New York. A28-F.
RICCIARDI, C. A.
Am. ex. 1935 New York. M.
RICCIARELLI, DANIELLO. *see* Volterra.
RICCIO, IL, ANDREA BRISCO. *see* Brisco, A.
RICCIO, FELICE. *see* Brusasorci.
RICCIO DA SIENA. *see* Neroni, Bartolommeo.
RICE, ANNE ESTELLE.
Eng. ad. 1934 London. M.
RICE, LUCY WILSON.
Mrs. C. D. Rice.
Am. b. Troy, Ala. 1874; ad. 1934 Austin, Tex. A.
RICE, MARGHUERITE SMITH. (S)
Mrs. Fred Jonas Rice.
Am. b. St. Paul, Minn. 1897; ad. 1934 Buffalo, N. Y. A.
RICE, NAN.
Mrs. Hugh Rice.
Am. b. Winnipeg, Can. 1890; ad. 1934 Chicago. A.
RICE, NITA.
Am. ex. 1934 Brooklyn, N. Y. M.
RICE, WILLIAM CLARK. (Mu)
Am. New York. 1875-1928 Same. A025.
RICE, WILLIAM MORTON JACKSON.
Am. Brooklyn, N. Y. 1854-1922. A022-F.
RICE, WILLIAM SELTZER. (Et)
Am. b. Manheim, Pa. 1873; ad. 1934 Oakland, Calif. A-F.
RICE, WILLIAM W. (Eg)
Am. ac. 1846-1860. F-7.
RICE-MEYROWITZ, JENNY DELONY.
Am. b. Wash., Ark. 1866; ad. 1935 Little Rock, Ark. A-F-W.
RICH, ALFRED WILLIAM.
Eng. b. Gravely 1856-1921 Tewkesbury. B-T.
RICH, JAMES ROGERS.
Am. Boston 1847-1910 Same. A08.
RICH, JOHN HUBBARD.
Am. b. Boston 1876; ad. 1934 Hollywood, Calif. A.
RICH, WALDO LEON.
Am. b. Schuylerville, N. Y. 1853-1930 Saratoga Springs, N. Y. A027.
RICHARD, ALEXANDRE LOUIS MARIE.
Fr. Millau 1782-1859 Toulouse. B-T.
RICHARD, FLEURY FRANÇOIS.
Fr. Lyons 1777-1852 Ecully. C-F.
RICHARD, JACOB.
Am. b. Ukrainia 1883; ad. 1934 Chicago. A.
RICHARDOT, JACQUES. (S)
Fr. Lunéville 1743-1806 Andenne. T.
RICHARDS, ANNA MARY.
Am. b. Germantown, Pa. 1870. 829.
RICHARDS, DAVID. (S)
Am. Wales 1829-1897 Utica, N. Y. A01-T.
RICHARDS, ELLA E.
Am. b. Virginia; ad. 1934 New York. A-F.
RICHARDS, FREDERICK THOMPSON. (Cart)
Am. Phila., Pa. 1864-1921 Same. A018-F.
RICHARDS, GEORGE MATHER.
Am. b. Darien, Conn. 1880; ad. 1934 New Canaan, Conn. A-F.
RICHARDS, HARRIET ROOSEVELT.
Am. b. Hartford, Conn.; ad. 1934 New Haven, Conn. A.
RICHARDS, JOHN INIGO.
Eng. b. 1740; d. 1810 in London. B-DNB-T.
RICHARDS, JOHN N.
Am. ex. 1935 Toledo, O. M.

RICHARDS, Lee Greene.
Am. b. Salt Lake City, Utah 1878; ad. 1934 Same. A.
RICHARDS, Lucy Currier. (S)
Mrs. F. P. Wilson.
Am. b. Lawrence, Mass.; ad. 1934 Norwalk, Conn. A.
RICHARDS, Myra Reynolds. (S)
Am. b. Ind., Ind. 1882. A20-Cs-F.
RICHARDS, Orren C.
Am. b. So. Boston, Mass. 1842. B-F-T-15.
RICHARDS, Richard Peter.
Eng. Liverpool 1839-1877 Pisa, It. B-T.
RICHARDS, Samuel.
Am. Spencer, Ind. 1853-1893 Denver, Colo. 181.
RICHARDS, Thomas Addison.
Am. London 1820-1900 Annapolis, Md. A02-B-C-DAB-F-T-4-11-15.
RICHARDS, Walter Du Bois.
Am. ad. 1935 Cleveland, O. M.
RICHARDS, William Trost.
Am. Phila., Pa. 1833-1905 Newport, R. I. A06-B-C-DAB-E-F-T-W3-4-11-15-46-234.
RICHARDSON, Andrew.
Am. 1799-1876 New York. F-T.
RICHARDSON, Benjamin J. (Et)
Am. London 1835-1926 Brooklyn, N. Y. A023.
RICHARDSON, Bertha G.
Am. ad. 1934 Toledo, O. M.
RICHARDSON, Catherine Priestly.
Am. b. New York 1900; ad. 1934 Brookline, Mass. A-F.
RICHARDSON, [Mrs.] Cherry Emma.
Am. b. 1859; ex. 1932 Dallas, Tex. M.
RICHARDSON, Clara Virginia.
Am. b. Phila., Pa. 1885. A28-F.
RICHARDSON, Earle Wilton.
Am. b. New York 1913; ad. 1934 Same. M.
RICHARDSON, Edward M. (S)
Eng. b. 1812; d. 1869 in London. B-DNB-T.
RICHARDSON, Francis Henry.
Am. Boston 1859-1934 Ipswich, Mass. A-B-F-M-T-W-Obit. Art Digest, 5-1-1934.
RICHARDSON, Frederic Stuart.
Eng. Clifton 1855-1934 Bristol. Wa1929.
RICHARDSON, Frederick. (Ill)
Am. b. Chicago 1862; ad. 1934 New York. A-F-W.
RICHARDSON, George.
Eng. 1736?-1817? London. B-DNB-T.
RICHARDSON, Harry C. (Ill)
Am. ad. 1934 New York. M.
RICHARDSON, Herbert. (Ill)
Am. ad. 1934 New York. M.
RICHARDSON, John F.
Am. ad. 1934 Nashville, Tenn. M.
RICHARDSON, Jonathan [The Elder]. (P-Author).
Eng. London 1665-1745 Same. B-Bd-E-DNB-T-803.
RICHARDSON, Jonathan [The Younger].
Eng. 1694-1771 London. B-DNB-T.
RICHARDSON, Margaret Foster.
Am. b. Winnetka, Ill. 1881; ad. 1934 Boston, Mass. A-W.
RICHARDSON, Marion.
Am. b. Brooklyn, N. Y. 1877; ad. 1934 New York. A.
RICHARDSON, [Mrs.] Mary Curtis.
Am. New York 1848-1931 San Fran., Calif. A028.
RICHARDSON, Mary Neal.
Am. b. Mt. Vernon, Me. 1859; ad. 1934 Boston, Mass. A.
RICHARDSON, Theodore J.
Am. Readfield, Me. 1855-1914 Minn., Minn. A012-F.
RICHARDSON, Thomas Miles [The Elder].
Eng. Newcastle 1784-1848 Same. B-DNB-T.
RICHARDSON, Thomas Miles [The Younger].
Eng. Newcastle 1813-1890 London. B-T.
RICHARDSON, Volney Allen.
Am. b. Attica, N. Y. 1880; ad. 1934 Buffalo, N. Y. A.
RICHARDSON, William.
Eng. ac. 1842-1877 in London. B-T.
RICHARDT, Joachim Ferdinand.
Dan. Seeland 1819-1895 Oakland, Calif. T.
RICHÉ, Louis (S)
Fr. b. Paris 1887; ad. Same. B-T.
RICHER, Paul M. L. Pierre. (S)
Fr. b. Chartres 1849. B-T.
RICHERT, Charles Henry.
Am. b. Boston 1880; ad. 1934 Arlington, Mass. A.
RICHET, Léon.
Fr. Solesmes 1844/7-1907 Paris. B-DBA-T.
RICHET, Teo.
Am. ad. 1934 New York. M.
RICHETON, Léon. (S)
Fr. France 1854-1934 London. M-T-Obit. Art News, 10-27-1934.
RICHEY, Oakley E.
Am. b. Hancock Co., Ind. 1902; ad. 1934 Ind., Ind. A.
RICHIER [or Richir], Herman Jean Joseph.
Belg. Ixelles 1866; ad. 1934 Brussels. B-T-Wa.
RICHIER, Jacob.
Fr. St. Michiel 1585/6-1639/40 Grenoble. B-T.
RICHIER, Jean I. (S)
Fr. St. Michiel 1581-1624 Same. B-T.
RICHIER, Jean II. (S)
Fr. b. St. Michiel; d. 1625 Metz. T.
RICHIER, Ligier [or Léger]. (S)
Fr. Lagonville 1500-1567/72. B-Hs-T.
RICHMOND, Agnes M.
Am. b. Alton, Ill.; ad. 1934 Brooklyn, N. Y. A.
RICHMOND, Evelyn K.
Am. b. Boston, 1872; ad. 1934 Santa Barbara, Calif. A.
RICHMOND, Gaylord D.
Am. b. Missouri 1903; ad. 1934 Altadena, Calif. M.
RICHMOND, George.
Eng. Brompton 1809-1896 London. B-Bd-C-DNB-T.
RICHMOND, Leonard.
Eng. ad. 1934 London. T-Wa.
RICHMOND, Thomas [The Elder]. (Min)
Eng. Kew 1771-1837 London. B-DNB-T.

RICHMOND, Thomas [The Younger].
Eng. London 1802-1874 Keswick. B-T.
RICHMOND, [Sir] William Blake.
Eng. London 1843-1921 Hammersmith. B-DNB-E-T.
RICHOMME, Joseph Théodore. (Eg)
Fr. Paris 1785-1849 Same. B-T.
RICHOMME, Jules.
Fr. Paris 1818-1903. B-C-T.
RICHTER, Adrian Ludwig.
Ger. Dresden 1803-1884 Same. B-C-E-T-880.
RICHTER, Christian. (Min)
Swe. Stockholm 1678-1732 London. B-DNB-T.
RICHTER, David [The Elder].
Swe. Stockholm 1662-1735 Vienna, Aus. B-T.
RICHTER, David [The Younger]. (S)
Swe. Stockholm 1664-1741. T.
RICHTER, Edouard Frédérick Wilhelm.
Fr. ac. 1884-1913 in Paris. B.
RICHTER, Emil Otto.
Ger. b. Löbnitz 1867; ad. 1934 Berlin. T.
RICHTER, Gustav Karl Ludwig.
Ger. Berlin 1823-1884 Same. B-C-T.
RICHTER, Henry James.
Eng. London 1772-1857 Marylebone. B-DNB-T.
RICHTER, Herbert Davis. (Et)
Eng. b. Brighton 1874; ex. 1934 in London. Wa.
RICHTER, Johan Heinrich
Ger. Coblenz 1803-1845 Same. B-T.
RICHTER [or Rychter], Josef.
Ger. Dresden 1780-1837 Warsaw, Pol. B-T.
RICHTER, Klaus.
Ger. b. Berlin 1887; ex. 1930 Same. T.
RICHTER, Otto Donner von.
see Donner von R.
RICHTER, Roman.
Ger. ac. 1630. M.
RICHTER, Wilmer S.
Am. ad. 1934 Brookline, Pa. M.
RICI. *see* Ricci; Riccio; Rizi.
RICIARELLI. *see* Volterra.
RICKETSON, Walton. (S)
Am. b. New Bedford, Mass. 1839; ad. 1925 Same. A23-F.
RICKETTS, Charles.
Eng. Geneva, Swi. 1866-1931 London. B-T-Wa1929-544-825.
RICKEY, George.
Am. ex. 1935 New York. M.
RICKLY, Jessie Beard.
Am. ad. 1934 St. Louis, Mo. A.
RICO Y ORTEGO, Martin.
Sp. Madrid 1833-1908 Venice, It. B-T.
RICOIS, François Edmé.
Fr. Courtalain 1795-1881 Paris. B-T.
RICOURT, Charles. (S)
Fr. b. Lille 1749; ac. 1795 Paris. B-T.
RIDDEL, James.
Scot. Glasgow 1858-1928. Wa1929-Y01929.
RIDDELL, [Mrs.] Annette Irwin.
Am. b. Oswego, N. Y.; ad. 1934 Laguna Beach, Calif. A.
RIDDELL, William M.
Am. b. Chicago 1877; ad. 1934 Laguna Beach, Calif. A.
RIDDICK, [Mrs.] M. E.
Am. ad. 1934 Norwalk, Conn. M.
RIDEL, Léopold.
Fr. ac. 1885 in Laval. B.
RIDEL, Louis Marie Joseph.
Fr. b. Vannes 1866; ad. 1934 Paris. B-DBA-T.
RIDER, Alexander.
Am. ac. 1810-1825 in Phila., Pa. F-2-6.
RIDER, Arthur G.
Am. b. Chicago 1898. A28.
RIDER, Charles Joseph.
Am. b. Trenton, N. J. 1880; ad. 1934 San Pedro, Calif. A.
RIDINGER [or Reidinger], Johan Elias.
Ger. Ulm 1695/8-1767 Augsburg. B-C-T-722.
RIDLEY, Matthew White.
Eng. Newcastle 1837-1888 London. B-T.
RIDOLFI, Carl.
It. Lonigo 1594-1658 Venice. T.
RIDOLFI, Claudio.
It. Verona 1570-1644 Corinaldo. B-T.
RIDOLPHINUS DA PISTOJA. (S)
It. ac. 12th Cent. in Pistoja. Hs.
RIEBER, Winifred.
Mrs. Charles H. Rieber.
Am. ex. 1934 New York. M.
RIEDEL, August Henrick [or Joseph].
Ger. Bayreuth 1799-1883 Rome, It. B-C-T.
RIEDEL, Gottlieb Friedrich.
Ger. Dresden 1724-1784 Augsburg. T.
RIEDER [or Reader], Marcel.
Fr. b. in Thann 1852. B-T.
RIEFSTAHL, Wilhelm Ludwig Friederich.
Ger. Neu Strelitz 1827-1888 Munich. B-C-T.
RIEGER, Albert.
Aus. Trieste 1834-1905 Vienna. B-T.
RIEKER, Albert George. (S)
Am. b. Stuttgart, Ger. 1890; ad. 1934 New Orleans, La. A.
RIEMENSCHNEIDER, Hans Tilman. (S)
Ger. Osterode 1460-1531 Würzburg. B-Hs-T-541.
RIEMERSCHMID, Richard.
Ger. b. in Munich 1868. B-T.
RIEPENHAUSEN, Ernest Ludwig. (Eg)
Ger. Göttingen 1765-1840 Same. B-T.
RIEPENHAUSEN, Franz.
Ger. Göttingen 1786-1831 Rome, It. B-C-T.
RIEPENHAUSEN, Johann.
Ger. Göttingen 1788/9-1860 Rome, It. B-C-T.
RIEPP, Johann Balthaser.
Ger. 1703-1764 in Germany. T.
RIESENBERG, Sidney H.
Am. b. Chicago 1885; ad. 1934 Yonkers, N. Y. A.
RIESENER, Henri François.
Fr. Paris 1767-1828 Same. B-T.
RIESENER, Louis Antoine Léon.
Fr. Paris 1808-1878. B-T.
RIESS, Wilhelm J.
Am. Berlin, Ger. 1856-1919 Chicago. A016.
RIETER, Heinrich.
Swi. Winterthur 1751-1818 Berne. B-T.
RIETSCHEL, Ernest Friedrich August. (S)
Ger. Pulsnitz 1804-1861 Dresden. B-E-Hs-T.
RIETSCHOOF, Jansz Claes.
Dut. Hoorn 1652-1719 Same. B-T.

RIETTI, ARTURO.
Aus. b. Triest 1863. B-T.
RIFFLE, ELBA LOUISA.
Am. b. Winimac, Ind. 1905; ad. 1934 Same. A.
RIGAL, LOUIS. (Mu)
Am. ac. 1934 New York. M.
RIGAUD Y ROS, HYACINTHE.
Fr. Perpignan 1659-1743 Paris. B-C-E-T-722-897.
RIGAUD, JACQUES.
Fr. Marseilles 1681-1754 Paris. B-T.
RIGAUD, JOHN FRANCIS.
Eng. Turin, It. 1742-1810 London. B-DNB-T.
RIGAUD, PIERRE GASTON.
Fr. b. Bordeaux 1874. DBA-T.
RIGAUD, STEPHEN FRANCIS DUTILH.
Eng. London 1777-1861 Same. B-DNB-T.
RIGBY, CUTHBERT.
Eng. b. Liverpool 1850. B-T.
RIGBY, JOSEPH P. (Cart)
Am. Youngstown, O. 1874-1934 Swissvale, Pa. M-Obit. N. Y. papers, 7-14-1934.
RIGGS, ROBERT. (Eg)
Am. ad. 1934 Phila., Pa. M.
RIGO, JULES ALFRED VINCENT.
Fr. Paris 1810-1892 Same. B-T.
RIGOLOT, ALBERT GABRIEL.
Fr. Paris 1862-1932 Same. B-DBA-T.
RIJ-ROUSSEAU [née Jeanne Caffier].
Fr. b. Cande; ex. 1925 in Paris. DBA.
RIJN, or RYN. *see* Rembrandt, H. van.
RILEY, FRANK H.
Am. b. St. Joseph, Mo. 1894; ad. 1934 Highland Park, Ill. A.
RILEY, GARADA CLARK.
Am. b. Chicago, Ill. 1894; ad. 1934 Highland Park, Ill. A.
RILEY [or Ryley], JOHN.
Eng. London 1646-1691 Same. B-Bd-DNB-T-702.
RILEY, MARY G.
Am. b. Wash., D. C.; ad. 1934 Same. A-F.
RILEY, NICOLAS F.
Am. ad. 1934 New York. M.
RILLAERT, JAN VAN.
Flem. Antwerp, 1495-1568 Louvain. B-T.
RIMINALDI, ORAZIO.
It. Pisa 1586-1630/1 Same. B-T.
RIMINI, LATTANZIO DA.
see Lattanzio, R.
RIMMER, ALFRED. (Author-Ill)
Eng. Liverpool 1829-1893 Chester. B-DNB-T.
RIMMER, CAROLINE HUNT. (S)
Am. Randolph, Mass. 1851-1918 Boston. M.
RIMMER, WILLIAM. (S)
Am. Liverpool, Eng. 1816-1879 So. Milford, Mass. DAB-E-F-Hs-T-Ta-15-235-701.
RINALDI, RINALDO. (S)
It. Padua 1793-1873 Rome. B-T.
RINCÓN, ANTONIO DEL.
Sp. Guadalaxara 1446-1500. B-T-722.
RINEHART, WILLIAM HENRY. (S)
Am. Frederick, Md 1825-1874 Rome, It. DAB-F-Hs-T-Ta-15-175.
RING, ALICE BLAIR.
Am. b. Knightville, Mass. 1869; ad. 1934 Pomona, Calif. A.
RING, HERMANN TOM.
Ger. Münster 1521-1597/9. B-T.
RING, LAURITZ [or Lars] ANDERSON.
Dan. Seeland 1854-1933 Roskilde. B-T.
RING, LUDGER TOM [The Elder].
Ger. Münster 1496-1547. B-T.
RING, LUDGER TOM [The Younger].
Ger. Münster 1522-1583/4 Brunswick. B-T.
RING, NICOLAUS TOM.
Ger. 1564-1622. T.
RING [or Ryngt], PIETER DE.
Dut. Leyden 1615-1660 Same. B-C-T.
RINGIUS, CARL SIGFRID.
Am. b. Bastad, Swe. 1879; ad. 1934 Hartford, Conn. A.
RINKEN, SHIBA [Hogen].
Jap. J., Vol. 1, page 73.
RIODAN, ROGER. (Ill)
Am. Ireland 1848-1904 New York. A05.
RION, [Mrs.] HANNA.
Am. So. Car. 1875-1924 Bermuda. A021.
RIOS, LUIGI DA.
It. Caneda 1844-1892 Venice. B-T.
RIOULT, LOUIS EDOUARD.
Fr. Montdidier 1780-1855 Paris. B-T.
RIP, WILLIAM CORNELIS.
Dut. b. Rotterdam 1856. B-T.
RIPLEY, AIDEN LASSELL.
Am. b. Wakefield, Mass. 1896; ad. 1934 Lexington, Mass. A.
RIPLEY, LUCY PERKINS. (S)
Am. b. Winona, Minn.; ad. 1934 Westbury, L. I., N. Y. A-F-W.
RIPLEY, ROBERT LE ROY ["Rip"]. (Cart)
["Believe It or Not" Series.]
Am. b. Santa Rosa, Calif. 1893; ad. 1935 New York. W.
RIPLEY, THOMAS EMERSON.
Am. b. Portland, Vt. 1865; ad. 1934 Santa Barbara, Calif. A.
RIPPINGILLE, EDWARD VILLIERS.
Eng. Norfolk 1798?-1859 Birmingham. B-DNB-T.
RIPPL-RÓNAI, JÓZSEF.
Hun. Kaposvár [Ungarn] 1861-1927 Same. T.
RISCHGITZ, PAUL EDOUARD.
Eng. Ghent, Belg. 1828-1909 London. T-Y01910.
RISHER, ANNA PRISCILLA.
Am. b. Dravosburgh, Pa. 1875; ad. 1934 Laguna Beach, Calif. A.
RISING, JOHN.
Eng. 1756-1815 London. B-DNB-T.
RISQUE, CAROLINE EVERETT. (S)
Am. b. St. Louis, Mo. 1886; ad. 1934 Clayton, Mo. A.
RISS, FRANÇOIS.
Fr. Moscow, Rus. 1804-1866 Paris. B-T.
RISSANEN, JUHO VILHO.
Fin. b. Kuopio, Finland 1873. DBA-T.
RISWOLD, GILBERT P. (S)
Am. b. Sioux Falls, So. Dak. 1881; ad. 1935 Chicago. A12-F.
RITCHIE, ALEXANDER.
Am. b. Scotland 1863; ad. 1934 Hicksville, L. I., N. Y. A.
RITCHIE, ALEXANDER HANDYSIDE. (S)
Scot. 1804-1870 Edinburgh. DNB-T.

RITCHIE, Alexander Hay. (Eg)
Am. Glasgow, Scot. 1822-1895 New Haven, Conn. C-DAB-F-T-7-15-40-55.
RITCHIE, John.
Br. 1809-1850. DNB-T.
RITCHIE, Lord.
Scot. ac. Dundee 1932. M.
RITMAN, Louis.
Am. b. Russia 1889; ad. 1934 Chicago. A.
RITSCHEL, William.
Am. b. Nüremberg, Ger. 1864; ad. 1934 Carmel, Calif. A-F-W-757.
RITSON, Jonathan. (Carver)
Eng. Whitehaven 1776-1846 Petworth. DNB-T.
RITSUO, Ogawa [Haritsu].
Jap. Ise 1662-1747 Tokio. J-T.
RITT, Augustin.
Rus. Leningrad 1756-1799. B-T.
RITTENBERG, Henry R.
Am. b. Libau, Rus. 1879; ad. 1934 New York. A-F-W.
RITTER, Alonzo W.
Am. b. Hagerstown, Md. 1898; ad. 1934 Same. A.
RITTER, Anne Gregory.
Am. b. Plattsburg, N. Y. 1868. A28.
RITTER, Edouard.
Aus. Vienna 1808-1853 Same. B-T.
RITTER, Henry.
Can. Montreal 1816-1853 Düsseldorf, Ger. B-C-E-T.
RITTER, Louis.
Am. 1854-1892 Cinn., O. M.
RITTER, Paul.
Ger. Nüremberg 1829-1907 Berlin. B-T.
RITZ, Raphaël.
Ger. Brig 1829-1894 Sitten. B-T.
RITZBERGER, Albert.
Ger. Pfaffstadt 1853-1915. T.
RITZEROW, Antoine.
Ger. b. Grabow 1877; ad. 1934 Munich. T.
RIVALTA, Augusto. (S)
It. Alessandria 1837/8-1925 Florence. B-T.
RIVALTZ, Antoine.
Fr. Toulouse 1677-1735 Same. B-T.
RIVALTZ, Jean Pierre.
Fr. Labastide 1625-1706 Toulouse. B-T.
RIVÉ, Pierre Louis de la.
Swi. Geneva 1753-1817. B.
RIVERA, Diego M. (Mu)
Mex. b. Guanojuato 1886; ac. 1935 Mexico. T-545-783-791-908.
RIVERS, Rosetta R.
Am. ad. 1935 Macon, Ga. M.
RIVIÈRE, Benjamin Jean Pierre Henri.
Fr. b. Paris 1864. B-DBA-T.
RIVIÈRE, Briton.
Eng. London 1840-1920 Same. B-C-DNB-E-T.
RIVIÈRE, Dahnac.
see Dagnac-Rivière.
RIVIÈRE, Henry Parsons.
Eng. b. 1811; d. 1888 London. B-DNB-T.
RIVIÈRE, Hugh Goldwin.
Eng. b. Bromley 1869; ad. 1934 London. B-T-Wa.
RIVIÈRE, Théodore Auguste. (S)
Fr. Toulouse 1857-1912 Paris. B-T-798.
RIVOIRE, Françoise.
Fr. Lyons 1842-1919 Grand St. Léger. B-T.
RIVOIRE, Raymond. (S)
Fr. b. Cusset 1884; ad. 1934 Paris. B-DBA-T.
RIX, Julian Walbridge.
Am. Peacham, Vt. 1850-1903 New York. A05-DAB-F.
RIXENS, Jean André.
Fr. St. Gaudens 1846-1924 Paris. B-T.
RIZA, Aqa. (Min)
Per. ac. 16-17th Cent. in Persia. T.
RIZA Y ABBASSI, Ali. (Min)
Per. ac. 16-17th Cent. in Persia. M-T.
RIZI [or Riccio], Antonello.
It. or Sp. d. 1610 Messina, It. T-722.
RIZI [or Ricci], Francesco.
Sp. Madrid 1608-1685. B-C-T-722.
RIZI [or Rici or Ricci], Fray Juan Andrés.
Sp. Madrid 1595/1600-1681 Monte Cassino, It. B-T-722.
RIZO [or Riccio], Andrea.
It. Padua 1470-1532 Same. T.
RIZOS, Jacques.
Gr. b. Athens; ac. 1900 Paris. B.
RIZZO, Antonio. (S)
It. d. 1499 in Venice. Hs-T.
RIZZONI, Alexandre.
Rus. Riga 1836-1902 Rome, It. B-T.
ROBAUDI, Alcite Theophile.
Fr. Nice 1850-1928. B-DBA-T.
ROBB, Brian.
Eng. ex. 1934 London. M.
ROBB, Elizabeth B.
Am. ad. 1934 Emsworth, Pa. A.
ROBBE, Henri.
Belg. Courtrai 1808-1887 Brussels. B-T.
ROBBE, Louis Marie Dominique Romain.
Belg. Courtrai 1806-1887 Brussels. B-T.
ROBBIA, [Fra] Ambrogio della. (S)
It. ac. 1504 in Siena. Hs-T.
ROBBIA, Andrea della. (S)
It. 1435-1525 Florence. B-E-Hs-T-V-546.
ROBBIA, Giovanni della. (S)
It. 1469-1529? Florence. B-E-Hs-T-V-546.
ROBBIA, Girolamo della. (S)
It. 1488-1566 Florence. B-E-Hs-T-V-546.
ROBBIA, Luca della. (S)
It. 1399-1482 Florence. B-E-Hs-T-V-546.
ROBBIA, Mattia della. (S)
It. ac. 1527-1530. Hs-T.
ROBBIE. *see* Robie.
ROBBINS, Ellen.
Am. 1828-1905. F.
ROBBINS, Horace Wolcott.
Am. Mobile, Ala. 1842-1904 New York. A05-C-F-3-15.
ROBBINS, John Williams.
Am. b. Windham, Conn. 1856; ad. 1934 Boston. A28-F-W.
ROBERT, Alexandre Nestor Nicolas.
Belg. Hainaut 1817-1890 Brussels. B-T.
ROBERT, Aurèle.
Swi. Eplatures 1805-1871. B-T.
ROBERT, Hubert [des Ruines].
Fr. Paris 1733-1808 Same. B-C-E-T-192-549-722.

ROBERT, Louis Léopold.
Swi. Neuchâtel 1794-1835 Venice, It. B-C-E-T-722.
ROBERT, Louis Valentin Elias. (S)
Fr. Éstampes 1821-1874 Paris. B-T.
ROBERT, Marius Hubert. (Mu)
Fr. ac. 1934 Paris. M.
ROBERT, Nicolas.
Fr. Langres 1614-1685 Paris. T.
ROBERT, Paul Ponce Antoine.
Fr. b. 1686; d. 1733 in Paris. B-T.
ROBERT, Théophile.
Fr. b. 1879. T-550.
ROBERT-FLEURY, Joseph Nicolas.
Fr. Cologne, Ger. 1797-1890 Paris. B-C-T.
ROBERT-FLEURY, Tony.
Fr. Paris 1838-1912 Same. B-C-E-T.
ROBERTI, Domenico.
It. Rome 1642-1707 Same. B-T.
ROBERTI, Ercole de.
It. Ferrara 1440/5-1495/6. T-V.
ROBERTS, Alfred.
Eng. ex. 1934 London. M.
ROBERTS, Alice Mumford. *see* Culin, A. M.
ROBERTS, Blanche Gilroy. (S)
Am. b. Phila., Pa. 1871; ad. 1935 Bronx, N. Y. A12-F.
ROBERTS, David.
Scot. Edinburgh 1796-1864 London. B-Bd-C-DNB-E-T.
ROBERTS, Elizabeth Wentworth.
Am. Phila., Pa. 1871-1927 Concord, Mass. A024-B-F-T.
ROBERTS, Ellis William.
Eng. Stoke 1860-1930 London. T-Wa1929-Y01931.
ROBERTS, Henry Benjamin.
Eng. Liverpool 1831-1915 Leyton. B-T.
ROBERTS, Howard. (S)
Am. Phila., Pa. 1843-1900 Paris. A02-F-T-Ta-15.
ROBERTS, Jack. (Ill)
Fr. b. Paris 1894. DBA-T.
ROBERTS, James [The Elder].
Eng. ac. 1766-1809 in Westminster. B-DNB-T.
ROBERTS, James [The Younger].
Fr. ac. 1818-1846 in Paris. B-T.
ROBERTS, Jessie M.
Am. ad. 1934 Cinn., O. M.
ROBERTS, John. (Eg)
Am. Scotland 1768-1803 New York. F-2-6-7-45.
ROBERTS, John Taylor. (S)
Am. b. Germantown, Pa. 1878; ad. 1915 Phila., Pa. A12.
ROBERTS, Josephine Seaman.
Am. b. Los Angeles, Calif.; ac. 1934 Same. A.
ROBERTS, Thomas.
Ir. Waterford, Ir. 1749-1794 Lisbon, Por. B-DNB-T.
ROBERTS, Thomas Sautelle.
Ir. Waterford, Ir. 1760?-1826. B-DNB.
ROBERTS, Tom.
Aust. b. Dorchester, Eng. 1856. B-T.
ROBERTS, [Mrs.] Violet Kent.
Am. b. The Dalles, Ore. 1880; ad. 1934 Wash., D. C. A.
ROBERTS, William.
Eng. 1788-1867. DNB-825.
ROBERTS, William Patrick.
Eng. b. London 1895; ad. 1934 Same. T-Wa.
ROBERTSON, Alexander. (Min)
Am. Aberdeen, Scot. 1772-1841 New York. B-F-T-2-6-182-184.
ROBERTSON, Andrew. (Min)
Scot. Aberdeen 1777-1845 London. B-Bd-DNB-T.
ROBERTSON, Archibald. (Min)
Am. Monymusk, Scot. 1765-1835 New York. B-DNB-F-T-2-6-45-182-786.
ROBERTSON, Charles.
Eng. d. 1891 in Walton. B-T.
ROBERTSON, Charles.
Ir. Dublin 1759/60-1821 London. B-T.
ROBERTSON, Eric Harold Macbeth.
Scot. b. Dumfries 1877. Wa-Y1927.
ROBERTSON, Forbes.
Am. b. 1853. M.
ROBERTSON, George.
Eng. London 1742/8-1788. B-Bd-DNB-T.
ROBERTSON, George Edward.
Eng. Chelsea 1864; ad. 1934 London. T-Wa.
ROBERTSON, George J.
Am. b. England; d. 1870 Rockford, Ill. M.
ROBERTSON, Percy. (Et)
Eng. b. Bellagio, It. 1869; ad. 1934 London. T-Wa.
ROBERTSON, Sarah Margaret Armour.
Can. b. Montreal 1891; ad. 1935 Same. M.
ROBERTSON, Tom.
Scot. b. Glasgow 1850; ad. 1934 Eastbourne. B-T-Wa.
ROBERTSON, Walford Graham.
Eng. b. London 1867; ad. 1934 Witley. T-Wa.
ROBERTSON, Walter.
Am. Dublin, Ir. 1760-1802 Futlehpore, India. B-F-T-2-6-182-786.
ROBERTUS [da Lucca]. (S)
It. ac. 12th Cent. in Lucca. Hs-T.
ROBESON, Edna Amelia. (Min)
Am. b. Davenport, Ia. 1887; ad. 1934 Woodstock, N. Y. A.
ROBETTA, Christoforo di Michele. (Eg)
It. Florence 1462-1522? Same. T.
ROBIDA, Albert. (Ill)
Fr. Compiègne 1848-1926 Neuilly. B-T.
ROBIE [or Robbie], Jean Baptiste.
Belg. Brussels 1821-1910. B-T.
ROBIN, Jean Baptiste Claude.
Fr. Paris 1734-1818 Chousy. B-T.
ROBINET, Paul Gustave [The Elder].
Fr. Magny-Vernois 1845-1932. B-DBA-T.
ROBINET, Paul Gustave [The Younger].
Fr. b. Poissy 1877. B-T.
ROBINET, Pierre Alfred. (S)
Fr. Paris 1814-1879. B-T.
ROBINS, Louisa.
Am. ad. 1934 Buffalo, N. Y. M.
ROBINS, Susan B. P.
Am. b. Boston 1849; ad. 1935 Same. A12-F.
ROBINS, William Palmer.
Eng. b. London 1882; ad. 1934 Sutton. T-Wa.
ROBINSON, Adah Matilda.
Am. b. Richmond, Ind. 1882; ad. 1934 Tulsa, Okla. A.

ROBINSON, Albert Henry.
Can. b. Hamilton, Ont. 1881; ad. 1935 Montreal, Que. M.
ROBINSON, Alexander Charles.
Am. b. Portsmouth, N. H. 1867; ad. 1934 Paris. A-F-W.
ROBINSON, Alonzo Clark. (S)
Am. b. Darien, Conn. 1876. A28.
ROBINSON, Boardman. (Ill)
Am. b. Somerset, Nova Scotia 1876; ad. 1934 Colorado Springs, Colo. A-F-W-46-701-779-783.
ROBINSON, Charles.
Eng. b. 1870; ex. 1934 London. T.
ROBINSON, Charles Dorman.
Am. Maine 1847-1933 San Rafael, Calif. F-WX1.
ROBINSON, Charles Hoxsey.
Am. b. Edwardsville, Ind. 1862; ad. 1934 Morro Bay, Calif. A.
ROBINSON, David. (Ill)
Am. b. Warsaw, Pol. 1886; ad. 1934 Silvermine, Conn. A-F.
ROBINSON, Delia Mary.
Am. b. Waterloo, Neb.; ad. 1934 Same. A.
ROBINSON, Douglas F.
Eng. London 1864-1929. B-T.
ROBINSON, Florence Vincent.
Am. b. Boston 1874; ad. 1934 New York. A-F-W.
ROBINSON, Francis Stanislaus.
Eng. b. Manchester 1885. Wa1929.
ROBINSON, Frederic Cayley.
Eng. Brentford 1862-1927 London. B-T-Y01928-825.
ROBINSON, George Crosland [Captain].
Eng. ac. 1882-1930 in London. B-T-Y01931.
ROBINSON, Gertrude Pew. (Min)
Am. ad. 1935 New York. M.
ROBINSON, Gregory.
Eng. ex. 1934 London. M.
ROBINSON, Increase.
Am. b. Chicago 1890; ad. 1934 Same. A.
ROBINSON, Irene Bowen.
Mrs. W. W. Robinson.
Am. b. So. Bend, Wash.; ad. 1934 Los Angeles, Calif. A.
ROBINSON, John.
Eng. Bath 1715-1745 London. DNB-T.
ROBINSON, [Sir] John Charles.
Eng. Nottingham 1824-1913 Dorset. B-T.
ROBINSON, John Henry. (Eg)
Eng. Bolton 1796-1871 Petworth. B-DNB-T.
ROBINSON, Kathleen Beverley. (S)
Am. b. Aurora, Can. 1882; ad. 1915 Chicago. A12.
ROBINSON, Mary Pomeroy.
Am. ad. 1934 New York. M.
ROBINSON, Mary Turlay.
Am. b. So. Attleboro, Mass.; ad. 1934 New York. A.
ROBINSON, Nancy Bell.
Am. b. Big Cove, Pa.; ad. 1934 Phila., Pa. A.
ROBINSON, R.
Eng. ac. 1797-1802 in London. B-T.
ROBINSON, Ruth C. *see* Treganza, Mrs. R. R.
ROBINSON, Theodore.
Am. Irasburg, Vt. 1852-1896 New York. B-C-E-F-T-46-71-701.
ROBINSON, Thomas.
Am. Nova Scotia 1835-1888 Prov., R. I. F-15.
ROBINSON, William.
Eng. Leeds 1749-1839 Same. DNB-T.
ROBINSON, William Heath.
Eng. Hornsey 1872; ad. 1934 Maidstone. T-Wa.
ROBINSON, William Howard.
Eng. b. Iverness; ad. 1934 London. Wa.
ROBINSON, William S.
Am. b. East Gloucester, Mass. 1861; ad. 1934 Old Lyme, Conn. A-F-W
ROBINSON, William T.
Am. b. Somerville, Mass. 1852; ad. 1934 Walden, Mass. A-F.
ROBIQUET, Pierre Victor. (Ill)
Fr. b. Paris 1879. DBA-T.
ROBITSCHER, [Miss] Bianca Bondi. (Eg)
Am. Dresden, Ger. 1844-1924 Elmhurst, L. I., N. Y. A022.
ROBSON, George Fenwell.
Eng. Durham 1788-1833 London. B-DNB-T.
ROBUS, Hugo. (S)
Am. b. Cleveland, O. 1885; ex. 1934 New York. M.
ROBUSTI, Domenico. *see* Tintoretto, D. R.
ROBUSTI, Giacomo. *see* Tintoretto, G. R.
ROBUSTI, Jacobo. *see* Tintoretto, J. R.
ROBUSTI, Marietta Tintorella.
It. Venice 1560-1590. B-C-722.
ROCCA, Michele [Parmigiano].
It. Parma 1670/5-1751 Venice. B-T.
ROCHARD, François Théodore.
Fr. Paris 1798-1858 Notting Hill, Eng. B-DNB-T.
ROCHARD [or Rochart], Simon Jacques. (Min)
Fr. Paris 1788-1872 Brussels, Belg. B-DNB-T.
ROCHE. *see also* Delaroche.
ROCHE, Alexander.
Scot. Glasgow 1863-1921 Edinburgh. B-T.
ROCHE, Marcel.
Fr. b. Paris 1890. DBA-T.
ROCHE, M. Paul. (Et)
Am. Cork, Ir. 1885; ad. 1934 Balt., Md. A-F.
ROCHE, Pierre. (S)
Fr. b. 1885; d. 1922 in Paris. B-T.
ROCHE, Samson Towgood. (Min)
Ir. Waterford 1748-1838/9. B-T.
ROCHEGROSSE, Georges Marie.
Fr. b. Versailles 1859. DBA-T.
ROCHELLE, Eugene. (Ill)
Am. 1876-1914 New York. A0X1.
ROCHET, Louis. (S)
Fr. Paris 1813-1880 Same. B-Hs-T.
ROCHLING, Karl.
Ger. b. Sarrebruck 1855. B.
ROCHOLL, Rudolf Theodor.
Ger. b. Sachsenberg 1854-1933 Düsseldorf. B-T.
ROCHUSSEN, Charles [or Karel].
Dut. Rotterdam 1814-1894 Same. B-T.

ROCKEY, A. B.
Am. b. Mifflinsburg, Pa. 1799; ac. 1830 Phila., Pa. F.
ROCKWELL, Evelyn Enola.
Am. b. Chicago 1887; ad. 1934 Forest Hills, L. I., N. Y. A.
ROCKWELL, Mary Chauplin.
Am. b. Roseville, N. J.; ad. 1934 New York. M.
ROCKWELL, Maxwell Warren. (Ill)
Am. b. 1876; d. 1911 New York. A010.
ROCKWELL, Norman. (Ill)
Am. b. New York 1894; ad. 1934 New Rochelle, N. Y. A28-F-W.
ROCLE, Margaret K.
Am. b. Watkins, N. Y. 1897; ad. 1934 Chula Vista, Calif. A.
ROCLE, Marius Romain.
Am. b. Brussels, Belg. 1897; ad. 1934 Chula Vista, Calif. A.
RODAKOWSKI, Henryk Hipolit.
Pol. Lemburg 1823-1894 Cracow. B-T.
RODARI Family. (S)
It. ac. 15-16th cent. in Italy. T.
RODDY, Edith Jeanette.
Am. b. Meadville, Pa.; ad. 1934 Syracuse, N. Y. A.
RODE, Christian Bernhard.
Ger. Berlin 1725-1797 Same. B-T.
RODE, Herman [or Hermen].
Ger. ac. 1485-1504 Lübeck, Ger. T.
RODELLA, Gustavo. (Et)
It. b. 1891; ex. 1934 Chicago. M.
RODERIGO. *see* Rodriguez.
RODGERS, [Mrs.] Isabel.
Am. ad. 1934 Lansdowne, Pa. M.
RODGERS, Richard H. (Ill)
Am. ad. 1933 New York. M.
RODIANI, Honorata [or Onorata].
It. d. 1452 Castelleone. T.
RODIN, Auguste René François. (S)
Fr. Paris 1840-1917 Meudon. B-Bd-C-DBA-E-Hs-T-547-548-813-849-884.
RODIONOV, M. S. (Et)
Rus. b. 1885; ad. 1935 Moscow. T.
RODRIGUEZ, Alfonso.
Sp. Messina 1578-1648 Same. B-T.
RODRIGUEZ, Bernardino Givan.
It. Messina 1606-1687. B-T.
RODRIGUEZ, Blanez Bonedetto.
Sp. Granada 1650-1737 Same. B-T.
RODRIGUEZ DE MIRANDA, De Pedro.
Sp. Madrid 1696-1766. B-T.
ROE, Fred.
Eng. b. 1887; ad. 1934 London. T-Wa.
ROE, Frederic Gordon.
Eng. b. Chelsea 1894; ad. 1934 London. Wa.
ROEBER [or Roeher], Fritz.
Ger. Elberfeld 1851-1924 Düsseldorf. T.
ROEBINGER, Charles William.
Am. b. Cinn., O. 1876. A28.
ROECKER, Henry Leon.
Am. b. Burlington, Ia. 1860; ad. 1934 Winthrop Harbor, Ill. A-F.
ROECUS. *see* Rhoecus.
ROED, Jörgen Pedersen.
Dan. Ringsted 1808-1888 Copenhagen. B-C-T.
ROEDER, Elsa. (Ill)
Am. Balt., Md. 1885-1914 Orange, N. J. A0X1.
ROEDER, Max.
Ger. b. Munich 1866. T.
ROEDERSTEIN, Ottillie Wilhelmine.
Swi. b. Zurich 1859. T.
ROEGELS [or Rögels], Andreas.
Ger. Barmen 1870-1917 Munich. T.
ROEGGE, Ernest Frederich Wilhelm.
Ger. Osnabrück 1829-1908 Munich. B-T.
ROEHN, Adolphe Eugène Gabriel.
Fr. Paris 1780-1867 Malakoff. B-T.
ROEHN, Jean Alphonse.
Fr. Paris 1799-1864 Same. B-T.
ROEHRICHT, Wolf. *see* Röhricht, W.
ROÉLAS, Juan de las [Clerigo].
Sp. Sèville 1558/60-1625 Olivares. B-C-722.
ROELOFS, Willem [The Elder].
Dut. Amsterdam 1822-1897 Berchem. B-T.
ROENTGEN, Abraham.
Ger. 1711-1793. T.
ROENTGEN, David.
Ger. 1743-1807 Wiesbaden. T.
ROEPEL, Conraet [or Koenraad].
Dut. The Hague 1678-1748 Same. B-C-T.
ROERBY, Martinus Christian.
Nor. 1803-1848 Copenhagen, Denmark. T.
ROERBYE. *see* Rorby.
ROERICH, Nicolas Konstantin.
Am. b. Leningrad, Rus. 1874; ad. 1935 New York. E-T-W-912.
ROESCH, Kurt Albert Ferdinand.
Ger. b. Berlin 1905; ad. 1934 Bronxville, N. Y. M.
ROESE, Herbert. (Ill)
Am. ad. 1934 New York. M.
ROESELER [or Roesler], August.
Ger. b. Hamburg 1866. T.
ROESSING, Karl.
Ger. b. 1897 in Germany; ad. 1935 Linz, Aus. M.
ROESTRATEN, Pieter Gerrits van.
Dut. Haarlem 1627-1700 London. B-DNB-T.
ROETTIERS, James [The Elder]. (Med)
Eng. London 1663-1698 Bromley. DNB-T.
ROETTIERS, James [The Younger]. (Med)
Eng. Bromley 1698-1772 Brussels, Belg. DNB-T.
ROETTIERS, John. (Med)
Flem. Antwerp 1631-1703 London. DNB-T.
ROETTIERS, Norbert. (Med)
Flem. Antwerp 1665/6-1727 Choisy, Fr. DNB-T.
ROFFIAEN, Jean François Xavier.
Belg. Ypres 1820-1898 Ixelles. B-T.
ROGELET DE LA PASTURE.
see Weyden, Roger van der.
ROGER, Eugène.
Fr. Sens 1807-1840 Paris. B-T.
ROGER, Suzanne.
Fr. b. Paris 1900. DBA-T-797.
ROGER-BLOCHE, Paul. (S)
Fr. b. Paris 1865. B-DBA-T-798.
ROGERS, [Mrs.] Adele.
Am. b. Mt. Vernon, N. Y.; ad. 1934 Provincetown, Mass. A.
ROGERS, [Miss] Barksdale. (Ill-S)
Am. b. Macon, Ger.; ad. 1934 New York. A.

ROGERS, Charles B.
Am. ad. 1934 Great Bend, Kan. A.
ROGERS, Franklin Whiting.
Am. b. Cambridge, Mass. 1854; ad. 1915 Bingham, Mass. A12-F-T-15.
ROGERS, Gretchen W.
Am. ad. 1934 Boston, Mass. A.
ROGERS, Jane.
Am. b. New York 1896; ad. 1934 Same. A.
ROGERS, John. (S) [Rogers Groups]
Am. Salem, Mass. 1829-1904 New Canaan, Conn. A05-E-F-Hs-T-46-668.
ROGERS, John Arthur. (Et)
Am. ad. 1934 Daytona Beach, Fla. A.
ROGERS, Margaret Esther.
Am. b. Birmingham, Eng. 1872; ad. 1934 Santa Cruz, Calif. A.
ROGERS, Mary.
Am. Pittsburgh, Pa. 1882-1920 New York. A018.
ROGERS, Mary G.
Am. ad. 1934 New York. A.
ROGERS, Nathaniel. (Min)
Am. Bridgehampton, L. I., N. Y. 1788-1844 Same. F-2-6.
ROGERS, Randolph. (S)
Am. Waterloo, N. Y. 1825-1892 Florence, It. F-Hs-T-15.
ROGERS, Robert S.
Am. ad. 1935 Atlanta, Ga. M.
ROGERS, William. (Eg)
[First English copper-plate engraver.]
Eng. b. London 1545; ac. 1580-1610 Same. B-DNB-T-751-880.
ROGERS, William Allen. (Cari)
Am. Springfield, O. 1854-1931 Wash., D. C. A028-F-T-W16.
ROGERS, William Gibbs. (Carver)
Eng. Dover 1792-1875 London. DNB-T.
ROGERS, William J. (Et)
Am. ex. 1934 New York. M.
ROGERT, Alene.
Am. ad. 1934 Wyoming, O. M.
ROGHMAN [or Rogman], Roelant.
Dut. Amsterdam 1597-1686 Same. B-T.
ROGUET, Louis. (S)
Fr. St. Junien 1824-1850 Rome, It. B-T.
ROHDEN, Johann Martin von.
Ger. Cassel 1778-1868 Rome, It. T.
ROHL-SMITH, Carl. *see* Smith, C. R.
ROHLAND, Caroline Speare.
Am. b. Boston 1885; ad. 1934 Woodstock, N. Y. A.
ROHLAND, Paul.
Am. b. Richmond, Va. 1884; ad. 1934 Woodstock, N. Y. A.
ROHLFS, Christian. (Eg)
Ger. b. Nieudorf 1849. B-DBA-T-775.
ROHN, Ray. (Ill)
Am. b. 1888; d. 1935 Phila., Pa. A-Obit. N. Y. papers, 7-9-1935.
RÖHRICH [or Röhricht], Franz Wolfgang.
Ger. Nüremberg 1787-1834 Same. B-T.
RÖHRICHT, Wolf.
Ger. b. 1886; ad. 1934 Berlin. M.
ROIG, Salvator de.
Sp. ac. 1466 in Zaragoza. T.
ROINÉ, Jules Edouard. (S)
Am. Nantes, Fr. 1857-1916 New York. A12-T.
ROJANKOVSKY, Fedor. (Ill)
Fr. ad. 1934 Paris. M.
ROJDESTVENSKI, Basil B.
Rus. ad. 1934 Moscow. M.
ROKES. *see* Sorgh, H. M.
ROKOTOV, Fedor Peter Stepanovitch.
Rus. b. 1730/5; d. 1808/12 Leningrad. T.
ROLAND, Charles Auguste.
Fr. Metz 1797-1859 Remilly. B-T.
ROLAND, Philippe Laurent. (S)
Fr. Lille 1747-1816 Paris. B-T.
ROLAND DE LA PORTE, Henri Horace.
Fr. Paris 1724-1793. B-T.
ROLANDO, Paolo Emilio.
Am. b. Rome, It. 1884; ad. 1934 Wash., D. C. A.
ROLANDO, Virginia Moorhead.
Mrs. Paul Emilio Rolando.
Am. b. North East, Pa. 1898; ad. 1934 Wash., D. C. A.
ROLFE, Edmund.
Am. Detroit, Mich. 1877-1917 Woodstock, N. Y. A014.
ROLFE, Henry Leonidas.
Eng. ac. 1847-1881 in London. T.
ROLFSEN, Alf.
Nor. b. Oslo 1895; ad. 1935 Same. T.
ROLI [or Rolli], Giuseppe Maria.
It. Bologna 1645-1727 Same. B-T.
RÖLING, Gerard V. A.
Dut. ad. 1934 Amsterdam. M.
ROLL, Alfred Philippe.
Fr. Paris 1847-1919. B-C-E-T.
ROLLAND, Benjamin de.
Fr. Gaudeloupe 1777-1855 Grenoble. B-T.
ROLLE, A. H. O.
Am. b. Minn. 1875; ad. 1934 Wash., D. C. A.
ROLLER, Samuel K.
Am. b. New Market, Va.; ad. 1934 New York. M.
ROLLETT, Herbert.
Eng. Gainsborough 1872-1932. Wa1929-Y01933.
ROLLIN [or Rollini], Jean.
Fr. ac. 17th Cent. in Avignon. B-T.
ROLLINS, Warren E.
Am. b. Carson City, Nev.; ad. 1933 New Mexico. A18-M.
ROLLINSON, William. (Eg)
Am. Dudley, Eng. 1762-1842 New York. F-T-2-7.
ROLLO, Jo.
Am. b. Ragusa, It. 1904; ad. 1934 Woodstock, N. Y. A.
ROLPH, John A. (Eg)
Am. England 1799-1862 Brooklyn, N. Y. F-2-7.
ROLSHOVEN, Julius C.
Am. Detroit, Mich. 1858-1930 New York. A028-B-F-T-W16-46.
ROLT, Vivian.
Eng. b. Stow 1874. Wa1929.
ROMAGNESI, Antoine Joseph Michel. (S)
Fr. Paris 1782-1852 Same. B-T.

ROMAGNOLI, Giovanni.
It. b. Faenza 1893; ex. 1933 Chicago. M-T.
ROMAIN, Jules. *see* Guilo, R.
ROMAKO, Anton.
Aus. Atzgersdorf 1832-1889 Venice, It. B-T.
ROMAN. *see* Romans.
ROMAN-EGYPTIAN PORTRAITURE.
First Century A.D.
ROMANDON [or Ramandon], Abraham.
Ger. d. 1687? in Berlin. T.
ROMANELLI, Ferdinando. (S)
It. ac. 1853 in Italy. M.
ROMANELLI, Giovanni Francesco.
It. Viterbo 1610-1662 Same. B-C-T-722.
ROMANELLI, Pasquale. (S)
It. Florence 1812-1887. B-T.
ROMANELLI, Raffaello. (S)
It. Florence 1856-1928. B-T.
ROMANELLI, Romano. (S)
It. b. Florence 1882; ad. 1934 Same. T.
ROMANINO, Giorolamo Romani.
It. Brescia 1480/7-1566? B-Bd-T.
ROMANO, Antoniazzo.
It. 1435?-1511. B-T.
ROMANO, Emanuele. (Ill)
It. ex. 1935 New York. M.
ROMANO, Espinsosa Caceda. (S)
Peruvian. b. San Matéo, Peru 1897. DBA.
ROMANO, Giovanni Christopher. (S)
It. Rome 1470-1512 Loreto. Hs-T.
ROMANO, Guilio Pippi.
see Giulio Romano, P.
ROMANO, Nicholas.
Am. b. Montoro, It. 1889; ad. 1934 Phila., Pa. A.
ROMANO, Paolo Taccone. (S)
see Taccone, Paolo.
ROMANO, Romanelli. (S)
see Romanelli, R.
ROMANO, Umberto.
Am. b. Italy 1905; ad. 1934 New York. A.
ROMANOVSKY, Demetri.
Am. b. Russia; ad. 1934 New York. M.
ROMANS, Bernard. (Eg)
Am. b. Holland 1720? d. 1784 at sea. F-T-2-7-147.
ROMANS [or Roman], Jacobus. (S)
Dut. The Hague 1640-1716. B-T.
ROMBAUX, Egidius. (S)
Belg. b. Schaerbeck 1865. B-T.
ROMBOUTS [or Rombout], Gillis Agidius.
Dut. Haarlem 1630-1678. B-T.
ROMBOUTS [or Rombout], Salomon.
Dut. b. 1652; d. 1702 Haarlem. B-T.
ROMBOUTS [or Rombouts], Théodore.
Flem. Antwerp 1597-1637 Same. B-C-T-722.
ROMERSWAEL, Marinus van.
see Marinus, van R.
ROMEU, Jaime.
Sp. ac. 1437-1475 in Zaragaza. T.
ROMEYN [or Romyn], Willem van.
Dut. Haarlem 1624-1693/4. B-C-T-722.
ROMNEY, George.
Eng. Dalton 1734-1802 Kendal. B-Bd-C-DNB-E-T-551-722-727.
ROMNEY, John. (Eg)
Eng. b. 1786; d. 1863 in Chester. B-DNB-T.
ROMNEY, Peter. [Brother of G. R.]
Eng. b. 1743; d. 1777 Stockport. B-DNB-T.
RONAULT, Georges.
Fr. b. Paris 1871. DBA.
RONCALLI, Cristoforo.
It. Pomerance 1552-1626 Rome. B-C-T.
RONDANI [or Rondono], Francesco Maria.
It. Parma 1490-1548 Same. B-C-T.
RONDEL, Frederick.
Am. Paris 1826-1892 U. S. B-C-T.
RONDEL, Henri.
Fr. Avignon 1857-1919 Paris. B-T.
RONDINELLO, Nicolò [or Nicolaus].
It. b. Ravenna; ac. 1480-1500 Venice. B-Bd-T-V.
RONEY, Harold Arthur.
Am. b. Sullivan, Ill. 1899; ad. 1934 San Antonio, Tex. A.
RONGIER, Jeanne.
Fr. b. Mâcon; ac. 1869-1900 in Paris. B-T.
RONNEBECK, Arnold. (S)
Am. b. Nassau, Ger. 1885; ad. 1934 Denver, Colo. A.
RONNEBECK, Louise Harrington Emerson. (Mu)
Mrs. Arnold Ronnebeck.
Am. b. Phila., Pa. 1901; ad. 1934 Denver, Colo. M.
RONNER, Emma Alice Henriette.
Belg. b. Brussels 1857. B-T.
RONNER-KNIP, Henriette.
Dut. Amsterdam 1821-1909 Brussels, Belg. T.
RONOT, Charles.
Fr. Belan 1820-1895 Dijon. B-T.
RONZONE, Benjamin.
Am. b. 1849; d. 1927 Brooklyn, N. Y. A024.
ROOD, Henry, Jr.
Am. b. Pleasantville, N. Y.; ad. 1934 Jackson Heights, N. Y. A.
ROOK, Edward Francis.
Am. b. New York 1870; ad. 1934 Old Lyme, Conn. A-F-W.
ROOKE, Nöel. (Eg)
Eng. b. London 1881; ad. 1934 Same. Wa.
ROOKE, Thomas Mathews.
Eng. Marylebone 1842-1893 London. B-T.
ROOKER, Edward. (Eg)
Eng. London 1711/2-1774 Same. DNB-T.
ROOKER, Michael Angelo. (Eg-P)
Eng. London 1743-1801 Same. B-DNB-T.
ROOM, Henry.
Eng. b. 1802; d. 1850 in London. B-DNB-T.
ROOME [or Roem], Family. (S)
It. ac. 14-16th Cent. in Italy. T.
ROOME, Jean van, II.
Belg. ac. 1506-1530 in Brussels. T.
ROORE [or Rorus], Jacques Ignatius de.
Flem. Antwerp 1686-1747 The Hague, Holland. B-T.
ROOS [or Rosa], Dietrich Théodor.
Ger. Wesel 1638-1698. B-T-722.
ROOS, Jan.
Flem. Antwerp 1591-1638 Genoa, It. B-T.
ROOS, Johann Heinrich.
Ger. Otterberg 1631-1685 Frankfort. B-C-T-722.
ROOS, Johann Melchior.
Ger. Frankfort 1659-1731. B-C-T.
ROOS, Philip Peter [Rosa di Tivoli].
Ger. Frankfort 1657-1705/6 Rome, It. B-T.

ROOSEVELT, Samuel Montgomery.
Am. New York 1863-1920 Same. A017-F.
ROOT, Robert Marshall.
Am. b. Shelbyville, Ill. 1863; ad. 1934 Same. A-F.
ROOTIUS, Jacob.
Dut. Hoorn 1635-1681/2 Same. B-Bd-T.
ROOTIUS, Jan Albertsz.
Dut. Hoorn 1615-1674 Same. B-Bd-T.
ROPE, Ellen Mary. (S)
Eng. b. Blaxhall 1855; ad. 1934 London. T-Wa.
ROPER, M. Secor.
Mrs. George Wisham Roper.
Am. b. Morristown, N. J. 1886; ad. 1934 Norfolk, Va. A.
ROPER, Murray T.
Am. ad. 1935 Sunnyside, L. I., N. Y. M.
ROPES, George.
Am. Salem, Mass. 1788-1819 Same. 169.
ROPES, Joseph.
Am. Salem, Mass. 1812-1885 New York. F-T-3-4-45-169.
ROPS, Félicien.
Belg. Namur 1833-1898 Éssonnes, Fr. B-DBA-E-T.
ROQUEPLAN, Camile Joseph Étienne.
Fr. Mallemart 1800-1855 Paris. B-C-T-722.
ROQUES, Guillaume [Joseph].
Fr. Toulouse 1754-1847 Same. B-T.
RORBY, Christian Martinus Wesiellorf.
Nor. Drammen 1803-1848 Copenhagen. B-T.
RORIMER, Louis.
Am. b. Cleveland, O. 1872; ad. 1934 Same. W.
RORITZER [or Roriczer], Family.
Ger. ac. 15-16th Cent. in Germany. T.
RORKE, Edward.
Am. b. 1856; d. 1905 Brooklyn, N. Y. A06.
ROSA. *see also* Roos.
ROSA [or Rosis], Carlo de.
It. b. Aquila; d. 1678 Bitonto. T.
ROSA, Ercole. (S)
It. Severino 1846-1893 Rome. T.
ROSA, Francesco di [Pacicco].
It. Naples 1600-1654 Same. B-T.
ROSA, Salavatore.
It. Renella 1615-1673 Rome. B-Bd-C-E-T-722.
ROSA DA TIVOLI. *see* Roos, Philip Peter.
ROSALBA, Carriera. *see* Carriera, R.
ROSALES, Eduardo.
Sp. Madrid 1837-1873 Rome, It. B.
ROSANDIĆ, Toma. (S)
Jugo-Slavian (Modern). 798.
ROSANKOVA-DRABKOVA, Marta.
Czec. b. Prague 1885. M.
ROSASPINA, Francesco.
It. b. 1762; d. 1842 in Bologna. B.
ROSE, [Sir] Francis.
Scot. b. Scotland; ex. 1934 New York. M.
ROSE, George L.
Am. b. Newport, R. I., 1861; ad. Upper Montclair, N. J. A.
ROSE, Guy.
Am. b. San Gabriel, Calif. 1867; d. 1925. A023-F-W14.
ROSE, Iver.
Am. b. 1899; ad. 1935 New York. M.
ROSE, [Mrs.] Leize.
Am. ad. 1934 New York. M.
ROSE, Robert Traill.
Eng. b. Newcastle 1863. Wa1929.
ROSE, Ruth Starr.
Mrs. W. Searls Rose.
Am. b. Eau Claire, Wis. 1887; ad. 1934 Caldwell, N. J. A-F.
ROSE, William S.
Eng. b. 1810; d. 1875 Edenbridge, Eng. B.
RÖSEL, August Johann von Rosenhof.
Ger. b. 1705; d. 1759 in Nüremberg. B.
ROSELAND, Harry.
Am. b. Brooklyn, N. Y. 1868; ad. 1934 Same. A-B-F-W.
ROSELLI. *see* Rosselli.
ROSELLO DI JACOPO, Franchi.
see Franchi, R. di J.
ROSEMALE, Dommicus Ambrosius.
Dut. Utrecht 1620-1699 Same. B.
ROSEMAN, Isa.
Rus. b. Russia 1877. DBA.
ROSEN, Charles.
Am. b. Westmoreland Co., Pa. 1878; ad. 1934 Woodstock, N. Y. A-F-W.
ROSEN, Georg Johann Otto Graf von.
Swe. b. Paris 1843. B.
ROSEN, Jan Henryk. (Mu)
Pol. b. 1891. M.
ROSEN, [Countess] Maud von. (S)
Swe. ad. 1935 Djurthatlu, Swe. M.
ROSENBAUER, William Wallace. (S)
Am. b. Chambersburg, Pa. 1900; ad. 1934 Kansas City, Mo. A.
ROSENBAUM, Caroline.
Am. ad. 1934 Orlando, Fla. M.
ROSENBERG, Ceil.
Am. b. 1907; ex. 1934 Chicago. M.
ROSENBERG, George Frederic.
Eng. Bath 1825-1869 Same. B-DNB.
ROSENBERG, Henry M.
Am. b. New Brunswick, N. J. 1858; ad. 1934 Dartmouth, N. S. A-F.
ROSENBERG, James N.
Am. b. Allegheny City, Pa. 1874; ad. 1934 New York. A-F.
ROSENBERG, Louis Conrad. (Et)
Am. b. Portland, Ore. 1890; ad. 1935 Fairfield, Conn. A028-F-830.
ROSENBERG, Samuel.
Am. b. Phila., Pa. 1896; ad. 1934 Pittsburgh, Pa. A-F.
ROSENBERG, Samuel Martin.
Am. b. Wash., D. C. 1893; ad. 1934 Springfield, Mass. A.
ROSENFELD, Edward.
Am. b. Balt., Md. 1906; ad. 1934 Same. A.
ROSENFELDER, Karl Ludwig Julius.
Ger. Breslau 1813-1881 Königsberg. B.
ROSENFIELD, Lester.
Am. b. Minn., Minn. 1886; ad. 1915 Duluth, Minn. A12.
ROSENGREN, Herbert.
Am. b. Kewanee, Ill. 1908; ad. 1934 Rockford, Ill. A.
ROSENKRANZ, Clarence C.
Am. b. Hammondsport, N. Y.; ad. 1934 St. Paul, Minn. A-F.

ROSENMEYER, Bernard Jacob.
Am. b. New York 1870; ad. 1935 Tenafly, N. J. A28-F.
ROSENSHINE, Annette. (S)
Am. b. San Fran., Calif. 1880; ad. 1934 Same. A.
ROSENSON, Olga.
Am. ad. 1934 Brooklyn, N. Y. M.
ROSENSTAND, Vilhelm Jakob.
Dan. b. Copenhagen 1838; ad. 1859-1886 in Italy. B-C.
ROSENSTOCK, Isadore.
Ger. b. Strasburg 1880. DBA.
ROSENTHAL, Albert.
Am. b. Phila., Pa. 1863; ad. 1934 Same. A-F-W-7.
ROSENTHAL, David.
Am. b. Cinn., O. 1876; ad. 1915 Same. A12-F.
ROSENTHAL, Doris.
Am. b. Riverside, Calif.; ad. 1934 Norwalk, Conn. A.
ROSENTHAL, Louis. (S)
Am. b. Lithuania 1887; ad. 1934 Balt., Md. A-Cs-F.
ROSENTHAL, Martin.
Am. ex. 1934 New York. M.
ROSENTHAL, Max. (Et)
Am. Turck, Rus.-Pol. 1833-1918 Phila., Pa. A015-F-7.
ROSENTHAL, Michael.
Am. b. Russia 1887; ad. 1935 Brooklyn, N. Y. F-M.
ROSENTHAL, Mildred.
Mrs. Hyman Mildred.
Am. b. Panama; ad. 1934 San Fran., Calif. A.
ROSENTHAL, Toby Edward.
Am. New Haven, Conn. 1848-1917 Berlin, Ger. A015-B-C-E-F.
ROSENTSU, Nagasawa.
Jap. 1654-1799 Japan. J., Vol. 2, page 99.
ROSEVEAR, Kenneth.
Am. ex. 1935 New York. M.
ROSEX, Nicoletto. *see* Modena.
ROSIER, Amédée.
Fr. b. Meaux 1831; ac. 1889 in Paris. B.
ROSIER, Jean Guillaume.
Belg. b. Lanaken 1858. B.
ROSIN, Harry. (S)
Am. b. 1897; ex. 1934 Phila., Pa. M.
ROSLIN, Alexandre.
Swe. Malnoé 1718-1793 Paris. B-683.
ROSLYN, Louis Frederick. (S)
[or Fritz Roselieb.]
Eng. b. London 1878; ad. 1934 Same. B-Wa.
ROSS, Benn.
Am. ad. 1935 New York. M.
ROSS. *see also* Roos. *see* Rosa.
ROSS, [Mrs.] Catherine Terry. (S)
Am. ad. 1934 Nyack, N. Y. M.
ROSS, Charles B.
Am. Chicago 1878-1933 Port Wash., N. Y. A030.
ROSS, Denman Waldo.
Am. b. Cinn., O. 1853; ex. 1934 Cambridge, Mass. A28-F-M.
ROSS, Frederick Webb. (Mu)
Am. b. Shelbyville, Ind. 1896; ad. 1934 Ridgefield, Conn. M.
ROSS, Gordon. (Ill)
Am. ad. 1934 New York. A12-M
ROSS, Harry Leith.
see Leith-Ross, H.
ROSS, Herbert W.
Am. b. Louisville, Ky. 1895; ex. 1933 in Paris. DBA.
ROSS, John. (S)
Scot. 1855-1929. Y01930.
ROSS, Joseph Halford.
Scot. b. Ross 1866. Wa1929.
ROSS, Joseph Thorburn.
Scot. Berwick 1849-1903 Edinburgh. B-DNB.
ROSS, Karl.
Ger. Holstein 1816-1837 Munich. B.
ROSS, Mabel.
Am. b. Boston 1906; ad. 1934 Springfield, Mass. A.
ROSS, Raymond L.
Am. b. Cattarugnus, N. Y. 1880; ad. 1934 Wash., D. C. A.
ROSS, Robert Thorburn.
Scot. Edinburgh 1816-1876. B.
ROSS, Sanford.
Am. b. Newark, N. J.; ad. 1934 Rumson, N. J. M.
ROSS, Theodor. *see* Ross, T.
ROSS, Vera [Mrs. Weekly].
Eng. b. London; ad. 1934 Chiswick. Wa.
ROSS, [Sir] William Charles. (Min)
Eng. London 1794-1860 Same. B-Bd-DNB.
ROSSE, Hermann.
Am. b. The Hague, Holland 1887; ad. 1934 Pomona, N. Y. A.
ROSSEAU, Percival Leonard.
Am. b. Point Coupeé, La. 1859; ad. 1934 Old Lyme, Conn. A-F-W.
ROSSELLI, Cosimo di Lorenzo [Filippo].
It. Florence 1438/9-1507 Same. B-E-722.
ROSSELLI, Matteo.
It. Florence 1578-1651. B-722.
ROSSELLINO, Antonio [Proconsolo]. (S)
It. Florence 1427?-1479? B-E-Hs-V-553.
ROSSELLINO, Bernardo. (S)
It. Florence 1409-1464. E-Hs-V.
ROSSELLO DI JACOPO. *see* Franchi, R. di J.
ROSSER, Milburn. (Ill)
Am. ad. 1935 New York. M.
ROSSET, Joseph. (S)
Fr. St. Claude 1706-1786 Same. B.
ROSSET-GRANGER, Paul Edouard.
Fr. b. Vincennes; ad. 1878 Paris. B.
ROSSETTI, Antonio. (S)
It. b. Milan 1813; [No death date]. B.
ROSSETTI, Dante Gabriel [Charles]. (P and Poet)
Eng. London 1828-1882 Birchington. B-Bd-C-DNB-T-191-554-710-844-922.
ROSSETTI, Lucy Madox [née Brown].
Eng. 1843-1894 Côte d'Azur, Fr. B-DNB.
ROSSI, Alberto.
It. b. Turin; ac. 19th Cent. in Milan. B.
ROSSI, Clarence.
Am. ad. 1934 Stratford, Conn. M.
ROSSI, Francesco dei Rossi.
see Salviati, Il. Cecchinno del.
ROSSI, John Charles Felix. (S)
Eng. 1762-1839 in London. B-DNB.
ROSSI, Joseph.
It. b. 1892. DBA.

ROSSI, Luigi.
It. Lugano 1853/4-1923 Same. B-DBA.
ROSSI, Nicolò Maria de.
It. Naples 1650-1700. B.
ROSSI, Pasquale [or Pasqualino].
It. Venice 1641-1700/25. B.
ROSSI, Properzia de. (S)
It. Bologna 1490-1530. Hs-V.
ROSSINI, Pellegrino di Mariano.
see Pellegrino di M.
ROSSIRE, [Mrs.] Beatrice.
Am. ad. 1934 New York. M.
ROSSITER, Thomas Pritchard.
Am. New Haven, Conn. 1818-1871 Cold Springs, N. Y. B-Bd-C-F-3-4-15.
ROSSMANN, Henry.
Am. ad. 1934 New York. M.
ROSSO, Il. Giovan Battista de Rossi.
It. Florence 1494-1541. B-V-722.
ROSSO, Medardo. (S)
It. Turin 1858-1928. B-Hs.
ROSSUM [or Rossem], Jan van.
Dut. ac. 1645/73 in Amsterdam. B.
ROSSY, Louis Joseph.
Fr. b. Valenciennes 1817; ac. 1846 in Paris. B.
ROSZAK, Theodore J.
Am. b. Inowroclaw, Pol. 1907; ad. 1935 Chicago. A.
ROTA. *see also* Rotta.
ROTA, Giuseppe. (Min)
It. ac. 1806-1821 in Italy. B.
ROTA, Martino.
It. Sebenico 1540-1592. B.
ROTAN, Walter. (S)
Am. ex. 1934 New York. M.
ROTARI, Pietro [Compte].
It. Verona 1707-1762 Leningrad, Rus. B-722.
ROTENBERG, Harold.
Am. ad. 1935 Boston. M.
ROTERS, Carl G.
Am. ex. 1933 in New York. A24-M.
ROTH, Bresslern. *see* Bresslern, R.
ROTH, Ernest David. (Et)
Am. b. Stuttgart, Ger. 1879; ad. 1934 New York. A-F-W16.
ROTH, Francis X.
Am. ad. 1934 New York. M.
ROTH, Frederick George Richard. (S)
Am. b. Brooklyn, N. Y. 1872; ad. 1934 Englewood, N. J. A-F-Cs-W.
ROTH, Herbert ["Herb"]. (Cari)
Am. ad. 1934 Larchmont, N. Y. A.
ROTH, James Buford.
Am. b. California, Mo. 1910; ad. 1934 Kansas City, Mo. A.
ROTH, Philipp.
Ger. b. Darmstadt 1841. B.
ROTHBART, Ferdinand.
Ger. Roth 1823-1889 Munich. B.
ROTHBORT, Samuel.
Am. b. Poland 1882; ad. 1934 Hempstead, L. I., N. Y. A.
ROTHENSTEIN, [Sir] William ["Will"].
Eng. b. Bradford 1872; ad. 1934 London. B-Wa-555-825.
ROTHENSTEIN, William Michael.
Eng. b. Hampstead 1908; ad. 1934 London. Wa.
ROTHERMEL, Dorothy. (Ill)
Am. ad. 1934 Langhorne, Pa. M.
ROTHERMEL, Peter Frederick.
Am. Nescopack, Pa. 1817-1895 Phila., Pa. B-Bd-C-F-4-15.
ROTHERY, Albert.
Am. b. Matteawan, N. Y. 1851; ad. 1915 Omaha, Neb. A12.
ROTHKOWITZ, Marcus.
Am. b. Lithuania 1903; ad. 1935 Brooklyn, N. Y. M.
ROTHSCHILD, Blanche.
Am. ad. 1934 New York. M.
ROTHSCHILD, Nathaniel.
Fr. ac. 1864-1879 Paris. B.
ROTHSCHILD, Elizabeth.
Am. ad. 1934 Brooklyn, N. Y M.
ROTHWELL, Elizabeth L.
Am. b. California, Pa.; ad. 1934 Pittsburgh, Pa. A.
ROTHWELL, Richard.
Ir. Athlone 1800-1868 Rome, It. B.
ROTIER, Peter.
Am. b. Baldwin, Wis. 1888; ad. 1934 Milwaukee, Wis. M.
ROTIG, Georges Frédéric.
Fr. b. Havre 1873; ad. 1934 Paris. B-DBA.
RÖTING [or Roeting], Julius.
Ger. Dresden 1821-1896 Düsseldorf. B.
ROTTA, Antonio.
It. b. Garizia 1828; ac. 1891 Berlin, Ger. B.
ROTTA, Silvio Guilio.
It. Venice 1853-1913. B.
ROTTENHAMMER, Jacob [or Johann].
Ger. Munich 1564-1623 Augsberg. B-C-722.
ROTTENHAMMER, Thomas.
Ger. ac. 1620 in Munich. B.
ROTTLUFF, Karl Schmidt.
see Schmidt-Rottluff, K.
ROTTMANN, Karl.
Ger. Heidelberg 1797/8-1850 Munich. B-C-722.
ROTTMAYR, van Rosenbrunn, J. F. M.
Aus. Laufen 1652-1730 Vienna. B.
ROTY. (Medalist-S)
Fr. Paris 1846-1911 Same. DBA-Hs.
ROUARGUE, Adolphe.
Fr. Paris 1810-1870 Same. B.
ROUARGUE, Émile. (Eg)
Fr. ac. 1858 in Paris. B.
ROUART, Ernest.
Fr. b. Paris 1874. DBA.
ROUART, Henri Stanislas.
Fr. Paris 1833-1912 Same. B-DBA.
ROUAULT, Georges.
Fr. b. 1871. M.
ROUBA, Michal.
Pol. ad. 1934 Wilno; ex. 1934 Pittsburgh, Pa. M.
ROUBAUD, Benjamin [or Benjain].
Fr. Roquevaire 1811-1847 Alger. B.
ROUBAUD, François.
Rus. 1860-1920. M.
ROUBAUD, François Félix. (S)
Fr. Cerdon 1825-1876 Lyons. B.
ROUBILIAC, Louis François. (S)
Fr. Lyons 1695-1762 London. B-E-Hs.
ROUBILLE, Auguste Jean Baptiste.
Fr. b. Paris 1872. B-DBA.

ROUCHITZ, F. E.
Rus. ac. 1870 in Moscow. B.
ROUDEBUSH, John H. (S)
Am. b. New York 1871; d. 1925 Jamaica, W. I. F-Ta.
ROUFFET, Jules.
Fr. Paris 1862-1931. DBA.
ROUGE, Guillaume le.
Fr. ac. 14-15 Cent. in Tours and Paris. M.
ROUGELOT, Benoit [or Benedict]. (S)
Fr. Tournus 1855-1894 Paris. B.
ROUGERNON, Jules [or Jean] James.
Fr. Gevray 1841-1880. B.
ROUGERON, Marcel Jules.
Am. b. Paris 1875; ad. 1934 New York. A.
ROUGET, Georges.
Fr. Paris 1784-1869 Same. B.
ROUILLARD, Jean Sébastien.
Fr. Paris 1789-1852 Same. B.
ROULAND, Orlando.
Am. b. Pleasant Ridge, Ill. 1871; ad. 1934 New York. A-F.
ROULLET [or Rollet], Jean Louis.
Fr. Arles 1645-1699 Paris. B.
ROULLET, Marie Anatole Gaston.
Fr. Ars. 1847-1925 Paris. DBA.
ROUS, Helen.
Am. ex. 1934 Woodstock, N. Y. M.
ROUSSE, Adolphe Marie Ernest.
Fr. Plaine 1844-1887 Pornic. B.
ROUSSEAU, Charles. (S)
Fr. b. 1691 in France. B.
ROUSSEAU, Charles.
Belg. b. Bruges 1862. B.
ROUSSEAU, Henri Julien Félix. [Called Douanier Rousseau.]
Fr. Labal 1844-1910 Paris. B-DBA-552-700.
ROUSSEAU, Jacques. (S)
Fr. Paris 1681-1741 Angers. B.
ROUSSEAU, Jacques.
Fr. Paris 1626/30-1693/4 London. B-DNB-E.
ROUSSEAU, Jules Antoine. (S)
Fr. ac. Versailles 17th Cent. B-E.
ROUSSEAU, Percival.
Fr. ex. 1934 New York. M.
ROUSSEAU, Philippe.
Fr. Paris 1816-1887 Acquigny. B-C.
ROUSSEAU, Pierre Étienne Théodore.
Fr. Paris 1812-1867 Barbizon. B-Bd-C-E-827-870-873.
ROUSSEAU DE LA ROTTIÈRE, Jean Siméon.
Fr. b. 1747; ac. 1792 in Paris. E.
ROUSSEAU, Victor. (S)
Belg. b. Hainaut 1865. B-E-Hs.
ROUSSEAUX, Émile Alfred.
Fr. Abbeville 1831-1874 Paris. B.
ROUSSEFF, W. Vladimir.
Am. b. Silistria, Bulgaria 1890; ad. 1934 Fish Creek, Wis. A.
ROUSSEL, Hippolyte Paul René. (S)
Fr. Paris 1867-1928 Same. DBA.
ROUSSEL, K. Xavier.
Fr. b. Lorry-les-Metz 1867; ad. 1934 Seine-et-Oise. B-DBA.
ROUSSEL, Théodore.
Fr. ac. 19th Cent. in France. M.
ROUSSELET, Gilles.
Fr. Paris 1610-1686 Same. B.
ROUSSELET, Jean. (S)
Fr. Paris 1656-1693 Gobelins. B.
ROUSSY, Toussaint.
Fr. b. Cette 1847. B.
ROUVEYRE, André. (Ill)
Fr. b. Paris 1879. DBA.
ROUX. *see also* Le Roux.
ROUX, Louis François Prosper.
Fr. Paris 1817-1903. B.
ROUX, Paul Louis Joseph.
Fr. ac. 19th Cent. in Paris. B.
ROVEZZANO, Benedetto da. (S)
It. 1476-1856. Hs.
ROWBOTHAM, Thomas Charles Leeson [The Younger].
Ir. Dublin 1823-1875/6 London. B-DNB.
ROWE, Clarence Herbert. (Et)
Am. Phila., Pa. 1878-1930. A027-F.
ROWE, Corinne Finsterwald.
Am. b. Marion, Wis. 1894; ad. 1934 Hampton, Conn. A.
ROWE, J. Staples.
Am. b. 1856; d. 1905 New York. A06-F.
ROWE, Louise Jopling.
see Jopling-Rowe [Mrs.]
ROWE, Sidney Grant.
Eng. 1861-1928. B-Wa1929-Y01929.
ROWE, William B. (Mu)
Am. ad. 1934 Buffalo, N. Y. M.
ROWELL, Fanny Taylor.
Mrs. Horace C. Wait.
Am. Princeton, N. J. 1865-1928. A025-F.
ROWELL, Louis.
Am. New York 1873-1928 Asheville, N. C. A025.
ROWLAND, Earl.
Am. b. Trinidad, Colo.; ad. 1934 Los Angeles, Calif. A.
ROWLAND, Edith.
Eng. ad. 1934 Woodford, Essex. Wa.
ROWLAND, Stanley Chamberlain. (Mu)
Eng. b. Hampton 1877; ex. 1934 New York. M-Wa.
ROWLANDS, [Mrs.] Constance Ethel. (Ill)
Br. b. Fukuoka, Jap. 1891; ad. 1934 Winscombe, Eng. Wa.
ROWLANDSON, George Derville.
Br. b. India 1861; ac. 1933 London. Wa1929.
ROWLANDSON, Thomas. (Cari)
Eng. London 1756-1827 Same. B-Bd-C-DNB-E-556-844-880.
ROWLES, [Mrs.] Lilian May Bevis.
Eng. b. Newport; ad. 1934 East Sheen. Wa.
ROWLEY, R.
Am. b. 1826. [No death date.] Fa-M.
ROWNTREE, Ralph.
Am. ad. 1934 New York. M.
ROWORTH, Edward.
Br. ac. 1934 So. Africa. M.
ROWSE, Samuel Worcester.
Am. Bath, Me. 1822-1901 Morristown, N. J. A04-C-F-4-15-45.
ROXAS, José de.
Sp. ac. 1810-1817. Fa.
ROY, Donatien.
Fr. b. Nantes 1854. B.
ROY, Jean Baptiste de.
Belg. Brussels 1759-1839. B.

ROY, Marius.
Fr. b. Lyons, 1833; ac. 1880 in Paris. B.
ROY, Pierre.
Fr. b. Nantes 1880; ad. 1934 Paris. M.
ROYALL, Mary Buckner.
Mrs. William Lawrence Royall.
Am. ex. 1935 New York. M.
ROYBET, Ferdinand Victor Léon.
Fr. Uzès 1840-1920 Paris. B-DBA.
ROYCE, Woodford.
Am. b. Willimantic, Conn. 1902; ad. 1934 Woodstock, N. Y. A.
ROYEN [or Roye], Willem Frederich van.
Dut. Haarlem 1654-1723 Berlin, Ger. B.
ROYER, Henri Paul.
Fr. b. Nancy 1869. B-DBA.
ROYER, Jacob S.
Am. b. Waynesboro, Pa. 1883; ad. 1934 Dayton, O. A.
ROYER, Lionel Nöel.
Fr. Château-du-Loir 1852-1926 Neuilly. B-DBA.
ROYER, Pierre.
Fr. ac. 1774-1796 in Paris. B.
ROYLANCE, Edna. (Et)
Am. ad. 1934 New York. M.
ROYLE, Herbert.
Eng. b. Manchester; ac. 1929 London. B-Wa1929.
ROYLE, Stanley.
Eng. b. Stalybridge 1888; ad. 1934 Sheffield. Wa.
ROYMERSWALE, Marinus van.
see Marinus van R.
ROZAIRE, Arthur D.
Can. Montreal 1879-1922 Los Angeles, Calif. M.
ROZEN, Jerome G.
Am. ac. 1933. M.
ROZIER, Dominique Hubert.
Fr. Paris 1840-1901 Same. B.
ROZIER, Jules Charles.
Fr. Paris 1821-1882 Versailles. B.
RUBBO, A. Datillo.
It. b. Naples 1871; ac. 1897 Sydney, Aust. M.
RUBEN, Christian.
Ger. Tréves 1805-1875 Inzersdorf. B.
RUBENS, Bartholomé.
see Vermejo, B.
RUBENS, Sir Perter Paul.
Flem. Siegen, Ger. 1577-1640 Antwerp. B-Bd-C-E-128-191-557-558-559-560-561-722-790-902-903.
RUBINS, David K. (S)
Am. ad. 1935 Tenafly, N. J. M.
RUBINS, Harry W. (Et-P)
Am. Buffalo, N. Y. 1865; ad. 1934 Minn., Minn. A.
RUBIO, Antonio Perez.
Sp. 1822-1887. B.
RUBIO, Luigi [or Louis Chevalier].
It. b. Rome; d. 1882 Florence. B.
RUBIO, Timeteo Perez.
Sp. ac. 1931 in Spain. M.
RUBLYOV [or Rublev], Andrei [or Andrey].
[Most prominent ancient Russian painter.]
Rus. 1370-1430. M.
RUCKLE, Thomas C.
Am. ac. 1834 in Balt., Md. Fa.
RUCKSTUHL, Frederic Wellington. (S)
Am. b. Alsace 1853; ad. 1934 Brooklyn, N. Y. A-F-Hs-W.
RUDAUX, Edmond Adolphe.
Fr. b. Verdun 1840. B.
RUDDER, Stephen William Douglas.
Am. Salem, Ind. 1906-1932 Chicago. A030.
RUDE, François. (S)
Fr. Dijon 1784-1855 Paris. B-E-Hs-562.
RUDE, Sophie [née Frémiet].
Fr. Dijon 1797-1867. B.
RUDELL, Peter Edward.
Ger. 1854-1899. A01-B.
RUDERT, Anton.
Am. ac. 1934 New York. M.
RUDISILL, Margaret.
Am. Montgomery Co., Ind. 1857-1933 Ind., Ind. A030.
RUDISUHLI, Hermann Jakob Lorenz.
Swi. b. St. Galle 1835; ac. 1875 in Paris. B.
RUDOLPH, Harold.
Am. ac. 1871/4 in New Orleans, La. 144-183.
RUDOLPH, [Mrs.] Pauline Dohn.
Am. b. Chicago; ad. 1934 Winnetka, Ill. A-F.
RUDOLPH, Wilhelm.
Ger. b. 1889 in Germany. M.
RUDY, Charles. (S)
Am. b. York, Pa. 1904; ad. 1934 New York. A.
RUE, Louis Félix de la. (S)
Fr. Paris 1720/5-1765/80 Same. B.
RUEGG, Verena.
Am. b. San Fran., Calif. 1905; ad. 1934 Hollywood, Calif. A.
RUEL [or Rüll], Johan Baptist.
Flem. Antwerp 1606-1680/3. B.
RUEL, Pierre Léon Horace.
Fr. ac. 1868 in Paris. B.
RUELAS, Juán de.
Sp. 1558-1625. M.
RUELLAN, Andrée. (Eg)
Am. ex. 1934 New York. M.
RUFFALO, Gasper John.
Am. b. Chicago 1908; ad. 1934 Same. A.
RUFINO, Tamayo.
Mex. ex. 1931 New York. M.
RUGENDAS, Georg Philipp [The Elder]. (Et)
Ger. Augsburg 1666-1742. B-C-722.
RUGENDAS, Johann Lorenz.
Ger. Augsburg 1775-1826. B.
RUGENDAS, Johann Moritz.
Ger. Augsburg 1802-1858 Weilheim. B.
RUGER, Julius.
Am. Germany 1841-1906 Buffalo, N. Y. A06.
RUGGERI, Quirino.
It. ex. 1935 Rome. M.
RUGGIERI [or Ruggeri], Guido.
It. b. Bologna 1550. B.
RUHLAND, Edwin.
Am. New York 1890-1922 Flushing, L. I., N. Y. A019.
RUHLMANN, Émile Jacques.
Fr. Paris 1869-1933. DBA.
RUIPEREZ, L.
Sp. ac. 19th Cent. in Spain. M.
RUISCH, Rachel.
Dut. 1684-1730. 722.
RUISDAEL. *see* Ruysdael.

RUIZ DE LA IGESIA, Francisco Ignacio.
Sp. Madrid 1648-1704 Same. B.
RUIZ, Pablo. *see* Picasso, P.
RUIZ DE SARABIA, Andrés.
Sp. b. Sèville d. Lima, Peru, 17th Cent. Fa.
RUL, Henri.
Belg. b. Antwerp 1862. B.
RULE, [Mrs.] Fay Shelly. (Min)
Am. b. Chattanooga, Tenn. 1889; ad. 1934 Same. A.
RUMAN, Alexandria Victoria [Princess].
Ger. ex. 1932 in Houston, Tex. M.
RUMLEY, Lucille.
Am. b. Preble Co., O. 1901; ad. 1934 Richmond, Ind. A.
RUMMELL, John.
Am. b. Springville, N. Y. 1861; ad. 1934 Buffalo, N. Y. A.
RUMMELL, Richard.
Am. b. 1848; d. 1924 Brooklyn, N. Y. A021.
RUMMLER, Alex J.
Am. b. Dubuque, Ia. 1867; ad. 1934 Norwalk, Conn. A-F.
RUMP, Christian Gottfried.
Dan. Hillerod 1816-1880 Fredericksborg. B-C.
RUMPF, Anton Karl. (S)
Ger. 1838-1911. Fa.
RUMPF, Peter Philipp.
Ger. Frankfort 1821-1896 Same. B.
RUMPH, Alice Edith.
Am. ed. 1934 New York. A.
RUMPLER, Franz.
Bohemian. b. in Tachau 1848. B.
RUMSEY, Charles Cary. (S)
Am. Buffalo, N. Y. 1879-1922 Floral Park, L. I., N. Y. A019-F.
RUMSEY, Daniel Lockwood. (S)
Am. b. 1900 Buffalo, N. Y.; ad. 1934 Same. M.
RUNCIMAN, Alexander.
Scot. Edinburgh 1736-1785. B-DNB-E.
RUNCIMAN, John.
Scot. Edinburgh 1744-1768 Naples, It. B-DNB.
RUNDLE, Henry M.
Am. ad. 1935 Moorestown, N. J. M.
RUNDLE, Valiquette Morrison.
Am. b. San Diego, Calif. 1907; ad. 1934 Lincoln, Neb. A.
RUNGE, Otto Philipp.
Ger. Wolgast 1777-1810 Manburg. B.
RUNGIUS, Carl Clemens Moritz.
Am. b. Berlin, Ger. 1869; ad. 1934 New York. A-F-W-46.
RUNK, Ferdinand.
Ger. Freiburg 1746-1834 Vienna, Aus. B.
RUOPPOLI, Giuseppe.
It. Naples 1600-1659 Same. B.
RUOTOLO, Onorio. (S)
Am. b. Italy 1888; ad. 1935 New York. W.
RUPERT, Prince du Rhin.
Ger. Prague 1619-1682 London. B.
RUPPRECHT, Friedrich Carl.
Ger. Obezeun 1779-1831 Bamberg. B.
RUSH, John. (S)
Am. Phila., Pa. 1781-1853 Same. M.
RUSH, Olive.
Am. b. Fairmont, Ind.; ad. 1934 Santa Fé, N. M. A-F-W-181.
RUSH, William. (S)
Am. Phila., Pa. 1756-1833 Same. E-Hs-F-Ta-701.
RUSHBURY, Henry. (Et)
Eng. b. Harborne 1889; ad. 1934 Colchester. Wa-825-830.
RUSHTON, Dorothy Marion.
Eng. Greenhithe 1884; ad. 1934 London. Wa.
RUSHTON, William C.
Eng. d. 1921. B-Y01922.
RUSIÑOL, Santiago.
Sp. b. 1861; d. 1931 in Barcelona. B-Fa.
RUSKIN, John. (P-Author)
Eng. London 1819-1900 Brantwood. B-DNB-565-566-790.
RUSS, Horace Alexander.
Am. b. Logtown, Miss. 1889; ad. 1934 New Orleans, La. A.
RUSS, Karl.
Aus. Vienna 1779-1843 Same. B-C.
RUSS, Robert.
Aus. b. Vienna 1847. B.
RUSSEL, Anthony.
Eng. 1660/3-1743. B-DNB.
RUSSEL [or Rousseel], Théodore.
Flem. Bruges 1614-1669 London. B-DNB.
RUSSELL, Albert Cuyp. (Eg)
Am. b. 1838; d. 1917 Roxbury, Mass. A015.
RUSSELL, Charles Marion. (P-S)
Am. St. Louis, Mo. 1865-1926 Great Falls, Mont. A023-F-W14.
RUSSELL, George Horne.
Can. Banff, Scot. 1861-1933 St. Stephen, N. B. M-893.
RUSSELL ["AE"], George William. (Poet-P)
Ir. Ireland 1867-1935 Bournemouth, Eng. E-Obit. N. Y. papers, 7-18-1935.
RUSSELL, Grace.
Am. ex. 1935 New York. M.
RUSSELL, Gyrth.
Eng. b. Dartmouth, Nova Scotia 1892; ad. 1934 London. Wa.
RUSSELL, Herald Alain [Captain].
Eng. b. France 1893; ad. 1934 Woolstone, Eng. Wa.
RUSSELL, [Rev.] John.
Eng. Guilford 1745-1806 London. B-Bd-DNB-E.
RUSSELL, Morgan.
Am. ad. 1934 Los Angeles, Calif. M.
RUSSELL, Moses B.
Am. ac. 1834/54 in Boston. F.
RUSSELL, Walter. (P-S)
Am. b. Boston 1871; ad. 1934 New York. A-F-W.
RUSSELL, Walter Westley.
Eng. b. London 1867. B-825.
RUSSELL, William.
Eng. b. 1780; d. 1870 in London. B-DNB.
RUSSIAN Artists. *see* books 895-912.
RUSSMANN, Felix.
Am. b. New York 1888; ad. 1934 Chicago. A.
RUSSOLO, Luigi.
It. b. Portognaro 1885. M.
RUST, John Adolph.
Dut. ac. 1821/8 in Amsterdam. B.
RUSTICI [or Rustichino], Francesco.
It. Siena 1595-1625. B-Bd-V.

RUSZCZYC, FERDYNAND.
Pol. b. 1870 in Poland. M.
RUTELLI, MARIO. (S)
It. b. Palermo 1859; ad. 1878 Paris. B.
RUTHART, KARL ANDREAS.
Ger. Allemagne 1640-1672 Rome, It. B-C.
RUTHERSTON, ALBERT DANIEL. (Ill)
Eng. b. Bradford 1881; ad. 1934 Oxford. Wa.
RUTHRAUFF, FREDERICK GRAY.
Am. Findlay, O. 1878-1932 Ogden, Utah. A029.
RUTHS, JOHANN VALENTIN GEORG.
Ger. Hamburg 1825-1905 Same. B.
RUTLAND, CHARLES. (S)
Eng. b. Cheltenham 1859. Wa1929.
RUTLAND, EMILY. (Ill)
Am. ad. 1935 Robstown, Tex. M.
RUTLAND [Duchess of], VIOLET.
Eng. b. Wigan; ad. 1934 London. Wa.
RUTLEDGE, BERTHA V.
Am. b. Topeka, Kan. 1890; ad. 1934 Same. A.
RUTTER, THOMAS WILLIAM.
Eng. b. Richmond 1874; ad. 1934 Northampton. Wa.
RUYL, LOUIS H.
Am. b. Brooklyn, N. Y. 1870; ad. 1935 New York. A28-F.
RUYLL, ANTONIO.
Sp. ac. 1430-1435 in Spain. M.
RUYSBRACK, JEAN MICHEL. (S)
Flem. Antwerp 1692-1770 Same. B.
RUYSCH [or Ruisch], RACHEL.
Dut. Amsterdam 1664/5-1750 Same. B-C-829.
RUYSDAEL, JACOB ISAACKSZ VAN.
Dut. Haarlem 1625/9-1682 Same. B-Bd-C-E-563-564.
RUYSDAEL, JACOB SALOMONSZ II.
Dut. Haarlem 1630/5-1681 Same. B-C-722.
RUYSDAEL, SALOMON VAN.
Dut. Haarlem 1600?-1670 Same. B-Bd-C-722.
RUYTEN [or Ruyters], JAN MICHAEL.
Belg. Antwerp 1813-1881. B.
RUYVEN, PIETER JANSZ. *see* Reuven, P. J.
RUZICKA, ANTONIN JOSEPH.
Am. Racine, Wis. 1891-1918 France. A016.
RUZICKA, RUDOLPH. (Ill)
Am. b. Czec. 1883; ad. 1935 Dobbs Ferry, N. Y. A28-F-W.
RYALL, HENRY THOMAS. (Eg)
Br. 1811-1867. DNB.
RYAN, CHARLES J.
Eng. ac. 1885 in London. B.
RYAN, KATHLEEN.
Ir. b. Athlone 1900; ad. 1934 Mayo. Wa.
RYAN, VIVIAN D.
Eng. ac. 1929 in London. Wa1929.
RYCKAERT [or Rickaet], DAVID I.
Flem. Antwerp 1560-1607 Same. B-C-449.
RYCKAERT [or Rickaet], DAVID II.
Flem. Antwerp 1586-1642 Same. B-C-449.
RYCKAERT [or Rickaet], DAVID III.
Flem. Antwerp 1612-1661 Same. B-C-449-722.
RYCKAERT, MARTIN.
Flem. Antwerp 1587/91-1631/8. B.
RYCKÈRE [or Rycker], ABRAHAM DE.
Flem. Antwerp 1566-1599. B.
RYCKÈRE [or Rycke], BERNARD DE.
Flem. Courtrai 1535-1590. B-C.
RYCKMAN [or Ryckemans], NICOLAS.
Flem. Antwerp 1595-1620. B.
RYDÉN, HENNING. (S)
Am. b. Sweden 1869; ad. 1934 New York. A.
RYDER, ALBERT PINKHAM.
Am. New Bedford, Mass. 1847-1917 Elmhurst, L. I., N. Y. A014-B-C-E-F-W9-1-46-51-71-138-237-567-701-762-779-790-835.
RYDER, CHAUNCEY FOSTER.
Am. b. Danbury, Conn. 1868; ad. 1934 New York. A-F-W.
RYDER, PLATT LOWELL.
Am. Brooklyn, N. Y. 1821-1896 Saratoga, N. Y. B-C.
RYDER, THOMAS. (Eg)
Br. 1746-1810. DNB.
RYDER, VAN. *see* Van Ryder.
RYDER, WORTH.
Am. b. Kirkwood, Ill. 1884; ad. 1934 Berkeley, Calif. A.
RYERSON, MARGERY AUSTEN. (Et)
Am. b. Morristown, N. J. 1886; ad. 1935 New York. A-F-W.
RYERSON, MARY McILVAINE. (S)
Am. b. Phila., Pa.; ad. 1934 New York. A.
RYLAND, HENRY.
Eng. Bedfordshire 1859-1924. Y01925.
RYLAND, ROBERT KNIGHT. (Mu)
Am. b. Grenada, Miss. 1873; ad. 1934 Brooklyn, N. Y. A-F-W.
RYLAND, WILLIAM WYNNE. (Eg)
Eng. London 1732-1783. B-DNB-E
RYLEY [or Riley], CHARLES REUBEN.
Eng. London 1752-1798 Same. B-DNB.
RYLEY, JOHN. *see* Riley, J.
RYLOFF, ARKADI.
Rus. b. 1870. M.
RYMSDYK, ANDREW VAN. (Eg)
Eng. d. 1780. DNB.
RYMSDYK, JAN VAN. (Eg)
Eng. b. Holland; ac. 1767-1778 in Bristol, Eng. B-DNB.
RYN. *see* Rembrandt, von Ryn.
RYN, JAN VAN.
Flem. Dunkirk, Fr. 1610-1678 Same. B.
RYN [or Rhyn], TITUS VAN.
Dut. 1641-1668. B.
RYNE, JOHANNES VAN.
Dut. 1712-1760. B.
RYSBRACK, JOHANNES MICHIEL. (S)
Flem. Antwerp 1692/4-1770 England. B-DNB-Hs-568.
RYSBRACK, PETER.
Flem. Antwerp 1655-1729 Brussels. B-C.
RYSBRACK, PETER ANDREAS.
Flem. Paris 1690-1748 London. B.
RYSEN [or Ryzen], WARNARD [or Warner].
Dut. Bommel 1600/25-1665 Espagne. B.
RYSSELBERGHE, THÉODORE VAN.
Belg. Ghent 1862-1926. B.
RYTHER, AUGUSTINE. (Eg)
Br. ac. 1576-1590. DNB.
RYTHER, MARGARET.
Am. ad. 1935 New York. M.

RYUTOKU, Ono.
Jap. ac. 1932. M.
SA, Aernance de. (S)
Por. b. Avintes; ac. 1900 in Paris. B.
SAABYE, A. (S)
Dan. b. Schirchise; ac. 1900 in Paris. B.
SAAGMOLEN [or Zogmoolen], Martinus.
Dut. Oldenburg 1620-1669 Amsterdam. B.
SAAL, Geor Eduard Ott.
Ger. Coblenz 1818-1870 Baden-Baden. B.
SAALBURG, Leslie. (Ill)
Am. ex. 1934 New York. d. 4/11/73 - PARIS M.
SAAVEDRA Y CASTILLO, Antonio.
Sp. Cordova 1603-1667 Orleans, Fr. B.
SABATELLI, Luigi.
It. Florence 1772/3-1850 Milan. B.
SABATINI, Raphael.
Am. b. Phila., Pa. 1898; ad. 1934 Same. A.
SABATTÉ, Fernand. (P-S)
Fr. b. Aiguillon 1874; ex. 1930 London. DBA.
SABBAGH, Georges Hanna.
Egyptian. b. Alexandria, Egypt 1877. DBA.
SABBATINI, Andrea [Salerno].
It. Bologna 1480-1545 Gaëte. B.
SABBATINI, Lorenzo [Il. Lorenzino].
It. Rome 1530-1577 Bologna. B.
SABLET, François Jean [Romain].
Swi. Morges 1745-1819 Nantes, Fr. B.
SABLET, Jacob Henri [Jacques].
Swi. Morges 1749-1803 Paris. B.
SABOGAL, José.
Peruvian. b. Cajabrama 1888; ad. 1935 Lima. M.
SABON, Laurent.
Fr. b. Nimes 1852. B.
SABURO, Osaki.
Jap. ac. 1932. M.
SABURO, Ota.
Jap. ac. 1932. M.
SABUROSUKE, Okada.
Jap. b. 1869. M.
SAC, Ollet.
Am. b. Albuquerque, N. M. 1900; ad. 1934 New Orleans, La. A.
SACCAGGI, Césare.
It. ac. 1900 in Paris. B.
SACCHI, Andrea.
It. Rome 1594/9-1661 Same. B-C-E-722.
SACCHI DI PAVIA [or Pavese], Pier Francesco.
It. ac. 1512-1527 in Milan. B-Bd.
SACKETT, Clara Elizabeth.
Am. b. Westfield, N. Y.; ad. 1934 New York. A.
SACKETT, Richard Roman.
Am. b. Bentonville, Ark. 1909; ad. 1934 Minn., Minn. A.
SACKS, Joseph.
Am. b. Shavli, Rus. 1887; ad. 1934 Phila., Pa. A-F.
SACKS, Walter T.
Am. ad. 1934 Rochester, N. Y. M.
SADDLER, John. (Eg)
Eng. b. 1813; d. 1892 Wokingham, Eng. DNB.
SADDLER [or Sadler], Thomas.
Eng. ac. 1670-1700. B-DNB.
SADEE, Philippe Lodowyck Jacob.
Dut. The Hague 1837-1904. B.
SADELER, Aegidius [The Younger].
Flem. Antwerp 1570-1629 Prague, Czec. B-Bd.
SADELER, Jan [or Hans] I.
Flem. Brussels 1500-1600/10 Venice, It. B.
SADELER, Jan [or Hans], [The Younger].
Flem. b. 1600; d. 1666 Munich, Ger. B.
SADELER, Raphael [The Elder].
Ger. Antwerp, Belg. 1555/61-1616/28 Munich. B.
SADLER, Walter Dendy.
Eng. Dorking 1854-1923 St. Ives. B.
SAECKER, Austin.
Am. b. Appleton, Wis. 1896; ad. 1934 Same. A.
SAEDELEER, Valerius de.
Belg. b. 1869; ad. 1934 Flanders. M.
SAEMUNDSSON, Nina. (S)
Icelandic. b. Iceland; ac. 1931. M.
SAENREDAM, Jan.
Dut. Zaandam 1565-1607 Assendelft. B.
SAENREDAM, Pieter Jansz.
Dut. Assendelft 1597-1667 Haarlem. B-C.
SAFT-LEVEN, Cornelis.
Dut. Gorkum 1607-1681/2 Rotterdam. B-C-722.
SAFT-LEVAN, Herman [The Elder].
Dut. d. 1627 in Rotterdam. B.
SAFT-LEVAN, Herman [The Younger].
Dut. Rotterdam 1609-1685 Utrecht. B-C-722.
SAGE, Cornelia Bentley.
Mrs. William Warren Quinton.
Am. b. Buffalo, N. Y. 1876; ad. 1934 Hollywood, Calif. A-F-W.
SAGE, Jean. (Ill)
Am. ad. 1935 Hackensack, N. J. M.
SAHLER, Helen. (S)
Am. b. Carmel, N. Y. 1877; ad. 1934 New York. A-Ca-F-W.
SAID, Claus. (Eg)
Am. b. Memphis, Tenn. 1902; ad. 1934 Same. M.
SAILMAKER, Isaac.
Dut. or Eng. 1633-1721. B.
SAIN, Edouard Alexandre.
Fr. b. 1830; d. 1910 in Paris. B-DBA.
SAIN, Paul Jean Marie.
Fr. b. Avignon; d. 1908. B.
SAINT and ST. Combined.
SAINT-ANDRÉ, Simon Bernard de.
Fr. Paris 1614-1617. B.
SAINT-AUBERT, Antoine François.
Fr. Cambrai 1715-1788 Same. B.
SAINT-AUBIN, Augustin de. (Eg)
Fr. Paris 1737-1807 Same. B-900.
ST. AUBIN, Catherine. (Et)
Br. d. 1836. DNB.
SAINT-AUBIN, Charles Germain de.
Fr. Paris 1721-1786 Same. B.
SAINT-AUBIN, Gabriel Jacques de.
Fr. Paris 1724-1780 Same. B.
SAINT-CLAIR, Norman.
Am. b. 1864; d. 1912 Los Angeles, Calif. A010.
SAINT-CYR, Yvonne de.
Fr. b. Paris; ad. 1934 Same. DBA.

SAINT-DANIEL.
Fr. b. Saint-Lo 1778; d. 1847. B.
ST. DEBICKI.
Pol. ac. 1900. M.
SAINT-EVRE, GILBERT.
Fr. Bault 1791-1858 Paris. B.
SAINT-GAUDENS, ANETTA JOHNSON. (S)
Mrs. Louis Saint-Gaudens.
Am. b. Flint, O. 1869; ad. 1934 Windsor, Vt. A-Cs-F.
SAINT-GAUDENS, AUGUSTUS. (S)
Am. Dublin, Ir. 1848-1907 Cornish, N. H. A06-B-E-F-Hs-15-18-19-26-35-46-104-128-172-175-191-236-701-779-798-815-826-932-946.
SAINT-GAUDENS, CARLOTTA. (Min)
Mrs. Homer Saint-Gaudens.
Am. Rochester, N. Y. 1884-1927. A20-F.
SAINT-GAUDENS, LOUIS. (S)
Am. New York 1854-1913 Cornish, N. H. A0X1-F-71.
SAINT-GAUDENS, PAUL. (S)
Am. b. Flint, O. 1900; ad. 1934 Windsor, Vt. A-Cs.
SAINT-GERMIER, JOSEPH.
Fr. b. Toulouse 1860. B.
SAINT-JEAN, SIMON.
Fr. Lyons 1808-1860 Same. B.
ST. JOHN, J. ALLEN.
Am. b. Chicago 1872; ad. 1934 Same. A.
ST, JOHN, LOLA ALBERTA.
Am. b. Albany, Ind. 1879; ad. 1934 Same. A.
ST. JOHN, [Mrs.] SUSAN HELY.
Am. b. 1833; d. 1913 Boston, Mass. A0X1.
SAINT-LANNE, LOUIS. (S)
Am. ad. 1934 New York. A-B-F.
SAINT, LAWRENCE. (Et)
Am. b. Sharpsburg, Pa. 1885. A28-F.
ST. LEGER, ISABELLA HENRIETTA.
Am. d. 1926 in New York. A024.
SAINT-MARCEAUX, RENÉ DE. (S)
Fr. b. Reims 1845. B-Hs.
SAINT-MARCEL, CHARLES EDMÉ CABIN.
Fr. Paris 1819-1890 Fontainebleau. B.
SAINT-MÉMIN, CHARLES BALTHAZER JULIEN FÉVRET DE. (Eg)
Fr.-Am. Dijon 1770-1852 Same. F-2-7-45-182-185-786.
SAINT-NON, JEAN CLAUDE RICHARD. (Eg)
Fr. Paris 1730-1791 Same. B.
SAINT-OURS, JEAN PIERRE PAUL.
Swi. Geneva 1752-1809 Same. B.
SAINT-PIERRE, GASTON CASIMER.
Fr. Nimes 1833-1916. B-C-DBA.
SAINT-QUENTIN, JACQUES PHILLIPPE JOSEPH DE.
Fr. b. 1738; d. 1760/80 in Paris. B.
SAINT-SIMON, CHRISTOPHE. (S)
Fr. b. Angers 1679; ac. 1747. B.
SAINTIN, JULES ÉMILE.
Fr. Lemée 1829-1894 Paris. B.
SAINTIN, LOUIS HENRI.
Fr. Paris 1846-1889. B.
SAIVE DE NAMUR, JEAN BAPTISTE [The Elder].
Fr. Namur 1540-1624. B.
SALA, GEORGE AUGUSTUS HENRY. (Ill-Writer)
Eng. London 1828-1896 Same. B-DNB.
SALA, JÚAN.
Sp. b. Barcelona 1895; ad. 1934 Paris. B-DBA.
SALA, PAOLO.
It. Milan 1859-1924. B.
SALA, RAFAEL.
Sp. ex. 1931 New York. M.
SALAI [or Salario], ANDREA.
It. 1483-1520 Milan. B-C-722.
SALAMANCA, ANTONIO.
It. b. Rome; ac. 1545/8. B.
SALANSON, EUGÈNIE MARIE.
Fr. b. Albert; ac. 1864-1892 in Montreal, Can. B-M.
SALATHÉ, FRÉDÉRIC.
Swi. Basle 1793-1860. B.
SALAZAR, TONO. (Cari)
Am. ad. 1934 New York. M.
SALDIBAR, P. (S)
Am. b. 1907; ad. 1934 West Haven, Conn. M.
SALEMME, ANTONIO. (S)
Am. b. Gaeta, It. 1892; ad. 1934 New York. A-Cs-F.
SALENTIN, HUBERT [or Henri].
Ger. Zulpich 1822-1910 Düsseldorf. B-C.
SALG, BERT N. (Ill)
Am. ad. 1934 Congers, N. Y. M.
SALGADO, JOSÉ VELLOVO.
Por. b. Lisbon; ac. 1900 Paris. B.
SALIBA, ANTONIO DE.
It. ac. 1480-1535. M.
SALIETTI, ALBERTO [or Umberto].
It. b. Ravenna 1892; ad. 1934 Milan. M.
SALIMBENI. *see also* San Severino.
SALIMBENI, VENTURA DI ARCANGELO.
It. Siena 1568-1613 Same. B-C-722.
SALING, HENRY FREDERICK.
Am. b. Hartford, Conn. 1901; ad. 1934 Same. A.
SALING, PAUL E.
Am. b. Germany 1876; ad. 1934 Hartford, Conn. A.
SALISBURY, [Mrs.] ALTA WEST.
Am. Darnestown, Md. 1879-1933 New Rochelle, N. Y. A030-F.
SALISBURY, FRANK O.
Eng. b. Harpenden 1874; ad. 1935 London. Wa.
SALLE, FRANÇOIS.
Fr. b. Bourges; ac. 19th Cent. B.
SALLES, JULES.
Fr. Nimes 1814-1898 Same. B.
SALLES-WAGNER, ADÉLAIDE.
Ger. Dresden 1823/5-1894 Nimes, Fr. B.
SALMEGGIO, ENEA [Talpino].
It. Bergamo 1538-1626 Same. B.
SALMON, ROBERT W.
Am. b. England; ac. 1829/40 in Boston. F-2-4.
SALMSON, HUGH FREDERICK.
Swe. Stockholm 1843-1894 Lund. B.
SALMSON, JEAN JULES. (S)
Fr. Paris 1823-1902 Coupvray. B.
SALOMÉ, ÉMILE.
Fr. Lille 1833-1881 Salomé. B.
SALOMON, ADAM. (S)
Fr. ac. 19th Cent. in France. B.

SALOMON, Bernard. (Eg)
Fr. Lyons 1520-1570 Same. B.

SALOMON, S. J. *see* Solomon, S. J.

SALOUN, Ladislav. (S)
Czec. b. Prague 1870. E-798.

SALT, Henry. (Ill)
Eng. Litchfield 1785-1827. B.

SALTER, George.
Am. ad. 1935 New York. M.

SALTER, William.
Eng. b. 1804; d. 1873 in London. B-DNB.

SALTHEVEN. *see* Saft-Leven.

SALTONSTALL, Elizabeth.
Am. b. Chestnut Hill, Mass. 1900; ad. 1934 Same. M.

SALTZA, Charles Frederick von.
Swe. 1858-1905. M.

SALTZMAN, Mary Peyton Eskridge.
Am. b. Ft. Leavenworth, Kan. 1878; ad. 1934 Wash., D. C. A.

SALVADOR CARMONA, Manuel.
see Carmona, M. S.

SALVATOR. *see* Rosa, S.

SALVATOR, Victor D. (S)
Am. b. Italy 1885; ad. 1934 New York. A-Cs-F-W.

SALVENDY, Frieda.
Czec. ad. 1934 Vienna, Aus. M.

SALVI, Giovanni Battista. *see* Sassoferrato.

SALVIATI, Antonio.
It. Verona 1816-1890. M.

SALVIATI, Il. Francesco [de Rossi].
It. 1510-1563. B-C-V-722.

SALVIATI, Giuseppi Porta [The Younger].
It. Garfagnano 1518/20-1575/85 Venice. 722.

SALZBRENNER, Albert.
Am. ad. 1935 New York. M.

SALZILLO, Francesco. (S)
see Zarcillo y Alcarez, F.

SAMACCHINI, Orazio.
It. Bologna 1552-1575 Same. B-722.

SAMBERGER, Leo.
Ger. b. Ingolstadt 1861. B.

SAMBOURNE, Edward Limley. (Cart)
Eng. London 1844-1910 Kensington. B-DNB-E.

SAMBROOK, Russell.
Am. ac. 1934. M.

SAMMONS, Frederick Harrington Cruikshank.
Am. Bath, Eng. 1853-1917 Chicago. A014-F.

SAMOKICH, Nicolas.
Rus. b. Russia 1860; ac. 1890 Paris. B.

SAMPLE, Paul Starrett. D. 2/28/74
Am. b. Louisville, Ky. 1896; ad. 1934 Pasadena, Calif. A.

SAMPSON, Melcene.
Am. ad. 1935 Okla. City, Okla. M.

SAMSTAG, Gordon.
Am. b. New York 1906; ad. 1934 Same. A.

SAMUEL, George.
Eng. ex. 1786-1823 in London. B-DNB.

SAMUEL, Richard.
Eng. ex. 1722-1786 in London. B-DNB.

SANBORN, Earl Edward.
Am. b. Lyme, N. H. 1890; ad. 1934 Annisquam, Mass. A.

SÁNCHEZ DE CASTRO, Júan.
Sp. ac. 1454/80 in Sèville. B-774.

SÁNCHEZ, Harriette de.
Am. ex. 1935 New York. M.

SÁNCHEZ, Júan II.
Sp. ac. 1513-1543 Sèville. B-774.

SÁNCHEZ, Pedro.
Sp. ad. 1934 Valencia; ex. 1934 Pittsburgh, Pa. M.

SÁNCHEZ, Pedro I.
Sp. ac. 1500 in Sèville. B-774.

SÁNCHEZ-COELLO. *see* Coello, Alonzo.

SÁNCHEZ-PERRIER, Emilio.
Sp. Sèville 1853-1907. B.

SANDAART, Joachim.
Ger. 1606-1688. 722.

SANDBY, Paul. (Eg)
Eng. Nottingham 1725-1805/9 London. B-DNB-E-364-722-844.

SANDBY, Thomas.
Eng. Nottingham 1721-1798 Windsor. B-DNB.

SANDELS, Gösta.
Swe. 1887-1919. DBA.

SANDEMAN, Archibald.
Eng. ex. 1934 London. M.

SANDERCOCK, Henry Ardmare.
Eng. ac. 1865-1883 in London. B.

SANDERS, Adam Achod. (S)
Am. b. Sweden 1889; ad. 1934 Brooklyn, N. Y. A-Cs.

SANDERS, Bernard. (Et)
Am. b. New York 1904; ad. 1935 Bronx, N. Y. M.

SANDERS, Bertha D.
Am. b. Illinois; ac. 1915 in New York. A12.

SANDERS, George L.
Scot. Kinghorn 1794-1846 London. B-DNB.

SANDERS, Herkules.
Dut. b. 1606; d. 1663 Amsterdam. B.

SANDERS, Joan Manning.
see Manning-Sanders, J.

SANDERS [or Saunders], John [The Younger].
Eng. b. 1750; d. 1823 in Bristol. B-DNB.

SANDERS, P. C., II.
Am. ad. 1935 San Antonio, Tex. M.

SANDERSON, Charles Wesley.
Am. Brandon, Vt. 1838-1905 Boston. A05-F-15.

SANDERSON, Henrietta.
Am. ad. 1934 Pompton Plains, N. Y. M.

SANDFORTH, Lettice. (Eg)
Eng. ex. 1935 London. M.

SANDHAM, J. Henry.
Br. Montreal, Can. 1842-1910 London. A010-C-DNB-F-47.

SANDONA, Matteo.
Am. b. Schio, It. 1883; ad. 1934 San Fran., Calif. A-F.

SANDOR, Mathias.
Am. Hungary 1857-1920 New York. A017-F.

SANDRART, Jakob von.
Ger. Frankfort 1630-1708 Nüremberg. B.

SANDRART, Joachin von.
Ger. Frankfort 1606-1688 Nüremberg. B-C-E.

SANDREUTER, Hans.
Swi. Basel 1850-1901 Riehen. B.

SANDRO DI MASSARELLO.
It. ac. 1304 in Italy. Fa-M.
SANDROCK, LEONHARD.
Ger. b. 1867 in Germany. Fa-M.
SANDYS, ANTHONY FREDERICK AUGUSTUS.
Eng. Norwich 1829-1904 London. B-DNB-E.
SANDYS, EMMA.
Eng. Norwich 1834-1877. B.
SANDZÉN, MARGARET.
Am. ad. 1934 Lindsborg, Kan. M.
SANDZÉN, SVEN BIRGER.
Am. b. Bildsberg, Swe. 1871; ad. 1934 Lindsborg, Kan. A-F-W.
SANFORD, EDWARD FIELD, JR. (S)
Am. b. New York 1886; ad. 1934 Same. A-Cs-F-W.
SANFORD, ISAAC. (Eg)
Am. ac. 1783-1822 in Hartford, Conn. F-2-6-7.
SAN GALLO, ANTONIO DA [The Elder].
It. Florence 1455-1534. V.
SAN GALLO, ANTONIO [The Younger].
It. Florence 1485-1546 Terni. V.
SAN GALLO, ARISTOTILE [Bastiano].
It. ac. 1525 in Florence. V.
SAN GALLO, FRANCESCO DI. (S)
It. b. 1493; d. 1570 in Rome. Hs-V.
SAN GALLO, GUILIANO DA.
It. Florence 1445/52-1516. V.
SANGER, GRACE H. H. COCHRANE.
Am. b. Newark, N. J. 1881; ad. 1934 Ruxton, Md. A.
SANGER, WILLIAM.
Am. b. Berlin, Ger. 1875; ad. 1934 Albany, N. Y. A-F.
SANGERNEBO, ALEXANDER. (S)
Am. Russia 1856-1930 Ind., Ind. A028-F.
SANGERNEBO, EMMA EYLES. (S)
Mrs. Alexander Sangernebo.
Am. b. Pittsburgh, Pa. 1877; ad. 1934 Ind., Ind. A-F.
SAN GIMIGANO. *see* Tamagni.
SANGLAN, E. (S)
Fr. ac. 19th Century. M.
SANGREE, [Mrs.] THEODORA.
Am. b. Harrisburg, Pa. 1901; ad. 1935 New York. M.
SANGSTER, SAMUEL. (Eg)
Br. 1804?-1872. DNB.
SAN MARCO, FRA BARTOLOMMEO DI.
[Baccio della Porta].
It. Florence 1475-1517. V.
SANO, E. B.
Belg. b. Paris; d. 1878 Antwerp. M.
SANO [or Ansano], DI PIETRO.
see Pietro Sano di Menico.
SANRAKU, KANO.
Jap. J., Vol. 1, page 88.
SANSALVADORE, PIERO.
It. b. Turin 1892; ad. 1934 London. M.
SANSENEY. *see* Senseney.
SANSETSU, KANO [Chiga].
Jap. Hizen 1589-1651. J., Vol. 1, page 130.
SAN SEVERNIO [or Salimbeni], LORENZO DA [The Elder].
It. 1374-1420. B.
SAN SEVERINO, LORENZO DA [The Younger].
It. Umbrian; ac. 1481; d. 1503. B.
SANSON, JUSTIN CHRYSOSTOME. (S)
Fr. b. Nemours 1833. B.
SANSOVINO, ANDREA CONTUCCI DEL MONTE. (S)
It. Sansovino 1460-1529 Loreto. E-Hs-V.
SANSOVINO, JACOPO [Tatti]. (S)
It. Sansovino 1477-1570 Venice. B-E-Hs-V.
SANT'AGATA, FRANCESCO DA. (S)
It. ac. 1520-1530. M.
SANT, JAMES J.
Eng. London 1820-1916. B-C.
SANTA CROCE, FRANCESCO RIZZO DA.
It. ac. 1517-1545 in Venice. B-Bd-C.
SANTA CROCE, GIROLAMO DA.
It. Santa Croce 1480?-1556. B-Bd-C.
SANTAGOSTINO [or Santagato], GIACOMO ANTONIO.
It. Milan 1588-1648. B.
SANTA MARIA, MAGUITA. (Min)
Am. ad. 1934 Phila., Pa. M.
SANTERRE, JEAN BAPTISTE.
Fr. Magny 1658-1717 Paris. B-C-E-722.
SANTI, ANDRIOLO. (S)
It. d. 1377 in Venice. Hs.
SANTI, GIOVANNI.
It. Colbordolo 1435?-1494 Urbino. B-Bd-C-722.
SANTI [or Sanzio], RAPHAELLO.
see Raphael Sanzio [or Santi].
SANTI DI TITO. *see* Tito, S. di.
SANTIS, GUGLIELMO DE.
It. b. Rome 1829. B.
SANTORO, RUBENS.
It. b. Mongrassono 1843; ex. London and Paris. B.
SANTOS, TORRELLA ANGELES.
Sp. ad. 1934 San Sebastien. M.
SANTVOORT, DIRCK DIRCKSZ VAN.
Dut. Amsterdam 1610-1680 Same. B-C.
SANZIO, GIOVANNI. *see* Santi, G.
SANZIO, RAFFAELLO. *see* Raphael, S.
SAPAJOU. (Cari)
[Real name George Sapojnikov.]
Rus. ad. 1932 Shanghai, China. 873.
SARACENO [or Sazucino], CARLO.
It. Venice 1585-1625. B.
SARAZIN [or Sarrazin], JACQUES. (S)
Fr. Noyon 1588-1660 Paris. B-E-Hs.
SARD, MICHELE.
Fr. ex. 1935 New York. M.
SARDEAU, HÉLÈNE. (S)
Am. b. Belgium; ad. 1935 Croton, N. Y. M.
SARE, [Mrs.] HILDA M.
Eng. b. Hitchin; ad. 1934 Norbury. Wa.
SARFF, WALTER.
Am. ex. 1934 Woodstock, N. Y. M.
SARG, MARY.
Am. b. 1913; ad. 1935 New York. M.
SARG, TONY. (Ill)
Am. b. Guatelmala 1880; ad. 1935 New York. A28-F.
SARGEANT, GENEVE RIXFORD.
Am. b. San Fran., Calif. 1868; ad. 1934 Same. A12-F-M.
SARGENT, HENRY.
Am. Gloucester, Mass. 1770-1845 Boston. B-Bd-C-F-2-4-6-169.

SARGENT, JOHN SINGER.
Am. Florence, It. 1856-1925 London.
A022-B-C-DAB-E-F-W13-1-5-15-46-51-55-70-105-127-128-138-172-176-178-192-238-239-240-241-242-243-244-697-700-701-721-736-748-762-779-781-807-826-878-947.

SARGENT, LOUIS AUGUSTUS.
Eng. b. London 1881; ad. 1934 Same. Wa.

SARGENT, MARGARET W. (S)
Am. b. Wellesley, Mass. 1892; ad. 1934 Same. A-F.

SARGENT, NATALIE. (Ill)
Am. ad. 1934 Phila., Pa. M.

SARGENT, PAUL TURNER.
Am. b. Hutton, Ill. 1880; ad. 1934 Charleston, Ill. A.

SARGENT, WALTER.
Am. Worcester, Mass. 1868-1927 No. Scituate, Mass. A024-F.

SARISKY, MICHAEL ALOYSIUS.
Am. b. Hungary 1906; ad. 1934 Cleveland, O. A.

SARKA, CHARLES N. (Mu)
Am. b. Chicago 1879; ad. 1934 New York. A-F.

SARKADI, LEO.
Am. ad. 1935 New York. M.

SARKISIAN, SARKIS.
Am. ad. 1935 Detroit, Mich. M.

SARLUIS, LÉONARD.
Fr. b. The Hague, Holland 1874. DBA.

SAROLDI, ENRICO.
It. ac. 1930. M.

SARONY, NAPOLEON. (Eg)
Am. ac. 1889-1926 in New York. F.

SARRABAT, ISAAC. (Eg)
Fr. ac. 1680 in France. B.

SARRABEZOLLES, CARLO. (S)
Fr. b. Toulouse 1888. DBA.

SARRAT, VERGÉ. *see* Vergé-Sarrat, Henri.

SARRAZIN. *see* Sarazin.

SARRE, CARMEN.
Am. ad. 1935 New Orleans, La. M.

SARRO, RODNEY DE. (Cart)
Am. ad. 1934 Chicago. M.

SARTAIN, EMILY. (Eg)
Am. Phila., Pa. 1841-1927 Same.
A024-B-Bd-C-F-W14-7-15.

SARTAIN, HARRIET.
Am. b. Phila., Pa.; ac. 1931. A28-B-F.

SARTAIN, JOHN. (Eg)
Am. London 1808-1897 Phila., Pa.
A01-B-Bd-E-2-6-7-15-40-179-182.

SARTAIN, SAMUEL.
Am. Phila., Pa. 1830-1906 Same. A06-F-7-40.

SARTAIN, WILLIAM.
Am. Phila., Pa. 1843-1924 New York.
A021-B-Bd-C-F-W14-7-15-46.

SARTE, MARIE MADELEINE DEL.
Fr. b. Paris; ac. 1866 Same. M.

SARTO, ANDREA DEL.
[Agnolo or Vannucchi.]
It. Florence 1486/7-1531 Same.
B-Bd-C-E-V-722.

SARTORIO, GUILO ARTISTIDE. (S)
It. Rome 1861-1932. B-Wa1929-Y01933.

SARTORIUS, FRANCIS [The Elder].
Eng. London 1734-1804. B-DNB.

SARTORIUS, JOHN.
Eng. London 1700? d. 1780? in London. B-DNB.

SARTORIUS, JOHN N. [or F.].
Eng. London 1755-1828/31.. B-DNB.

SASS, HENRY.
Eng. London 1788-1844. B-DNB.

SASS [or Sasse], RICHARD.
Eng. England 1774-1849 Paris. B-DNB.

SASSETTA, STEFANO DI GIOVANNI.
It. Siena 1392-1450. B-C-V-784.

SASSO, ANTONIO.
It. ac. 1859 in Florence. M.

SASSOFERRATO, GIOVANNI BATTISTA SALVI.
It. Sassoferrato 1605-1685 Rome. B-Bd-C.

SATINAS, F. PABLO.
Sp. ac. 19th Cent. in Spain. M.

SATOMI, MUNETSUGU.
Jap. b. Osaka 1900; ad. 1934 Paris. DBA.

SATRA, AUGUST.
Am. Bohemia 1877-1919 U. S. M.

SATTERLEE, WALTER.
Am. Brooklyn, N. Y. 1844-1908 New York.
A07-B-C-E-F-15.

SATURNINO DE GATTI.
It. Umbrian 1463-1521? M.

SAUBÈS, DANIEL.
Fr. Guiches 1855-1922 Paris. DBA.

SAUERLÄNDER, WILLI.
Ger. ac. 1928 in Alttann. M.

SAUGER, AMÉLIE.
Fr. ac. 1934 in Paris. DBA.

SAUL.
Am. b. Russia 1904; ad. 1934 New York. A.

SAUL, J. H. LOUIS. (Et)
Am. d. 1925 Astoria, L. I., N. Y. A022.

SAUL, MAURICE BOWER.
Am. b. Phila., Pa. 1883; ad. 1934 Moylan, Pa. A.

SAULO, GEORGES ERNEST. (S)
Fr. b. Angers; ac. 1893 in Paris. B.

SAULO, MAURICE. (S)
Fr. b. Paris 1901. DBA.

SAUNDERS, CLARA ROSSMAN.
Am. b. Cinn., O.; ad. 1934 Wash., D. C. A.

SAUNDERS, HENRI DMOCHOWSKI. (S)
Pol. 1810-1863. M.

SAUNDERS, JOSEPH. (Eg)
Eng. ac. 1832-1836 in London. B.

SAUNDERS, KENDALL.
Am. b. Templeton, Mass. 1886; ac. 1926 New York. A12-F.

SAUNDERS, L. PEARL.
Am. b. Tenn.; ad. 1934 Nashville, Tenn. A-F.

SAUNDERS, THEODORE [Raymond Vielant].
Am. b. Denver, Colo. 1908; ad. 1934 Chicago. A.

SAUNDERS, XANTIPPE.
Am. b. 1852; d. 1922 Louisville, Ky. M.

SAUNIER, CHARLES.
Fr. Monthéry 1815-1889 Paris. B.

SAUNIER, NOËL.
Fr. Vienna, Aus. 1847-1890 Paris. B.

SAUPIQUE, GEORGES. (S)
Fr. b. Paris 1889. DBA.

SAUTAI, PAUL ÉMILE.
Fr. Amiens 1842-1901. B-C.

SAUTER, Georg.
Ger. b. Rothenbach 1866. B.
SAUVAGE, Pieter [or Piat] Joseph.
Flem. Tournai 1744-1818 Same. B.
SAUVAIGE, Louis Paul.
Fr. Lille 1827-1885 Trouville. B.
SAUVE, Jean Jacques Théodore.
Fr. Paris 1792-1869 Same. B.
SAUX, Henrietta Browne Sophie.
see Browne, H. S.
SAUZAY, Adrien Jacques.
Fr. Paris 1841-1928. B-C-DBA.
SAVA, Anastas Botzaritch. (S)
Eng. b. Belgrade 1896; ad. 1934 London. Wa.
SAVAGE, Edward.
Am. Princeton, Mass. 1761-1817 Same. F-2-6-7-40-45-182-786.
SAVAGE, Eugene Francis.
Am. b. Covington, Ind. 1883; ad. 1934 Ossining, N. Y. A-F-W-181-779.
SAVAGE, Frances [Mrs. Curtis]. (S)
Am. ad. 1934 New York. M.
SAVAGE, John. (Eg)
Eng. ac. 1690-1700 in London. B-DNB.
SAVAGE, [Mrs.] Marguerite Downing.
Am. b. Bay Ridge, L. I., N. Y. 1879; ad. 1934 Worcester, Mass. A-F.
SAVAGE, Steele. (Et)
Am. ad. 1934 New York. M.
SAVAGE, Thomas.
Am. ad. 1935 Fort Dodge, Ia. M.
SAVERY, Roelandt Jacobsz.
Flem. Courtrai 1576-1639 Utrecht, Holland. B-C-569-722.
SAVERYS, Albert.
Belg. ad. 1934 Deynze; ex. 1934 Pittsburgh, Pa. M.
SAVIGNAC, Raymond.
Fr. b. St. Étienne 1886. DBA.
SAVILLE, Bruce Wilder. (S)
Am. b. Quincy, Mass. 1893; ad. 1934 Santa Fé, N. M. A-Cs-F-W.
SAVINI, Alfonso.
It. b. Bologna; ac. 19th Cent. in Italy. B.
SAVOLDO, Giovanni Girolamo.
It. Brescia 1480-1548/9 Venice. B-Bd-C-V.
SAVONAZZI, Emilio.
It. Bologna 1580-1660 Camerino. B-C.
SAVREUX, Maurice.
Fr. b. Lille 1884. DBA.
SAVRY, Hendrick.
Dut. Haarlem 1823-1907 Same. B.
SAWADA, Mme.
Jap. ex. 1935 New York. M.
SAWKINS, J. G.
Am. ac. 1930. M.
SAWTELLE, A. Elizabeth.
Am. ad. 1934 Washington, D. C. A.
SAWTELLE, Mary Berkeley.
Mrs. Charles G. Sawtelle.
Am. b. Wash., D. C. 1872; ad. 1934 New York. A.
SAWYER, Conway. (S)
Am. b. New York; ad. 1935 Wilmington, Del. M.
SAWYER, Edith.
Am. b. So. Coventry, Conn.; ad. 1934 Brooklyn, N. Y. A.
SAWYER, Edward Warren. (S)
Am. Chicago 1876-1932 France. A029-Cs-F.
SAWYER, Helen Alton.
Mrs. Jerry Farnsworth.
Am. b. Wash., D. C. 1900; ad. 1934 North Truro, Mass. A.
SAWYER, Leila G.
Am. ad. 1934 New York. M.
SAWYER, Philip Ayer.
Am. b. Chicago 1877; ad. 1934 Tiskilwa, Ill. A.
SAWYER, Wells M.
Am. b. Iowa 1863; ad. 1934 New York. A-F.
SAXON, James.
Eng. b. Manchester; ex. 1795-1817 London. B-DNB.
SAXTON, John Gordon.
Am. b. Troy, N. Y. 1860; ad. 1934 Seaford, N. Y. A-F.
SAY, Frederick Richard.
Eng. ac. 1826-1858. B-DNB.
SAY, William. (Eg)
Eng. Norwich 1768-1834 London. B-Bd-DNB.
SAYER, Edmund Sears.
Am. b. Meadville, Pa. 1878; ad. 1934 Wash., D. C. A.
SAYER, Henry Lyman.
Am. b. 1875; d. 1918 Phila., Pa. A015-F.
SAYER [or Sayers], James. (Cari)
Eng. Yarmouth 1748-1823 London. B-DNB-E.
SAYLOR, James C.
Am. ad. 1934 Riverdale, N. Y. M.
SCACCO, Cristoforo.
It. ac. 1499 in Verona. B.
SCAFFI, Luigi.
It. ac. 19th Cent. in Florence. B.
SCALBERT, Jules.
Fr. b. Douai; ac. 1876-1891 in Paris. B.
SCALELLA, Jules.
Am. b. Phila., Pa. 1895; ad. 1934 So. Ardmore, Pa. A.
SCALETTI, Leonardo.
It. ac. 1484. Fa-M.
SCANDINAVIAN Artists.
see book No. 683.
SCANLAN, Robert Richard.
Br. ac. 1826-1876. Fa-M.
SCARAVAGLIONE, Concetta. (S)
Am. b. New York 1900; ad. 1934 Same. A.
SCARCELLA [or Scarsllino], Ippolito.
It. Ferrara 1551-1620/1. B-C.
SCARDINO, Antonio.
It. ac. 1852 in Naples. M.
SCARPAZA, Vittore. *see* Carpaccio, V.
SCARPITTA, G. Salvatore Cartaino. (S)
Am. b. Palermo, It. 1887; ad. 1934 Los Angeles, Calif. A-F-W.
SCARSELLA. *see* Scarcella.
SCATTOLA, Ferruccio.
It. b. Venice, It. 1873; ac. 1932 Rome, It. M.
SCHAAF, Anton. (S)
Am. b. Milwaukee, Wis. 1869; ad. 1934 New York. A-Cs-F-W.
SCHAAL, Louis Jacques Nicolas.
Fr. Paris 1800-1859 Same. B.

SCHAAL, SOLANGE.
Fr. b. St. Germain 1899. DBA.
SCHABELITZ, RUDOLPH FREDERICK. (Ill)
Am. b. Stapleton, S. I., N. Y. 1884; ad. 1934 New York. A-F.
SCHACHT, LOUISE.
Am. ad. 1934 Brooklyn, N. Y. M.
SCHADOW, FÉLIX.
Ger. Berlin 1819-1861 Same. B-T.
SCHADOW, FRIEDRICH WILHELM VON.
Ger. Berlin 1789-1862 Düsseldorf. B-C-E-722.
SCHADOW, JOHANN GOTTFRIED. (S)
Ger. Berlin 1764-1850 Same. B-E-Hs.
SCHADOW, RUDOLPH. (S)
Ger. Rome, It. 1786-1822 Same. E-Hs.
SCHAEFELS, HENRI FRANÇOISE.
Belg. Antwerp 1827-1904 Same. B-C.
SCHAEFELS, LUCAS.
Belg. Antwerp 1824-1885. B.
SCHAEFER, HANS. (S)
Am. b. Sternberg, Czec. 1875; ad. 1934 New York. A.
SCHAEFFER, AUGUST.
Aus. b. Vienna 1833; ac. 1873/92. B-C.
SCHAEFFER [or Schafer], HENRY THOMAS.
Eng. ac. 1873-1901 in London. B.
SCHAEFFER, MEAD. (Ill)
Am. b. 1898; ad. 1934 New York. A-W.
SCHAETTE, LOUIS.
Am. b. Chicago; d. 1917 New York. A014.
SCHAEUFFELIN, HANS LEONHARD.
see Schaüffelein, H. L.
SCHAFER, GEORGE LESLIE.
Am. b. Wilmington, Ill. 1895; ad. 1934 Same. A.
SCHAFF, ANTON. *see* Schaaf, A.
SCHAFFGOTSCH, COUNT.
Ger. ex. 1930 in Munich. M.
SCHAFFNER, MARTINO.
Ger. Ulm 1480-1551 Augsburg. B-C-722.
SCHALCKEN [or Shalkin], GODFRIED.
Dut. Dordrecht 1643-1706 The Hague. B-C-E-722.
SCHALDACH, WILLIAM J. (Et)
Am. b. Elkhart, Ind. 1896. A28.
SCHALL, FREDERICK PHILIP.
Am. b. Chicago 1877; ac. 1915 New York. A12.
SCHALL, JEAN FRÉDÉRIC.
Fr. Strassburg 1753-1835 Paris. B.
SCHALLINGER, MAX.
Am. ex. 1934 Baltimore, Md. M.
SCHAMBERG, MORTON LIVINGSTON.
Am. b. Phila., Pa. 1881; ac. 1926 New York. A12-F.
SCHANKER, LOUIS.
Am. b. New York 1903; ad. 1935 Same. M.
SCHANZENBACHER, NELLIE.
Am. b. Louisville, Ky.; ad. 1934 Same. A.
SCHAR, AXEL EUGÈNE.
Am. b. Oslo, Nor. 1887; ad. 1934 Duluth, Minn. A.
SCHARBOROUGH, ALONZO.
Am. ad. 1934 Staten Island, N. Y. M.
SCHARF, GEORGE [The Elder]. (Min)
Ger. Mainburg 1788-1860 London. B-DNB-E.
SCHARF, [Sir] GEORGE [The Younger]. (Ill)
Eng. London 1820-1895 Same. B-DNB-E.
SCHARFF, EDWIN.
Ger. b. 1887. Fa.
SCHARL, JOSEPH.
Ger. ex. 1930 in Munich M.
SCHARY, SAUL. (Et)
Am. b. Newark, N. J. 1904; ad. 1934 New York. A.
SCHATTENSTEIN, NIKOLAUS [or Nikol].
Am. b. Russia 1877; ad. 1934 New York. A-F.
SCHATZ, BORIS. (S)
Bulgarian 1863-1932. Y01933.
SCHAUER, MARTHA K.
Am. b. Troy, O. 1889; ad. 1934 Dayton, O. A.
SCHÄUFFELEIN, HANS LÉONARD. (Min)
Ger. Nüremberg 1480/90-1539/40 Nördlingen. B-C.
SCHAUMANN, RUTH. (S)
Ger. b. 1899. M.
SCHEDONE. *see* Schidone.
SCHEEMAEKERS, PEETER [The Elder]. (S)
Flem. Antwerp 1640-1714 Arendonk. B.
SCHEEMAEKERS, PEETER [The Younger]. (S)
Flem. Antwerp 1691-1771 Same. B-DNB-E-Hs.
SCHEEMAKERS, THOMAS. (S)
Br. 1740-1808. DNB.
SCHEFFAUER, P. J. (S)
Ger. 1756-1808. Hs.
SCHEFFER, ARY.
Fr. Dordrecht, Holland 1795/7-1858 Argenteuil. B-C-E-474-570-722.
SCHEFFER, HENRI.
Fr. The Hague, Holland 1778-1862 Paris. B-C.
SCHEFFLER, RUDOLF.
Am. b. Zwickau, Saxony 1884; ad. 1934 Brooklyn, N. Y. A.
SCHEIBE, RICHARD. (S)
Ger. b. 1879; ex. 1933 in Chicago. M.
SCHEIBNER, [Mrs.] VIRA MCILLRATH.
Am. b. Cleveland, O. 1889; ad. 1934 St. Augustine, Fla. A.
SCHEIDACKER, HANNS T.
Am. ad. 1934 Brooklyn, N. Y. M.
SCHEITS [or Schentz], MATHIAS.
Ger. Hamburg 1640-1700 Same. B-C.
SCHELER, ARMIN A.
Am. ad. 1935 New Rochelle, N. Y. M.
SCHELFHOUT, ANDREAS.
Dut. The Hague 1787-1870. B-C.
SCHELFHOUT, LODEWIJK.
Dut. b. 1881 in Holland. Fa.
SCHELL, FRANK [or Francis H.] (Et)
Am. b. 1830; d. 1909 Germantown, Pa. A07.
SCHELL, FRANK CRESSON. (Ill)
Am. b. Phila., Pa. 1857; ad. 1934 Same. A20-F-W.
SCHELL, FRED B.
Am. d. 1905 Chicago. B.
SCHELL, GERTRUDE.
Am. ad. 1934 Germantown, Pa. M.
SCHELL [or Schel], SEBASTIAN.
Ger. Innsbruck, Aus. 1479-1554. M.
SCHELLIN, ROBERT.
Am. b. Akron, O. 1910; ad. 1934 Milwaukee, Wis. A.

SCHELLINKS, WILLEM.
Dut. Amsterdam 1627/32-1678 Same. B-C.
SCHELVER, AUGUST FRANZ.
Ger. b. Osnabrück 1805; d. 1844 Munich. C.
SCHENAU, JOHANN ELEAZAR ZEIZIG.
Ger. Zittau 1737/40-1806 Dresden. B-C.
SCHENCK, AUGUST FRIEDRIC ALBRECHT.
Dan. Glückstadt 1828-1901 Ecouen, Fr. B-C.
SCHENCK, PHOEBE JOSEPHINE.
Am. b. Cleveland, O. 1883; ad. 1915 New York. A12.
SCHENDEL, PETRUS VAN.
Belg. Ter Heyden 1806-1870 Brussels. B-C.
SCHENK [or Schenck], PIETER.
Dut. Elberfeld 1645/61-1715 Amsterdam. B.
SCHEPP, FLORENCE L.
Am. ad. 1934 New York. M.
SCHEPS, HENRY.
Am. ad. 1934 Chicago. M.
SCHERRER, JEAN JACQUES.
Fr. b. Lutterbach; ac. 1887-1901 Paris. B.
SCHERRES, KARL.
Ger. Königsberg 1833-1908 Berlin. B-C.
SCHERREWITZ, JOHAN.
Dut. b. Holland 1868. B.
SCHETKY, CAROLINE. (Min)
Mrs. T. M. Richardson.
Am. ac. 1813 in Boston. F-2-6.
SCHETKY, JOHN ALEXANDER.
Scot. Edinburgh 1785-1824. B-DNB.
SCHETKY, JOHN CHRISTIAN.
Scot. Edinburgh 1778-1874 London. B-C-DNB-E.
SCHEURENBURG, JOSEF.
Ger. Düsseldorf 1846-1914. B-C.
SCHEURER, KASPAR JOHANN NEPOMUK.
Ger. Aix 1810-1887 Düsseldorf. B.
SCHEURICH, PAUL. (S)
Ger. ac. 1929 in Germany. M.
SCHEVILL, WILLIAM V.
Am. b. Cinn., O. 1864; ad. 1934 New York. A-F-W.
SCHEX, JOSEPH.
Ger. d. 1894 in Düsseldorf. B.
SCHIATTESI, ARTEMISIA. *see* Gentileschi, A.
SCHIAVO, PAOLO DI. *see* Stefano, P. di.
SCHIAVONE, ANDREA MELDOLLA.
It. Dalmatia 1522?-1582 Venice. B-C-722.
SCHIAVONE, GREGORIO [Dalmaticus].
It. Delmatia 1420-1470 Padua. B-C.
SCHIAVONETTI, LUIGI. (Eg)
It. Bassano 1765-1810 London. B-DNB-E.
SCHIAVONETTI, NICOLÒ. (Eg)
It. Bassano 1771-1813 London. B-DNB.
SCHIAVONI, GIOVANNI.
Ger. 1804-1848? Fa.
SCHIAVONI, NATALE.
It. Chioggia 1777-1858 Venice. B-C.
SCHICHTMEYER, JOHANNES. (S)
Ger. ac. 1900 in Berlin. B.
SCHICK, GOTTLIEB.
Ger. Stuttgart 1779-1812 Same. B-C.
SCHIDONE, BARTOLOMMEO.
It. Modena 1570-1615. B-C-722.
SCHIEDGES, PETER PAUL.
Dut. The Hague 1813-1876 Same. B.
SCHIELE, EGON.
Ger. 1890-1918. Fa.
SCHIEVELBEIN, FRIEDRICH HERMANN. (S)
Ger. Berlin 1817-1867 Russia. B-Hs.
SCHIFFER, ETHEL BENNETT.
Mrs. W. B. Schiffer.
Am. b. Brooklyn, N. Y. 1879; ad. 1934 New Haven, Conn. A-F.
SCHILDKNECHT, EDMUND GUSTAV.
Am. b. Chicago; ad. 1934 Ind., Ind. A.
SCHILDKNECHT, RUTH STEBBINS.
Am. ad. 1935 Ind., Ind. M.
SCHILLE, ALICE.
Am. b. Columbus, O.; ad. 1934 Same. A-F-W-46.
SCHILLING, ALEXANDER.
Am. b. Chicago 1859. A20.
SCHILLING, ARTHUR OSCAR.
Am. b. Germany 1882; ad. 1934 Rochester, N. Y. A.
SCHILLING, JOHANNES. (S)
Ger. Mittweida 1828; [No death date]. B-Hs.
SCHILLING, JOST.
Ger. ac. 1596. Fa.
SCHINDLER, JAKOB EMIL.
Aus. Vienna 1842-1892. B-C.
SCHINDLER, OSKAR.
Ger. b. 1869; ac. in Dresden. B.
SCHINKEL, KARL FRIEDRICH.
Ger. b. Neuruppin 1781; d. 1841 in Vienna, Aus. B-C-722.
SCHIRM, KARL C.
Ger. b. Wiesbaden 1852. B.
SCHIRMER, AUGUST FRIEDRICH WILHELM.
Ger. Berlin 1802-1866 Italy. B-C-E.
SCHIRMER, JOHANN WILHELM.
Ger. Jülich, Prussia 1807-1863 Carlsruhe. B-C-E-722.
SCHIWETZ, EDWARD M.
Am. b. Cuero, Tex. 1898. M.
SCHJÖLBERG, GUIDO. (Et)
Nor. ex. 1934 Chicago; ad. 1935 Oslo, Nor. M.
SCHLABITZ, ADOLF.
Ger. b. Wartenberg 1854. B.
SCHLADERMUNDT, HERMAN T. (Mu)
Am. b. Milwaukee, Wis. 1863; ad. 1934 Bronxville, N. Y. A-F-W.
SCHLAFFER, LISA.
Am. b. Brooklyn, N. Y. 1907; ad. 1934 Forest Hills, L. I., N. Y. A.
SCHLAIKJER, JES WILLIAM.
Am. b. Brooklyn, N. Y. 1897; ad. 1934 New York. A-F.
SCHLECHT, CHARLES. (Eg)
Am. b. Stuttgart, Ger. 1843; ac. 1905 New York. F-7.
SCHLEGEL, FRIEDRICH.
Ger. ac. early part of 19th Cent. M.
SCHLEGELL, GUSTAV VON.
Am. b. St. Louis, Mo.; 1877; ad. 1934 St. Paul, Minn. A-F.
SCHLEGELL, WILLIAM VON.
Am. ad. 1935 Harrison, N. Y. M.
SCHLEIBNER, KASPER.
Ger. b. 1863. Fa-M.
SCHLEICH, EDUARD.
Ger. Harbach 1813-1879 Munich. B-C.
SCHLEIN, CHARLES.
Am. b. Russia 1900; ad. 1934 New York. A.
SCHLEISSNER, CHRISTIAN ANDREAS.
Dan. Lyngby 1810-1882 Charlottenburg. B-C.

SCHLEMMER, FERDINAND LOUIS.
Am. b. Crawfordsville, Ind. 1893; ad. 1934 Same. A.
SCHLEMMER, OSKAR.
Ger. b. 1888; ex. 1933 New York. Fa.
SCHLESWIG-HOLSTEIN, ALEXANDRA VON
Ger. b. 1893; came to U. S. 1926. M.
SCHLESINGER, FÉLIX.
Ger. b. Hamburg 1833. B-C.
SCHLESINGER, HENRI GUILLAUME.
Fr. Frankfort, Ger. 1813/4-1893 Paris. B-C.
SCHLEY, MATHILDE G.
Am. b. Horicon, Wis. 1874; ad. 1934 Chicago. A.
SCHLICHTEN, JAN PHILIPP VAN.
Dut. Holland 1681-1745 Mannheim, Ger. B-C.
SCHLICHTEN, JOHANN FRIEDRICH.
Ger. Mannheim 1725-1795. B.
SCHLÖEPKE, THEODOR.
Ger. Schwerin 1812-1878 Same. C.
SCHLÖESSER [or Schlösser], KARL.
Ger. b. Darmstadt 1836; ac. 1861 Paris. B-C.
SCHLOMKA, ALFRED.
Fr. ac. 1886-1889 in Paris. B.
SCHLOTH, LUCAS FERDINAND. (S)
Swi. Basel 1818-1891 Thale, Ger. B.
SCHLÜTER, ANDREAS. (S)
Ger. Hamburg 1664-1714 Berlin. E-Hs.
SCHMALZ, HERBERT GUSTAVE.
Eng. b. London 1856. B-C.
SCHMAND, J. PHILLIP.
Am. b. Germania, Pa. 1871; ad. 1934 New York. A.
SCHMEDTGEN, WILLIAM HERMAN. (Ill)
Am. b. Chicago 1862. A12-F.
SCHMID, FRÉDÉRIC.
Swi. b. Basel; ad. 1934 London. Wa.
SCHMID, MATTHIAS.
Swi. Tyrol 1835-1923. B-C.
SCHMID, WILHELM.
Swi. b. 1892. Fa.
SCHMIDT, ALBERT H.
Am. b. Chicago 1883; ex. 1935 Santa Fé, N. M. A12-M.
SCHMIDT, GEORG FRIEDRICH.
Ger. Berlin 1712-1775 Same. B.
SCHMIDT, HAROLD VAN. (Ill)
Am. ad. 1935 Westport, Conn. M.
SCHMIDT, KARL.
Am. b. Worcester, Mass. 1890; ad. 1934 Same. A.
SCHMIDT, KATHERINE.
Am. b. Xenia, O. 1898; ad. 1934 New York. A-F.
SCHMIDT, MARTIN JOACHIM [or Johan].
Aus. Austria 1718-1801 Krems. B-C.
SCHMIDT, MAXMILLIAN ["Max"].
Ger. Berlin 1818-1901 Same. B-C.
SCHMIDT, OSCAR F.
Am. ad. 1934 New York. M.
SCHMIDT, OTTO. (Ill)
Am. b. Phila., Pa.; ad. 1934 Same. A.
SCHMIDT, PAUL.
Am. b. Phila., Pa. 1893; ad. 1935 Oakland, Calif. M.
SCHMIDT, RUDOLPH.
Am. ac. 1911. M.
SCHMIDT, WERNER PAUL.
Ger. ex. 1930 in Munich. M.
SCHMIDT, WILLEM HENDRIK.
Dut. Rotterdam 1809-1849 Delft. B-C.
SCHMIDT-ROTTLUFF, KARL.
Ger. b. 1881; ad. 1934 Berlin. DBA.
SCHMIED, FRANÇOIS LOUIS.
Swi. b. 1873 Switzerland. M.
SCHMITSON, TEUTWART.
Ger. Frankfort 1830-1863 Vienna, Aus. B-C.
SCHMITT, ALBERT FELIX.
Am. b. Boston 1873; ad. 1934 Biarritz, Fr. A-F.
SCHMITT, CARL.
Am. b. Warren, O. 1889; ad. 1934 Norwalk, Conn. A.
SCHMITT, ROBERT.
Am. ad. 1934 Norwalk, Conn. M.
SCHMITZ, BRUNO. (S)
Ger. b. 1856; ac. 1890 in Berlin. Hs.
SCHMITZ, CARL L. (S)
Am. ad. 1934 New York. M.
SCHMITZBERGER, JOSEPH.
Ger. b. Munich 1851. B.
SCHMOHLE, FRED C. (S)
Am. Germany 1847-1922 Los Angeles, Calif. A019.
SCHMUTZER, FERDINAND. (Et)
Aus. Vienna 1870-1928. B.
SCHMUTZER, JACQUES [or Jakob] MATHIAS.
Aus. Vienna 1733-1811. B.
SCHNAKENBERG, HENRY ERNEST.
Am. b. New Brighton, S. I., N. Y. 1892; ad. 1934 New York. A-F-571-779.
SCHNEBBELIE, JACOB. (Et)
Eng. London 1760-1792 Same. B-DNB.
SCHNEBBELIE, ROBERT BREMME.
Eng. d. 1849 in London. B-DNB.
SCHNEGG, GASTON. (S)
Fr. b. Bordeaux; ac. 1900 in Paris. B.
SCHNEIDER, ARTHUR.
Am. ac. 1926 in Chicago. A12-F.
SCHNEIDER, ELSBETH.
Am. ad. 1934 Chico, Calif. M.
SCHNEIDER, [Mme.] FÉLICE.
Fr. St. Cloud 1831-1888. B.
SCHNEIDER, JOHANN CASPAR.
Ger. Mentz 1753-1819 Same. B-C.
SCHNEIDER, OTTO H.
Am. b. Muscatine, Ia.; ad. 1935 Ocean Beach, Calif. M.
SCHNEIDER, OTTO J. (Et)
Am. b. Atlanta, Ill. 1875; ad. 1934 Chicago. A-F-46.
SCHNEIDER, ROSE.
Am. ad. 1934 San Diego, Calif. M.
SCHNEIDER, SUSAN HAYWARD.
Mrs. Karl Schneider.
Am. b. Pana, Ill.; ad. 1934 Phila., Pa. A.
SCHNEIDER, THEOPHILE.
Am. b. Freiburg, Ger. 1872; ad. 1934 Boston, Mass. A-F.
SCHNEIDER, WILLIAM G.
Am. Monroe, Wis. 1863-1912 New York. A010.
SCHNELLE, WILLIAM G.
Am. b. Brooklyn, N. Y. 1897; ad. 1934 Woodhaven, L. I., N. Y. A.
SCHNETZ, JEAN VICTOR.
Fr. Versailles 1787-1870 Paris. B-C.

SCHNIER, Jacques. (S)
Am. Rumania 1898; ad. 1934 San Fran., Calif. A-Cs.
SCHNITZLER, August R.
Am. ad. 1934 Irvington, N. J. M.
SCHNITZLER, J. Michael.
Bav. Neustadt 1782-1861 Munich, Ger. C.
SCHNITZSPAN, Leo L.
Am. ad. 1934 New York. M.
SCHNORR VON KAROLSFELD, Julius Ritter.
Ger. Leipzig 1794-1872 Dresden. B-C-E-722.
SCHOBEL, Georg.
Ger. ac. 1897 in Berlin. B.
SCHOCZYLAS, Ladislas. (Carver)
Pol. d. 1934 in Warsaw.
Obit. N. Y. papers, 4-10-1934.
SCHÖDL, Max.
Aus. Vienna 1834-1921. B-C.
SCHOEFF, J.
Dut. ac. 1640-1660 at The Hague. C.
SCHÖEN [or Sehon], Erhard.
Ger. d. 1542 in Nüremberg. B-Bd.
SCHÖEN, Martin. *see* Schongauer.
SCHOENEWERK, Alexandre. (S)
Fr. Paris 1820-1885/6. B.
SCHOEVAERDTS, Mathys [or Mathieu].
Flem. b. Brussels 1665. B.
SCHOFF, Stephen Alonzo. (Eg)
Am. Danville, Vt. 1818-1905 Brandon, Vt. B-F-7-40.
SCHOFIELD, Flora I.
Am. b. Lanark, Ill. 1879; ad. 1934 Chicago. A.
SCHOFIELD, Louis Sartain. (Eg)
Am. b. 1868; ac. 1926 Wash., D. C. F-7.
SCHOFIELD, Walter Elmer.
Am. b. Phila., Pa. 1867; ad. 1934 New York. A-B-F-W-46.
SCHOFIELD, William Bacon. (S)
Am. Hartford, Conn. 1864-1930 Worcester, Mass. A027-F.
SCHOLTZ, Julius.
Ger. Breslau 1825-1893 Dresden. B-C.
SCHOLZ, Richard.
Ger. b. Hanover 1860. B.
SCHÖN, Erhard. *see* Schöen, E.
SCHÖN, Otto.
Ger. b. 1893. Fa.
SCHONGAUER [or Schön], Martin. (Eg)
Ger. Colmar 1440/5-1488/91 Same.
B-Bd-C-E-572-722-801-923.
SCHONHARDT, Henri. (S)
Am. b. Prov., R. I. 1877; ad. 1934 Same. A-B-F-W.
SCHONHERR, Karl Gottlob.
Ger. Lengefeld 1824-1906 Dresden. B-C.
SCHÖNHOFER, Sebald. (S)
Ger. ac. 1350 in Nüremberg. M.
SCHÖNLEBER, Gustav.
Dut. Besighheim 1851-1917. B-C.
SCHÖNLEBER, Hans Otto.
Ger. 1889-1930. M.
SCHOOFF, Johan Pietersz.
Flem. b. 1609; d. 1660 at The Hague, Holland. B.
SCHOOK, F. De Forest.
Am. b. Michigan 1872; ad. 1934 Lombard, Ill. A.
SCHOONJANS, Anton [Parhasius].
Flem. Antwerp 1650-1716 Vienna, Aus. B.
SCHOONOVER, Frank Earle. (Ill)
Am. b. Oxford, N. J. 1877; ad. 1934 Wilmington, Del. A-F-W.
SCHOOTEN [or Verschooten], Joris van.
Dut. Leyden 1587-1650/1 Same. B-C.
SCHOPFER, Hans [The Elder].
Ger. ac. 1531-1564 in Germany. B.
SCHOPFER, Hans [The Younger].
Ger. b. Munich; d. 1610 Same. B-C.
SCHOPIN, Heinrich Frédéric.
Ger. Lübeck 1804-1881. B.
SCHOREEL, Jan van.
Dut. Schoreel 1495-1567. 722.
SCHORN, Karl.
Ger. Düsseldorf 1800-1850 Munich. C.
SCHORSTEIN, Lucien de.
Fr. b. Paris; ad. 1934 Same. DBA.
SCHOTEL, Johannes Christianus.
Dut. Dordrecht 1787-1838 Same. B-C.
SCHOTEL, Petrus Jan.
Dut. Dordrecht 1808-1865 Dresden, Ger. B-C.
SCHOTT, Max.
Am. ac. 1907 in New York. B.
SCHOTT, Walter. (S)
Ger. b. Ilsenburg 1861. B.
SCHOTZ, Benno. (S)
Esthonian. b. 1891; ad. 1934 Glasgow, Scot. Wa.
SCHOUKHARFF, Basil.
Rus. b. Moscow 1877; ad. 1934 Paris. DBA.
SCHOULER, Willard C.
Am. b. Arlington, Mass. 1852; ad. 1926 Same. A12-F.
SCHOUMAN, Aert.
Dut. Dordrecht 1710-1792 The Hague. B.
SCHOUMAN, Martinus.
Dut. Dordrecht 1770-1848 Breda. B-C.
SCHRACK, Joseph Earl.
Am. ad. 1935 New York. M.
SCHRADER, Julius Friedrich Antonio.
Ger. Berlin 1815-1900 Same. B-C.
SCHRAM, Abraham John.
Am. b. Grand Rapids, Mich. 1891; ad. 1934 Wash., D. C. A-F.
SCHRAMM-ZITTAU, Rudolf.
Ger. b. Zittau 1874. B.
SCHRAUDOLPH, Claudius [The Elder].
Ger. Obersdorf 1813-1891 Same. B-C.
SCHRAUDOLPH, Claudius [The Younger].
Ger. Munich 1843-1891 Stuttgart. B-C.
SCHRAUDOLPH, Johann.
Ger. Obersdorf 1808-1879 Munich. B-C.
SCHRECKENGOST, Viktor. (S)
Am. b. Sebring, O. 1906; ad. 1934 Cleveland, O. A.
SCHREIBER, Charlotte.
Can. England 1834-1922 Canada. M.
SCHRIEBER, Georges.
Am. b. Brussels, Belg. 1904; ad. 1934 New York. A.
SCHREIBER, Gladys. (Ill)
Am. ad. 1934 New York. M.
SCHREUSS, Charles.
Fr. b. 1864. M.
SCHREYER, Adolf [or Adolphe].
Ger. Frankfort 1828-1899 Kronberg. B-Bd-C-E.

SCHREYVOGEL, Charles.
Am. New York 1861-1912 Hoboken, N. J. A010-B-F-245.
SCHRIMPF, [Prof.] Georg.
Ger. b. Munich 1889; ad. 1934 Berlin. M.
SCHRODER, Albert.
Ger. ac. 1877-1881 in Munich. B.
SCHRÖDTER, Adolf.
Ger. 1805-1875 Karlsruhe, Ger. B-C.
SCHROEDER, Henry. (Eg)
Br. 1774-1853. DNB.
SCHROFF, Alfred Hermann.
Am. b. Springfield, Mass. 1863; ad. 1934 Eugene, Ore. A.
SCHROTER, Bernhard.
Ger. b. Meissen 1848. B.
SCHROTH, Dorothy L.
Am. b. San Fran., Calif. 1906; ad. 1934 Same. A.
SCHRYVER, Louis de.
Fr. b. Paris; ac. 1876-1900. B.
SCHUBERT, Marie. (Ill)
Mrs. M. Frobisher.
Am. ad. 1934 New York. M.
SCHUBIN. *see* Choubine.
SCHUCH, Karl.
Ger. Vienna, Aus. 1846-1903 Same. B.
SCHUCH, Werner Wilhelm Gustav.
Prussian. Hildesheim 1843-1918. B-C.
SCHUCHARDT, Carl W.
Am. ad. 1935 Milwaukee, Wis. M.
SCHUFFENECKER, Claude Émile.
Fr. Fresne St. Manès 1851-1934. B-DBA.
SCHÜHLEIN [or Schüchlin], Hans. (S)
Ger. Ulm 1440-1502/5 Same. B-C-722.
SCHUHMACHER, W.
Dut. ad. 1934 Amsterdam. M.
SCHUKIN, S. S.
Rus. ex. 1935 New York. M.
SCHÜLDT, H.
Ger. ex. 1934 New York. M.
SCHULENBERG, Adele. (S)
Mrs. Charles K. Gleeson.
Am. b. St. Louis 1883; ad. 1934 Kirkwood, Mo. A.
SCHULER, Hans. (S)
Am. Alsace-Lorraine 1874; ad. 1934 Balt., Md. A-B-Cs-F-W-46.
SCHULER, Howard J.
Am. ad. 1934 Toledo, O. M.
SCHULER, Jules Théophile.
Fr. Strassburg 1821-1878 Same. B.
SCHULLER, Joseph Carl Paul.
Fr. ac. 1880-1895 in Paris. B.
SCHULMAN, Abram Gustav.
Am. b. Königsberg, Ger. 1881; d. 1935 Phoenix, Ariz.
A12-F-Obit. N. Y. papers, 6-6-1935.
SCHULTE, Antoinette.
Am. b. New York 1897; ad. 1934 Same. A.
SCHULTHEISS, Karl Johann Jacob.
Swi. Neuenburg 1775-1855 Zurich. B.
SCHULTZ, Albert B. (Ill)
Am. d. 1913 in New York. A0X1.
SCHULTZ, Carl Fredrich.
Ger. Selchow 1796-1866 Neu-Rippin. C.
SCHULTZ, George F.
Am. b. Chicago 1869; ad. 1934 Chicago. A-B-F-W9.
SCHULTZ, Harold.
Am. b. Grafton, Wis. 1907; ad. 1934 Chicago. A.
SCHULTZ, Harry.
Am. b. Russia 1900; ad. 1931 New York. A28.
SCHULTZ, Isabelle. (S)
Am. b. Balt., Md. 1896; ad. 1934 Same. A.
SCHULTZBERG, Anshelm Léonard.
Swe. b. Falun 1862. B.
SCHUMACHER, Karl Georg Christian.
Ger. Doberan 1797-1869 Dresden. C.
SCHUMACHER, William Émile.
Am. b. Boston, Mass. 1870; ad. 1915 Paris. A12.
SCHUMANN, Paul R.
Am. b. Germany 1876; ad. 1934 Galveston, Tex. A.
SCHUMWAY, Henry C. (Ill)
Am. Middletown, Conn. 1807-1884 New York. B-Bd.
SCHUPPEN [or Scuppen], Jacob van.
Flem. Fontainebleau, Fr. 1670-1751 Vienna, Aus. B.
SCHUPPEN, Pierre Louis van. (Eg)
Flem. Antwerp 1623/7-1702 Paris. B-Bd.
SCHURMAN, Anna Maria van.
Ger. Cologne 1607-1678 Wiewarden. B.
SCHUSSELE, [Mrs.] Cecilia Muringer.
Am. France 1841-1916 Phila., Pa. A013.
SCHUSSELE, Christian.
Am. Alsace, Fr. 1824-1879 Merchantville, N. J. C-F.
SCHUSTER, Donna N.
Am. ad. 1934 Los Angeles, Calif. A-F.
SCHUSTER-WOLDAN, Raffael.
Ger. b. Striegan 1870. B.
SCHUT, Cornelis.
Flem. Antwerp 1597-1655 Same. B-C-722.
SCHÜTZ, Anton Joseph Friedrich. (Et)
Am. b. Germany 1894; ad. 1935 Lynbrook, L. I., N. Y. A28.
SCHÜTZ, Christian George.
Ger. Flörsheim 1718-1791 Frankfort. B-C.
SCHÜTZ, Wilhelm.
Ger. b. 1840; d. 1898 Munich. B-C.
SCHUTZENBERGER, Louis Frédéric.
Fr. Strassburg 1825-1883 Paris. B-C.
SGHUYLER, Remington.
Am. b. Buffalo, N. Y. 1887; ad. 1934 Westport, Conn. A.
SCHÜZ, Theodor.
Ger. Thumlingen 1830-1900 Düsseldorf. B-C.
SCHVALBE, Orest Adamovitch.
see Kiprensky, O. A.
SCHWAB, Eloisa.
Am. b. Havana, Cuba 1894; ad. 1934 New York. A-F.
SCHWABE, Charles [or Carlos].
Ger. b. Altona 1866. B.
SCHWABE, Randolph.
Eng. b. Manchester 1885; ad. 1934 London. Wa.
SCHWACHA, Georg, Jr.
Am. ad. 1934 East Orange, N. J. M.

SCHWANEKAMP, Elsa. (S)
Am. ad. 1935 Eggertsville, N. Y. M.
SCHWANEKAMP, William J. (Et)
Am. b. Buffalo, N. Y. 1893; ad. 1934 Same. A.
SCHWANFELDER, Charles Henry.
Eng. Leeds 1773-1837. B-DNB.
SCHWANKOVSKY, Frederick John de St. Vrain, Jr.
Am. b. Detroit, Mich. 1885; ad. 1934 Laguna Beach, Calif. A.
SCHWANTHALER, Ludwig Michael. (S)
Ger. Munich 1802-1848 Same. B-E-Hs.
SCHWARCZ, Dorothea R.
see Greenbaum, D. S.
SCHWARTZ. *see also* Schwarz.
SCHWARTZ, Andrew Thomas. (Mu)
Am. b. Louisville, Ky. 1867; ad. 1934 Chicago. A-W.
SCHWARTZ, Christoph.
Ger. b. 1550; d. 1592 in Munich. B-C.
SCHWARTZ, Frans.
Dan. b. Copenhagen 1850. C.
SCHWARTZ, Manfred.
Am. b. Germany 1908; ad. 1934 Brooklyn, N. Y. A.
SCHWARTZ, William S.
Am. b. Russia 1896; ad. 1934 Chicago. A.
SCHWARTZE, Johan Georg.
Dut. Amsterdam 1814/5-1874. B-C.
SCHWARTZE, Therese [or Teresa].
Dut. Amsterdam 1852-1918. B-C-E.
SCHWARZ, Frank H.
Am. b. New York 1894; ad. 1934 Same. A28.
SCHWARZ, Felix Conrad.
Am. b. New York 1906; ad. 1934 Wash., D. C. A.
SCHWARZ, Frank H.
Am. b. New York 1894; ad. 1934 Same. A.
SCHWARZ, Margaret. (S)
Am. b. New York 1900. Cs.
SCHWARZ, Rudolf. (S)
Am. Vienna, Aus. 1866-1912 Ind., Ind. F-Ta-181.
SCHWARZ, William Tefft.
Am. b. Syracuse, N. Y. 1889; ad. 1934 Merion, Pa. A.
SCHWARZBECK, Fritz. (S)
Ger. ad. 1935 Darmstadt. M.
SCHWARZOTT, Maxmilian. (S)
Am. ac. 1898-1926 in New York. A12-F-Ta.
SCHWARZSCHILD, Alfred.
Ger. b. Frankfort; ac. 1903 in Paris. B.
SCHWATHE, Hans. (S)
Aus. b. 1870. M.
SCHWAZ, Hans Maler Zu. *see* Maler.
SCHWEGLER, Jakob.
Swi. b. 1793; d. 1866 in Lucerne. B.
SCHWEICHARDT, Hendrik William.
Ger. Brandenburg 1746-1797 London. B-DNB.
SCHWEIG, Aimee Gladstone.
Am. b. St. Louis, Mo. 1897; ad. 1934 Same. A.
SCHWEITZER, Gaston Auguste. (S)
Fr. b. Monteuil 1879. DBA.
SCHWEITZER, Gertrude.
Am. b. New York 1901; ad. 1934 Hillside, N. J. A.
SCHWEIZER, J. Otto. (S)
Am. b. Zurich, Swi. 1863; ad. 1934 Phila., Pa. A-Cs-F-W.
SCHWENINGER, Karl [The Elder].
Aus. Vienna 1818-1887. B.
SCHWICHTENBERG, [Miss] Martel.
Ger. ad. 1934 Capetown, So. Africa. M.
SCHWIEDER, Arthur I.
Am. b. Bolivar, Mo. 1884; ad. 1934 New York. A.
SCHWIND, Moritz Ludwig Ritter von.
Aus. Vienna 1804-1871 Munich, Ger. B-C-E-722.
SCHWITTERS, Kurt.
Ger. b. Hanover 1887. M.
SCILLA [or Silla], Agostino.
It. Messina 1629/39-1700 Rome. B.
SCIORTINO, Antonio. (S)
It. b. Malta 1881. M.
SCOLES, John. (Eg)
Am. ac. 1793-1844 in New York. F-2-7-147.
SCOPAS [or Skopas]. (S)
Gr. ac. 360 B.C. in Athens. E-Hs-817.
SCOREL [or Scoreel], Jan van.
Dut. Schoorl 1475-1562 Utrecht. B-Bd-C.
SCORZA, Sinibaldo. (Min)
It. b. 1589; d. 1631 Genoa. B-C.
SCOTT, Adam Sheriff.
Scot. b. Perth 1887; ad. 1935 Montreal, Can. M.
SCOTT, Anna Page.
Am. b. Dubuque, Ia.; d. 1925 Same. A022.
SCOTT, Bertha.
Am. b. Frankfort, Ky. 1884; ad. 1934 Same. A.
SCOTT, Catherine.
Am. b. Ottawa, Kan. 1900; ad. 1934 Same. A.
SCOTT, Charles Thomas. (S)
Am. b. Chester Co., Pa. 1876; ad. 1926 Phila., Pa. A12-F.
SCOTT, David.
Scot. Edinburgh 1806-1849 Same. B-C-DNB-E-812.
SCOTT, Dorothy Carnine.
Mrs. Ewing C. Scott.
Am. b. Hannford, N. D. 1903; ad. 1934 Sweet Briar, Va. A.
SCOTT, [Mrs.] Emily Maria Spaford.
Am. Springwater, N. Y. 1832-1915 New York. A012-F-46.
SCOTT, Eric Glidden.
Am. b. Bega, Aust. 1893; ad. 1934 Paris. A.
SCOTT, Frank Edwin.
Am. Buffalo, N. Y. 1863-1929 Paris. A027.
SCOTT, Georges.
Fr. b. Paris 1873. DBA.
SCOTT, Geraldine Armstrong.
Am. b. Elkhart, Ind. 1900; ad. 1934 Kokomo, Ind. A.
SCOTT, Harold W.
Am. ad. 1934 Croton Falls, N. Y. M.
SCOTT, James.
Am. b. Racine, Wis. 1889; ad. 1934 Milton, N. Y. A.
SCOTT, James P.
Aust. d. 1932. Y01933.
SCOTT, Jeannette.
Am. b. Kincardine, Ont., Can. 1864; ad. 1934 Skaneateles, N. Y. A-F-W.

SCOTT, JOHN. (Eg)
Eng. Newcastle 1774-1827 Chelsea. B-DNB.
SCOTT, JOHN W. A.
Am. Roxbury, Mass. 1815-1907 Cambridge, Mass. A06-F.
SCOTT, JULIAN.
Am. Johnson, Vt. 1846-1901 Plainfield, N. J. A04-B-C-F-4-15.
SCOTT, KATHERINE H.
Am. b. Burlington, Ia.; ad. 1934 West Chester, Pa. A.
SCOTT, MARIE.
Am. ad. 1934 Los Angeles, Calif. M.
SCOTT, MARY FLORENCE.
Am. ad. 1935 Sanford, Fla. M.
SCOTT, RALPH C.
Am. b. Elliston, Newfoundland 1896; ad. 1934 Prov., R. I. A.
SCOTT, ROBERT. (Eg)
Scot. Lanack 1777-1841. B-DNB.
SCOTT, SAMUEL.
Eng. London 1703/10-1772 Bath. B-C-DNB.
SCOTT, TOM [or Thomas].
Scot. Selkirshire 1854-1927. B.
SCOTT, WALTER.
Scot. b. Edinburgh 1906; ad. 1934 Same. Wa.
SCOTT, WILLIAM BELL. (P and Poet)
Scot. Edinburgh 1811-1890 Parkill. B-Bd-DNB-E.
SCOTT, WILLIAM EDOUARD.
Am. b. Ind., Ind. 1884; ad. 1934 Chicago. A-F-W16.
SCOTT, WILLIAM WALLACE.
Am. Roxbury, Mass. 1822-1905 New Rochelle, N. Y. A06-F.
SCOUGAL [or Scougall], JOHN.
Scot. Leith 1645?-1730? Edinburgh. B-DNB.
SCRIBNER, ELIZABETH.
Mrs. Sidney Jones.
Am. b. New York; ad. 1934 Same. A.
SCRIVEN, EDWARD. (Eg)
Br. 1775-1841. DNB.
SCROPE, WILLIAM.
Eng. 1772-1852. B-DNB.
SCRYMSER, CHRISTABEL.
Am. b. Brooklyn, N. Y. 1885; ad. Rockville Center, L. I., N. Y. A.
SCUDDER, ALICE RAYMOND.
Am. b. New Orleans, La.; ad. 1934 Pasadena, Calif. A.
SCUDDER, JANET. (S)
Am. Terre Haute, Ind. 1875; ad. 1934 Paris. A-Cs-DBA-F-W-46-181-757-829-932.
SCUTT, WINIFRED.
Am. ex. 1934 New York. M.
SCYLLIS. [*see also* Dipoenus.] (S)
Fr. ac. 580 B.C. E.
SEABORNE, WILLIAM. (S)
Am. b. 1849; d. 1917 New York. A014.
SEABROOKE, ELLIOTT.
Eng. ex. 1933 in London. Wa1929.
SEACORD, ALICE NICHOLSON.
Mrs. Jay Gould Seacord.
Am. b. Milwaukee, Wis. 1888; ad. 1934 Chicago. A.
SEALE, A. BARNEY. (S)
Eng. ad. 1934 London. M.
SEAMAN, [Mrs.] BUEHA L.
Am. b. New York 1878; ad. 1934 Catskill, N. Y. M.
SEARCY, ELIZABETH. (Et)
Am. b. Memphis, Tenn.; ad. 1934 Same. A.
SEARL, LEON A. (Cart)
Am. b. 1882; d. 1919 Flushing, L. I., N. Y. A016.
SEARLE, ALICE T. (Min)
Am. b. Troy, N. Y. 1869; ad. 1926 Brooklyn, N. Y. A12-B-F.
SEARLE, JOHN.
Am. ac. 1822 New York. M.
SEARS, CHARLES PAYNE.
Am. New York 1864-1908 Atlantic Highlands, N. J. A07-B.
SEARS, ELINOR LATHROP.
Am. b. Hartford, Conn. 1899; ad. 1934 Lyme, Conn. A.
SEARS, PHILIP SHELTON. (S)
Am. b. Boston 1867; ad. 1934 Brookline, Mass. A-Cs-F-W.
SEARS, SARAH CHOATE.
Mrs. J. Montgomery Sears.
Am. b. Cambridge, Mass. 1858; ad. 1934 Boston. A-B-F-W.
SEARS, TABER. (Mu)
Am. b. Boston 1870; ad. 1934 New York. A-F-W-46.
SEATON, C. H.
Am. Monson, Mass. 1865-1926 Virginia. A026-F.
SEATON, JOHN THOMAS.
Scot. ac. 1761-1806 in Edinburgh. B-DNB.
SEAVER, ELSBETH. (S)
Am. ad. 1934 Cleveland, O. M.
SEAWELL, HENRY WASHINGTON.
Am. b. San Fran., Calif.; ad. 1934 Same. A.
SEBASTIANI, LAZARO BASTANNA.
It. 1430-1512. Bd-C-V.
SEBASTIANI DEL PIOMBO [Luciani].
It. Venice 1485?-1547 Rome. B-Bd-C-E-V-722.
SEBEN, HENRI VAN.
Belg. b. Brussels 1827. [No death date.] B.
SEBRON, HIPPOLYTE VICTOR VALENTIN.
Fr. Caudebec 1801-1879. B-C.
SECOR, DAVID PELL.
Am. Brooklyn, N. Y. 1824-1909 Bridgeport, Conn. A07.
SEDDON, THOMAS.
Eng. London 1821-1856 Cairo, Egypt. B-C-DNB-E.
SEDLACEK, [Dr.] FRANZ.
Aus. b. 1891; ad. 1934 Vienna. M.
SEEBOLD, MARIE M.
see Molinary, [Mrs.] Andrés.
SEEDS, ELISE.
Am. b. Phila., Pa.; ad. 1934 Hollywood, Calif. M.
SEEGER, HERMANN LUDWIG.
Ger. b. Potsdam 1810. [No death date.] B.
SEEGER, KARL LUDWIG.
Ger. Alsey 1808/9-1866 Darmstadt. B-C.
SEEGMILLER, WILHELMINE.
Am. 1866-1913. M.
SEEHAS, CHRISTIAN LUDWIG.
Ger. b. 1754; d. 1802 in Schwerin. C.
SEEKATZ, JOHANN KONRAD.
Ger. Gronstadt 1719-1768 Darmstadt. B-C.
SEEL, ADOLF.
Ger. b. Wiesbaden 1829; ac. 1850-1878. B-C.

SEELER, KATHERINE SCHIEFER.
Am. ad. 1935 Cleveland, O. M.
SEELY, WALTER FREDERICK.
Am. b. Maine 1886; ad. 1934 Los Angeles, Calif. A.
SEEMAN [or Zeeman], ENOCH.
Br. Danzig, Ger. 1694-1744 London. B-DNB.
SEEMAN, REINIER NOOMS. *see* Zeeman, R. N.
SEEUW, MARINUS DE.
see Marinus van Reymerswale.
SEEVAGEN, LUCIEN.
Fr. b. Chaumont 1887; ad. 1935 Paris. M.
SEEWALD, RICHARD.
Ger. b. 1889 in Germany. M.
SEGAL, ARTHUR.
Ger. b. 1875 in Germany. M.
SEGAL, BERNARD.
Am. ad. 1935 Cinn., O. M.
SEGAL, DOROTHY.
Am. ad. 1935 Hartford, Conn. M.
SEGAL, RUTH.
Mrs. Louis Segal.
Am. ad. 1934 Mt. Vernon, N. Y. M.
SEGALL, JULIUS.
Am. d. 1925 Milwaukee, Wis. A022.
SEGALL, LASAR.
Rus. b. Vilna 1890. DBA.
SEGANTINI, GIOVANNI. (P-S)
It. Arco 1858-1899 Savignino. B-E-573.
SÉGÉ, ALEXANDRE.
Fr. Paris 1817-1885 Coubron. B-C.
SEGHERS. *see* Zeghers.
SEGNA DI BUONAVENTURA.
It. ac. 1298-1330 in Siena. B.
SEGNOLO, GIAPECO DI [Coporali]. (Min)
It. ac. 1471-1478 in Perugia. M.
SÉGOFFIN, VICTOR JOSEPH JEAN AMBROSE. (S)
Fr. Toulouse 1867-1925 Paris. B-DBA-798.
SEGONSAC, ANDRÉ ALBERT MARIE DUNOYER.
Fr. b. Boussy 1885; ad. 1934 Paris. DBA-797-947.
SEGUIER, JOHN.
Eng. London 1785-1856 Same. B-DNB.
SEGUIER, WILLIAM.
[First keeper of the Nat. Gallery, London.]
Eng. London 1771-1843 Brighton. B-DNB.
SÉGUIN-BERTAULT, PAUL.
Fr. b. Chateaurenault 1869. DBA.
SÉGURA, JEAN JOSÉ.
Mex. b. Guadalajara 1901. DBA.
SEIBOLD, CHRISTIAN.
Ger. Mentz 1697/03-1768 Vienna, Aus. B-C.
SEIDEL, EMORY P. (S)
Am. b. 1881; ad. 1934 Chicago. A.
SEIDENBERG, RODERICK. (Et)
Am. b. 1889. M.
SEIFERT, ALFRED.
Ger. Horovic 1850-1901 Munich. B.
SEIFERT, FRANZ. (S)
Ger. b. 1866 in Germany. M.
SEIGNAC, GUILLAUME.
Fr. b. Rennes; ac. 1903 in Paris. B.
SEIGNAC, PAUL.
Fr. Bordeaux 1826-1903/4. B.
SEIHO, TAKEUCHI.
Jap. ac. 1933 in Kyoto. M.
SEIKI, YOKOYAMA.
Jap. ac. 1850. J., Vol. 2, page 104.
SEILER, CARL WILHELM ANTON.
Ger. Wiesbaden 1846-1921. B.
SEIPP, ALICE.
Am. b. New York 1889; ad. 1934 Scranton, Pa. A-F-W.
SEISENGGER, JACOB.
Aus. Linz 1505-1567 Same. B-C.
SEISSER, MARTIN B.
Am. b. Pittsburgh, Pa. 1845. F-15.
SEITHER, [Mrs.] ANNE BARBER.
Am. b. Phila., Pa.; ac. 1915 Same. A12.
SEITZ, ANTON.
Ger. Roth 1829-1900 Munich. B-C.
SEITZ, OTTO.
Ger. Munich 1846-1912. B-C.
SEKKEI, YAMAGUCHI.
Jap. J., Vol. 2, page 76.
SELDEN, [Miss] DIXIE.
Am. b. Cinn., O.; ad. 1934 Same. A.
SELDEN, HENRY BILL.
Am. Erie, Pa. 1886-1934 New London, Conn. A-F-Obit. N. Y. papers, 1-27-1934.
SELDON, REEDA.
Am. ad. 1934 New York. M.
SELFRIDGE, REYNOLDS L.
Am. b. Jasonville, Ind. 1898; ad. 1934 Ind., Ind. A.
SELIGMAN, EDGAR.
Eng. ex. 1934 in London. M.
SELIGMANN, KURT.
Swi. b. Basel 1900. DBA.
SELINCOURT, GEOFFREY DE.
Eng. ex. 1934 in London, Eng. M.
SELINGER, JEAN PAUL.
Am. Boston 1850-1909 Same. A07-F.
SELL, CHRISTIAN.
Ger. Altona 1831-1883 Düsseldorf. B-C.
SELLAJO, ANDREA [or Jacopo] DEL.
It. Florence 1441/6-1493 Same. B.
SELLARI, GIROLAMO. *see* Carpi, G. da.
SELLERS, MARY.
Am. b. Pittsburgh, Pa. 1869; ad. 1934 Same. A.
SELLIER, CHARLES FRANÇOIS [or Auguste].
Fr. Nancy 1830-1882 Same. B-C.
SELLORS, EVALINE C. (S)
Am. ad. 1934 Fort Worth, Tex. M.
SELLSTED, LARS GUSTAV.
Am. Sweden 1819-1911 Buffalo, N. Y. A09-C-F-15-246.
SELOUS [or Slous], HENRY COURTENAY.
Eng. b. 1803; d. 1890 Beaworthy, Eng. B.
SELVA, ROBERTO DE LA. (Carver)
Mex. b. Nicaragua, C. A.; ex. 1935 New York. M.
SEM [George Goursat]. (Cart)
Fr. b. 1863; d. 1934 Paris. M-Obit. N. Y. papers, 11-26-1934.
SEMENOWSKI, EISMAN.
Pol. ac. 1891-1911. B.
SEMINI, ANDREA [Vecchio].
It. Genoa 1526-1595 Same. B-C.
SEMINI, OTTAVIO.
It. Genoa 1520-1604 Milan. B-C.
SEMITECOLÒ, NICCOLÒ.
It. d. After 1400 in Venice. B.

SEMOLEI, Il.
see Franco, Giovanni Battista.
SEMON, John.
Am. b. 1852; d. 1917 Cleveland, O. A015.
SEN, Lalit M.
Indian (American). ex. 1930 New York. 411.
SENARE, Jacobus Albertus.
Belg. Loo 1755/8-1829 Paris. B-C.
SENAT, Prosper Louis.
Am. Germantown, Pa. 1852-1925 Same. A022-F.
SENAVE, Jacobus Alburtus.
Belg. Loo 1758-1829 Paris. B-Bd-C.
SENECAL, Ralph L.
Am. b. Bolton, Can. 1883; ad. 1934 Palmer, Mass. A.
SENEFELDER, Aloys. (Eg)
[Reputed to have invented Lithography.]
Ger. Prague, Czec. 1771-1834 Munich. B.
SENET, Rafael.
Sp. b. 1856. Fa.
SENIOR, Mark.
Eng. b. Heaton 1864. B.
SENIOR, Oliver.
Eng. b. Nottingham 1880; ad. 1934 Eastbourne. Wa.
SENNHAUSER, John. (Et)
Am. ad. 1935 New York. M.
SENNO, Pietro.
It. 1845?-1904. M.
SENSENEY, George Eyster. (Et)
Am. b. Wheeling, W. Va. 1874; ad. 1934 Holyoke, Mass. A28-F-W.
SENUS, Willem van. (Eg)
Dut. b. 1770; d. 1851 in Amsterdam. B.
SENYARD, George.
Am. d. 1924 Olmstead Falls, O. A021-F.
SEPESHY, Zoltan L.
Am. b. Kassa, Hun. 1898; ad. 1934 Bloomfield Hills, Mich. A-F.
SEQUEIRA, Domingos Antonio de.
Por. Lisbon 1768-1837 Rome, It. B-C-E.
SERAFINI, Serafino dei.
It. Modena 1340/4-1393+. B-Bd.
SEREDY, Kate.
Am. ad. 1935 Ridgefield, N. J. M.
SERENDAT DE BELZIM, Louis.
Fr. b. Port Louis 1854. DBA.
SERGEANT, Edgar.
Am. b. New York 1877; ad. 1934 Nutley, N. J. A.
SERGELL, Johan Tobias. (S)
Swe. Stockholm 1740-1814 Same. B-E-Hs.
SERGENT, Antoine Louis Françoise.
Fr. Chartres 1751-1817 Nice. B.
SEROV [or Seroff], Valentin Alexandrovitch.
Rus. Moscow 1865-1911. B.
SERPELL, Susan Watkins.
Mrs. Goldsborough Serpell.
Am. Calif. 1875-1913. A014-F.
SERPOTTA, Giacoma.
It. 1656-1732. M
SERRA, Enrique.
It. 1859-1918. B.
SERRA, Jaime.
Sp. ac. 14th Cent. in Spain. M.
SERRA, Pere [or Pedro] of Barcelona.
Sp. ac. 1373-1399 in Barcelona. M.
SERRAO, [Mrs.] Luella Varney. (S)
Am. b. Angola, N. Y. 1865; ad. 1926 Cleveland, O. A20-F.
SERRE [or Serra], Michel Gaspard Jacques.
Fr. Spain 1653/8-1733 Marseilles. B-C.
SERRES, Dominique [The Elder].
Eng. Auch, Ger. 1722-1793 London. B-Bd-C-DNB.
SERRES, Dominique [The Younger].
Eng. b. 1778; d. 1804 London. B.
SERRES, John Thomas [Giovanni].
Eng. London 1759-1825 Same. B-DNB.
SERRES, [Mrs.] Olivia. (P-Writer)
Eng. 1772-1834. B-DNB.
SERRES, Raoul Jean.
Fr. ac. 1898-1906 in Paris. B.
SERRUR, Henry Auguste Calixte César.
Fr. Lambersart 1794-1865 Paris. B.
SERRUYS, Yvonne. (S)
Fr. b. Menin 1874. DBA.
SERT, José Maria. (Mu)
Sp. b. 1876. M.
SERVAES, Albert.
Belg. ad. 1934 Saint Martin, Belg. DBA.
SERVANDONY, Jean Nicolas [or Jerome].
Fr. Lyons 1695-1766 Paris. B.
SERVEAU, Clément.
Fr. b. Paris 1886; ad. 1935 Same. DBA.
SERVIN, Amédée Elie.
Fr. Paris 1829-1886. B-C.
SERVOLINI, Luigi. (Eg)
It. b. Italy 1906; ex. 1934 Chicago; ad. 1935 Leghorn, It. M.
SERWOUTERS, Pieter van.
Dut. Antwerp, Belg. 1586-1657 Amsterdam. B.
SESSHIU.
Jap. 1420-1506. J., Vol. 1, page 71.
SESSLER, Alfred.
Am. ad. 1935 Milwaukee, Wis. M.
SESSLER, Stanley Sascha.
Am. b. Russia 1905; ad. 1934 South Bend, Ind. A.
SESSON [Sataké Heizo].
Jap. ac. middle 16th Cent. in Japan. J., Vol. 1, page 111.
SESTO, Cesare da.
It. Sesto 1480-1521/3 Milan. B-C-722.
SETCHEL, Sarah.
Eng. b. 1803; d. 1894 Sudbury. B-DNB.
SETON, Ernest Thompson. (Ill)
Am. b. So. Shields, Eng. 1860. A28-F-46.
SETTANNI, Luigi.
Am. b. Torremaggiore, It. 1908; ad. 1934 Phila., Pa. A.
SETTEI, Tsukioka.
Jap. J., Vol. 1, page 148
SETTIGNANO, Desiderio da.
see Desiderio da S.
SEURAT, Georges Pierre.
Fr. Paris 1859-1891 Same. B-DBA-574-700-820-847
SEVCIK, Karl. (Ill)
Am. ad. 1934 Chicago, Ill. M.
SEVERANCE, Julia Gridley. (S)
Am. b. Oberlin, O. 1877; ad. 1934 Same. A.
SEVERDONCK, François van.
Belg. Brussels 1809-1889. B.

SEVERDONCK, Joseph van.
Belg. b. 1819; d. 1905 Brussels. B-C.
SEVERINI, Gino.
Fr. b. Cortona, It. 1883; ad. 1934 Paris. DBA-575-797.
SEVERN, Joseph.
Eng. England 1793-1879 Rome, It. B-DNB-E.
SEVERN, Walter.
Eng. Frascati, It. 1830-1904 London. DNB.
SEWALL, Blanche Harding.
Mrs. Cleveland Sewall.
Am. b. Fort Worth, Tex. 1889; ad. 1934 Houston, Tex. A.
SEWARD, Coy Avon.
Am. b. Chase, Kan. 1884; ad. 1934 Wichita, Kan. W.
SEWELL, Alice.
Am. b. Hillsboro, Ore.; ad. 1934 Same. A.
SEWELL, Helen Moore. (Ill)
Am. b. Mare Island, Calif. 1896; ad. 1934 Ridgewood, N. J. A.
SEWELL, Lydia Amanda Brewster.
Mrs. Robert V. V. Sewell.
Am. No. Elba, N. Y. 1859-1926. A026-F.
SEWELL, Robert Van Vorst. (Mu)
Am. New York 1860-1924 Florence, It. A022-B-F-46.
SEXTON, Frederick Lester.
Am. b. Cheshire, Conn. 1889; ad. 1935 New Haven, Conn. A.
SEYBOLD. *see* Seibold, Christian.
SEYDEL, Albert. (Mu)
Belg. ad. 1934 New York. M.
SEYFFERT, Leopold Gould.
Am. b. California, Mo. 1887; ad. 1934 New York. A-F-W-1.
SEYMOUR, Celia Burnham.
Am. b. Buffalo, N. Y. 1872; ad. 1915 New York. A12.
SEYMOUR, George L.
Eng. ac. 1876 in London. B.
SEYMOUR, James.
Eng. London 1702-1752 Same. B-DNB.
SEYMOUR, Joseph H. (Eg)
Am. ac. 1791-1882 in Phila., Pa. F-2-7-147.
SEYMOUR, Munsey.
Br. Calcutta, India 1837-1912 Barton, Vt. M.
SEYMOUR, Ralph Fletcher. (Ill)
Am. b. Milan, Ill. 1876; ad. 1931 Chicago. A28-F.
SEYMOUR, Robert. (Ill)
Eng. London 1800?-1836. B-DNB.
SEYMOUR, Samuel. (Eg)
Am. b. England; ac. 1797-1822 in Phila., Pa. F-2-7-40.
SEYMOUR-HADEN, Francis. (Ill)
Eng. b. London 1818. B-830.
SEYSSAUD, René.
Fr. ac. 19th Cent. in France. B-M.
SHACKELFORD, Shelby.
Am. b. Halifax, Va. 1899; ad. 1934 New York. A.
SHACKLETON, Charles.
Am. b. Mineral Point, Wis.; d. 1920 New Canaan, Conn. A017.
SHACKLETON, John.
Eng. ac. 1730-1767 in London. B-DNB.
SHACKLETON, Kathleen.
Eng. ex. 1935 London. M.
SHACKLETON, William.
Eng. Bradford 1872-1933. B-Wa1929-825.
SHADE, William August.
Am. New York 1848-1890 Switzerland. M.
SHADOW. *see* Schadow.
SHAFER, L. A.
Am. b. Geneseo, Ill. 1866; ad. 1934 New Rochelle, N. Y. A-F.
SHAFFRAN, Jascha.
Am. ad. 1935 Memphis, Tenn. M.
SHAGALL, Mark. *see* Chagall, M.
SHAHN, Ben.
Am. b. Russia 1898; ad. 1934 New York. A.
SHALDERS, George.
Eng. b. 1825/6; d. 1873 Portsmouth. B-DNB.
SHALER, Frederick R.
Am. Findlay, O. 1880-1916 Italy. A014-F.
SHALLUS, Francis. (Eg)
Am. Phila., Pa. 1773-1821 Same. F-2-7.
SHANE, Frederick.
Am. b. Kansas City, Mo. 1906; ad. 1934 Same. A.
SHANNON, Charles Hazelwood.
Eng. b. Sleaford 1863; ad. 1934 Kew. B-E-Wa.
SHANNON, Howard Johnson. (Ill)
Am. b. Jamaica, L. I., N. Y. 1876; ad. 1934 Same. A-F.
SHANNON, [Sir] James Jebusa.
Am. Auburn, N. Y. 1862-1923 London. A020-B-E-F-W10-46-178.
SHAPI, Jack. (Ill)
Am. b. New York 1906; ad. 1934 Same. M.
SHAPLEIGH, Frank Henry.
Am. b. Boston, Mass. 1842. C-F-15.
SHARADIN, Henry William.
Am. b. Kutztown, Pa. 1872; ad. 1934 Same. A.
SHARAKU, Tōshūsai.
Jap. ac. 1795 in Japan. J-581.
SHARE, Henry Pruett. (Ill)
Am. Los Angeles, Calif. 1853-1905 Flatbush, N. Y. A05.
SHARMAN, John.
Am. ad. 1934 Belmont, Mass. A-F.
SHARP. *see also* Sharpe.
SHARP, Everett Hill.
Am. b. Foster, Ky. 1907; ad. 1934 Muncie, Ind. A.
SHARP, Joseph Henry.
Am. b. Bridgeport, O. 1859; ad. 1934 Pasadena, Calif. A-F-W-46.
SHARP, Miles Balmford.
Eng. b. Brighouse 1897; ad. 1934 Nuneaton. Wa.
SHARP, William. (Eg)
Eng. London 1749-1824 Chiswick. B-DNB-E.
SHARPE [or Sharp], Charlotte.
Mrs. Best Morris.
Eng. b. London; ex. 1817-1849 Same. B-DNB.
SHARPE [or Sharp], Dorothea.
Eng. ad. 1934 Blewbury. Wa.
SHARPE [or Sharp], Eliza.
Eng. 1796-1874 Chelsea. B-DNB.
SHARPE, Julia Graydon.
Am. b. Ind., Ind.; ad. 1934 Same. A.

SHARPE, Louis [Mrs. Seyffarth].
Eng. London 1798-1843 Dresden, Ger. B-DNB.
SHARPE, Mary Anne.
Eng. b. London; ex. 1819-1867 Same. B-DNB.
SHARPE, Matthew.
Am. ex. 1933 in New York. M.
SHARPLES, Ellen.
Mrs. James Sharples, Jr.
Eng. Birmingham 1769-1849 Bristol. B-F-6-45-577.
SHARPLES, Felix T.
Am. England 1789-1844 No. Car. F-45.
SHARPLES [or Sharpe], James.
Eng. 1825-1893. B.
SHARPLES, James [The Elder].
Am. Lancashire, Eng. 1750-1811 New York. B-Bd-C-DNB-F-2-45-179-182-577.
SHARPLES, James [The Younger].
Eng. b. 1789; d. 1839 Bristol, Eng. B-DNB-F-577.
SHARPLES, Rolinda.
Eng. New York 1797-1838 Bristol, Eng. B-DNB-577.
SHARPLESS, Ada May. (S)
Am. b. Hilo, Hawaii 1904; ad. 1934 Santa Ana, Calif. A.
SHARRER, Madeleine S.
Am. b. Colo. Springs, Colo. 1898; ad. 1934 New Orleans, La. M.
SHATTUCK, Aaron Draper.
Am. Francestown, N. H. 1832-1928 Granby, Conn. A025-C-F-W16-3-4-15.
SHAVER, John H.
Am. ad. 1934 New York. M.
SHAW, Annie Cornelia.
Am. Troy, N. Y. 1852-1887 Chicago. C-F-15.
SHAW, Arthur Winter.
Eng. b. Kent 1869; ad. 1934 Barham. Wa.
SHAW, Charles G.
Am. ex. 1935 New York. M.
SHAW, Elsa Vick.
Am. ad. 1935 Cleveland, O. M.
SHAW, Frederick A. (S)
Am. b. 1855; d. 1912 Brookline, Mass. A010.
SHAW, Glenn Moore.
Am. b. Olmsted Falls, O. 1891; ad. 1934 Lakewood, O. A.
SHAW, Harriette Mc Creary.
Mrs. Thomas W. Shaw.
Am. b. Fayetteville, Ark. 1865; ad. 1934 Seattle, Wash. A-W.
SHAW, Harry M.
Am. ex. 1934 New York. M.
SHAW, Hollis B.
Am. ad. 1934 New York. M.
SHAW, John Byam Lister.
Br. Madras, India 1872-1919 London. DNB-576.
SHAW, Joshua. (Eg)
Am. Bellingborough, Eng. 1776-1860 Burlington, N. J. B-F-2.
SHAW, Robert. (Et)
Am. Wilmington, Del. 1859-1912 Same. A010.
SHAW, Ruth Faison.
[Originator of Finger Painting.]
Am. ad. 1935 New York. M.
SHAW, Stephen William.
Am. Windsor, Vt. 1817-1900 San Fran., Calif. A02.
SHAW, Sydney Dale.
Am. b. Walkley, Eng. 1879; ad. 1934 New York. A-F-15.
SHAW, William.
Am. b. 1842; d. 1909 Jamaica, L. I., N. Y. A08.
SHAYER, William J. [The Elder].
Eng. Southampton 1788-1879 Shirley. B.
SHEAFER, Frances Burwell.
Mrs. Samuel Waxman.
Am. b. Penn.; ad. 1934 Cambridge, Mass. A.
SHEAN, Charles M. (Mu)
Am. b. Brooklyn, N. Y.; d. 1925 Same. A022-F-W13.
SHEARER, Christopher H.
Am. b. Reading, Pa. 1840; d. 1926 Tuckerton, Pa. A023-B.
SHEARN, Clarence.
Am. ad. 1934 Charleston, S. C. M.
SHEDONE. *see* Schidone.
SHEE, [Sir] Martin Archer.
Ir. Dublin 1769-1850 Brighton, Eng. B-C-DNB-E-722.
SHEELER, Charles.
Am. b. Phila., Pa. 1883; ad. 1935 Ridgefield, Conn. A12-F-M.
SHEERER, Mary C.
Am. b. Kentucky; ad. 1934 New Orleans, La. M.
SHEETS, Millard.
Am. Pomona, Calif. 1907; ad. 1934 Claremont, Calif. A.
SHEETS, Nan.
Mrs. Fred C. Sheets.
Am. b. Albany, Ill. 1885; ad. 1934 Okla. City, Okla. A-F.
SHEFFER, Glen C.
Am. b. Angola, Ind. 1881; ad. 1934 Chicago. A.
SHEFFIELD, George.
Eng. Wigton 1839-1892 Wilmslow. B-DNB.
SHEFFIELD, Isaac.
Am. Guilford, Conn. 1798-1845. F-2.
SHEGOGUE, James Hamilton.
Am. Charleston, S. C. 1806-1872 Warrenville, Conn. F-3.
SHELDON, Charles Miles.
Am. Laurenceburg, Ind. 1866-1928 London. A025-F-W14-Y01929.
SHELDON, Roy Van Auken. (S)
Am. b. St. Louis, Mo.; ad. 1935 New York. Cs.
SHELDON, Rufus.
Am. d. 1917 in Pittsfield, Mass. A014.
SHELDON-WILLIAMS, [Mrs.]
Eng. ex. 1935 London. M.
SHELL, Gertrude.
Am. ad. 1935 Phila., Pa. M.
SHELLEY, Samuel. (Min)
Eng. London 1750-1808 Same. B-DNB.
SHELLHASE, George. (S)
Am. ex. 1933 in White Plains, N. Y. M.

SHELTON, William Henry.
Am. Allen's Hill, N. Y. 1840-1932 Morristown, N. J. A029.
SHÊN CHOU.
Chinese. ac. 16th Cent. in China. E.
SHÊN NAN-PUN.
Chinese. ac. 1731-1733 in China. E.
SHENTON, Edward. (Ill)
Am. ad. 1934 Phila., Pa. M.
SHENTON, Henry Chawner [The Elder]. (Eg)
Eng. Westchester 1803-1866 London. B-DNB.
SHENTON, Henry Chawner [The Younger]. (Eg)
Eng. 1825-1846. DNB.
SHENTON, William Kernot. (S)
Eng. 1836-1877. DNB.
SHEPARD, Bertha S.
Am. ad. 1934 New York. M.
SHEPARD, Clarence.
Am. b. Cortland, N. Y. 1869; ad. 1934 Kansas City, Mo. A.
SHEPARD, Ernest Howard. (Ill)
Eng. b. 1879; ad. 1934 Guilford. Wa.
SHEPARD, Mary. (Ill)
Am. ad. 1934 New York. M.
SHEPARD, Ralph C.
Am. ad. 1934 New York. M.
SHEPHEARD, George.
Eng. b. 1770? d. 1882 London. B-DNB.
SHEPHEARD, George Walwyn.
Eng. b. 1804; ac. 1830/52 London. B-DNB.
SHEPHERD, Charles.
Am. b. England; d. 1924 Brooklyn, N. Y. A021.
SHEPHERD, Don.
Am. ad. 1934 Westport, Conn. M.
SHEPHERD, F. H. S.
Eng. ac. 19th Cent. in London. M.
SHEPHERD, George.
Eng. ac. 1800-1830 in London. B-DNB.
SHEPHERD, George Sydney.
Eng. London 1805-1858. B-DNB.
SHEPHERD, J. Clinton. (P-S)
Am. b. Des Moines, Ia. 1888; ad. 1934 New York. A.
SHEPHERD, Nina.
Am. b. Des Moines, Ia.; ad. 1934 Springfield, Mo. A.
SHEPHERD, Stanley Raymond.
Eng. b. London 1906; ad. 1934 Harrow. Wa.
SHEPHERD, Thomas Hosmer.
Eng. ac. 1817-1840 in London. B-DNB.
SHEPHERD, William James Affleck.
Eng. b. London 1867; ad. 1934 Surrey. Wa.
SHEPPARD, J. Warren.
Am. b. Brooklyn, N. Y. 1882; ad. 1934 Same. A.
SHEPPARD, [Mrs.] Nancy.
Scot. Nusseerabad 1890; ad. 1934 London. Wa.
SHEPPARD, Oliver.
Ir. b. Tyrone 1865; ad. 1934 Dublin. B-Wa.
SHEPPARD, Peter Clapham.
Can. b. Toronto 1882; ad. 1935 Same. M.
SHEPPARD, Robert. (Eg)
Br. ac. 1730-1740. DNB.
SHEPPARD, Warren W.
Am. Greenwich, N. Y. 1858; ad. 1934 Brooklyn, N. Y. A-B-F-W.
SHEPPARD, William.
Br. ac. 1759-1806. DNB.
SHEPPARD, William Ludlow.
Am. Richmond, Va. 1833-1912 Same. A010.
SHEPPERSON, Claude Allin.
Eng. b. Beckenham 1867; d. 1921 in Chelsea. M.
SHERBORN, Charles William. (Eg)
Eng. London 1831-1912 So. Kensington. DNB.
SHERIDAN, Frank J., Jr. (Ill)
Am. ad. 1934 New York. A.
SHERIDAN, John E. (Ill)
Am. b. Tomah, Wis.; ad. 1934 New York. A.
SHERINGHAM, George. (Ill)
Eng. b. London 1884; ad. 1934 Same. Wa.
SHERLOCK, William.
Ir. b. Dublin 1738; ac. 1759-1806 London. B-DNB.
SHERLOCK, William P.
Br. ac. 1800-1820 in London. B-DNB.
SHERMAN, Charles H.
Am. ad. 1934 New York. M.
SHERMAN, Clifford C. (Cart)
Am. b. 1878; d. 1920 Springfield, Ill. A017.
SHERMAN, Elizabeth Evelyn.
Am. b. Chicago 1896; ad. 1934 Coronado, Calif. M.
SHERMAN, Jessie Gordon.
Am. b. Lenox, Mass.; ad. 1934 Boston. A.
SHERMAN, Stowell Bradford.
Am. b. Prov., R. I. 1886; ad. 1934 Same. A.
SHERMAN, Welby.
Eng. ac. 1827. [No death date.] M.
SHERRIN, David.
Eng. b. 1868; ad. 1935 Kent, Eng. B-M.
SHERWIN, Charles. (Eg)
Br. ac. 1780. DNB.
SHERWIN, John Keyse. (Eg)
Eng. London 1751?-1790. B-DNB-E.
SHERWIN, William. (Eg)
Eng. Wellington 1650-1715. B-DNB.
SHERWOOD, Mary Clare.
Am. b. Lyons, N. Y. 1868; ad. 1934 Vicksburg, Miss. A.
SHERWOOD, Rosina Emmet.
Mrs. Arthur M. Sherwood.
Am. b. New York 1854; ad. 1934 Stockbridge, Mass. A-B-C-F-W-46.
SHERWOOD, Ruth. (S)
Am. b. Chicago 1890; ad. 1934 Same. A-Cs-F.
SHERWOOD, William Anderson. (Et)
Am. b. Balt., Md. 1875; ad. 1934 Bruges, Belg. A-F.
SHEVCHENKO.
Rus. ex. 1935 London. M.
SHIAVONI, Félice.
It. Trieste 1803-1868. B-C.
SHIBANOV, Michael.
Rus. ac. 1787. M.
SHIDELER, Paul. (Et)
Am. b. Ind., Ind. 1888; ad. 1934 Same. A.
SHIDONE. *see* Schidone.

SHIELDS, Emma Barber.
Am. b. 1863; d. 1912 in New York. A010.
SHIELDS, Frederick James.
Eng. b. Hartlepool 1833; d. 1911 in Wimbledon. DNB.
SHIELDS, Phyllis.
Am. ad. 1934 Ocean Park, Calif. M.
SHIELDS, Thomas W.
Am. Scotland 1850-1920 Brooklyn, N. Y. A017.
SHIFFER, J. Bernard Van Rossum. (Ill)
Am. ad. 1934 Boston, Mass. M.
SHIFRIN.
Rus. ad. 1935 Moscow. M.
SHIKO, Watanabé.
Jap. J., Vol. 2, page 11.
SHILL, F. Hutton.
Am. b. Omaha, Neb. 1872; ac. 1915 Silvan Springs, Ark. A12.
SHILLING, Alexander.
Am. b. Chicago; ad. 1934 New York. A-F-W14.
SHINDLER, A. Zeno.
Am. ac. 1853-1860 in Phila., Pa. F-45.
SHINN, Alice R.
Am. ad. 1934 New York. M.
SHINN, Everett.
Am. b. Woodstown, N. J. 1876; ad. 1934 New York. A-F-W14.
SHINN, Florence Scovel. (Ill)
Am. b. Camden, N. J.; ad. 1915 New York. A12-W8-46.
SHIPLEY, Georgiana.
Mrs. Francis Hare Naylor.
Eng. ex. 1781 London; d. 1806 Lausanne, Swi. B-DNB.
SHIPLEY, William.
Eng. b. 1714; d. 1803 in Manchester. B-DNB.
SHIRLAW, Walter.
Am. Paisley, Scot. 1838-1909 Madrid, Sp. A08-B-C-F-1-7-15-39-46.
SHISHKIN, Ivan.
Rus. 1821-1899 Russia. M.
SHIUBUN [of Sokokuji].
Jap. ac. 15th Cent. in Japan. J., Vol. 1, page 89.
SHIUGETSU [Takaji Gonnokami].
Jap. ac. 1470 in Japan. J., Vol. 1, page 107.
SHIVA, Ramon.
Am. b. Spain 1893; ad. 1934 Chicago. A.
SHIVELY, Douglas.
Am. ex. 1935 Santa Cruz, Calif. M.
SHIVELY, Paul. (Ill)
Am. b. 1897; ex. 1935 New York. M.
SHOEMAKER, Edna Cooke. (Ill)
Mrs. Orlando Shoemaker.
Am. b. Phila., Pa. 1891; ad. 1934 Same. A.
SHOESMITH, Kenneth D. (Posters)
Eng. b. Yorkshire; ad. 1934 London. Wa.
SHŌHAKU, Soga.
Jap. b. 1559; d. 1635 in Kyoto. J., Vol. 1, page 130.
SHŌHIN, [Miss] Noguchi.
Jap. ac. 1920 in Tokyo. [Deceased.] M.
SHOKLER, Harry.
Am. b. Cinn., O. 1896; ad. 1934 Brooklyn, N. Y. A.
SHŌKWADO [Shōjo-o].
Jap. Yamato 1584-1639. J., Vol. 1, page 65.
SHONNARD, Eugenie Frederica. (S)
Am. b. Yonkers, N. Y. 1886; ad. 1934 New York. A-Cs-F.
SHOOSMITH, Thurston Laidlaw.
Eng. Northampton 1865-1934 Same. M-Wa-Obit. Art News, 3-16-1935.
SHOPE, Henry Brengle. (Et)
Am. Balt., Md. 1862-1929 France. A026-F.
SHOPEN, Kenneth George.
Am. b. Elgin, Ill. 1902; ad. 1934 Chicago. A.
SHOR, Sara. (Ill)
Rus. ex. 1935 London. M.
SHORE, Arnold.
Aust. ac. 1933 in Australia. M.
SHORE, Henrietta M.
Am. b. Toronto, Can.; ad. 1934 Carmel, Calif. A-F-W-578.
SHORELY, George H.
Am. b. Hoosick Falls, N. Y. 1870; ad. 1934 New York. A.
SHORT, [Sir] Frank. (Et)
Eng. b. Stourbridge 1857; ad. 1934 London. B-E-Wa-364-830.
SHORT, Richard.
Welsh. b. Wales 1841; d. 1916 Cardiff. B-M.
SHORTER, Edward Swift.
Am. b. Columbus, Ga. 1900; ad. 1934 Macon, Ga. A.
SHOUDY, Theodore.
Am. ad. 1934 New York. M.
SHOVEN, Hazel Brayton.
Am. b. Jackson, Mich. 1884; ad. 1934 San Diego, Calif. A.
SHOVER, Edna Mann. (Ill)
Am. b. Ind., Ind. 1885; ad. 1934 Same. A.
SHOYEN, [Miss] Uyemura.
Jap. b. Kyoto 1875. M.
SHRADER, Edwin Roscoe.
Am. b. Quincy, Ill. 1879; ad. 1934 Los Angeles, Calif. A-F-W.
SHRADY, Henry Mervin. (S)
Am. New York 1871-1922 Same. A019-F-Ta-W14-46.
SHULGOLD, William Robert.
Am. b. Russia; ad. 1934 Pittsburgh, Pa. A-F.
SHULKIN, Anatol.
Am. b. 1899; ad. 1935 New York. M.
SHULL, James Marion. (Ill)
Am. b. Ohio 1872; ad. 1934 Maryland. A28-W.
SHULZ, Ada Walter.
Mrs. Adolph R. Shulz.
Am. Terre Haute, Ind. 1870-1928 Nashville, Ind. A025.
SHULZ, Adolph Robert.
Am. b. Delavan, Wis. 1869; ad. 1934 Nashville, Ind. A-F-W-46-181.
SHULZ, Alberta R.
Am. ad. 1934 Nashville, Ind. M.
SHUMAN, Anna M.
Am. Pittsburgh, Pa. 1890-1919. A018.
SHUMATE, Ella A.
Am. ad. 1934 Lebanon, Ind. M.
SHUMWAY, Henry Colton. (Min)
Am. Middletown, Conn. 1807-1884 New York. C-F-2-3-6-15.
SHUNKO, Katsugawa.
Jap. d. 1827. J., Vol. 2, page 48.

SHUNKO, YAMAMOTO.
Jap. ac. 1900. J., Vol. 2, page 89.
SHUNMAN, KUBO.
Jap. 1757-1820. J., Vol. 2, page 50.
SHUNSHO, KATSUGAWA.
Jap. 1726-1792. J., Vol. 2, page 38.
SHUNZAN, KATSUGAWA.
Jap. ac. 1820. J., Vol. 2, page 49.
SHUNZAN, YAGIOKA.
Jap. ex. 1930 in Tokyo. M.
SHURTLEFF, ROSWELL MORSE.
Am. Ringe, N. H. 1838-1915 New York. A012-B-C-F-3-15.
SHUSTER ["Will"], WILLIAM HOWARD.
Am. b. Phila., Pa. 1893; ad. 1934 Santa Fé, N. M. A-F.
SHUTE, BEN E.
Am. ad. 1935 Atlanta, Ga. M.
SHUTTLEWORTH, CLAIRE.
Am. b. Buffalo, N. Y.; d. 1930 Same. A028.
SIBBEL, JOSEPH. (S)
Am. b. Germany; d. 1907 New York. A06-F-Ta.
SIBEL, MURIEL VINCENT. (Et)
Am. b. Brooklyn, N. Y. 1898; ad. 1934 Boulder, Colo. A.
SIBERECHTS [or Sibrecht], GUIELLIMUS JAN.
Flem. Antwerp 1627-1703 London. B-C-722.
SIBONI, EMMA. (Min)
Am. b. Denmark 1877; ad. 1934 Wash., D. C. A.
SIBSON, THOMAS.
Eng. Cumberland 1817-1844 Malta. B-DNB.
SICARD, FRANÇOIS. (S)
Fr. Tours 1862-1934 Paris. B-DBA-798.
SICARD [or Sicardy], LOUIS.
Fr. Avignon 1746-1825. B.
SICHEL, ERNEST.
Eng. b. Bradford; ac. 1885 in London. B.
SICHEL, HAROLD M. (Ill)
Am. ad. 1934 New York. M.
SICHEL, NATHANIEL.
Ger. Mentz 1845-1907. B-C.
SICHEM [or Voschem], CHRISTOPHER VAN. (Eg)
Dut. ac. 1573-1601 in Delft. B.
SICHULSKI, [Prof.] CASIMIR.
Pol. ad. 1935 Cracow; ex. 1934 Pittsburgh, Pa. M.
SICKERT, BERNARD.
Eng. 1863-1932 London. Wa1929-Y01933.
SICKERT, WALTER RICHARD.
Eng. b. Munich, Ger. 1860; ad. 1934 London. E-Wa-818-825-871.
SIDANER. *see* Le Sidaner.
SIDES, HILDA MARY.
Eng. b. London 1871; ad. 1934 Bedford. Wa.
SIDI-BE, KALIFALA.
African Negro. ad. 1935 Senegal, West Africa. M.
SIDLEY, SAMUEL.
Eng. Manchester 1829-1896. B-DNB.
SIEBERLING, GERTRUDE.
Mrs. Frank A. Sieberling.
Am. ad. 1934 Akron, O. M.
SIEBERT, EDWARD SELMAR.
Am. b. Wash., D. C. 1856; ad. 1926 Rochester, N. Y. A20-F.
SIEDENBURG, MILDRED.
Am. ad. 1934 New York. M.
SIEFFERT, PAUL R. E.
Fr. b. Paris 1874. B-DBA.
SIEGEL, WILLIAM. (Ill)
Am. ex. 1935 New York. M.
SIEGELMAN, IRMA.
Am. ad. 1934 New York. M.
SIEGEN VON SECHTEN, LUDWIG. (Eg)
Produced, in 1642, the earliest known Mezzotint; now in Boston Museum of Art.
Dut. Sechten 1609-1680 Wofenbuttel. B-Bd.
SIEGERT, AUGUST FRIEDRICH.
Ger. Neuwied 1820-1883 Düsseldorf. B-C.
SIEL. *see* Müeller von Seil.
SIELKE, LEO, JR.
Am. b. 1880; d. 1930 in New York. A027.
SIEMER, CHRIS. (Mu)
Am. ac. 1933. M.
SIEMERING, LEOPOLD RUDOLF. (S)
Ger. Berlin 1835-1905 Same. B-Hs.
SIEMIRADZKI, HENDRIK.
Pol. Grodno 1843-1902. B-C.
SIENA, BRESCIANINO. *see* Brescianino da S.
SIENA, GUIDO DA. *see* Guido da S.
SIENA, MATTEO DA. *see* Matteo di G.
SIEVERS, FREDERICK WILLIAM. (S)
Am. b. Fort Wayne, Ind. 1872; ad. 1934 Richmond, Va. A-F-W.
SIEVIER, ROBERT WILLIAM. (Eg-S)
Eng. London 1794-1865. B-DNB.
SIFER WAS. (Illuminator)
Br. ac. 15th Cent. M.
SIGALON, XAVIER.
Fr. Uzès 1788-1837 Rome, It. B-C-E-722.
SIGNAC, PAUL.
Fr. b. Paris 1863; d. 1935 Same. B-DBA.
SIGNORACCIO, PAOLO DEI.
see Paolimo da Pistoja.
SIGNORELLI, LUCCA [D'Egido di Ventura].
It. Cortona 1441/4-1523/4 Same. B-Bd-C-E-V-722-784.
SIGNORI, SERGE.
Fr. ad. 1934 Paris. M.
SIGNORINI, GIOVANNI [Telemaco].
It. Florence 1835-1901. B.
SIGNORINI, GIUSEPPE.
It. 1857-1933. Fa-M.
SIGRIST, PROSPER M.
Am. ad. 1934 Toledo, O. M.
SI-KIN, KÜ-TSZE.
Chinese. ac. 15th Cent. in China. M.
SILANION. (S)
Gr. ac. 4th Cent. B.C. E-Hs.
SILAS, ELLIS.
Eng. ac. 1929 in London. Wa1929.
SILAS, [Mrs.] LILIAN.
Eng. ad. 1934 Bedford, Eng. Wa.
SILBER, ESTHER [Reed].
Am. b. St. Louis, Mo. 1900; ad. 1934 Same. A.
SILBER, JONAS. *see* Master, J. S.
SILBERMAN, SARAH GETTLEMAN. (S)
Am. b. Odessa, Rus. 1909; ad. 1934 Atlantic City, N. J. A.
SILBERT, BEN.
Am. b. Russia 1895; ex. 1935 Milwaukee, Wis. M.
SILHOUETTES *see* books 773-795.

SILK, Henry.
Eng. ad. 1935 in London. M.
SILOÉ, Gil de. (S)
Sp. ac. 1480 in Spain. Hs.
SILSBEE, Martha.
Am. b. Salem, Mass. 1858; ad. 1926 Boston. A12-F.
SILSBY, Clifford F.
Am. b. New Haven, Conn. 1896; ad. 1934 Los Angeles, Calif. A.
SILSBY, Wilson. (Et)
Am. ad. 1934 Hollywood, Calif. M.
SILVA, Francis Augustus.
Am. New York 1835-1886 Same. F-15.
SILVA, William Posey.
Am. b. Savannah, Ga. 1859; ad. 1934 Carmel, Calif. A-F-W.
SILVEIRA, Bento Coelho de.
Por. d. 1708 in Portugal. M.
SILVER, Rose.
Am. b. New York 1902; ad. 1934 Seattle, Wash. A.
SILVERMAN, Elijah.
Am. ex. 1935 New York. M.
SILVERMAN, Miles.
Am. ad. 1934 Toledo, O. M.
SILVERS, Herbert Ferber.
Am. b. New York 1906; ad. 1934 Same. A.
SILVERSTRE, Israel. (Ill)
Fr. Nancy 1621-1691 Paris. B.
SILVESTRE, Louis de [The Younger].
Fr. Paris 1675-1760 Same. B-C.
SILVESTRE, Nicolas Charles de.
Fr. Paris 1698-1767 Valenton. B.
SILVESTRE, Paul. (S)
Fr. b. Toulouse 1884. DBA.
SILVETTE, Brooks Johnson.
Mrs. Herbert Silvette.
Am. b. Willoughby Beach, Va. 1906; ad. 1934 University, Va. A.
SILVETTE, David.
Am. b. 1909; ad. 1934 Richmond, Va. M.
SILVETTE, Ellis M.
Am. ad. 1933 New York. M.
SILVETTE, Marcia.
Am. ad. 1935 Richmond, Va. M.
SILVIUS, Paul T.
Am. b. Hampton, Ia. 1899; ad. 1934 Los Angeles, Calif. A.
SIMARD, Marie Louis. (S)
Fr. b. Paris; ad. 1934 Same. DBA.
SIMART, Pierre Charles. (S)
Fr. Troyes 1806-1857 Paris. B.
SIMAY [or Sima], Imre.
Czec. ac. 1910-1930. Fa-M.
SIMBOLI, Raymond S.
Am. ad. 1934 Pittsburgh, Pa. M.
SIMKHOVITCH, Simkha.
Am. b. Leningrad, Rus. 1893; ad. 1934 Greenwich, Conn. A.
SIMKINS, Martha.
Am. b. Texas; ad. 1934 Woodstock, N. Y. A.
SIMM, Franz Xaver.
Aus. b. Vienna 1853. B.
SIMMONDS, William George. (S)
Eng. b. Constantinople, Turkey 1876; ad. 1934 Stroud, Eng. Wa-798.
SIMMONS. *see also* Simons.
SIMMONS, Cordray.
Am. ex. 1934 New York. M.
SIMMONS, Edward Emerson. (Mu)
Am. Concord, Mass. 1852-1931 Balt., Md. A028-B-C-E-F-W16.
SIMMONS, Franklin. (S)
Am. Webster, Me. 1839-1913 Rome, It. A0X1-B-F-15.
SIMMONS, Freeman Willis.
Am. Fredonia, Pa. 1859-1926. A024.
SIMMONS, Henry England.
Am. ad. 1934 New York. M.
SIMMONS, John.
Eng. Nailsea 1715-1780 Bristol. B.
SIMMONS, Marion Louise.
Am. b. Rumson, N. J. 1903; ad. 1934 Same. A.
SIMMONS, Teresa C. (Et)
Am. ad. 1934 Roxbury, Conn. M.
SIMMONS, Will. (Et)
Am. b. Elche, Sp. 1884; ad. 1935 Roxbury, Conn. A28-F-M.
SIMMONS, William Henry. (Eg)
Eng. London 1811-1882 Same. B-DNB.
SIMON, Abraham. (Med-S)
Eng. Yorkshire 1622?-1692? DNB-E.
SIMON, Friedrich Rudolf.
Swi. Berne 1828-1862 Hyèrs. B.
SIMON, Grant Miles.
Am. b. Phila., Pa. 1887; ad. 1934 Same. A.
SIMON, Herman C.
Am. b. 1867. M.
SIMON, Howard. (Eg)
Am. ad. 1934 New York. A.
SIMON, Jacques Paul.
see Simon-Reims, J. P.
SIMON, Jacques Roger.
Fr. b. Paris 1875. B-DBA.
SIMON, Jean [or John]. (Eg)
Fr. Normandie 1675-1751/5 London. B-DNB.
SIMON, Lucien.
Fr. b. Paris 1861; ad. 1934 Same. B-DBA-Ms.
SIMON, Pierre [The Elder]. (Eg)
Fr. Paris 1640-1710 Same. B-Bd.
SIMON, Pierre [The Younger]. (Et)
Eng. London 1750-1810. B.
SIMON, Thomas. (Med)
Eng. Yorkshire 1623?-1665 London. DNB-E.
SIMON, T. Frank. (Et)
Czec. ac. 1930. Auc. sale 1934 New York. M.
SIMON-REIMS, Jacques Paul. (S)
Fr. b. Reims 1890; ex. 1935 Paris. DBA.
SIMONAU, François.
[Called the "Flemish Murillo."]
Belg. Bornheim 1783-1859 London. B.
SIMONE DA BOLOGNA. *see* Bologna, S. da.
SIMONE, Edgardo. (S)
Am. b. 1890; ex. 1933 Wash., D. C. M.
SIMONE DI MEMMI DI MARTINI.
see Martini, S.
SIMONET, Jean Baptiste. (Eg)
Fr. Paris 1742-1810 Same. B-Bd.
SIMONET, Sebastian.
Am. b. Stillwater, Minn. 1898; ad. 1934 Same. A.
SIMONET Y LOMBARDO, Enrique.
Sp. ac. 1900 in Paris. B.

SIMONETTI, ATTILIO.
It. b. Rome; ac. 1875 in Naples. B-C.
SIMONI, GUSTAVO.
It. b. Rome 1846. B.
SIMONIDY, MICHEL.
Rumanian. b. Bucharest 1871; d. 1933. B.
SIMONS. *see also* Simmons.
SIMONS, ARMORY COFFIN.
Am. b. Charleston, S. C. 1869; ad. 1934 Hollywood, Calif. A-B-Cs-F.
SIMONS, GEORGE.
Am. b. 1834; d. 1917 Long Beach, Calif. A015-Y01918.
SIMONS, PINCKNEY MARCIUS.
see Marcius-Simons.
SIMONSEN, NIELS.
Dan. Copenhagen 1807-1885 Same. B-C.
SIMONSON, LEE. [Theatre]
Am. ad. 1934 New York. M-911.
SIMONT, JOSEPH. (Ill)
Am. ad. 1934 New York. A.
SIMPKIN, ALFRED N. (Ill)
Am. ad. 1934 New York. M.
SIMPSON, ALICE M.
Am. b. Newark, N. J.; ad. 1934 New York. A.
SIMPSON, C. HELEN. *see* Whittemore, C. H.
SIMPSON, CHARLES WALTER.
Eng. b. Surrey 1885; ad. 1934 London. Wa.
SIMPSON, [Mrs.] CLARA DAVIDSON.
see Davidson, C. D.
SIMPSON, [Mrs.] EDNA HUESTIS. (Min)
Am. b. Troy, N. Y. 1882; ad. 1934 New York. A.
SIMPSON, H. W. (Et)
Eng. ex. 1935 Chicago; ad. 1935 Leicester, Eng. M.
SIMPSON, JOHN.
Eng. London 1782-1847 Same. B-C-DNB.
SIMPSON, JOSEPH. (Et)
Scot. b. Carlisle 1879; ad. 1934 London. Wa.
SIMPSON, MARION.
Mrs. Lesley Simpson.
Am. b. Kansas City, Mo. 1899; ad. 1934 Berkeley, Calif. A.
SIMPSON, MARTHA.
Am. b. Chicago; ad. 1934 New York. M.
SIMPSON, MAXWELL STEWART.
Am. b. Elizabeth, N. J. 1896; ad. 1934 Same. A.
SIMPSON, THOMAS HENRY.
Eng. b. Whitby 1875; ad. 1934 Streatham. Wa.
SIMPSON, WILLIAM. (P-Writer)
Scot. Glasgow 1823-1889 Willesden. B-DNB.
SIMPSON, WILLIAM MARKS, JR. (S)
Am. b. Norfolk, Va. 1903; ad. 1934 Same. A.
SIMS, CHARLES.
Eng. London 1873-1928. B-825.
SIMS, FLORENCE. (Min)
Am. b. Birmingham, Ala. 1891; ad. 1934 New Haven, Conn. A.
SIMSON, THEODORE SPICER.
see Spicer-Simson, T.
SIMSON, WILLIAM.
Scot. Dundee 1800-1847 London. B-E.
SINCLAIR, ALFRED.
Eng. b. Liverpool 1866; ac. 1887 Adelaide, So. Aust. M.
SINCLAIR, ARCHIE.
Am. b. Pitlochry, Perthshire, Scot. 1895; ad. 1934 Portland, Ore. A.
SINCLAIR, BERNICE.
Am. b. Knox, Ind. 1887; ad. 1934 Fort Wayne, Ind. A.
SINCLAIR, ELLEN CHISHOLM.
Am. ad. 1935 Phila., Pa. M.
SINCLAIR, GERRIT V.
Am. b. Grand Haven, Mich. 1890; ad. 1934 Milwaukee, Wis. A-F.
SINCLAIR, HELEN.
Br. b. Durban, Natal; ac. 1929 Same. M.
SINCLAIR, IRVING.
Am. ad. 1934 San Fran., Calif. M.
SINDELAR, THOMAS A. (Ill)
Am. b. Cleveland, O. 1867; ad. 1926 New York. A12-F.
SINDGREN, AMÉLIE.
Swe. b. Stockholm 1814; ac. 1856 Same. [No death date.] B.
SINDING, OTTO.
Nor. 1842-1909. M.
SINDING, STEPHAN. (S)
Nor. 1846-1922. B-Hs-778.
SINGER, WILLIAM EARL.
Am. ad. 1934 Chicago, Ill. M.
SINGER, WILLIAM H., JR.
Am. b. Pittsburgh, Pa. 1868; ad. 1934 Nordfjord, Nor. A-F-W-46.
SINGLETON, HENRY.
Eng. London 1766-1839 Same. B-C-DNB.
SINIBALDI, JEAN PAUL.
Fr. Paris 1857-1909. B.
SINKEL, HENRICUS JOHANNES.
Dut. Almelo 1835-1908. B-C.
SINKS, ALOIS E.
Am. 1848-1881. M.
SINN, ALBERT.
Am. ad. 1934 Chicago, Ill. M.
SINNOCK, JOHN RAY. (Med)
Am. b. Raton, N. M. 1888; ad. 1934 Phila., Pa. A-Cs.
SINTEMIS, RENÉE. (S)
Ger. b. Glatz [Silvésia] 1888. DBA.
SINT-JANS GEERTZEN TOT.
Dut. ac. 15th Cent. in Haarlem. 700.
SINZ, WALTER A. (S)
Am. b. Cleveland, O. 1881; ad. 1934 Same. A.
SIPPE, HEILIGEN.
see Master of the Holy Kinship.
SIQUEIROS, DAVID ALFARO. (Mu) D 1/7/74
Mex. ex. 1935 New York. M.
SIRANI, ELISABETTA.
It. Bologna 1638/9-1665 Same. B-C-722-829.
SIRANI, GIOVANNI ANDREA.
It. Bologna 1610-1670 Same. B-C-722.
SIRONI, MARIO.
It. b. 1893. Fa-M.
SISLEY, ALFRED.
Fr. Paris 1839/40-1899 Moret. B-DBA-E-847.
SISSON, FREDERICK R.
Am. b. Prov., R. I. 1893; ad. 1934 Same. A.
SISTI, ANTHONY.
Am. b. New York 1901; ad. 1934 Buffalo, N. Y. A.

SITCHKOV, Vladimir.
Rus. b. 1875; ad. 1935 Moscow. M.
SITHIUM, Miguel.
Sp. ac. 1481-1515+ in Spain. M.
SITTIG, Augusta.
Am. ad. 1934 Brooklyn, N. Y. M.
SITTON, John Melza. (Mu)
Am. ad. 1934 New York. M.
SITZMAN, Edward R.
Am. b. Cinn., O. 1874; ad. 1934 Ind., Ind. A.
SKÂNBERG, Carl E.
Swe. 1850-1883. B-580.
SKARBINA, Franz.
Ger. Berlin 1849-1910. B-C.
SKEAPING, [Mrs.] Jocelyn Barbara. (S)
Eng. b. Wakefield 1903; ad. 1934 London. Wa.
SKEAPING, John.
Eng. b. Liverpool; ad. Same. Wa.
SKEAPING, John Rattenbury. (S)
Eng. b. Woodford 1901; ad. 1934 London. Wa.
SKEATS, Leonard Frank.
Eng. b. Southampton 1874; ad. 1934 Bath. Wa.
SKEELE, Anna Katherine.
Am. b. Wellington, O. 1896; ad. 1934 Monrovia, Calif. A.
SKELTON, Joseph Ratcliffe.
Eng. b. Newcastle; ad. 1934 London. Wa.
SKELTON, Leslie James.
Am. Montreal, Can. 1848-1929 Colorado Springs, Colo. A026-F-W14.
SKELTON, Ralph Fisher.
Am. b. Port Byron, Ill. 1899; ad. 1929 London. Wa1929.
SKELTON, William. (Eg)
Eng. London 1763-1848. B-DBA.
SKIDMORE, Lewis Palmer.
Am. b. Bridgeport, Conn. 1877; ad. 1934 Atlanta, Ga. A.
SKIDMORE, Thornton D. (Ill)
Am. b. Brooklyn, N. Y. 1884; ad. 1934 New York. A28.
SKILLIN, Simeon. (Carver)
Am. ac. Boston, Mass. 1800. [No death date.] M.
SKINNER, Charlotte B.
Mrs. William Lyle Skinner.
Am. b. San Fran., Calif. 1879; ad. 1934 Same. A.
SKINNER, Frances Van Arsdale.
Am. ad. 1935 Newtonville, Mass. M.
SKIPPE, Jean.
Eng. ac. 1770-1811. B.
SKIPWORTH, Frank Markham.
Eng. ac. 1917-1927 in London. B.
SKIRVING, Archibald. (Min)
Scot. b. Haddington 1749; d. 1819 Inverest. B-DNB.
SKOCZLAS, Wladyslaw. (Eg)
Pol. 1883-1934 Warsaw.
DBA-Obit. Art Digest, 5-15-1934.
SKOGGARD, Arvid. (S)
Swe. b. Norrland 1886; ad. 1934 Floral Park, L. I., N. Y. M.
SKÖLD, Otte.
Swe. b. 1894; ad. 1934 Stockholm. DBA-M.
SKOLFIELD, Raymond White.
Am. b. Portland, Me. 1909; ad. 1934 Brooklyn, N. Y. A.
SKOOG, Karl Frederick. (S)
Am. b. Sweden 1878; ad. 1934 Boston, Mass. A-Cs-F-W.
SKOOVGOARD, Peter Kristian.
Dan. b. Hammerhus 1817; d. 1875/6 in Copenhagen. B-C.
SKOPAS. *see* Scopas.
SKOU, Sigurd.
Nor.-Am. b. in Norway; d. 1929 in Paris. A026-F.
SKOUGER, Martha Gilbert.
Am. b. Brooklyn, N. Y. 1885; ad. 1934 Same. A.
SKRENDA, Al. (Ill)
Am. ad. 1934 New York. M.
SKUPAS, Anthony.
Am. b. 1907; ex. 1934 Chicago. M.
SLADE, Anthony.
Eng. b. London 1908; ad. 1934 Hove. Wa.
SLADE, Caleb Arnold.
Am. b. Acushnet, Mass. 1882; ad. 1934 Truro, Mass. A-F-W-46.
SLADE, Cora L.
Mrs. Abbott E. Slade.
Am. ad. 1934 Fall River, Mass. A.
SLADE, Robert.
Am. New York 1861-1912 Milwaukee, Wis. M.
SLAGER, W. D.
Am. ad. 1934 Toledo, O. M.
SLATER, Edwin C.
Am. b. New Jersey 1884; ad. 1934 Greenwich, Conn. A.
SLATER, Walter James.
Eng. Manchester 1845-1923. B-Y01924.
SLAUGHTER, Stephen.
Eng. ac. 1730-1750; d. 1765 Kensington, Eng. DNB.
SLAVONA, Maria.
Ger. b. Lübeck 1865; ad. 1934 Berlin. M.
SLEETH, L. MacDonald. (S)
Mrs. Francis V. Sleeth.
Am. b. Croton, Ia. 1864; ad. 1934 Wash., D. C. A-F.
SLEIGH, Bernard [or Barnay]. (Eg)
Eng. Birmingham 1872; ad. 1934 London. Wa.
SLÉNDZINSKI, Ludomir.
Pol. b. 1889; ad. Wilnö, Pol. M.
SLEVOGT, Max.
Ger. Landshut 1868-1932. B-Y01933.
SLICK, Edwin.
Am. ex. 1935 Hagerstown, Md. M.
SLINGELAND, Pieter Corneliez van.
Dut. Leyden 1640-1691 Same. B-C-722.
SLINGHUFF, Kathleen. (S)
Am. ex. 1935 Balt., Md. M.
SLOAN, [Mrs.] Alice.
Am. ex. 1934 East Hampton, L. I., N. Y. M.
SLOAN, James Blanding.
Am. b. Corsicana, Tex. 1886; ad. 1934 Same. A.
SLOAN, John.
Am. b. Lock Haven, Pa. 1871; ad. 1935 New York. A-F-W-I-46-248-582-701-779-783.

SLOAN, Marianna.
Am. b. Lock Haven, Pa.; ad. 1934 Phila., Pa. A.
SLOANE, George.
Am. ad. 1915 Boston, Mass. A12.
SLOANE, Marian Parkhurst.
Mrs. George Sloane.
Am. b. Salem, Mass.; ad. 1934 Boston. A-F-W.
SLOBE, Laura.
Am. ad. 1935 in Chicago, Ill. M.
SLOCOMBE, Frederick Albert. (Et)
Eng. ac. 1886-1909 London. B.
SLOCUM, Rosalie.
Am. ex. 1935 New York. M.
SLODTZ, René Michel [or Michel Ange]. (S)
Fr. Paris 1705-1764. B-E-Hs.
SLODTZ, Sébastien. (S)
Fr. Anvers 1655-1726 Paris. B.
SLODTZ, Sébastien Antoine. (S)
Fr. Paris 1695-1754 Same. B.
SLOMAN, Joseph.
Am. b. Phila., Pa. 1883; ad. 1934 Union City, N. J. A-F.
SLOPER, Norma Wright.
Am. b. New Haven, Conn. 1892; ad. 1934 New Britain, Conn. A.
SLUITER, Willy.
Dut. ac. 1900 in Paris. B.
SLUSSER, Jean Paul.
Am. b. Wauseon, O. 1886; ad. 1934 Ann Arbor, Mich. A-F.
SLUTZ, Helen Beatrice.
Am. b. Cleveland, O.; ad. 1934 Evanston, Ill. A.
SLUYTER [or Sluter], Claes Nicolaes. (S)
Dut. ac. 1375-1405. B-Hs-583.
SLUYTERS, Jans.
Dut. b. 1881; ad. 1934 Amsterdam. M.
SMALL, Eugene Walter.
Am. New York 1871-1934 Same.
M-Obit. N. Y. papers, 5-8-1934.
SMALL, Frank O. (Ill)
Am. b. Boston, Mass. 1860; ad. 1915 Same. A12.
SMALL, William.
Scot. b. Edinburgh 1843. B-Wa1929.
SMALLEY, Janet. (Ill)
Am. ad. 1935 New York. M.
SMALLFIELD, Frederick.
Br. b. 1829. [No death date.] M.
SMARGIASSI, Gabriel.
Fr. ac. 1827-1837 in Paris. B.
SMART, Borlase. (Author-P)
Eng. b. Kingsbridge 1881; ad. 1934 St. Ives, Cornwall, Eng. M-Wa.
SMART, Douglas Ion. (Et)
Eng. b. 1879; ad. 1934 London. Wa
SMART, Edgar Rovley. (Et)
Eng. Manchester 1887-1934 Sweden.
Wa1929-Obit. Art News, 3-17-1934.
SMART, Edmund Hodgson.
Eng. b. England 1873; ad. 1934 Los Angeles, Calif. W-Wa.
SMART, John.
Scot. Leith 1838-1899 Edinburgh. B.
SMART, John. (Min)
Eng. Norfolk 1740/1-1811 London. B-DNB-E.
SMED, Peer. (S)
Am. ad. 1934 Woodhaven, L. I., N. Y. M.
SMEDLEY, Will Larrymore.
Am. b. Sandyville, O. 1871; ad. 1934 Chatauqua, N. Y. A-F.
SMEDLEY, William Thomas.
Am. Chester Co., Pa. 1858-1920 Bronxville, N. Y. A017-B-C-E-F-Y01921-46.
SMET, Gustave. *see* De Smet, G.
SMETHAN, James. (Ill-Author)
Eng. 1821-1889. B-DNB.
SMEYERS, Egide Joseph [The Younger].
Flem. Mechlin 1694-1774 Same. B.
SMEYERS, Gilles.
Flem. Mechlin 1635-1710 Same. B-C-722.
SMIBERT [or Smybert], John.
Am. Edinburgh, Scot. 1684/8-1751 Boston, Mass. B-Bd-C-DNB-F-1-2-182.
SMIBERT, Nathaniel.
Am. Boston 1734-1756 Same. C-F-2.
SMILLIE, George Frederick Cumming. (Eg)
Am. New York 1854-1924 Wash., D. C. A20-F-W14.
SMILLIE, George Henry.
Am. New York 1840-1921 Bronxville, N. Y. A018-B-C-F-15.
SMILLIE, Helen Sheldon Jacobs.
Am. New York 1854-1926 Same. A023-F-W13.
SMILLIE, James. (Eg)
Am. Edinburgh, Scot. 1807-1885 Poughkeepsie, N. Y. B-F-2-7-15-40-880.
SMILLIE, James David.
Am. New York 1833-1909 Same. A07-B-C-E-F-7-15-40-46.
SMILLIE, William Main. (Eg)
Am. New York 1835-1888 Same. F-7.
SMIRKE, Robert.
Eng. Wigton 1752-1845 London. B-C-DNB-E-272-722.
SMIT, Aermont.
Dut. Amsterdam 1641-1678 Same. B-C.
SMITH, Albert Alexander.
Am. b. New York 1896; ad. 1934 Paris. A.
SMITH, Albert Delmont.
Am. New York 1886; ad. 1934 Same. A.
SMITH, Alfred.
Fr. b. Bordeaux 1854. DBA.
SMITH, Alfred E.
Am. Lynn, Mass. 1863; ad. 1935 Boston, Mass. A12-F.
SMITH, Alive Ravenal Huger. (Ill)
Am. b. Charleston, S. C. 1876; ad. 1934 Same. A-F-W.
SMITH, Allen.
Am. b. 1810; d. 1890 in Cleveland, O. F.
SMITH, Amanda Banks.
Am. b. 1846; d. 1924 Greenwich, Conn. A021.
SMITH, André. (Et)
Am. ad. 1934 Stony Creek, Conn. A.
SMITH, Anita Miller.
Am. b. Torresdale, Pa. 1893; ad. 1934 Woodstock, N. Y. A.
SMITH, Anker. (Eg)
Eng. London 1764-1835. B-DNB.
SMITH, Anne Dorrien.
Br. ex. 1935 London. M.

SMITH, Anne Fry.
Am. b. Phila., Pa. 1890; ad. Oreland, Pa. A.
SMITH, Archibald Carey.
Am. New York 1837-1911 Bayonne, N. J. A010-C-F-15.
SMITH, Arthur Reginald.
Eng. b. Skipton 1872; d. 1934. Wa.
SMITH, Benjamin. (Et)
Eng. d. 1833 in London. DNB.
SMITH, Bernice C.
Am. ad. 1934 New York. M.
SMITH, Calvert.
Am. ad. 1934 New York. M.
SMITH, Calvin Rae.
Am. New York 1850-1918 Brooklyn, N. Y. A015-C.
SMITH, Carl Frithjof.
Am. b. Cinn., O. 1868; ad. 1934 Pasadena, Calif. A-F-W.
SMITH, Carl Rohl. (S)
Dan. d. 1900 in Copenhagen. A02-B-T.
SMITH, Carlton Alfred.
Eng. b. London 1853; ad. 1929 Same. B-Wa1929.
SMITH, Charles.
Scot. Orkneys 1749-1824 Lille, Fr. B-DNB.
SMITH, Charles John. (Eg)
Eng. Chelsea 1803-1838. B-DNB.
SMITH, Charles L. A.
Am. b. New York 1871; ad. 1934 Los Angeles, Calif. A.
SMITH, C. Moore.
Am. ad. 1934 Mt. Vernon, N. Y. M.
SMITH, Charles Timothy.
Am. ad. 1935 Pittsburgh, Pa. M.
SMITH, Charles W. (Ill)
Am. ad. 1934 Jackson Heights, N. Y. M.
SMITH, Clemie C.
Am. b. Tiskilwa, Ill.; ad. 1934 Omaha, Neb. A.
SMITH, Colvin.
Scot. Brechin 1795-1875 Edinburgh. DNB-E.
SMITH, C. Loraine.
Eng. ac. 1794-1806. M.
SMITH, Dan. (Et)
Am. Izigtut, Greenland 1865-1934 New York. M-Obit. N. Y. papers, 12-12-1934.
SMITH, David Murray.
Scot. b. Edinburgh; ad. 1934 Surrey, Eng. M.
SMITH, De Kost [or Cost].
Am. b. Amenia, N. Y. 1864; ad. 1934 Same. A28.
SMITH, Dorothy Hope.
Am. b. 1879. M.
SMITH, Duncan. (Mu)
Am. Charlottesville, Va. 1877-1934 Same. A-F-M-Obit. N. Y. papers, 11-10-1934.
SMITH, Edward. (S)
Ir. b. 1746; d. 1812 Dublin. B.
SMITH, E. Galusha.
Am. b. Morris, Ill. 1849. [Deceased.] A20.
SMITH, Edward Gregory.
Am. b. Grand Rapids, Mich. 1880; ad. 1934 Old Lyme, Conn. A-F.
SMITH, Edward Herndon.
Am. b. Mobile, Ala. 1891; ad. 1934 Same. A.
SMITH, E. Innis Dorrien.
Br. ex. 1935 London. M.
SMITH, Edward Robinson.
Am. Beirut, Syria 1854-1921 Stamford, Conn. A018.
SMITH, Edwin James.
Am. b. Omaha, Neb. 1899; ad. 1934 Same. A.
SMITH, Edwin Whitney. (S)
Eng. b. Bath 1880; ad. 1934 London. Wa.
SMITH, Elmer Boyd. (Ill)
Am. b. St. John, N. B., Can. 1860; ad. 1934 Wilton, Conn. A-F-W.
SMITH, Ernest Browning.
Am. b. Brimfield, Mass. 1866; ad. 1934 Los Angeles, Calif. A.
SMITH, Eva Florence.
Am. b. Mansfield, O.; ad. 1934 New York. M.
SMITH, Francis [or Francesco].
Eng. b. Italy; ac. 1770-1802 in London. B-DNB.
SMITH, Francis Berkeley. (Ill)
Am. b. Astoria, L. I., N. Y. 1868; ad. 1934 Paris. A.
SMITH, F. Carl. *see* Smith, C. F.
SMITH, Francis Drexel.
Am. b. Chicago 1874; ad. 1934 Colo. Springs, Colo. A-F.
SMITH, Francis Hopkinson.
Am. Balt., Md. 1838-1915 New York. A012-C-F-15-46.
SMITH, Frank Hill.
Am. Boston, Mass. 1841-1904 Same. A05-C-F-15-47.
SMITH, Frank Vining.
Am. ad. 1934 Boston. M.
SMITH, Frederick William. (S)
Eng. ex. 1818-1835 in London. B-DNB.
SMITH, F. M. Bell. *see* Bell-Smith.
SMITH, Gabriel. (Eg)
Eng. London 1724-1783. B-DNB.
SMITH, Gean.
Am. b. N. Y. State 1851; d. 1928 Galveston, Tex. A026.
SMITH, George.
Eng. Chichester 1713-1776 London. B-DNB.
SMITH, George.
Eng. London 1829-1901 Same. B.
SMITH, George Girdler. (Eg)
Am. Danvers, Mass. 1795-1859 Boston. F-2-7-169-184.
SMITH, George Melville.
Am. b. 1879; ex. 1934 in Chicago. M.
SMITH, Gertrude Binney.
Am. b. 1873; d. 1932 Beverly, Mass. A029.
SMITH, [Mrs.] Gertrude Roberts.
Am. b. Cambridge, Mass. 1869; ad. 1934 New Orleans, La. A.
SMITH, Gladys K.
Am. b. Phila., Pa. 1888; ad. 1934 Same. A.
SMITH, Grainger.
Eng. b. Hull 1892. Wa1929.
SMITH, Granville Walter.
see Granville-Smith, W.
SMITH, Gregory.
Am. ad. 1935 Old Lyme, Conn. M.

SMITH, Harriet Frances.
Am. b. Worcester, Mass. 1873; ad. 1934 W. Roxbury, Mass. A.
SMITH, Harry Knox.
Am. b. Phila., Pa. 1879; ad. 1934 New York. A-F.
SMITH, Hely Augustus Morton.
Eng. b. Dorset 1862; ad. 1934 London. Wa.
SMITH, Henry Pember.
Am. Waterford, Conn. 1854-1907 Asbury Park, N. J. A06-B-C-F.
SMITH, Herbert Luther.
Eng. 1811-1870. B.
SMITH, Hervey [Captain].
Br. ac. 1759-1770. Fa-M.
SMITH, Holmes.
Am. b. Keighley, Eng. 1863; ad. 1934 St. Louis, Mo. A.
SMITH, Hope.
Am. b. Prov., R. I. 1879; ad. 1934 Same. A.
SMITH, Howard Everett.
Am. b. West Windham, N. H. 1885; ad. 1934 Boston. A-F-W.
SMITH, Hugh Bellingham.
Eng. ac. 1891-1921 in London. B.
SMITH, Irwin Elwood.
Am. b. Parsons, Kan. 1893; ad. 1934 Topeka, Kan. A.
SMITH, Isabel E. (Min)
Mrs. F. Carl Smith.
Am. b. Cinn., O.; ad. 1934 Pasadena, Calif. A-F-W.
SMITH, Ishmael. (S)
Am. b. Barcelona, Sp. 1886; ad. 1934 New York. A.
SMITH, Jack Wilkinson.
Am. b. Paterson, N. J. 1873; ad. 1934 Alhambra, Calif. A-F.
SMITH, Jacob Getlar.
Am. b. New York 1898; ad. 1934 Sunnyside, L. I., N. Y. A.
SMITH, James B.
Am. early 19th Cent. in New York. M.
SMITH, James Calvert.
Am. ad. 1934 Falls Village, Conn. M.
SMITH, James P. (Min)
Am. b. 1803; d. 1888 Phila., Pa. F-6.
SMITH, Jesse Willcox. (Ill)
Am. b. Phila., Pa.; d. 1935 Same.
Obit. N. Y. papers, 5-4-1935-A-F-W-46.
SMITH, John. (Eg)
Eng. 1652?-1742. B-DNB.
SMITH, John. (S)
Ir. b. Dublin; d. 1812 Same. B.
SMITH, John [The Younger].
Eng. Chichester 1717-1764/9 Same. B-Bd-DNB.
SMITH, John ["Warwick Smith"].
Eng. b. 1749; d. 1831 in London. B-DNB.
SMITH, John Francis.
Am. b. Chicago; ad. 1934 San Diego, Calif. A.
SMITH, John Orrin. (Eg)
Eng. 1799-1843. DNB.
SMITH, John Raphael.
Eng. Derby 1752-1812 Doncaster. B-Bd-DNB-E.
SMITH, John Reubens. (Eg)
Am. England 1770/5-1849 New York. F-2-6-7.
SMITH, Joline Butler.
Am. ad. 1915 New Haven, Conn. A12.
SMITH, Joseph E.
Am. ad. 1934 New Orleans, La. M.
SMITH, Joseph Lindon.
Am. b. Pawtucket, R. I. 1862; ad. 1934 Dublin, N. H. A-F-W.
SMITH, Judson de Jonge.
Am. b. Grand Haven, Mich. 1880; ad. 1934 Woodstock, N. Y. A.
SMITH, Jules Andre. (Et)
Am. b. Hong Kong, China 1880; ad. 1931 Pine Orchard, Conn. A28-F-W16.
SMITH, Leonard John.
Scot. b. Aberdeen 1885; ad. 1934 London. Wa.
SMITH, Letta Crapo.
Am. Flint, Mich. 1862-1921 Boston, Mass. A023-F-W14-46.
SMITH, Leyland Croft.
Am. b. Opelika, Ala. 1910; ad. 1934 Same. A.
SMITH, Linus Burr.
Am. b. Minn., Minn. 1899; ad. 1934 Manhattan, Kan. A.
SMITH, Louise Jordan.
Am. Warrenton, Va. 1873-1928 Lynchburg, Va. A026.
SMITH, Marcella [Claudia Heber].
Am. b. East Molesey, Surrey, Eng. 1887; ad. 1934 Wash., D. C. A.
SMITH, Margery Hoffman.
Am. b. Portland, Ore. 1888; ad. 1934 Same. A.
SMITH, [Mrs.] Marrow Stuart.
Am. b. Staunton, Va. 1889; ad. 1934 Norfolk, Va. A.
SMITH, Marshall J., Jr.
Am. b. New Orleans, La.; d. Covington, Ky. F-183.
SMITH, Matthew.
Eng. b. Halifax, N. S. 1879; ad. 1934 London. Wa1929-825.
SMITH, May Mott. *see* Mott-Smith, M.
SMITH, [Mrs.] Minnie Walker.
Am. b. New Haven, Conn. 1883; ad. 1934 Same. A.
SMITH, Myrtis.
Am. ad. 1934 Memphis, Tenn. M.
SMITH, Oliver Phelps. (Mu)
Am. b. Hartford, Conn. 1867; ad. 1934 Mt. Vernon, N. Y. A.
SMITH, Percy John. (Et)
Eng. ad. 1934 London. Wa.
SMITH, R. Harmer.
Am. b. Jersey City, N. J. 1906; ad. 1934 Same. M.
SMITH, Reginald.
Eng. Bristol 1855-1925 London. B.
SMITH, Robert Brooks.
Am. Brooklyn, N. Y. 1857; ad. 1934 Jersey City, N. J. M.
SMITH, Robert J.
Am. ad. 1934 Dayton, O. M.
SMITH, Rosamond Lombard.
see Bouvé, [Mrs.] R. S.
SMITH, Russell.
Am. Glasgow, Scot. 1812-1897 Weldon, Pa. F.

SMITH, Sarah K.
Am. b. Rio Vista, Calif.; ad. 1934 Wheaton, Ill. A.
SMITH, Sidney. (Cart)
Am. b. Bloomington, Ill. 1877; ad. 1934 Chicago. W.
SMITH, Sidney L. (Et)
Am. Foxboro, Mass. 1845-1919 Boston. F-7.
SMITH, Stephen Catterson.
Eng. Slupton 1806-1872 London. B-DNB.
SMITH, Sydney Ure.
Aust. ac. 1933 in Australia. M.
SMITH, Thomas [Major].
Am. ac. 1680-1693 in Boston. F.
SMITH, Thomas ["Smith of Derby"].
Eng. d. 1767/9 in Bristol. B-DNB.
SMITH, Thomas Herbert.
Am. b. New York 1877; ad. 1934 Wilton, Conn. A.
SMITH, [Mrs.] Thomas Herbert.
Am. ad. 1934 Wilton, Conn. M.
SMITH, Thomas Lochlan.
Am. Glasgow, Scot. 1835-1884 New York. C-F-15-182.
SMITH, Vernon.
Am. ad. 1935 Orleans, Mass. M.
SMITH, [Mrs.] Violet Thompson. (Min)
Am. b. Annapolis, Md. 1882; ad. 1934 W. Haddonfield, N. J. A.
SMITH, Virginia Jeffrey.
Am. b. Rochester, N. Y.; ad. 1934 Same. A.
SMITH, Wallace Herndon.
Am. b. St. Louis, Mo. 1901; ad. 1934 Same. A.
SMITH, Walter Granville.
see Granville-Smith, W.
SMITH, William.
Eng. Guildford 1707-1764 Shopmyke. B-DNB.
SMITH, William A.
Am. ad. 1934 Toledo, O. M.
SMITH, William Collingwood.
Eng. Greenwich 1815-1887 London. B.
SMITH, Woodward.
Aust. ac. 1933 in Australia. M.
SMITH, W. St. Thomas.
Ir.-Can. b. Belfast, Ir. 1862; ad. 1935 St. Thomas, Ont., Can. M.
SMITH, Wuanita. (Ill)
Am. b. Phila., Pa. 1866; ad. 1934 Same. A-F.
SMITH, Xanthus.
Am. Phila., Pa. 1838-1929 Weldon, Pa. A027.
SMITH-HALD, Frithjof.
Nor. b. Norway; d. 1903 Chicago. M.
SMITHARD, G. S.
Br. d. 1919 Johannesburg, So. Africa. Y01920-M.
SMITHBURN, Florence Bartley.
Am. b. New Augusta, Ind.; ad. 1934 Same. A.
SMITHER, John [or James]. (Eg)
Am. ac. 1768-1800 in Phila., Pa. F-2-7-147-184.
SMITS, Jakob.
Dut. Rotterdam 1855-1928. B-584.
SMITZ [or Smits], Caspar [or Gaspar].
Dut. ac. 1689-1707 in Dublin, Ir. B-DNB.
SMOOT, Margaret. (S)
Am. b. Lakeport, Calif. 1907; ad. 1934 Maitland, Fla. A.
SMUL, Ethel L.
Am. ex. 1935 New York. M.
SMUTNY, Joseph S.
Am. Bohemia 1855-1903 New York. A04.
SMYTH [or Smith], Edward. (S)
Ir. b. Ireland 1746/9; d. 1812 Dublin. B-DNB.
SMYTH, Eugene Leslie.
Am. New York 1857-1932 Townshend, Vt. M-Obit. N. Y. papers, 5-6-1932.
SMYTH, John. (S)
Eng. 1775?-1834? DNB.
SMYTH, Margarita Pumelly.
Am. b. Newburgh, N. Y. 1873; ad. 1926 Watertown, Mass. F-WXI.
SMYTH, Montague.
Eng. b. London; ad. 1934 Same. Wa.
SMYTH, Samuel Gordon. (Mu)
Am. b. Phila., Pa. 1891; ad. 1934 Upper Darby, Pa. A-F.
SMYTHE, Lionel Percy.
Scot. Edinburgh 1840-1918 London. B.
SNAPERS, Pieter.
Flem. Antwerp 1592-1667 Brussels. B-C-722.
SNEAD, Louise Willis. (Min)
Mrs. Harry Vairm Snead.
Am. b. Charleston, S. C.; ad. 1934 New York. A.
SNEDEKER, Virginia.
Am. ex. 1935 New York. M.
SNELL, Florence Francis.
Mrs. Henry Bagley Snell.
Am. b. London, Eng.; ad. 1934 New Hope, Pa. A.
SNELL, Henry Bayley.
Am. b. Richmond, Eng. 1858; ad. 1934 New Hope, Pa. A-B-F-W.
SNELL, Lulu M.
Am. ad. 1934 Toledo, O. M.
SNELL, Patricia Von Hoyt.
Am. ad. 1934 New Dorp, S. I., N. Y. M.
SNELLINCK [or Snellincx], Jan I.
Flem. Mechlin 1544/9-1638 Antwerp. B-C-722.
SNOW, Edward Taylor.
Am. Phila., Pa. 1844-1913 Same. A0XI.
SNOWDEN, Elsie Brooke.
Am. b. Ashton, Md. 1887; ad. 1934 Same. A.
SNOWDEN, George Holburn. (S)
Am. b. Yonkers, N. Y. 1902; ad. 1934 New York. A.
SNYDER, Clarence W.
Am. b. Phila., Pa. 1873; ad. 1934 Same. A.
SNYDER, Corydon G.
Am. ad. 1934 Chicago, Ill. A.
SNYDER, Eugene G.
Am. ad. 1934 Toledo, O. M.
SNYDER, Frans.
Flem. Antwerp 1579-1657 Same. B-Bd-C-E-722.
SNYDER, Harold E. (Ill)
Am. ad. 1934 Phila., Pa. M.
SNYDER[or Snayers], Hendrick.
Flem. b. Antwerp 1612; [No death date] B.
SNYDER, Margaret E.
Mrs. Edward Danell.
Am. ad. 1934 New York. M.

SNYDER, William Henry.
Am. b. Brooklyn, N. Y. 1829-1910 Same. A09.
SNYDERS, Pieter [or Petrus].
Flem. Antwerp 1681-1752 Same. B-Bd-C.
SO-AMI [Shinso].
Jap. J., Vol. 1, page 93.
SOBEI, Kinkozan.
Jap. ex. 1927 in Tokyo, Jap. M.
SOBLE, Jack [John J.]
Am. b. Russia 1893; ad. 1934 New York. A.
SOBUN, Morikawa.
Jap. ac. 19th Cent. in Japan. J., Vol. 2, page 105.
SODERBERG, Yngve Edward. (Et)
Am. b. Chicago 1896; ad. 1935 Mystic, Conn. A28.
SÖDERNARK, Johan Per.
Swe. Stockholm 1822-1848. B-C.
SÖDERSTON, Herman.
Am. Sweden 1862-1926 New Haven, Conn. A023-F.
SÖDERSTON, Leon.
Am. ad. 1935 Yonkers, N. Y. M.
SÖDERSTROM, Clare.
Am. b. Omaha, Neb.; ad. 1934 W. Los Angeles, Calif. M.
SODINI, Dante. (S)
It. Florence 1858-1935 Same. B-M-Obit. N. Y. papers, 2-2-1935.
SODOMA, Il.
[Giovanni Antonio de Bazzi.]
It. Vercelli 1477-1549 Siena. B-Bd-C-E-V-722.
SOELEN, Theodore. *see* Van Soelen, T.
SOELLNER, Oscar Daniel.
Am. b. Chicago 1890; ad. 1934 Dixon, Ill. A.
SOEST [or Zoest], Conrad von.
Ger. ac. 1405-1422. M.
SOEST, Gérard von.
Ger. Westphalia 1637-1681 London. B.
SOEST, Louis van.
Dut. b. The Hague 1867. B.
SOEST, Meister von.
Ger. ac. 1250-1270. M.
SOFFICI, Audenzo.
It. b. 1879; ac. 1934 in Florence. M-866.
SOGA, Keisai.
Jap. ac. 1815-1842 in Japan. M.
SOGGI, Niccolò.
It. Arvezzo 1480-1551 Same. C-V.
SOGLIANO, Giovanni Antonio.
It. Florence 1492-1544 Same. B-V.
SOGLOW, Otto. (Cart)
Am. b. New York 1900; ad. 1934 Same. M.
SOHIER, Alice Ruggles.
Am. b. Quincy, Mass. 1880; ad. 1934 Concord, Mass. A.
SOHN, August Wilhelm.
Ger. Berlin 1829-1899 Bonn. B-C.
SOHN, Hedda. (Ill)
Am. ad. 1934 New York. M.
SOHN, Karl Ferdinand.
Ger. Berlin 1805-1867 Cologne. B-C.
SOIRON, F. D. (Eg)
Eng. ac. 1790 in London. B.
SOJARA, Il. *see* Gatti, Bernardino.
SOKOKUJI [or Shokokuji].
Jap. d. 1781 in Japan. J., Vol. 1, page 88.
SOKOL, Koloman. (Eg)
Am. b. Czec.; ad. 1934 New York. M.
SOKOLE, Miron.
Am. ad. 1935 New York. M.
SOKOLOV, Peter I.
Rus. 1828-1889. B-M.
SOKOLSKY, Sulamith.
Am. ad. 1934 New York. M.
SOLA, Antonio. (S)
Sp. ac. 19th Cent. in Madrid. B.
SOLANA, José Gutiérrez.
Sp. b. 1886; ad. 1934 Madrid. M.
SOLANA, Júan.
Sp. ac. 1402 in Spain. M.
SOLANA, Nicolás.
Sp. ac. 1401-1407. 774.
SOLARI, Christoforo. (S)
It. Milanese. Hs.
SOLARI, Mary.
Am. b. 1849; d. 1929 in Memphis, Tenn. A027.
SOLARIO, Andrea da.
It. Solario 1460/5-1515/30 Pavia. B-Bd-C-722.
SOLARIO, Antonio [Lo Zingaro].
It. Civita 1382?-1455 Naples. E.
SOLDI, Andrea.
It. Florence 1682-1768/9. B.
SOLDI, Émile Arthur. (S)
Fr. Paris 1846-1906. B.
SOLDWEDEL, Frederic.
Am. b. New York 1886; ad. 1934 Same. F-M.
SOLE, Giovanni Giuseppe dal.
It. Bologna 1654-1719 Same. B.
SOLER, Urbici. (S)
Mex. ex. 1934 Mexico City. M.
SOLIMENA, Francesco [Ciccio].
It. Naples 1657-1747 Same. B-C-722.
SOLIS, Francisco de.
Sp. Madrid 1629-1684 Same. B-C.
SOLIS, Virgil. (Eg)
Ger. Nüremberg 1514-1562. B-Bd.
SOLMAN, Joseph.
Am. b. Russia 1909; ad. 1934 New York. M.
SOLOMAN, Abraham.
Eng. London 1823-1862 France. B-C-DNB.
SOLOMAN, Maude Beatrice.
Mrs. Joseph Solomon.
Am. b. Seattle, Wash.; ad. 1934 New York. A.
SOLOMON, Simeon.
Eng. London 1840-1905 Same. B-DNB.
SOLOMON, Solomon Joseph.
Eng. London 1860-1927. B-C-Wa01929.
SOLOMONS, Estella Frances.
Ir. b. Dublin; ex. 1935 London. Wa.
SOLON, Harry.
Am. b. San Fran., Calif. 1873. A.
SOLON, Léon Victor. (S)
Am. b. England 1872; ad. 1934 New York. F-W.
SOMER, Paulus van I.
Flem. Antwerp 1576-1621 London. B-DNB.
SOMER, Paulus van III.
Dut. Amsterdam 1649-1694 London. B-DNB.

SOMERS, Helene.
Am. ad. 1935 Brooklyn, N. Y. M.
SOMERS, Louis Jean.
Belg. Antwerp 1813-1880 Same. B-C.
SOMERSCALES, Thomas Jacques.
Eng. Hull 1842-1928. B-Wa01929.
SOMERVILLE, Charles.
Scot. b. Falkirk 1870; ad. 1934 Ashford. Wa.
SOMERVILLE, Howard.
Scot. b. Dundee; ad. 1934 London. Wa.
SOMM, Henri. (Cari)
Fr. b. 1810; d. 1889 in Paris. B.
SOMMER, Edwin G.
Am. b. Roseville, N. J. 1899; ad. 1934 Macedonia, O. A.
SOMMER, William.
Am. b. Detroit, Mich. 1867; ad. 1934 Macedonia, O. M.
SOMOV, Konstantin Andreevich.
Rus. b. Leningrad 1869; ad. 1935 Paris. DBA-E.
SOMPEL [or Sompelen], Pieter van. (Eg)
Flem. Antwerp 1600-1643. B.
SON [or Zoon], Jan Frans van.
Flem. Antwerp 1658-1718/23 London. B-C-DNB.
SON, Joris [or Georg] van.
Flem. Antwerp 1623-1667 Same. B-C.
SONDERLAND, John Baptist Wilhelm.
Ger. Düsseldorf 1804/5-1878. B-C.
SONDERMANN, Hermann.
Ger. Berlin 1832-1901 Düsseldorf. B-C.
SONDHEIMER, Rosalee. (S)
Am. ad. 1934 Memphis, Tenn. M.
SONJE, Jan Gabrielsz.
Dut. Delft 1625-1707 Rotterdam. B-C.
SONN, Albert H.
Am. b. Newark, N. J. 1869; ad. 1934 Same. A.
SONNE, Jörgen Valentin.
Dan. Zealand 1801-1890. B-C.
SONNICHSEN, Yngvar.
Am. b. Oslo, Nor. 1875; ad. 1934 Seattle, Wash. A-F-W.
SONNTAG, William Louis.
Am. Pittsburgh, Pa. 1822-1900 New York. A02-B-C-F-4-15-46.
SONREL, Elizabeth.
Fr. b. Tours; ac. 1893-1910 in Paris. B.
SOOLEMAKER [or Solemacher], Jan Frans.
Flem. Antwerp 1635?-1665/6 Italy. B-C.
SOOY, Louise Pinkney.
Am. b. Blairstown, Ia. 1889; ad. 1934 Los Angeles, Calif. A.
SOPER, Eileen Alice.
Eng. b. Enfield 1905; ad. 1934 Welwyn. Wa.
SOPER, Thomas George.
Eng. b. London 1870; ad. 1934 Welwyn. B-Wa.
SOPHER, Aaron. (Et)
Am. ex. 1934 Baltimore, Md. M.
SÖRENSEN, Carl Frederick.
Dan. Besserly 1818-1879 Copenhagen. B-C.
SÖRENSEN, Carl Sofus Wilhelm. (S)
Am. b. Denmark 1864; ad. 1915 Chicago. A12.
SÖRENSEN, Hendrik.
Nor. ad. 1935 Oslo. M.
SÖRENSEN, Olga.
Dan. b. Denmark. DBA.
SORENSEN, Rex. (S)
Am. b. Omaha, Neb. 1908; ad. 1934 Oak Grove, Ore. M.
SORENSON-DIEMAN, Clara Barth Leonard. (S)
Am. b. Ind. 1877; ad. 1926 Cedar Rapids, Ia. A20-F-181.
SORGH [or Zorg], Hendrik Maertensz.
Dut. Rotterdam 1611/21-1670/8. B-C-722.
SORINE [or Sorin], Savely.
Am. b. Poltask, Rus. 1886; ac. 1934 U. S. DBA-912.
SORALLA Y BASTIDA, Joaquin.
Sp. Valencia 1862/3-1923 Madrid. B-E-748.
SORIA, Martin de.
Sp. ac. 1483-1499 in Spain. M.
SORKAU, Albert.
Fr. b. Toul 1874. DBA.
SOSEN, Mori. [Morikata].
Jap. 1747-1821. J., Vol. 2, page 95.
SOTAN, Oguri.
Jap. d. 1464/70. J., Vol. 1, page 91.
SOTATSU, Towaraya. (Mu)
Jap. J., Vol. 2, page 49.
SOTOMAYÓR, Fernando Alvárez.
Sp. b. 1875 in Spain. M.
SOTTEK, Frank.
Am. b. Toledo, O. 1874; ad. 1934 Same. A.
SOTTER, George William.
Am. b. Pittsburgh, Pa. 1879. A28-F-W.
SOUCHON, François.
Fr. Allais 1787-1857 Lille. B-C.
SOUDBININ, Seraphin. (S)
Rus. ex. 1924 New York. M.
SOUDEIKIN, Sergei Yurievich.
Am. b. Russia; ad. 1934 New York. M-912.
SOUGEZ, Madeleine.
Fr. b. Bordeaux 1891; ad. 1934 Paris. DBA.
SOULACROIX, Joseph Frédéric Charles.
Fr. b. Montpelier 1825; ac. 1850 in Paris; [No death date] B.
SOULARY, Claude.
Fr. Lyons 1792-1870 St. Étienne. B.
SOULAS, Louis Joseph.
Fr. b. Orléans 1905. DBA.
SOULE, Charles.
Am. b. Freeport, Me. 1809; [No death date]. M.
SOULEN, Henry J. (Ill)
Am. ex. 1933 New York. M.
SOULES, Eugène Edouard.
Fr. ac. 1831-1876 in Paris. B.
SOUMY, Joseph Paul Marius.
Fr. Puy 1831-1863 Lyons. B.
SOUNES, William Henry. (S)
Eng. London 1830-1873 Sheffield. B.
SOURDY, Louise.
Fr. b. Paris 1900. DBA.
SOUSA-CARDOZO, Amadeo de.
Por. 1887-1918. M.
SOUTER, John B. (Et)
Eng. ad. 1934 London. Wa.
SOUTHALL, Joseph Edward.
Eng. b. Nottingham 1861; ad. 1934 Birmingham. B-Wa.
SOUTHAMPTON [Lady].
Eng. ex. 1934 in London. M.

SOUTHER, John K.
Am. b. 1870; d. 1909 Wash., D. C. A08.
SOUTHER, Lyna Chase.
Mrs. Latham T. Souther.
Am. b. St. Louis, Mo. 1880; ad. 1934 Springfield, Ill. A.
SOUTHWARD, George.
Am. Salem, Mass. 1803-1876 Same. F-6-169.
SOUTHWICK, Elsie Whitmore. (Min)
Am. b. Prov., R. I.; ac. 1924. A12-46.
SOUTHWICK, Jeanie Lea.
Am. b. Worcester, Mass.; ad. 1934 Same. A-F.
SOUTHWICK, Katherine.
Mrs. Burton Keeler.
Am. b. Buxton, Me. 1887; ad. 1934 Scarsdale, N. Y. A.
SOUTHWORTH, Fred W.
Am. b. Canada 1860; ad. 1934 Tacoma, Wash. A.
SOUTHWORTH, Nathaniel. (Min)
Am. Scituate, Mass. 1806-1858 Dorchester, Mass. 6.
SOUTHWORTH, William.
Am. ac. 1850 in Phila., Pa. F.
SOUTINE, Haim.
Lithuanian. b. Smilovitchi 1894. DBA-797.
SOUTMAN, Pieter Claesz.
Dut. Haarlem 1580-1657. B-C.
SOUVERBIE, Jean.
Fr. b. Bilancourt 1891; ex. 1933 Chicago. DBA.
SOUZOUKI, Ruytchi.
Jap. ac. 1927 in Paris. DBA.
SOWDEN, John.
Eng. b. Bradford 1838. [No death date.] M.
SOYER, Elizabeth Emma [née Jones].
Eng. London 1813-1842 Same. B-DNB.
SOYER, Isaac.
Am. ad. 1934 New York. M.
SOYER, Moses.
Am. b. 1898; ad. 1935 New York. M.
SOYER, Paul Constant.
Fr. Paris 1823-1903. B-C.
SOYER, Raphael.
Am. b. Russia 1899; ad. 1934 New York. A.
SOZONOV, V.
Rus. ad. 1934 London. M.
SOZU, Yeishin.
[Called the "Fra Angelico of Japan."]
Jap. Buddhist Priest Fujiwara Period. (794-1186). M.
SPACKMAN, Cyril Saunders. (S)
Am. b. Cleveland, O. 1887; ad. 1934 London. A-F-Wa.
SPADA, Lionello.
It. Bologna 1576-1622 Parma. B-C-722.
SPADARA, Micco. *see* Garguilio, D.
SPADER, William Edgar.
Am. b. Brooklyn, N. Y. 1892; ad. 1934 New York. A-F.
SPADINI, Armando.
It. Florence 1883-1925 Rome. E.
SPAEDONCK, Cornelis van.
Dut. Tilburg 1756-1840 Paris. B.
SPAENDONCK, Geradus van.
Dut. Tilburg 1746-1822 Paris. B-C-722.
SPAETH, [Mrs.] Carola.
Am. b. Phila., Pa. 1883; ad. 1934 Princeton, N. J. A.
SPAETH, Janet. (S)
Am. ex. 1934 New York. M.
SPAETH, Marie Haughton.
Mrs. J. Duncan Spaeth.
Am. b. Hanover, N. H.; ad. 1934 Princeton, N. J. A-F.
SPAFARD, Myra B.
Am. b. Manchester, Mich.; ac. 1931. A28.
SPAGNA, Lo.
[Giovanni di Pietro.]
It. (Umbrian) 1450/60-1529/30. B-C-E-722.
SPAGNA, Vincent.
Am. b. Italy; ex. 1935 New York. M.
SPAGNOLETTO. *see* Ribera, José.
SPAGNULO, Lo. *see* Crespi, G. M.
SPALDING, Elizabeth.
Am. b. Erie, Pa.; ad. 1934 Denver, Colo. A.
SPANG, Frederick A.
Am. Norristown, Pa. 1834-1891 Reading, Pa. M.
SPANGENBERG, Gustav Adolf.
Ger. Hamburg 1828-1891 Berlin. B-C.
SPANGENBERG, Louis.
Ger. Hamburg 1824-1893 Berlin. B-C.
SPANIEL, Otaka. (S)
Croatian. (Modern) 798.
SPANISH Artists.
see books 699-719-774-805-819; *also* consult the Hispanic Society of America, New York.
SPANTON, Mabel Henry.
Eng. b. Hanley 1874; ex. 1934 London. DBA-Wa.
SPANZOTTI, Gian Martino [Piedmontese].
It. ac. 1480-1524/8 in Casale. B.
SPARHAWK-JONES, Elizabeth.
Am. b. Balt., Md. 1885; ad. 1934 Phila., Pa. A-F-WX1-757.
SPARK, Joseph.
Am. b. Jersey City, N. J. 1896; ad. 1934 Detroit, Mich. A.
SPARKS, Arthur Watson.
Am. Wash., D. C. 1870-1919 Phila., Pa. A016-F.
SPARKS, Will.
Am. b. St. Louis, Mo. 1862; ad. 1934 San Fran., Calif. A-F-W.
SPARRE, Louis [Count].
Swe. b. 1863. Fa-M.
SPARROW, Louise Winslow Kidder. (S)
Mrs. Herbert George Sparrow.
Am. b. Malden, Mass. 1884; ad. 1934 Wash., D. C. A-W.
SPAULDING, Henry Plympton.
Am. b. Cambridge, Mass. 1868; ad. 1934 Brookline, Mass. A.
SPEAKMAN, Anna Weatherly Parry. (Ill)
Mrs. T. Henry Speakman.
Am. b. Springfield, Ill.; ad. 1934 Stamford, Conn. A.
SPEAKMAN, Russel Lindsay.
Mrs. Harold Speakman.
Am. b. Topeka, Kan.; ad. 1934 Redding Ridge, Conn. A.
SPEAR, Arthur Prince.
Am. b. Wash., D. C. 1879; ad. 1934 Boston. A-F-W.

SPEAR, F. H. (Et)
Eng. ad. 1934 London. M.
SPEAR, THOMAS T.
Am. b. 1803. [No death date.] M.
SPEARS, ETHEL.
Am. b. Chicago 1903; ad. 1934 Same. A.
SPEED, HAROLD.
Eng. b. London 1873. Wa.
SPEED, JOHN. (Cartographer)
Eng. ac. 1610 London. M.
SPEICHER, EUGENE EDWARD.
Am. b. Buffalo, N. Y. 1883; ad. 1935 New York. A-F-W-1-46-105-172-585-694-779.
SPEIGHT, FRANCIS.
Am. b. Windsor, N. C. 1896; ad. 1935 New York. A.
SPELLMAN, COREEN MARY.
Am. ad. 1934 Forney, Texas. A.
SPELLMAN, JOHN A.
Am. b. Owatonna, Minn. 1880; ad. 1934 Oak Park, Ill. A-F.
SPENCE, BENJAMIN EDWARD. (S)
Eng. Liverpool 1822-1866 Leghorn, It. B-DNB.
SPENCE, PERCY F. S.
Aust. b. Sydney, N. S. W. 1868. B.
SPENCE, ROBERT. (Et)
Eng. b. 1871; ad. 1934 London. Wa.
SPENCE, WILLIAM. (S)
Eng. Chester 1793-1849 Liverpool. B.
SPENCELAYH, CHARLES.
Eng. b. Rochester 1865; ad. 1934 Kent. Wa.
SPENCELEY, J. WINFRED. (Eg)
Am. b. Boston, Mass. 1865; ac. 1905 Same. F-7.
SPENCER, EDNA ISBESTER. (S)
Am. b. St. John, N. B. Can.; ad. 1934 Waban, Mass. A.
SPENCER, EMMELINE.
Am. ad. 1934 Toledo, O. M.
SPENCER, FREDERICK R.
Am. Lenox, N. Y. 1806-1875 Wampoville, N. Y. B-Bd-F-15.
SPENCER, GERVASE [or Jarvis]. (Min)
Eng. ac. 1735-1763 in London. B-DNB.
SPENCER, GILBERT.
Eng. b. Cookman 1892; ad. 1934 London. Wa-825.
SPENCER, GUY RAYMOND. (Cart)
Am. b. Jasper Co., Mo. 1878; ad. 1934 Omaha, Neb. A12-W.
SPENCER, HENRY CECIL.
Am. b. Mangum, Okla. 1903; ad. 1934 College Station, Tex. A.
SPENCER, HOWARD BONNELL.
Am. b. Plainfield, N. J.; ad. 1934 New York. A.
SPENCER, JEAN V.
Am. ad. 1935 Trenton, N. J. M.
SPENCER, JIM-EDD. (Ill)
Am. ad. 1934 Kansas City, Mo. A29.
SPENCER, LAVINA BINGHAM.
see Bingham, L. [Countess].
SPENCER, LEONTINE.
Am. ad. 1934 Brooklyn, N. Y. M.
SPENCER, [Mrs.] LILLIE MARTIN.
Am. England 1847-1902 New York. A04.
SPENCER, MARGARET FULTON.
Am. b. Phila., Pa. 1882; ad. 1934 New Hope, Pa. A-DBA.
SPENCER, MARY.
Am. b. Fitchburg, Mass.; ad. 1934 Brooklyn, N. Y. A.
SPENCER, NILES.
Am. b. Pawtucket, R. I. 1893; ad. 1934 New York. A.
SPENCER, NOËL WOODWARD. (Et)
Eng. b. Nuneaton 1900; ad. 1934 Birmingham. Wa.
SPENCER, ROBERT.
Am. Harvard, Neb. 1879-1931 New Hope, Pa. A028-DBA-F-W16.
SPENCER, STANLEY. (Mu)
Eng. ad. 1934 Cookham. Wa-825.
SPENCER, W. CLYDE.
Am. Peoria, Ill. 1874-1915 New York. A012.
SPENCER-PRYSE, [Captain] GERALD.
Eng. b. 1881; ad. 1934 London. Wa.
SPENLOVE-SPENLOVE, FRANK.
Eng. Stirling, N. B. 1866-1933 London. B-M-Wa1929-Obit. Studio, 8-1933.
SPERANZA, GIOVANNI.
It. Venice 1480-1536. B-C-V.
SPERLING, HECKEL CATHERINE.
Ger. 1699-1741. M.
SPERLING, JOHANN CHRISTIAN.
Ger. Halle 1691-1746 Anspach. B-C.
SPERRY, ARMSTRONG. (Ill)
Am. ad. 1934 Silvermine, Conn. M.
SPICER, HENRY. (Min)
Eng. Reepham 1741/3-1804 London. B-DNB.
SPICER-SIMSON, MARGARET SCHMIDT. (Min)
Mrs. Theodore Spicer-Simson.
Am. b. Wash., D. C. 1874; ad. 1915 Paris. A12.
SPICER-SIMSON, THEODORE. (S)
Am. b. Havre, Fr. 1871; ad. 1934 New York. A-Cs-F-W.
SPICUZZA, FRANCESCO J.
Am. b. Sicily 1883; ad. 1934 Milwaukee, Wis. A-F.
SPIEGEL, DORIS. (Ill)
Am. ad. 1935 New York. M.
SPIERINCKX, PETER NICOLAS.
Flem. Antwerp 1635-1711 Same. B-C.
SPIERS, HARRY.
Am. b. Selsea, Essex, Eng. 1869; ad. 1934 Boston, Mass. A-F.
SPILBERG [or Spielberg], JOHANNES.
Ger. Düsseldorf 1619-1690 Same. B.
SPILSBURY, F. B.
Eng. ac. 1795 in England. B.
SPILSBURY, JOHN. (Eg)
Eng. 1730?-1795? B-DNB.
SPILSBURY, JONATHAN. (Eg)
Eng. London; ac. 1760-1807 Same. B-DNB.
SPILSBURY, MARIA [Mrs. Taylor].
Eng. London 1777-1820 Ireland. B-DNB.
SPINELLO DI LUCA [Aretino].
It. Arezzo 1330/3-1410 Same. B-Bd-C-E-V-78.
SPIRIDON, IGNACE.
It. ac. 1900 in Paris. B.

SPITGERBER, August.
Ger. b. Steingaden 1844. B.

SPITZER, Adele R. (S)
Mrs. Oscar Spitzer.
Am. ad. 1934 New York. M.

SPITZER, Lydia.
Am. ad. 1934 Toledo, O. M.

SPITZWEG, Karl.
Ger. Munich 1808-1885 Same. B-C.

SPIVAK, H. David.
Am. b. Phila., Pa. 1893; ad. 1934 Denver, Colo. A.

SPIZZIRRI, Luigi.
Am. b. Spezzano, It. 1894; ad. 1934 Phila., Pa. A.

SPLIVATO, Wilna. (S)
Am. ex. 1933 in Paris. M.

SPONGBERG, Grace.
Am. ad. 1935 Chicago, Ill. M.

SPOONER, Charles. (Eg)
Br. d. 1767 in England. DNB.

SPOONER, Charles H.
Am. Phila., Pa. 1836-1901 Same. A04.

SPOTH-BENSON, Eda.
Am. b. Brooklyn, N. Y. 1898; ad. 1934 New York. A.

SPRAGUE, Florence. (S)
Am. b. Paulina, Ia.; ad. 1934 Des Moines, Ia. A.

SPRAGUE, Robert B.
Am. b. Dayton, O. 1904; ad. 1934 Same. A.

SPRAGUE-SMITH, Isabelle Dwight.
Mrs. Charles Sprague-Smith.
Am. b. Clinton, N. Y. 1861; ad. 1934 New York. A.

SPRANGER, Bartholomeus [Schilden].
Flem. Antwerp 1546-1627 Prague, Czec. B-C.

SPREAD, Henry Fenton.
Am. b. Kinsale, Ir. 1844; ad. 1926 Chicago. F-15.

SPRETER, Roy F. (Ill)
Am. ad. 1934 New York. M.

SPRINCHORN, Carl.
Am. b. Broby, Swe. 1887; ad. 1934 New York. A-F-W16.

SPRING, Alphons.
Ger. Libau, Rus. 1841/3-1908 Bad Oeynhaussen, Ger. B.

SPRING, Edward Adolphus. (S)
Am. b. New York 1837. [No death date.] F-15.

SPRING, E. W.
Am. ad. 1934 Toledo, O. M.

SPRINGER, Carl.
Am. b. Fultonham, O. 1874; d. 1935 Delaware, O. Obit. N. Y. papers, 8-13-1935 A-F.

SPRINGER, Charles Henry.
Am. Prov., R. I. 1857-1920. A018.

SPRINGER, Cornelis.
Dut. Amsterdam 1817-1891 Hilversum. B-C.

SPRINGER, Eva.
Am. b. Cimarron, N. M.; ad. 1934 Wash., D. C. A.

SPRINGINKLEE, Hans. (Eg)
Ger. ac. 1520-1540 in Nüremberg. B.

SPRINGWEILER, Erwin.
Am. ex. 1935 New York. M.

SPRONG, Gérard. *see* Verspronck, G.

SPRUANCE, Benton M. (Et)
Am. ad. 1934 New York. A.

SPRUNGER, Arthur L.
Am. b. Berne, Ind. 1897; ad. 1934 Goshen, Ind. A.

SPUNK, Robert Godfrey.
Am. Ger. 1862-1912 Ridgefield, N. J. A010.

SPURGEON, Edna.
Am. Harlan, Ia. 1903; ad. 1934 Galva, Ia. A.

SPURRIER, Steven. (Ill)
Eng. b. London 1878; ad. 1934 Same. Wa-778.

"SPY." (Cartoonist)
see Udvardy, Imre László.
see Ward, [Sir] Leslie.

SPYCK, Hendryck van der.
Dut. ac. 1667 The Hague. B.

SQUARCIONE, Francesco.
It. Padua 1394-1474 Same. B-Bd-C.

SQUIRE, Maud Hunt. (Et)
Am. b. Cinn., O. 1873; ad. 1934 France. A-F.

SQUIRES, C. Clyde. (Ill)
Am. b. Salt Lake City, Utah 1883; ad. 1934 New York. A.

SQUIRES, Lawrence.
Am. Salt Lake City, Utah 1887-1928. A026.

SQUIRRELL, Leonard Russell. (Et)
Eng. b. Ipswich 1893; ad. 1934 Same. Wa.

ST. *see* Saint.

STAAL, Pierre Gustave Eugène.
Fr. Vertus 1817-1882 Ivey. B.

STAATS, Henry Philip.
Am. ad. 1934 Kent, Conn. M.

STABB, Charles I.
Eng. ac. 1908-1927. M.

STABLI, Adolph.
Swi. Winterhur 1843-1901 Munich, Ger. B.

STACEY, Anna Lee.
Mrs. John Franklin Stacey.
Am. b. Glasgow, Mo.; ad. 1934 Chicago. A-F-W.

STACEY, J. George.
Am. b. Fayette, N. Y. 1863; ad. 1934 Geneva, N. Y. A.

STACEY, John Franklin.
Am. b. Biddeford, Me. 1859; ad. 1934 Chicago. A-F-W.

STACEY, Lynn Nelson.
Am. b. Wash., D. C. 1903; ad. 1934 Des Moines, Ia. A.

STACKPOLE, Ralph. (S)
Am. b. Williams, Ore. 1885; ad. 1934 San Fran., Calif. A-F.

STACKPOOLE, Frederick. (Eg)
Eng. b. 1813; d. 1907 London. DNB.

STACQUET, Henri.
Belg. Belgium 1838-1906 Paris. B.

STACY, William.
Am. d. 1919 Burlington, Vt. A016.

STADLER, Joseph Constantin. (Eg)
Eng. ac. 1780-1812 in London. B.

STAFFORD, Mary.
Mrs. John R. Frazier.
Am. b. Chicago 1895; ad. 1934 Prov., R. I. A.

STAFFORD, P. Scott.
Am. ad. 1934 New York. M.

STAGG, Clarence Alfred.
Am. b. Nashville, Tenn. 1902; ad. 1934 Same. A.
STAGG, Hamilton. (Eg)
Eng. ex. 1933 in London. M.
STAGG, [Mrs.] Jessie A. (S)
Am. b. England; ad. 1934 New York. A28-Cs.
STAGG, William.
Eng. d. 1928 Bristol. Wa01929.
STAHL, M. Louise.
Am. b. Cinn., O.; ac. 1931. A28.
STAHR, Paul C. (Ill)
•Am. b. New York 1883; ad. 1934 Same. A-F.
STAIGG, Richard Morrell.
Am. Leeds, Eng. 1820-1881 Newport, R. I. C-F-4-6-15-45.
STAIR, [Mrs.] Ida M. (S)
Am. Logansport, Ind. 1857-1908 Denver, Colo. A023-181.
STALBEMT [or Staelbent], Adriaen van.
Flem. Antwerp 1580-1662 Same. B-C.
STALDER, Mary.
Am. ad. 1934 New York. M.
STALEY, Clarence W.
Am. b. Sanborn, Ind. 1892; ad. 1915 Martinsville, Ind. A12.
STALLAERT, Joseph.
Belg. Brabant 1825-1903 Brussels. B-C.
STAMATO, Frank. (S)
Am. b. 1897; ad. 1934 Phila., Pa. A.
STANFIELD, George Clarkson.
Eng. London 1828-1878. B-C-DNB.
STANFIELD, Marion Baar.
Am. b. New York 1895; ad. 1934 Same. A.
STANFIELD, William Clarkson.
Eng. Durham 1793-1867 London. B-Bd-C-DNB-E.
STANGÉ, Émile.
Am. b. Jersey City, N. J. 1863; ad. 1934 No. Hackensack, N. J. A.
STANGÉ, Madeleine Liebert von.
Ger. ex. 1934 New York. M.
STANHOPE, J. R. Spencer.
Eng. London 1829-1908 Florence, It. B-C.
STANILAND, Charles Joseph.
Eng. b. 1838; ac. 1896, London. [No death date.] M.
STANISIA, Sister.
Am. b. Chicago 1888; ad. 1934 Same. A.
STANISLAWSKI, Jan.
Pol. b. Poland 1860; d. 1906 Paris. B.
STANLAWS, Penrhyn [Adamson].
Am. b. Dundee, Scot. 1877; ad. 1934 New York. A-F-W.
STANLEY, George M. (S)
Am. b. Louisiana 1903; ad. 1934 Los Angeles, Calif. Cs.
STANLEY, James M.
Am. Canandaigua, N. Y. 1814-1872 Detroit, Mich. 46.
STANLEY, Jane C. Mahon.
Mrs. Louis Crandall Stanley.
Am. b. Detroit, Mich. 1863; ad. 1934 Ann Arbor, Mich. A.
STANLEY, Montague. (Actor-P)
Scot. Dundee 1809-1844 Bute. B-DNB.
STANNARD, Alfred.
Eng. Norwich 1806-1899. B-DNB.
STANNARD, Alfred George.
Eng. b. Norwich 1828; ex. 1851-1864 London; d. 1885. B.
STANNARD, Henry.
Eng. 1844-1920. Y01920.
STANNARD, Henry John Sylvester.
Eng. b. London 1870; ad. 1934 Bedford. Wa.
STANNARD, Joseph.
Eng. Norwich 1797-1830 Same. B-DNB-E.
STANNARD, Theresa Sylvester.
Eng. b. Flintwick 1898; ad. 1934 Bedford. Wa.
STANTON, Clark.
Eng. Birmingham 1832-1894. B.
STANTON, Elizabeth Cady.
Mrs. William H. Blake.
Am. b. New York 1894; ad. 1934 Same. A-F.
STANTON, Gideon Townsend.
Am. b. Morris, Minn. 1885; ad. 1934 New Orleans, La. A.
STANTON, [Sir] Herbert Hughes.
see Hughes-Stanton, H.
STANTON, Lucy Mary.
Am. Atlanta, Ga. 1875-1931 Athens, Ga. A028-F-W16-46.
STANTON, Samuel Ward.
Am. Newburgh, N. Y. 1870-1912 at sea. A010.
STANWYCK, Gary. (Actress-P)
Am. ex. 1934 New York. M.
STANZIONI, Massimo.
It. Naples 1585-1656 Same. B-C.
STAPELFELDT, Karsten. (Ill)
Am. ad. 1934 New York. M.
STAPLES, Clayton Henri.
Am. b. Osceola, Wis. 1892; ad. 1934 Wichita, Kan. A.
STAPLES, Owen.
Can. b. Stoke-under-Hann, Somerset, Eng. 1866; ad. 1935 Toronto, Ont. Can. M.
STAPLES, Robert Posonby.
Eng. b. 1853; ac. 1929 Cooktown, Eng. Wa1929.
STAPPEN [or Pierre], Charles van der. (S)
Belg. Brussels 1843-1910. B-Hs-798.
STAR [or Staren], Dirck van. (Eg)
Dut. ac. 1520-1550 in Holland. B.
STARK, Arthur James.
Eng. Chelsea 1831-1902 Surrey. DNB.
STARK, Forrest F. (S)
Am. b. Milwaukee, Wis. 1903; ad. 1934 Ind., Ind. A.
STARK, James.
Eng. Norwich 1794-1859 London. B-Bd-DNB-E.
STARK, Joseph August.
Aus. Gratz (Styria) 1782-1838 Same. B-C.
STARK, Otto.
Am. Ind., Ind. 1859-1926 Same. A023-F-181.
STARK, Robert. (S)
Eng. ac. 1883 in London. B-Hs.
STARKENBORGH, Jacobus Nicolas.
Dut. b. Holland 1822. [No death date.] B-M.

STARKS, Chloe Lesley.
Am. b. Ohio 1866; ad. 1915 Palo Alto, Calif. A12.
STARKWEATHER, William Howard Bloomfield.
Am. b. Edinburgh, Scot. 1879; ad. 1934 Brooklyn, N. Y. A-F-W.
STARNINA, Gherado.
It. Florence 1354?-1408 Same. B-C-V.
STARONOSSOV, P.
Rus. ad. 1934 Moscow. M.
STARR, Louisa.
Mrs. Enrico Francesco Canziani.
Eng. London 1845-1909 Same. B.
STARR, Maxwell B.
Am. b. Odessa, Rus. 1901; ad. 1934 New York. A.
STARRETT, Henrietta McCaig. (Ill)
Am. ad. 1935 Phila., Pa. M.
STARRETT, Virginia Frances. (Ill)
Am. b. 1901; d. 1931 Pasadena, Calif. A028.
STATON, Joseph. (Glass-P)
Eng. ac. 1800 in London. M.
STATTLER, Albert Cornel.
Pol. Cracow 1800-1882 Warsaw. B-C.
STAUFER, Joseph K.
Am. ad. 1934 Fieldston, N. Y. M.
STAUFFER, Edna Pennypacker.
Am. Phoenixville, Pa.; ad. 1934 New York. A.
STAUFFER, Karl.
Swi. Trübschachen 1857-1891 Florence, It. B-Bd.
STAVENITZ, Alexander R. (Eg)
Am. ad. 1934 New York. M.
STAVEREN, Johan Adriaensz van.
Dut. Leyden 1625-1668/9. B-C.
STCHEDRIN, Sylvester F. [The Younger].
Rus. b. 1791; d. 1830 Russia. M.
STCHUKIN, Stephen S.
Rus. b. 1758; d. 1828 Russia. M.
STEA, Cesare. (S)
Am. b. Bari, It. 1893; ad. 1934 New York. A-Cs-F.
STEAD, Fred.
Eng. b. Shipley 1863; ad. 1934 Bradford. Wa.
STEARNS, Frederic Wainwright.
Am. ad. 1934 Phila., Pa. A.
STEARNS, Junius Brutus [The Younger].
Am. Burlington, Vt. 1810-1885 Brooklyn, N. Y. C-F.
STEBBINS, Emma. (S)
Am. New York 1815-1882 Same. F-Hs-Ta-15.
STEBBINS, Marcia.
Am. ex. 1935 New York. M.
STEBBINS, Roland Stewart.
Am. b. Boston 1883; ad. 1934 Madison, Wis. A.
STEDMAN, Jeannette.
Am. b. 1880; d. 1924 Chicago. A021.
STEDMAN, Margaret Weir. (Min)
Am. ad. 1934 Haddonfield, N. J. M.
STEDMAN, Myrtle Kelly.
Am. b. Charleston, Ill. 1908; ad. 1934 Houston, Tex. A.
STEDMAN, Wilfred Henry.
Am. b. Liverpool, Eng. 1892; ad. 1934 Houston, Tex. A.
STEEL, James W. (Eg)
Am. Phila., Pa. 1799-1879 Same. F-7-40.
STEELE, Brandt Theodore.
Am. b. Battle Creek, Mich. 1870; ad. 1934 Ind., Ind. A-F.
STEELE, Christopher [or Edward].
["Count Steele."]
Eng. b. Egremont 1720; ac. 1756 in London. B-DNB.
STEELE, Frederic Dorr. (Ill)
Am. b. Marquette, Mich. 1873; ad. 1935 New York. A28-F-W.
STEELE, Theodore Clement.
Am. Owen Co., Ind. 1847-1926 Bloomington, Ind. A023-B-F-W14-181.
STEELE, Thomas Sedgwick.
Am. Hartford, Conn. 1845-1903 Swampscott, Mass. A04.
STEELE, Zulma.
Mrs. Neilson T. Parker.
Am. b. Appleton, Wis. 1881; ad. 1934 Woodstock, N. Y. A.
STEELER, Joseph Karl. *see* Stieler, J. K.
STEELINK, Willem.
Dut. b. Amsterdam 1856. B.
STEELL, Gourlay.
Scot. Edinburgh 1819-1894 Same. B-C.
STEEN, Franciscus van den.
Flem. Antwerp 1604-1672 Vienna, Aus. B.
STEEN, Jan Havicksz.
Dut. Leyden 1626?-1679 Same. B-Bd-C-E-722.
STEENE, William. (P-S)
Am. b. Syracuse, N. Y. 1888; ad. 1934 Chapel Hill, N. C. A-F-W.
STEENWYCK, Hendrik van [The Elder].
Flem. Steenyck, Holland 1550-1604 Frankfort, Ger. B-C-722.
STEENWYCK, Hendrik van [The Younger].
Flem. Frankfort 1580-1649 London. B-C-722.
STEENWYCK, Herman [or Harmen].
Dut. Delft 1612-1656. B-Bd.
STEENWYCK, Pieter van.
Dut. ac. 1632-1654 in Holland. B-Bd.
STEER, Henry Reynolds. (Ill)
Eng. London 1858-1928. B-Wa01929.
STEER, Paul Wilson.
Eng. b. Birkenhead 1860; ad. 1934 Chelsea. B-E-Wa-825-871.
STEERE, Lora Woodhead. (S)
Am. b. Los Angeles, Calif.; ad. 1934 Hollywood, Calif. A.
STEES, Sevilla L.
Am. b. Phila., Pa.; ad. 1934 Same. A.
STEFANI. *see* Stefano.
STEFANO D'AREZZO.
It. ac. 1373. Fa-M.
STEFANO, Della Bella. *see* Bella.
STEFANO DA FERRARA.
It. Ferrara 1480-1551 Same. C.
STEFANO FIORENTINO [Vecchio].
see Master of the St. Nicolas Frescoes.
STEFANO DA FOSSANO, Amnrogio.
see Borgognone, A.
STEFANO, Francesco di. *see* Cesellino, F.

STEFANO DI GIOVANNI [Ponte].
see Sassetta, S. di G.
STEFANO DI NICCOLÒ.
It. ac. 1441. Fa-M.
STEFANO, PAOLI DI [Badaloni].
[Called also Paolo Schiavo.]
It. Florence 1397-1478 Pisa. 889.
STEFANO, PIEVANO.
It. ac. 1381. Fa.
STEFANO, TOMMASCO DI [Giottino].
It. Naples 1230/1-1310. B.
STEFANO, VENEZIANO.
It. ac. 1353-1381 in Venice. V.
STEFANO, VINCENZO DE.
It. b. Verona 1859; ac. 1887 Venice. B.
STEFANO DA ZEVIO [The Younger].
It. Zevio 1393-1450 Verona. B-C.
STEFFAN, JOHANN GOTTIFRIED.
Swi. Switzerland 1815-1905 Munich, Ger. B-C.
STEFFECK, CARL CONSTANTINE HEINRICH.
Ger. Berlin 1818-1890 Königsberg. B-C.
STEGGLES, H.
Br. ac. 1931. Fa-M.
STEGGLES, W. J.
Br. ac. 1931. Fa-M.
STEHL, EDWARD RICHARD.
Am. b. 1844; d. 1919 Sea Cliff, N. Y. A016.
STEICHEN, EDUARD J.
Am. b. Milwaukee, Wis. 1879. A20-B-F.
STEIG, WILLIAM. (Ill)
Am. b. New York 1907; ad. 1934 Same. M.
STEIGER, HARWOOD M.
Am. b. Macedon, N. Y. 1900; ad. 1934 New York. A-F.
STEIN, JANET O.
Am. ad. 1935 New York. M.
STEINBERG, NATHANIEL P.
Am. b. Jerusalem, Palestine 1898; ad. 1934 Chicago. A.
STEINBRÜCK, EDUARD.
Ger. Magdeburg 1803-1882 Landeck. B-C.
STEINBRUECKS, VICTOR.
Am. ex. 1934 Seattle, Wash. M.
STEINER, LILLI.
Am. ex. 1934 New York. M.
STEINERT, [Mrs.] SYLVIA CURTIS.
Am. b. Paris, Fr. 1899; ad. 1934 Same. M.
STEINHAUSER, WILHELM AUGUST. (Et)
Ger. Sorau 1846-1924. B-C.
STEINHEIL, ADOLPH CHARLES EDOUARD.
Fr. d. 1908 in Paris. B.
STEINHEIL, LOUIS CHARLES AUGUSTE.
Fr. Strasburg 1814-1885 Paris. B-C.
STEINHOF, EUGENE G. (S)
Am. ad. 1935 New York. M.
STEINLE, JOHANN EDUARD VON.
Aus. Vienna 1810-1886 Frankfort, Ger. B-C.
STEINLEN, ALEXANDRE THÉOPHILE.
Fr. Lausanne, Swi. 1859-1923 Paris. B-DBA-579-586.
STEINWYCKE. *see* Steenwyck.
STEKETEE, HELEN.
Am. ad. 1934 Grand Rapids, Mich. M.
STEKETEE, SALLIE HALL.
Mrs. Paul Frederick Steketee.
Am. Brazil, Ind. 1882; ad. 1934 Grand Rapids, Mich. A.
STELLA, FRANÇOIS VAN DER [The Elder].
Flem. Mechlin 1563/5-1605 Lyons, Fr. B.
STELLA, FRANÇOIS DE [The Younger].
Fr. Lyons 1603-1647 Paris. B-C.
STELLA, JACQUES.
Fr. Lyons 1595/6-1657 Paris. B-Bd-C-722.
STELLA, JOSEPH.
Am. b. Italy 1880; ad. 1934 New York. A-F.
STELLAR, HERMINE.
Am. b. Austria; ad. 1934 Chicago. A.
STELLING, DOROTHY.
Am. ex. 1935 Santa Cruz, Calif. M.
STEMLER, OTTO ADOLPH.
Am. b. Cinn., O. 1872; ad. 1934 Same. F-W.
STENBACH, SABINE VON. (S)
[Legendary daughter of Edwin von Steinbach.]
Ger. ac. 14th Cent. in Germany. M.
STENBERRY, ALGOT.
Am. ad. 1934 New York. M.
STENGEL, GEORGE J.
Am. b. Newark, N. J. 1872; ad. 1934 Ridgefield, Conn. A.
STENGELIN, ALPHONSE.
Fr. b. Lyons 1852. B-DNB.
STEPHAN, ELMER A.
Am. b. Pittsburgh, Pa. 1892. A28.
STEPHAN, JOHN.
Am. b. Maywood, Ill. 1906; ad. 1934 Chicago. A.
STEPHANOFF, FRANCIS PHILIP.
Eng. London 1788-1860. B.
STEPHANOFF, JAMES.
Eng. London 1787-1874 Bristol. B.
STEPHANUS [Pupil of Pasiteles]. (S)
Roman. ac. First Cent. B.C. in Rome. Hs.
STEPHEN, JESSIE.
Am. b. Delaware, O. 1891; ad. 1934 Wayne, Neb. A.
STEPHENS. *see also* Stevens.
STEPHENS, ALICE BARBER. (Ill)
Mrs. Charles H. Stephens.
Am. Salem, N. J. 1858-1932 Moylan, Pa. A029-B-F-W-46.
STEPHENS, CHARLES ARTHUR LLOYD.
Am. d. 1914 Brooklyn, N. Y. A0X1.
STEPHENS, CHARLES H. (Ill)
Am. d. 1931 Pittsburgh, Pa. A029.
STEPHENS, CLARA JANE.
Am. ad. 1934 Portland, Ore. A.
STEPHENS, DANIEL OWEN.
Am. b. Phila., Pa. 1873; ad. 1934 Pittsburgh, Pa. A.
STEPHENS, EDWARD BOWRING. (S)
Eng. Exeter 1815-1886. DNB.
STEPHENS, GEORGE FRANK. (S)
Am. b. Rahway, N. J. 1859; ad. 1933 Arden, Del. A28-F-W.
STEPHENS, WILLIAM REYNOLDS.
see Reynolds-Stephens, W.
STEPHENSON, JAMES. (Eg)
Eng. Manchester 1828-1886 London. B-DNB.
STEPPE, ROMAIN.
Belg. ac. 1933. M.
STERBA, ANTONIN.
Am. b. Hermanec, Czec. 1875; ad. 1934 Chicago. A.
STERCHI, EDA ELIZABETH.
Am. b. Olney, Ill.; ad. 1934 Same. A.

STERL, Robert Herman.
Ger. 1867-1932. M.
STERLING, Lindsey Morris. (S)
Am. b. Mauch Chunk, Pa. 1876; ad. 1926 Phila., Pa. A20-Cs-F.
STERLING, [Mrs.] Lindsey Morris. (S)
Am. Mauch-Chunk, Pa. 1876-1931 Englewood, N. J. A029-F.
STERN, Leonard X.
Am. ad. 1935 Cleveland, O. M.
STERN, Marguerite Louis Delphine [née Fould]. (S)
Fr. b. Marnes-la-Coquette 1866. DBA.
STERNAD, Rudoff. (Min)
Aus. ac. 1933 in Vienna. M.
STERNAMAN, Mary Lou.
Am. ex. 1935 Santa Cruz, Calif. M.
STERNBERG, David.
Rus. ad. 1934 Moscow. M.
STERNBERG, Harry. (Et)
Am. b. New York 1904; ad. 1935 Same. A28.
STERNBERG, [Mrs.] L. B.
Am. ad. 1935 Buffalo, N. Y. M.
STERNBERG, Wassily.
Rus. 1818-1845. B-M.
STERNE, Maurice. (P-S)
Am. b. Libau, Rus. 1877; ad. 1935 New York. A-Cs-F-W-1-46-105-700-779-813.
STERNER, Albert Edward.
Am. b. London 1863; ad. 1935 Astoria, L. I., N. Y. A-B-F-W-46-587.
STERNER, Karl.
Aus. b. 1885; ad. 1934 Vienna. M-Ms.
STERNFIELD, Edith A.
Am. b. Chicago 1898; ad. 1934 Grinnell, Ia. A.
STERRETT, Cliff. (Cart)
Am. b. Fergus Falls, Minn. 1883; ad. 1934 New York. W.
STETCHER, Karl.
Am. Germany 1831-1924 Wichita, Kan. A021-F.
STETSON, Charles Walter.
Am. Tiverton, R. I. 1858-1911 Rome, It. A09-F.
STETSON, Dale.
Am. b. 1905; ad. 1935 New York. M.
STETSON, Katherine Beecher. (S)
Am. b. Prov., R. I. 1885; ad. 1934 Pasadena, Calif. A-Cs-F.
STETTHEIMER, Florine.
Am. ex. 1934 New York. M.
STETTINER, Jacques.
Fr. b. Paris 1904. DBA.
STEUART, Le Conte.
Am. ad. 1934 Kaysville, Utah. A.
STEUART, M. Louisa.
Am. b. Balt., Md.; ad. 1934 Same. A.
STEUBEN, Alexandre Joseph.
Fr. Paris 1814-1862 Same. B-C.
STEUBEN, Charles Auguste Henri.
Ger. Bauerbach 1788-1856 Paris. B-C.
STEVAERTS. *see* Palamedèsz.
STEVENS. *see also* Stephens.
STEVENS, Alfred Émile Léopold Victor.
Belg. Brussels 1828-1906 Paris. B-Bd-C-E-922.
STEVENS, Alfred George. (S)
Eng. Blanford 1818-1875 London. DNB-E-Hs-864-922.
STEVENS, Antoine Palamèdes.
see Palamèdesz.
STEVENS, Charles K. (Ill)
[Originator of colored book-jackets.]
Am. New York 1877-1934 Same. M-Obit. Art Digest, 3-1-1934.
STEVENS, [Mrs.] Clara Harch.
Am. b. Harrodsburg, Ky. 1854; ad. 1934 Lake Bluff, Ia. A.
STEVENS, Dorothy. (Et)
Am. b. Toronto, Can. 1888; ad. 1926 Same. A20-F.
STEVENS, Edith Briscoe.
Am. Phila., Pa. 1896-1931 Gloucester, Mass. A028.
STEVENS, Francis.
Eng. b. 1781; d. 1822/3 in Exeter. B-DNB.
STEVENS, George Washington.
Am. b. Utica, N. Y. 1866; ad. 1926 Toledo, O. A12-F.
STEVENS, Helen B. (Et)
Mrs. T. W. Stevens.
Am. b. Chicago 1878; ad. 1934 Same. A-F-46.
STEVENS, Hugo.
Am. ex. 1933 New York. M.
STEVENS, John Calvin.
Am. b. Boston 1855; ad. 1934 Portland, Me. A.
STEVENS, Joseph Edouard.
Belg. Brussels 1819/21-1892 Same. B-C.
STEVENS, Kelly Haygood.
Am. b. Mexia, Tex. 1896; ad. 1934 Same. A.
STEVENS, Lawrence Tenney. (S)
Am. b. Brighton, Mass. 1896; ad. 1934 Bedford Hills, N. Y. A-Cs.
STEVENS, Lucy Beatrice. (Ill)
Am. b. New York 1876; ad. 1934 Pomfret, Conn. W.
STEVENS, Marian.
Am. ad. 1934 New York. M.
STEVENS, Richard. (Ill)
Am. ad. 1934 San Fran., Calif. M.
STEVENS, Thomas Wood. (Mu)
Am. b. Daysville, Ill. 1880; ad. 1934 Chicago. A-F.
STEVENS, Vera.
Am. b. Hustontown, Pa. 1895; ad. 1934 Provincetown, Mass. A.
STEVENS, Will Henry.
Am. b. Vevay, Ind. 1887; ex. 1934 New York. A-F.
STEVENS, William Charles.
Am. Barre, Mass. 1854-1917. A015-F.
STEVENS, William Dodge. (Ill)
Am. b. Tidioute, Pa. 1870; ad. 1934 New York. A-F.
STEVENS, William Lester.
Am. b. Rockport, Mass. 1888; ad. 1934 Same. A-F-W.
STEVENS-MAGZHAN, Peeter [Stephani].
Flem. Mechlin 1540-1620 Prague, Czec. B.
STEVENSON, Beulah Eisle.
Am. b. Brooklyn, N. Y.; ad. 1934 Same. A-F.

STEVENSON, David Watson. (S)
Scot. Ratho 1842-1904 Edinburgh. B-DNB.
STEVENSON, Dorothea.
Am. b. Dallas, Tex. 1910; ad. 1934 Okla. City, Okla. A.
STEVENSON, Elaine Louise.
Am. b. Port Huron, Mich. 1891; ad. 1934 Kalamazoo, Mich. A.
STEVENSON, Florence Ezzell.
Mrs. Earle Dodds Stevenson.
Am. b. Russellville, Ala. 1894; ad. 1934 Chicago. A.
STEVENSON, Gordon.
Am. b. Chicago 1892; ad. 1934 New York. A-F.
STEVENSON, Richard Macaulay.
Scot. b. Glasgow 1860. B.
STEVENSON, Robert Alan Mowbray.
Br. 1847-1900. DNB.
STEVER, Gustav Curt.
Rus. Riga 1823-1877 Düsseldorf, Ger. B-C.
STEVERS. *see* Palamèdesz.
STEVINSON, James Alexander. (S)
Eng. b. Chester 1881; ad. 1934 London. Wa.
STEWARDSON, Edmund Austin. (S)
Am. Phila., Pa. 1860-1892 Newport, R. I. B-F-Ta.
STEWARDSON, Thomas.
Eng. Kendal 1781-1859 London. B-DNB.
STEWART, Albert T. (S)
Am. b. Kensington, Eng. 1900; ad. 1934 New York. A-Cs.
STEWART, Anthony. (Min)
Scot. Crieff 1773-1846 London. B-DNB.
STEWART, Charles Edward.
Scot. b. Glasgow; ad. 1934 Bucks, Eng. Wa.
STEWART, [Miss] Cumbrae.
Eng. ad. 1934 Chelsea. Wa.
STEWART, Ethelyn S.
Am. ad. 1934 Arlington, N. J. M.
STEWART, Frances de F.
Am. ad. 1934 New York. M.
STEWART, Frank Algernon.
Eng. b. Croydon 1877; ad. 1934 Rathlin. M.
STEWART, [Mrs.] Grace Bliss.
Am. b. Atchison, Kan. 1885; ad. 1934 New York. A-F-W.
STEWART, James. (Eg)
Scot. Edinburgh 1791-1863 Cape Colony, So. Africa. B-DNB.
STEWART, Julius L.
Am. Phila., Pa. 1855-1920 Paris. A12-B-C-E-F-W10-46.
STEWART, Le Conte.
Am. b. Glenwood, Utah 1891; ad. 1934 Kaysville, Utah. F-M.
STEWART, William. (Ill)
Eng. b. Greenwich 1886; ad. 1934 Edinburgh, Scot. Wa.
STEWART, William A.
Eng. b. Ilkley 1882; ad. 1934 Jerusalem, Palestine. M.
STEYN, Stella.
Ir. b. Dublin; ex. 1930 London. M.
STEYNBERG, C. S. (S)
Br. ac. 1934 So. Africa. M.
STICKROTH, Harry I.
Am. b. 1844; d. 1922 Chicago. A019-F.
STIELER [or Steeler], Joseph Karl.
Ger. Mayence 1781-1858 Munich. B-C.
STIEPEVICH, V. G.
Rus. ac. 1890. M.
STILES, Samuel. (Eg)
Am. East Windsor, Conn. 1796-1861 New York. F-2-7.
STILKE, Hermann.
Ger. Berlin 1803-1860 Same. B-C.
STILL, Clifford E.
Am. ad. 1935 Pullman, Wash. M.
STILLMAN, Ary.
Am. b. Russia 1891; ex. 1935 New York. DBA-M.
STILLMAN, William James.
Am. Schenectady, N. Y. 1828-1901 England. E.
STILLSON, Blanche.
Am. b. Ind., Ind.; ad. 1934 Same. A.
STILLWELL, Charles B.
Am. ad. 1934 New York. M.
STILWELL, Wilber Moore.
Am. b. Covington, Ind. 1908; ad. 1934 Kansas City, Mo. A.
STIMMER, Tobias.
Swi. Switzerland 1534/9-1582/92 Strassburg, Ger. B-C.
STIMPSON, Helen Townsend.
Am. b. New York; ad. 1934 Hartford, Conn. A.
STIMSON, Anna Katherine. (S)
Am. b. New York 1892; ad. 1934 Phila., Pa. A.
STIMSON, John Ward.
Am. Paterson, N. J. 1850-1930. A26-F-W16.
STINCHFIELD, Estelle.
Am. ad. 1934 Denver, Colo. M.
STINSON, Harry Edward. (S)
Am. b. Wayland, Ia. 1898; ad. 1934 Iowa City, Ia. A.
STITES, John Randolph.
Am. b. Buffalo, N. Y. 1836; ac. 1884. [No death date.] C.
STITT, Herbert D.
Am. b. Hot Springs, Ark. 1880; ad. 1934 Pikesville, Md. A-F.
STIVERS, Harley Ennis. (Ill)
Am. b. Nokomis, Ill. 1891; ad. 1934 New York. A.
STOBBAERT, Jean Baptiste.
Belg. Antwerp 1838-1914. B-C.
STOCK, Ernest.
Am. ad. 1934 Boston, Mass. M.
STOCK, Henri Charles.
Fr. ac. 1838-1884 in Bordeaux. B.
STOCK, Henry John.
Eng. London 1853-1930. Wa1929-Y01931.
STOCK, Ignatius van der.
Dut. ac. 1660 in Brussels, Belg. B.
STOCK, Joseph.
Am. ac. 1840. [No death date.] M.
STOCKBRIDGE, Dana W.
Am. Haverhill, Mass. 1881-1922. A020-F.
STOCKER, Hans.
Swi. b. Basel 1896. DBA.
STOCKLEY, Busdriver.
Br. ex. 1934 in London. M.
STOCKLEY, Henry.
Eng. ex. 1935 London. M.

STOCKMAN, [Mrs.] HELEN PARK.
Am. b. Englewood, N. J. 1896; ad. 1934 Same. A-F.
STOCKS, ARTHUR.
Eng. London 1846-1889 Same. B-DNB.
STOCKS, KATHERINE M.
Eng. ac. 1879 in London. B.
STOCKS, LUMB. (Eg)
Eng. Lightcliffe 1812-1892 London. B-DNB.
STODART, EDWARD JACKSON. (Eg)
Eng. b. Barnsbury 1879; ad. 1934 Surrey. Wa.
STODDARD, ALICE KENT.
Am. b. Watertown, Conn.; ad. 1934 Phila., Pa. A-F-W.
STODDARD, FREDERICK LINCOLN. (Mu)
Am. b. Coaticook, Que., Can. 1861; ad. 1934 Gloucester, Mass. A-F.
STODDARD, MUSETTE O.
Am. ad. 1934 Nashville, Ind. M.
STODDARD, VINE.
Am. ex. 1935 New York. M.
STOEBEL, JOHAN ANTHONIE BATHASAR.
Dut. The Hague 1821-1905 Leyden. B.
STOENESCU, EUSTACE GRIGORIE.
Rumanian. b. 1884; ac. 1914 in Paris. B.
STOFFE, JAN JACOBSZ VAN DER.
Dut. Leyden 1611-1682. B.
STOHR, JULIA COLLINS.
Mrs. Peter C. Stohr.
Am. b. Toledo, O. 1866; ad. 1934 Lovell, Me. A.
STOHR, JULIE.
Mrs. J. S. Roe.
Am. b. St. Paul, Minn. 1895. A28.
STOIJANA, GEORGE [or Gjura]. (Mu)
Am. ad. 1934 Los Angeles, Calif. M.
STOKES. ADRIAN S.
Eng. b. Southport 1854; ad. 1934 London. Wa.
STOKES, FRANK WILBERT.
Am. b. Nashville, Tenn.; ad. 1934 New York. A-F-W16.
STOKES, GEORGE VERNON. (Et)
Eng. b. London 1873; ad. 1934 Deal. Wa.
STOKES, HELEN PHELPS.
Am. ad. 1934 New York. M.
STOKES, MARIANNE.
Mrs. Adrian Stokes.
Eng. ac. 1884 in London. B.
STOLITZA, EUGÈNE ANANIEFF.
Rus. b. 1870 in Russia. B.
STOLL, JOHN THEODOR EDWARD.
Am. b. Goettingen, Hanover, Ger. 1889; ad. 1934 San Fran., Calif. A.
STOLL, ROLF.
Am. b. Heidelberg, Ger. 1892; ad. 1934 E. Cleveland, O. A.
STOLLER, ALEXANDER. (S)
Am. ad. 1935 Chicago, Ill. M.
STOLTENBERG, HANS JOHN.
Am. b. Flensburg, Ger. 1879; ad. 1934 Wauwatosa, Wis. A.
STOLTENBERG, MATHAIS.
Ger. ac. 1830-1853 in Germany. M.
STOMER [or Stoom], MATHAUS I.
Flem. ac. 1615-1630 in Rome, It. B.
STOMME [or Stom], JAN JANZ DE.
Dut. Groeningen 1643-1657. B.
STOMME VAN KAMPEN.
see Avercamp, Hendrick van.
STONE, ALICE BALCH.
Mrs. Robert Bowditch Stone.
Am. b. Swampscott, Mass. 1876; ad. 1934 Boston. A.
STONE, [Mrs.] ALICE WADSWORTH.
Am. West Eaton, N. Y. 1855-1917 Brooklyn, N. Y. A015.
STONE, FRANK.
Eng. Manchester 1800-1859 London. B-C-DNB-E.
STONE, FRANK FREDERICK. (S)
Am. b. London 1860; ad. 1934 Los Angeles, Calif. A.
STONE, GEORGE M.
Am. Topeka, Kan. 1858-1911. A12.
STONE, HENRY ["Old Stone"].
Eng. b. 1600; d. 1653 in London. B-DNB-E.
STONE, HORATIO. (S)
Am. Jackson, N. Y. 1808-1875 Italy. B-Bd-Cs-F.
STONE, IDA A.
Am. ad. 1934 New York. M.
STONE, JOHN. (S)
Eng. d. 1667. E.
STONE, J. M.
Am. b. Dana, Mass. 1841; d. Australia. B-F-15.
STONE, [Mrs.] MADELINE MASTERS. (S)
Am. d. 1932 Wash., D. C. A029.
STONE, MARCUS.
Eng. London 1840-1921 Same. B-C-E.
STONE, MARIE W.
Am. d. 1920 San Fran., Calif. A017.
STONE, MAYSIE. (S)
Am. ad. 1934 New York. M.
STONE, NICHOLAS [The Younger]. (S)
Eng. d. 1647. E.
STONE, NICOLAS [The Elder]. (S)
Eng. Woodbury 1586-1647 London. E-Hs.
STONE, ORRIN FURSE.
Am. ad. 1934 Pasadena, Calif. A.
STONE, SEYMOUR MILLAIS.
Am. b. Poland 1877; ad. 1934 New York. A-F-W.
STONE, STANFORD BYRON.
Am. b. Denver, Colo. 1906; ad. 1934 New York. A.
STONE, TOM.
Can. ad. 1935 Toronto, Ont. M.
STONE, VIOLA PRATT.
Mrs. Joseph H. Stone.
Am. b. Omaha, Neb.; ad. 1934 Long Beach, Calif. A.
STONE, WALTER KING. (Ill)
Am. b. Barnard, N. Y. 1875; ad. 1934 Ithaca, N. Y. A-F-W.
STONE, WILLIAM OLIVER.
Am. Derby, Conn. 1830-1875 Newport, R. I. B-Bd-C-F-3-4-15.
STONEHILL, GEORGE.
Am. ex. 1935 New York. M.
STONELAKE, FRANK.
Eng. 1879-1929. M.
STONER, HARRY. (Mu)
Am. b. Springfield, O. 1880; ad. 1934 New York. A.

STONER, OLIVER.
Am. b. Pleasantville, Pa.; ad. 1934 Phila., Pa. A.
STOOP, DIRK [or Daniel] RODRIGUEZ.
Dut. Utrecht 1610-1686 Same. B-C.
STOOPS, HERBERT M. (Ill)
Am. ad. 1934 New York. M.
STOPFORD, WILLIAM HENRY.
Eng. 1842-1890. B.
STORCK. *see* Stork.
STORER, HENRY SARGANT. (Eg)
Eng. Cambridge 1795-1837 London. B-DNB.
STORER, JAMES SARGANT. (Eg)
Eng. Cambridge 1771-1853 London. B-DNB.
STOREY, GEORGE ADOLPHUS.
Eng. London 1834-1919. C.
STORK [or Storck], ABRAHAM.
Dut. Amsterdam 1630/5-1710 Same. B-Bd-C-722.
STORK [or Storck], JAN [or Jacobus].
Dut. ac. 1660-1684 in Amsterdam. B.
STORK, LISL.
Mrs. C. Stork.
Am. b. Salzburg, Aus. 1888; ad. 1934 Phila., Pa. A.
STORK [or Storck], TIEN. (Cari)
Am. ac. 1917. M.
STORM, ANNA ALFRIDA.
Am. b. Sweden 1896; ad. 1934 Greeley, Colo. A.
STORM, CHARLES VAN GRAVESANDE.
see Gravesande, C. S. van.
STORM, GEORGE.
Am. Johnstown, Pa. 1830-1913 Lancaster, Pa. A0X1.
STORRS, FRANCIS HUDSON.
Mrs. William M. Storrs.
Am. b. New York; ad. 1934 Hartford, Conn. A.
STORRS, JOHN H. (S)
Am. b. Chicago 1885; ad. 1934 Same. A-Cs-F.
STORY, [Mrs.] ELIZABETH JESSIE. (Et)
Eng. b. Oxford; ad. 1934 London. Wa.
STORY, GEORGE HENRY.
Am. New Haven, Conn. 1835-1923 New York. A020-C-F-15.
STORY, INA PERHAM.
Am. ex. 1934 New York. M.
STORY, JULIAN.
Am. Walton, Eng. 1857-1919 Phila., Pa. A016-B-E-F.
STORY, MARION. (Min)
Am. d. 1907 Port Chester, N. Y. A06.
STORY, THOMAS WALDO. (S)
Am. Rome, It. 1855-1915 New York. A013-B-F-Hs-Ta.
STORY, WILLIAM WETMORE.
Am. Salem, Mass. 1819-1895 Italy. F-Hs-15-45-588.
STOSS [or Stwosz], VEIT. (S)
Ger. Cracow, Pol. 1447-1542 Nüremberg, Ger. B-Bd-E-Hs.
STOTHARD, ALFRED JOSEPH. (Med)
Eng. 1793-1864. M.
STOTHARD, CHARLES ALFRED. (Et)
Eng. London 1786-1821 Devonshire. B-DNB.
STOTHARD, THOMAS. (Ill)
Eng. London 1755-1834 Same. B-Bd-C-DNB-E-589.
STOTT, EDWARD.
Eng. Rockdale 1859-1918. B-825.
STOTT, WILLIAM OF OLDHAM.
Eng. Oldham 1858-1900 at sea. B-C.
STOUFFER, J. EDGAR. (S)
Am. ad. 1934 Balt., Md. M.
STOUT, IDA McCLELLAND. (S)
Am. b. Decatur, Ill.; d. 1927 Rome, It. A025.
STOVER, ALLAN JAMES.
Am. b. West Point, Miss. 1887; ad. 1934 Corvalis, Ore. A.
STOVER, WALLACE.
Am. b. Elkhart, Ind. 1903; ad. 1934 Same. A.
STOW, JAMES. (Eg)
Eng. Maidstone 1770-1823. B-DNB.
STOWELL, M. LOUISE.
Am. b. Rochester, N. Y.; ac. 1931. A28.
STOWITTS, HUBERT J.
Am. b. Rushville, Neb. 1892; ad. 1934 Hollywood, Calif. M.
STRAAT, HJ.
Swe. *see* book 824.
STRACHAN, A. CLAUDE.
Eng. ac. 1891 in Liverpool. B.
STRACHEY, HENRY.
Eng. b. 1863; ad. 1934 Clinton, Eng. Wa.
STRADANUS, JOHANNES [Della Straet].
Flem. Bruges 1523/36-1605 Florence, It. B-C-803.
STRAGLAITA, CARLO.
It. ac. 19th Cent. in Milan. B.
STRAHALN, FRANK. (Mu)
Am. b. Vienna, Aus. 1879; ad. 1934 Dallas, Tex. A.
STRAHAN, ALFRED WINFIELD.
Am. b. Balt., Md. 1886; ad. 1934 Same. A.
STRAIN, DANIEL J.
Am. b. New Hampshire; d. 1925 Boston. A20-F-47.
STRAIN, FRANCES.
Am. b. Chicago, Ill. 1898; ad. 1934 Same. A.
STRANDENAES, BRYN.
Am. ad. 1934 New York. M.
STRANG, IAN.
Eng. b. London 1886; ad. 1934 Same. Wa.
STRANG, RAY C. (Ill)
Am. ad. 1934 New York. M.
STRANG, WILLIAM.
Scot. Dumbarton 1859-1921 Bournemouth. DNB-E-825.
STRANGE, [Sir] ROBERT. (Eg)
Scot. Orkney 1721-1792 London. B-DNB-E.
STRASSER, ROLAND.
Aus. ex. 1934 London. M.
STRATER, HENRY.
Am. b. Louisville, Ky. 1896; ad. 1934 Ogun quit, Me. A.
STRATHMAN, KARL.
Ger. b. 1866. M.
STRATONIKOS. (S)
Gr. (Pergamon); ac. 175 B.C. Hs.
STRATTON, FRED.
Eng. ad. 1934 London. Wa.

STRATTON, Howard Fremont.
Am. ad. 1935 Phila., Pa. M.
STRAUCH, George.
Ger. Nüremberg 1613-1675. B-C.
STRAUCH, Herman.
Am. ad. 1934 Nashville, Tenn. M.
STRAUCH, Lorenz.
Ger. Nüremberg 1554-1630. B-C.
STRAUCHEN, Edmund R.
Am. ad. 1934 Cinn., O. M.
STRAUSS, Betty.
Am. ad. 1934 New York. M.
STRAUSS, Carl Sumner. (Et)
Am. ad. 1934 Switzerland. A.
STRAUSS, Malcolm Mitteldorfer.
Am. b. Richmond, Va. 1880; ad. 1934 Same. A.
STRAUSS, Raphael.
Am. Cinn., O. 1830-1919. M.
STRAUTIN, Wally.
Mrs. Edward Strautin.
Am. ad. 1935 New York. M.
STRAWBRIDGE, Anne West.
Am. b. Phila., Pa. 1883; ad. 1934 Same. A.
STRAWBRIDGE, Edward R.
Am. b. Phila., Pa. 1903; ad. 1934 Chestnut Hill, Pa. M.
STREAN, Maria Judson. (Min)
Am. b. Wash., Pa.; ad. 1934 New York. A.
STREATER, Robert.
Eng. London 1624-1680 Same. C-DNB.
STREATFIELD, Josephine.
Am. b. London 1882; ad. 1934 New York. A.
STREATOR, Harold A.
Am. b. Cleveland, O.; ad. 1926 Morristown, N. J. A12-F.
STREBELLE, Rodolphe Armand.
Belg. ad. 1934 Brussels. M.
STRECHINE, Stephanie von.
Ger. b. 1858. M.
STRECKER, Herman. (S)
Am. Phila., Pa. 1836-1901 Reading, Pa. A04.
STREEK, Juriaan van.
Dut. Amsterdam 1632?-1678. B-C.
STREET, Frank. (Ill)
Am. ad. 1934 Leonia, N. J. A.
STREET, J. Fletcher. (Mu)
Am. ad. 1934 Phila., Pa. M.
STREET, Naomi Scudder.
Am. ad. 1934 Huntington, L. I., N. Y. M.
STREET, Robert.
Am. b. 1796; ac. 1840 in Phila., Pa. F.
STREETER, Julia Allen.
Mrs. George L. Streeter.
Am. b. Detroit, Mich. 1877; ad. 1934 Balt., Md. A.
STREETES [or Stretes], William [or Guillim].
Eng. b. Holland; ac. 1556 in London. B-C-DNB.
STREETON, Arthur.
Aust. b. Geelong, Victoria 1867; ad. 1935 Melbourne. B-M.
STREIGHT, Howard.
Am. d. 1912 San José, Calif. A010.
STRICKLAND, William. (Eg)
Am. Phila., Pa. 1787-1854 Nashville, Tenn. F-2-7.

STRIFFLER, Albert Christian.
Am. b. 1861; d. 1918 Brooklyn, N. Y. A015.
STRIGEL, Bernhard.
Ger. Memmingen, 1460/1-1527 Same. B-C.
STRIJ. *see* Stry.
STRINGFIELD, Vivian F.
Am. b. Calif.; ad. 1934 Los Angeles, Calif. A.
STROBEL, Johann Anthoine Balthasar.
Dut. Gravenhage 1821-1905 Leyden. B.
STROBEL, Oscar.
Am. b. Cinn., O. 1891; ad. 1934 Hollywood, Calif. A.
STROBENTZ, Frederick [or Fritz].
Hun. b. Budapest 1856. B.
STROBERLE, João Glamma.
Por. Lisbon 1708-1792 Oporto. B-C.
STROBL, S. (S)
Hun. b. Asorajk; ex. 1934 London. M.
STROEHLING, P. E.
Rus. ac. 1803-1826 in London. B.
STROMBERG, [Baron] A. von.
Ger. ac. 1930. M.
STRONACH, Ancell.
Scot. b. Dundee 1901; ad. 1934 Glasgow. Wa.
STRONG, Constance Gill.
Am. b. New York 1900; ad. 1934 Gary, Ind. A.
STRONG, Elizabeth.
Am. b. Hartford, Conn. 1855; ad. 1934 Carmel, Calif. A.
STRONG, Joseph D.
Am. Bridgeport, Conn. 1852-1900 San Fran., Calif. A02.
STRONG, Ray Stanford.
Am. b. Covallis, Ore. 1905; ad. 1934 San Fran., Calif. A.
STRONGYLION. (S)
Gr. ac. 5th Cent. B.C. in Athens. E-Hs.
STROTHER, David Hunter.
Am. 1816-1888. F.
STROTHER, Sanford. (Ill)
Am. ad. 1934 East Orange, N. J. M.
STROTHMANN, F. (Ill)
Am. ad. 1934 New York. M.
STROUD, Clara.
Am. ad. 1934 Point Pleasant, N. J. M.
STROUD, [Mrs.] Ida Wells.
Am. b. New Orleans, La. 1869; ad. 1934 Newark, N. J. A.
STROZZI, Bernardo [Il. Capuccino].
It. Genoa 1581-1644 Venice. B-C-722.
STRUBEN, Edith.
Br. ad. 1934 So. Africa. M.
STRUBING, Louisa Hayes.
Am. b. Buffalo, N. Y. 1881; ad. 1934 Eggertsville, N. Y. A.
STRUCK, Hugo.
Ger. ac. 1900 in Paris. B.
STRUDWICK, Clement.
Am. b. Columbia, Tenn.; ad. 1934 Durham, N. C. A.
STRUDWICK, John Melhuish.
Eng. b. London 1849. B-C.
STRUNK, Herbert. (S)
Am. b. Shakopee, Minn. 1891; ad. 1934 Lava, N. Y. A.

STRUTT, Alfred William.
Eng. b. 1856; d. 1924 in London. B-Y01925.
STRUTT, Arthur John.
Eng. Chelmsford 1819-1888 Rome, It. B.
STRUTT, Jacob George.
Eng. England 1790-1864 Rome, It. B-DNB.
STRUTT, Joseph. (Eg)
Eng. 1749-1802. DNB.
STRUTT, William Thomas. (Min)
Eng. 1777-1850. B-DNB.
STRUTZEL, Léopold Otto.
Ger. b. Dessau 1855. B.
STRUVEN, [Mrs.] Gertrude Stanwood.
Am. b. West Newbury, Mass. 1874; ad. 1934 Wilmette, Ill. A.
STRUYS, Alexandre [Théodorus Honoré].
Belg. b. Berchem 1852. B-C.
STRY [or Strij], Abraham van I.
Dut. Dordrecht 1753-1826 Same. B-C.
STRY [or Strij], Jacobus van.
Dut. Dordrecht 1756-1815 Same. B-C.
STRYCKER, Jacobus Gerritsen.
Am. Holland 1619-1687 New York. F.
STRYJENSKA [Madame], Zofja.
Pol. b. 1897 in Poland. M.
STRYOWSKI, Wilhelm August.
Ger. b. Danzig 1834; ac. 1882. B-C.
STUART, Charles.
Eng. ac. 1845-1854 in London. B.
STUART, Frederick T.
Am. b. 1837; d. 1913 Brookline, Mass. A0X1-F-7.
STUART, Gilbert.
Am. Narragansett, R. I. 1755-1828 Boston. B-Bd-C-DNB-E-F-1-2-4-5-6-45-46-85-138-160-169-179-182-188-189-191-249-250-590-701-748-786-922.
STUART, James.
Eng. London 1713-1788 Same. B-DNB.
STUART, James B.
Am. d. 1915 Madison, Wis. A013.
STUART, James Everett.
Am. b. Dover, Me. 1852; ad. 1934 San Fran., Calif. A-F-W.
STUART, Jane E.
Am. b. 1810/2; d. 1888 Newport, R. I. F-2.
STUART, John. (Min)
Eng. ac. late 18th Cent. in England. M.
STUART, Kenneth.
Am. ex. 1933 New York. M.
STUART, R. James.
Am. ad. 1934 New York. M.
STUART-HILL, A.
Eng. ad. 1935 Chelsea; ex. 1934 Pittsburgh, Pa. M.
STUBBLE, Henry.
Eng. ac. 1785-1791 in London. B.
STUBBS, George.
Eng. Liverpool 1724-1806 London. B-C-DNB-591-735.
STUBBS, George Townley. (Eg)
Eng. Liverpool 1756-1815 London. DNB-591.
STUBBS, James Henry Phillipson. (Eg)
Eng. Marylebone 1810-1864 London. B-Bd.
STUBBS, Mary Helen.
Am. b. Greenville, O. 1867; ad. 1934 Chicago. A.

STUBER, Dedrick Brandes.
Am. b. New York 1878; ad. 1934 Los Angeles, Calif. A.
STUCK, Franz Ritter von.
Ger. Bavaria 1863-1928. B-E-Y01929.
STUCKELBERG, Johann Melchior Ernest.
Swi. Basel 1831-1903 Same. B-C.
STUCKGOLD, Stanislas.
Pol. d. 1933 Paris. DBA.
STUDD, Arthur Haythorne.
Eng. 1864-1919. M.
STUERBOUT, Thierry [or Dirk].
see Bouts, Dirk.
STUEVER, Celia M. (Et)
Am. b. St. Louis, Mo.; ac. 1931. A28.
STUFFERS, Anthony. (Ill)
Am. Holland 1894-1920 Chicago. A017.
STUHR, Johann Georg.
Ger. Hamburg 1640-1721 Same. B-C.
STULL, Henry.
Am. Hamilton, Can. 1851-1913 New Rochelle, N. Y. A0X1.
STUMP, Samuel John.
Eng. d. 1863 in London. B-DNB.
STURGES, Dwight Case. (Et)
Am. b. Boston; ad. 1934 Same. A28-F-W.
STURGES, Katherine. (Ill)
Am. ad. 1934 Roslyn, L. I., N. Y. A.
STURGES, Lee. (Et)
Am. b. Chicago 1865; ad. 1934 Melrose Park, Ill. A28-F-W.
STURGES, Lillian.
Am. b. Wilkes-Barre, Pa.; ad. 1934 Pittsburgh, Pa. A.
STURGIS, Mabel Russell.
Am. b. Boston, Mass. 1865; ad. 1934 Same. A.
STURM, Fritz.
Ger. b. Rostock 1834; ac. 1885 Berlin. B-C.
STURM, Justin. (S)
Am. b. Nebraska 1899; ex. 1935 New York. M.
STURM, Paul. (S)
Ger. b. Leipzig 1859. B.
STURM, William F. (Eg)
Am. b. New York; d. 1912 Hoboken, N. J. A010.
STÜRMER, Karl.
Ger. Berlin 1803-1881. B-C.
STURSA, Jan. (S)
Czec. Moravia 1880-1923. E-798.
STURT, John. (Eg)
Br. 1658-1730. DNB.
STURTEVANT, Edith Louise.
Am. b. Utica, N. Y. 1888; ad. 1934 Easton, Pa. A.
STURTEVANT, Helena.
Am. Middletown, R. I. 1872; ad. 1934 Newport, R. I. A.
STURTEVANT, Louisa Clark.
Am. b. Paris 1870; ad. 1934 Newport, R. I. A.
STUVEN [or Stuvens], Ernest.
Ger. Hamburg 1657-1712 Rotterdam, Holland. B-C.
STYKA, Adam.
Pol. b. Kielce 1890. DBA.
STYKA, Jan.
Pol. Lemberg 1858-1925 Rome, It. B-DBA.

STYKA, Tadé.
Pol.-Fr. b. Paris 1889; ad. 1934 New York. DBA-M.
STYLES, George William.
Am. b. Sutton, Eng. 1887; ad. 1934 Detroit, Mich. A.
STYPPAX. (S)
Gr. ac. 5th Cent. B.C. in Cyprus. Hs.
STYRES, J. R. L.
Am. ac. 1932. M.
SU HAN-CHEN.
Chinese. ac. 12th Cent. in China. M.
SUARDI, Bartolommeo [Bramantino].
It. Milan 1450/5-1528/30 Same. B-Bd-C-T-V.
SUAVIUS [or Susterman], Lambert.
Ger. Liège, Belg. 1520?-1567 Frankfort. B.
SUBLEYRAS, Pierre Hubert.
Fr. Uzès 1699-1729 Rome, It. B-C-E-722.
SUCHARDA, Stanislav. (S)
Pol. ac. in Prague, Czec. 798.
SUCHET, Joseph François.
Fr. 1824-1896. M.
SUDEYKIN, Sergie.
Rus. b. Smolensk 1884; ad. 1935 New York. M.
SUE, Gabriel.
Fr. b. Marseilles 1867. DBA.
SUESS, Hans. *see* Kulmbach, H.
SUEUR. *see* Le Sueur.
SUGAR, Sam. (Ill)
Am. ad. 1934 New York. M.
SUHR, Frederic J. (Ill)
Am. b. Brooklyn, N. Y. 1885; ad. 1934 New York. A.
SUHR, William.
Am. b. Kreutzburg, Ger. 1896; ad. 1934 Detroit, Mich. A.
SUHRLANDT, Johann Heinrich.
Ger. Schwerin 1742-1827 Ludwigslust. B-C.
SUHRLANDT, Rudolf Friedrich Karl.
Ger. Ludwigslust 1781-1862 Schwerin. B-C.
SUIJDERHOEF, Jonas. (Eg)
Dut. 1613-1686. M.
SUISHŌ, Nishiyama.
Jap. ex. 1935 New York. M.
SUKENOBU, Nishikawa.
Jap. 1675-1754/5. J., Vol. 2, page 36.
SULLIVAN, D. Frank.
Am. b. 1812; ad. 1934 Pittsburgh, Pa. A.
SULLIVAN, Edmund J. (Ill)
Eng. b. London 1869; ex. 1929 Same. B-Wa1929.
SULLIVAN, Francis.
Am. b. 1861; d. 1925 New York. A022-F.
SULLIVAN, Lillie. (Ill)
Am. d. 1903; Wash., D. C. A04.
SULLIVAN, Louise Karrer.
Mrs. William Sullivan.
Am. b. Port Huron, Mich. 1876; ad. 1934 Boston. A.
SULLIVAN, Luke. (Eg)
Ir. Ireland 1705-1771 London. B-DNB.
SULLIVAN, Pat. (Cart)
Am. Sydney, N.S.W. Aust. 1887-1933 New York. A030.
SULLY, Jane Cooper [Mrs. Darley].
Am. b. 1807; d. 1877 in Phila., Pa. F-2.
SULLY, Lawrence.
Am. Ireland 1769-1804 Richmond, Va. F-2-6.
SULLY, Robert Matthew.
Am. Petersburg, Va. 1803-1855 Madison, Wis.
SULLY, Thomas.
Am. Horncastle, Eng. 1783-1872 Phila., Pa. B-Bd-C-DNB-E-F-1-2-15-30-46-144-182-183-188-189-251-252-253-701.
SULLY, Thomas Wilcocks, Jr.
Am. Phila., Pa. 1811-1847 Same. F-2-6.
SULTAN MUHAMMAD.
Pers. ac. 1550 in Persia. M.
SUMMERS, Charles. (S)
Eng. London 1827-1878. B-DNB.
SUMMERS, Ivan F.
Am. b. Mt. Vernon, Ill.; ad. 1934 Woodstock, N. Y. A.
SUMMERS, William Henry. (Cart)
Am. b. Springarten, Ill. 1897; ad. 1934 E. Cleveland, O. M.
SUMMY, Katherine Strong.
Am. b. Wash., D. C. 1888; ad. 1934 Same. A.
SUMNER, L. W. Y.
Am. b. Middletown, Conn.; ad. 1934 Greenwich, Conn. A.
SUNDBLOM, Haddon. (Ill)
Am. ad. 1934 Chicago. M.
SUNDER, Lucas. *see* Cranach [The Elder].
SUNMAN [or Sonmans], William.
Dut.-Eng. b. Holland; d. 1708 London. B-DNB.
SUNYER, Jouquím.
Sp. b. Vilenora y Gestru 1875; ad. 1934 Barcelona. DBA-M.
SURAND, Gustave P. A.
Fr. ac. 1884-1910 in Paris. B.
SURENDORF, Charles Frederick.
Am. b. Richmond, Ind. 1906; ad. 1934 Wash., D. C. A.
SURVAGE, Léopold.
Rus. b. Moscow 1879; ad. 1934 Paris. DBA.
SUS, Gustave.
Ger. Rumbeck 1823-1881 Düsseldorf. B-C.
SUSAN, Robert.
Am. ac. 1929 in Phila., Pa. A20-F.
SÜSS, Hans. *see* Kulmbach, Hans von.
SUSTERMANS, Justus [or Joost].
Flem. Antwerp 1597-1681 Florence, It. B-C-722-890.
SUSTRIS. *see* Zustris.
SUTHERLAND, Claire D.
Am. ad. 1934 New York. M.
SUTHERLAND, Graham Vivian. (Et)
Eng. b. London 1903; ad. 1934 Kent. Wa.
SUTHERLAND, Thomas. (Eg)
Eng. ac. 1785-1825 in London. B.
SUTRO, Florence Edith Clinton.
Am. England 1875-1906 New York. A06.
SUTTERMANS. *see* Sustermans.
SUTTON, Alice Marion.
Am. b. Cambridge, Mass. 1907; ad. 1934 Same. A.
SUTTON, George Miksch.
Am. b. Bethany, Neb. 1898; ad. 1934 Same. A.

SUTTON, Harry, Jr.
Am. b. Salem, Mass. 1897; ad. 1934 Boston. A-F.
SUTTON, H. W.
Eng. ac. 1932. M.
SUTTON, Jessie Butler.
Am. b. Columbus, O. 1901; ad. 1934 Cleveland Heights, O. M.
SUTTON, Ruth Haviland.
Am. b. Springfield, Mass. 1898; ad. 1934 Same. A.
SU TUNG-po.
Chinese. 1036-1101. M.
SUVÉE, Joseph Benôit.
Belg. Bruges 1743-1807 Rome, It. B-C.
SUYDAM, Edward Howard.
Am. b. Vineland, N. J. 1885. A28-F.
SUYDAM, James Augustus.
Am. New York 1817-1865 No. Conway, N. H. B-Bd-C-F-2-15.
SUYDERHOEF, Jonas. (Eg)
Dut. Leyden 1613-1686 Haarlem. B.
SUZANNE, François Marie. (S)
Fr. ac. 1750-1802 in Paris. B.
SUZOR-COTÉ, Aurele de Foy. (P-S)
Can. b. Arthabaska, Que. 1869; ad. 1935 Montreal, Can. B-M.
SUZUKI, Kwason.
Jap. ac. 1900 in Japan. J., Vol. 2, page 105.
SVABINSKY, Max.
Czec. b. Moravia 1873; ac. 1900 in Paris. B-E.
SVENDSEN, Charles C.
Am. b. Cinn., O. 1871; ad. 1934 Same. A.
SVENDSEN, Svend.
Am. b. Christiania, Nor. 1864; ad. 1915 Chicago. A12.
SVOBODA, Joséf Cestmir. (Ill)
Am. b. Czec. 1899; ad. 1934 New York. A.
SVOBODA, Vincent A.
Am. ad. 1934 New York. M.
SVOR, Anders. (S)
Nor. ac. in Christiania. B-798.
SWADA [Miss].
Jap. ex. 1935 New York. M.
SWAIN, Frank William.
Am. b. Oakland, Calif. 1892; ac. 1934 Cinn., O. A28-F.
SWAIN, Joseph. (Eg)
Eng. Oxford 1820-1909 Ealing. DNB.
SWAIN, William.
Am. b. 1803; d. 1847 New York. F-169.
SWAINE, Francis.
Eng. London 1740-1782 Same. B-DNB.
SWAINE, John. (Eg)
Eng. Stanwell 1775-1860 London. B-DNB.
SWAINE, John Barak. (Et)
Eng. 1815?-1838. DNB.
SWALLEY, John F.
Am. b. Toledo, O. 1887; ad. 1934 Same. A.
SWAN, Cuthbert Edmund.
Ir. Ballyragget 1873-1931. Wa1929.
SWAN, Emma Levina.
Am. Prov., R. I. 1853-1927 Same. A026.
SWAN, James.
Scot. b. Hawick 1864; ad. 1934 Grosse Ile., Mich. M.
SWAN, John Macallan. (P-S)
Eng. Old Brantford 1847-1910 Niton. B-DNB-E-Hs.
SWAN, Joseph A.
Am. ex. 1934 Cinn., O. M.
SWAN, Paul.
Am. b. Illinois; ac. 1929 New York. F.
SWAN, Robert John.
Eng. b. London 1888; ad. 1934 Chelsea. Wa.
SWANEVELT, Herman van.
Dut. Woerden 1600/20-1655 Paris. B-C-722.
SWANN, Don. (Et)
Am. ad. 1935 Balt., Md. M.
SWANSON, Bennet A.
Am. b. 1899; ad. 1934 St. Paul, Minn. A.
SWANSON, Jonathan M.
Am. b. Chicago 1888; ad. 1934 New York. A.
SWANTEES, Ethel.
Am. ex. 1935 New York. M.
SWANWICK, Joseph Harold.
Eng. 1866-1929. B-Wa1929-Y01930.
SWART, Jan [Giovanni de Frisia].
Ger. b. Groningen 1469; d. 1535 in Gouda, Holland. B-C.
SWARTZ, Harold. (S)
Am. b. San Marcial, New Mex. 1887; ad. 1934 Los Angeles, Calif. A-W.
SWAYNE, Hugh Nelson.
Am. b. Hickman, Ky. 1903; ad. 1934 Same. A.
SWEBACH, Bernard Edouard.
Fr. Paris 1800-1870 Versailles. B.
SWEBACH, Jacques François Joseph [Fontaine].
Fr. Metz 1769-1823 Paris. B-C.
SWEDISH Artists. *see* book 824.
SWEENEY, Dan. (Ill)
Am. ad. 1934 New York. M.
SWEENEY, Sarah C.
Am. b. Nashville, Tenn. 1876; ad. 1915 New York. A12.
SWEERTS [or Swarts], Michael.
Dut. Amsterdam 1614/20-1656. B.
SWENGEL, Faye.
Am. ad. 1934 Lumberville, Pa. M.
SWENSON, Gottfrida.
Am. b. Sweden 1882; ad. 1934 Duluth, Minn. A.
SWENSON, Ole.
Am. b. Kansas City, Mo. 1907; ad. 1934 Same. A.
SWERTS, Jan.
Belg. Antwerp 1825-1879 Prague, Czec. B-C.
SWETT, C. A. (Eg)
Am. ac. 1839-1862 in Boston. F.
SWETT, William Otis, Jr.
Am. b. Worcester, Mass. 1859; ad. 1934 Dover Plains, N. Y. A-F.
SWIECINSKI, Georges Clément de. (S)
Fr. b. Radaus 1878. DBA.
SWIFT, Ivan.
Am. b. Wayne, Mich. 1873; ad. 1934 Detroit, Mich. A-F-W.
SWIGGETT, [Mrs.] Grace Kiess.
Am. b. Cinn., O.; ad. 1934 Wash., D. C. A.
SWINDELL, Bertha. (Min)
Am. b. Balt., Md. 1874; ad. 1934 Same. A.

SWINNERTON, JAMES G. (Ill)
Am. b. Calif.; ad. 1934 Palo Alto, Calif. F-M.
SWINSTEAD, A. LESTER.
Eng. ad. 1934 London Wa.
SWINSTEAD, CHARLES HILLYARD.
Br. 1850-1921. B-Y01922.
SWINSTEAD, ERIC HUBERT.
Eng. b. Stoke-Newington 1882. Wa1929.
SWINSTEAD, FRANK HILLYARD.
Eng. b. Chelsea 1862. Wa1929.
SWINTON, ALFRED.
Am. England 1826-1920 Hackensack, N. J. A017.
SWINTON, JAMES RANNIE.
Eng. 1816-1888. B-DNB.
SWINTON, MARION.
Am. ad. 1935 Hackensack, N. J. M.
SWISHER, ALLAN LEE.
Am. Gypsum, Kan. 1888; ad. 1935 New York. A12-F.
SWOPE, H. VANCE.
Am. Indiana 1879-1926. A024-F.
SWOPE, KATE F.
Mrs. Charlton A. Swope.
Am. b. Louisville, Ky.; ad. 1926 New York. A12-F.
SWORD, JAMES BRADE.
Am. Phila., Pa. 1839-1915. A013-C-F.
SWYNNERTON, ANNIE LOUISA.
Mrs. Joseph William Swynnerton.
Eng. Manchester 1845-1933 Hayling Island. B-M-Obit. N. Y. papers, 10-25-1933.
SWYNNERTON, JOSEPH WILLIAM. (S)
Eng. ac. 1873 in London. B.
SYENES, ANDRÉ DUGO.
Hun. b. Szolnok 1895. DBA.
SYER, JOHN [The Younger].
Eng. Atherton 1815-1885 Exeter. B.
SYKES, [Mrs.] ANNIE G.
Am. b. Brookline, Mass.; d. 1931 Cinn., O. A028-F.
SYKES, CHARLES HENRY. (Cart)
Am. b. Athens, Ala. 1882; ad. 1934 Phila., Pa. A28-F-W.
SYKES, GODFREY. (Mu)
Eng. Malton 1825-1866 London. B-DNB.
SYKES, MALTBY.
Am. ad. 1934 Birmingham, Ala. M.
SYKES, S. D. GILCHRIST.
Am. b. Cheshire, Eng.; ad. 1934 Brookline, Mass. A.
SYLVESTER, FREDERICK OAKES.
Am. Brockton, Mass. 1869-1915 St. Louis, Mo. A012-F-46.
SYLVESTER, HARRY ELLIOTT.
Am. North Easton, Mass. 1860-1921 Boston. A018.
SYLVESTER, [Mrs.] IDA POND.
Am. b. New York; ad. 1934 Passaic, N. J. A.
SYLVESTER, JOSEPH NÖEL.
Fr. b. Béziers 1847; ac. 1869-1883 in Paris. B-C.
SYME, JOHN.
Scot. Edinburgh 1795-1861 Same. B-DNB.
SYME, PATRICK. (P-Author)
Scot. Edinburgh 1774-1845 Dollar. B-DNB.
SYMINGTON, JAMES.
Am. b. Baltimore, Md. 1841; ad. 1915 New York. A12.
SYMMES, AGNES LOUISE.
Am. b. University, Va. 1889; ad. 1934 Same. A.
SYMONDS, WILLIAM ROBERT.
Eng. b. Suffolk 1851. B-Wa1929.
SYMONS, GEORGE GARDNER.
Am. Chicago, Ill. 1863-1930 Hillside, N. J. A027-F-W14-46-757.
SYMONS, MARK LANCELOT.
Eng. London 1887-1935 Barkham. Wa.
SYMONS, WILLIAM CHRISTIAN.
Eng. b. 1845; d. 1911 in London. B-DNB.
SYNGE, EDWARD M. (Et)
Eng. 1860-1913. M.
SYPIORSKI, ANTOINE DE.
Fr. b. St. Dizier 1890. DBA.
SYRLIN, JÖRG [The Elder]. (S)
Ger. [Swabian] ac. 1460-1491. Hs-Ms.
SYRLIN, JÖRG [The Younger].
Ger. [Swabian] b. 1455; d. 1521. Ms.
SZANKOWSKY, BOLESLAV VON.
Pol. b. 1873 in Poland. M.
SZANTO, LOUIS.
Am. b. Hungary 1893; ad. 1935 New York. M.
SZCZEPKOWSKI, JAN. (Carver)
Pol. b. 1878 in Poland. M.
SZE, [Miss] MAIMIE.
Chinese. ad. 1934 New York. M.
SZEKELY, JOSEPH.
Am. ad. 1935 New York. M.
SZERNER, WLADYSLAW.
Pol. b. 1836. [No death date.] M.
SZINYEI-MERSE, PAUL [or Pal].
Hun. 1845-1920 Paris. B-E.
SZOEKE, ANDREW. (Ill)
Am. ad. 1934 New York. M.
SZÖNYI, ISTVÁN.
Hun. b. 1884; ex. 1934 London. M.
SZPINGIER, ZYGMUNT.
Pol. b. 1901 Warsaw. M.
SZUKALSKI, STANISLAS. (S)
Pol. b. Warta 1895; ad. 1934 Hollywood, Calif. M.
SZYNDLER, PANTALÉON.
Pol. Warsaw 1876-1905 Same. B.

TAAKE, DAISY. (S)
Am. b. St. Louis, Mo. 1886; ad. 1934 Same. A.
TAANMAN, JACOB.
Dut. Zaandam 1836-1923 Amsterdam. B.
TABAR, FRANÇOIS GERMAIN LÉOPOLD.
Fr. Paris 1818-1869 Argenteuil. B-C.
TABARY, ÉMILE.
Fr. ac. 1808 in Paris. [No death date.] B.
TABER, EDWARD MARTIN.
Am. New York 1863-1896 Wash, Conn. I-71.
TACCA, PIETRO. (S)
It. Carrara 1580-1650. B-Hs.
TACCONI, FRANCESCO.
It. Cremona 1464-1490 Same. B-C.
TACK, AUGUSTUS VINCENT.
Am. b. Pittsburgh, Pa. 1870; ad. 1935 New York. A-B-F-W.

TADAMA, Fokko.
Am. b. Bandar, India 1871; ad. 1926 Seattle, Wash. A20-B-F.
TADD, J. Liberty.
Am. England 1863-1917 Phila., Pa. A014.
TADDEO, Bartolo. *see* Bartolo.
TADDEO, Gaddi. *see* Gaddi.
TADEME, Alma. *see* Alma-Tadema.
TADOLINI, Scipione. (S)
It. Rome 1822-1893. B.
TAFFS, C. H. (Ill)
Am. ad. 1934 New York. A.
TAFI, Andrea [Ricchi]. (Mosaic)
It. b. Florence; ac. 1320 Same. B.
TAFLINGER, Elmer E.
Am. b. Ind., Ind. 1891; ad. 1934 Same. A.
TAFT, Lorado. (S-and Author)
Am. b. Elmwood, Ill. 1860; ad. 1935 Chicago. A-B-Cs-E-F-Hs-Ta-W-46-757-768-798-813-815.
TAGE, Emp.
Am. ex. 1935 New York. M.
TAGGART, Edwin Lynn.
Am. b. Richmond, Ind. 1905; ad. 1934 Same. A.
TAGGART, George Henry.
Am. b. 1865; ad. 1934 Port Washington, N. Y. A-F.
TAGGART, John C.
Am. ac. 1855. M.
TAGGART, Lucy M.
Am. b. Ind., Ind.; ad. 1934 Same. A.
TAGGART, Richard T.
Am. b. Ind., Ind. 1904; ad. 1934 Altadena, Calif. A.
TAGLIANI, Ludovico.
It. b. Florence; ac. early 19th Cent. B.
TAGORE, [Sir] Rabindranath.
Br. b. 1861; ad. 1934 Calcutta, India. M.
TAHY, Joannes de.
Hun. ac. 20th Cent. M.
TAI CHIN.
Chinese. Ming Dynasty (1368-1644). E.
TAIGADO, Iké [Akihira].
Jap. 1723-1776. J., Vol. 2, page 78.
TAIKWAN, Yokoyama.
Jap. b. Tokyo 1868; ac. 1934 Same. M.
TAILLASSON, Jean Joseph.
Fr. Blaye 1746-1808 Paris. B-C.
TAILLIS, [Comtesse] L. Gourgand du.
Fr. ac. 1926. Fa.
TAIN-Y-HAN.
Chinese. b. Kinhiang 1904; ad. 1934 Paris. DBA.
TAINTOR, [Mrs.] Daisy Josephine.
Am. b. Ft. Wayne, Ind.; ad. 1934 New York. A.
TAIT, Agnes.
Mrs. William McNulty.
Am. b. New York 1896; ad. 1935 Same. A28-M.
TAIT, Arthur Fitzwilliam.
Am. Liverpool, Eng. 1819-1905 Yonkers, N. Y. A05-B-C-E-F-15.
TAIT, [Mrs.] Bess Norriss.
Aust. b. Melbourne 1878; ad. 1934 Chelsea, Eng. Wa.
TAIT, John Robinson.
Am. Cinn., O. 1834-1909 Balt., Md. A07-B-C-F-15.
TAITE, Alice Maud. *see* Fanner, A. M.
TAKAMURA, Ko-Oun. (S)
Jap. ac. 1900 in Tokyo. M.
TAKANEN, Johannes. (S)
Fin. ac. 19th Cent. in Finland. B.
TAKEKOSHI, Kenzo. (Et)
Jap. d. 1930 in Tokyo. M.
TAKESHI, Hayashi.
Jap. ac. 1932 in Japan. M.
TAKUMA, Tamé-Uji.
Jap. ac. 10th Cent. in Japan. M.
TALARN, Gabriel.
Sp. ac. 1402 in Spain. M.
TALBOT, [Mrs.] Cornelia Brackenridge.
Am. Natrona, Pa. 1888-1925 Same. A022.
TALBOT, George Quartus Pine.
Eng. Bridgewater 1853-1888 Grasmere. M.
TALBOT, Grace Helen. (S)
Am. b. No. Billerica, Mass. 1901; ad. 1934 France. A-Cs-F.
TALBOT, Jean.
Fr. b. Bordeaux 1894. DBA.
TALBOT, Jesse.
Am. b. 1806; d. 1879 Brooklyn, N. Y. B.
TALBOTT, Katherine. (S)
Am. b. Wash., D. C. 1908; ad. 1934 Berkeley, Calif. A.
TALBURT, Harold M. (Ill)
Am. ad. 1935 New York. M.
TALCOTT, Allen Butler.
Am. Hartford, Conn. 1867-1908 Lyme, Conn. A07-B-F.
TALCOTT, Sarah Whiting.
Am. b. West Hartford, Conn. 1852; ad. 1934 Elmwood, Conn. A.
TALCOTT, V. Huntington. (S)
Am. ad. 1934 New York. M.
TALCOTT, William.
Am. ac. 1820-1836. M.
TALIAFERRO, Elizabeth Stewart.
Mrs. W. F. Taliaferro.
Am. b. Newark, N. J. 1869; ad. 1934 Nuttall, Va. A.
TALLBERG, Axel. (Et)
Swe. Geffie 1860-1928, Stockholm. Wa01929.
TALLMAGE, Thomas Eddy. (Et)
Am. b. Wash., D. C. 1876. A28-F.
TALLMAN, [Mrs.] Essie.
Am. ex. 1935 Davenport, Ia. M.
TALLMAN, Martha Griffith.
Mrs. Walter R. Tallman.
Am. Wales 1859-1930 New York. A028-F.
TALMAGE, Algernon M.
Eng. b. 1871; ad. 1934 London. Wa.
TALMAN, John.
Eng. d. 1726 in London. D-DNB.
TALPINO. *see* Salmeggio, Enea.
TALUET, Ferdinand [The Elder]. (S)
Fr. Angers 1820-1904. B.
TAMAGNI DA SAN GIMIGANO, Vincenzo.
It. San Gimigano 1492-1530. B.
TAMARA DE LEMPICKA.
see Lempicka, T. de.
TAMAYO, Rufino.
Mex. b. Mexico 1900; ex. 1935 Cinn., O. M-791.
TAMBURINA, Antonio.
It. ac. 1888. M.
TAMBURINI, Arnoldo.
It. b. Florence 1843. B.

TAMBURNI, José Maria.
Sp. b. 1854; ac. in Barcelona. M.
TAMOTZU, Chuzo. (Eg)
Jap.-Am. b. Japan 1891; ad. 1934 New York. A.
TANAKA, Yashuski.
Jap.-Am. ac. 1918-1927 in France. M.
TANBERG, Ella Hotelling.
Mrs. Ella Hotelling.
Am. b. Jonesville, Wis.; d. 1928 Hollywood, Calif. A026-F.
TANDLER, Rudolph Frederick.
Am. b. Grand Rapids, Mich. 1887; ad. 1934 St. Louis, Mo. A.
TANDY, John.
Eng. b. London 1905; ad. 1934 Same. Wa.
TANDY, Russell H. (Ill)
Am. ad. 1934 New York. M.
TANEFF, Nickola.
Bulgarian. b. 1881. M.
T'ANG YIN.
Chinese. Ming Dynasty (1368-1644). E.
TANGUE, Henry Herbert La.
see La Tangue, H. H.
TANGUY, Yves.
Fr. b. Paris 1900. M.
TANKEI. (S)
Jap. ac. 13th Cent. (Feudal Period). Hs.
TANNAHILL, Mary H.
Am. b. Warrenton, N. C.; ad. 1934 Provincetown, Mass. A-F.
TANNAHILL, Sallie B.
Am. b. New York 1881; ad. 1935 Same. A28-F.
TANNER, Benjamin. (Eg)
Am. New York 1775-1848 Balt., Md. F-2-7-40.
TANNER, Henry Ossawa.
Am. b. Pittsburgh, Pa. 1859; ad. 1935 Paris. A-B-E-F-W-2-7-254-757-801.
TANNER, Henry S. (Eg)
Am. New York 1786-1858 Same. F-2-7.
TANNER, John Sigismund. (Med)
Br. d. 1775. DNB.
TANNER, Virginia B.
Am. ex. 1934 New York. M.
TANOUX, Henri Adrien.
Fr. b. Marseilles; ac. 1905 in Paris. B.
TANTARDINI, Antonio. (S)
It. Milan 1829/33-1879/82. B.
TANYU, Kano.
Jap. Kyoto 1602-1674. J., Vol. 1, page 41.
TAPIRO, José.
Sp. ac. 1865-1900 in Spain. B.
TAQUOY, Maurice.
Fr. b. Mareuil-sur-Ay; ad. 1934 Paris. DBA.
TARAVAL, Jean Hugues.
Fr. Paris 1728-1785 Same. B.
TARBELL, Edmund Charles.
Am. b. West Groton, Mass. 1862; ad. 1934 Boston. A-B-E-F-W-1-46-701.
TARDIEU, Victor François.
Fr. b. Lyons 1870; ac. 1907 in Paris. B-DBA.
TARLETON, Mary Livingston. (S)
Am. b. Stamford, Conn.; ad. 1934 Great Neck, L. I., N. Y. A-F.
TARRANT, Margaret Winifred.
Eng. ad. 1934 Surrey. Wa.
TAS, Jeane.
Am. ex. 1935 New York. M.
TASKER, William.
Br. 1808-1852. M.
TASKEY, Harry Le Roy.
Am. b. Rockford, Ind. 1892; ad. 1934 New York. A.
TASSAERT, Nicolas François Octave.
Fr. Paris 1800-1874 Same. B-C.
TASSEL, Richard. (S)
Fr. Langres 1580-1660 Same. B.
TASSIE, James. (Modeler)
Scot. Glasgow 1735-1799. B-DNB.
TASSIE, William. (Modeler)
Eng. London 1777-1860. B-DNB.
TASSY, Charles Robert.
Fr. b. Paris 1882. DBA.
TATE, Christopher. (S)
Br. 1811-1841. DNB.
TATE, Patricia Marshall.
Mrs. Qistein Lie-Nielsen.
Am. ad. 1935 Boston, Mass. M.
TATE, William.
Eng. b. 1750? d. 1806 Bath. B-DNB.
TATNALL, Henry Lea.
Am. Brandywine, Del. 1829-1885 Wilmington, Del. F.
TATTEGRAIN, François.
Fr. Péronne 1852-1916. B-C-DBA.
TATTERSALL, George ["Wildrake"]. (Eg)
Eng. 1817-1849. B-DNB.
TATTI, Jacopo. *see* Sansavino, J.
TAUBES, Frederick.
Aus. b. Lwow 1900; ad. 1934 New York. M.
TAUCH, Waldine Amanda. (S)
Am. b. Schulenburg, Tex. 1894; ad. 1934 New York. A-Cs.
TAUNAY, Charles Auguste. (S)
Fr. Paris 1769-1824 Rio de Janiero, Brazil. B.
TAUNAY, Nicolas Antoine.
Fr. Paris 1755-1830 Same. B-C-722.
TAURISKOS [of Tralles]. (S)
Gr. ac. 80 B.C. in Rhodes. C-Hs.
TAURIS.
Per. ac. 16th Cent. in Persia. M.
TAUSZKY, David Anthony.
Am. b. Cinn., O. 1878; ad. 1934 New York. A.
TAUZIN, Mario.
Fr. ex. 1935 Paris. M.
TAVERNER, William.
Eng. 1703-1772. B.
TAVERNIER, Hippolyte.
Fr. b. Francheville 1884; ex. 1934 London. DBA.
TAVERNIER, Jules.
Fr. ac. 1865-1870 in Paris. B.
TAVERNIER, Melchior.
Belg. Antwerp 1594-1641 Paris. B.
TAVERNIER, Paul.
Fr. ac. 1876-1905 in Paris. B-C.
TAVSHANJIAN, Artemis. (Min)
Mrs. Charles A. Karagheusian.
Am. b. Englewood, N. J. 1904; ad. 1934 New York. A.
TAYLER, Albert Chevalier.
Eng. Leytonstone 1862-1925 London. B.
TAYLER, Frederick.
Eng. Borham Wood 1802-1889 London. B-DNB.

TAYLOR, ANNA HEYWARD.
Am. b. Columbia, S. C. 1879; ad. 1935 Charleston, S. C. A28.
TAYLOR, BERNARD DOUGLAS.
Eng. Elland 1881-1928. Wa01929.
TAYLOR, [Mrs.] CAROL. (S)
Am. ad. 1934 New York. M.
TAYLOR, CECELIA EVANS. (S)
Am. b. Chicago 1897; ad. 1934 Williamsville, N. Y. A.
TAYLOR, CHARLES ANDREW.
Am. b. Phila., Pa. 1910; ad. 1934 Same. A.
TAYLOR, CHARLES JAY. (Ill)
Am. New York 1855-1929 Pittsburgh, Pa. A026-F-W14.
TAYLOR, CHARLES WILLIAM. (Eg)
Eng. b. Wolverhampton 1878; ad. 1934 Essex. Wa.
TAYLOR, CORA BLISS.
Am. b. Cinn., O. 1895; ad. 1934 Chicago. A.
TAYLOR, [Mrs.] E. A. *see* King, Jessie M.
TAYLOR, EDGAR J.
Am. b. Brooklyn, N. Y. 1862. A28.
TAYLOR, EDWIN C.
Am. b. Detroit, Mich. 1874; ad. 1934 New Haven, Conn. A.
TAYLOR, ELIZABETH.
Am. ad. 1934 New Berlin, Ill. A.
TAYLOR, EMILY HEYWARD DRAYTON.
Mrs. J. Madison Taylor.
Am. b. Phila., Pa. 1860; ad. 1934 Same. A-F-W.
TAYLOR, ERNEST ARCHIBALD.
Scot. b. Greenock; ac. 1929. Wa1929.
TAYLOR, ETHEL C.
Am. ad. 1934 New York. A.
TAYLOR, FARWELL M.
Am. b. Okla. 1905; ad. 1934 San Fran., Calif. A.
TAYLOR, FRANK WALTER. (Ill)
Am. Phila., Pa. 1874-1921 Same. A018-F.
TAYLOR, FRED.
Eng. b. London 1875; ad. 1935 Same. Wa.
TAYLOR, H. WESTON. (Ill)
Am. b. Chester, Pa. 1881; ad. 1934 Same. A.
TAYLOR, HELEN CAMPBELL.
Am. b. Chicago 1900; ad. 1934 Same. A.
TAYLOR, HELEN JACKSON.
Am. b. Kenilworth, Ill. 1903; ad. 1934 Barrington, Ill. A.
TAYLOR, HENRY FITCH.
Am. Cinn., O. 1853-1925 Plainfield, N. J. A022-F-W13.
TAYLOR, HENRY KIND.
Eng. ac. 1857-1869. B.
TAYLOR, HENRY WHITE.
Am. b. Otisville, N. Y. 1899; ad. 1934 Paoli, Pa. A.
TAYLOR, HILDA.
Am. ad. 1935 New York. M.
TAYLOR, HORACE.
Am. b. 1864; d. 1921 Swamp Lake, Wis. A018.
TAYLOR, IDA C.
Am. b. Le Roy, N. Y.; ad. 1934 Same. A.
TAYLOR, ISAAC [The Elder]. (Eg)
Eng. Worcester 1730-1807 Edmonton. B-DNB.
TAYLOR, ISAAC [The Younger]. (Eg)
Eng. London 1759-1829 Ougar. B-DNB.
TAYLOR, ISAAC [The Third]. (Eg-Author)
Eng. 1787-1865. DNB.
TAYLOR, ISIDORE JUSTIN SEVERIN. (Eg)
Fr. b. 1789; d. 1879 in Paris. B.
TAYLOR, JACK W. (Eg)
Am. ex. 1934 New York. M.
TAYLOR, JAMES. (China P. and Ill)
Eng. Worcester 1745-1797 London. B-DNB.
TAYLOR, JAMES E. (Ill)
Am. Cinn., O. 1839-1901 New York. A04.
TAYLOR, [Mrs.] JESSE MARION.
see King, J. M.
TAYLOR, JOHN.
Eng. 1745?-1806. B-DNB.
TAYLOR, JOHN ["Old Taylor"].
Eng. London 1739-1838 Same. B-DNB.
TAYLOR, JOHN C. E.
Am. b. New Haven, Conn. 1902; ad. 1934 Hartford, Conn. A.
TAYLOR, JOHN W.
Am. ex. 1935 Andover, Mass. M.
TAYLOR, JOSEPH RICHARD. (S)
Am. b. Lincoln Co., Wash.; ad. 1934 Norman, Okla. A.
TAYLOR, LEONARD CAMPBELL.
Eng. b. Oxford 1874; ad. 1934 London. B-Wa.
TAYLOR, MARY SMYTH PERKINS.
Mrs. William F. Taylor.
Am. Phila., Pa. 1875-1931 Same. A028-F.
TAYLOR, PAUL FORRESTER.
Am. b. Phila., Pa. 1898; ad. 1934 Same. A.
TAYLOR, PETER [or Patrick].
Scot. 1756-1788. B-DNB.
TAYLOR, PRENTISS. (Eg)
Am. ad. 1934 New York. M.
TAYLOR, RALPH.
Am. b. Russia 1896. A.
TAYLOR, R. PERMELIA.
Am. ex. 1935 New York. M.
TAYLOR, REBECCA LINDON.
Am. ex. 1933 New York. M.
TAYLOR, REBECCA SMITH.
Am. ac. 1933. M.
TAYLOR, RENWICK.
Am. b. 1898; ad. 1934 Brooklyn, N. H. A.
TAYLOR, ROBERT B.
Am. ad. 1934 Toledo, O. M.
TAYLOR, ROLLA S.
Am. b. Galveston, Tex.; ad. 1934 San Antonio, Tex. A.
TAYLOR, ROY W. (Cart)
Am. b. 1882; d. 1914 Wash., D. C. A012.
TAYLOR, SCOTT. (S)
Am. ad. 1935 Paris, Fr. M.
TAYLOR, SIMON. (Botanical-P)
Eng. d. 1772/98. B-DNB.
TAYLOR, THOMAS.
Am. Scotland 1854-1915 Brooklyn, N. Y. A012.
TAYLOR, THOMAS.
Eng. b. Bishop 1817; d. 1880. B.
TAYLOR, WILLIAM BENJAMIN SARSFIELD.
Ir. b. Dublin 1781; d. 1850. B-DNB.
TAYLOR, WILLIAM FRANCIS.
Am. b. Hamilton, Ont. Can. 1883; ad. 1934 Lumberville, Pa. A.
TAYLOR, WILLIAM H.
Can. b. Port Stanley, Falkland Islands, So. Amer.; ac. 1933 Canada. M.

TAYLOR, William Ladd.
Am. b. Grafton, Mass. 1854; d. 1926. A024-F-W14-46-47.
TAYLOR, William Nicholson.
Am. b. Cinn., O. 1882; ad. 1934 New York. A.
TAYLOR, Will Samuel. (Mu)
Am. b. Ansonia, Conn. 1882; ad. 1934 Prov., R. I. A-F-W.
TAYLOR, Wynne Byard. (S)
Mrs. Edward A. Taylor.
Am. ad. 1934 Southport, Conn. M.
TCHEKHONINE, Serge.
Dan. b. Novgorod, Russia 1878. DBA.
TCHELITCHEW, Pavel [or Paul].
Rus. b. Moscow 1898; ex. 1934 New York. M-797.
TCHOUKIN, S. S.
Rus. 1754/8-1828. B.
TEAGUE, Donald. (Ill)
Am. b. Brooklyn, N. Y. 1897; ad. 1934 New Rochelle, N. Y. A.
TEASDALE, Mary.
Am. b. Salt Lake City, Utah; ad. 1915 Same. A12.
TEDESCO, Piero di Giovanni. (S)
It. ac. 14th Cent. in Florence. Hs.
TEDICE, Enrico di. *see* Enrico di T.
TEED, Douglas Arthur.
Am. b. Utica, N. Y. 1864. [Deceased.] A20.
TEED, H. Samuel.
Eng. London 1883-1916 in war. M.
TEEL, Lewis W.
Am. ad. 1934 El Paso, Tex. M.
TEERLING [or Teerlinc], Levina. (Min)
Flem. ac. 1545/90 in Bruges. B.
TEESDALE, Christopher H.
Am. b. Eltham, Eng. 1886; ad. 1934 Cleburne, Tex. A.
TEE-VAN, Helen Damrosch.
Mrs. John Tee-Van.
Am. b. New York 1893; ad. 1934 Same. A.
TEFFT, Carl E. (S)
Am. b. Brewster, Me. 1874. A12-F-Ta.
TEGNE, Donald. (Ill)
Ad. 1934 New Rochelle, N. Y. M.
TEGNER, Rudolph. (S)
Dan. ac. 1900-1934 in Copenhagen. B-798.
TEICHNER, Joseph.
Am. b. Gyoma, Hun. 1888; ad. 1934 New York. A.
TEIGEN, Peter.
Am. b. Minn., Minn.; ad. 1935 Princeton, N. J. M.
TEIJI, Tsuda. (S)
Jap. b. Tatsuno 1896; ad. 1934 Osake. M.
TEJADE, Carlos S. de.
Sp. ac. 1933. M.
TELAKOWSKA, [Miss] Wanda. (Eg)
Pol. b. Sosnowiec 1905; ad. 1934 Warsaw. M.
TELECLES. (S)
Gr. ac. 560 B.C. in Samos. M.
TELLANDER, Frederic.
Am. b. 1878; ad. 1934 Chicago. A.
TELLING, Elizabeth. (Et)
Am. b. Milwaukee, Wis. 1882; ex. 1935 New York. A28-F.
TEMPEL, Abraham Lamberts van den.
Dut. Leeuwarden 1622/3-1672 Amsterdam. B-C-722.
TEMPERILLI, Il. *see* Caselli, Christoforo.
TEMPESTA, Antonio.
It. Florence 1555-1630 Rome. B-C-722.
TEMPESTA, Il. Cavaliere.
see Molyn, Pieter de [The Younger].
TEMPESTI, Giovanni Baptista.
It. Volterra 1730-1804 Pisa. B.
TEMPLE, Vere.
Eng. ad. 1934 London. M.
TEMPLE-BIRD, [Mrs.] Kathleen.
Eng. b. Ipswich; ad. 1934 London. Wa.
TEN EYCK, John Adams.
Am. Bridgeport, Conn. 1893-1932 Stamford, Conn. A029-F.
TEN KATE, Herman Frederick Carel.
Dut. The Hague 1822-1891 Same. B-C.
TEN KATE, Hendrik Gerrit.
Dut. Amsterdam 1803-1856 Same. B.
TEN KATE, Johan Mari Henri.
Dut. b. The Hague 1831. [No death date.] B.
TEN KATE, Sube J.
Dut. b. 1858; ac. 1900 in Amsterdam. B.
TENERANI, Pietro da Torano. (S)
It. Carrara 1798-1869. B-Hs.
TENG CHUN.
Chinese. ac. Sung Dynasty. M.
TENGGREN, Gustaf. (Ill)
Am. ad. 1934 Rhinbeck, N. Y. M.
TENGELER, J. W.
Dut. ac. 1771. M.
TENIERS, David [The Elder].
Flem. Antwerp 1582-1649 Same. B-Bd-C-E-722.
TENIERS, David [The Younger].
Flem. Antwerp 1610-1690 Brussels. B-Bd-C-E-722.
TENIERS, David III.
Flem. Antwerp 1638-1685 Brussels. B-E.
TENNANT, Allie Victoria. (S)
Am. b. St. Louis, Mo.; ad. 1934 Dallas, Tex. A.
TENNANT, John F.
Eng. 1796-1872. B.
TENNIEL, [Sir] John. (Cart)
Eng. Kensington 1820-1914 London. B-DNB-E.
TEPPER, Natalie A.
Am. b. New York 1892; ad. 1934 Brooklyn, N. Y. M.
TEPPER, Saul. (Ill)
Am. b. New York 1899; ad. 1934 Same. A.
TER BORCH [or Terburg], Géraerd [The Younger].
Dut. Zwolle 1617-1681 Deventer. B-Bd-C-E-592-722.
TER BORCH [de Dude], Gérard.
Dut. Zwolle 1584-1662. B-592.
TERBRUGGHEN [or Verbruggen], Henrik.
Dut. Utrecht 1588-1629 Same. B.
TERECHKOVITCH, Kostia [or Constantin].
Rus. b. Moscow 1902; ex. 1934 in London. DBA-797.
TER MEULEN. *see* Meulen.
TERRAIRE, Clovis Frédéric.
Fr. ac. 1905 in Paris. B.

TERRASSE, M. J. A. Edouard.
Fr. b. Puy 1856. B.
TERRELL, Allen Townsend. (S)
Am. ad. 1934 Riverhead, N. Y. M.
TERRENI [or Ferri], Antonio. (Et)
It. ac. 18th Cent. in Florence. M.
TERRIZZI, Anthony T. (S)
Am. ad. 1915 New York. A12.
TERRY, Luther.
Am. Enfield, Conn. 1813-1869 Italy. F-3-4-15.
TERWEN [or Terwee], Jan Aerts. (S)
Dut. Dordrecht 1511-1589. Hs.
TESCHENDORFF [or Teschen], Emil.
Ger. Stettin 1833-1894 Berlin. B-C.
TESSAU, Mori.
Jap. d. 1841. J., Vol. 2, page 98.
TESSIER, Louis Adolphe.
Fr. b. Anvers; ac. 1886-1909 in Paris. B.
TESTA, Pietro [Lucchesino].
It. Lucca 1617-1650 Rome. B-C-722.
TESTELIN [or Tettelin], Henri.
Fr. Paris 1616-1695 The Hague, Holland. B-C-722.
TESTELIN [or Tettelin], Louis [The Elder].
Fr. Paris 1615-1655 Same. B-C-722.
TETZEL, George James.
Am. ad. 1935 New York. M.
TEUINISSEN [or Authonisz], Cornelis.
Dut. 1499-1553. M.
TEVIS, E. E. (Ill)
Am. ad. 1933 New York. M.
TEW, Maguerite R. (S)
Am. b. Magdalena, New Mex. 1886; ad. 1934 Los Angeles, Calif. A.
TEWSBURY, Fanny Wallace.
Am. b. Boston; ad. 1934 Newton, Mass. A.
TEXIER, Jean Ernest. (S)
Fr. Paris 1829-1861 Same. B-Hs.
THACHER, Elizabeth.
Am. b. Brookline, Mass. 1899; ad. 1934 Same. A.
THACKERA, James. (Eg)
Am. Phila., Pa. 1767-1848 Same. F-2-7.
THACKERA, William W. (Eg)
Am. Phila., Pa. 1791-1839 Same. F-2-7.
THACKERAY, William Makepeace. (Novelist and Illustrator)
Eng. Calcutta, India 1811-1863 Kensington, Eng. B-DNB.
THAIN, Howard A.
Am. b. Dallas, Tex. 1891; ad. 1934 New York. A.
THALINGER, E. Oscar.
Am. b. Alsace-Lorraine 1885; ad. 1934 St. Louis, Mo. A.
THANGUE, Henry Herbert.
see La Tangue, H. H.
THAULOW, Fritz [or Frits].
Nor. Christiania 1847-1906 Volendam, Holland. B.
THAW, Florence.
Mrs. Alex Blair Thaw.
Am. b. New York 1864; ad. 1934 Wash., D. C. A.
THAYER, Abbott Handerson.
Am. Boston 1849-1921 Monadnock, N. H. A018-B-C-E-F-1-15-46-71-255-256-257-701.
THAYER, [Mrs.] Emma Beach.
Am. 1850-1924. A021-F.
THAYER, Ethel Randolph.
Am. b. Boston 1904; ad. 1934 Same. A.
THAYER, Gerald Handerson.
Am. b. Cornwall, N. Y. 1883; ac. 1926 Monadnock, N. H. A20-F.
THAYER, Gladys.
Mrs. David Reasoner.
Am. b. So. Woodstock, Conn. 1886; ex. 1935 New York. A12-F-M.
THAYER, Polly.
Am. ad. 1935 Boston, Mass. M.
THAYER, Raymond L.
Am. b. Sewickley, Pa. 1886; ad. 1934 New York. A.
THAYER, Sanford.
Am. ac. 1930 in Syracuse, N. Y. F-M.
THAYER, Theodora W. (Min)
Am. Milton, Mass. 1868-1905 New York. A06-F-46.
THEAKSTON, Joseph. (S)
Eng. York 1772-1842 Pimlico. B-DNB.
THÉAULON [or Théolon], Étienne.
Fr. b. 1739; d. 1780 Paris. B.
THECLA, Julia.
Am. ad. 1934 Chicago, Ill. M.
THEDY, Marc.
Ger. b. Munich 1858. B.
THEED, William [The Elder].
Eng. 1764-1817. B-DNB.
THEED, William [The Younger]. (S)
Eng. Trentham 1804-1891. DNB-Hs.
THEIS, [Mrs.] Gladys Huling.
Am. b. Bartlesville, Okla. 1903; ad. 1934 Wash., D. C. A.
THEISS, John William.
Am. b. Zelionople, Pa. 1863; ad. 1934 Springfield, Ohio. A.
THELEN-RUDEN. *see* Ruden, T.
THEOBALD, Elizabeth Sturtevant. (S)
Mrs. Samuel Theobald, Jr.
Am. b. Cleveland, O. 1876; ad. 1934 New York. A-F.
THEOBALD, Samuel, Jr.
Am. b. Balt., Md. 1872; ad. 1934 New York. A.
THEOCLES. (S)
Gr. ac. 550 B.C. in Sparta. M.
THEODORICH OF PRAGUE.
Hun. ac. 1348-1375 in Prague, Czec. B.
THEODOROPOULO, A. (Eg)
Gr. ex. 1935 Athens, Gr. M.
THEODOROS. (S)
Gr. ac. 575 B.C. in Athens. B-C-Hs.
THÉOLON. *see* Théaulon.
THEON.
Gr. ac. 4th Cent. B.C. in Samos. B-C-E.
THEOTOCOPULI, Domenico.
see Greco, El.
THEOTOCOPULI, Jörge Manuel.
Son of El. Greco [Domenico T.].
Sp. 1578-1631. M.
THERIAT, Charles James.
Am. b. New York 1860; ad. 1933 Paris. B-F-W.
THESIGER, Ernest.
Eng. b. London 1879; ad. 1934 New York. Wa.

THETFORD, William E.
Am. London 1813-1903 Brooklyn, N. Y. A05.
THEUERKAUFF, Carl Rudolph.
Am. Germany 1875-1926 Rochester, N. Y. A023-F.
THEUS, Jeremiah.
Am. Switzerland 1719-1774 Charleston, S. C. B-F-2-25-182.
THEVENAZ, Paul.
Am. Geneva, Swi. 1891-1921 U. S. A018.
THEVENET, Jacques.
Fr. b. Montquin 1891. DBA.
THEVENOT, François.
Fr. b. Paris 1856. B-DNB.
THEW, Garret.
Am b. Sharon, Conn. 1892; ad. 1934 Westport, Conn. A.
THEW, Robert. (Eg)
Am. ac. 1850-1865. F-7.
THEW, Robert. (Eg)
Eng. Patrington 1758-1802 Stevenage. B-DNB.
THIEDE, Henry A. (Ill)
Am. b. Germany 1871; ad. 1934 Chicago. A.
THIEL, Julius Arthur.
Ger. b. Dresden 1841; ac. 1887 London. B.
THIELE, Friedrich Johann Alexander.
Ger. Erfurt 1747-1803 Dresden. B-C.
THIELE, Ivan.
Fr. b. Strassburg 1877. DBA.
THIELEN, Jan Philip van [Rigouldts].
Flem. Mechlin 1618-1667 Boisschot. B-C-722.
THIELLEY, Claude.
Fr. Rully 1811-1891. B.
THIEM, Herman C.
Am. b. Rochester, N. Y. 1870; ad. 1934 Same. A.
THIEME, Anthony.
Am. b. Rotterdam, Holland 1888; ad. 1935 Boston. A.
THIERSCH, Ludwig.
Bav. b. Munich, Ger. 1825; ac. 1861 in Berlin. B-C.
THIL, Jean Charles de.
Ger. Nüremberg 1624-1676. B.
THIL, Jeanne.
Fr. b. Calais 1887. DBA.
THIRION, Eugène Romain.
Fr. Paris 1839-1898. B-C.
THIRTLE, John.
Eng. Norwich 1774-1839 Same. B-DNB.
THOBURN, Jean.
Am. Calcutta, India 1887-1934 Pittsburgh, Pa. A.
THOELE, Lillian Caroline Anna.
Am. b. St. Louis, Mo. 1894; ad. 1934 Same. A.
THOENER, Charles H.
Am. b. 1884; d. 1924 Yonkers, N. Y. A023.
THOLEN, William Bastien.
Dut. Amsterdam 1860-1931 The Hague. B-M.
THOM, James. (S)
Scot. Ayrshire 1799-1850 New York. B-DNB.
THOM, James [or John].
Scot. b. Edinburgh 1785; ac. 1815 London. B-DNB.
THOM, James Crawford.
Am. New York 1835-1898 Atlantic Highlands, N. J. B-C-F-15.
THOMA, Hans.
Ger. Bernau 1839-1924 Carlsruhe. B-E.
THOMAS, Alexandre.
Ger. Prussia 1804/10-1894 Brussels, Belg. B.
THOMAS, Allan A. F. (Ill)
Am. b. Jackson, Mich. 1902. A.
THOMAS, Byron.
Am. b. Balt., Md. 1902; ad. 1934 New York. A.
THOMAS, Cecil. (S)
Eng. b. London 1885; ad. 1934 Same. Wa.
THOMAS, Conrad Arthur. (Mu)
Am. Dresden, Ger. 1858-1932 No. Pelham, N. Y. A029-F.
THOMAS, D. F. (Min)
Am. d. 1924 in Baldwin Park, Calif. A023.
THOMAS, [Mrs.] Elizabeth Finley.
Am. b. St. Paul, Minn.; ac. 1930 New York. A12-M.
THOMAS, Ellen.
Am. b. Augusta, Ga. 1895; ad. 1934 Same. M.
THOMAS, Emma Warfield.
Am. b. Phila., Pa.; ad. 1934 Same. A.
THOMAS, Estelle L.
Am. b. New York; ad. 1934 Pittsburgh, Pa. A.
THOMAS, Eugène Émile. (S)
Fr. Paris 1817-1882 Neuilly. B.
THOMAS, Genevieve. (S)
Am. ad. 1934 New York. M.
THOMAS, George Grosvenor.
Scot. 1856-1923. M.
THOMAS, George Havard. (S)
Eng. Sorento, It. 1893-1933 London. M-Wa1929-Obit. Art News, 12-30-1933.
THOMAS, George Housman.
Eng. London 1824-1868 Boulogne, Fr. B-C-DNB.
THOMAS, Henry Atwell.
Am. New York 1834-1904 Brooklyn, N. Y. A05.
THOMAS, Howard.
Am. b. Mt. Pleasant, O. 1899; ad. 1934 Milwaukee, Wis. A.
THOMAS, Isaiah. (Eg)
Am. b. 1749; d. 1831 Worcester, Mass. F-2.
THOMAS, James Havard. (S)
Eng. Bristol 1854-1921. B-E.
THOMAS, Jan [The Younger].
Flem. Ypres 1617-1673/8 Vienna, Aus. B-C.
THOMAS, John. (S)
Eng. Chalfont 1813-1862 Birmingham. B-DNB.
THOMAS, John Evan. (S)
Eng. Brecon 1809-1873 London. B-DNB.
THOMAS, Lenore. (Carver)
Am. ex. 1935 New York. M.
THOMAS, Lillian M. (Min)
Am. ad. 1934 Phila., Pa. M.
THOMAS, Margaret.
Eng. ac. 1863-1880 in London. B.
THOMAS, Muriel.
Am. ex. 1935 New York. M.

THOMAS, Paul.
Fr. b. Paris 1859. B-DBA.
THOMAS, Paul Kirk Middlebrook.
Am. b. Phila., Pa. 1875; ad. 1934 New York. A-F-W.
THOMAS, Percy. (Et)
Br. 1846-1922. Y01923.
THOMAS, Roland.
Am. b. Kansas City, Mo. 1883; ad. 1934 Same. A020-F.
THOMAS, Ruth.
Am. b. Wash., D. C. 1893; ad. 1934 Newport, R. I. A.
THOMAS, Steffen Wolfgang George. (S)
Am. b. Fuerth, Ger. 1906; ad. 1934 Atlanta, Ga. A.
THOMAS, Stephen Seymour.
Am. b. San Antonio, Tex. 1868; ad. 1934 Los Angeles, Calif. A12-B-F-W13.
THOMAS, [Mrs.] Vernon. (Ill)
Am. b. Evanston, Ill. 1894; ad. 1934 Chicago. A.
THOMAS, Victor. (Eg)
Fr. Paris 1750-1812. B.
THOMASON, Francis Q.
Am. b. Van Buren, Ark.; ad. 1926 Phila., Pa. A12-F.
THOMASSIN, Simeon. (Eg)
Fr. Troyes 1652-1732 Paris. B.
THOMPKINS, Clementina.
see Tompkins, C.
THOMPSON. *see also* Thomson.
THOMPSON, Albert.
Am. b. Woburn, Mass. 1853; ac. 1881. C-F-15.
THOMPSON, Alfred Wadsworth.
Am. Balt., Md. 1840-1896 Summit, N. J. B-Bd-C-F-15-39.
THOMPSON, Cephas [The Elder].
Am. Middleboro, Mass. 1775-1856 Same. B.
THOMPSON, Cephas Giovanni [The Younger].
Am. Middleboro, Mass. 1809-1888 New York. B-C-F-2-4-15.
THOMPSON, Charles. (Eg)
Eng. London 1791-1843 Germany. B-DNB.
THOMPSON, Charles Thurston. (Eg)
Eng. Perkham 1816-1868 Paris. B-DNB.
THOMPSON, [Mrs.] Edity Blight.
Am. b. Phila., Pa. 1884; ad. 1934 Westbury, L. I., N. Y. A-DBA-F.
THOMPSON, Elizabeth [Lady Butler].
Eng. b. Switzerland 1844; ex. 1920 London. B.
THOMPSON, Ellen Kendall Baker.
Mrs. Harry Thompson.
Am. b. Fairfield, N. Y.; d. 1913 England. A0X1.
THOMPSON, Ernest Heber. (Et)
Aust. Dunedin, N. Z.; ad. 1934 London. Wa.
THOMPSON, Ernest Thorne. (Et)
Am. b. St. John, N. B. Can. 1897; ad. 1934 New Rochelle, N. Y. A.
THOMPSON, George Albert.
Am. b. New Haven, Conn. 1868; ad. 1934 Mystic, Conn. A-F.
THOMPSON, Georgette Rosamund.
Am. b. New Orleans, La. 1905; ad. 1934 Same. A.
THOMPSON, Harry Ives.
Am. West Haven, Conn. 1840-1906 Same. A20-F-3.
THOMPSON, Jacob.
Eng. Penrith 1806-1879 Cumberland. B-DNB.
THOMPSON, Jerome.
Am. Middleboro, Mass. 1814-1886 Glen Gardner, N. J. B-C-F-4-15.
THOMPSON, John. (Eg)
Eng. Manchester 1785-1866 Kensington. B-DNB.
THOMPSON, John Edward.
Am. b. Buffalo, N. Y. 1882; ad. 1934 Denver, Colo. A.
THOMPSON, Juliet.
Am. b. New York; ad. 1934 Same. A.
THOMPSON, Kate E.
Am. b. Middletown, N. Y. 1872; ad. 1934 Pompton Plains, N. J. A.
THOMPSON, Kenneth.
Am. ex. 1935 New York. M.
THOMPSON, Launt. (S)
Am. Ireland 1833-1894 Middletown, N. Y. E-F-Hs-Ta.
THOMPSON, Leslie Prince.
Am. b. Medford, Mass. 1880; ad. 1934 Boston. A-F-W.
THOMPSON, Louise Guthrie.
Am. b. Okla. 1902; ad. 1934 Los Angeles, Calif. A.
THOMPSON, Martin E.
Am. b. 1786; d. 1877 New York. B.
THOMPSON, Marvin Francis.
Am. b. Rushville, Ill. 1895; ad. 1934 Chicago. A.
THOMPSON, Mills. (Mu)
Am. b. Wash., D. C. 1875; ad. 1934 Saranac, N. Y. A-F-W.
THOMPSON, Myra.
Am. b. Manry Co., Tenn. 1860; ad. 1915 Spring Hill, Tenn. A12.
THOMPSON, Nellie Louise.
Am. b. Boston, Mass.; ad. 1934 Same. A-F.
THOMPSON, Thomas.
Am. England 1767?-1852 U. S. M.
THOMPSON, Thomas [or John] Clement.
Ir. Belfast 1780-1857 Cheltenham, Eng. B.
THOMPSON, Walter W.
Am. b. Newton, Mass. 1881; ad. 1934 New York. A.
THOMPSON, William.
Br. 1730?-1800. DNB.
THOMPSON, William John.
Am. Savannah, Ga. 1771-1845 Edinburgh, Scot. B-Bd-F-6-179.
THOMPSON, Woodman.
Am. b. Pittsburgh, Pa. 1889; ad. 1934 New York. A.
THOMS, [Dr.] Herbert.
Am. ad. 1935 New Haven, Conn. M.
THOMSEN, Frederick Carlton. (S)
Am. b. 1907; ad. 1934 Greenwich, Conn. M.
THOMSEN, René Charles.
Fr. ad. 1927 Paris. DBA.
THOMSEN, Sandor von Colditz. (S)
Am. Chicago 1879-1914 Same. A012.

THOMSON, ALFRED REGINALD. (Mu)
Br. b. Bangalore, India 1895; ad. 1934 London. Wa.
THOMSON, GEORGE.
Am. b. Claremont, Ont. Can. 1868; ad. 1934 Owen Sound, Can. A.
THOMSON, HENRY.
Eng. London 1773-1843. B-DNB.
THOMSON, HENRY GRINNELL.
Am. b. New York 1850; ad. 1934 Wilton, Conn. A.
THOMSON, HUGH. (Ill)
Ir. Coleraine 1860-1920 Wandsworth, Eng. B-DNB.
THOMSON, JAMES. (Eg)
Eng. Northumberland 1788-1850 London. B-DNB.
THOMSON, [Rev.] JOHN.
Scot. Dailly 1778-1840 Duddingstone. B-DNB-E.
THOMSON, [Mrs.] JOSEPHINE N.
Am. Ind., Ind. 1872-1928 New York. A026.
THOMSON, LESLIE.
Scot. b. Aberdeen 1851. B.
THOMSON, [Miss] LETTICE.
Eng. ex. 1934 London. M.
THOMSON, RODNEY. (Ill)
Am. ad. 1934 New York. M.
THOMSON, TOM.
Can. b. Owen Sound 1877; d. 1917. M.
THOMSON, WILLIAM T.
Am. b. Phila., Pa. 1858; ad. 1934 Same. A.
THOR, WALTER.
Ger. b. Neusalz 1879. B.
THORBURN, ARCHIBALD.
Scot. b. 1860 Scotland. Wa1929.
THORBURN, ROBERT. (Min)
Scot. Dumfries 1818-1885 Tunbridge Wells, Eng. B-C-DNB.
THOREAU, SOPHIA.
Am. ac. 1839. [No death date.] M.
THOREN, OTTO VON.
Aus. Vienna 1828-1889 Paris. B-C.
THORLEY, AGNES M. (Mu)
Am. ex. 1935 New York. M.
THORNDIKE, CHARLES.
Am. ad. 1934 Silvermine, Conn. M.
THORNDIKE, CHARLES HALL.
Am. b. Paris 1875; ad. 1915 Same. A12.
THORNDIKE, GEORGE QUINCY.
Am. Boston 1825-1886 Same. B-F-4-15.
THORNE, ANNA LOUISE.
Am. b. Toledo, O. 1878; ad. 1934 Same. A.
THORNE, DIANA.
Am. b. Canada 1895; ad. 1935 New York. A28.
THORNE, THOMAS ELSTON.
Am. b. Lewiston, Me. 1909; ad. 1934 Portland, Me. A.
THORNE, WILLIAM.
Am. b. Delavan, Wis. 1884; ad. 1934 Same. A-B-F-W.
THORNE-WAIT, ROBERT.
Eng. b. Cheltenham 1842; ad. 1934 Bournemouth. B-Wa.
THORNHILL, [Sir] JAMES. (Mu)
Eng. Dorset 1675-1734 Thornhill. B-C-DNB-E.
THORNLEU, GEORGE WILLIAM.
Fr. ac. 1878-1888 in Paris. B.
THORNLEY, B. JAMES.
Am. ad. 1934 White Plains, N. Y. M.
THORNTON, ALFRED HENRY ROBINSON.
Br. b. Delhi, India 1863; ad. 1934 Painswick, Eng. Wa.
THORNTON, AMY G.
Am. b. 1845; d. 1913 Brooklyn, N. Y. A0X1.
THORNTON, KATHLEEN E.
Eng. London 1901-1927. Wa01929.
THORNTON, WILLIAM. (Eg)
Am. West Indies 1761-1827 Phila., Pa. F-6-7-45.
THORNYCROFT, HELEN.
Eng. ac. 1864-1910 in London. B.
THORNYCROFT, MARY FRANCIS [Mrs. Thomas]. (S)
Eng. London 1814-1895. B-DNB.
THORNYCROFT ROSALIND. (Ill)
Am. ad. 1934 New York. M.
THORNYCROFT, THERESA G.
Eng. ac. 1874 in London. B.
THORNYCROFT, THOMAS. (S)
Eng. b. 1815; d. 1885 London. B-DNB.
THORNYCROFT, WILLIAM HANO. (S)
Eng. London 1850-1925 Oxford. B-E-Hs.
THORPE, FREEMAN.
Am. Ohio 1844-1922 Hubert, Minn. A019-F.
THORPE, POLLY.
Am. ad. 1935 Stamford, Conn. M.
THORS, JOSEPH.
Eng. ac. 1863-1884 in London. B.
THORSEN, LARS.
Am. Norway 1876; ad. 1934 Noank, Conn. A.
THORWALDSEN, ALBERT [or Alberto] BERTEL. (S)
Dan. Copenhagen 1770-1844 Same. B-E-Hs-593-594-710.
THOURON, HENRY JOSEPH.
Am. Phila., Pa. 1851-1915 Rome, It. A013-F.
THRASHER, HENRY DICKINSON. (S)
Am. Cornish, N. H. 1883-1918 France. A015.
THRASHER, LESLIE.
Am. b. Piedmont, W. Va. 1889; ad. 1934 New York. A.
THRASYMEDES. (S)
Gr. ac. 4th Cent. B.C. Paros. E.
THROCKMORTON, CLEON FRANCIS.
Am. b. Atlantic City, N. J. 1897; ad. 1934 New York. A.
THRUPP, FREDERICK. (S)
Br. 1812-1895. DNB.
THUILLIER, PIERRE.
Fr. Amiens 1799-1858 Paris. B-C.
THULDEN [or Tulden], THEODORUS VAN.
Dut. Bois-le-Duc, Fr. 1607-1676 Same. B-C.
THULSTRUP, THUR DE.
Am. Sweden 1848-1930 New York. A027-F-W16.
THUM, PATTY PRATHER.
Am. Louisville, Ky. 1853-1926 Same. A023-F-W13.
THUMAN, PAUL FRIEDRICH.
Ger. b. Tschacksdorf 1834; d. 1908 Berlin. B-C.
THURBER, ALICE HAGERMAN.
Mrs. Thomas L. Thurber.
Am. b. Birmingham, Mich. 1871; ad. 1934 Same. A.

THURBER, Caroline.
Mrs. Dexter Thurber.
Am. b. Oberlin, O.; ad. 1934 Brookline, Mass. A-F-W.
THURBER, James.
Am. ex. 1934 New York. M.
THURLO, Frank.
Am. Newburyport, Mass 1828-1913. A0X1.
THURLOW, Helen. (Ill)
Am. ad. 1934 Norwalk, Conn. A.
THURN, Ernest.
Am. b. Chicago 1889; ad. 1934 East Gloucester, Mass. A.
THURNER, Gabriel Édouard.
Fr. Mulhouse 1840-1907 Paris. B.
THURSTON, [Mrs.] Jane Mc Duffie.
Am. b. Ripon, Wis. 1887; ad. 1934 Pasadena, Calif. A.
THURSTON [or Thuston], John. (Ill)
Eng. Scarboro 1774-1822 London. B-DNB.
THYS, Gysbrecht.
Flem. Antwerp 1616-1684 Same. B.
THYS [or Tyssens], Peter [The Elder].
Dut. Antwerp 1624-1677/9 Same. B-C.
TIARINI, Alessandro.
It. Bologna 1577-1668 Same. B-C-722.
TIBALDI DE PELLEGRINI, Domenico Pellegino.
It. Bologna 1532/40-1582/3. B-722.
TIBALDI, Pellegrino da Bologna.
It. Bologna 1527/32-1592/7 Milan. B-C-722.
TIBBS, Charlotte E.
Am. ad. 1934 Biloxi, Miss. M.
TIBERTI, Alessandro.
It. b. Taizzano 1872. B.
TIBURTIUS, Hans. (Et)
Ger. b. 1892. M.
TICE, Clara.
Am. ad. 1934 New York. M.
TICHY, Hans.
Aus. ex. 1928 in Vienna (Deceased). B.
TIDDEN, John Clark.
Am. b. Yonkers, N. Y. 1889. A28.
TIDEMAND, Adolf.
Nor. Mandal 1814-1876 Christiania. B-C.
TIDEY, Alfred. (Min)
Eng. Worthing 1808-1892 Acton. B-Bd-DNB.
TIDEY, Henry.
Eng. Worthing 1814-1872 London. B-Bd-DNB.
TIEBOUT, Cornelius. (Eg)
Am. New York 1777-1830 Kentucky. B-F-2-7-40-184.
TIECK, Christian Friedrich. (S)
Ger. Berlin 1776-1851 Same. B-Hs.
TIELING [or Fieling], Lodewyk.
It. ac. 17th-18th Cent. in Italy. B.
TIELT, Pierart dou.
Fr. ac. 14th Cent. in Tournai, It. M.
TIEPOLO, Giovanni Battista.
It. Venice 1693/6-1770 Madrid, Sp. B-Bd-C-E-191-595-596-722.
TIEPOLO, Giovanni Domenico.
It. Venice 1727-1804. B-596-722.
TIEPOLO, Lorenzo.
It. Venice 1737?-1772 Espagne. B.
TIFFANY, Louis Comfort.
Am. New York 1848-1933 Same. A030-B-C-E-F-W-15-46-258.
TIFFANY, William Shaw.
Am. b. 1824; d. 1907 New York. A06-B-F.
TILBORCH [or Tilburg], Egidius [or Gillis] van [The Elder].
Flem. Antwerp 1578-1632. B.
TILBORCH [or Tilburg], Egidius [or Gillis] van [The Younger].
Flem. Brussels 1625?-1678? Same. B-C-722.
TILDEN, Alice Foster.
Am. b. Brookline, Mass.; ad. 1934 Milton, Mass. A.
TILDEN, Anna Meyer.
Am. b. Waupun, Wis. 1897; ad. 1934 Hinsdale, Ill. A.
TILDEN, Douglas. (S)
Am. b. Chico, Calif. 1860; d. 1935 Berkeley, Calif. Obit. N. Y. papers, 8-8-1935.
TILENS [or Tilen], Jan [or Hans].
Flem. Antwerp 1589-1630 Same. B-C.
TILGNER, Victor. (S)
Ger. b. 1844; d. 1896 Germany. B-Hs.
TILIUS [or Fielius], Jan.
Dut. b. Bois-le-Duc 1660-1719 Same. B.
TILL, Johann.
Aus. Vienna 1827-1894 Same. B.
TILLAC, Jean Paul.
Fr. ac. 1906 in Paris. B.
TILLEMANS [or Tilmans], Peter.
Flem. Antwerp 1684-1734 Norton, Eng. B-DNB.
TILLEMANS [or Tilmans], Simon Peter [Schenk].
Ger. Bremen 1601-1670 Vienna, Aus. B.
TILLERY, Mary H.
Am. b. Scotland Neck, N. C.; ad. 1934 Raleigh, N. C. A.
TILLIER, Paul Prosper.
Fr. b. Boupère 1834. [No death date.] B.
TILLINGHAST, Mary Elizabeth.
Am. b. New York; d. 1912 Same. A010-F-46.
TILLOTSON, Alexander.
Am. b. Waupun, Wis. 1897; ad. 1934 Milwaukee, Wis. A.
TILLY, Eugène James (Et)
Br. b. Walkern 1870; ad. 1934 Sutton, Eng. Wa.
TILSON, Henry.
Eng. b. Yorkshire 1659; d. 1695/6. B-DNB.
TILTON, Florence.
Am. Vermilion, S. D. 1894; ad. 1934 Normal, Ill. A.
TILTON, John Rollin.
Am. Loudon, N. H. 1828-1888 Rome, It. B-C-F-4-15.
TIMANTHES.
Gr. ac. 400 B.C. in Cythnus. B-C-E.
TIMBAL, Louis Charles.
Fr. Paris 1821/2-1880 Same. B-C.
TIMBRELL, Henry. (S)
Ir. Dublin 1806-1849 Rome, It. B-DNB.
TIMBRELL, James C.
Eng. b. 1810; d. 1850 in Portsmouth, Eng. B-DNB.
TIMKEN, Georgia. *see* Fry, G. T.
TIMLIN, William M.
Br. ac. 1934 in So. Africa. M.
TIMMERMANS, Louis.
Fr. Brussels, Belg. 1846-1910. B.

TIMMINS, Harry L. (Ill)
Am. b. Neb. 1887; ad. 1934 New York. M.
TIMMONS, Edward J. Finley.
Am. b. Janesville, Wis. 1882; ad. 1934 Chicago. A.
TIMOMACHUS.
Gr. ac. 136 B.C. in Byzantium. B-C-E.
TIMOTEO DA URBINO.
see Vite da Urbino, T.
TIMOTHEUS [or Timotleos]. (S)
Fr. ac. 350 B.C. in Athens. E-Hs.
TINDALL, William Edwin.
Eng. b. Scarborough 1863; ad. 1934 Yorks. B-Wa.
TINELLI, Cavalière Tiberio.
It. Venice 1586-1638. B.
TINO DI CAMAINO. *see* Camaino, T.
TINTORETTA, Maria.
It. Venice 1560-1590 Same. C-722.
TINTORETTO, Domenico Robusti.
It. Venice 1562-1637 Same. B-Bd-C-E-597.
TINTORETTO, Il [Jacopo Giacomo Robusti].
It. Venice 1512/18-1594 Same. B-Bd-C-E-78-597-722-790.
TINWORTH, George. (S)
Eng. Walworth 1843-1913 Kew. B-DNB-Hs.
TIRMAN, Henriette.
Fr. b. Charleville; ad. 1934 Paris. DBA.
TISCH, Annette Pauline.
Am. b. New York; ad. 1934 Same. A.
TISCHBEIN, Anton Wilhelm.
Dut. b. 1734; d. 1804 Hanau, Ger. B.
TISCHBEIN, August Anton.
Ger. Rostock 1805; ac. 1845 in Trieste, It. C.
TISCHBEIN, Johann Friedrich August.
Dut. Maestricht 1750-1812 Heidelburg, Ger. B-C.
TISCHBEIN, Johann Heinrich [The Elder].
Ger. Hainau 1722-1789 Cassel. B-C.
TISCHBEIN, Johann Heinrich Wilhelm.
Ger. Hainau 1751-1829 Entin. B-C.
TISCHLER, Victor.
Aus. b. Vienna 1890. DBA.
TISDALE, Elkanch. (Eg)
Am. b. Lebanon, Conn. 1771; [No death date]. F-2-3-6-7-147-179.
TISIO [or Tisi], Benvenuto. *see* Garofalo, Il.
TISSIER, Jean Baptiste Ange.
Fr. Paris 1814-1876 Same. B.
TISSIER, Jeanne.
Fr. b. Moulins 1888. DBA.
TISSOT, James Joseph Jacques.
Fr. Nantes 1836-1902 Paris. B-C-E.
TITCOMB, Mary Bradish.
Am. b. New Hampshire; d. 1927 Marblehead, Mass. A026.
TITCOMB, Virginia Chandler. (S)
Am. b. Otterville, Ill.; ac. 1926 Brooklyn, N. Y. F-W7.
TITCOMB, William Holt Yates.
Eng. Cambridge 1858-1930. Wa1929-Y01931.
TITI [or Tito], Santi di.
It. San Sepolcro 1536-1603 Florence. B-V.
TITIAN [or Tiziano] Vecelli [or Vecellio].
It. Pieve di Cadore 1477/89-1576 Venice. B-Bd-C-E-V-78-710-722-790-898-950.
TITLOW, Harriet Woodfin.
Am. b. Hampton, Va.; ad. 1934 Jersey City, N. J. A.
TITO, Ettore.
It. b. Venice 1859; ad. 1935 Same. B.
TITO, Santi di.
It. Borgo 1536-1603 Florence. B-722.
TITSWORTH, Julia.
Am. b. Westfield, Mass. 1878; ad. 1935 New York. A12-F.
TITTLE, Walter Ernest. (Ill)
Am. b. Springfield, O. 1883; ad. 1934 New York. A-F-W.
TITUS, Aimé Baxter.
Am. b. Cinn., O. 1883; ad. 1934 San Diego, Calif. A.
TITUS, Walton Craig.
Am. ad. 1934 New York. M.
TIVOLI, Rosa da. *see* Roos, Philipp Peter.
TIVOLI, Serafino de.
It. b. Leghorn 1826; [No death date]. B.
TIZIANO, Girolamo di.
[or Dente, Girolamo di.]
It. b. 1510; ac. 1568 Venice. T-V.
TIZIANO, Vecelli. *see* Titian, V.
TOBAR, Don Alfonso Miguel de.
Sp. Higuera 1678-1758 Madrid. B-C.
TOBEY, Barney.
Am. b. New York 1926; ad. 1935 Same. M.
TOBIAS, Morton.
Am. ex. 1935 New York. M.
TOBIN, George Timothy.
Am. Weybridge, Vt. 1864; ad. 1934 New Rochelle, N. Y. A28-F-W.
TOBLER, Victor.
Ger. b. Trogen, Swi. 1846; ac. 1870 Munich. B-C.
TOCQUÉ [or Toucquet], Jean Louis.
Fr. Paris 1676-1772 Same. B-C-722.
TOD DER MARIA, Master of.
see Cleves, Joos van [The Elder].
TODD, Arthur Ralph Middleton.
Eng. ad. 1934 London. Wa.
TODD, Charles Stewart.
Am. b. Owensboro, Ky. 1885; ad. 1915 Cinn., O. A28.
TODD, Henry George.
Eng. Ipswich 1847-1898 Same. B.
TODD, Henry Stanley.
Am. b. St. Louis, Mo. 1871; ad. 1934 Huntington, L. I., N. Y. F-W.
TODD, Murray F. (Et)
Eng. ad. 1932 London. M.
TODD, Nell Margaret.
Am. b. Minn., Minn. 1882; ad. 1915 Same. A12.
TODESCHINI [Cipper].
see Cipper, Giacomo Francesco.
TOEPFFER, Adam Wolfgang.
see Topffer, A. W.
TOEPUT [or Pozzoserrato], Ludwig. (Eg)
Flem. b. 1550; d. 1610. B.
TOERRING, Helene. (Min)
Am. ad. 1934 Phila., Pa. M.
TOFANO, Édouard.
It. ac. 1900 in Paris. B.
TOFEL, Jennings.
Am. ex. 1935 New York. M.
TOFT, Albert. (S)
Eng. Birmingham 1862-1900. B-E-Hs.
TOFT, Peter.
Dan. b. Kolding; d. 1901 in London. M.

TOGAN, UNKOKU.
Jap. ac. 1573-1591. J., Vol. 1, page 113.
TOGORES, JOSÉ DE.
Sp. ad. 1935 Barcelona; ex. 1934 Pittsburgh, Pa. M.
TOJETTI, EDWARD.
Am. Rome, It. 1852-1930 San Fran., Calif. A029.
TOJETTI, VIRGILIO.
Am. Rome, It. 1849-1901 New York. A04-B-C.
TOKITA, KAMEKICHI.
Jap. ad. 1934 Seattle, Wash. M.
TOL, CLAES JACOBSZ.
Dut. ac. 1636 in Utrecht, Holland. B.
TOL, DOMINICUS VAN.
Dut. Bodengraven 1631/42-1676 Leyden. B-C-722.
TOLEDO, JUÁN DE [El. Capitan].
Sp. Lorca 1611-1665 Madrid. B-C.
TOLEGIAN, MANUEL J.
Am. ad. 1935 New York. M.
TOLLES, SOPHIE MAPES.
Am. b. New York; ac. 1883 Same. [No death date]. C-F.
TOLLET, TONY.
Fr. b. Lyons 1857. DBA.
TOLMAN, ROBERT.
Am. ad. 1935 New York. M.
TOLMAN, RUEL PARDEE.
Am. b. Brookfield, Vt. 1878. A28.
TOLMAN, STACY.
Am. b. Concord, Mass. 1860; ad. 1934 Pawtucket, R. I. A.
TOLSON, MAGDALENA WELTY.
Mrs. Norman Tolson.
Am. b. Berne, Ind. 1888; ad. 1934 Chicago. A.
TOLSON, NORMAN.
Am. b. Distington, Cumberland, Eng. 1883; ad. 1934 Chicago. A.
TOLSTOI, [Count] FEDOR.
Rus. b. 1783; d. 1873. Fa.
TOM, JAN BEDYS.
Dut. Boskoop 1813-1894 Leyden. B-C.
TOMA, GIOVACCHINO.
It. Naples 1838-1891 Same. B.
TOMA, MATTHIAS RUDOLF.
Aus. Vienna 1792-1845 Same. B-C.
TOMASO, RICO. (Ill)
Am. b. Chicago 1898; ad. 1934 New York. A.
TOMÈ, LUCA DI [Nuto].
It. ac. 1355-1392 in Siena. M.
TOMÈ, NARCISO.
Sp. b. Toro; ac. 1721 in Toledo. B-Hs.
TOMKINS, PELTRO WILLIAM. (Eg)
Eng. London 1759-1840 Same. B-DNB.
TOMLIN, BRADLEY WALKER.
Am. b. Syracuse, N. Y. 1899; ad. 1934 New York. A.
TOMLINSON, HENRY WELLING.
Am. b. Balt., Md. 1875. A28.
TOMLINSON, REGINALD R.
Eng. b. Overton 1885; ad. 1934 London. Wa.
TOMLINSON-BALDWIN, JEAN.
It. b. Florence 1889. DBA.
TOMMASI, ADOLFO.
It. b. Leghorn 1851. B.
TOMMASI, PUBLIO DE.
It. b. Rome 1849; ac. 1844 Same. B.
TOMMASO DA MODENA. *see* Modena, T.
TOMMASO DI NICCOLÒ.
It. ac. 1355 in Florence. M.
TOMME, LUCA DI. *see* Tomé, L.
TOMPKINS, ABIGAIL BROWN.
Am. ac. 1924; [No death date]. M.
TOMPKINS, CLEMENTINA.
Am. b. Georgetown, D. C. 1848-1913 New York. A028-C-F-15.
TOMPKINS, FRANK HECTOR.
Am. Hector, N. Y. 1847-1922 Brookline, Mass. A019-F.
TOMS, PETER.
[Painted drapery for Joshua Reynolds.]
Eng. d. 1776/7. B-DNB.
TOMSON, ARTHUR.
Eng. Chelmsford 1859-1905 Robertsbridge. B-DNB.
TOMSON, CLIFTON.
Eng. 1775-1835 Nottingham. B.
TONETTI, FRANÇOIS MICHEL LOUIS. (S)
Am. Paris 1863-1920 New York. A017-F-Ta.
TONETTI, MARY LAWRENCE. (S)
Mrs. F. M. L. Tonetti.
Am. ac. 1915 in New York. A12.
TONGE, LAMMERT VAN DER.
Eng. ac. 1915. M.
TONGE, ROBERT.
Eng. Longton 1823-1856 Egypt. B.
TONITA PENA [Quah Ah].
Indian (American). ex. 1932 New York. 411.
TONKIN, [Mrs.] LINLEY MUNSON.
Am. b. Sherman, Tex.; d. 1932 Denton, Tex. A.
TONKS, [Prof.] HENRY.
Eng. b. Solihull 1862; ad. 1934 Chelsea. Wa.
TONSBERG, GERTRUDE MARTIN.
Am. b. Boston 1903; ad. 1934 Same. A.
TOORENVLIET, JACOB [or Jason].
Dut. Leyden 1641-1719 Same. B-C.
TOOROP, CHARLES.
Dut. b. 1891 Holland. M.
TOOROP, JAN THEODOOR.
Dut. Java 1859-1928 Amsterdam. B.
TOOVEY, RICHARD GIBBS HENRY.
Eng. Brussels, Belg. 1861-1927 London. Wa01929.
TOPCHEVSKY, MORRIS.
Am. b. Poland 1898; ad. 1934 Chicago. A.
TOPFFER, ADAM WOLFRANG.
Eng. Geneva, Swi. 1766-1847 Morillon, Eng. B.
TOPFFER, JEAN CHARLES. (S)
Swi. Geneva 1832-1905 Paris. B.
TOPFFER, RODOLPHE.
Swi. Geneva 1799-1846 Same. B.
TOPHAM, FRANCIS WILLIAM.
Eng. Leeds 1808-1897 Cordova, Sp. B-C-DNB.
TOPHAM, FRANK WILLIAM WARWICK.
Eng. London 1838-1924. B-C-Y01925.
TOPPAN, CHARLES. (Eg)
Am. Newburyport, Mass. 1796-1874 Italy. F-2-7-169.
TOPPELIUS, WALDEMAR.
Rus. ac. 1898 in Russia. M.

TOPPI, Mario.
It. ex. 1934 New York. M.
TOPPING, James.
Am. b. Cleator Moor, Eng. 1879; ad. 1934 Oak Park, Ill. A.
TOQUÉ, Louis. *see* Tocqué.
TORBIDO, Francesco [Il. Moro].
It. Verona 1486-1546 Same. B-C.
TORBY, [Count] Michael.
ex. 1934 in London. M.
TOREL, William. (S)
Br. ac. 1272-1291. B.
TORESANI, Andrea.
It. Brescia 1727-1760 Venice. B.
TORGGLER, Hermann.
Br. b. 1878. M.
TORI [Suiko Period]. (S)
Jap. ac. 7th Cent. in Japan. Hs.
TORII, Genjin.
Jap. ex. 1934 New York. M.
TORITTI, Giuseppe. (S)
It. b. Venice 1743; [No death date]. B.
TORO, J. (S)
Fr. b. 1671/2; d. 1731 in Toulon. B.
TORRANCE, James. (Ill)
Scot. 1859-1916. M.
TORRE, Alessandro della. *see* Casolani.
TORRE, Flamino [Degli Ancinelli].
It. Bologna 1621-1661 Modena. B.
TORRE Y LOPEZ, Antonio de la.
Sp. ac. 19th Cent. in Madrid. B.
TORRENT, Ramón.
Sp. b. 1323?; d. 1370 in Spain. M.
TORRENTIUS, Jan Simmonsz.
Dut. Amsterdam 1589-1644 Same. B-722.
TORRENTS, Stanislas.
Fr. ac. 1864-1886 in Marseilles. B-C.
TORRES, Clemente de.
Sp. Cadiz 1665-1730 Same. B-Bd.
TORREY, Charles Cutler. (Eg)
Am. d. 1827 Nashville, Tenn. F-7-169.
TORREY, Elliot Bouton.
Am. b. East Hardwick, Vt. 1867; ad. 1934 San Diego, Calif. A-W.
TORREY, Franklin. (S)
Am. Boston, Mass. 1829-1912 Florence, It. A010.
TORREY, Fred M. (S)
Am. b. Fairmont, W. Va. 1884; ad. 1934 Chicago. A-F-798.
TORREY, George Burroughs.
Am. b. New York 1863; ad. 1934 Same. A12-F-W.
TORREY, Helen. (Ill)
Am. ad. 1935 New York. M.
TORREY, Mabel Landrum. (S)
Am. b. Sterling, Colo. 1886; ad. 1934 Chicago. A.
TORREY, Manasseh Cutler.
Am. b. Salem, Mass.; d. 1837 New York. F-2-6-169.
TORRIGIANI, Bartolommeo.
It. d. 1693 in Naples. B.
TORRIGIANI, Pietro [or Pedro]. (S)
It. Florence 1492-1522 Sèville, Sp. B-DNB-E-Hs-V.
TORTEBAT, Jean.
Fr. Paris 1652-1718 Same. B.
TORY [or Toury], Geoffroy. (Ill)
Fr. Bourges 1485-1554 Bernard. B.
TOSCA, [Miss] Olinsky.
Am. ad. 1935 Lyme, Conn. M.
TOSCHI, Paolo. (Eg)
It. Parma 1788-1854 Same. B.
TOSHINBU, Okumura.
Jap. ac. 1727 in Japan. J., Vol. 2, page 39.
TOSI, Arturo.
It. b. 1871; ac. 1930 in Leghorn. M.
TOTO, Anthony.
Eng. b. Florence, It.; ac. 1518/43 England. B-DNB.
TOTSUGEN, Tanaka.
Jap. d. 1823 in Japan. J., Vol. 1, page 78.
TOTTEN, Vichen von Post. (S)
Mrs. George Oakley Totten.
Am. b. Sweden 1886; ad. 1934 Wash., D. C. A-Cs.
TOUCQUET, Louis. *see* Tocqué, L.
TOUDOUZE, Édouard Alexandre Simon.
Fr. Paris 1848-1909. B.
TOULGOVAT, Pierre. (S)
Fr. ad. 1932 Paris. M.
TOULMOUCHE, Auguste.
Fr. Nantes 1829-1890 Paris. B-C.
TOULOUSE-LAUTREC, Henri de.
Fr. Albi 1864-1901 Malromé. B-DBA-598-700.
TOUR. *see* La Tour.
TOURNAI, Julius.
Ger. b. 1861 in Germany. M.
TOURNIÈRES, Robert Levrac.
see Levrac-Tournières, R.
TOURNON, Georges.
Fr. ad. 1934 Paris. DBA.
TOURNY, Joseph Gabriel. (Eg)
Fr. Paris 1817-1880 Montpelier. B.
TOURS, Gerhard de. (Illuminator)
Fr. ac. 10th Cent. in France. B.
TOUSSAINT, François Christoph Armand.
Fr. Paris 1806-1862 Same. B-M.
TOUSSAINT, Pierre.
Fr. ac. 1865 in Paris. B.
TOVÁR, Alonso Miguel de.
Sp. Sèville 1678-1758. B.
TOVEY, Samuel Griffiths.
Eng. Bristol 1808-1873 Same. M.
TOWERS, James.
Eng. Liverpool 1853; ad. 1934 Purley. B-Wa.
TOWN, Ithiel.
Am. b. Thompson, Conn. 1784; d. 1844. M.
TOWNE, Charles [The Elder].
Eng. b. 1760; d. 1850? in London. B-DNB.
TOWNE, Charles [The Younger].
Eng. London 1780-1850 Same. B.
TOWNE, Francis.
Eng. 1740-1816 London. B-844.
TOWNE, Joseph. (Modeler)
Eng. 1808-1879. DNB.
TOWNLEY, Charles.
Eng. London 1746-1800. B.
TOWNLEY, Clifford.
Am. ad. 1934 City Island, N. Y. M.
TOWNLEY, [Mrs.] Frances Brown.
Am. b. Waterbury, Conn. 1908; ad. 1934 New York. A.
TOWNSEND, Alfred O.
Eng. Bristol 1846-1917. B.

TOWNSEND, Arthur O.
Am. ad. 1935 New York. M.
TOWNSEND, Ernest N.
Am. b. New York 1893; ad. 1934 Same. A.
TOWNSEND, Ethel Hore. (Min)
Mrs. John Townsend.
Am. b. Staten Island, N. Y. 1876; ad. 1934 Glen Ridge, N. J. A.
TOWNSEND, Frances B.
Am. b. Boston, Mass.; d. 1916. A016.
TOWNSEND, Harry Everett.
Am. b. Wyoming, Ill. 1879; ad. 1934 Norwalk, Conn. A-F.
TOWNSEND, Helen Elizabeth.
Am. b. Effingham, Ill. 1893; ad. 1934 Wash., D. C. A.
TOWNSEND, Lee. (Ill)
Am. b. Wyoming, Ill. 1895; ad. 1934 New York. A.
TOWNSHEND, George. (Cari)
Eng. 1724-1807. B.
TOWNSHEND, Henry James.
Eng. Taunton 1810-1866. B.
TOWNSLEY, Channel Pickering.
Am. b. Sedalia, Mo. 1867; ad. 1926 London. A12-F.
TOYOHARU, Utagawa.
Jap. 1735-1814. J., Vol. 2, page 60.
TOYOHIRO, Utagawa.
Jap. 1763-1828. J., Vol. 2, page 61.
TOYOKUNI, Gosotei II.
Jap. 1777-1835. M.
TOYOKUNI, Kunisada.
Jap. ac. 19th Cent. M.
TOYOKUNI, Utagawa.
Jap. 1769-1825. J., Vol. 2, page 50.
TOYONOBU, Ishikawa.
Jap. 1711-1785. J., Vol. 2, page 39.
TOZZI, Mario.
It. b. Urbino 1895; ad. 1935 Paris. DBA.
TRACHSEL, Albert.
Swi. Berne 1863-1929 Geneva. B-DBA.
TRACY, Glen.
Am. b. Hudson, Mich. 1883; ad. 1934 Cinn., O. A.
TRACY, Henry Prevost.
Am. b. 1888; d. 1919 Denver, Colo. A016.
TRACY, John M.
Am. b. Rochester, O. 1844. M.
TRACY, Lois Bartlett.
Am. ad. 1934 Winter Park, Fla. M.
TRADER, Effie Corwin. (Min)
Am. b. Xenia, O. 1874; ad. 1934 Cinn., O. A.
TRAFTON, Howard A.
Am. ad. 1934 New York. M.
TRAIES, William.
Eng. Crediton 1789-1872 Exeter. B.
TRAIN, H. Scott. (Ill)
Am. ad. 1934 Astoria, L. I., N. Y. A.
TRAINI, Francesco.
It. b. Pisa; ac. 1341/6 in Florence. B-V.
TRANCHANT, Pierre Jules.
Fr. b. Paris 1882; ex. 1934 Madrid, Sp. B-DBA.
TRAPPES, Francis M.
Eng. ex. 1868-1885 in London. B-DNB.
TRASHER, Harry Dickinson. (S)
Am. b. Plainfield, N. J. 1883; ad. 1915 Baltic, Conn. A12.

TRAÙ, Giovanni. (S)
It. ac. 1475 in Italy. Hs.
TRAUT, Hans.
Ger. ac. 1477-1505 in Nüremberg. B-C.
TRAUT, Wolfgang. (Eg)
Ger. ac. 1510/20 in Nüremberg. B-M.
TRAUTMAN, Johann Georg.
Ger. b. 1713; d. 1769/72 in Frankfort. B-C.
TRAVAUSE, Pierre. (S)
Fr. Corsaint 1822-1869 Paris. B.
TRAVER, George A.
Am. Corning, N. Y. 1864-1928 New York. A025-F.
TRAVER, Marion Gray.
Am. b. Elmhurst, L. I., N. Y. 1896; ad. 1934 New York. A.
TRAVER, Warde.
Am. b. Ann Arbor, Mich. 1880; ad. 1926 New York. F.
TRAVI, Antonio.
It. Sestri 1613-1669 Genoa. B-C.
TRAVIÈS DE VILLERS, Charles Joseph.
Fr. Winterthur, Swi. 1804-1859 Paris. B.
TRAVIS, Diane.
Am. b. New York 1892; ad. 1934 Tulsa, Okla. A.
TRAVIS, Kathryne Hail.
Am. b. Ozark, Ark.; ad. 1934 Dallas, Tex. A.
TRAVIS, Olin Herman.
Am. b. Dallas, Tex. 1888; ad. 1934 Same. A-F.
TRAVIS, Paul Bough.
Am. b. Wellsville, O. 1891; ad. 1934 Cleveland, O. A.
TRAVIS, William D. T.
Am. b. 1839; d. 1916 Burlington, N. J. A013.
TRAYER, Jean Baptiste Jules.
Fr. Paris 1824-1908/9. B-C.
TREADWELL, Helen. (Mu)
Am. ex. 1934 New York. M.
TREASE, Sherman.
Am. b. Galena, Kan. 1889; ad. 1934 San Diego, Calif. A.
TREBILCOCK, Paul.
Am. b. Chicago 1902; ad. 1934 Same. A-W.
TREFETHEN, Jessie B.
Am. Portland, Me.; ad. 1934 Oberlin, O. A.
TREGANZA, [Mrs.] Ruth Robinson.
Am. b. Elmira, N. Y. 1877. A28.
TREGO, William Brooke Thomas.
Am. Yardley, Pa. 1859-1909 No. Wales, Pa. A07-B-F.
TREGOR, Nison. (S)
Am. b. Vilma, Rus.; ad. 1934 U. S. 912.
TRELLIARD, Jacques André.
Fr. 1712-1794. B.
TREMBATH, James. (Ill)
Am. ad. 1934 Phila., Pa. M.
TRÉMOLLIÈRE, Pierre Charles.
Fr. Cholet 1703-1739 Paris. B-C-722.
TRENCH, [Miss] Marianne L.
Eng. b. Guilford 1888; ad. 1934 Same. Wa.
TRENCHARD, Edward.
Am. Phila., Pa. 1850-1922 West Islip, N. Y. A019-F.
TRENCHARD, Edward C. (Eg)
Am. b. Phila., Pa. 1784; d. 1824. F-2-7.

TRENCHARD, JAMES. (Eg)
Am. b. New Jersey 1747; d. in England. F-2-7-147.
TRENKWALD, JOSEF MATHIAS VON.
Aus. Prague, Czec. 1824-1897. B-C.
TRENTACOSTE, DOMENICO. (S)
It. b. 1856; d. 1933 Palermo. B.
TRENTANOVE, GAETANO. (S)
Am. b. Florence, It. 1858; ad. 1900 Wash., D. C. F-Ta.
TRENTANOVE, RAIMONDO. (S)
It. Faenza 1742-1832 Rome. Ms.
TRENTO, ANTONIO DA. *see* Antonio da T.
TRESHAM, HENRY.
It. Dublin 1749-1814 London. B-DNB.
TREU [or Trey], JOHANN NIKOLAUS.
Ger. Bamberg 1734-1786/98 Würzburg. B-C.
TREU [or Trey], JOSEPH CHRISTOPH.
Ger. Bamberg 1738-1798 Same. B-C.
TREU [or Trey], KATHARINA.
Ger. Bamberg 1743-1811 Mannheim. B-C.
TREVISANI, FRANCESCO.
It. b. 1656; d. 1746 in Rome. B-C.
TREVISO, GIROLAMO DA [Trevigi].
It. ac. 1470-1475. B-V.
TREVITTS, JOSEPH.
Am. ad. 1934 Manistee, Mich. M.
TRIBOLO, IL. (S)
[Niccoló dei Pericoli.]
It. Florence 1485-1550. B-Hs-V-599.
TRICCA, M. A.
Am. ad. 1935 New York. M.
TRICKER, FLORENCE.
Am. b. Phila., Pa.; ad. 1934 Swarthmore, Pa. A.
TRIEBEL, FREDERICK ERNEST. (S)
Am. b. Peoria, Ill. 1865; ad. 1934 College Point, L. I., N. Y. A-F-Ta-W.
TRIGGS, FLOYD WILDING. (Cari)
Am. Winnebago, Ill. 1872-1919 Stamford, Conn. A016.
TRIGT, HENDRIK ALBERT VAN.
Dut. Dordrecht 1829-1899 Heiloo. B-C.
TRILLEAU, GASTON. (Ill)
Fr. ad. 1934 Paris. DBA.
TRIMOLET, ANTHELME.
Fr. Lyons 1798-1866 Same. B.
TRIMOLET, LOUIS JOSEPH.
Fr. Paris 1812-1843 Same. B.
TRINO, FRANCESCO DA.
[or Pier Francesco Guala.]
It. d. 1760 in Trino. B-Bd.
TRINQUESSE, LOUIS R.
Fr. ac. 1758-1779 in Paris. B-C.
TRIOSON, GIRODET. *see* Girodet de Roucy, T.
TRIQUET, JULES OCTAVE.
Fr. b. Paris 1867. B.
TRIQUETI, HENRI BARON DE. (S)
Fr. Conflans 1802-1874 Windsor, Eng. B-Hs.
TRISCOTT, SAMUEL PETER ROLT.
Am. Gosport, Eng. 1846-1925 Maine. A022-F-W13.
TRISTAN, LUIS.
Sp. Toledo 1586-1640 Same. B-C-722.
TRNKA, [Mrs.] ANNA BELLE WING.
Am. Buffalo, N. Y. 1876-1922. A020.
TROCCOLI, GIOVANNI BATTISTA.
Am. b. Lauropoli, It. 1882; ad. 1934 Newton Center, Mass. A.
TRODOUX, HENRI ÉMILE ADRIEN. (S)
Fr. b. Leningrad; ac. 1874 in Paris. B.
TROGER, PAUL.
Aus. Zell 1698-1762 Vienna. B-C.
TROLSTOI, THEODORE PETROVITCH.
Rus. Leningrad 1783-1873. B.
TROMBETTA, EZECHIELE. (S)
It. ac. 19th Cent. in Milan. B.
TROMKA, A.
Am. ad. 1934 New York. M.
TROMMER, MARIE.
Am. b. Russia; ad. 1934 Brooklyn, N. Y. A.
TROOG [or Trood], W. H.
Eng. b. 1848; d. 1899 in London. B.
TROOST, CORNELIS.
[Called the "Dutch Hogarth."]
Dut. Amsterdam 1697-1750 Same. B-Bd-C-722.
TROTT, BENJAMIN. (Min)
Am. b. 1770; d. 1839 Boston, Mass. F-2-6-25-179-182.
TROTTER, NEWBOLD HOUGH.
Am. Phila., Pa. 1827-1898 Atlantic City, N. J. A01-C-F-15.
TROUBETZKOY, PAUL. (S)
Am. b. Maggiore, It. 1866; ad. 1934 Paris. A-B-F-Hs-798.
TROUBETZKOY, PIERRE.
Am. b. Milan, It. 1864; ad. Cobham, Va. A-F-W.
TROUILLEBERT, PAUL DÉSIRÉ.
Fr. Paris 1829-1900 Same. B-DBA.
TROUK, ADELL HENRY.
Am. Vienna, Aus. 1856-1934 New Haven, Conn. M-Obit. N. Y. papers, 1-21-1934.
TROUT, ELIZABETH DOROTHY BURT.
Am. b. Fort Robinson, Neb. 1896; ad. 1934 Wash., D. C. A.
TROWBRIDGE, ALEXANDER B.
Am. ad. 1935 Wash., D. C. M.
TROWBRIDGE, SAMUEL BRECK PARKMAN.
Am. New York 1862-1925 Same. A022.
TROWBRIDGE, SHERMAN. (Et)
Am. ex. 1934 New York. M.
TROWBRIDGE, VAUGHAN.
Am. b. New York 1869; ad. 1926 Paris. A20-F-W14.
TROY [or Troye], EDWARD.
Am. Switzerland 1808-1874 Georgetown, Ky. F-2.
TROY [or Troye], FRANÇOIS DE.
Fr. Toulouse 1645-1730 Paris. B-C-722.
TROY, JEAN FRANÇOIS DE.
Fr. Paris 1679-1752. B-C-E-722.
TROYES [School of].
Fr. ac. 16th Cent. in France.
TROYON, CONSTANT.
Fr. Sèvres 1810-1865 Paris. B-Bd-C-DBA-E-843.
TRUAX, SARAH E.
Am. b. Iowa; ad. 1934 San Diego, Calif. A.
TRUBACH, ERNEST SERGEIFF.
Am. b. Russia 1907; ad. 1934 New York. A.
TRUBEE, JOHN.
Am. ex. 1935 New York. M.
TRÜBNER, HEINRICH WILHELM.
Ger. Heidelberg 1851-1917 in Carlsruhe. B.
TRUCHET, LOUIS ABEL. *see* Abel-Truchet, L.

TRUCKSEES, [Mrs.] Frances Hoar.
Am. ad. 1934 Boulder, Colo. M.
TRUCKSEES, Frederick Clement.
Am. b. Browsburg, Ind. 1895; ad. 1934 Boulder, Colo. A.
TRUE, Allan Tupper.
Am. b. Colorado Springs, Colo. 1881; ad. 1934 Littleton, Colo. A-F-W.
TRUE, Grace Hopkins.
Mrs. E. D. A. True.
Am. b. Frankfort, Mich. 1890; ad. 1934 Detroit, Mich. A.
TRUE, Joseph. (S)
Am. ac. 1816-1886. M.
TRUE, Virginia.
Am. b. St. Louis, Mo. 1900; ad. 1934 Boulder, Colo. A.
TRUESDELL, Edith Park.
Am. b. Derby, Conn. 1888; ad. 1934 Los Angeles, Calif. A.
TRUESDELL, Gaylord Sangston.
Am. Waukegan, Ill. 1850-1899 New York. A01-B-Bd-F.
TRUEWORTHY, J. (Min)
Am. ad. 1934 Pasadena, Calif. M.
TRUMAN, Edward.
Am. ac. 1741. *see* book 2.
TRUMBULL, Edward.
Am. b. 1884. M.
TRUMBULL, Gordon.
Am. Stonington, Conn. 1841-1903 Hartford, Conn. A05-C-F-3-15.
TRUMBULL, John.
Am. Lebanon, Conn. 1756-1843 New York. B-Bd-C-E-F-1-2-3-4-6-45-46-138-160-179-182-184-188-189-259-260-261-701-786.
TRUMM, Peter. (Eg)
Ger. ex. 1933 in New York. M.
TRUMP, Rachel Bulley.
Mrs. Charles C. Trump.
Am. b. Canton, O. 1890; ad. 1934 Merion, Pa. A-F.
TRUMPORE, William L.
Am. b. 1867; d. 1917 Jersey City, N. J. A015.
TRUNK, Herman.
Am. b. New York; ad. 1934 Brooklyn, N. Y. A.
TRUPHÈME, Auguste Joseph.
Fr. b. Aix 1836; ac. 1886 Paris. B-C.
TRUTAT, Félix.
Fr. Dijon 1824-1848 Same. B-600.
TRUTOWSKY, Konstantin Alexandrovitch.
Rus. Kursk 1827-1893. B.
TRYON, Benjamin F.
Am. b. New York 1824. [No death date.] F-15.
TRYON, Dwight William.
Am. Hartford, Conn. 1849-1925 So. Dartmouth, Mass. A022-B-C-E-F-W14-1-3-46-262-601.
TSA, Toke.
Indian (American). ex. 1930 New York. 411.
TS'AO FUH-LING.
Chinese. ac. 3rd Cent. in China. M.
TS'AO PA.
Chinese. ac. 8th Cent. in China. E.
TSCHACBASOV, Nahum.
Am. ex. 1935 New York. M.
TSCHAGGENY, Charles Phillogène.
Belg. Brussels 1815-1894 Same. B-C.
TSCHAGGENY, Edmond Jean Baptiste.
Belg. Neuchâtel, Swi. 1818-1873 Brussels. B.
TSCHAUTSCH, Albert.
Ger. b. Seelow 1843. B-C.
TSCHERUKINE, Georges.
Rus. ad. 1934 Paris. M.
TSCHUDI, Lill.
Swi. b. Schwanden 1911; ad. 1934 Same. M.
TSCHUDY, Herbert Bolivar.
Am. b. Plattsburg, O. 1874; ad. Brooklyn, N. Y. A-F.
TSCHUDY, Rudolf.
Am. Switzerland 1855-1923 Cinn., O. A020-F.
TSUNENOBU, Kano.
Jap. Kyoto 1636-1713. J., Vol. 1, page 136.
TUAILLON, Louis. (S)
Ger. b. Berlin 1862. B-Hs.
TUBBY, Josiah.
Am. ad. 1934 Portland, Me. M.
TUBY, Jean Baptiste. (S)
It. Rome 1630/5-1700. B.
TUCK, [Mrs.] A. J. M.
Am. ad. 1935 Tuxedo Park, N. Y. M.
TUCK, Marie.
Aust. b. So. Aust. 1872. M.
TUCKER, Allen.
Am. b. Brooklyn, N. Y. 1866; ad. 1934 New York. A-F-46-602-701.
TUCKER, Arthur. (Et)
Eng. Bristol 1863-1929. B-Wa1929.
TUCKER, Benjamin.
Am. Newburyport, Mass. 1768-1796? F-6-169.
TUCKER, Cornelia. (S)
Am. b. Loudenville, N. Y. 1897; ad. 1934 Sugar Loaf, N. Y. A-F.
TUCKER, Robert.
Eng. b. 1807; d. 1891 in Bristol, Eng. B.
TUCKER, William E. (Eg)
Am. Phila., Pa. 1801-1857 Same. F-2-7-40.
TUCKERMAN, Lilia McCauley.
Mrs. Wolcott Tuckerman.
Am. ad. 1934 Carpinteria, Calif. A.
TUCKERMAN, Stephen Salisbury.
Am. Boston, Mass. 1830-1904 England. A05-C-F-15.
TUDOR, Rosemund.
Am. b. Buzzards Bay, Mass. 1875; ad. 1934 Redding, Conn. A.
TUITE, [Colonel] M. A.
Eng. ex. 1934 London. M.
TUKE, Henry Scott.
Eng. b. York 1858. B-Wa1929.
TULDEN, Théodor van.
Flem. 1607?-1676? 722.
TULLEY, Sidney S.
Can. Toronto, Ont. 1860-1911. M.
TULLOCH, William Alexander.
Am. b. Venezuela, So. Am. 1887; ad. 1934 New York. A.
TUNG CHI-CH'ANG.
Chinese. 1554-1636. E.
TUNG YUAN.
Chinese. ac. 10th Cent. in China. E.

TUNIS, Edwin. (Et)
Am. ad. 1934 Baltimore, Md. A.
TUNNICLIFFE, Charles Frederick. (Eg)
Eng. b. Macclesfield 1901; ad. 1934 Same. Wa.
TUPPER, Alexander Garfield.
Am. b. Gloucester, Mass. 1885; ad. Same. A.
TURA, Cosino [Cosmè de Ferrara].
It. Ferrara 1420/32-1495 Same. B-Bd-C.
TURA, Segna di.
see Segna di Buonaventura.
TURCAN, Jean. (S)
Fr. ac. 1878 in Paris. B.
TURCAS, Jules [or John].
Am. Cuba 1854-1917 New York. A014-F.
TURCHI, Alessandro [Orbetto].
It. Verona 1582-1648 Rome. B-C-722.
TURINO, Giovanni di. (S)
Am. Italy 1841-1899 U. S. A01-Hs.
TURKENTON, [Mrs.] Netta Craig.
Am. b. Georgetown, D. C. 1844; ad. 1934 Wash., D. C. A.
TURMAN, William T.
Am. b. Graysville, Ind. 1867; ad. 1934 Terre Haute, Ind. A.
TURMEAU, John. (Min)
Eng. London 1777-1846 Liverpool. B-DNB.
TURNBULL, Andrew Watson.
Eng. ad. 1934 Richmond. Wa.
TURNBULL, Gale.
Am. b. Long Island City, N. Y. 1889; ad. 1934 Paris. A.
TURNBULL, Grace H.
Am. b. Balt., Md.; ad. 1934 Same. A.
TURNBULL, Ruth. (S)
Am. b. 1912. Cs.
TURNER, A. D.
Am. d. 1919 in Albany, N. Y. A016.
TURNER, Alfred M.
Am. England 1852-1932 West Brighton, N. Y. A020.
TURNER, Charles. (Eg)
Eng. Woodstock 1773/4-1857 London. B-DNB-E.
TURNER, Charles Yardley. (Mu)
Am. Balt., Md. 1850-1919 New York. A016-B-C-F-Y01920-46.
TURNER, David [or Daniel].
Eng. ac. 1782-1817 in London. B.
TURNER, E. P.
Am. ac. 1927 New York. M.
TURNER, F. C.
Eng. ac. 1810-1846 in London. B.
TURNER, Francis Lee.
Mrs. E. K. Turner.
Am. b. Bridgeport, Ala. 1875; ad. 1934 Atlanta, Ga. A.
TURNER, Helen M.
Am. b. Louisville, Ky. 1858; ad. 1934 New York. A-F-W-46.
TURNER, James. (Eg)
Am. ac. Boston 1744; d. 1759 Phila., Pa. F-2-7-147.
TURNER, J. Horsfall.
Eng. ex. 1934 London. M.
TURNER, Joseph Mallord William.
[Produced over 19,000 items of art.]
Eng. London 1775-1851 Same. B-Bd-C-DNB-E-604-727-790-820-844-870-880-909-917-922.
TURNER, Lottie B.
Am. ac. 1915 in Brooklyn, N. Y. A12.
TURNER, Marion Jane.
Am. ad. 1934 Chester, Pa. M.
TURNER, Matilda Hutchinson.
Am. b. Jerseyville, Ill.; ad. 1934 Phila., Pa. A.
TURNER, Raymond.
Am. ad. 1935 New York. M.
TURNER, Richard Sydney. (Cart)
Am. b. 1873; d. 1919 Newburgh, N. Y. A016.
TURNER, Ross Sterling.
Am. Westport, N. Y. 1847-1915 Nassau, Bahamas. A012-B-F-46-47-169.
TURNER, William ["Turner of Oxford"].
Eng. Oxon 1789-1862 Oxford. B-DNB.
TURNER, William Greene. (S)
Am. b. 1832; d. 1917 Newport, R. I. A015.
TURNERELLI, Edward Tracy. (Et)
Eng. London 1813-1896 Leamington. DNB.
TURNERELLI, Peter. (S)
Ir. Belfast 1774-1839 London. DNB.
TURNEY, Olive.
Am. b. Pittsburgh, Pa. 1847; ad. 1934 Same. A.
TURNEY, Winthrop Duthie.
Am. b. New York 1884; ad. 1934 Brooklyn, N. Y. A.
TURONE [or Turoni], Maestro.
It. ac. 16th Cent. in Verona. B.
TURPIN DE CRISSÉ, Lancelot Théodore.
Fr. Paris 1781-1859 Same. B-C.
TURRELL, Arthur James. (Et)
Eng. b. 1871; ad. 1929 London. Wa1929.
TURRELL, Charles James. (Min)
Am. London 1845-1932 White Plains, N. Y. A020-B-Y01933.
TURZAK, Charles.
Am. ad. 1934 Chicago, Ill. A.
TUSCHER, Karl Marc.
Ger. Nüremberg 1705-1751 Copenhagen, Denmark. B-C.
TUSHINGHAM, Sidney. (Et)
Eng. b. Burslem 1884; ad. 1934 London. Wa.
TUSSAUD, John Theodore. (S in Wax)
Eng. b. Kensington 1858; ad. 1934 Herts. Wa.
TUSSAUD, Madame. (S in Wax)
[Marie Gresholtz.]
Founder of the Tussaud Wax Figures.
Swi. Berne 1760-1851 London. DB.
TUTHILL, Corinne.
Am. ad. 1934 Florence, Ala. M.
TUTILO [Monk of St. Gall]. (S)
Fr. d. 908 A.D. in Lorrain. B-Hs.
TUTTLE, Adrianna.
Am. b. Madison, N. J. 1870; ad. 1934 Newark, N. J. A.
TUTTLE, Francis M.
Am. ac. 1900 in Geneva, N. Y. M.
TUTTLE, Henry Emerson. (Et)
Am. b. Lake Forest, Ill. 1890; ad. 1935 New Haven, Conn. A28.
TUTTLE, Isabel Hollister.
Am. ad. 1935 New Haven, Conn. M.

TUTTLE, Macowin.
Am. b. Muncie, Ind. 1861; d. 1935 Buck Hill Falls, Pa.
A-M-Obit. N. Y. papers, 3-28-1935.
TUTTLE, Mary McArthur Thompson.
Am. b. Hillsboro, O. 1849; ad. 1915 Same. A12-F.
TUTTLE, [Mrs.] Mildred Jordan.
Am. b. Portland, Me. 1874; ad. 1934 Clinton, Conn. A.
TUTTLE, Ruel Crompton.
Am. b. Windsor, Conn. 1866; ad. 1934 Greenfield, Mass. A-F.
TWACHTMAN, Alden.
Am. ad. 1935 Greenwich, Conn. M.
TWACHTMAN, John Henry.
Am. Cinn., O. 1853-1902 Gloucester, Mass.
A05-B-C-F-1-15-46-51-71-105-138-172-605-691-701-762-779.
TWARDZIK, Hendryk F.
Am. b. Osuiencium, Pol. 1900; ad. 1934 Boston, Mass. A.
TWEED, John. (S)
Scot. Glasgow 1869-1933 London.
Wa1929-Obit. N. Y. papers, 11-13-1933.
TWEEDIE, William Menzies.
Scot. Glasgow 1826-1878. B.
TWELVETREES, C. R. (Ill)
Am. ad. 1934 New York. M.
TWIBILL, George W.
Am. Penn. 1766-1836 New York. F-2-6.
TWIG-SMITH, W.
Am. b. Nelson, N. Z., Aust. 1883; ad. 1934 Honolulu, Hawaii. A.
TWINING, Yvonne.
Am. b. New York 1907; ad. 1934 So. Egremont, Mass. M.
TWITCHELL, Asa Weston.
Am. Swansea, Mass. 1820-1904 Slingerlands, N. Y. M.
TWORKOV, Jack.
Am. b. Russia 1900; ad. 1934 Provincetown, Mass. A.
TWYMAN, Joseph.
Am. England 1842-1904 Chicago. A05.
TYLER, [Mrs.] Alice Kellogg.
Am. Chicago 1874-1900 Same. A02.
TYLER, Audubon. (Ill)
Am. ad. 1933 New York. M.
TYLER, Bayard Henry.
Am. Oneida, N. Y. 1855-1931 Yonkers, N. Y. A028-F-W16.
TYLER, Carolyn D. (Min)
Am. b. Chicago; ad. 1934 Same. A.
TYLER, Ernest Franklin.
Am. b. New Haven, Conn. 1879; ad. 1934 New York. A.
TYLER, Griswold.
Am. b. Boston, Mass. 1883; ad. 1934 Same. A.
TYLER, James Gale.
Am. Oswego, N. Y. 1855-1931 Pelham, N. Y. A028-B-F-W16.
TYLER, Jean. (S)
Am. ad. 1935 Cleveland, O. M.
TYLER, Stella Elkins. (S)
Am. ad. 1935 Newtown, Pa. M.
TYLER, William. (S)
Br. d. 1801. DNB.
TYNG, [Mrs.] Lucien Hamilton.
Am. New York 1874-1933 Nassau, Bahamas. A030.
TYR, Gabriel.
Fr. 1817-1868. B-C.
TYRASA.
Rus. ad. 1935 Leningrad. M.
TYRE, Philip S.
Am. b. Wilmington, Del. 1881; ad. 1934 Phila., Pa. A.
TYRON, Carroll.
Am. ad. 1935 Phila., Pa. M.
TYRONE [Tom Tyrone Comfort].
Am. b. Port Huron, Mich. 1909; ad. 1934 Los Angeles, Calif. M.
TYSON, Beatrice.
Eng. ex. 1934 London. M.
TYSON, Carroll Sargent, Jr.
Am. b. Phila., Pa. 1878; ad. 1934 Same. A-F.
TYSON, Dorsey Potter.
Am. b. 1891; ad. 1934 Balt., Md. M.
TYSON, Mary.
Am. ex. 1935 Andover, Mass. M.
TYSSENS, Peter. *see* Thys. P.
TYTLER, George. (Ill)
Eng. d. 1859 in London. B.
TYTUS, Robb de Peyster.
Am. b. Ashville, N. C.; d. 1913 Saranac Lake, N. Y. A0X1.

UBALDINI, Petruccio. (Illuminator)
It. Tuscany 1524?-1600? England. B-DNB.
UBELESQUI, Alexandre.
Fr. Paris 1649-1718. B.
UBERTI, Farinato. *see* Farinato, U.
UBERTINI, Baccio and Francesco.
see Bacchiaca.
UCCELLO, Paolo di Dono.
It. Florence 1396/7-1475 Same.
B-Bd-C-V-78-722-783.
UCEDA, Pedro de.
Sp. d. 1714 in Sèville. Bd.
UCHTERVELDT, Jacob. *see* Ochtervelt, J.
UDEN, Lucas van.
Flem. Antwerp 1595-1672 Same. B-C-722.
UDINE, Giovanni da.
[Nanni or Ricamatori.]
It. Udine 1487-1564 Siena. B-V-722.
UDINE, Martino da.
see Pelligino da San Daniele.
UDWARDY ["Spy"] Imre László. (Cart)
Eng. b. Budapest 1885; ad. 1934 Northwood, Eng. Wa.
UFER, Walter.
Am. b. Louisville, Ky. 1876; ad. 1934 Taos, N. M. A-F-W-1-46.
UGGIONE, Marco d'. *see* Oggiono, M.
UGO, Antonio. (S)
It. b. Palermo 1870. B.
UGOLINO, Andrea di. *see* Pisano, A.
UGOLINO DA SIENA [or di Neri].
It. d. 1339/49 in Siena. B-C.
UGONIA, Giuseppe. (Eg)
It. ad. 1934 in Brisighella. M.
UHDE, Karl Hermann Fritz von.
Ger. b. 1848; d. 1911 Munich. B-C-E.
UHL, S. Jerome, Sr.
Am. b. 1842; d. 1916 Cinn., O. A013.

UHLE. ALBRECHT BERNHARD.
Am. b. Chemnitz, Saxony 1847; d. Phila., Pa. A12-F.
UHLER, RUTH PERSHING.
Am. b. Gordon, Pa. 1898; ad. 1934 Houston, Tex. A.
UKIL, R. (Mu)
India. ac. 1932 in British India. M.
ULBER, ALTHEA.
Am. b. Los Angeles, Calif. 1898; ad. 1934 Same. A.
ULEN, PAUL V.
Am. b. Frankfort, O. 1893; ad. 1934 Cleveland, O. M.
ULFSTEN, NICOLAY.
Nor. b. Bergen 1855. B.
ULFT, JACOB VAN DER.
It. Gorkum, Holland 1627-1689 Italy. B-C-722.
ULIANOV, N.
Rus. b. 1875; ac. 1935 Russia. M.
ULKE, HENRY.
Am. Germany 1821-1910 Wash., D. C. A08-F.
ULLMAN, ALICE WOODS. (Ill)
Mrs. Eugene Paul Ullman.
Am. b. Goshen, Ind.; ad. 1926 Provincetown, Mass. A12-F.
ULLMAN, BENJAMIN.
Fr. Blotzheim, Ger. 1829-1884 Paris. B-C.
ULLMAN, EUGENE PAUL.
Am. b. New York 1897; ad. 1934 Paris. A-F-DBA.
ULLMAN, JULIUS.
Am. b. Bavaria 1863; ad. 1934 Seattle, Wash. M.
ULLMAN, RAOUL ANDRÉ.
Fr. b. Paris 1867. B.
ULLRICH, ALBERT H.
Am. b. Berlin, Ger. 1869; ad. 1934 Wilmette, Ill. A.
ULLRICH, CHARLES FREDERICK.
Am. New York 1858-1908 Berlin, Ger. A07-C-F-46.
ULLRICH, HANS JACOB.
Swi. Zurich 1798-1877 Same. B-C.
ULOCRINO. *see* Briosco, Andrea.
ULP, CLIFFORD MCCORMICK.
Am. b. Olean, N. Y. 1885; ad. 1934 Rochester, N. Y. A-F-W.
ULREICH, EDWARD BUK.
Am. b. Hungary; ad. 1934 New York. A.
ULREICH, NURA WOODSON.
Mrs. Edward Buk Ulreich.
Am. b. Kansas City, Mo.; ad. 1934 New York. A.
UMBACH, JONAS [The Elder].
Ger. Ausburg 1624-1700. B.
UMBRICHT, HONORÉ LOUIS.
Fr. b. Obernai 1860. B-C-DBA.
UNBEKANNTER. *see* Master Unbekannter.
UNDERWOOD, ANN.
Eng. b. Grimstead 1876; ad. 1934 Same. Wa.
UNDERWOOD, CLARENCE F.
Am. Jamestown, N. Y. 1871-1929 New York. A026-F-W14.
UNDERWOOD, LEON.
Am. ex. 1935 Seattle, Wash. M.
UNDERWOOD, LEON GEORGE CLAUDE. (P-S)
Eng. b. 1890; ad. 1934 London. Wa.
UNDERWOOD, THOMAS. (Eg)
Am. b. 1790/5; d. 1849 Lafayette, Ind. F-2-7.
UNGAR, VALERIA.
Am. ad. 1935 New York. M.
UNGER, HANS [or William].
Ger. b. Bautzen 1872. B.
UNGER, JOHANNA.
Ger. Hanover 1837-1871 Pisa, It. B-C.
UNOLD, MAX.
Ger. b. 1885; ac. 1935 in Germany. M.
UNPO, O-OKA.
Jap. ac. 19th Cent. in Japan. J., Vol. 2, page 88.
UNSWORTH, EDNA GANZHORN.
Am. b. Balt., Md. 1890; ad. 1934 Long Beach, Calif. A.
UNTERBERGER, CHRISTOPH.
Aus. Tyrol 1732-1797 Vienna. B-C.
UNTERBERGER, FRANZ RICHARD.
Swi. b. Innsbruck 1838; ac. 1874 Brussels, Belg. B-C.
UNTERSBERGER, IGNAZ.
Aus. Cavalese 1743-1797 Vienna. B-C.
UNTHANK, GERTRUDE.
Am. b. Economy, Ind. 1878; ad. 1934 Superior, Wis. A.
UPHAM, JOHN WILLIAM.
Eng. Offwell 1772-1828 Weymouth. B.
UPJOHN, ANNA MILO.
Am. ad. 1934 New York. M.
UPRKA, FRANTIŠEK. (S)
Jugo-Slavia. (Modern.) *see* book 798.
UPRKA, JOZA [or Josph].
Czec. b. Moravia 1862. M.
UPSHUR, MARTHA ROBINSON.
Mrs. Francis W. Upshur.
Am. b. Richmond, Va. 1885; ad. 1934 Same. A.
UPTON, FLORENCE K.
Am. b. Flushing, L. I., N. Y.; d. 1922 London. A20-F.
UPTON, JOHN A.
Br. b. Eng. 1850; d. Adelaide, Aust. M.
URBAIN, ALEXANDRE.
Fr. b. Sainte-Marie 1875. DBA.
URBAN, GRETH.
Am. b. Vienna, Aus. 1909; ad. 1935 New York. DBA.
URBAN, JOSEPH.
[Decorative Theatrical Artist.]
Am. Vienna 1872-1933 New York. A030-W17.
URBANO DA CORTONA.
see Cortona, Urbano di Pietro.
URBINO, BRAMANTE DA.
It. Urbino 1444-1514 Rome. V.
URBINO, RAPHAEL. *see* Raphael.
UREFPAU, ANDRÉ DE. (Min)
Fr. ad. 1934 Paris. M.
URIA AZA, TYNO.
Sp. b. Ribadasella 1905. DBA.
URICH, LOUIS J. (S)
Am. b. Paterson, N. J. 1879; ad. 1934 Elmhurst, L. I., N. Y. A-Cs.
URQUHART, ANNIE MACKENZIE.
Scot. b. Glasgow; ad. 1934 London. Wa.

URQUHART, Edith Mary.
Scot. b. Edinburgh; ad. 1934 Chelsea, Eng. Wa.
URQUHART, Murray McNeel Caird.
Scot. b. Kirkcudbright 1880; ad. 1934 London. Wa.
URSULESCU, Mihai M. (Eg)
Am. b. Echka, Rumania; ad. 1935 Detroit, Mich. M.
URWICK, Walter Chamberlain.
Eng. b. London 1864; ac. 1929. B-Wa1929.
URY. *see* Müller-Ury.
URY, Lesser.
Ger. 1862-1931. Ms-Y01932-775.
USHAKOV, Simeon.
Rus. ac. 1663-1696 in Russia. M.
USHER, J. (Ill)
Am. ad. 1935 New York. M.
USHER, Leila. (S)
Am. b. Onolaska, Wis. 1859; ad. 1934 New York. A-Cs-F.
USHER, Ruby W. (Min)
Am. ad. 1934 Summit, N. J. M.
USSI, Stefano.
It. Florence 1822-1901 Same. B-C.
USUI, Bumpei.
Am. ad. 1934 New York. M.
UTAMARO, Kitagawa.
Jap. b. Kayayoye 1754; d. 1806. E-J., Vol 2, page 18.
UTERBERGER, Franz R.
see Unterberger, F. R.
UTILI DA FAENZA, Giovanni Battista.
see Bertucci, G. B. da F.
UTRECHT, Adriaen van.
Flem. Antwerp 1559-1652 Same. B-C-722.
UTRECHT, Jacob van [Claessens].
Dut. b. Utrecht; ac. 1506-1524. B-C.
UTRILLO, Maurice.
Fr. b. Paris 1883; ad. 1934 Same. B-DBA-606-607-797.
UTTER, André.
Fr. b. Paris 1886. DBA.
UWINS, Thomas.
Eng. London 1782-1857 Staines. B-C-DNB-722.
UYTENAEL [or Uitenvael], Joachim.
Dut. Utrecht 1566-1638 Same. B-C.
UYTENBROECH, Moses van.
Dut. b. 1570; d. 1648 The Hague. B-C.
UZELAC, Milivoy.
Jugo-Slavia. b. Mostar 1897. DBA.

VAARBERG, H.
Belg. ac. 1860. M.
VAARDT [or Waart], Jan vander.
Dut. Haarlem 1647-1721 London. B-DNB.
VACCARO, Andrea.
It. Naples 1598-1670 Same. B-C.
VACHER, Charles.
Eng. Westminster 1818-1883 Kensington. B-DNB.
VACHER, Sydney. (Et)
Eng. b. 1854; d. 1934. M.
VADDER, Lodewyck de.
Flem. Brussels 1605-1655 Same. B-C.
VAEDEC, Rudolph. (S)
Hun. ac. 1900. M.
VAENIUS [or Venius]. *see* Veen.
VAFFLARD, Pierre Antoine Augustin.
Fr. Paris 1777-1838 Same. B-C.
VAGA, Perino del.
see Buonaccorsi, P. del Vaga.
VAGAGGINI, Merno.
It. b. Florence 1892. M.
VAGIS, Polygnotus. (S)
Am. b. Greece 1896; ex. 1934 New York. M.
VAGNETTI, Gianni.
It. b. Florence 1899; ac. 1935. M.
VAGO, Sandor.
Am. b. Hungary 1887; ad. 1934 Cleveland, O. A.
VAIL, Eugène Laurent.
Am. b. Saint-Servan, Fr. 1857; ad. 1934 Paris. A12-B-DBA-F-46.
VAILLANT, Bernard.
Flem. Lille, Fr. 1627/34-1675 Leyden. B.
VAILLANT, Jacques.
Flem. Lille, Fr. 1631-1691 Berlin. B.
VAILLANT, Jacques Gaston Émile.
Fr. b. Melun 1879. DBA.
VAILLANT, Louis David. (Mu)
Am. b. Cleveland, O. 1875; ad. 1934 New York. A-F-W.
VAILLANT, Maximilien.
Fr. b. Douai 1891. DBA.
VAILLANT, Pierre Henri.
Fr. b. Paris 1878. B-DBA.
VAILLANT, Wallerant.
Flem. Lille, Fr. 1623-1677 Amsterdam. B-C.
VAINI, Pietro.
Am. Rome, It. 1847-1875 New York. B-C-F-15.
VALADE, Jean.
Fr. Poitiers 1709-1787 Paris. B.
VALADON, Jules Emmanuel.
Fr. Paris 1826-1900 Same. B-C.
VALADON, Suzanne.
Fr. b. Limoges 1867. DBA-797.
VALCKENBORCH. *see also* Valkenburg.
VALCKENBORCH, Frederick van.
Flem. Mechlin 1570-1623/5 Nüremberg, Ger. B.
VALCKENBORCH, Lucas van.
Flem. Mechlin 1530/40-1625 Brussels. B-C.
VALCKENBORCH, Marten van.
Flem. Mechlin 1533/42-1604 Frankfort, Ger. B-C.
VALCKERT, Werner [or Warnard] van.
Dut. Amsterdam 1580-1655. B-C.
VALDENUIT.
Fr. or Am. b. France; ac. 1797 in New York. F-2-7-45.
VALDÉS, Lucas de.
Sp. Sèville 1661-1724 Cadiz. B.
VALDÉS-LEAL, Don Juán de.
Sp. Cordova 1630-1690 Sèville. B-Bd-C-722.
VALENCIENNES, Pierre Henri.
Fr. Toulouse 1750-1819 Paris. B-C-722.
VALENKAMPH, Theodore Victor Carl.
Am. Sweden 1868-1924 Gloucester, Mass. A021.
VALENSI, Henry.
Fr. b. Alger 1883. DBA.

VALENTIEN, ANNA MARIE. (S)
Mrs. Albert R. Valentein.
Am. b. Cinn., O. 1862; ad. 1934 San Diego, Calif. A-17.
VALENTIN, FRANÇOIS.
Fr. Gungamp 1738-1805 Quimper. B.
VALENTIN DE BOULLONGUE, JEAN.
Fr. Coulommiers 1591-1634 Rome, It. B-C-722.
VALENTINE, ALBERT R.
Am. Cinn., O. 1862-1925. A022-F.
VALENTINE, EDWARD.
Am. ex. 1934 New York. M.
VALENTINE, EDWARD VIRGINIUS. (S)
Am. Richmond, Va. 1838-1930 Same. A027-F-Ta-W16.
VALENTINE, FRANCIS B.
Am. b. Buffalo, N. Y. 1897; ad. 1934 Same. A.
VALENTINE, JANE H.
Am. b. Bellefonte, Pa. 1866; ad. 1934 Phila., Pa. A.
VALENTINE, WILLIAM.
Can. England 1798-1849 Halifax, N. S. F-6.
VALENTINI, VALENTINO.
It. b. Florence 1858. B.
VALENZA [or Valencia], JACOPO DA.
It. ac. 1485-1502. B-C.
VALERIO, P. F.
Am. ad. 1934 New York. M.
VALERIO, SILVIO B.
Am. ad. 1935 New York. M.
VALERIO, THÉODORE.
Fr. b. 1819; d. 1879 Vichy. B.
VALERO, CRISTÓBAL.
Sp. d. 1789 in Valencia. B-C.
VALESIO, GIOVANNI LUIGI.
It. Bologna 1579-1640 Rome. B.
VALINOTTI, DOMENICO.
It. ad. 1934 Turin, It. M.
VALKENBORCH. *see* Valckenborch.
VALKENBURG, HENDRIK.
Dut. Deventer 1826-1896. M.
VALKENBURG, THEODOR DIRK [Thiery].
Dut. Amsterdam 1675-1725 Surinam. B-C.
VALLANCE, JOHN. (Eg)
Am. Scotland 1770-1823 New York. F-2-7-147.
VALLANCE, WILLIAM FLEMING.
Scot. Paisley 1827-1904. B-C-DNB.
VALLAYER-COSTER, ANNE.
Fr. Paris 1744-1818 Same. M.
VALLE, [Mme.] MAUDE RICHMOND FLORENTINO.
Am. ad. 1934 Denver, Colo. A.
VALLEJO, ANTONIUS FRANCISCUS.
Mex. ac. 1766 in Mexico. M.
VALLERY-RADOT, JACQUES.
Fr. ad. 1935 Paris. M.
VALLÉS, BARTOLOMÉ.
Sp. ac. 1482-1486 in Spain. M.
VALLÉS, GIL.
Sp. ac. 1483-1538 in Spain. M.
VALLET, ALEXIS.
Fr. b. Verrière 1869. B.
VALLET, ÉDOUARD ["Ed"].
Swi. b. 1876; ad. 1934 Geneva. B-DBA.
VALLET, JEAN PIERRE.
Fr. b. 1809; d. 1886 in Paris. B.
VALLFOGONA, PERE JOHAN DE. (S)
It. ac. 1426-1445 in Italy. Hs.
VALLIN, JACQUES ANTOINE.
Fr. Paris 1760-1831. B.
VALLOTTON, FÉLIX ÉDOUARD.
Fr. Lausanne, Swi. 1865-1925 Paris. B-DBA.
VALLS, DOMINGO.
Sp. ac. 1366-1398 in Spain. M.
VALMIER, GEORGES. (Cubist)
Fr. b. Augoulême 1885. DBA.
VALSOLDO, IL.
see Paracca, Giovanni Antonio.
VALTAT, LOUIS.
Fr. b. Dieppe 1869. DBA.
VALTON, CHARLES. (S)
Fr. b. Pau; ex. 1900 in Paris. B.
VAN-VAN DE-VAN DEN-VAN DER.
Note: see also the specific names, particularly for Dutch and Flemish Artists.
VAN ABBÉ, SALOMON.
Eng. b. Amsterdam, Holland 1883; ad. 1934 London. Wa.
VAN AEKEN. *see* Bosch.
VAN ALLEN, GERTRUDE E.
Am. b. Brooklyn, N. Y. 1897; ad. 1934 Port Wash., N. Y. A.
VAN BEEK, WILLIAM. (S)
Am. ex. 1934 New York. M.
VAN BENSCHOTEN, CLARA D.
Am. ad. 1934 New York. M.
VAN BENTHUYSEN, WILL.
Am. Leavenworth, Kan. 1883-1929 New York. A026.
VAN BEUREN, NAN GREACEN.
Am. b. Giverny, Fr. 1908; ad. 1934 New York. M.
VAN BOSKERCK, ROBERT WARD.
Am. Hoboken, N. J. 1855-1932 New York. A029-C-F-W.
VAN BUREN, RAEBURN. (Ill)
Am. b. Pueblo, Colo. 1891; ad. 1934 Chicago. A28.
VAN BUREN, STANBERY.
Am. b. Zanesville, O.; ac. 1915 Columbus, O. A12.
VAN BUSKIRK, CARL.
Am. Cinn., O. 1887-1930 New York. A027.
VAN CEULEN, CORNELIUS JANSSENS.
see Janssens van Ceulen.
VAN COTT, DEWEY.
Am. Salt Lake City, Utah 1898-1932 Mt. Vernon, N. Y. A029.
VAN COTT, FERN H.
Mrs. Dewey Van Cott.
Am. b. 1899; ad. 1934 New Britain, Conn. A.
VAN COURT, FRANKLIN.
Am. b. Chicago 1903; ad. 1934 Same. A.
VAN DELFT, JAN. *see* Vermeer.
VAN DELFT, JOHN H.
Am. d. 1913 Brooklyn, N. Y. A0X1.
VAN DEN BERGH, VIKKE.
Fr. b. Mechlin, Belg. 1876; ac. 1935 Paris. DBA.
VAN DER DOES, JEAN.
Am. ex. 1935 New York. M.
VAN DER STAPPEN, CHARLES. (S)
Belg. Brussels 1843-1910. E.

VAN DER VEER, MARY.
Am. b. Amsterdam, N. Y. 1865; ad. 1934 Same. A.
VAN DER VELDE, HANNY.
Mrs. A. W. Van der Velde.
Am. b. Rotterdam, Holland 1883; ad. 1934 Royal Oak, Mich. A.
VAN DER WEYDEN, HARRY.
Am. b. Boston, Mass. 1868; ad. 1935 Rye, Sussex, Eng. A28-B-F-W10-757.
VAN DOESBURG, THÉO.
Dut. Utrecht 1883-1931. DBA.
VAN DONGEN. *see* Dongen.
VAN DRESSER, WILLIAM. (Et)
Am. b. Memphis, Tenn. 1871; ad. 1934 Palm Beach, Fla. A.
VAN DUZEE, KATE KEITH.
Am. b. Dubuque, Ia. 1874; ad. 1934 Same. A.
VAN DYCK, [Sir] ANTHONY [or Anthonis].
Flem. Antwerp 1599-1641 London.
B-Bd-C-DNB-E-191-192-722-902-903-951.
VAN DYCK, PETER.
Eng. b. Pays-Bas 1729; ac. 1767 in London. B-DNB.
VAN DYCK, PHILIP.
[Called the "Little Van Dyck."]
Dut. Amsterdam 1680-1753 The Hague. B-C-E-722.
VAN ELTEN, HENDRICK DIRK KRUSEMAN.
Am. b. Alkmaar, Holland 1829-1904 Paris. A05-B-C-F-15-46.
VAN EYCK, HUBERT [or Huybrecht].
[Art of painting in oils attributed to him.]
Flem. Maaseyck 1366?-1426 Ghent.
B-Bd-C-E-V-191-608-609-610-611-722.
VAN EYCK, JAN.
Flem. Maaseyck 1380/90-1440 Bruges.
B-Bd-C-E-V-191-609-610-611-722.
VAN EYCK, LAMBERT.
Flem. ac. 1431. B-T.
VAN EYCK, MARGARETHA. (Min)
Flem. ac. 1440 in Ghent. B-T.
VAN GOGH, VINCENT.
Dut. Zundert 1853-1890 Antwerp.
B-612-613-700-783-790-811-847.
VAN GORDER, LUTHER EMERSON.
Am. Pittsburgh, Pa. 1861-1931 Toledo, O. A028.
VAN GORP, HENRI NICOLAS.
Fr. Paris 1756-1819. B.
VAN GOYEN. *see* Goyen.
VAN HAELEWYN, H. S.
Am. ad. 1934 Wilton, Conn. M.
VAN HOOK, NELL.
Am. b. Virginia 1897; ad. 1934 Atlanta, Ga. A.
VAN INGEN, HENRY A.
Am. Holland 1833-1899 U. S. A01.
VAN INGEN, WILLIAM BRANTLEY. (Mu)
Am. b. Phila., Pa. 1858; ad. 1934 New York. A-F-W-46.
VAN LAER, ALEXANDER THEOBALD.
Am. Auburn, N. Y. 1857-1920 Ind., Ind. A017-F.
VAN LAER, BELLE. (Min)
Am. b. Phila., Pa. 1862; ad. 1935 Johnsville, Pa. A12-F.
VAN LESHOUT, ALEXANDER J. (Et)
Am. b. Harvard, Ill. 1868. A20.
VAN LOO. *see* Loo.
VAN LOON, HENDRIK WILLEM. (Author-Ill)
Dut.-Am. b. Rotterdam 1882; ad. 1934 Riverside, Conn. M-W.
VAN MARCKÉ DE LUMMEN, ÉMILE.
Fr. Sèvres 1827-1890 Hyers. B.
VAN OSS, THOMAS WILLEM.
Eng. b. Walberswick 1901; ex. 1934 London. Wa.
VAN PAPPELENDAN, LAURA.
Am. b. Iowa; ad. 1934 Chicago. A.
VAN ROEKENS, PAULETTE.
Am. b. Chateau-Thierry, Fr. 1898; ad. 1934 Langhorne, Pa. A-F.
VAN RYDER, JACK.
Am. b. Continental, Ariz. 1898; ad. 1934 Elgin, Ariz. A.
VAN RYN, AGNES POTTER.
Am. b. London 1892; ad. 1934 Cinn., O. A.
VAN RYN. *see* Rembrant.
VAN SCRIVEN, PEARL AIMAN.
Am. b. Montgomery Co., Pa. 1896; ad. 1934 Phila., Pa. A.
VAN SHECK, SIDNEY W. JIROUSEK.
Am. b. Prague, Czec.; ad. 1934 Auburn, Ala. A.
VAN SLOUN, FRANK J.
Am. b. St. Paul, Minn.; ad. 1934 San Fran., Calif. A.
VAN SLYCK, WILMA LUCILE.
Am. b. Cinn., O. 1898; ad. 1934 Same. A.
VAN SOELEN, THEODORE.
Am. b. Minn. 1890; ad. 1935 Corwall, Conn. A.
VAN SOEST. *see* Soest.
VAN STAR. *see* Vallert.
VAN STOCKUM, HILDA. (Ill)
Am. ad. 1934 New York. M.
VAN STRY [or Stij]. *see* Stry.
VAN TYNE, PETER.
Am. b. Flemington, N. J. 1857; ad. 1934 Trenton, N. J. A.
VAN VEEN, PIETER.
Dut. Leyden 1562-1629 The Hague. B.
van VEEN, PIETER. (J. L.)
Dut.-Am. b. The Hague 1875; ad. 1934 New York. A-F.
VAN VEEN, STUYVESANT.
Am. b. New York 1910; ad. 1934 Same. A.
VAN VLECK, [Mrs.] NATALIE JOHNSON.
Am. ad. 1934 New York. M.
VAN WAGENEN, ELIZABETH VASS.
Am. b. Savannah, Ga. 1895; ad. 1934 Danville, Va. A.
VAN WART, AMES. (S)
Am. b. New York 1884; ad. 1935 Same. A12-F.
VAN WASSENHOVE. *see* Justus of Ghent.
VAN WERVEKE, GEORGE. (Ill)
Am. ad. 1934 New York. A.
VAN WOUW, ANTON. (S)
Br. b. So. Africa; ad. 1935 Johannesburg, Trans. M.
VAN ZANDT, [Mrs.] HILDA.
Am. b. Henry, Ill. 1892; ad. 1934 San Pedro, Calif. A.
VANAISE, GUSTAVE.
Belg. Ghent 1854-1901/4 St. Gilles. B-C.

VANCE, Fred Nelson. (Mu)
Am. Crawfordsville, Ind. 1880-1926 Nashville, Ind. A024-F.
VANDAEL. *see* Dael, Jan Frans van.
VANDERBANK. *see* Banck, John and Peter.
VANDERCOOK, Margaret Metzger. (S)
Am. b. New York 1899; ad. 1934 Same. A.
VANDERHAMEN Y LEON.
see Hamen y Leon, Juan Van der.
VANDERLYN, John.
Am. Kingston, N. Y. 1775-1852 Same. B-Bd-C-E-F-1-2-4-6-45-144-182-183-701.
VANDERLYN, Pieter.
Am. Holland 1676/80-1778 New York. F.
VANDERMER. *see* Vermeer.
VANDERPOEL, Emily Noyes.
Mrs. John A. Vanderpoel.
Am. b. New York; ad. 1934 Same. A.
VANDERPOEL, John H.
Am. Holland 1857-1911 St. Louis, Mo. A09-B.
VANDERPOEL, Matilda.
Am. b. Holland; ad. 1934 Chicago. A.
VANDEVELDE. *see* Velde, Van de.
VANGELISTI, Vincenzio. (Eg)
It. Florence 1728/45-1798. B.
VANKA, Maximilian.
Yugo-Slav. b. Zagreb 1890; ad. 1935 New York. M.
VANLOO. *see* Loo.
VANMOUR, Jean Baptiste.
Flem. Valenciennes, Fr. 1671-1737 Constantinople, Turkey. B.
VANNI, Andrea Di.
It. 1332-1414. Bd.
VANNI, Francesco [The Elder].
It. ac. 1370-1395 in Italy. Fa.
VANNI, Francesco [The Younger].
It. Siena 1563/5-1609/10 Same. B-C-722.
VANNI, Lippo di.
It. ac. 1341-1375 in Siena. B-784.
VANNI, Rafaello.
It. Siena 1596-1657. B.
VANNI, Turino di.
It. ac. 1395 in Pisa. B-C.
VANNUCCI, Pietro.
see Perugino, Pietro di Christoforo.
VANNUETELLI, Scipione.
It. Rome 1834-1894 Same. B-C.
VANQUEZ, Diaz.
see Diaz, Daniel Vanquez.
VANUDEN, Lucas.
Flem. Antwerp 1595-1672. M.
VANVITELLI, Kaspar van Wittel.
Dut. Utrecht 1674-1736 Rome, It. B.
VARATORI, Allesandro. *see* Padovanino.
VARELA, Francisco.
Sp. b. Sèville; d. 1656 Same. Bd.
VARGA, Nargit.
Am. ex. 1934 New York. M.
VARGAS, Louis de.
Sp. Sèville 1502-1568 Same. B-C.
VARGISH, Andrew.
Am. ad. 1934 Union City, N. J. A.
VARIAN, Dorothy.
Am. b. New York 1895; ad. 1934 Woodstock, N. Y. A.
VARIAN, George Edmund. (Ill)
Am. Liverpool, Eng. 1865-1923 Brooklyn, N. Y. A020-F.
VARIAN, Lester E.
Am. b. Denver, Colo. 1881; ad. 1934 Same. A28.
VARIN, Jean. (S)
Fr. Liège, Belg. 1596-1672 Paris. B.
VARIN, Quentin.
Fr. Amiens 1580-1645. B-C-722.
VARIN, Raoul. (Eg)
Fr. b. Reims; ex. 1892 in Paris. B.
VARLEY, Cornelius.
Eng. Hackney 1781-1873 Highbury. B-C-DNB-E.
VARLEY, Frederick Horsman.
Can. b. Sheffield, Eng.; ad. 1935 Vancouver, B. C. M.
VARLEY, John.
Eng. 1850-1933. M-Obit. Studio, 10-1933.
VARLEY, John, Jr.
Eng. d. 1899 in London. B.
VARLEY, John, Sr.
Eng. Hackney 1778-1842 London. B-C-DNB-E.
VARLEY, William Fleetwood.
Eng. Hackney 1785-1856 Ramsgate. B-DNB.
VARNUM, William Harrison.
Am. b. Cambridge, Mass. 1878; ad. 1934 Madison, Wis. A-F-W.
VAROTARI. *see* Padovanino, Alessandro.
VASARI, Antonio [The Elder].
[Father of Giorgio Vasari.]
It. ac. in Florence about 1510 +. V.
VASARI, Emillio.
It. b. Florence; ac. 1904 in Paris. B-DNB.
VASARI, Giorgio. (Author and Artist)
It. Arezzo 1511-1574 Florence. B-Bd-C-E-V-192-722.
VASARI, Giorgio [The Elder].
[Grandfather of Giorgio Vasari.]
It. d. 1481 in Arezzo. B-V.
VASCO. *see* Fernandez.
VASILKOWSKY, Serge.
Rus. b. 1854; d. 1920 Russia. M.
VASNETZOFF, Apollinarius M.
Rus. b. 1856; ad. 1935 Leningrad. B.
VASNETZOFF, V. M.
Rus. b. 1848. B.
VASQUEZ. *see* Vazquez.
VASS, Elemér.
Hun. b. 1892; ex. 1934 London. M.
VASSALLETTO, I. (S)
It. ac. 1220-1276 in Italy. Hs.
VASSALLETTO, II. (S)
It. ac. 1220-1276 in Italy. Hs.
VASSE, Louis Claude. (S)
Fr. Paris 1716-1772 Same B.
VASSELON, Marius.
Fr. ac. 1902 in St. Étienne. B.
VASSILACCHI, Antonio.
It. Milo 1556-1629 Venice. B.
VASSILIEFF, Nicolai Ivanovitch.
Am. b. Russ.; ad. 1934 New York. 912.
VASSILIEFF, Th. A.
Rus. ac. 1850-1873. B.
VASSOS, John. (Ill)
Am. ad. 1934 New Canaan, Conn. M.
VASTAGH, György.
Hun. Szegedin 1834; ac. 1900 Paris. B-C.
VAUCHELET, Théophile Auguste.
Fr. Passy 1802-1879. B-C.

VAUDECHAMP, Jean Joseph.
Fr. 1790-1866. B-F-144-183.
VAUGHAN, Malcolm. (Ill)
Am. ad. 1934 New York. M.
VAUGHAN, S. Edson.
Am. b. San Diego, Calif. 1901; ad. 1935 Santa Barbara, Calif. M.
VAUTHIER, Moreau. (S)
Fr. d. 1893. Hs.
VAUTHIER, Pierre Louis.
Fr. b. Brazil; d. 1902 in Paris. B.
VAUTHRIN, Ernest Germain.
Fr. ac. 1915 in Paris. M.
VAUTIER, Benjamin Louis Marc.
Ger. Morges 1829-1898 Düsseldorf. B-C.
VAUTIER, Otto.
Ger. b. Düsseldorf 1863. DBA.
VAUTRINOT, Madolin.
Am. b. 1914; ad. 1935 Egg Harbor, N. J. M.
VAWTER, John William. (Ill)
Am. b. Boone Co., Va. 1871; ad. 1934 Nashville, Ind. A-F-W.
VAWTER, [Mrs.] Mary H. Murray.
Am. b. Balt., Md. 1871; ad. 1934 Nashville, Ind. A.
VAYANA, Nunzio.
Am. b. Castelvetrano, It. 1887; ad. 1934 Ogunquit, Me. A.
VAYSON, Paul.
Fr. b. Gordes 1842; d. 1911. B-C.
VAZQUEZ, Alonzo [or Ildefonso].
Sp. ac. 1600-1649 in Sèville. B.
VAZQUEZ, Juán Bautista.
Sp. d. 1579 in Sèville. B.
VAZQUEZ, Ubeda Carlos.
Sp. b. 1869. M.
VAZQUEZ-DIAZ, Daniel.
Sp. b. 1882; ad. 1934 Madrid. M.
VEBER, Jean. (Cari)
Fr. Paris 1864-1928. B-DBA.
VECCHIA, Pietro della.
It. Venice 1605-1678 Same. B-C-722.
VECCHIETTA, Il. [Lorenzo di Pietro]. (P-S)
It. b. 1412; d. 1480 in Siena. B-C-Hs.
VECCHIO, Il.
see Palma Jacopo, Il. Vecchio.
see also Zacchia da Lucca, Lorenzo.
VECELLIO [or Vecelli], Francesco.
It. Cadore 1483-1559 Same. B-722.
VECELLIO [or Vecelli], Marco.
It. Venice 1545-1641. B-722.
VECELLIO [or Vecelli], Orazio.
It. Venice 1515/28-1576 Same. B-C-722.
VECELLIO [or Vecelli], Tiziano. *see* Titian.
VEDDER, Dorothy.
Mrs. James Monahan.
Am. Wallace, Idaho 1897-1934 New York. M.
VEDDER, Elihu.
Am. New York 1836-1923 Rome, It. A022-B-C-E-F-1-4-5-46-71-263-748-880.
VEDDER, Simon Harmon.
Am. b. Amsterdam, N. Y. 1866; ad. 1915 London. A12-B.
VEEN, Martin van. *see* Heemskerck, M.
VEEN, Otto [or Otho] van.
Dut. Leyden 1556/8-1629 Brussels, Belg. B-C.
VEEN, Pieter. *see* Van Veen, P.
VEERENDAEL, Nicolas van. *see* Verendael, N.
VEILLON, Auguste Louis.
Swi. Bex 1834-1890 Geneva. B-C.
VEIT, Philipp. (Mu)
Ger. Berlin 1793-1877 Mentz. B-C-E.
VEITH, Édouard.
Aus. ac. 1900 in Paris. B.
VELA, Vincenzo. (S)
It. b. 1822; d. 1891 in Italy. B-Hs.
VELASCO, Antonio Palomino.
Sp. b. 1653; d. 1725 in Spain. M.
VELASCO, Luis de.
Sp. d. 1606 Toledo, Sp. B-C.
VELASCO DE COIMBRA.
Por. ac. 1530-1540 in Portugal. B-Bd.
VELASQUEZ, Diego Rodriguez de Silva y.
Sp. Sèville 1599-1660 Madrid. B-Bd-C-E-191-192-615-616-722-790-823.
VELDE, Adriaen van de.
Dut. Amsterdam 1636/9-1672. C-E-722.
VELDE, Cornelis van de.
Dut. ac. 1710-1729 in London. B.
VELDE, Esaias van de [The Elder].
Dut. Amsterdam 1590-1630 The Hague. B-C-722.
VELDE, Henri van de.
Dut. b. 1896; ex. 1933 New York. Fa.
VELDE, Jan II van de.
Dut. 1593-1641. B-C.
VELDE, Jan III van de.
Dut. 1620-1660. B.
VELDE, Peter van de.
Flem. Antwerp 1634-1687. B.
VELDE, Willem van de [The Elder].
Dut. Leyden 1610/1-1693 London. B-C-DNB-722.
VELDE, Willem van de [The Younger].
Dut. Amsterdam 1633-1707 London. C-DNB-E-722.
VELDENAER, Johann [Giov. di Westphalia].
Dut. ac. 1447-1483 in Holland. B.
VELLERT, Dirick Jacobszoon [Van Star]. (Eg)
Flem. ac. 1511-1544 in Belg. M.
VELSEY, Seth M. (S)
Am. b. Logansport, Ind. 1903; ad. 1934 Dayton, O. A-Cs.
VELTEN, Wilhelm.
Rus. or Ger. b. Leningrad, Rus. 1846. B.
VÉLY, Anatole.
Fr. Ronsoy 1838-1882 Paris. B-C.
VENA, Angelo.
Argentine. ac. 19-20 Cent. Fa.
VENANT [or Van Nant], François [or Vernando].
Dut. Middelburg 1592-1631. B.
VENDRAMINI, Francesco. (Eg)
It. b. Italy; ac. 1805 in Leningrad, Rus. DNB.
VENDRAMINI, Giovanni. (Eg)
It. Roneode 1769-1839 London. B-DNB.
VENETO, Bartolommeo.
It. b. 1490; d. 1555 in Italy. B-M.
VENETZIANOFF, Alexei Gavrilovitsch.
Rus. Nejine 1775/80-1846 Tver. B.
VENEZIANO, Antonio. *see* Antonio, V.
VENEZIANO, Bonifazio.
It. b. 1491; d. 1553 in Italy. B-C-V-722.
VENEZIANO, Domenico di Bartolommeo.
It. b. 1390; d. 1461 in Venice. B-Bd-C-V.

VENEZIANO, Lorenzo.
It. ac. 1357-1379 in Venice. B-V.
VENEZIANO, Paolo. *see* Master Paolo.
VENEZIANO, Stefano.
It. ac. 1353-1381 in Venice. B-V.
VENIUS, Otho.
Flem. b. 1556; d. 1629 in Belg. 722.
VENNE, Adriaen Pietersz van der.
Dut. Delft 1589-1662 The Hague. B-C-722.
VENNENAN, Charles Ferdinand.
Flem. Ghent 1803-1875 Brussels. B-C.
VENTURA, Agnolo di. (S)
It. ac. 1330 in Siena. Hs.
VENTURA, Stefi.
Aus. b. Vienna; ad. 1934 Same. DBA.
VENUSTI, Marcello.
It. Como 1515-1579 Rome. B.
VERA, Paul Bernard.
Fr. b. Paris 1882. DBA.
VERARD, Antonio.
Fr. d. 1573 in Paris. B.
VER BECK, William Francis [Frank]. (Ill)
Am. Mansfield, O. 1858-1933 Essex, Eng. A030-F-W.
VERBEECK, François Xavier Henri.
Flem. b. Antwerp 1686; d. 1755. B-C.
VERBEECK, Pieter Cornelis.
Dut. b. Haarlem 1599; d. 1658. B-C.
VERBEEK, Gustave.
Am. ex. 1935 New York. M.
VERBOECKHOVEN, Charles Louis.
Belg. Warneton 1802-1889 Brussels. B-C.
VERBOECKHOVEN, Eugéne Joseph.
Belg. Warneton 1799-1881 Brussels. C-E.
VERBOOM, Adriaen Hendriksz.
Dut. b. Rotterdam 1628; d. 1670. B-C.
VERBRUGGE, Jan Carel.
Flem. Bruges 1756-1831 Same. B-C.
VERBRUGGEN, Gaspar Pieter [The Elder].
Flem. Antwerp 1635-1687 Same. B-C.
VERBRUGGEN, Gaspar Pieter [The Younger].
Flem. Antwerp 1664-1730 Same. B.
VER BRYCK, Cornelius.
Am. New Jersey 1813-1844 Brooklyn, N. Y. F.
VER BRYCK, William.
Am. b. New York 1823; d. 1899. A01.
VERBURGH, Dionys.
Dut. ac. 1708 in Leyden. B.
VERBURGH, Médard.
Belg. b. Roulers 1886. DBA.
VERBUYS [or Verbius], Arnoldus Libertin.
Dut. b. Dordrecht 1645/55; d. 1729. B.
VERCHURING, Hendrik.
Dut. 1620-1690 Holland. M.
VERDI, Francesco Ubertini dei.
see Bacchiaca, Francesco.
VERDIER, François [Van Hamken].
Fr. Paris 1651-1730 Same. B-C-722.
VERDIER, Marcel Antoine.
Fr. Paris 1817-1856 Same. B-C.
VERDILHAN, Mathieu.
Fr. b. 1876; d. 1929 in France. M.
VERDOEL [or Verdael], Adriaen.
Dut. Overmans 1620-1681/95. B-C.
VERDUSSEN, Jan Picter.
Flem. Antwerp 1700-1773 Avignon, Fr. B-C.
VERDUSSEN, Peeter.
Flem. Antwerp 1662-1710. C.

VEREISKY, George. (Et)
Rus. ad. 1935 Leningrad.
VERELST [or Elst], John [or Jan].
Dut. ac. 1691 in London. B.
VERELST [or Elst], Pieter Harmansz.
Dut. Dordrecht 1614/8-1665/8 Antwerp, Belg. B-C-702.
VERELST [or Elst], Simon Peetersz.
Dut. The Hague 1637/44-1710/21 London. B-C-DNB-702.
VERELST [or Elst], Willem.
Flem. b. Belgium; ac. 1740 in London. B-DNB.
VERENDAEL [or Veerendael], Nicholas van.
Flem. Antwerp 1640-1691 Same. B-C.
VERESMITH [or Werhrschmidt], Daniel.
Br. d. 1932. Y01933.
VERESTCHAGIN, [Basil] Vassili Vasilievitch.
Rus. b. Russia 1842; d. 1904 at sea. C-E.
VERGARA, Joseph.
Sp. Valencia 1726-1799 Same. B.
VERGÉ-SARRAT, Henri.
Fr. b. 1844; ac. 1927 in Paris. DBA.
VERGER, Peter. (Eg)
Am. ac. 1796 in New York. F-2-7-40-147.
VERGOS, Jaime II [Huguet-Vergos].
Sp. ac. 1459-1503 in Catalonia. M.
VERGOS, Pablo.
Sp. d. 1495 in Catalonia. M.
VERGOS, Raphael.
Sp. ac. 15th Cent. in Spain. Fa.
VERHAEGEN, Louis M. (S)
Am. ac. 1890 in New York. M.
VERHAEGEN, Pierre Jan Joseph.
Flem. b. 1728; d. 1811 in Louvain, Belg. B-C-722.
VERHAEGEN, Theodor. (S)
Flem. Mechlin 1701-1759. B-Hs.
VERHAEGT [Van Haecht], Tobias.
Flem. Antwerp 1561-1631 Same. C.
VERHAERT, Pierre.
Belg. Antwerp 1852-1908. B.
VERHAS, Jan François.
Belg. Termonde 1834-1896 Brussels. B-C.
VERHEYDEN, Franciscus [or François].
Belg. Louvain 1806-1899 Brussels. B-C.
VERHEYDEN, Frans Pietersz.
Dut. The Hague 1657-1711 Same. B.
VERHEYDEN, Isidoor.
Belg. Antwerp 1846-1905/6 Brussels. B.
VERHEYDEN, Jan Hendrik.
Dut. Utrecht 1778-1846 Same. B-C.
VERHEYDEN, Matthaus.
Dut. Breda 1700-1776. B.
VERHEYDEN, Pieter van der.
Flem. Antwerp 1530-1572. B.
VERHULST, Rombout. (S)
Dut. Mechlin, Belg. 1624-1696 The Hague. B-Hs.
VERKOLYE [or Verkolje], Jan [or Johannes].
Dut. Amsterdam 1650-1693 Delft. B-C-722.
VERKOLYE [or Verkolje], Nicolaes.
Dut. Delft 1673-1746 Amsterdam. B-C-722.
VERLA [or Verlo], Francisco.
It. ac. 1490-1520 in Florence. B.
VERLAT, Charles Michel Marie.
Belg. Antwerp 1824-1890 Same. B-C-E.
VERLET, Charles Raoul. (S)
Fr. Angoulême 1857-1923. B-DBA-798.

VERMARE, André. (S)
Fr. b. Lyons 1869. DBA.
VERMEER VAN HAARLEM [The Elder].
Dut. Haarlem 1628-1691. Fa.
VERMEER VAN HAARLEM [The Younger].
Dut. Haarlem 1656-1705. Fa.
VERMEER, Johannes.
[Called Jan Vermeer van Delft.]
Dut. Delft 1632-1675? Same.
B-Bd-C-E-191-192-617-748.
VERMEHREN, Johan Frederik Nikolai.
Dan. Ringsted 1823-1910. B-C.
VERMEJO, Bartolomé Cárdenas.
Sp. ac. 1440-1500 in Spain. T-774.
VERMERSCH, Ambros.
Flem. Ghent 1810-1854. B.
VERMEULEN. *see also* Meulen.
VERMEULEN, Andries.
Dut. Dordrecht 1763-1814 Amsterdam. B-C.
VERMEULEN, Cornelis Martinus.
Flem. Antwerp 1644-1702 Samé. B.
VERMEYEN, Jan Cornelis [El. Mayo].
Dut. Haarlem 1500-1559 Brussels, Belg. B-C.
VERMILYE, Anna Josephine. (Et)
Am. ad. 1934 Westfield, N. J. A.
VERMOSKIE, Charles.
Am. ad. 1934 Stoughton, Mass. M.
VERNANSAL, Guy Louis [The Elder].
Fr. Fontainebleau 1648-1729 Paris. B-C.
VERNER, Elizabeth O'Neill. (Et)
Am. b. Charleston, S. C.; ad. 1934 Same. W.
VERNER, Frederick Arthur.
Can. b. Sheridan, Ont. 1836; d. 1928. M.
VERNET, Carle [Antoine Charles Horace].
Fr. Bordeaux 1758-1836 Paris. C-E-722.
VERNET, [Claude] Joseph.
Fr. Avignon 1712/14-1789 Paris.
B-Bd-C-E-722.
VERNET, [Émile Jean] Horace.
Fr. Paris 1789-1863 Same. C-E-722.
VERNHES, Henri-Édouard. (S)
Fr. b. Bozoulz 1854; ac. 1900 Paris. B.
VERNIER, Émile Louis.
Fr. b. 1831; d. 1887 Paris. B-C.
VERNON, Beatrix Charlotte.
Br. b. New Zealand 1887; ad. 1934 London.
Wa.
VERNON, H. J.
Br. ac. 1840-1860. M.
VERNON, Paul.
Fr. b. Paris; ac. 1874 Same. B.
VERNON, Thomas. (Eg)
Eng. b. Staffordshire 1824?; d. 1872 in London. B-DNB.
VEROCCHIO. *see* Verrocchio.
VERON, Alexander René.
Fr. b. Montbazon 1826; d. 1897. B.
VERONA, Liberale. *see* Liberale da V.
VÉRONÈSE, Bonifazio I.
It. Venice 1490/1-1540 Verona. B-Bd-V-618.
VÉRONÈSE, Bonifazio di Pitati II.
It. Verona 1487-1575 Venice. B-Bd-V-618.
VÉRONÈSE Il., Paolo [Caliari].
It. Verona 1528-1588 Same.
B-Bd-C-E-V-78-619-722.
VERPILLEUX, Émile Antoine. (Et)
Eng. b. London 1888; ac. 1930 Same. M.

VERRALL, Hugh.
Eng. ex. 1935 London. M.
VERREES, J. Paul.
Am. b. Belgium 1899; ac. 1924 New York.
A20.
VERRILL, Alpheus Hyatt. (Ill)
Am. b. New Haven, Conn. 1871; ad. 1934 New York. W.
VERRIO, Antonio. (Mu)
It. Otranto 1639?-1707 London. B-DNB.
VERROCCHIO, Andrea del [Cioni]. (P-S)
It. Florence 1435-1488 Venice.
B-C-E-Hs-V-620-621.
VERROCCHIO—Pseudo.
[Real name not known. Imitator of Andrea Verrocchio; above.]
It. ac. 1470-1490 in Venice. M.
VERSCHOOTEN. *see* Schooten.
VERSCHURINGH, Hendrik [The Elder].
Dut. Gorcum 1627-1690 Dordrecht. B-C.
VERSCHUUR, Wouterus [or Wouter].
Dut. Amsterdam 1812-1874 Vorden. B-C.
VERSHAEREN, Johannes Antoinius.
Flem. Antwerp 1803-1863 Same. B-C.
VERSHUIER, Liève Pietersz. (P-S)
Dut. Rotterdam 1630?-1686 Same. B.
VERSPRONCK [or Versprong], Gérard.
Dut. Haarlem 1600-1651 Same. B-722.
VERSPRONCK [or Versprong], Johannes Cornelisz.
Dut. Haarlem 1597-1662 Same. B-C.
VER STEEG, Florence Biddle.
Am. b. St. Louis, Mo. 1871; ad. 1934 Same.
A.
VERSTEEG, Maggiel.
Dut. Dordrecht 1736-1843 Same. B-C.
VERSTILLE, William. (Min)
Am. b. 1755?; d. 1803 in Boston, Mass.
F-2-6-169
VERSTRAETE, Theodor.
Belg. Ghent 1840-1907 Antwerp. B.
VERTANGHEN, Daniel.
Dut. The Hague 1598-1681/4 Amsterdam.
B-C.
VERTÈS, Marcel. (Ill)
Hun. b. Budapest 1895; ad. 1934 Paris. DBA.
VERTIN, Pieter Geradus.
Dut. The Hague 1819-1893 Amsterdam. B.
VERTUE, George. (Eg)
Eng. London 1684-1756 Same. B-DNB-E.
VERTUNNI, Achille.
It. Naples 1826-1897. B-C.
VERVEER, Elchanon.
Dut. The Hague 1826-1900 Same. B.
VERVEER, Salomon Leonardus.
Dut. The Hague 1813-1876 Same. B-C.
VERWÉE, Alfred Jacques.
Belg. b. 1838; d. 1905 in Brussels. B-C.
VERWÉE, Louis Pierre.
Belg. Courtrai 1807-1877/82. B.
VERWILT, Francis.
Dut. Rotterdam 1623-1691. B.
VESTER, Willem.
Dut. Heemstede 1824-1871 Haarlem. B.
VESTIER, Antoine.
Fr. Avallon 1740-1824 Paris. B-C.
VETH, Jan Pieter.
Dut. Dordrecht 1864-1925. B.

VETTER, [Mrs.] CORNELIA COWLES.
Am. b. Hartford, Conn. 1881; ad. Same. A-F.
VETTER, [Prof.] HÉGÉSIPPE JEAN.
Fr. Paris 1820-1890. B-C.
VEYRASSAT, JULES JACQUES.
Fr. Paris 1828-1893 Same. B-C-DBA.
VEZIN, CHARLES.
Am. b. Phila., Pa. 1858; ad. 1934 Old Lyme, Conn. A-F.
VIANDEN, HENRY.
Am. Germany 1814-1899 Milwaukee, Wis. M.
VIARDOT, LÉON.
Fr. Dijon 1805-1900 Paris. B-C.
VIBBERTS, [Mrs.] EUNICE WALKER.
Am. b. New Albany, Ind. 1899; ad. 1934 Scarsdale, N. Y. A.
VIBBERTS, GRACE C.
Am. ad. 1934 New Britain, Conn. M.
VIBERT, JAMES. (S)
Fr. b. Carouge 1872. B-DBA.
VIBERT, JEHAN GEORGES.
Fr. Paris 1840-1902 Same. B-Bd-C.
VIBERT, PIERRE EUGÈNE.
Fr. b. Carouge 1875. B-DBA.
VICAIRE, MARCEL. (S)
Fr. b. Paris 1893. DBA.
VICAJI, DOROTHY E.
Eng. ad. 1934 Hampstead. Wa.
VICE, HERMAN STODDARD.
Am. b. Jefferson, Ind. 1884; ad. 1934 Chicago. A.
VICENTINO, GIUSEPPE NICCOLÒ. [Rospiglioni.]
It. ac. 1510-1540 in Bologna. B-V.
VICKERS, ALFRED.
Eng. Newington 1786-1868. B-DNB.
VICKERS, ALFRED GOMERSAL.
Eng. Lambeth 1810-1837 Pentonville. B-DNB.
VICKERS, S. J.
Am. ex. 1935 New York. M.
VICO [or Vicus], ENÉA.
It. Parma 1520-1563/7 Same. B.
VICTOORS [or Fictoor], JAN.
Dut. Amsterdam 1620-1676. B-Bd-C-722.
VICTORIA, PRINCESS [Queen of England].
Eng. b. 1819; d. 1901 in London. B-DNB.
VIDAL, FRANCISCO.
Arg. b. Cordoba, Arg.; ad. 1933 Buenos Aires. M.
VIDAL, GÉRARD. (Eg)
Fr. Toulouse 1742-1804 Paris. B.
VIDAL, VINCENT.
Fr. Aude 1811-1887 Paris. B-C.
VIDAR, FREDE.
Am. b. Denmark 1911; ad. 1935 San Fran., Calif. M.
VIDAURRETA Y ALMADA, VALENTIN.
Mex. b. Culiacan, Sinaloa 1905; ad. 1934 Albuquerque, N. M. M.
VIEIRA, FRANCESCO DE MATTOS [The Elder].
Por. Lisbon 1699-1783 Same. B.
VIEIRA, FRANCISCO [The Younger].
Port. Oporto 1765-1805 Lisbon. B.
VIELLARD, FABRIEN. *see* Launay, F.
VIEN, MARIE JOSEPH [Count].
Sp. Montpelier 1716-1809 Paris. B-C-E-722.
VIERGE, DANIEL [Ortiz]. (P-Et)
Sp. Madrid 1851-1904 Bologna, It. B-E.
VIERRA, CARLOS.
Am. b. 1876; ad. 1935 Santa Fé, N. M. A16.
VIEUX, LE. *see* Vecchio, Il.
VIGARNI, FELIPE. (S)
Sp. d. 1543 in Spain. Hs.
VIGÉE, LOUIS.
Fr. b. 1727; d. 1767 in France. B.
VIGÉE-LEBRUN, MARIE LOUISE ELIZABETH.
Fr. Paris 1755-1842 Same. B-Bd-C-E-622-722-756-829.
VIGELAND, ADOLF GUSTAV. (S)
Nor. b. Mandel 1869. B-E-Hs-798.
VIGER-DURIGNEAU, JEAN LOUIS VICTOR.
Fr. Orne 1819-1879 Paris. B-C.
VIGNA, GLORIANO.
Am. b. Paterson, N. J. 1900; ad. 1934 Same. A.
VIGNE, FÉLIX DE.
Belg. Ghent 1806-1862 Same. B-C.
VIGNE, PAUL DE. (S)
Belg. Ghent 1843-1901 Brussels. B-E-Hs.
VIGNON, CLAUDE.
Fr. Tours 1593-1670 Paris. B-C.
VIGNON, CLAUDE FRANÇOIS.
Fr. Paris 1593-1670 Same. B-C.
VIGNON, PHILIPPE.
Fr. b. Paris 1634; d. 1701. B.
VIGNON, VICTOR PAUL.
Fr. b. 1847; d. 1909 Paris. B.
VIGOUREUX, PIÈRRE. (S)
Fr. b. Avallon 1884. DBA.
VILADOMET, ANTONIO.
Sp. Barcelona 1678-1758 Same. B-Bd.
VILADRICH, MIGUEL.
Sp. b. 1889 in Spain. M.
VILLA, GEORGES. (Ill)
Fr. b. Montmédy 1883. DBA.
VILLAIN, EUGÈNE MARIE FRANÇOIS.
Fr. b. Paris 1821; ac. 1844 Same. B-Ms.
VILLARD, ANTOINE.
Fr. b. Mâcon 1867. DNB.
VILLAVICENCIO, DON PEDRO NUÑEZ DE.
Sp. Sèville 1635-1700 Same. C.
VILLEDIEU, [Mlle] MARIE.
Fr. ac. 1900 in Paris. B.
VILLEGAS Y CORDERO, JOSÉ.
Sp. Sèville 1848-1921 Rome, It. B-C.
VILLEGAS MARMOLEGO, PEDRO [The Elder].
Sp. Sèville 1520-1597. B-722.
VILLENEUVE, JULIEN VALLOU DE.
Fr. b. 1795; d. 1866. M.
VILLENEUVE, LOUIS JULES FRÉDÉRIC.
Fr. Paris 1796-1842 Same. B.
VILLERS, GASTON DE. [Gaston Bernheim-Jeune.]
Belg. b. Brussels 1870. DBA.
VILLOLDO, JUÁN DE.
Sp. b. 1480 in Spain. 722.
VILLON, DUCHAMP RAYMOND. (S)
Fr. Dampville 1876-1918. DBA.
VILLON, JACQUES GASTON DUCHAMP.
Fr. b. Dampville 1875. DBA.
VILMOS, ABA NOVAK.
see Aba-Novak, V.
VINALL, JOSEPH WILLIAM TOPHAM. (Et)
Eng. b. Liverpool 1873; ad. 1934 London. Wa.
VINCELET, VICTOR.
Fr. ac. 1870 in Paris. B.

VINCENT, François André.
Fr. Paris 1746-1816. B-Bd-C-722.
VINCENT, George.
Eng. Norwich 1796-1831 Same. B-DNB-E.
VINCENT, Harry Aiken.
Am. Chicago 1867-1931. A028-F-W16.
VINCENT DE BEAUVAIS.
see Beauvais, V.
VINCHON, Auguste Jean Baptiste.
Br. or Fr. Paris 1789-1855 Ems, Ger. B-C.
VINCI, Leonardo da. *see* Leonardo da Vinci.
VINCK, Franz Kaspar Hubert.
Belg. Antwerp 1817-1903 Berchem. B-C.
VINCKEBOONS [or Vinck-Boons], David.
Dut. Mechlin, Belg. 1578-1629 Amsterdam. B-C-722.
VINCOTTE, Thomas. (S)
Belg. b. 1850 in Belgium. Hs.
VINEA, Francesco.
It. Forli 1846-1904 Florence. B-C.
VINER, Giuseppe.
It. b. 1875; d. 1925 in Italy. M.
VINES, Hernando.
Sp. b. 1904 in Spain. M.
VINICKY, Charles.
Am. ad. 1934 Bronx, N. Y. M.
VINIT, Pierre.
Fr. b. Paris 1870. DBA.
VINIZIANO. *see* Veneziano.
VINKELES [Reiner], Johannes.
Dut. Amsterdam 1741-1816 Same. B.
VINNE, Vincent Laurensz van der.
Dut. Haarlem 1629-1702 Same. B-C.
VINOGRADOV, Sergey.
Rus. b. Moscow 1869; ac. 1906. B.
VINTER, John Alfred.
Eng. ac. 19th Cent. in London. B-DNB.
VINTON, Frederic Porter.
Am. Bangor, Me. 1846-1911 Boston, Mass. A09-B-C-E-F-15-46-47.
VINTON-BROWN, [Mrs.] Pamela.
Am. b. Boston, Mass. 1888; ad. 1934 Woodstock, N. Y. A.
VIOLAND, Benoit.
Fr. ac. 1650 in Grenoble. B.
VIOLET, Pierre. (Min)
Fr. France 1749-1819 London. B-DNB.
VIOLLET-LE-DUC, Adolphe Étienne. (S)
Fr. Paris 1817-1878 Same. B-C.
VIOLLIER, Edmond.
Fr. b. Lyons 1865. DBA.
VIOLLIER, Jean Louis. *see* Voilles, J. L.
VIRAC, Raymond Pierre.
Fr. b. Madrid, Sp. 1892. DBA.
VIRGIL MASTER SHOP.
[Made a specialty of scenes from Virgil.]
It. ac. about 1450 in Florence. M.
VIRGIN among VIRGINS.
see Master of the Virgo Inter Virgines.
VISCHER [or Vissher], Cornelis [The Elder].
Flem. Gouda 1520-1586. B.
VISCHER [or Vissher], Cornelis [The Younger].
Dut. 1618/29-1658/62. B.
VISCHER, Hermann [The Elder]. (S)
Ger. ac. 1453/7 in Nüremberg. E-Ms.
VISCHER, Hermann [The Younger].
Ger. d. 1516. Ms.
VISCHER, Peter [The Elder]. (S)
Ger. Nüremberg 1455-1529 Same.
VISCHER, Peter [The Younger]. (S)
Ger. Nüremberg 1487-1528. B-Hs-Ms.
VISHNEVETSKY, F.
Rus. b. 1801; d. 1863 Russia. M.
VISPO, Bambino.
see Master of the Bambino Vispo.
VISPRE, François Saverino.
Fr. Paris 1730-1790 London. B.
VISSHER. *see* Vischer.
VISTYN, James.
Am. ad. 1934 Cleveland, O. M.
VITE [or Vito], Timoteo della.
It. Ferrara 1467/9-1523 Urbino. B-C-722.
VITELLI, Gaspar van. *see* Wittel, G. van.
VITERBO, Andrea Maratto di.
It. ac. 1483 in Viterbo. B-V.
VITERBO, Dario. (S)
It. b. Florence 1890. DBA.
VITERBO, Pier Francesco da.
It. ac. 1503 in Italy. V.
VITI, Eugènio.
It. b. 1881; ad. 1935 Naples; ex. 1934 Pittsburgh, Pa. M.
VITI, Timoteo. *see* Vite.
VITO. *see* Vite.
VITRINGA, Wingerus [or William].
Dut. Leewarden 1652/7-1721 Wirdum. B.
VITTORIA, Alessandro [della Volpe]. (S)
It. 1525-1608. Hs-Ms-V.
VIVARES, François. (Eg)
Fr. France 1709-1780 London. B-DNB.
VIVARES, Thomas. (Eg)
Eng. b. London 1735; ac. 1770/90 Same. B-DNB.
VIVARINI, Alvise [or Luigi] [The Elder].
It. ac. 1414 in Florence. 722.
VIVARINI, Alvise [or Luigi] [The Younger].
It. Murano 1446/7-1502 Same. B-Bd-E-722.
VIVARINI, Antonio da Murano.
It. Murano 1400-1470? Venice. B-Bd-E-722.
VIVARINI, Bartolommeo da Murano.
It. b. Murano; ac. 1450?-1499? Venice. B-Bd-E-722.
VIVASH, [Mrs.] Ruth Athey.
Am. b. St. Louis, Mo. 1892; ac. 1934 Brooklyn, N. Y. A.
VIVIAN, Calthea Campbell.
Am. b. Fayette, Mo.; ad. 1934 Berkeley, Calif. A.
VIVIAN, George.
Eng. Bath 1798-1873 London. M.
VIVIANI [or Viocano], Ottavio [Cordazzo].
It. b. Brescia 1599; d. 1674 Rome or Naples. B.
VIVIEN, Thomas Joseph.
Fr. Lyons 1657-1734/5 Rome, It. B-C-722.
VIVIN, Louis.
Fr. b. 1861. DBA.
VIZETELLY, Frank. (Ill)
Eng. London 1830-1883? Sudan, Africa. B-DNB.
VIZETELLY, Henry. (Eg)
Eng. London 1820-1894 Fareham. B-DNB.
VLACHOPOULOS, Xénophon.
Gr. b. Athens 1900. DBA.
VLAMINCK, Maurice de.
Fr. b. Paris 1876; ad. 1934 Same. DBA-797.
VLERICK, Peeter.
Flem. Cortrai 1539-1581 Tournai. B-C.

VLEUGHELS [or Wieughels], JACQUES PHILIPPE.
Belg. Antwerp 1619-1694 Paris. B-Bd.
VLEUGHELS [or Wieughels], NICOLAS.
Fr. Paris 1668/9-1737 Rome, It. B-C-722.
VLIEGER, SIMON JACOBSZ DE.
Dut. Rotterdam 1601-1652 Weesp. B-C-722.
VLIET, HENDRIK CORNELISZ VAN DER.
Dut. Delft 1611/12-1675 Same. B-C.
VLIET, JAN JORIS VAN DER.
Dut. b. Delft 1610; ac. 1635. B.
VLIET, WILLEM VAN DER.
Dut. Delft 1584-1642 Same. B-C.
VLOORS, ÉMILE.
Belg. b. Borgerhaut 1871. B.
VODKINE. *see* Petro-Vodkin.
VOELCKER [or Volcker], GOTTFRIED WILHELM.
Ger. Berlin 1775-1849 Same. B-C.
VOENIUS. *see* Veen, Otto van.
VOERMAN, JAN.
Dut. b. Kampen 1857. B.
VOERST, ROBERT VAN.
Flem. Deventer, Holland 1596/7-1636 England. B-DNB.
VOET [or Vouet], JACOB FERDINAND.
Flem. Antwerp 1639-1691/2 Rome, It. B-C.
VOET, KAREL BORCHAERT.
Dut. Zwolle 1670?-1743/5 The Hague. B-C.
VOGEL [or Voegel], CHRISTIAN LEBRECHT.
Ger. Dresden 1759-1816 Same. B-C.
VOGEL, HERMANN.
Fr. ac. 1889-1911 in Paris. B.
VOGEL, HUGO [Prof.].
Ger. b. Magdeburg 1855. B-C.
VOGEL, LUDWIG.
Swi. Zurich 1788-1879 Same. B-C.
VOGEL, VALENTINE.
Am. b. St. Louis, Mo. 1906; ad. 1934 Same. A.
VOGEL VON VOGELSTEIN, CARL CHRISTIAN.
Ger. Saxony 1788-1868 Munich. B-C.
VOGELAER, KAREL VAN [Distelbloom].
Dut. Holland 1653-1695 Rome, It. B.
VOGHTER [or Vogtherr], HEINRICH [The Elder].
Ger. Strassburg 1490-1537 Zani. B.
VOGLER, PAUL.
Fr. ac. 20th Cent. in Paris. B.
VOGNILD, EDNA.
Mrs. Enoch M. Vognild.
Am. b. Chicago; ac. 1931. A28-F.
VOGNILD, ENOCH M.
Am. Chicago 1880-1928 Woodstock, N. Y. A026.
VOGNILD, [Mrs.] TED.
Am. b. Chicago; ad. 1934 Same. A.
VOGT, ADOLFE.
Ger. Lieberstein 1843-1871 Canada. B.
VOGT, LOUIS CHARLES.
Am. b. Cinn., O. 1864. A12-F.
VOILLEMOT, ANDRÉ CHARLES.
Fr. Paris 1822/3-1893 Same. B-C-DBA.
VOILLES [or Viollier], JEAN LOUIS.
Fr. Paris 1744-1796 Russia. B.
VOIRIOT, GUILLAUME.
Fr. ac. 1759-1791 in Paris. B.
VOIRON, LÉON JOSEPH.
Fr. Nancy 1833-1887. B.
VOIS [or Voys], ARIE DE [or Adrian].
Flem. Utrecht 1631-1680/90 Leyden, Holland. B-C-803.
VOISIN, HENRI.
Fr. b. St. Mandé 1861. DBA.
VOLAIRE [or Volere], JACQUES ANTOINE.
Fr. Toulon 1735-1820 Naples, It. B.
VOLCKER, HANS.
Ger. ac. 1893 in Munich. B.
VOLK, ADALBERT J. [or "V. Blada"]. (Et)
Am. b. Germany 1828; d. 1912 Balt., Md. M.
VOLK [Stephen A.], DOUGLAS.
Am. Pittsfield, Mass. 1856-1935 Fryeburg, Me. A-B-C-F-M-W-15-Obit. N. Y. papers, 2-7-1935. Obit. Art Digest, 2-15-1935.
VOLK, LEONARD W. (S)
Am. b. Wellstown, N. Y. 1828; d. 1895. E-F-T-15.
VOLK, VICTOR.
Am. b. Milwaukee, Wis. 1906; ad. 1934 Same. A.
VOLKER, HANS. *see* Volcker, H.
VOLKERLING, FREDERICK. (S)
Ger. ac. in Leipzig. 798.
VOLKERS, ÉMIL.
Ger. Birkenfeld 1831-1898 Düsseldorf. B-C.
VOLKERT, EDWARD CHARLES.
Am. Cinn., O. 1871-1935 Same. A-F-M-W-Obit. N. Y. papers, 3-6-1935. Obit. Art Digest, 6-1-1935.
VOLKHARDT, FREDERICK A.
Am. ex. 1935 Santa Cruz, Calif. M.
VOLKHART, GEORG WILHELM.
Ger. Herdicke 1815-1876 Düsseldorf. B-C.
VOLKHART, MAX.
Ger. Düsseldorf 1848-1924. B.
VOLKMAN, HANS RICHARD VON.
Ger. Halle 1860-1927. B.
VOLKMAN, WILHELM [or Arthur]. (S)
Ger. b. Leipzig 1851. B.
VOLKMAR, ANTONIE.
Ger. b. Berlin 1827. [No death date.] B-C.
VOLKOV, EFIM.
Rus. b. 1844; d. 1920 Russia. M.
VOLLERDT [or Vollaert], JOHANN CHRISTIAN.
Ger. Leipzig 1708/9-1769 Dresden. B-C.
VOLLEVENS, JOHANN [The Elder].
Dut. b. 1649; d. 1728 The Hague. B.
VOLLEVENS, JOHANN [The Younger].
Dut. b. The Hague 1685; d. 1758. B.
VOLLMAR, LUDWIG.
Ger. Sackingen 1842-1884 Munich. B.
VOLLMER, ADOLF FRIEDRICH.
Ger. Hamburg 1806-1875 Same. B-C.
VOLLMER, GRACE LIBBY.
Am. b. Hopkinton, Mass.; ad. 1934 Laguna Beach, Calif. A.
VOLLMERING, JOSEPH.
Ger.-Am. Germany 1810-1887 New York. B-C-F.
VOLLNER, EDNA.
Am. ex. 1933 in Paris. M.
VOLLON, ALEXSIS.
Fr. b. Paris 1865. B-DBA.
VOLLON, ANTOINE.
Fr. Lyons 1833-1900 Paris. B-C.
VOLLWEIDER, AUGUST.
Ger. b. Baden-Baden 1835; ac. 1867. C.

VOLMAR. *see also* Vollmar.
VOLMAR, Georg Johann.
Ger. Mengen 1770-1831/2 Berne, Swi. B-C.
VOLMAR, Joseph Simon. (S)
Swi. Berne 1796-1865 Same. B.
VOLPATO, Giovanni. (Eg)
It. Bassano 1733-1803 Rome. B.
VOLPE, Anton. (S)
Am. b. 1853; d. 1910 New York. A08.
VOLSCHENK, J. E. A.
Br. ac. 1934 in So. Africa. M.
VOLTERRA [or Ricciarelli], Daniello da.
It. Volterra 1509-1566 Rome. C-E-V-722.
VOLTERRA, Francesco Neri da.
It. ac. 1341-1370 in Florence. B-C-V.
VOLTERRANO, Il. *see* Franceshini, Baldassare.
VOLTRI, Niccolò da.
It. ac. 1400 in Genoa. C.
VOLTZ, Friedrich Johann.
Ger. Nördlingen 1817-1886 Múnich. B-C.
VOLTZ, Ludwig.
Ger. b. Augsburg 1825. [No death date.] B-C.
VOLZ, Gertrude [Crosby].
Am. b. New York 1898; ad. 1934 Same. A.
VOLZ, Wilhelm. (S)
Ger. Carlsruhe 1855-1901 Munich. B.
VON. *see also* specific names.
VON BEUST, Anton.
Am. ad. 1934 Orange, N. J. M.
VONCH [or Vonk], Elias.
Dut. Amsterdam 1605-1652 Same. B.
VONCK [or Vonk], Johann.
Dut. Amsterdam 1630; ac. 1660 Same. B.
von DACHENHAUSEN, Friedrich Wilhelm.
Am. b. Wash., D. C. 1904; ad. 1934 Same. A.
VON DER LANCKEN, Francis.
Am. b. Brooklyn, N. Y. 1872; ad. 1934 Chautauqua, N. Y. A.
VON DER MUHLL, H. Robert. (P-S)
Fr. b. Mulhouse 1898. DBA.
VONDROUS, John C.
Am. b. Bohemia 1884; ad. 1935 New York. A28-F.
von EISENBARTH, August.
Am. b. Hungary 1897; ad. 1934 New York. A.
VON GOTTSCHALCK, Oscar Hunt.
Am. b. Prov., R. I. 1865; ad. 1934 Hackensack, N. J. A12-W.
VON HOFSTEN, Hugo Olof.
Am. b. Sweden 1865; ac. 1931 Winnetta, Ill. A28-F.
von NEUMANN, Robert.
Am. b. Rostock, Ger. 1888; ad. 1934 Milwaukee, Wis. A.
VONNOH, Bessie Potter. (S)
Am. b. St. Louis, Mo. 1872; ad. 1934 New York. A-B-Cs-F-W-932.
VONNOH, Robert William.
Am. Hartford, Conn. 1858-1933 Nice, Fr. A030-B-C-E-F-W17-46-Obit. N. Y. papers, 1-15-1934.
VON SALTZA, Carl Frederick.
Am. Sweden 1858-1905 New York. A06-F.
von SCHMIDT, Harold. (Ill)
Am. b. Alameda, Calif. 1893; ad. 1934 Westport, Conn. A.
VON SCHNEIDAU, C.
Am. Smoland, Swe. 1893; ad. 1934 Los Angeles, Calif. A.
VONWYL [or Von Wyl], Jakob.
Swi. Lucerne 1595-1621. B-C.
VOOGD, Hendirk.
Dut. Amsterdam 1766-1839 Rome, It. B-C.
VOORDECKER, Henri.
Belg. Brussels 1779-1861 Same. B.
VOORHEES, Clark Greenwood.
Am. New York 1871-1933 Old Lyme, Conn. A030-F-W.
VOORHEES, Hope Hazard.
Am. b. Coldwater, Mich. 1891; ad. 1934 Detroit, Mich. A.
VOORHEES, James P. (S)
Am. b. 1855; ac. Wash., D. C. M.
VOORHESS, Louis T.
Am. b. Michigan; ad. 1934 High Point, N. C. A.
VOORHOUT, Johannes.
Dut. Withoorn 1647-1723 Amsterdam. B-C.
VOORT [or Voerst], Cornelis van der.
Flem. Antwerp 1576-1624 Amsterdam. B-C.
VOORT, Michiel Frans van der.
Flem. Antwerp 1714-1777 Same. B-C.
VOOS, Clara.
Am. ex. 1934 New York. M.
VORGANG, Paul.
Ger. b. Berlin 1860; ac. 1896 Same. B.
VORIS, Millie Roesgen.
Am. b. Dudleytown, Ind. 1869; ad. 1934 Columbus, Ind. A.
VOROBIEFF, M. V.
Rus. b. 1789; d. 1855 in Russia. B.
VOROBIEFF, S. M.
Rus. b. 1817; d. 1888 in Russia. B.
VORSTERMANS, Johannes.
Flem. Bommel 1643-1699. B-C.
VORSTERMANS, Lucas Émile [The Elder].
Flem. Antwerp 1578/95-1675 Bommel. B.
VORTRIEDE, Loretta H.
Am. ad. 1934 Maumee, O. M.
VOS, Cornelis de [The Elder].
Flem. Hulst 1585?-1651 Antwerp. B-C-722.
VOS, Hubert.
Am. Maastricht, Holland 1855-1935 New York. A-B-F-M-Obit. N. Y. papers, 1-8-1935.
VOS, Marius. (S)
Am. ad. 1935 Paris. M.
VOS, Martin [or Marten] de [The Elder].
Flem. Antwerp 1532/6-1603 Same. B-C-722.
VOS, Paulus [or Pauwell] de.
Flem. Hulst 1590-1678 Antwerp. B-C-722.
VOS, Simon de.
Flem. Antwerp 1603-1676 Same. B-C-722.
VOSBERG, Heinrich.
Ger. Leer 1833-1891 Munich. B.
VOSMAER, Jacob. *see* Wouters, J.
VOSPER, Sydney Curnow.
Eng. b. Plymouth 1866; ad. 1934 London. Wa.
VOSS, Clara.
Am. ad. 1935 New Haven, Conn. M.
VOSS, [Mrs.] Elsa Horne. (S)
Am. ad. 1934 Westbury, L. I., N. Y. M.
VOSS, Karl. (S)
Ger. b. Cologne 1820. [No death date.] M.

VOTRUBA, Fritz. (S)
Aus. ac. 1934 in Vienna. M.
VOUET. *see also* Voet.
VOUET, Claude.
Fr. b. 1636; d. 1710 in Paris. B.
VOUET, L. Aubin.
Fr. Paris 1595/9-1641 Same. B.
VOUET, Simon.
Fr. Paris 1590-1649 Same. B-C-E-722.
VOYEZ, Nicolas Joseph. (S)
Fr. Abbeville 1742-1806 Paris. B.
VOYS, Ary de.
Dut. Leyden 1641-1698. B-722.
VOZECH, Anthony. (S)
Am. ad. 1934 Berwyn, Ill. M.
VRANCX [or Franck], Sébastiaan.
Flem. Antwerp 1573/8-1647 Same. B-C-E-722.
VREELAND, Francis William.
Am. b. Seward, Neb. 1879; ad. 1934 Hollywood, Calif. A.
VREEM, Anthony.
Flem. Dordrecht, Holland. 1640-1681. B.
VREL [or Vrelle], Jacobus [or Jan].
Dut. ac. 1650-1670 in Holland. B.
VRELANT [or Vredelant], Guillaume. (Min)
Dut. Utrecht 1410-1481 Bruges, Belg. B.
VRIENDT, Albrecht François Lieven de.
Belg. Ghent 1843-1900 Antwerp. B-C-E.
VRIENDT, Cornelis Floris de.
see Floris de Vriendt, C.
VRIENDT, Juliaen Joseph de.
Belg. b. Ghent 1842. B-E.
VRIES, Abraham de.
Dut. Rotterdam 1590-1650 The Hague. B-C.
VRIES, Adriaen de.
Dut. The Hague 1560-1643. B-Bd-C-Ms.
VRIES, Jan Reynier de.
Dut. ac. 1645-1657 in Haarlem. B.
VRIES, Jan [or Hans] Vredeman.
Dut. Leeuwarden 1527-1604/8 Antwerp, Belg. B-C.
VRIES, Roelof [or Roelant] Jansz van.
Dut. Haarlem 1631-1681 Amsterdam. B-C.
VRIES [or Frisius], Simon de.
Dut. Leeuwarden 1580-1628 The Hague. B.
VROLYK, Johann Martinus.
Dut. The Hague 1845-1899 Same. B.
VROMANS, Nicolas. (Snake Painter)
Dut. b. 1655/60; d. 1719 Holland. C.
VROOM, Cornelis Hendriksz.
Dut. Haarlem 1600-1661. B.
VROOM, Hendrik Corneliszen.
Dut. Haarlem 1566-1640 Same. B-C.
VROOM, Matthaus.
Dut. ac. 1620-1632 in Antwerp, Belg. B.
VUCHINICH, Vuk. (S)
Am. b. Jugoslavia 1901; ad. 1934 New York. A-Cs.
VUCHT, Jan van der.
Dut. Rotterdam 1603-1637 The Hague. B.
VUERCHOZ, Gérard. (S)
Swi. ac. 1913. Fa.
VUEZ [or Duez or Huez or Wuez], Arnould.
Fr. St. Omer 1642-1719 Lille. B-C.
VUILLARD, Jean Édouard.
Fr. b. Cuiseaux 1867; ad. 1935 Paris; ex. 1934 Pittsburgh, Pa. B-DBA-M.
VUILLEFROY, Félix Dominique de.
Fr. Paris 1841-1910 Same. B-C-DBA.
VUILLEMENOT, Fred A.
Am. b. Ronchamp, Fr. 1890; ad. 1934 Toledo, O. A.
VUILLERMET, Charles.
Swi. ac. 1930 in Geneva. B.
VUILLIER, Gaston Charles.
Fr. b. Perpignan 1847. B.
VUKOVIC, Marko.
Am. ex. 1934 Cinn., O. M.
VULITCH, Antoinette de.
Fr. ac. 1926. Fa.
VULPE, Gabriele de.
It. ac. 1535 in Parma. B.
VYALOV, Constantin.
Rus. b. 1900 in Russia. Fa.
VYBOUD, Auguste Jean. (Eg)
Fr. ac. 1896-1903 in Paris. B.
VYSEKAL, Édouard Antonin.
Am. b. Kutna Hora, Czec. 1890; ad. 1934 Los Angeles, Calif. A-F.
VYSEKAL, Luvena Buchanan.
Mrs. Édouard Antonin Vysekal.
Am. b. Le Mars, Ia.; ad. 1934 Los Angeles, Calif. A-F.
VYTLACIL, Elizabeth Foster.
Mrs. Vaclav Vytlacil.
Am. b. St. Paul, Minn. 1899; ad. 1934 Paris. A.
VYTLACIL, Vaclav.
Am. b. New York 1893; ad. 1934 Paris. A-DBA.
WAAG [or Waaij], Nicolas van der.
Dut. b. Amsterdam 1855; ac. 1910 Same. B.
WAAGEN, Adalbert.
Ger. b. Munich 1834; ac. 1869 Same. [No death date.] C.
WAAGENS, M. A. (S)
Ger. b. 1869 in Germany. M.
WAARD [or Waert], Anthony de.
Dut. The Hague 1689-1751 Same. B.
WAAY [or Way], Nicolaas van der.
Dut. b. 1855 in Holland. M.
WABBE, Jacob.
Dut. b. Hoorn; ac. 17th Cent. B.
WACH, Karl Wilhelm.
Ger. Berlin 1787-1845 Same. B-C.
WACHELIN [or Wachte], Johannes. (Eg)
Ger. ac. 1508-1520 in Strasburg. B.
WACHSMUTH, Ferdinand.
Ger. Mülhouse 1802-1869 Versailles. B-C.
WACHTEL, Elmer.
Am. Balt., Md. 1864-1929 Mexico. A026-F.
WACHTEL, Marion Kavannaugh.
Mrs. Elmer Wachtel.
Am. b. Milwaukee, Wis. 1875; ad. 1934 Pasadena, Calif. A-F.
WACHTER, Georg Friedrich Eberhard.
Ger. Balingen 1762-1852 Stuttgart. B-C.
WACIK, Franz. (Mu)
Aus. ac. 1934 in Vienna. M.
WACK, Henry Wellington.
Am. b. Balt., Md. 1873; ad. 1934 New York. A-F.
WACKER, Rudolf.
Aus. b. Bregenz 1893; ad. 1935 Same. M.
WACKERMAN, Dorothy. *see* Hutton, D. W.

WADDELL, Martha E.
Am. b. Ontario, Can. 1904; ad. 1934 Youngstown, O. A.
WADE, Caroline D.
Am. b. Chicago, Ill. 1857. A28-F.
WADE, Robert.
Am. b. Haverhill, Mass. 1882; ad. 1934 Bradford, Mass. A.
WADE, Thomas.
Eng. b. 1828; d. 1891 in London. B.
WADEN, Robert.
Aust. b. So. Aust. 1900; ad. 1935 Victor Harbor, So. Aust. M.
WADHAM, J. W.
Eng. ac. 1925 in London. Y1925.
WADMAN, Lolita.
Mrs. David Granahan.
Am. b. Minn., Minn. 1908; ad. 1934 Same. M.
WADSWORTH, Adelaide E.
Am. Boston, Mass. 1844-1928. A026.
WADSWORTH, Daniel.
Am. ac. 1806-1848 in Conn. M.
WADSWORTH, Edward.
Eng. b. 1889; ad. 1934 Sussex. Wa-825.
WADSWORTH, Frank Russell.
Am. Chicago 1874-1905 Spain. A06-F.
WADSWORTH, Wedworth. (Ill)
Am. Buffalo, N. Y. 1846-1927 Durham, Conn. A024-F.
WAEL [or Waal], Cornelis de.
Flem. Antwerp 1592-1669 Genoa, It. B-C.
WAEL [or Waal], Lucas Janszen de.
Flem. Antwerp 1591-1676 Same. B.
WAGEMAN, Thomas Charles.
Eng. b. 1787; d. 1863 in London. B.
WAGEMANS, Maurice.
Belg. Brussels 1877-1927. B.
WAGENBAUR, Max Josef.
Bav. Bavaria 1744-1829 Munich. B-C.
WAGENHALS, Katherine H.
Am. b. Ebensburg, Pa. 1883; ad. 1926 San Diego, Calif. A12-F.
WAGER-SMITH, [Miss] Curtis. (Ill)
Am. b. Binghamton, N. Y.; ad. 1934 Willow Grove, Pa. A.
WAGMÜLLER, Michael. (S)
Ger. Munich 1839-1881. Hs.
WAGNER, Adélaide Salles.
see Salles-Wagner, A.
WAGNER, Alexander von.
Hun. b. Budapest 1838; ac. 1866 Munich. B-C.
WAGNER, B. Collet.
Am. b. Grenoble, Fr. 1873; ad. 1934 San Marino, Calif. A.
WAGNER, Edward Q.
Am. b. 1855; d. 1922 Detroit, Mich. A019-F.
WAGNER, Elise [Puyroche].
Ger. Dresden 1828-1895 Lyons, Fr. B-C-T.
WAGNER, Ferdinand [The Elder].
Ger. b. 1819/20; d. 1881 in Augsburg. B-C.
WAGNER, Ferdinand [The Younger].
Ger. b. Passau 1847. B-C.
WAGNER, Frank Hugh.
Am. b. Milton, Ind. 1870; ad. 1934 Chicago. A.
WAGNER, Fred.
Am. b. Valley Forge, Pa. 1864; ad. 1934 Phila., Pa. A-F.
WAGNER, Jacob.
Am. Bavaria 1852-1898 Dedham, Mass. M.
WAGNER, Johann George [The Younger].
Ger. Meissen 1744-1766. B.
WAGNER, Johann Martin von.
Ger. Würzburg 1777-1858 Rome, It. B-C.
WAGNER, Johann Peter Alexander. (S)
Ger. b. 1730; d. 1809 in Würzburg. Hs.
WAGNER, Joseph. (Eg)
Ger. Thalendörf 1706-1780 Munich. B.
WAGNER, Maria Dorothea [Dutrich].
Ger. Weimar 1728-1788 Meissen? B-C.
WAGNER, Mary North. (Min)
Am. b. Milford, Ind. 1875; ad. 1934 Chicago. A.
WAGNER, Otto.
Ger. Turgan 1803-1861 Dresden. B.
WAGNER, Paul.
Ger. ac. 1889 in Germany. M.
WAGNER, Pierre Frédéric.
Fr. b. Paris 1897. B-DBA.
WAGNER, Robert Leicester ["Rob"].
Am. b. Detroit, Mich. 1872; ad. 1934 Beverly Hills, Calif. A-F-W14.
WAGNER, S. Peter.
Am. b. Md.; ad. 1934 Rockville, Md. A.
WAGONER, Harry B.
Am. b. Rochester, Ind. 1889; ad. 1934 Altadena, Calif. A.
WAGREZ, Jacques Clément.
Fr. Paris 1850-1908. B-C.
WAHANIK, Elisa.
Am. ad. 1935 Seattle, Wash. M.
WAHLBERG, Alfred.
Swe. Stockholm 1834-1906. B-C.
WAHLBOM, Johann Wilhelm Carl.
Swe. Colmar, Ger. 1810-1853 London. B.
WAID, D. Everett.
Am. ad. 1934 New York. M.
WAINEWRIGHT, Thomas Francis.
Eng. ac. 1831-1883 in London. B.
WAINEWRIGHT, Thomas Griffith.
Eng. ex. 1825 in London. [No death date.] B.
WAINWRIGHT, Beatrice [Mrs. Roberts].
Eng. b. Leicester; ad. 1934 Chelsea. Wa.
WAINWRIGHT, Samuel H., Jr.
Am. b. Japan; ex. 1934 New York. M.
WAINWRIGHT, William John.
Eng. Birmingham 1855-1931. B-Wa1929-Y01932.
WAITE, Emily Burling.
Mrs. Arthur William Manchester.
Am. b. Worcester, Mass. 1887; ad. 1934 Same. A-F.
WAITE, James Clarke.
Eng. b. London; ac. 1873-1885 Same. B.
WAITE, Robert Thorne.
see Thorne-Waite, R.
WAITT, Marian Martha Parkhurst.
Am. b. Salem, Mass. 1875; ad. 1915 Somerville, Mass. A12.
WAKELIN, Roland.
Aust. ex. 1935 Sydney, N. S. Wales. M.

WAKEMAN, MARION FREEMAN.
Mrs. Seth Wakeman.
Am. b. Montclair, N. J. 1891; ad. 1934 Northampton, Mass. A.
WAKEMAN, ROBERT CARLTON. (S)
Am. b. Norwalk, Conn. 1889; ad. 1934 Same. A.
WAKEN, MABLE J.
Am. b. Chicago, Ill. 1879; ad. 1934 Same. A.
WAKUN, ISHIBASHI.
Jap. ac. 1900 in Japan. J., Vol. 2, page 89.
WALBERG, CARL.
Am. ex. 1935 Pittsburgh, Pa. M.
WALCH, JAKOB.
Ger. ac. 15th Cent. in Nüremberg. B.
WALCOTT, BELLE HAVENS.
Mrs. Harry Mills Walcott.
Am. b. Havens Corners, O. 1870; ad. 1934 Rutherford, N. J. A.
WALCOTT, [Mrs.] CHARLES D.
Am. ad. 1935 Wash., D. C. M.
WALCOTT, HARRY MILLS.
Am. b. Torrington, Conn. 1870; ad. 1934 Rutherford, N. J. A-B-F-W.
WALCOTT, WILLIAM. (Et)
Eng. Russia 1874; ad. 1934 Chelsea. Wa-830.
WALCUTT, WILLIAM.
Am. 1819-1895. M.
WALDECK, CARL GUSTAVE.
Am. St. Charles, Mo. 1866-1931. A028-F-W16.
WALDECK, NINA V.
Am. b. Cleveland, O. 1868; ad. 1934 Olmsted Falls, O. A.
WALDEN, LIONEL.
Am. Norwich, Conn. 1861-1933 Chantilly, Fr. A030-B-F-W-46.
WALDIE, JANE [Mrs. Watts].
Br. 1793-1826. DNB.
WALDMÜLLER, FERDINAND GEORGE. (Min)
Aus. Vienna 1793-1865 Same. B-C.
WALDO, ALLIE DEAN.
Am. ad. 1934 Toledo, O. M.
WALDO, EUGENE LOREN.
Am. b. New York 1870; ad. 1934 Ponca City, Okla. A.
WALDO, SAMUEL LOVETT.
Am. Windham, Conn. 1783-1861 New York. B-Bd-C-E-F-1-2-3-4-15-144-182-183.
WALDORF, ANTOINE.
Dut. The Hague 1803-1806 Amsterdam. B-C.
WALE, SAMUEL.
Eng. d. 1786 in London. B-DNB-803.
WALENN, FREDERICK DUDLEY.
Eng. ac. 1929 London. Wa1929.
WALES, GEORGE CANNING. (Et)
Am. b. Boston 1868; ad. 1934 Brookline, Mass. A28-F-W.
WALES, JAMES.
Scot. Peterhead 1747/8-1795/6 India. B-DNB.
WALES, ORLANDO G.
Am. b. Phila., Pa.; ad. 1933 Allentown, Pa. A-M.
WALES, SUSAN MAKEPIECE LARKIN.
Am. Boston, Mass. 1839-1927 Same. A026-F.
WALES-SMITH, ARTHUR DOUGLAS. (Ill)
Eng. b. Darjeeling, India 1888; ad. 1934 Lymington, Eng. Wa.
WALHAIN, CHARLES ALBERT. (P-S)
Fr. b. Paris 1877; ac. 1900/5 Same. B-DBA.
WALINSKY, ROSA NEWMAN. (S)
Am. ex. 1935 New York. M.
WALKER, ALANSON BURTON. (Ill)
Am. b. Binghamton, N. Y. 1878; ad. 1934 New Canaan, Conn. A.
WALKER, ALEXANDER. (Et)
Scot. ac. 1929 Glasgow. Wa1929.
WALKER, ANTHONY. (Eg)
Eng. 1726-1765. DNB.
WALKER, ARTHUR GEORGE. (S)
Eng. b. Hackney 1861; ad. 1934 Parkstone. Wa.
WALKER, MRS. A. STEWART. *see* Walker, Sybil.
WALKER, BERNARD FLEETWOOD.
Eng. b. Birmingham 1892; ex. 1934 London. Wa.
WALKER, CHARLES ALVAH. (Et)
Am. Loudon, N. H. 1848-1920 Brookline, Mass. A017-F.
WALKER, DUGALD STEWART. (Ill)
Am. b. Richmond, Va.; ad. 1934 New York. A-F-W.
WALKER, EDWARD.
Eng. b. Bradford 1879; ad. 1934 Scarborough. Wa.
WALKER, ELIZABETH [née Reynolds].
Eng. London 1800-1876 Same. B-DNB.
WALKER, ETHEL.
Scot. b. Edinburgh 1867; ad. 1934 Chelsea, Eng. Wa-825.
WALKER, FERDINAND GRAHAM.
Am. Mitchell, Ind. 1859-1927 New Albany, Ind. A024-F-W14-181.
WALKER, FRANCIS ANTILL. (Min)
Am. b. 1872; d. 1916 Brooklyn, N. Y. A013.
WALKER, FREDERICK.
Eng. b. Liverpool 1841-1874 Denbigh. B.
WALKER, FREDERICK. (Ill)
Eng. London 1840-1875 St. Fillans. B-Bd-C-DNB-E 880.
WALKER, GENE ALDEN.
Am. ad. 1934 Warren, Pa. M.
WALKER, HAROLD E.
Am. b. Scotch Ridge, O. 1890; ad. 1934 Toledo, O. A.
WALKER, HENRY OLIVER.
Am. Boston 1843-1929 Belmont, Mass. A026-E-F-W14-46.
WALKER, HOBART ALEXANDER.
Am. b. Brooklyn, N. Y. 1869; ad. 1934 Maplewood, N. J. A.
WALKER, HORATIO.
Am. b. Listowell, Ont. Can. 1858; ad. 1934 Ile d'Orleans, Que., Can. A-B-E-F-W-1-46.
WALKER, JAMES. (Eg)
Eng. 1748-1808? B-DNB.
WALKER, JAMES.
Am. England 1819-1889 Watsonville, Calif. F.
WALKER, JAMES WILLIAM.
Eng. Norwich 1831-1898 Norfolk. B.
WALKER, JOHN. (Eg)
Eng. ac. 1795 in London. B-DNB.

WALKER, JOHN CRAMPTON.
Ir. b. Dublin 1890; ad. 1934 Same. Wa.
WALKER, JOHN LAW.
Am. b. Glasgow, Scot. 1899; ad. 1934 Burbank, Calif. A.
WALKER, JOHN P.
Am. b. 1855; d. 1932 Richmond, Va. A029.
WALKER, JOHN ROWSON.
Eng. Nottingham 1796-1873. B.
WALKER, LEONARD.
Eng. b. Ealing 1877; ad. 1934 London. Wa.
WALKER, LISSA BELL.
Am. ad. 1934 Charlottesville, Va. M.
WALKER, MARGARET BEVERLEY.
Mrs. Hugh Vincent Walker.
Am. b. Darlington, S. C. 1883; ad. 1935 Greenville, S. C. M.
WALKER, MARIAN D. BAUSMAN. (S)
Mrs. Otis L. Walker.
Am. b. Minn., Minn. 1889; ad. 1934 Casper, Wyo. A.
WALKER, NELLIE VERNE. (S)
Am. b. Red Oak, Ia. 1874; ad. 1934 Chicago. A-Cs-F-W-46.
WALKER, ROBERT.
Am. ad. 1935 New York. M.
WALKER, ROBERT.
Eng. b. 1599; d. 1658/60 in London. B-C-DNB-E.
WALKER, ROBERT MCALLISTER.
Eng. b. Fleetwood 1875; ad. 1934 Bothwell. Wa.
WALKER, RYAN. (Cart)
Am. Springfield, Ky. 1870-1932. A12-W17.
WALKER, SOPHIA A.
Am. ad. 1935 New York. M.
WALKER, SYBIL.
Mrs. A. Stewart Walker.
Am. ad. 1934 New York. M.
WALKER, T. DART.
Am. Goshen, Ind. 1869-1914 New York. A0X1.
WALKER, WILLIAM.
Eng. Hackney 1780-1863. B.
WALKER, WILLIAM. (Eg)
Eng. b. 1729; d. 1793. DNB.
WALKER, WILLIAM. (Eg)
Scot. Edinburgh 1791-1867 London. B-DNB.
WALKER, WILLIAM EYRE. (Et)
Eng. b. Manchester 1847; ac. 1929. B-Wa1929.
WALKER, WILLIAM HENRY. (Cart)
Am. b. Pittston, Pa. 1871; ad. 1934 Flushing, L. I., N. Y. A-F-W.
WALKINSHAW, JEANIE WALTER.
Mrs. Robert Walkinshaw.
Am. b. Balt., Md.; ad. 1934 Seattle, Wash. A.
WALKOWITZ, ABRAHAM.
Am. b. Tuiemen, Siberia 1880; ad. 1934 Brooklyn, N. Y. A.
WALL, A. BRYAN.
Am. b. Allegheny City, Pa.; ad. 1934 Pittsburgh, Pa. A-F.
WALL, BERNARDT. (Et)
Am. b. Buffalo, N. Y. 1872; ad. 1934 Lime Rock, Conn. M.
WALL, HERMANN C. (Ill)
Am. b. Germany 1875; ad. 1915 Wilmington, Del. A12.
WALL, WILLIAM ALLEN.
Am. New Bedford, Mass. 1801-1885 Same. F-2.
WALL, WILLIAM G.
Am. b. Dublin, Ir. 1792; d. *after* 1862 U. S. F-2.
WALLACE, ETHEL A.
Am. b. Chesterfield, N. J.; ad. 1934 New Hope, Pa. A.
WALLACE, FRANK.
Am. ad. 1935 Sydney, Aust. M.
WALLACE, FREDERICK ELLWOOD.
Am. b. Haverhill, Mass. 1893. A28.
WALLACE, HAROLD FRANK.
Eng. b. York 1881; ad. 1934 Pelsall. Wa.
WALLACE, JOHN LAURIE.
Am. b. Garvagh, Ir. 1864; ad. 1934 Omaha, Neb. A.
WALLACE, OREN J. (S)
Am. ac. 1932 U. S. M.
WALLACE, [Mrs.] OTTILIE. (S)
Scot. b. Edinburgh 1875; ad. 1934 London. Wa.
WALLACE, ROBIN.
Eng. b. Kendal 1897; ad. 1934 London. Wa.
WALLANDER, JOSEF WILHELM.
Swe. Stockholm 1821-1888. B-C.
WALLASTON. *see* Wollaston.
WALLEN, J. J.
Fr. ac. 19th Cent. in France. B.
WALLER, FRANK.
Am. New York 1842-1923 Morristown, N. J. A020-C-F-15.
WALLER, [Mrs.] MARY LEMON.
Eng. ad. 1934 London. Wa.
WALLER, MERVYN NAPIER.
Aust. b. Penshurst, Victoria 1893. M.
WALLER, SAMUEL EDMUND.
Eng. Gloucester 1850-1903. B-C-DNB.
WALLET, ALBERT CHARLES.
Fr. b. Valenciennes 1852; ad. 1900 Paris. B.
WALLET, PAUL LOUIS ALEXANDRE.
Fr. b. Amiens 1818; ac. 1870 in Paris. B.
WALLEY, ABIGAIL B. P.
Am. b. Boston, Mass. 1845. A28.
WALLIN, DAVID.
Swe. ad. 1935 Stockholm; ex. 1934 Pittsburgh, Pa. M.
WALLIS, ALFRED.
Eng. ex. 1935 London. M.
WALLIS, FRANK.
Am. ad. 1934 New York. M.
WALLIS, GEORGE.
Eng. Wolverhampton 1811-1891 Wimbledon. B.
WALLIS, HENRY. (Ill)
Eng. b. 1805? d. 1890 in London. B-DNB.
WALLIS, KATHERINE ELIZABETH. (S)
Can. b. Peterboro, Ont. 1861; ad. 1935 Paris. M.
WALLIS, ROBERT. (Eg)
Eng. London 1794-1878 Brighton. B-DNB.
WALLIS, ROSA.
Eng. b. Stretton 1857; ad. 1934 London. Wa.

WALLIS, W. Cyril.
Eng. ex. 1934 London. M.
WALLS, William.
Scot. b. Dunfermline 1860. Wa1929.
WALMSLEY, Thomas.
Ir. Dublin 1763-1805 Tath. B-DNB.
WALSCAPELE, Jacob van.
Dut. ac. 1667-1718 in Amsterdam. B-C.
WALSH, Christine [Mrs. Frank W.].
Am. ad. 1934 New Orleans, La. M.
WALTENSFERGER, Charles E.
Am. Detroit, Mich. 1871-1931 Same. A028.
WALTER, Adam B. (Eg)
Am. Phila., Pa. 1820-1875 Same. F-7-40.
WALTER, Christian J.
Am. b. Pittsburgh, Pa. 1872; ad. 1934 Same. A.
WALTER, Edgar. (S)
Am. b. San Fran., Calif. 1877; ad. 1935 Same. A12-B-F-Ta.
WALTER, Joseph. (Mu)
Am. b. Galtuer, Aus. 1865; ad. 1934 Dubuque, Iowa. A.
WALTER, Joseph.
Eng. Bristol 1783-1856. B.
WALTER, Martha.
Am. b. Phila., Pa.; ad. 1934 Melrose Park, Pa. A-F-W-46.
WALTER, Pierre François Prosper.
Fr. Nancy 1816-1852/5. B.
WALTER, Solly. (Ill)
Am. Vienna, Aus. 1846-1900 Honolulu, Hawaii. A020.
WALTER, Valerie H. (S)
Am. b. Balt., Md.; ad. 1934 Same. A-F.
WALTER, William Francis.
Am. b. Wash., D. C. 1904; ad. 1934 Same. A.
WALTERS, Carl. (S)
Am. b. Fort Madison, Ia. 1883; ad. 1934 Woodstock, N. Y. A.
WALTERS, Émile.
Am. b. Winnipeg, Can. 1893; ad. 1934 New York. A-F-W.
WALTERS, Evan.
Welsh. b. Wales 1893; ad. 1934 London. Wa.
WALTERS, George Stanfield.
Eng. ac. 1860-1893 London (Deceased). M.
WALTERS, Jessica.
Eng. ex. 1934 London. M.
WALTERS, Kenneth.
Am. ad. 1935 Cleveland, O. M.
WALTERS, Samuel.
Eng. London 1811-1882 Bootle. B.
WALTHARD, Friedrich.
Swi. Berne 1818-1870 Same. B-C.
WALTHER, Adolf Wilhelm.
Ger. b. Saxony 1826; ac. 1878 in Dresden. B-C.
WALTHER, Charles H.
Am. b. Balt., Md. 1879; ad. 1934 Same. A.
WALTHER, Frederick. (Min)
Am. ad. 1934 Phila., Pa. M.
WALTHER, Karl.
Ger. ad. 1935 Berlin; ex. 1934 Pittsburgh, Pa. M.
WALTHER-FIRLE. *see* Firle, W.

WALTMAN, Harry Franklin.
Am. b. Ohio 1871; ad. 1934 Dover Plains, N. Y. A-F-W.
WALTNER, Charles Albert. (Eg)
Fr. Paris 1846-1925. B-DBA-Y01926.
WALTON, Allan.
Eng. b. Cheshire 1892; ad. 1934 Same. Wa.
WALTON, Cecil [Mrs. Robertson].
Scot. b. Glasgow 1891; ad. 1934 Edinburgh. Wa.
WALTON, Edward Arthur.
Scot. b. 1860; d. 1922 Scotland. B.
WALTON, Elijah.
Eng. Birmingham 1832-1880. B-DNB.
WALTON, Frank.
Eng. ac. 1840-1927 in London. B-C.
WALTON, Henry [The Elder].
Eng. 1720-1790. B.
WALTON, Henry [The Younger].
Eng. 1746-1813. M.
WALTON, William.
Am. Phila., Pa. 1843-1915. A013.
WAMSLEY, Frank C. (S)
Am. b. Locust Hill, Mo. 1879; ad. 1934 Hollywood, Calif. A.
WANDS, Alfred James.
Am. b. Cleveland, O. 1902; ad. 1934 Denver, Colo. A-F.
WANDSCHNEIDER, Wilhelm. (S)
Ger. b. Berlin; ac. 1914 St. Louis, Mo. M.
WANE, Richard.
Eng. Manchester 1852-1904 Egremont. B.
WANG, Chien.
Chinese. ac. 17th Cent. in China. E.
WANG HUI.
Chinese. ac. 17th Cent. in China. E.
WANG MÊNG.
Chinese. Yuan Period (1260-1368). E.
WANG SHIH-MIN.
Chinese. ac. 17th Cent. in China. E.
WANG WEI. (Painter and Poet)
Chinese. ac. 699-759 in China. E.
WANG YUAN-CH'I.
Chinese. ac. 17th Cent. in China. E.
WANKER, M. Walling.
Am. ex. 1935 Portland, Ore. M.
WAPPERS, Gustave Egide Charles.
Belg. Antwerp 1803-1874 Paris. B-C-E.
WARD, Bernard Evans.
Am. London 1857-1933 Akron, O. A030.
WARD, Charles Caleb.
Am. ex. 1890 New York. M.
WARD, Charles D.
Eng. b. Taunton 1872; ad. 1934 Blewsbury. Wa.
WARD, [Mrs.] Charlotte Blakeney.
Eng. ad. 1934 London. Wa.
WARD, Edgar Melville.
Am. Urbana, O. 1839-1915 New York. A012-C-F-15.
WARD, Edmund F.
Am. b. White Plains, N. Y. 1892; ad. 1934 Same. A.
WARD, Edward Matthew.
Eng. London 1816-1879 Windsor. B-C-DNB-E.
WARD, Elsie. (S)
Am. ac. 1925 in Denver, Colo. F-Ta.

WARD, George Raphael. (Eg)
Eng. 1798-1879. B-DNB.
WARD, Henrietta Mary Ada.
Mrs. Edward Matthew Ward.
Eng. London 1832-1924. C.
WARD, Herbert T. (S)
Am. London 1863-1919 France. A016-B-DBA.
WARD, Irving.
Am. b. 1867; d. 1924 Balt., Md. A021-F.
WARD, James.
Eng. London 1769-1859 Cheshnut. B-Bd-C-DNB-E-722.
WARD, James F.
Am. ad. 1934 Brooklyn, N. Y. M.
WARD, John Quincy Adams. (S)
Am. Urbana, O. 1830-1910 New York. A08-E-F-Hs-15-46-71-623-701-932.
WARD, J. Stephen.
Am. b. St. Joseph, Mo. 1876; ad. 1934 Jacksonville, Ore. A.
WARD, [Sir] Leslie. (Cart)
[Also known as "Spy".]
Eng. London 1851-1922 Same. M.
WARD, Leslie Moffat.
Eng. b. Worcester 1888; ad. 1934 Bournemouth. Wa.
WARD, Louis.
Am. ex. 1934 New York. M.
WARD, Lynd Kendall. (Eg)
Am. b. Chicago 1905; ad. 1934 Palisade, N. J. A28.
WARD, [Mrs.] Mabel Raymond. (Et)
Am. b. New York 1874; ad. 1915 Same. A12.
WARD, Martin Theodore.
Eng. b. 1799? d. 1874 in York, Eng. B-DNB.
WARD, Nina B.
Am. b. Rome, Ga.; ad. 1926 Phila., Pa. A12-F.
WARD, Ralph.
Am. ex. 1934 New York. M.
WARD, Ruth Porter.
Am. b. Statesville, N. C.; ad. 1934 Wash., D. C. A.
WARD, Vernon de Beauvoir.
Eng. b. Hampstead 1905; ad. 1934 Same. Wa.
WARD, William. (Eg)
Eng. London 1766-1826 Same. B-DNB-E.
WARD, William Dudley B.
Can. b. Graveley Bank, Eng.; d. 1935 Toronto, Can. M.
WARD, William James. (Eg)
Eng. London 1800?-1840. B-DNB.
WARD, Winifred. (S)
Am. b. Cleveland, O. 1889; ad. 1926 Phila., Pa. A12-F.
WARDLE, Arthur.
Eng. b. London 1864; ex. 1934 Same. B-Wa1929.
WARDMAN, John William.
Am. Leeds, Eng. 1901; ad. 1934 Los Angeles, Calif. A.
WARE, Florence Ellen.
Am. b. Salt Lake City, Utah 1891; ad. 1934 Same. A.
WARE, John.
Am. ac. 1732-1798 New York. M.
WAREHAM, John Hamilton Dee.
Am. b. Grand Lodge, Mich.; ad. 1934 Cinn., O. A.
WARFIELD, Mabel.
Am. b. New Orleans, La. 1905; ad. 1934 Same. A.
WARGNY, Armand.
Am. ad. 1934 New York. M.
WARHANIK, Elizabeth C.
Mrs. C. A. Warhanik.
Am. b. Phila., Pa. 1880; ad. 1934 Seattle, Wash. A.
WARIN, Jean. (S)
Fr. 1604-1672. M.
WARING, John Burley.
Eng. Lyme 1823-1875 Hastings. B.
WARING, Laura Wheeler.
Mrs. Walter E. Waring.
Am. b. Hartford, Conn.; ad. 1934 Phila., Pa. A.
WARING, Leila. (Min)
Am. ad. 1934 Charleston, S. C. A.
WARLOW, Herbert Gordon.
Eng. b. Sheffield 1885; ad. 1934 London. Wa.
WARNACUT, Crewes.
Am. b. Osman, Ill. 1900; ad. 1934 Inwood, Ind. A.
WARNBERGER, Simon.
Ger. Pullak 1769-1847 Same. B-C.
WARNEKE, Heinz. (S)
Am. b. Bremen, Ger. 1895; ad. 1934 New York. A-Cs.
WARNER, Earl A. (Ill)
Am. b. 1883; d. 1918 Battle Creek, Mich. A015.
WARNER, Everett Longley.
Am. b. Vinton, Ia. 1877; ad. 1934 Pittsburgh, Pa. A-F-W.
WARNER, [Mrs.] Mary Loring.
Am. b. Sheffield, Mass. 1860; ad. 1934 Middletown, Conn. A-F.
WARNER, Nell Walker.
Am. b. Nebraska 1891; ad. 1934 La Crescenta, Calif. A.
WARNER, Olin Levi. (S)
Am. West Sheffield, Conn. 1844-1896 New York. E-F-Hs-15-46-71-701.
WARNER, Victor Bell.
Am. b. Ipswich, Eng. 1908; ad. 1934 New York. A.
WARNER, William. (Eg)
Am. Phila., Pa. 1813-1848 Same. F-2-7-40.
WARNERSSEN, Peter.
Dut. ac. 1500 in Holland. M.
WAROQUIER, Henry de.
Fr. b. Paris 1881; ad. 1934 Same. DBA.
WAROQUIER, Louis de.
Fr. ac. 1844-1848 in Paris. B.
WARREN, Asa Coolidge.
Am. Boston 1818-1904 New York. A05-F-7.
WARREN, A. W.
Am. b. Coventry, Eng.; d. 1873 New York. F.
WARREN, Charles Turner. (Ill)
Eng. London 1767-1823 Wandsworth. B-DNB.

WARREN, Dudley Thompson. (S)
Am. b. East Orange, N. J. 1890; ad. 1934 Roanoke, Va. A.

WARREN, Elisabeth Boardman.
Mrs. Tod Lindemuth.
Am. b. Bridgeport, Conn. 1886; ad. 1934 Provincetown, Mass. A28.

WARREN, Ferdinand E. (Ill)
Am. b. Independence, Mo. 1899; ad. 1935 Brooklyn, N. Y. A.

WARREN, Frederic Bryant.
Am. b. No. Adams, Mass.; d. 1919 Flushing, L. I., N. Y. A016.

WARREN, Harold Broadfield.
Am. b. Manchester, Eng. 1859; ad. 1934 Cambridge, Mass. A-F-W.

WARREN, Henry.
Eng. London 1794-1879 Same. B.

WARREN, Leon.
Am. ad. 1934 Jackson Heights, L. I., N. Y. M.

WARREN, Mallory Page.
Am. ad. 1935 San Antonio, Tex. M.

WARRICK, Mete Vaux [Mrs. Fuller]. (S)
Am. b. Phila., Pa. 1877; ad. 1934 Farmingham, Mass. A-F-46.

WARSAW, Albert Taylor.
Am. b. New York 1899; ad. 1934 Same. A.

WARSHAWSKY, Abel George.
Am. b. Sharon, Pa. 1883; ad. 1934 Paris. A-DBA-F-W.

WARSHAWSKY, Alexander.
Am. b. Cleveland, O. 1887; ad. 1934 Paris. A.

WARTHMÜLLER, Robert.
Ger. Landsberg 1859-1895 Berlin. B.

WARWICK, Edward.
Am. b. Phila., Pa. 1881; ad. 1934 Same. W.

WARWICK, [Mrs.] Ethel Herrick.
Am. b. New York; ad. 1934 Phila., Pa. A.

WASEY, Jane. (S)
Mrs. Domenico Mortellito.
Am. ex. 1935 New York. M.

WASHBURN, Cadwallader. (Et)
Am. b. Minn., Minn.; ad. 1934 Englewood, N. J. A-F-W-46.

WASHBURN, Louis Bunnell.
Am. b. Dimock, Pa. 1875; ad. 1934 Jacksonville, Fla. A.

WASHBURN, Mary N.
Am. Greenfield, Mass. 1861-1932 Same. A029-F.

WASHBURN, Roy Engler.
Am. b. Vandalia, Ill. 1895; ad. 1934 Chicago. A.

WASHINGTON, Elizabeth Fisher.
Am. b. Siegfried's Bridge, Pa.; ad. 1934 Phila., Pa. A.

WASHINGTON, Georges.
Fr. Marseilles 1827-1900 Paris. B.

WASHINGTON, William. (Et)
Eng. b. Marple, Eng. 1885; ad. 1934 London. Wa.

WASLEY, Frank.
Eng. b. 1854. B.

WASSENBERGH, Jan Abel.
Dut. Groningen 1689-1750 Same. B.

WASSENHOVE, van. *see* Justus of Ghent.

WASSER [or Waser], Anna.
Swi. Zurich 1679-1713. B.

WASSON, George Savery.
Am. b. Groveland, Mass. 1855; ac. 1926 in Maine. F-W8-15.

WATANABÉ KYAZAN.
Jap. J., Vol. 2, page 76.

WATELET, Charles Joseph.
Belg. b. Beaurain 1867; ad. 1925 Paris. B-DBA.

WATELET, Claude Henri.
Fr. Paris 1718-1786. B.

WATELET, Louis Étienne.
Fr. Paris 1780-1866 Same. B-C.

WATELIN [or Wattelin], Louis François Victor.
Fr. Paris 1838-1907. B-C.

WATENPHUL, Max Peiffer.
Ger. ad. 1934 Hattingen-Ruhr, Ger. M.

WATERBURY, Florence.
Am. ad. 1934 Convent, N. J. M.

WATERHOUSE, John Williams.
Eng. Rome, It. 1849-1917 London. B-C-E.

WATERLOO [or Waterlo], Anthonie.
Flem. Lille, Fr. 1609/10-1676/7 Utrecht, Holland. B-C-722-803.

WATERLOW, [Sir] Ernest Albert.
Eng. London 1850-1919 B-C-DNB-E.

WATERMAN, Marcus.
Am. Prov., R. I. 1834-1914 Moderno, It. A12-C-F-15-47.

WATERS, George Fite. (S)
Am. b. San Fran., Calif. 1894; ad. 1934 Hossegor [Landes], Fr. A-Wa.

WATERS, George W.
Am. Coventry, Eng. 1832-1912 Elmira, N. Y. F.

WATERS, R. Kinsman.
Am. b. Columbus, O. 1887; ad. 1934 Same. A.

WATERS, Sadie P.
Am. St. Louis, Mo. 1869-1900. 829.

WATERSON, David.
Scot. b. 1870; ad. 1934 Brechin, Scot. Wa.

WATHEN, James. (Ill)
[Known as "Jimmy Sketch."]
Eng. d. 1928 Hereford, Eng. B.

WATKINS, Bartholomew Colles.
Ir. Dublin 1833-1891 Glenmore. B.

WATKINS, Bernard C. (Ill)
Am. ad. 1934 Paterson, N. J. M.

WATKINS, [Mrs.] Catherine W.
Am. b. Hamilton, Ont., Can.; ad. 1934 Los Angeles, Calif. A.

WATKINS, Franklin Chenault.
Am. b. New York 1894; ad. 1934 Phila., Pa. A.

WATKINS, Susan.
Am. b. California 1875. B-F-46.

WATKINS, William Reginald.
Am. b. Manchester, Eng. 1890; ad. 1934 Balt., Md. A.

WATROUS, Elizabeth Snowden Nicolas.
Mrs. Harry Willson Watrous.
Am. New York 1858-1921 Same. A018-F.

WATROUS, Harry Willson.
Am. b. San Fran., Calif. 1857; ad. 1934 New York. A-F-W.

WATROUS, Marie Day.
Am. b. Pittsfield, Mass.; ad. 1934 Paris. DBA.

WATSON, Adele.
Am. b. Toledo, O. 1873; ad. 1934 Pasadena, Calif. A.

WATSON, Amelia Montague.
Am. b. East Windsor Hill, Conn. 1856; ad. 1934 Same. A-F-W.

WATSON, [Miss] Angele Hamendt.
Am. b. Belgium; ad. 1935 New York. M.

WATSON, Caroline. (Eg)
Eng. London 1758-1814 Pimlico. B-DNB.

WATSON, Charles A.
Am. Balt., Md. 1857-1923 Easton, Md. A021-F.

WATSON, Charles John. (Et)
Eng. Norwich 1846-1927. B-Y01928.

WATSON, Dawson. *see* Dawson-Watson.

WATSON, Dudley Crafts.
Am. b. Lake Geneva, Wis. 1885; ad. 1934 Ravinia, Ill. A-F-W.

WATSON, Earnest W. (Eg)
Am. b. Conway, Mass.; ad. 1935 Brooklyn, N. Y. A29.

WATSON, Edith Sarah.
Am. b. East Windsor Hill, Conn. 1861; ad. 1934 Same. W.

WATSON, Elizabeth H.
Am. ad. 1934 Phila., Pa. A.

WATSON, Elizabeth V. Taylor.
Am. b. New Jersey; ad. 1934 Boston, Mass. A.

WATSON, [Mrs.] Ella.
Am. Worcester, Mass. 1850-1917 Somerville, Mass. A014.

WATSON, Forbes.
Am. ad. 1935 New York. M.

WATSON, George.
Scot. b. 1767; d. 1837 Edinburgh. B-C-DNB.

WATSON, George Spencer.
Eng. London 1869-1934 Same. B-Wa1929-Obit. Art News, 5-5-34.

WATSON, Harry.
Eng. b. Scarborough 1871; ad. 1934 London. Wa.

WATSON, Henry Summer. (Ill)
Am. Bordentown, N. J. 1868-1933 New York. A030-W17.

WATSON, Homer Ramsford.
Can. b. Doon, Can. 1855; ad. 1934 Same. B.

WATSON, James. (Eg)
Ir. Ireland 1740-1790. B-DNB.

WATSON, John.
Am. Scotland 1685-1768 Perth Amboy, N. J. B-C-F-2-4-6-182.

WATSON, John Dawson.
Eng. Sedbergh 1832-1892 Conway. B-DNB.

WATSON, Morris.
Am. ex. 1934 in New York. M.

WATSON, Musgrave Lewthwaite. (P-S)
Eng. Carlisle 1804-1847 London. B-DNB.

WATSON, Nan.
Am. b. Edinburgh, Scot.; ad. 1934 New York. A.

WATSON, [Mrs.] Ruth Crawford.
Am. b. Decatur, Ala. 1892; ad. 1934 Same A.

WATSON, Samuel. (S)
Eng. Heanor 1663-1715 Same. B-DNB.

WATSON, Sydney Robert.
Eng. b. Enfield 1892; ad. 1934 Leicester. Wa.

WATSON, Thomas. (Eg)
Eng. London 1743-1781 Bristol. B-DNB.

WATSON, Walter J.
Eng. b. Cheshire 1879. Wa1929.

WATSON, William [The Younger].
Eng. ac. 1886-1921 London. B-Y01922.

WATSON, William Peter.
Eng. b. So. Shields; d. 1932. Wa1929-Y01933.

WATSON, William Smellie.
Scot. Edinburgh 1796-1874 Same. B-C.

WATSON-GORDON. *see* Gordon, W.

WATT, Barbara Hunter.
Am. b. Wellesley, Mass.; ad. 1934 Same. A.

WATT, G. Fiddes.
Scot. b. Aberdeen 1873; ad. 1934 Kensington. Wa.

WATT, James Henry. (Ill)
Eng. London 1799-1867 Same. B-DNB.

WATT, William G. (Eg)
Am. New York 1867-1924 Same. A20-F.

WATTEAU, François Louis Joseph [The Younger].
Fr. Valenciennes 1758-1823 Lille. B.

WATTEAU, Jean Antoine
Fr. Valenciennes 1684-1721 Nogent. B-Bd-C-E-624-625-722-790-847-878-952.

WATTEAU, Louis Joseph [The Elder].
Fr. Valenciennes 1731-1798 Lille. B.

WATTIER, Charles Émilie.
Fr. Paris 1800-1868 Same. B-C.

WATTS, Arthur George. (Ill)
Eng. b. Chatham 1883; d. 1935 Swi. Wa-Obit. N. Y. papers, 7-21-1935.

WATTS, Frederick Waters.
Eng. b. 1800; d. 1862 in London. B.

WATTS, George Frederick. (P-S)
Eng. London 1817-1904 Compton. B-Bd-C-DNB-E-Hs-748-922-953.

WATTS, James Lawrence. (S)
Br. b. 1849; d. 1925. Y01926.

WATTS, James Thomas.
Eng. b. Birmingham; ad. 1929 Liverpool. B-Wa1929.

WATTS, J. W. (Eg)
Am. ac. 1850 in Boston; [No death date]. F-7.

WATTS, Simon. (Eg)
Eng. ac. 1736-1775 in London. B.

WATTS, William. (Eg)
Eng. London 1752-1851 Cobham. B-DNB.

WATTS, William Clothier.
Am. b. Phila., Pa.; ad. 1934 Carmel, Calif. A.

WAUDBY, Roberta F. C. (Ill)
Am. ad. 1934 New York. M.

WAUGH, Coulton.
Am. b. England 1896; ad. 1934 Provincetown, Mass. A.

WAUGH, Frederick Judd.
Am. b. Bordentown, N. J. 1861; ad. 1934 Provincetown, Mass. A-F-W-46-757.

WAUGH, Ida.
Am. b. Phila., Pa.; d. 1919 New York. A016-F.

WAUGH, Samuel B.
Am. Mercer, Pa. 1814-1885 Janesville, Wis. F.
WAUGH, Sidney Biehler. (S)
Am. b. Amherst, Mass. 1904; ad. 1934 New York. A.
WAUTERS, Charles Augustin.
Belg. Boom 1811-1869 Mechlin. B-C.
WAUTERS, Émile Charles.
Belg. Brussels 1845-1933 Paris. B-C-DBA-E.
WAUTERS [or Wouters], Franz.
Flem. Lierre 1612/4-1659 Antwerp. B.
WAY, Andrew John Henry.
Am. Wash., D. C. 1826-1888 Balt., Md. C-F-15.
WAY, Charles Jones.
Can. Dartmouth, Nova Scotia 1835-1919 Switzerland. B-Y01920.
WAY, Edna Martha.
Am. b. Manchester, Vt.; ad. 1934 Athens, O. M.
WAY, Nicolaas. *see* Waay.
WAY, William Cossens.
Eng. b. Newcastle; ac. 1867/86. B.
WAYCOTT, Hedley.
Am. ad. 1934 Peoria, Ill. M.
WAYER, Mathieu de. (Carver)
Ger. ac. 1563. M.
WDOWISZEWSKI, Czeslaw.
Pol. ex. 1934 Toledo, O. M.
WEAR, Maud Marian.
Eng. b. London 1873; ad. 1934 Sussex. Wa.
WEATHERBY, Evelyn Mae.
Am. ad. 1934 Toledo, O. M.
WEAVER, Annie Vaughn. (Ill)
Am. 1935 Selma, Ala. M.
WEAVER, Beulah Barnes.
Am. b. Wash., D. C. 1886; ad. 1934 Same. A.
WEAVER, B. Maie.
Am. b. New Hartford, Conn. 1875; ad. 1934 Westfield, Mass. A.
WEAVER, Inez Belva.
Mrs. H. H. Weaver.
Am. b. Marshal Co., Ia. 1872; ad. 1934 Stromsberg, Neb. A.
WEAVER, John Pyefinch.
Eng. b. 1814. [No death date.] DNB.
WEAVER, Margarita Weigle.
Mrs. John Weaver.
Am. b. Brandon, Vt. 1889; ad. 1934 Same. A.
WEAVER, P. T.
Am. ac. 18 Cent. F-2.
WEAVER, Thomas.
Eng. b. 1775; d. 1845 in England. M.
WEBB, Aileen [Mrs. Vanderbilt].
Am. ad. 1934 New York. M.
WEBB, Archibald Bertram.
Eng. b. Ashford 1887; ad. 1934 Perth, W. Aust. Wa.
WEBB, A. C.
Am. b. Nashville, Tenn. 1888; ad. 1934 New York. A28.
WEBB, Charles Meer.
Eng. London 1830-1895 Düsseldorf, Ger. B.
WEBB, Clifford Cyril. (Et)
Eng. b. London 1895; ad. 1935 Same. Wa.
WEBB, Dora Elizabeth.
Eng. b. London; ad. 1934 Birmingham. Wa.
WEBB, E. W.
Eng. ac. 1819-1850; [No death date]. M.
WEBB, Jacob Louis.
Am. Wash., D. C. 1856-1928 New York. A026-F.
WEBB, James.
Eng. b. 1825; d. 1895 London. B.
WEBB, Mahala Theodore. (S)
Eng. b. Stamford 1888; ad. 1934 Melton Mowbray. Wa.
WEBB, Paul.
Am. ad. 1934 Norwalk, Conn. M.
WEBB, Thomas ["Tom"]. (Ill)
Am. ad. 1935 New York. M.
WEBBER. *see also* Weber.
WEBBER, Charles T.
Am. Cinn., O. 1825-1911 Same. M.
WEBBER, John.
Eng. Berne, Swi. 1751-1793 London. B-DNB.
WEBBER, Wesley.
Am. Gardiner, Me. 1841-1914 Boston. A012-F.
WEBER. *see also* Webber.
WEBER, Adolphe.
Fr. b. Boulay 1842; ac. 1867 Paris. B-C.
WEBER, Alfred [Charles].
Fr. Paris 1862-1922. DBA.
WEBER, Audry.
Eng. ex. 1934 London. M.
WEBER, August.
Ger. Frankfort 1817-1873 Düsseldorf. B-C.
WEBER, August James.
Am. b. Marietta, O. 1889; ad. 1934 Same. A.
WEBER, Carl.
Am. Phila., Pa. 1850-1921 Ambler, Pa. A018-F.
WEBER, Elsa. (Et)
Am. b. Charleston, S. C.; ac. 1924 New York. A20.
WEBER, Frederick Theodore. (Et)
Am. b. Columbia, S. C. 1883; ad. 1935 New York. A-F.
WEBER, Max.
Am. b. Russia 1881; ad. 1934 Great Neck, L. I., N. Y. A-F-W.
WEBER, Max.
Ger. b. 1847 in Germany. M.
WEBER, Otto.
Ger. Berlin 1832-1888 London. B-DNB.
WEBER, Paul.
Ger.-Am. Darmstadt, Ger. 1823-1916 Phila., Pa. B-C-F-15.
WEBER, Rudolph. (Ill)
Am. Swi. 1858-1933 New York. A030.
WEBER, Sybilla Mittell.
Am. b. New York 1892; ad. 1934 Same. A.
WEBER, Theodor Alexander.
Ger. Leipzig 1838-1907. B-C.
WEBER, Walter Alois. (Ill)
Am. b. Chicago 1906; ad. 1934 Highland Park, Ill. M.
WEBER, William.
Am. Germany 1865-1905 Kansas City, Mo. A05.
WEBER-FULOP [Mme.].
Aus. b. Vienna; ex. 1934 New York. M.
WEBSTER, Bernice M.
Am. ad. 1935 New York. M.

WEBSTER, E. AMBROSE.
Am. b. Chelsea, Mass. 1869; ad. 1934 Provincetown, Mass. A.

WEBSTER, FREDERICK. (S)
Am. b. Grand Rapids, Mich. 1869; ad. 1915 Evanston, Ill. A12.

WEBSTER, H. DANIEL. (S)
Am. Frankville, Ia. 1880-1912 Texas. A012.

WEBSTER, HAROLD TUCKER. (Cart)
Am. b. Parkesburg, W. Va. 1885; ad. 1934 Stamford, Conn. W.

WEBSTER, HERMAN ARMOUR. (Et)
Am. b. New York 1878; ad. 1934 Paris. A-DBA-F-W-46.

WEBSTER, MARGARET LEVERICH.
Am. b. Belleville, N. J. 1906; ad. 1934 Florham Park, N. J. A.

WEBSTER, MARY HORTENSE. (S)
Am. b. Oberlin, O.; ad. 1934 Chicago. A.

WEBSTER, ROLAND HARDING.
Eng. b. Chester 1873; ad. 1934 Ellesmere. Wa.

WEBSTER, THOMAS.
Eng. Pimlico 1800-1886 Cranbrook. B-Bd-C-DNB-E.

WEBSTER, WALTER ERNEST.
Eng. b. Manchester 1878; ad. 1934 London. B-Wa.

WECHTLIN, JOHANN [or Hans] Ulrich.
Ger. 1460-1526. M.

WECKESSER, AUGUST.
Swi. Winterthur 1821-1899 Rome, It. B.

WEDDERSPOON, RICHARD GIBSON.
Am. b. Red Bank, N. J.; ad. 1934 Syracuse, N. Y. A.

WEDEPOHL, THEODOR.
Am. Westphalia, Ger. 1863-1931 New York. A028.

WEDERKINCH, HOLGER (S)
Dan. b. Femo, Denmark 1886; ac. 1929 London. DBA-Wa1929.

WEDGEWOOD, JOSIAH. (Potter)
Eng. Staffordshire 1730-1795 Burslem. DNB-E.

WEDIN, ELOF.
Am. ex. 1934 Minn., Minn. M.

WEEDON, AUGUSTUS WALFORD.
Eng. London 1838-1908. B.

WEEKES, HENRY. (S)
Eng. Canterbury 1807-1877 London. B.

WEEKS, CAROLINE.
Am. ac. 1860-1870. F.

WEEKS, EDWIN LORD.
Am. Boston 1849-1903 Paris. A05-B-Bd-C-E-F-15-46.

WEEKS, HENRY. (S)
Eng. b. 1807; d. 1877 London. B-DNB.

WEELE, HERMAN JOHANNES VAN DER.
Dut. b. Middleburg, Zeeland 1852. B.

WEENIX, JAN BAPTIST [The Elder].
Dut. Amsterdam 1621-1660 Utrecht. B-C-E-722.

WEENIX [or Weeninx] JAN [The Younger].
Dut. Amsterdam 1640-1719 Same. B-C-722.

WEERT, ANDRIAEN DE.
Flem. Brussels 1536-1566 Cologne, Ger. B.

WEERTS, JEAN JOSEPH.
Fr. Roubaix 1847-1927. B-C-DBA.

WEGELIN, ADOLF.
Ger. Cleves 1810-1881 Cologne. B-C.

WEGENER, JOHANN FRIEDRICH WILHELM.
Ger. Dresden 1812-1879 Gruna. B-C.

WEGENROTH, STOW. (Eg)
Am. ad. 1935 New York. M.

WEGMAN, BERTHA.
Swi. b. Soglio 1847; ac. 1900 in Paris. B.

WEGUELIN, JOHN REMHARD.
Eng. Sussex 1849-1927 London. B-C-Y01928.

WEHLE, HEINRICH THEODOR.
Aus. Förstagen 1778-1805 Kroba. B.

WEHLE, JOHANNES ROBERT.
Ger. b. Radeburg 1848. B.

WEHN, JAMES A. (S)
Am. b. Ind., Ind.; ad. 1934 So. Seattle, Wash. A.

WEHNER, GEORGE.
Am. ex. 1935 New York. M.

WEHNERT, EDWARD HENRY.
Eng. London 1813-1868 Same. B-DNB.

WEHR, JULIAN. (Ill)
Am. ex. 1935 New York. M.

WEI-CH'IH I-SING.
Chinese. ac. 630 A.D. in China. E.

WEIDITZ, HANS. (Eg)
Ger. ac. 1516-1536 in Augsberg. M.

WEIGALL, HENRY.
Eng. b. 1829; d. 1925 in London. B.

WEIGAND, KONRAD.
Ger. Nüremberg 1842-1897 Munich. B-C.

WEIGEL, CHRISTOPH. (Cari)
Ger. Redivitz 1654-1726 Nüremberg. B.

WEIGELE, HENRI. (S)
Fr. b. Schierbrok, Ger.; ac. 1902/27. B.

WEIGHT, CAREL VICTOR MORLAIS.
Eng. b. London 1898; ad. 1935 Same. Wa.

WEIL, [Mrs.] CARRIE H. (S)
Am. b. New York 1888; ad. 1934 Same. A.

WEIL, [Mrs.] SYLVA. (Ill)
Am. ad. 1934 New York. M.

WEILAND, JAMES.
Am. b. Toledo, O. 1877; ad. 1934 Lyme, Conn. A-F.

WEILL, EDMOND.
Am. b. New York 1877; ad. 1934 Brooklyn, N. Y. A.

WEINBERG, [Mrs.] ÉMILIE SIEVERT.
Am. b. Chicago; ad. 1934 San Fran., Calif. A.

WEINEDEL, CARL. (Min)
Am. b. 1795; d. 1845 New York. F-2-6.

WEINER [or Weyneers], HANS.
Ger. Weilham 1570-1617. B.

WEINER, LOUIS.
Am. b. Vinntza, Rus. 1892; ad. 1934 Chicago. A.

WEINERT, ALBERT. (S)
Am. b. Leipzig, Ger. 1863. A-Cs-F-Ta-W.

WEINGAERTNER, HANS.
Am. b. Germany 1896; ad. 1935 Lyndhurst, N. J. A.

WEINIK, SAMUEL.
Am. b. Newark, N. J. 1890; ad. 1934 Bronx, New York. A.

WEINMAN, ADOLPH ALEXANDER. (S)
Am. b. Carlsruhe, Ger. 1870; ad. 1934 Forest Hills, L. I., N. Y. A-Cs-F-W-46.

WEINMAN, ALBERT. (S)
Am. b. 1860; d. 1931 East Rockaway, L. I., N. Y. A028.
WEINRICH, AGNES.
Am. b. Iowa; ad. 1934 Provincetown, Mass. A.
WEINZHEIMER, FREDERICK AUGUST.
Ger. b. Galzheim, Rhineland 1882; ad. 1934 Florence, It. M.
WEIR, DOROTHY.
Mrs. Mahonri M. Young.
Am. b. New York 1890; ad. 1935 Same. A.
WEIR, HARRISON WILLIAM.
Eng. Lewes 1824-1906 Appledore. B-DNB.
WEIR, HELEN STEWART.
Br. b. New York; ad. 1934 London. Wa.
WEIR, IRENE.
Am. ad. 1934 Katonah, N. Y. A-F.
WEIR [or Weyer], JACOB.
Ger. ac. 1648-1670 in Hamburg. B-C.
WEIR, JOHN FERGUSON. (P-S)
Am. West Point, N. Y. 1841-1926 Prov., R. I. A023-B-C-E-F-Ta-W14-1-3-4-5-15.
WEIR, JULIAN ALDEN.
Am. West Point, N. Y. 1852-1919 New York. A016-C-E-F-1-15-46-104-192-264-701-748-757.
WEIR, LILLIAN.
Am. b. Fort Wadsworth, N. Y. 1883; ad. 1915 New York. A12.
WEIR, ROBERT WALTER.
Am. New Rochelle, N. Y. 1803-1899 New York. B-Bd-C-E-F-2-4-15.
WEIR, WILLIAM JOSEPH.
Am. b. Ballina, Ir. 1884; ad. 1934 Chicago. A.
WEIROTTER, FRANZ EDMUND.
Aus. Innsbruck, Swi. 1730-1771 Vienna. B-C.
WEIRTER, LOUIS. (Et)
Eng. 1871-1932. Y01933.
WEIS, JOHN ELLSWORTH.
Am. Higginsport, O. 1892; ad. 1934 Cinn., O. A-F.
WEISBRODT, H. W. (Eg)
Am. b. 1856; d. 1927 in Cinn., O. A024.
WEISE, ROBERT.
Ger. b. Stuttgart 1870. B.
WEISEL, DEBORAH D.
Am. Doylestown, Pa.; ad. 1934 Springfield, Mo. A.
WEISENBORN, RUDOLPH.
Am. ad. 1934 Chicago. A.
WEISENBURG, HELEN MILLS.
Am. ad. 1934 Balt., Md. A.
WEISER, JOSEF EMANUEL.
Ger. Patschkau 1847-1911. B-C.
WEISGERBER, ALBERT.
Ger. St. Ingbert 1878-1915. B.
WEISHAUPT, VICTOR.
Ger. b. Munich 1848. B-C.
WEISMAN, JACQUES.
Fr. b. Paris 1878. DBA.
WEISMAN, JOSEPH.
Am. b. Schenectady, N. Y. 1907; ad. 1934 Los Angeles, Calif. A.
WEISS, BARTHOLOMANUS IGNAZ.
Ger. Munich 1730-1815 Same. B.
WEISS, CARL JACOB HERMANN.
Ger. Hamburg 1822-1897. B.
WEISS, DAVID. (Eg)
Swi. Stiegno 1775-1844 Vienna, Aus. B.
WEISS, ERNEST RUDOLF. (Et)
Ger. b. Lahr 1875. B.
WEISS [or Weis], FERDINAND FRIEDRICH WILHELM.
Ger. Magdeburg 1814-1878 Berlin. B-C.
WEISS, JOSÉ [or John].
Eng. Paris 1859-1929 London. B.
WEISS, JOSEPH ANDREAS.
Bav. Bavaria 1814-1887 Munich, Ger. B-C.
WEISS, WILLIAM L.
Am. ad. 1934 East Gloucester, Mass. M.
WEISS, WOJCIECH.
Pol. b. 1875. M.
WEISSENBRUCK, JAN [or Johannes].
Dut. The Hague 1822/3-1880 Same. B-C.
WEISSENBRUCK, JOHANN HENDRIK.
Dut. The Hague 1824-1903 Same. B.
WEISSER, [Mrs.] FRED W.
Am. b. Guadalupe Co., Tex. 1890; ad. 1934 San Antonio, Tex. A.
WEISZ, ADOLPHE.
Fr. ac. 1875-1900 in Paris. B-C.
WEISZ, EUGEN.
Am. b. Hungary; ad. 1934 Wash., D. C. A.
WEITSCH, FRIEDRICH GEORG.
Ger. Brunswick 1758-1828 Berlin. B-C.
WELBY, [Lady] DÉSIRÉE. (S)
Eng. ad. 1934 London. Wa.
WELCH, HORACE DEVITT.
Am. b. 1888. M.
WELCH, JACK. (Ill)
Am. ad. 1934 New York. M.
WELCH, MABEL R. (Min)
Am. b. New Haven, Conn.; ad. 1935 New York. A-F-46.
WELCH, THOMAS B.
Am. Charleston, S. C. 1814-1874 Paris. F-2-7-40.
WELCH, KEMP. *see* Kemp-Welch.
WELDEN, JEAN DOUGLAS. [Mrs. Archibald.]
Am. ad. 1934 Stamford, Conn. M.
WELDON, CHARLES DATER. (Ill)
Am. b. Mansfield, O.; d. 1935 East Orange, N. J. Obit. N. Y. papers, 8-10-1935. A-B-F-W.
WELDORP, ANTHONIE.
Dut. The Hague 1803-1866 Amsterdam. B.
WELIE, ANTOON VAN.
Dut. b. 1867. M.
WELLA, [Mrs.] H. EMILY.
Am. Delaware, O. 1846-1925 Rochester, N. Y. A022.
WELLENS, HELEN MILLER.
Am. b. 1879; d. 1924. Fa.
WELLER, CARL F.
Am. Stockholm, Swe. 1853-1920 Wash., D. C. A017.
WELLER, DANIEL.
Am. b. 1860; d. 1923 Salt Lake City, Utah. M.
WELLER, THEODOR LÉOPOLD.
Ger. Mannheim 1802-1880. B-C.
WELLMORE, E. (Eg)
Am. ac. 1835-1850 in New York. F-2-6-7-40-45.
WELLS, [Mrs.] ALICE RUSMORE. (Min)
Am. ad. 1934 Plainfield, N. J. A.

WELLS, Amy Watson.
Am. b. Lynchburg, Va. 1899; ad. 1934 Morrisville, Pa. A.
WELLS, Archibald.
Scot. b. Glasgow 1874; ad. 1934 Rye, Scot. Wa.
WELLS, Benjamin B.
Am. ad. 1935 Hackensack, N. J. M.
WELLS, Cady.
Am. b. Southbridge, Mass. 1904; ad. 1934 Santa Fé, N. M. A.
WELLS, Charles S. (S)
Am. b. Glasgow, Scot. 1872; ad. 1934 Minn., Minn. A.
WELLS, Denys George.
Eng. b. Bedford 1881; ad. 1934 New Malden. Wa.
WELLS, [Mrs.] Eloise Long.
Am. b. Alton, Ill. 1875; ad. 1934 St. Louis, Mo. A.
WELLS, F. Marion. (S)
Am. b. 1848; d. 1903 San Fran., Calif. A04-F-Ta.
WELLS, Henry Tanworth.
Eng. London 1828-1903. B-C-DNB.
WELLS, James Lesesne.
Am. b. Atlanta, Ga. 1903; ad. 1934 Wash., D. C. A.
WELLS, John Archibald.
Eng. ac. 1920. Fa-M.
WELLS, Leonard Harry.
Eng. b. Nottingham 1903; ad. 1934 London. Wa.
WELLS, Lucy D.
Mrs. William A. Wells.
Am. b. Chicago 1881; ad. 1934 Seattle, Wash. A.
WELLS, [Mrs.] Madeline Rachel.
Br. b. India; ad. 1934 London. Wa.
WELLS, Newton Alonzo.
Am. b. Lisbon, N. Y. 1852; ad. 1926 Chicago. A12-F.
WELLS, Reginald Fairtax. (S)
Eng. b. Rio de Janeiro, Brazil 1877; ad. 1934 Sussex, Eng. Wa.
WELLS, William Frederick.
Eng. London 1762-1836. B-DNB.
WELLSTOOD, James. (Eg)
Am. Jersey City, N. J. 1855-1880 Same. F-7.
WELLSTOOD, John Geikie. (Eg)
Am. b. Edinburgh, Scot. 1813-1899 New York. F.
WELLSTOOD, William. (Eg)
Am. b. Edinburgh, Scot. 1819-1900 New York. F-7-40.
WELONSKI, Pio [or Pius]. (S)
Pol. b. Warsaw 1879; d. 1931. B.
WELSCH, Paul.
Fr. b. Strasbourg 1889; ad. 1934 Paris. A.
WELSH, Herbert.
Am. b. Phila., Pa. 1851; ad. 1926 Same. A12-F.
WELSH, Horace Devitt.
Am. b. Phila., Pa. 1888; ad. 1934 New York. A28-F-W.
WELSH, William P.
Am. b. Lexington, Ky. 1889; ad. 1934 Chicago. A.
WELTI, Albert.
Swi. b. Zurich 1862. DBA.
WELTI, Jacques Albert.
Swi. b. Zurich 1894. DBA.
WEMMELL, Charles W.
Am. Brooklyn, N. Y. 1839-1916 Same. A013.
WEMYSS, D. R.
Am. ad. 1935 Louisville, Ky. M.
WÊN CHÊNG-MING.
Chinese. ac. 16th Cent. in China. E.
WEN T'UNG.
Chinese. Sung Dynasty [960-1260]. E.
WENBAN, Sion Langley.
Am. Cleveland, O. 1848-1897 Munich, Ger. B.
WENBAUM, Albert.
Fr. ad. 1934 Paris. DBA.
WENCK, Paul. (Ill)
Am. b. 1892; ad. 1935 Mt. Vernon, N. Y. M.
WENCKER, Joseph.
Fr. Strasbourg 1848-1919. B-C.
WENDEL, Theodore.
Am. ad. 1934 Ipswich, Mass. A-F.
WENDLING, Gustav.
Ger. b. 1862; ad. 1900 Paris. B.
WENDT, Julia M. Bracken. (S)
Mrs. William Wendt.
Am. b. Apple River, Ill. 1871; ad. 1934 Los Angeles, Calif. A-B-F-T-Ta-W-46.
WENDT, William.
Am. b. Germany 1865; ad. 1934 Los Angeles, Calif. A-F-W-46-757.
WENGENEROTH, [Mrs.] Isabelle Stow.
Am. b. Toledo, O. 1875; ad. 1934 Bayport, L. I., N. Y. M.
WENGENROTH, Stow.
Am. b. New York 1906; ad. 1934 Bayport, L. I., N. Y. M.
WENGER, John.
Am. b. Russia 1887; ad. 1934 New York. A-F.
WENGLEIN, Joseph.
Ger. Munich 1845-1919. B-C.
WENLOCK, [Lady] Mary.
Br. d. 1932. Y01933.
WENNER, Violet.
Am. ex. 1935 Wash., D. C. M.
WENRICH, John. (Ill)
Am. b. Cumberland, Md. 1894; ad. 1934 New York. M.
WENTLAND, Frank A.
Am. b. Rolling Prairie, Ind. 1897; ad. 1934 Mich. City, Ind. A.
WENTSCHER, Julius.
Ger. b. Grandenz 1842. B.
WENTWORTH, Almond Hart.
Am. b. Milton Mills, N. H. 1872; ad. 1934 West Haven, Conn. A.
WENTWORTH, Cecile de.
Am. b. New York; d. 1933 Nice, Fr. B-F-WX1-46-Obit. Art News, 9-16-1933.
WENTWORTH, Daniel F.
Am. b. Norway, Me. 1850; ad. 1934 New Milford, Conn. A.
WENTWORTH, Harriet Marshall.
Am. ad. 1934 Phila., Pa. M.
WENTWORTH, Thomas Hanford.
Am. 1781-1849 New York. M-7.

WENTZ, HENRY FREDERICK.
Am. b. The Dalles, Ore.; ad. 1934 Portland, Ore. A-F.
WENZELL, ALBERT BECK.
Am. Detroit, Mich. 1864-1917 Englewood, N. J. A014-F-46.
WENZLER, H. A.
Am. b. Denmark; d. 1871 New York. F-4-6.
WERBE, ANNA LAVICK.
Am. b. 1888; ad. 1934 Detroit, Mich. A.
WERDEN, MASTER OF.
see Master of the Life of the Virgin.
WERENSKIÖLD, ERIK. (P-S)
Nor. b. Vinger 1855. B.
WERFF, ADRIAAN VAN DER.
Dut. Kralinger 1659-1722 Rotterdam. B-Bd-C-722.
WERFF, PIETER VAN DER.
Dut. Kralinger 1665-1722 Rotterdam. B-C.
WERGELAND, OSCAR ARNOLD.
Nor. Christiania 1844-1910. B.
WERIMERS, GUILLAUME. (Tapestry)
Flem. ac. 1737. M.
WERN, TOM.
Br. ac. 1929 in Wales. Wa1929.
WERNER, ANTON ALEXANDER VON.
Ger. b. 1843; d. 1915 in Berlin. B-C-E.
WERNER, FRITZ.
Aus. b. Vienna 1898; ad. 1934 New York. M.
WERNER, FRITZ.
Ger. Berlin 1825/8-1908. B-C.
WERNER, JOSEPH [The Younger].
Swi. Berne 1637-1710/6 Same. B-C.
WERNER, KARL FRIEDRICH HEINRICH.
Ger. Weimar 1808-1894 Leipzig. B-C-Ms.
WERNTZ, CARL N.
Am. b. Sterlihg, Ill. 1874; ad. 1935 Chicago. A-F.
WERTEN, MARYA.
Pol. ad. 1934 Buffalo, N. Y. M.
WERTHEIMER, GUSTAV.
Aus. Vienna 1847-1904 Paris. B-C.
WERTINGER, HANS.
Ger. b. 1491; d. 1533 Landshut. B.
WERTMÜLLER, ADOLF ULRIC.
Am. Stockholm, Swe. 1751-1811 Wilmington, Del. B-C-F-2-6-786.
WERTZ, HARRY HOWARD.
Am. b. Bascom, O. 1892; ad. 1934 New York. M.
WERVE, CLAUX [or Claus] DE. (S)
Fr. ac. 1385-1439. Hs.
WERY, ÉMILE AUGUSTE.
Fr. ac. 1906 in Reims. B.
WERY, FERNAND.
Belg. ac. 1930. M.
WESCOTT, ALISON FARMER.
Mrs. Paul Wescott.
Am. ad. 1935 Pottstown, Pa. M.
WESCOTT, PAUL.
Am. ad. 1935 Pottstown, Pa. M.
WESEL, HERMAN WYNRICH VON.
Flem. 1360?-1414. Bd.
WESSEL, HERMAN H.
Am. b. Vincennes, Ind. 1878; ad. 1934 Cinn., O. A.
WESSELHOEFT, MARY FRASER.
Am. b. Boston, Mass. 1873. A28.
WESSELS, GLENN.
Am. ad. 1935 San Fran., Calif. M.
WESSER, MAGRAW.
Am. ad. 1934 Brooklyn, N. Y. M.
WESSINBRANCH, J. H.
Am. Duluth, Minn. 1822-1880. M.
WEST, [Sir] BENJAMIN.
Am.-Eng. Springfield, Pa. 1738-1820 London. B-Bd-C-DNB-E-F-1-2-4-5-6-30-45-138-182-265-266-267-268-269-625-701-722-757-789.
WEST, BENJAMIN FRANKLIN.
Am. b. Salem, Mass. 1818; [No death date]. 169.
WEST, BERNICE. (S)
Am. b. New York 1906; ad. 1934 Same. A.
WEST, FRANCIS ROBERT. (Crayon)
Ir. b. 1749?; d. 1809 Dublin. B-DNB.
WEST, GERTRUDE.
Eng. b. Birmingham 1872; ad. 1934 London. Wa.
WEST, [Mrs.] GLADYS.
Am. b. Phila., Pa. 1897; ad. 1934 Same. A.
WEST, JAMES G.
Am. ex. 1933 in Cleveland, O. M.
WEST, JOSEPH.
Eng. b. Farnhill 1882; ad. 1934 Keighley. Wa.
WEST, JOSEPH WALTER.
Eng. Hull 1860-1933. B-Wa1929.
WEST, KATHERINE ANNE.
Eng. b. London 1904. Wa1929.
WEST, LEVON. (Et)
Am. b. Centerville, S. D. 1900; ad. 1935 New York. A28-W-627-830.
WEST, PETER B.
Am. Bedford, Eng. 1837-1913 Albion, N. Y. A0X1-F-15.
WEST, RAPHAEL LAMAR.
[Son of Benjamin West.]
Eng. London 1769-1850. DNB-2.
WEST, RICHARD WILLIAM.
Scot. b. Aberdeen 1887; ad. 1934 Same. Wa.
WEST, ROBERT.
Br. d. 1770. DNB.
WEST, ROBERT LUCIUS.
Ir. 1774-1849. B-DNB.
WEST, SARAH JESSIE.
Am. b. Toledo, O.; ad. 1915 Put-in-Bay, O. A12.
WEST, [Mrs.] SOPHIE.
Am. Paris 1825-1914 Pittsburgh, Pa. A0X1.
WEST, THOMAS ALFRED.
Eng. b. Manchester; ad. 1934 Liverpool. Wa.
WEST, WILLIAM EDWARD.
Am. Lexington, Ky. 1788-1857 Nashville, Tenn. F-2-4-6-45.
WEST, WILLIAM ["Waterfall"].
Eng. Bristol 1801-1861 Chelsea. B.
WESTALL, RICHARD.
Eng. Hertford 1765-1836 London. B-C-DNB-E-722.
WESTALL, WILLIAM.
Eng. Hertford 1781-1850 St. John's Wood. B-DNB.
WESTBROOK, LLOYD LEONARD.
Am. b. Olmsted Falls, O. 1903; ad. 1934 Same. A.
WESTCOTT, PHILLIP.
Eng. Liverpool 1815-1878 Manchester. B.

WESTERBAEN, JAN JANSZ [The Elder].
Dut. The Hague 1600-1686 Same. B.
WESTERBAEN, JAN JANSZOON [The Younger].
Dut. The Hague 1631/2-1672. B.
WESTERBEEK, CORNELIUS.
Dut. ac. 19th Cent. in Amsterdam. B.
WESTERFELDT, PATRICK MC LOSKSY.
Am. New York 1854-1907 Asheville, N. C. A06-F.
WESTERFIELD, JOSEPH MONT.
Am. b. Hartford, Ky. 1885; ad. 1915 Louisville, Ky. A12.
WESTERHOHM, VICTOR.
Rus. ac. 1900 in Paris. B.
WESTERLUND, STIRLING C.
Am. ad. 1934 Long Beach, Calif. M.
WESTERMAN, HARRY JAMES. (Cart)
Am. b. Parkesburg, W. Va. 1877; ad. 1934 Columbus, O. A28-F-W.
WESTMACOTT, [Sir] RICHARD [The Elder]. (S)
Eng. London 1775-1856 Same. B-DNB-E-Hs.
WESTMACOTT, RICHARD [The Younger]. (S)
Eng. London 1799-1872 Kensington. B-DNB.
WESTMAN, SWEN R.
Swe. b. Stockholm 1887. DBA.
WESTON, HAROLD.
Am. b. Merion, Pa. 1894; ad. 1934 St. Huberts, N. Y. A.
WESTON, HARRY ALLAN.
Am. Springfield, Ill. 1885-1931 New York. A028.
WESTON, WILLIAM PEREY.
Can. b. London, Eng. 1879; ad. 1935 Vancouver, B. C., Can. M.
WESTOVER, RUSSELL CHANNING. (Cart)
Am. b. Los Angeles, Calif. 1886; ad. 1934 New Rochelle, N. Y. W.
WESTWOOD, PERCY JAMES. (Et)
Eng. b. London 1878; ex. 1934 Same. Wa.
WET [or Wette], GERRIT DE.
Dut. Amsterdam 1616-1679 Same. B.
WET [or Wette], JACOB WILLEMSZ.
Dut. Haarlem 1610?-1671? B-C.
WET [or Wette], JAN DE.
Ger. b. Hamburg 1617? B-C.
WETHERALD, HARRY W.
Am. b. Prov., R. I. 1903; ad. 1934 Same. A.
WETHERBEE, GEORGE FAULKNER.
Am. Cinn., O. 1851-1920 London. A12-B-F.
WETHERILL, ELISHA KENT KANE.
Am. Phila., Pa. 1874-1929 Aberdeen, S. C. A026-F.
WETHERILL, MARIA LAWRENCE.
see Lawrence-Wetherill, M.
WETMORE, MARY MINERVA.
Am. b. Canfield, O.; ad. 1934 Champaign, Ill. A.
WETZEL, GEORGE JULIUS.
Am. b. New York 1870; ad. 1934 Douglastown, N. Y. A.
WEXELSEN, CHRISTIAN DOLPHIN.
Nor. Tholen 1830-1883. B.
WEYDEN, GOSWIN [or Goosen] VAN DER.
Flem. Brussels 1465-1538 Antwerp. B.
WEYDEN, HARRY VAN DER.
see Van Der Weyden, H.
WEYDEN, ROGER [or Rogier] VAN DER [Pasture].
Flem. Tournay 1399/1400-1464 Brussels. B-Bd-C-E-V-628-629-722.
WEYDEN, ROGIER VAN DER [The Younger].
Flem. d. 1543 in Antwerp. B.
WEYL, MAX.
Am. Mühlen, Würtemberg, Ger. 1837-1914 Wash., D. C. A0X1-F.
WEYLER [or Weyller], JEAN BAPTISTE.
Fr. Strasbourg 1749-1791 Paris. B.
WEYSSENHOFF, HENRI.
Pol. b. Pokrevno; ac. 1900 Paris. B.
WHAITE, HENRY CLARENCE.
Eng. Manchester 1828-1912 Conway. B.
WHALEY, EDNA REED.
Mrs. Marcellus S. Whaley.
Am. b. New Orleans, La. 1884; ad. 1934 Columbia, N. C. A.
WHALL, CHRISTOPHER WHITWORTH.
Br. d. 1924. Y01925.
WHARBURTON, JAMES. (Eg)
Am. b. 1827; d. 1898 Pawtucket, R. I. A01.
WHARTON, ALENE GRAY.
Am. ad. 1935 Nashville, Tenn. M.
WHARTON, PHILIP FISBOURNE.
Am. Phila., Pa. 1841-1880 Media, Pa. B-C-F-15.
WHATLEY, HENRY.
Eng. Bristol 1842-1901 Same. M.
WHEATLEY, E. GRACE.
Eng. ad. 1930 London. M.
WHEATLEY, FRANCIS.
Eng. London 1747-1801 Same. B-Bd-C-DNB-E.
WHEELAN, ALBERTINE RANDALL.
Am. b. San Fran., Calif. 1863; ad. 1935 New York. A26-M.
WHEELER OF BATH.
Eng. b. 1820; d. 1885. M.
WHEELER, CHARLES.
Aust. b. Dunedin, N. Z. 1881. M.
WHEELER, CHARLES THOMAS. (S)
Eng. b. Wolverhampton 1892; ad. 1934 London. Wa.
WHEELER, CLIFTON A.
Am. b. Hadley, Ind. 1883; ad. 1934 Ind., Ind. A-F-181.
WHEELER, DORA. *see* Keith, D. W.
WHEELER, JAMES J.
Br. ac. 1850 [Auc. sale New York 1934]. M.
WHEELER, JANET D.
Am. b. Detroit, Mich.; ad. 1934 Long Beach, Calif. A-F-W.
WHEELER, KATHLEEN.
Mrs. W. R. H. Crump.
Am. b. Reading, Eng. 1884; ad. 1934 Somerset, Md. A.
WHEELER, NINA BARR.
Am. ad. 1934 New York. M.
WHEELER, TEX HUGHLETTE. (S)
Am. ad. 1935 Tucson, Ariz. M.
WHEELER, W. R.
Am. b. Scio, Mich. 1832; ac. 1855 Hartford, Cohn. [No death date.] F-3-6.
WHEELER, ZONA LORRAINE.
Am. b. Bridgeport, Kan. 1913; ad. 1934 Same. A.

WHEELOCK, WARREN.
Am. b. Sutton, Mass. 1880; ad. 1934 New York. A-F.
WHEESSEL, JOHN. (Eg)
Eng. ac. 1799 in England. M.
WHELAN. *see also* Wheelan.
WHELAN, BLANCHE.
Am. b. Los Angeles, Calif.; ad. 1934 Same. A.
WHELAN, MICHAEL LEO.
Ir. b. Dublin 1892; ad. 1934 Same. Wa.
WHETSEL, [Mrs.] GERTRUDE P.
Am. b. McCune, Kan. 1886; ad. 1934 Los Angeles, Calif. A.
WHICHELO, C. JOHN M.
Eng. ex. 1810-1865 in London. DNB.
WHIPPLE, BEATRICE.
Am. ad. 1934 Cranford, N. J. M.
WHIPPLE, CHARLES AYER. (Mu)
Am. Southboro, Mass. 1859-1928 Wash., D. C. A025.
WHIPPLE, DOROTHY WIELAND.
Am. ad. 1934 Toledo, O. M.
WHISLER, HOWARD FRANK.
Am. b. New Brighton, Pa. 1886; ad. 1934 New York. A.
WHISTLER, JAMES ABBOTT MCNEILL. (P-Et)
Am. Lowell, Mass. 1834-1903 London. A04-B-Bd-C-E-F-1-4-5-15-46-96-127-138-178-270-271-272-273-274-275-630-701-748-757-779-781-783-825-830-922-947.
WHISTLER, REX JOHN.
Eng. b. 1905; ad. 1934 London. Wa.
WHITAKER, FREDERIC.
Am. b. Prov., R. I. 1891; ad. 1934 Cranston, R. I. A.
WHITAKER, GEORGE WILLIAM.
Am. Fall River, Mass. 1841-1916 Prov., R. I. A013.
WHITCOMB, SUSAN.
Am. ac. 1842 in Brandon, Vt. M.
WHITCOMBE, THOMAS.
Eng. London 1760-1824. B.
WHITE, BELLE CADY.
Am. b. Chatham, N. Y.; ad. 1934 Brooklyn, N. Y. A.
WHITE, CHARLES HENRY. (Et)
Am. b. Hamilton, Ont. Can. 1878; ad. 1926 New York. A12-F.
WHITE, CLARENCE SCOTT.
Am. b. Boston 1872; ad. 1934 Belmont, Mass. A-F.
WHITE, EDWIN D.
Am. So. Hadley, Mass. 1817-1877 Saratoga Springs, N. Y. B-C-F-3-4-15.
WHITE, ELIZABETH.
Am. b. Sumter, S. C. 1893; ad. 1934 Same. A.
WHITE, EMMA LOCKE RIANHARD.
Mrs. F. Winthrop White.
Am. b. New Brighton, S. I., N. Y. 1871; ad. 1934 Same. A.
WHITE, ETHELBERT.
Eng. Isleworth 1891; ad. 1935 Hampstead. Wa-825.
WHITE, GEORGE. (Eg)
[First to use the etched line to strengthen Mezzotint.]
Eng. London 1684?-1732. B-DNB-E.
WHITE, GEORGE GORGAS. (Ill)
Am. b. Phila., Pa.; d. 1898 New York. A01.
WHITE, G. HARLOW.
Eng. London 1817-1888. B.
WHITE, GILBERT.
Am. ex. 1934 New York. M.
WHITE, HELÈNE MAYNARD. (S)
Am. b. Balt., Md. 1870; ad. 1934 Detroit, Mich. A12-F-W.
WHITE, HENRY COOKE.
Am. b. Hartford, Conn. 1861; ad. 1934 Waterford, Conn. A.
WHITE, INEZ MARY PLATFOOT.
Am. b. Ogden, Utah 1889; ad. 1934 Omaha, Neb. A.
WHITE, JACOB CAUPEL.
Am. b. New York 1895; ad. 1934 Same. A.
WHITE, JANE.
Am. ad. 1935 Montclair, N. J. M.
WHITE, JESSIE ALINE.
Am. b. Wessington, S. D. 1889; ad. 1934 Dallas, Tex. A.
WHITE, JOHN.
Scot. b. Edinburgh 1851; ad. 1934 Beer, Scot. Wa.
WHITE [or With], JOHN.
[First English water colour painter.]
Eng. ac. 1585-1593 in Plymouth. 279-844.
WHITE, JOHN BLAKE.
Am. b. 1782; d. 1859 Charleston, S. C. B-Bd-C-F-2-6-15.
WHITE, MARGARET WOOD.
Mrs. Victor Gerald White.
Am. b. Chicago 1893; ad. 1935 Woodmere, L. I., N. Y. A.
WHITE, MARY JANE.
Am. b. Columbia City, Ind. 1907; ad. 1934 Same. A.
WHITE, [Mrs.] MAZIE JULIA BARKLEY.
Am. b. Fort Scott, Kan. 1871; ad. 1934 Clifton, N. J. A.
WHITE, NELSON COOKE.
Am. b. Waterford, Conn. 1900; ad. 1934 Same. A-F.
WHITE, NONA L.
Am. b. Illinois 1859; ad. 1934 Pasadena, Calif. A.
WHITE, ORRIN AUGUSTINE.
Am. b. Hanover, Ill. 1883; ad. 1934 Pasadena, Calif. A-F-W.
WHITE, PAUL M.
Am. ad. 1934 New York. M.
WHITE, ROBERT. (Eg)
Eng. London 1645-1703 Same. B-DNB-E.
WHITE, THEODORE.
Am. ex. 1935 New York. M.
WHITE, THOMAS GILBERT. (Mu)
Am. b. Grand Haven, Mich. 1877; ad. 1934 Paris. A-DBA-W-46.
WHITE, VERA M.
Am. ad. 1935 Ardmore, Pa. M.
WHITE, VERNER MOORE.
Am. Richmond, Va. 1863-1923 Chautauqua, N. Y. M.
WHITE, VICTOR GERALD.
Am. b. Dublin, Ir. 1891; ad. 1935 Woodmere, L. I., N. Y. A.

WHITE, Walter Charles Louis.
Am. b. Sheffield, Eng. 1876; ad. 1934 St. Albans, N. Y. A-F.
WHITE, William Fletcher.
Am. b. Hudson, N. Y. 1885; ad. 1934 New York. A.
WHITECHURCH, Robert. (Eg)
Am. b. London 1814; ac. 1883 Wash., D. C. F-7-40.
WHITEHEAD, Margaret Van Cortlandt.
Am. ad. 1934 Greenwich, Conn. A.
WHITEHEAD, Tom.
Eng. b. Brighouse 1886; ad. 1934 Halifax, N. S. Wa.
WHITEHEAD, Walter. (Ill)
Am. b. Chicago 1874; ad. 1934 Plainfield, N. J. A-F.
WHITEHORN, James.
Am. Wallingford, Vt. 1803-1888 New York. C-F-2-15.
WHITEHURST, Camelia.
Am. b. Balt., Md.; ad. 1934 Same. A-F-W.
WHITEMAN, Samuel Edwin.
Am. b. Phila., Pa. 1860; d. 1922. A020-B-F.
WHITESIDE, Frank Reed.
Am. Phila., Pa. 1866-1929 Same. A026-F-W14.
WHITESIDE, Henry Leech.
Am. b. Brownsville, Pa. 1891; ad. 1934 Wilmington, Del. A.
WHITFIELD, Emma Morehead.
Am. b. Greensboro, N. C. 1874; d. 1932 Richmond, Va. A029.
WHITING, Almon Clark.
Am. b. Worcester, Mass. 1878; ad. 1934 New York. A-F-W.
WHITING, Frederic.
Eng. b. 1874; ad. 1934 London. Wa.
WHITING, John Downes.
Am. b. Ridgefield, Conn. 1884; ad. 1934 New Haven, Conn. A28-F-W.
WHITING, Onslow.
Eng. ad. 1934 Manaccan, Cornwall, Eng. Wa.
WHITLEY, Gladys Ethel. (Min)
Eng. b. London 1886; ad. 1934 Sussex. Wa.
WHITLOCK, Mary Ursula.
Am. ad. 1934 New York. M.
WHITMAN, Sarah de St. Prix Wyman.
Am. Balt., Md. 1842-1904 Boston. A05-F.
WHITMER, [Mrs.] Helen Crozier.
Am. b. Darby, Pa. 1870; ad. 1934 La Grangeville, N. Y. A.
WHITMORE, Robert Houston.
Am. b. Dayton, O. 1890; ad. 1934 Yellow Springs, O. A-F.
WHITNEY, Anne. (S)
Am. Watertown, Mass. 1822-1915 Boston. A012-F-Ta.
WHITNEY, Beatrice.
Mrs. Van Ness.
Am. b. Chelsea, Mass. 1888; ad. 1934 Brookline, Mass. A-F.
WHITNEY, Charles Frederick.
Am. b. Pittston, Mass. 1858; ad. 1934 Danvers, Mass. A.
WHITNEY, Elias J. (Eg)
Am. ac. 1800 in New York. [No death date.] F.
WHITNEY, Gertrude Vanderbilt. (S)
Mrs. Harry Payne Whitney.
[Founder of the Whitney Museum of American Art.]
Am. b. in New York 1876; ad. 1934 Same. A-Cs-Hs-W-46.
WHITNEY, [Mrs.] Helen Reed.
Am. b. Brookline, Mass. 1878; ad. 1934 Rose Valley, Pa. A.
WHITNEY, Isabel L. (Mu)
Am. b. Brooklyn, N. Y.; ad. 1934 New York. A.
WHITNEY, Josepha.
Am. b. Wash., D. C. 1872; ad. 1934 New York. A.
WHITNEY, Philip R.
Am. b. Council Bluffs, Ia. 1878; ad. 1934 Rose Valley, Pa. A.
WHITNEY-SMITH, Edwin. (S)
Eng. b. Bath 1880; ad. 1934 Hampstead. Wa.
WHITON, [Mrs.] Margaret Low. (S)
Am. ad. 1934 Westport, Conn. M.
WHITTAKER [or Whitaker], James William.
Eng. Manchester 1828-1876. B-DNB.
WHITTAKER, John Bernard.
Am. b. Ireland 1836; ac. 1876 New York. [No death date.] F.
WHITTAKER, Mary Wood.
Am. d. 1926 Brooklyn, N. Y. A023.
WHITTEMORE, Constance. (Ill)
Am. ad. 1934 New York. M.
WHITTEMORE, Frances Davis.
Mrs. L. D. Whittemore.
Am. b. Decatur, Ill.; ad. 1934 Topeka, Kan. A.
WHITTEMORE, [Mrs.] Grace Corner.
Am. b. Columbia Co., Pa. 1876; ad. 1934 E. Orange, N. J. A.
WHITTEMORE, Helen Simpson.
Mrs. William John Whittemore.
Am. b. Horsham, Eng.; ad. 1934 New York. A.
WHITTEMORE, M. Eleanor. (Min)
Am. ad. 1933 New York. M.
WHITTEMORE, William John.
Am. b. New York 1860; ad. 1935 Same. A-F-W-46.
WHITTINGTON, [Mrs.] Marjory.
Eng. b. London; ad. 1934 Same. Wa.
WHITTREDGE, Worthington.
Am. Springfield, O. 1820-1910 Summit, N. J. A08-B-C-F-1-4-15-46.
WHOOD, Isaac.
Eng. London 1689-1752. B-DNB.
WHORF, John.
Am. b. 1903; ad. 1935 New York. M.
WHYDALE, Ernest Herbert. (Et)
Eng. b. Elland 1886; ad. 1934 Roylston. Wa.
WHYMPER, Charles.
Eng. b. London 1853. Wa1929.
WHYMPER, Edward. (Eg)
Eng. b. 1840; d. 1911 Chamonix. DNB.
WHYMPER, Josiah Wood. (Eg)
Eng. Ipswich 1813-1903 Haslemere. B.
WICAR [or Vicar], Jean Baptiste Joseph.
Fr. Lille 1762-1834 Rome, It. B-C.
WICHGRAF, Fritz.
Ger. b. Potsdam 1853. B.

WICKARD, J. MURRY.
Am. ex. 1934 in Chicago. M.
WICKENBERG, PER [or Peter] GABRIEL.
Swe. Stockholm 1808/12-1846 Paris. B-C.
WICKENDEN, ROBERT.
Eng. b. Rochester 1861. B.
WICKENDEN, ROBERT J.
Am. England 1870-1931 Brooklyn, N. Y. A028.
WICKER, [Mrs.] MARY H.
Am. b. Chicago, Ill.; ad. 1934 Same. A.
WICKES, WILLIAM JARVIS.
Am. b. Saginaw, Mich. 1897; ad. 1934 Same. A.
WICKEY, HARRY HERMAN. (Et)
Am. b. Stryker, O. 1892; ad. 1934 Cornwall Landing, N. Y. A28-17.
WICKHAM, JULIA M.
Am. ad. 1934 Cutchogue, L. I., N. Y. M.
WICKHAM, MICHAEL.
Br. ad. 1934 London. M.
WICKISER, RALPH.
Am. ad. 1935 Oyster Bay, L. I., N. Y. M.
WICKS, HEPPIE EN EARL.
Am. b. Le Roy, N. Y. 1869; ad. 1934 Same. A-F.
WICKSTEAD, PHILIP.
Eng. b. London; ac. 1780. Bd-M.
WICKWIRE, JERE RAYMOND.
Am. b. Cortland, N. Y. 1883; ad. 1934 Same. A.
WIDFORSS, GUNNAR MAURITZ.
Am. Stockholm, Swe. 1879-1934 Grand Canyon [Nat. Park], Ariz. A-M-Obit. Art Digest, 1-1-1935.
WIDHOPFF, D. O.
Fr. Odessa, Rus. 1867-1933 Paris. DBA.
WIDLISKA, LEOPOLD.
Am. ad. 1934 New York. M.
WIECHMANN, MARGARET HELEN. (S)
Am. b. New York 1886; ad. 1915 Same. A12.
WIECZOREK, MAX.
Am. b. Breslau, Ger. 1863; ad. 1934 Los Angeles, Calif. A-F-W14.
WIEGAND, GUSTAVE ADOLPH.
Am. b. Bremen, Ger. 1870; ad. 1935 New York. A-F-W.
WIEGELE, FRANZ.
Aus. ac. 1934. M.
WIEGMAN, MARIE ELIZABETH [Hanche].
Ger. Silverberg 1826-1893 Düsseldorf. B-C.
WIEGMAN, MATHIEU.
Dut. ac. 1914-1930. M.
WIENAND, FRITZ. (S)
Ger. b. Pforzheim 1901. DBA.
WIERIX, HIERONYMUS.
Flem. Antwerp 1548/53-1619. B.
WIERIX, JAN [or Jerome].
Flem. Antwerp 1549?-1615? B.
WIERTZ, ANTONIE JOSEPH.
Belg. Dinant 1806-1865 Brussels. B-Bd-C.
WIERUSZ, KOWALSKI.
see Kowalski-Wierusz.
WIESCHEBRINK, FRANZ.
Ger. Munich 1818-1884 Düsseldorf. B-C.
WIESE, KURT. (Ill)
Am. ad. 1935 New York. M.
WIESELTHIER, VALLY. (S)
Auss. b. 1895; ex. 1934 Chicago. M.
WIESSLER, WILLIAM, JR.
Am. b. Cinn., O. 1887; ad. 1934 Same. A.
WIETÜCHTER, GUSTAV.
Ger. b. 1873 in Germany. M.
WIGAND, A. ALBRIGHT.
Mrs. Otto Charles Wigand.
Am. ad. 1934 Stapleton, S. I., N. Y. A-F.
WIGAND, OTTO CHARLES.
Am. ad. 1934 Stapleton, S. I., N. Y. A-F.
WIGGIN, JESSIE DUNCAN. (S)
Am. b. Boston, Mass. 1872; ad. 1934 New York. M.
WIGGINS, CARLETON.
Am. Turners, N. Y. 1848-1932 New York. A029-B-C-F-W16-46.
WIGGINS, GUY.
Am. b. Brooklyn, N. Y. 1883; ad. 1934 Lyme, Conn. A-B-F-W.
WIGGINS, [Mrs.] MYRA ALBERT.
Am. b. Salem, Ore. 1869; ad. 1934 Seattle, Wash. A.
WIGGINS, SIDNEY MILLER.
Am. b. New Haven, Conn. 1881; ad. 1934 Yonkers, N. Y. A.
WIGGLESWORTH, FRANK.
Am. b. Boston, Mass. 1893; ad. 1934 Same. A.
WIGHT, FREDERICK.
Am. ad. 1934 Augusta, Ga. M.
WIGHT, MOSES.
Am. Boston, Mass. 1827-1895 Same. C-F-4-15.
WIGHTMAN, THOMAS. (Eg)
Am. England 1800-1888 Boston, Mass. F-2-7.
WIGHTMAN, WINIFRED URSULA.
Br. b. Leningrad, Rus. 1881; ad. 1934 London. Wa.
WIJANTS, JAN. *see* Wynants.
WIKEN, DICK. (S)
Am. ex. 1935 Milwaukee, Wis. M.
WIKSTROM, BROR ANDERS.
Am. Sweden 1854-1909 New York. A07-144-183.
WILBERG, CHRISTIAN JOHANNES.
Ger. Havelberg 1839-1882 Paris. B-C.
WILBUR, DOROTHY THORNTON.
Am. b. Fincastle, Va.; ad. 1934 Wash., D. C. A.
WILBUR, ELEANOR E.
Am. b. 1844; d. 1912 Cambridge, Mass. A0X.
WILBUR, MARGARET CRAVEN. (S)
Am. ad. 1934 New York. M.
WILBY, MARGARET C.
Am. ad. 1934 Detroit, Mich. M.
WILCOCKS, EDNA MARRETT.
Am. b. Portland, Me. 1887; ad. 1934 Altadena, Calif. A.
WILCOX. *see also* Willcox.
WILCOX, FRANK NELSON.
Am. b. Cleveland, O. 1887; ad. 1934 Same. A-F.
WILCOX, JOHN ANGE JAMES. (Eg)
Am. b. Portage, N. Y. 1835; ac. 1860 Boston. [No death date.] F-7.

WILCOX, Lois.
Am. b. Pittsburgh, Pa.; ad. 1934 Sweet Briar, Va. A-F.
WILCOX, Ray.
Am. b. Elmira, N. Y. 1883; ad. 1934 Tenafly, N. J. A.
WILCOX, Ruth.
Am. b. New York 1908; ad. 1934 Tenafly, N. J. A.
WILCOX, Ruth Turner.
Am. b. New York 1888; ad. 1934 Tenafly, N. J. A.
WILCOX, Urquhart.
Am. b. New Haven, Conn. 1876; ad. 1934 Buffalo, N. Y. A.
WILD, Charles.
Eng. London 1781-1835 Same. B-DNB.
WILD, Frank Percy.
Eng. b. Leeds, 1861. Wa1929.
WILD, Winifred Eveline.
Eng. b. Chalfont; ad. 1934 Boscombe. Wa.
WILD-WALL, Curt.
Ger. b. 1898 ad. 1935 Dresden, Ger.
WILDE, Gerald.
Eng. ex. 1934 London. M.
WILDE, Hamilton G.
Am. [No dates.] F-4.
WILDE, Ida M. (Min)
Am. ad. 1934 Springfield, Mass. M.
WILDE, Lois.
Am. ex. 1934 Minn., Minn. M.
WILDE, Samuel de.
Eng. b. 1747; d. 1832. B.
WILDENRATH, Jean Alida.
Am. b. Denmark 1892; ad. 1934 New York. A.
WILDENS, Jan.
Flem. Antwerp 1586-1653 Same. B-C-722.
WILDER, André.
Fr. b. Paris 1871. DBA.
WILDER, Arthur B.
Am. b. Poultney, Vt. 1857; ad. 1934 Woodstock, Vt. A.
WILDER, Bert.
Am. b. Taunton, Mass. 1883; ad. 1934 Homer, N. Y. A.
WILDER, Clifford.
Am. ad. 1934 Birmingham, Ala. M.
WILDER, James A.
Am. ad. 1934 Honolulu, Hawaii. M.
WILDER, Louise Hibbard. (S)
Mrs. Bert Wilder.
Am. b. Utica, N. Y. 1898; ad. 1934 Homer, N. Y. A.
WILDER, Ralph Everett. (Cari)
Am. b. Worcester, Mass. 1875; d. 1924. A12-W8.
WILDER, Thomas.
Am. ac. 1842. Fa.
WILDERMUTH, D.
Am. ad. 1934 Toledo, O. M.
WILDHACK, Robert J. (Ill)
Am. b. Pekin, Ill. 1881. A28.
WILDMAN, William Ainsworth.
Eng. b. Manchester 1882; ad. 1934 London. Wa.
WILDT, Adolfo. (S)
It. Milan 1868-1931.
B-M-Obit. Art News, 3-28-1931.

WILENCHICK, Clement.
Am. ad. 1934 New York. M.
WILENSKI, Reginald Howard.
Eng. b. London 1887; ad. 1934 Same.
Wa-454-566-843-847-855.
WILES, Francis. (S)
Ir. b. 1889; ad. 1934 Dublin. Wa.
WILES, Gladys Lee.
Am. b. New York; ad. 1934 Same. A-W.
WILES, Irving Ramsay.
Am. b. Utica, N. Y. 1861; ad. 1934 New York. A-E-F-W-1-46.
WILES, Lemuel Maynard.
Am. Perry, N. Y. 1826-1905 New York.
A05-C-F-15.
WILEY, Frederick J. (Mu)
Am. ad. 1934 New York. A.
WILEY, Hedwig.
Am. b. Phila., Pa.; ad. 1934 Same. A.
WILEY, Lucia. (Eg)
Am. ex. 1935 Seattle, Wash. M.
WILFORD, Loran Frederick.
Am. b Wamego, Kan. 1892; ad. 1934 Springdale, Conn. A.
WILGUS, William John.
Am. ac. 1838. F-Fa-276.
WILHELM. *see* Master Wilhelm.
WILHELM, A. Wayne.
Am. ad. 1934 Woodstock, N. Y. M.
WILHELM, E. Paul. (S)
Ger. b. 1905 Tibet, East Prussia; ad. 1935 Dayton, O. M.
WILHELMSON, Carl.
Swe. b. Fiskebackskil 1866; d. 1928. B-DBA.
WILIMOVSKY, Charles A.
Am. b. Chicago 1885; ad. 1934 Same. A-F.
WILKES, Susan H.
Am. ad. 1934 Nashville, Tenn. M.
WILKIE, [Sir] David.
Scot. Cults 1785-1841 at sea.
B-Bd-C-DNB-E-631-722-812-909.
WILKIE, Henry Charles.
Eng. b. 1864; ad. 1934 London. Wa.
WILKIE, Leslie Andrew.
Aust. b. Melbourne, Victoria 1879; ad. 1935 Adelaide, So. Aust. M.
WILKIE, Robert.
Scot. b. Sinclairtown, Kirkcaldy 1888; ad. 1934 Glasgow. Wa.
WILKIN, Charles.
Eng. London 1750-1814 Same. B.
WILKIN, Frank W. (Min)
Eng. ac. 1806-1842 in London. B.
WILKIN, Henry.
Eng. London 1801-1852 Brighton. B.
WILKIN, Mildred Pierce.
Am. b. Kansas 1896; ad. 1934 Chino, Calif. A.
WILKINS, Emma C.
Am. ad. 1935 Savannah, Ga. M.
WILKINSON, Alfred Henry. (S)
Eng. b. Birmingham 1884; ad. 1934 London. Wa.
WILKINSON, Charles A.
Eng. b. London; ac. 1881 Same. B.
WILKINSON, Edward.
Am. b. Manchester, Eng.; ad. 1934 Houston, Tex. A.

WILKINSON, J.
Br. ac. 1775. M.
WILKINSON, J. WALTER. (Ill)
Am. b. 1892; ad. 1935 Balt., Md. M.
WILKINSON, NORMAN.
Eng. b. Cambridge 1878; ad. 1929 Highgate. Wa1919.
WILKINSON, REGINALD CHARLES.
Eng. b. London 1881; ad. 1934 Sussex. Wa.
WILKINSON, RUTH LUCILLE.
Am. b. Des Moines, Ia. 1902; ad. 1934 Iowa City, Ia. A.
WILKS, SARA. Am. ac. 1775. M.
WILL, AUGUST.
Am. Germany 1834-1910 Jersey City, N. J. A08.
WILL, BLANCA.
Am. b. Rochester, N. Y. 1881; ad. 1934 Same. A-F.
WILLAERT, FERDINAND.
Belg. b. Ghent 1861. B-DBA.
WILLAERTS, ABRAHAM.
Dut. Utrecht 1603/13-1669/71 Same. B-C.
WILLAERTS, ADAM.
Flem. Antwerp 1577-1662/6 Utrecht, Holland. B-C.
WILLAERTS, ISAAC.
Dut. b. Utrecht 1620; d. 1693. B.
WILLARD, ARCHIBALD M.
[Painted "Spirit of '76".]
Am. b. 1837; d. 1918 Cleveland, O. A016-277.
WILLARD, ASAPH. (Eg)
Am. ac. 1816-1828. F-2-7.
WILLARD, FRANK HENRY. (Cart)
Am. b. Anna, Ill. 1893; ad. 1934 Chicago. W.
WILLARD, HOWARD. (Ill)
Am. ad. 1934 New York. M.
WILLARD, THEODORA.
Am. b. Boston, Mass.; ad. 1915 Same. A12.
WILLARD, WILLIAM.
Am. b. 1865. M.
WILLAUME, LOUIS.
Fr. b. Lagny 1874. DBA.
WILLCOX, GEORGE BURRELL.
Eng. b. 1811; d. 1852 in London. B.
WILLE, AUGUST VON.
Ger. Cassel 1829-1887 Düsseldorf. B-C.
WILLE, FRITZ JULIUS VON.
Ger. b. Weimar 1860. B.
WILLE, JOHANN GEORGE. (Eg)
Ger. Koningsberg 1715-1808 Paris. B.
WILLE, PIERRE ALEXANDRE.
Fr. Paris 1748-1821. B.
WILLEBORT, THOMAS [Bosschaert].
Flem. Bergh, Holland 1614-1654 Antwerp. B-C.
WILLEMENT, THOMAS. (Heraldic P.)
Eng. b. 1786; d. 1871 Faversham. B-DNB.
WILLEMS, FLORENT JOSEPH MARIE.
Belg. Liège 1823-1905 Neuilly, Fr. B-C-E.
WILLEMS, MARCUS.
Flem. Mechlin 1527-1561 Same. B.
WILLERS, ERNST.
Ger. Oldenburg 1802-1880 Munich. B-C.
WILLET, ANNIE LEE.
Mrs. William Willet.
Am. b. Bristol, Pa. 1867; ad. 1934 Phila., Pa. A20-F-W.
WILLET, WILLIAM. (Mu)
Am. New York 1868-1921 Phila., Pa. A018-F-46.
WILLETT, ARTHUR REGINALD. (Mu)
Am. b. England 1868; ad. 1934 New York. A.
WILLETT, JACQUES I.
Am. b. Baku, Rus. 1882; ad. 1934 New York. A-912.
WILLETTE, LÉON ADOLPHE. (Ill)
Fr. Châlons 1857-1926 Paris. B-DBA-E.
WILLIAM OF BRUGES.
Flem. ac. 16th Cent. in Bruges. Fa.
WILLIAM OF COLOGNE.
see Master William of Cologne.
WILLIAM OF WESTMINSTER.
Eng. Benedictine Monk; ac. 13th Cent. M.
[Reputed to have executed, by command of King Henry III, the oldest existing painting in English art.]
WILLIAMS, ADELE.
Am. ad. 1934 Richmond, Va. A.
WILLIAMS, ALEXANDER.
It. b. 1846; d. 1930 Dublin. Wa1929-Y01931.
WILLIAMS, ALFRED.
Eng. Newark, Eng. 1832-1905 France. B-DNB.
WILLIAMS, ALFRED WALKER.
Eng. ac. 1843-1891 in London. B.
WILLIAMS, ALYN. (Min)
Am. b. Wales 1865; ad. 1934 Wash., D. C. A-F-Wa1929.
WILLIAMS, ARTHUR GILBERT.
Br. ac. 1838-1894. Fa.
WILLIAMS, BERKELEY, JR.
Am. b. Richmond, Va. 1904; ad. 1934 Same. A.
WILLIAMS, CHARLES D. (Ill)
Am. b. New York 1880; ad. 1934 Same. A.
WILLIAMS, CHARLES SNEED.
Am. b. Evansville, Ind. 1882; ad. 1934 Chicago. A-F-181.
WILLIAMS, CHARLES WARNER. (S)
Am. b. Henderson, Ky. 1903; ad. 1934 Chicago. A.
WILLIAMS, CHRISTOPHER DAVID.
Welsh. Maesteg 1873-1934 London. Wa1929-Obit. N. Y. papers, 7-22-1934.
WILLIAMS, [Mrs.] CLARA ELSENE.
see Peck, C. E.
WILLIAMS, DWIGHT.
Am. Camillus, N. Y. 1856-1932 Cazenovia, N. Y. A029-F-W-16.
WILLIAMS, E. E.
Br. b. 1793; d. 1822. DNB.
WILLIAMS, EDWARD [The Younger].
Eng. Lambeth 1782-1855 Barnes. B-C.
WILLIAMS, EDWARD K.
Am. b. Greensburg, Pa. 1870; ad. 1934 Nashville, Ind. A.
WILLIAMS, ELEANOR PALMER.
Mrs. Carroll R. Williams.
Am. b. Balt., Md.; ad. 1934 Phila., Pa. A.

WILLIAMS, Esther.
Am. b. Boston 1907; ad. 1934 Same. A.
WILLIAMS, Florence White. (Ill)
Am. b. Putney, Vt.; ad. 1934 Chicago. A.
WILLIAMS, Frederic Allen. (S)
Am. b. West Newton, Mass. 1898; ad. 1934 New York. A-Cs-F.
WILLIAMS, Frederick Ballard.
Am. b. Brooklyn, N. Y. 1871; ad. 1934 Glen Ridge, N. J. A-F-W-46.
WILLIAM, Frederick Dickinson.
Am. Boston 1829-1915 Brookline, Mass. A012-F-15.
WILLIAMS, Gaar. (Cart)
Am. b. 1881; d. 1935 Chicago, Ill. M-Obit. N. Y. papers, 6-16-1935.
WILLIAMS, George Alfred. (Ill)
Am. Newark, N. J. 1875-1932 Kennebuck, Me. A029-F-W16.
WILLIAMS, George Augustus.
Eng. ac. 1841-1885 in London. B.
WILLIAMS, [Mrs.] Gertrude Alice Meredith.
Eng. d. 1934 North Tawton, Devon, Eng. Obit. Art News, 4-7-1934.
WILLIAMS, Gluyas. (Ill)
Am. b. San Fran., Calif. 1888; ac. 1934 Boston. A28-W.
WILLIAMS, Harold T.
Am. ad. 1934 Silvermine, Conn. M.
WILLIAMS, Henry.
Am. Boston, Mass. 1787-1830 Same. F-2-6.
WILLIAMS, [Dr.] Henry Smith.
Am. ad. 1934 Roxbury, Conn. M.
WILLIAMS, Howe.
Am. b. Massillon, O.; ad. 1934 Tempe, Ariz. A.
WILLIAMS, Hubert John.
Eng. b. Beckenham 1905; ad. 1934 Anerley. Wa.
WILLIAMS, Hugh William ("Grecian")
Scot. Galles 1773-1829 Edinburgh. B-DNB.
WILLIAMS, Irene Pownoll.
Eng. ac. 1934 Cheltenham. Wa.
WILLIAMS, Isaac L.
Am. Phila., Pa. 1817-1895 Same. C-F-15.
WILLIAMS, James Francis.
Scot. Perthshire 1775-1846 Glasgow. B.
WILLIAMS, James Robert. (Cart)
Am. b. Halifax, N. S. 1888; ad. 1934 Prescott, Ariz. W.
WILLIAMS, John [Anthony Pasquin]. (Eg)
Am. b. England 1750; d. 1818 Brooklyn, N. Y. B.
WILLIAMS, John Alonzo. (Ill)
Am. b. Sheboygan, Wis. 1869; ad. 1934 New York. A-F-W.
WILLIAMS, John Haynes.
Eng. Worcester 1834-1908 Eastbourne. B-C.
WILLIAMS, John Scott. (Ill)
Am. b. Liverpool, Eng. 1877; ad. 1934 New York. A28-F-M.
WILLIAMS, Joseph Lionel.
Eng. d. London 1874. B.
WILLIAMS, Juliet Nora.
Eng. ad. 1934 Midhurst, Sussex. Wa.
WILLIAMS, Kate A.
Am. ad. 1934 New York. A.
WILLIAMS, Keith Shaw.
Am. b. Marquette, Mich. 1906; ad. 1934 New York. A.
WILLIAMS, L. Gwendolen.
Eng. b. Liverpool; ad. 1934 London. Wa.
WILLIAMS, Lawrence S.
Am. b. Columbus, O.; ad. 1934 Tenafly, N. J. A.
WILLIAMS, Lois K.
Am. ad. 1935 New York. M.
WILLIAMS, Louis.
Am. b. Boston 1904; ad. 1935 Haverhill, Mass. M.
WILLIAMS, Louis Sheppard. (Eg)
Am. b. Bridgeton, N. J. 1865; ad. 1915 Wash., D. C. A12.
WILLIAMS, Louise Houston.
Am. b. Garnett, Kan. 1883; ad. 1934 Anacortes, Wash. A.
WILLIAMS, Lucy O.
Am. ad. 1934 Forrest City, Ala. M.
WILLIAMS, Margaret Lindsay.
Welsh. b. Cardiff; ad. 1934 Dinas Powis, Wales. Wa.
WILLIAMS, Mary Rogers.
Am. Hartford, Conn. 1857-1907 Florence, It. A06.
WILLIAMS, May.
Am. b. Pittsburgh, Pa.; ad. 1934 Same. A.
WILLIAMS, Mildred Emerson.
Am. b. Detroit, Mich. 1892; ad. 1934 Same. A-F.
WILLIAMS, Morris Meredith.
Eng. b. Cambridge 1881; ac. 1910-1927. M.
WILLIAMS, Pauline Bliss.
Am. b. Springfield, Mass. 1888; ad. 1934 Same. A.
WILLIAMS, Penry.
Eng. b. England 1789; d. 1885 Rome, It. B-C-DNB.
WILLIAMS, Peter.
Rus. ad. 1934 Moscow; ex. 1929 Pittsburgh, Pa. M.
WILLIAMS, Ramond Hendry.
Am. b. Ogden, Utah 1900; ad. 1934 Lincoln, Neb. A.
WILLIAMS, Robert [or Roger]. (Eg)
Eng. ac. 1680-1704 in London. DNB.
WILLIAMS, Ruth Campbell.
Am. ad. 1934 Cleveland, O. M.
WILLIAMS, [Mrs.] Ruth Moore.
Am. ad. 1934 New York. M.
WILLIAMS, Salomon.
Ir. d. 1824 in Dublin. B.
WILLIAMS, Samuel. (Eg)
Eng. Colchester 1788-1853 London. B-DNB.
WILLIAMS, Terrick.
Eng. b. Liverpool 1860; ad. 1934 Kensington. B-Wa.
WILLIAMS, Thomas. (Eg)
Eng. b. 1800; d. 1840 London. B-DNB.
WILLIAMS, Virgil.
Am. ac. 1870. Fa.
WILLIAMS, Walter Reid. (S)
Am. b. Ind., Ind. 1885. A28-F.
WILLIAMS, Wheeler. (S)
Am. b. Chicago 1897; ad. 1934 New York. A-Cs.

WILLIAMS, William.
Br. b. 1758; d. 1794. B.
WILLIAMS, William Joseph.
Am. New York 1759-1823 Charleston, S. C. F-786.
WILLIAMS-LYOUNS, Herbert Francis. (Eg)
Eng. b. Plymouth 1863; ad. 1934 Kingsbridge. Wa.
WILLIAMSON, Ada C.
Am. ad. 1934 Phila., Pa. A-F.
WILLIAMSON, Albert Curtis.
Can. b. Brampton 1869; ad. 1934 Toronto. M.
WILLIAMSON, Daniel Alexander.
Eng. Liverpool 1822-1903 Broughton. B.
WILLIAMSON, Harold.
Eng. b. Manchester 1898; ad. 1934 Bournemouth. Wa.
WILLIAMSON, Harold Sandys.
Eng. b. Leeds 1892; ad. 1934 London. Wa.
WILLIAMSON, James W. (Ill)
Am. ad. 1935 Greenwich, Conn. M.
WILLIAMSON, John.
Am. Scotland 1826-1885 Glenwood, N. Y. C-F-4-15.
WILLIAMSON, John.
Eng. Ripon 1751-1818 Liverpool. B.
WILLIAMSON, J. Maynard, Jr.
Am. b. Pittsburgh, Pa. 1892; ad. 1926 Same. A12-F.
WILLIAMSON, Samuel.
Eng. Liverpool 1792-1840 Same. C.
WILLIAMSON, Shirley.
Mrs. Edward Lincoln Williamson.
Am. b. New York; ad. 1934 Palo Alto, Calif. A-F.
WILLIAMSON, W. M.
Eng. ac. 1853-1875 in London. B.
WILLIG, R. (S)
Eng. ac. 1890 in Liverpool. B.
WILLIGEN, Claes Jansz van.
Dut. Rotterdam 1630-1676. B.
WILLING, John Thomson. (Ill)
Am. b. Toronto, Can. 1860; ad. 1934 New York. A28-F-17.
WILLING [or Wielingh], Nicolas.
Dut. The Hague 1640-1689 Berlin, Ger. B.
WILLINK, Karel.
Dut. b. 1900 in Holland. M.
WILLIS, Albert Paul.
Am. b. Phila., Pa. 1867; ad. 1934 Same. A-F.
WILLIS, Alice M.
Am. b. St. Louis, Mo. 1888; ad. 1915 Same. A12.
WILLIS, Edmund Aylburton.
Am. Bristol, Eng. 1808-1899 Brooklyn, N. Y. A01-Bd.
WILLIS, Eola.
Am. b. Dalton, Ga.; ad. 1934 Charleston, S. C. A.
WILLIS, Ethel Mary.
Eng. b. London 1874; ad. 1934 Cheswick. Wa.
WILLIS, Frank. (Et)
Eng. Windsor 1865-1932. Wa1929-Y01933.
WILLIS, Henry Brittan.
Eng. Bristol 1810-1884 London. B-DNB.
WILLIS, John Henry.
Br. b. Tavistook 1887; ad. 1934 London. Wa.
WILLIS, [Miss] Patty.
Am. ad. 1935 Charlestown, W. Va. M.
WILLIS, Ralph Troth. (Mu)
Am. b. Freestone Point, Va. 1876; ad. 1934 Encinitas, Calif. A.
WILLIS, Samuel William Ward. (S)
Eng. b. London 1870; ad. 1935 Same. Wa.
WILLISON, George.
Scot. b. 1741; d. 1797 Edinburgh. B-DNB.
WILLMAN, Michael Lucas Léopold.
Ger. Konigsberg 1630-1706. B-C.
WILLMORE, Arthur. (Eg)
Eng. Birmingham 1814-1888 London. B-DNB.
WILLMORE, James Tibbitts. (Eg)
Erdington 1800-1863 London. B-DNB-E.
WILLOUGHBY, Esther.
Eng. b. Croydon; ad. 1934 London. Wa.
WILLOUGHBY, [Mrs.] Vera.
English. ad. 1934 London. Wa.
WILLROIDER, Joseph.
Ger. Villach 1838-1860 Munich. B-C.
WILLROIDER, Ludwig.
Ger. Villach 1845-1910. B.
WILLS, [Sir] Gilbert Allan Hamilton. (S)
Eng. b. 1880; ad. 1934 Moreton-in-Marsh, Eng. Wa.
WILLS, Helen Newington.
Mrs. Frederick S. Moody, Jr.
Am. b. Centerville, Calif. 1906; ad. 1934 San Fran., Calif. W17.
WILLS, Thomas Alexander Dodd.
Eng. b. London 1873. Wa1929.
WILLSON. *see also* Wilson.
WILLSON, James Mallory.
Am. b. Kissimmee, Fla. 1890; ad. 1934 West Palm Beach, Fla. A.
WILLSON, Martha Butterick. (Ill)
Mrs. Howard D. Day.
Am. b. Prov., R. I. 1885; ad. Same. A.
WILLUMSEN, Jens Ferdinand.
Dan. b. 1863 in Denmark. M.
WILMARTH, Euphemia B.
Am. d. 1906 in Pasadena, Calif. A06.
WILMARTH, Lemuel Everett.
Am. Attleboro, Mass. 1835-1918 Brooklyn, N. Y. A015-C-F-15.
WILMER, William A. (Eg)
Am. d. 1855 in Phila., Pa. F-2-7-10.
WILMES, Frank.
Am. b. Cinn., O. 1858; ad. 1934 Same. A.
WILMOT, Florence Freeman.
Eng. b. Lea Hall; ad. 1934 Stratford. Wa.
WILSHIRE, William Pitt.
Aust. b. 1807. [No death date.] M.
[First artist born in Australia.]
WILSON. *see also* Willson.
WILSON, Alexander. (Eg)
Am. Paisley, Scot. 1766-1818 Phila., Pa. B-F-2-7-632-922.
WILSON, Andrew.
Scot. Edinburgh 1780-1848 Same. B-DNB.
WILSON, [Miss] Ashton.
Am. b. Charleston, W. Va. 1880; ad. 1934 New York. A.
WILSON, Bassett.
Eng. ex. 1934 in London. M.

WILSON, Benjamin.
Eng. Leeds 1721-1788 Bloomsbury. B-DNB.
WILSON, Charles Edward.
Eng. b. Whitwell; ad. 1934 Addiscombe. Wa.
WILSON, Charles Heath.
Eng. London 1810-1882 Florence, It. B.
WILSON, Charles Theller.
Am. b. 1855; d. 1920 New York. A017.
WILSON, Claggett.
Am. b. Wash., D. C. 1887; ad. 1934 Boston. A-F.
WILSON, David Forrester.
Scot. Glasgow 1873-1934 Same. Wa-Obit. Apollo 2-1935.
WILSON, Edward Arthur. (Et)
Am. Scot.; b. Glasgow 1886; ad. 1935 Jackson Heights, N. Y. C. A28-F-W.
WILSON, Francis Vaux.
Am. b. Phila., Pa. 1874; ad. 1935 Old Lyme, Conn. A28-M.
WILSON, Frederick.
Am. b. England 1858; ad. 1915 Briarcliff Manor, N. Y. A12.
WILSON, [Capt.] George.
Eng. b. Lille, Fr. 1882; ad. 1934 London. Wa.
WILSON, Gilbert Brown.
Am. b. Terre Haute, Ind. 1907; ad. 1934 Same. A.
WILSON, Helen.
Am. b. Lincoln, Neb. 1884; ad. 1934 Same. A.
WILSON, Helen Mary Graham.
Eng. b. London 1903; ad. 1934 Hampstead. Wa.
WILSON, Henrietta.
Am. b. Cinn., O.; ad. 1934 Same. A.
WILSON, Hugh Cameron.
Scot. b. Glasgow; ad. 1934 Same. Wa.
WILSON, James Frederick.
Eng. b. Newport 1887; ad. 1934 Ilford, Essex. Wa.
WILSON, John [or Jock].
Eng. b. 1774; d. 1855 Folkestone. B-DNB.
WILSON, L. Alice.
Am. ad. 1934 Pelham, N. Y. M.
WILSON, [Mrs.] Lucy Adams.
Am. b. Warren, O. 1855; ad. 1934 Miami, Fla. A.
WILSON, [Mrs.] Margaret Evangeline.
Eng. b. Boscombe 1890; ad. 1934 West Indies. Wa.
WILSON, Mary.
Am. ad. 1934 New York. M.
WILSON, Mary G. W.
Scot. b. Falkirk; ad. 1934 Same. Wa.
WILSON, Matthew.
Am. London 1814-1892 Brooklyn, N. Y. F-6-15.
WILSON, May.
Eng. b. Sheffield; ad. 1934 Oakham. Wa.
WILSON, Melva Beatrice.
Am. Madison, Ind. 1866-1921 New York. A018.
WILSON, Muriel.
Eng. ex. 1934 in London. M.
WILSON, R. A. (Et)
Eng. ad. 1934 London. M.
WILSON, Richard.
Br. Pinegas, Eng. 1714-1782 Llanberis, Wales. B-Bd-C-DNB-E-722.
WILSON, Robert Burns.
Am. Parker, Pa. 1851-1916 Brooklyn, N. Y. A013.
WILSON, Rosa Cecil O'Neil. (Ill)
Am. b. Wilkes-Barre, Pa.; ad. 1934 Saugatuck, Conn. A-F.
WILSON, Sidney Ernest. (Eg)
Eng. b. Isleworth 1869; ad. 1934 Harpenden. Wa.
WILSON, Solomon.
Am. b. Vilno, Pol. 1894; ad. 1934 New York. A.
WILSON, Stanley R.
Eng. b. Camberwell 1890; ad. 1934 London. Wa.
WILSON, Vernon.
Am. ex. 1935 Pittsburgh, Pa. M.
WILSON, William J.
Am. b. Toledo, O. 1884; ad. 1934 Long Beach, Calif. A.
WILLIAMS, Winslow.
Am. ad. 1934 New York. M.
WILT, Thomas van der.
Dut. Piershil 1650/9-1730/3 Delft. B-C.
WILTON, Joseph. (S)
Eng. London 1722-1803. DNB-Hs.
WILTZ, Arnold.
Am. b. Berlin, Ger. 1889; ad. 1934 Woodstock, N. Y. A.
WILTZ, E. Madeline Shiff.
Mrs. Arnold Wiltz.
Am. b. Denver, Colo.; ad. 1934 Woodstock, N. Y. A.
WILWERDING, Walter Joseph. (Ill)
Am. b. Winona, Minn. 1891; ad. 1934 Minn., Minn. W.
WIMAR, Charles F.
Am. Germany 1828-1863 St. Louis, Mo. M.
WIMMER, Rudolf.
Ger. b. Gottsdörf 1849. B.
WIMPERIS, Edmund Monson.
Eng. Chester 1835-1900 London. B-M.
WINANTS, Jan. *see* Wynants, J.
WINCHELL, Elizabeth Burt.
Mrs. John Patten Winchell.
Am. b. Brooklyn, N. Y. 1890; ad. 1934 Brunswick, Me. A.
WINDBY, Frederic Charles.
Eng. b. Newport 1875; ad. 1934 London. Wa.
WINDISCH, Marion Linda. (S)
Mrs. Alden Cody Bentley.
Am. b. Cinn., O. 1904; ad. 1934 New York. A.
WINDUS, William Lindsay.
Eng. Liverpool 1822-1907 London. B-DNB.
WINEBRENNER, Harry Fielding. (S)
Am. b. Summersville, W. Va. 1884; ad. 1934 Santa Monica, Calif. A-F.
WINEGAR, Anna.
Am. ad. 1934 Bronxville, N. Y. M.
WINGART, Constance.
Am. ex. 1935 St. George, S. I., N. Y. M.
WINGATE, [Sir] James Lawton.
Scot. b. 1846; d. 1924. B.
WINGE, Marten Eskil.
Swe. Stockholm 1825-1896. B-C.

WINGERT, EDWARD OSWALD.
Am. b. Phila., Pa. 1864; ad. 1934 Same. A.
WINGFIELD, JAMES DIGMAN.
Eng. b. 1800; d. 1872. B.
WINGHE, JODOCUS VAN.
Flem. Brussels 1544-1603 Frankfort, Ger. B-C.
WINGHEN [or Wing], JEREMIAS VON.
Ger. Frankfort 1587-1658. B.
WINHOLTZ, CALEB.
Am. ad. 1935 St. Paul, Minn. M.
WINKLER, AGNES CLARK.
Mrs. G. A. M. Winkler.
Am. b. Cinn., O. 1893; ad. 1934 Chicago. A.
WINKLER, JOHN W.
Am. b. Austria 1890; ad. 1931 Berkeley, Calif. A28-F.
WINKLER, KURT. (Eg)
Ger. ad. 1934 Dresden. M.
WINKS, LUCILLE CONDIT.
Am. b. Sterton, La.; ad. 1934 Salisbury, N. C. A.
WINNE [or Vinne], LIÉVIN.
Belg. Ghent 1832-1880 Brussels. B-C.
WINNER, MARGARET F.
Am. b. Phila., Pa. 1866; ad. 1934 Same. A.
WINNER, WILLIAM E.
Am. ac. 1843-1881 in Phila., Pa. F-M.
WINSLOW, EARL B.
Am. b. Northville, Mich. 1884; ad. 1934 New York. A-F.
WINSLOW, [Mrs.] ELEANOR C. A.
Am. b. Norwich, Conn. 1877; ad. 1934 New York. A.
WINSLOW, GEORGE. (S)
Am. ad. 1934 Santa Fé, N. M. M.
WINSLOW, HENRY. (Et)
Am. b. Boston, Mass. 1874; ad. 1934 London. A-F-Wa.
WINSLOW, [Mrs.] LORETTA E.
Am. ad. 1934 South Orange, N. J. M.
WINSTANLEY, GERRARD.
Eng. ac. 1698-1756. DNB.
WINSTANLEY, HAMLET.
Eng. Warrington 1698-1756 Same. DNB.
WINSTANLEY, JOHN.
Am. b. Louisville, Ky.; ad. 1934 City Island, N. Y. A.
WINSTANLEY, WILLIAM.
Am. b. England; ac. 1775-1806 in Phila., Pa. F-2-182.
WINT, PETER DE. *see* De Wint, P.
WINTER, ALICE BEACH.
Mrs. Charles Allan Winter.
Am. b. Green Ridge, Mo. 1877; ad. 1934 East Gloucester, Mass. A-F-W.
WINTER, ANDREW.
Am. b. Sindi, Esthonia 1892; ad. 1934 New York. A-F.
WINTER, CHARLES ALLAN.
Am. b. Cinn., O. 1869; ad. 1934 East Gloucester, Mass. A-F-W.
WINTER, EZRA AUGUSTUS.
Am. b. Manistee, Mich. 1886; ad. 1934 New York. A-F-W-1-46.
WINTER, GEORGE.
Am. England 1810-1876 Lafayette, Ind. F-181.
WINTER, HEINRICH.
Ger. b. Frankfort 1843. C.
WINTER [or Wintter], JOSEPH GEORG.
Ger. Munich 1720/30-1789. B.
WINTER, LOUIS DE.
Belg. b. Antwerp 1819; ac. 1856. [No death date.] C.
WINTER, LUMEN. (Ill)
Am. ad. 1934 Brooklyn, N. Y. M.
WINTER, MARY.
Am. ad. 1935 New York. M.
WINTER, PHARAON ABDON LÉON DE.
Fr. Bailleul 1849-1924. B.
WINTER, VINAL. (S)
Am. ad. 1934 New York. M.
WINTER, WILLIAM TATTON.
Br. b. 1855; d. 1928. Y01929.
WINTERHALDER, ERWIN. (S)
Am. b. Zurich, Swi. 1879. Cs.
WINTERHALTER, FRANÇOIS XAVIER.
Ger. Baden-Baden 1806-1873 Frankfort. B-C.
WINTERHALTER, HERMANN.
Ger. St. Blaise 1808-1891 Carlsruhe. B.
WINTERICH, JOSEPH. (S)
Am. Neuwied, Ger. 1861-1932 Coblenz, Ger.; ac. 1920 Cleveland, O. A029.
WINTERS, ELLEN. (P-S)
Am. ad. 1934 New York. M.
WINTERSTEIN, ERHARD.
Ger. b. Dresden 1841. B.
WINTOUR, JOHN CRAWFORD.
Scot. b. 1825; d. 1882 in Edinburgh. B.
WINTRINGHAM, FRANCES M.
Am. b. Brooklyn, N. Y. 1884; ad. 1934 Same. A.
WINZER, CHARLES F. (Et)
Eng. b. Warsaw, Pol. 1886; ex. 1934 London. DBA.
WIRE, MELVILLE THOMAS.
Am. b. Austin, Ill. 1877; ad. 1934 Albany, Ore. A.
WIREMAN, EUGENIE M.
Am. b. Phila., Pa.; ad. 1934 Same. A.
WIRES, [Mrs.] ALDEN CHOATE.
Am. b. Oswego, N. Y. 1903; ad. 1934 Rockport, Mass. A.
WIRES, HAZEL K.
Am. b. Oswego, N. Y. 1903; ad. 1934 Rockport, Mass. A.
WIRGMAN, FRANCES.
Eng. b. Birkenhead; ad. 1934 Southport. Wa.
WIRGMAN, THEODORE BLAKE.
Eng. b. 1849; d. 1925. Y01926.
WIRTH, ANNA MARIA. (Ill)
Am. b. Johnstown, Pa. 1868; ad. 1934 Same. M.
WISCHNIOWSKY, JOSEPH.
Ger. ac. 1856 in Germany. M.
WISE, ETHEL BRAND. (S)
Mrs. L. E. Wise.
Am. New York 1888-1933 Syracuse, N. Y. A030.
WISE, [Mrs.] FLORENCE BARAN.
Am. b. Farmingdale, N. Y. 1881; ad. 1934 Cranston, R. I. A.
WISE, LOUISE WATERMAN.
Mrs. Stephen Wise.
Am. b. New York; ad. 1934 Same. A-F.

WISE, Percy Arthur.
Eng. b. Solihull; ad. 1934 Dorset. Wa.
WISE, [Mrs.] Sarah Morris Green. (S)
Am. Onarga, Ill. 1877-1919 New York. A016.
WISE, Vera.
Am. ad. 1935 Kansas City, Mo. M.
WISELTIER, Joseph.
Am. Paris 1889-1933 Hartford, Conn. A030.
WISER, Guy Brown.
Am. b. Marion 1895; ad. 1934 Columbus, O. A.
WISLICENUS, Hermann.
Ger. Eisenach 1825-1885/99. B-Bd-C.
WISNER, Frances.
Am. b. Pana, Ill. 1906; ad. 1934 Seattle, Wash. M.
WISNIESKI, Oskar.
Ger. Berlin 1819-1891 Same. B-C.
WISSING, Willem.
Dut. Amsterdam 1656-1687 Burleigh. B-C-DNB-702.
WIT, Dom Gregorius de.
Dut. ex. 1930 in Munich, Ger. M.
WIT, Jacob de.
Dut. Amsterdam 1695-1754. B-C-722.
WITHERINGTON, William Frederick.
Eng. London 1785-1865 Same. B-C-DNB.
WITHERS, Alfred.
Eng. b. London 1856. B.
WITHERS, Dod. *see* Dods-Withers, Isabelle.
WITHERS, George.
Am. b. Wichita, Kan. 1911; ad. 1934 Kansas City, Mo. A.
WITHERS, Loris A.
Am. ad. 1934 Port Wash., L. I., N. Y. M.
WITHERS, Walter.
Eng. b. Staffordshire 1857; ad. 1933 Sydney, N. S. W., Aust. B.
WITHERSPOON, Mary Eleanor.
Am. b. Gainesville, Tex. 1906; ad. 1934 Ft. Worth, Tex. A.
WITHERSTINE, Donald Frederick. (Et)
Am. b. Herkimer, N. Y. 1896; ad. 1934 Provincetown, Mass. A.
WITHOOS, Matthias.
Dut. Amersfoort 1627-1703 Hoorn. B-C.
WITHOOS, Peter.
Dut. Amersfoort 1654-1693 Amsterdam. B.
WITKOWSKI, Karl.
Am. Austria 1860-1910 Newark, N. J. A08.
WITSEN, Willem.
Dut. Amsterdam 1860-1923. B.
WITT, Johann. (Ill)
Ger. Lübeck 1834-1886 Zurich. B.
WITT, John Harrison.
Am. Dublin, Ind. 1840-1901 New York. A04-C-F.
WITTE, Emanuel de.
Dut. Alkmaar 1607-1692 Amsterdam. B-C-722.
WITTE, Gaspar [or Jaspar] de.
Dut. Antwerp, Belg. 1624-1681 Same. B-C.
WITTE, Jacob de.
Dut. Amsterdam 1695-1754. M.
WITTE, Pieter de [Pietro Candido].
see Candido, Pietro.
WITTENBERG, Jan.
Dut. b. 1886; ad. 1935 Doorn, Holland. M.
WITTERS, Nell.
Am. b. Grand Rapids, Mich.; ad. 1934 New York. A28-F.
WITTEWRONGE, [Sir] Charles Bennet Lawes.
see Lawes-Wittewronge.
WITTIG, Edward. (S)
Pol. b. 1881 in Poland. M.
WITTKAMP, Johan Barnard.
Belg. Risenbeck, Westphalia 1820-1885 Antwerp. B-C.
WITTLE, Gaspar van [Vitelli].
Dut. Utrecht 1674-1736 Rome, It. B.
WITTMER, Johann Michael.
Bav. Bavaria 1802-1880 Rome, It. B-C.
WITZ, Conrad.
Swi. ac. 1400-1447 in Nantes, Fr.; d. 1447. B.
WITZINGER, Hans.
Swi. ac. 1443 in Geneva. B.
WIVELL, Abraham.
Eng. Marylebone 1786-1849 Birmingham. B-DNB.
WIWULSKI, A. (S)
Pol. ac. Cracow, Poland. 798.
WLEROCK, Robert. (S)
Fr. b. Mont-de-Marsan 1882. DBA.
WLEUGHELS, Nicolas. *see* Vleughels, N.
WO PEEN.
Indian (American). ex. 1932 New York. 411.
WOCHER, F. W.
Am. b. Kansas City, Mo. 1869; ad. 1934 Yonkers, N. Y. M.
WODZINOVSKI, Vincent.
Pol. b. Poland 1866. B.
WOEIRIOT [or Voiriot], de Bouzey, Pierre. (S)
Fr. Reims 1531/2-1589. B.
WOELFLE, Arthur William.
Am. b. Trenton, N. J. 1873; ad. 1934 New York. A-F-W.
WOENSAM [or Wonsam], Anton von Worms.
Ger. b. Worms; ac. 1528-1541 in Cologne. B-C.
WOHLEGEMUTH, Michael.
see Wolgemut, M.
WOICESKE, R. William. (Et)
Am. b. Bloomington, Ill.; ad. 1935 Woodstock, N. Y. A28-M.
WOISERI, J. L. Bouquet de. (Eg)
Am. ac. 1800. F-2-147.
WOLCHONOK, Louis.
Am. b. New York 1898; ad. 1934 Same. A.
WOLCOTT, Elizabeth Tyler. (Ill)
Am. ex. 1935 White Plains, N. Y. M.
WOLCOTT, Harold.
Am. ex. 1935 White Plains, N. Y. M.
WOLCOTT, Katherine.
Am. b. Chicago 1880; ad. 1934 Same. A.
WOLCOTT, Rosamond. (Et)
Am. ad. 1935 New Rochelle, N. Y. M.
WOLDAN, Raffael Schuster.
see Schuster-Woldan, R.
WOLF, August.
Ger. b. Weinheim 1842. C.
WOLF, Friedrich.
Ger. Dresden 1833-1884 Same. B.

WOLF, Hamilton Achille.
Am. b. New York 1883; ad. 1934 Berkeley, Calif. A.
WOLF, Henry. (Eg)
Am. Alsace 1852-1916 New York. A013-B-F-8.
WOLF, Johann Andreas.
Ger. Munich 1652-1716 Same. B-C.
WOLF, Joseph.
Anglo-Ger. Mörz 1820-1899 London. B-DNB-E.
WOLFE, Ada A.
Am. b. Oakland, Calif.; ad. 1934 Minn., Minn. A.
WOLFE, Edward.
Br. b. So. Africa; ad. 1934 London. M.
WOLFE, George.
Eng. Bristol 1834-1890 Clifton. B.
WOLFE, J. Karl.
Am. b. Brookhaven, Miss. 1904; ad. 1934 Jackson, Miss. A.
WOLFE, Natalie. (S)
Mrs. D. D. Michael.
Am. b. San Fran., Calif. 1896; ad. 1934 Same. A.
WOLFENSBERGER, Johann Jakob.
Swi. b. 1797; d. 1850 in Zurich. B.
WOLFF, Émil. (S)
Ger. Berlin 1802-1879 Rome, It. B.
WOLFF, Gustave H. (S)
Am. b. Germany 1863; d. 1935 Berlin. A-M-Obit. Studio, 4-1935.
WOLFF, Robert Jay. (S)
Am. b. Chicago 1905; ad. 1934 Same. A.
WOLFFORDT, Artus.
Flem. Antwerp 1581-1641 Same. C.
WOLFSON, William. (Et)
Am. b. Pittsburgh, Pa. 1894; ad. 1935 Same. A28-F.
WOLGEMUT, Michael.
Ger. Nüremberg 1434-1519 Same. Bd-C-E-722.
WOLLASTON, John [The Elder].
Eng. London 1672-1760? B.
WOLLASTON, John [The Younger].
Am. b. England; ac. 1750/67 New York. B-F-182.
WOLLEN, William Barnes.
Eng. b. Leipzig, Ger. 1857; ac. 1926 London. B.
WOLLES, Lucien.
Belg. b. Brussels 1862; ac. 1905 Paris. B.
WOLLHEIN, Gert Heinrich.
Ger. b. 1894; ad. 1934 Montroughe [Seine], Fr. M.
WOLMARK, Alfred Aaron.
Eng. b. Warsaw, Pol. 1877; ad. 1934 London. Wa-825.
WOLSELEY, Garnet Ruskin.
Eng. b. London 1884; ad. 1934 Chelsea. Wa.
WOLSTENHOLME, Dean [The Elder].
Eng. b. 1757; d. 1837 London. B-735.
WOLSTENHOLME, Dean. [The Younger].
Eng. b. London 1798; d. 1883. B-735.
WOLTER, [Prof.] H. J.
Dut. ad. 1935 Amsterdam; ex. 1934 Pittsburgh, Pa. M.
WOLTERS, Henrietta [née van Pee]. (Min)
Dut. Amsterdam 1692-1741 Same. B.
WOLTRECK, F. (S)
Fr. b. 1800. [No death date.] B.
WOLTZE, Berthold.
Ger. Havelberg 1829-1896 Weimar. B-C.
WOMRATH, Andrew Kay. (Ill)
Am. b. Phila., Pa. 1869; ad. 1934 Kent, Conn. A.
WONDER, Pieter Christoffel.
Dut. Utrecht 1777/80-1852 Amsterdam. B-C.
WONG, TYRUS, Y.
Chinese. ad. 1934 Los Angeles, Calif. M.
WONSETHER, John Charles.
Am. b. Camden, N. J. 1900; ad. 1934 Collingswood, N. J. A.
WOOD, Christopher. (Potter)
Eng. b. 1902; d. 1931 London. Wa1929.
WOOD, Edith Longstreth.
Mrs. William S. Wood.
Am. b. Germantown, Pa.; ad. 1934 Phila., Pa. A.
WOOD, Elizabeth Wyn. (S)
Can. b. Orilla, Ont. 1903; ad. 1934 Toronto, Ont. M.
WOOD, Ella Miriam.
Am. ex. 1935 New Orleans, La. M.
WOOD, Ethelwyn A.
Am. b. Germantown, Pa. 1902; ad. 1934 Lake Worth, Fla. A.
WOOD, Francis Derwent. (S)
Eng. Keswick 1872-1926 London. B-Hs.
WOOD, Frank Watson.
Scot. b. Berwick 1862; ex. 1934 Sunderland, Eng. Wa1929.
WOOD, Franklin T. (Et)
Am. b. Hyde Park, Mass. 1887; ad. 1935 Rutland, Mass. A28-F.
WOOD, George Bacon, Jr.
Am. Phila., Pa. 1832-1910 Mass. C-F-15.
WOOD, Grant.
Am. b. Anamosa, Ia. 1892; ad. 1935 Cedar Rapids, Ia. A-F-779.
WOOD, Harrie Morgan.
Am. b. Rushford, N. Y. 1902; ad. 1934 New York. A.
WOOD, John.
Eng. London 1801-1870 Same. B-DNB.
WOOD, John George.
Eng. ac. 1792-1838 in London. B.
WOOD, John Warrington. (S)
Eng. Warrington 1839-1886 Rome, It. B.
WOOD, Joseph. (Min)
Am. Clarkstown, N. Y. 1778-1852 Wash., D. C. F-2-6-45.
WOOD, Kathryn Leone.
Am. b. Kalamazoo, Mich.; ad. 1934 Los Angeles, Calif. A.
WOOD, Lawson. (Ill)
Eng. b. Highgate 1878; ad. 1934 London. M.
WOOD, Lewis John.
Eng. b. 1831; d. 1901 in London. B.
WOOD, Marshall. (S)
Eng. ex. 1854 in London; d. 1882. DNB.
WOOD, Mary Earl.
Am. b. Lowell, Mass.; ad. 1934 Boston. A.
WOOD, Molly Wheeler.
Am. ad. 1934 Phila., Pa. M.

WOOD, NAN.
Mrs. Charles Morgan Wood.
Am. b. Dayton, O. 1873; ad. 1934 Ipswich, Mass. A.
WOOD, OGDEN.
Am. New York 1851-1912 Paris. A0X.
WOOD, RALPH. (Pottery)
Eng. ac. 1770 in London. M.
WOOD, ROBERT SYDNEY RENDLE.
Eng. b. Plymouth 1895; ad. 1934 Belfast, Ir. Wa.
WOOD, RUTH MARY. (Ill)
Eng. b. So. Shields 1899; ad. 1934 Devon. Wa.
WOOD, SHAKSPERE. (S)
Eng. b. England 1827; d. 1886 Rome, It. B-DNB.
WOOD, STANLEY.
Am. b. Bordentown, N. J. 1894; ad. 1934 Carmel, Calif. A.
WOOD, STARR. (Ill)
Eng. b. London; ad. 1934 Same. Wa.
WOOD, THOMAS.
Eng. London 1800-1878. B.
WOOD, THOMAS WATERMAN.
Am. Montpelier, Vt. 1823-1903 New York. A04-C-F-3-15-39.
WOOD, URSULA. (Et)
Eng. ac. 1934 London. Wa.
WOOD, VIRGINIA H.
Mrs. C. F. Goddard.
Am. ad. 1934 New York. M.
WOOD, WALLACE.
Eng. b. London 1894; ad. 1934 Same. Wa.
WOOD, WILFRIED RENÉ.
Eng. b. Manchester 1888; ad. 1934 Hampstead. Wa.
WOOD, WILLIAM.
Eng. Ipswich 1768-1809 London. B.
WOOD, WILLIAM JOHN.
Can. b. Ottawa, Ont. 1877; ad. 1935 Midland, Ont. M.
WOOD, WILLIAM R. C.
Am. Wash., D. C. 1875-1915 Balt., Md. A012-F.
WOOD, WILLIAM THOMAS.
Eng. b. Ipswich 1877; ad. 1934 London. Wa.
WOODBURY, CHARLES HERBERT.
Am. b. Lynn, Mass. 1864; ad. 1934 Boston. A-B-E-F-W-46.
WOODBURY, MARCIA OAKES.
Mrs. Charles H. Woodbury.
Am. b. So. Berwick, Me. 1865-1913 Ogunquit, Me. A0X1-F.
WOODCOCK, HARTWELL L.
Am. Belfast, Me. 1853-1929 Same. A027.
WOODCOCK, PERCY FRANKLIN.
Can. b. Athens, Can. 1855; ad. 1935 Montreal, B-M.
WOODFORD, JAMES A. (S)
Scot. ad. 1934 London. M.
WOODFORDE, SAMUEL.
Br. Castle Cary 1763-1817 Italy. B-C-DNB.
WOODHOUSE, WILLIAM.
Eng. b. Morecambe 1857. Wa1929.
WOODINGTON, WILLIAM FREDERICK. (P-S)
Eng. Sutton 1806-1893 Brixton. B-DNB.
WOODLOCK, DAVID.
Ir. b. Golden 1842; ad. 1929 Liverpool, Eng. Wa1929.
WOODMAN, CHARLES HENRY.
Eng. b. 1823; d. 1888. M.
WOODMAN, EDITH.
see Burroughs, E. W.
WOODMAN, RICHARD [The Elder]. (Eg)
Eng. ac. 1810 in London. B.
WOODMAN, RICHARD [The Younger]. (Eg)
Eng. London 1784-1859 Same. B-DNB.
WOODROFE, LOUISE M.
Am. b. Champaign, Ill.; ad. 1934 Urbana, Ill. A.
WOODROFFE, ELEANOR G.
Am. ad. 1934 Niantic, Conn. M.
WOODROFFE, PAUL VINCENT.
Br. b. India 1875; ad. 1934 Campden, Eng. Wa.
WOODRUFF, B. D.
Am. ad. 1934 Toledo, O. M.
WOODRUFF, CLAUDE WALLACE. (Ill)
Am. ad. 1934 Decatur, Ill. A.
WOODRUFF, CORICE. (S)
Mrs. Henry S. Woodruff.
Am. b. Ansonia, Conn. 1878; ad. 1934 Minn., Minn. A.
WOODRUFF, EUGENIE GRAY.
Mrs. John Woodruff.
Am. ad. 1934 New York. M.
WOODRUFF, HALE ASPACIO.
Am. b. Cairo, Ill. 1900; ad. 1934 Atlanta, Ga. M.
WOODRUFF, JOHN KELLOGG. (P-S)
Am. b. Bridgeport, Conn. 1879; ad. 1934 Grand View, N. Y. A.
WOODRUFF, WILLIAM. (Eg)
Am. ac. 1817-1824 in Phila., Pa. F-2-7.
WOODS, ALBERT.
Eng. b. Preston; ad. 1934 London. Wa.
WOODS, BEATRICE.
Am. ad. 1935 Cinn., O. M.
WOODS, ENOCH S. (S)
Am. ac. late 19th Cent. in Hartford, Conn. M.
WOODS, HAROLD JAMES.
Eng. b. Sandown 1894; ad. 1934 Portsmouth. Wa.
WOODS, HENRY.
Eng. Warrington 1846-1921 Venice, It. B-C.
WOODS, JOHN GOODRICH WEMYSS.
Eng. ad. 1934 Seaford, Eng. Wa.
WOODS, LILLA SORRENSON.
Mrs. E. B. Woods.
Am. b. Portage, Wis. 1872; ad. 1934 Hanover, N. H. A.
WOODSON, MARIE L.
Am. b. Selma, Ala. 1875; ad. 1934 Denver, Colo. A.
WOODVILLE, RICHARD CATON, JR.
Eng. London 1855-1927. M.
WOODVILLE, RICHARD CATON, SR.
Am. Balt., Md. 1825-1855 London. B-F-1-4.
WOODWARD, DEWING.
Am. b. Williamsport, Pa. 1876; ad. 1934 Coral Gables, Fla. A.
WOODWARD, ELIZA.
Eng. b. 1842; ad. 1929 Birmingham. Wa1929.

WOODWARD, Ellsworth.
Am. b. Bristol Co., Mass. 1861; ad. 1934 New Orleans, La. A-F-W-183.
WOODWARD, George Montard. (Cari)
Eng. b. 1760?; d. 1809 in London. B-DNB.
WOODWARD, Helen M.
Am. b. Newtown, Ind. 1902; ad. 1934 Ind., Ind. A.
WOODWARD, Hildegard.
Am. ad. 1934 Boston, Mass. M.
WOODWARD, John Douglas.
Am. Virginia 1848-1924 New Rochelle, N. Y. A021.
WOODWARD, Lella Grace.
Am. b. Coldwater, Mich. 1858; ad. Forest Glen, Md. 1915 A12.
WOODWARD, Mabel May.
Am. b. Prov., R. I. 1877; ad. 1934 Same. A.
WOODWARD, Robert Strong.
Am. b. Northampton, Mass. 1885; ad. 1934 Shelburne Falls, Mass. A-F.
WOODWARD, Stanley Wingate.
Am. b. Malden, Mass. 1890; ad. 1934 Newton, Mass. A-F.
WOODWARD, Thomas.
Eng. Pershore 1801-1852 Worcester. B-DNB.
WOODWARD, Wilbur Winfield.
Am. St. Omer, Ind. 1851-1882 Lawrencebury, Ind. 181.
WOODWARD, William.
Am. b. Seekonk, Mass. 1859; ad. 1934 Biloxi, Miss. A-F-W-183.
WOODWELL, Joseph R.
Am. Pittsburgh, Pa. 1843-1911 Same. A09-F-46.
WOOG, Raymond.
Fr. b. Paris 1875; ac. 1924 Same. DBA.
WOOLDRIDGE, Harry Ellis.
Eng. London 1845-1917 Same. DNB.
WOOLEN, W. B.
Eng. b. Leipzig, Ger. 1851. M.
WOOLEY, William. (Eg)
Am. ac. 1800. F-7-147.
WOOLF, Michael Angelo.
Am. London 1837-1899 U. S. A01-B.
WOOLF, Samuel Johnson.
Am. b. New York 1880; ad. 1934 Same. A-F-W.
WOOLFE, [Mrs.] Annette.
Am. ad. 1934 New York. M.
WOOLLARD, Dorothy Edith Griffiths. (Et)
Eng. ad. 1934 London. Wa.
WOOLLARD, Florence Eliza.
Eng. b. Clapham 1878; ad. 1934 Same. Wa.
WOOLLATT, Edgar.
Eng. b. Nottingham 1871; ad. 1929 Same. Wa1929.
WOOLLATT, Leighton Hall. (P-S)
Eng. b. Nottingham 1905; ad. 1934 Same. Wa.
WOOLLETT, Sydney. (S)
Am. ad. 1935 Boston, Mass. M.
WOOLLETT, William. (Eg)
Eng. Maidstone 1735-1785 London. B-DNB-E.
WOOLLEY, Sarah Albertson.
Am. b. Roslyn, L. I., N. Y.; ex. 1934 Buck Hill Falls, Pa. M.
WOOLLEY, Virginia.
Am. b. Selma, Ala. 1884; ad. 1934 Laguna Beach, Calif. A.
WOOLLEY, William. (Eg)
Am. ac. 1800. F-7-147.
WOOLMER, Alfred Joseph.
Eng. Exeter 1805-1892. B.
WOOLMER, Ethel.
Eng. ex. 1935 London. M.
WOOLMER, Thomas. (S-Poet)
Eng. Hadleigh 1825-1892 Hendon. B-E-Hs.
WOOLRYCH, Bertha Hewit.
Mrs. F. Humphry W. Woolrych
Am b. Ohio 1868; ad. 1934 St. Louis, Mo. A.
WOOLRYCH, Francis Humphry William.
Am. b. Sydney, N. S. W. Aust. 1868; ad. 1934 St. Louis, Mo. A-F-W.
WOOLSEY, Carl E.
Am. b. Chicago Heights, Ill. 1902; ad. 1934 Taos, N. M. A.
WOOLSEY, Wood W.
Am. b. Danville, Ill. 1899; ad. 1935 Martinsville, Ind. A.
WOOTTAN, John.
Eng. b. 1668?; d. 1765 in London. B-C-DNB.
WOPFNER, Joseph.
Aus. b. Schwaz 1843. B-C.
WORCESTER, Albert.
Am. b. West Compton, N. H. 1878; ad. 1926 Detroit, Mich. F.
WORES, Theodore.
Am. b. San Fran., Calif. 1860; ad. 1934 Same. A-F.
WORKMAN, David Tice. (Et)
Am. b. Wapheton, N. D. 1884; ad. 1926 Minn., Minn. A12-F.
WORKMAN, Harold.
Eng. b. Oldham 1897; ad. 1934 Southborne. Wa.
WORKMAN, Norah.
Ir. b. Belfast 1871; ad. 1929 Same. Wa1929.
WORLIDGE, Thomas.
Eng. b. 1700; d. 1766 London. B-DNB.
WORMS, Anton Woensam von. (Eg)
Ger. d. 1541. Fa.
WORMS, Jules.
Fr. Paris 1832-1924. B-C.
WOROBIEFF, Maxime Nikiforovich.
Rus. b. 1787; d. 1855 in Leningrad. B-C.
WORRALL, Ella.
Eng. b. Liverpool 1863; ad. 1934 Same. Wa.
WORRALL, J. E.
Eng. Liverpool 1829-1913 Same. M.
WORRALL, James.
Am. ac. 1805-1815 in Virginia. F-2.
WORSDALE, James.
Eng. b. 1692?; d. 1767 in London. B-DNB.
WORSFOLD, Maud Beatrice.
Eng. ad. 1934 London. Wa.
WORSWICK, Lloyd. (S)
Am. b. Albany, N. Y. 1899; ad. 1934 New York. A-Cs-F.
WORTH, Thomas. (Cari)
Am. b. New York 1834; ac. 1860 Same; [No death date]. F-15.
WORTHINGTON, Elizabeth.
Am. ex. 1935 New York. M.

WORTHINGTON, Harry Edward.
Eng. b. Worthing 1867. Wa1929.
WORTHINGTON, Pearl Hill.
Am. b. Lock Haven, Pa. 1889; ad. 1934 New Rochelle. N. Y. A.
WORTHINGTON, William Henry. (Eg)
Eng. London 1795-1839 Same. B.
WORTHLEY, Caroline Bonsall.
Mrs. Irvington Tupper Worthley.
Am. b. Cinn., O. 1880; ad. 1934 Phoenixville, Pa. A.
WORTMAN, Denys. (Cart)
Am. b. Saugerties, N. Y. 1887; ad. 1935 New York. A29.
WOSTENHOLME. *see* Wolstenholme.
WOTHERSPOON, W. W.
Am. New York 1821-1888. M.
WOU, Claes Claesz.
Dut. b. 1592; d. 1665 in Holland. Fa.
WOUTERS, Frans.
Flem. Lierre 1614-1659 Antwerp. B-C.
WOUTERS, Jakob [Vosmaer].
Dut. Leyden 1584-1641 Delft. B.
WOUTERS, Rik.
Belg. b. 1882; d. 1916. M.
WOUTERSZ, Johannes [J. W. Snap].
Dut. ac. 1542 in Amsterdam. B.
WOUW, Antoine van. (S)
Dut. b. Amsterdam 1863; ad. 1935 Johannesburg, Transvaal, S. A. M.
WOUWERMAN, Jan.
Dut. Haarlem 1629-1666 Same. B-C-722.
WOUWERMAN, Philip.
Dut. Haarlem 1619-1668. B-Bd-C-E-722-902.
WOUWERMAN, Pieter.
Dut. Haarlem 1623-1682 Amsterdam. B.
WOZENCROFT-EVANS, Vyvyan Grace Selina.
Eng. b. Hampton 1909; ad. 1929 Same. Wa1929.
WRAGE, Jochim Heinrich.
Ger. b. Hitzhusen 1843. B-C.
WRAY, Henry Russell.
Am. Phila., Pa. 1864-1927 Colorado. A025-F.
WRBA, Georg. (S)
Ger. b. Munich 1872. B-798.
WREDE, Christian. (S)
Ger. ad. 1935 Munich. M.
WREN, [Sir] Christopher. (Eg)
Eng. East Knoyle 1632-1723 London. B-Bd-DNB-689.
WRENN, Charles Lewis.
Am. b. Cinn., O. 1880; ad. 1934 New York. A.
WRENN, Elizabeth Jencks. (S)
Am. b. Newburgh, N. Y. 1892; ad. 1934 Balt., Md. A.
WRENN, Harold Holmes.
Am. b. Norfolk, Va. 1887; ad. 1934 Balt., Md. A.
WRIGHT, Alice Maud. (Ill)
Eng. b. Hoxton; ad. 1934 Highgate. Wa.
WRIGHT, Alice Morgan. (S)
Am. b. Albany, N. Y. 1881; ad. 1934 Same. A-Cs-F.
WRIGHT, [Mr.] Alma Brockerman.
Am. b. Salt Lake City, Utah 1875; ad. 1934 Same. A.
WRIGHT, Bertha Eugénie Stevens.
Mrs. Lawrence Wright.
Am. b. Astoria, L. I., N. Y.; ad. 1934 Merrick, L. I., N. Y. A.
WRIGHT, [Mrs.] Catherine Morris.
Am. b. Phila., Pa. 1899; ad. 1934 Glenside, Pa. A.
WRIGHT, Charles Cushing. (Eg)
Am. b. Damariscotta, Me.; d. 1853 New York. F-2-7.
WRIGHT, Charles H.
Am. b. Knightstown, Ind. 1870; ad. 1934 New York. A.
WRIGHT, Charles Lennox.
Am. b. Boston 1876; ad. 1934 Bayside, L. I., N. Y. F.
WRIGHT, [Mrs.] E. Hilda.
Aust. b. Victoria; ad. 1934 Delegate, N. S. W., Aust. Wa.
WRIGHT, Ethel.
Eng. b. London; ad. 1934 Same. Wa829.
WRIGHT, Ferdinand de.
Finnish. b. Finland; ac. 1889 in Paris. B.
WRIGHT, Frank Arnold. . (S)
Eng. b. London 1874; ad. 1934 Surrey. Wa798.
WRIGHT, F. E.
Am. b. So. Weymouth, Mass. 1849; ad. 1925 Boston. F15.
WRIGHT, Fred W.
Am. b. Crawfordsville, Ind. 1880; ad. 1934 New York. A-F.
WRIGHT, George Frederick.
Am. Wash., Conn. 1828-1881 Hartford, Conn. C-F-3.
WRIGHT, George Hand. (Ill)
Am. b. Fox-Chase, Pa. 1872; ad. 1934 So. Norwalk, Conn. A-F-W.
WRIGHT, Grant.
Am. b. Decatur, Mich. 1865; ad. 1934 Weehawken, N. J. A.
WRIGHT, Irene Clara. (Min)
Eng. b. London; ad. 1934 Same. Wa.
WRIGHT, James Couper. (Glass-P)
Am. ad. 1934 Santa Barbara, Calif. M.
WRIGHT, James Henry.
Am. b. 1813; d. 1883 in Brooklyn, N. Y. F.
WRIGHT, John.
Eng. ac. 1790; d. 1820 in London. B.
WRIGHT, John Buckland. (Eg)
Aust. b. New Zealand 1897; ad. 1934 Paris; ex. 1935 London. M.
WRIGHT, J. Dunbar.
Am. b. 1862; d. 1917 Port Jervis, N. Y. A014.
WRIGHT, John Massey.
Eng. b. 1777; d. 1866 in London. B-DNB.
WRIGHT, John Michael ["J. M. Ritus"].
see Wright, J. M.
WRIGHT, John William.
Eng. London 1802-1848 Same . B-DNB.
WRIGHT, Joseph [Die Sinker].
[First Die Sinker at Philadelphia Mint.]
Am. Bordentown, N. J. 1756-1793 Phila., Pa. B-Bd-DNB-F-2-6-7-182-184-786.
WRIGHT, Joseph of Derby.
Eng. Derby 1734-1797 Same. B-C-DNB.
WRIGHT, Joseph Michael.
Scot. b. Scotland 1625; d. 1700 London. B-DNB-E.

WRIGHT, Margaret Hardon. (Et)
Mrs. James Hayden Wright.
Am. b. Newton, Mass. 1869. A28.

WRIGHT, M. Louise.
Mrs. John Wright.
Am. b. Phila., Pa. 1875; ad. 1934 London. A-F-46.

WRIGHT, Miriam Noel. (S)
Am. d. 1930 Milwaukee, Wis. AC27.

WRIGHT, Nora.
Eng. ad. 1934 Horncastle. Wa.

WRIGHT, [Mrs.] Patience. (Wax-S)
Am. Bordentown, N. J. 1725-1786 London. DNB-F-Hs-Ta.

WRIGHT, Philip Cameron. (Ill)
Am. b. Phila., Pa. 1901; ad. 1934 Jackson Heights, N. Y. A.

WRIGHT, Richard.
Eng. Liverpool 1735-1775? Isle of Man. B-DNB.

WRIGHT, Rufus.
Am. b. Cleveland, O. 1832; [No death date]. C-F-15.

WRIGHT, R. Stephens. (Et)
Am. ad. 1935 Chicago; ex. 1935 New York. M.

WRIGHT, Stanton Macdonald.
Am. b. Virginia 1890; ad. 1934 Santa Monica, Calif. M.

WRIGHT, Thomas M.
Eng. Birmingham 1792-1849 London. B-DNB.

WRIGLEY, Thomas.
Eng. b. Manchester 1883; ad. 1934 Norfolk. Wa.

WRIGLEY, [Mrs.] Viola B.
Am. ad. 1934 White Plains, N. Y. M.

WRINCH, Mary Evelyn.
Can. b. Kirby-le-Soken, Essex, Eng. 1887; ad. 1934 Toronto, Can. M.

WTTENWAEL, Joachim Anthonisz.
Dut. Utrecht 1566-1638 Same. B.

WU CHANG-SHIH.
Chinese. ad. 1935 Shanghai. M.

WU CHÊN.
Chinese. 1280-1354. E.

WU LI.
Chinese. ac. 17th Cent. E.

WU TAO-TZU.
Chinese. d. 760? E.

WU WEI.
Chinese. Ming Dynasty (1368-1644) E.

WUCHTERS [or Wugters], Abraham.
Dut. Holland 1610/15-1683 Soroe, Denmark. B-C.

WUERMER, Carl.
Am. b. ~~Munich~~, Ger. 1900; ad. 1934 New York. A-F-W.

WUERPEL, Edmund Henry.
Am. b. St. Louis, Mo. 1866; ad. 1934 Clayton, Mo. A-F-W.

WUERTZ, Émil H. (S)
Am. b. Germany; d. 1898 Chicago, Ill. F.

WUESTEN, Johannes. (Eg)
Ger. b. 1896; ex. 1934 Chicago, Ill.; ad.1935 Dresden, Ger. M.

WULFF, Timothy Milton.
Am. b. San Fran., Calif. 1890; ad. 1934 Same. A.

WULFFAERT, Adrianus.
Belg. b. Ter Goes, Zeeland 1804; ac. 1830 Bruges. M.

WUNKEI. (S)
Japanese. [Feudal Period]; ac. 13th Cent. Hs.

WÜNNERBERG, Carl.
Ger. b. Düsseldorf 1850. B-C.

WUNSCH, Marie Maizi.
Ger. Weinhaus 1862-1898 Meran, Aus. B.

WUPPER, Josephine.
Am. ex. 1935 Milwaukee, Wis. M.

WURMSER, Nicolas.
Ger. ac. 1348-1360 in Strassburg. B-C.

WURZINGER, Carl.
Aus. Vienna 1817-1883 Dubling. B-C.

WÜST, Alexander.
Belg. Dordrecht, Holland 1837-1876 Antwerp. B.

WÜST [or Wüsten], Johann Heinrich.
Swi. Zurich 1741-1821 Same. B-Bd-C.

WÜSTEN, Johannes.
Ger. b. 1896 in Germany. M.

WUTHENAU, Alexander von.
Ger. b. Germany; ad. 1934 Wash., D. C. M.

WUTKY, Michael.
Aus. Krems 1738/9-1822/3 Vienna. B-C.

WYANT, Alexander Helwig.
Am. Port Washington, O. 1836-1892 New York. B-C-E-F-1-15-46-127-280-701.

WYATT, A. C.
Am. b. England; d. 1933 Montecito, Calif. A030.

WYATT, Colin. (S)
Eng. ex. 1935 London. M.

WYATT, Henry.
Eng. Thickbroom 1794-1840 Prestwich. B-DNB.

WYATT, Matthew Cotes. (S)
Br. b. 1777; d. 1862. DNB.

WYATT, Richard James. (S)
Eng. b. 1795; d. 1850. DNB-Hs.

WYATT, Thomas.
Eng. Thickbroom 1799?-1859 Lichfield. B-DNB.

WYCK. *see also* Van Wyck.

WYCK, John [or Jan]
Eng. Haarlem, Holland 1652-1702 London. B-DNB.

WYCK, Thomas.
Dut. Beverwyck 1616-1677 Haarlem. B-C-722.

WYCKOFF, Joseph.
Am. b. Ottawa, Kan. 1883; ad. 1934 New York. A.

WYCKOFF, Marjorie Annable. (S)
Am. b. Montreal, Que., Can. 1904; ad. 1934 Buffalo, N. Y. A.

WYCZÓLKOWSKI, Léon.
Pol. b. Miastkowo-Koscielme 1852; ad. 1934 Poznàn, Pol. M.

WYER, Raymond.
Am. b. London; ad 1915 Muskegon, Mich. A12.

WYETH, Henriette.
[Mrs. Peter Hurd.]
Am. b. Wilmington, Del. 1907; ad. 1934 Chadds Ford, Pa. M.

WYETH, NEWELL CONVERS. (Ill)
Am. b. Needham, Mass. 1882; ad. 1934 Chadds Ford, Pa. A-F-W-46.
WYL [or Weyl], JAKOB VON.
Swi. Lucerne 1586-1620/1 Rome, It. B.
WYLD, WILLIAM.
Eng. London 1806-1889 Paris. B-C.
WYLE, FLORENCE. (S)
Can. b. Trenton, Ill. 1881; ad. 1934 Toronto, Can. M.
WYLIE, KATE.
Scot. b. Skelmorlie; ad. 1934 Glasgow. Wa.
WYLIE, MARION.
Am. b. Wash., D. C. 1913; ad. 1934 Los Angeles, Calif. M.
WYLIE, ROBERT.
Br.-Am. Isle of Man 1839-1877 Pont Avens, Fr. B-C-E-F-15.
WYLLIE, CHARLES WILLIAM.
Br. ac. 1871-1923. B.
WYLLIE, [Lt.-Col.] HAROLD.
Eng. b. London 1880; ad. 1934 Same. Wa.
WYLLIE, WILLIAM LIONEL.
Eng. Portsmouth 1851-1931 London. B-Wa1929.
WYMAN, LOIS PALMER.
[Mrs. Kendall.]
Am. ad. 1935 New Haven, Conn. M.
WYNANTS [or Wijnants], JAN.
Dut. Haarlem 1615/20-1679/82 Amsterdam. B-Bd-C-722.
WYNDHAM, GUY RICHARDS CHARLES.
Eng. b. Canterbury 1896; ad. 1934 London. Wa.
WYNFIELD, DAVID WINKLE.
Eng. b. 1837; d. 1887 in London. B-C.
WYNGAERDE, FRANÇOIS VAN DEN.
Flem. Antwerp 1612-1660. B.
WYNGAERDE, FRANS VAN DEN.
Flem. ac. 1561-1572. B.
WYNRICH, HERMANN.
Ger. ac. before 1400-1413/4. M.
WYNTRACK, DIRK.
Dut. Drenth 1625-1678/87 The Hague. B-C.
WYON, ALLAN GAIRDNER. (S)
Eng. b. London 1882; ad. 1934 Same. Wa.
WYON FAMILY. (Engravers of Seals)
Alfred-Benjamin-Joseph-Leonard-Thomas-and William.
Eng. ac. 18-19 Cent. in Bristol, Eng. DNB.
WYRASCH [or Wursch], JOHANN MELCHIOR JOSEPH.
Swi. b. 1732; d. 1789 in Besançon. B.
WYSE, HENRY TAYLOR.
Scot. b. Glasgow 1870. B.
WYSPIANSKI, STANISLAW.
Pol. Crakow 1869-1907 Same. B.
WYTMAN, MATHEUS.
Dut. b. 1650; d. 1689 in Utrecht. B-C.
WYVILL, [Mrs.] ELIZABETH.
Eng. ad. 1934 York, Eng. Wa.
WYWICZKI, MICHAEL GORSKY.
Pol. ac. 1861 in Poland. M.

XAVERY, FRANCISCUS.
Flem. ac. 1761-1768 The Hague. B.
XAVERY, JACOB IV.
Dut. The Hague 1736-1769. B.
XAVERY, JEAN BAPTISTE. (S)
Dut. Antwerp, Belg. 1697-1742 The Hague. B.
XCERON, JOHN [or Jean].
Gr.-Am. b. Mégalopolis, Gr. 1890; ex. 1935 New York. DBA-M.
XENO OF SICYON.
Gr. Pupil of Neocles. Dates uncertain, but mentioned by Pliny. C.
XENOKRATES. (S)
Gr. ac. 4th Cent. in Pergamon. Hs.
XENOPLON VLACHOPOULOS. *see* Vlachopoulos.
XIMENES, ETTORE. (S)
It. Parma 1855-1927. B-E-Hs.
XIMENES [or Ximenez], FRANCISCO.
Sp. Torragone 1598-1666. B.
XIMENEZ, DONOSO JOSEF [or Juán].
Sp. b. 1628; d. 1690 in Madrid. B.
XIMENEZ DE ILLESCAS, BARNABÉ.
Sp. Lucena 1613-1671 in Andujar. B.
XYLANDER, VILHELM FERDINAND.
Dan. b. Copenhagen 1840; ac. 1868 Munich, Ger. C.

YAFFEE, EDITH WIDING.
Am. b. Helsingfors, Finland 1895; ad. 1934 Wash., D. C. A.
YAFFEE, PAUL. (S)
Am. ex. 1934 in Balt., Md. M.
YAGLIJIAN, EDMUND.
Am. ad. 1934 New York. M.
YAGO, RAFAEL SANCHIS.
Sp. b. Valencia 1891; ad. 1934 Castellon. M.
YAGOUB, SIDI-BEN.
Br. ac. 1923 in India. Fa.
YALE, LEROY MILTON. (Et)
Am. Vinyard Haven, Mass. 1841-1906. A06-F.
YALLAND, THOMAS KING.
Eng. Bristol 1845-1934. Wa01934.
YAMADA DO-AN [Mimbu Taiyū].
Jap. ac. 1550. J., Vol. 1, page 111.
YAMAGISHI, KAZUE. (Eg)
Jap. ex. 1934 Chicago, Ill.; ad. 1935 Tokyo, Jap. M.
YAMASAKI, C.
Jap. ad. 1935 New York. M.
YAN D'ARGENT, ERNEST.
Fr. b. 1850; d. 1908 in Paris. Fa.
YANDELL, [Miss] ENID. (S)
Am. Louisville, Ky. 1870-1934 Boston, Mass. A-Cs-F-W46-829-Obit. N. Y. papers, 6-13-1934.
YÃNEZ [or Yãnes], HERNANDO.
Sp. b. Almedina; ac. 1531/60. B-C.
YARBROUGH, VIVIAN SLOAN.
Am. b. Whitesboro, Tex. 1893; ad. 1934 Ft. Worth, Tex. A.
YARD, MARGARET MOFFAT.
Am. ac. 1926. Fa.
YARROW, WILLIAM HENRY KEMBLE.
Am. b. Glenside, Pa. 1891; ad. 1934 New York. A-F.
YARZ, EDMOND.
Fr. b. Toulouse; ac. 1876-1903 in Paris. B-C.
YASUNOBU, KANO.
Jap. ac. 17th Cent. in Japan. J., Vol. 1, page 131.

YATES, CULLEN.
Am. b. Bryan, O. 1886; ad. 1934 Shawnee, Pa. A-F-W-46.
YATES, JOHN.
Eng. b. Blackburn 1885; ad. 1934 Same. Wa.
YATES, [Mrs.] JULIE CHAMBERLAIN. (S)
Am. d. 1929 New York. A027.
YATES, MARY.
Eng. b. Kent 1891; ad. 1934 Ambleside. Wa.
YATES, RUTH. (S)
Am. ad. 1934 Scarsdale, N. Y. M.
YATES, THOMAS.
Eng. ac. 1788-1796 in London. B.
YAZAKI, CHIYOJI.
Jap. b. 1874; ex. 1924 in Paris. Fa.
YEADON, DICK.
Eng. b. Brierfield 1896; ad. 1934 Kendal. Wa.
YEAGER, EDGAR LOUIS.
Am. b. Detroit, Mich. 1904; ad. 1934 Same. A.
YEAGER, JOSEPH. (Eg)
Am. ac. 1816-1845 in Phila., Pa. F-2-7.
YEAMES, WILLIAM FREDERICK.
Eng. Russia 1835-1918 Teignmouth, Eng. B-C.
YEATMAN, ALICE MARY.
Eng. b. Sunderland; ad. 1934 Same. Wa.
YEATS, JACK BUTLER [The Younger].
Ir. b. Dublin; ad. 1934 Same. Wa.
YEATS, JOHN BUTLER [The Elder].
Am. Ireland 1839-1922 New York. A019-B-F-Y01923.
YEEND-KING, HENRY JOHN.
Eng. London 1855-1924. B-Y01925.
YEEND-KING, LILIAN.
Eng. b. Paris, Fr. 1882; ad. 1934 Sussex, Eng. Wa.
YEISHI, CHOBUNSAI [Hosoda].
Jap b. 1746; d. 1829. J., Vol. 2, page 54.
YEITOKU, KANO.
Jap. b. 1543; d. 1590. J., Vol. 1, page 113.
YEIZAN, KIKUGAWA.
Jap. ac. 1800-1830. M.
YELLAND, RAYMOND D.
Am. London, Eng. 1848-1900 Oakland, Calif. A02-C-F-15.
YELLOWLEES, WILLIAM.
[Called the "Little Raeburn."]
Scot. Scotland 1796-1859 London. B.
YEN HUI.
Chinese. Vuen Dynasty [1280-1368]. E.
YEN LI-PÈN.
Chinese. b. 600; d. 673. E.
YENCESSE, OVIDE. (S)
Fr. b. Dijon 1869. DBA.
YENS [or Jens], KARL JULIUS HEINRICH. (Mu)
Am. b. Altona, Ger. 1868; ad. 1934 Laguna Beach, Calif. A.
YEO, RICHARD. (Med)
Eng. b. 1720; d. 1779. B-DNB.
YEOMANS, WALTER C. (Et)
Am. ad. 1935 Cornwall Bridge, Conn. M.
YERBYSMITH, ERNEST A. (S)
Am. ac. 1934 Glendale, Calif. M.
YERUSHALMY, DAVID. (S)
Am. b. Jerusalem, Palestine 1893; ad. 1934 Chicago. A.
YÉSHIN, SODZU.
Jap. Yamato 942-1017. J., Vol. 1, page 46.
YETTS, WALTER PERCIVAL. (Mu)
Eng. b. Reading 1878; ad. 1934 London. Wa.
YEWELL, GEORGE HENRY.
Am. Havre de Grace, Md. 1830-1923 Lake George, N. Y. A020-C-F-4-15.
YKENS, FRANS [The Younger].
Flem. Antwerp 1601-1683/93 Same. B-C.
YKENS, PIETER [The Younger].
Flem. Antwerp 1648-1695/6 Same. B-C.
YLEN, JEAN D'.
Fr. ac. 1920 in Paris. Fa.
YOGETSU.
Jap. ac. 1500. J., Vol. 1, page 110.
YOGHJIAN, EDMUND.
Am. ad. 1934 New York. M.
YOHN, FREDERICK COFFAY. (Ill)
Am. Ind., Ind. 1875-1933 Norwalk, Conn. A030-F-W17-46.
YON, EDMOND CHARLES JOSEPH.
Fr. Paris 1836-1897. B-C.
YŌSAI, KIKUCHI.
Jap. 1781-1878. E-J., Vol. 1, page 43.
YOSHIDA, MUNSTOSHI.
Jap. ac. 1900 in Paris. B.
YOSHITA, H.
Jap. ac. 1930. Fa.
YOSHITORA.
Jap. ac. 1890. J., Vol. 2, page 72
YOUNG, ARETTA.
Am. Idaho 1864-1923 Provo, Utah. A020.
YOUNG, ARTHUR ["Art"]. (Cart)
Am. b. Illinois 1866; ad. 1934 Bethel, Conn. A28.
YOUNG, ARTHUR RAYMOND.
Am. b. New York 1895; ad. 1934 Same. A28.
YOUNG, AUGUST.
Am. Germany 1839-1913 Brooklyn, N. Y. A0X1.
YOUNG, BESSIE INNES.
Scot. b. Glasgow; ad. 1934 Same. Wa.
YOUNG, BLAMIRE.
Eng. Yorkshire 1865; ac. 1933 Australia. Y1921.
YOUNG, CHARLES JAC. (Et)
Am. b. Bavaria 1880; ad. 1934 Weehawken Heights, N. J. A-F.
YOUNG, CHARLES MORRIS.
Am. b. Gettysburg, Pa. 1869; ad. 1934 Radnor, Pa. A-F-W.
YOUNG, CRAWFORD.
Am. ad. 1934 Norwalk, Conn. M.
YOUNG, ÉDUARD.
Aus. b. Prague, Czec. 1823; ac. 1873 in Vienna. C.
YOUNG, ELEANOR.
Am. ad. 1934 New York. M.
YOUNG, ELLSWORTH.
Am. ad. 1934 Oak Park, Ill. A.
YOUNG, ESTHER CHRISTENSEN. (Ill)
Mrs. Charles J. Young.
Am. b. Milwaukee, Wis. 1895; ad. 1934 Ardmore, Pa. A.
YOUNG, F. CLIFFORD.
Am. b. New Waterford, O. 1905; ad. 1934 New York. A.
YOUNG, FRANCES PRICE.
Am. b. Winterset, Ia. 1901; ad. 1934 Hibbing, Minn. A.

YOUNG, HARVEY B.
Am. Port Mils, Vt. 1840-1901 Colo. Springs, Colo. A04-15.
YOUNG, HELEN.
Am. b. So. Otselic, N. Y. 1888; ad. 1934 Mt. Vernon, N. Y. A.
YOUNG, JAMES H. (Eg)
Am. ac. 1817-1845 in Phila., Pa. F.
YOUNG, JAMES HARVEY.
Am. b. Salem, Mass. 1830; ac. 1867 in Boston. F-15-47-169.
YOUNG, JOHN. (Eg)
Eng. b. 1755; d. 1825 in London. B-DNB.
YOUNG, JOHN HENRY.
Aust. b. New Zealand; ad. 1929 London. Wa1929.
YOUNG, [Lady] KATHLEEN HILTON [Scott]. (S)
Eng. b. England; ad. 1934 London. Wa.
YOUNG, LOUIS C.
Am. Grand Rapids, Mich. 1864-1915 Pelham, N. Y. A012.
YOUNG, MAHONRI MACKINTOSH. (P-S)
Am. b. Salt Lake City, Utah 1877; ad. 1934 New York. A-E-F-W-46-55-779.
YOUNG, [Mrs.] MAHONRI.
see Weir, Dorothy.
YOUNG, QUINTER.
Am. ex. 1935 Cinn., O. M.
YOUNG, SIBYL.
Eng. b. Kent 1901; ad. 1934 Norfolk. Wa.
YOUNG, SUSANNE BOTTOMLEY.
Am. b. New York 1891; ad. 1934 Garden City, L. I., N. Y. A.
YOUNG, THOMAS A.
Am. London 1837-1913 Brooklyn, N. Y. A0X1.
YOUNG, TOBIAS.
Eng. d. 1824 in Southampton. B.
YOUNG-HUNTER, JOHN.
Am. b. Glasgow, Scot. 1874; ad. 1934 New York. A-W-Wa.
YOUNGERMAN, REYNA ULLMAN.
Am. b. New Haven, Conn. 1902; ad. 1934 Hamden, Conn. A.
YOUNGMAN, ANNIE MARY.
Eng. b. 1860; d. 1919. Y01920.
YOUNGMAN, HAROLD JAMES. (S)
Eng. b. Bradford 1886; ad. 1934 Chelsea. Wa.
YOUNGMAN, JOHN MALLOWS.
Eng. b. 1817; d. 1899 in London. B.
YOUON, CONSTANTIN FEODOROVITCH.
Rus. b. 1876; ad. 1926 Moscow. M.
YOURIEVITCH, SERGE. (S)
Rus. ad. 1934 Paris. DBA-798.
YOURIST, MANUEL.
Am. ad. 1934 Toledo, O. M.
YPEREN [or Ypres], KAREL.
Flem. Ypres 1510-1563/4 Coutrai. B.
YRONDY, CHARLES GASTON. (S)
Fr. b. Paris 1885. DBA.
YRURTIA, ROGELIO. (S)
Fr. b. Buenos Aires, Arg. 1879. DBA.
YSENBRANDT. *see* Isenbrandt.
YSENDYCK [or Isendyck], ANTONIUS VAN.
Flem. Antwerp 1801-1875. B-C.
YSERN Y ALIÉ, PERE [or Pierre].
Sp. b. Barcelona 1876. DBA.
YU LING.
Chinese. ac. 1700. M.
YUDOVIN, SOLOMON. (Eg)
Rus. ac. 20th Cent. in Russia. M.
YUKIHIDÉ, TOSA [Kasuga].
Jap. ac. 15th Cent. in Japan. J., Vol. 1, page 71.
YUKIN, P. J.
Rus. ac. 20th Cent. in Russia. M.
YUKINOBU, KIYOHARA.
Jap. b. 1643; d. 1682. J., Vol. 1, page 139.
YULE, WILLIAM J.
Scot. Dundee 1868-1900 Nordrach. B.
YUMEDONO, HORYUJI. (S) Jap. M.
YÜN SHOU-P'ING [or Nan-t'ien].
Chinese. ac. 17th Cent. in China. E.
YUNK, ENRICO.
It. Turin 1849-1878 Pisa. C.
YUNK, LURINO.
It. Turin 1840-1887 Pisa. B.
YUON, CONSTANTIN.
see Youon, Constantin Fedorovitch.
YUSEN, MORI.
Jap. ac. 1830 in Japan. J., Vol. 2, page 98.
YUSHO, KAIHOKU.
Jap. J., Vol. 1, page 101.
YVERNI, JACQUES.
Fr. ac. 15th Cent. in France. M.
YVON, ADOLPHE.
Ger. Eschweiler 1817-1893 Paris. B-C.
YWYNS, MICHIEL. (S)
Dut. ac. 1514-1518 in Middelburg. B.

ZAAK, GUSTAV.
Ger. b. Stechau 1845. B.
ZABARELLI, ADRIANO [Il. Paladino].
It. Florence 1610-1680. B.
ZABOLY, [Mr.] BELA PAL. (Ill)
Am. b. Cleveland, O. 1910; ad. 1934 Same. A.
ZABRISKIE, WILLIAM B.
Am. b. 1840; d. 1933 in Hackensack, N. J. A030.
ZACCHIA DA LUCCA, LORENZO.
It. ac. 1558. Wi.
ZACCHIA, PAOLO [Il. Vecchio].
It. ac. 1520/30 in Florence. B.
ZACCONE, FABIAN.
Am. ad. 1935 West New York, N. J. M.
ZACHERTOWNA, ELWINA. (S)
Pol. ad. 1934 Warsaw. M.
ZACHO, CHRISTIAN.
Dan. b. Grenaa 1843. B-C.
ZACHTLEVEN. *see* Saft-Leven.
ZACKHEIM, BERNARD.
Am. ex. 1935 San Fran., Calif. M.
ZADIG, BERTRAND. (Et)
Am. b. Budapest, Hun. 1904. A28.
ZADIG, WILLIAM. (S)
Swe. b. Malmo 1884. DBA.
ZADKINE, OSSIP. (S)
Rus.-Fr. b. Smolensk, Rus. 1890; ex. 1934 London. DBA-Ta-855.
ZAENGLEIN, HILDA.
Am. ex. 1935 New York. M.
ZAFFONI, GIOVANNI MARIA [Calderari].
It. Friuli 1534-1570. B.
ZAGANELLI, BERNARDINO.
It. b. Cotignola; ac. 1460-1509. B-C-V.

ZAGANELLI, Francesco.
It. b. Cotignola 1465-1531. B-C-V.
ZAGO, Santo.
It. ac. 1550 in Venice. B.
ZAGORSKY, N. P.
Rus. b. 1849; d. 1893. B.
ZAHN, Johann Karl Wilhelm.
Ger. Rodenberg 1800-1871 Berlin. B.
ZAHRTMAN, Kristian.
Dan. Rönne 1843-1917. B-C.
ZAICHIU, Hara.
Jap. J., Vol. 1, page 142.
ZAINER, Gunther.
Ger. ac. 1485 in Germany. M.
ZAIS, Giuseppe.
Ger. b. 1709; d. 1784 in Trévise. B-M.
ZAISS, Leonard. (P-S)
Am. b. 1892; d. 1933 in Harrison, N. Y. A030.
ZAK, Eugène.
Pol.-Fr. Paris 1884-1926 Same. DBA-736.
ZAKARIAN, Zachaire.
Turkish. b. Constantinople; ac. 1900 in Paris. B.
ZAKAROV, P. Z.
Rus. b. 1816; d. 1852. Fa.
ZAKHAROV, Adrien Dmitrievitch.
Rus. b. 1761; d. 1811. Fa.
ZAKHAROV, Feodor.
Rus. b. Russia 1882; ad. 1935 New York. M.
ZALA, György. (S)
Hun. ac. 1900 in Paris. B.
ZAMAÇOIS, Éduardo.
Sp. Bilboa 1842-1871 Madrid. Bd-C.
ZAMBONI, Giovanni Battista Cremonni.
It. Cento 1550-1610 Bologna. B-T-722.
ZAMOYSKI, Auguste de. (S)
Pol. b. 1893 in Poland. DBA.
ZAMPA, Francesco. (S)
It. ac. 15th Cent. in Italy. Fa.
ZAMPIERI, Domenico. *see* Domenichino, Z.
ZAN, Bernard. (Eg)
Ger. ac. 1580 in Nüremberg. B.
ZANCARLI [or Giancarli], Poliphilos.
It. ac. 1624 in Italy. B.
ZANCHI, Antonio.
It. Este 1631/9-1722 Venice. B.
ZANDOMENEGHI, Frédérico.
It. b. 1849; d. 1917 in Italy. B.
ZANDOMENEGHI, Luigi. (S)
It. b. 1778; d. 1850 in Venice. B.
ZANETTI, Antonio Maria [Girolamo].
It. Venice 1680-1757 Same. B.
ZANETTI, Antonio Maria [Giovane].
It. Venice 1716-1778 Same. B.
ZANETTI, Domenico.
It. ac. 1738 in Italy. B.
ZANINI, Gigiotto.
It. b. Virgo di Fossa; ad. 1934 Milan. M.
ZANOBI DI BENEDETTO. *see* Strozzi.
ZANOBI. *see* Macchiavelli.
ZAORTIGA, Bonanat.
Sp. ac. 1403-1413 in Spain. M.
ZÁPATER, Juán José.
Sp. b. 1866 in Spain. M.
ZAPPI, Lavinia. *see* Fontana, L.
ZARAGOZA, Lorenzo.
Sp. ac. end of 14th Cent. in Spain. M.
ZARCILLO Y ALCAREZ, Francisco. (S)
Sp. Murcia 1707-1781. E-Hs.
ZARING, [Mrs.] Louise Eleanor.
Am. b. Cinn., O.; ad. 1934 Greencastle, Pa. A.
ZARRAGA, Angel.
Mex. b. Mexico 1866. DBA.
ZARSKY, Ernest. (Eg)
Am. b. Germany 1864; ad. 1934 East Cleveland, O. A.
ZARUBIN, Victor.
Rus. b. 1875; ac. 1935 Russia. M.
ZÄSINGER, Martin [or Matheus]. (Eg)
[*also* called Master MZ.]
Ger. ac. 1500 in Munich. B.
ZATSINGER. *see* Zäsinger.
ZATZKA, Fritz.
Aus. ac. 20th Cent. in Austria. M.
ZAUFFELY. *see* Zoffany.
ZAVATTORI [or Zavattari], Gregorio.
It. ac. 1453-1475 in Milan. B.
ZAVERY, Gerherd Joseph.
Flem. b. Antwerp; ac. 1741 The Hague, Holland. B.
ZAYAS, G. de. (Ill)
Am. ad. 1935 New York. M.
ZEEGELAAR, Gerrit van.
Dut. Loenen 1719-1794 Wageningen. C.
ZEEMAN [or Seeman], Renier Nooms.
Dut. Amsterdam 1612/23-1668/73. B-C-722.
ZEGHERS [or Seghers], Daniel [Jesuit].
Flem. Antwerp 1570-1661 Same. B-C-722.
ZEGHERS [or Seghers], Geeraard.
Flem. Antwerp 1589/91-1651 Same. B-C-722.
ZEGHERS [or Seghers], Hendrik.
Flem. b. Antwerp 1780. [No death date.] B
ZEGHERS [or Seghers], Hercules Pietersz.
Dut. Utrecht 1589-1640/5. B-C.
ZEGHERS [or Seghers], Jan Baptiste.
Flem. Antwerp 1624-1670/1. B
ZEHENDER, Karl Friedrich.
Swi. Berne 1818-1870 Montreux. B.
ZEHENDER, Karl Ludwig.
Swi. Bomont 1751-1814 Berne. B.
ZEHENTMAYR, Thomas.
Ger. 1550?-1623. M.
ZEIDLER, Avis.
Am. b. Madison, Wis. 1908; ad. 1934 San Fran., Calif. A.
ZEIGLER. *see also* Ziegler.
ZEIGLER, Lee Woodward.
Am. b. Balt., Md. 1868; ad. 1934 Newburgh, N. Y. A-F-W.
ZEISING, Walter.
Ger. b. 1876 in Germany. M.
ZEITBLOOM, Bartholomaus.
Ger. Ulm 1450?-1518/21. B-C-722.
ZEITLIN, Alexander. (S)
Am. b. Tiflis, Rus. 1872; ad. 1934 New York. A.
ZELGER, Jakob Joseph.
Swi. Stanz 1812-1888. B-C.
ZELL, Ernest Negley.
Am. b. Dayton, O. 1874; ad. 1934 Columbus, O. A-F.
ZELLER, August. (S)
Am. Bordentown, N. J. 1863-1918 Pittsburgh, Pa. A015.

ZELLER, Johann Conrad.
Swi. Hirslanden 1807-1856 Zurich. B-C.
ZELLER, Magnus.
Ger. ac. 20th Cent. in Germany. M.
ZELOTTI, Giambattista.
It. Verona 1532-1592 Same. C-722.
ZENALE, Bernardino Martini.
It. Treviglio 1436-1526 Milan. B-C-V.
ZENISEK, Franz [Frantisck].
Czecho-Slovakian. b. 1849. Fa.
ZENOBIO, Luca da Ca'. *see* Carlevaris.
ZENSABURO, Kojima.
Jap. ac. 1932. M.
ZENTARO, Kojima.
Jap. b. 1892. M.
ZEPPENFELD, Victor.
Ger. b. Greiz 1834; ac. 1871. [No death date.] C.
ZERBE, Karl. D. 11/29/72
Am. b. Germany; ad. 1934 Cambridge, Mass. M.
ZERNORA, Katherina.
Rus. ad. 1934 Moscow; ex. 1931 Pittsburgh, Pa. M.
ZERZAVY [or Zrzavy], Jan.
Czec. b. Vadin 1890. DBA.
ZESHIN, Shibata.
Jap. 1806-1891. J., Vol. 2, page 104.
ZETSCHE, Éduard.
Aus. b. Vienna 1844. B.
ZETTLER, Emil Robert. (S)
Am. b. Chicago 1878; ad. 1934 Same. A-F-W.
ZEUNER [or Zeurner].
Dut. ac. 1802 in Amsterdam. [No death date.] B.
ZEUXIS [or Zeuxippus].
Gr. Heraclea 464-390 B.C. B-C-E.
ZEVIO, Stefano da. *see* Stefano, Z.
ZEZZOS, Alessandro.
It. b. Venice; ac. 1889 Same. B.
ZICHY, Mihaly [or Michael] von.
Hun. Zala 1827-1906. C.
ZICK, Alexander.
Ger. b. Berlin 1845; ac. 1886 Same. B.
ZICK, Januarius.
Ger. Munich 1733/5-1797/1812. B-C-722.
ZIEGFIELD, Edwin.
Am. b. 1905; ad. 1934 Minn., Minn. M.
ZIEGLER, Archibald. (Mu)
Eng. b. London 1903; ad. 1934 Chelsea. Wa.
ZIEGLER, Claude [or Charles] Jules.
Fr. Langres 1804-1856 Dijon. B-C-722.
ZIEGLER, Eustace Paul.
Am. b. Detroit, Mich. 1881; ad. 1934 Seattle, Wash. A.
ZIEGLER, Frederick J. (S)
Am. b. New York 1886; ad. 1935 Woodmere, L. I., N. Y. Cs.
ZIEGLER, Henry. (Et)
Am. b. Sherman, Tex. 1889. M.
ZIEGLER, Henry Bryan.
Eng. London 1789-1874. B.
ZIEGLER, Samuel P.
Am. b. Lancaster, Pa. 1882; ad. 1934 Ft. Worth, Tex. A.
ZIEM, Félix François Georges Philbert.
Fr. Beaume 1821-1911 Paris. B-Bd-C-DBA-E.
ZIER, François Édouard ["Ed"].
Fr. b. 1856; d. 1929 in Paris. B.
ZIER, Victor Casimir.
Pol. b. Warsaw 1822; ac. 1883. [No death date.] B-C.
ZIERMANN, Karl.
Ger. Saalfeld 1850-1881 Berka. B-C.
ZIESENIS, Johannes. (S)
Dut. Amsterdam 1770-1820 The Hague. B.
ZIESENIS, Johann Georg.
Dan. Copenhagen 1716-1777 Hanover, Ger. B-C.
ZILCKEN, Charles Louis Philippe.
Dut. The Hague 1857-1930. B.
ZILLE, Heinrich. (Et)
Ger. b. 1864; d. 1929 in Berlin. M.
ZILVE, Alida. (S)
Am. b. Amsterdam, Holland; ad. 1934 Brooklyn, N. Y. A-Cs-F.
ZIM, Marco. (Et)
Am. ad. 1934 New York. M.
ZIMM, Bruno Louis. (S)
Am. New York 1876; ad. 1934 Woodstock, N. Y. A-F-Ta-W.
ZIMMELE, Margaret Scully. (S)
Am. b. Pittsburgh, Pa. 1872; ad. 1934 Wash., D. C. A-F.
ZIMMER, Marion Bruce.
Am. ad. 1934 Syracuse, N. Y. M.
ZIMMER, Wilhelm.
Ger. b. Apolda 1853. B-C.
ZIMMERMAN, August Albert.
Ger. Zittau 1808-1888 Munich. B-C.
ZIMMERMAN, Carl.
Am. ad. 1935 Cinn., O. M.
ZIMMERMAN, Clemens von.
Ger. Düsseldorf 1788-1869 Munich. B-C.
ZIMMERMAN, Ernest [or Karl, or Georg].
Ger. Munich 1852-1901 Same. B-C.
ZIMMERMAN, Eugène ["Zim"]. (Cari)
Am. Basel, Swi. 1862-1935 Horseheads, N. Y. A28-F-M-W-Obit. N. Y. papers, 3-26-1935.
ZIMMERMAN, Frederick Almond.
Am. b. Canton, O. 1886; ad. 1934 Pasadena, Calif. A.
ZIMMERMAN, Friedrich.
Swi. b. 1823; d. 1884 in Geneva. B-C.
ZIMMERMAN, Harold S.
Am. ad. 1935 Orville, O. M.
ZIMMERMAN, Lillian Hortense. (S)
Am. b. Milwaukee, Wis.; ad. 1934 Same. A.
ZIMMERMAN, Mason W.
Am. b. Phila., Pa. 1861; ad. 1934 Same. A-F.
ZIMMERMAN, Reinhard Sebastian.
Ger. Hagenau 1815-1893 Munich. B-C.
ZIMMERMAN, Richard August.
Ger. Zittau, Saxony 1820-1875 Munich. B-C.
ZIMTZOWITZ, Temina. (Mu)
Am. ex. 1935 New York. M.
ZINCKE, Christian Friedrich.
Ger. Dresden 1683/4-1767 England. B.
ZINCKE, Paul Francis ["Old Zincke"].
Eng. b. 1750; d. 1830 London. Wi.
ZINGALE, Santos.
Am. b. Milwaukee, Wis. 1908; ad. 1935 Same. A.
ZINGARO, Lo ["The Gipsy"].
see Solario, Antonio.

ZINGG [or Zink], ADRIAN.
Swi. St. Gall 1734-1816 Leipzig, Ger. B.
ZINGG, JULES.
Fr. b. Montbéliard 1882. DBA.
ZINKEISEN, DORIS CLARE.
Scot. ad. 1934 London. Wa.
ZIPPA [or Zipper], GIACOMO FRANCESCO.
see Cipper, G. F.
ZIPPRICH, ANTHONY E.
Am. ex. 1935 New York. M.
ZIROLI, ANGELO. (S)
Am. b. Italy 1899; ad. 1934 Chicago. A.
ZIROLI, NICOLA VICTOR.
Am. Campobasso, It. 1908; ad. 1934 Chicago. A.
ZISLIN, HENRI. (Ill)
Fr. b. Mülhouse 1875. DBA.
ZITO. (Cari). ac. 1934. M.
ZO, HENRI.
Fr. Bayonne 1873-1933. B-DBA.
ZO, JEAN BAPTISTE ACHILLE.
Fr. Bayonne 1826-1901 Same. B-C.
ZOAN, ANDREA. (Eg)
It. ac. 1475-1505 in Venice. M.
ZOBEL, GEORGE. (Eg)
[Made marble dust pictures.]
Eng. b. 1840; d. 1881 in London. B.
ZOCCHI, ÉMILIO. (S)
It. b. Florence 1835. [No death date.] B.
ZOCCHI, GIUSEPPE.
It. Tuscany 1711-1767. B.
ZOELLNER, RICHARD.
Am. ad. 1935 Cinn., O. M.
ZOFF, ALFRED.
Aus. b. Vienna 1843. B.
ZOFFANY [or Zauffely], JOHANN.
Eng. Frankfort, Ger. 1733/5-1810 London. B-Bd-C-DNB-E-633.
ZOGBAUM, RUFUS FARCHILD.
Am. Charleston, S. C. 1849-1925 New York. A022-F.
ZOIR, CARL ÉMILE.
Swe. b. 1867. Ms.
ZOLL, FRANZ JOSEPH.
Ger. Baden-Baden 1770-1833 Munich. B-C.
ZOLNAY, GEORGE JULIAN. (S)
Am. b. Hungary 1863; ad. 1934 Wash., D. C. A-F-Ta-W.
ZOMER [or Somer], JAN PIETERSZ.
Dut. Amsterdam 1641-1726. B.
ZONA, ANTONIO.
It. Venice 1810/5-1892. B-C.
ZOPPI, ANTONIO.
It. b. Navarre; ad. 1934 Florence. M.
ZOPPO, MARCO.
It. Bologna 1433-1498. B-Bd-C-V-722.
ZOPPO, PAOLO.
It. ac. 1492-1530 in Bergamo. B-V.
ZORACH, MARGUERITE.
Am. b. Santa Rosa, Calif. 1888; ad. 1935 New York. A-701.
ZORACH, WILLIAM. (P-S)
Am. b. Russia 1887; ad. 1935 New York. A-Cs-F-104-105-138-700-701-703-779.
ZORG. *see* Sorgh.
ZORGA, CHARLES DALLA.
It. b. 1902 in Italy. Fa.
ZORN, ANDERS LEONARD. (Et)
Swe. Mora, 1860-1920 Stockholm, Swe. B-DBA-E-192-830-880.
ZORNES, MILFORD.
Am. b. Camargo, Okla. 1908; ad. 1934 Claremont, Calif. M.
ZORNLIN, GEORGIANA MARGARETTA.
Eng. b. 1800; d. 1881 in London. B.
ZOTOV, A.
Rus. ac. late 19th Cent. in Russia. M.
ZOTTO, ANTONI DA. (S)
It. ac. 1879 in Venice. B.
ZOZZORA, FRANK.
Am. b. Sassano, It. 1902; ad. 1934 Madison, Wis. A.
ZSCHOCKE, ALEXANDER.
Ger. ac. 1929 in Germany. M.
ZSISSLY.
Am. b. Chicago 1897; ad. 1934 Naperville, Ill. A.
ZUBER, JEAN HENRI.
Fr. Rixhelm 1844-1909. B-C.
ZUBER-BÜHLER, FRITZ.
Swi. b. Locle; ac. 1850/86 in Paris. B-C.
ZUBIAURRE, RAMÓN DE.
Sp. b. 1882; ex. 1934 New York. M.
ZUBIAURRE, VALENTIN DE.
Sp. b. 1879; ad. 1934 Madrid. B.
ZUCCARELLI, FRANCESCO.
It. Pitigliano 1701-1788 Florence. B-C-E.
ZUCCARO [or Zucchero], FEDERIGO.
It. St. Agnolo 1542/3-1609 Ancona. B-Bd-C-E-V-722.
ZUCCARO [or Zucchero], TADDEO.
It. St. Agnolo 1529-1556 Rome. B-C-E-V-722-803.
ZUCCATI [or Zuccato], FRANCESCO and VALERIO.
It. both ac. 1579 in Venice. B-C.
ZUCCATI [or Zuccato], SEBASTIANO.
It. ac. 1495. B-V.
ZUCCHI, ANTONIO PIETRO.
It. Venice 1726-1795 Rome. B-DNB.
ZUCCHI, GIUSEPPE. (Eg)
It. ac. 1770 in London. DNB.
ZUCCHI, JACOPO DEL.
It. Florence 1541-1604.
ZUCCO, FRANCESCO.
It. Bergamo 1600-1627 Same. B.
ZUCCOLI, LUIGI.
It. b. Milan; ac. 1860-1876 Same. B.
ZUCKER, JACQUES.
Am. ad. 1935 New York. M-892.
ZÜGEL, HEINRICH JOHANN VON.
Ger. b. Murrhard 1850; ad. 1930 Munich. B-C-M.
ZUHR, HUGO.
Fin.-Swe. b. Finland 1895; ac. 1934 Sweden. DBA.
ZULOAGA Y ZABALETA, IGNACIO.
Sp. b. Eibar, Sp. 1870. B-DBA-E-634.
ZULOW, FRANZ.
Aus. ac. 1931 in Austria. M.
ZUMBO, GAETANO GIULIO. (S)
It. b. 1656; d. 1701 in Italy. Fa.
ZUMBUSCH, KASPAR VON. (S)
Ger. b. 1830; d. 1915 Dieppe. B-Hs.
ZUMBUSCH, LUDWIG VON.
Ger. b. Munich 1861. B.

ZUMPE, Johannes.
Ger. Leipzig 1819-1864 Dresden. B.
ZÜND, Robert.
Swi. Lucerne 1827-1909. B-C.
ZÜNDT, Mathias.
Dut. b. 1498; d. 1586 in Holland. M.
ZURBARÁN, Francisco de.
Sp. Fuente de Cantos 1598-1662 Madrid. B-Bd-C-E-635-722-823.
ZURCHER, Hans.
Swi. b. Zug. 1880. B.
ZURCHER, Jakob.
Swi. b. Swi. 1834; d. 1884 Rome, It. B.
ZURICHER, Ulrich Wilhelm.
Swi. b. Berne 1877. B.
ZURLAUBEN, Béat Fidèle.
Ger. b. 1720; d. 1799 in Germany. Fa.
ZUSTRIS [or Sustris], Lambert Frederic.
Dut. Amsterdam 1526-1599? Munich, Ger. C-722.
ZUYLER, J. H. van.
Dut. ac. 1644 in Holland. Wi.
ZWAERDECROON, Bernardus.
Dut. Utrecht 1617-1654 Same. B.
ZWART, Wilhelmus H. P. J. de.
Dut. b. The Hague 1862; ac. 1910 Paris. B.
ZWENGAUER, Anton [The Elder].
Ger. Munich 1810-1884 Same. B-C.
ZWIETEN [or Swieten], Cornelis van.
Dut. ac. 1648-1671 in Leyden. B.
ZWILLER, Marie Augustin.
Fr. b. Didenheim 1850. B-DBA.
ZWINGER, Anna Felicitas [Prissler].
Ger. b. 1740; d. 1808. Fa.
ZWINTSCHER, Oscar.
Ger. Leipzig 1870-1916. B-Ms.
ZWOBADA, Jacques. (S)
Fr. b. Neuilly 1900. DBA.
ZWOLLE [or Zwoller, or Zwoll].
see Master I.A.M. of Zwolle.
ZWORYKINE, Boris Vassilievitch.
Rus. b. 1872 in Russia. M.
ZYDERWELD, Willem.
Dut. Amsterdam 1796-1846 Same. B.
ZYGLINSKI, Franciszek.
Pol. Warsaw 1816-1849 Same. B.
ZYGMUNT, Waga III.
Pol. b. 1566; d. 1632 in Warsaw. B.
ZYL [or Zyll], Dirk [or Thierry] van.
Dut. ac. 1660 in Utrecht. B.
ZYL [or Zyll], Gerard Pietersz van.
[Called the "Little Van Dyck".]
Dut. Leyden 1607/19-1665 Amsterdam. B-C.
ZYL [or Ziel], Roeloff van.
Dut. ac. 1611-1624 in Utrecht. B.
ZYLVELT [or Sylvett], Antony.
Dut. b. Amsterdam 1643. [No death date.] B.
ZYSSET, Jakob.
Swi. ac. 1680 in Berne. B.
ZYZYWI, Karlus.
Turkish. b. Constantinople 1883. DBA.